The New World Dictionary-Concordance to the New American Bible

The work on The New World Biblical Dictionary and Concordance for the New American Bible has been done, and superbly so, by a group of priest-scholars in Rome, Italy. Their writing reflects the new trends in biblical thinking in the Christian churches today. Their opinions on difficult problems in the Scriptures are restrained, conservative in the sense of conserving values, and yet advances in terms of their reflection of the new principles of Scriptural study as set forth in an encyclical of Pope Pius XII and the documents of the second Vatican Council. However, those who wrote this book make no statements that are not backed up by solid research and sound scholarship.

This book has been compiled as a tool for the study of the New American Bible. Because of new and different spellings and word usage in this translation, older dictionaries and concordances are no longer serviceable. Realizing this, the publishers commissioned this work several years ago in order that readers would have an up-to-date and practical biblical reference designed specifically for this magnificent new translation. The New American Bible, the reader of it will note, abounds in footnotes which explain with great clarity more difficult verses of the Scriptures. These footnotes, coupled with the in-depth treatment of biblical topics in this dictionary, will give the reader all the reference material he needs to make a thorough study of the Scriptures.

The making of a Bible dictionary and concordance is a tedious, painstaking task. To all who had a hand in this one—scholars, writers, editors and proof-readers—we express our deep sense of gratitude for making this work possible and for their contribution to the broader and deeper study of the sacred Scriptures.

The New World Dictionary-Concordance

to the New American Bible

 WORLD

Nihil Obstat | M.R.P. Thomas Tuomey, O.S.A., S.T.D.

Imprimatur | ✠Hector Cunial, Archiep. Soleropolitan. Vicesgarens e
Vicarialu Urbis, die 1.4.70

Library of Congress Catalog Card Number: 72-77415
International Standard Book Number: 0-529-04540-0

Printed in Canada

TIME CHART OF BIBLE HISTORY

| | **3000 BC** | **2500** | **2000** |

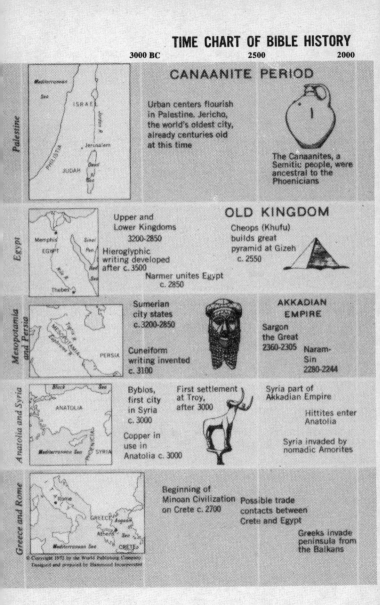

Palestine

CANAANITE PERIOD

Urban centers flourish in Palestine. Jericho, the world's oldest city, already centuries old at this time

The Canaanites, a Semitic people, were ancestral to the Phoenicians

Egypt

Upper and Lower Kingdoms 3200-2850

Hieroglyphic writing developed after c. 3500

Narmer unites Egypt c. 2850

OLD KINGDOM

Cheops (Khufu) builds great pyramid at Gizeh c. 2550

Mesopotamia and Persia

Sumerian city states c.3200-2850

Cuneiform writing invented c. 3100

AKKADIAN EMPIRE

Sargon the Great 2360-2305

Naram-Sin 2280-2244

Anatolia and Syria

Byblos, first city in Syria c. 3000

Copper in use in Anatolia c. 3000

First settlement at Troy, after 3000

Syria part of Akkadian Empire

Hittites enter Anatolia

Syria invaded by nomadic Amorites

Greece and Rome

Beginning of Minoan Civilization on Crete c. 2700

Possible trade contacts between Crete and Egypt

Greeks invade peninsula from the Balkans

© Copyright 1971 by the World Publishing Company
Designed and prepared by Hammond Incorporated

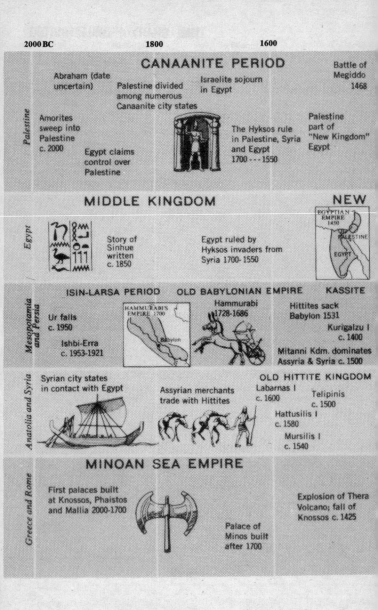

2000 BC	1800	1600

Palestine

CANAANITE PERIOD

Abraham (date uncertain)

Palestine divided among numerous Canaanite city states

Israelite sojourn in Egypt

Battle of Megiddo 1468

Amorites sweep into Palestine c. 2000

Egypt claims control over Palestine

The Hyksos rule in Palestine, Syria and Egypt 1700 --- 1550

Palestine part of "New Kingdom" Egypt

Egypt

MIDDLE KINGDOM

NEW

Story of Sinhue written c. 1850

Egypt ruled by Hyksos invaders from Syria 1700-1550

EGYPTIAN EMPIRE 1450

PALESTINE

EGYPT

Mesopotamia and Persia

ISIN-LARSA PERIOD

OLD BABYLONIAN EMPIRE

KASSITE

Ur falls c. 1950

Ishbi-Erra c. 1953-1921

HAMMURABI'S EMPIRE 1700

Babylon

Hammurabi 1728-1686

Hittites sack Babylon 1531

Kurigalzu I c. 1400

Mitanni Kdm. dominates Assyria & Syria c. 1500

Anatolia and Syria

Syrian city states in contact with Egypt

Assyrian merchants trade with Hittites

OLD HITTITE KINGDOM

Labarnas I c. 1600

Telipinis c. 1500

Hattusilis I c. 1580

Mursilis I c. 1540

Greece and Rome

MINOAN SEA EMPIRE

First palaces built at Knossos, Phaistos and Mallia 2000-1700

Palace of Minos built after 1700

Explosion of Thera Volcano; fall of Knossos c. 1425

TIME CHART OF BIBLE HISTORY

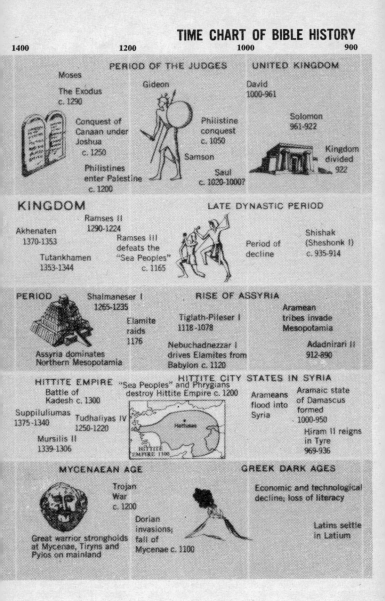

1400	1200	1000	900

PERIOD OF THE JUDGES — UNITED KINGDOM

Moses

The Exodus
c. 1290

Gideon

Conquest of
Canaan under
Joshua
c. 1250

Philistine
conquest
c. 1050

Samson

Philistines
enter Palestine
c. 1200

Saul
c. 1020-1000?

David
1000-961

Solomon
961-922

Kingdom
divided
922

KINGDOM — LATE DYNASTIC PERIOD

Akhenaten
1370-1353

Ramses II
1290-1224

Ramses III
defeats the
"Sea Peoples"
c. 1165

Tutankhamen
1353-1344

Period of
decline

Shishak
(Sheshonk I)
c. 935-914

PERIOD — RISE OF ASSYRIA

Shalmaneser I
1265-1235

Elamite
raids
1176

Tiglath-Pileser I
1118-1078

Nebuchadnezzar I
drives Elamites from
Babylon c. 1120

Assyria dominates
Northern Mesopotamia

Aramean
tribes invade
Mesopotamia

Adadnirari II
912-890

HITTITE EMPIRE — HITTITE CITY STATES IN SYRIA

"Sea Peoples" and Phrygians
destroy Hittite Empire c. 1200

Battle of
Kadesh c. 1300

Suppiluliumas
1375-1340

Tudhaliyas IV
1250-1220

Mursilis II
1339-1306

Arameans
flood into
Syria

Aramaic state
of Damascus
formed
1000-950

Hiram II reigns
in Tyre
969-936

HITTITE
EMPIRE 1100

Hattusas

MYCENAEAN AGE — GREEK DARK AGES

Trojan
War
c. 1200

Dorian
invasions;
fall of
Mycenae c. 1100

Great warrior strongholds
at Mycenae, Tiryns and
Pylos on mainland

Economic and technological
decline; loss of literacy

Latins settle
in Latium

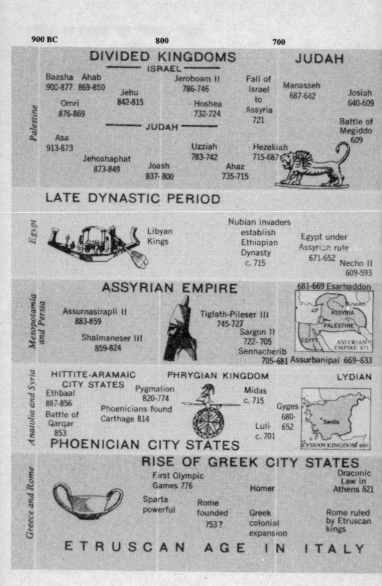

900 BC   **800**   **700**

DIVIDED KINGDOMS   JUDAH
──── ISRAEL ────

Baasha   Ahab   Jeroboam II   Fall of
900-877   869-850   786-746   Israel   Manasseh
            Jehu   to   687-642   Josiah
Omri   842-815   Hoshea   Assyria   640-609
876-869   732-724   721

            ──── JUDAH ────   Battle of
Asa   Megiddo
913-873   Uzziah   Hezekiah   609
          Jehoshaphat   783-742   715-687
          873-849   Joash   Ahaz
                       837-800   735-715

LATE DYNASTIC PERIOD

                              Nubian invaders
                              establish
          Libyan   Ethiopian   Egypt under
          Kings   Dynasty   Assyrian rule
                              c. 715   671-652
                                                          Necho II
                                                          609-593

ASSYRIAN EMPIRE   681-669 Esarhaddon

                                                         ASSYRIA
Assurnasirapli II   Tiglath-Pileser III   PALESTINE
883-859   745-727   EGYPT
                                      Sargon II   ASSYRIAN
          Shalmaneser III   722-705   EMPIRE 671
          859-824   Sennacherib
                              705-681 Assurbanipal 669-633

HITTITE-ARAMAIC   PHRYGIAN KINGDOM   LYDIAN
CITY STATES
Ethbaal   Pygmalion   Midas
887-856   820-774   c. 715
                 Phoenicians found   Gyges
Battle of   Carthage 814   680-
Qarqar   652   •Sardis
853   Luli-
PHOENICIAN CITY STATES   c. 701   LYDIAN KINGDOM 600

RISE OF GREEK CITY STATES
                   First Olympic   Draconic
                   Games 776   Law in
                                         Homer   Athens 621
                   Sparta
                   powerful   Rome
                               founded   Greek   Rome ruled
                               753?   colonial   by Etruscan
                                          expansion   kings

E T R U S C A N   A G E   I N   I T A L Y

Palestine · *Egypt* · *Mesopotamia and Persia* · *Anatolia and Syria* · *Greece and Rome*

600   **500**   **400**   **300**

CAPTIVITY

Fall of
Judah to
Babylonia
587

Cyrus of Persia
permits Jews to
return to Zion
538

Ezekiel

Temple
rebuilt
520-515

JEWS UNDER PERSIAN RULE

Ezra returns to
Jerusalem and reforms
society according to
Mosaic Law
458

Nehemiah
rebuilds the
walls of Jerusalem
c. 440

With the defeat
of the Persians
by Alexander the Great,
Palestine passes
under Greek rule
332

LATE DYNASTIC PERIOD

Hophra
(Apries)
588-569

Egypt under
Persian rule
525-404

Many Jews settle in Egypt
after the fall of the Temple
in 587

Last
native
dynasties

Persian
rule
342-332

Alexander the
Great conquers
Egypt 332

NEW BABYLONIAN EMPIRE

Fall of
Nineveh
612

Nebuchadnezzar II
605-562

Cyrus
550-530

Darius I
522-486

Xerxes I
486-465

PERSIAN EMPIRE

PERSIAN EMPIRE 500
PALESTINE
PERSIA
EGYPT
INDIA

Alexander
the Great
conquers
Persian Emp.
334-331

KINGDOM

Croesus
560-547

Lydians
devise
coinage
c. 600

Syria &
Anatolia
fall to
Persia
546-538

PERSIAN RULE

Phoenicians provide
navy for Persian
attack on Greece

Alexander
successfully
besieges Tyre
332

Solon's
judicial reforms
in Athens
c. 590

Roman
Republic
established
509

PERSIAN WARS

(499-479)
Marathon
490

Thermopylae
& Salamis
480

GOLDEN AGE

Pericles
461-429

Peloponnesian
Wars
431-404

Socrates'
death
399

RISE OF MACEDON

Philip II
359-336

Alexander
the Great
336-323

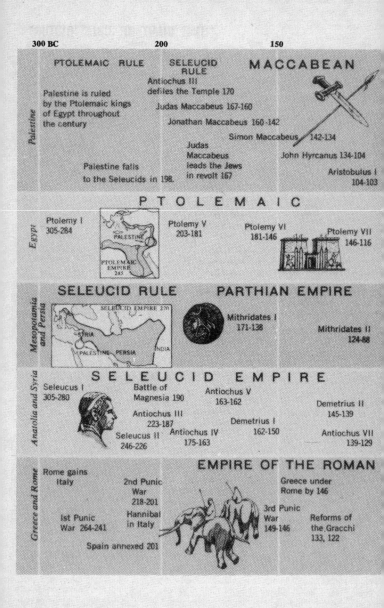

300 BC	200	150

Palestine

PTOLEMAIC RULE   SELEUCID RULE   MACCABEAN

Antiochus III defiles the Temple 170

Palestine is ruled by the Ptolemaic kings of Egypt throughout the century

Judas Maccabeus 167-160

Jonathan Maccabeus 160-142

Simon Maccabeus 142-134

Judas Maccabeus leads the Jews in revolt 167

John Hyrcanus 134-104

Palestine falls to the Seleucids in 198.

Aristobulus I 104-103

Egypt

PTOLEMAIC

Ptolemy I 305-284

Ptolemy V 203-181

Ptolemy VI 181-146

Ptolemy VII 146-116

PTOLEMAIC EMPIRE 245

Mesopotamia and Persia

SELEUCID RULE   PARTHIAN EMPIRE

SELEUCID EMPIRE 270

SYRIA   PALESTINE   PERSIA   INDIA

Mithridates I 171-138

Mithridates II 124-88

Anatolia and Syria

SELEUCID EMPIRE

Seleucus I 305-280

Battle of Magnesia 190

Antiochus V 163-162

Demetrius II 145-139

Antiochus III 223-187

Demetrius I 162-150

Seleucus II 246-226

Antiochus IV 175-163

Antiochus VII 139-129

Greece and Rome

EMPIRE OF THE ROMAN

Rome gains Italy

2nd Punic War 218-201

Greece under Rome by 146

1st Punic War 264-241

Hannibal in Italy

3rd Punic War 149-146

Reforms of the Gracchi 133, 122

Spain annexed 201

100   **50**   **BC | AD**   **50**

PERIOD   ROMAN   RULE

Alexander   Hyrcanus II
Jannaeus   63 -- 40
103 -- 76

  Alexandra   Herod the Great   Herod Antipas
  76 -- 67   37 ---- 4   4 BC --- AD 39

    Aristobulus II   Pontius Pilate
    67 -- 63   Birth of   27 -- 37
      Christ 5

      Pompey conquers   Death of Christ 30
      Palestine for Rome
      63

E G Y P T   ROMAN   RULE

Ptolemy VIII   Cleopatra VI
116 --- 81   51 --- 30

  Ptolemy XI   Caesar
  80 -- 51   in Egypt
    47   30 Egypt made Roman province.

P A R T H I A N   E M P I R E

Phrates III   War with Rome
70 -- 57   55 -- 38
  Battle of Carrhae   PARTHIA
  53   Phrates IV,
    Orodes I   38 -- 32,   PALESTINE
    57 -- 38   defeats Antony   PARTHIAN   PERSIA
    in 36   EMPIRE A.D. 2

ROMAN RULE

Mithridatic Wars   Cappadocia   Paul's first
89-84, 83-81, 75-65   annexed by   and second
  Battle of Zela   Rome 18   missionary
  Syria annexed   47   journeys in
  by Pompey 64   Most of Anatolia   Asia Minor
    under Rome   46 -- 53
  Antiochus XIII   by 6
  68 - 67

REPUBLIC   ROMAN   EMPIRE

Sulla dictator
82-79

  Death of   Battle of
  Caesar 44   Actium 31   Southern Britain
      conquered 43
  Caesar conquers   Augustus — First
  Gaul 58-51   Emperor 27 BC - AD 14

AD 50	100	150	200

Palestine

Herod Agrippa II
50 - - - - 100

Jewish-Roman
War
66 - -73

Destruction of
Jerusalem
70

Fall of Masada
73

ROMAN RULE

Palestine under direct rule of
Roman Procurators

Bar Cochba Revolt
132 - - 135

Jews expelled from
Jerusalem 135

The Jews concentrate
in Galilee following
their banishment
from the vicinity
of Jerusalem

Egypt

ROMAN RULE

Significant Christian center
established in Alexandria
c. 50

Egyptian
Christians
persecuted c. 200

Mesopotamia and Egypt

PARTHIAN EMPIRE

Vologases
51 - - 80

War with
Rome 56-63

War with
Rome 113-117

Osroes
(Chosroes)
89 - - 128

War with
Rome 162-165

War with
Rome
195 - - 202

Vologases III
148-192

Anatolia and Syria

ROMAN RULE

Paul's third
journey in
Asia Minor
54 - - 58

ROMAN EMPIRE
117 A.D.

Greece and Rome

Nero
54-68

Burning of
Rome, persecution
of Christians
64

Peter & Paul
die in Rome
c. 67?

Hadrian
117-138

Marcus Aurelius
161-180

Rescript against
Christians 177

ROMAN EMPIRE

Aaron, First high priest of the Hebrews, elder brother of Moses and Miriam (Ex. 6:20; 7:7; 15:20). He was the son of Amram and Jochebed. In the earliest traditions of the Pentateuch Aaron the Levite is appointed by God to be Moses' spokesman with Pharaoh (Ex. 4:14-16; 5:1-4) and with the Hebrew people in Egypt (Ex. 4:27-31). In the story of the plagues Aaron was Moses' companion, but the part he played was limited (Ex. 8:8; 9:27; 10:16). In the traditions concerning Israel's wanderings in the desert, Aaron is still associated with Moses as his subordinate. With Hur he supported Moses' outstretched arms on the mountain while Joshua fought the Amalekites (Ex. 17:10-12). He also shared, with all the elders of Israel, Moses' meal with Jethro his father-in-law (Ex. 18:12). In the story of the covenant with God on Mount Sinai, the position of Aaron is somewhat ambiguous. He accompanied Moses, who scaled the mountain to meet God (Ex. 19:24; 24:1-2; 24:9-11). While Moses passed forty days on the mountain, to Aaron and Hur was entrusted the care of the people. During this period he was partly responsible, at least through weakness, for the idolatry of the people in constructing the golden calf (Ex. 32:1-4, 15-24). Afterwards he excused himself with Moses and escaped punishment. With Miriam he opposed Moses over the Cushite woman he had married (Num. 12:1), but God justified Moses and punished Miriam.

The priestly traditions of the Pentateuch have preserved and developed the stories concerning the priestly ministry of Aaron. He was consecrated priest by Moses through anointing (Lev. 8:1-12) and he donned the sacred vestments which were made in accordance with precise divine instructions (Ex. 28). Thus Aaron and his sons, who were also consecrated priests, were entrusted with the care of the tabernacle and of the worship. The priesthood of Aaron was unequivocally confirmed by God on the occasion of the revolt of Korah and his followers, who contested the prerogatives of the priestly tribe of Levi (Num. 16 and 17). The other biblical books recall Aaron as the first high priest, from whom came the Israelite priests of the succeeding centuries (1 Chron. 6:3). The two older sons, Nadab and Abihu, were excluded from the priesthood, and the priestly line was perpetuated through Eleazar and Ithamar. Eleazar was inducted into his priestly functions by Moses (Num. 20:28; Deut. 10:6) after Aaron's death, which took place on Mt. Hor, before, therefore, he could view the Promised Land. This was in punishment for his incredulity at Meribah (Num. 20:23-28; 33:38-39). The Epistle to the Hebrews contrasted the Levitical priesthood of the Old Testament, typified in the person of Aaron (Heb. 5:4; 7:11), with the priesthood of Christ, underscoring the transitory and provisional nature of the former and the limits and deficiencies under which it functioned, in contrast to the perfect priesthood and self-oblation of Christ (Heb. 9:1-14).

Aaron's rod, In some of the episodes narrated in the books of Exodus and Numbers, Aaron's rod is the instrument of prodigies which were meant to convince Pharaoh of the authentically divine mission of Moses and Aaron (Ex. 7:9-10). Thus Aaron threw his rod on the ground and it became a serpent which ate up the serpents into which the Egyptian magicians had transformed their rods. Aaron, at Moses' orders, used his rod to strike the water of the river and change it into blood (Ex. 7:17); to make frogs swarm over all the land of Egypt (Ex. 8:5); to strike the dust of the ground and change it into gnats or mosquitoes (Ex. 8:12). Later on, the branch bearing the name of Aaron sprouted alone among the branches representing the twelve tribes, thus putting to silence those who were complaining against the priesthood of the house of Levi, which Aaron's branch represented. Aaron's branch was placed before the ark as a sign to the rebels that God had chosen the tribe of Levi (Num. 17). Hebrews 9:4

records that the branch that miraculously blossomed was kept in the Holy of Holies together with the ark of the covenant.

Ab, The name of the fifth month in the Hebrew calendar. *See* MONTH.

Abaddon (a-bad′dun), "Place of destruction." In the Old Testament the term was a poetic name for the realm of the dead (Job 26:6; Prov. 15:11; Ps. 88:12). In rabbinical literature it came to mean a part of Sheol to which sinners were condemned. In Revelation 9:11 the term has been personified to "the angel of the abyss."

Abagtha, One of the seven eunuchs who served Persian King Ahasuerus as chamberlains (Esth. 1:10).

Abana (ab′-a-na), **Abanah,** One of the rivers which cut across the region of Damascus, today called the Barada. It is mentioned in 2 Kings 5:12 in the answer which Naaman the Syrian gave to the prophet Elisha to whom he went to be cured of his leprosy. Elisha told him to go and wash himself seven times in the Jordan.

Abarim (ab′-a-rim), Mountains in the extreme west of Moab, which form the eastern boundary of the valley of the Jordan and the Dead Sea. The Israelites camped there before entering Palestine (Num. 33:47) and from one of its peaks, Mount Nebo, Moses contemplated the Promised Land (Deut. 32:49) before he died. The Abarim are also mentioned in Jeremi: h 22:20.

Abba, The special name by which the Christians are inspired to address God by the Spirit that is given them at baptism (Rom. 8:15; Gal. 4:6). Abba means father; it is the Aramaic form used in popular language by children when addressing their fathers. Jesus adopted this expression to pray to God, his Father (Mk. 14:36) and he taught the disciples to do likewise (Lk. 11:11). Although the Fatherhood of God was not unknown in Jewish spirituality and theology of the time, it was expressed in more reserved and formalistic terms, and the use of common language was avoided. Jesus wished that between his disciples and his Father there should unfold that same immediacy, trust, intimacy and abandonment that exists between a child and its father. St. Paul in preserving the Aramaic word echoes the newness introduced by Jesus, and underlines that the possibility of addressing God as Father flows from the saving mission of the Son of God, who pours into us his own Spirit, making us adoptive children of God.

Abdi, 1. A Levite, grandfather of Ethan (1 Chron. 6:44). 2. A Levite in the reign of Hezekiah (2 Chron. 29:12). 3. One of the sons of Elam (Ezra 10:26).

Abdon, 1. One of the minor judges, son of Hillel of Pirathon. He was judge over Israel for 8 years, and after his death was buried in Pirathon. Of him it is recounted that he had 40 sons and 30 grandsons, who according to Judges 12:13-15, rode on 70 asses, betokening great wealth.

2. Abdon is the name of three other biblical personages: the son of Jeiel and his wife Maacah, a distant ancestor of Saul (1 Chron. 8:30; 9:36); a minister of the court of Josiah of Judah (2 Chron. 34:20) and a descendant of Benjamin (1 Chron. 8:23).

3. A Levite city of the region assigned to the tribe of Asher (Josh. 21:30; 1 Chron. 6:74).

Abednego, The Babylonian name for Azariah, one of the prophet Daniel's three companions at the court of Nebuchadnezzar (Dan. 1:7). For refusing to worship the golden statue he was thrown into the fiery furnace with Shadrach (Hananiah) and Meshach (Mishael) but with them was miraculously saved (Dan. 1:7; 3:12-97; 1 Mac. 2:59).

Abel, According to Genesis 4:2 Abel was the second son of Adam and Eve. He was a shepherd and offered to the Lord in sacrifice some of the first-born of his flocks. God looked favorably on Abel's offering but not so on what Cain his brother offered (Gen. 4:5). Cain, jealous of his brother, killed him even though he was quite innocent. The reason for the preference of Abel's sacrifice is probably rooted in the ancient Israelite tradition which gave preference in cultural matters to the nomadic pastoral life over the settled farm life. In Mt. 23:35, Lk. 11:51, Heb. 11:4, 1 Jn. 3:12 he is called "the just one," his sacrifice is celebrated. his spirit of faith given as a model. *See* CAIN.

Abel-Beth-Maacah (may′-a-kah), A city of David's kingdom, north of Lake Huleh in northern Palestine. Sheba took refuge there after his abortive attempt at revolt against David (2 Sam. 20:14-18). It is also mentioned among the cities conquered by Ben-Hadad of Damascus together with Baasha king of Israel (1 Kgs. 15:20; 2 Chron. 16:4) and by Tiglath-pileser III in the time of Pekah (2 Kgs. 15:29).

Abel-Keramim (ker′-a-mim), A locality of eastern Jordan, probably in the district of the present Amman. Judges 11:32-33 tells us that Jephthah severely defeated the Ammonites, harassing them from Aroer through twenty towns all the way to Minnith and Abel-keramim.

Abel-Meholah (ma-ho′-lah), A city of Transjordania, on the eastern frontier of the fifth district, according to the administrative division introduced by Solomon (1 Kgs. 4:12). The name occurs in the account of the campaign of Gideon against the Midianites (Judges 7:22). Its claim to fame lies in its being the birthplace of Elisha (1 Kgs. 19:16) where also he was designated to be successor to the prophet Elijah (1 Kgs. 19:19-21).

Abel-Shittim, *See* SHITTIM.

Abia, A Greek form of the name of King Abijah, which is read in Jesus' genealogy according to Matthew 1:7. *See* ABIJAH.

Abiathar (a-by′-a-thar), A priest, son of Ahimelech of the family of Eli (1 Kgs. 2:27) and a descendant of Ithamar, son of Aaron. He was the one survivor of the wholesale slaughter of the priests of Nob ordered by Saul (1 Sam. 22:20). When he fled to David he took with him the ephod (1 Sam. 23:6). Abiathar was David's priest during the period of his disagreements with Saul (1 Sam. 23:8-12; 30:7-8) and after the conquest of Jerusalem he appears in the list of the ministers of the king as priest and counsellor (2 Sam. 20:25; 1 Chron. 15:11; 27:34). He remained loyal to David throughout the rebellion of Absalom, and together with Zadok wished to accompany David in his flight, bringing with him the ark, but David ordered them to remain on in Jerusalem with it (2 Sam. 15:24-29). In the contention over the succession to David, Abiathar took the side of Adonijah against Solomon, who was supported by Zadok (1 Kgs. 1:6, 7). When Solomon succeeded to the throne he banished Abiathar to Anathoth, sparing his life in gratitude for the services given to his father David in the past (1 Kgs. 2:26). In this banishment the historian saw the execution of God's sentence against the house of Eli for its infidelities in the exercise of the priesthood (1 Sam. 2:27-36).

Abib, The Canaanite name for the first month (March-April) of the ancient Israelite calendar (Ex. 13:4; 34:18).

Abiel, The father of Kish and grandfather of King Saul (1 Sam. 9:1; 14:51).

3

Abiezer (ab′-i-ee′-zer), 1. A descendant of Manasseh according to the genealogies of 1 Chron. 7:18, Jos. 17:2, and Num. 26:30. To Abiezer's clan belonged the family of Gideon (Jgs. 6:11, 24; 8:2, 32).

2. An Abiezer of Anathoth appears among the thirty warriors of the personal guard of David (2 Sam. 23:27; 1 Chron. 11:28). To him, according to 1 Chron. 27:12, was given the ninth division of 24,000 men who served during the ninth month of the year.

Abigail, 1. The wife of Nabal, and a woman of intelligence and beauty, according to 1 Sam. 25:3. Nabal was a Calebite of Maon, a rich landlord with possessions at Carmel, a town in the territory of Judah, a man described in the Bible as "harsh and ungenerous" (1 Sam. 25:3). Nabal refused to help David, but Abigail placated David's anger (1 Sam. 25:4-35). About ten days after this episode Nabal suddenly died and David married Abigail (1 Sam. 25:38-43). Abigail followed David during his stay in Philistia in the service of Achish (1 Sam. 27:3) and afterwards at Hebron where David was made king of Judah (2 Sam. 2:2). Their son Chileab was born at Hebron (2 Sam. 3:3) and is apparently identical with the Daniel mentioned in 1 Chronicles 3:1.

2. A sister of King David (1 Chron. 2:16; 2 Sam. 17:25), wife of Ithra (1 Chron. 2:16, 17) and mother of Amasa, to whom David committed the generalship of his army in place of Joab (2 Sam. 19:13).

Abihail (ab′-a-hail), 1. The father of Esther (Esth. 2:15; 9:29). 2. The name of several persons in the Old Testament (Num. 3:35; 1 Chron. 2:29; 5:14; 2 Chron. 11:18).

Abihu (a-by′-hue), Son of Aaron and Elisheba (Ex. 6:23; 1 Chron. 6:3). With his brother Nadab and seventy elders of Israel he accompanied Moses and Aaron on Mount Sinai when he went to meet the Lord (Ex. 24:1, 9). He was consecrated priest with the other sons of Aaron: Nadab, Ithamar and Eleazar (Ex. 28:1; Num. 3:2-3). Abihu and Nadab, according to Lev. 10:1-3, committed irregularities while offering incense before the Lord and for this were punished by being burned alive by the fire that emerged from the presence of the Lord (*see also* Num. 3:4; 26:61). As they had no children, the priestly line of Aaron was continued only through the families of Ithamar and Eleazar.

Abijah, 1. The second son of the prophet Samuel, who was named by his father to be judge in Israel together with his older brother Joel (1 Sam. 8:1-2). The injustices committed by the two brothers in the exercise of their office provoked the indignation of the people, who brought their complaints to Samuel and demanded that he select a king to rule over them instead of judges (1 Sam. 8:4-5).

2. According to 1 Chronicles 24:3-19 David divided the priestly families into 24 classes who took turns in the temple service. The eighth class had the name of Abijah (v.10), and to it belonged Zechariah, father of John the Baptist (Lk. 1:5).

3. King of Judah (c. 915-913 B.C.) son and successor to Rehoboam. His mother's name was Maachah, daughter of Abishalom (1 Kgs. 15:1). The author of 1 Kgs. 15:1-8, who always calls him Abijam, gives a negative judgment on his reign from the religious point of view, but otherwise gives no information on his kingship. 2 Chron. 13:3-19 however tells us that he was in battle against Jeroboam king of Israel on Mount Zemaraim in the highlands of Ephraim. Abijah defeated Jeroboam and conquered several towns which he annexed to his kingdom, such as Bethel, Jeshanah and Ephron. According to 2 Chron. 13:21 Abijah had 14 wives from whom he had 22 sons and 16 daughters.

4. Son of Jeroboam I, king of Israel (931-910/9). While still very young he fell gravely ill, so Jeroboam sent his wife, in disguise so that she could not be recognized, to the prophet Ahijah of Shiloh, who had predicted Jeroboam's accession to the throne of Israel. The queen pleaded for the life of the child. Ahijah had been warned beforehand by God and thus recognized the king's wife. He announced that the Lord, in punishment for the apostasy of Jeroboam, had decreed the child's death, and indeed the expiration of the whole house. As predicted, Abijah died the moment his mother crossed the threshold of her house when she returned from her visit to Ahijah (1 Kgs. 14:1-18).

5. Daughter of Zechariah, mother of King Hezekiah of Judah (2 Kgs. 18:2; 2 Chron. 29:1). Her name was shortened to Abia or Abi.

Abilene (ab-a-lee′-ne), A mountain region north of Mt. Hermon and west of Damascus. In the first century, at the time of Christ, it was a tetrarchy governed by Lysanias, according to Luke 3:1. After the death of Herod I the Great (4 B.C.) Abilene was incorporated into the Roman province of Syria under the rule of a tetrarch. Later during the reign of Herod Agrippa (37-44 A.D.) it was incorporated into Palestine. The principal city of the region is Abila, where an inscription has been found which confirms the information given by Luke.

Abimelech (a-bim′-e-lek), 1. A Canaanite king of Gerar in S. Palestine. According to Gen. 20:1-18 Abimelech took into his harem Sarah, the wife of Abraham, whom Abraham had passed off as his sister. He was however warned in a dream and restored Sarah to Abraham. A variant of this story, which this time takes place between Abimelech and Isaac, is found in Gen. 26:1-16. Abimelech and his general Phicol had disagreements with Abraham (Gen. 21:23-32) and Isaac (Gen. 26:26-33) over the possession and use of water-sources in Beersheba, but in both cases the problems were resolved peacefully through agreements.

2. The son of Gideon and of one of his Canaanite concubines from the city of Shechem (Jgs. 8:31). Although Shechem was a Canaanite city, it was under Gideon's domination. With the encouragement and financial help of the citizens of Shechem, Abimelech killed off his 70 brothers, save Jotham, so that his reign might be undisputed (Jgs. 9:1-5). He was then made king by the people of Shechem, but Jotham, when he heard of it, managed to turn the Shechemites against him (Jgs. 9:7-21). The people gathered under Gaal son of Ebed against Zebul, who was in charge of the city by order of Abimelech. When Abimelech got news of the revolt, he lay in wait and ambushed the people, broke into the city, destroyed it and sowed it with salt (Jgs. 9:26-45). He also burned down the temple of El-berith where the survivors had taken refuge (Jgs. 9:46-49). Soon afterwards, during the assault on the city of Thebez, Abimelech was crushed by a millstone thrown at him by a woman, and he died (Jgs. 9:50-55). After the death of Uriah in battle, Joab recorded the tragic end of the reign of Abimelech in his message to David (2 Sam. 11:22).

Abinadab (a-bin′-a-dab), 1. The ark of the covenant, after it had been recovered from the Philistines into whose hands it had fallen (1 Sam. 4-6), remained in the house of Abinadab in the district of Kiriath-jearim for twenty years (7:1-2). Eleazar, Abinadab's son, was deputed by the local people to take care of the ark. David came to Abinadab's house to take the ark to Jerusalem, but during the journey Uzzah, another son of Abinadab, who was guiding the cart on which the ark was being transported, steadied it with his hand. The anger of God, the story goes, blazed up against Uzzah for showing such irreverence to the ark, and he was struck dead on the spot. The transferral of the ark was interrupted and it

5

remained for three months in the house of Obed-Edom, from where finally it was brought to Jerusalem (2 Sam. 6:1-19).

2. One of David's brothers, a son of Jesse, who served with two other brothers in Saul's army (1 Sam. 16:8; 17:13).

Abinoam (a-bin′-o-am), A son of Saul (1 Sam. 31:2), father of Barak, who with the prophetess Deborah, overcame the Canaanite king Sisera (Jgs. 4-5).

Abiram (a-by′-ram), 1. The son of Eliab, of the tribe of Reuben, who with his brother Dathan gave strong support to Korah in his rebellion against Moses and Aaron. The rebels were swallowed up in a fissure that opened in the earth (Num. 16; Ps. 106:17).

2. The first-born son of Hiel, who lived in the time of Ahab, king of Israel (874-853 B.C.). Hiel set about reconstructing Jericho, and the first book of Kings 16:34 says: "He lost his first-born son, Abiram, when he laid the foundation, and his youngest son, Segub, when he set up the gates, as the Lord had foretold through Joshua, son of Nun." 1 Kings 16:34 attributes their death to the curse pronounced by Joshua after the conquest of the city (Josh. 6:26).

Abishag (ab′-i-shag), The name of the young woman from the town of Shunem, who nursed the aged David and kept him warm (1 Kgs. 1:1-4). Adonijah, Solomon's rival for the succession to the throne of David, wanted to marry her, but Solomon felt an implied threat to his succession or to his prerogatives, which included possession of his father's harem. So Solomon took this occasion to rid himself of a possibly dangerous rival, and had Adonijah slain (1 Kgs. 2:13-25).

Abishai (a-by′-shy), first-born son of Zeruiah, the sister of David, brother of Joab and Asahel (1 Chron. 2:16). He occupies an important place in the military history of the kingdom of David, and remained loyal to the king even when the latter was in serious trouble. Abishai accompanied David in the daring nocturnal raid on Saul's camp, which could have made Saul a prisoner in David's hands. David however spared him and forbade Abishai to harm the king (1 Sam. 26:1-12). He took part in the battle of Gibeon, together with Joab and Asahel, against the supporters of Saul's son (2 Sam. 2:18). In this battle Asahel died at the hands of Abner (2 Sam. 2:19-23). Abishai and Joab avenged Asahel's death by treacherously killing Abner (2 Sam. 3:23-30) against the will of David (2 Sam. 3:31-39). Next in command to Joab, Abishai was in charge of David's army, and took part in the principal military expeditions of his reign: against Ammon (2 Sam. 10:9-14), against the Philistines (2 Sam. 21:15-17) and against Edom (1 Chron. 18:12-13). He took David's side in the internal troubles of the kingdom: he was with him on his flight from Jerusalem during the rebellion of Absalom (2 Sam. 16:5-14), and with Joab and Ittai he defeated the rebels in the battle of Mahanaim (2 Sam. 18). Wth Joab he was entrusted by David with putting an end to the rebellion of Sheba (2 Sam. 20). A man of uncommon talents, he was chief of the so-called group of Thirty, "David's warriors" about whom were recounted prodigious feats of strength and courage (2 Sam. 23:18-19; 1 Chron. 11:20-21). Nothing is known of his death.

Abital (a-by′-tal), A wife of King David and mother of his son Shephatiah (2 Sam. 3:4; 1 Chron. 3:3).

Abiud (a-by′-ud), Son of Zerubbabel; an ancestor of Jesus in Matthew 1:13.

Abner, Son of Ner, and therefore cousin of King Saul and head of his army (1 Sam. 14:50-51). There is little information on his activities during the lifetime of Saul (a war against the Philistines in 1 Sam. 17:55-57; a campaign against David in 1 Sam. 26:5), even though he was a person of rank and influence in the king's court (1 Sam. 20:25). After Saul's death, Abner took with him Ishbaal, Saul's only son still alive, led him to Mahanaim, a town east of the Jordan, and proclaimed him king of Israel (2 Sam. 2:8-10). Abner was in command of the army of Ishbaal against David and took part in the battle of Gibeon, in which he killed Asahel, brother of Joab, head of David's army (2 Sam. 2:12-32). Abner was offended by the reproof of Ishbaal for having consorted with one of Saul's concubines, and so decided to support David in bringing all Israel under his control (2 Sam. 3:7-11). He began treating with David (2 Sam. 3:12-16) and made great efforts to convince the Israelites and especially the tribe of Benjamin to which Saul's family belonged, of the necessity of submitting to David and uniting all Israel (2 Sam. 3:17-19). He was finally received by David to whom he revealed his intentions and the steps he had taken in this direction (2 Sam. 3:20-21). When Joab heard that David had received Abner peacefully, he decided to kill him, because he feared him as a rival, and also because he wished to avenge (*see* AVENGER) the death of his brother, Asahel. With the assistance of another brother Abishai, Joab treacherously murdered Abner in Hebron (2 Sam. 3:23-27), a deed that David bitterly deplored (2 Sam. 3:28-29). David composed an elegy on the death of Abner (2 Sam. 3:33-34).

abominable

by observing the *a.* customs	they do *a.* deeds Ps. 14:1, Ps. 53:1
Lev. 18:30	made of them their *a.* images
You shall not eat any *a.* thing	Ezek. 7:20
Deut. 14:3	

abomination

for it is an *a.* to the Lord	sacrifice of the wicked is an *a.*
Deut. 7:25	Prov. 21:27
Everyone who is dishonest is an *a.*	shall be the horrible *a.* Dan. 9:27
Deut. 25:16	setting up the horrible *a.*
the perverse man is an *a.*	Dan. 11:31
Prov. 3:32	the horrible *a.* is set up
seven things are an *a.* to him	Dan. 12:11
Prov. 6:16	

Abraham, Terah's son, the fist and greatest of the patriarchs of Israel and "father of a multitude of nations" (Gen. 17:4). The clan of Terah stemmed from Ur in Mesopotamia (Gen. 11:28). Terah took with him his son Abram and Abram's wife Sarah, together with his grandson Lot when he crossed over to Haran in northern Mesopotamia (Gen. 11:31). In Haran Abraham received the command from God to abandon his homeland and the house of his father and to set out towards the land of Canaan. He also received the promise that he would become for all nations of the earth a source of blessing (Gen. 12:1-3). God's initiative and Abraham's response form the theme of the patriarchal history of Genesis. On God's part the accounts portray the riches of promise and consequent fulfilment, while Abraham's faith and trusting self-surrender are exalted (Gen. cc. 12-25). Abraham set out on his journey, crossed Palestine to the desert in the south, stopping off at Shechem where God appeared to him to renew his promises, and at Bethel where he erected an altar and called upon the name of God (Gen. 12:8). The most ancient version of the promises can be read in Genesis 15. The first oracle promises progeny as numerous as the stars of the sky, and the author underlines Abraham's faith in a text which was to become a favorite Pauline quotation (Rom. 4 and Gal. 3), for he read into it the first revelation of the principle of salvation through faith and not through our own efforts. The second oracle preserved there is concerned with the future possession of the promised land of Canaan, of which the beneficiaries would be the descendants of Abraham (Gen. 15:7-21). On this occasion God formalized his covenant with Abraham, using the rites with which pacts or treaties were concluded among the peoples of that time (Jer. 34:8 ff.) so as to give Abraham a tangible guarantee of the truth of the promises and the fidelity of God in fulfilling them. The priestly account of these facts, which is of more recent date, contains some new elements (Gen. 17): God changed the name of Abram into Abraham "for I am making you the father of a host of nations" (Gen. 17:5). In reality both names mean the same thing: "exalted is my father (God)," and are in fact dialect forms of the same word. This is then a popular etymology, through which the compiler-narrator wished to emphasize the glorious destiny to which God had called Abraham.

As a further clause and at the same time a tangible sign of the alliance with God, He gave Abraham the law of circumcision. For future generations this will become the sign of their belonging to Abraham and therefore of their having a share in the goods promised to him (Gen. 17:9-14).

The traditions gathered in chapters 16, 18, 21, and 22 deal with the birth of the son of promise. As Sarah was sterile, Abraham, at his wife's suggestion, took her slave Hagar to have a son by her, who would then pass juridically for the son of Abraham and Sarah (Gen. 16:1-4). This custom was sanctioned by the laws of the time and is attested to in the traditions concerning Jacob (Gen. 30). It is contained, for example, in the laws found in the city of Nuzi, which date from the first half of the second millenium before Christ, and regulated the lives of the people of northern Mesopotamia, from which the clan of Abraham stemmed. The son of this union was Ishmael (Gen. 16:11), but he did not become the heir to the promises, as Sarah herself had a son, Isaac, whose birth was predicted in Gen. 18:10-15; 21:1-7. To put an end to the rivalries between Isaac and Ishmael, Abraham again acceded to Sarah's wish and dismissed Hagar who departed with her son Ishmael. He too was to have a glorious future because he was Abraham's son, but was not to become heir to the promises.

In the traditions preserved about Abraham there is also the cycle which treats of the destruction of Sodom and the other cities of the Pentapolis ("five cities") of the Dead Sea area. These traditions really refer to Lot, Abraham's grandson, from whom he had separated to put an end to the rivalries that had arisen between their respective shepherds (Gen. 13:5-13). Sarah died at Hebron and was buried in the cave of Machpelah, which had been bought for this purpose by Abraham from a Hittite living in the place (Gen. 25:1-20). Afterwards Abraham took another wife named Keturah, from whom he had several sons (Gen. 25:1-4). Abraham died at Hebron and was buried with Sarah in the cave of Machpelah (Gen. 25:5-11).

The promises made to Abraham are the beginning of the story of salvation, and the development of this history is no more than the unfolding of the promises (Pss. 105, 106). The covenant of Sinai is based on the liberation of the people from Egypt which constituted them into God's people. The Sinai covenant recalled the pact with Abraham (Ex. 6:1-8). As St. Paul contemplated the whole history of salvation in the light of the promises fulfilled in Christ, he concluded that what was pledged to Abraham was the salvation brought about by Christ, who was the heir and son of Abraham (Gal. 3:15-18). All who believe, as did Abraham, become heirs to the fulfilment of the promises in Christ (Gal. 3:28-29). On the other hand, in Paul's view, there is no other way to salvation except that inaugurated by Abraham. In contrast to the Jews who rejected the gift who was Christ, and who thought they could stand before God justified on their own works alone, Paul opposed the faith of Abraham by which he surrendered himself to the saving action of God in trust and self-opening, and so was able to dare all things, not for a salary as recompense to his works, but in the sure hope of the free gift of grace. Thus the faithful, who make Abraham's sentiments and attitudes their own in their relationship with God, become Abraham's true children and the real heirs to the promises made to him (Rom. 4).

Abraham's Bosom, According to first century Jewish eschatology, the bosom of Abraham was the place where the just were gathered after death, while between them and the condemned stretched a deep abyss. The expression, which can only be found in Luke 16:22-23, could have been suggested by the common theme of the celestial banquet, which was the usual way of describing the lot of the just after death. According to the customs of the time, the guest of honor at table was given a place beside the host, where he reclined so that by leaning back he could rest his head on his host's breast, as one can read in John 13:25.

Abram, When God made a covenant with Abram (Gen. 17:1-19), he changed his name to Abraham, to show him that he wished to make him "the father of a host of nations" (Gen. 17:5). In reality, both forms of the name mean the same thing: "the exalted is my father (God)." Both forms are dialectal. Gen. 17:5 is therefore a popular etymology, used by the writer to express in an understandable way and with pastoral effect the glorious destiny to which God was calling Abraham.

abroad

he scattered them all over the earth	water sources be dispersed *a*
Gen. 11:9	Prov. 5:16

Abronah (a-bro′-nah), A stopping-place of the Israelites en route to Canaan under Moses (Num. 33:34, 35), north of Ezion-geber.

Absalom, Son of David and Maacah, the daughter of Talmai, king of Geshur (2 Sam. 3:3). Absalom killed his half-brother Amnon in revenge for the violation of his full sister Tamar, and then fled to Geshur where he remained for three years (2 Sam. 13). At Joab's pleading, David forgave him and so he returned from exile (2 Sam. 14). He was then called back to court but not admitted to the presence of the king (2 Sam. 14:28) for two years, and then again, only after Joab had interceded for him (2 Sam. 14:33). He nurtured ambitions to supplant his father David, and so he plotted against him by seeking to draw the people to himself and speaking evil of David (2 Sam. 15:1-6). Eventually David had to flee Jerusalem, taking with him his personal guard and his most intimate collaborators (2 Sam. 15:13-37). Absalom insulted him further by publicly taking possession of his harem (2 Sam. 16:20-23). Finally Absalom decided to cross the Jordan with an army and deal a decisive blow to David. David however had information from Hushai, Absalom's counsellor who was loyal to David, and so had the opportunity to prepare himself to do battle (2 Sam. 17). The definitive battle took place in the forest of Ephraim (2 Sam. 18:6) and Absalom was defeated. Absalom, pursued by his father's forces, was caught by his hair on the branches of an oak tree, and contrary to David's orders (2 Sam. 18:5) was slain by Joab (2 Sam. 18:9-18). On hearing of Absalom's death, David wept (2 Sam. 19:1-9).

Abubus (a-boo′-bus), The father of Ptolemy, who murdered Simon the Maccabee (1 Mac. 16:16).

abundance
with joy and gratitude for *a.*   an *a.* of lasting peace   Jer. 33:6
                    Deut. 28:47

abundant
and from their *a.* yield of milk   with delight at her *a.* breasts
                    Isa. 7:22   Isa. 66:11

Accad, A city of the plain of Shinar, which with Babel, Erech and Calneh
belonged to the kingdom of Nimrod (Gen. 10:10). It was the capital of the
kingdom of Sargon I and retained this preeminence throughout the duration of this dynasty (c. 2350-2150 B.C.). The city, whose site on the Euphrates River is unknown, gave its name to the region, which lay north of
Sumer.

acceptable
they will be *a.* offerings on my altar   and acts uprightly is *a.* to him
                    Isa. 60:7   Acts 10:35
                    In an *a.* time I have heard you   2 Cor. 6:2

acceptance
to find *a.*, it must be   Lev. 22:21

Acco, A port city on the coast of Palestine, eight miles north of Mt. Carmel, in the bay of the same name. It is mentioned in Judges 1:31-32 as
part of the territory of Asher. Under the name of Ptolemais (from Ptolemy
II Philadelphus 283-246 B.C., king of Egypt) it occurs sometimes in the
history of the Maccabees as one of the cities allied against them (1 Mac.
5:15), and there also were held various meetings between Jonathan Maccabeus and the Syrian authorities (1 Mac. 10:51-56; 11:21-24). The last of
these meetings culminated in the imprisonment of the Jewish chieftain.
Paul came to Ptolemais during his third missionary journey (Acts 21:7).
In the middle ages it was known as Acre, and today its name is Akka.

accuse
Let not the king *a.* his servant   the one to *a.* you is Moses
                    1 Sam. 22:15   Jn. 5:45

Achaia (a-kay′-a), A region in Greece to the south of the gulf of Corinth.
It was conquered by the Romans in 146 B.C. and made a senatorial province in 27 B.C. under the government of a proconsul, which office, at the
time of Paul, was being filled by Gallio, brother of Seneca (Acts 18:12). It
was visited by Paul in the second (Acts 17:15; 18:18) and third apostolic
journeys (Acts 19:21).

Achaicus (a-kay′-a-cus), A Christian of Corinth (1 Cor. 16:17).

Achan (ay′-kan), Son of Carmi of the tribe of Judah (Josh. 7:1) who violated Joshua's prohibition and took silver, gold and a scarlet cloak as
spoils from Jericho, which had been given up to anathema, or total destruction. When in consequence the Israelites were thrown back in the
first attack against Ai, Joshua led Achan and all the people belonging to
him to the Vale of Achor, where they were stoned to death (Josh. 7).

Achbor, An official of king Josiah sent to consult the prophetess Huldah
concerning the Book of the Law found in the Temple (2 Kgs. 22:12, 14).

Achior (ay′-ki-or), The "leader of all the Ammonites," according to
Judith 5:5, who tried to dissuade the Assyrian Holofernes from marching
against Israel by recounting God's works in their favor (Judith 5:5-21).
After Holofernes' death at the hands of Judith, Achior believed in the
God of Israel, had himself circumcised and united with the people of Is-
rael (Judith 14:10).

Achish (ay′-kish), Philistine king of the city of Gath, with whom David took refuge while fleeing from Saul, and whom he served as a vassal for a time (1 Sam. 27). Achish gave David the city of Ziklag as a residence (1 Sam. 27:6). David made frequent raids on the non-Israelite tribes in the south of Palestine, sparing neither man nor woman and taking all the spoils he could find. Achish became convinced that David was hated by his own people and would become his ever-loyal subject (1 Sam. 27:8-12). However, when the Philistines were preparing to enter into combat with Saul on the mountains of Gelboe, David was excluded, for the other Philistine confederates still looked on him with suspicion (1 Sam. 29:1-10). There is a second account of the relationship between David and Achish in 1 Sam. 21:11-16.

Achor (ay′-kor), The name of the valley southwest of Jericho where Achan was stoned for having taken spoils from Jericho which were destined to anathema, or total destruction (Josh. 7:24-26). It formed one of the northern boundaries of the territory of the tribe of Judah (Josh. 15:7).

Achsah (ak′-sah), Caleb's daughter given in marriage to Othniel as a prize for the conquest of the city of Kiriath-sephir (Debir) at the time of the conquest of Palestine by the Israelites (Jgs. 1:12-15; Josh. 15:16-19).

Achshaph (ak′-shaf), A Canaanite city which entered into the alliance formed by Jabin king of Hazor against Joshua and the Israelites (Josh. 11:1-5). Joshua defeated the alliance in the battle near the waters of Merom (Josh. 11:6-9). Achshaph was situated in the territory of Asher, in northern Palestine (Josh. 19:25).

Achzib, A place name: a city of Judah (Josh. 15:44); a village in Galilee (Josh. 19:29; Jgs. 1:31).

acknowledge

his brothers he would not *a*.	you who are near, *a*. my might
Deut. 33:9	Isa. 33:13
a. that your own right hand	All who see them shall *a*. them
Job 40:14	Isa. 61:9
before men I will *a*.	Mt. 10:32

Acrostic, A short literary composition so constructed that the first letters of each line read into a word when taken together, or so that each line begins with a letter of the alphabet in order. This is a very antique literary device, found not only in Greek and Roman times but also in the Bible, for example Pss. 9-10; 25; 34; 37; 111; 112; 119; 145; Lam. 1-4; Prov. 31:10-31; Nah. 1:2-8.

Acts of the Apostles, The fifth historical book of the New Testament. St. Luke, its author, intended it to be a continuation of his gospel (Lk. 1:1-4 and Acts 1:1-2). The theme of the book is given in Jesus' command to the Apostles recorded in Acts 1:8: "You will receive power when the Holy Spirit comes down on you; then you are to be my witnesses in Jerusalem, throughout Judea and Samaria, yes, even to the ends of the earth." Thus the book narrates the ascension of Jesus Christ (1:9-11) and leads on to the outpouring of the Holy Spirit at Pentecost (1:12-14) and the fruit of this outpouring in the great missionary activity of the Church which, starting in Jerusalem arrived at Rome, the capital of the empire. In the first part of the book Peter is the principal actor, and the stage is the first Jewish-Christian community. The twelve are there around him with John receiving special mention (chapter 1-9). The second part of the book describes the mission to the Gentiles, and is centered on Paul, whose conversion is described on three different occasions (9:1-31; 22:5-16; 26:10-18), even though the first steps towards the mission among the non-Jews were taken by Peter who was commanded by God to baptize the centurion Cornelius (9:32-11:18). The center of the mission among the Gentiles was Antioch, where the church was founded by the Christians who fled Palestine because of the persecution of the Jews (11:19-30) in which Stephen had lost his life (6:8-8:3). Paul was called by Barnabas from Tarsus to Antioch where they organized the first missionary journey (13:1-14:28). On their return they found the Church in an uproar as the Jewish Christians wished to have the converted Gentiles undergo the rite of circumcision. Paul and Barnabas went up to Jerusalem to examine the question with the Apostles (c. 15). Paul's second missionary journey brought him as far as Greece (Athens and Corinth) and again concluded in Antioch (15:36-18:22). The third missionary journey (18:23-20:4) was interrupted at Jerusalem (20:5-21:14) where Paul had gone with the gifts of the Gentiles for the poor of the churches of Palestine. He was accused and brought to trial by the Jews but he appealed as a Roman citizen to Caesar, and so was brought to Rome (21:15-28:31). The book concludes unexpectedly with the account of Paul's imprisonment in Rome. In reality, however, in the humble and hidden form of the words of the prisoner in the last verses of the book (28:30-31) can be seen the fulfilment of Christ's command and commission given at the beginning in 1:8.

Unanimous tradition from the second century on attributes the book of Acts to St. Luke, Paul's companion. This seems to be confirmed by internal evidence, especially in those parts where the author recounts episodes in Paul's journeys where the first person is used, indicating that Luke himself was part of the adventure (16:10-17; 20:5-16; 21:1-18; 27:1-28:16). The date of composition is difficult to establish as we have no information other than that supplied by the book itself. It was certainly written after Mark and Luke. On account of the seemingly sudden interruption of the work at the end, some think that it was written after the first imprisonment of Paul in Rome (62-64 A.D, *see* PAUL), but perhaps the interruption is not so abrupt as it seems to some today, and may indeed have been intended this way by the author. Scholars place the composition date between 70 and 90 A.D.

Because of its emphasis on the Spirit, the book is often called the Gospel of the Spirit and Luke's Gospel, therefore, the Gospel of the Son.

Adadah (ad'-a-dah), A town in the extreme southern territory of Judah (Josh. 15:22).

Adah (ay'-dah), 1. One of the two wives of Lamech (Gen. 4:19, 20).

2. Wife of Esau (Gen. 36:2, 4, 10, 12, 16).

Adaiah (a-day'-yah), (1) Grandfather of Josiah (2 Kgs. 22:1); (2) A son of Ethan (1 Chron. 6:26); (3) The name of several other men in the Old Testament (1 Chron 8:21; 9:12; 2 Chron. 23:1; Ezra 10:29, 39; Neh. 11:5.)

Adalia (a-day'-li-a), A son of Haman the vizier of king Ahasuerus (Esth. 9:8). *See* HAMAN.

Adam, The name of the first man (Gen. 2:25). *See* MAN.

Adam, A city on the east bank of the Jordan. When the Israelites with Joshua set out to pass over the Jordan, the waters coming downstream stood and rose up in a solid mass far off at Adam, while those flowing down to the Dead Sea were wholly cut off (Josh. 3:16).

Adar (ay'-dar), The twelfth month of the Hebrew calendar, corresponding to February-March.

Adasa (ad'-a-sa), A town between Jerusalem and Beth-horon where Judas Maccabeus defeated the Seleucid army commanded by Nicanor (1 Mac. 7:40-45).

Adbeel, The third of twelve sons of Ishmael and chieftain of a clan (Gen. 25:13).

Addi, An ancestor of Jesus in Luke 3:28.

adjure
How many times must I *a*.   I *a*. you by the Jesus whom
         1 Kgs. 22:16   Acts 19:13

Admah, A city of the Pentapolis which took part in the alliance against the kings of the East (Gen. 14) and was destroyed together with Sodom and Gomorrah (Deut. 29:23; Hos. 11:8).

Admatha, An official in the court of king Ahasuerus (Esth. 1:14).

admonish
and I will *a*. you   Ps. 81:9   exhort you to *a*. the unruly
Lord and *a*. you   1 Thess. 5:12   1 Thess. 5:14

Adonai (a-doe'-ny), *See* GOD; LORD.

Adoni-Bezek (a-doe'-ny-beez'-ek), A Canaanite king of Bezek, defeated by the tribe of Judah. He managed to escape but was overtaken and his thumbs and big toes cut off, as he had already done to seventy kings. He was taken to Jerusalem where he died (Jgs. 1:5-7).

Adonijah, Son of David and of Haggith, born at Hebron (2 Sam. 3:4), a rival of Solomon in the struggle for succession which disturbed the last days of David's life. He was supported by Joab and Abiathar, but Solomon prevailed with the help of Nathan and Zadok (1 Kgs. 1:5-31). On hearing the news of Solomon's consecration, he took refuge in the sanctuary, and Solomon spared his life (1 Kgs. 1:41-53). After the death of David, Adonijah used the good graces of Bathsheba, Solomon's mother, to ask for the hand of Abishag, the young Shunamite girl who had comforted David in his old age. Solomon interpreted this request as an invasion of his rights of succession and inheritance, and a sign of Adonijah's continuing ambitions for the throne, so he ordered his death (1 Kgs. 2:13-25) and had Abiathar his supporter sent into exile.

Adoniram, Son of Abda, an official of David and Solomon, entrusted with the supervision of the forced labor needed to work on Solomon's vast building projects (2 Sam. 20:24 where he is called Adoram; 1 Kgs. 4:6; 5:13, 14). When the northern tribes rebelled, Rehoboam sent Adoniram, his task-master, to regain control, but he was stoned to death by them. This rebellion lead to the definitive break between Israel and Judah (1 Kgs. 12:18; 2 Chron. 10:18).

Adoni-Zedek (a-doe'-ny-zee'-dek), A Canaanite king of Jerusalem who formed part of an alliance of five kings of the region who opposed Joshua after the defection of the city of Gibeon, which allied itself with the Israelites (Josh. 10:1).

adorn
so as to *a*. in every way   Tit. 2:10

adornment
their *a*. should be good deeds
            1 Tim. 2:10

Adrammelech (a-dram'-a-lek), 1. The name of a god (probably identicawith Hadad) adored by the people of Sepharvaim, who were settled by the Assyrians in Samaria after the conquest of the city in 722 B.C. (2 Kgs. 17:31).

2. Son of Sennacherib. In the year 681 B.C. he killed his father while the latter was praying in the temple of Nisroch (2 Kgs 19:37).

Adramyttium (ad-ra-mit′-i-um), A seaport on the NW shore of Asia Minor, modern Edremit. Paul embarked in a ship of Adramyttium to reach Myra when he was taken captive to Rome (Acts 27:2).

Adriel (ay′-dri-el), The husband of Merab, Saul's elder daughter. Merab was first promised to David (1 Sam. 18:17-19).

Adullam, A town southwest of Jerusalem in the territory of Judah (Josh. 15:35) conquered by Joshua (Josh. 12:15). David dwelt in a cave in Adullam during the hostilities with Saul (1 Sam. 22:1-2) and during some campaigns against the Philistines (2 Sam. 23:13). Adullam was fortified by Rehoboam before the invasion by Pharaoh Shishak (2 Chron. 11:7). It was among the towns reconstructed after the return from exile (Neh. 11:30).

Adultery, Adultery consists in a sexual relationship between a married and an unmarried person or between married persons not married to each other. In the Bible it was a violation of the husband's rights over his wife. Adultery arose when a relationship was had with a girl affianced to another (Deut. 22:23), but if she were a slave, the offense did not merit death by execution (Lev. 19:20). The law demanded death by stoning for both parties (Ezek. 16:40; John 8:3). The Decalogue forbade adultery, even desire for it (Ex. 20:14, 17; Deut. 5:18, 21).

The New Testament reiterated the condemnation (Matt. 5:27-28; 19:18; Mark 10:19; Luke 18:20). Jesus however showed clemency to the woman taken in adultery in John 8:1 ff. On the disputed meaning of the clause in Matt. 5:32; 19:9, *see* DIVORCE.

Israel's disloyalty to the Lord is called adultery by Jer. 2:20 ff., 3:8; Ezek. 16:1 ff.; Hos. 2:4, etc., while the intimate and faithful union of Christ with his Church is described by Paul in terms of a holy marriage (Eph. 5:25).

Adummim, "The ascent of Adummim," a pass in the road from Jerusalem to Jericho (Josh. 15:7; 18:17).

advantage

what *a.* have I more than	Job 35:3	and man has no *a.*	Eccl. 3:19
	What is the *a.*, then,	Rom. 3:1	

Aeneas, The name of the paralytic whom Peter cured in Lydda (Acts 9:33-35).

Aenon (ee′-non), A locality on the west bank of the Jordan, near Salim and south of Scythopolis, rich in water resources, where John the Baptist baptized (Jn. 3:23).

Aesora (i-sor′-a), A variant name of the city of Hazor (Judith 4:4) *See* HAZOR.

affliction

the *a.* of my people	Ex. 3:7	the bonds of *a.*	Job 36:8
the bread of *a.*	Deut. 16:3	the furnace of *a.*	Isa. 48:10

afraid

but I was *a.*	Gen. 3:10	for he was *a.* to look	Ex. 3:6
ʹher Moses became *a.*	Ex 2:14	they were very much *a.*	Lk. 2:9

Agabus (ag'-a-bus), A Jewish-Christian prophet of Jerusalem who, while at Antioch, predicted a great famine. This prediction proved true during Claudius' reign (49 A.D., Acts 11:28). Later he predicted to Paul his imminent imprisonment at Jerusalem by taking Paul's girdle and binding his own feet and hands with it (Acts 21:10-11).

Agag (ay'-gag), King of Amalek, defeated by Saul, who however spared his life, despite the command of Samuel to destroy everything and everybody. When Samuel reproved Saul, the prophet himself slew Agag (1 Sam. 15:8-33; *see* Esth. 3:1, 10; 9:24).

Agape (a-gah'-pay), 1. A Greek word for charity. *See* LOVE.

2. A name given in Jude 12 to the brotherly feasts of the early Christians.

age

at a contented old *a.*	Gen. 15:15	he was about thirty years of *a.*	
either in this *a.*	Matt. 12:32		Lk. 3:23
a son in her old *a.*	Lk. 1:36	He is of *a.*—ask him	Jn. 9:23

aghast
They look *a.* at each other
  Isa. 13:8

Agora (ag'-o-ra), The town square, center of town life in Grecian times, the place of assembly, meetings and market (Acts 16:19; 17:17; Mt. 11:16; 20:3; Mk. 6:56).

Agrapha, Words attributed to Jesus but not recorded in the Gospels. The only one that has scriptural authority is contained in Acts 20:35. Some appear as variants in biblical manuscripts and others are recorded in the works of the early Church Fathers and in the apocryphal Gospels. Genuine agrapha are very rare and it is very hard to determine whether those transmitted in the aprocrypha are genuine.

Agrippa, The Agrippa of Acts 25:13-26:32 was Agrippa II, great-grandson of Herod the Great, and son of Herod Agrippa I. *See* HEROD.

Agur (ay'-gur), Son of Jakeh and author of a small collection of proverbs that are contained in Prov. 30:1-33.

Ahab, King of Israel (869-850 B.C.), son and successor of Omri. He was a most able politician and governor, who kept the dynasty intact and forged realistic relationships with the neighboring kingdoms. The sources are not entirely clear, nor is history's judgment univocal on Ahab's reign. He suffered the invasion of his territories by Ben-hadad king of Syria who laid siege to Samaria, but Ahab by an astute military maneuver managed to defeat him (1 Kgs. 20:1-21). After a year Ben-hadad made another attempt with the same result: he was defeated at Aphek, and was forced to restore the cities taken during the reign of Omri, and enter into commercial contracts favoring the Israelites (1 Kgs. 20:26-34). Less evident, but nonetheless important was Ahab's part in the coalition between Damascus, Israel and Harmath which in the year 854 B.C. went into battle against Shalmaneser III at Karkar. Ahab's contribution was 2,000 chariots and 10,000 foot soldiers. The outcome of the battle was uncertain, and Shalmaneser was only temporarily stopped. Relationships with the kingdom of Judah improved during this period. Jehoshaphat of Judah (871-848) was an ally of Ahab against the Syrians, and this alliance was sealed by the marriage of Athaliah, daughter of Ahab, to Jehoram, son of Jehoshaphat (2 Kgs. 8:18). These political and military successes are somewhat obscured in the biblical account of his reign, as the author of 1 Kings is above all interested in the developments from the religious point of view. And in this light the reign of Ahab received a negative judgment, for Ahab married Jezebel, the daughter of Ethbaal, king of Tyre (1 Kgs. 16:31). This politically advantageous alliance brought with it official approval for the cult of Baal and Astarte, which was zealously advanced by the queen. The prophet Elijah was the champion of Yahwistic faith against the Canaanite cult (1 Kgs. 17:1-22, 38) and consequently suffered much from the persecutions of Jezebel (19:1-18). He remained constant however in the defense of the traditions of Israel (1 Kgs. 18), and continued to denounce the excesses of Ahab and his unrestrained ambition (1 Kgs. 21). Ahab died from the wounds received in the war against the Syrians in the conquest of Ramoth-gilead (1 Kgs. 22:29-39).

Ahasuerus (a-hazh′-oo-er′-us), King of Persia (485-465 B.C.), son and successor of Darius I, better known as Xerxes which is the form of the name adopted in the Greek sources. He repudiated his wife Vashti and took for himself the young Jewess Esther, according to the account given in the biblical book of Esther.

Ahava (a-hay′-va), A town in Babylonia and a settlement of exiled Jews (Ezra 8:15, 21, 31).

Ahaz, King of Judah (735-715 B.C.), son and successor of Jotham. He refused to share in an alliance with Rezin king of Syria and Pekah king of Israel against Tiglath-pileser III (2 Kgs. 16:1-6). To force him to join, Rezin and Pekah invaded the kingdom of Judah and attacked Jerusalem but failed to take it. Isaiah counseled political neutrality but Ahaz refused his advice and invited in Tiglath-pileser III (2 Kgs. 16:7-9) to whom he then became a vassal in the full sense of the word. This political move carried with it religious consequences, for political vassalage also implied the acceptance of foreign religious cults (2 Kgs. 16 10-18).

Ahaziah (ay′-a-zy′-ah), 1. King of Israel (850-849 B.C), son and successor of Ahab (1 Kgs 22:52-54). Together with Jehoshaphat of Judah, he undertook certain sea-going commercial projects, with ships built in Ezion-geber, but they were not successful (2 Chron. 20:35; 1 Kgs. 22:48). A fatal fall in his palace put an end to a brief reign. In his injuries he sought help from Baalzebub, the god of the city of Ekron. The prophet Elijah thereupon announced to Ahaziah that death had been decreed as the penalty for his idolatrous action (2 Kgs. 1:2-18).

2. King of Judah (842 B.C.), son and successor of Jehoram of Judah. He formed an alliance with his uncle, King Jehoram of Israel, and waged war against the Syrians. Subsequently Jehoram was slain and Ahaziah severely wounded in a rebellion led by Jehu. Ahaziah managed to escape but died of his wounds at Megiddo. After his death all his sons, except Joash, were slain on the orders of his mother, Athalia, who seized the throne. She ruled for six years and was herself murdered, after which Joash became king (2 Kgs. 8:24-11:21).

Ahiam (a-hy′-am), One of the Thirty warriors of David (2 Sam. 23:33; 1 Chron. 11:35).

Ahijah (a-hy′-jah), A prophet of Shiloh who predicted that after the death of Solomon the kingdom would be split in two; Judah and Israel. He announced to Jeroboam that he would be king over Israel (1 Kgs. 11:29). When later he was asked by Jeroboam's wife about the future of her ailing son Abijah, he predicted his death and the tragic end of the whole house of Jeroboam (1 Kgs 14:1).

Ahikam (a-hy′-kam), An official of king Josiah sent to consult the prophetess Huldah concerning the Book of Law (2 Kgs. 22:12, 14). Ahikam rescued Jeremiah from death during the reign of Jehoiakim (Jer. 26:24). His son Gedaliah was appointed governor of Judah by Nebuchadnezzar (2 Kgs. 25:22).

Ahikar (a-hy'-kar), A nephew of Tobit, chancellor of Esarhaddon, king of Nineveh (Tob. 1:21 ff). He became Tobit's helper, when the latter became blind (Tob. 2:10) and rejoiced with him at his cure (Tob. 11:18). There exists an apocryphal work which describes the misadventures of Ahikar; to this work Tob. 14:10 alludes.

Ahimaaz (a-him'-a-az), 1. The father of Ahinoam, wife of Saul (1 Sam. 14:50).

2. Son of the priest Zadok (2 Sam. 15:27). He remained loyal to David during Absalom's rebellion, and together with Jonathan, son of Abiathar, was commissioned to report back to David whatever plans of Absalom that Hushai the counsellor and David's spy could discover (2 Sam. 15:36; 17:15-21). Ahimaaz was the first to bring David news of the death of Absalom, but when he saw the consternation of the king, he preferred to keep the news secret (2 Sam. 18:19-32).

Ahiman (a-hy-man), One of the three legendary giants among the Anakim of Hebron (Num. 13:22; Josh. 15:14; Jgs. 1:10).

Ahimelech (a-him'-e-lek), The son of Ahitub, of the house of Eli, and priest of Nob. He helped David while he was fleeing from Saul, giving him at David's request the "showbread" (hallowed "bread of the presence") to feed him and his companions. He also gave him Goliath's sword (1 Sam. 21:1-10; Mt. 12:1-8; Mk. 2:23-28; Lk. 6:1-5). Doeg the Edomite told Saul of the help given by Ahimelech to David, so Saul ordered Ahimelech and all eighty-five of his companions to be slaughtered (1 Sam. 22:6-18).

Ahinadab (a-hin'-a-dab), One of the twelve officers of King Solomon who provided food for the royal household (1 Kgs. 4:14).

Ahinoam (a-hin'-o-am), 1. The daughter of Ahimaaz, wife of Saul (1 Sam. 14:50).

2. One of David's wives, the mother of the king's first-born son Ammon who was born at Hebron (2 Sam. 2:2). She accompanied David during his stay among the Philistines (1 Sam. 25:43; 27:3). She was taken prisoner by the Amalekites but David freed her (1 Sam. 30:5).

Ahio (a-hy'-o), The son of Abinadab and brother of Uzzah (2 Sam. 6:3-4).

Ahiram, Head of a clan of the tribe of Benjamin (Num. 26:38).

Ahithophel (a-hith'-o-fel), A native of Giloh, a locality in the territory of Judah. He was a counsellor of David, but nevertheless supported the rebellion of Absalom (2 Sam. 15:12). It was on Ahithophel's advice that Absalom publicly violated his father's harem (2 Sam. 16:20-22). His further counsel was for Absalom to authorize him to take command of the army and pursue David, but Hushai's word prevailed. The latter was secretly on David's side, and so suggested to Absalom to delay the pursuit until a more numerous army could be prepared and commanded by Absalom himself (2 Sam. 17:1-14). When Ahithophel saw that his plan had come to nothing, and that the revolt was doomed to failure, he committed suicide (2 Sam. 17:23).

Ahitub (a-hy'-tub), The father of Ahimelech, the priest of Nob who helped David (1 Sam. 22:9).

Ahuzzath, The adviser of King Abimelech of Gerar (Gen. 26:26-31).

Ai (ay'-eye, or eye), A city in the territory of Ephraim to the east of Bethel. In the vicinity, between Ai and Bethel, Abram camped and erected there an altar (Gen. 12:8; 13:3). According to Josh. 7-8 it was conquered and put to flames by the Israelites at the command of Joshua. Today the place is known as et-Tell.

Aiah (ay'-ya), The father of Rizpah, Saul's concubine (2 Sam. 3:7; 21:8-11).

Aijalon (ay'-ja-lon), A city located in the Shephelah (which *see*) listed as belonging to the tribe of Dan (Josh. 19:42; 21:24), and afterwards numbered among the Levitical cities of Ephraim (1 Chron. 6:54) and of Benjamin (1 Chron. 8:13). Its important position on one of the principal roads leading to the coast explains how it often found itself involved in wars. Thus it figures in Joshua's victory over the coalition of Canaanite cities around Jerusalem (Josh. 10:12), and in Saul's victory over the Philistines (1 Sam. 14:31). It was fortified by Rehoboam (2 Chron. 11:10) and was again captured by the Philistines during the kingship of Ahaz (2 Chron. 28:18).

Akeldama (a-kel'-da-ma), An Aramaic name for a field set aside for the burial of strangers, and situated near Jerusalem. According to Acts 1:19, where the word is interpreted as 'Field of Blood,' the name derives from the fact that it was bought by Judas with the thirty pieces of silver that he received for betraying Jesus. Matthew 27:3-10 tells us that it was bought by the priests with the silver pieces that Judas threw back at them. Before this event, according to Matthew, the place had been known as THE POTTER'S FIELD.

Akkub, 1. Son of Elioenai (1 Chron. 3:24).

2. Father of temple gatekeepers (Ezra 2:42; Neh. 7:45).

3. Father of temple slaves (Ezra 2:45).

4. A Levite (Neh. 8:7).

Akrabattene (ak'-ra-bat'-en-e), A fortress in S. Judaea where Judas Maccabeus defeated the Idumeans (1 Mac. 5:3).

Alabaster, In ancient times, this was a white, translucent marble found only in Egypt, whereas today it is a form of gypsum. It is mentioned in Mt. 26:7; Mk. 14:3; Lk. 7:37, in the story of the anointing of Jesus with precious ointment by Mary of Bethany (Mt.-Mk.) or by the sinful woman (Lk.). The reference is to a particular type of bottle, made of this material, and used as a container for perfumes. It had no handles and the neck of the bottle had to be broken in order to empty the contents. Both the bottle and the perfume used by Mary were expensive.

Alcimus (al'-si-mus), An apostate Jew of the priestly line, and leader of the Hellenistic faction, which opposed the Maccabean revolt and denounced Judas Maccabaeus to King Demetrius (1 Mac. 7:5-7). He was confirmed as high priest by the king, and then allied himself with Bacchides, the head of the Syrian army in Palestine, causing 60 Hasideans to be put to death treacherously (1 Mac. 7:8-20). As he was preparing to set about destroying the wall of the inner court of the temple, he was mysteriously struck down with paralysis, from which he died in the second month of the year 153 B.C. (1 Mac 9:54-57).

Alema (al'-a-ma), A Hellenistic city in Transjordan. The Jewish population of this and the other five cities of the region was liberated by Judas

Maccabeus when imprisoned by the Gentile inhabitants (1 Mac. 5:26-45).

Aleph, The first letter of the Hebrew alphabet.

Alexander, 1. Alexander III king of Macedonia (356-323 B.C.), son and successor of Philip of Macedonia. He determined to put an end to the Persian threat and carried the war accordingly right into the Persian empire. Thus began a momentous career which in an incredibly brief time made Alexander the ruler of a vast empire which reached from Greece to India and from Asia Minor to Egypt. His conquests are referred to in 1 Mac. 1:1-9; 6:2. According to Josephus Flavius, a first century Jewish writer, Alexander, after defeating Darius, and while he was besieging Tyre, wrote to the high priest in Jerusalem, demanding that the Holy City submit to him. His demand was rejected and he marched against Jerusalem. The high priest went out to meet Alexander as he approached the city and appeased the king's hostility so effectively that Alexander entered the Temple and adored the God of the Jews. When he had been shown some passages of Dan (8:5, 21 f.; 11:3 f.) which were interpreted as referring to him, Alexander guaranteed to all Jews within his dominions the freedom to observe their own laws. Most scholars however consider Josephus' report to be without historical foundation.

2. Alexander Balas, King of Syria (150-145 B.C.), a usurper who claimed to be the son of Antiochus IV Epiphanes. Jonathan Maccabeus took Alexander's side against Demetrius I Soter and for this was rewarded with the high priesthood and nomination as governor of Judea (1 Mac. 10:1-11, 19).

3. Other men named Alexander are found in Mk. 15:21; Acts 4:6, 19:33; 1 Tim. 1:20; 2 Tim. 4:14.

Alexandria, A seaport of Egypt, founded by Alexander the Great in 331 B.C., and with Antioch and Rome, one of the principal cities of the Roman empire. There flourished in the centuries immediately before Christ and in the first centuries of the Christian era a Jewish community which maintained full cultural and cultic communications with Jerusalem, and became a point of fusion between Judaism and Hellenism. In Alexandria, to serve the liturgical needs of the Jewish community, the celebrated Greek translation of the Bible known as the Septuagint (or 'Seventy') was made during the third to first centuries B.C. Some Old Testament books such as the Book of Wisdom and the Book of Ecclesiasticus were authored or translated in Alexandria. Alexandria is mentioned in the New Testament as the birthplace of Apollo the Jew (Acts 18:24). The Alexandrine Jews had their own synagogue at Jerusalem, and its members are mentioned among the opponents of Stephen the Martyr (Acts 6:9). Tradition has it that the evangelist Mark brought Christianity to Alexandria, and that he became first bishop of the city.

alien; aliens
When an *a.* resides with you	any *a.* residing with you
Lev. 19:33	Num. 15:14
You shall treat the *a.* Lev. 19:34	and for the resident *a.* Num. 15:15
from the hands of *a.* Ps. 144:7	

Allegory, A continued metaphor, i.e. a literary composition in which the various terms and details are to be interpreted, not in their original meaning, but in a transferred sense. An allegory is distinguishd from a parable, which is a comparison or developed similitude in which the general sense of the whole story, not each and every individual detail, is directed towards illustrating a truth. Among the more famous biblical allegories are the canticle of the vine (Isa. 5:1-6), the story of the eagles (Ezek. 17:1-10) and some discourses of the Lord in John's Gospel (Jn. 10:1-16; 15:1-10). For the most part the parables of the Gospels contain allegorical elements, although, as a whole, they cannot be given purely allegorical interpretations. Even in New Testament times, as is evident from Mt. 13:18-23, the parables began to be interpreted along allegorical lines. Allegorical interpretation as a method to be applied in principle to the whole of Scripture, and particularly to the Old Testament, began in Judaic tradition, especially at Alexandria with Philo Judaeus. One can find traces of this method of interpretation in Gal. 4:24. Many Fathers of the Church adopted this method of interpretation and used it generously, particularly in homilies to the people and in writings with a pastoral slant.

Alleluia, A transcription of the Hebrew phrase **hallelu-yah,** which means "praise the Lord."

Alliance, *See* COVENANT.

Allon-Bacuth (bak′-uth), "The oak of the weeping," a place near Bethel where Deborah, Rebekah's nurse, was buried (Gen. 35:8).

Almighty, The usual translation of the Hebrew word El-Shaddai, the name for God in various biblical texts. The word **almighty** derives from the Greek translation of the Hebrew Bible known as the Septuagint, which used the word **Pantocrator,** which means almighty, all-powerful, omnipotent.

Almon-diblathaim (dib′la-thay′-im), A place in the desert where the Israelites encamped en route to Canaan (Num. 33:46, 47).

Alms, Alms and almsgiving are particularly praised in the Books of Tobit and Sirach. Tobit 4:7 states that alms free one from sin and death. It is better to give alms than to store up treasure (Tob. 12:8; *see* 2:16; 12:9; 14:15). For Sirach alms atone for sin (12:3), and are something by which a man will be long remembered (Sir. 3:15; 31:11; *see* Dan. 4:24). In the New Testament Christ warns his followers against vanity in almsgiving, while nevertheless exhorting to it (Matt. 6:2, 3, 4; Lk. 11:41; 12:43) and the Acts reserve praise for almsgivers (Acts 9:36; 10:4, 31). Paul brought alms for his nation (Acts 24:17) but, like Jesus, warns against vainglory in giving (1 Cor. 13:3). Alms are no substitute for charity, and all the alms in the world are useless, from the Christian point of view, unless they are an expression of love (1 Cor. 13:3).

Aloes, An aromatic substance which comes from southeast Asia and is used as perfume. It was used, together with myrrh, to embalm the body of Jesus (Jn. 19:39).

alone

the man to be *a*.	Gen. 2:18	Moses *a*. is to come close Ex. 24:2
you cannot do it *a*.	Ex. 18:18	and I *a*. have escaped Job 1:15

Alphaeus (al-fee′-us), 1. The father of James the Less, Apostle (Mt. 10:3; Mk. 3:18; Lk. 6:15; Acts 1:13).

2. The father of Levi, who became St. Matthew, Apostle (Mk. 2:14).

Altar, The place of sacrifice. It occupies a place of prime importance among all the cult utensils and instruments of the Israelite ritual. The most ancient legislation on the altar prescribed that it should be of earth or unhewn stones, and resting on the earth, without steps (Ex. 20:24-25). In the Old Testament we read other descriptions of the altar. The altar of holocausts was placed in the courtyard of the priests of the Temple of Solomon. It was a bronze altar of enormous proportions (1 Kgs. 8:64; 2 Chron. 4:1). It remained in the Temple until the time of King Ahaz

(735-715) who substituted it with another one constructed after a model he had seen at Damascus (2 Kgs. 16:10-16). Inside the Temple, in the front chamber, was the altar of incense (1 Kgs. 6:20; 1 Chron. 28:18; 2 Chron. 26:16-20), overlaid with gold, on which incense was burned. The altar of incense also had its place in Herod's temple, according to Luke's account of the annunciation of the birth of John the Baptist to Zechariah his father (Lk. 1:11). Among the various altars can be included the table on which were placed the twelve breads of the presence. This was in the front chamber of the temple. On the Tabernacle altars of the desert *see* Ex. 25-27.

Alush (ay′-lush), A stopping-place of the Israelites in the wilderness during the journey to Canaan (Num. 33:13, 14).

Amalekites, A seminomadic tribe, which got its name from its founding ancestor Amalek, who was held to have been descended from Esau (Gen. 36:12). The tribe wandered mostly to the south of Palestine in the desert of Sinai. The Bible always portrays it as hostile to the Israelites. They had no sooner escaped from Egypt when they had to defend themselves from Amalekite attacks (Ex. 17:8) and later on during the journey through the desert (Num. 14:45). During the early years of King Saul, the prophet Samuel ordered him to exterminate the Amalekites and their king Agag. Samuel won a decisive victory over them, but failed to carry out the extermination order, for which he was severely punished (1 Sam. 15:1-35). The Amalekites raided Ziklag, the city given to David by Achish the Philistine, burned it and made off with all the women and children. David pursued them, vanquished them and retrieved all the spoils, including their flocks and herds (1 Sam. 30). After the defeat the Amalekites fade from history.

Amana (a-may′-na), A mountain of the Anti-Lebanon range (Song of Songs 4:8).

Amariah (am-a-ry′-ah), 1. According to 1 Chron. 6:7, Amariah, son of Meraioth, was in the line of the high priest and father of Ahitub, whose son was Zadok.

2. Seven other people bear this name in the Bible: among them, a Levite (1 Chron. 23:19), the high priest at the time of Jehoshaphat (2 Chron. 19:11), and the grandfather of the prophet Zephaniah (Zeph. 1:1).

Amarna, *See* TELL-AMARNA.

Amasa (a-may′-sa), The son of Jether and Abigail, the sister of David. He supported Absalom against David and was appointed by him over the army to replace Joab, David's general, who had taken flight with King David (2 Sam. 17:25). Amasa was defeated by David's supporters, and repenting of his disloyalty, he sought to win back for David all those who had supported Absalom (2 Sam. 19:14). He remained head of David's army (2 Sam. 20:4) but Joab, in the act of kissing him in greeting, sank his sword into him and killed him in punishment for his previous disloyalty to the king (2 Sam. 20:7 ff.).

Amasai (a-may′-sy), 1. The chief of the Thirty warriors among David's army (1 Chron. 12:18), but not to be found in the more authentic listings of the Thirty at 2 Sam. 23:18-39 and 1 Chron. 11:20-46.

2. The name is borne by several other men in the Old Testament (1 Chron. 15:24; 2 Chron. 29:12).

Amasiah (am-a-sy′-ah), An officer of the army of King Jehoshaphat of Judah (2 Chron. 17:16).

amazement
will call forth *a*.,   Deut. 28:37

Amaziah (am-a-zy′-ah), King of Judah (800-783 B.C.), son and successor of Joash (2 Kgs. 14:1). He had his father's assassins executed, but spared the lives of their sons (2 Kgs. 14:5-6). He conquered the Edomites (2 Kgs. 14:7) but was eventually himself conquered and taken prisoner by Jehoash, the king of Israel (2 Kgs. 14:8-16).

Amaziah is also the name of a priest of Bethel at the time of Amos the prophet (Amos 7:10).

ambassador
I am an *a*. in chains   Eph. 6:20

Amen, A Hebrew word which means "truly" or "it is true," and is used as an expression of acceptance of a commission (1 Kgs. 1:36) or of approval of what has just been said, as for example, in the conclusion to hymns, prayers or doxologies (Ps. 41:44; 1 Chron. 16:36, and frequently in the New Testament, e.g. Rom. 1:25; 9:25; Rev. 5:14). In Rev. 3:14 Christ is declared to be the Amen of God, because in Him all the words of God to men found reality in flesh and blood. Jesus uses Amen in the Gospels, generally repeating it, to solemnize some saying and underscore its importance (Mt. 5:18, 26; Jn. 1:51, etc.).

Amittai (a-mit′-tie), The father of the prophet Jonah (2 Kgs. 14:25; Jonah 1:1).

Ammiel (am′-i-el) 1. Leader among Israelites (Num. 13:12).

2. Personal name mentioned several other places in Old Testament (2 Sam. 9:4; 1 Chron. 3:5; 26:5).

Ammihud (am-my′-hud), Personal name (Num. 1:10; 34:20,28; 1 Chron. 9:4).

Amminadab, Father of Elisheba, wife of Aaron (Ex. 6:23). His name figures in David's genealogy (Ruth 4:19-22) and in that of Jesus (Mt. 1:4; Lk. 3:33).

Ammizabad (a-miz′-a-bad), The son of Benaiah (1 Chron. 27:6).

Ammonites, An Aramaean tribe, racially related to the Hebrews, who occupied that part of Transjordan between the rivers Arnon and Jabbok (Josh. 12:2 ff). The lengendary origins of these descendants of Ammon, son of Lot and of one of his daughters, are found in Gen. 19:38. The Ammonites did not permit the Hebrews to cross their territories when they were on their way with Moses towards the promised land (Deut. 2:19-37). During the early period of the judges, the Ammonites united with the king of Moab and seized Jericho, but were driven across the Jordan by the judge Ehud (Jgs. 3:13) and were again vanquished by Jephthah (Jgs. 10:6). One of Saul's first victories was the defeat of the Ammonite king Nahash (1 Sam. 11:1-15). Since Nahash had been a friend of David, the latter sent his sympathies to Hanun, the son of Nahash when his father died. But the Ammonites abused the Israelite envoys and war broke out. David's army occupied Ammonite territory and conquered its capital, Rabbath-Ammon (2 Sam. 10). It was in this war that Uriah, the husband of Bathsheba, was slain (2 Sam. 11).

After the Babylonian Exile the Ammonites tried to hinder the Israelites' efforts to rebuild the walls of Jerusalem (Neh. 4:3) and they were still a people to be reckoned with in the times of Judas Maccabeus, who was put to his mettle to subdue them (1 Mac. 5:6). The prophetic books contain several anti-Ammon oracles (Jer. 49:1-5; Ezek. 25:5; Amos 1.13-15; Zeph. 2:8-11).

Amnon, First-born son of David. His mother was Ahinoam, and Hebron his birthplace. He raped his half-sister Tamar, for which her full brother Absalom slew him in revenge (2 Sam. 13).

Amon (am′-on), King of Judah (642-640 B.C.), son and successor of Manasseh, whose politics of dependence on the Assyrians he also continued. Like his father, a bloodthirsty man, he also gave himself to the idolatrous worship of the Assyrians (2 Kgs. 21:19-22). He was assassinated in a conspiracy by his own officials (2 Kgs. 21:23, 24; 2 Chron. 33:24 ff.).

Amorites, One of the peoples who occupied Palestine before the arrival of the Israelites (Gen. 10:16; Ex. 3:8). Sometimes the word **Amorite** is used in a larger sense to mean all those who lived in Palestine in pre-Israelite times (Gen. 15:16). Abraham and the other patriarchs had dealings with the Amorites (Gen. 14:13; 48:22); their homeland was in the region between Syria and Babylonia. The Amorite king of Heshbon in Transjordan, Sihon, was overthrown by the Israelites, and again by Moses, for having refused to allow them to pass peacefully through their territories to Canaan (Num. 21:21-31). Even after the Israelite occupation, however, the Amorites remained. At Gibeon Joshua defeated the coalition of the Amorite kings of Jerusalem, Hebron, Jarmuth, Lachish and Eglon (Josh. 10:1-19).

Amos, The Book of, The prophet Amos, a native of the village or Tekoa, six miles south of Bethlehem, was a shepherd and a tender of fig-bearing sycamore trees (Amos 7:14). Amos appeared at Bethel, the shrine of the northern kingdom about 750 B.C., during the prosperous reign of Jeroboam II, to announce the doom of the northern kingdom (Amos 5:2). Amos mentions no specific enemy as the agent of the destruction, but Assyria carried out the threat. Amos is the first prophet to announce the end of the northern kingdom.

The five visions related in chapters 7-9 likely constituted Amos' call to prophetic work. It is not certain that he preached other than in Bethel. His work there was interrupted by Amaziah, the high priest, who charged him with treasonable statements and demanded that he return to his home in the south.

Amos proclaimed Yahweh as the international God of justice. In the first section of his book he announces that God will punish the six neighbors that immediately surround Israel for their atrocities of war, as well as punish Israel for her sins. Sin is the Lord's affair wherever it occurs. God cares for all nations (Amos 9:7).

Israel's position was a position of responsibility rather than one of privilege alone. Despite the privileges of election, exodus, and temple worship, since the responsibility had not been discharged, Israel must be punished (Amos 3:2). Worship apart from justice is an abomination (Amos 5:21).

Amos is the first of the prophets to use the term "Day of the Lord." The people understood this day to be the day of the defeat of their enemies and of Hebrew exaltation. Amos declared that it was an inevitable day of doom (Amos 5:18).

Amos envisioned that some small remnant would survive the calamity (Amos 3:12). A Messianic age would come in which the fallen tabernacle of David would be rebuilt (Amos 9:11; *see* Acts 15:16-17).

23

Amoz, The father of the prophet Isaiah (Isa. 1:1).

Amphipolis, A Macedonian city, visited by Paul and Silas during Paul's second missionary journey (Acts 17:1).

Ampliatus, A Christian of Rome, to whom Paul sends greetings in Romans 16:8.

Amram, According to Ex. 6:18-20, the grandson of Levi, the husband of Jochebed, the father of Moses, Aaron and Miriam (Num. 26:58-59).

Amraphel, King of Shinar (Babylonia) who invaded Palestine with three other kings from the East and five from the city-states of the Pentapolis. They were defeated by Abraham (Gen. 14). Some have tried to identify Amraphel with Hammurabi, king of Babylon, but this attempt has now been abandoned.

Anab (ay′-nab), A city of Judah, from which Joshua expelled the Anakim (Josh. 11:21; 15:50).

Anael (an′-i-el), Brother of Tobit (Tob. 1:21).

Anakim (an′-a-kim), One of the peoples who occupied Palestine before the arrival of the Israelites. Popular fantasy gave to this people the stature of giants (Num. 13:28; Deut. 2:21; 9:2) and held them to be descended from the Nephilim, the sons born of marriages between the sons of God and the daughters of men (Num. 13:33; Gen. 6:4). They had the cities of Hebron, Debir and Anab, from which Joshua expelled them. The survivors took refuge in the Philistine cities of Gaza, Gath and Ashdod (Josh. 11:21, 22).

Anamim, An unknown ethnic group listed among the sons of Egypt and Ham in the Table of Nations (Gen. 10:13; 1 Chron. 1:11).

Anammelech (a-nam′-a-lek), One of the gods of the Sepharvaim, a people conquered by the Assyrians, colonies of whom were planted in Samaria by Sargon II after the destruction of the city (722 B.C.). In honor of this god the Sepharvites burned their own children (2 Kgs. 17:31 where he is called Hadad).

Ananias (an′-a-ny′-as), Greek form of Hebrew Hananiah. 1. According to Tobit 5:13, the archangel Raphael appeared to Tobit in the form of a youth who claimed to be Azariah, son of Hananiah.

2. Husband of Sapphira who with his wife was punished with death for lying and fraud against the Christian community of Jerusalem (Acts 5:1-10).

3. A Christian of Damascus who received a command from the Lord in a vision to go and visit Paul and lay hands on him to cure his blindness and fill him with the Holy Spirit (Acts 9:10-16).

4. The high priest before whom Paul appeared in Jerusalem (Acts 23:2) and who later again accused Paul before the Roman procurator Felix (Acts 24:1).

Anath (ay′-nath), The father of Shamgar, one of the minor judges (Jgs. 3:31; 5:6).

Anathoth (an′-a-thoth′), A Levite town of the tribe of Benjamin, 5 miles north of Jerusalem (Josh. 21:18; 1 Chron. 7:8). Here were the estates of Abiathar, David's high priest, afterwards deposed by Solomon (1 Kgs. 2:26). It was also the birthplace of Jeremiah the prophet (Jer. 1:1).

Anchor, Symbol of hope, according to Heb. 6:19, 20: "Like a sure and firm anchor, that hope extends beyond the veil through whicn Jesus, our forerunner, has entered on our behalf, being made high priest forever according to the order of Melchizedek."

Andrew, One of the twelve disciples, brother of Peter, native of Bethsaida in Galilee (Jn. 1:44). He was a follower of John the Baptist, one of the first two to meet Jesus, to whom he introduced his brother Peter (Jn. 1:35-44). According to Mk. 1:16 Andrew received his definitive vocation to follow Jesus while he was with Peter on the banks of the Sea of Galilee. It was Andrew who procured for Jesus the bread and fishes for the miracle of the multiplication of the loaves and fishes (*see* Jn. 6:9), and he was Philip's intermediary to Jesus on behalf of some Gentiles who wished to have an interview with him (Jn. 12:22). In the New Testament aprocryphal Acts of Andrew, it is narrated that he preached in Asia Minor and Greece, where, in the city of Patras, he suffered martyrdom by being crucified on an X-shaped cross.

Andronicus, 1. An official of Antiochus IV Epiphanes to whom was committed the government of Antioch in the king's absence. At the instigation of Menelaus the usurper, Andronicus effected the death of Onias the legitimate high priest. He was later punished with death by Antiochus IV (2 Mac. 4:30-38).

2. A Roman Christian, who together with Junias, was called by Paul his "kinsmen and fellow prisoners" (Rom. 16:7).

Aner (ay'-ner), An Amorite who accompanied Abraham to rescue Lot (Gen. 14:13, 24).

Angels, From the Greek **aggelos** meaning messenger. When compared with that of other ancient religions such as Mesopotamian and Persian, the angelology of the Bible is very sober. The most characteristic aspects of Bible angels are: a. The angels, called in the original text "God's sons" and also "saints," make up the heavenly court of God, who appears as a king surrounded by his ministers and courtiers (1 Kgs. 22:19; Pss. 29:1; 82; 89:7) who praise him (Pss. 103:20; 148:2). They fulfill particular functions, such as accuser before the divine tribunal (Job 1-2). b. In postexilic Judaism angelology underwent an enrichment probably following the model of other religions, and, above all, the Persian religion. The Bible however scarcely alludes to this development, which is more abundantly reflected in the non-biblical apocalyptic literature. For example, certain personages emerge in clearer outline, even with names, such as Gabriel who interprets the vision of Daniel (Dan. 8:16; 9:21; *see* Zech. 1-6), Raphael, Tobiah's protector (Tob. 12:15) and Michael, the protector of the people of Israel in the vision of Dan. 10:13, 21. c. The 'angel of the Lord' often appears in the Genesis traditions on the patriarchs and in other historical books of the Bible. This 'angel' is always in the singular. This seems to be a very ancient part of the biblical tradition and independent of the more recent concept of the 'court of angels' in 1 Kings 22:19. The 'angel of the Lord' intervenes in the episode of Hagar (Gen. 16) and appears in various episodes of Jacob's life (Gen. 31:11; 32:24), as well as in the Exodus (Ex. 14:19), and to him is confided the guidance of the people through the desert (Ex. 32:2). He always appears in fulfilment of some task given him by God in relationship to man, and at times the 'angel' seems to be confused with God himself (*see* Gen. 21:18; 31:13). This would lead one to believe that the 'angel of the Lord' is rather a concrete form of conceiving of God's intervention in human affairs, a way of getting around the difficulty of expressing God's direct intervention. d. There are no important innovations in the New Testament angelology. The New Testament offers no light on the nature or competence of the

angels. They are ministers or messengers of God to announce, e.g. the
birth of John the Baptizer (Lk. 1:11) or that of Jesus (Gabriel, Lk. 1:26)
or the instructions to Joseph on protecting the child Jesus (Matt. 1:20;
2:13, 19). They aid Jesus after His forty days' fast (Matt. 4:11; Mk. 1:13).
The angels accompany the dead to the destiny reserved for them after
death (Lk. 16:22) and in the last judgment (Matt. 13:41, 49; 16:27;
24:31). In the Acts angels intervene to guide and assist the apostles in
their missionary activities (Acts 5:19; 10:3; 12:7; 17:23). On some errors
concerning angels in the Pauline churches of Asia *see* COLOSSIANS, EPISTLE
TO. The belief in guardian angels is deduced from Jesus' words in Matt
18:10.

Anger, As a human passion, anger is severely condemned by Jesus in
Matt. 5:22. Here he takes his listeners beyond mere extrinsic correctness
in human relationships and shows how the will of God revealed in the
commandments reaches down to the very core of the person to eradicate
all that is alien to God's love. Not only is anger the source from which
flow injuries to one's neighbor, but it excludes that interior communion
with one's neighbor that must mark the Christian. The severe admonish-
ment of the Lord is echoed in the preaching of the apostles (Eph. 4:26;
Col. 3:8; 1 Tim. 2:8; Tit. 1:7).

This severe teaching of the Lord seems to be in contrast to the frequent
mention in the Bible of the anger of God. While this is an obvious
anthropomorphism (*see* ANTHROPOMORPHISM), the question nevertheless
arises as to its meaning. God's anger is how anthropomorphic language
sums up God's aversion to sin. In concrete and plastic terms it expressed
God's incompatibility with sin. God's anger blazes against the people of
Israel because of its incredulity and unfaithfulness (Num. 11:1; Deut.
1:34; 9:8) and especially against its leaning to idolatry (Jer. 4:4; 7:20;
32:31; Hos. 5:10; 8:5). The anger of God is translated into implacable
punishment rushing out like a fire that destroys (Isa. 65:5; Jer. 17:4; Ezek.
21:36). God's anger is placated by humiliation, repentance and prayer
(Pss. 6:2; 38:2), especially through the intercession of those whom God
himself has appointed as his ministers, e.g. Moses (Ex. 32:11; Deut. 9:19)
and the prophets (Jer. 7:6; 14:11; 15:1; 18:20; Ezek. 9:8, 13; 13:4, 5;
Amos 7:3, 6). In the New Testament the anger of God as exemplary punishment for sin is above all associated with the last judgment (Matt.
24:51; Rom. 3:5; 12:19, and especially in Rev. 11:18; 14:19; 16:1, etc.).

anguish
We saw the *a.* of his heart   like the *a.* of a mother   Jer. 4:31
                Gen. 42:21 affliction and *a.* will come
a. overpower him   Job 15:24   Rom. 2:9
my loins are filled with *a.* Isa. 21:3

Anna, 1. Wife of Tobit (Tob. 1:9, 20).

2. The prophetess who recognized in the child Jesus the Messiah, when
his parents brought him to the temple to be presented to the Lord (Lk.
2:36-38).

3. According to the apocryphal proto-gospel of James, Anna was also the
name of Mary's mother.

Annas, The high priest of the Jews from 15 to 5 B.C., and father-in-law of
Caiaphas, the high priest who condemned Jesus (Lk. 3:2; Acts 4:6). After
being taken prisoner at Gethsemane, Jesus was brought first of all before
Annas to be interrogated (Jn. 18:13), even though at that time the latter
had no official capacity.

Annunciation, The announcement made to Mary by the angel Gabriel that she was to become the mother of the Messiah. According to Lk. 1:26-38 this took place at Nazareth, in the house of Mary, who had not yet been joined in marriage to Joseph.

Anointing, The custom of anointing people and things with oil is very ancient, and is found among many ancient peoples. It had different applications. It was a cosmetic practice of daily grooming or at least used before particularly joyful or festive occasions (Ruth 3:3; Judith 16:10; Deut. 28:40). It was also used as an expression of esteem with guests (Lk. 7:46). To it were also attributed therapeutic effects (Isa. 1:6; Mk. 6:13).

Anointing also had religious significance as a rite of consecration. Through anointing, certain objects were dedicated to the service of the cult, so that to use them for profane purposes was thereafter forbidden. In the Old Testament the altar was anointed (Ex. 29:35) as were the utensils used in worship (Ex. 40:10). So too was the Tabernacle (Lev. 8:10) and the ark of the covenant (Ex. 30:26). Anointing was also the essential rite of consecration of kings: through it, in a certain way, the king became a sharer in the sanctity of God and his person was therefore inviolable (1 Sam 24:7, 11; 26:9, 11, 13; 2 Sam. 1:14, 16). The rite of anointing appears from the beginning in the monarchy of Israel. Saul was anointed by Samuel (1 Sam. 9:16; 10:1). David was anointed king of Judah at Hebron (2 Sam. 2:4) and later as king of Israel (2 Sam. 5:3; 1 Sam. 16:13). There is more information in 2 Sam. 19:11 (the usurper Absalom), 2 Kgs. 9:3, 6 (Jehu of Israel) etc. In the priestly ritual of Exodus 29:4-7 and Leviticus 8:6-12, anointing is also the essential act of the consecration of the high priest. Aaron and his sons were consecrated priests by Moses through anointing (Lev. 8:12). The same rite was to be observed for Aaron's successors. In the New Testament, James 5:14 prescribes that in the case of sickness elders of the church should be called to pray over the sick person and anoint him with oil in the name of the Lord. This rite, according to James, will save the man and forgive his sins. Catholic tradition has seen in this text the scriptural foundations of the Sacrament of the Sick.

answered

The Hittites *a*. Abraham		Then Satan *a*. the Lord	Job 1:7
	Gen. 23:5	But Satan *a*. the Lord	Job 1:9
the God who *a*. me	Gen. 35:3	the evil spirit *a*.	Acts 19:15
	He *a*. with a question	Acts 21:13	

Anthropomorphism, The representation or conception of the divinity under human forms, or as having human attributes and being subject to human passions. The Bible and especially the Old Testament very frequently use anthropomorphisms to speak about God. If on the one hand the Bible underlines the transcendence of God, who is spirit and not flesh, who is invisible and whose presence no creature can bear without dying, on the other hand it speaks of God as if he had a body and members such as arms, a face and so on. Moreover God's reactions are described in the psychological framework of a man. Not only does anthropomorphic language not demand, it positively excludes, a literal interpretation. It is however not only legitimate to use this type of language, in fact, it cannot be avoided. Human statements about God are always analogous, that is, partly true. The later abstract and refined concepts of developed theology have their importance for a rational development of revelation. This however does not do away with the usefulness and indeed necessity of anthropomorphic language. This answers man's need for a more intuitive, more symbolic and imaginative way of conceiving of God. Even if it seems to compromise the divine transcendence, it has the advantage of bringing out how immediately near God is, how involved and concerned for human happenings, how intense his love for man and his wish to save him. Moreover a whole field of religious experience cannot be conceived or expressed except with the use of anthropomorphisms, as is abundantly attested to in religious literature.

Antichrist, In the visions of the end of history which anticipate Jewish apocalyptic history, a fixed element in the unrolling of the ultimate events is the almost general apostasy which comes to a head in the decisive encounter between the forces of good and evil. This is the prelude to the divine victory. Against this backdrop must be understood the figure of the Antichrist. Apocalyptic literature gives no clear countenance to the agent who will rise in opposition to God, and the same vague expressions mark the apocalyptic discourse in the gospel tradition (Mk. 13:21-22; Matt. 24:23, 24). 2 Thess. 2:3-12 is more precise in its description, but here the name of Antichrist is missing. He is called a 'man of lawlessness,' sustained by Satan, who will oppose whatever bears the name of God. He will make use of all kinds of prodigies to seduce those who will be condemned, but in the end will himself be destroyed by the Lord "with the breath of his mouth" (2:8; *see* Isa. 11:4). The name Antichrist is read only in 1 John 2:18; 2:22; 4:3 and 2 John 7, where, however, the person who will not acknowledge the coming of Jesus Christ in the flesh is called the Antichrist. (*See* JUDGMENT.) Here John, as is his wont, has actualized the figure, just as he actualizes eschatology. The Antichrist becomes the Antichrists (1 John 2:18), namely those who deny that "Jesus is the Christ" (2:22).

Anti-Lebanon, The mountain range which rises parallel to the Lebanon range, and to the east. *See* LEBANON.

Antioch, 1. A city of Syria (today Antakia), founded by Seleucus I Nicator around 300 B.C. and called Antioch in memory of the founder's father, Antiochus. With Rome and Alexandria it formed one of the three principal cities of the Roman Empire. Antioch had been the capital of the Seleucid empire which arose after Alexander's empire had been divided, at his death, among his generals. For this reason one finds Antioch frequently mentioned in accounts of the struggle between faithful Jews who wished to preserve their traditions intact, and the hellenizing intentions of the Seleucid kings. Antioch was the seat of the first Gentile Christian church, and there for the first time Christ's followers were called Christians (Acts 11:19-26). It was the greatest center of missionary activity among the Gentiles in apostolic times, thanks to the work of Paul (Acts 13:1; 14:25; 18:22). At Antioch took place the dramatic disagreement between Peter and Paul, recorded in Gal. 2:11.

2. A town in Pisidia (Asia Minor) founded by Seleucus I in 280 B.C., visited by Paul on his first missionary journey (Acts 13:14-51; 14:20, 21) and where he suffered persecution at the hands of the Jews (2 Tim. 3:11).

Antiochis (an-ty′-o-kis), A concubine of King Antiochus IV Epiphanes (2 Mac. 4:30).

Antiochus (an-ty′-o-kus), 1. Antiochus IV Epiphanes, the Seleucid king of Syria (175-164 B.C.), son of Antiochus III the Great, and successor to his brother Seleucus IV Philopater. He took advantage of the dissensions among the Jews and decided to extend as far as Palestine his plan of uniting all his dominions under one law, religion and habit of life drawn from the Greek cultural patrimony. The measures taken for this purpose provoked large segments of the Jewish population, first into disdain and then into armed revolt headed by Mattathias, the father of the Maccabees (1 Mac. 1:10-6:17).

2. Antiochus V Eupator (164-161 B.C.), son and successor to Antiochus IV who was dethroned and assassinated by Demetrius I Soter (1 Mac. 6:17-7:1-4) together with Lysias, who was a regent appointed by Antiochus IV.

3. Antiochus VI (145-142 B.C.), son of Alexander Balas; he had as regent Tryphon. He confirmed Jonathan as high priest. He was assassinated by Tryphon who usurped the throne (1 Mac. 13:31, 32).

4. Antiochus VII (139-129 B.C.), son of Demetrius II. He succeeded to the throne, thanks to the support of Simon Maccabeus, whose help he obtained through false promises. After he became king he forgot the favors and the promises and wished to subjugate Judea and make it part of his dominions. He had Judea invaded but his army was routed by Judas and John Hyrcanus, sons of Simon Maccabeus (1 Mac. 15-16).

Antipas (an′-ti-pas), *See* HEROD ANTIPAS.

Antipater (an-tip′-a-ter) 1. Father of Herod I the Great.

2. Son of Jason, ambassador of Jonathan Maccabeus to Rome and Sparta (1 Mac. 12:16; 14:22).

Antipatris (an-tip′-a-tris), A town on the plain of Sharon N. of Jaffa (Acts 23:31).

Antonia (an-toe′-ni-a), A fortress at the NW corner of the court of the Jerusalem Temple. It was rebuilt by Nehemiah after the exile (Neh. 2:8; 7:2), at a later time restored by the Hasmonean chieftains, and completely transformed by Herod I, who gave it the name **Antonia** in honor of Mark Antony. It was occupied, at the time of the Roman governors, by a garrison for the surveillance of the city and the Temple (Acts 21:31-36; 22:24). An extensive flagstone pavement has recently been discovered in Jerusalem; this originally belonged to the central courtyard of the fortress. This is possibly the "**lithostrotos**" (stone pavement or mosaic) where, according to John 19:13, took place the trial of Jesus before Pilate. The question cannot be decided until more precise information is had on where Pilate established his court when he resided in Jerusalem, for he might also have stayed in Herod's palace. *See* GABBATHA.

anxiety

your water shaking with *a*.	eat their bread in *a*.	Ezek. 12:19
Ezek. 12:18		

Apelles (a-pel′-iz), A Christian of Rome greeted by Paul (Rom. 16:10).

Aphairema (a-far′-e-ma), A district of Samaria in Maccabbean times (1 Mac. 10:38; 11:34).

Aphek (ay′-fek), Name of several cities in Palestine.

a city north of Sidon	Josh. 13:4 a city north of Joppa	1 Sam. 4:1
Aphek an Asherite city	a city beyond Jordan	1 Kgs. 20:26
Josh. 19:30		

Apis (ay′-pis), The sacred bull of the Egyptians worshipped in Memphis (Jer. 46:15).

Apocalypse, *See* REVELATION.

Apocalyptic Literature, A literary genre that was common in Judaism from the second century B.C. to the second century A.D., and from which several of the apocryphal writings of the Old Testament have come down to us. Its principle common characteristics are the following:

1. As the name indicates (**apocalypsis** means revelation), apocalyptic writing is the literature of revelation. Its intention is to transmit to the reader the revelations ordinarily had by great personages of the history of Israel such as Moses, Ezra, Baruch, and Enoch. It is different however from the prophetic literature, which is also literature of revelation, in that for the prophets the organ of transmission of the revelation is the word of God, while for the apocalypses it is above all in vision that revelation takes place. These can be symbolic visions but at other times it is a question of a direct vision of divine things. It is on this point that the common theme of the ascents of famous personages is built. There, by exception, they are invited to contemplate with their own eyes the habitation of God and his heavenly court, the most secret mechanisms of creation, and above all, what God has in store for the future. In this sense, too, apocalyptic writing can be called the literature of revelation, for often sacred history does not appear only as the succession of God's interventions to bring to realization his salvific designs, but as the successive manifestation at the opportune moments, and especially in the future, of the realities created at the beginning, before the world came to be, such as the Messiah, the law, the glory of the saints and so on. These realities await the moment of their manifestation before the eyes of men.

2. For the most part apocalyptic literature is pseudonymous, that it, attributed to persons of the past. This attribution was meant above all to serve as a guarantee of the truth of these revelations. Thus what follows in presentation under the form of a vision of the future is what has in reality taken place in the past, at the time of the true author. Past history however is presented under symbolic forms, at times bizarre and complex. In these it is easy to identify the web of events known from history. The symbols used in this part also serve to describe the true future of the author, which is almost without exception the imminent end of the world.

3. The principal theme of apocalyptic literature is eschatology, that is, the last stage of the history of humanity and of the world, and its future consummation in the kingdom of God or the future world. The intention of the authors of the apocalyptic writings is above all to sustain the faith of their Jewish contemporaries in the definitive and absolute victory of God over evil, over Satan and over the historical empires that oppress and persecute the just, and especially the people of Israel.

In fact, apocalyptic literature was born in circumstances of particular gravity for the safety and permanence of the Jewish nation, that is, during the Seleucid persecution and the Roman domination.

It is in the light of this fundamental intention of the author that the writings should be understood. This particularly holds true for some elements which might provoke from today's reader a more severe judgment. The certainty of triumph by God is based on the experience of his fidelity to his promises in the past. Apocalyptic literature has recourse to pseudonymity, for in this way it can convince the reader of the fulfilment of promises and of how God has kept his word. On the other hand, seeing that the apocalyptic vision of the future arose from a meditation on the past, it is useless to go in search of information or detailed descriptions of future events, especially of eschatological events. The writers were in no position to know. Under the form of those terrible and minute descriptions, however, the authors expounded the meaning of the future in the whole context of sacred history. History tends to its fulfilment which will bring with it the triumph of God and the happiness of those faithful to God, even though the authors who reaffirmed this were in the dark as to the circumstances in which this triumph would take place, including the circumstance of time. It seems that this is the interpretation that must be given, with due reservations, to the canonical apocalyptic writings, Daniel, Revelation and the passages of the New Testament which contain themes taken from this literary tradition. *See* APOCRYPHAL BOOKS.

Apocryphal Books, Jewish and ancient Christian writings, similar in title and subject to the canonical books, but to which the Church never attributed definite canonical authority. Some of these books were accepted as inspired in several regions of the Church, and by some ecclesiastical writers. Protestants generally consider as apocryphal some books that are listed as canonical, or authentically scriptural, by the Catholic Church; these are the so-called deuterocanonical books; and to the works of the Old Testament which Catholics consider to be apocryphal, they give the name "pseudepigrapha." Although apocryphal works are neither inspired nor canonical, they are of great value in investigating the religious doctrine of Judaism at the time of the birth of Christianity. They are also sources for definite streams of doctrine, at times heretical, within Christianity itself in the first centuries.

The principal aprocryphal books of the Old Testament are: 3 and 4 Esdras, often quoted by the Fathers; together with 3 and 4 Maccabees and the Prayer of Manasses they have often been published as an appendix to the Latin Vulgate translation. Other apocrypha are the Apocalypse of Baruch, the books of Enoch, the Testament of the Twelve Patriarchs, the book of Jubilees, the Psalms of Solomon, the Odes of Solomon, the Ascension of Moses, the Martyrdom of Isaiah and the Letter of Aristeas.

New Testament apocryphal works can be divided according to the type of New Testament canonical works they intend to imitate. The apocryphal gospels, for example, are the Gospel of James, the Gospel of Thomas, the Gospel of the Hebrews. There are then the Acts of John, of Paul, of Peter, of Andrew, of Thomas, and of Philip, while there are letters of Paul and Seneca, an epistle to the Laodiceans, and another apocryphal one to the Corinthians. There is an apocalypse of Peter, of Paul and of Thomas.

Apollonia, A city of Macedonia which Paul and Silas passed through on the second missionary journey (Acts 17:1).

Apollonius, 1. A native of Tarsus, governor of Coelesyria and Phoenicia under Seleucus IV. He collaborated in despoiling the treasury of the Temple of Jerusalem carried out by Heliodorus (2 Mac. 3:5; 2 Mac. 4:4).

2. Governor of Coelesyria under Alexander Balas. He was defeated by Jonathan and Simon Maccabee in the battle that took place between Joppa and Ashdod (around 165 B.C.; 1 Mac. 10:67-89).

3. Son of Gennaeus, governor of one of the districts of Palestine at the time of Lysias and Antiochus V (2 Mac. 12:2).

Apollos, A Jew of Alexandria, a man eloquent and versed in the Scriptures (Acts 18:24). He taught and announced at Ephesus with exactitude the things regarding Jesus, even though he knew only the baptism preached by John. Priscilla and Aquila gave him deeper instruction on Christianity (Acts 18:24-26). Then he went over to Greece where he settled in Corinth and immediately distinguished himself for his zeal and doctrine, and especially in the debate with the Jews (Acts 18:27-28). We can deduce from 1 Cor. the great impact that Apollos' preaching made among the Christians of that church, seeing that one of the factions in that church claimed Apollos' authority, even though he is in no way blamed for these divisions (1 Cor. 3:3-9; 4:6). Some authors however wish to see in these passages a debate of Paul with Apollos (*see* 1 Cor. 2:1 and 2 Cor. 11:6): Paul speaks in deprecatory terms of his purely human wisdom and eloquence. Apollos left Corinth and in 1 Cor. 16:12 Paul states that he invited him to return to the city, but that his invitation was not accepted. Apollos is mentioned in Titus 3:13.

Apollyon, "destroyer," Greek name of "the angel of the abyss" (Rev. 9:11). *See* ABADDON.

Apostles, Etymologically the word comes from the Greek **apostellein,** to send. An apostle, then, is somebody sent. With the exception of John 13:16 and Philippians 2:25 (and probably also 2 Cor. 8:23) where the term is used generically of a messenger sent, the word "apostle" in the New Testament is reserved for the designation of a particular function in the service of the mission of Jesus and of the Church. The way in which the word is used however is not totally univocal and in fact sometimes departs a little from the use Christian tradition made of the term and the meaning it has today.

1. The synoptic gospels and Acts (with the exception of Acts 14:4, 14 where Paul and Barnabas are also called apostles) reserve the title of apostle to the group of the Twelve. We can see from Paul's letters and from Acts 4:4, 14 that without detriment to the exceptional position of this group, there was a time when the term had not yet acquired this exclusive sense. The Twelve, whose names with slight variations have been handed down in four lists (Matt. 10:2-4; Mk. 3:16-19; Lk. 6:13-16; Acts 1:13), were chosen by Jesus from among the larger group of disciples, because "He named twelve as his companions whom he would send to preach the good news" (Mk. 3:14). Luke 6:13 also adds that Jesus himself gave them the name of apostle, but it seems that the title as such is of ecclesiastical origin and that Jesus called them the Twelve (Mk. 3:14) with evident symbolic reference (Matt. 19:28; Lk. 22:30). The mission of which Mark 3:14 speaks took place while Jesus was still living, and as part of his mission as preacher of the coming of the kingdom of God. The so-called mission discourses (Matt. 10; Lk. 9:1-6; 10:1-16; Mk. 6:7-13) contain the instructions given to them by Jesus for this mission. The actual form in which these discourses appear, however, especially in Matt. 10, comes from the light of the missionary experience of the Church and combines other sayings of Jesus directed towards the mission of the disciples after his departure. Jesus entrusts to them his very own mission and message, and confers on them the power to carry out his work, with miracles and exorcisms, which show that the kingdom of God is already here and active (Matt. 10:8; 11:5; Mk. 6:13). They are to carry out this mission "in his name." This on the one hand clearly appoints them his legates, and on the other makes Jesus the source of their authority, and in fact likens their authority to his own: "He who welcomes you welcomes me" (Matt. 10:40). John does not use the term apostle but nevertheless has the same notion of the position of the Twelve in relationship to Jesus and before the world. He develops the notion of mission with exclusive reference to the mission of the Apostles in the preaching of the word of Jesus after his exaltation (Jn. 13:20; 17:18; 20:21).

The position of the Twelve in the Church after Pentecost is described for us in the Acts. Here the Apostles appear first and foremost as witnesses of the resurrection of Christ (Acts 4:33; 1:21, 22). Now the concept of witness includes not only the personal verification of what is witnessed to in the apparitions, but also the explicit mandate to render testimony to this event: the Apostles are qualified witnesses, chosen and designated by God for this purpose (Acts 59:29-32). They are in this way the centers of cohesion in the Christian community (Acts 2:42 ff.) and constitute the link with the community of disciples who lived around Jesus (Acts 1:21, 22). They proclaim that Word and confirm it with prodigies (Acts 5:12) and exercise a real authority for the effective advancement of the Church (Acts 4:34-37; 5:1-11). Because of this they can give authoritative solutions to questions, even in the interpretation of the gospel, which arise in the community (Acts 15). They can impose hands to constitute new ministers to be associated, with definite functions, with their own apostolic ministry (Acts 6:1-7). The Twelve take on the care of, and feel immediately responsible for, the new communities which for various reasons, and particularly because of the persecution of the Jews, are founded away from Judea, throughout Palestine and even as far away as Antioch (Acts 11:12).

Paul had to argue vehemently his position as apostle against those judaizing Christians who questioned it (Gal. 1-2). It is clear from this debate that while Paul did not reserve the name apostle exclusively to the Twelve, he did recognize their exceptional position within the group of the "Apostles." Paul contended that to him should be accorded the same position within the Church as was given to the Twelve, those who were the "acknowledged pillars" (Gal. 2:9). He makes particular reference to Peter, James and John, whom he had met in Jerusalem. This claim was received without contest in the meeting in Jerusalem, as narrated in Gal. 2:1-10. Paul based his claim on the mission he had received directly from Jesus in the vision he had had at the moment of his conversion. For this reason when he lists the apparitions of the risen Lord he does not hesitate to include, albeit in the last place, his own experience (1 Cor. 15:1-9).

It is however also true that Paul speaks of others who do not belong to the group of the Twelve as apostles. For instance he calls Andronicus and Junias apostles (Rom. 16:7). At other times he refers to apostles with nothing in the text to suggest that he is speaking exclusively of the Twelve (1 Cor. 4:9-13; 9:5; 15:7). It is difficult to say what was the authority and position of these "apostles" in the Church. The Pauline letters do not contain clear references on this point. One might think that the basic distinction was made on the basis of the immediate origin of one's mission being from Jesus (Gal. 1:1). In other texts however it would seem to be the name for all those who had seen the Lord (1 Cor. 15:7). This would explain why Barnabas was called apostle (1 Cor. 9:4-6; Gal. 2:9; Acts 14:4, 14).

There is then some obscurity on the precise meaning given at first to the term apostle. It was to become with time, and already in Luke and the Acts, the exclusive title of the Twelve and Paul. In itself the term means 'sent,' and could therefore be extended to all who had a mission, either received directly from Jesus or from the "Apostles" or from the church. This however does not mean that the altogether unique position of the Twelve was passed over or compromised: they remained the qualified witnesses of Jesus on whom the church was built and in whom it holds together.

appeal
I *a*. to the emperor Acts 25:11 I was forced to *a*. Acts 28:19
but *a*. to him as 1 Tim. 5:1

appearance
the *a*. of fire Num. 9:15 with changed *a*. Job 14:20
Do not judge from his *a*. and his *a*. beyond that of mortals
1 Sam. 16:7 Isa. 52:14
because man sees the *a*. nor *a*. that would attract us
1 Sam. 16:7 Isa. 53:2

appetite
he steals to satisfy his *a*. if you have a ravenous *a*.
Prov. 6:30 Prov. 23:2

Apphia (aff'-i-a), A Christian woman mentioned by Paul among those to whom his letter to Philemon was addressed (v. 2), and held by some scholars to be Philemon's wife.

apple, apples

the *a.* of his eye	Deut. 32:10	like golden *a.*	Prov. 25:11
the *a.* of your eye		refresh me with *a.*	S. of S. 2:5
	Ps. 17:8, Prov. 7:2	Under the *a.* tree	S. of S. 8:5
		and the *a.*, all the trees	Joel 1:12

approach

a. a close relative	Lev. 18:6	You shall not *a* a woman
		Lev. 18:19
	he shall *a.* me	Jer. 30:21

Aquila (ac**′**-quil-a), A Jewish Christian, husband of Priscilla, who was with Paul in Corinth and accompanied him to Ephesus. He and Paul were of the same trade, tentmakers. Aquila, with his wife, taught Apollos more perfectly the way of the Lord. *See* Acts 18:2, 26; Rom. 16:3.

Arab, A town of Judah (Josh. 15:52).

Arabah, In the Hebrew this word frequently denotes a parched desert land. In Josh. 18:18 it probably refers to the desert land south of the Dead Sea, extending to the Gulf of Aqaba.

Arabia, This may mean where Arabia is now located, or it may include the desert region extending from Egypt and bordering Palestine on the south and east. *See* 1 Kgs. 10:15; Gal. 4:25.

Arad, A Canaanite city of southern Palestine in the Negeb, whose king attacked the Israelites on their way to the Promised Land and succeeded in taking some of them prisoners. The Israelites made a vow against him and his city and completely destroyed it (Num. 21:1-3). It was later inhabited by the Kenite tribe (Jgs. 1:16). In Joshua 12:14, the conquest of Arad is attributed to Joshua.

Aram, Aramaeans, A west semitic people. In the genealogy of peoples given in Gen. 10:22, 23, Aram, from whom the Aramaeans take their name, is the son of Shem and grandson of Noah. According to Gen. 22:20, 21 however he is the son of Kemuel and grandson of Nahor, Abraham's brother. From the twelfth century B.C. on, the more abundant and precise information available concerning this people shows them organized into little city-states in Syria and northern Mesopotamia. These little city-states were frequently divided by private ambition for leadership and so never succeeded in forming an empire. They had frequent dealings with Israel, and particularly with the northern kingdom. The most important of these was the kingdom of Damascus, which for some time was subject to David (2 Sam. 8:5) but was independent towards the end of Solomon's reign (1 Kgs. 11:23-25). At the invitation of Asa of Judah (912/11-871/70 B.C.). Ben-hadad invaded the kingdom of Israel. Later he imposed severe economic conditions on Omri of Israel (876-869), a situation reversed by Ahab of Israel (869-850 B.C.) who defeated Ben-hadad twice and made him prisoner (1 Kgs. 20). The flourishing kingdom of Damascus at last fell prey to the expanding Assyrian empire of Tiglath-pileser III, who in 734 B.C. conquered it and made it part of the empire. Other Aramaean states mentioned in the Bible are: Zobah, whose king Hadadezer was defeated by David (2 Sam. 8:3-7); Beth-Rehob and Maacah, who linked up with Zobah and the Ammonites in the same battle, only to be defeated by David.

The early history of this people is quite obscure, but it is generally held that there are ethnic relationships between them and the patriarchs of

Israel. According to Deut. 26:5 the father of Israel (Jacob) was a wander-ing Aramaean. The region from which the patriarchs came is often calleu Paddan-Aram (the plain of Aram, e.g. Gen. 25:20; 31:18) and Aram naharaim (i.e. Aram of the two rivers, Gen. 24:10), while Genesis also records relationships between Jacob and Laban, who was known as the Aramaean (Gen. 25:20; 28:5). The Aramaeans then are probably part of the wave of west Semites who, at the end of the third millenium and the beginning of the second, passed from the Arabian desert into upper and lower Mesopotamia and Syria, little by little settling down to a less no-madic life.

Aram-naharaim (nay′-a-ray′-im), *See* ARAM.

Ararat, A region north of Assyria in what is now Armenia. On the moun-tains of this territory Noah's ark came to rest when according to Gen. 8:4 the waters of the flood receded. The Assyrians who assassinated King Sennacherib in 681 B.C. took refuge in Ararat according to 2 Kgs. 19:37; Isa. 37:38.

Aratus, A Stoic poet (c. 310-245 B.C.), author of a poem entitled **Phae-nomena** from which Paul cited a verse in his discourse on the Areopagus of Athens, Acts 17:28.

Araunah, A Jebusite citizen of Jerusalem, whose threshing floor David bought to construct an altar (2 Sam. 24:18). David had offended God by taking a census of the people, and was punished by a plague which killed seventy thousand of them. David saw an angel standing near the thresh-ing floor of Araunah the Jebusite, and from Gad, the prophet, he received the command to build an altar there. He bought the place with the oxen and equipment for fifty shekels of silver and there offered holocausts and sacrifices (2 Sam. 24:5-25).

Arba, The father of Anak (Josh. 15:13) and the greatest man among the Anakim (Josh. 14:15). *See* ANAKIM.

Arbela, A city of Galilee where the Syrian army under Bacchides and Alcimus camped in the campaign against Judas Maccabeus, in the spring of 160 B.C.

Archangel, A particular category of angels, about whom the Bible tells us very little. The only mention of them is in 1 Thessalonians 4:16 and Jude 9. The first text tells us that an archangel will announce the coming of Christ while the second is a quotation from an apocalyptic writing of the Jews called **The Assumption of Moses** where Michael is called an archan-gel. Christian tradition included Raphael, Gabriel and Oriel among the archangels. The extra-biblical Jewish traditions give other numbers and names.

Archelaus (ar′-ka-lay′-us), The son of Herod I the Great and Malthace, and brother of Herod Antipas. According to Matt. 2:22 he was king of Judea at the time the Holy Family returned from Egypt. His reign was short (4 B.C.-6 A.D.). He was first of all deprived by Augustus of the title king, which had been conferred on him by his father's will, and made instead ethnarch of Judea, Samaria and Idumaea. He aroused the suspi-cions of the Emperor and so was banished to Vienne in France. His ter-ritories then passed under the control of a Roman governor.

Archippus (ar-kip′-us), One of the people to whom the letter to Philemon was sent (Philem. 2) and also mentioned by Paul in Colossians 4:16 with the mandate to look carefully to the ministry entrusted to him.

Areli, A son of Gad (Gen. 46:16; Num. 26:17).

Areopagite (ar'-e-op'-a-jite'), A member of the supreme court of Athens, which held its sessions on the hill of Areopagus. According to Acts 17:34 one of the tribunal members called Dionysius the Areopagite converted to the faith upon hearing Paul's discourse in that place.

Areopagus (ar'-e-op'-a-gus), The name of a hill near the Acropolis of Athens, and hence the name of a tribunal which held its sessions there. The jurisdiction of this tribunal varied from time to time, and while Paul was there, the competency of the court was so limited as to be almost symbolic on account of the political conditions in Greece at the time. According to Acts 17:19, the Athenians brought Paul to the Areopagus to hear him expound his doctrine at firsthand. Since the term is ambiguous, it is not possible to say whether he was brought into court or simply to the hill Areopagus. Paul's polished discourse, preserved in Acts 17:22-31 is a model of the manner in which the gospel message was presented to Gentiles who were ignorant of the biblical traditions. Paul however failed to be convincing, and was interrupted by his audience. The fruits of his Athenian mission were, according to Acts 17:34, scarce. Among the few notable converts were Dionysius the Areopagite and Damaris (Acts 17:34).

Aretas (ar'-e-tus), The name of several Nabataean kings.

1. Aretas I, who is mentioned in 2 Mac. 5:8. Jason had unsurped the high priesthood (2 Mac. 4:7) and when the death of Antiochus IV was wrongly reported, Jason tried to take over Jerusalem but failed and fled for refuge to the kingdom of Aretas. He was accused however in Aretas' court and had to flee from there into Egypt.

2. Aretas IV (9 B.C. -40 A.D.) the Nabataean king who controlled Damascus when Paul labored there after his conversion (2 Cor. 11:32, 33; Acts 9:20-25). When Paul was accused by the Jews before the governor of the city, he escaped through the window of a house that formed part of the wall, being let down in a basket. Aretas waged war on Herod Antipas to vindicate his daughter whom Herod repudiated to marry Herodias (c. 35-37 A.D.).

Argob, A region in the land of Bashan in Transjordan, which formed part of the sixth administrative district of Solomon. It comprised up to sixty cities (1 Kgs. 4:13). Before the Israelites arrived in Canaan, it belonged to the kingdom of Og (Deut. 3:4). It was conquered by Jair, son of Manasseh and assigned by Moses to this tribe (Deut. 3:13, 14).

Aridatha (ar'-i-day'-tha), A son of Haman the vizier of King Ahasuerus (Esth. 9:8). *See* HAMAN.

Ariel, 1. Probably the name of the altar of holocausts in the Temple (Isa. 29:9; Ezek. 43:15), and through metonymy, the symbolic name for Jerusalem in an oracle which threatens imminent punishment on the Holy City (Isa. 29:1, 2, 7).

2. The name of different personages of the Old Testament: one of the heads of Ezra's committee for the return from exile (Ezra 8:16); also a Moabite whose two sons were killed by Benaiah, one of David's Thirty (2 Sam. 23:20).

Arimathea (ar'-i-ma-the'-a), The native city of the Joseph who buried the body of Jesus in a new sepulcher of his own (Matt. 27:57-60). *See* RAMAH.

Arioch (ar'-i-ok), 1. According to Gen. 14:1, 9, king of Ellasar, one of the four kings who joined in a punitive campaign against the five cities of the Pentapolis. They took Lot and his family as prisoners but they were overtaken and defeated by Abraham with the help of some allies (Gen. 14:13 ff.). Some scholars have sought to identify him with Warad-Sin, king of Larsa in Mesopotamia, but this opinion has recently been abandoned.

2. According to Dan. 2:14, captain of the guard of Nebuchadnezzar of Babylonia.

arise

A., lift up the boy	Gen. 21:18
	A., my beloved, my beautiful one,
	S. of S. 2:13

Aristarchus, A Christian of Thessalonica. He was with Paul in Ephesus, when, together with Gaius, they were involved in the popular upheaval caused by Demetrius, a silversmith of the city (Acts 19:23-29). He accompanied Paul throughout the rest of the third apostolic journey until they came to Jerusalem (Acts 20:4). He probably suffered Roman custody and imprisonment with the apostle (Acts 27:2; Col. 4:10; Philem. 24).

Aristobulus (ar-is-tob′-u-lus), 1. A Jew of the priestly family, resident of Alexandria, teacher of king Ptolemy VI Philometer (181-145 B.C.). To him was addressed a letter of Judas Maccabeus in which he invited the Jews of Alexandria to celebrate the feast of the Dedication of the Temple after it had been profaned under Antiochus IV Epiphanes (2 Mac. 1:10-2:18).

2. In Rom. 16:11 Paul salutes the Christians of the house of Aristobulus, who is otherwise unknown.

Arius (ar′-i-us), Arius I, king of Sparta (309-265 B.C.). He wrote to the High Priest Onias offering friendship and a sharing of property of the peoples, seeing that they were brothers stemming from the same patriarch Abraham (1 Mac. 12:7, 19-23).

Ark of the Covenant, The chest or box that God, on Mt. Sinai, ordered Moses to make. According to Ex. 25:10-26, it was constructed of acacia wood, overlaid outside and inside with gold, and its measurements were about three and three quarter feet long and two and one quarter feet high and wide. It could be carried by two acacia wood poles which were inserted in four golden rings attached to the ark's four corners. A solid gold slab rested on top of the ark, and upon this slab, known as the **kapporit** or propitiatory, were two golden cherubims.

The ark was kept, according to Ex. 26:33; 40:21, in the Tent or Tabernacle which also held the tablets of the law given by God to Moses (Ex. 25:16; 40:20; Deut. 10:1-5). It was the seat or center of the benevolent presence of God to his people. 1 Sam. 4:4 states that God was seated between the cherubims of the ark, which was then called the footstool for the feet of the Lord (1 Chron. 28:2; Ps. 99:5; *see* Num. 10:33-35).

When the Israelites had entered Palestine the ark passed from Gilgal (Josh. 7:6) to Bethel (Jgs. 20:27) and then to Shiloh, where it was at the time of Samuel (1 Sam. 3:3). It was captured by the Philistines in the battle of Aphek (1 Sam. 4:11) and taken to Ashdod, Gath and Ekron (1 Sam. 5:3-6). It was restored to the Israelites after God had punished the Philistines severely for retaining it. It remained for some time in Kirjath-jearim in the house of Abinadab. David took it from there and installed it permanently in the new capital of his kingdom, Jerusalem (2 Sam. 6). Later the ark was placed in the innermost sanctuary of the Temple by Solomon, where it remained until the destruction of the Temple and of the city in 587 B.C. According to one not-so-reliable tradition, the ark was saved by Jeremiah on the eve of the destruction of the city and hidden on

Mt. Nebo (2 Mac. 2:4) but it was more probably destroyed together with the Temple.

Armageddon, According to Rev. 16:16, the place where the kings of the earth will convene at the call of the unclean spirits who go out from the Beast, from the Dragon and from the False Prophet· "the devils then assembled the kings in a place called in Hebrew Armageddon." This is the transcription of a Hebrew name, but given the approximate character of this transcription, the origin of the name is obscure. Some think this is an allusion to the city and mountain of Megiddo, the scene of many important battles recorded in the Old Testament (Jgs. 5:19; 2 Kgs. 23:29). Others believe that the name contains no precise geographical allusion but would be a defective transcription of **har-mo'ed**, meaning the 'mountain of meeting' (*see* Isa. 14:13).

Armenia, *See* ARARAT.

Armoni, A son of Rizpah, Saul's concubine (2 Sam. 21:8).

Army, Up to the time of the monarchy there was no stable and organized Israelite army. During its nomadic period, and that of the judges, the army was but the people in arms. In a time of crisis men from one or more tribes were called, and they furnished their own arms, mainly swords and slings. The constant threat from the Philistines was a decisive factor in the founding of the monarchy and in the reorganization of the army. Saul not only levied soldiers on a more rigid pattern from the tribes, but also gathered a central force of professional soldiers around him (1 Sam. 13:2; 14:52). David did likewise, and after the break with Saul and the flight to the Cave of Addullam, he had with him 400 men (1 Sam. 22:2), a number which later increased to 600 (1 Sam. 25:13). David was now in a powerful military position, able to offer his services even to the Philistines (1 Sam. 27:2). When he had become king of Judah David increased this army and added to it a special personal guard recruited among the Cherelites and Pelethites, who were Philistines (1 Kgs. 1:8, 32). These served not merely as his bodyguard but also to consolidate the central authority. To the larger army gathered from the tribes David gave a new shape, dividing it, according to 1 Chron. 27, into twelve divisions of 24,000 troops each. These gave service by rote, a month each for the twelve months of the year. Solomon introduced cavalry and chariots, for which he had stalls and carriage-houses constructed in supply centers strategically distributed throughout the national territory (1 Kgs. 24:6; 9:19; 10:26).

Arni, An ancestor of Jesus (Lk. 3:33).

Arnon, The biblical name for the actual Wadi-el-Mojib, a river that runs in a deep canyon from the highlands of Transjordan to spill into the eastern shore of the Dead Sea. It was the natural frontier between the lands of Moab to the south and the Amorite kingdom of Sihon to the north. After the Israelite conquest, the Arnon became the southern limit of the territory assigned to the tribe of Reuben (Num. 21:13, 24, 26, 28; Deut. 2:24-26; 3:8, 16; Josh. 12:1; 13:9-15).

Arod, A son of Gad (Gen. 46:16).

Aroer, 1. A city situated at the northern limit of the valley of the river Arnon in the territory of the Amorite kingdom of Sihon (Deut. 4:48; Josh. 12:2). It was conquered by the Israelites and assigned to the tribe of Reuben in Josh. 13:16, but to the tribe of Gad in Num. 32:34. It belonged to the Israelites up to the time of David (2 Sam. 24:5) but was later conquered by King Mesha of Moab, and was still Moabite in the time of Jeremiah (Jer. 48:19).

2. A city of the territory of the tribe of Gad in Transjordan, near Rabbah, the capital of the Amorite kingdom (Jgs. 11:33; Josh. 13:25). Some scholars believe that this and the previous town are one and the same.

3. A city mentioned in 1 Sam. 30:28. From the context it follows that this town must be sought in the territory of Judah, and seems to be the same as the town of Adadah, mentioned in Josh. 15:22.

Arpad, A city of northern Syria, today called Tell-Erfad, near Aleppo. It was conquered and destroyed by the Assyrians (2 Kgs. 18:34; 19:13; Isa. 10:9; 36:19; 37:13; Jer. 49:23).

Arphaxad (ar-fak′-sad), 1. According to the table of nations of Gen. 10, Arphaxad was the third son of Shem, the grandson of Noah (Gen. 10:22) and grandfather of Heber, one of the founding fathers of the Hebrews, from whom they take their name (Gen. 11:10-13; 1 Chron. 1:17-18). His name is also read in Luke's genealogy of Jesus (Lk. 3:36).

2. According to Judith 1:1-5, it is the name of the king of the Medes, the founder of the city of Ecbatana, who was later conquered by Nebuchadnezzar, king of Niniveh.

arrow

Run and fetch the *a.*	1 Sam. 20:36	they place the *a.* on a string	
Jonathan had shot the *a.*			Ps. 11:2
	1 Sam. 20:37	a sword or a sharp *a.*	Prov. 25:18
The *a.* is farther on	1 Sam. 20:37	nor shoot an *a.* at it	Isa. 37:33

Artemas (ar′-te-mas), One of St. Paul's companions, whom the apostle expected to send to Crete to replace Titus, who was to meet him at Nicopolis (Tit. 3:12).

Artemis (ar′-te-mis), A Greek goddess corresponding to Diana of the Roman religion. In Greek mythology she was the daughter of Zeus and the sister of Apollo, and was represented as a virgin huntress. She was venerated as the protector of young marriageable women, and of women during childbirth. The cult of Artemis at Ephesus departed not a little from this image and was more a fertility cult to the mother-goddess. The mother-goddess, symbol of the fertility of the earth, of animals and of men, was well known among the peoples of the Middle East and Asia Minor. According to Acts 19:27-40, Paul's success at Ephesus threatened grave damage to the commerce in statues and images of the goddess which abounded there. The silversmiths of the city, headed by one Demetrius, organized a civil commotion against Paul and his companion for doing damage to the goddess' fame. Two of his companions, Gaius and Aristarchus, were brought before the authorities of the city, but they managed to escape without harm, thanks to the intervention of one of the chiefs. After this commotion Paul left Ephesus (Acts 20:1).

Arumah (a-roo′-mah), A place in central Palestine where Abimelech settled after he had been driven out from Shechem (Jgs. 9:41).

Arvad, A Phoenician city on a small island of the same name on the coast of Syria, north of Beirut. In ancient times, from the fifteenth century B.C. to the Greco-Roman epoch, it was a very active commercial center. According to Ezek. 27:8, 11 it was famous for its expert sailors and brave warriors. Its people, according to the genealogy of Genesis 10:18, were Canaanite.

Arza, The chamberlain of King Elah of Israel, in whose house the latter was murdered by Zimri (1 Kgs. 16:9).

Asa, 1. King of Judah (913-873 B.C.), son and successor to Abijah. He took stringent measures against the idolatrous cults, banishing the sacred prostitutes and destroying the idols, without even sparing the goddess Ashera which had the protection of the queen mother Maacah (1 Kgs. 15:11-15). Baasha, king of Israel, began to war against Asa, and commenced fortifying the city of Ramah on the borders of Judah. For this reason Asa took the gold and silver of the temple and the royal palace and gave it to Ben-hadad, king of Damascus, asking him to break his alliance with Baasha and make one with him. Ben-hadad sent his army against Israel and Baasha was constrained to abandon his anti-Judah projects. Asa took the material for the fortification of Ramah and with it fortified the cities of Geba and Mizpah on the northern borders of his kingdom (1 Kgs. 15:18-22). According to 2 Chron. 16:7-9, Asa was reproved by Hanani for his alliance with Ben-hadad. 2 Chron 14:8-14 records his victory over Zerah the Ethiopian.

2. Son of Elkanah, Levite and father to Obadiah (1 Chron. 9:16).

Asahel, Nephew of David, son of Zeruiah and brother to Joab and Abishai, and one of the Thirty warriors of David's army (2 Sam. 23:24; 1 Chron. 2:15; 11:26). He was killed by Abner in the battle of Gibeon between the supporters of Saul's descendants and those loyal to David (2 Sam. 2:18-23). His death was later revenged by Joab who treacherously killed Abner in Hebron (2 Sam. 3:27-30).

Asaiah (a-zay'-yah), 1. A servant to King Josiah (2 Kgs. 22:12, 14).

2. Name of at least two other men in Old Testament (1 Chron. 4:36; 9:5).

Asaph (ay'-saf), According to 1 Chron. 6:15-33, a Levite of the family of Gershon. He was appointed by David to take charge, with Ethan and Herman, of the Levite chanters of the Tabernacle, and later, under Solomon was in charge of the Temple at Jerusalem. One of the music guilds at the Temple was called the "Sons of Asaph" (1 Chron. 25:1-2), which is mentioned in the list of the Jews who returned with Zerubbabel from exile (Ezra 2:41; Neh. 7:44). Psalms 50, 73 to 83 are attributed to the Sons of Asaph, but probably only belonged to their repertoire, and were not necessarily composed by them.

ascend
Who can *a.* the mountain   Ps. 24:3   I will *a.* above the tops   Isa. 14:14
          the Son of Man *a.* to   Jn. 6:62

Ascents, Songs of, *See* PSALMS.

Asenath (as'-e-nath), Joseph's wife, daughter to Potiphera, the Egyptian priest of the god On, and mother of Ephraim and Manasseh (Gen. 41:45, 50-52; 46:20).

Ashan (ay'-shan), A Levitical town of Judah (Josh. 21:16), formerly of Simeon (Josh. 19:7).

Ashbel, A son of Benjamin (Gen. 46:21; Num. 26:38).

Ashdod, One of the five cities forming the Philistine Pentapolis (Josh. 13:3) in the territory assigned, theoretically, to the tribe of Judah (Josh. 15:46-47), but only occupied by the Israelites in the time of Uzziah, king of Judah (783-742; 2 Chron. 26:6). To the temple of Dagon in Ashdod the Philistines brought the captured ark of the covenant, setting it down beside Dagon, only to find Dagon thrown down and shattered. Then came the plague of tumors, so that panic gripped the Philistines and they transferred the ark to Gath (1 Sam. 5:1-8; 6:17). Ashdod suffered but brief years of Israelite domination. In its new-found liberty it revolted against Sargon II, king of Assyria (711), who however reconquered it. From then on Ashdod remained faithful to Assyria until this empire came to an end. It became a provincial capital in the Persian empire, and was opposed to the rebuilding of the walls of Jerusalem undertaken by Nehemiah (Neh. 4:1). The Maccabees sacked the city on several occasions (Judas: 1 Mac. 4:15; Jonathan: 1 Mac. 10:77-85 and John Hyrcanus: 1 Mac. 16:10). According to Acts 8:40, the region of Ashdod, called Azotus in Hellenistic times, was evangelized by Philip. Today the city's name is Eshdud.

Asher, The eighth of the sons of Jacob, born of Zilpah, the slave of his first wife Leah (Gen. 30:13). Asher is the founding father of the tribe of Asher. Its territory was a strip of land about 60 miles long and 15 miles wide on the Mediterranean coast north of Mt. Carmel (Josh. 19:24-31). Its geographical position explains in part its isolation and scanty participation in the events of ancient Israelite history. People from the tribe of Asher did take part in Gideon's undertakings (Jgs. 6:35; 7:23) but the tribe did not accept Deborah's invitation to fight against the Canaanites of the north (Jgs. 5:17). In the blessings of Jacob (Gen. 49:20) and Moses (Deut. 33:24-25) Asher is remembered for its prosperity.

Asherah, A Canaanite goddess, wife of the god El, who was supreme in the Canaanite pantheon. When the Old Testament refers to Ashera, it is more probably an allusion to Baal's consort, which is why she is associated with the rites of fertility in Canaanite cult practice. The texts that speak of Asherah usually refer to a cult object, a kind of wooden stake erected in the soil, and probably carved in the shape of a woman, an image or symbol of the goddess (*see* Judges 6:26-30; 1 Kings 15:33; 2 Kings 13:6; 17:16; 18:4; 21:7; 23:6).

ashes

I am but dust and *a.*	Gen. 18:27	reformed in sackcloth and *a.*	
for removing the *a.*	Ex. 27:3		Matt. 11:21
as he sat among the *a.*	Job 2:8	the sprinkling of a heifer's *a.*	
with the dust and *a.*	Job 30:19		Heb. 9:13

Ashima (a-shy′-ma), The name of a god venerated by the people of Hamath whom the Assyrians settled in Samaria after the destruction of the city and the exile of the people of the north (722 B.C.: 2 Kgs. 17:30).

Ashkelon (ash′-ke-lon), One of the five cities forming the Philistine Pentapolis (Josh. 13:3). It is situated in the territory of Judah, which tribe according to Judges 1:18 conquered it. It was certainly Philistine at the time of the Judges (Samson, Judges 14:19) and of Kings Saul and David (1 Sam. 6:17; 2 Sam. 1:20). It is the object of several prophetic utterances threatening dire punishment on it and on the other Philistine cities (Amos 1:8; Jer. 25:20; 47:5; Zech. 9:5; Zeph. 2:4).

Ashkenaz (ash′-ka-naz), According to Jer. 51:27, a northern kingdom associated with Ararat and Minni, identified by some authors with the Scythians. In the table of nations, Ashkenaz is the son of Gomer and grandson of Japheth (Gen. 10:3).

Ashpenaz (ash′-pa-naz), The name of the chief eunuch of Nebuchadnezzar in the Book of Daniel (Dan. 1:3).

Ashtaroth (ash′-ta-roth), A city of Transjordan in the region of Bashan. residence of Og, king of the Amorites, defeated by the Israelites (Deut. 1:4; 3:10; Josh. 12:4). It was assigned to the tribe of Manasseh (Josh. 13:31), and was a Levitical city of the family of Gershom (1 Chron. 6:56).

Ashteroth-karnaim (kar-nay′-im), A locality east of the sea of Galilee, inhabited by the Rephaim, the almost legendary inhabitants of pre-Israelite Palestine, who were defeated by Chedorlaomer and his allies (Gen. 14:5). Some authors identify Ashteroth-karnaim with Ashtaroth.

Ashtoreth, *See* ASTARTE.

Asia, In the Bible it can mean: 1. In the books of the Maccabees, the kingdom of the Seleucids (1 Mac. 8:6; 2 Mac. 3:3).

2. In the New Testament, it is the Roman province of Asia, which comprised the most westerly part of Asia Minor, with its capital first in Pergamum and later in Ephesus.

Asiarch, The title of some officials in the city of Ephesus, known to us from Acts 19:31 and from some inscriptions. There is no certain information on what precisely their function was. They are thought to be the priests of the cult of the Roman emperor in Asia, elected annually to preside at the solemnities in honor of the emperor.

Asmodeus (az-mo-dee′-us), The name of the demon who, according to the account in Tobit 8:3, killed Sarah's seven husbands. Tobiah then married her and defeated the demon, thanks to the instructions given him by Raphael (Tob. 8:2, 3) to place the fish's heart and liver on the burning incense, the stench of which drove the demon to Egypt.

Aspatha (as-pay′-tha), One of the ten sons of Haman the vizier of king Ahasuerus (Esther 9:7). *See* HAMAN.

assembly

the whole *a.* of Israel present		by the public *a.*	Prov. 5:14
	Ex. 12:6	the whole *a.* in chaos	Acts 19:32
extol him in the *a.*	Ps. 107:32	settled in the lawful *a.*	Acts 19:39

Assos, A port city in the gulf of Adramythium, where Paul embarked for his last journey to Jerusalem (Acts 20:13). It is situated on the west coast of Asia Minor, opposite the island of Lesbos.

Assyria, A region that extends from the eastern bank of the middle course of the Tigris to Armenia to the north, the mountains of Zagros to the east and Babylonia to the south. It takes its name from its ancient capital Assur. The history of these eastern Semites that relates to the history of Israel begins around the year 1000 B.C. Before that, with its alternating periods of precarious independence, Assyria was at the mercy of its powerful neighbors, the Babylonians and the Mitanni. From that time on however, thanks to the organizing ability and military prowess of its kings, it became one of the greatest empires in history. Salmanassar III (858-824 B.C.) followed out the lead of Ashurnasirpal II (883-858 B.C.) and carried the limits of the empire to the Persian gulf to the south and to Syria to the west. To stop the advance of the Assyrians, the Aramaeans of Syria united to do battle with Salmanassar III in Karkar (853 B.C.). At this battle Ahab of Israel was also present, as was Hamath (848 B.C.). Even though the outcome of the battle was uncertain, the Aramaean coalition did succeed in checking the Assyrians, who did not appear again in the area until the time of Tiglath-pileser III (745-727 B.C.). He managed to conquer Damascus (734 B.C.). Ahaz of Judah was invited to enter into a coalition with the Aramaeans together with Pekah of Israel, but Ahaz refused. Then Pekah invaded the land of Judah to bring pressure on Ahaz, but he called to his aid Tiglath-pileser III, declaring himself the latter's vassal (Isa. 7; 2 Kgs. 15-16). Salmanassar V (727-721 B.C.) decided to complete the assimilation of the western regions. He captured the kingdom of the north and laid siege to Samaria, which fell, it seems, to his successor Sargon II (722-705 B.C.; 2 Kgs. 17). Sargon II deported the

Israelite population of the north and established in their place colonies from Hamath, Avva and other regions. A further Assyrian campaign in the west was undertaken by Sennacherib (705-681 B.C.). He took over almost all the territory of Judah but did not succeed in capturing Jerusalem (2 Kgs. 18-19). Assyria reached the limits of her territorial aspirations when Egypt submitted through the efforts of Esarhaddon (681-669 B.C.) and Ashur-banipal (668-630 B.C.). The zenith of its splendor however almost coincided with its disintegration, which took place with shattering rapidity. Nabopolassar of Babylonia and Cyassaus king of the Medes conquered and razed to the ground Niniveh the capital in 612. The last Assyrian king was finally defeated in 609 and with this was ended Assyrian independence and history.

Astarte, A Canaanite fertility goddess, particularly venerated at Sidon (2 Kgs. 23:13), one of the most popular figures among the idolatrous cults from time to time adopted by the Israelites (Jgs. 10:6; 1 Sam. 7:3; 12:10), together with the god Baal. Her cult was introduced to Jerusalem by Solomon (1 Kgs. 11:5). In the Bible her name reads Astoret, i.e. with the vowels of the word **boset,** meaning abomination, which had to be read out in public recitation instead of her proper name.

astonishment
of terror, *a.* and mockery   At this the family's *a.*   Mk. 5:42
          2 Chron. 29:8

Asyncritus (a-sing′-cri-tus), A Christian of Rome greeted by Paul (Rom. 16:14).

Atad (ay′-tad), A locality in southern Palestine where the funeral cortege bearing Jacob's body to Palestine stopped. Later it was called Abel-mizraim (Gen. 50:10-11).

Atargatis (a-tar′-ga-tis), A goddess of fertility venerated in Syria, wife of the god Attis, in Greek, Adonis. 2 Mac. 12:26 speaks of the temple dedicated to her in Carnaim in Transjordan.

Ataroth (at′-a-roth), 1. A city in the territory of Gad (Num. 32:3, 34).

2. A city of Ephraim, on the eastern border of their lands (Josh. 16:7).

3. The name of two other cities, mentioned but not identified in Josh. 16:2 (*see* Josh. 16:5; 18:13) and in 1 Chron. 2:54.

Athaliah (ath′-a-ly′-ah), Wife of Jehoram, king of Judah (849-842 B.C.), daughter of Ahab, king of Israel (869-850), and mother of Ahaziah, king of Judah (841). After the death of Ahaziah, who reigned but a few months, Athaliah decided to exterminate the whole royal line. Joash, son of Ahaziah, alone escaped the massacre. He hid in the temple under the protection of the High Priest Jehoiada. In the seventh year of Athaliah's reign (837) Jehoiada, backed by the royal guard, proclaimed Joash king in the temple and Athaliah was killed (2 Kgs. 11:1-16).

Athenobius (ath′-e-no′-bi-us), A legate of Antiochus VII Sidetes to Simon Maccabeus (1 Mac. 15:32-36).

Athens, By the first century A.D. Athens had long since lost its preeminence as capital of the ancient world. Though subject to Rome, it was still considered one of the principal centers of philosophy and the arts, excelling all its rivals, such as Alexandria, by the splendor of its traditions. St. Paul visited Athens during his second missionary journey and there met with the Epicurean and Stoic philosophers. He spoke at the Areopagus without however convincing his audience to any great extent. One famous convert was however Dionysius the Areopagite (Acts 17:10-34).

Atonement, Expiation, in the sense of the Hebrew word **kapper** of which it is a translation. To expiate was to perform those rites and actions which led to the elimination of the obstacles to intimacy with God created by sin. Expiation brought about reconciliation between man and God.

The idea of expiation permeated Old Testament theology, as can be gathered from the importance attached to expiatory sacrifices in the Jewish ritual. It is important to note that expiation in the Old Testament is never aimed at God as if through it His anger could be appeased or His favor cultivated. The Jews expiated their sins, which were the blocks put in the way of God's unwithdrawn goodness to man, and which therefore had to be removed. The way to removing these obstacles was through the blood of the victims of sacrifice. According to Lev. 17:11, the life of the body was considered to be in the blood, and God is said to have given blood so that the people could perform the rite of atonement for their lives at the altar: "for it is blood that atones for a life." When a leader of the people or a private individual inadvertently did something forbidden by the law, this was expiated by a victim, part of whose blood was spread by the priest on the horns of the altar of holocausts (Lev. 4:22-35). When however expiation must be made for the whole people, then the blood was also sprinkled on the veil at the entrance to the inner sanctuary of the temple.

These rites clearly suggest that the victim and its blood were not intended to be substitutions for the sinner, in the sense that the victim was subjected to the punishment due to the sinner's sin. Rather the life-blood of the victim was considered to have the power of purifying the altar and the tabernacle, the symbol of God and the place of His benevolent presence to man. With the pouring of the life-blood was removed all that impeded the flow of God's goodness to man.

In the post-exilic period the day of expiation was one of the great Jewish feast days. It was celebrated on the tenth of the month Tishri (September-October). On that day was performed a solemn rite of expiation for the sanctuary, the priests and the people. The ceremony is described in Lev. 16: the high priest entered the Holy of Holies wearing the consecrated linen and washed for this unique annual solemnity. He burned incense and sprinkled the propitiation, or throne of mercy, with the blood of the young bull that had been immolated for his own sins and those of the priests, and with the blood of the goat for the sins of the people. In the second part of the rite the high priest placed his hands on the head of the second goat, confessing all the faults, transgressions and sins of the sons of Israel. The goat was then sent into the desert for Azazel, who probably was a demon who inhabited the desert. *See* AZAZEL.

According to Heb. 9 this rite was a type of the expiation achieved by Christ, even though in many points the two do not bear comparison. Christ atoned, not in the flesh of animals, nor in a man-made sanctuary, but in His own humanity. Moreover, His atonement in one not-to-be-repeated act brought about an eternal redemption. The New Testament often alludes to the provisional nature of the Old Testament expiation rites to underscore the unique power of Christ's death and resurrection. According to Rom. 3:25, God appointed Jesus to sacrifice His life so as to win reconciliation through faith: this is an evident allusion to the Old Testament expiatory rites described in Lev. 16. The repeated insistence on the blood of Christ (Eph. 2:13; 1 Pet. 2:24; Rom. 3:25, etc.) was meant to bring home to the faithful how Christ brought to fulfilment what was anticipated in the Old Testament, an expiation worked out through the horror of death, and the glory of what it led to, namely, the resurrection. Through this redemptive act, everybody has access to the Father who, through it, has pledged to all men an eternal inheritance.

Attalia (at-a-ly′-a), A port city on the southern coast of Asia Minor, founded by Attalus II, king of Pergamum (159-138 B.C.). It was here that St. Paul embarked to return to Antioch at the end of his first missionary journey (Acts 14:25).

Attalus (at′-a-lus), Name of three kings of Pergamum. The King Attalus of whom 1 Mac. 15:22 speaks as among the addressees of a letter from Rome in favor of the Jews is to be identified with either the second or third king of the same name (159-138 B.C. or 138-133 B.C.).

Augustus, Gaius Julius Caesar Octavianus, Roman Emperor at the time of Our Lord's birth (Luke 2:1). The title "Augustus" was given him by the Roman senate (27 B.C.) and it was borne also by his successors. Augustus deposed Archelaus, Herod's son, and placed Judea, Samaria and Idumaea under the authority of a Roman governor.

authentic
a. worshippers will worship
Jn. 4:23

Avenger, The usual translation of the Hebrew term **go'el,** which was a typical juridical institution of primitive, and especially, nomadic societies. It was based on the principle of cohesion between the blood-members of the tribe. Israel retained the institution even after settling in Canaan. The avenger, who is the nearest relative in accordance with the order precisely established in Lev. 25:49, has definite rights and duties, essentially aimed at protecting the group to which he belongs, and indirectly geared towards the protection of the members of that group. The principal duty of the avenger is to repay the murder of a family member by killing the aggressor, or a member of his family. This blood-revenge is however strictly regulated by Israelite law to contain it within reasonable limits. Death was the repayment for death, but lesser injuries were vindicated less drastically. Exodus 21:23-25 stipulates: a life for a life, an eye for an eye, tooth for tooth, hand for hand, foot for foot, burn for burn, wound for wound, stroke for stroke. The law moreover foresees the case of unintentional killing and ordains the establishment of refuge cities whither a person could flee to appeal to a board who would determine the degree of guilt (Num. 35:9-34; Deut. 19:1-13). Israelite law would not accept a fine in compensation for willful killing, basing its stand on the inalienable right of God over the life of every man (Gen. 9:6; Num. 35:31-34). An Old Testament example of blood-revenge according to the **go'el** institution is the death of Abner to vindicate the killing of Asahel (2 Sam. 2:22-23; 3:22-30). The **go'el** institution is also operative in the so-called Levirate law which obliged a brother to marry the widow of his deceased brother if the brother died without male issue, to ensure that the family name would perdure (Deut. 25:5-10).

The book of Ruth illustrates another case of **go'el**: if an Israelite must sell his patrimony, the **go'el** has first right on it so that the property will stay in the family (Lev. 25:25 and Jer. 32:6 f.). This right may however be ceded in favor of the next nearest relative (Ruth 3:12; 4:14).

Avva, The city of origin of one of the groups which the king of Assyria settled in Samaria to replace the dispossessed and exiled Israelites (722 B.C., 2 Kings 17:24).

Avvim (av′-vim), A people who lived in the region of Gaza in Palestine even before the Israelites came (Deut. 2:23; Josh. 13:3).

Ayin (a-yeen′), The 16th letter of the Hebrew alphabet (a guttural sound without parallel in English).

Azariah (az′-a-ry′-ah), 1. King of Judah (783-742), often called Uzziah. *See* 2 Kings 14:22; 15:1-7; 2 Chronicles 26:1-23.

2. The name of one of Daniel's three companions, also called Abednego (Dan. 1:6), who were cast into the fiery furnace and escaped unharmed (Dan. 3:12).

3. The name of 20 other Old Testament personalities, among whom were the following: a. The son of Obed, prophet of Judah, who encouraged Asa, king of Judah (913-873 B.C.) to undertake a religious reform (2 Chron. 15:1-8). b. Son of Jehoshaphat, king of Judah (873-849), killed by his brother Jehoram to make secure his succession to the throne (2 Chron. 21:2-4).

4. The name with which the archangel Raphael introduced himself to Tobiah. (Tob. 5:13; 6:7; 9:2).

Azazel (a-zay′-zel, or az′-a-zel), On the Day of Atonement the high priest imposed his hand upon a goat while confessing the sins of the people. Then the goat was sent into the desert "for Azazel" (Lev. 16:8-10; 20-28). What "for Azazel" means is uncertain. Some scholars hold it refers to the function of the goat (the goat that departs), while another interpretation would have it that Azazel is the name of some demon of the desert.

Azekah (a-zee′-ka), A city of Judah (Josh. 15:35), northeast of Lachish. As the coalition forces of the Canaanite kings fled before Joshua's army, a huge shower of hailstones pelted them all the way to Azekah. More deaths resulted from this than from Israel's sword (Josh. 10:10 ff.). Azekah is also the scene of a struggle between Saul and the Philistines (1 Sam. 17:1).

Azor (ay′-zor), Ancestor of Jesus according to the genealogy of Mt. 1:13, 14.

Azotus, *See* ASHDOD.

B

Baal (ba′-al), Hebrew and other semitic languages have in common the word Baal, meaning lord, master, which is also equivalent to such modes of address as "Your Excellency." With time this name, for all practical purposes, became identified with the god of rain, the storm god and the god of fertility in the Canaanite pantheon. This god's proper name was Hadad. Baal represented the active element in fertility and was by far the most popular among the Canaanite gods, though not the supreme one; the latter's name was El, the father of the gods. Baal is frequently associated with Anat, his sister and wife in Canaanite mythology. Among the religious texts discovered at Ras Shamra, the ancient Ugarit, there are three tablets with poems celebrating the deeds of prowess of Baal. The first poem treats of the battle between Baal and Yamm (the sea) to whom El had conceded power over the earth and over Baal. Baal is unhappy with the situation and, helped by Qothar–we–Kharis, the artisan and wise god, he engages in battle with Yamm, whom he overcomes with a blow to the head. In this way Baal secures his dominion over the earth against any danger from the waters of the open sea. Many of the elements of these semite myths were used to express the Biblical account of creation, as the work of the Lord (*see* Ps. 148:5; Isa. 40:26, etc.).

Another poem sings of Baal's victory over Mot or Death. Baal is invited by Mot to come down into the depths of the earth. There is a lacuna in the text and then occurs El's mourning over the death of Baal. Anat, Baal's companion, now begins an anxious search for her husband. She asks Mot to free his prisoner, but Mot refuses. Finally Anat is victorious and so

Baal returns to life and recovers his dominion over the earth. This myth obviously represents the cycle of the year's seasons, with winter's death and spring's resurgence.

The worship of Baal was a great and powerful rival to the worship of Israel's God through Old Testament history up to the Exile. At times the worship of the Lord seemed to be submerged by the increasing favor granted to the worship of Baal, and to be transformed into a dangerous syncretism, so severely and decidedly denounced by the prophets. According to Judges 6:25-30 Gideon's father built an altar to Baal, who was venerated by the neighboring peoples. It was however during the time of Ahab of Israel that Baal worship had its greatest vogue (869-850 B.C.). He had married Jezebel, the daughter of the king of Tyre. She gave open protection to the worship of the Canaanite god, keeping her own priests and prophets and persecuting those loyal to the Lord. Elijah was an object of her special hatred (1 Kgs. 16-18).

The Books of Kings also record the periodic attempts of various kings to eradicate or contain the spread of Baalism. Asa of Judah (913-873), Jehu of Israel (842-815), Hezekiah (715-687), Josiah (641/40-609), supported by the zeal of prophets like Elisha, Isaiah, Jeremiah etc., were among the most determined religious reformers of Israelite history.

Baalah (ba′-al-ah), The earlier name of Kiriath-jearim (Josh. 15:9; 1 Chron. 13:6). *See* KIRIATH-JEARIM.

Baal-Berith (ba′-al-be′-rith), A god venerated in the city of Shechem (Jgs. 9:4) and adored also by the Israelites after the death of Gideon, according to Judges 8:33.

Baal-Gad (ba′-al-gad), A town west of Mount Hermon. The territory conquered by Joshua extended as far as Baal-gad (Josh. 11:17; 12:7; 13:5).

Baal-Hanan (ba′-al-ha′-nan), A king of Edom (Gen. 36:38, 39).

Baal-Hazor (ba′-al-ha′-zor), A locality 7½ miles south of Shiloh, where Amnon, David's son, was killed by his half-brother Absalom in revenge for the violation of his sister Tamar (2 Sam. 13:23).

Baalim, Plural of the Hebrew Baal. *See* BAAL.

Baalis (ba′-al-is), King of Ammon, who sent a certain Ishmael to kill Gedaliah, the governor of Judea, whom Nebuchadnezzar had appointed from Babylon after the destruction of Jerusalem (587 B.C.; Jer. 40:13-16). Afterwards he gave asylum to Gedaliah's assassins (Jer. 41).

Baal-Peor (ba′-al-pe′-or), A divinity venerated at Peor or Beth-peor. Here the Israelites worshiped idolatrously when they camped in Shittim, almost on the eve of passing over the Jordan into the land of Canaan. For this sin the people were gravely punished (Num. 25:1-9; Deut. 4:3; Ps. 106:28).

Baal-Perazim (ba′-al-per′-a-zim), A place near Jerusalem where David defeated the Philistines (2 Sam. 5:20; Isa. 28:21).

Baalzebub (ba′-al-ze′-bub), A god venerated in the city of Ekron, one of the five cities forming the Philistine Pentapolis. Ahaziah, king of Israel (850-849), fell from the balcony of his palace and injured himself, and so sent some servants to consult with Baalzebub about his cure. For this Elijah reproved him and predicted his death (2 Kgs. 1).

Baal-Zephon (ba′-al-ze′-fon), One of the first stop-overs made by the

Israelites on their flight from Egypt, even before they crossed the Red Sea (Ex. 14:2).

Baanah (ba′-an-ah), A Benjaminite who with his brother Rechab killed Ishbaal, the last descendant of the house of Saul. The brothers brought Ishbaal's head to David, hoping for reward, but their reward was death (2 Sam. 4:2-12).

Baasha (ba′-ash-a), King of Israel (900-877). He killed his predecessor Nadab, son of Jeroboam I, and all his family. Later Baasha received from the prophet Jehu the warning that the same lot would befall his own family (1 Kgs. 15:27-34; 16:1-7). He waged war on Asa of Judah (913-873) but Asa struck an alliance with Ben-hadad, king of Damascus, who invaded Israel from the north, obliging Baasha to abandon his Judean projects (1 Kgs. 15:16-22).

Babel, Tower of, The last episode of primitive history narrated in Genesis 11 is the story of the construction of the city or tower of Babel. This story sets out to explain the dispersion of peoples and the diversity of tongues. It gives an ideal picture of the beginnings of settled life in terms of a humanity that still formed one social entity, both ethnically and linguistically. The scene is set in the east on the plain of Shinar. The people were becoming aware of the new horizons that were offered by the change over from nomadic to settled existence, and of the value of united forces. For this reason they determined to build a city to prevent dispersion, and a tower reaching up to heaven to ensure that their name would be remembered forever. The Bible text does not compel one to interpret their plans as being similar to those of the Titans of Greek mythology, who wished to assault the very divinity. Nevertheless the account sees in their efforts an immoderate ambition and an exaggerated affirmation of man, exaggerated because it neglected or ignored his absolute dependence on God. Neither humanism nor human effort is here condemned, but only the immoderate exaltation of the human as the supreme value.

The story is itself an etiology, an explanation of causes, of the surprising fact of the diversity of tongues, taken together with a popular etymology of the word **Babel** which means "gate of God." These two elements were combined very probably because at the time the real aspirations of Babylonia to be the capital of the world were being all too painfully experienced by many peoples. The Bible account would afford a theological explanation of why these aspirations proved vain, and why they will always be shattered.

The tower referred to in the account is clearly a ziggurat, a lofty pyramidal structure, built in successive stages, equipped with outside stairs and topped with a small shrine. It was man's vocalizing in brick and mortar his religious aspirations to come near to God, and to have God come near to man's world. The scripture account blames the effort, even if it is not a product of Titanism in the strict sense, for challenging God, for which reason its builders were punished. The whole account is however steeped in anti-Babylonian polemic, which leads one to suppose that the story grew among those peoples who were subjected to the harsh yoke of Babylonian aspirations. How the story came to Israel, or whether it is original with the Bible, is not known. Immediately following this judgment on sin, Abraham is introduced and the divine initiative puts a decisive end to the division between man and God.

baby

there was a *b.* boy, crying	Ex. 2:6	and the *b.* lying in the manger
the *b.* leapt in her womb	Lk. 1:41	Lk. 2:16
the *b.* leapt in my womb	Lk. 1:44	

Babylonia, A region in Mesopotamia bordered to the north by Assyria, by the Arabian desert to the west, by the Persian highlands to the east, and by the Gulf of Persia to the south. The name derives from the city of Babylon, on the left bank of the Euphrates. It is a most fertile and rich area, and in ancient times there was a continual succession of peoples and cultures which in turn had their influence on Israel. The earliest known inhabitants were the Sumerians, whose flourishing civilization has left its mark on the whole of the cultural, religious, artistic and literary history of the area. (The first dynasty of Ur lasted from c. 2700 to 2500 B.C.) There followed the Accadic period, when the Sumerians were supplanted by this strong semite people, first in the north and then in the south (2350-2150 B.C.). It was not until about 2050 that the Sumerians succeeded in reestablishing themselves. During the period 1950 to 1686 B.C. Babylon appears for the first time as the capital of the whole Babylonian empire through the achievements of the 1st dynasty of Babylon, whose most celebrated sovereign was Hammurabi (1728-1686). There followed a dark age in its history. The Kassites first overran it (1550-1150) and then the Assyrians (1150-612). Babylonia only re-won its importance at the head of the empire in the 7th century B.C. Already in 721 the Aramaeans (or Chaldeans) had succeeded in creating a kingdom in Babylon, which enjoyed a brief independence under Merodach-baladan (2 Kgs. 20:12). In 625 Nabopolassar ascended the throne, and taking advantage of the internal divisions in the Assyrian empire and relying on the help of Cyaxerxes, he rebelled against Assyria and captured Nineveh, the Assyrian capital (612). Nabopolassar was followed on the throne by the exceptionally gifted King Nebuchadnezzar II (605-562) who captured Jerusalem (587) and deported large portions of the people of Judea to Babylonia. This is known as the Babylonian exile or captivity (2 Kgs. 24 and 25). The Babylonian empire came to a definitive end at the hands of the Persians whose king, Cyrus, took Babylon in 539 and Babylonia was reduced to the stature of a Persian province.

Babylonia figures in the Bible as a type, and later as a symbol, of a power adverse to God and His people, and its name is found in the cryptic language of apocalyptic literature and in the veiled references of Christians suffering persecution at the hands of the Romans (Rev. 16:19; 17:5; 18:10; 1 Pet. 5:13).

Bacchides (bak′-i-dees), General of the Seleucid army under Demetrius I Soter (161-150 B.C.). He was sent into Judea to make Alcimus high priest (1 Mac. 7:8). After the defeat and death of Nicanor, another Seleucid general, he returned to Judea to fight Judas Maccabeus, whom he conquered first in Arbela, and later in Elasa, where the Jewish hero died (1 Mac. 9:1-27). The struggle continued with Judas' successor, his brother Jonathan (1 Mac. 9:43-53), who, after numerous armed battles with the Seleucid general, at last defeated him decisively, and got from him a favorable peace (1 Mac. 9:58-73).

bad

very *b*. figs, so *b*.	Jer. 24:2	a decayed tree bears *b*. fruit
but the *b*. ones very *b*.	Jer. 24:3	Matt. 7:17

Bagoas (ba-go′-as), A eunuch of the court of Holofernes, who was entrusted with the personal affairs of the king (Judith 12:11), and discovered the body of the king after he had been slain by Judith (Judith 14:14-18).

Bahurim (ba-hu′-rim), A locality in the neighborhood of Jerusalem, where Shimei cursed David as he fled from Absalom (2 Sam. 16:5-13; 19:16-23).

baker

and *b*. gave offense	Gen. 40:1	When the chief *b*. saw	Gen. 40:16
the *b*. of the king of Egypt		*b*. desists from stirring	Hos. 7:4
	Gen. 40:5		

Balaam (ba′-lam), A non-Israelite seer, son of Beor and native of Pethor. According to Num. 22-24, while the Israelites were camped on the plains of Moab before crossing the Jordan, Balak king of Moab sent for Balaam to pronounce curses on the Israelites. Balaam however found himself interiorly compelled to bless the people he was called on to curse. The words the Bible puts in the mouth of Balaam belong to the most ancient texts in the Bible, and reach back into the twelfth century B.C. The first oracle (Num. 23:7-10) is a short poem in honor of Israel, praised for being selected by Yahweh as the chosen people among all the nations of the world. The second (23:18-24) is a proclamation of the saving presence of God in the midst of His people Israel, to which He guarantees protection and strength, making it immune to every misfortune or accident. In the third (24:3-7) Balaam gives a brief description of his experience as seer, and then predicts the future victory of Israel over all her enemies and her coming prosperity. In the fourth (24:15-24) there is first an introduction like that to the third, and then he predicts a royal line for Israel which will extend its dominion over the surrounding peoples, Moab and Edom. This oracle is certainly connected with the foundation of the Davidic dynasty. The story of Balaam is often told in the Bible as a manifestation of the power of God and the special protection He accords His people (Deut. 23:4-6; Josh. 24:9-10). Balaam however is also recorded as a type of the false prophets and false doctors who lead the people astray from the ways of the Lord (2 Pet. 2:16; Jude 11; Rev. 2:14). A tradition with a variance about Balaam is read in Num. 31:8; 16; Josh. 13:22.

Baladan (bal′-a-dan), The father of King Merodach-baladan of Babylon (2 Kgs. 20:12). *See* MERODACH-BALADAN

Balak (ba′-lak), King of Moab who called the seer Balaam, son of Beor, of Pethor, to curse the Israelites while they were encamped on the plains of Moab before crossing the Jordan. Balaam however, despite himself, felt impelled to bless the Israelites instead of cursing them, thus negating Balak's plans (Num. 22-24).

Balances, The type of balances, or scales, used in antiquity did not differ much from the type used today. Before Roman times people did not know of the balance made of a plate with an extended bar giving the graduated scale. The prophets are frequent and severe in their condemnation of those who interfere with the weights or the scales (e.g. Ezek. 45:10; Hos. 12:7; Amos 8:5; Mic. 6:11), and similar warnings are found in the juridical texts (Lev. 19:35; Deut. 25:13-16).

bald, baldhead

because of his *b*. crown	Lev. 13:40	Go up, *b*., they shouted	
because of his *b*. forehead			2 Kgs. 2:23
	Lev. 13:41	Every head has been made *b*.	
sore of the *b*. spot	Lev. 13:43		Jer. 48:37

Balm, Balsam, A sweet-smelling resinous substance probably obtained from the mastix tree, a bushy evergreen commonly grown in Gilead in Old Testament times. It is mentioned frequently as having commercial value (Gen. 37:25; Ezek. 27:17) and curative properties (Jer. 8:22; 46:11; 51:8).

Balthasar (bal-thaz′-ar), The name of one of the three Magi in late Christian tradition. *See* MAGI.

Bamoth (ba′-moth), A stopping-place of the Israelites en route to Canaan under Moses (Num. 21:19, 20).

Bamoth-Baal (ba′-moth-ba′-al), A locality in the region of Moab, where Balak, king of Moab, brought Balaam to view the Israelites camped in the vicinity (Num. 22:41), with the intention of rendering his curses more efficacious. Later the land passed over to the tribe of Reuben (Josh. 13:17).

Bani (ba′-ni), 1. The Gadite (2 Sam. 23:36), one of David's mighty men.

2. Descendant of Perez (1 Chron. 9:4).

3. Name of several other men in Old Testament (Ezra 2:10; 10:29; Neh. 9:4, 5; 11:22).

Baptism, No sacrament receives such vast and varied treatment at the hands of the authors of the New Testament as the sacrament of baptism. Yet none of the authors has devoted a passage of any length, much less a systematic study, to baptism as such.

It is evident from St. Luke's Acts of the Apostles that the decisive importance of baptism was recognized in the church from the very beginning. The outpouring of the Spirit drove the apostles from the upper chamber of prayer into the streets of Jerusalem to announce the good news, and that day around 3000 were baptized (Acts 2:38-41). John and Peter completed baptism in the name of Jesus in Acts 8:12-17. Acts 9:18 recounts how Paul was baptized. The doors of the church were thrown open to the Gentiles with the vision of Peter and the baptism of Cornelius, Acts 10. The baptisms of Lydia and her household and of the jailer and his household are recounted in Acts 16:14, 15 and 29-33.

The Christian rite of baptism was not wholly unprepared for. The Qumran documents tell us of a community that made much of washings and purifications. Leviticus 11-15; 22:1-8, Numbers 19:11-22 list the pure and impure animals and the acts that rendered a person impure, even though these acts might have no moral significance. For all these acts which rendered a man legally impure there were prescribed acts of purification, most of which were performed by washing in water By New Testament times the Jews themselves used baptism as a rite of initiation equal in importance to circumcision.

John the Baptizer, in contrast to what went before, baptized others, while in other baptisms, the person administered baptism to himself. Moreover John's baptism was essentially prophetic; it spoke of what was to come. It called for **metanoia**, that is, conversion, moral goodness, and not just ritual purification. John's baptism was for the forgiveness of sins; for this Ezekiel had prepared by prophesying that God would come to bring about the great washing with pure water, to give his people a new heart (Ezek. 18:31; 36:25-26).

John openly preached that the one to come after him would baptize, not just with water for the sake of reform, but with the Holy Spirit and with fire (Matt. 3:11; *see* Jn. 1:27; Lk. 3:16). The full import of this prophecy was seen by the Christian community after the Spirit had descended in tongues of fire on Pentecost day (Acts 2:1-3).

Christ by His death and resurrection radically redeemed the whole world. Those, like the apostles, who had been in contact with His saving humanity throughout His life received the fruits of this contact with the descent of the promised Spirit (Jn. 14:16 ff.; 16:7 ff.). Before Christ withdrew His visible presence, He pledged to remain on within His church (Matt. 28:20; Jn. 15:1-11), and this He accomplishes through the vital activity of

His Spirit (1 Jn. 3:24). Invisibly present, Christ gives regenerative power to His words and actions when they are spoken and performed by His mystical body, the Church. Through the waters of baptism and the words of invocation people who had no opportunity of coming into saving contact with Christ's visible humanity are now immersed in His saving acts.

Romans 6:1-11 sums up what happens in baptism. The sin-bound Christian over whom the water is poured is immersed in Christ's redemptive death, and comes from the water alive with Christ's new life. With Christ, the new Christian no longer lives to himself but to God. The Holy Spirit, poured abundantly into the hearts of the baptized (Rom. 5:5) entitles them to cry out with Jesus, "Abba, Father" (Rom. 8:15; Gal. 4:4-7) with the full privilege of sonship. The Christian becomes coheir with Christ to the kingdom of heaven (Rom. 8:17; Gal. 3:16).

With baptism the Spirit dissolves the chain that binds man in sin and transfers him from darkness to the kingdom of God's beloved Son (Col. 1:13). Sin is washed away and the person is flooded with the life-giving Spirit (Titus 3:5). The Christian draws near to God in the full assurance of faith that his heart is sprinkled clean from an evil conscience and his body washed with pure water (Heb. 10:22). Ephesians 5:25-26 tells us that Christ died voluntarily so that he might make the Church His bride holy by cleansing her with water and with the word. Baptism buries man in his sins with Christ so that he can rise to share Christ's risen life (Col. 2:12).

In baptism the Christian is radically redeemed, or rather, the redemptive vigor of Christ catches him up, drives out all sin, and makes the former sinner now a sharer in His surrender and resurrection. The realities into which the Christian is introduced, however, are only visible to the eyes of faith (Heb. 11:1), and so behind the water and the word one must look for the redeeming Christ, active and alive in the work of the community. While still in the state of pilgrimage, it remains possible for the Christian, by a perverse act, to cut himself off from the redeeming Christ. Paul warns the Corinthians to steer clear of what would reduce them once again to the slavery of sin (1 Cor. 6:9 ff.). If the Christian allows God to enfold him in His love, then he is assured that nothing can snatch him from grace (Rom. 8:31-39). The realities however are at work in him, moving him towards the full fruits of redemption in his own resurrection (1 Cor. 15).

Christian life is nothing other than the living out of the realities of baptism —a life like Christ's, lived out in our flesh by the Holy Spirit (*see* Rom. 12:1 ff.; 1 Jn. 3:24). Its chief mark is love (Rom. 13:8-10 Matt. 22:40; Gal. 5:22; 1 Cor. 13; Rom. 5:5), and by love is the indwelling of Christ recognized (Jn. 13:35).

Barabbas (ba-rab′-bas), A notorious murderer and robber, whose release the people preferred to that of Christ, when Pilate offered them a choice on the feast-day. Pilate, the Roman prefect, was convinced that Christ was innocent, and he thought by this ruse to avoid sentencing him to death. According to the custom, the Roman governor would release a prisoner at the Passover, and thinking that he would secure Christ's release, Pilate confronted the people with a choice between Christ and this notorious criminal. The ruse failed (Matt. 27:15-26; Mk. 15:7-15; Lk. 23:17-25; Jn. 18:39-40).

Barachel (bar′-ak-el), Father of Elihu, the young man who was angry with Job's friends for their interpretation of his suffering (Job 32:2).

Barak (ba′-rak), The son of Abinoam from Kedesh in Naphtali (Jgs. 4:5). Deborah, the prophetess, sent for Barak to inform him that the Lord had ordered the men of Zebulun and Naphtali to unite against the Canaanite kings of the north. With the 10,000 men who answered his call Barak defeated Sisera who was general of the army of Jabin, king of Hazor, in the vicinity of Mt. Tabor. Heb. 11:32 praises Barak for his faith, while Sam. 12:11 records him as one of the saviors of Israel.

Bar-Jesus, Also called Elymas, the false prophet and magician who lived at the court of Sergius Paulus, the proconsul in Paphos, Cyprus. When Elymas tried to dissuade Sergius from accepting the faith, Paul struck him blind. This miracle so impressed Sergius that he consented to be baptized by Paul (Acts 13:6-11).

Bar-Jonah, Simon Peter's surname, according to Matt. 16:17.

barley

Now the flax and *b*.	Ex. 9:31 God twenty *b*. loaves	2 Kgs. 4:42
with a homer of *b*.	Lev. 27:16 Put in wheat and *b*.	Isa. 28:25

Barnabas, A name, meaning 'son of consolation,' given by the apostles to Joseph, a Levite from Cyprus, one of the first Christians of the community at Jerusalem, to which also he made over his goods (Acts 4:36). He was related to John Mark the Evangelist (Col. 4:10). He was held in high esteem as a man of faith and was filled with the Holy Spirit (Acts 11:24). He managed to dissipate the suspicions the Christians had of Paul, their former persecutor, when he first arrived at Jerusalem (Acts 9:27). Later, while working in Antioch in Syria, Barnabas sought out Paul, who was then at Tarsus, and both men pursued a successful apostolate there. Both returned to Jerusalem, bringing the alms from the church at Antioch to the poor of the holy city (Acts 11:19-30). They brought with them John Mark. From Antioch the three set out on the first great missionary journey. John Mark left them at Perge, and Paul and Barnabas completed the rest of the journey by themselves (Acts 13-14). When they returned to Antioch, they found a bitter dispute in progress over circumcision for non-Jewish converts. Opposing such a practice, Paul and Barnabas went to Jerusalem to have the question settled authoritatively by the apostles. Their opinion was strenuously upheld by Peter and the others (Acts 15; Gal. 2:1-10). Upon their return to Antioch Paul and Barnabas decided to visit once more the churches founded by them during their first journey. Barnabas wished to take John Mark with them once more, but Paul opposed this on account of Mark's having abandoned them during their first journey Barnabas then took Mark with him to Cyprus while Paul and Silas went off together. Despite this disagreement, Paul speaks with esteem and love of Barnabas.

barren

Sarai was *b*.	Gen. 11:30 The *b*. wife bears seven	1 Sam. 2:5
your land will be *b*.	Ex. 23:26 May that night be *b*.	Job 3:7
	and the *b*. womb Prov. 30:16	

barrier

by breaking down the *b*. Eph. 2:14

Barsabbas (bar′-sab-as), 1. Joseph Barsabbas, surnamed Justus, the disciple proposed along with Matthias to fill the vacancy created by the defection of Judas in the apostleship (Acts. 1:23).

2. Judas Barsabbas, a Christian of Jerusalem, who was appointed to accompany Paul, Barnabas and Silas to Antioch after the Council of Jerusalem (Acts 15:22).

Bartholomew, One of the twelve Disciples. Nothing more is known of him. He appears in the lists of the twelve selected by Jesus (Matt. 10:2-4; Mk. 3:15-19; Lk. 6:14-15; Acts 1:13). Bartholomew and Philip are linked

Bartimeus

together in all the gospel lists. This, coupled with the fact recorded by
John (1:47) that Philip brought Nathanael to Jesus, has led to speculation
that Bartholomew and Nathanael are one and the same person.

Bartimeus (bar-ti-me´-us), The blind man whose sight Jesus restored outside Jericho (Mk. 10:46-52). According to Matthew 20:29-34, on that occasion two blind people were cured.

Baruch, Book of, The canonical book of Baruch consists of:

a. An historical introduction wherein Baruch is said to have composed the
book during the Babylonian exile (1:1-14).

b. A confession of the sins of the people and a prayer for restoration of
the kingdom soon (1:15-3:8).

c. A panegyric on the wisdom that is obvious in the law of Israel (3:9-4:4).

d. Jerusalem's lamentation for the tragedy that has befallen her, and
words of consolation that the city addresses to her children (4:5-5:9).

e. As an appendix there is a letter from Jeremiah to the people in exile on
the dangers of idolatry (c. 6).

The book is preserved in Greek only, but this is probably a translation of
a Hebrew original. Scholars generally hold that the book is not authored
by one but by several people. The variety of subject-matter and composition suggest a collection of poems of different authors. It was probably put
together during the Maccabean period and before the end of the first century B.C. It was never accepted into the Hebrew canon, nor is it accepted
as canonical by non-Catholics. Under the name, or rather pseudonym,
Baruch have come down two apocryphal apocalyptic works, the Apocalypse of Baruch, composed around 100 A.D. and the Greek Apocalypse of
Baruch, still more recent (c. 150 A.D.).

Baruch (ba´-rook), Son of Neriah (Jer. 32:12), the companion and scribe
of the prophet Jeremiah. At Jeremiah's dictation, Baruch put down on
paper the prophecies of destruction pronounced by the prophet from the
beginning of his ministry. Afterwards the volume was read to the people
in the temple and to King Jehoiakim in his palace. He was enraged at the
threats contained in it, and tore it up with his own hands and threw it into
the fire bit by bit as it was read to him (Jer. 36). Once more Jeremiah
dictated the same oracles to Baruch (Jer. 36:27-32). Baruch kept the deed
of ownership to the field of Anathoth, which Jeremiah bought as a symbol
of the restoration of Israel after the exile (Jer. 32). In Jer. 45:1-5 is found
an oracle of Jeremiah in favor of his faithful servant. After the destruction
of Jerusalem and the killing of Gedaliah, the governor of Judah appointed
by the Chaldeans, the surviving leaders of the Hebrews accused Baruch of
prompting Jeremiah to stop the people from emigrating into Egypt, so
that they might thus fall a prey to sword or exile by the Chaldeans (Jer.
42). Despite Jeremiah's insistence that this was Yahweh's command,
Johanan and the army leaders led the remnant, taking Jeremiah and Baruch with them, into Egypt (Jer. 43:4-7).

Barzillai (bar-zil´-la-i), 1. A rich landowner of Rogelim in Gilead, Transjordan, who together with Shobi and Machir, helped David and his troops
in Mahanaim while he was fleeing from his son Absalom (2 Sam. 17:27-
29). After his victory over Absalom, David wanted to recompense Barzillai and invited him to live at court with him. Barzillai refused on account
of his age (80), but asked that his son Chimham should take his place
(2 Sam. 19:31-39). Before dying David commended the sons of Barzillai
to Solomon on account of the kindness of their father (1 Kgs. 2:7).

54

2. A priestly family which claimed descendance from one of the daughters of Barzillai. Unable to prove their priestly origin, they were removed from the priesthood (Ezra 2:61; Neh. 7:63).

Basemath (bas′-e-math), An Ishmaelite woman, wife of Esau and mother of Reuel (Gen. 36:3, 17).

Bashan (ba′-shan), A volcanic region in Transjordan which extends north of the river Yarmuk to Mt. Hermon. In the Old Testament it is often celebrated for its fertility and for the abundance and opulence of its flocks and herds (Deut. 32:14; Jer. 50:19; Ezek. 39:18; Amos 4:1; Ps. 22:12, etc.). King Og of Bashan was defeated by the Israelites and his people exterminated while Moses was still alive, just before they crossed the river (Num. 21:32-35; Deut. 3:1-11). The region was assigned to the tribe of Manasseh (Num. 32:33; Josh. 13:30; 17:1). It was still Israelite territory in Solomon's time (1 Kgs. 4:13), but later it was conquered by Hazael, king of Damascus, during the time of Jehu of Israel (2 Kgs. 10:33) and reconquered by Jeroboam II (2 Kgs. 14:25), finally falling into the hands of Tiglath-pileser, emperor of Assyria (2 Kgs. 15:29). During the Roman period the region of Bashan was included in the kingdom of Herod together with Trachonitis, Batanea, Galaunitis and Araunitis. At the time of Christ, Philip was tetrarch of Trachonitis and Iturea (Luke 3:1).

Baskama (bas′-ka-ma), The place of the death and burial of Jonathan Maccabeus (1 Mac. 13:23). The site has not been identified.

Basket, Containers made of woven fiber or cane, and very common in Old Testament times. They were manufactured in a great variety of sizes and shapes and were used to keep and carry food in (Gen. 40:16; Ex. 29:3; Jgs. 6:19, etc.), to convey bricks and also mortar in construction, and were big enough to contain a man, as is evidenced by Paul's escape in one from the walls of Damascus (2 Cor. 11:33). 2 Kings 10:7 tells of the seventy sons of Ahab whose heads were sent in baskets to Jehu at Jezreel. Two noted prophetic visions allude to baskets of fruit (Jer. 24:2; Amos 8:2).

basket, baskets

pecking at them out of the *b.*		other *b.* contained very bad figs	
	Gen. 40:17		Jer. 24:2
out of the *b.*	Ex. 29:23	I was lowered in a *b.*	2 Cor. 11:33
freed from the *b.*	Ps. 81:7	filled twelve *b.*	Matt. 14:20
One *b.* contained excellent figs			
	Jer. 24:2		

Bath, A liquid measure, equal, according to Ezekiel 45:11, 14, to an ephah, which was a dry measure. The bath is reckoned at about 41 quarts but calculations are approximate.

Bathing, The Bible mentions bathing as a hygienic measure (2 Sam. 11:2; Dan. 13:15) often accompanied by anointing (2 Sam. 12:20; Esth. 2:12), as a measure used in particular circumstances or to show hospitality (Gen. 24:32; 18:4; 19:2; Lk. 7:44). In Jewish ritual however the bath was one of the principal means of purification from cultic impurities. Priests, for example, had to wash themselves before exercising their functions so as to cleanse themselves from every possible impurity (Lev. 8:6; 16:4; Ex. 30:17; 21). Even wars were considered sacred, and so all those preparing to take part in them had to purify themselves by bathing (Num. 31:16-24). Special ablutions were also prescribed for the utensils or persons who had comeintocontactwithsacredthings(Lev.16:23-28;Num.19:7-10,etc.).

Bathsheba, Daughter of Eliam, wife of Uriah the Hittite, who was a captain in David's army. While her husband was away at the siege of Rabba, David set eyes on her, invited her to his palace and seduced her (2 Sam. 11:2-5). When Bathsheba became pregnant, David tried to arrange things so that it would appear that Uriah had made her so. His strategy failed (2 Sam. 11:6-13), so David sent Uriah back to camp with sealed instructions for Joab, the general, to place Uriah where he would certainly be killed. When this happened as planned, David married Bathsheba (2 Sam. 11:14-27). Their first son died, as Nathan the prophet had foretold when he reproved David for his crime (12:1-23). David's second son by Bathsheba was Solomon, who later was named heir to the throne, thanks to the opportune maneuverings of his mother and Nathan (2 Sam. 12:24, 25; 1 Kgs. 1:11). Afterwards she pleaded with her son on behalf of Adonijah, who wished to have Abishag as his wife. Solomon was offended by the request and had Adonijah killed (1 Kgs. 2:12).

Bath-Shua, Wife of Judah and mother of Onan, Er and Shelah (Gen. 38:2,12; 1 Chron. 2:3).

battle
On the seventh day *b.* 1 Kgs. 20:29 who will get ready for *b.*
from the fury of *b.*   Isa. 21:15   1 Cor. 14:8
In *b.* I should march   Isa. 27:4

Bdellium (del'-li-um), An aromatic resin, yellow in color, which is collected from a tree native to southern Arabia (Gen. 2:12). Manna was compared with bdellium for its color (Num. 11:7).

Bealiah (be-a-li'-ah), A Benjaminite who served in the band of David at Ziklag (1 Chron. 12:6).

Bear, The animal of this name in the Bible is identified by zoologists as **ursus syriacus**, richer in fur than the European bear. It was a rather common animal in Palestine in Old Testament times, to judge from the numerous references made to it. It was known to be fierce, unsparing of men or animals (1 Sam. 17:34-37; 2 Kgs. 2:24), especially when it was deprived of its young (2 Sam. 17:8; Hos. 13:8). It was also known by its growl (Isa 59:11) and appears as a symbolic animal in prophetic visions (Dan. 7:5; Rev. 13:2).

Beard, For the Hebrew, and indeed generally among semitic peoples, a full beard marked a man's dignity; to cut his beard was to insult and degrade him (2 Sam. 10:4; Isa. 50:6). The law prescribed that a leper must shave his beard (Lev. 14:9). Men took great care of their beards, anointing them with ointments (Ps. 133:2) while a disordered beard was a sign of bereavement or sorrow (Jer. 41:5; 48:37).

beard
all the hair of his head, his *b.,*   hair from my head and *b.* Ezra 9:3
              Lev. 14:9 It shall also shave off the *b.*
nor trim the edges of your *b.*   Isa. 7:20
              Lev. 19:27

beasts
Wild *b.* honor me   Isa. 43:20 If I fought those *b.* 1 Cor. 15:32
or has been killed by wild *b.*
              Ezek. 44:31

Beatitude, A literary form which consists in proclaiming the happiness of a person or category of persons by using the fixed formula "Blessed are they who . . ." followed by the specification of the motive or circumstance which entitles him to be called blessed. In Greek such a person is called **makarismos** or **makarios,** blessed, or happy (*see* Rom. 4:6, 9). Indeed, it is a very frequent literary form in the Old Testament and is clearly of religious inspiration. Those are declared blessed, for example, who receive from God pardon for their sins (Ps. 32:1, 2), those who fear God (Pss. 112:1; 128:1), those who walk in the way of the Lord (Ps. 1) and meditate on his words (Ps. 29:9), those who trust in God (Ps. 16:20) etc. In the New Testament, especially in the gospels and in Revelation (*see* Rev. 1:3; 14:13; 16:15; 19:9; 20:6; 22:7, 14) the form serves to proclaim the happiness of those who have shared in the eschatological salvation (*see* Matt. 13:16, 17; Lk. 10:23, 24). The beatitudes list the conditions of those who aspire to the salvation which Jesus brings: faith and what it involves (Matt. 11:6; Lk. 7:23, Jn. 20:29), vigilance (Matt. 24:46; Lk. 12:37, 43), the observance of the commandments of Jesus (Jn. 13:17). Other beatitudes strive for the effect of paradox, contrasting true happiness according to the norms of the one supreme good which is the kingdom and the following of Christ with what the world holds for happiness (Lk. 14:14; Acts 20:35; James 1:12; 1 Pet. 3:14; 4:14). Luke underlines the contrast when to the four beatitudes of the Sermon on the Mount he adds four laments or "woes" (6:24-26) which correspond to the four preceding beatitudes.

beautiful

saw how *b*. the woman was   Ah, you are *b*., my beloved
                    Gen. 12:14   S. of S. 1:15
Rachel was well-formed and *b*.   Ah, you are *b*., my beloved,
                    Gen. 29:17   S. of S. 4:1
            How *b*. upon the mountains   Isa. 52:7

Beautiful Gate, A gate of the Jerusalem Temple, the scene of the healing of a paralytic by Peter and John (Acts 3:2, 10).

Becher (be′-ker), A son of Benjamin (Gen. 46:21; 1 Chron. 7:6).

Bectileth, An unidentified plain in Cilicia occupied by Holofernes (Judith 2:21).

bed, beds

and sat up in *b*.   Gen. 48:2   on his *b*. by pain   Job 33:19
My *b*. shall comfort me   Job 7:13   Reflect, upon your *b*., in silence
as they slumber in their *b*.   Ps. 4:5
                    Job 33:15

Beeliada (be-e-li′-ad-ah), A son of King David born in Jerusalem (1 Chron. 14:7).

Beelzebul (be-el′-ze-bul), In the New Testament Beelzebul is the name of a demon to whom the Pharisees attributed the exorcisms worked by Jesus (Matt. 10:25; 12:24, 27; Mk. 3:22; Lk. 11:15).

Beeri (be-e′-ri), 1. The father of prophet Hosea (Hos. 1:1).

2. The name of the Hittite father-in-law of Esau (Gen. 26:34)

Beeroth (be-e′-roth), A town 9 miles north of Jerusalem in the territory of Benjamin (Josh. 18:25). Together with three other Hivite peoples, the inhabitants made a pact of friendship with the Israelites on their arrival at the territory of Joshua (Josh. 9:17). Baanan and Rechab, two freebooting chieftains of Saul from Beeroth, killed off his last male descendant, Ishbaal, and brought his head to David, courting favor, but were executed for their efforts (2 Sam. 4:2-12).

Beeroth Bene-jaakan (be-e′-roth-ben-e-ja′-a-kan), A place where the Israelites camped on their journey through the desert (Deut. 10:6; Num. 33:31).

Beer-sheba, A city and oasis of the Negeb, a desert region south of Palestine, today called Bir-es-Seba. It lies about 30 miles to the south of Hebron. It figures often in the story of the patriarchs. Genesis 21:25-33 preserves the tradition of the pact between Abraham and Abimelech, king of Gerar, concerning the use and ownership of the wells of the region. In this text Beer-sheba is interpreted as the well of the oath, or the well of the seven, depending on the Hebrew sense. The seven would refer to the seven lambs sacrificed to sanction the pact made. A similar tradition about Isaac is found in Gen. 26:26-33. Abraham settled there for some time (Gen. 22:19) and later Isaac did likewise (Gen. 26:25). Here God renewed the promises made to Abraham and Isaac (Gen. 26:23, 24) and to Jacob (46:1). At the time of the patriarchs, Beer-sheba had a sanctuary to the god El-Olam (Gen. 21:33) and later an Israelite sanctuary which was still frequented in the time of Amos (Amos 5:5). After the conquest it was assigned to the tribe of Judah (Josh. 15:28) even though Joshua 19:2 puts it in the lands of Simeon. Throughout the whole history of Israel until the Exile, Beer-sheba was the southern limit of Israelite territory, and indeed of its territorial ambitions (Jgs. 20:1; 1 Sam. 3:20; 2 Sam. 17:11, etc.).

beginning

In the *b.*, when God created	Gen. 1:1	In the *b.* was the Word	Jn. 1:1
		He was present to God in the *b.*	
the *b.* of wisdom	Ps. 111:10		Jn. 1:2
The *b.* of wisdom is	Prov. 9:10	he who is the *b.*	Col. 1:18

Behemoth, A monstrous animal of astonishing size and strength, described in Job 40:15-24. The text probably refers to the hippopotamus.

Bekah, A weight measure equal to half a sanctuary shekel (Ex. 38:26), reckoned to be about 6 grams.

Bel, A name for Marduk, god of the city of Babylonia (Isa. 46:1; Jer. 50:2; 51:44). According to Dan. 14:2-21, Daniel uncovered the fraud perpetrated by the priests of Bel in Babylon and was permitted by the king to destroy the idol of the god.

Bela, 1. Son of Beor; first king of Edom (Gen. 36:32-33; 1 Chron. 1:43-44).

2. First son of Benjamin (Gen. 46:21; Num. 26:38; 1 Chron. 7:6; 8:1).

3. Name of one of the five cities forming the Pentapolis, also called Zoar (Gen. 14:2-8).

Belial (be′-le-al), From the Hebrew **beliyya'al,** which means worthless or useless. The term is used in the Old Testament in expressions like the son or the daughter of Belial to indicate a perverse or dissolute person (Deut. 13:14; Jgs. 19:22; and 2 Sam. 20:1, etc.). In apocryphal Jewish literature it is the proper name for the prince of demons, the archenemy of the Messiah—another name for Satan. This is the sense of the word in 2 Cor. 6:15.

believe

suppose they will not *b.* me		To know and *b.* in me	Isa. 43:10
	Ex. 4:1	we can see it and *b.* in him	
so that they may *b.*	Ex. 4:5		Mk. 15:32
And if they will not *b.*	Ex. 4:9	the man who refuses to *b.*	
I could not *b.*	Job 9:16		Mk. 16:16

bells

with gold *b*. between them	*b*. of pure gold were also made
Ex. 28:33	Ex. 39:25
upon the *b*. of the horse Zech. 14:20	

belly

On your *b*. shall you crawl	and your *b*. to swell	Num. 5:21
Gen. 3:14	and her *b*. will swell	Num. 5:27
Whether it crawls on its *b*.	God shall compel his *b*.	Job 20:15
Lev. 11:42		

Beloved Disciple, An unnamed disciple of Jesus mentioned in John 13:23; 19:26; 21:7, 20, and traditionally identified with John the Apostle, the author of the fourth gospel.

Belshazzar (bel-shaz′-ar), The son of Nabonidus, the last king of Babylon. He reigned together with his father and was governor of the capital of the empire. He is presented as son of Nebuchadnezzar and last king of Babylonia in Daniel 5, where also is given a detailed account of the banquet he offered for 1,000 of his noblemen. During this banquet the sacred vessels plundered from the temple of Jerusalem were sacrilegiously used for serving wine. While they were drinking, the fingers of a human hand appeared and wrote words on the plaster directly behind the lampstand. When Belshazzar's own seers could not interpret them, Daniel was called and read in them the ruin of the kingdom, which began that very night with the murder of Belshazzar, and the take-over of the kingdom by Cyrus the Mede.

Belteshazzar (bel-te-shaz′-ar), The name given to Daniel by the chief eunuch Ashpenaz in the court of Nebuchadnezzar, king of Babylonia (Dan. 1:7; 2:26; 4:5).

Benaiah (ben-ay′-ah), The son of Jehoiada who was in command of the Cherethites and Pelethites, the personal bodyguards of David (2 Sam. 8:18; 20:23; 1 Chron. 18:17). For his bravery he is numbered among the thirty warriors of David's army (2 Sam. 23:20-23). He remained loyal to Solomon in his struggle against Joab and Adonijah (1 Kgs. 1:38). He put Joab to death at the order of the king, and took his place as general of the army (1 Kgs. 2:25-36).

Benedictus, Zacharias' canticle sung by him at the birth of his son John the Baptist (Lk. 1:68-79).

Ben-hadad (ben-ha′-dad), 1. Ben-hadad I, king of Damascus. When Baasha king of Israel (900-877) declared war on Asa of Judah (913-873) the latter called Ben-hadad to his aid and struck an alliance with him. Ben-hadad invaded Israel from the north, forcing Baasha to renounce his plan of war against Judah (1 Kgs. 15:16-22). During the reign of Ahab, Ben-hadad once more invaded Israel and laid siege to its capital Samaria, but he was repulsed (1 Kgs. 20:1-20). A little later he again attempted an invasion but was defeated by the Israelites under Ahab at Aphek and made prisoner. He was released after drawing up a commercial agreement very favorable to the Israelites (1 Kgs. 20:26-34). 2 Kings 6:24-7:26 tells of yet another siege of Samaria by Ben-hadad. According to 2 Kings 8:7-15, Ben-hadad was killed by Hazael, who succeeded him to the throne. According to some scholars, Ahab's rival was not Ben-hadad I, but Ben-hadad II.

2. Ben-hadad, king of Damascus, son and successor to Hazael, defeated three times by Jehoash, king of Israel (2 Kgs. 13:14-25; 801-786 B.C.) and again by Jeroboam II (786-746 B.C., 2 Kgs. 14:25-28; Amos 1:4).

Benjamin, Son of Jacob and Rachel, and founding father of the tribe bearing his name. He was born between Bethel and Ephrath, the youngest of Jacob's sons, and together with Joseph, his father's favorite (Gen. 35:16; 44:20, 27-29). He often figures in the story of Joseph. He remained behind with his father when his brothers went down into Egypt where they met Joseph, whom they had sold, but who had by now risen to power. Joseph insisted that Benjamin also come (Gen. 42:15). At the sight of Benjamin, Joseph was moved to tears and withdrew, but eventually made known his true identity to his brothers (Gen. 43:29).

The tribe of Benjamin occupied the strip of land west of the Jordan with Ephraim to the north and Judah to the south (Josh. 18:11) and was considered the least of the twelve tribes (1 Sam. 9:21). Ehud the judge belonged to the tribe of Benjamin, and fought strenuously against the Moabites and slew their king Eglon (Jgs. 3). To this tribe also belonged Saul, first king of Israel (1 Sam. 9:1). The tribe remained faithful to Saul and supported his son Ishbaal against David (2 Sam. 2:8 ff.) until Abner finally persuaded them to submit to David (2 Sam. 3:19). After the division that took place at the death of Solomon, most of Benjaminite territory was included in the kingdom of Judah. (1 Kgs. 12:21-24). According to Romans 11:1 and Philippians 3:5 Paul was from the tribe of Benjamin.

The tablets of the second millenium B.C. discovered at Mari mention a tribe of Benjamin, which however has nothing to do with the Israelite tribe of the same name. Benjamin is in fact a geographical designation meaning "an inhabitant of the south," which explains how the name fitted diverse tribes and peoples.

Ben-Oni, "The son of my sorrow," Rachel's name for her son, who was later called Benjamin by Jacob (Gen. 35:18).

Ben Sira, *See* ECCLESIASTICUS.

Beor (be′-or), Father of Balaam, a seer of the city of Pethor who was invited by Balak, king of Moab, to come and curse the Israelites who were overrunning the land (Num. 22:5).

Bera (be′-rah), The king of Sodom defeated by Chedorlaomer and his allies (Gen. 14:2).

Berechiah (ber-a-ki′-ah), 1. The father of the prophet Zechariah (Zech. 1:1, 7).

2. The name of several other men in the Old Testament (1 Chron. 6:24; 15:23; 2 Chron. 28:12; Neh. 3:4).

Beriah (be-ri′-ah), 1. Son of Asher (Gen. 46:17).

2. Son of Ephraim (1 Chron. 7:23).

3. Personal name (1 Chron. 7:13; 23:10).

Bernice, The daughter of Herod Agrippa I, sister of Agrippa II, wife of Herod the king of Chalcis, who was her father's brother. After his death in 48 A.D., Bernice lived in incest with her brother Agrippa II. She married Polemon, king of Cilicia, but returned to live again with her brother. Paul, a prisoner at Caesarea, was brought before Agrippa and Bernice by Festus, the Roman governor, to plead his case (Acts 25:13, 23; 26:30). According to Tacitus, Bernice later became mistress to Titus the emperor.

Beroea (be-re′-a) 1. A city in Macedonia (today called Verria) east of Thessalonica. Paul and Silas, on their return journey from Thessalonica, came here and preached in the city's synagogue, but when the Jews of Thessalonica heard this, they went there to make trouble and stir up the people so that Paul departed for Athens, leaving Silas and Timothy at Beroea to rejoin him later (Acts 17:10-14).

2. A name for the city of Aleppo in Syria during the Hellenistic era (2 Mac. 13:4).

Berothai (ber′-o-thie), A city of the Aramaean kingdom of Zobah (located in modern Lebanon) pillaged by David (2 Sam. 8:8).

beside
Happy are you who sow *b*.   Isa. 32:20

besiege
and *b*. David   1 Sam. 23:8   who *b*. you outside the walls
                                                Jer. 21:4

Bestiality, Sexual intercourse between a man or a woman and an animal, punishable by death in Israelite law (Ex. 22:18; Lev. 20:15, 16).

Beth, The second letter of the Hebrew alphabet (b). Its original form was that of a crude house. In the sense of "house" or "place of," beth enters into many compound place names, as in Bethany ("house of the poor"), Bethel ("house of God"), etc.

Bethabara (beth-ab′-ar-ah), *See* BETHANY, 2.

Bethany, 1. A town near Jerusalem, about 1¾ miles east, on the eastern slope of the Mount of Olives, today known as el-Azariyeh. It was the birthplace of Lazarus, Martha and Mary (Jn. 11:1; 12:1) and of Simon the leper (Mark 14:3). During the week preceding his passion, Jesus spent his nights at Bethany while his days were spent preaching in Jerusalem (Matt. 21:17; Mark 11:11). It was from Bethany that Jesus set out with his disciples on his triumphant entry into Jerusalem (Mark 11:1; Lk. 19:28).

2. The village "beyond the Jordan" where John the Baptist baptized, according to John 1:28. We have no more information of a place of this name beyond the Jordan. Some old manuscripts have Bethabara instead of Bethany, and this reading is preferred by some scholars.

Beth-Aven, 1. A town of Benjamin (Josh. 18:12) near Bethel (Josh. 7:2).

2. "House of Wickedness," the name given by the prophet Hosea (10:5) to the city of Bethel on account of the idolatrous practices carried on there by the Israelites.

Beth-Barah, A town in the Jordan Valley, site unknown, seized by Gideon when pursuing the Midianites (Jgs. 7:24).

Beth-Eden, An Aramaic city-state in northern Mesopotamia (Amos 1:5; 2 Kgs. 19:12; Isa. 37:12).

Bethel, A city in central Palestine, fourteen miles north of Jerusalem, today called Beitin. Abraham erected an altar between Bethel and Ai (Gen. 12:8; 13:3), and according to Genesis 28:10-22 (*see* Gen. 35:1-13) Jacob give it its name. Previously it had been called Luz. There Jacob erected a column to commemorate the theophany and the promises given by God. The city was conquered by the Ephraimites (Jgs. 1:22-26) and assigned to this tribe (Josh. 16:2; 18:13; 1 Chron. 7:28). Bethel was situated on the border between Ephraim and Benjamin (Josh. 16:1; 18:11-13). For a certain period during the reign of the judges, the ark of the covenant was kept at Bethel and there the people assembled (Jgs. 20:18, 25-28; 21:2). It was also one of the places where Samuel judged Israel (1 Sam. 7:16). After the schism that took place at the death of Solomon, Jeroboam of Israel (922-901) established at Bethel a worship center rivalling that of Jerusalem (1 Kgs. 12:29-33). The cult of the golden calf, though not intended in an idolatrous sense at the beginning, nevertheless gave rise to suspicions of idolatry and merited serious condemnations from the prophets (Amos 3:14; 4:4; 5:5; Hos. 4:15; 5:8; 10:5). Amos exercised his prophetic ministry at Bethel, but was expelled by the priest Amaziah (Amos 7:10-12). More exposed geographically than Jerusalem, it often changed hands in the wars between the two rival kingdoms. At the beginning of the schism, it belonged to Israel (1 Kgs. 12:29). It passed over to Judah under Ahijah (2 Chron. 13:19) but became Israelite once more under Baasha (1 Kgs 15:22; 2 Chron. 16:6). After the destruction of the northern kingdom it was inhabited by foreign colonists, and there too a priest of the Lord established himself (2 Kgs. 17:28). Josiah, king of Judah, managed to annex Bethel to his kingdom shortly before the exile (2 Kgs. 23:15). After the exile, Benjamin's sons settled there (Neh. 11:31). During the Maccabean period it was fortified by Bacchides, the general of the Seleucid army (1 Mac. 9:50).

Bethesda, The name of the five-porched, spring-fed pool at Jerusalem where Jesus cured the paralytic (Jn. 5). Some manuscripts name it Bethzatha, and this is used in many editions of the New Testament. John 5:4 is a later gloss to the text: the movement of the water was probably due to the intermittent rise and fall of the level of the pool. Excavation has uncovered the spot, which consisted of two ponds surrounded by five colonnades.

Beth-Horon (beth-ho′-ron), The name of two cities, upper and lower Beth-horon, 3 miles apart, situated in the land of Ephraim, near its border with Benjamin (Josh. 16:5; 18:13). Because of its strategic position dominating one of the principal roads from the coast to the central mountainous region, it was the scene of much military action at the time of the Israelite conquest of Palestine (Josh. 10:10-12), during the struggle with the Philistines (1 Sam. 13:18; 14:23) and in the Maccabean period (1 Mac. 7:39-45). It was fortified by Solomon (1 Kgs. 9:17) and Bacchides, the Seleucid general who opposed the Maccabeans (1 Mac. 9:50).

Bethlehem, 1. A town of Judah, five miles south of Jerusalem, on the road between Jerusalem and Hebron (Jgs. 19:1, 2, 9-11; Gen. 35:19). It is identified with Ephrath, the birthplace of Benjamin, and the place where Rachel died (Gen. 35:19; 48:7), though the tradition on which this is founded is not at all certain. It was the birthplace of David (1 Sam. 15:1; 17:12; Ruth 4:22; Mic. 5:1) and Samuel anointed him king of Israel there. The Philistines occupied it for some time (2 Sam. 23:14). It was among the cities fortified by Rehoboam (2 Chron. 11:6) but Bethlehem's main claim to fame is as the birthplace of Jesus (Matt. 2:1-16; Lk. 2:4-15; Jn. 7:42).

2. A city in the territory of Zebulun (Josh. 19:15), birthplace of Ibzan, one of the minor judges (Jgs. 12:8-10).

Beth-Peor, A site on the plain of Moab in the land of the Moabites, east of the Jordan (Deut. 3:29; Josh. 13:20). The Israelites camped in the valley there, before crossing the Jordan, and there Moses was buried (Deut. 34:6).

Bethphage (beth′-fa-je), A small village on the road from Bethany to Jerusalem. From here Jesus sent his disciples for the ass on which he triumphantly entered Jerusalem (Matt. 21:1; Mk. 11:1; Lk. 19:29).

Beth-rehob, An Aramaean city of southern Syria which sent forces to support the Ammonites against David's army (2 Sam. 10:6).

Bethsaida (beth-sa′-dah), A city on the northern coast of the Sea of Galilee, and east of the Jordan. It was the birthplace of the apostles Peter, Andrew and Philip (Jn. 1:44; 12:21) and the scene of the cure of the blind man (Mk. 8:22). In the desert just beyond Bethsaida Jesus miraculuously fed the five thousand (Mk. 6:45; Lk. 9:10). For their refusal to believe in him Jesus condemned the people of Bethsaida (Matt. 11:20-24; Lk. 10:13-15). The tetrarch Philip made it his capital, giving it the name Bethsaida Julias in honor of the daughter of Augustus.

Beth-shan, An ancient Canaanite city at the eastern limits of the plain of Esdraelon, not far from the Jordan. It remained Canaanite even after the Israelite conquest of Palestine (Jgs. 1:27; Josh. 17:16), and was afterwards assigned to the tribe of Manasseh (Jgs. 1:27) and Issachar (Josh. 17:11). In Saul's time, Beth-shan was in the hands of the Philistines and after the defeat and death of Saul, his body and those of his sons were hung from the walls of this city (1 Sam. 31:10-12). In Hellenistic times it was called Scythopolis. Today it is only a huge mound, much excavated, at the opening of the Valley of Jezreel where it approaches the deep Jordan River valley. Its strategic location and commanding position explain its long history and the many battles for its possession.

Beth-shemesh (beth-shem′-esh), 1. An Amorite city in Palestine which retained its independence even after the Israelite conquest, and probably up to the time of the monarchy (Jgs. 1:35). It is located on the border between the lands of Judah and those of Dan, west of Jerusalem (Josh. 15:10). It was among the Levitical cities of the tribe of Judah (Josh. 21:16; 1 Chron. 6:44) and to it was brought the ark of the covenant after it had been restored to the Israelites by the Philistines (1 Sam. 6:9-20). It was the scene of a battle between Jehoash of Israel (801-786 B.C.) and Amaziah of Judah (800-783; 2 Kgs. 14:11-13; 2 Chron 25:21-23). It was conquered by the Philistines in the time of Ahaz of Judah (735-715 B.C.; 2 Chron. 28:18).

2. A city in the territory of Issachar (Josh. 19:22).

3. A Canaanite city in the land of Naphtali (Josh 19:38) but not occupied by that tribe (Jgs. 1:33).

Beth-shittah, A location in Transjordan where the Midianites took refuge after their defeat by judge Gideon (Jgs. 7:22).

Bethuel (beth-u′-el), According to Gen. 22:20-24, he was the younger son of Nahor, brother of Abraham, and father of Rebekah, Jacob's wife.

Bethulia, The home of Judith (Judith 6:7, 10; 4:7), in Samaria, near Dothan. Probably a fictitious location. Bethul is mentioned in Josh. 19:4, as belonging to the tribe of Simeon, but its location is not the same as the Bethulia of the book of Judith.

Beth-zur, A Canaanite fortress town in the territory of Judah (Josh. 15:18) occupied by the Caleb clan (1 Chron. 2:45). It was further fortified by Rehoboam, and assumed a particular importance during the Maccabean wars. In the battle of Beth-zur, Judas Maccabeus defeated the Seleucid army of Lysias (1 Mac. 4:29; 2 Mac. 11:5). After this victory, Judas fortified the city to block the incursion of the Idumaeans (1 Mac. 4:61; 6:7, 26). Later it was occupied by the Seleucids (1 Mac. 6:31-49) and fortified by Bacchides (1 Mac. 9:52) until finally it was subjected to the Jews under Simon Maccabeus (1 Mac. 11:65; 14:7-33).

better

Far *b.* for us to be the slaves		the gleaning of Ephraim *b.* Jgs. 8:2
	Ex. 14:12	they looked healthier and *b.* fed
Would it not be *b.*	Num. 14:3	Dan. 1:15

Beulah, A symbolic name, meaning "the married," applied to Jerusalem in Isa. 62:4, in anticipation of her glorious restoration after the Exile.

Bezalel (bez′-a-lel), Son of Uri, of the tribe of Judah, a skilled metal, stone and wood-worker appointed by God, with Oholiab as his assistant, to construct the tabernacle in the desert (Ex. 31:2; 35:30 ff.).

Bezek (be′-zek), A town of southern Palestine, conquered by the tribe of Judah. The Canaanite king of the town, Adonizedek, fled, but he was overtaken, his thumbs and big toes cut off, and he was brought to Jerusalem, where he died (Jgs. 1:4-7). Another town of the same name is mentioned in 1 Sam. 11:8.

Bible, The collection of sacred books which were written through the inspiration of the Holy Spirit and recognized by the Church as such. The name comes from the Latin **biblia** which is a transcription from the neutral plural Greek, **ta biblia,** and thus transcribed is used as a singular feminine noun. The Greek word means "The Books." The Bible comprises the Old and the New Testaments (*see* TESTAMENT). The Old Testament consists of those books written before Christ's coming. The New Testament is the testimony of the salvation brought about by the life, death and resurrection of Jesus Christ.

In Christian tradition it is customary to divide the books of the Old and the New Testaments according to their literary genre into historical, prophetic and didactic works, but the division is only approximative. The Hebrew Bible is divided into three parts, Torah or Law, Prophets or **Nebu'im,** and Writings or hagiographa **(Ketubim).** The Torah comprises the five first books of the Bible from Genesis to Deuteronomy, and is thus in Greek called the Pentateuch (*see* PENTATEUCH). The Prophets are in their turn divided into the earlier prophets (from Joshua to 2 Kings) and the later prophets: Isaiah, Jeremiah, Ezekiel and the twelve minor prophets. The Writings are the Psalms, Proverbs, Job, Song of Songs, Ruth, Lamentations, Ecclesiastes, Esther, Daniel, Ezra-Nehemiah, and 1 and 2 Chronicles.

From the point of view of canonicity (*see* CANON), there is a distinction between proto-canonical and deutero-canonical works. According to the Catholic church, both groups are equally canonical and inspired. The distinction is made on the historical basis of their admission into the canon. In the case of the deutero-canonical works some doubts were entertained in a few areas of the ancient church, and so their sacred and inspired character was not universally recognized until later, around the fourth or fifth centuries. The deutero-canonical works of the Old Testament are not accepted as canonical nor inspired by the non-Catholic Christian churches. The deutero-canonical works of the Old Testament are: Baruch, Tobit, Judith, 1 and 2 Maccabees, Wisdom and Sirach (Ecclesiasticus). The New Testament deutero-canonical works are Hebrews, James, 2 Peter, 2 and 3 John, Jude and Revelation. Protestants recognize no such distinction among the New Testament books.

The books, with the exception of Obadiah and Philemon, are divided into chapters and verses. This division was not originally found in the Bible nor does it always correspond to the development of the subject in hand. Stephen Langton carried out the division into chapters in the Latin version in 1228, and from here it went back into the original and into other versions. The division into verses of the Old Testament was the work of Santes Pagnini OP (d. 1541), and was introduced into the Latin edition in 1528. For the New Testament this was done by Robert Estienne in the Greek edition he brought out in 1555.

Bigtha, One of the seven eunuchs who served King Ahasuerus as chamberlains (Esth. 1:10).

Bildad, One of the three friends who came to console Job (Job 2:11) and one of the speakers in the book's dialogue (8:1; 18:1; 25:1). He is called the Shuhite, a place otherwise unknown.

Bilhah, The slave given by Laban to his daughter Rachel (Gen. 29:29), mother of Dan (Gen. 30:5) and Naphtali (Gen. 30:8) through Jacob. Later she had intercourse with Reuben, a son of Jacob and Leah (Gen. 35: 22).

bind

Violet ribbons shall *b*. the rings
Ex. 28:28
Will a rope *b*. him in the furrow
Job 39:10
but he will *b*. our wounds
Hos. 6:1
B. him hand and foot   Matt. 22:13

bird, birds

let *b*. fly beneath the dome
Gen. 1:20
all kinds of winged *b*.   Gen. 1:21
and every kind of *b*.   Gen. 7:14
We were rescued like a *b*.
Ps. 124:7
spread before the eyes of any *b*.
Prov. 1:17
Ephraim flies away like a *b*.
Hos. 9:11
B. are of their kind, fish are
1 Cor. 15:39

Birsha, The king of Gomorrah defeated by Chedorlaomer and his allies (Gen. 14:2-11).

birthright

First give me your *b*.   Gen. 25:31
What good will any *b*. do
Gen. 25:32
So he sold Jacob his *b*.   Gen. 25:33
his *b*. was given   1 Chron. 5:1
the *b*. had been Joseph's
1 Chron. 5:2
Esau, who sold his *b*. for a meal
Heb. 12:16

Bishop, *See* HIERARCHY.

bite

no charm will work when they *b*.
Jer. 8:17
teeth have something to *b*.   Mic. 3:5
the serpent there to *b*. them
Amos 9:3

Bithynia (bith-in′-e-ah), A region northwest of Asia Minor, and a Roman province, together with Pontus, from 64 B.C. During the second apostolic journey, Paul and Timothy intended to visit this province but "when they came to Mysia they tried to go on into Bithynia, but again the Spirit of Jesus would not allow them" (Acts 16:7). The Christians of Bithynia are mentioned among those to whom the first epistle of Peter was addressed (1 Pet. 1:1).

bitter

burst into loud, *b*. sobbing
Gen. 27:34
making life *b*. for them   Ex. 1:14
unleavened bread and *b*. herbs
Ex. 12:8
so *b*. were they over the fate
1 Sam. 30:6
and life to the *b*. in spirit   Job 3:20

Bitumen (bit-too′-men), A black mineral resin which abounds around the Dead Sea area (Gen. 14:10), used of old to make ships waterproof (Gen.

6:14; Ex. 2:3), and as cement in the construction of buildings (Gen. 11:3).

Blasphemy, Blasphemy is an insult offered to God in speech. It runs counter to the third prohibition of the Decalogue (Ex. 20:7; Deut. 5:11), and is again expressly reproved in Lev. 24:14-16 under pain of stoning (Jn. 10:30-33). Jesus was on different occasions accused of blasphemy. Those who did not believe in him would give no other interpretation to his words, especially to his explicit declarations of equality with the Father (Jn. 5:17, 18; 10:33) and of his power to forgive sins (Matt. 9:3; Mk. 2:7; Lk. 5:21). The undeniable works of power such as exorcisms and miraculous cures had then to be attributed to the devil, whose instrument Jesus would then be. This interpretation was qualified by Jesus as "that, I assure you, is why every sin, every blasphemy, will be forgiven men, but blasphemy against the Spirit will not be forgiven"—an unpardonable sin, since it obstinately refused to accept Jesus for what he was, that is, the only name given to men by which they can be saved (Matt. 12:31; Mk. 3:28-30; Lk. 12:20; *see* Acts 4:12). The accusation of blasphemy easily led to the sentence of death pronounced on Jesus by the Sanhedrin (Matt. 26:65, 66; Mk. 14:63, 64; Lk. 22:70-71). In fact the answer of Jesus to the question of Caiaphas contained a clear affirmation of his equality with God. His answer was in fact the fusion of two texts of the Old Testament, Ps. 110:1 and Dan. 7:13. The first speaks of the enthronement of the Messiah at the right hand of God but it was commonly interpreted in a metaphorical sense, as a figurative way of describing the Messiah at the head of God's people. When however it was put together with Dan. 7:13, which speaks of the coming of the Son of Man in the clouds of heaven, it implied that Jesus would be enthroned in heaven at the right hand of God, and would therefore be a real exaltation to a condition of perfect equality with God, sharing with him the same universal and divine dominion. This characteristic fusion of texts was one of the most widespread confessions of faith in the divinity of Christ in the apostolic church (*see* Mk. 16:19; Acts 2:34; 7:56; Rom. 8:34; Col. 3:1; Heb. 8:1; 1 Pet. 3:22; Rev. 3:21).

blasphemy, blasphemies

this day of *b*.	2 Kgs. 19:3	out of heart proceed *b*. Mk. 7:22
manner of *b*. forgiven	Matt. 12:31	*b*. names Rev. 13:1
	b. against God Rev. 13:6	

Blastus, The chamberlain of king Herod Agrippa I (Acts 12:20).

blemish

a year-old male and without *b*.	but it must be without *b*. Lev. 3:6
	Ex. 12:5 who was without *b*. from the
but it must be without *b*. Lev. 3:1	2 Sam. 14:25

Blessing, The first mention of God's blessing in the Bible is had in the creation story, when a fundamental characteristic of the blessing appears: it is God's delight with the vitality of creation as it increases and multiplies (*see* Gen. 9:1). The blessing embraces other aspects of life until it becomes synonymous with happiness or well-being, understood not exclusively in the worldly sense, but, as always in the Old Testament, with deep religious resonances, since material well-being derives from submission to God's designs and since he is the only source of all that is good. An example of this is the covenant blessing in Deut. 28:1-14 and the typical wisdom tradition which makes wisdom herself the source of happiness and every good thing without contrasting the various levels and aspects of human life. Gen. 12:1-3 describes the call of Abraham, and the accompanying blessing which has no immediate result but is nevertheless

a harbinger, and indeed the very source of the good things pledged to
Abraham and his seed, which are destined to include every saving gift,
and, according to the authoritative interpretation of Paul (Gal. 3:8-14),
proffer Christian salvation itself. The story of the patriarchs is centered on
the transmission and faithful fulfilment of the blessing contained in the
promises and repeated to Isaac (Gen. 26:3-4) and Jacob (Gen. 28:13;
32:29). Abraham is chosen so that through him the blessing can embrace
all the nations of the earth (Gen. 12:3), just as, in another sense, Isaac
(Gen. 28:14), Jacob (Gen. 30:27), Joseph (Gen. 39:5) and Israel itself
(Josh. 19:24) became the instruments of blessing.

The divine blessing is transmitted in worship through the use of appropri-
ate formulae pronounced by legitimately designated persons. The priest
with upraised hands used to bless the worshipping assembly (Lev. 9:22;
2 Chron. 30:27) and even the king, on given occasions, would bless the
people (1 Kgs. 8:14; 2 Sam. 6:18). The words of blessing are contained in
Num. 6:23-27. Besides the cultic blessings, the Bible describes the father
blessing his sons, and particularly his first-born before dying (Gen. 27:28,
29). Blessings were frequent too in Christian worship (*see* Gal. 6:18; Phil.
4:23; 1 Cor. 16:23; 2 Cor. 13:13). The gospels record several blessings by
Jesus: that of the children with the imposition of hands (Mk. 10:13-16;
Matt. 19:13-15; Lk. 18:15-17), in the act of multiplying the bread (Matt.
14:19; Mk. 6:41; Lk. 9:16), during the breaking of bread with the disciples at Emmaus (Lk. 24:30), at the institution of the Eucharist (Matt.
26:26; Mk. 14:22) and at the moment of the Ascension (Lk. 24:50).

blind

and makes another *b*.	Ex. 4:11	the *b*. and the lame will drive
he who is *b*., or lame	Lev. 21:18	2 Sam. 5:6
who misleads a *b*. man		the *b*. recover their sight
	Deut. 27:18	Matt. 11:5
	they are *b*. leaders of the *b*.	Matt. 15:14

Blindness, An affliction often mentioned in the Old and the New Testament. The Mosaic law contains some dispositions aimed at protecting the
blind, explicitly forbidding others to place obstacles in their path (Lev.
19:14), or lead them astray (Deut. 27:18). Tob. 6:9 prescribes the gall of a
fish for use as an eye ointment. In the New Testament the blind appear as
poor and mendicant (Matt. 20:30; 21:14, etc.). Jesus had a special care
for the blind, and the gospels have preserved several accounts of cures of
the blind by Jesus (Jn. 9; Matt. 9:27; Mk. 8:22; Matt. 20:30; Mk. 10:46;
Lk. 18:35, and in general, Matt. 11:5 and Lk. 7:22). As in the religious
language of all times, blindness is also used in a metaphorical sense to
indicate an interior disposition of spiritual hard-heartedness or a willed
lack of sensitivity to the works and the wishes of God (Isa. 42:18; 43:8;
56:10; Rom. 2:19; 2 Cor. 4:4; 2 Pet. 1:19). In this sense the Pharisees are
reproved by Jesus (Matt. 23:17; 15:14; Lk. 6:39).

Blood, Field of, English translation of Akeldama. *See* AKELDAMA.

Blood, In the anthropology of the Bible, while breath was considered the
principal life-source, the author found no embarassment in holding the
blood to be the vehicle or seat of the life force. "The life of a living body is
in its blood" affirms Leviticus 17:11 (*see* Gen. 9:5; Deut. 12:23), and the
killing of men or animals is commonly described as 'spilling their blood.'
God is the only absolute lord of life, and his rights he defends inexorably:
the spilling of blood is an insult to God's sovereignty and demands reparation (Gen. 4:10; 21:9). With the shattering of the harmony that flowed
from God's creative word at the beginning, God established fixed norms
within which violence must be kept. These norms form the fundamental

stipulations of God's pact with Noah: the blood of man will be vindicated without the possibility of compromise (Gen. 9:6) while the butchering of animals is permitted. To eat the blood however is forbidden (Gen. 9:4). It must be poured out like water into the earth. This prohibition was a most ancient taboo which lasted until the end of Old Testament history (*see* Acts 15:20) and was understood in the laws of Gen. 9 and Deut. 12 as a recognition of God's absolute dominion over life. In ancient Israel it seems that every slaughter of animals had a sacrificial character, and the blood was poured out at the extremes of the altar. After the centralization of cult in Jerusalem, animals were butchered apart from worship, but it was still necessary to pour the blood out on the earth (Deut. 12:15, 16).

Animal blood had a particular function in the ritual of the sacrifices of expiation. Since life was in the blood, God gave it to Israel as a means of bringing about expiation (Lev. 17:11). This must not be understood in the sense that the killing of an animal substituted for the death of the sinner, with the canceling out of his sin and the placating of the divine anger. The blood, because it contained life, was understood to purify the sin and make it possible for the sinner once more to approach God and receive his benevolence. The blood was sprinkled on the veil that hung in front of the Holy of Holies, and it was rubbed on the horns of the altar (*see* Lev. 4:6, 25). On the great Day of Atonement the 'propitiation,' or seat of God's mercy, (the ark) was sprinkled with blood (Lev. 16).

The New Testament often tells of the blood Christ shed in expiation for sin (Rom. 3:25; 5:29; Eph. 1:7; 2:13, etc.). This is expressed in the account of the institution of the Eucharist (Matt. 26:28, and parallel texts, and Jn. 6). These expressions must be understood in the sense of the terminology of expiation and blood used in the whole Bible, as expressive of the saving value of the death and resurrection of Christ. It must not be understood in the sense of punishment undergone in place of sinners to placate an angry God, but rather that through his death and resurrection Christ became a 'vivifying spirit,' giving us as a gift the Holy Spirit who overcomes sin in us. Blood is repeatedly referred to, not simply to bring home the great suffering in the redemption (Eph. 1:18; 1 Pet. 1:7), but also constantly to re-evoke what this led to, namely the resurrection. A highly developed theology of the blood of Jesus is already found in the letter to the Hebrews (cc. 9-10), in which the author has drawn up in a complete and coherent manner the parallelism between the ritual of the Old Testament and the death and resurrection of Christ. Jesus, through his own blood, that is, through his self-gift in death, has penetrated into the Holy of Holies and achieved an eternal redemption, blotting out with his blood what blocked men from him, and making it possible for them too to live in the true and living God (9:11 ff.; *see* 9:20, 22; 10:4, 19; 13:20). Revelation theology puts the blood shed by Christ in particular relief, as a vivid expression of his death which brought about universal expiation and purification (Rev. 5:9; 1:5; 7:14).

Boanerges (bo-an-er′-jees), Aramaic for "the sons of thunder," the nickname given by Jesus to the brothers James and John, sons of Zebedee, probably on account of their impetuosity (Mk. 3:17), or perhaps connected with their request (Lk. 9:54) to send lightning down on the Samaritans.

Boaz, 1. Son of Salmon and kinsman of Naomi, who married Ruth, exercising his rights according to levirate law (Ruth 2-4; Deut. 25:5). Their son, Obed, was the grandfather of David. Boaz is included in the genealogy of Jesus (Matt. 1:5; Lk. 3:32).

2. The name of one of the two columns which stood before the door of Solomon's Temple (1 Kgs. 7:21). *See* JACHIN AND BOAZ.

Body of Christ, One of the most fruitful and original themes of Paul's theology of the Church is that of the Church as Christ's body. This appears for the first time in 1 Corinthians and occurs again in Romans. It is developed with new elements, that of the head and the fullness (**pleroma**) in Colossians and Ephesians. It is this theme that affected strongly the theological thinking of Paul. To understand the genuine sense intended by the apostle, it is necessary to beware of two easy equivocations.

First, the expression "Body of Christ" is not to be understood in the sense of Greek anthropology, as a distinct body that is separable from the soul. It must be taken in the sense of Paul's use of language (*see* Rom. 6:12; 1 Cor. 6:18). The body is the human being in its concrete existence, his whole being with the accent placed on the physical and material component of his external appearance. The "Body of Christ" then is the concrete humanity of Christ in his present glorious condition.

Secondly, the expression "Body of Christ" does not primarily and directly mean a "social" body or organism, a group of members in a society organized together with different functions and tasks. Comparing society or the whole of humanity to an organic body is a very ancient practice, and was in use among the Stoics. Paul was certainly aware of this usage and exploited it to make a secondary and derived application of it to express his insight into "His body, the church" (Col. 1:24). Here however 'body' must always be understood in a constant and essential reference to the individual and physical humanity of Jesus now glorified.

In fact the origin of this expression must be sought in the Pauline idea of the union and intimacy between individual Christians and Christ. This union is not a mere affectionate or moral union. The Christian through faith and baptism is 'incorporated into Christ,' that is, the Christian is inserted into Christ's death and resurrection. The Christian with Christ dies to sin to rise with him to a new life that is animated by the same Spirit who animates the humanity of the glorified Christ (Rom. 6:1-11). On the basis of this real and vital communion between the Christian and Christ, the Christian, for Paul, "clothed" with Christ (Gal. 3:27), carries within himself the image of the heavenly Adam (1 Cor. 15:49), puts on the New Man (Eph. 4:24) and is, in effect, a new creature (2 Cor. 5:17; Gal. 6:15), a 'member of Christ' seeing that he is animated by the same life (1 Cor. 6:15), noting that "whoever is joined to the Lord becomes one spirit with him" (1 Cor. 6:17).

This incorporation of the individual Christian into the glorified humanity of Christ is placed in particular relief and at the same time nourished and increased in eucharistic communion. The Christians who receive the sacramental body of the Lord are ever more intimately united in this Body of Christ. The eucharist however announces a further development of the theme, namely the reciprocal union of all Christians who receive "the cup of blessing" (1 Cor. 10:16, 17). To illustrate this reciprocal union between Christians, Paul was to use the classical comparison of a society with an organic body (1 Cor. 12:12-27; Rom. 12:4-5). One must not however forget that in Paul's application of the comparison there is a profound change, for with Paul it is no mere metaphoric expression for a social phenomenon, but is built on the radical fact of the union and incorporation of the individual Christians into Christ, who together then form his 'Body,' and not just a body of Christ (1 Cor. 12:27). "You, then, are the body of Christ. Every one of you is a member of it."

In the epistles to the Ephesians and Colossians there are new harmonies to the same theme. First, while keeping to what has already been expounded, there is an explicit identification between the Church and the Body of Christ (Col. 1:18, 24; Eph. 1:22; 5:23-30). This novelty was in part due to the semantic change that the term **ekklesia**, church, underwent. Besides meaning the local communities, this came also to mean the church universal (*see* 1 Cor. 1:2; 4:17).

The relationships between Christ and the Church which is his body are explained with greater precision thanks to the combination of this theme with that of Christ, Head of the Church (*see* HEAD). The theme of Christ as Head of the Church has a different origin from that of the Church as Christ's Body. The 'Head' theme was used simply to announce the primacy and universal dominion acquired by Christ through his exaltation to the right hand of the Father "and the immeasurable scope of his power in us who believe. It is like the strength he showed in raising Christ from the dead and seating him at his right hand in heaven, high above every principality, power, virtue and domination, and every name that can be given in this age or in the age to come" (Eph. 1:20-22; Col. 2:10). However by coming into contact with the theme of the Body of Christ, the title of Head applied to him was understood in the sense of vital principle, mover and sustainer of the whole organism, as was the opinion of contemporary Greek scientific knowledge (Col. 2:19; Eph. 4:16).

In Ephesians and Colossians the Church is related to Christ as a body to its head which is for it the vital and directive principle. The logic of the images used places a distinction between Christ and the Church, not so as to make the Church autonomous or self-sufficient but to express with greater force the radical and vital dependence which makes the body of Christians what it is.

In an exhortation to Christian couples, Paul urges them to imitate the example of Christ who loved the Church and immolated himself to make it holy and pure, and he goes on to add: "observe that no one ever hates his own flesh; no, he nourishes it and takes care of it as Christ cares for the church" (Eph. 5:21-33).

The Church then exists as the Body of Christ. The individual Christian who is inserted into his glorified humanity lives from the supernatural life that has its fullness in Christ. This remains the essential and fundamental element in the theme of the Body of Christ and of Paul's theology of the Church. By adding the image of Christ as Head of the Church, in so far as he is its vital source, Paul does not extenuate the realism of the preceding image. Rather he secures for the individual and physical humanity of the glorified Christ the place that is properly his without danger of it being dissolved into a pseudomystical identification with individual Christians. *See* HEAD, PLEROMA.

Bondage, *See* SLAVERY.

bones

This one, at last is *b*. of my *b*.	a lion he breaks all my *b*.
Gen. 2:23	Isa. 38:13
you must bring my *b*. Gen. 50:25	now filled with *b*. Ezek. 37:1
Then they took their *b*.	can these *b*. come to life
1 Sam. 31:13	Ezek. 37:3
with *b*. and sinews Job 10:11	

Book, Its most ancient form was that of a scroll, made of leaves of papyrus or skin glued together in varying lengths and widths, and wound around a rod. Only one side was used for writing usually but *see* Ezek. 2:9. The modern book form stems from the second century A.D. and its first examples are Bible manuscripts.

Booths, Feast of, *See* TABERNACLES, FEAST OF.

border, borders

the Canaanite *b*.extended
Gen. 10:19

on the *b*. of the land of Edom
Num. 20:23

bosom

Put your hand in your *b*. Ex. 4:6

He put it in his *b*. Ex. 4:6

put your hand back in your *b*.
Ex. 4:7

and slept in his *b*. 2 Sam. 12:3

buried my guilt in my *b*. Job 31:33

Carrying them in his *b*. Isa. 40:11

boundary

the eastern to the western *b*.
Ezek. 48:1-7

Bow, Among the arms of warfare, besides the sword and sling, the Bible frequently mentions the bow (Gen. 48:22; Josh. 24:12; 2 Kgs. 6:22; Hos. 1:7; 2:20). The bow was made of wood bent by a cord. Its resilience and resistance was augmented by the use of knitted sinews and horn. At the beginning it seems to have been the distinctive weapon of the chieftains and kings (1 Sam. 20:20; 2 Sam. 1:22; 2 Kgs. 9:24; 13:15), but little by little its use spread, probably after the introduction of the war-chariot and the adoption of Assyrian war tactics (2 Chron. 26:14; 1 Chron. 8:40; 12:2; 2 Chron. 14:7; 17:17).

bow

I set my *b*. in the clouds Gen. 9:13

As the *b*. appears in the clouds
Gen. 9:16

the *b*. of bronze shall pierce
Job 20:24

bow

to him alone shall *b*. down
Ps. 22:30

Bozrah, A city of Edom, residence of King Jabob (Gen. 36:33; 1 Chron 1:44) often named in the prophetic oracles against Edom (Amos 1:12; Isa. 34:6; 63:1; Jer. 49:13, 22). It was famous for its cloth weaving and dyeing, and for its trade.

branches

on the vine were three *b*.
Gen. 40:10

and his *b*. shall be green Job 15:32

or five on its fruitful *b*. Isa. 17:6

Then comes the cutting of *b*.
Isa. 18:5

I am the vine, you are the *b*.
Jn. 15·5

brave

the *b*. man with the heart
2 Sam. 17:10

those who are with him are *b*.
2 Sam. 17:10

bread

brought out *b*. and wine
Gen. 14:18

gave him some *b*. Gen. 25:34

hire themselves out for *b*.
1 Sam. 2:5

b. gotten secretly is pleasing
Prov. 9:17

I myself am the living *b*. Jn. 6:51

Breastplate, Part of the sacred vestments of the high priest, described in detail in Exodus 28:15-30. It should be made of gold, purple and crimson dye stuffs, and fine linen. It was square and folded over, with four sets of three precious stones each, mounted in gold settings with the name of one of the twelve tribes on each setting. It was attached in front by a system of gold rings and cords, while to the pectoral itself was attached the Urim and the Thummin. It was worn when the priest entered the sanctuary, so that by means of the engraved names he might continually call to mind the twelve tribes, whose representative before God he was (*see* Ex. 28:30; 39:8-21).

breath

into his nostrils the *b*. of life	if you take away their *b*.
Gen. 2:7	Ps. 104:29
the faintest *b*. of life. Gen. 7:22	in whose nostrils is but a *b*.
By the *b*. of God they perish	Isa. 2:22
Job 4:9	

bribe

Never take a *b*. for a *b*. blinds	whom I have accepted a *b*.
Ex. 23:8	1 Sam. 12:3

Brick, Bricks used for building in Palestine, Egypt and Mesopotamia were a mixture of clay and straw dried in the sun or baked in the furnace (*see* Ex. 1:14; 5:6 f.). Given the scarcity of stone, especially in Mesopotamia, bricks were used for the construction even of immense buildings (Gen. 11:3).

bronze

forge instruments of *b*. and iron	gold, silver or *b*. Ex. 31:4
Gen. 4:22	articles of silver, gold and *b*.
gold, silver and *b*. Ex. 25:3	2 Sam. 8:10
and cast five *b*. pedestals	*b*. for what will be made of *b*.
Ex. 26:37	1 Chron. 29:2
the bow of *b*. Job 20:24	

brook

are undependable as a *b*. Job 6:15

Brother, In Hebrew 'ah, ordinarily translated 'brother,' but in practice it expresses kinship in a larger sense, and less precisely than in English, on account of the absence of Hebrew terms for the different levels and degrees of relationship. Not only the sons of the same father, but all the male members of the same family complex were called brothers. The members of the group or clan were considered to have descended from the same common ancestor, who remained on in memory and legend as the group's center of cohesion (Num. 16:10). Even today the word 'brother' admits of a larger meaning, so that friends, allies, colleagues, and fellow citizens can be embraced in the same brotherhood: it was no different in ancient times (*see* 2 Sam. 1:26; 1 Kgs. 9:13; Num. 8:23-26; 2 Chron. 29:34; 1 Sam. 30:23). All the members of the Chosen People are called brothers, not simply because Abraham is their common father, but even more especially because they are sons of God and his creatures (Mal. 2:10). The revelation of God's fatherhood, the common awareness of sharing the same saving gift which is Christ, the new commandment of love given by Christ, are some of the resonances that gave the first Christians the feeling that they were brothers. This is attested to in the New Testament (*see* Acts 1:16; Rom. 1:13; 1 Cor. 15:58; Phil. 4:1, etc.).

A particular problem arises with regard to the New Testament reference to Jesus' brothers. "He was still addressing the crowds when his mother and his brothers appeared outside to speak with him" (*see* Matt. 12:46; 13:55; Mk. 3:31; 6:3; Lk. 8:19; Jn. 2:12; 7:3, 5, 10; Acts 1:14; 1 Cor. 9:5; Gal. 1:19). We are supplied with the names of four of them: James, Joseph, Jude and Simon (Matt. 13:55; Mk. 6:3). The most ancient Christian tradition has taken these passages to mean brother in the larger sense, and not as Mary's children. They were more distant relatives. Even though most non-Catholic interpretation rejects this interpretation, it is far from arbitrary. The New Testament, written in Greek, was composed by Semites, and the Aramaic background breaks through in very many places, so that the Greek word **adelphos** is more or less used in the larger sense of the Hebrew **'ah** given above. There are also other reasons bearing out this interpretation. The brothers of Jesus are never called the sons of Mary and Joseph. James and Joseph, it is true, are called sons of Mary, but she is distinct from Jesus' mother (Matt. 27:56; Mk. 15:40), while James is said to be the son of Alpheus. This James, the brother of Jesus, is to be identified with James the Minor, one of the apostles (Matt. 10:3 and parallel texts). Finally, in the hypothesis that there were other sons, it would be quite difficult to explain why Jesus on the cross confided Mary to John's care (Jn. 19:26). The theory that would have these brothers of Jesus as children of a previous marriage of Joseph is not accepted by Catholic scholars.

brother

I have become the *b*. of jackals	mother, son, daughter, *b*.
Job 30:29	Ezek. 44:25
b. is born for the time of stress	This Mary whose *b*. Lazarus
Prov. 17:17	Jn. 11:2

Brothers of the Lord, *See* BROTHER.

build

let us *b*. ourselves a city Gen. 11:4	Unless the Lord *b*. the house
Let us *b*. with you Ezra 4:2	Ps. 127:1
I did not want to *b*. on Rom. 15:20	

Bul, Canaanite name for the eighth month of the old Hebrew calendar (1 Kgs. 6:38), known later as Marheswan. It corresponds roughly to October/November.

Bull, In the Old Testament the bull is mentioned particularly with regard to sacrifice. Bull sacrifices were prescribed on the most solemn feasts, such as the Passover (Num. 28:16-25), on the feast of Pentecost and during the feast of Weeks (Num. 28:26-31), on the feast of Tabernacles (Num. 7), at the consecration of priests (Ex. 29:1-37) and in many expiation sacrifices (Lev. 4:16). The bull was admired in the whole Middle East as a symbol of power and fertility, and to it was often given a divine title, e.g. in Babylonia (Marduk), in Egypt (Osiris) and in Canaan (El, the supreme god of the Canaanite pantheon). The term is applied in a figurative sense to the Lord in ancient texts, such as Gen. 49:24, where the original Hebrew **'abir** originally meant 'the bull,' and in poetic writings (Isa. 1:24; 49:26; Ps. 132:2, 5). It is also given to several personages in the Bible on account of their strength and vigor (Deut. 33:17; Isa. 10:13; 34:7; Jer. 50:27).

bull, bulls

and sacrifice young *b*. as peace	had sacrificed a young *b*.
Ex. 24:5	1 Sam. 1:25
Procure a young *b*. and two	Their *b*. gender without fail
Ex. 29:1	Job 21:10

Burial, Throughout their whole history, the Israelites buried their dead and attached the greatest importance to this last act of reverence to their departed dear ones. To be abandoned without burial, a prey to the beasts of the fields and the birds of the air, was feared as the greatest of all misfortunes, from which even the enemy, as far as possible, was spared. Ahijah the prophet predicted to Jeroboam's wife that for the latter's unfaithfulness to God, "when one of Jeroboam's line dies in the city, dogs will devour him; when one of them dies in the field, he will be devoured by the birds of the sky." (1 Kgs. 14:11; *see* Jer. 16:4; 22:19; 1 Kgs. 2:31; 2 Kgs. 9:36). In contrast to the Greeks and to the pre-Israelite inhabitants of Palestine, cremation was not practiced among them, except as an exceptional measure and a most serious punishment (Gen. 38:24; Lev. 20:14; Josh. 7:25). One notable exception to this rule was the cremation of Saul and his sons before burying their bones (1 Sam. 31:12). Particular importance was attached to being buried with one's own ancestors (*see* 1 Kgs. 13:22).

The care taken of the body of the deceased must have been very simple. Old Testament information on this point is scarce. It is certain that embalming was not a regular practice. Where it is mentioned in the Bible, it is said to be an Egyptian usage, and took 40 days to complete (*see* Gen. 50:2, 3, 26). From the New Testament we know that before burial the body was washed (Acts 9:37), anointed with ointment (Jn. 12:7; 19:39; Mk. 16:1; Lk. 24:1), and rolled up in linen strips, even though it is not quite clear what system of binding or bandaging was used (*see* Matt. 27:59; Lk. 23:53; Mk. 15:46). The face was covered with a handkerchief (Jn. 20:7).

The Israelite tomb was excavated out of rock, or a natural cavern used for burial (Gen. 23). The bodies were placed on benches, or later in niches cut out of the walls. Ordinarily in Old Testament times, beside the body were placed personal objects and some dishes. On Jesus' tomb *see* Matt. 27:60, 66; 28:2; Mk. 15:46; 16:3; Lk. 24:2; 23:53; Jn. 19:41; 20:1. This type of tomb was expensive and could be afforded only by prosperous families, who procured for themselves burial sites worthy of their rank (Isa. 22:16). The more modest families and the poor buried their dead in the ground, and in Jerusalem, in the Valley of Kidron, there was an area reserved for the burial of strangers and those executed (Jer. 26:23).

Tombs were excavated outside the walls of the city, with the exception of the tomb of the kings of Judah, which was in the old city of David (1 Kgs. 2:10; 11:43; 14:31; 2 Kgs. 16:20). The erection of monuments over the tombs came only at a later period (1 Mac. 13:27, 30). Prior to this period, simple commemorative pillars were used (Gen. 35:20; 2 Sam. 18:18).

burn, burns

That *b.* and consumes his briers		but the chaff he will *b.* Matt. 3:12
Isa. 10:17		and bundle them up to *b.*
it will *b.* without being quenched		Matt. 13:30
Jer. 7:20		

buy

Go down there and *b.* some		We will *b.* the lowly man
Gen. 42:2		Amos 8:6
B. for yourself my field	Jer. 32:7	While they went off to *b.* it
Please *b.* my field	Jer. 32:8	Matt. 25:10

Buzi (boo′-zi), The father of the prophet Ezekiel (Ezek. 1:3).

Byblos (bib′-los), A Greek name for the ancient Gebal, a Phoenician city, on the Mediterranean coast 25 miles north of Beirut. Ezekiel 27:9 notes its workmen's fame as ship-builders. They collaborated with those of Hiram, king of Tyre, and of Solomon in the preparation of the materials for the construction of the Temple (1 Kgs. 6:32). The Greek name, "Byblos," comes from **biblos**, "book." Here was manufactured, from reeds from Egypt, the papyrus (ancient paper) on which records, correspondence, documents and "books" were written. The word "Bible" is directly derived from Byblos.

C

Caesarea (sez′-a-ree′-a), Chief port-city of Palestine at the time of Christ, located on the coastal road from Tyre to Egypt, 23 miles south of the promontory of Mount Carmel, 64 miles northwest of Jerusalem. Caesarea was constructed (25-13 B.C.) by Herod the Great on former lightly populated marshlands along the Mediterranean. An effective harbor was created by skillful use of mole and breakwater, and Caesarea quickly gained most of the traffic between Jerusalem and the Mediterranean world. Vast public works, including a huge amphitheater, agora, theater, a palace, a temple of Caesar, and numerous statues, all in the Hellenistic style, made Caesarea, almost overnight, a commercial, political and artistic success. Caesarea was the headquarters of the Roman governors of Palestine and the administrative center of Herod's dominions. Its population was mostly Gentile, with a significant Jewish minority. Philip the Evangelist lived there; he brought the gospel to Caesarea (Acts 8:40) and entertained Paul and his companions in his home (Acts 9:30; 21:8). Peter preached to a Gentile congregation there (Acts 10:34, 44, 48). Paul went through Caesarea several times on his missionary journeys (e.g. Acts cc. 18-22). It was to Caesarea that he was sent for trial by Felix (Acts 23:23-33); he was imprisoned there for two years (Acts 24:27), and made his second defense there before Festus and Agrippa II (Acts 25-26). From Caesarea he was sent by ship to Rome in the custody of a centurion (Acts 27:1).

Caesarea Philippi (sez′-a-ree′-a fil′-a-py), A town near one of the headwaters of the Jordan River, at the foot of Mount Hermon, built by Philip, tetrarch of Iturea and Trachonitis, a son of Herod the Great, in honor of Philip's patron, the Roman Caesar-Emperor, Tiberius. Philip added his own name to "Caesarea" to distinguish it from other cities of the same name. The site, previously known as Paneas, had a long history as a favorite seat of the Hellenistic nature-cult god, Pan. The locality was the scene of Peter's great confession of Christ (Matt. 16:13; Mk. 8:27).

Caiaphas (kay′-a-fas), Surname of Joseph, high priest at the time of the ministry of John the Baptist (Lk. 3:2) and of the trial of Jesus. The years of his high priesthood were 18-36 A.D. He was appointed by Valerius Gratus and deposed by Vitellius, Roman governors. Caiaphas was the son-in-law of Annas and succeeded him in the office. He was perhaps the first to suggest that Jesus be killed to prevent trouble with Rome (Jn. 11:49ff). The plans for arresting Jesus were made in his home (Matt. 26:3ff); the hearing before the Sanhedrin was held there (Matt. 26:5ff; Mk. 14:53; Lk. 22:54); it was Caiaphas who pressed on Jesus the question about his messianic claim (Matt. 27:62ff; Mk. 14:6ff). He also played an active role in bringing charges against Peter and John (Acts 4:6).

Cain, According to Genesis 4:1 Cain was the first-born of Adam and Eve. He murdered his brother Abel. The second half of Gen. 4:1 is a play on words lost in translation. The name "Cain" probably means "smith." The episode about Cain and Abel often poses problems to the reader unaccustomed to ancient texts, such as who could kill Cain, seeing that nobody other than his family existed, and other similar questions. In reality these questions immediately show that the text is being taken for something it is not.

The most common interpretation holds that the Cain story is an ethnological etiology, that is, a narrative that seeks to explain or represent in a very concrete way the condition of life and some characteristics of a human group by projecting these elements back to a common ancestor. Cain then is the fictitious ancestor of the Kenite tribe known also from other passages in the Bible (Jgs. 4:11). The nomadic Kenite tribe associated with the Israelites in the desert although it did not form part of the confederation of the twelve tribes (Jgs. 1:16; 1 Sam. 15:6).

As the story is told in the Bible, it is very probably an adaptation of a Kenite tradition, in which obviously their ancestry would have been given anything but a negative judgment. In Gen. 4:1-15 however the account gives a black picture of what originally would have been an exaltation of the ferocity and pitiless revenge of Cain. This hypothesis is confirmed by the song of Lamech (Gen. 4:23-24) where the original spirit of the Kenite tradition on Cain can be discovered: Cain is an implacable vindicator, the sign of the Lord is tattooed on his face as a warning to all to keep their distance and not provoke the ferocity of the Kenite, whose life of wandering is not that of the assassin fleeing justice but the proud and high condition of the true nomad who despises the settled peoples. It would seem that the Kenites knew the name of God, Yahweh, even before the Israelites (*see* YAHWEH).

The Israelite author has reversed the story in the face of its originators, giving it a radically contrary judgment. How did the biblical author make Cain the son of Adam? An answer is perhaps found in Gen. 5:9 where a certain Kenan, which is but a variant of the name Cain, is made son of Enosh. In Hebrew Enosh means 'man,' like 'adam;' and so the Kenites could be said to have exalted their pride to the point where they claimed to be the sons of the son of the first man. Thus the anachronisms that surprise the present-day reader were already present in the original account, but they were anachronisms with a meaning as the story's point was to explain the historical condition in life of the human group, Kenites, who lived in a fully historical epoch (*see* also GENEALOGY; NOMADISM).

The episode of Cain is also referred to in Hebrews 11:4; 1 John 3:12; Jude 11.

cake
take one unleavened *c.*   Lev. 8:26   a. *c.* of pressed figs   1 Sam. 30:12
Ephraim is a hearth *c.*   Hos. 7:8

Caleb (kay′-leb), One of the 12 spies sent by Moses to scout the land of Canaan from Israel's wilderness encampment (Num. cc. 13-14), and subsequently the lieutenant of Joshua and the conqueror of Hebron and inheritor of the surrounding south-Judah countryside. When the spies reported, the majority dwelt upon the fortified cities and the large-sized warlike men they had observed. Caleb in contrast described the land in glowing terms—"flowing with milk and honey"—and argued that since "the Lord is with us" an immediate attack should be made. Joshua concurred. The majority viewpoint, however, prevailed, and the people's timidity was viewed as rebellion against the Lord and disbelief in his presence (Num. 14:9). Because of their disbelief the adult wilderness generation—all except Joshua and Caleb, "who has followed Yahweh fully" (14:24)—were excluded from entrance into the Promised Land. Later Caleb had to defeat the resident people of Hebron and south Judah, the Anakim or giants. Actually Othniel took Hebron and thereby won Caleb's daughter Achsah as wife.

Older sources call Caleb the son of Jephunneh the Kenizzite (Num. 32:12) and also the brother of Kenaz, Othniel's father (Josh. 15:17; Jgs. 1:13). Kenaz was an Edomite chief or tribe (Gen. 36:11; 1 Chron. 1:53). So very possibly Caleb and Kenaz were Kenizzites or Horites who penetrated the folk of the tribe of Judah; Caleb for example made several marriages (1 Chron. 2:18f, 24, 42-50; 4:15). But Caleb is also said to be the son of Hezron (1 Chron. 2:18, 24; *see* 2:4-5), and the P source (Num.

13:6) provides him with a family tree going back to Judah. Whatever his ancestry, Caleb epitomizes fearless faith in the God of Israel and in his promises.

Caligula (cal-lig′-u-la), Gaius Julius Caesar Germanicus surnamed Caligula, Roman Emperor from 37 to 41 A.D. He ordered that a statue of himself as Zeus be made, which would be erected in the Jerusalem Temple. *See* ABOMINATION OF DESOLATION.

call

what he would *c.* them	Gen. 2:19	Then *c.* me and I will respond	
I did not *c.* you	1 Sam. 3:5		Job 13:22
C. now!	Job 5:1	Woe to those who *c.* evil good	
			Isa. 5:20

Go, *c.* your husband Jn. 4:16

Camel, There is frequent mention of the camel in Scripture as a beast of burden (e.g. Gen. 37:25), as well as for riding on, and as constituting no small item in the wealth of the early Hebrews. This was the one-humped or Arabian camel. The dromedary type of this species was swift (1 Sam. 30:17). The evidence of the date of the camel's domestication is mixed. Genesis 24 contains many circumstantial references to them, and bones of camels have been found in domestic settings in Mari dating in the 18th century B.C. But the art and literary evidences from Egypt and Mesopotamia do not antedate 1100 B.C. Perhaps the resolution is that large-scale camel nomadism (e.g. Midianites, Jgs. 6:5) came only at the later date. Abraham had camels in Egypt (Gen. 12:16) and in Canaan (24:10). Jacob owned and used them (30:43; 31:17) and made a gift of them to Esau (32:15). The Amalekites used them in the days of Saul and David (1 Sam. 15:3; 27:8; 30:17). Camels carried the gifts of the Queen of Sheba to Solomon (1 Kgs. 10:2). Job is pictured as owning 3000 before his testing, 6000 afterwards. The flat foot of the camel enables it to walk on sand without sinking in. On journeys it can survive on desert plants and do without water for several days and for as much as 20 days in cool weather.

camp

had been leading Israel's *c.*		the Lord had come into the *c.*	
	Ex. 14:19		1 Sam. 4:6
in the *c.* of the Hebrews mean		Gods have come to their *c.*	
	1 Sam; 4:6		1 Sam. 4:7

can

c. I alone bear the crushing		*C.* your servant taste what he	
	Deut. 1:12		2 Sam. 19:36
C. I bring him back again		*C.* a thing insipid be eaten Job 6:6	
	2 Sam. 12:23	*C.* the papyrus grow up without	
C. I distinguish between good			Job 8:11
	2 Sam. 19:36	*C.* the reed grass flourish without	
			Job 8:11

Cana (kay′-na), A Galilean town, Khirbet Qana, 9 miles north of Nazareth, on the east-west road between Magdala on the Sea of Galilee and Ptolemais on the Mediterranean. Here was held the wedding feast at which Jesus turned the water into wine (Jn. 2:1-11). It was the home of Nathanael (Jn. 21:2).

Canaan, The land of Canaan is the most ancient and the most common biblical designation for the strip of land that stretches from the sea to the desert and from the southern border of Syria to Egypt (*see* e.g. Gen. 15:18-20). Here it was that the Israelite tribes settled. Originally the name was a geographical designation which also served to denote the semitic people who had settled there in the long-distant past, and certainly before the end of the third millenium B.C. Some of them had been pushed out and confined to determined areas by succeeding waves of semitic peoples (the Amorites) and non-semites such as the Hittites, the Hurrites, the Philistines, etc. during the second millenium. In the Bible the term Canaanite is used for the residue of the most ancient semitic people (thus in the lists of peoples dislocated by the incoming Israelites in Gen. 15:20; Ex. 3:8; Deut. 7:1; 20:17; Josh. 3:10, etc.), and probably too for the non-Israelite population of Palestine in general (Gen. 12:6; 13:17). At the time of the Israelite arrival the Canaanites (in the first meaning of the word) occupied the coastal plain of Palestine and the Jordan valley (Num. 13:29; Deut. 1:7; 11:30; Josh. 11:3). There were also enclaves however in the central regions (Josh. 17:11-13).

In the Table of Nations Canaan is the son of Ham (Gen. 10:6) and on him is placed the curse pronounced by Noah against Ham (Gen. 9:25-27).

cannot

poor and *c.* afford so much	these I *c.* bear Isa. 1:13
Lev. 14:21	its billows roar, they *c.* pass
barred my way and I *c.* pass	Jer. 5:22
Job 19:8	

Canon, From the Greek **kanon,** which etymologically means a reed, but in use meant a yardstick, or measure, or norm (Gal. 6:16). In today's theological language the canon is the authentic list of recognized sacred books, that is, books written under the inspiration of the Holy Ghost and as such received by the Church. The canon of sacred books was solemnly defined on April 8, 1546, by the Council of Trent. Vatican I confirmed this on April 24, 1870. These definitions repeat the lists of sacred books established in previous non-ecumenical councils, such as the first, third and fourth councils of Carthage, held in the years 393, 397 and 419 in the west, and the Trullan Synod in 692 in the east. Moreover, they were contained in the non-dogmatic decree on the Jacobites in the ecumenical council of Florence (1441). The canonical books of the Catholic Church and the separated eastern churches are:

Old Testament: Genesis, Exodus, Leviticus, Numbers, Deuteronomy, Joshua, Judges, Ruth, 1 and 2 Samuel, 1 and 2 Kings, 1 and 2 Chronicles, Ezra, Nehemiah (also called 2 Ezra), Tobit, Judith, Esther, 1 and 2 Maccabees, Job, Psalms, Proverbs, Ecclesiastes (also called Koheleth), Wisdom, Sirach (also called Ecclesiasticus), Song of Songs (also called Canticle of Canticles), Isaiah, Jeremiah, Lamentations, Baruch, Ezekiel, Daniel, Hosea, Joel, Amos, Obadiah, Jonah, Micah, Nahum, Habakkuk, Zephaniah, Haggai, Zechariah, Malachi.

New Testament: The Four Gospels according to Matthew, Mark, Luke and John; The Acts of the Apostles; 14 letters traditionally ascribed to St. Paul: Romans, 1 and 2 Corinthians, Galatians, Ephesians, Philippians, Colossians, 1 and 2 Thessalonians, 1 and 2 Timothy, Titus, Philemon, Hebrews; 7 Catholic Epistles: James, 1 and 2 Peter, 1, 2 and 3 John, Jude; and finally, the Book of Revelation, also called the Apocalypse.

The Council definitions of the Canon intend only to list the books with their traditional titles, without pretending to resolve questions of a critical nature about authorship. Today, for example, modern scholars find it difficult to attribute the letter to the Hebrews to Paul. Catholics, too, may debate this question, but the canonicity, and thus too the inspiration of the book, may not be doubted. The Council of Trent stated that all the books of the Old and New Testament must be received with equal devotion and reverence.

A distinction is made between protocanonical and deuterocanonical books: this refers, not to inspiration, but to the stage at which the books were universally recognized as canonical; for doubts were entertained in some churches about certain books right up to the fifth century. In the west, for instance, doubts were cast on the letter to the Hebrews, as its Pauline authorship was questioned. In the east, Revelation was not fully received, for it seemed to some to be millenaristic in tone. The deuterocanonical works of the New Testament are: Hebrews, James, 2 Peter, 2 and 3 John, Revelation.

The Christian Church accepted as sacred books of the Old Testament those contained in the Greek translation known as the Septuagint (LXX), made by the Alexandrine Jews. This edition, however, contained seven books not recognized by the Jews in Palestine, who fixed their canon at the end of the first century at the celebrated Council of Jamnia. On this account questions arose in regard to the inspiration of these seven books: Tobit, Judith, Wisdom, Sirach (Ecclesiasticus), Baruch, 1 and 2 Maccabees, together with some portions of other books which were found in the Greek translation (Daniel 3:24–90: the canticle of the three youths in the furnace; and cc. 13 and 14; also Esther 10:4–16, 24). The deuterocanonical works of the Old Testament are not received into the canon of the Protestant churches.

Capernaum (ka-per′-nay-um), Kaphar-Nahum, "the town of Nahum," now identified with Tell Hum, a town on the northern shore of the Sea of Galilee. This busy little lake port was the center of the Galilean ministry of Jesus (*see* Matt, 9:1). Its harbor was lively with fishing craft, which were protected by breakwaters from sudden storms. It was apparently a Roman military post with a customs house on the road from Damascus to Jerusalem. The ruins include a fine white limestone synagogue, now partly restored, dating from the 3rd century A.D.

Caph, The 11th letter of the Hebrew alphabet (k).

Capharsalama (caf′-ar-sal′-a-ma), A place northwest of Jerusalem where Judas Maccabeus won a victory over the Seleucid general Nicanor (1 Mac. 7:31).

Caphtor, In biblical tradition Caphtor was the place of origin of the Philistines (Jer. 47:4; Amos 9:7). From Egyptian sources it is clear that the island of Crete is meant by the name; but there is no evidence of a Philistine occupation of Crete. Perhaps "Caphtor" was used broadly for the Aegean area, whence the Philistines emerged.

capital

a bronze *c*. five cubits high	the *c*. topping each was
2 Kgs. 25:17	2 Chron. 3:15

captain

I am the *c*. of the host Josh. 5:14	The *c*. of the host of the Lord
	Josh. 5:15

captive, captives

their little ones as *c*. Num. 31:9	the enemies who took them *c*.
a comely woman among the *c*.	1 Kgs. 8:48
Deut. 21:11	making *c*. of its captors Isa. 14:2

captivity, *See* EXILE.

carbuncle

your gates of *c*. Isa. 54:12	

carcass
c. of an unclean animal   Lev. 5:2

Carchemish (kar'-kem-ish), Capital of the Hittite empire, on the upper Euphrates. It was the scene of Nebuchadnezzar's defeat of Pharaoh Neco (605 B.C.).

care, cared, cares

You have lavished all this *c.*		where he *c.* for him	Lk. 10:34
	2 Kgs. 4:13	worldly *c.*	Lk. 21:34
c. abound within me	Ps. 94:19	take *c.* of the church	1 Tim. 3:5

Carkas, One of the seven eunuchs who served king Ahasuerus as chamberlains (Esth. 1:10).

Carmi, The father of Achan, who violated the ban laid by Joshua on Jericho (Josh. 7:1, 18; 1 Chron. 2:7).

Carpenter, Carpenter is the translation given to **tekton** which was the name given to the trade of Joseph, Mary's husband (Matt. 13:55) and of Jesus (Mk. 6:3). On both occasions it is used with the article, *the* carpenter, which could mean that he was the only carpenter in the village. Carpenter means a man who can turn his hand to anything, a kind of general handyman often found in farming countrysides. To him the people come to make and repair farm implements or domestic appliances, and his trade could also include putting up small, simple houses of stone.

carpenter, carpenters

as well as *c.* and masons		The *c.* stretches a line	Isa. 44:13
	2 Sam. 5:11	Is this not the *c.*	Mk. 6:3
pay them out to the *c.*	2 Kgs. 22:6		

carry, carried

c. them to a place outside the		and *c.* them along to the camp	
	Lev. 10:4		Josh. 4:8

Carshena (car-she'-nah), A prince of Media and Persia under King Ahasuerus (Esth. 1:14).

cattle

all kinds of *c.*	Gen. 1:25	idols are upon beasts and *c.*	
grazing land for *c.*	Isa. 7:25		Isa. 46:1

Cave, Caves were used for shelter, as places of refuge, and for burial. Palestine's limestone and sandstone hills provide many natural caves, and artificial ones were easy to dig. Lot, afraid to live in Zoar, took to a cave (Gen. 19:30). The Edomites lived largely in caves at Petra, down to Roman times. Uses of caves for refuge are told often in the O.T. (e.g. Josh. 10:16; Jgs. 6:2; 1 Sam. 13:6; 22:1; 24:3; 2 Sam. 23:13). Abraham bought a cave for Sarah's sepulcher. For Lazarus' tomb *see* John 11:38; for Jesus' *see* John 19:41.

Cedar, Cedars of Lebanon especially. In O.T. times this was the most sought-after material for the construction of fine buildings and objects appropriately made of wood. David and Solomon imported vast quantities (2 Sam. 5:11; 7:2, 7; 1 Kgs. cc. 5-7; etc.). Solomon's "House of the Forest of Lebanon" had 3 rows of 15 cedar pillars each. Cedar was used in the interiors of palaces, temples and courts; as masts for ships (Ezek. 27:5); in chests, musical instruments, coffins. Poets and prophets employed the cedar as a symbol of strength, worth, incorruptibility. Trunks of Lebanese cedar attain a girth of 40 feet, and the flat branches a spread of almost 300 feet in circumference.

Cedron, *See* KIDRON.

Censer, A brazen vessel for burning incense (Lev. 10:1; 16:12). For his Temple Solomon had gold ones made (1 Kgs. 7:50; 2 Chron. 4:22; now translated by NAB, "fire pans." *See* also Heb. 9:4; Rev. 8:3-5).

Census, Caesar Augustus several times decreed an enrollment or census of the people within his vast empire. One of these was ordered in 8 B.C. This is the one mirrored in Luke 2:1-5. 5 B.C. is a more likely year for the birth of Jesus than 8 B.C., but perhaps the bureaucratic machinery necessary to take an enrollment in an outlying province like Palestine could not be set in motion for 2 or 3 years. It has been held that Rome did not require a subject to return to his original home for such enrollments, but recently a discovered Roman census edict dating from 104 A.D. in the province of Egypt made just that stipulation.

In the O.T. enrollments were by tribe, family and lineage (Num. 1:18). They were taken for taxation purposes (Ex. 30:13-16; Num. 3:40-51); for military drafting (Num. 1:3; 26:2; 2 Sam. 24:9); and for apportioning duties in cult-worship among the Levites (Num. 3:4). It is very difficult to make any sense out of the figures offered as the results of the three recorded censuses of Israelites of military age, for they are clearly exaggerations and in one case contradictory (Num. 1:46; 11:21; 26:2; 51; 2 Sam. 24:9; 1 Chron. 21:5). Josephus in his *Antiquities* says that David used the wrong method of taking a census, and hence was punished by the Lord: he should have levied a half-shekel tax (*see* Ex. 30:11-16), and thus avoided the taboo on head-counting per se.

Centurion, A Roman officer, several honorably mentioned (Matt. 8:5-13; Lk. 7:2-10; Matt. 27:54; Lk. 23:47; Acts 27:43). A centurion commanded, nominally, "a century," 100 foot soldiers. Normally there were 10 centurions in a cohort, and 60 in a legion. They were picked for leadership and steadiness. The senior centurion of a legion had power and prestige, and all centurions were responsible military men, professionals, like top sergeants.

Cephas, *See* PETER.

chaff, *See* WINNOWING.

chain, chains

put a gold *c.* about his neck		cordlike *c.* to the filigree	Ex. 28:14
	Gen. 41:42	I wear these *c.*	Acts 28:20
two *c.* of pure gold	Ex. 28:14	even in my *c.*	2 Tim. 1:16

Chalcol (kal′-kol), Son of Mahol, one of the legendary wise men whose wisdom was surpassed only by Solomon's (1 Kgs. 5:11).

Chaldea (kal-dee′-a), *See* BABYLONIA.

change

they might *c.* their minds		Can the Ethiopian *c.* his skin	
	Ex. 13:17		Jer. 13:23
Such men *c.* the night into day		unless you *c.* and become like	
	Job 17:12		Matt. 18:3
When there is a *c.* of priesthood	Heb. 7:12		

Chariot, War chariots were in common use among the enemies of Israel from the time they were employed by the Pharaoh of the Exodus (Ex. 14). They were not adopted by the Israelites until the days of David, who captured some (2 Sam. 8:4), and Solomon, who built chariot cities in strategic spots. They constituted the "heavy artillery" of an army. The

Israelite chariots of Solomon and his successors, as well as the horses, were imported chiefly from Egypt. They were two-wheeled, their wooden bodies semicircular, reinforced with metal plates, and mounted from behind. In battle they normally carried two persons, the driver on the left, an archer beside him. They were drawn by two or more horses. In open terrain chariots were devastating. Barak's strategy (Jgs. 4) was to lure Sisera's into the soggy bottom-lands of the river Kishon, where they became mired. Chariots could also be used for hunting, for patrolling royal estates, and for transporting kings, princes and generals (e.g. Absalom, Jehu). Poets and prophets found chariots effective symbols of power (Pss. 20:7; 104:3; Jer. 51:21; Zech. 6:1).

Charisma, The Greek word **charisma** (from **charis,** grace) had the generic sense of a gratuitous gift. In this sense it is used to denote Christian salvation which is the gratuitous gift of eternal life (Rom. 5:15; 6:23). It has however a more precise meaning in other texts (1 Cor. 12:4, 23, 30, 31; Rom. 12:6). Charisms are special gifts which the Holy Spirit distributes to the faithful for the good of the whole community (*see* 1 Cor. 12:4-7). Paul in 1 Cor. 12:8-10, 28-30 and Rom. 12:6-8 lists some of these gifts. Not all however had unusual or extraordinary manifestations. Some charisms such as that of the apostolate, teaching, assistance, government (1 Cor. 12:28, 29) respond more to what one today might call a vocation, obviously brought about and sustained by the Spirit for the service of the Church. One can only offer an approximative interpretation of some of these gifts, as the name given them by the apostle is too generic for more concrete definition. As an example, speaking with wisdom and knowledge seems to be related to that more profound knowledge of the Christian mysteries of which Paul speaks in other places. (*See* KNOWLEDGE.) On the charism of prophecy *see* PROPHECY. At Corinth the abundance and variety of charisms had created a rather delicate situation. There the gift of glossolalia was highly esteemed and avidly sought after. From the description afforded by the apostle in 1 Cor. 14:6-25, it seems that the gift came with a kind of ecstatic rapture during which enigmatic words or sounds were uttered, which then of course required someone with a charism for interpreting them. Paul exhorts the community to proceed with order and harmony in whatever has to do with charisms. All charisms are the Spirit's work, but there is among the Spirit's gifts a hierarchy of value which is to be respected, and especially so in the Christian assembly (1 Cor. 14:26-39). Prophecy is the most precious and the most useful for the good of the community, and therefore to this one should aspire. Love however is above all charisms. Without love every charism is empty and love will remain when all charisms will have outlived their usefulness (1 Cor. 13).

Charity, *See* LOVE.

Chebar (kee′-bar), A canalized river passing by Babylon and joining the Euphrates at Erech. By the Chebar Ezekiel saw visions (Ezek. 1:3; 3:15,23; 10:15,22; 43:3).

Chederlaomer (ked′-er-la-oh′-mer), King of Elam, a land east of Babylonia, on the Persian Gulf. At one time he held most of the Fertile Crescent to Egypt in his sway. The "Five Kings" of the five Dead Sea cities rebelled against him (Gen. 14). Chederlaomer's associates in the campaign (14:1) were vassal "kings" of petty city-states in the S. Palestine region, but are otherwise unidentifiable.

Chemosh (kee′-mosh), The national deity of Moab (Num. 21:29; Jgs. 11:24). Solomon, perhaps for political reasons or as a favor to a Moabite wife, built an altar to Chemosh (1 Kgs. 11:7), destroyed only some 300 years later by Josiah (2 Kgs. 23:13). As with the worship of Molech, live children were on occasion sacrificed by burning.

Chenaanah (ke-na′-a-nah), The father of the prophet Zedekiah (1 Kgs. 22:11, 24).

Cherethites and Pelethites (ker′-e-thites; pel′-e-thites), Groups of mercenary soldiers, who formed David's personal guard. Their chief was Benaiah (2 Sam. 8:18; 20:23). They were Philistines (Ezek. 25:16). They accompanied David when he was forced to abandon Jerusalem to his son Absalom (2 Sam. 15:18). They took part in the campaign against the rebellious Sheba (2 Sam. 20:7) and they supported the election of Solomon as David's successor to the throne (1 Kgs. 1:38-44).

Cherith (ker′-ith), A stream east of Jordan whither God sent Elijah during the drought in the reign of Ahab (869-850 B.C.; 1 Kgs. 17:2-7). There he quenched his thirst and the ravens brought him bread.

Cherub, Cherubim, Christian tradition adopted this name from the Old Testament to designate a special category of angels together with the Seraphim and the Thrones.

In the Old Testament the cherubim (plural form) are beings distinct from the category of angels, and have their own well defined functions. On the cover of the ark of the Lord were two cherubim of gold with wings extended to cover the propitiatory (Ex. 25:10-22; 37:7-9). On the cherubim of the ark the invisible God sat enthroned. For this reason he was called "the Lord of hosts, who is enthroned upon the cherubim" (1 Sam. 4:4; 2 Sam. 6:2; Pss. 80:2; 99:1). In the innermost room of the Temple of Solomon, that is in the **Debir** (*see* TEMPLE), were two wooden cherubim covered with gold, with wings extended "so that one wing of each cherub touched a side wall while the other wing, pointing toward the middle of the room, touched the corresponding wing of the second cherub" (1 Kgs. 6:23-28). The walls on all sides of both the inner and the outer rooms had carved figures of cherubim, palm trees and open flowers (1 Kgs. 6:29).

Nothing is said in these texts about how these cherubim looked. We can gather some idea of this however from the description of the cherubim who support and transport the throne of God in the vision of Ezekiel (*see* Ezek. 9:3; 10:1). They are living beings with human and animal traits. Ezekiel is obviously inspired by the figures of the cherubim of the Temple and the ark which supported the throne of the invisible God. The cherubim then would not be much different from animal figures, perhaps that of a lion or bull, with wings and the face of a man, which in Egypt and Mesopotamia were guardian spirits at the entrance to their temples and on the royal thrones. The task of being guardian spirits is explicitly assigned to them in Genesis 3:24. When Adam and Eve were expelled from paradise the Lord "stationed the cherubim and (or with) the fiery revolving sword to guard the way to the tree of life."

Chesed (ke′-sed), Son of Nahor, Abraham's brother (Gen. 22:22).

Chidon (ki′-don), The threshing floor where Uzzah was struck dead after touching the ark of the Lord (1 Chron. 13:9).

children
in pain shall you bring forth *c.* Gen. 3:16
has kept me from bearing *c.* Gen. 16:2
not counting the *c.* Ex. 12:37
to take the food of the *c.* Mk. 7:27
Rachel bewailing her *c.* Matt. 2:18
God can raise up *c.* to Abraham Matt. 3:9
c. will turn against parents Matt. 10:21

Chileab (kil′-e-ab), Second son of David, of Abigail (2 Sam. 3:3; called Daniel in 1 Chron. 3:1).

Chilion (kil′-i-on), A son of Elimelech and Naomi; he married Orpah and soon died (Ruth 1:2,5).

Chimham (kim′-ham), Son of Barzillai. The father was generous to David at Mahanaim; the son in lieu of his father (2 Sam. 19:37-40) returned to Jerusalem with the aging king, where he seems to have been granted a pension (1 Kgs. 2:7; *see* also Jer. 41:17).

Chinnereth, Chinneroth (kin′-e-reth, roth), A fortified town on the northwest shore of the Sea of Galilee. It gave its name to the lake in olden times, which was later called Gennesaret and finally the Sea of Galilee.

Chislev (kiz′-lev), The ninth month of the Hebrew year, November-December (Neh. 1:1; Zech. 7:1).

Chloe, A woman whose servants told Paul of divisions within the church at Corinth (1 Cor. 1:11).

Chorazin (ko-ray′-zin), A town in Galilee c. 2½ miles north of Capernaum. Because it remained unrepentant Jesus denounced it (Matt. 11:21; Lk. 10:13). In the ruins of a local synagogue archaeologists found a "Moses seat" (Matt. 23:2).

chose

wives as many of them as they *c*.	Saul *c*. three thousand men
Gen. 6:2	1 Sam. 13:2
Lot, therefore, *c*. for himself	But he *c*: the tribe of Judah
Gen. 13:11	Ps. 78:68
For love of your fathers he *c*.	And he *c*. David his servant
Deut. 4:37	Ps. 78:70

Christ, Body of, *See* BODY OF CHRIST.

Chronicles, Books of, With Ezra and Nehemiah the two books of Chronicles form one historical work (*see* 2 Chron. 36:22-23, which is repeated in Ezra 1:1-3). The Hebrew title for the work is the "Book of Facts and Days," that is, the annals. The Septuagint named them the books of **paraleipomenon** (from the Greek **paraleipo,** to omit) as it was thought that their scope was to fill in what had been left out of the books of Kings and Samuel, which turns out, however, to be an erroneous opinion. The present title stems from the title proposed by St. Jerome for his Latin translation: "Chronicle of the whole of divine history."

In fact the book takes in the whole sacred history from the creation of Adam until the edict of Cyrus which put an end to the exile (537 B.C.). It can be divided into three principal sections:

a. From Adam to David (1 Chron. 1-9): this contains everything from Genesis up to 2 Samuel spelled out in genealogies that substantially follow those scattered here and there throughout the books mentioned.

b. The reigns of David and Solomon (1 Chron. 10–2 Chron. 9): the narrative part begins with the reign of David who is the material and formal center of the Chronicler's history.

c. The history of the kings of Judah from Solomon up to the exile (2 Chron. 10-36). The author omitted all the history of the schismatic kingdom of the north, whose kings make only sporadic appearances whenever they figure in the history of Judah.

The description of the content of the book already affords us an idea of its scope and its theological intentions. The author certainly belonged to the priestly environment of Jerusalem, and so saw in David the most perfect realization of theocracy as the political, religious and civil constitution of

Israel. This then remained an example to imitate, and placed the foundations for the whole future history of the people of Israel. Moreover it constituted the divine pledge of restoration and even of greater things in the future. The author's description of David's kingdom and reign is as theological as it is historical. He discreetly passes over those elements that might obscure or contradict the normative character of that period, such as David's adultery, the internal struggle for succession to the throne, the rebellions of Absalom and Sheba, and so on. On the other hand he attributes personally to David all the institutions that sustain the theocratic structure, much as the Priestly author attributed to Sinai and to the revelation to Moses the whole legislative and cultic apparatus of Israel.

Particular emphasis is placed on the oracle of Nathan, the **magna charta** of David's theocracy. The author is particularly interested in the work of David to institute and organize the cult in Jerusalem. He goes beyond the account of 1 Kings and indeed beyond the historical truth when he makes David the founder and organizer of the whole Jerusalem liturgy, to be carried out in a temple for which David, according to the author, had left the most detailed plans without however having undertaken its construction. Solomon faithfully carried out David's plans; in fact David was blocked by God from bringing the plans to execution because "you may not build a house in my honor, for you are a man who fought wars and shed blood" (1 Chron. 28:3).

The reasons given here reveal another constant in the religious mentality of the author. He was profoundly convinced that God was Lord of peoples and history, in the course of which he does not cease to exercise judgment. In every episode or circumstance that departs from the ideal plan of God the author sees the effects of human infidelity. Like 1-2 Kings, Chronicles is a religious interpretation of the past, and not just a neutral chronicle of events (*see* e.g. 2 Chron. 33:1-20 compared with 2 Kgs. 21:1-18; 2 Chron. 35:19-22 compared with 2 Kgs. 23:29-30).

When then 1-2 Chronicles is read, the mentality and theology of the author should be kept in mind. This however is generally so obvious that there is no difficulty in distinguishing between this and the historical matter that is grist to his mill. Despite the recent epoch in which the book was written, it contains precious information and traditions which complement and at times correct to advantage the version of the facts given in 1-2 Kings. It would therefore seem that the author used well-informed sources, some of which he cites. Besides the books of the Bible which were used but are not quoted, the author drew his information from the annals of the Kings of Judah and Israel, books that were also used in 1-2 Kings (*see* 2 Chron. 16:11; 25:26, etc.), as well as from some works attributed to prophets such as Samuel (1 Chron. 29:29), Nathan (1 Chron. 29:29; 2 Chron. 9:29), Gad (1 Chron. 29:29), Iddo (2 Chron. 9:29; 12:15), Shemaiah (2 Chron. 12·15), Jehu (2 Chron. 20:34), Hozai (2 Chron. 33:19), Isaiah (2 Chron. 32:32; 26:22) and Ahijah the Shilonite, which were probably collected into a historical work of prophetic inspiration. He also quotes the Lamentations of Jeremiah for the death of Josiah, which however are different from the canonical book of Lamentations (2 Chron. 35:22; *see* LAMENTATIONS).

The book certainly comes after Ezra and Nehemiah. The genealogies reach to the sixth generation after Zerubbabel (1 Chron. 3:19-21). It is however before Sirach which seems to depend on 1-2 Chronicles in what it tells of some personages of the past (Sir. 44-50). It was probably written during the third century B.C.

Chronology, 1. Old Testament. The Pentateuch contains much chronological data that is set down with what seems to be great precision. These statements are especially evident in the genealogies, which lead the reader down through history from the creation of the world to the death of Moses (e.g. Gen 5; 11:10–26; 17:1; 25:7, etc.) The precision of the dates, however, should not be allowed to deceive one: they are not historical facts as we know them, but the results of artificial and imaginative calculations to which no key has been discovered. This is more than evident for the period from the creation until the flood, and from the flood to Abraham—a period that can only with difficulty be called "history" in the proper sense of the term. The dates offered by Genesis for the era of the patriarchs are no longer credible. Non-biblical documents describing the movements of seminomad peoples in the region of Syria-Palestine help us give the biblical account its proper setting. However, a comparison between the Bible and other documents allows us to establish only that the period of the patriarchs fits well into the Palestinian situation in the second quarter of the second millenium before Christ, that is, 1750 to 1500 B.C.

The Bible supplies two coordinates for dating the Exodus. According to Exodus 12:40 the Jews lived in Egypt for 430 years. 1 Kings 6:1 tells us that the dedication of the Temple of Solomon took place 480 years after the Exodus. Both of these dates, however, are artificial. The first one is had by doubling the 215 years that elapsed between Abraham and the departure of Jacob for Egypt. The second figure is obtained by multiplying 40 years by 12 generations. For the dating of the Exodus it is a help to compare the information in Exodus 1 with Egyptian history: the "new king who did not know Joseph" is Ramses II (reigned 1290–1224 B.C.), so that, with all probability, the Exodus can be put into the first half of the thirteenth century B.C. *See* also MERNEPTAH.

A brief summary of events after the Exodus, through the period of the Judges, and up to the breakup of the United Kingdom, offers these approximate dates: Canaan entered by the Israelites, 1250 B.C. The period of the Judges, 1250–1020. Saul, 1020–1000; David, 1000–960; Solomon, 960–921. The kingdom divided, 921 B.C.

1 and 2 Kings establish a chronology of the kings of Judah and Israel by synchronizing the reigns of the kings of the two countries, e.g. "Ahab, the son of Omri, began to reign over Israel in the thirty-eighth year of Asa king of Judah" (1 Kgs. 16:29). This synchronization allows one to establish a reasonably close chronology for the history of the two kingdoms, by no means exact and perfect, by combining the dates given in the extant texts. Much of the incoherence can be resolved if two factors are kept in mind. First, there was the diversity in computing the beginning of a year (i.e. March/April or September/October) in the different kingdoms, and a change took place in the calendar system after the Exile. Secondly, there is the proven fact of co-reigns—proven in some cases, probable in others. But in the O.T. the regnal years of co-kings (usually an aging and ill king and a son-regent) are often spoken of as running consecutively instead of in part concurrently.

But a third factor tosses another imprecise element into the computations. This imprecision is the way the years of a reign were counted. Assume King A became king on New Year's Day of a new decade. In our ten-year hypothetical instance he reigns 5½ years. King B reigns 2¾ years, from the middle of year 6 to the end of the third month of year 9. King C reigns from the third of year 9 to, say, the third month of year 11. Do all these reigns, as computed by some of the authors of the historical books of the O.T., add up to 10¼ years? Unfortunately, no. Under one system of dating, called antedating, King A is credited with 6 years. King B is also credited with year 6, years 7 and 8 of course, and also for year 9, when he ruled but 3 months; he is credited with 4 years. King C, ruling 9 months in year 9, is credited with a year there, another year for year 10, and still another year for his 3 months of rule in year 11—3 years in all. Under this system these 3 kings are said to have ruled 13 years, where only 10 years and 3 months elapsed. The antedating system resulted in counting one year too many in each reign.

In the other system, called postdating, used at other times or in other countries, the chroniclers did not start calculating a king's reign until the first New Year after the death of his predecessor. This avoided the extra year that antedating added to the length of each reign. Reigns which were too short to extend to the next New Year were not counted at all. For a while Judah followed the postdating system and Israel the antedating, but each kingdom later reversed its basis. Furthermore, New Year was changed from autumn (Tishri) to spring (Nisan) before the Exile. Such are the thorny thickets that confront the chronologist of O.T. times.

In the midst of all this imprecision on the part of Hebrew scribes, a few dates can be pinned down as absolute on the evidence of Assyrian and Babylonian documents, which employed a sounder method. One evidence found in these documents is a mention of an eclipse of the sun, known today to have occurred on June 15, 763 B.C. Other ancient non-Hebrew documents cast confirming witness to the establishment of these dates:

853 B.C. Shalmaneser III (859–824) battles Ahab of Israel and his Syrian allies at Qarqar in the sixth year of his reign.

841 B.C. Shalmaneser III in his eighteenth year receives tribute from Jehu of Israel.

743 and 738 B.C. Tiglath-pileser III (745–727) is paid tribute by Menahem of Israel.

722/21 B.C. Sargon II captures Samaria in his accession year–that is, between the time of his accession and the next following New Year.

701 B.C. Sennacherib (705–681) in his fourth year besieges Jerusalem and Hezekiah.

609 B.C. Josiah is killed at Megiddo by forces under Pharaoh Neco of Egypt.

597 B.C., March 16. Nebuchadnezzar II (605–562) captures Jerusalem on the second day of Adar in his seventh year.

Out of such evidences do scholars pursue the task of fitting the O.T. data into a scheme in agreement with secular records.

Other important dates for the history of Judah after the Exile are: the decree of repatriation of the Jews of Babylonia, issued by Cyrus in 539 B.C. For the chronology of the activities of Ezra and Nehemiah, *see* EZRA. The Maccabean revolt against the Seleucids began in 168 B.C. For the chronology of the Hasmonean dynasty, *see* HASMONEAN.

2. New Testament. The most useful chronological data are found in Luke and the Acts of the Apostles. Luke 3:1 dates the beginning of John the Baptist's work in the fifteenth year of the emperor Tiberius, that is, in 27 or 29 A.D., depending on whether Luke counted from the date Tiberius assumed sole rule or the year when Caesar Augustus took him into the ruling collegium. At that time Jesus was about thirty years old. It is certain that the date of the beginning of the Christian era is at least four and perhaps seven years after the birth of Christ; in other words, Jesus was born 7–4 B.C. For the chronology of the Passion, *see* PASSION. For the life and missionary activity of Paul, *see* PAUL.

Church, Church translates the Greek **ekklesia.** The word has a long history in Greek culture and in Hellenistic Judaism. **Ecclesia** comes from the verb **kaleo,** which means **to call** or **convoke.** In classical usage **ecclesia** is the assembly of the people, called together or come together to deliberate on problems of a public nature (*see* Acts 19:29-40). In itself it did not have religious overtones. The word however was chosen by the translators of the Septuagint to express certain terms of the Old Testament such as **'edah** and **qahal** which designated the cultic assemblies of the people of Israel (*see* Deut. 9:10; 18:16; 1 Kgs. 8:65) and the people itself. In the Greek translation of the Septuagint the church of God means the people of Israel, not formally as an ethnic unity, but as God's people, called, convoked, formed by him as the object of his designs (*see* Acts 7:38).

The first question that biblical ecclesiology must pose is that of the relationship between Jesus and the Church. Some have wished to drive a wedge between Jesus' concept of his mission and work and the Church as we have it today. The Church today, for these authors, would be the result of Jesus' teaching, but unforeseen by him, even if it was not explicitly excluded in his intentions. The center of attention in Jesus' preaching would then have been exclusively the advent of the kingdom of God, and not the establishment of a church. This thesis would at first sight seem to be validated by the extreme scarcity of texts relative to the church in the gospels. In fact the word **ecclesia** is only read twice, in Matt. 16:18 and 18:17, and certainly the second of these does not go back in its present form to Jesus himself. The first text remains, however, and resists any attempt to disprove its authenticity or antiquity.

In this text Jesus speaks of **his** church. Here the word should be understood in the sense given above, and in the context of the eschatological expectations of biblical tradition. Biblical eschatology has as one of its fundamental elements the constitution of the community of those who will be sharers in salvation. The aim of God's intervention through his Messiah is precisely to establish the new people of God, the community of saints. The Messiah cannot be separated from the people who are to be the beneficiaries of his work. This is the logical conclusion of one of the fundamental categories of the history of salvation in which God's words and interventions are directed to a people (*see* Isa. 9; 11; Jer. 23:5; Ezek. 34). From this point of view the person of the Messiah is inseparable from his church, that is, from the people who are to reap the advantages of the salvation he brings, and who will be established by the Messiah as God's saved people. If then Jesus believed himself to be the person through whom God was bringing the history of salvation to its completion (*see* JESUS CHRIST), the establishment of a church is not only compatible with his thought, but also a necessary part of his work.

From this it follows that the eschatological people of God could not exist in its most genuine sense except on the basis of Jesus' death and resurrection. It had its beginnings however in the group of those who followed Jesus during his life, and had thus enjoyed the preliminaries of salvation. They thus formed the nucleus around which the church was established (Acts 1 and 2). It follows, secondly, that the concepts of Kingdom of God and Church are not identical, even though they cannot in fact be separated. The Kingdom of God is definitive salvation. The Church is the community of those who share in this definitive salvation, that is, they have a part in its goods. The Church shares the tension which animates the very realization of the Kingdom of God, that is, the Church is wholly directed towards the eschatological consummation of the Kingdom. The Church in this sense is not a definitive reality, but rather a pilgrim people sighing for its final home after having passed through the purification of the judgment.

In the apostolic writings of the New Testament the Church is placed in the most intimate relationship with Christ. This is nothing more than a reflection of the change that took place from the gospel of the Kingdom preached by Jesus to the gospel of Jesus Christ preached by the Church (*see* KINGDOM OF GOD). The relationship between Christ and the Church is on the level of life, and finds its most celebrated expression in the Pauline doctrine of the Church as Christ's body (*see* BODY OF CHRIST).

The word **ecclesia** moreover serves to designate the local Christian community, especially when this was united around the Table of the Lord. The Church grew around those who were the official witnesses of Jesus. Luke has sketched in deft words a picture of the essential Christian community: "They devoted themselves to the apostles' instruction and the communal life, to the breaking of bread and the prayers" (Acts 2:42). Faith and baptism fused the individual into the community, that is, it numbers them among the saints, the people made up of those redeemed by the Lord (Acts 2:41). The witness of the apostles, received with faith, brings increase to the Church. Through it God continues to call new members and multiply the new people. Luke has traced out the history of this witness in Acts (Acts 1:8; *see* APOSTLE; HIERARCHY; PETER).

The Church, even the local church, is God's Church, that is, it is made up of a portion of his people over which he watches through the pastors whom he has appointed (Acts 20:28). In the church and for its good the Spirit distributes different gifts, all aimed at building up the church: the apostolate, teaching, prophecy and other charisms (1 Cor. 12; *see* CHARISM). The church is compared to a building, the foundations of which are the apostles and the prophets, with Christ the cornerstone (*see* CORNERSTONE). In him the whole Church hangs together and is raised to form a holy Temple of the Lord. It is into him that Christians have been built like living stones, through the breathing of the Spirit, so as to make up the dwelling place of God (Eph. 2:19-22).

For John the Church is the flock, gathered together by Jesus through his self-sacrifice (Jn. 10:1-15). The vital insertion of the individual members into Christ comes to the fore in the allegory of the vine and the branches, which is John's parallel to Paul's doctrine on Christ's body (Jn. 15:1-5). Christ confided the care of his flock to Peter after he had drawn from him the triple profession of love (Jn. 21). In Revelation, Jesus asks for an account of things from the angels of the seven churches to which the book is written, that is, from the bishops for their flocks (Rev. 1-3). In the rest of the book the reader assists at the triumphal consummation of the Church's journey, decked out in all the usual splendor of apocalyptic visions. To that glorious conclusion the Church today wends its pilgrim way.

Chuza (koo′-za), Steward of Herod Antipas, husband of the Joanna who ministered to Jesus (Lk. 8:3) and was one of the discoverers of the empty tomb (Lk. 24:10).

Cilicia, In the first century A.D. Cilicia was a Roman province at the northeast corner of the Mediterranean. Its chief city was Tarsus, birthplace of Paul. The Cilician Gates northwest of Tarsus were a famous pass through the Taurus Mountains into central Turkey—a path used by all the armies of expanding empires, eastbound or westbound. Paul used this route to get to the communities in the interior where he founded churches, and to revisit them (Acts 15:40; 18:23).

Cinnamon, One of the spices brought by trade caravans from India or Persian Gulf ports, obtained from a tree native to Ceylon, raised also in India and East Indies islands. The labor involved, from tree to consumer in Palestine, made it expensive as well as enjoyable to the senses. Beyond its culinary uses it was used in preparing holy oil (Ex. 30:23); in perfuming a bed (Prov. 7:17). A poet used it as a figure of speech of the bride (S. of S. 4:14) and a seer listed it as a trade item of detested Babylon-Rome (Rev. 18:1).

Circumcision, A most ancient and widespread rite of initiation in which the foreskin of the penis is cut off. Usually carried out at the age of puberty, the Israelites alone performed it on the eighth day after birth. It became the particular characteristic of the covenant people, although they were aware that it was also practiced among other peoples (*see* Jer. 9:24-25, where Egypt is mentioned as a country where circumcision is practiced, while Josh. 5:9 and Ex. 32:21-30 indicates the opposite). The semite people of Canaan practiced it, and the Bible records that the patriarchs and the Israelites themselves adopted the practice after their arrival in Palestine (Gen. 17:9-14, 23-27; Josh. 5:2-9). The Philistines, on the other hand, were uncircumcised, and were often designated simply as the "uncircumcised" (1 Sam. 14:6; 31:4).

Exodus 4:24-26 speaks of the circumcision of Moses' son. It was then a rite of conjugal initiation and admittance to the full life of the tribe, and took place when the boy was grown. Israelite law, however, as has been noted, prescribed circumcision on the eighth day after birth (Lev. 12:3; Gen. 17:12). This seems to be a later development, which however conserved the idea of full admittance to the tribe (Ex. 12:47-48). Even though circumcision always had a religious significance, the later development of this meaning does not seem to antedate the exile. During this period the Israelites were deprived of their cultural and institutional inheritance, and living among the Babylonians, the observance of the sabbath and circumcision became the distinctive marks of God's people (Ex. 31:12-17). Genesis 17:9-14 gives a synthesis of the religious thought behind the rite of circumcision. It was to be a sign of the covenant between God and his people, whether they were born Jews or brought into the people from outside. Thus God's covenant demands that "every male among you shall be circumcised."

Under this aspect it had a function analogous to the faith of Abraham in Genesis 15:6, and St. Paul (Rom. 4) could say that circumcision was the seal of justice obtained through acceptance of the faith. It becomes the external sign of the alliance struck between God and Abraham and his descendants.

In the New Testament, circumcision is recorded as the sign of belonging to the chosen people (Acts 10:45; 11:2). Jesus was circumcised on the eighth day (Lk. 2:21) as was Paul (Phil. 3:5). As Christianity spread, the problem arose about the necessity of circumcision for Gentile converts. In the practical order the problem was resolved by the visible outpouring of the Holy Spirit which ratified their admission (*see* the case of Cornelius, Acts 10:11). The question was kept alive however by some Jewish Christians at Antioch who held that circumcision was still necessary for admittance to the kingdom (Acts 15; Gal. 1-2). Even though the Council of Jerusalem resolved the question by denying the necessity of circumcision, the problem continued to occupy the Pauline churches for several years, as the letters to Romans and Galatians testify. Paul argues that justification is from God's graciousness, not from works of man such as circumcision, and to bolster his case he invokes the example of Abraham (Rom. 4) who was justified by faith (Gen. 15:6) while circumcision only served as the external seal placed on the justification already received. In this way, whether they are circumcised or not, the true sons of Abraham are those who, like him, are justified by faith. They come into the possession of the promises made to him. Paul condemns those who trust in the mere external rite, incapable of itself of producing justification, and instead he proposes baptism, which he calls "Christ's circumcision which strips off the carnal body completely" (Col. 2:11; Eph. 2:11).

In a figurative sense, uncircumcision meant a particular privation (Ex. 6:12, 30) while in a religious sense, it meant the obtuseness of man to the voice of God (Jer. 9:25; 6:10; Lev. 26:41; Deut. 10:16).

Cistern, Artificial reservoirs created to exploit the resources of spring water and gather the rainwaters. They were excavated in the rock or ground and lined with lime to seal them against seepage (Jer. 2:13). The cisterns placed in the courtyards of homes would also gather the rains from the roofs. A courtyard cistern was Jeremiah's prison (Jer. 38:6-13). The cistern water was then used to irrigate the gardens and water the flocks (2 Chron. 26:10). They were also indispensable for the provision of water during sieges when the wells outside the city walls would be cut off by the besieging army. Hezekiah foresaw the siege of Jerusalem and had a tunnel bored to draw the water of the founatin of Gihon, along the hill of Jerusalem, to a cistern placed inside the walls of the city. (*See* SILOAM).

citadel
I was in the *c.* of Susa when   the gates of the temple *c.* Neh. 2:8
                           Neh. 1:1

Cities of Refuge, *See* REFUGE, CITIES OF.

City, From Lev. 25:31 it can be concluded that a city was a group of dwellings and other buildings circled by a wall, while a village was unwalled. The city served the largely agricultural population, located in such a way as to serve conveniently as a market town, and ideally on a hilltop for defense, with an adjacent supply of water. Besides the outer wall for defense, a city could be equipped with a tower or citadel as a refuge in case the outer rim was surmounted. Various types of cities are mentioned throughout the Old Testament. Before the Exodus the Jews were forced to build Pithom and Raamses, store-cities for the Pharoah. Solomon deployed his chariots and horses in Megiddo, Hazor and Gezer, which he had fortified for the defense of Israelite territory. There were also royal cities (Josh. 10:2; 1 Sam. 27:5) and cities of refuge, namely Kedesh, Shechem, Hebron, Bezer, Ramoth-gilead and Golan. The term city did not necessarily denote grandeur and it seems many cities were but glorified villages or even just fortresses. There was however a tendency to crowd the city as much as possible, and so houses and tents would seem to be heaped on top of one another. The streets were an accumulation of potsherds and other refuse trodden down to form a rough hard surface. One area in which there was considerable ingenuity was the waterworks, necessary for life, and especially necessary during times of siege. Isaiah mentions Siloam, a tunnel bringing water from the spring of Gihon, and Hezekiah built a tunnel to carry water to a pool on the left slope of the hill of Zion.

City of David, *See* JERUSALEM.

Claudius Lysias (lis′-e-as), The tribune of the cohort stationed at Jerusalem (Acts 23:26). When Paul was in danger of being lynched because it was stated he had brought uncircumcised people into the Temple, Lysias intervened with his soldiers and centurions to free him from those who were beating him and brought him into the fortress. Before going into the fortress, and with Lysias' permission, Paul addressed the crowd to identify himself and explain the mission he was on. The crowd interrupted the speech and so the tribune commanded that Paul be led into the fortress. There he ordered him to be examined under the lash so as to discover why the Jews wished to kill him. While Paul was being prepared for the scourging, he revealed that he was a Roman citizen. The centurion gave this information to Lysias who immediately grew afraid because of what he had done. However he wanted the truth of the matter and so had Paul brought before the chief priests and the council (Acts 21:31-22:30). Once more however the tribune had to intervene with his soldiers to guarantee the Apostle's safety. Then, when news came of a plot against Paul's life, Lysias decided to have him transferred to Caesarea where he would be in the custody of the governor (Acts. 23:1-30).

Clean, Unclean, Legislation regarding purity and impurity occupies a large space in Israelite ritual. These categories belong to one of the most ancient strata of Israelite religion. It is probable that those who gave to this legislation its definitive form were unable to understand the genuine primitive meaning of these dispositions.

In Israelite legislation the notions of pure and impure are cultic rather than ethical categories. They do not therefore presume to pass judgment on the moral dispositions of those who approach the worship of God. Pure or impure in practice meant to be fit or unfit legally to enter into the sphere of worship. The absence of all moral connotation is evident in the fact that impurity was contracted by external contact with persons who were in the state of impurity, that the impurity disappeared of itself after a certain space of time, that impurity could be washed away by ablutions that were merely external, that some impurities are absolutely unavoidable, and finally impurity attached also to animals and things.

There were thus pure and impure animals (*see* Lev. 11; Deut. 14). The criterion for distinguishing them was purely arbitrary. An animal was pure if it had hooves, provided it was cloven-footed and chewed the cud. Fishes that had both fins and scales were pure, etc. Pure animals could be used for food, and the victims for sacrifice were always chosen from among them.

On the impurity arising from leprosy *see* LEPROSY. All sexual functions made a person impure for some time: birth (Lev. 12), intercourse (Lev 15:18), menstruation (Lev. 15:19), pollution (Lev. 15:2, 16). Any contact or approach to a corpse made people and things impure (Num. 19).

The person qualified to determine impurity and purity was the priest (Lev. 13:12). Means for removing impurity were, according to the case, sacrifices (Lev. 14:10 ff.) and ablutions with water. Sometimes lustral water is prescribed, that is, water prepared according to the rite described in Numbers 19:1-10, but the legislation is not coherent on this point (*see* Lev. 22:4-6; Num. 6:9-12).

What considerations made the Israelites declare one thing pure and another impure? The answer is not easy. On the one hand it is clear that no one reason will satisfy all the lists and cases. On the other hand a great part of this legislation is an archaic inheritance which was conserved by the typical inertia of the liturgical-cultic environment without eventually even being understood. In the evolution of the Israelite religion the concept of purity became a simple judgment of cultic qualification or disqualification, without any other formal content. Here it is of interest to note that the notion of impurity was used as an arm against the religions of the people with whom Israel lived and so as a practical means to underline the separation of Israel in its historical context and in its belonging to the Lord. In the distinction between pure and impure animals one can find archaic traces of hygienic and sanitary dispositions, and also very clear polemical measures against non-Israelite cults. The animals that were excluded as impure were those venerated or associated with the gods of the neighboring peoples. In the impurity connected with touching corpses and with the sexual functions is latent the emotional charge that would accompany these experiences, but the legislation served to keep far from the cult funeral rites and the whole sexual sphere.

By New Testament times the legislation and the casuistry concerning purity and impurity had reached inflationary proportions. It had become a matter of formal obedience to the law for the law's sake, with no meaning, which was corrupting the sincere ethical effort of Pharisaism. Jesus' attitude towards this formalism was decidedly negative. "Nothing that enters a man from outside can make him impure; that which comes out of him, and only that, constitutes impurity" (Mk. 7:15). These words were audacious for the era in which they were pronounced, and Jesus took pains to explain them later to the disciples (Mk. 7:17-23). They find their echo in Peter's vision at Joppa (Acts 10:1-15), which opened the way to the admission of Gentiles to the Church (Acts 10:17-48).

Already in the Old Testament the notion of purity and impurity served to illustrate, in a transferred sense, what should be the internal dispositions of the person who wished to approach God, what were those that separated one from God, and what was the action of God in remitting sins (*see* Jer. 2:22; 4:14; Mal. 3:12). The Psalmist prays to God: "Cleanse me of sin with hyssop, that I may be purified; wash me, and I shall be whiter than snow" (Ps. 51). Ezekiel announces that God "will sprinkle clean water upon you to cleanse you from all your impurities, and from all your idols I will cleanse you" (Ezek. 36:25). In these and other texts purity and impurity have become ethical categories. This meaning was perpetuated in the New Testament and in Christian tradition.

cleanse

to *c.* the Lord's house
2 Chron. 29:15

the Lord's house to *c.* it
2 Chron. 29:16

c. you from all your impurities
Ezek. 36:25

from all your idols I will *c.* you
Ezek. 36:25

Cleopas (cle′-o-pas), One of the disciples who met the risen Christ on the way to Emmaus (Lk. 24:18).

Clopas, Husband of Mary, one of the women who stood at the foot of the Cross of Jesus (Jn. 19:25). Many identify him with Alphaeus, father of James the Less (Mk. 3:18; Matt. 10:3; Lk. 6:15; Acts 1:13).

cloth

spread an all-violet *c.*   Num. 4:6

they spread a violet *c.*   Num. 4:7

violet *c.* to cover the lampstands
Num. 4:9

he left the *c.* behind   Mark 14:52

sews a piece of unshrunken *c.*
Matt. 9:16

by nothing but a linen *c.*
Mark 14:51

Clothing, In Genesis 2:25 it is recorded that the man and his wife were both naked and were not ashamed. This does not mean the absence of inordinate sexual impulses but rather a state of mutual respect, esteem, and confidence. Only in the case of Bathsheba is there a relationship between inordinate desires and nakedness which was otherwise considered something repugnant or ignominious (*see* e.g. Gen. 9:21; Ex. 20:26; 28:42-43; Ezek. 44:18; Sir. 45:8; 2 Sam. 10:4-5). Adulterous women were pilloried naked (Hos. 2:5; Nah. 3:5; Jer. 13:26). Prisoners of war were often stripped, perhaps for the booty of their garments as well as for the disgrace of their defeat (Isa. 20:4; 47:3).

Clothing consisted of the **ezor** which was either a short skirt or a girdle (Jer. 13:1; Isa. 5:27; Ezek. 23:15; 2 Kgs. 1:8). The tunic of wool or linen, sleeved or sleeveless, reached down beyond the knees and would be tucked up for work or travel (Ex. 12:11; 2 Kgs. 4:29). An outer cloak was worn over the tunic. This cloak was not worn at work but was used for warmth at night (Matt. 24:18; *see* Ex. 22:25 ff.; Deut. 24:13). The girdle was a belt of leather or other material which besides binding the clothes to the body also held weapons, tools and even money and other objects. A further garment, the **me'il**, was worn by people in authority such as kings (1 Sam. 18:4; 24:5, 11) and the high priest (Ex. 28:31 ff; Lev. 8:7). Jesus wore a cloak and a seamless tunic, woven throughout, which were given, as was the law, to his executioners (*see* Jn. 19:23). In the Sermon on the Mount Jesus tells his followers to let the person who wants your cloak have your tunic too (Matt. 5:40, Lk. 6:29). For festive occasions festive clothes were worn (*see* Matt. 22:11 ff; Lk. 15:22). Women also wore the tunic and cloak, a little different in style. To interchange garments between the sexes was forbidden by the law (*see* Deut. 22:5).

Cloud, Clouds are mentioned in the Bible almost exclusively as part of the cosmic scenario that stages the manifestations of God (Ex. 19:16; Jgs. 5:4; *see* THEOPHANY). At times the clouds have the role of transport on which God comes to the help of the person who calls upon him (Pss. 18:10; 68:5). The cloud that fills the sanctuary in the desert (Ex. 40:36-37) or the Temple of Solomon (1 Kgs. 8:10) is the symbol and the external manifestation of the presence of God and of his taking possession of these his dwellings. Here the cloud is a visible manifestation of the glory of God (*see* GLORY). The pillar and the cloud of fire have identical functions in the tradition on the Exodus (Ex. 13:21). All this is nothing more than a stylized version of the traditional representation of the revelation of God's glory, reproduced artificially with incense in Israelite ritual (Lev. 16:2, 13; Ps. 98:6-7).

The clouds are also the means of transport of the Son of Man, whose divinity is in this way at least insinuated (Matt. 26:64; Mk. 14:62).

cloud, clouds

enveloped in a dense black *c.* Deut. 4:11	*C.* hide him so that he cannot Job 22:14
rain and thickening *c.* 2 Sam. 22:12	I will command the *c.* Isa. 5:6 a bright *c.* overshadowed
his head reach to the *c.* Job 20:6	Matt. 17:5

cock

before the *c.* crows tonight Matt. 26:34	the *c.* will not crow Jn. 13:38 that moment a *c.* began to crow
Before the *c.* crows twice Mk. 14:72	Jn. 18:27

Coele-Syria (see′-li-seer′-i-a), Greek, literally "hollow Syria," the region between the Lebanon and Anti-Lebanon Mountains. Superficially this valley appears on relief maps to be a northern continuation of the Jordan Rift, but a geological complexity separates the two. Furthermore, Coele-Syria's Litani River valley is much higher, for a long way c. 3000 feet above sea level, and 3287 feet above it at Baalbek. At the southern end of Coele-Syria the Litani runs through a narrow gorge and cuts directly westwards to the Mediterranean. In the period following the death of Alexander, the Ptolemies and Seleucids (whichever controlled it) created a province called the same, but with expanded borders including portions of Palestine, especially those east of the Jordan, and lands also towards the Euphrates to the northeast. This is the sense of the use of "Coele-Syria" in 1 and 2 Maccabees. Roman administrative districts were more sharply defined and differently named. Much of the Seleucid "Coele-Syria" was in the tetrarch of Philip, Trachonitis and Iturea, in the time of Jesus.

Colossae, An ancient city of Phrygia, located on the Lycus River, a tributary of the Meander, about 80 miles east of Ephesus. It is mentioned only in the introduction to Paul's letter to the Colossians (Col. 1:2). *See* COLOSSIANS, EPISTLE TO THE.

Colossians, Epistle to the, This is the one letter written by Paul to a community that was not personally founded by him (Col. 2:1; *see* COLOSSAE). It belongs to the group of letters known as the Captivity Epistles, written as it was by Paul while he was in jail (4:10, 18). Colossians, Philemon and Ephesians belong to the same captivity which was probably the first of the two he underwent at Rome, and therefore between 62-63 A.D. (*see* Acts 28:30-31).

The reason why Paul wrote was the danger of heresies and doctrinal deviations that was arising in his churches of Asia Minor (Colossae, Laodicea, Ephesus, *see* Col. 4:16). Paul was informed of these dangers by Epaphras, his disciple, and founder of the church of Colossae (Col. 1:7, 8; 4:12, 13; *see* EPAPHRAS). We have no other information on the precise nature of the doctrinal deviations except what can be gleaned from the letter itself and from the letter to the Ephesians, which is very similar. So a problem arises in defining what the errors were, as Paul's refutation seems to go further than the actual proportions of the errors and to draw from them conclusions that are perhaps logical but may not have been explicitly professed. There are no doubts on two points, it seems: a. The Colossians had an immense cult and veneration for the angels (2:18) which seriously compromised the absolute primacy of Christ in the order of creation and salvation. These angels were identical with the "cosmic forces" (Col. 2:20; *see* Gal. 4:3) and had, they believed, an intermediate rank between God and the world over which they exercised real power, thus heavily influencing the personal destiny of men.

b. Given their fear and worship of these beings, the Colossians engaged in ascetical observances in food and calendar (2:16, 20-23) of Jewish inspiration. This was a new enslavement to the law and to the angels who supposedly governed the world, and so contained an implicit denial of the unique value of the salvation brought about by Christ.

Paul refutes these errors by showing the absolute primacy of Christ in every order, so that even the presumed power of the angels is subject to him. Through his death and resurrection Christ has deprived them of their instrument of power, the law (Col. 2:14-15), and has incorporated them, as vanquished, in his triumphal procession.

Christ in fact is the image of the invisible God and the first-born of all creation (*see* FIRST-BORN), for in him everything was created (Col. 1:15-16). He is also the first-born from the dead, head of the body of the Church, in whom everything has been brought together in reconciliation (Col. 1:17-20). There is no power that is not subject to Christ's dominion, and so to him alone should the Colossians adhere. From him in fact as head, the whole body (*see* BODY OF CHRIST) receives nourishment and cohesion so as to grow in God (Col. 2:16-19). Paul concludes, as usual, by giving counsel and recommendations for the moral conduct of Christians (3:5-4:6) and finishes up with some personal notes (4:7-9) and greetings

(4:10-18).

The errors of the church of Colossae gave Paul an opportunity of developing with greater precision and profundity many of the major themes of the preceding letters. These errors obliged Paul to meditate more deeply on the cosmic repercussions of Christian salvation, and so think out the depth of the mystery of Christ in its relationship with creation, the Church and the universe.

The doctrine on angels which appears in Colossians and Ephesians is in all probability a concession to his readers with the purpose of setting the stage for the development of the discussion. Other concepts and vocabulary (*see* PLEROMA) seem also to be derived from the terminology of his adversaries, but they are transformed and reshaped in the synthesis that Paul offers in opposition to the errors. Colossians and Ephesians rest on the great christological and ecclesiological themes of the previous letters. In this new synthesis however these themes are profoundly enriched. There is then a continuity and progress between Romans, 1 and 2 Corinthians and Colossians-Ephesians, nor should one go in search of any other author for Colossians and Ephesians than Paul himself.

comforted
you have *c*. me, your servant   Then David *c*. his wife
                        Ruth 2:13   2 Sam. 12:24
                and *c*. him for all the evil   Job 42:11

comforts
For the Lord *c*. his people   As a mother *c*. her son, so will I
            Isa. 49:13; 52:9   Isa. 66:13

commander
be our *c*..that we may be able   you are to anoint as *c*.
                        Jgs. 11:6   1 Sam. 9:16
made him their leader and *c*.   appointed him *c*.   1 Sam. 13:14
                        Jgs. 11:11

companion
but the *c*. of fools   Prov. 13:20 but the glutton's *c*. disgraces
                                                                Prov. 28:7
                though she is your *c*.   Mal. 2:14

complain
brothers come to *c*. to us   *c*. in the bitterness of my soul
                        Jgs. 21:22   Job 11:11

condemn
my own mouth might *c*. me   and be the ones to *c*. it
                        Job 9:20   Matt. 12:41
will you *c*. the supreme Just One   They will *c*. him to death
                        Job 34:17   Mk. 10:34
those who would *c* him   Ps. 109:31 Son into the world to *c*. the
                                                                Jn. 3:17
                Nor do I *c*. you   Jn. 8:11

condemning
and *c*. the guilty party   Deut. 25:1

confidence
On what do you base this *c*.   His *c*. is but a gossamer thread
                        2 Kgs. 18:19   Job 8:14
Is not your piety a source of *c*.   drawing near him with *c*.
                        Job 4:6   Eph. 3:12
                then, surrender your *c*.   Heb. 10:35

Confirmation, A sacrament of Christian initiation intimately related to Baptism. Indeed, often they are mentioned in the same sentence of the New Testament as if they did not exist as separate sacraments (e.g. in the Pauline epistles). The most explicit texts witnessing to the distinction between this sacrament and Baptism are Acts 8:4-20; 19:1-7 and Heb. 6:1-6. In these places is mentioned an imposition of hands conferring the Holy Spirit, distinct and separable from the baptismal rites. The first text tells us that when the apostles heard that the Samaritans had received the word of God, they sent Peter and John to impose hands on them that they might receive the Holy Spirit, for hitherto "they had only been baptized in the name of the Lord Jesus" (Acts 8:16, 17). This interpretation is confirmed by the story of Simon the Magician (Acts 8:18-19). In Acts 19:1-7, Paul imposed hands on the disciples of John the Baptizer so that they might receive the Holy Spirit, whom they had not even heard of up to that point. Hebrews 6:1-6 has a synthesis of early Christian catechesis, where too a distinction is drawn between Baptism and the laying on of hands, and the stages of initiation are numbered as being brought to the light, tasting the gift from heaven, receiving a share of the Holy Spirit, etc. Cornelius' conversion in Acts 10:44-47 is a special case in which the Holy Spirit descended as at Pentecost to move Peter to confer Baptism on him (Acts 10:44-47).

confirmed

I bore to Christ has been so *c.*   it was *c.* to us by those   Heb. 2:3
                    1 Cor. 1:6

confuse
and there *c.* their language
                    Gen. 11:7

Coniah, The King Jehoiakim of Judah (Jer. 22:24, 28; 37:1). *See* JEHOIA-KIM.

Conscience, The practical judgment or decision, from the moral point of view, on what should be done or not done. Stoic ethical doctrine developed the notion and philosophy of this central core of all morality, and even gave the faculty its name (Greek **syneidesis**) by which it is also known in the New Testament. Paul made use of the term to throw light on the problem of the liceity of eating what had been offered to the idols and later sold by the city butchers. The Corinthians asked Paul's direction on this point. Paul in answer first established a general principle: since idols are nothing in themselves, there is really nothing against eating meat that has been sacrificed to them. However he immediately speaks about the individual conscience and what it dictates to each. If then a person does not have this right conscience and nevertheless eats meat sacrificed to idols, his conscience is contaminated (1 Cor. 8:7). Others however who like Paul have a right conscience on this matter should not just arrogantly proceed without regard to other people. They too can be obliged to limit their liberty so as not to perturb the conscience of the weak (1 Cor. 8:8-13; *see* 1 Cor. 10:23-33). Paul discusses an analogous case in Romans 14:14-23, proposing the same solution with different terms. Here too is a general principle (Rom. 14:14) which however, in the exercise, can be limited in the application one makes of it to a given case, lest scandal should arise, or a weaker brother might be drawn to do what his own conscience does not approve.

Conscience, the innermost sanctuary of the person where alone he stands before God, condemns or approves, and so is an interior law, written on the heart (Rom. 2:14-16).

consolation

give him the cup of *c*. to drink   for your *c*: is now   Lk. 6:24
           Jer. 16:7   do we share abundantly in his *c*.
and awaited the *c*. of Israel   2 Cor. 1:5
         Lk. 2:25   it is for your *c*.   2 Cor. 1:6
       so you will share in the *c*.   2 Cor. 1:7

consume

your enemies will *c*. the crop
         Lev. 26:16

convert

and land to make a single *c*.   who had been a *c*. to Judaism
         Matt. 23:15   Acts. 6:5

Copper, According to Ezekiel 27:12-13, copper was imported from Tarshish (southern Spain), Tubal and Meshech (mountainous regions in modern Turkey), and Javan (Greece). Deut. 8:9 recounts the riches to be found in the soil of Palestine, among which copper is mentioned, which was found especially in the valley of the Arabah. The ruins of the copper foundries established by Solomon have been discovered at Ezion-geber, on the gulf of Aqabah.

Corban, Transcription of the Hebrew term for a gift consecrated to God in the priestly ritual (Lev. 1:2; 22:27, Num. 7:25, etc.). In Matthew 27:6 it is the name of the temple treasury. Mark 7:11 condemns a typical case of Pharasaical hypocrisy: a person was considered dispensed from the obligation to care for his own parents if he declared his goods **Corban,** that is, made over to God, even though he might have no true intention of doing this.

Coriander, The fruit of an umbelliferous plant (**Coriandrum sativum**), globular and externally smooth, aromatic and used in medical and food preparations. Manna, according to Ex. 16:31 and Num. 11:7, was like the coriander seed, white in color.

Corinth, A Greek city on the isthmus of the same name which links the Peloponnesian peninsula to the continent. Its situation made it a necessary port of call on the east-west route, and consequently one of the chief commercial centers of the ancient world, and the principal one in Greece. The city possessed two ports, Lechaeon to the west and Cenchreae to the east of the isthmus. Corinth, in the ancient world, was also famous, or infamous, for loose living, which explains in part the problems of the first Christian community there, and the list of abuses that Paul found it necessary to condemn (1 Cor. 5:1-9; 6:9, 15-20), and which also, perhaps, prompted him to list the vices of the pagans in Romans 1:24-32, a letter written from Corinth. The city was destroyed by the Romans when they had defeated the Achaian league (146 B.C.) and it remained in ruins until 44 B.C. when Caesar erected there a Roman colony, called Laus Julia Corinthos, which became the capital of the senatorial province of Achaia, and the proconsul's residence. According to Acts 18:1-18, Paul visited Corinth on his second missionary journey, and there met Aquila and Priscilla, with whom he lived and worked as a tentmaker. He preached in the synagogue there, where Crispus, its leader, converted to the faith. After his first disagreements with the Jews there, he moved to a house next door to the synagogue, the property of Titus Justus. After a year and a half of apostolic labor, Paul was accused, without success, before the proconsul Gallius. He remained on at Corinth for some time, and then embarked, with Aquila and Priscilla, for Syria. Paul's dealings with the church at Corinth were numerous and exciting, as his two letters to the faithful there testify. Acts 18:27-19:1 tells us that, after Paul's departure, Apollos worked there, information that is confirmed by 1 Corinthians 1:12.

Corinthians, Epistles to the, The two epistles to the Corinthians are all that remains of a more abundant correspondence between Paul and the faithful at Corinth. This correspondence took place during one of the most difficult periods of the Apostle's life. These letters give us direct and precious information on the life and problems of an ethnic-Christian community in one of the most characteristic cities of the Hellenistic world. For Corinth was a crossroads for different civilizations and many peoples, a center of riches and of moral decadence. (*See* CORINTH.) The epistles treat of concrete problems, moral, doctrinal and disciplinary in the church at Corinth. As is Paul's wont, he resolves these problems in the light of the great principles of his theology. So the letters combine wise practical norms and profound doctrinal insights, bearing witness to Paul's spirit that was at one and the same time realist and contemplative.

While Paul was at Ephesus, where he stayed for three years during his third apostolic journey (Acts 19:1-20:1), he received from Corinth disturbing news that moved him to pen a first letter that today is lost (unless it is preserved in 2 Cor. 6:14-7:1; *see* below). In this letter he recommended severity with those Christians whose conduct was unworthy of Christians (1 Cor. 5:9-13). A little later Stephanas, Fortunatus and Achaicus all arrived from the church at Corinth, probably bringing to Paul a letter with various questions that were preoccupying the community there (1 Cor. 7:1; 16:17). At the same time Paul came to know, through the servants of a Corinthian woman named Chloe, that there were divisions and rivalry in the church at Corinth between different groups, some of whom claimed for their authority Paul, others Apollos, others again Cephas, or even Christ (1 Cor. 1:11-12). There were moreover other public abuses. Paul decided to write once more to answer the questions that had been put to him in writing and to remedy the situation of which he had been informed by word of mouth. This is 1 Corinthians, written at Ephesus towards Easter of 57 A.D.

After the usual introduction (1:1-9), Paul goes on to treat of the abuses he had heard about by word of mouth (1:10-6:20). These were divisions in the community (1:10-4:21), an unheard-of tolerance in a grave case of public incest (5:1-8) and other serious deficiencies in some Christians (5:9-13). Paul also reproves the ease with which Christians went before pagan tribunals to resolve controversies between them instead of leaving the judgment up to the community (6:1-11). Finally Paul gives the lie to a tendentious and erroneous interpretation of his doctrine on the liberty of the Christian, which is by no means libertinage or lack of restraint, but the service of the Lord (6:12-20).

Next he sets out to answer the questions on which he had been asked by letter (7:1). The first had to do with marriage and virginity and is resolved without detriment either to the holiness of marriage or the excellence of virginity. Paul advises that each person should remain on in the state in which he or she had found his Christian vocation. He proposes celibacy as a more excellent way because it permits a total dedication to the Lord, but he adds that it would be presumption to choose it if one could not observe it (c. 7). The second question was on the liceity of eating meat immolated to idols, which was often then sold at a cheap rate by the butchers of the city. The Christian, is Paul's response, knows that idols are nothing, and therefore in principle meat sacrificed to them is no different from any other meat. However one must take into account the conscience of others, who might be led into error or scandal if a Christian were to follow his conscience. This solution is then confirmed by Paul's own example (cc.

8-10). The last part (cc. 11-15) probably does not contain answers to questions proposed to the Apostle, but is rather a list of recommendations by Paul himself. Chapters 11-14 seek to correct abuses taking place in the Christian assemblies. Let the women come veiled as tradition teaches them (11:2-16), but above all let order reign in the celebration of the fraternal agape and the eucharist (11:17-34). The charisms (*see* CHARISMA) posed a delicate problem. Since they arise from the same Spirit they should not cause rivalry nor discord. There is however between them a hierarchy of values to be respected for the good of the community they are destined to serve. Love however is better than all charisms, and without it every charism would be vain (cc. 12-14). Finally Paul severely corrects doubts that had arisen on the reality of the resurrection. Christ arose as the first-born from the dead, and so too will all arise. Resurrection however is not a simple reanimation of a corruptible organism. It is the complete transformation of man to the image of the glorious Christ (c. 15). The letter concludes with an invitation to contribute to a collection Paul was organizing among the Gentile churches to help the Jewish-Christian churches of Palestine, as evidence of communion and unity (16:1-4). He then announces his plans for the future (16:5-14).

These plans were never realized, due to circumstances beyond Paul's control. This created a misunderstanding between Paul and the Corinthian community, which accused Paul of being two-faced (2 Cor. 1:12-17). This is the first indication of a sudden worsening of relationships between the Apostle and his church, which embittered Paul's heart and spurred him to write what is one of the most severe and yet most moving of his writings.

It is not easy to reconstruct the episodes of this new and graver crisis. We have only indications and allusions scattered through the letter, and these are open to different interpretations. One can however hold the following as sufficiently well-founded: when Paul came to know that at Corinth there was open conspiracy against his authority, he decided to go there. It was a brief and unsuccessful visit, but he promised to return shortly in a calmer mood (2 Cor. 1:15-2:1). In the interval however things got worse and Paul, probably through one of his representatives, was very seriously offended (2 Cor. 2:5-10). So he decided to postpone his projected visit and substitute it with a severe letter written 'with many tears' (2 Cor 2:4), which today is lost, or else preserved as 2 Cor. 10-13. This letter had the desired effect. The guilty one was punished and relationships between Paul and the community notably improved (2 Cor. 2:5-11). Paul had to abandon Ephesus after much suffering (Acts 19:23-40; 2 Cor 1:8-11) and went towards Macedonia where he found Titus, who from Corinth had brought information about the submission and pacification of the community (2 Cor. 7:5-15). From Macedonia Paul wrote the second letter to the Corinthians, the fourth in chronological order, towards the end of 57 A.D.

There is much discussion today on whether the second letter to the Corinthians as we have it today was the one written by Paul from Macedonia. There is in fact a violent contrast between the first part, especially cc. 1-6, and cc. 10-13. The first chapters presuppose reconciliation and intend to wipe out all misunderstanding, while cc. 10-13 breathe the fire of the most heated moments of the crisis. Not a few scholars therefore would see these latter chapters as what remains of the letter of "tears" (2 Cor. 2:4). In 6:13 the discussion is brusquely interrupted, to be taken up anew in 7:2. So 2 Cor. 6:14-7:1 would be the remains of the first letter written by the Apostle before our 1 Corinthians (*see* 1 Cor. 5:9-13). In 9:1 Paul once more takes up the subject matter of 8:1 ff. These would then be two independent writings on the same subject with c. 8 forming part of the original 2 Corinthians and c. 9 part of an instruction on the collection to be made, addressed to all the churches of Achaia.

This reconstruction is certainly only a hypothesis. It is not however unfounded. In fact the second letter to the Corinthians as it now stands presents characteristics which, while they do not exclude Paul as author, seem to exclude unity of composition.

Cornelius, A Roman centurion of the Italian cohort stationed in Caesarea (Acts 10:1). Cornelius was the first pagan to be received into the church. The episode of his conversion and baptism is recounted with many details in Acts 10:1-11:18. Cornelius was a proselyte of the class of the "God-fearing" (Acts 10:2; *see* PROSELYTE). In a vision he was directed to summon Peter to his home. Peter was at Joppa. At the same time Peter had a vision, the sense of which became clear when he was invited to the house of a pagan. In fact the point of the vision was the message to Peter not to call anything that God had purified unclean. In other words it did away with the Jewish practice, to which Peter had faithfully adhered, of not mingling with uncircumcised pagans because they were unclean. Peter therefore went to Cornelius' home and preached Jesus to him and his family. Even before he had finished preaching, the Holy Spirit descended on Cornelius and his family with manifestations similar to those experienced by the apostles at Pentecost (Acts 10:44-46; *see* Acts 2:4). Peter thus decided to baptize them (Acts 10:1-48). When he returned to Jerusalem Peter was reproved by some Jewish Christians for having entered the house of a pagan and for having eaten with them. Peter explained the supernatural motives that had led him to such action (the visions he and Cornelius had had) and to baptize them (the descent of the Spirit). When they heard this, they acquiesced, giving praise to God for the conversion (Acts 11:1-18).

The episode of Cornelius' conversion gives the solution for the two most serious conflicts that arose in the apostolic Church: the problem of the obligation of the law for the Gentiles who had come into the Church (*see* Acts 15:7-11) and the problem of the relationships between Jewish Christians and ethnic Christians in the Church (*see* Acts 15:28-29; Gal. 2:11-14).

Cornerstone, The precise meaning of the word translated from the Greek and Hebrew is not altogether clear. Ordinarily it is interpreted to mean the foundation stone that joins two walls at the corner and so gives cohesion to the whole building. Others would have it that the cornerstone is the one that closes the vault of the ceiling, and so gives solidity and finality to a construction. In both instances, the intent of the word is clear, namely, to express in figurative terms the fundamental role played by or given to a certain part of the whole, such as that of the leaders among the people (*see* Jgs. 20:2; 1 Sam. 14:38; Isa. 19:13; Zech. 10:4). God will plant as a foundation for Zion a proved and solid cornerstone (Isa. 28:16). Ps. 118:22 uses the same metaphor to mark the election of Israel, the cornerstone rejected from the building and taken up by God to confute the plans of her enemies. Jesus applied Ps. 118:22 to himself to announce his exaltation, which will annul and overturn the homicidal plans of his adversaries (Matt. 21:42; Mk. 12:10; Lk. 20:17). This exegesis, which also calls upon Isa. 28:16 (*see* 1 Pet. 2:4-8), is continued in the apostolic teaching (Acts 4:11; 1 Pet. 2:7). In expressing the Church in terms of building up an edifice, Paul shows Christ to be the cornerstone (Eph. 2:6): the building which is raised up on the foundation of the apostles and the prophets has Christ as a cornerstone.

101

corruptible
This *c.* body must be clothed   When the *c.* frame takes on
        1 Cor. 15:53   1 Cor. 15:54

Cos, An island in the Aegean sea off the southwest coast of Asia Minor, a stage on Paul's last journey to Jerusalem (Acts 21:1).

could
C. we find another   Gen. 41:38

Council, Council ordinarily translates the Greek **synedrion,** the Aramaic form of which is **sanhedrin,** the name by which the supreme tribunal of Judea was known in Hellenistic (1 Mac. 11:23; 12:6; 14:28; 2 Mac. 4:44) and Roman times (Acts 9:2; 26:12, etc.). Sometimes local tribunals were also called **synedria** (*see* Mk. 13:9; Matt. 5:21; 10:17). The **synedrion** was also called senate (**gerousia,** Acts 5:21) or **presbyterion** (Acts 22:5).

As a national institution, the Sanhedrin does not appear before the second century B.C. and its composition and competence underwent change throughout its history. It was under the presidency of the high priest, currently in power, and it consisted of the past four high priests and representatives of the families from which the high priest was ordinarily chosen, as well as the elders or representatives of the principal lay families. From the reign of Alexandra (76-67 B.C.), protectress of the Pharisees, it also included a group of scribes of Pharisaic bent (*see* Mk. 11:27; 15:1; Lk. 20:1; Acts 23:6-10). The number of members was theoretically limited to seventy-one (*see* Num. 11:10-24).

In New Testament times the authority of the council was limited to Judea, even though its moral authority extended to the Diaspora (Acts 9:2; 22:5; 26:12), and it was competent in all the questions regarding Judean law. It had power to arrest with its own police. It is not certain whether it could carry out capital sentences without their being ratified by the Roman prefect. The information in John 18:31 seems to be in contrast with Acts 7:57, which tells of the death of Stephen. However this case could perhaps be explained by the agitated circumstances in which it took place. The council under the presidency of Caiaphas condemned Jesus to death for blasphemy (Mk. 14:53-65; Matt. 26:57-66; Lk. 22:54-71; Jn. 18:12-27). Though it is not possible to reconstruct in detail how the trial was carried out (Matthew and Mark speak of two sessions, Luke of only one), it would seem that from the juridical point of view it was not seriously vitiated in form (*see* PASSION). Peter and John were also brought before the Sanhedrin (*see* Acts 4:5-18; 5:17-38), as was Paul (Acts 22:30).

Council of Jerusalem, The name given, by analogy with the later councils of the Church, to the meeting of the Apostles Peter, James, John, Paul and Barnabas and ecclesiastics of Jerusalem to resolve the question of whether the new Christians, coming from paganism, would have to accept the old law. Were they to be bound by the old Jewish traditions, into which Christ was born and from which the church grew (Acts 15; Gal. 2)? The meeting took place in 49 or 50 A.D., after Paul's first missionary journey (Acts 15:1-2). According to Gal. 2:1-10 Paul's position against circumcision as a necessary initiation rite was completely accepted by Peter, James and John, who also recognized the validity of Paul's apostleship and came to an agreement in principle on what territory should be each person's apostolate. Acts 15 records the intervention of Peter and James in favor of Paul's thesis, to which some practical norms are added to ease relationships between Jewish and pagan converts (Acts 15:28-29). These extra norms however were not known to Paul, and seem to have derived from another meeting. Luke notes them at this point perhaps because of the similarity of the material discussed.

counselor

David's *c.*	2 Sam. 15:12	was also the king's *c.*
a prudent *c.*	1 Chron. 26:14	1 Chron. 27:33
was *c.* and scribe	1 Chron. 27:32	Or has your *c.* perished Mic. 4:9

Covenant, Covenant ordinarily translates the Hebrew **berith,** which is translated in Greek as **diatheke,** and means testament (*see* TESTAMENT). The word **berith** is taken from profane language where it is used to designate every type of contract or alliance between private individuals, tribes or peoples (*see* Gen. 21:22; 25:26; 1 Sam. 11:1; 18:3, etc.). It passed over into religious language however to signify the historical relationships which God deigned to establish with the people of Israel and with the whole of humanity.

The Bible speaks of different covenants between God and man, but the meaning of the term is not always the same. These different covenants have in fact varying internal structures. It is, however, always necessary to note that the biblical concept of alliance or covenant applied to the relationships between God and man is quite different from the type of accord through negotiation which culminates in a contract between equals, such as happens in business affairs.

The covenant of God with Abraham (Gen. 15) is an absolute and unconditioned promise confirmed by oath expressed by God in rites that were used by men to sanction a solemn obligation (Gen. 15:7-21; Jer. 34:8-10). It is not, however, bilateral in obligations. God alone, by his promises, pledges himself. This promise, however, demands that man respond with faith: "Abram put his faith in the Lord, who credited it to him as an act of righteousness" (Gen. 15:6; Rom. 4; *see* FAITH). The version given in the priestly tradition of the Pentateuch of the same event (Gen. 17) is not substantially different: circumcision is not what God demands in exchange for his promised gifts, but rather a sign that man himself has responded in faith, and, because it is something visible and external, it is a sign that the covenant has taken place (*see* CIRCUMCISION; SIGN).

To this type of covenant-oath also belongs God's covenant with Noah. This also consists in the solemn pledge freely entered into by God not to send another flood on the earth nor ever again to change the rhythm of nature and the seasons of the year. The sign of this covenant-oath is the rainbow, which will remind God of the word he has given, and man of the guarantee or pledge of God's promise (*see* Gen. 9:8-17; 8:21-22).

In the Old Testament however the pact par excellence between God and Israel is that sanctioned on Sinai, whose mediator was Moses (Ex. 19-33). The Sinai covenant is inseparable from the liberation from Egypt brought about by God in the Exodus. This covenant is, on the one hand, placed in relationship with the past, as the fulfilment of the promise made to Abraham. On the other hand it looks to the future, as the decisive passage towards the possession of the land of Canaan, which was also promised to Abraham (Ex. 3:7-8; 6:2-8). Over and beyond this the Exodus in itself is the action through which God had acquired for himself a people of his own from amongst all the peoples of the earth (Ex. 19:5-7; *see* ELECTION, EXODUS). The covenant of Sinai defines and sanctions in a solemn way the relationship that arose between God and Israel by means of the Exodus.

The structure of the Sinai covenant is similar in many points to a type of alliance between unequal partners, that is, between a sovereign king and a vassal king. This type of pact was in use in international political relationships in the middle east during the second millenium B.C. Recent studies on these similarities have opened the way to a more precise understanding of the religious economy of the Old Testament. The most important texts on the Sinai covenant (Ex. 19:34 ff.; Josh. 24 and the book of Deuteronomy) are so composed as to remind one of the documents of extra-biblical pacts to which we have been alluding. After the mention of God's name and titles (Ex. 20:1; Josh. 24:2) there is a listing of the benefits granted by God to Israel, his people (Josh. 24:2-14). This part is called the historical prologue and is very important. It not only is meant to awaken in the people sentiments of gratitude and therefore a favorable disposition in accepting the law, but it also serves as the basis for God's right in demanding from the people he redeemed an acceptance of his will as expressed in the law. With an evident logical nexus the text goes on to proclaim the stipulations of the covenant in which can be distinguished the request for exclusive worship of God (first precept of the Decalogue, Ex. 20:2; Josh. 24:14) and the concrete and multiple demands made by the various codes of laws (Decalogue, Book of the Covenant, Ex. 1-23, Deuteronomic Code, etc.), all handed down in the context of the Sinai covenant. God then promises blessings on those who will observe his covenant and curses on those who will be its transgressors (Deut. 27:11-28:68; *see* BLESSING; CURSE). In the end the heavens and the earth are called to witness the covenant entered upon (Isa. 1:2; Mic. 6:1-2; Ps. 50; *see* WITNESS). The document of the covenant contains stipulations about the pact itself: the document should be read periodically (Deut. 31:10), the vassal king should pay regular visits to the sovereign king and bring gifts (*see* Ex. 34:23, etc.), the document of the pact should be placed in the Temple at the feet of the divinity. In Israel the tables of the law were placed in the ark of the covenant, which is also the seat of the invisible presence of God who sits enthroned upon the cherubim (*see* ARK OF THE COVENANT, CHERUB).

The plan of the Sinai covenant can be seen as a bilateral agreement, but one must immediately note that this bilaterality is altogether different from the rights and duties that would arise between two equal partners. First of all the person who establishes the covenant is God. He alone imposes the stipulations without discussion. In the context of the covenant, law and grace integrate one another: the law finds its justification in preceding history, which is summed up in the historical prologue, and which affirms the right of God to demand a total service and a dedication that is exclusive, seeing that this is a people which, by saving them, he has made his very own. God's blessing, which takes up the content of the promises given to the patriarchs, is gratuitous, that is, it is not given in exchange for the observance of the law, even though the only people to benefit from it would be those remaining faithful to the covenant. The law defines the demands on the people of Israel, not to win God's benefits, which are totally gratuitous, but to show that they have accepted the covenant and are God's people. Moreover the law establishes how the people should comport themselves to be able to live with God and so be able to enjoy for the future his gratuitous salvific action.

In succeeding history however the Sinai covenant proved to be an unstable institution because Israel showed herself incapable of remaining loyal to what was covenanted. The uninterrupted experience of sin in the history of the people induced the prophets to proclaim that in the context of the covenant Israel was inevitably doomed to malediction and judgment. Finally the destruction of Samaria and the exile of Judah, which brought to nothing the gift of the promised land, put the seal on the curse of the covenant. The prophet Jeremiah declared that the Sinai covenant had been irremediably shattered (Jer. 31:32; *see* Ezek. 16:59). At the same time however the same prophets turned to the future with a hope founded in the word of God and in a new definitive saving intervention on his part, taking the shape of a new covenant. The theme of the new covenant proposed by Jeremiah (Jer. 31:31-34) was to be taken up by Deutero-Isaiah and Ezekiel (Isa. 55:3; 59:21; 61:8; Ezek. 33:26-28; 36:25-28). The newness of the covenant promised for the future consisted chiefly in its interiority, not to be understood in the psychological sense, but as a renewal of the heart of man. God would bring about a profound remission of sin (Jer. 31:33; Ezek. 36:25, 29) and would write his law on man's heart, that is, he would bring it about that in each person an interior force would carry him spontaneously to obedience and knowledge of God (Jer. 31:33; 24:7; 32:39). On the theme of the new heart, *see* Jer. 4:4; Ezek. 36:26-27; Ps. 51:12; *see* HEART.

The new covenant was in fact sanctioned by the sacrifice of Jesus (Matt. 26:28; Mk. 14:24; Lk. 22:20; 1 Cor. 11:25; *see* LORD'S SUPPER). The words pronounced by Jesus over the chalice of the Eucharist contain an evident allusion to the words of Moses on Sinai (Ex. 24:4-8), but to them Jesus adds mention of the expiatory value of the blood he was to shed. In this way he claims for his own the mission of universal salvation entrusted to the Servant of Yahweh (Isa. 53; *see* SERVANT OF THE LORD), who was destined to become by virtue of his passion "a covenant of the people, a light for the nations" (Isa. 42:6). The sacrifice of the new covenant then is not just a simple communion rite, but an expiation, or better, an efficacious sacrifice of communion, capable of truly bringing humanity to God precisely because it is capable of bringing about a true and radical expiation of sins. This was to be developed beautifully in Hebrews 9, where the mission of Jesus as mediator of the new covenant is explained in the light of the sacrificial rite of the Day of Atonement (*see* ATONEMENT, DAY OF).

St. Paul particularly emphasized the interiority of the new covenant. He underscored the interior renewal of man, taking his inspiration from Jer. 31:31. The apostles were the ministers of the new covenant, which was not a covenant of the letter but of the Spirit (2 Cor. 3:6). The new law is the Holy Spirit (Rom. 8:2) who moves Christians from within and brings them to the liberty of the children of God (*see* Rom. 8:14; Gal. 4:21; *see* LIBERTY).

covet

not *c*. your neighbor's house	They *c*. fields	Mic. 2:2
Ex. 20:17	"You shall not *c*."	Rom. 7:7
c. your neighbor's wife	you shall not *c*.	Rom. 13:9
Ex. 20:17; Deut. 5:21		

cow, cows

their *c*. calve and	Job 21:10	*c*. and the bear shall be neighbors
		Isa. 11:7

You *c*. of Bashan   Amos 4:1

craftily
This one dealt *c*. with our people
Acts 7:19

Crates (cra′-teez), The head of the Cypriot mercenaries who came to Palestine to help Sostratus, Seleucid governor of Jerusalem (2 Mac. 4:29).

crawl

On your belly shall you *c*.	reptiles that *c*. upon the ground
Gen. 3:14	Ezek. 38:20

Creation, The peoples of ancient civilizations from Egypt to Mesopotamia, among whom Israel lived, believed that the world was the work of the gods they venerated. From their writings we can gather eloquent testimony to the importance of this fact in their general outlook on man and nature. The biblical doctrine on creation cannot be isolated from this context. Indeed it must be taken to be the mature result of a long and complex process of assimilation and criticism of the concepts of the cultural environment into which the people of Israel were inserted. This process was of course governed by the norms of the Israelite religious heritage, by which also it was enlightened. This held especially for the nature of God and their experience of being saved by him in the Exodus.

In oriental religions the doctrine on creation was above all expressed in mythical accounts (*see* MYTH). These accounts were less interested in the reconstruction of the creative act as such than in the periodic regeneration of time and nature through the mythical re-evocation of the primordial event, that is, of the first constitution of things. By being re-evoked the primordial event was able once more to actuate its saving power and thus ensure the consistency of the rhythm of nature through another annual cycle. Creation is the fruit of a victory that was won in the world of the gods (e. g. Marduk won over Tiamat in Mesopotamia; Baal over Yamm in Ugarit; *see* BAAL, MARDUK) in which nature was involved. In fact nature is nothing more than an epiphany of the divine world.

The religion of Israel however does not go along with, nor can it be resolved into, a religious interpretation of nature. It originates from the historical election of the people by God, an election that was inserted in the event of the Exodus (*see* ELECTION; EXODUS). This means that in the Bible testimony on creation the accent is not on the fact that the world is the work of God, but on the fact that God, Israel's Savior, is also the creator of the world. Secondly, creation enters the cycle of the history of salvation and is seen as the first manifestation of the same goodness, fidelity and omnipotence of God which Israel experiences throughout her own history. Creation then is the first saving action of God, the beginning of the history of salvation and therefore the first act in a whole list of deeds that God performed in Israel's favor (Ps. 136). It is described along the lines of the historical actions of God, using for this purpose partial themes gathered from the oriental myths, but radically changing their meaning. The use of mythical themes is understandable seeing that the myths thought of creation as a victory over the sea and the abyss of waters, so offering a fairly close parallelism to the historical Exodus which was also a victory of God over the sea (Isa. 51:10; Pss. 73; 89; 93; 104).

In creation God for the first time put his omnipotence at the service of his saving design (*see* Rom. 1:16). Creation was therefore a pledge for the future, which was appealed to as a motive of hope for salvation during the calamities that befell the individual (Ps. 76) and the whole people, as for example in the Exile (Isa. 41:4; 44:24-28; 45:12, 13; 43:5, 6; 45:18, 19; Ps. 89). God's reign over nature is based on the creation seen as a victory (Pss. 93; 104) after the example of God's reign over Israel, established in his victory over Egypt, Israel's oppressor (Ex. 15; Pss. 46; 98). God's fidelity is manifested in the perpetually undisturbed order of creation (Pss. 111; 146; 148) just as it is also shown in the fulfilment of his promises (Ps. 105). This fidelity is so much more worthy of praise in view of the fact that the world's consistency is continually threatened by the powers that were conquered and tamed at the instant of creation (*see* the Priestly version of the flood, *see* FLOOD). God's goodness (**hesed,** *see* MERCY) is the force that guarantees the covenant, and that dominates all the relationships between God and his creatures (Pss. 33:5; 119:64; 145:9) and can be praised as the ultimate and only reason for all the works of God in nature and in history (Ps. 136). From all this it becomes clear that biblical tradition elaborated its doctrine on creation by extending to it concepts already forged to understand and express the experience of the saving God in history.

The mythical theme of God's struggle with the sea, personified in monstrous creatures with their own names, can also be read in extra-biblical sources (e. g. Leviathan, Isa. 27:1; Rehab, Isa. 51:9; *see* LEVIATHAN; RAHAB). In the book of Job these have become a mere poetic fiction (Job 38:8; 9:13). In other poetic and prophetic texts from a more ancient age this is one element in a legacy of cosmological concepts that is placed, in a secondary role, at the service of Israel's faith in God. This borrowing from the surrounding cultures however was not done without important modifications. Strictly speaking, one cannot speak in the Bible of a struggle between God and the sea, but only of God's victory. In other words, there is no trace in the Bible of the dramatics found for example in the Canaanite poems (*see* BAAL) where for an instant it seems that the consistency of the universe was held in suspense and that all depended on the outcome of the fight. In the Bible these monstrous creatures are not really God's adversaries. They stand patiently in front of God with the only and exclusive function of awaiting his victorious command.

In Gen. 1, which is the Priestly account of creation (*see* PENTATEUCH), the traditional mythical elements have already lost all personification and have become almost scientific cosmological terms, suitable for describing the primordial chaos which is the point of departure for the creative process (Gen. 1:2). Creation is described as a journey from this original chaos, which in the semitic mentality is the closest approximation to the philosophical notion of non-entity, to a world ordered and perfect, 'good,' where life is possible (*see* Gen. 1:2 and Isa. 40:15, 17; 44:9; 41:29). This concept neither excludes nor is it opposed to the idea of creation as production from nothing (2 Mac. 7:28); rather it is its equivalent in a different order of ideas. In fact, both these concepts establish that from which creation began as the negation of created reality: from the denial of the notion of being, one arrives at the notion of nothingness, and from the denial of concrete consistency in the universe one arrives at imagining an empty desolation. This desolate waste could be defined as a representation of that which in philosophical categories is called nothingness.

The salient features of Gen. 1 are: the scheme of the week of creation and the theme of creation through a word. The first is a chapter in priestly theology meant to explain the Israelite institution of the sabbath (Ex. 20:8-11; 31:16, 17; *see* SABBATH). The second is a development of the experience of the efficacy of the prophetic word (Isa. 48:13; Pss 33:6, 9; 148:5; *see* WORD). Genesis moreover wishes to emphasize the transcendency of God the creator who in no way gets entangled in nature. Between God and his work there is only the untouched but nevertheless unbreakable link of his will expressed in his word.

The doctrine on creation gets new light in the wisdom tradition. God creates through his wisdom, which takes on the shape of a person with a view to creation (Prov. 8:22-31; *see* WISDOM, PERSONIFICATION OF). This tradition is important, for it laid the foundations for the Johannine and Pauline doctrine of creation 'in him' (Col. 1:16) or 'through him' (John 1:3). Christ is the first-born of every creature. (*See* FIRST-BORN). Everything was created in him and in him all things hold together (Col. 1:15; Heb. 1:2). The salvation aspect of this creative activity of the preexisting Word is evident in the relationship that both John and Paul place between creation and salvation by the same incarnate Word. The work of redemption is like a new creation (2 Cor. 5:17; Gal. 6:15; Eph. 2:10, 15) from which not even inanimate nature is excluded. It became subjected to corruption on account of the sin of the first man (Rom. 8:18-25) but the history of salvation will be completed with the revelation of a new heaven and a new earth (2 Pet. 3:13; Rev. 21:1; 21:5).

Cremation, *See* BURIAL.

Crescens (cres′-sens), A companion of Paul, who was with him during his second Roman imprisonment (2 Tim. 4:10).

Crete, An island in the Mediterranean, south of Greece, where flourished the Minoan civilization in the second millenium B.C. In Old Testament Hebrew, the island is called Caphtor, even though the name seems to have included the whole Aegean region. From here came the so-called Sea People, among whom were numbered the Philistines. In the Hellenistic period, and perhaps even before that, there were Jewish colonies on the island (1 Mac. 15:23), and Cretan Jews were in Jerusalem on the day of Pentecost (Acts 2:11). Paul visited Crete, but the circumstances of the visit are unknown, and he left Titus there to take care of the new Christian community which was being upset by resident Jews (Titus 1:5). In Titus 1:12 Paul cites a Cretan poet called Epimenides who said of his people that they were nothing but "liars, beasts and lazy gluttons." This is considered an excessively harsh criticism. Near Crete Paul suffered shipwreck on his way to Rome as a prisoner (Acts 27:7-21).

crippled
he used to sit *c*.   Acts 14:8

Crispus, A Corinthian Jew, chief of the city synagogue, converted with all his family to the faith through the preaching of Paul (Acts 18:8), and one of the few converts who was baptized by Paul himself (1 Cor. 1:14).

Crocodile, The only mention of the crocodile in the Bible is in Job 41, where it is described in hyperbolic terms and named Leviathan, one of the maritime monsters in Canaanite mythology. The tone of the description given by the author of Job is explainable once it is remembered that crocodiles were almost unknown in the Palestine of the period, even though there is evidence of them in the marshy river mouths of the Mediterranean up to the second millenium B.C.

Cross, An instrument for execution consisting of an upright beam left permanently in the ground surmounted by a cross-beam or **patibulum,** which might also be attached a little below the top of the upright. The condemned prisoner himself carried the **patibulum** to the place of execution, where he was stripped naked. His arms were bound to the cross-beam and his legs to the upright with either nails or rope or both. He was left suspended until he died of thirst or starvation.

Crucifixion was unknown in Israel during Old Testament times (*see* HANGING). It was however used by the Persians, from whom the Greeks and Romans adopted it. According to Roman law crucifixion was reserved for slaves and non-Roman citizens for particularly grave crimes.

Jesus was condemned to die on the cross by the prefect Pontius Pilate (Matt. 27:26 and parallel texts). The execution of the sentence was confided to a group of Roman soldiers under the command of a centurion (Matt. 27:54). After being subjected to flagellation and derision in the **praetorium** Jesus was loaded with the **patibulum** and led to Golgotha (Jn. 19:17) together with two other condemned prisoners (Lk. 23:32). On the journey, however, a man had to be forced to carry Jesus' cross behind him. This was Simon of Cyrene, who happened to be passing at the time (Lk. 23:26). Jesus was stripped and nailed to the cross (Jn. 20:25-27) after having refused to drink the proferred wine and myrrh, a narcotic used in Judea to attenuate the sufferings of the condemned. Jesus' clothes were distributed among the soldiers who had carried out the sentence, as was their right in Roman law (Matt. 27:32-36). At the top of the cross, above Jesus' head, the **titulus** was attached, giving the reason for his condemnation written in Aramaic, Greek and Latin (Matt. 27:37). To speed up the

death of the condemned, which could last more than one day, it was customary to break their legs. Jesus' death however occurred earlier than
usual, so his legs were not broken; but to ensure his death a soldier
pierced his side with a lance, and blood and water flowed from it (Jn.
19:31-37). The body was taken down from the cross before sunset, as
bodies could not remain exposed during the sabbath. Joseph of Arimathea, a disciple of Jesus, took care to provide the body of Jesus with decent burial. He asked and obtained from Pilate permission to have the
body, which was then placed in a new tomb of his own (Jn. 19:38-42).

crucified

to be handed over to be *c*.	Two insurgents were *c*. along
Matt. 26:2	Matt. 27:38
he handed him over to be *c*.	the one who was *c*. Mk. 16:6
Matt. 27:26	handed Jesus over to be *c*.
	Jn. 19:16

There they *c*. him   Jn. 19:18

Cubit, A measure of length, theoretically reaching from the elbow to the
extremity of the middle finger. From contrasting measures referred to in
the Old Testament, one can deduce that there were varying estimates of a
cubit's length (2 Chron. 3:3; Ezek. 40:5) which varied from 15 to 22
inches.

Cummin, A plant whose seeds were used as spice or relish. These were
extracted by a kind of flail (Isa. 28:25, 27). Jesus condemned the Pharasaical hypocricy in tithing even this small plant while neglecting the
weightier matters of the law (Matt. 23:23).

Cuneiform, A type of writing obtained through the use of the **euneus** or
wedge, a reed stylus almost triangular in shape which was impressed in
varying combinations on a still damp clay tablet, and later baked dry,
either in the sun or the furnace. This ensured an almost timeless indelibili-
ty. This was the most widely used writing system in the Near East up to
about 500 B.C. The most ancient documents of the oriental civilizations
are conserved in cuneiform. It was probably invented by the Sumerians,
later adopted by the Akkadians, Assyrians and Babylonians in Mesopotamia, by the Hittites and Canaanites towards the west, by the Persians
and other peoples as well, such as Elamites, Hurrites, etc. Cuneiform was
not always employed in the same way. The Sumerian script is ideograph-
ic, with each symbol representing a word. With the Akkadians it was syl-
labic, each symbol representing a syllable, even though some of the
Sumerian ideographs were retained. In Canaan (Ras Shamra) and in
Persia two different cuneiform alphabetic systems were developed, in
which each letter or symbol represented a different phonetic element.

Cup, The chalice or cup is often used in the metaphorical language of the
Bible; especially in a religious sense it is a symbol of the lot assigned by
God to individuals and nations. God himself is the heritage, the cup of the
faithful (Ps. 16:5), for whom he prepares a table and makes the cup brim
over (Pss. 23:5; 116:13). The cup of God's anger is a symbolic expression
for the chastisement which awaits the wicked (Pss. 11:6; 75:8; Isa. 51:17,
22, etc.), and which will fall upon the nations to repay them for their
actions (Jer. 25:14-29; Jer. 51:7), and will even pursue the chosen race
(Ezek. 23:31-33). Revelation uses the same expression for the eschatological punishment (14:10; 16:19; 17:4; 18:6). The chalice Jesus was destined to taste was his passion and death (Matt. 20:22-23; Mk. 10:38,39),
which he prayed, in the garden, to be spared (Matt. 26:39; Mk. 14:36,
Lk. 22:42); nevertheless he accepted it because it came to him from the

hands of the Father (Jn. 18:11). On the eucharistic cup *see* Matt. 26:27;
Mk. 14:23; Lk. 22:17; 1 Cor. 10:16, 21; 11:25-27.

cup

Pharoah's *c*. was in my hand	Gen. 40:11	If they refuse to take the *c*.	Jer. 25:28
the *c*. of his wrath	Isa. 51:17	gives a *c*. of cold water	Matt. 10:42
the *c*. of his staggering	Isa. 51:22		Matt. 10:42
I took the *c*.	Jer. 25:17	Then he took a *c*.	Matt. 26:27
she held a gold *c*.	Rev. 17:4	the *c*. I shall drink	Mk. 10:38

Curse, The curse or malediction is the opposite of a blessing. It is a solemn declaration through which a person is cut off from every sphere of beneficent influence and abandoned to the power of evil. In its stricter sense the curse is no mere desire but a kind of peremptory sentence which brings about through its own power what it dictates. In many instances in Scripture (*see* PSALMS), the curse amounts to a strong, formal and ritualistic desire that divine justice will overcome evil. In the magic-filled mentality of ancient peoples the curse worked automatically and irresistibly if it was pronounced in accordance with the established rites. It was as feared as the force of arms when employed as a means of offense, defense or revenge.

Balak, king of Moab, summoned from Mesopotamia the sorcerer Balaam to curse the Israelites and thus bring them to powerlessness when they invaded his lands on the way to Canaan (Num. 22:2-8). God however proved himself more powerful than any magic and caused Balaam to pronounce blessings rather than curses on Israel. When Balak rebuked Balaam for his betrayal, the latter had to confess: "Is it not what the Lord puts in my mouth that I must repeat with care?" (Num. 23:12).

The curse, without any magical context, is an integral part of the economy of the Sinai covenant (*see* COVENANT). Curses are threatened on those who will prove unfaithful to the covenant. The content of the malediction is spelled out in the long list of calamities in Deut. 28:15-68, but in synthesis it is nothing more than the radical exclusion of the guilty person from the sphere of God's saving action and his abandonment to the punishment of the divine anger, which expresses God's incompatibility with sin. Here too the curse works in a peremptory and inevitable manner, but there is no magic automatism. God's word is here efficacious: he does not speak in vain but brings to completion what he threatens.

Curses in the sense of radical exclusion from divine favor are called down on those guilty of the specific crimes listed in Deuteronomy 27:14-26. This text brings forward an element of the rite of renewal in the covenant. The Levites proclaim a list of twelve maledictions, a kind of decalogue, to which the people respond Amen. Here is an example of a particular type of apodictic law (*see* LAW) in which the curse has the function of punishment for non-observance. It is not just any punishment but a radical and complete punishment, nor is its imposition confided to any tribunal, but to God himself. For this reason the punishment is inevitable, for nobody can escape God. Thus for example runs the malediction: "Cursed be he who slays his neighbor in secret" (Deut. 27:24). The execution of the punishment is implicitly left up to God, not to an automatic magical process inherent in the curse itself. This holds also in other curses, which are, in practice, precepts, and sentences against their transgressors. Here the unfailing application of the punishment is assured. Joshua curses the person who would ever try to reconstruct the city of Jericho, which was doomed to extermination (Josh. 6:26). This curse was realized, according to 1 Kgs. 16:34, in the case of Hiel and his sons at the time of King Ahab.

Saul cursed the person who should take food before an end was put to the pursuit of the fleeing Philistines (1 Sam. 14:24-26). His son Jonathan was involuntarily involved in this curse, even though he had been the hero of that memorable day. Joshua cursed the Gibeonites for having acted with fraud against Israel (Josh. 9:23) and Nehemiah cursed those who had married foreign wives (Neh. 13:25).

After the first sin God cursed the serpent (Gen. 3:14) but neither the man nor the woman. This means that the condemnation of the serpent is total while Adam and Eve, though direly punished, can nevertheless hope in the future. These hopes have no other foundation than the gratuitous goodness of God, who in fact manifested to Abraham his design to bless all the tribes of the earth (Gen. 12:1-3).

curse

those who bless you and *c.* those   this water then that brings a *c.*
                    Gen. 12:3   Num. 5:22
          into her with all its bitter *c.*   Num. 5:24

curtains

no one to raise its *c.*   Jer. 10:20 their tent *c.* and all   Jer. 49:29

Cush, The biblical name for the region south of Egypt, later called Ethiopia. In the genealogy of Genesis 10:6 Cush descends from Cam together with Misraim (Egypt), Put (Somaliland) and Canaan.

Cushan-rishathaim (coo′-shan-rish′-a-thay′-im), King of Edom, who oppressed the Jews for eight years until defeated by Othniel. Other readings would have him king of Aram-naharaim (Aram of the two rivers, Mesopotamia; Jgs. 3:8-10).

Cushi (coosh′-eye), Father of the prophet Zephaniah (Zeph. 1:1).

custodian

Hegai, *c.* of the women   Esth. 2:8 Shaashgaz, *c.* of the   Esth. 2:14

custody

put them in *c.*   Gen. 40:3   who kept him in *c.* till   Lev. 24:12
the chief baker in *c.*   Gen. 41:10 they kept him in *c.*   Num. 15:34

custom, customs

observing the abominable *c.*   in all the various Jewish *c.*
                    Lev. 18:30   Acts 26:3
which means they advocate *c.*   our ancestral *c.*   Acts 28:17
                    Acts 16:21

cut, cutting

with the wood that he had *c.*   she ought to *c.* off her hair
                    Gen. 22:3   1 Cor. 11:6
and *c.* down their sacred poles   perverse tongue will be *c.* off
                    Ex. 34:13   Prov. 10:31
and then *c.* up into threads   *c.* it off and throw it away
                    Ex. 39:3   Matt. 5:30
like the calf which they *c.* in two   *c.* off his ear   Mk. 14:47
                    Jer. 34:18   If you were *c.* off   Rom. 11:24

Cuth (cooth), An ancient city of Mesopotamia, about 19 miles north of Babylon, the native place of some of the bands of colonists who were settled in Samaria by Sargon II (722 B.C., 2 Kgs. 17:24, 30) after he had conquered the city.

Cymbal, A percussion instrument. Psalm 150:5 distinguishes the clashing and the clanging cymbals. They were used to accompany the liturgical chant in the Temple (2 Sam. 6:5; 1 Chron. 15:16, 19, 28; 16:5-42, etc.).

cymbals

tambourines, sistrums and *c.*   stationed there with *c.* to praise
2 Sam. 6:5   Ezra 3:10
a noisy gong, a clanging *c.* 1 Cor. 13:1

Cypress, The cypress tree, rising majestically to a tapering height of 90 feet, grew abundantly on the mountains of Lebanon (Isa. 41:19; 60:13). The timber makes excellent building material.

Cyprus, An island in the eastern Mediterranean, famous for its copper mines from which it gets its name (latin **cuprum** means copper). In the Hebrew Old Testament it is known as Elisha (Gen. 10:4; 1 Chron. 1:7), and its inhabitants are called Kittim (Isa. 23:1, 12; Ezek. 27:6). During the Hellenistic period, Cyprus was under the domination of the Ptolemies of Egypt (294-58 B.C.), and even then the island had a flourishing Jewish colony (1 Mac. 15:15-23). From 58 B.C. it was, with Cilicia, a Roman province under the authority of a proconsul (Acts 13:7). The gospel was preached in the island by Christians who abandoned Jerusalem on account of the persecution which followed the martyrdom of Stephen (Acts 11:19-20). Later Paul and Barnabas, whose native place it was, visited it during their first missionary journey. They preached in the principal towns from Salamis to Paphos. Here they converted the proconsul Sergius Paulus, and met the magician Bar-Jesus who tried to block the proconsul's conversion (Acts 13:4-13). After the Council of Jerusalem and the dispute between Barnabas and Paul, the former, in the company of John Mark, returned to the island (Acts 15:39).

Cyrene (sy-ree´-ne), Capital city of Cyrenaica (Libya). The city was founded by Greek colonists in 630 B.C., captured by Alexander the Great (331 B.C.), fell to the kingdom of the Ptolemies, and finally, after a brief period of independence, became a Roman province. During the Hellenistic period several Jewish colonies were settled there by the Ptolemies. The Jews of Cyrene had their own synagogue in Jerusalem (Acts 6:9), and their presence in the city on the day of Pentecost is recorded in Acts 2:10. Cyrene was also the native place of Simon, who was forced to carry Jesus' cross to Calvary (Matt. 27:32; Mk. 15:21), and of Lucius, one of the prophets and teachers in the church at Antioch (Acts 13:1).

Cyrus, Cyrus II the Great (ruled 559-529 B.C.), founder of the Persian empire, was son and successor to Cymbyses (600-559 B.C.). His kingdom was vassal to the Medes, but in 553 B.C. Cyrus refused obedience to Astyages, king of the Medes, whose ministers took the part of Cyrus, who then easily defeated Astyages and took the capital city Ecbatana. Croesus, king of Lydia, formed an alliance with Babylonia and Egypt against the growing threat of the Medes and Persians, now united under Cyrus, who soon showed his imperial ambitions. He wished to extend the confines of the empire towards Cappadocia. After an indecisive battle with Croesus, Cyrus boldly led his army against Lydia's capital, Sardis, and took Croesus prisoner. He soon added the Greek colonies of Asia Minor to his conquests, and then returned towards the falling Babylonian empire to consolidate his victories from that quarter. In 539 B.C. he took Babylonia without difficulty, thanks to the treachery of the Babylonians themselves who betrayed Nabonidus. Cyrus treated the newly conquered peoples with a tolerance hitherto unknown in the East. The Assyrians had been wont to oppress and deport conquered peoples, but Cyrus introduced a regime of respect even for conquered kings and peoples. In line with this policy he issued an edict repatriating the exiled Jews, permitting them to rebuild the Temple and bring back to Jerusalem the sacred vessels plundered by Nebuchadnezzar (2 Chron. 36:22; Ezra 1:1-7). The Babylonians themselves took advantage of the same clemency, restoring their god Marduk who had been supplanted by the reform of Nabonidus, who established the god Sin in its stead, not without serious opposition by Marduk's priests. While the Babylonian poets celebrated Cyrus as God's chosen leader appointed to vindicate the insults offered to Marduk, Deutero-Isaiah, the prophet of the exile, sings the same theme in his works, lauding Cyrus and attributing his prodigious career and victories to the protection of Yahweh, who willed to make Cyrus his anointed, the instrument of the chosen people's liberation from Babylonia (Isa. 41:2-5, 25; 44:24, 28; 45:1-5, 13; 48:14-15). Cyrus died in the battle against Queen Tomyris and the Massagetae in 529 B.C.

D

D, The abbreviation for Deuteronomy, the third source or stratum of the Pentateuch. *See* DEUTERONOMY; PENTATEUCH.

Daberath (dab′-er-ath), A Levitical city in the territory allotted to Issachar (Josh. 21:28).

Dagon (day′-gon), A semitic god, known in Ugarit and Mesopotamia, whose cult was adopted by the Philistines after its arrival in Palestine. The popular account of the exploits of Samson has it that he was brought into Dagon's temple to perform feats for the three thousand people gathered there to worship. However, he put his arms around the two main pillars supporting the building and pushing with all his might and calling on the name of the Lord, he brought the whole temple down, killing that day more than he had killed during his life: for he too died in the collapse (Jgs. 16:22-30). When the Philistines captured the ark of the covenant in the battle of Aphek, they brought it into the temple of Dagon in Ashdod (1 Sam. 5:1-5). Dagon's cult continued up to the time of the Maccabees. The temple of Dagon was destroyed by Jonathan Maccabeus (1 Mac. 10:84).

daily

they offered the *d.* holocausts	Give us each day our *d.* bread
Ezra 3:4	Lk. 11:3
Give us today our *d.* bread	neglected in the *d.* distribution
Matt. 6:11	Acts 6:1
Encourage one another *d.*	Heb. 3:13

Daleth, The fourth letter of the Hebrew alphabet (d).

Dalmanutha (dal-ma-nu′-tha), According to Mark 8:10, the name of the region to which Jesus retired with his disciples after the second miracle of the loaves. He reached it by boat, so one supposes that it was situated on the Sea of Galilee. However the reference is uncertain and the place unidentified. Matthew 15:39 refers to a Magdala or Magadan at this point, also unidentified.

Dalmatia, A region in ancient Illyria, on the eastern Adriatic shore. It was a Roman province in 10 A.D., and was visited by Titus, according to 2 Tim. 4:10.

Dalphon, One of the ten sons of Haman the vizier of King Ahasuerus (Esther 9:7). *See* HAMAN.

Damaris (dam′-a-ris), An Athenian woman, one of the few converts Paul made during his brief stay in Athens (Acts 17:34).

Damascus, A city of Syria, east of the mountains of anti-Lebanon, in a plain made fertile by the rivers Abana (today Barada) and Pharpar (2 Kgs. 5:12). On account of its position on the main arteries connecting Egypt and Asia Minor with Mesopotamia, Damascus was one of the principal commercial centers of antiquity. The kingdom of Damascus had frequent but not always friendly dealings with Israel. Kings Ben-hadad, Hazael, and Ben-hadad II often figure in the military history of the North (1 Kgs. 15:18; 19:15; 20:22; 2 Kgs. 5-7; 8:7-15; 10:32-33). Continually under threat from the westward ambitions of the Assyrians, Damascus entered into an alliance with other Aramaean kingdoms and thus succeeded in blocking the Assyrian advance at Karkar (853 B.C.) only to be taken, a century later, by Tiglath-pileser III (733 B.C., 2 Kgs. 16:9-12; Isa. 8:4; 10:9; 17:1-3) who made it an Assyrian province. After a brief spell of independence (Jer. 49:23-27), it passed into the possession of the Chaldeans, Persians, and Seleucids (1 Mac. 11:62; 12:32). In New Testament times Damascus was Nabatean (2 Cor. 11:32). It had one of the first Christian communities, the victim of Paul's persecuting zeal before his conversion, which took place on the road to the city (Acts 9; 22:5-11; 26:12).

damned
the evildoers shall rise to be *d*.
                              Jn. 5:29

Dan, Jacob's fifth son, born of Bilhah, Rachel's slave (Gen. 30:6; 35:25; 46:23; Ex. 1:4), founding father of the tribe of Dan (Gen. 49:16; Deut. 33:22; Jgs. 5:17). This tribe first tried to settle on the coastal plains of Palestine (Jgs. 1:34-36) but failed. They then migrated to the extreme north and established themselves in the territory whose capital was Laish, later renamed Dan (Josh. 19:40-48). Judges 17-18 tells the story of this migration in detail. Their intent is to explain the origins of the sanctuary in the city of Dan, which together with that of Bethel, was to become the official sanctuary of the northern kingdom after the schism of Jeroboam (1 Kgs. 12:29 ff.; Amos 8:14). The city of Dan is often mentioned as the northern limit of Israelite territory, while Beersheba was its southern limit (Jgs. 20:1; 1 Sam. 3:20; 2 Sam. 3:10, etc.). For a time Dan was occupied by the Aramaeans of Damascus (1 Kgs. 15:20).

Dancing, Dancing to the accompaniment of the tambourine and other musical instruments, and often together with song (Ex. 15:20; 2 Sam. 6:5; 1 Sam. 18:6-7) is frequently recorded as the symbol and expression of joy and festivity. (Eccles. 3:4; Jgs. 21:21). Groups of dancing girls receive David upon his return from the triumph over Goliath (1 Sam. 18:6-7), and the daughter of Jephtha came out to meet him, dancing to the timbrels, when he returned from his victory over the Amorites (Jgs. 11:34; *see* also Judith 3:10; Ps. 30:12). Dances also formed part of the liturgical functions, such as the vineyard festival at Shiloh (Jgs. 21:16-24), David's dance in front of the ark (2 Sam. 6), and the worshipful dancing that took place around the golden calf (Ex. 32:19). The prophets of Baal, and even Israel's prophetic groups, used dance to induce ecstatic trances (*see* 1 Sam. 10:10; 19:20; 1 Kgs. 18:26; Ps. 149:3). The New Testament account of the beheading of John the Baptist (Matt. 14:6; Mk. 6:22) records an example of the customs in the Hellenized courts of the Middle East.

Daniel, A quasi-lengendary figure, whose name appears in the Canaanite writings of Ugarit, and whose fame and integrity are linked with those of Noah and Job in Ezekiel 14:14-20; 28:3.

Daniel, Book of, According to the Christian canon, the fourth of the major prophets, included in the Hebrew canon among the "Writings" or

"Hagiographa." Although it was traditionally listed among the great prophetic writings of Israel, the book, because of its literary genre and the date of its composition, belongs rather to Jewish apocalyptic literature. Moreover it is the only book of this literature numbered among the canonical Old Testament works.

The book recounts some episodes and visions that happened to a Jew by the name of Daniel, who was deported to Babylonia in 605 B.C. and, together with three other Jews, Hananiah, Mishael and Azariah, was educated in the court of the king of Babylonia c. 1). The episodes recounted in cc. 2-6 are among the best known of cred history. Daniel and his companions are thrown into a burning rnace for having refused to adore an idol, but they come from it miracu.ously unharmed (c. 3). Daniel interprets a dream of king Nebuchadnezzar (3:13-4:34). During a banquet celebrated by Belshazzar, Daniel interprets the mysterious words that appeared in writing on the wall of the banquet-hall, and which announced the imminent end of the Babylonian empire and the conquest of the city (5:1-6:1). Chapter 5:2-29 recounts an episode similar to c. 2: Daniel is responsible for having transgressed an order of king Darius I (522-485 B.C.) stating that during thirty days no prayers or petitions were to be made to God but only to the king. Daniel is thrown into the lions' den from which he escapes without injury.

The second part of the book (cc. 7-12) is told by Daniel in the first person, except for 7:1-2 and 10:1. It contains four visions with their relative interpretations: the vision of the son of man (c. 7), the vision of the ram (c. 8), the prophecy of the seventy weeks (c. 9), the vision of the ruin of the empire with the persecution of the faithful Jews and the final triumph of God (cc. 10-12). The Greek texts contain three deuterocanonical additions: 3:21-45: the canticle of the three youths in the furnace in Babylonia, the story of Susanna, saved by Daniel from the accusation of adultery by the lecherous old men, and c. 14, Daniel with the priests of the god Bel.

The book is written partly in Hebrew (1:1-2:4a; 8:1-12:13), partly in Aramaic (2:4b-7:28) while the deuterocanonical additions are in Greek. The book as it stands today was composed during the last years of the reign of Antiochus IV Epiphanes, king of the Seleucids, probably between 167 and 163 B.C. The historical background and the allusions contained in the visions place us in the period of the persecutions of Antiochus IV Epiphanes which provoked the revolt of the Maccabees (1 Mac. 2:54-60). The four empires are often mentioned in the visions of the book (cc. 2 and 7). These are the Babylonian, Mede, Persian and Seleucid empires. The recent date of the work explains why the book was not placed among the prophets, but rather in the most recent part of the Hebrew canon, the so-called "Writings" or "Hagiographa," together with Ecclesiastes, Job, etc. The actual book itself however is not an original or new work. Its author gathered and reworked very ancient material. The episodes of the first part (cc. 1-6), despite some historical inexactitudes, seem to go back, in their most ancient form, to the Persian period. The vision material depends on the apocalyptic tradition which succeeded to, and took the place of, the prophetic charism. The visions have clearly been reworked to adapt them to new historical conditions, in accordance with the method often used by Revelation. (*See* APOCALYPTIC LITERATURE.) Even though therefore its present redaction goes back no further than the second century B.C., a long history preceded it, which is, however, difficult to reconstruct in detail.

Daphne, One of Antioch's suburbs; famous for its Temple of Apollo which had rights of sanctuary. Onias the high priest took refuge there from Menelaus who had become high priest dishonestly and had plundered Solomon's temple of the sacred vessels to buy Andronicus' favor. Menelaus persuaded Andronicus to kill Onias. For this purpose Andronicus treacherously coaxed Onias from the sanctuary, and then slew him (2 Mac. 4:30-35).

Darda, Son of Zerali and of Judah, noted for his wisdom in which only Solomon surpassed him (1 Kgs. 5:11; 1 Chron. 2:6).

dare, dared
and *d.* look no more   Acts 7:32 I will not *d.* speak of anything
                                                                Rom. 15:18

Daric, A Persian coin made of 8.5 grams of gold (Ezra 2:69; Neh. 7:70-72).

Darius (da-ry'-us), Darius I Hystaspis, known as Darius the Great, king of Persia (522-485 B.C.) the great organizer of the empire. He permitted the Jews to take up once more the work of constructing the temple at Jerusalem (Ezra 4:25; 5:1 f.) and this was brought to a conclusion in the sixth year of his reign (Ezra 6:15). It was during his reign that Zechariah and Haggai exercised their prophetic ministry (Zech. 1:1; Hag. 1:1; 2:10). Daniel in 5:31; 6:1, 25: 11:1 speaks of Darius the Mede, conqueror of the Chaldeans and organizer of the new empire, in all of which Daniel plays an important role. What the book of Daniel tells, however, is incompatible with what is established from other sources in regard to the history of the Persian empire. The editor of the book of Daniel, who lived in the 2nd century B.C. seems badly informed in Persian history. With what little he knew he reconstructed the scenery of Daniel's life in a manner that only slightly corresponds to what actually happened.

Darkness, *See* LIGHT.

Darkon, Ancestor of a family of Solomon's servants (Ezra 2:56; Neh. 7:58).

Date, *See* PALM TREE.

Dathan (day'-than), Son of Eliab of the tribe of Reuben. With Abiram he headed a revolt against Moses during the Israelites' stay in the desert (Num. 16:12). Numbers 16 puts together the traditions on two different events: the revolt of Korah and the Levites against Moses and principally against Aaron on account of the latter's cultic prerogatives (16:3-11) and the revolt of Dathan and Abiram who contested Moses' leadership and accused him of leading the people to their ruin (16:12-14). This distinction is sufficiently confirmed by the repetitions which are read in Num. 16, and insinuated by the mention of Dathan and Abiram only in Deuteronomy 11:6; Psalm 106:17. Sirach 45:18 already knows of the fusion of the two events as they are read in Num. 16.

Dathema (dath'-e-ma), A fortress in Transjordan besieged by the Seleucid army and relieved by Judas Maccabeus (1 Mac. 5:9).

daughter
sister, but only my father's *d.*   Now Saul's *d.* Michal
              Gen. 20:12   1 Sam. 18:20
Whose *d.* are you   Gen. 24:23 rebellious *d.*   Jer. 31:22
when it was time for Saul's *d.*   capital city of *d.* Egypt   Jer. 46:19
              1 Sam. 18:19 Herodias' *d.* performed a dance
                                                              Matt. 14:6

David, Son of Jesse of the tribe of Judah. The family of Jesse, which lived in Bethlehem, descended from Ruth and Boaz (*see* Ruth 4:18-22). There were six other sons and two daughters (1 Chron. 2:13-16; 1 Sam. 16:10-11; 17:12). David was anointed king by Samuel after Samuel's conflict with Saul (1 Sam. 15:28; 16:13). He was taken to the court of the king as a harpist, with the task of alleviating with his music the states of melancholy into which Saul would lapse (1 Sam. 16:14-23). According to 1 Sam. 17 Saul knew David after the latter's victory over Goliath, the Philistine giant of Gath. This information is in contrast with 1 Sam. 16:14-23, and is made even more uncertain by the attribution of the killing of Goliath to a certain Elhanan (2 Sam. 21:20). Some authors think that Elhanan was David's name before he became king. In any case, David was further distinguished for his military qualities. His warrior exploits were crowned by success which won for him the favor of the people and the jealousy of Saul (1 Sam. 18:6-16). Neither marriage with Saul's daughter Michal (1 Sam. 18:17-30) nor the intercession of Jonathan, Saul's son and David's intimate friend (*see* 1 Sam. 19:1-8), could reconcile Saul with David (1 Sam. 19:9-20; 20:42). David fled from Saul, taking with him mercenaries and offering his services to the Philistines of Gath (1 Sam. 21). He succeeded however in avoiding situations in which he would have to fight against Israel (1 Sam. 21-27; 30). When he heard of the death of Saul and Jonathan in the battle of the Mountains of Gilboa (2 Sam. 1:17-27), David made for Hebron where he was anointed king of Judah (2 Sam. 2:4). In the meantime the tribes of the north supported Ishbaal, Saul's son, who was being ably managed by Abner, the general of Saul's army (2 Sam. 2:8-10). The battle of Gibeon between David's army under Joab and Ishbaal's under Abner did not resolve the situation (2 Sam. 2:12-23). Abner later turned against Ishbaal and entered into negotiations with David in order to turn over to him the tribes of the north. These negotiations fell through when Joab treacherously killed Abner in revenge for the death of his brother Asahel, slain by Abner at Gibeon (2 Sam. 3:27). Ishbaal was then treacherously killed, without however David having had any part in it (2 Sam. 4:9-12). Finally the elders of Israel came to Hebron and struck a pact with David who thus became king of Israel (2 Sam. 5:1-5).

David chose Jerusalem as capital of his kingdom. The city had remained in the hands of the Jebusites even after the conquest of Joshua, but now it fell to David (2 Sam. 5:6-16). David established the royal palace in Jerusalem, making use of materials and craftsmen from Hiram, king of Tyre (2 Sam. 5:11 ff.). Once he had done away with the dangers from the Philistines (2 Sam. 5:17-25) he was able to get to work on knitting the nation together and strengthening the position of the monarchy, while at the same time aggregating some further territories to the land. David had the ark of the covenant brought to Jerusalem, thus making the royal city also the religious center of the ancient Confederation of the Twelve Tribes (2 Sam. 6). He had intentions of constructing a temple but was advised not to by an oracle of the prophet Nathan. This oracle also contained a promise of perpetuity for the dynasty of the throne of Judah, to become the basis of the whole messianic hope of biblical tradition (2 Sam. 7). By taking advantage of the political decadence of Egypt and Mesopotamia, David succeeded in affirming the Israelite position in the neighboring kingdoms of Moab (2 Sam. 8:2), among the Aramaeans of Damascus (2 Sam. 8:3-14) as well as among the Ammonites and the Edomites (2 Sam. 12:26-31).

The last years of David's reign were perturbed by the rivalries and jealousies of his sons born from different wives. These conflicts are recounted in the "History of the succession of David," one of the most beautiful works of Israelite history, today included in 2 Sam. 9-20. These struggles also had significant political consequences. Absalom, son of David and Maacah, (1 Chron. 3:2; 2 Sam. 3:2-5) who had killed his half-brother Amnon in revenge for the latter's violation of Absalom's full sister Tamar (2 Sam. 13), sought to usurp his father's throne, and so prepared a revolt. This revolt met with success at first, and David was obliged to flee Jerusalem (2 Sam. 15-16). He once more entered the city after the defeat and death of Absalom which he bitterly mourned (2 Sam. 18-19). He was however again faced with revolt, this time by Sheba, a Benjamite who wished to exploit the traditional attachment of the tribes to the memory of Saul (2 Sam. 20). The rivalries over the succession continued almost to the vigil of the king's death. David named Solomon his successor. He had been born from Bathsheba, the wife of Uriah. Solomon counted on the support of Nathan, Zadok and Benaiah, despite another attempt at usurpation by Adonijah, David's son by Haggith (1 Chron. 3:2; 1 Kgs. 1).

David was to go down in biblical tradition as the "king according to the heart of the Lord." Despite some shadows on his character, the figure of David has always attracted readers of the Bible for the nobility of his character, which found, in the anonymous author of the books of Samuel, a delicate panegyrist and a devoted admirer. David was endowed with political acumen and uncommon military talents. Thanks however above all to the oracle of Nathan, David also became the type of true king of God's people, and in his ideal figure converged the hopes of the people in the coming of a king, a son of David, who would be God's instrument in the saving of his people.

David, City of, *See* JERUSALEM.

dawn
night until the following *d.*   nor gaze on the eyes of the *d.*
            Jgs. 19:25   Job 3:9
            the *d.* of youth is fleeting   Eccles. 11:10

Day, In early Israel the day was computed from morning to morning (Jgs. 19:5-9; 1 Sam. 19:11; Num. 11:32; Gen. 19:34). After the exile the Babylonian system of computation was adopted which started the day at sunset (*see* Gen. 1:5-8, 13, 19, 23; Ex. 12:18; Lev. 23:32). Thus the sabbath rest commenced on the evening of Friday according to our computation (*see* Mk. 15:42; 16:1; Lk. 23:54-56). The days of the week were designated by ordinal numbers, except for the sabbath (Mk. 16:2; Lk. 24:1, etc.). In New Testament times the Hebrews adopted the Greek usage of dividing the sunlight period into 12 hours, again known by ordinal numbers, and with varied duration according to the seasons (*see* Matt. 20:3-6; Mk. 15:25, 33 ff.; Jn. 1:39; 4:6, 52; 19:14; Acts 2:15; 10:9). The night was divided into four watches (Lk. 12:38; Matt. 14:25; Mk. 13:35).

Day of the Lord, The idea of the Day of the Lord was one of the most ancient forms of Israelite eschatological hope. It was not always, and especially in the more ancient texts, considered to be the inauguration of another transcendent world and the end of the present age. This was to come later. Nevertheless it can be called eschatological because it was expected as the decisive and definitive intervention of God in favor of Israel, even though it was to happen in history. The oldest mention of this theme in the Bible (Amos 5:18-20) was certainly polemical. Amos takes exception to the concept of the Day of the Lord which only nourishes hopes of splendor and glory for Israel. According to the prophet, Israel's election will only turn out to be a motive for more severity and rigor in the judgment of God (Amos 3:1-2). The Day of the Lord will be 'darkness and not light' (*see* also Amos 6:3; 8:9). Other pre-exilic prophets tread the same path as Amos: the Day of the Lord will be a judgment that will not spare Israel (Isa. 2:11-17; 13:9-10 and especially Zeph. 1:7-11; 1:12-18; 2:1-3). With the post-exilic prophets the Day of the Lord is presented as the definitive and eschatological intervention of God, without however the polemic against the unfounded confidence of Israel that marked Amos, Isaiah and Zephaniah. The Day of the Lord will comprise different acts culminating in the salvation of the elect people, following the judgment of the nations that oppress the Lord's people (Joel 2-4). In Zechariah 14 the Day of the Lord ends with the universalistic vision of the peoples who come to Jerusalem each year to celebrate the Feast of Tabernacles and adore God the King (*see* also Mal. 3:2).

In the New Testament the eschatological terms are put in a christological key so that the Day of the Lord becomes the Day of the Son of Man, in which he will be revealed in all his glory to judge the world (Lk. 17:24-30). For Paul the Day of the Lord is the second coming of Christ (*see* PAROUSIA), his coming in glory to bring the present age to its close and make the definitive passage into the future world (1 Cor. 1:8; 5:5; 2 Cor. 1:14; Phil. 1:6, 10; 2:16; 1 Thess. 5:2; 2 Thess. 2:2). The terminology of the Old Testament is maintained in the eschatology of John's Revelation (Rev. 16:14).

Deacon, From the Greek **diakonos,** minister or servant. Today it is the name of one of the major clerical orders and therefore designates a specific function in the church. The term is used in this sense only in Philippians 1:1 and in 1 Timothy 3:8-13, even though it occurs very frequently in the apostolic Fathers of the first and second centuries. In Philippians Paul salutes the bishops and deacons of the church of Philippi, but nothing more is known of their specific function except that they were subject to the bishops as their ministers. In 1 Timothy Paul enumerates the qualities that deacons should have, which would seem to indicate that they looked after the administration of church funds and carried out other practical duties. Tradition has seen in Acts 6 the story of the institution of the diaconate in the Church. According to this passage, this measure came about to meet particular difficulties of the Jewish-Christian church in Jerusalem. Its Hellenistic members complained that they were being neglected (6:1). To remove these difficulties and take care of their needs, seven were chosen and installed in office through the imposition of the apostles' hands (Acts 6:5-7). While this passage seems to speak only of administrative functions, at least some of those chosen later carried on a truly apostolic activity, preaching and baptizing. At this point they are not called deacons (*see* 6:8-7:6; 8:26-40).

The term **diakonos** is also used in its genuine sense of servant or minister, e.g. the servants or ministers of Jesus, of God, of the New Testament (2 Cor. 11:23; 11:15; 3:6; 6:4), to show the service given to the gospel cause. In Romans 16:1 Phoebe is called "deaconess of the church of Cenchreae." Given the variety of meanings the word **diakonos** can have, it is not easy to determine what precisely Phoebe's functions were. Deaconesses were probably Christian women entrusted with particular services in the Christian community, such as are described in 1 Timothy 3:11, even though deaconesses are not mentioned there.

Deaconess, *See* DEACON.

Dead Sea, The depression at the mouth of the Jordan. In the Bible it is called the Salt Sea (Gen. 14:3; Num. 34:3; Deut. 3:17; Josh. 3:16; 12:3; 15:2; 18:19), East Sea (Ezek. 47:18; Joel 2:20; Zech. 14:8) or the Sea of Arabah, Arabah being the name for the whole depression which continues on to the Gulf of Aqabah (Deut. 3:17; 4:49; Josh. 3:16; 12:3). In Genesis 14:3 the valley which cradles the Dead Sea is called the Valley of

Siddim. The battle between the kings of the east and the Pentapolis confederation took place there. The most southerly part of the Dead Sea (south of the peninsula of Lisan, which juts out from the eastern shore) is a recent geological formation. The memory of this fact gave rise to the account of the destruction of Sodom and Gomorrah (Gen. 14). The level of the waters lies 1290 feet beneath sea-level, and the sea bed lies at 1300 feet. The sea has no outlet, and so is subject to intense evaporation leaving the waters with an unusually high percentage of salts of magnesium, sodium and calcium. This makes any water or marine life impossible. During messianic times the waters of the sea would be purified by the flow from the fount of the Temple in Jerusalem according to Ezekiel 47:8-12; Zechariah 14:8. The sea is 53 miles long and 10 miles across at its widest point. Besides the Jordan it also receives the waters of the Môjib (the Biblical Arnon) on its eastern shores, and other smaller streams.

Dead Sea Scrolls, These are the manuscripts discovered from 1947 on in different caves just northwest of the Dead Sea, in the neighborhood of a locality known as Khirbet Qumran (*see* QUMRAN, KHIRBET), from the river of the same name that runs into the Dead Sea. The manuscripts belonged to the library of people who had lived in community in the area. They had probably been hidden in the caves for safekeeping during the war with the Romans in 70 A.D. which ended with the destruction of Jerusalem. An examination of the writings themselves confirms this opinion, as they stem from the second and first centuries B.C. After the year 70 the place was no longer occupied by these people, and so the manuscripts lay forgotten in the caves until they were discovered by chance by some Ta'amireh Bedouins in 1947.

Biblical texts: Remains of all the canonical books of the Hebrew canon with the exception of Esther were discovered. The most important manuscripts are the two rolls of Isaiah, one of them complete, and the other containing a third of the text. The study of these texts, which antedate by several centuries the most ancient biblical manuscripts hitherto known, substantially confirms the consonant text fixed by the Massoretes, even though in quite a few points the Septuagint is closer.

Apocryphal works: Among the apocryphal works already known, the **Testament of the Twelve Patriarchs,** the **Book of Jubilees** and some parts of the **Book of Enoch** are represented.

Books belonging to the Sect: The **Manual of Discipline,** that is, the rule of the sect, has given us an insight into the doctrines and practices of the "Community of the Covenant," as they called themselves at Khirbet Qumran. They have commonly been identified as Essenes, who up to this were only known from references in Philo and Flavius Josephus. Similar are the **Damascus Document** and the **Zadokite Document,** known from manuscripts discovered in the genizah of Cairo, and which reflect a different stage of the same sect. Different **Pesarim** or midrashic commentaries on the Bible are explanations of the Bible texts in the service of the history of the sect. They are the principal sources of information on the origin and especially on the tragic adventures of the life of the sect's founder, the so-called Master of Justice. A **Pesar** on Habakkuk 1-2, Nahum and different psalms (Ps. 37) have been found. The book of the **War of the Sons of Light against the Sons of Darkness** describes the strategy and gives the norms for the imminent and decisive battle in which the forces for good will stand against the forces of evil, and in which the members of the sect will have a role of the first order to fill. The **Hodayoth** or hymns are lyrical religious compositions which imitate the canonical psalms. They are attributed to the Master of Justice, the founder of the sect. *See* ESSENES, QUMRAN.

deaf

and makes another *d*. and dumb	to my weeping be not *d*. Ps. 39:13
Ex. 4:11	On that day the *d*. shall hear
You shall not curse the *d*.	Isa. 29:18
Lev. 19:14 the *d*. hear	Matt. 11:5
brought him a *d*. man Mk. 7:32	

Death, The biblical ideas on death, as could be expected, follow on the Israelite reflection on life and the emergence of the doctrine of the resurrection (*see* LIFE, RESURRECTION). In the Old Testament books that know of no possibility of a true life after death, there can be distinguished at least two concepts of death, two ways of confronting the problem and two attitudes to be taken towards it.

The most widespread, even in more recent works like Sirach, is that of courageous resignation. He takes into account the set limits of human existence and thus makes no question of death if it arrives when life has run its course and the vitality of the organism is at an ebb (Job 21:28; 29:18-20). In the lovely expression of 2 Sam. 14:14; "We must indeed die; we are then like water that is poured out on the ground and cannot be gathered up." From this point of view it is not death itself that is of concern, but death "in the noontime of life" (Isa. 38:10) that becomes an enigma, especially when it hits the just and leaves the sinner (Job 21). In fact the theory of retribution, of early Wisdom inspiration, seems able to grapple only with the problem of premature death by making it the consequence of sin (Prov. 5:21-23). Job's friends pushed this theory (*see* Job 4:7-9; 8:8-20).

The author who wished to give a rational basis to this attitude was Ben Sira. God created man from the earth and to the earth he had him return. He gives to man a determined measure of days (Sirach 17:1, 2). Ben Sira forces himself to see the normalcy of this condition, just one more case of the law that governs the universe: "All flesh grows old, like a garment; an age-old law is: All must die. As with the leaves that grow on a vigorous tree: one falls off and another sprouts, so with the generations of flesh and blood: one dies and another is born" (Sir. 14:17, 18; *see* also 40:11; 41:1-4, and above all 17:26: "For not immortal is any son of man. Is anything brighter than the sun? Yet it can be eclipsed").

The second attitude to death takes up the problem in its most enigmatic terms. Death is seen framed, not in a universe of natural facts, but as the heaviest burden that weighs down human existence, which itself is already afflicted with fatigue, pain, inclination to evil, the hostility of the surrounding world and the unbalance of human relationships themselves (Gen. 3:14-19). Death is the punishment for sin, the evident sign of a rupture between God and man, which took place at the beginning and is therefore a common patrimony (Gen. 2-3; *see* FALL, THE). This way of looking at death was to prove very fruitful in the future. Even though it seemed to slip into the area of the forgotten during the centuries, it reemerged in a more precise and complete form in Wisdom 1-5, and in the light of the doctrine of the resurrection. God did not make death nor does he rejoice in the destruction of the living (Wis. 1:13). "God formed man to be imperishable, the image of his own nature he made him. But by the envy of the devil, death entered the world, and they who are in his possession experience it" (Wis. 2:23, 24).

In these texts the word death has a density of meaning that goes beyond the biological fact of death. Death is the sign of the hopeless end, or better, physical death itself is the entry to eternal perdition. For this reason the author avoids the term death when he speaks of the departure of the just (*see* Wis. 5:7, 10, 11, 14, 17).

The book of Wisdom anticipates some of the central themes of the New Testament. For Paul too death entered the world as the consequence of the sin of the first man (Rom. 5:12). In this text death has the precise meaning of damnation. Christ however has conquered death by rising from the dead (Rom. 6:9) and in him all the faithful are called to resurrection (1 Cor. 15:22). Those who believe and are baptized receive the Spirit of him who raised Jesus from the dead, and he will also raise us with him (Rom. 8:11). Victory over death will be complete at the end of time when the dead will arise glorious and immortal (1 Cor. 15:25). In the meantime Christians die a physical death, which however is not true death: it is a falling asleep in the Lord (1 Thess. 4:13-18). In death the body is sowed like a seed to flower in incorruption and immortality (1 Cor. 15:35-44). From this death Rev. 2:11; 20:6, 14; 21:8 distinguishes the "second death" which is eternal damnation on the day of judgment.

Death of Jesus, Jesus himself spoke of his tragic death, above all in the so-called prophecies of the passion (Mk. 8:31; Matt. 16:21; Lk. 9:22; Mk. 9:31; Matt. 17:22; Lk. 9:44; Mk. 10:33, 34; Matt. 20:17f.; Lk. 18:37), and in other sayings on the Son of Man (Mk. 10:45; Matt. 20:28; Mk. 9:12; 14:21, 41; *see* SON OF MAN). Often attempts have been made to see in these texts hindsight, or prophecies after the event. Even though this thesis seems the most obvious and easy, it is nevertheless extremely improbable.

In fact, that Jesus should speak of his impending death is anything but improbable, as natural perspicacity alone could with all certainty predict a tragic and violent end to his ministry. Jesus was accused of blasphemy (Mk. 2:7; Jn. 5:18; 10:33), of not observing the sabbath (Mk. 2:23; 3:1-6) and of magic (Mk. 3:22; Matt. 9:34)—all of them grave accusations, with death as their penalty. Indeed Jesus' life was more than once threatened, and actual attempts were made on it (Lk. 4:29; Jn. 8:59). The so-called prophecies of the passion have value not so much for the foresight of the event itself, but for the interpretation which Jesus gave to this necessary part of his mission.

The prevision of his death could not but provoke in Jesus a definite attitude of mind, since it related directly to the consciousness he had of his mission as founder of the kingdom of God. Jesus even spoke in public of his death. He denounced the incredulity of Israel with its age-old reluctance to hear the voice of God, a reluctance expressed in the persecution of the prophets who had been sent to them in the past. Jesus places his own murder as the climax of this age-long rebellion (Matt. 23:19 ff.; Lk. 13:34, 35). When the Pharisees sent by Herod exhort him with threats to abandon Galilee, Jesus answers: "I must proceed on course today, tomorrow and the day after, since no prophet can be allowed to die anywhere except in Jerusalem" (Lk. 13:33). In the parable of the murderous vineyard workers (Matt. 21:33; Mk. 12:1; Lk. 20:9), Jesus places the killing of the son as the climax of the rebellion of Israel and announces the judgment that will fall on it.

Within the circle of his disciples however, Jesus spoke more directly of his death. To them he reveals that he is destined to fulfill the mission of the Servant of the Lord described in Isaiah 53, that is, to give his life as the means of redemption for all (Mk. 10:45; 2 Tim. 2:11). Jesus uses the title of Son of Man to signify that the glory and saving dominion brought to completion by the Son of Man will be the fruit of his obedience and fidelity even to death (*see* Phil. 2:5 ff.; *see* LORD'S SUPPER; SACRIFICE; SERVANT OF THE LORD; SON OF MAN).

These words of Jesus (Mk. 10:45) are the source of the biblical doctrine on the soteriological value of Christ's death. At times the attention of the evangelists stays on the external aspect of Jesus' death, that is, on the external circumstances that led to it and to his executioners. Then the death of Jesus is presented as the vain attempt of men to suffocate the voice of God and to bring to nothing his plans. This vain attempt of men was brought to nothing by the omnipotence of God who raised Jesus from the dead and had him sit at his right hand in glory (*see* Acts 2:22-25; 3:13-15; 4:11 which cites Ps. 118:22). ·

In the whole story of salvation, however, in its deepest aspect the death of Christ with his resurrection is the salvation of the world. Jesus died for our sins and arose for our justification (Rom. 4:25). Jesus' obedience to the death, even to the death on the cross (Phil. 2:8) is the act which does away with the heritage of sin and death introduced into the world by the disobedience of the first man (Rom. 5:12-21). The Christian is baptized into the death of Christ, and is therefore involved in the act which brings him from death to sin to newness of life (Rom. 6:1-11). Death is the consummation of the love of Christ, who, having loved those who were his own in the world, loved them to the extreme of love (Jn. 13:1), for no greater love exists than that which gives its life for those it loves (Jn. 15:13). Jesus' death is his Pasch, that is, his passage from this world to the Father (Jn. 13:1). It is the reconciliation of God with the world (2 Cor. 5:18), victory over sin (Rom. 8:3), death and the law (Rom. 7:1-6).

By dying on the cross Jesus perfectly expiated for sin, something sought after but unachieved in the Old Testament (Heb. 9). He is in fact priest and victim, and has carried out his self-oblation in a most perfect act that needs no repetition, for there is nothing further to be added. Christians who celebrate the eucharist enter into communion with that oblation and reap the fruits of that salvation (*see* EUCHARIST). On the historical aspects of the death of Jesus *see* PASSION.

Debir (dee′-bur), A Levitical city (Josh. 21:15; 1 Chron. 6:44) of Judah (Josh. 15:49), also called Kiriath-sepher (Josh. 15:15; Jgs. 1:11), 12 miles southwest of Hebron. It was inhabited by the Anakim at the time of the Israelite invasion (Josh. 11:21). Its conquest is attributed to Joshua (Josh. 10:38; 11:21) and to the Calebite tribe of Othniel, which was associated with the tribe of Judah (Jgs. 1:11-15; Josh. 15:15-17).

Deborah, 1. Rebekah's nurse. She accompanied her charge when the latter was given in marriage to Isaac (Gen. 24:59) and died in Canaan near Bethel, where she was buried (Gen. 35:8).

2. A prophetess and judge over Israel, wife of Lapidoth (Jgs. 4:4). Deborah was the inspirer of the Israelite reaction to the oppression of Jabin, the Canaanite king of Hazor. She gathered an army of 10,000 men of the tribes of Naphtali and Zebulun, which she entrusted to Barak. The Israelites took advantage of the nature of the terrain which was little suited to Jabin's chariots (Jgs. 5:19-22) and so brought off a victory. Sisera, head of the Canaanite army, managed to flee but was killed by Jael in whose tent he had taken refuge (Jgs. 4:6-24). The so-called canticle of Deborah (Jgs. 5) is an epic composition and stems almost from the same era. It is noted for its literary merits and also important as one of the most ancient examples of Israelite literature. Moreover it forms one of the few contemporary historical sources for the period of the judges.

Decalogue, The Decalogue, that is, the "ten words" or commandments, is a collection of ten apodicitic laws (*see* LAW) which biblical tradition puts at the center of the stipulations of the Covenant of Sinai (*see* COVENANT). The Decalogue is found in Exodus 20:2-17 and Deuteronomy 5:6-21. The former belongs to the account itself of the Sinaitic Covenant, while the

latter forms part of one of the discourses of Moses in the book of
Deuteronomy. There are only minor differences between the two versions, e.g. in the explanation of the sabbath observance, which in
Deuteronomy has a humanitarian purpose while in Exodus it is placed in
relationship to the six days of the account of creation. The tenth precept
in Exodus places first the house and then lists its various elements: wife,
slaves, animals, etc., while Deuteronomy 5 gives first place to the wife and
then mentions the house with its slaves and animals.

As the Decalogue now reads, both in Exodus 20:2-17 and Deuteronomy
5:6-21, it contains explanatory additions inserted at a later period. At the
beginning the Decalogue consisted of ten brief categorical precepts, of the
type still preserved in Exodus 20:13-15 and Deuteronomy 5:17-20, such
as, "You shall not kill; you shall not steal." These brief precepts are easily
separated from the later additions, e.g. "You shall not have others besides
me," "You shall not carve idols for yourselves," "You shall not take the
name of the Lord in vain," etc. Even if the form that today is read in
Exodus 20 and Deuteronomy 5 is more recent in time, it does allow us to
reconstruct a more ancient version of the commandments, which can justly be termed Mosaic. There are no reasons strong enough to call into
doubt the tradition that sees in the commandments one of the most important parts of the Mosaic patrimony. Perhaps in Moses' time there did
not exist such a Decalogue, that is, such a collection of ten laws. The
Decalogue seems to have arisen from a choice made with pedagogic purposes in mind from a more ample series of similar precepts. The choice
however did intend to retain what was considered fundamental and inalienable in the demands of the God of Israel. In this hypothesis the
Decalogue is a compendium of the fundamental obligations undertaken
to fulfill the commitment assumed by Israel to serve their Lord.

Decapolis, A region of Transjordan which encompassed the territory of
the confederation of the ten Hellenistic cities formed under the auspices
of the Romans in 63 B.C. These cities were founded after the conquest of
Alexander the Great, during the Seleucid period. Some of them fell under
Jewish dominion during the Hasmonaean period. They were made free
cities by the Romans, in direct dependence on the Roman legate of the
province of Syria. The Romans knew their importance not only for the
defense of the limits of the Empire—situated as they were on its desert
frontiers—but also as a solid support for Rome in the east on account of
their Hellenistic tradition and character. In 75 A.D. Pliny included in the
Decapolis the following cities: Hippo, Gadara, Pella, Philadelphia, Gerasa, Dion, Canatha, Damascus, Raphana and Scythopolis, which last was
the only one on the Palestinian side of the Jordan. The confederation
however did not always embrace the same cities, and at times there were
more than ten. Gospel tradition records two miracles worked by Jesus in
the Decapolis region—Mark 7:31-37, the cure of the deaf and dumb person; and Mark 5:1-20, the cure of the demoniac of Gerasa. *See* also Matthew 4:23, 24.

deceit, deceive

came to *d.* you	2 Sam. 3:25	on whom you rely *d.* you
Do not let Hezekiah *d.* you		Isa. 37:10
	Isa. 36:14	*d.* upon *d.* Jer. 9:5
Do not *d.* yourselves Jer. 37:9		

decree

King Cyrus issued a *d.*	Ezra 5:13	Thus, when the *d.* Esth. 1:20
whether a *d.* really was issued		and *d.* had been obeyed Esth. 2:8
	Ezra 5:17	Caesar Augustus published a *d.*
I have issued this *d.*	Ezra 7:13	Lk. 2:1

Dedan (dee′-dan), An Arab tribe living in the confines of Edom (Jer. 49:8; Ezek. 25:13). It was known for its commercial talents (Ezek. 27:20) and its caravans (Ezek. 38:13). Two genealogies are given for it. In the Table of Nations it appears among the descendants of Cush (Gen. 10:7; 1 Chron. 1:9). In Gen. 25:3, 1 Chron. 1:32 it appears as the offspring of Jokshan and descendant of Abraham by his second wife Keturah.

Dedication, Feast of, A feast celebrated annually to commemorate the purification of the Temple in 164 B.C. after it had been profaned by Antiochus IV Epiphanes. In 167 B.C. he had an abominable idol erected on the altar of holocausts (Dan. 9:27; 11:31), to which on the 25th Chislev, sacrifices were solemnly offered (1 Mac. 1:54-59). Three years later on the same day, Judas Maccabeus, having recovered the city and the Temple, solemnly dedicated the new altar of holocausts, and the worship in the Temple was once more practiced. Judas Maccabeus ordered that each year the day of dedication of the altar should be celebrated for eight days, beginning with the 25th Chislev (1 Mac. 4:36-59; 2 Mac. 10:1-8). The Feast of the Dedication was still celebrated at the time of Jesus (Jn. 10:22). Flavius Josephus (1st century A.D.) calls it the Feast of Lights, referring to the custom of lighting lamps and putting them on the doors of the houses of the city. A characteristic custom of the feast was the procession with palms and tree branches to the Temple where hymns were sung (Ps. 30 and Pss. 113-118; *see* Ps. 118:27). There sacrifices were offered. The Bible does not give many details on how the feast was celebrated. In 2 Mac. 1:9; 10:6 it is said to be celebrated like the Feast of Tents, but perhaps the similarity is limited to the joy of the feast and its eight-day duration.

dedication
celebrated the *d.* of his house — Ezra 6:16
the feast of the *D.* — Jn. 10:22

deep
God cast a *d.* sleep on the man — Gen. 2:21
How very *d.* are your thoughts — Ps. 92:6

deer
as they do the gazelle or the *d.* — Deut 12:15
red *d.*, the gazelle, the roe *d.* — Deut. 14:5

defeated
came down and *d.* them — Num. 14:45
we *d.* him and his sons — Deut. 2:33
who *d.* them and occupied — Jgs. 11:21
which was *d.* at Carchemish — Jer. 46:2

defiled
Shechem had *d.* his daughter — Gen. 34:5
their sister Dinah had been *d.* — Gen. 34:13
they have *d.* your holy temple — Ps. 79:1
You entered and *d.* my land — Jer. 2:7
I am not *d.* — Jer. 2:23
Israel is *d.* — Hos. 5:3

Degrees, Songs of, *See* PSALMS.

Delaiah (del-ai′-ah), Personal name: (1 Chron. 24:18; Ezra 2:60; Neh. 6:10; 7:62; Jer. 36:12).

delicate
most refined and *d.* woman — Deut. 28:56
dainty and *d.* — Isa. 47:1
O lovely and *d.* daughter — Jer. 6:2

delight, delights

Your commands are my *d.*   I found *d.* in the sons of men
Ps. 119:143   Prov. 8:31
and I was his *d.* day by day   my love, my *d.*   S. of S. 7:7
Prov. 8:30

Delilah, A woman of Sorek, with whom Samson fell in love. She was then used by the Philistines to discover the secret of the extraordinary strength of Samson in order to nullify it (Jgs. 16:4-21).

deliver

will *d.* up to you   Deut. 7:16   *d.* him into the king's grasp
and will *d* them   Jgs. 4:7   1 Sam. 23:20
bind you and *d.* you over   but *d.* us from the evil one
Jgs. 15:13   Matt. 6:13

delivered

I have *d.* him into your hand   Lord, our God, *d.* into our hands
Deut. 3:2   Deut. 3:3

Delos, An island of the Aegean Sea (1 Mac. 15:23).

Deluge, *See* FLOOD.

Demas (dee′-mas), 1. A collaborator of Paul (Philem. 24; Col. 4:14) who later abandoned him "for love of this world" (2 Tim. 4:10).

2. In the apocryphal works of the New Testament the name of the good thief to whom paradise was promised in Luke 23:43. He is also called Dysmas, and his companion, Gestas.

Demetrius (di-mee′-tre-us), 1. Demetrius I Soter, Seleucid king of Syria (162-150 B.C.), son of Seleucus IV Philopator (181-175 B.C.). At the death of his father he was sent as hostage to Rome, but upon hearing the news of the death of his uncle Antiochus IV Epiphanes (175-164 B.C.) he fled. He succeeded in killing off the young Antiochus V Eupator, son and successor of Antiochus IV, and his general Lysias, and so acquired for himself the Seleucid throne (1 Mac. 7:1-49). Alcimus, head of the philo-Hellenistic Jews, accused Judas Maccabeus to Demetrius. The king sent an army under Bacchides to carry out a punitive and intimidating campaign against the Jews and to install Alcimus as high priest (1 Mac. 7:5-20). Alcimus however was defeated by the superior Maccabean force, and once more asked Demetrius for help. He sent another army under Nicanor, who however was defeated and killed in a battle with Judas Maccabeus (1 Mac. 7:21-50). On hearing the news of Nicanor's defeat Demetrius once more sent Bacchides, who prevailed on the numerically inferior army that opposed him, and in this battle Judas Maccabeus lost his life (1 Mac. 9:1-31). A pretender to the throne of Demetrius arose in the person of Alexander Balas. Jonathan Maccabeus, who succeeded his brother as head of the revolt, took the latter's part. Alexander then nominated Jonathan as high priest. Backed by the Jews, Alexander entered into war against Demetrius, who was defeated and killed in battle (1 Mac. 10:1-50).

2. Demetrius II Nicator, Seleucid king of Syria (142-139 B.C.), son of Demetrius I. With the help of Ptolemy VI king of Egypt (181-145 B.C.), Demetrius II succeeded in recovering the throne which Alexander Balas had usurped (1 Mac. 11:1-13). Demetrius did not keep the promises he had made to Jonathan Maccabeus (1 Mac. 11:38-52), so he went over to the side of his rival, Antiochus VI, who was counting on the support of Tryphon (1 Mac. 11:57-62). Tryphon however wanted the throne for

himself, and so decided· to get rid of Antiochus' most dangerous ally, Jonathan Maccabeus, who was treacherously killed in Ptolemais (1 Mac. 12:39-53). Simon Maccabeus succeeded his ·brother, taking the part of Demetrius II from whom he obtained the freedom of Judea (1 Mac. 13:31-53). Demetrius II was made prisoner by Arsaces, king of the Parthians, Tryphon's ally (1 Mac. 14:1-3). He rewon his freedom and the throne in 129 B.C., but after a brief reign (129-125 B.C.), he died in a battle against a rival supported by Ptolemy VII Phiscon (145-116 B.C.).

3. A Christian praised in 3 John 12.

4. A silversmith at Ephesus who manufactured silver miniatures of the temple of Diana of the Ephesians. Moved with zeal for the worship of the goddess, and by fear lest his market suffer, he fomented a riot against Paul and his companions. As a consequence Paul had to interrupt his preaching at Ephesus and depart for Macedonia (Acts 19:24-20:1).

demolish

and *d.* all their high places	we *d.* sophistries	2 Cor. 10:4
Num. 33:52		

Demon, Demonology, Demonology is an attempt at a partial explanation of the problem of evil, which demands the existence of a special category of superhuman beings who are evil and hostile to men, and equipped with powers not given to men. With these powers they are responsible for the physical and moral calamities that befall the world of man. Demonology is late in the biblical tradition, and in the general outlines in which it was assumed by Christian tradition, it went back no further than the Exile. It established itself chiefly in the intertestamentary period, as is attested to by the apocryphal works of the Old Testament. In the older books the mention of demons is very rare, and it is always a question of marginal elements that are not original but taken from other eastern religious traditions, especially those of Mesopotamia and Canaan. Even though they lived in a cultural environment that was saturated with demonological beliefs, speculations and practices, the Israelites refused to accept this exotic world or to make it their own—at least in so far as official orthodoxy was concerned. This held even when Israel found it difficult to offer a good explanation of evil. The reason for this refusal was the characteristic intolerance of the God of Israel, expressed in the first precept of the decalogue, with its consequent prohibition of magical practices. This allowed no room for a being or category of beings who might be responsible for evil if they were to exist alongside God and independent of him. This is why, even when Israel acquired a more consistent demonology, she was careful to avoid every suspicion of dualism, always placing the personal sin of these beings at the beginnings of their actual condition.

Among the demons of which the most ancient texts speak are: the **se'irim**, literally, the 'hairy ones,' who inhabit the desolate cities (Isa. 13:21; 34:14). Leviticus 17:7 prohibits offering sacrifices to the **se'irim**. This should probably be understood as a prohibition to sacrifice to foreign gods, according to the identification that was to develop in later Jewish tradition (in 2 Chron. 11:15 the golden calves erected by Jeroboam in Bethel and Dan are put on the same level as the **se'irim**). Next come the **sedim**: Deuteronomy 32:17 and Psalm 106:37 speak of sacrifices offered to these demons, but these texts are probably to be understood in the sense given above. The **lilith** is a female demon also known from Akkadic texts (Isa. 34:14). The **ceseph** is the Canaanite god of plagues (Deut. 32:24; Ps. 76:3; Ps. 78:48). She appears in Habakkuk 3:5 with **deber** ("pestilence") personified. In Psalm 91:5 other demons appear as personifications of the effects they produce.

The most original contribution of Israel in this field was the figure Satan, who originally belongs to another level of considerations (*see* SATAN). In the Old Testament some other demons are also called by name: Asmodeus, in the story of Tobit (Tob. 3:8; *see* ASMODEUS), Azazel (Lev. 16:8, 26; *see* AZAZEL). In the intertestamentary period demonology attracted the attention of the apocalyptic circles. This interest was facilitated by the flow of the Iranian and Hellenistic religions, which partially inherited Mesopotamian demonology. Just as in the case of the world of angels, so too the sphere of demons is described in detail and different attempts are made to organize its members with an accurate distribution of tasks which include, among other things, causing calamities and disasters, provoking diseases and seducing men from the sphere of good and the service of God. Despite this influence of Iranian dualism, Israel gave her own historical explanation to the evil of these beings, whom she saw as angels fallen from God's friendship. To this purpose Israel exploited some biblical texts which seemed to insinuate just such a partial corruption of the angelic court: Genesis 6:1-5 was to become the favorite text, to which later was added Isaiah 14:4-20, which is, however, in reality an oracle against Babylonia.

It is this world of concepts, which by now had reached a higher level of spirituality, that lies at the base of New Testament demonology. Besides Satan (and Beelzebub, the "prince of demons," Mk. 3:22, *see* BAALZEBUB, SATAN), the gospel tradition speaks of spirits, unclean spirits, evil ones, who can take possession of man (Mk. 1:23-26; 5:2-13; 9:17-29 and parallel texts; Matt. 4:24; 8:16; 9:32; Lk. 4:33; 7:21; Acts 5:16; 8:7; 16:16-18) and animals (*see* Mk. 5:12). To their action are attributed many diseases which afflict men (Lk. 13:11; Mk. 9:17-29; Matt. 12:22). The exorcisms worked by Jesus as the signs of the actual presence of the eschatological kingdom of God in his person and work show that the last hours of the reign of Satan are here and that his reign has been shattered and his power stripped from him with the arrival of the stronger one (Mk. 3:27 and parallels: Lk. 10:17; Matt. 12:28; Lk. 11:20).

St. Paul often presents the saving event of the death and resurrection of Jesus with a cosmic apparatus that also includes the heavenly beings. These are recalled with the names of some of their categories and orders, such as principalities, powers, thrones, dominations and so on. They occupy an ambiguous position however. They are clearly hostile to Christ and to Christians in Romans 8:38 and Ephesians 1:21, 3:10, 6:12. They are the princes of darkness against whom Christians have to fight. In Colossians 2:15 Christ by his death is said to have taken away their power. In Philippians 2:10, 1 Corinthians 2:6-8 they appear in a less negative light. They are created in Christ (Col. 1:16), they have Christ as head (Col. 2:10). This ambiguity is more evident in Ephesians and Colossians and is explained by the errors in those churches which Paul is opposing. For the authority and influence of these beings was being so exalted as to call into question Christ's own primacy. So Paul set about putting into clear light the absolute primacy of Christ (Col.) and ended up by emphasizing the negative character of these rivals (Eph.).

Under the guise of this complex demonology with its different mythical, folkloristic elements and its prescientific explanations for natural phenomena and diseases, the conviction is expressed that a personified evil has somehow been introduced into God's good creation. The gospel story itself cannot be explained without this transcendental dimension. If on the one hand we must strip this doctrine of its bizarre elements and proceed with a sobriety unknown in the past, on the other it cannot be denied that at the origin of this doctrine is a valid insight that Christian tradition has taken seriously.

Demophon (dem′-o-fon), A Seleucid governor of a district of Palestine in Maccabean times (2 Mac. 12:2).

Demythologizing, Demythologizing is the programmatic motto of a modern direction in biblical theology inaugurated by the German exegete Rudolf Bultmann. Bultmann poses to himself a problem of extreme actuality: how can we render the Christian message in a way that makes it intelligible to the man of today? According to Bultmann the New Testament presents the Christian message wrapped up in a mythical language which makes it incomprehensible and unacceptable to the man of today. This mythical language essentially consists in the fact that the divine intervention in the world appears as a reality or a visible and verifiable action in the world and in history before it encounters the believer. "The myth," writes Bultmann, "objectifies what is beyond and brings it into this world to put it at our disposal." If then the Christian message is to keep its value it must be demythologized. This demythologizing process is not an attempt at modernizing the Christian faith at any cost, which would be absurd. Demythologizing only has meaning in so far as it responds to the true and deep meaning of the myth. In fact "the true meaning of the myth is not to give an objective image of the universe. What is expressed in the myth is rather the way in which man understands himself in the world." The myth then should not be understood as a picture of the universe but as the vehicle of a certain understanding of man. The myth should be interpreted from the anthropological, or better still, from the existential point of view. At this point Bultmann turns to the existentialist philosophy of Heidegger to make his own the philosophy of human existence elaborated by this philosopher.

We cannot here expound the results that Bultmann gets from his application of demythologizing to the New Testament. Suffice it to say that for him the historical Jesus (*see* JESUS CHRIST) is cut off from the interests of the faith, which is exclusively concerned with the announcement of the death and resurrection of Christ. Neither however are these two events to be interpreted as objective saving events, that is, as a death that really occurred for our sins (even though it is historically verifiable that Jesus died on the cross) and as a return of Jesus to life. This would be to regress to an objectifying vision of God's action. Bultmann holds that all discussion of a history of salvation is absurd (*see* SALVATION HISTORY).

Bultmann's program arises from a real problem in Christanity today, but it is unacceptable to a great part of Protestant theology and to Catholic theology. It is true that the New Testament contains and uses the representations and ideas of the time, and that today these have no meaning for us but must be reinterpreted so as to discover and retain that which the authors wished to express. Bultmann however carries his demythologizing to such limits that the Christian message comes out of it radically changed. Once all links with the historical Jesus have been snapped, and the whole importance of the message reduced to the death and resurrection, the Christian message becomes more or less an existential ideology, and no longer a meeting in faith with the person Jesus Christ. Thus Christ passes from being the true center of the message to becoming a mere occasion for the word of preaching.

Denarius (de-nar′-i-us), A Roman coin of 3.8 grams of silver. It was the laborer's daily wage (Matt. 20:1-16).

dens

and remain quietly in their *d*.   While they crouch in their *d*.
     Job 37:8   Job 38:40
    crouch in their *d*.   Ps. 104:22

depth, depths

or walked about in the *d*.   because the soil had no *d*. Mk. 4:5
     Job 38:16   neither height nor *d*. nor
in the *d*. of the sea   Matt. 18:6   Rom. 8:39

Derbe (der′-be), A city in Lycaonia in Asia Minor, which from 25 B.C. belonged to the Roman province of Galatia. It was the native place of Gaius, a companion of Paul on his journey from Macedonia to Asia Minor (Acts 20:4). The city was visited by Paul on his first and second apostolic journeys (Acts 14:6, 20; 16:1).

Descent into Hell, This article of the Apostle's Creed cannot be found literally applied to Christ in the New Testament. The language is nevertheless biblical, and the truth depends in its elements on the New Testament message. Descent into 'hell' is the equivalent of death, for in this phrase 'hell' should not be taken in the sense of later theology as the place of torment for the damned, but in the neutral sense of the habitation of the dead, like Sheol of the Old Testament. The primary sense of the term is then that Christ really died, as in Acts 2:24-31, where Psalm 16:10 is given a christological interpretation. The theme of 'descent' is sometimes referred to the incarnation (Eph. 4:8-10, which cites Ps. 68:19 according to the Targum), at others to death, that is, to descent to the dwelling-place of the dead which preceded the triumph of the resurrection (Rom. 10:6, quoting Deut. 30:2). In the Jewish-Christian tradition the descent of Christ into Hades has a salvific character, for with it comes the liberation of the just of the Old Testament. Thus they begin to benefit from the fruits of the redemption. The article of the Creed, then, on Christ's descent into hell brings out his saving effect for the whole reach of salvation history which tended towards Christ as its fulfilment.

Despite some similarities in vocabulary, the obscure text of 1 Peter 3:19, 20 should not be understood in this sense. This text records the journey of Enoch to Hades to announce the final judgment to the fallen angels (Gen. 6:1-5). This is told in the apocryphal work of 1 Enoch 12. The point is to underline how Jesus, even though he died and descended into hell, was already death's victor, and so even his descent was but a proclamation of his imminent full victory in the resurrection.

Desert, Not only was the desert for Israel a memory of the past, but a daily spectacle, for the narrow fertile zone was bound from south to east by desert. The horrors of the desert are reflected in the descriptions of the punishments God threatens (Hos. 2:5; Jer. 4:26) and especially in the curses of the Covenant (Deut. 28:23, 24). These horrors can be appreciated in contrast by reading the exaggerated praises for the land of Palestine, despite its very modest water resources (*see* PALESTINE; Deut. 8:7-10).

The time spent by Israel in the desert remained in memory as the formative period of her history. It was the time when the people were proved (Deut. 8:2-6), and when God was sorely tried (Ex. 17:1-7; Num. 20:1-11; Acts 7:11; 1 Cor. 10:5; Heb. 3:8). It was above all, however, the time during which Israel was able to experience the continual providence of God for his people (Deut. 11:5) while at the same time answering with fidelity to the voice of God (Jer. 2:2, 3). Hosea presents the future conversion of Israel as a return to that ideal period when a mystical marriage took place between the Lord and his people (Hos. 2:16-22).

desert
Who made the world a *d.*
Isa. 14:17
from Sela across the *d.* Isa. 16:1
and scattered over the *d.* Isa. 16:8

will the *d.* become an orchard
Isa. 32:15
Then Jesus was led into the *d.*
Matt. 4:1
sent him out toward the *d.* Mk. 1:12

desire
So shall the king *d.* your beauty
Ps. 45:12
The *d.* of the wicked shall perish
Ps. 112:10

name and your title are the *d.*
Isa. 26:8
I continue to cherish the *d.*
Rom. 15:23

desolate
enrich the waste and *d.* ground
Job. 38:27

Let their encampment become *d.*
Ps. 69:26
the city sits *d.* on the ground Isa. 3:26

despair
owes kindness to one in *d.*
Job 6:14

laughs at the *d.* of the innocent
Job 9:23
full of doubts, we never *d.* 2 Cor. 4:8

despise
I *d.* my life Job 9:21
should the wicked man *d.* God
Ps. 10:13

wisdom and instruction fools *d.*
Prov. 1:7
Men *d.* not the thief Prov. 6:30
and *d.* the other Matt. 6:24

destroy
Will you *d.* the whole city
Gen. 18:28
We are about to *d.* this place
Gen. 19:13

And he *d.* you from the face of
Deut. 6:15
but all the wicked he will *d.*
Ps. 145:20

detail
God's new way in greater *d.*
Acts 18:26

determine, determined
This made the disciples *d.*
Acts 11:29

No, I *d.* that while I was
1 Cor. 2:2

Deuterocanonical, Inspired and canonical books about whose acceptance into the canon of sacred books some doubts were entertained for a time, and in certain regions of the ancient Church. The Church accepts both the proto- and the deuterocanonical works with the "same reverence and piety." The distinction then has nothing to do with the grace of inspiration, but merely recalls the vicissitudes of the books' final, full and universal acceptance into the canon on the part of the Church. The deuterocanonical books of the Old Testament are not admitted by the Jews or the non-Catholic churches into their canons. These are: the book of Baruch (with the letter of Jeremiah), Tobit, Judith, 1 and 2 Maccabees, Wisdom (Ecclesiasticus). To these are added some fragments preserved only in the Septuagint, but considered canonical by the Catholic Church: Esther 10:4-16, 24; Daniel 3:24-90; 13:1-14:42. The deuterocanonical books of the New Testament are: Hebrews, James, 2 Peter, 2-3 John, and Revelation. The so-called deuterocanonical fragments, at times held in doubt because of their absence from some mss., are Mark 16:9-20, Luke 22:43, 44 and John 7:53-8:11.

Deuteronomy, The fifth book of the Pentateuch. The title is given it in the

Greek translation of the Septuagint (Deut. 17:18) where it is interpreted as 'second law,' that is, the law given by Moses to complete that promulgated on Sinai. In the place cited, however, it only means a second copy of the same law, promulgated in Deuteronomy.

Deuteronomy is a peculiar book in the Pentateuch. It is presented in the form of a long discourse given by Moses on the plains of Moab (Deut. 1:1-5), just as the Israelites were about to pass over the Jordan to occupy the land of Canaan. Into the discourse, and forming a good part of it, there is a long series of laws (Deut. 12-26; besides, in Deut. 5 there is a repetition of the Decalogue of Ex. 20). Then follow instructions given by Moses on the way in which the Covenant is to be renewed at Shechem (Deut. 27), a long list of blessings and maledictions (Deut. 28) and a final exhortation (Deut. 29-30). The book closes with the canticle of Moses (Deut. 31-32), the blessings pronounced by Moses on the tribes (Deut. 33) and the account of Moses' death on Mount Nebo (Deut. 34).

No modern reader could be deceived by the literary fiction adopted by the author. It is obvious that it is not Moses that speaks. The code of laws, for example, reflects the economic, social and family conditions of a society that has been sedentary for a long time, with centrally constituted authority. In other words, what is here mirrored is a community much more developed than that which appears in Ex. 21-23, the "Book of the Covenant." *See* LAW. The literary fiction however is legitimate, seeing that the author wished to take up and make live the Mosaic patrimony in view of new and changed circumstances. Like the other sources of the Pentateuch then (*see* PENTATEUCH), Deuteronomy is the final result of a long process of rethinking and adaptation of Israelite traditions, especially those to do with the Covenant. Its peculiar literary form saved it from the fate of the other sources, Priestly, Elohistic and Yahwistic, and it has come down as a coherent and integral whole.

Behind the present Deuteronomy, then, lies a long tradition, which is ordinarily sought after in the Levitical circles of the northern kingdom. The rhetorical and paraenetic style of the discourse and also that of the laws is an echo of the practice of preaching on the law, the election and the Covenant, which can be situated in the sanctuaries of Israel. Deuteronomy uses a few essential themes with infinite variations on them, and is the clearest exponent of the theology of the Sinai Covenant as this has been set out in the article on the Covenant (*see* COVENANT).

The book of Deuteronomy had different editions. The first ordering of its content took place in the northern kingdom before 722 B.C. After the ruin of Samaria, it emigrated to Judah and there seems to have inspired the reforming efforts of King Hezekiah (715-687 B.C.). Later it was lost, then rediscovered in the Temple during the repairs ordered by King Josiah (622 B.C.; *see* 2 Kgs. 22:3-20). Then it became the **charta magna** of the religious reform of Josiah (2 Kgs. 23:1-27) and furnished some of the central themes for the prophecy of Jeremiah. During the exile it received its definitive redaction and served as an introduction to the long historical work which reaches from Joshua to 2 Kings and which was elaborated by a school of thought that took its inspiration from the central themes of Deuteronomy. Later it was definitively detached from this synthesis and with the addition of the final chapters, from 31:14 on, was put together with the other Mosaic traditions to form the Pentateuch.

Devil, *See* SATAN.

devil

to be tempted by the *d*.	Matt. 4:1	father you spring from is the *d*.
he was tempted by the *d*.	Lk. 4:2	Jn. 8:44

devour, devours

locusts will *d*. the crop Deut. 28:39 each *d*. the flesh of his neighbor
strangers *d*.   Isa. 1:7   Isa. 9:18

Dew, Moisture deposited from the air, especially during the cool of the
night. It appears as tiny droplets on flowers, grass, and surfaces generally
in the morning. It is particularly intense in Palestine during the summer
on account of the sudden drop in night temperature after the heat of the
day. In some places it is the only source of moisture for the arid fields.

dew

the *d*. of the heavens   Gen. 27:28 neither *d*. nor rain upon you
far from the *d*. of the heavens   2 Sam. 1:21
                           Gen. 27:39 who has begotten the drops of *d*.
In the morning a *d*. lay all about   Job 38:28
                           Ex. 16:13 like a cloud of *d*.   Isa. 18:4
when the *d*. fell upon the camp   For your *d*. is a *d*. of light
                           Num. 11:9   Isa. 26:19

Diadem, A turban-like crown to denote royalty in Old Testament times.
The Greeks called it a **diadema** (*see* 2 Sam. 1:10; 12:30; Job 29:14; S. of S.
3:11). In the restored Israel, according to Isaiah 62:3, Jerusalem was to be
a crown of splendor in the hand of the Lord, a princely diadem in the
hand of God. The dragon in the Revelation vision of the woman clothed
with the sun had a diadem on each of its seven heads (Rev. 12:3). The
beast had one on each of its ten horns (13:1). The rider on the white horse
in the battle at the end had on his head many diadems, being king of kings
(19:12).

Diana, *See* ARTEMIS.

Diaspora (dy-as′-po-ra), A Greek word meaning dispersion, and used to
designate the Jewish communities who had settled outside Palestine (Jn.
7:35; 1 Pet. 1:1; James 1:1). The first emigrations of Jews from Palestine
were the result of the mass deportation ordered by Sargon king of Assyria
in 722 B.C. when he conquered Samaria. Nebuchadnezzar conquered
Jerusalem in 587 B.C. and again deported large segments of the population. Those deported from Samaria did not succeed in preserving their
identity, and there remain no traces of them in history. The Jews who
were deported by Nebuchadnezzar, on the other hand, were the future
restorers of the religious life and traditions in Judea under the Persians
(*see* EXILE). Not all Jews returned home. Many who remained on in Babylonia established flourishing communities which endured until the Arab
conquest in the seventh century A.D.

There were Jewish colonies in Egypt at least since the sixth century, but
the founding of Jewish communities throughout the eastern Mediterranean world and on to Rome began in the Hellenistic age (2 Mac.
13:23). Although spiritually bound to the Holy City and to the land of
Palestine, these communities gave a more liberal tone to their religious
views and put into motion an intense proselytic effort (*see* PROSELYTE).
For the most part the uses and customs of these communities were recognized by the authorities of the various places, and so they constituted a
kind of city within the city. Their religious exclusiveness together with
their commercial ability and their agility in attracting the favor of the
powerful often made them the objects of anger and envy, with the result
that they suffered frequent expulsions and confiscations, which however
were ably manipulated and thus mitigated by the Jews themselves.

The spread of Judaism throughout the Mediterranean world was one of the circumstances which most helped the preaching of Christianity. as is illustrated by the apostolic methods of St. Paul (*see* PAUL).

Diatessaron (dy-a-tess´-a-ron), A harmony of the four gospels, forming a single continuous account, composed by Tatian the Syrian around 170 A.D.

Diblaim (dib´-la-im), Father of Gomer, wife of the prophet Hosea (Hos. 1:3).

Dibon, A city of Moab north of the river Arnon, today Dhiban. It was occupied first by Sihon, an Ammonite king, and later conquered by the Israelites (Num. 21:23-30). It was assigned to the tribe of Gad (Num. 32:3, 34; 33:45) and perhaps for some time belonged to the territory of Reuben (Josh. 13:17). Dibon makes another appearance, as a Moabite city, in the oracles of Isaiah and Jeremiah against Moab (Isa. 15:1-9; Jer. 48:18, 22).

Didrachma (dy-drac´-ma), A Greek coin, valued at two drachmas. This was the amount every Israelite was bound to pay yearly as a tax to the Temple (Matt. 17:24).

Didymus (did´-a-mus), In Greek, this means twin, and is the Greek name for the apostle Thomas (Jn. 11:16; 20:24; 21:2).

die

also might *d.* like his brothers	When will he *d.*	Ps. 41:6
Gen. 38:11	will *d.* from lack of discipline	Prov. 5:23
he will *d.* as soon as he sees		
Gen. 44:31	for a man to eat and never *d.*	
he shall *d.*	1 Kgs. 1:52	Jn. 6:50

different

with others of a *d.* species	shall you keep two *d.* measures	
Lev. 19:19		Deut. 25:14
two *d.* kinds of seed	Lev. 19:19	in your harlotry you were *d.*
of two *d.* kinds of thread		Ezek. 16:34
Deut. 22:11		

difficulty

with *d.* will a rich man enter	Again with *d.* we moved along
Matt. 19:23	Acts 27:8

Diklah, An Arabian people or region listed among the sons of Shem in the Table of Nations (Gen. 10:27; 1 Chron. 1:21).

diminish

The waters continued to *d.* until
Gen. 8:5

Dinah, Daughter of Jacob and Leah (Gen. 30:21; 46:15). According to Genesis 34, Dinah was kidnapped by Shechem, son of Hamor, a Hurrian of the city of Shechem. Hamor proposed that Jacob should consent to the marriage between Shechem and Dinah, thus establishing friendly relationships between the two people. Jacob consented on condition that they should accept circumcision. While the men of Shechem were still suffering from the effects of the operation, Simeon and Levi killed them to vindicate the honor of Dinah. This story presents in terms of a family conflict what was probably an abortive attempt on the part of the tribes of Simeon and Levi to establish themselves in the center of Palestine.

Dinhabah (din´-ha-bah), A city of Edom, with Bela, son of Beor its king (Gen. 36:32).

Dionysius (dy'-a-nish'-yus), 1. The Greek god of wine and patron of the dramatic arts, equivalent to the Roman Bacchus. Antiochus IV Epiphanes in his efforts to impose Greek culture on the cities of Judea obliged the people to take part, myrtle-browed, in the procession to honor the god (2 Mac. 6:7), and Nicanor, the general of Demetrius I threatened to destroy the temple at Jerusalem and to erect in its place a temple to Bacchus (2 Mac. 14:33).

2. An Athenian, a member of the Areopagus, who converted to Christianity when he heard Paul's teaching (Acts 17:34). According to one tradition he was the first bishop of the city, and various theological tracts of unknown authorship circulated under his name in the fourth and fifth centuries.

Dioscorinthius (dy'-os-co-rinth'-i-us), The first month of the Macedonian calendar corresponding to November/December (2 Mac. 11:21).

Diotrephes (dy-ot'-re-feez), A Christian who was severely rebuked for his ambition in 3 John 9, 10.

dirt
and *d.* shall you eat   Gen. 3:14   are *d.*, and to *d.* you shall return
Gen. 3:19

Disciple, Though disciples of Jesus are mentioned in both the gospels and the Acts of the Apostles, the meaning is different. In the Acts practically all the faithful are called the disciples of Jesus (*see* Acts 6:1, 2; 9:1, 19, 26; 13:52, etc.). In the gospels the disciples are those who "follow Jesus," a phrase which suggests a constant following of the Lord, a sharing in his lot and condition of life. These followers of Jesus are called disciples and Jesus is their Master or Rabbi, undoubtedly because of an analogy between Jesus and his disciples and that of the masters of the law and their disciples (*see* Matt. 22:16; Mk. 2:18; Lk. 5:33). The analogy was only external however, for there were deep differences in the substance of the relationship. On the one hand, although Jesus was called Rabbi, he was not a Rabbi. He had followed no ordinary course of instruction, had been a disciple to no Rabbi, and did not have, nor did he ask for, permission to teach from anybody (Matt. 13:54; Jn. 7:15). Even as he discussed the law and its interpretation, he did it in a way unheard of among the Rabbis who were his contemporaries (*see* Matt. 7:29; Mk. 1:22). In the same way, the analogies of Jesus with his disciples and those of other Rabbis should not gloss over the profound differences that distinguish the two: the initiative to become a disciple did not depend on the disciple but on Jesus who calls with authority those whom he wishes (*see* Matt. 4:18-22; Mk. 1:16-20; Lk. 5:1-11). Secondly, the purpose of the disciple was not to acquire an intellectual or moral formation: what makes a person a disciple is faith in the saving mission of Jesus. One is not, then, a disciple during the time of training and later a Rabbi. One is a disciple for ever, for the condition of disciple is complete in itself, summed up in surrender to the Person of Jesus who is the founder of the kingdom. Finally Jesus demands from the disciple a complete and radical dedication to the kingdom such as no Rabbi would ever dream of asking from a disciple (*see* Matt. 9:13 ff.; Lk. 9:57-60; Matt. 10:37; Lk. 14:26). From the circle of his disciples Jesus chose twelve, "those whom he wished," to send them to preach. (*See* Matt. 10; Mk. 6:7, 8; Lk. 9:1-6; *see* APOSTLE; TWELVE, THE.) It is not always clear to whom the evangelists are referring when they mention the disciples. The difficulty arises from the fact that the description given of the disciple, especially of the individual vocation, would seem to limit the number to modest proportions, while often the evangelists speak of a "multitude of disciples." A solution to this problem is perhaps to be found in the fact that these and similar usages are written into the introductions to frame some of the episodes or discourses of Jesus. It is probable, then, that the evangelists had in mind the meaning that "disciple" had in the apostolic church, and should in these cases be taken in the generic sense of the term of a person sympathetic to Jesus. Elsewhere however the name of disciple seems to be reserved only to the Twelve (*see* Mk. 6:35; Matt. 13:10; 14:15; Lk. 8:9). There is then in the gospels a fluctuating terminology in which the semantic evolution of the term "disciple" can be seen at work.

discipline

let you hear his voice to *d*. you
Deut. 4:36

He will die from lack of *d*.
Prov. 5:23

the reproofs of *d*.
Prov. 6:23

your trials as the *d*. of God
Heb. 12:7

If you do not know the *d*. of sons
Heb. 12:8

all *d*. seems a cause of grief
Heb. 12:11

disease

Asa contracted a serious *d*.
2 Chron. 16:12

with an incurable *d*.
2 Chron. 21:18

from a *d*. in your bowels
2 Chron. 21:15

disgrace

that would be a *d*. for us
Gen. 34:14

All the day my *d*. is before me
Ps. 44:16

Dispersion, *See* DIASPORA.

displaying

but rather in *d*. what he thinks
Prov. 18:2

dissembling

the Jews joined in his *d*.   Gal. 2:13

distinction

He made no *d*. between them
Acts 15:9

distinguish, distinguishes

the Lord *d*. between the Egyptians
Ex. 11:7

you may *d*. between the clean
Lev. 11:47

distributed

He *d*. the offerings made
2 Chron. 31:14

distribution

It was their duty to make the *d*.
Neh. 13:13

Divination, The practice of divination (predicting future events) was severely prohibited by the Mosaic law. In Deuteronomy 18:9 some practices of divination are recalled, and these are qualified as "abominations." These practices, the account goes on to say, belong to the peoples with whom Israel lives. God however had given to his people a legitimate means of communication with God, that is, the prophet, the heir to the office which Moses himself had on Sinai as intermediary of the revelation (Deut. 18:13-22). In Leviticus 19:31 the practice of divination is punishable by death. History however shows that such punishments were to no avail. In the account of Josiah's religious reforms, the extirpation of magicians and soothsayers is recorded (2 Kgs. 23:24). Saul is accused of having had recourse to soothsayers (1 Sam. 28:7) as did Manasseh (2 Kgs. 21:6; *see* also 2 Kgs. 17:17).

division, divisions

all that pertained to the *d.*	to spread, not peace, but *d.*
1 Chron. 27:1	Matt. 10:34
according to the *d.* 2 Chron. 35:5	

Divorce, According to Deuteronomy 24:1: "When a man, after marrying a woman and having relations with her, is later displeased with her because he finds in her something indecent," then he could repudiate her by handing her a bill of divorce. Once the repudiated woman marries another man, and later becomes free again, she cannot return to the first husband (Deut. 24:2-4). The husband who falsely accuses his wife of not being a virgin at the time of marriage loses the right to repudiate her (Deut. 22:13-19), as does the man who is forced to marry a woman because he has violated her (Deut. 22:28-29).

The vague expression "something indecent" (Deut. 24:1) was given different interpretations by the rabbis at the time of Jesus. Some proposed a rigid interpretation which limited the faculty to divorce to cases in which the woman was found guilty of adultery. Others were more liberal and allowed divorce for any reason whatsoever. This dispute was the background to the question placed by the Pharisees to Jesus in Matthew 19:3. Jesus, however, undercuts their question and reaches back to the original design of God for marriage, expressed in Genesis 2:24: What God has united, man must not separate. For that reason, "whoever divorces his wife and marries another commits adultery against her" (Mk. 10:1-12; Lk. 16:18; 1 Cor. 7:10-11). This absolute prohibition of divorce seems at first to be mitigated by the clause in Matthew 19:9 and 5:32, which is however unknown to all the other testimony on this word of Jesus.

This would seem to suggest that the clause ("lewd conduct is a separate case") was introduced to clarify the doctrine of Jesus in the face of difficulties or problems of the Christian communities to which the gospel was addressed. It is not however easy to determine what precisely that problem was or how that clause clarified it. The most probable opinion, it would seem, is the following: Matthew 19:9 and 5:32 do not speak of "adultery" but of "lewd conduct," that is, of sexual intercourse not permitted by the law. The Greek word for fornication, **porneia** is probably the translation of the Aramaic **zenut,** a term used by the rabbinic casuists to denote invalid marriages, that is, contracted with the impediments listed by Leviticus. Matthew 19:9 and 5:32 would then explicitly include these invalid marriages, without however making any exception to the indissolubility of valid marriages.

Dodanim, *See* RODANIM.

Dodo, Personal name (Jgs. 10:1; 2 Sam. 23:9; 1 Chron. 11:12; 2 Sam. 23:24; 1 Chron. 11:26).

Doeg, An Edomite, chief of Saul's shepherds (1 Sam. 21:8). He was at Nob when Ahimelech received David and gave him the breads of the presence to feed the men who had fled with him from Saul, and the sword that had belonged to Goliath (1 Sam. 21:1-10). Doeg reported this to Saul, who accused Ahimelech of high treason for having given help to the king's enemies. In vain Ahimelech tried to excuse himself with the plea that he was ignorant of the fact that David had fled the king. Saul ordered that Ahimelech and the other priests at Nob be executed. None of his soldiers, however, dared to lay hands on the priests, so Doeg came forward and slaughtered them himself (1 Sam. 22:6-18).

Dog, Not much information of a scientific sort can be garnered on this subject from the Bible. Dogs however are frequently mentioned, generally in a pejorative sense, as returning to their own vomit (Prov. 26:17) or eating what is unclean (Ex. 22:30) and even devouring human flesh (1 Kgs. 14:11). One must not give what is holy to dogs (Matt. 7:6) nor is it good to give the children's food to dogs, though they may have what falls from the table (Matt. 15:26; Mk. 7:27). To emphasize the misery of the poor man Lazarus, Luke tells us that the dogs came to lick his sores (Lk. 16:21). Paul warns the Philippians to keep an eye out for the dogs, i.e. for the evildoers, while Revelation warns that those excluded from life are the dogs and sorcerers and fornicators and murderers and idolaters, etc. Clearly, then, from the metaphorical use of the term, the dog was not held in high esteem by scripture writers.

Dok, The name of the small fortress where Simon Maccabeus, his two sons and some of his servants were treacherously killed during a banquet (1 Mac. 16:15, 16).

dominion

Let them have *d.* over the fish	the entire land under his *d.*
Gen. 1:26	1 Kgs. 9:19
Have *d.* over the fish of the sea	from the *d.* of Satan to God
Gen. 1:28	Acts 26:18

donkey

Both of you stay here with the *d.*
Gen. 22:5

door

the Lord will pass over that *d.*	away from me, and bar the *d.*
Ex. 12:23	2 Sam. 13:17
and there, at the *d.* or doorpost	at my neighbor's *d.* Job 31:9
Ex. 21:6	

Dophkah, A stage of the journey of the Israelites through the desert towards the land of Canaan. It was the first halt after setting out from Sinai (Num. 33:12).

Dor, An ancient city and seaport on the Mediterranean coast south of Mt. Carmel, today known as et-Tanturah. The city's king took part in the Canaanite coalition which opposed the Israelites and was conquered by Joshua (Josh. 11:2; 12:23) even though it seems that the city itself remained a Canaanite possession, (Jgs. 1:27) probably up to the time of the monarchy (1 Kgs. 4:11). It belonged to the territory of Asher but was occupied by the tribe of Manasseh (Josh. 17:11; 1 Chron. 7:29). Tryphon took refuge there, but was besieged by Antioch VII Sidetes, so he fled by sea (1 Mac. 15:11-14).

Dorcas, The Greek name (meaning "gazelle") of Tabitha, a Christian woman at Joppa distinguished for her alms and good works, and miraculously raised to life by Peter (Acts 9:36-42).

Dorymenes (dor-im′-e-neez), The father of Ptolemy Macron, who was one of the three generals sent by Lysias to put an end to the Maccabean revolt (1 Mac. 3:38).

Dositheus (doe-sith′-e-us), 1. A Maccabean captain (2 Mac. 12:19).

2. A powerful horseman (2 Mac. 12:35).

Dothan (doe′-than), A town in central Palestine, south of the plain of Esdraelon and north of Samaria, today called Tell Dotha (Judith 4:6; 7:3). It was in the neighborhood of Dothan that Joseph met his brothers who threw him into a waterless cistern and later sold him to the Ishmaelite merchants who carried him to Egypt (Gen. 37:17). Here too the Aramaeans attempted to take the prophet Elisha prisoner, but he prayed to the Lord to strike them blind, whereupon he led them meekly into the city of Samaria (2 Kgs. 6:8-23).

Douay Version, *See* ENGLISH VERSIONS OF THE BIBLE.

doubt, doubts

No *d.* you are the intelligent folk   full of *d.*   2 Cor. 4:8
    Job 12:2

dough

their *d.* before it was leavened   your first batch of *d.*   Num. 15:21
    Ex. 12:34   the women knead *d.*   Jer. 7:18
Since the *d.* they had brought   has its effect all through the *d.*
    Ex. 12:39   1 Cor. 5:6
a cake of your first batch of *d.*   to make of yourselves fresh *d.*
    Num. 15:20   1 Cor. 5:7

Dove, Any bird of the large *Columbidae* family, in biblical usage. When the dove did not return to the ark Noah deduced that the waters were receding (Gen. 8:8-12). Leviticus 5:7 and 12:8 prescribed as an offering for the first-born male, in poor families, two turtledoves or two young pigeons. This was carried out by Joseph and Mary in the case of Jesus (Lk. 2:22 ff.). The dove on account of its serenity and gentleness served prophet and poet in their metaphors. The beloved was beautiful in the Song of Songs, with dove-like eyes (1:15; 2:10, 14; 4:1; 5:12). After his recovery from illness Hezekiah sang that he was moaning like a dove (Isa. 38:14; *see* 59:11). Hosea however calls Ephraim a silly and senseless dove (Hos. 7:11). In the New Testament the Spirit descended on Jesus in the shape of a dove (Mk. 1:10; Jn. 1:32), and Jesus exhorts his followers to be simple like doves (Matt. 10:16).

Dowry, Goods or property brought by the bride to the marriage. In the ordinary course of events it was given by the father for the marriage and remained the property of the wife. The Old Testament does not contain any legal disposition in regard to dowry, and in the various stories, the details on dowries are scarce and obscure. The slaves given by their fathers to Rebekah (Gen. 24:59), to Rachel and Leah (Gen. 29:24, 29) are interpreted as dowry (*see* also Gen. 31:15). On marrying Solomon, Pharaoh's daughter received in dowry the city of Gezer (1 Kgs. 9:16), and Achsan, the daughter of Caleb received as dowry land with springs of water (Josh. 15:18-19; Jgs. 1:14-15).

Drachma, An ancient Greek silver coin weighing 4.3 gr. (*see* Lk. 15:8-9).

Dream, Among all ancient peoples dreams were considered favorite means that God used to communicate with men. The fact that the dream arose with total spontaneity from man's intimate core, or emerged from the margins of consciousness without force or reflection or meditation made it seem something that came from without, something placed there by Another in one's heart. Both in the Old and the New Testament dreams are used by God or angels to speak to man, guide and warn him (e.g. Gen. 20:3-7; 31:10-13; Job 33:14 ff.; Matt. 1:20). At other times dreams are taken as premonitions of the future (Gen. 37:5; 40; 41; Dan. 2). The Old Testament does not have anything in principle against this mentality: dreams were one of the means to get an answer from God (1 Sam. 28:6). In Numbers 12:6-8 there is a clear distinction between the prophets, to whom God speaks in dreams and visions, and Moses, with whom God spoke face to face. Even Jeremiah, who was implacably opposed to any kind of counterfeit prophecy, did not exclude dreams as a means of revelation, though he was obviously aware of the innumerable abuses and delusions to which dreams exposed one (Jer. 23:25-28; 27:9, 10; 29:9).

dream

came to Abimelech in a *d*.	I had another *d*.	Gen. 37:9
Gen. 20:3	Solomon awoke from his *d*.	
God answered him in a *d*.		1 Kgs. 3:15
Gen. 20:6	Like a *d*. he takes flight	Job 20:8
Once Joseph had a *d*. Gen. 37:5	appeared in a *d*.	Matt. 1:20

drink

and then let the boy *d*. Gen. 21:19	Samaritan and a woman, for a *d*.	
the Almighty let him *d*. Job 21:20		Jn. 4:9
and given them tears to *d*. Ps. 80:6	let him *d*. who believes in me	
Give me a *d*. Jn. 4:7		Jn. 7:38

dromedary, *See* CAMEL.

drunk

he became *d*.	Gen. 9:21	Drink, become *d*., and vomit
Eli, thinking her *d*. 1 Sam. 1:13		Jer. 25:27
	these men are not *d*. Acts 2:15	

Drunkenness, The moderate use of wine is often recommended in the Bible: God gives men bread to make them strong, oil to make them happy, and wine to make them cheerful (*see* Ps. 104:15; Prov. 31:6-7; Jgs. 9:13). Paul recommends that Timothy take a little wine for his stomach (Tim. 5:23). Immoderate use leading to intoxication is severely prohibited; it leads to confusion (Hos. 4:11), to a dulling of the conscience (Isa. 5:11-12; 56:11-12; Amos 6:6) and is also the source of economic and social ruin of families (Prov. 20:1; 23:20-21). The New Testament damns drunkenness as one of the sins that excludes us from eternal life (Rom. 13:13; 1 Cor. 5:11; 6:10; Gal. 5:21). Paul advises Titus and Timothy to select as ministers of the churches people not infected with this vice (Titus 1:7; 1 Tim. 3:3; *see* Lev. 10:8-9). *See* CUP.

Drusilla, Youngest daughter of Agrippa I, king of Judea (41-44 A.D.). She was betrothed to Epiphanes, king of Commagene, but the marriage did not take place because he refused to convert to Judaism. Later Azizus, king of Emesa married her, once he had himself circumcised. She deserted her husband to marry Felix, the Roman procurator of Judea (52-60 A.D.). Drusilla was with Felix when Paul was brought as a prisoner before the Roman governor in Caesarea (Acts 24:24).

dry

so that the *d*. land may appear	and pour it on the *d*. land Ex. 4:9	
Gen. 1:9	offered up *d*. or mixed with oil	
God called the *d*. land Gen. 1:10		Lev. 7:10
Everything on *d*. land Gen. 7:22		

Dumah, 1. An Arabian tribe in the genealogy of Ishmael, son of Abraham and Hagar (Gen. 25:14; 1 Chron. 1:30). The oracle of Isa. 21:11 is directed against Dumah. The Greek translation of the Bible (LXX) reads at this point Edom, and is probably correct.

2. A city of Judah south of Hebron (Josh. 15:52).

dumb

makes another deaf and *d*.	I kept *d*. and silent	Ps. 39:3
Ex. 4:11	the tongue of the *d*. will sing	
like a *d*. man who Ps. 38:14		Isa 35:6

Dung Gate, The gate in the walls of Jerusalem leading to the road to the valley of Hinnom (Neh. 3:13, 14; 12:31).

Dura, A plain in the province of Babylon where, according to Daniel 3:1, Nebuchadnezzar had a golden statue erected to be adored by all the people. The locality is unknown at present, and the attempt to identify it with the city of Dura on the Euphrates, a little over 200 m. north of Babylon, does not fit the text.

dust

and threw *d.* upon their heads		and there is gold in its *d.*	Job 28:6
	Job 2:12	and man would return to the *d.*	
bring me down to *d.* again			Job 34:15
	Job 10:9		

dwelling

shall be your *d.*	Gen. 27:39	the *d.* place of the wicked	
Listen from your heavenly *d.*			Job 21:28
	1 Kgs. 8:30	their *d.* through all generations	
your heavenly *d.* place			Ps. 49:12
	1 Kgs. 8:39, 43, 49		

Dye, Dyeing, A craft in which the peoples of the ancient Near East, including the Hebrews, excelled. Wherever lands and climate were right for sheep and goat herds, and where an ample and regular supply of water was at hand, there weaving and its related trade, dyeing, were likely to flourish. Preeminent among the dye merchants were those of Tyre, the Phoenician city on the Mediterranean north of Mount Carmel. Tyre possessed the secret of the production of the most popular color, purple, the color of kings (*see* Mk. 15:17), which members of the local dyers' guild obtained from the murex mollusc native to the waters of the Tyre-and-Sidon region. Many other colors could be produced from vegetable dyes obtained from plants found in the countryside or available through commerce. Almond leaves provided yellow, pomegranate bark black, red came from the madder plant, blue from various indigo-bearing flowers and weeds. Vegetable coloring brews were mixed with various inorganic solutions, "mordants," that bit into the fibers and were themselves insoluble, or nearly so. Dye vats uncovered at Tell Beit Mirsim (ancient Debir in the highlands of Judah, south of Hebron) show the clear remains of ancient dye vats of an ingenious sort, especially in their retention of the costly dye solutions for reuse. Dyeing was done at the thread stage, not with the fabric. It was a home craft, but there were guilds of dyers for mutual support within the cloth and clothing trade. Colored cloths are specified for the Tabernacle (Ex. 35:6, 23, 25, 35). See also Judges 5:30 and Acts 16:14. Isaiah drew a vivid figure based on the arts of dyeing and bleaching (1:18).

dysentery

with chronic fever and *d.*

                                        Acts 28:8

Dysmas (diz′-mas), The name of the Good Thief crucified with Jesus. The name appears only in late Christian tradition.

E

E, The abbreviation for Elohist, the second source or stratum in the Pentateuch. *See* PENTATEUCH.

each

and placed *e.* half	Gen. 15:10	*e.* of them had six wings	Isa. 6:2
Having greeted *e.* other	Ex. 18:7	to rest on *e.* of them	Acts 2:3

eagle

the *e.*, the vulture   Lev. 11:13   Behold, like an *e.* he soars

that swoops down like an *e.*   Jer. 48:40

               Deut. 28:49   your nest high as the *e.*   Jer. 49:16

ear

the barley was in *e.*   Ex. 9:31   he opens my *e.* that I may hear

my *e.* caught a whisper of it   Isa. 50:4

            Job 4:12   nor his *e.* too dull to hear   Isa. 59:1

          cutting off his *e.*   Matt. 26:51

Earth, Israel's idea of the cosmos, like that of eastern civilization in general, was prescientific, based on data and assessments that were elemental and barely developed into a system, and indeed quite frequently inconsistent with one another. The earth was a disc sustained on columns or solid foundations (Job 9:6; 38:4, 6; Ps. 104:5; Isa. 24:18; 40:21; Prov. 8:29) which were driven into the lower waters (Pss. 24:2; 136:6; Gen. 49:25). Creation, then, was often recounted in two stages: the establishment of the earth and its liberation from the waters that were contained within limits which they were henceforth forbidden to overflow (Pss. 104:5-7; 93; 24:2; Job 26:10; Prov. 8:29). In contrast with heaven, earth designates all the lower universe while heaven is God's dwelling-place (Pss. 104:3; 29:10; Isa. 40:22). The earth is his property (Ps. 24:1) and the footstool of his throne (Isa. 66:1), an expression which extends to the whole earth a function attributed to the ark of the covenant. (*See* ARK OF THE COVENANT.) This contrast between heaven and earth was extended to the order of morality and salvation to express how man who is corruptible and mortal is called to incorruptibility and immortality (1 Cor. 15:45-47; Col. 3:2-5).

earth

the *e.* was a formless wasteland   nor by the *e.* (it is his footstool)

            Gen. 1:2   Matt. 5:35

the *e.* was corrupt and full of   who is of the *e.* is earthly   Jn. 3:31

            Gen. 6:11

Earthquake, Palestine lies in a geologically unstable region and is therefore exposed to frequent shiftings of the earth's crust. Earthquakes then as now were a frequent occurrence. The Old Testament records only one, at the time of King Uzziah of Judah (783-742 *see* Amos 1:1; Zech. 14:5). Other similar events gathered in the Bible are of a different nature. Numbers 16:31 speaks of the earth swallowing up the rebellious Korah, Dathan and Abiron. Matthew 27:54, 28:2 recalls that the earth was shaken at the death and resurrection of Jesus. Acts 16:26 tells of a similar event during the imprisonment of Paul and Silas at Philippi, outside Palestine. Earthquakes are the cosmic accompaniment to visions of Yahweh (Ex. 19:18; Jgs. 5:4; Pss. 18:8; 68:9; Joel 4:16) and of the apocalyptic events of the last days (Isa. 24:18-19; Matt. 24:7; Mk. 13:8; Lk. 21:25-26; Rev. 6:12; 8:5; 11:13; 16:18).

earthquake

the wind there was an *e.*   two years before the *e.*   Amos 1:1

        1 Kgs. 19:11   there was a mighty *e.*   Matt. 28:2

With thunder, *e.*, and great noise

          Isa. 29:6

ease

you go outside to *e.* nature   my couch shall *e.* my complaint

            Deut. 23:14   Job 7:13

Easter, *See* PASSOVER.

Eastern Sea, A name for the Dead Sea (Ezek. 47:18; Joel 2:20; Zech. 14:8).

East Wind, For the Israelites it was a warm, dry, sandy wind typical of desert regions, known as sirocco or khamsin. In the Yahwist account of the Exodus it was a wind of this type which moved and dried the waters that blocked the flight of the Israelites (Ex. 14:21; *see* also Job 27:20-21; Jonah 4:8; Ezek. 27:26; Gen. 41:6). *See* EXODUS.

eat

"You are free to *e.* from any	*e.* the fruit of your handiwork
Gen. 2:16	Ps. 128:2
and dirt shall you *e.* Gen. 3:14	where I may *e.* the Passover
	Mk. 14:14

Ebal (ee′-bal), A mountain in central Palestine, 2950 feet high, north of and opposite Mount Gerizim. Between the two mountains there is a road which links Jerusalem with the north through Samaria. At the entrance to this passage was Shechem (today Tell Balata). According to the instructions of Moses (Deut. 11:29-32; 27:11-26) this was to be the place where the covenant should be solemnly renewed once the Israelites had entered into Palestine. Six tribes, Reuben, Gad, Asher, Zebulun, Dan and Naphtali should shout from Mt. Ebal curses against those who should transgress the covenant, while from the opposite Mount Gerizim the remaining six tribes should proclaim blessings. These dispositions of Moses were carried out as is described in Joshua 8:30-35. This episode probably reflects the rite of the periodic, perhaps annual, renewal of the covenant which was celebrated in all likelihood at Shechem during the feast of Tabernacles.

Ebed-melech (ee′-bed-mel′-ik), An Ethiopian eunuch of the court of Zedekiah, king of Judah (597-587 B.C.) who intervened with the king on behalf of Jeremiah when the prophet had been thrown into a cistern to die. Zedekiah, who had first consented to the punishment of the prophet, afterwards ordered Ebed-melech to free him (Jer. 38:1-13; *see* also Jer. 39:15-18).

Ebenezer, Literally "stone of help," a place that got its name from a commemorative pillar erected there by Samuel in memory of an Israelite victory over the Philistines. It lay "between Mizpah and Jeshanah" (1 Sam. 7:12). This location does not fully correspond with the Ebenezer near Aphek where the Israelites suffered a crushing defeat at the hands of the Philistines who on that occasion also captured the ark of the covenant (1 Sam. 4:1; 5:1).

Eber (ee′-ber), Son of Shem and founding father of the Israelites (Gen. 10:21-25, with a little variation in Gen. 11:14-26 and 1 Chron. 1:17-27). He is mentioned in the genealogy of Jesus in Luke 3:35.

Ecbatana (ec-bat′-a-na), The capital city of the Medes, conquered by Cyrus, king of Persia. It was the summer residence of the Persian kings. According to Ezra 6:2, at Ecbatana in the time of Darius I (522-485) was found Cyrus's decree on the repatriation of the Jews in Babylon. Raguel lived at Ecbatana with his daughter who married the young Tobias (Tob. 3:7; 14:12). The information in Judith 1:1-3 on the foundation of Ecbatana seems rather legendary.

Ecclesiastes, *See* QOHELETH.

Ecclesiasticus (Sirach), A deuterocanonical wisdom book of the Old Testament. The title **Ecclesiasticus** is only found in the Latin version of the Bible and in the writings of the Latin fathers. The name **Ecclesiasticus**

really covers all the books that are today known as deuterocanonical. This designates those books whose sacred character and inspiration was not yet universally accepted in the church, but which were nevertheless permitted to be read publicly in church. **Ecclesiasticus** is a Latin word meaning used by the church. This book alone among the others retained the name, perhaps because it was the most important of the series. It was in fact used in the ancient church as a manual of instruction for catechumens. Another reason for its retaining the name was perhaps its similarity with Ecclesiastes, the Latin title for another wisdom book, Qoheleth. Ecclesiasticus was not admitted to the Jewish or Protestant canon, but its canonicity was defined at the Council of Trent (1545-1563 A.D.).

Up to 1895 A.D. the only known edition of the book was the Greek translation made by the nephew of the author. In that year, in the synagogue at Cairo, were found fragments of various manuscripts of the original Hebrew. More were discovered in 1931, while still others came to light from the caves of Qumran. (*See* DEAD SEA SCROLLS.) In this way we have now about two thirds of the original text, which is different in the order of the chapters, and often in the material itself, from the Greek translation. The Latin text has still more additions.

In the Greek text the book has the title: "The Wisdom of the Son of Sira," or "of Jesua, the Son of Sira." In his prologue to the Greek translation the author's grandson calls him Jesus. At the end the name of the author appears again, with a different reading: "Jesus, son of Sira, Eleazar, of Jerusalem" in the Greek, and "Simeon, son of Jesus, son of Eleazar, son of Sira" in the Hebrew, 50:27.

The insertion of the name of Simeon in the Hebrew is not important. He was a man who was born and raised in the Holy City, who speaks with admiration and enthusiasm of the Temple and the cult (50:1-21). From his youth he gave himself to the study of the law and the prophets and the other sacred books of the Jews (Prologue 7-14; 51:13-21). He belonged to the class of scribes or wise men, whose praises he sings with a certain amount of complacency (38:24; 39:11).

He was animated by a sincere attachment to his religion, a fervent follower of the traditions sacred to Israel (cc. 44-50), who also however was remarkably open and appreciative of the new and good things culture had to offer. While remaining loyal to his own heritage, he knew how to take what was best from the surrounding Greek culture and customs. (*See* for example, 9:9; 32:1-8; 38:1-15; 39:32-35.) Through the counsels and admonitions that he penned in his book emerges the picture of a man of peaceful character who loved friendship (6:14-17; 22:24-27) and harmony in domestic life (7:20-30; 26:16-20).

He knows on all occasions how to take the middle path, avoiding concession to mere impulse and immoderation, but also steering clear of gratuitous or supererogatory sacrifices. His is the last voice of a rich tradition from which he draws generously (33:16-18), adding to it from his own sound judgment and nobility of soul.

The author does not develop his material in accordance with a preestablished plan. His exhortations, counsels and doctrine touch all the points that the formation of youth might demand, but it is fruitless to search for a progressive theme. At most one can distinguish five parts, each of which begins with a doctrinal introduction on the value of wisdom and on the words of God. Then follows in each case a list of concrete instructions. (*See* n. I, 1:1-16:23; II, 16:24-23:17; III, 24:1-32:13; IV, 32:14-42:14; V, 42:15-50:29)

The fifth part contains a historical section, the so-called 'Eulogy of the

Fathers,' a gallery of the illustrious names in sacred history, imperishable models of virtue, loyalty, wisdom and heroism (cc. 44-50). In this the author follows the account of the sacred books, but at times he offers a different version of the facts. The reason for this was partly to adapt his material to the scope of his writing and partly the Jewish interpretation of the time. The appendix is a hymn of thanksgiving which takes its inspiration from the thanksgiving psalms (c. 51).

The book was composed in the Hebrew language of Palestine. The author's grandson states that he came to Egypt in the 38th year of the reign of King Euergetes, that is, Ptolemy VII Euergetes, 170-117 B.C., or 132 B.C. After this the translation was made. The original was done around 50 years earlier, about 180 B.C. The date fits in with other inferences that can be drawn from the book. The author was a contemporary of Simon the High Priest. This must be Simon II, 218-198 B.C., during which time the Temple was repaired and embellished (*see* 50:1-3) and marvelously saved from the ambitions of Ptolemy Philometor (50:4). The silence of the author in regard to the hellenization policy of Antiochus IV Epiphanes (171-164 B.C.) and the Maccabean revolt also point to the date given.

Sirach 25:23 holds particular importance as it is one of the only two explicit references in the Old Testament to the Paradise story of Genesis 3. Sirach 25:23 belongs to a lengthy discourse of the author on the evils that can oppress man because of woman (Sir. 25:12-25). Among these evils the author includes the following: "In woman was sin's beginning and because of her we all die" (v. 23). The author is undoubtedly alluding to Genesis 3 or to some very similar story, while for the sake of the point he is making he passes over in silence the part of Adam in the origin of death.

It is a cause for wonder that the author does not insist elsewhere on this explanation of the origin of death. When he treats of the origin and condition of man, he offers very different considerations. It would therefore seem that Sirach, even though he was aware of the explanation of Genesis 3, did not find it completely to his theological taste. He used the story for his purpose almost incidentally, but it did not answer the problems to which Sirach addressed himself, nor was it in keeping with the general direction of his spirit.

The theme of Genesis 2, 3 is developed by Sirach in c. 16:24-27 and throughout c. 17. In 16:24-30 he writes of creation and in c. 17 of man. "The Lord from the earth created man, and in his own image he made him. Limited days of life he gives him and makes him return to earth again" (17:1, 2). Death is seen as a matter of fact, and nothing suggests that it could have been otherwise. It is framed in the dispositions of God who has given his universe a perfect order (16:27, 28).

Like other authors of the Old Testament, Sirach sees death as the end of life without any hope of resurrection: it is the human condition. (*See* DEATH.) We are far from the courageous thought of the author of Genesis 2, 3. (*See* FALL, THE.) Both authors scrutinize essentially the same problems: death, pain, the tragic condition of man. The Genesis author faces the problem in its most radical and enigmatic dimensions. He finds the solution of the problem in the sin of the first man. Sirach tries on the other hand to "dedramatize" the problem. He sees the tragedy of the situation but tries to convince himself of the normalcy of things (Sir. 41:4). While the death of a young person might cause scandal, the death of an old person provokes no particular problem. In 14:11-19 Sirach takes pains to frame death in the universal principle of order in creation: "As with the leaves that grow on a vigorous tree: one falls off and another sprouts—so

with the generations of flesh and blood: one dies and another is born"
(14:18). There are similar efforts in 40:11 and 17:26, 27.

In these attempts at an explanation one becomes aware of a certain preoccupation with apologetics, perhaps against those who dared blaspheme
the providence of God (*see* Sir. 16:16). One cannot say that Sirach is
opposed to Genesis 2, 3. They speak in different languages. Sirach lacks
the historic perspective of the story of Genesis 2, 3. In c. 17 he does not
really speak of the first man, but of man or of everyman. In this he is
nearer to Genesis 1. Then in a vein more pastoral than speculative, he
refuses to abandon the factual situation. Confronted with the enigma of
pain and death he attempts no radical explanations. Instead he suggests
attitudes of trust and wisdom, and in this case, submission to the universal
order that governs us, and resignation to the providence of God.

Eden, 1. The translation of Eden, or garden of Eden as garden of delight
(Gen. 2:8, 10) is read in the Septuagint, but is based on a wrong etymology. Eden is a geographical name, but it belongs to a legendary geography
which deludes every attempt to identify it with existing places. The garden
of Eden theme appears in two principal forms. In Ezekiel 28:13, 31:9,
36:35 and Isaiah 51:3 Eden is the garden of God, full of leafy trees where
the first man lived and from which he was expelled for his pride. In Genesis 2-3 the garden of Eden is not God's dwelling-place, but was planted by
God to serve as man's residence, to be conserved and cultivated by him
(2:15).

Genesis 2:8 places the garden in the east (*see* Gen. 3:24; 4:16). Verses 10
and 14 are probable additions to the original story and are the author's
attempt to identify more precisely this region. The garden of Eden should
be at the common source of the four great rivers which then divided as
they came out of Paradise. The Pishon would be the Indus, the Gihon the
Nile, the Hiddekel the Tigris and the Perat the Euphrates.

Allusions to the legendary fruitfulness and fertility of the garden of Eden
are read in some prophetic texts which describe the future restoration of
Israel (Isa. 51:3; Ezek. 36:35; *see* Joel 2:3; Gen. 13:10).

2. Eden or Beth-eden (Amos 1:5), probably to be identified with Bit-
Adini, known from Assyrian texts, an Aramaean kingdom in northern
Mesopotamia with its capital at Til-Barsip, which was conquered by Shal-
manesar V (*see* 2 Kgs. 19:12; Isa. 37:12; Ezek. 27:23).

Edna, Wife of Raguel and mother of Sarah, who married Tobias (Tob.
7:2, 15; 8:11-12).

Edom, Edomites (ee′-dom), The territory of Edom extended southeast
from the Dead Sea, between the river Zered to the north which separated
it from Moab, and the Gulf of Aqaba to the south, the depression of
Arabah westward, and the desert to the east. Archaeological research has
shown that it was unoccupied from the nineteenth to the thirteenth centuries B.C. In the thirteenth century B.C. a west semitic people ethnically
related to the Israelites settled there, as is recorded in the biblical traditions of Esau (Gen. 25:30; 36:1; 1 Chron. 1:35). Perhaps there was a
confederation of 12 tribes as in Israel (Gen. 36:20-30) but they had a
monarchic organization before Israel (Gen. 36:31-39).

While Israel was on her way to Canaan, the king of Edom refused to
permit them to pass through his territory, obliging them to go around the
land (Num. 20:14-20; 21:4). Deut. 2:2-8 however has a different tradition.

According to 1 Samuel Saúl defeated the Edomites, but the conquest of
the land was the work of David (2 Sam. 8:13-14) and it remained under

the domination of Israel until the time of Jehoram of Judah (849-842 B.C.; *see* 2 Kgs. 8:20-22).

Edom's independence however did not last long. Amaziah of Judah (800-783 B.C.) and later Uzziah (783-742) once more carried Israelite dominion as far as the Gulf of Aqaba over the whole of Edomite territory (2 Kgs. 14:7, 22).

Under Ahaz of Judah independence was once more achieved (735-715 B.C.; 2 Kgs. 16:6), but Edom was under vassalage to the Assyrians.

The Old Testament records the joy of Edom over the destruction of Jerusalem in 587 (Ps. 137:7; Lam. 4:21-22). Edom's history is also echoed in the prophets who have many oracles about, and hostile allusions to, Edom (*see* Amos 1:11-12; Obad.; Isa. 11:14; 21:11, 12; 34:5-17; Jer. 49:7-22; Ezek. 35).

During the Seleucid period the land of Edom was occupied by the Arab Nabataean people. The Arab kingdom of Idumea (which is the Greek for Edom) extended as far as Moab and southern Palestine with its capital at Petra. *See* NABATAEANS.

Edrei (ed′-re-eye), A city of Bashan, the residence of King Og (Deut. 1:4).

egg, eggs

nest with young birds or *e*. in it	As one takes *e*. left alone
Deut. 22:6	Isa. 10:14
flavor in the white of an *e*. Job 6:6	a scorpion if he asks for an *e*.
	Lk. 11:12

Eglah, One of David's wives, and mother of Ithream (2 Sam. 3:5; 1 Chron. 3:3).

Eglaim, A city in Moab (Isa. 15:8).

Eglon, 1. King of Moab who made incursions into Israelite territory and took possession of Jericho. He was killed treacherously by Ehud, judge over Israel (Jgs. 3:12-30).

2. A Canaanite city in central Palestine (today Tell-el-Hesi?). When the Gibeonites allied themselves with Joshua, the king of Jerusalem invited four other city kings, among them Eglon, to undertake a punitive expedition against Gibeon. The Gibeonites asked help from Joshua who defeated the alliance of the five (Josh. 10:1-27). Eglon was occupied by the tribe of Judah (Josh. 15:39).

Egypt, Egypt, the "gift of the Nile" according to the celebrated expression of Herodotus, was the cradle of one of the most ancient and flourishing civilizations that are known. Ancient Egypt comprised the strip of territory that channeled the Nile from the waterfalls at Aswan to where it disgorged, through the many streams of the delta, into the Mediterranean. The historic empire of Egypt arose from the fusion of the kingdoms of Upper and Lower Egypt. The distinction of the two kingdoms corresponded to their geographical configuration, but their fusion into one empire came, not so much from political vicissitudes as from the practical necessity of coordinating and organizing to the full the exploitation of what was to both countries their only vital source, namely, the irrigating waters of the great river. The Pharaoh, in whom both kingdoms converged, carried the emblems of both kingdoms, the white crown and lotus flower for the Upper, and the red crown and papyrus flower for the Lower Kingdom.

Manetho, an Egyptian historian of the Ptolemaic epoch (III c. B.C.), divided the history of his country into dynasties, and this system has been maintained even by today's historians. The first two dynasties (3300-2850) form the so-called archaic period. The Old Kingdom comprises dynasties III to V (2850-2052 B.C.), which reigned in Memphis. To this period belong the famous pyramids of Gizeh.

For the study of the Bible the New Kingdom (1610-1085 B.C.) holds great interest. The New Kingdom comprised dynasties XVIII to XX. After the domination of the Hyksos (*see* HYKSOS), Egypt awoke to a new spirit of expansion and conquest which eventually brought the limits of the Empire as far as the Euphrates under Thutmose III (1502-1448 B.C.). He however had no successors capable of sustaining the imperial ambitions in Asia, which became clear two centuries later under Seti I (1317-1301 B.C.) and Ramses II (1301-1234 B.C.). It is the common opinion of scholars today that the events narrated in Exodus 1-15 should be dated during the reign of Ramses II. The Israelites had been obliged to forced labor in the building projects of Ramses II (Ex. 1). The Exodus then was the attempt, which succeeded, to escape from this situation. The Bible obviously dresses the event in epic colors which greatly exaggerate the historical facts. In the miracle of the Sea of Reeds only a section of chariots belonging to one of the pontine garrisons, and not the whole army of the Pharaoh, was involved. (*See* EXODUS.) The New Kingdom came to an end as a result of a massive attack by the "Sea Peoples," probably inhabitants of Greece and the Mediterranean islands who had been driven out by Doric invasions. Ramses III (1195-1165) managed to contain the impetus of these invaders, but Egypt was obliged to renounce forever her imperial ambitions in Asia.

From the last period of ancient Egyptian history several personages hold interest for Bible studies. Shishak I (935-914 B.C.) offered sanctuary to Jeroboam, future king of Israel, and later invaded Palestine and sacked Jerusalem (918 B.C.) (*see* SHISHAK, 1 Kgs. 11:26-40; 14:25-28; 2 Chron. 12:2-9). Tirhakah advanced with his army as far as Judah to oppose Sennacherib, king of Assyria, who at that time was engaged in a campaign against Hezekiah (2 Kgs. 19:9; Isa. 37:9). Neco (609-594) carried out a campaign against the Babylonians. Josiah of Judah tried to stop Neco but he was defeated and killed at the battle of Megiddo. Neco made Josiah's son Eliakim king instead of Jehoahaz, and changed his name to Jehoiakim, to denote his position as a vassal (2 Kgs. 23:29-35; 2 Chron. 32:20-24). Neco was later defeated at Carchemish (605 B.C.) by Nebuchadnezzar. Later Hophra (588-569 B.C.) made a briefly successful attempt to back Zedekiah of Judah against Nebuchadnezzar. The latter was obliged to lift the siege of Jerusalem, but he returned as soon as Hophra departed (Jer. 37:5-11).

After the conquest of Jerusalem, part of the population of Judah sought to escape to Egypt for fear of reprisals from the Babylonians on account of the assassination of Gedaliah, governor of Judah (Jer. 41-44).

In 525 Cambyses king of Persia conquered Egypt which thereupon became a province of the Persian empire. In 332 B.C. it came under the dominion of Alexander who built the city of Alexandria in the delta which would give to Egypt, no longer a political but a cultural primacy. After the death of Alexander in 323 B.C. Egypt passed to his general Ptolemy, the founder of the Ptolemaic dynasty, which guided the destiny of Egypt until the Roman conquest. *See* PTOLEMY.

Egypt, Brook of, The brook of Egypt (or the river of Egypt in Gen. 15:18) is not the Nile but the wadi-el-Arish, which flows from the Sinai peninsula into the Mediterranean about half-way between Gaza and the extreme eastern portion of the Nile delta. It is the southern limit of the land of

Israel (Num. 34:5; 1 Kgs. 8:65; 2 Kgs. 24:7; Isa. 27:12; Ezek. 47:19; 48:28).

Ehud, A Benjaminite, son of Geza and judge of Israel, who freed Israel from the oppression of the Moabites who had settled in Jericho. He was appointed to take the tribute to Eglon king of Moab, but he carried with him a dagger strapped to his thigh. When he got the king alone he sank the dagger into him, locked the doors on the inside and escaped through the window. He occupied the ford on the Jordan and cut off the flight of the invaders who were annihilated by the Israelites (Jgs. 3:12-30).

eight

when he is *e.* days old	Gen. 17:12	you shall offer *e.* bullocks	
e. boards, with their sixteen			Num. 29:29
	Ex. 26:25	bedridden for *e.* years	Acts 9:33

eighteen

king of Moab for *e.* years		those *e.* who were killed	Lk. 13:4
	Jgs. 3:14	bondage of Satan for *e.* years	
for *e.* years they afflicted	Jgs. 10:8		Lk. 13:16

Ekron, A city of the Philistine Pentapolis (Josh. 13:3). When the Philistines captured the ark of the covenant they brought it to Ekron, but an epidemic afflicted the city, so they restored the ark to the Israelites (1 Sam. 5:10-6:16). Even though there is information of an Israelite conquest of the city in pre-monarchic times (Josh. 15:11, 45, 46; 19:43; Jgs. 1:18; 1 Sam. 7:14), it did not become Israelite property until the time of David (*see* 1 Sam. 17:52). In Ekron Baalzebub was worshipped. When King Ahaziah of Israel had recourse to Baalzebub he was rebuked by Elijah who announced to him his imminent death (2 Kgs. 1:2-16). Ekron was given by Alexander Balas (150-145 B.C.) to Jonathan Maccabeus to reward his fidelity during the internal wars of the Seleucid kingdom (1 Mac. 10:89).

El, The common semitic word for "God" and then the proper name of the Supreme God in the Canaanite Pantheon. *See* BAAL; GOD; PATRIARCHS, RELIGION OF THE; UGARIT.

Elah (ee′-lah), 1. King of Israel (877-876 B.C.), son and successor of Baasha. He was killed by Zimri, captain of half of his chariotry, who usurped the throne (1 Kgs. 16:8-10).

2. The father of Hoshea, last king of Israel (732-724 B.C.; 2 Kgs. 15:30; 17:1; 18:1-19).

Elam (ee′-lam), A region east of Babylon in the mountains of Zagros. In Genesis 10:22 Elam is numbered among the Semites, probably for its geographical proximity to Mesopotamia rather than for race or language reasons. The Elamites in fact belonged to the Armenoid group. The Elamites had no direct dealings with Israel and only get sporadic mention in the Bible (Isa. 11:11; 21:2; 22:6; Jer. 49:34-39; Ezek. 32:24). Susa, the territory's capital, was taken by Cyrus, who made it the chief city in the Persian empire. According to Acts 2:9 Jews from Elam were among those in Jerusalem on the day of Pentecost.

Elam, Personal name (1 Chron. 8:24; 26:3; Ezra 2:7; Neh. 12:42).

Elasa (el′-a-sa), A region near Beth-horon which was the scene of the battle in which Judas Maccabeus died (1 Mac. 9:5-18).

Elasah (el′-a-sa), Son of Shaphan who brought Jeremiah's letter to the exiles in Babylon (Jer. 29:3).

Elath (ee′-lath), A city often mentioned as being near Ezion-geber (Tell

Kheleifeh) on the Gulf of Aqaba. Excavations however seem to prove that it was really a later name of Ezion-geber, as there was no room for two cities in the vicinity.

Eldad, One of the seventy elders of Israel who received some of the spirit of Moses and prophesied (Num. 11:26-30).

Elder, In the tribal organization of ancient Israel, the authority which regulated the life of the group was invested in the "ancients," that is, in the heads of family or clan, who thus became the centers of cohesion in the whole group. The ancients exercised a collegial authority with functions of representation and government. In this way the ancients as authorized spokesmen for the whole community played decisive roles in some of the most important decisions of Israelite history. Thus their part was paramount in the institution of the monarchy (1 Sam. 8:4), in the election of David as king of Judah (*see* 2 Sam. 2:4) and later as king of the tribes of the north (2 Sam. 5:3). In the Pentateuch tradition and in that of the books of Joshua and Judges the elders frequently have their part to play; in the story of Moses (Ex. 3:16; 4:29), in the solemn ratification of the Covenant (Ex. 24:1-9), and afterwards with Joshua in the assembly at Shechem (Josh. 24). To them Joshua gave his farewell discourse (Josh. 23:1).

The ancients constitute the local authority (Josh. 9:11; Jgs. 8:5; 11:5; 1 Sam. 11:3) and it is they who confer the mandate on the chieftains who were occasionally chosen to coordinate the military efforts of the tribes (Jgs. 11:5). They accompanied these chieftains as a kind of consultative senate (Josh. 8:10; *see* Deut. 27:1), and during the monarchic period had their place alongside the king (2 Sam. 17:4; 2 Kgs. 10:1). The ancients also had a judiciary function to fulfill. Justice was administered at the gate of the city before a group of ancients (Ruth 4:1-11; 1 Kgs 21:8; 2 Kgs 10:1). What their powers were in this field is often recorded in the Deuteronomy code of laws (Deut. 19:12; 21:3; 22:15; 25:8).

This system for the exercise of authority is an obvious outgrowth of the type of society in which it appears and is bound therefore to undergo change in keeping with the changing society of which it is born. Two instances of this transformation in the Jewish system are the passage from nomadic to settled existence, and the evolution into a monarchic society. With the change from nomadic existence, the rigid tribal structure of the family as a center of cohesion gave way little by little to a concentration on the local community, the group of people living in the same place. Thus the representative function of the ancients became more and more the inheritance of the more prosperous heads of family and land proprietors, who thus emerged as a type of local aristocracy. Membership in this group also gave access to the group of 'ancients' or notable people of the place. With the advent of the monarchy came also the ceaseless tendency to centralization of power and the consequent subordination of local organizations to the central authority. The monarchy tended progressively to subject local bodies to an ever-increasing control.

Nevertheless the councils of ancients remained a part of Israelite history right up to the end, especially on a local level, but also on a national level thanks to its presence in the Sanhedrin. Thus it figures largely in the story of the Passion (Matt. 16:21; 21:23; 26:3; 26:57; 27:1; 27:12, 20, 41 and parallel texts) and in the account of the conflicts between the apostles and the Jewish authorities at Jerusalem (Acts 4:23; 23:14, 15; 24:1).

elder

your *e.* sister was Samaria   Oholah was the name of the *e.*
Ezek. 16:46   Ezek. 23:4
e. son was out on the land   Lk. 15:25

Elealeh (el′-e-ay′-la), A city of Transjordan in the territory of Reuben (Num. 32:3) and later under Moabite rule (Isa. 15:4; Jer. 48:34).

Eleazar (el′-e-ay′-zar), 1. Son of Aaron (Ex. 6:23) consecrated priest by Moses (Num. 3:1-4) and successor to Aaron as high priest (Num. 20:25-28). After the death of Nadab and Abihu, the other priest-sons of Aaron, Eleazar and Ithamar remained as heads of the priestly families (1 Chron. 24). Eleazar was present at the nomination of Joshua as successor of Moses (Num. 27:18-23) and with him carried out the distribution of Canaan among the tribes (Josh. 14:1; 17:4; 19:51; 21:1). He was the father of Phinehas (Ex. 6:25; Josh. 24:33), and from him also descended Zadok, Solomon's high priest (1 Chron. 6:35-38), and Ezra (Ezra 7:1-5).

2. Son of Abinadab, to whom was assigned the care of the ark during its stay at Kiriath-jearim after it had been given back by the Philistines (1 Sam. 7:1).

3. Son of Mattathias, brother of the Maccabees (1 Mac. 2:5). He died in the battle of Beth-zechariah; supposing that Antiochus V Eupator was on the royally caparisoned elephant, he ran under it and drove his sword into it, whereupon it collapsed on top of him, crushing him (1 Mac. 6:43-46).

4. An ancestor of Joseph (Matt. 1:15).

Election, The doctrine of God's election of Israel is expressed clearly, consistently, and adequately only from Deuteronomy on. The verb used is **bahar.** It is however sufficiently clear also in the ancient traditions on the patriarchs and on the Exodus: to these traditions the election doctrine gives meaning and purpose. The doctrine of the election highlights above all the gratuitousness and the freedom of God's saving initiative. It is then one of the essential elements of the story of salvation that constantly emerges under different aspects at all stages of that history.

To be a chosen people means to be the object of a saving initiative on the part of God. Choice was not made on the basis of the merits of the chosen; God chooses in a free and unexplainable love. Deuteronomy voices it without ambiguity: "He has chosen you from all the nations on the face of the earth to be a people, peculiarly his own. It was not because you are the largest of all nations that the Lord set his heart on you and chose you, for you are really the smallest of all nations. It was because the Lord loved you and because of his fidelity to the oath he had sworn to your fathers" (Deut. 7:7, 8; *see* 4:37; 9:5).

In this text there is a new element in the election: God, in choosing, freely commits himself to his people. In time this pledge by God is affirmed as a promise or oath that is unqualified and therefore irrevocable. It is an understanding of this irrevocability that prompts Paul when he speaks of the temporary separation of Israel, which will however be followed by its conversion, en masse, to the gospel. "In respect to the gospel, the Jews are enemies of God for your sake; in respect to the election, they are beloved by him because of the patriarchs" (Rom. 11:28, 29). In these celebrated chapters of the epistle to the Romans (cc. 9-11) Paul poses the problem of God's fidelity to his promises (Rom. 9:6) and to the choice of his people: "I ask, then, has God rejected his people? Of course not!" (Rom. 11:1). Despite appearances, and despite the rejection on their part of the gospel, God's word remains irrevocable. Paul launches his audacious vision to the future and to horizons of salvation that are totally based on the irrevocability and gratuitousness of God's choice which commits God's wisdom and omnipotence in ways that astonish Paul: "How deep are the riches and the wisdom and the knowledge of God! How inscrutable his judgments, how unsearchable his ways!" (Rom. 11:33; *see* vv. 34-36).

By virtue of the choice, Israel becomes God's special possession and a holy nation (Ex. 19:6; *see* Deut. 7:6; 14:2; 26:18; Ps. 135:4; Mal. 3:17). The two expressions are practically synonymous; they proclaim at the same time a blessing and a demand. The people will enjoy the inviolability of something that is God's: among the Covenant's blessings is read: "He (God) will establish you as a people sacred to himself, as he swore to you; so that, when all the nations of the earth see you bearing the name of the Lord, they will stand in awe of you" (Deut. 28:9, 10; *see* Jer. 14:9; Amos 9:12; Isa. 63:19; 2 Chron. 7:14). God watches over his possession and breaks out into implacable anger against those who threaten or injure it (Isa. 9:16 ff.; Zech. 1:14; 8:2).

But the zeal or jealousy of the Lord, that is, his passionate attachment to whatever he has made especially his own does not only blaze into anger against those who profane his possession from without, but above all is directed with indignation against the disloyalty of those who bear his name (Ex. 34:14; Deut. 4:24; 6:15; Josh. 24:19; Nah. 1:2). Holiness or belonging to God then brings with it a corresponding demand which is expressed in the law. The code of laws contained in Leviticus 17-26 offers, as justification for many of the concrete dispositions that it lays down, the demands of that holiness that is expected from a people belonging to a holy God: "To me, therefore, you shall be sacred; for I, the Lord am sacred, I, who have set you apart from the other nations to be my own" (Lev. 20:26), and more concisely: "Be holy, for I, the Lord, your God, am holy" (Lev. 19:2; *see* Ex. 22:30).

The election then is a pledge of salvation and an expression of God's goodness, but no guarantee against impurity. Indeed, it evokes from man a pledge of fidelity and obedience that is all the greater on account of the gratuitousness of the gift offered. The relationship between these two, God's self-giving and man's surrender to it, is expressed by Amos in a paradox: "You alone have I favored, more than all the families of the earth; Therefore I will punish you for all your crimes" (Amos 3:2). The same warning is found in the other prophets who try to shake the people from that false confidence in the certainty of salvation offered by God: while on God's part the promise and pledge is unwithdrawn, to it corresponds on man's part an obedience to his voice (Jer. 7:3-10).

The concept of a historical choice of a special people by God must be understood as a free, but not arbitrary, choice by God: it only gets its meaning in view of an unlimited spread of God's dominion over all the peoples of the earth. This world-wide dominion is explicitly affirmed in Exodus 19:5: "You shall be my special possession, dearer to me than all other people, though all the earth is mine." For Deuteronomy 32:8-10 the election of God's people in the desert was the realization of a choice made by the Most High: "When the Most High assigned the nations their heritage,/when he parceled out the descendants of Adam,/He set up the boundaries of the peoples/after the number of the sons of God;/While the Lord's own portion was Jacob,/His hereditary share was Israel" (*see* also Deut. 4:19-20).

When it is viewed in this larger context, the election of Israel appears as a divine initiative which transcends Israel itself, and cannot but have universal repercussions in the order of salvation. This conclusion is in fact drawn by the prophets who see in the future that the nations will share in the goods of Israel and come to acknowledge the sovereignty of God. (*See* GENTILES.) That salvation is for all is clearly seen in the instrument chosen by God to bring to accomplishment his saving designs (*see* Isa. 42:1-4; 49:1-5; *see* SERVANT OF THE LORD).

In a way that is less conspicuous but equally unequivocal, the whole wide scope of the choice of Israel by Yahweh is sufficiently affirmed in the account of the call of Abraham: "All the communities of the earth shall find blessing in you" (Gen. 12:3). This solemn declaration is in manifest contrast with the sorry conclusion to the episode of the Tower of Babel, which immediately precedes it (Gen. 11:1-9). (*See* TOWER OF BABEL.) Here the relationship between humanity and its creator God seemed definitively and incurably ruptured. Here however was immediately inserted the account of the call of Abraham and the promise of universal blessing that it contained: with it the sacred author lets it be understood, and with sufficient clarity, that the divine initiative that took its start with Abraham was to reestablish and give a positive and definitive solution to the relationships between men and God.

Elect Lady, A symbolic name for the church to which is addressed the Second Letter of John (2 Jn. 1:1).

El-Elyon (el′-el-yone′), "God the Most High," the God of Jebusite Jerusalem, worshiped by Melchizedech, king-priest of the city. *See* MELCHIZEDECH; PATRIARCHS, RELIGION OF THE.

elements
like slaves subordinated to the *e.*   natural *e.* to which you   Gal. 4:9
                                          Gal. 4:3

Eleutherus (a-loo′-ther-us), A river in Syria which flows from Lebanon to the Mediterranean (1 Mac. 11:7; 12:30).

eleven
and his *e.* children   Gen. 32:23   you shall offer *e.* bullocks
E. such sheets   Ex. 26:8   Num. 29:20
                    told all these things to the *E.*   Lk. 24:9

Elhanan (el-hay′-nan), One of David's warriors, son of Jair. In 2 Samuel 21:19 he is said to have killed the giant Goliath, while 1 Chronicles 20:5 attributes to him the killing of Lahmi, Goliath's brother. Moreover 1 Samuel 17 assigns the killing of Goliath to David. Scholars vary in their explanations of this inconsistency. Some hold that 2 Samuel 21:19 is historical and that making David the giant-killer is legendary, to adorn even more the figure and fame of the greatest king of Israel. Others hold 1 Samuel 17 to be authentic, except that here it was a question of an unnamed person who was later identified with Goliath. Others again would make Elhanan and David the same person. David would be the name taken by Elhanan when he became king.

Eli, A priest of the sanctuary of Shiloh (1 Sam. 1:9) to whom Hanna confided her son Samuel whom she had consecrated to the Lord (1 Sam. 1:9-2:11). At that time the Ark of the Lord was at Shiloh (1 Sam. 4:4). Eli's two priest sons, Hophni and Phinehas, were guilty of grave misdeeds in the exercise of the priesthood (1 Sam. 1:3; 2:12-17). Their father tried to correct them but to no avail (1 Sam. 2:22-26). Samuel (1 Sam. 3:1-18) or an unnamed prophet (1 Sam. 2:27-36) announced to Eli that God was about to punish his house. In fact both his sons were killed at the battle of Aphek against the Philistines, where they had carried the Ark. At the news of their death and of the capture by the enemy of the Ark, Eli fell backwards off his seat by the gate, broke his neck and died. He had ruled over Israel for forty years (1 Sam. 4:1-18).

Eliab, 1. Father of Dathan and Abiram of the tribe of Reuben who revolted against Moses in the desert (Num. 16:1).

2. The first-born of Jesse, and David's older brother (1 Sam. 16:6). He served in Saul's army (1 Sam. 17:13-28).

Eliakim (e-lie′-a-kim), 1. Son of Hilkiah and royal chamberlain during the reign of Hezekiah (2 Kgs. 18:18, 26, 37) and highly praised by Isaiah (Isa. 22:15-25).

2. The second son of Josiah king of Judah (640-609 B.C.). At the death of Josiah, his first-born Jehoahaz succeeded him, but he was made prisoner by the Pharaoh Neco of Egypt (2 Kgs. 23:34) who made Eliakim king of Judah, changing his name to Jehoiakim. Jehoiakim had to pay dearly in silver and gold for the privilege (2 Kgs. 23:34-35).

Eliam (e-lie′-am), Father of Bathsheba who was wife of Uriah. She was seduced and then married by David (2 Sam. 11:3; 1 Chron. 3:5).

Eliashib (e-lie′-shib), The high priest of Jerusalem in the time of Nehemiah (Ezra 10:6; Neh. 3:1).

Eliel (e-lie′-el), Personal name of several Old Testament men (1 Chron. 5:24; 11:46, 47; 12:12; 15:9, 11).

Eliezer (el′-i-ee′-zer), 1. Abraham's servant and his heir in the eventuality that no children were born to the patriarch (Gen. 15:2). He set off for Aram to find a wife for Isaac, his master's son, even though the servant mentioned in the chapter remains unnamed (Gen. 24).

2. Son of Moses and Zipporah (Ex. 18:4; 1 Chron. 23:15; 26:25).

3. Ancestor of Jesus in Luke 3:29.

Elihu (e-lie′-hue), 1. An Ephraimite, father of Jeroham, son of Tohu. He was an ancestor of Elkanah, husband of Hannah, by whom he had his son Samuel (1 Sam. 1-1). 1 Chron. 6:19 calls him Eliel and 1 Chron. 6:12 names him Eliab.

2. A "chief of thousands" who with others from Manasseh deserted Saul to join David at Ziklag (1 Chron. 12:21).

3. Son of Barachel the Buzite of the clan of Ram, who was angry with Job for thinking himself right and God wrong and equally angry with the three men, who were older than he, but who had been put to silence by Job's protestation of his own innocence. His speech seeks to clarify for Job God's providence and the meaning of his suffering (cc. 32-37). *See* JOB.

Elijah, A prophet of Tishbeh (location uncertain; possibly in Gilead), who exercised his ministry during the kingship of Ahab (869-850 B.C.) and Ahaziah (850-849 B.C.), kings of Israel. Elijah was the zealous defender of Yahwism against the religious syncretism favored and spread by Ahab and his wife Jezebel. 1 Kings 17-22 and 2 Kings 1 have conserved some traditions about Elijah and some of the episodes which were the fruit of this disagreement.

In 1 Kings 17 Elijah announced a drought which would last three years, in punishment for the idolatry of the people. By order of the Lord, Elijah settled down during this period, first at the river Cherith and then at Zarephath where he miraculously rewarded the widow who offered him hospitality, and whose son he raised to life.

In 1 Kings 18 is the tradition of the public challenge issued by Elijah to the prophets of Baal on Mt. Carmel, which ended with the slaughter of the latter at the river Kishon. Jezebel was angered at this and decided to get rid of Elijah (1 Kgs. 19). The prophet took flight towards Mt. Horeb where he was given a vision of Yahweh who ordered him to anoint Jehu king of Israel, Hazael king of Damascus, and Elisha as prophet and his successor.

On his return to Palestine he met Elisha and invited him to follow him by the symbolic gesture of throwing his own cloak around him.

In 1 Kings 21 occurs the episode of the vineyard of Naboth, which was adjacent to the palace. Ahab wished to have it to increase his gardens but Naboth refused to sell, for which Jezebel treacherously had him killed. At this Elijah announced to the king that God had decreed the imminent tragic end of his whole house (1 Kgs. 21:20-24).

In 2 Kings 1 Elijah announced the imminent death of Ahaziah who in his sickness had sent to consult Baalzebub, a deity of Ekron. The cycle of the traditions about Elijah concludes in 2 Kings 2:1-18 with the story of his being taken up to heaven in a fiery chariot.

Elijah was so striking a figure that his memory remained alive in later tradition. The legend of his being taken up in a fiery chariot, however, contributed not a little to this. He was expected to return at the end of time, and thus became an eschatological figure. This hope of Elijah's return is present in Malachi 3:23 and Sirach 48:10, and was particularly alive in New Testament times (Matt. 11:14; 17:10; Mk. 9:11; Jn. 1:21, 25). Jesus was himself identified with Elijah by some (Matt. 16:14; Mk. 8:28; Lk. 9:19), whereupon he declared that John the Baptist was the Elijah who was to come (Matt. 11:14; 17:11; Mk. 9:12). Elijah is mentioned elsewhere in the New Testament in Matt. 17:3; Mk. 9:4; Lk. 9:30 (the Transfiguration where Elijah appeared with Moses as symbols of the Law (Moses) and the Prophet (Elijah) giving witness to Jesus); Matt. 27:47-49; Mk 15:35; Lk. 4:25; Rom. 11:2; James 5:17.

Elika (e-lie′-ka), One of the Thirty warriors of David's army (2 Sam. 23:25).

Elim (ee′-lim), An encampment of the Israelites on their journey through the desert, situated between the Reed Sea and Sinai, an oasis of palms with abundant springs of water (Ex. 15:27; 16:1; Num. 33:9). It is traditionally identified with modern Wadi Gharandel.

Elimelech (e-lim′-e-lek), A Bethlehemite, husband of Naomi, who emigrated to Moab during the period of the Judges. His two sons Mahlon and Chilion married Moabite women, Orpah and Ruth. Elimelech and his sons died, and Naomi returned to Palestine with Ruth, where the latter married Boaz (Ruth 1-3).

Eliphaz (el′-e-faz), 1. First-born of Esau from his Hittite wife Ahad, ancestor of several Edomite clans (Gen. 36:4, 10-11; 1 Chron. 1:35-36).

2. Eliphaz of Teman was a friend of Job and one of the principal disputants with him (Job 2:11; 4:1; 15:1; 22:1; 42:7, 9).

Eliphelet (e-lif′-a-let), A son of King David (2 Sam. 5:16; 1 Chron. 3:6).

Elipheleth (e-lif′-a-leth), One of the Thirty warriors of David's army (1 Chron. 11:36).

Elisha (e-lie′-sha), The son of Shaphat of Abel Meholah. He was disciple and successor to the prophet Elijah. His prophetic mission was conferred on him by Elijah himself at the command of the Lord (1 Kgs. 19:15-21). Thereafter he accompanied Elijah and was a witness to Elijah's being snatched up to heaven in a whirlwind (2 Kgs. 2:1-18).

Elisha exercised his prophetic ministry in the kingdom of the north during the reigns of Ahaziah, Joram, Jehu, Jehoahaz and Joash, that is, from 850 until 790 approximately—Joash reigned from 801 until 786 B.C. It is no easy matter to form a precise picture of his activities. The traditions concerning Elisha that are gathered in 2 Kings 2-8 are, on the one hand, too fragmentary while, on the other, they show a marked tendency to revel in the marvelous and extraordinary so that the image of the prophet that they transmit is somewhat deformed and one-sided.

It can be held as certain, even if surprising, that Elisha played an important role in the political maneuverings of the kingdom of the north. He supported the politico-religious rebellion of Jehu against Ahab's dynasty (2 Kgs. 9), and that of Hazael which overthrew Ben-hadad of Damascus (2 Kgs. 8:7-15).

Already however he had appeared in the company of Joram of Israel and Jehoshaphat of Judah in their campaign against Moab, during which he intervened on several occasions with his gifts of clairvoyance and wonder-working, and announced to Joash the outcome of his campaigns against the Aramaeans (2 Kgs. 13:14-25).

In these traditions Elisha maintained a middle position between independence from, and an intransigent criticism of, his predecessor Elijah in regard to the monarchy, becoming a type of court prophet like Nathan in David's time. In the most significant event Elisha undoubtedly acted as spokesman for the prophetic circles who were opposed to religious syncretism such as had been introduced by Ahab. When then Jehu ordered the massacre of the royal family, this took on the character of a sacred vindication on account of Elisha's intervention.

The most surprising factor however in the Elisha tradition is the abundance of miracles. There is no doubt that Elisha had the gift of clairvoyance and that he had ecstatic experiences that were more remarkable than with any other Old Testament prophet (*see* 2 Kgs. 3:11-20; 5:21-27; 6:24-7:20; 8:1-15). 2 Kgs. 3:14, 15 mentions the use of music to provoke a trance in an instance unparalleled in the whole Old Testament, though there is plentiful documentation to this usage in other religions.

It is regrettable that the prophetic circles who kept alive the memory of Elisha interested themselves chiefly in these extraordinary phenomena. Some of these miracles are bizarre if not downright revolting, such as the story of the small boys who came out of the town and jeered at him, calling him "Baldhead," upon which he cursed them, with the result that two she-bears came out of the woods and mauled forty-two of them (2 Kgs. 2:23-25). One suspects that popular imagination generated for their hero an epic history that outstripped the facts. Some of the stories excessively mimic prodigies attributed also to Elijah, such as the reanimation of the Shunamite woman's son (2 Kgs. 4:8-37 and *see* 1 Kgs. 17:17-23), and the prodigious increase of the oil (2 Kgs. 4:1-7) and the multiplication of the twenty barley loaves (2 Kgs. 4:42-44 and *see* 1 Kgs. 17:8-16). They are the fruit of an understandable desire to put the disciple at the level of the master.

Elishah, A place in the island of Crete, listed among the sons of Japheth in the Table of Nations (Gen. 10:4; 1 Chron. 1:7).

Elishama (e-lish′-a-ma), 1. Grandfather of Joshua, head of the tribe of Ephraim in the census of the Israelite tribes in the desert (Num. 1:10; 2:18; 7:48, 53; 10:22).

2. Son of David born in Jerusalem (2 Sam. 5:16).

Elisheba (e-lish′-a-ba), Daughter of Aminadab and wife of Aaron (Ex. 6:23).

Elishua (el′-i-shoo′-a), One of the sons of King David born at Jerusalem (2 Sam. 5:15; 1 Chron. 14:5).

Eliud (e-lie'-ud), An ancestor of Jesus (Matt. 1:14, 15).

Elizabeth, The Greek form of the Hebrew Elisheba, the name of Zechariah's wife and mother of John the Baptizer, whom she miraculously conceived, according to the angel's announcement, even though she was advanced in years. She was a relative of Mary the mother of Jesus (Lk. 1:5-66).

Elizur (e-lie'-zur), The leader of the tribe of Reuben under Moses (Num. 1:5; 2:10; 7:30; 10:18).

Elkanah (el-kay'-nah), An Ephraimite, husband of Hannah and father of Samuel (1 Sam. 1-2; 1 Chron. 6:12, 19).

Elkosh, The land of the prophet Nahum (Nah. 1:1).

Ellasar (el'-a-sar), A city of King Arioch, who was one of the kings of the east who took part in the punitive expedition against the cities of the Pentapolis in the time of Abraham (Gen. 14:1). Its site is unknown; the attempt to identify it with the Babylonian city of Larsa has now been abandoned.

Elmadam, An ancestor of Jesus in Luke's genealogy, 3:28.

Elnathan, The father of Nehushta, king Jehoiakim's wife, and a prince of Judah under Jehoiakim (2 Kgs. 24:8; Jer. 26:22; 36:12).

Eloah, A Hebrew word for "God," a form of "El" used principally in poetry. *See* GOD.

Elohim (el'-o-him or el-o'-him), Plural of El, but also used of a single divine being, notably the God of Israel. *See* GOD.

Elohist, The conventional name given to the second source or stratum of the Pentateuch. *See* PENTATEUCH.

Elon, A minor judge who lived at Ayyalon (Judges 12:11-12).

El-Shaddai (el-shad'-eye), *See* PATRIARCHS, RELIGION OF THE.

Elul, The sixth month in the Hebrew calendar corresponding to August-September (1 Mac. 14:27; Neh. 6:15).

Elymais (el'-i-may'-is), A region of Persia (Tob. 2:10; 1 Mac. 6:1).

Elymas (el'-i-mas), Another name (Acts 13:8) for the Jewish false prophet and magician who sought to turn the proconsul Sergius Paulus away from the faith, when, at Cyprus, he sent for Paul and Barnabas to hear them. In Acts 13:6 he is called Bar-jesus. *See* BAR-JESUS.

embalm, embalmed

to *e*. his faher	Gen. 50:2	He was *e*. and laid to rest	
When they *e*. Israel	Gen. 50:2		Gen. 50:26

Embalming, The Jews did not have the custom of embalming bodies. *See* BURIAL. Exceptions to this rule are Jacob and Joseph who died in Egypt (Gen. 50:2-3, 26).

embrace, embraces

if you *e*. her	Prov. 4:8	to *e*., and a time to be far from *e*.	
accept the *e*. of an adulteress			Eccles. 3:5
	Prov. 5:20	his right arm *e*. me	S. of S. 2:6

embroider, embroidered

with cherubim *e*. on them	Ex. 26:1	with an *e*. gown	Ezek. 16:10
e. on cloth of fine linen	Ex. 28:6	strip off their *e*. garments	
			Ezek. 26:16

emerald

| a topaz and an *e*. | Ex. 28:17 | jasper, sapphire, garnet and *e*. |
| a topaz and an *e*. | Ex. 39:10 | Ezek. 28:13 |

Emim, A quasi-legendary population of Transjordan, also known as Rephaim, who were dispossessed by the Moabites on the latter's arrival (Deut. 2:10, 11; Gen. 14:5).

Emmanuel, A Hebrew name which means "God with us." It was the name to be borne by the baby whose birth was announced by Isaiah to Ahaz in Isa. 7:10-17. The historic backdrop of this celebrated oracle was the Syro-Ephraimite war (734-733 B.C.). Rezin king of Damascus and Pekah king of Israel invaded Judah and penetrated as far as Jerusalem in an attempt to force Ahaz to unite with them in coalition against Tiglath-pileser III of Assyria, or, in the case of his refusing to cooperate, to supplant him with a puppet. Isaiah sent an oracle to the king in which God commanded: "Take care you remain tranquil and do not fear," for the enemy kings would not only prove incapable of executing their plans, but within a short period they were destined to disappear with their peoples from any position of power (Isa. 7:1-10). This was tantamount to recommending neutrality and avoidance of a course of vassalage to Tiglath-pileser III which would carry with it detriment for the nation, both politically and religiously. Ahaz therefore should resist a little, for Tiglath-pileser would eventually, in his own interest, take action against his adversaries. Isaiah offered the king a sign as guarantee of the promise of salvation contained in the oracle, but the king adopted an attitude of fearfulness which was nothing more than distrust and incredulity toward what the prophet promised. Isaiah nevertheless persisted and offered once more a sign, no longer miraculous, but which reasserted the certainty of the promised salvation: before the baby to be born should reach the age of reason, the territories of the two threatening kings would be devastated and thus Judah would be free.

Without doubt the text is messianic (*see* Matt. 1:22, 23) but it is not clear in which sense the text is to be taken as messianic. First it is necessary to identify the persons to whom the prophet refers as the "maiden" **(almah)** and the child. It must be taken into account that the birth and growth of the child is proposed as the chronological term for the end of the Syro-Ephraimite war and the destruction of the two aggressor kings. On the other hand, even though the Septuagint translates the word **almah** as virgin, all scholars recognize that it does not mean virgin (which employs another Hebrew word), and that the sign offered by Isaiah does not therefore refer to a virginal birth. **Almah** means simply a girl of marriageable age (*see* Gen. 24:43; Prov. 30:19).

In Isaiah 8:8 the name Emmanuel reappears. The text is interpreted as referring to the invasion of Judah by Sennacherib's troops at the time of Hezekiah. In this text the name Emmanuel can be referred without difficulty to Hezekiah. This identification of Emmanuel with Hezekiah was for long difficult from the chronological point of view. Today, however, the chronology question has been reopened because of the clear need to re-think 2 Kings 16:2 and 18:2, which if taken exactly as they stand, would make Ahaz only eleven years older than his son.

For these reasons it is believed that Isaiah in 7:10-12 was thinking directly of the birth of Hezekiah. The **almah** is Ahaz's young wife. One more easily understands why Isaiah took this sign. He announced that God would prove faithful to his promises to David in regard to his dynasty. When this was being cast in doubt by the political and military projects of Israel and Damascus, God announced through Isaiah's mouth that not only should Ahaz have a successor, but that the threats from without should come to nothing even before this successor should reach the age of reason.

The text is then messianic: it is an announcement of a concrete realization of the promise made to David. But it is equally certain that the messianic import of the text is not thus exhausted: for the messianic hope underwent an evolution in which little by little it was enriched by the concrete experience of salvation history. For this evolution *see* MESSIANISM.

Emmaus (e-may′-us), A town of Judah in the vicinity of which Judas Maccabeus won a victory of the Seleucid general Gorgias (1 Mac. 3:40-57; 4:1-15). Mostly however it is known because of the apparition of the risen Lord to the two disciples which took place on the road there (Lk. 24:13-15). Its exact site is debatable: some place it at the modern Amwas, which was the Greek Nicopolis, 19 miles to the west of Jerusalem, but this does not correspond to the 60 stadia (7 miles) mentioned in Luke 24:13. Others prefer El-Qubeibeh which is about 7 miles west of Jerusalem where Crusaders in 1099 found an old Roman fort called Castellum Emmaus.

emptied, emptying

she quickly *e.* her jug	Gen. 24:20	priest came, *e.* the chest	
When they were *e.* their sacks			2 Chron. 24:11
	Gen. 42:35	shaken out and *e.*	Neh. 5:13

encourage, encouragement

E. him, for he is to give		*e.* and strengthen him	Deut. 3:28
	Deut. 1:38	destroy it. *E.* him	2 Sam. 11:25
		delight at the *e.*	Acts 15:31

end

put an *e.* to all mortals	Gen. 6:13	one *e.* of the heavens	Ps. 19:7
from one *e.* of Egypt's	Gen. 47:21	the *e.* of his talk	Eccles. 10:13

Endor, A city in the plain of Esdraelon near Mt. Tabor, today called Endur, in the land of Manasseh (Josh. 17:11). Here the Israelites won a notable victory over Sisera (Ps. 83:10). It was also the home of the necromancer whom Saul consulted to conjure up the spirit of Samuel (1 Sam. 28:7-11).

En-eglaim (en-eg′-la-im), An oasis on the shore of the Dead Sea (Ezek. 47:10).

enemy, enemies

take vengeance on his *e.*		the *e.* of the Lord	Ps. 37:20
	1 Sam. 18:25	the *e.* at the gate	Ps. 127:5
		when we were God's *e.*	Rom. 5:10

Engedi, A city in the desert of Judah, about half-way along the west coast of the Dead Sea (Josh. 15:62; Ezek. 47:10) beside a fertile oasis (S. of S. 1:14; Sir. 24:14) where David took refuge during the hostilities with Saul (1 Sam. 24:1).

English Bible, The complete Bible was done into English for the first time in a translation attributed to John Wycliffe, but perhaps better said to be done under his leadership. The first version, in a plodding heavy style, is attributed chiefly to Nicholas of Hereford, while its revision, around 1400 is said to be by John Purvey. It was a translation from the Latin.

Tyndale in 1525 published his New Testament translation, and before his execution in 1536 had succeeded in translating much of the Old Testament from the Hebrew and Greek. Tyndale's New Testament was heavily used in the Authorized Version of 1611.

There followed a succession of translations: Coverdale's Bible (1535), Matthew's Bible (1537), The Great Bible (1539), Taverner's revision of Matthew's Bible, the Geneva Bible (1557) and, under the leadership of Bishop Parker of Canterbury, the Bishops' Bible.

For their part the Catholics prepared the Rheims-Douay translation, of which the New Testament was published in 1582 at Rheims, while, for lack of financial resources, the Old Testament translation did not see the light until 1609-1610. For exaggerated apologetic purposes the version was made from the Latin Vulgate; the original texts however were used in the preparation of the New Testament translation. The translation was so scrupulously literal that it excessively anglicized the Latin.

King James I in 1604 called a conference of religious groups at which John Reynolds proposed a new translation of the Bible which would be acceptable to all. Fifty-four scholars were assembled on a tripartite board, Oxford, Cambridge and Westminster. The work of each section was to be corrected and revised by the other two, and so they set to work in 1607 and brought it to completion in 1610. The Bishops' Bible, Tyndale, Matthews, Coverdale and others were used, together with the Catholic Rheims New Testament. The result was a great success in filling the need for a contemporary, readable translation. The Authorized Version, with royal approval, and without notes so as to suit all religious leanings, was published in 1611.

Challoner, the vicar-apostolic of London, though not a scholar, did the best he could with the defects of the Rheims-Douay version. In 1750 and 1763 he revised the Old Testament and in 1749, 1750, 1752, 1763 and 1772 he revised the New Testament, in the main adopting more accurate readings from the Authorized Version.

With the vast steps forward in nineteenth century biblical research and scholarship, the defects of all the translations to date were more and more keenly felt, so that in 1870 the Convocation of Canterbury decided on the revision of the Authorized Version. The revised New Testament was published in 1881 and the Old Testament in 1885. The language was modernized and use was made of the increased knowledge of the original languages.

The Americans published their own Revised Version of the Bible in 1901 as the American Standard Bible, and a half-century later published a revision of this, which is universally praised, as the Revised Standard Version. The New Testament appeared in 1946 and the whole Bible in 1953.

For the Catholics the Confraternity of Christian Doctrine brought out a revised Rheims-Challoner New Testament in 1941, but since it used the Vulgate, and since the Encyclical **Divino Afflante Spiritu** (1943) advised the use of original texts, the need was felt for yet another translation and not just a revision depending on secondary texts. Both the Old Testament and the New have been superbly translated from the original texts and are now available to the public under the title of New American Bible.

Recent years have seen many excellent translations by independent scholars such as Moffatt (New Testament 1913, Old Testament 1935), Goodspeed (New Testament 1923, Old Testament 1931), Knox (New Testament 1945, Old Testament 1949), Kleist and Lilly (New Testament 1954).

Perhaps the most monumental of recent Catholic endeavors is The Jerusalem Bible, a work which draws on the French **La Bible de Jerusalem** for its notes, but is based on the original Greek and Hebrew texts for its translation. It is done into fluid English with accuracy in the hopes of meeting what the introduction terms the two principal dangers to Christianity today: irrelevancy, and its being consigned to the realm of mythology.

With the ever-increasing knowledge of the Bible and its times as guide, further new and hopefully ever more accurate translations of the Word of God are to be expected in coming years.

engraved
e. by God himself	Ex. 32:16	*e.* like seal engravings	Ex. 39:6
	E. with a diamond point	Jer. 17:1

En-hakkore (en-hak′-o-re), "The spring of the caller," near Lehi, from which Samson drank after a victorious encounter with the Philistines (Jgs. 15:19).

enjoy, enjoyment
pleasure and the *e.* of good		chosen ones shall long *e.*	
	Eccles. 2:1		Isa. 65:22
drink and *e.* the fruit	Eccles. 3:13	drink well. *E.* yourself	Lk. 12:19

En-mishpat, *See* KADESH.

enmity
e. between you and the woman
                                    Gen. 3:15

Enoch, 1. In the Yahwist genealogy for Cain, Enoch is his son, who in turn fathered Irad. Enoch is also the name that Cain gave to a town that he built (*see* Gen. 4:17, 18).

2. In the priestly genealogy for Adam, Enoch is son of Jared and father of Methuselah. The Bible states that, in all, Enoch lived for three hundred and sixty-five years, and walked with God. Then he vanished because God took him (Gen. 5:21-24). Sirach praises Enoch in the eulogy of the ancestors as a person who pleased the Lord and was taken up, an example for the conversion of all generations (Sir. 44:16; *see* 49:14). The epistle to the Hebrews upholds him as an example of faith: "By faith Enoch was taken away without dying" (Heb. 11:5).

Extra-biblical Jewish literature abounds with references to Enoch. He is one of the preferred figures in apocalyptic literature, and under his assumed name appear some of the most noted and important of the apocalyptic writings. In them he is admitted to the contemplation of the cosmological and eschatological mysteries which are the center of interest in these works. There are three books attributed to him. The first book of Enoch is a compilation of various writings of the second and first centuries before Christ. One of these, the Book of Parables has particular importance because it is the chief Jewish source for the concept of the Son of Man. (*See* SON OF MAN.) The epistle of Jude quotes this work briefly (Jude 14, 15). The complete work has only come down in an Ethiopian translation.

The second book of Enoch, or the Book of the Secrets of Enoch has come down only in a Slavic translation. It is a Jewish work written in Greek at the beginning of the Christian era.

The third book of Enoch is in Hebrew and comes from the second or third century after Christ.

The question is often asked: is Enoch dead, or still alive? And no ready answer is available. The question cannot be answered because it does not make sense. All scholars in fact admit that the point of the genealogy is to link up the creation story with that of the flood—while that of Genesis 10 is aimed at linking up the flood story with the traditions about Abraham. It is a variant version of similar lists of the names of pre-flood kings which are found in Sumero-Akkadic texts. The seventh of these kings, called En-me-dur-an-ki has some characteristics that are similar to those of Enoch, the seventh in the genealogy of Genesis 5. Both are called friends of God, both are presented as wise—Enoch in Sirach 44:16, in the Hebrew text, is said to be an example of wisdom for all generations.

The point at issue is absent however from the similarities: immortality. The only personage in the Mesopotamian legends to reach immortality was Utnapishtim, the hero of the Mesopotamian flood. (*See* FLOOD, THE.) It is probable that Enoch's immortality derived from this legendary Mesopotamian hero. But it is impossible to say when or by whom this fusion in Enoch of elements belonging to two different characters took place.

Enosh, Son of Seth. According to Genesis 4:26 he was the first to invoke the name of the Lord. Genesis 5:9 makes him the father of Kenan, who is none other than Cain. Since Enosh in Hebrew means "man" as does the name Adam, 5:9 could explain why the tradition about Cain was inserted by the Yahwist author after the paradise story. *See* CAIN; on the problem of a pre-Israelite cult of Yahweh *see* YAHWEH.

enough

E. now! Stay your hand	not be *e.* for you and us
2 Sam. 24:16	Matt. 25:9
not when they have *e.* Isa. 56:11	

En-rimmon, A city of Simeon (1 Chron. 4:32), later of Judah (Josh. 15:32), rebuilt by the exiles who returned from Babylon (Neh. 11:29).

En-Rogel (en-roe′-gel), A spring near Jerusalem, on the border between the territories of Judah and Benjamin (Josh. 15:7; 18:16). Jonathan and Ahimaaz, who remained loyal to David during Absalom's revolt, stayed there in order to keep the king informed of what was happening in the capital (2 Sam. 17:17). At this spring the usurper Adonijah celebrated his coronation (1 Kgs. 1:9). Today it is called Bir Ayyub and situated where the Kidron joins the Valley of Hinnom.

enter

about to *e.* Egypt Gen. 12:11	they *e.* the palace Ps. 45:16
he *e.* with you into judgment	*E.* through the narrow gate
Job 22:4	Matt. 7:13

envied, envious, envy

Philistines became *e.* of them	the *e.* of all Eden's trees
Gen. 26:14	Ezek. 31:9
They *e.* Moses in the camp	Out of *e.,*the patriarchs Acts 7:9
Ps. 106:16	

Epaenetus (e-pee′-ne-tus), A Christian greeted as "my beloved Epaenetus; he is the first offering that Asia made to Christ" (Rom. 16:6).

Epaphras (ep′-a-fras or e-paf′-ras), A Christian of Colossae, a prison companion of Paul when he wrote to the Colossians. He was probably the founder of the church at Colossae, Hierapolis and Laodicea (Col. 1:7; 4:12, 13; Philem. 23).

Epaphroditus (e-paf′-ro-dy′-tus), A Christian, a collaborator of Paul, who brought to him the gift of the church of Philippi (Phil. 2:25-30). Some identify him with Epaphras.

Ephah, A dry measure, equal to one tenth of a homer, the equivalent of around half a bushel (*see* Zech. 5:6-10; Jgs. 6:19; Ruth 2:17; 1 Sam. 1:24).

Ephesians, Epistle to, The epistle of Paul to the Ephesians gives rise to two important questions. The first is whether it was in fact written to the Ephesians, and the second is whether St. Paul really wrote it.

The question of whether it was written to the Ephesians arises from two considerations. First, the impersonal tone of the letter seems to exclude its coming from Paul to a community in which Paul lived for three years (*see* Acts 19:1-10). There is a total absence of reference to the concrete circumstances of the church at Ephesus, nor are there the final greetings that chracterize Paul's other letters. Some passages of the letter suggest that he is penning it to people he doesn't know but of whom he has heard: "for my part, from the time I first heard of your faith in the Lord Jesus" (Eph. 1:15). Others imply that through the written word only will they get to know the depths Paul saw in the mystery of Christ (3:2-4; *see* 4:21).

Secondly, the words 'in Ephesus' in the inscription are missing in some of the more ancient and more important manuscripts, such as the Chester Beatty papyrus (p 46), the most ancient of all; and in manuscripts B (Vaticanus) and S (Sinaiticus) of the fourth century, the words were added in at a later date. Marcion, a heretic of the second century, knows the letter as the Epistle of Paul to the Church of Laodicea (*see* Col. 4:16) while other ancient fathers such as Origen, Basil and Jerome of centuries 3-4 tell us that the words were absent from many manuscripts known to them. One can deduce then with certainty that the words 'in Ephesus' did not belong to the original text of the epistle.

How must one then explain an epistle without destinataries, the inscription not withstanding (1:1)? Two principal explanations emerge. One states that the letter was really sent to the church of Laodicea, and that it is no other than the letter Paul refers to in Colossians 4:16. This was the way Marcion knew it in the second century. Then the name Laodicea was cancelled as a consequence of Revelation 3:14-16 where the church is condemned for being neither cold nor hot, and in its place was substituted the name of one of Paul's churches to which there was no extant letter. Thus Ephesus was chosen. One can, however, question whether the condemnatory words of Revelation 3:14-16 could have such a disastrous effect. For this reason the second explanation is preferable.

This explanation is also based on Colossians 4:16, which reads: "Once this letter has been read to you, see that it is read in the assembly of the Laodiceans as well, and that you yourselves read the letter that is coming from Laodicea." This second letter is what is now known as the Epistle to the Ephesians, but it was not sent exclusively to the church of the Laodiceans. It was rather an encyclical letter, destined for several churches of Asia Minor, some of which were certainly not founded by Paul. This then would explain the impersonal tone of the letter. The letter was sent in as many copies as there were churches to which it was addressed (e.g. Laodicea, Hierapolis and even others). Ephesus probably did not figure among them. The letter was nevertheless brought to Ephesus, the most important center of the region, and from there it was sent out to the individual churches. The letter was subsequently copied and spread by Ephesus without the name of any destinataries, even to other places. Later the letter was assigned to that city because it had spread from there, and finally the city's name found its place in the inscription of the letter (1:1). While this explanation is more plausible, it is certainly not possible to prove all its assertions.

The question of Pauline authorship arises by virtue of internal reasons such as style, vocabulary and content. The style is emphatic, heavy and over-weighted with pleonasms; it is almost liturgical in tone. This impression becomes more marked when Ephesians is compared with Colossians, which treats of an analogous subject. The vocabulary is novel: there are 36 new words not found elsewhere in the New Testament. This however is not sufficient to deny Pauline authorship. A similar argument would exclude Paul from authorship of letters such as that to the Galatians and 1 Corinthians, which are certainly Paul's. More significant is the fact that Ephesians uses terms to indicate things for which Paul is accustomed to use other words. (Some have thought to discover inconsistency between this and other Pauline letters, but in reality, not one point can be quoted which cannot be demonstrated to be a legitimate and coherent evolution of the same doctrine.)

The authenticity is also questioned on another score, that of the extraordinary affinity of theme and development between it and the epistle to the Colossians. Some therefore claim that Ephesians is but an imitation of Colossians written by an unknown disciple of Paul. The similarity of the two cannot be denied. It has been calculated that only about 30 percent of the content of Colossians is without parallel in Ephesians, while only a half of Ephesians treats of subjects untouched by Colossians.

One must however recognize in the parts that are original to the letter to the Ephesians the strength of the thought which flows evenly from a pen perfectly at ease both when treating of subjects contained in Colossians and when writing new material for Ephesians. A recent commentator ironically remarks that to deny Pauline authorship to Ephesians leaves us with the greater problem of producing another Paul capable of writing it, who was completely at home in his theme and able to write variations on Pauline doctrine with such conviction. That an author of such stature should have remained unknown is unthinkable. At most one could concede a greater liberty of expression on the part of the secretary to whom Paul would have committed the actual writing of the letter. (*See* LETTER.) This too could explain the differences in style already alluded to. .

At the time of the writing of the epistle to the Ephesians Paul was a prisoner (*see* 4:1), very probably at Rome. Ephesians was written about the same time as the epistle to the Colossians; both were brought by Tychicus (Col. 4:7 and Eph. 6:21). In Ephesians Paul has in mind a larger audience and so he develops the thoughts that the crisis of the church of Colossae had provoked, without however the same concrete references that are found in the letter to the Colossians. The epistle to the Ephesians has the tone and character of a statement of program or a position in theology; it reads like a doctrinal synthesis. Together with the letter to the Romans it is, among all the authentic writings of Paul, the one that most approaches the typical epistle as distinct from a letter. *See* LETTER.

Ephesus, A city and port at the mouth of the river Cayster on the western coast of Asia Minor. It was the capital of the Roman province of Asia. Saint Paul visited the city during his second apostolic journey while returning from Corinth on the way to Jerusalem and Antioch. He preached in the synagogue and although asked by the Jews to remain, he departed very soon, promising to return (Acts 18:19-21). After his departure Apollos came there and was instructed in the way by Aquila and Priscilla. Apollos had only experienced the baptism of John, although he preached with enthusiasm and accuracy about Jesus. Apollos afterwards set out for Corinth (Acts 18:24-28).

Paul stayed at Ephesus for two years during his third missionary journey. He started to preach in the synagogue, but the hostility of the Jews forced him to choose another base of operations, the lecture room of Tyrannus (Acts 19:8-12). Paul had to abandon the city after the riot organized by Demetrius the silversmith, who felt that his trade—making miniature silver models of the shrine of Diana—was being discredited by Paul's teaching (Acts 19:23-20:1).

On his return from the third missionary journey Paul stopped at Miletus and sent for the elders of the church of Ephesus, where he held a farewell discourse that brought them to tears (Acts 20:17-38).

Although Acts does not recount it, it does seem that Paul was imprisoned at Ephesus for a while, during which he wrote his letter to the Philippians. (*See* PHILIPPIANS.) During his second visit to Ephesus he wrote the first letter to the Corinthians (*see* CORINTHIANS, EPISTLES TO; 1 Cor. 15:32-16:8).

On the people to whom the letter to the Ephesians was written *see* EPHESIANS, EPISTLE TO. To the church of the city is also addressed one of the seven letters of Revelation (1:11; 2:1). Tradition has it that the disciple John lived in Ephesus for a long time, together with the mother of Jesus. That Mary lived there is very doubtful, but John's residence there is attested to by ancient writers (Irenaeus of Lyons in the second century), although Ignatius of Antioch does not seem to have heard of it. *See* JOHN, GOSPEL OF.

Ephod (ee′-fod), In the Old Testament the word ephod is used to designate different objects that were used in the cult.

a. Ephod bad or linen ephod was a priestly vestment, a short tunic used in acts of worship: *see* e.g. 1 Sam. 2:18; 22:18; 2 Sam. 6:14.

b. From this is obviously derived the ephod which was the distinctive garment of the high priest. It is described in Ex. 28:6-14 and 39:2-7. It must be brightly colored in gold, purple, violet and crimson. Its front and back piece were joined by shoulder straps, on which were fastened twelve stones engraved with the names of the twelve tribes, six on each, so that "thus Aaron shall bear their names on his shoulders as a reminder before the Lord" (Ex. 28:12).

Two rosettes were also attached to the shoulder straps and from them hung the gold cords to which was attached the 'pectoral of judgment,' an ornate burse containing the sacred instruments known as the Urim and Thummim (*see* URIM and THUMMIM; Ex. 28:15-30; 39:8-21).

Ephod is probably a word taken from the Egyptian and meaning a special type of cloth. Hence the cloth gave its name to the vestment made from it, which in its final evolution became the high priest's sacred vestment. It is not however altogether clear how the name ephod came to be given to another greatly different object:

c. In some ancient texts of the book of Judges and the books of Samuel (Jgs. 8:27; 17:5; 18:14, 18, 20; 1 Sam. 23:6-10; 30:7) there is mention of a cultic object whose only clear use was the obtainment of oracles (1 Sam. 23:10; 30:8). It is of interest to note that in some of these texts ephod seems to be a corruption or correction of the word **aron**, ark. And on this probability is based a recent explanation of the enigma. During Israel's nomadic period there existed an ark with sacred instruments for divination. This institution evolved in two directions with the passage of time: the ark of the covenant and the ark of the oracles. The latter was eventually reduced in size and found its place on the breast of the priestly ephod. The word ark became synonymous with the ark of the covenant while the word ephod was extended to mean the ancient ark of the oracles, now carried, in fact, on the priest's ephod.

Ephphatha (ef′-a-tha), A Greek transcription of the Aramaic **'etpetah,** the passive form of the verb **petah,** to open, used by Jesus in the cure of the deaf mute in Mark 7:34.

Ephraim (ee′-fra-im), The second son of Joseph, the founding father of the Israelite tribe of the same name. His mother was Asenath, the daughter of Potiphera, priest of On, and he was born in Egypt (Gen. 41:52; 46:20). He was adopted by Jacob who preferred him, in his blessing, to the first-born Manasseh (Gen. 48:17-20; *see* Deut. 33:17). In reality Ephraim is the geographical name of the central mountainous region of Palestine from Bethel to Shechem (*see* Josh. 24:33; 1 Sam. 1:1). The name later attached itself to that part of Joseph's family which settled in the region. The territory extended to the north as far as the southern boundary of Jezreel, and to the south as far as Bethel (Josh. 16:4-10; 1 Chron. 7:20 ff.). It was the center of cohesion for the Israelite confederacy throughout the whole pre-monarchical period. From Ephraim came, among others, Joshua (Josh. 19:49, 50; 24:30) and Samuel (1 Sam. 1:1). After the schism it became the political and military center for the northern kingdom, and is often simply referred to by the prophets as Ephraim (e.g. Hos. 4:17; 5:3; Isa. 9:8; Jer. 7:15; 31:9; Ezek. 37:16). In the struggles at the time of the judges, Ephraim intervened at Gideon's request against the Midianite chieftains, Oreb and Zeeb. The Ephraimites seized the water points as far as Beth-barah and the Jordan, and captured Oreb whom they killed at Oreb's Rock, and Zeeb, whom they slew at Zeeb's Winepress. They then reproved Gideon for not having called them at the beginning of the campaign. Gideon's words however calmed their anger (Jgs. 7:24-8:2). A similar conflict arose between Ephraim and Jephthah, whom they rebuked for not inviting them to share in the war against the Ammonites. Jephthah and the Gileadites took up arms against the Ephraimites and routed them, cutting them off from the fords of the Jordan. They trapped the fugitive Ephraimites by asking them to pronounce "Shibboleth," meaning either an ear of corn or a flowing stream. As the Ephraimites were unable to pronounce the word properly, and pronounced it instead as "Sibboleth," they were easily identified and thereupon slaughtered (Jgs. 12:1-6).

Ephrath, Ephrathah, 1. The second wife of Caleb, mother of Hur and of Ashhur (1 Chron. 2:19, 24).

2. A village south of Bethel (Gen. 35:16), but north of Jerusalem, near Ramah (1 Sam. 10:3; Jer. 31:15). On the road between Bethel and Ephrath Rachel gave birth to Benjamin, but she died in childbirth and was buried on the roadside. Jacob raised a monument to her there. A gloss in Genesis 35:19 identifies Ephrath with Bethlehem south of Jerusalem (*see* Ruth 4:11; Micah 5:1). Moreover the families of David and of Elimelech, the husband of Naomi are called Ephrathites (1 Sam. 17:12; Ruth 1:2). This uncertainty in the location of the place seems to owe its origins to a migration of families from Ephrath to Bethlehem, in the vicinity of which, at a later period, Rachel's tomb was sought, since this from ancient times had been associated with the dwelling place of the Ephrathites.

Ephron, 1. The Hittite who sold Abraham the cave near Hebron in which he buried Sarah (Gen. 23; 25:9; 45:29; 50:13).

2. A mountain in the land of Judah (Josh. 15:9).

3. A town near Bethel (2 Chron. 13:19).

Epiphanes (e-pif′-a-nees), The title and royal name of Antiochus IV (175-164 B.C.) and of Antiochus VI (145-142 B.C.), Seleucid kings of Syria.

Epistle, The name commonly given to the twenty-one letters of the New

Testament, fourteen under Paul's name, one under James's, two under Peter's, three under John's and one under Jude's. An epistle, as opposed to a letter, was a treatise or essay for public reading with the greetings a literary device or form of dedication. A letter was more personal and concrete, with reference to definite situations. Using this distinction some scholars have called thirteen of Paul's writings and the second and third of John's epistles "letters"; the rest are epistles. *See* LETTER.

equal
Gold or crystal cannot *e.* it   thereby making himself God's *e.*
          Job 28:17   Jn. 5:18
as an *e.*   Isa. 46:5

Erastus, 1. A Christian who was one of Paul's collaborators, sent with Timothy from Ephesus to Macedonia (Acts 19:22) and who is also mentioned in 2 Tim. 4:20.

2. The city treasurer in Corinth, who sends greetings in Romans 16:24.

Erech, The biblical name of Uruk, an ancient Sumerian city in Lower Mesopotamia, today Warka (Gen. 10:10).

Eri, A son of Gad (Gen. 46:16; Num. 26:16).

Esarhaddon (ee′-sar-had′-don), King of Assyria (681-668 B.C.), son and successor of Sennacherib (705-681 B.C., *see* 2 Kgs. 19:37; Isa. 37:38; Ezra 4:2).

Esau, The first-born of Isaac and Rebekah and twin brother of Jacob. Esau appears again as the founding hero of the Edomites living in Seir (*see* EDOM; Gen. 36:9-43; Deut. 2:4-12). The Genesis traditions about Esau revolve around the central theme of his rivalry with Jacob. The theme undoubtedly transposes into familiar terms the historical conflicts that arose between the descendents of Jacob and the Edomites, who were related ethnically and who were geographical neighbors from the thirteenth century on. The rivalry of the brothers started in the maternal womb (Gen. 25:22) which was interpreted by Yahweh for her in that she would give birth to the founders of two rival peoples (*see* v. 23). The theme was developed theologically by St. Paul in Romans 9:10-13 to show forth the gratuitousness of the divine choice. Esau sold his birthright for a plate of lentil soup and bread (Gen. 25:29-34), and Jacob cunningly obtained Isaac's blessing instead of Esau. Jacob took refuge in Haran (Gen. 27:41-45). The story continues in Gen. 33 with the reconciliation of the two brothers after Jacob's return from Haran. Esau went to live in the mountains of Seir, southeast of the Dead Sea (Gen. 36:6-8).

Esdraelon (ez′-dra-ee′-lon), The Greek name for the plain of Jezreel (Judith 3:9). *See* JEZREEL.

Esdras, A Greek and Latin form of Ezra. This form of the word is used to designate the two apocryphal books which were handed down under the name of Ezra, so that they could be distinguished from the canonical works known as the two books of Ezra (the books of Ezra and Nehemiah). The third book of Esdras is a historical book alike in style and content to the canonical books of Ezra. The fourth book of Esdras is an apocalyptic work composed in the first century A.D. Jerusalem. It was widely used and venerated in the ancient church and even today it is customary to edit it as an appendix to the Latin Vulgate translation.

Esdris, An officer of the Seleucid army of Gorgias (2 Mac. 12:36).

Esek, "Contention," the name of a well dug by Isaac's servants (Gen. 26:20).

Eshcol, "The grape cluster," the name of a valley in S. Palestine from which the men sent by Moses to spy on the land brought back an enormous cluster of grapes (Num. 13:23-24).

Eshtaol (esh′-ta-ol), A town alloted to Dan (Josh. 19:41), then in Judah (Josh. 15:33). Samson was buried in the family tomb between Eshtaol and Zorah (Jgs. 16:31).

espoused

my wife Michal, whom I *e*.	Mary, his *e*. wife	Lk. 2:5
2 Sam. 3:14		

Essenes, A religious sect of Judaism at the time of the New Testament, known to us from the writings of Philo of Alexandria (1st c. A.D.) and Josephus Flavius. The name "Essenes" has not yet been completely explained. Several Greek and Hebrew words have been suggested as etymological sources. It would seem to be derived from the Hebrew **hasidim** meaning "the pious ones." (*See* HASIDIM.) The derivation implies an explanation of the historical origins of the sect. The most distinctive characteristic of this sect is its monastic bent. According to Pliny, its members lived in community without women, without love, without money. After a period of trial, they pledged themselves with solemn oaths to observe their rules. They did not marry and they lived under authority. They carried out, with extreme exactness, the demands of the law. They subjected themselves to complex purification rites, while at the same time they rejected the Temple sacrifices, probably because they considered illegitimate the priesthood then in function. They had their own secret doctrines which they pledged not to reveal. Flavius Josephus exaggerated somewhat the similitude between the Essenes and the Pythagorian communities, thus creating a false impression. He attributes to them a doctrine on the immortality of the soul which is more suggestive of Greece than of Israel.

According to the common opinion of the specialists, the "monks" of Qumran, whose library was discovered from 1947 on in caves along the north west coast of the Dead Sea, were Essenes. *See* DEAD SEA SCROLLS; QUMRAN.

establish, establishing

I will *e*. my covenant	Gen. 6:18	*e*. a house for you	2 Sam. 7:11
now *e*. my covenant	Gen. 9:9	until he re-*e*. Jerusalem	Isa. 62:7

Esther, Book of, A book of the Old Testament numbered among the 'scriptures' or 'hagiographa' of the Hebrew Canon. It is placed among the historical books with Tobit and Judith, and after Ezra-Nehemiah in the Vulgate.

The book recounts the story of an attempt at mass extermination of the Jews in Persia, which however came to nothing thanks to a Jewish woman named Hadassah, who was known in Persian as Esther.

Esther had been brought up by Mordecai, son of Jair, who had been deported from Jerusalem by Nebuchadnezzar king of Babylon. She is described as his uncle's daughter, therefore his cousin, and an orphan, "beautifully formed and lovely to behold" (Esth. 2:7). One text states that he had brought her up to be his daughter, but post-Christian Jewish tradition has it that she was brought up to be Mordecai's wife.

Following a royal edict Esther was taken into the harem of King Ahasuerus (Xerxes I) (486-465 B.C.), and she pleased him so much that he proclaimed her queen instead of Vashti (2:17).

While attached to the royal chancellory, Mordecai came to know of a conspiracy hatched by two of the king's eunuchs to kill the king. Through-

Esther, Mordecai passed the information to the king, who took action which ended with the execution of the conspirators (2:19-23).

Soon after, Haman was appointed by the king as his minister. All those employed at the chancellory were ordered to bow down and prostrate themselves before Haman, a gesture which Mordecai's Jewish religion would not allow him to do. Haman was seized with fury and decided to do away with the whole Jewish race on account of Mordecai's refusal to bow.

With the pogrom decided upon, the day was chosen by lot or pur (3:7) as the 14th day of the month called Adar in the twelfth year of the king. Mordecai let Esther know of Haman's designs on the Jewish race and asked her to plead for them with the king (c. 4).

In the meantime while Haman was having a gibbet prepared for Mordecai, the king remembered the Jew who had saved his life and ordered that he be given the honors and gifts due to such a favor. Esther finally asked for the life of the Jews and of Mordecai in Haman's presence. The king withdrew to consider the question while Haman prostrated himself on Esther's bed to plead for her intercession in his favor. The king caught him on the queen's bed and believing him to have tried to use violence on her, ordered him to be hanged on the gibbet that Haman had prepared for Mordecai.

The king spared the lives of Mordecai and of the Jews and gave him power to exercise summary justice on all those who ill-treated or oppressed the Jews. This was to take place on the 14th and 15th day of Adar, that is, precisely on the days decided on by Haman for their extermination. Finally Mordecai was himself appointed prime minister (cc. 5-10). It was to commemorate this liberation that the feast of Purim was established, for the 14th and 15th of Adar (9:20-32). On the historical relationships between this feast and the story of Esther *see* PURIM.

The book has come down in two versions, one briefer Hebrew version and the other in the Greek of the Septuagint. The material with which the Septuagint amplifies the Hebrew can be found in the Vulgate in 10:4-6, even though the Septuagint has the extra material scattered through the book. These chapters are deuterocanonical. Exegetes commonly hold that the more ancient and original version is the Hebrew. The additions in the Greek came somewhat after the event, and were an attempt to emphasize and highlight the religious import of the book, namely the divine protection of Israel.

It has often been pointed out that the name of God is not even mentioned in the Hebrew version. However it must be remembered that it was addressed to Jews accustomed to reading history in the light of God's secret action in favor of his people, which was present even in the most human of events. The Greek version, especially with its insertion of the prayers of Mordecai and Esther, gave the book a new outlook, which was also perhaps aimed at forwarding Jewish religious propaganda among the pagans.

There is no biblical or extra-biblical source to verify the facts narrated in the book of Esther. While the author was acquainted with the customs of the Persian court, he takes some notorious liberties in the use of names and dates which suggest he was writing a historical novel rather than strict history. If Mordecai was deported at the time of Nebuchadnezzar in 597 B.C. he would hardly be alive in the time of Xerxes I (486-465 B.C.). Moreover the latter's wife was Amestris, which seems to exclude the story of Vashti's being supplanted by Esther.

The policy of religious tolerance that marked Persian rule after Cyrus is hardly consonant with the decree to exterminate the Jews, while one can hardly credit its opposite, empowering the Jews with imperial approval to do away with 75,000 nobles of the empire. Whether there is some historical basis of lesser proportions is a question that cannot be answered. It is certain that the book is an invitation to believe in the providence of God for his people Israel, a providence made evident in the overthrow of Haman's plans against the Jews. The book seems to have emerged during a period in which this faith was in danger of giving way to oppression or persecution, thus bringing the very life of Judaism into jeopardy. The Maccabean epoch is a suitable framework for such a book, which would also explain the vivid national spirit that animates it. This too would fit in with the notice contained in the eleventh chapter of the Greek text, v. 3, that Mordecai's letter concerning the Purim was brought to Egypt by Dositheus, a priest and Levite, and Ptolemy his son in the fourth year of Ptolemy and Cleopatra, that is Ptolemy VIII Soter II (116-107 B.C.).

Etam (ee′-tam), The cave from which Samson was taken to be delivered to the Philistines (Jgs. 15:8, 11).

eternal
e. punishment and the just to *e*   words of *e*. life   Jn. 6:68
            Matt. 24:46   God's *e*. power   Rom. 1:20
        an *e*. weight of glory   2 Cor. 4:17

Etham (ee′-tham), A stage of the journey of the Israelites through the desert, still inside the Egyptian border (Ex. 13:20; Num. 33:6-8).

Ethan (ee′-than), 1. Son of Zerah, who was son of Judah and Tamar (1 Chron. 2:6).

2. Ethan the Ezrahite, a wise man with whom Solomon is favorably compared (1 Kgs. 5:11).

3. An ancestor of Asaph, one of the men appointed to lead the singing in the Temple by David (1 Chron. 6:24-28).

4. Son of Kishi, a Merarite, also appointed cantor in the Temple by David (1 Chron. 6:29).

There is great confusion about identifying these Ethans. Some would hold them all to be one person, while others would distinguish them in one way or another.

Ethanim (eth′-a-nim), The name of the seventh month of the Canaanite calendar corresponding to the later Hebrew Tishri and to our September-October (1 Kgs. 8:2).

Ethbaal, King of the Sidonians, father of Jezebel who was wife of Ahab, king of Israel (869-850 B.C.; 1 Kgs. 16:31).

Ethiopia, For the biblical period the name Ethiopia and Cush may be understood to cover more or less the same territory. At first the land of Cush covered the territory between the Second and Third Cataracts of the Nile, but later, during the New Kingdom or Empire period (from 1570 B.C. on) it seems to have included all known or imagined territory south of Egypt. It did not correspond to the modern kingdom of Ethiopia, but rather to ancient Nubia and modern Sudan. According to the genealogy of Genesis 10:6-8 Noah's son Ham sired Cush, who fathered Nimrod, "who was the first potentate on earth." Ethiopia was the Greek name for the same area.

Amos 9:7 refers to the Cushites as a people of no great concern to God. Isaiah in 18:1-7 contains an oracle against Cush, "a people tall and bronzed, from a people dreaded near and far, a nation strong and conquering, whose land is washed by rivers" (v. 2). The oracle probably refers to Egypt which was governed at the time by Pharaohs of Nubian ancestry. Isaiah 43:3 prophesies that Egypt, Cush and Seba will be given in exchange for Israel. Ezekiel pronounces against Egypt in c. 30: "The remnant of his people God will ransom from Cush, among other nations" (cf. Isa. 11:11).

Ethiopian Eunuch, The story of the Ethiopian eunuch is told in Acts 8:26-40. Philip received a message from the angel to set out at noon, an improbable time for a journey, on the road to Gaza, where he encountered the chief treasurer of the queen of Ethiopia, who, Luke states five times, was a eunuch. This led to a conversation which culminated in the baptism of the eunuch by Philip, whereupon the latter was snatched off by the spirit to Azotus.

Luke seems to have made a point of insisting that this was a eunuch and an Ethiopian. Deuteronomy 23:2 excluded eunuchs from the assembly of Yahweh, but Isaiah 56:3 included foreigners and eunucns in the promised kingdom. Moreover Isaiah 11:11 predicted that God would rescue the remnant of his people out of Cush, while Psalm 68:32 sings: "Let nobles come from Egypt; let Ethiopia extend its hands to God." In recounting the story, and in his emphasis, Luke points out how salvation is even for those who live in the farthest parts of the earth, and for those whom the strict letter of the law seemed to have excluded. *See* ETHIOPIA; EUNUCH.

Eubulus (you-bue′-lus), A Christian who salutes Timothy (2 Tim. 4:21).

Eucharist, Tradition and Christian theology has given the name Eucharist to the sacramental commemoration of the redemptive death of Christ. The word stems from the Greek word **eucharistein:** to give thanks. This commemorative rite which formed so much a part of the life of the apostolic Christian community was called by Paul "the Lord's Supper" (1 Cor. 11:20). The very name suggests the real context of the celebration, its historic origins and its essence which was to be a commemoration of the last supper celebrated by the Lord with his disciples before he went to his death: "Do this as a remembrance of me" (Lk. 22:19; 1 Cor. 11:24, 25). The name **eucharist** underscores one of the fundamental elements of the celebration, and is derived from the frequent mention of thanksgiving as part of the celebration of the Lord's Supper (*see* Matt. 26:27; Mk. 14:23; Lk. 22:17; 1 Cor. 11:24, and also in the story of the multiplication of loaves in Matt. 15:36; Mk. 8:6; Jn. 6:11). *See* LORD'S SUPPER.

Euergetes (you-er′-ja-tees), "Benefactor," the royal title of Ptolemy VII king of Egypt (Sir., prologue). *See* PTOLEMY.

Eumenes (you′-me-nees), Eumenes II, king of Pergamum (197-158 B.C.) who sided with the Romans against the Seleucid king Antiochus III the Great (1 Mac. 8:8).

Eunice, A Jewish-Christian woman of Galatia (Lystra or Derbe) who was married to a Gentile, and mother of Timothy, Paul's disciple (Acts 16:1). In 2 Tim. 1:5 Paul records the sincere faith of Eunice and of her mother Lois, who had instructed Timothy from his youth in the sacred scriptures.

Eunuch, A castrated male usually in charge of the women's quarters in ancient Eastern households. The Hebrew word **saris** however may be derived from the Akkadian meaning captain, officer or chief. They could hold eminent positions in the royal court. The chief treasurer of the queen of Ethiopia was a eunuch (Acts 8:27). Potiphar, Pharaoh's captain of the guard, is called a eunuch in Gen. 37:36, but in c. 39 he turns out to be married. The king's cupbearer and baker are also called eunuchs in Genesis 40:1. Perhaps the word simply means official of the court.

As a eunuch was defective, he was excluded from the covenant community: he "may not be admitted into the community of the Lord" (Deut. 23:2). Isaiah predicts that "some of your own bodily descendants shall be taken and made servants in the palace of the king of Babylon" (Isa. 39:7), and the historian Herodotus implies that captives were generally treated in this way. Deutero-Isaiah includes eunuchs however in the promised kingdom of the redeemed (Isa. 56:3-5).

Matthew 19:12 quotes Jesus as saying: "Some men are incapable of sexual activity from birth; some have been deliberately made so; and some there are who have freely renounced sex for the sake of God's reign. Let him accept this teaching who can." This text has been radically interpreted and applied on occasion, and notoriously so in the case of Origen. The more common interpretation takes it as an invitation to the ideal of voluntary celibacy or virginity such as Christ himself embraced. A third interpretation however keeps it in the context of the question of divorce (19:1-9) which Christ excluded. Those who voluntarily renounced sexual pleasures for the sake of the kingdom are those whose marriage has broken up through no fault of their own, and who nevertheless remain faithful to their vows as a sacramental image of God's faithfulness to his spouse, the Church, even when through weakness and sins she has slackened off in her correspondence to his graciousness in her regard.

Eupator (you′-pa′tor), The royal title of King Antiochus V (1 Mac. 6:17; 2 Mac. 10:10).

Euphrates, A river in Mesopotamia. According to the legendary geography of Genesis 2:10-14 the Euphrates was one of the four branches into which the river of Paradise divided. Scripture at times uses it as a symbol of the immense power of the Mesopotamian empires (Isa. 8:7; 27:12; Jer. 2:18). Again it expresses the northern limits of Israelite aspirations to territorial expansion, limits aspired to but only rarely reached during the time of the monarchy (Gen. 15:18; Deut. 1:7; 11:24; Josh. 1:4; 2 Sam. 8:3; 10:16; 1 Kgs. 5:4).

The Euphrates emerges in the mountains of Armenia from the union of two rivers, the Kara-su and the Murad-su. It first runs towards the Mediterranean, but at the level of Carchemish it turns suddenly and flows towards the Persian Gulf. Some believe—but the matter is disputed—that in ancient times the Euphrates poured directly into the gulf, but that as the shore-line moved south due to the alluvial formation, the Euphrates joined with the Tigris to irrigate this last region. The river below the junction is called today Shatt el-Arab. The principal tributary of the Euphrates is the Khabur, which enters above Dura-Europas, after which the Euphrates receives no further tributaries.

Eupolemus (you-pol′-e-mus), The ambassador of the Jews sent by Judas Maccabeus (161 B.C.) to make a pact with the Roman senate (1 Mac. 8:17; 2 Mac. 4:11).

Eutychus (you′-ti-kus), A young man in Troas who was raised to life by Paul (Acts 20:7-12).

Evangelist, As a term indicating the authors of the four gospels the word does not appear in the New Testament. The "evangelist" was apparently one who exercised a stable function or activity in the missionary work of the ancient church. In Eph. 4:11 there is a list of the gifts Christ gave for the building up of his body: the evangelists come third after apostles and prophets. The name derives from the Greek **evangelizo,** to announce good news, and so suggests a ministry of preaching. Its place in the list however indicates a position that was subordinate to that of the apostles. In the New Testament only Philip the deacon (Acts 21:8) and Paul's disciple Timothy are called evangelists. Perhaps these texts should be understood in the original sense of the word as 'preachers of the gospel,' and not in the technical sense of the function about which Ephesians 4:11 speaks.

Eve, The name of the first woman. The name was given her by Adam after the first sin, and for the biblical author means "mother of all the living," a popular etymology which makes the word **hawwah,** Eve derive from **hayah,** to live. On the creation of woman *see* WOMAN. On her part in the first sin *see* FALL, THE. References to Eve are found in Tobit 8:6, 2 Cor. 11:3 and 1 Tim. 2:13.

everlasting

of the *e.* mountains	Gen. 49:26	share in *e.* life	Mk. 10:17
possess *e.* life?	Matt. 19:16	age to come, *e.* life	Mk. 10:30

Evi, A Midianite king defeated and killed by the Israelites under Moses (Num. 31:8; Josh. 13:21).

evil

anything but *e.*   Gen. 6:5   prone the people are to *e.*
                                                            Ex. 32:22
I fear in *e.* days   Ps. 49:6

Evil-merodach (mer′-o-dak), King of Babylonia (562-560 B.C.), son and successor of Nebuchadnezzar (605-562 B.C.). In the year of his accession to the throne, he did a favor to Jehoiachin, king of Judah, who was then a prisoner in Babylon. He took him from prison, gave him the most honored place among the other kings who were with him in Babylon, admitted him to the royal table and granted him a pension for his maintenance (2 Kgs. 25:27-30). This is the consoling conclusion to the Second Book of Kings.

Evodia (ev-o′-dia), A Christian woman in the church of Philippi (Phil. 4:2; *see* Acts 16:12-25).

exchange

bread in *e.* for	Gen. 47:17	in *e.* for his very self?	Matt. 16:26
may not sell or *e.*	Ezek. 48:14	in *e.* for his life?	Mk. 8:37

exhortations

using *e.* of this sort   Lk. 3:18   with the power of *e.*   Rom. 12:8
Brothers, if you have any *e.*
                              Acts 13:15

Exile, In the year 587 B.C. the army of Nebuchadnezzar king of Babylonia took Jerusalem, destroyed the city and razed the Temple. The king decreed the mass deportation of the people of Judah to Babylonia. Thus began the long exile of the chosen people, far from the land of promise, which lasted until 538 B.C. when Cyrus II, king of Persia, who had captured Babylonia, ordered the repatriation of the exiles who were being held there. Among these were the Jews, who were permitted to rebuild their Jerusalem and the Temple.

The deportation of the people of Judah is only one example of the policy of conquest exercised by the Assyrians under Tiglath-pileser III and later adopted by the neo-Babylonians under Nebuchadnezzar. The Babylonian exile was not the only one suffered by the people of Palestine. In 732 B.C., during the reign of Pekah, king of Israel, Tiglath-pileser king of Assyria came and took all the territory of Naphtali, Gilead and Galilee, and de-

ported the inhabitants to Assyria, according to 2 Kings 15:29. In 722 the
king of Assyria, Sargon II took Samaria and deported the Israelites to
Assyria, settling them in Halah on the Habor, a river of Gozan in the
cities of the Medes and, "brought people from Babylon, Cuthah, Avva,
Hamath and Sepharvaim and settled them in the cities of Samaria in place
of the Israelites. They took possession of Samaria and dwelt in its cities"
(2 Kgs. 17:24).

The object of this deportation policy was evident. It was a radical attack
on the national consciousness of the conquered peoples in the hope of
eliminating any aspiration towards revolt. Thus it was hoped to secure the
cohesion, peace and submission of all the peoples and regions of the vast
Assyrian empire. It must be admitted that the policy succeeded in part, for
after the deportation of 722 B.C. all traces of the deported Samarian people were lost.

Judah had suffered another deportation even before 587 B.C. In 597 B.C.
Nebuchadnezzar placed Jerusalem uner siege. Jehoiachin, king of Judah
(598-597 B.C.) surrendered to the king of Babylonia, who took him captive. Nebuchadnezzar carried off all the treasures of the Temple and those
of the palace. He deported from Jerusalem all the officers, craftsmen and
smiths, together with Jehoiachin himself, his mother, his eunuchs and
functionaries, and the chief men of the land, and brought them to Babylon (*see* 2 Kgs. 24:10-17).

The people of Judah, even in exile, succeeded in maintaining their own
identity and national, racial and religious cohesion. Indeed scholars generally agree that the exile, despite the relatively scanty information that
has come down about it, was a period of fruitful silence, during which
were set the foundations for the national reconstruction and the change in
spirit that is markedly noticeable in later times. During the first years of
exile the people were guided from afar by Jeremiah (Jer. 29; 51:59-64),
and afterwards in Babylon itself the chief support and leadership came
from the prophetic ministry of Ezekiel and Deutero-Isaiah. *See* EZEKIEL;
ISAIAH.

The people in exile were able to make out fairly well in their new surroundings. They were free, and lived in their own colonies at Tel-Abib
(Ezek. 3:15) and in other places (Ezra 2:50). Many succeeded in carving
out a career in the commercial and economic life of the country. From the
religious point of view, as was to be expected, emphasis was placed on
those elements which distinguished the Jews from the surrounding peoples, such as the observance of the Sabbath (*see* SABBATH) and circumcision (*see* CIRCUMCISION). It was however above all the law that characterized the people, now that they were deprived of their own cult.

The exile was a time of great literary activity, not so much new creative
works as those of compilation, elaboration and re-interpretation of the
legislative, historical and prophetic literary heritage of the previous centuries in the light of the decisive event of the exile.

It is probably necessary to search in the years of exile for the origins of
one of the most successful and influential institutions of Judaism, that of
the synagogue, which became the place of common prayer, the soul and
center of cohesion of the local Jewish communities now far from the Temple. *See* SYNAGOGUE.

The exile also brought about a change of heart among the Jews. At the
beginning the exile had in fact appeared to be not just a defeat for the
people, but a defeat of their God Yahweh, as if he had failed to assert
himself and his superiority over the gods of the other nations. The exile
however caused the collapse of a false sense of security nurtured by the

people during the crisis that preceded their fall, based on a quasi-magical confidence in the inviolability of the Temple (*see* Jer. 7:1-15).

This initial disillusionment was gradually overtaken on the one hand by the thesis that this was but a punishment for sins that became evident in a long and implacable examination of conscience that covered the whole previous history contained in 1-2 Kings, and on the other by a more exact and intransigent formulation of monotheism, which was pushed ahead in a vehement polemic against idolatry. The oneness of God, creator and savior, lies at the center of Deutero-Isaiah's message (Isaiah 40-55).

Even under the weight of its own self-confessed guilt Israel did not lose hope in the restoration, a hope born of ancient but nevertheless irrevocable promises made by God. Now however they were appreciated in a new light, for now they were more clearly seen to be gratuitous, the fruit of a divine 'justice' which had no reason to be in man, but came totally from God's goodness. (*See* JUSTICE.) Moreover the people became more aware that God's ways are far above man's designs. The experience of the exile brought home to the people the meaning of the ancient promises and corrected the introverted vision that had falsely been formed around them. The messianic hope, which had been struck at the roots by the destruction of the Davidic dynasty, needed most of all to be revitalized, even if this had to take place through crisis and disillusionment (Ps. 89; *see* MESSIANISM). So there is presented a figure who is neither royal nor prophetic who in the hands of God will become an instrument of salvation through suffering. *See* SERVANT OF THE LORD.

Exodus, The word comes from the Greek **"exodus,"** exit, while as an event it comprises, in a broad sense, all that is described in Exodus 1-15, covering the liberation of the Israelites from the oppression of Egypt. In the account of the call of Moses the Exodus is presented not just as an isolated incident of God's goodness to his chosen race, now oppressed by the Egyptians. The liberation is announced in the full context of the salvation history of Israel, linked with the past of promise and pointing to the future of realization of the designs of God. God is about to intervene because He has freely pledged Himself to Abraham and to his descendants (6:5-6). He will now bring to fulfilment His promise to consign to Israel the land of Canaan (3:8; 6:8). In itself the Exodus states that God hereby acquires for Himself in an irrevocable manner His people whom He draws to Himself, and makes His own (6:7). The special relationship that arose between God and His people through this intervention was to be solemnly sanctioned in the Sinai covenant, towards which the Exodus was pointed. *See* COVENANT.

The Exodus was to be celebrated and commemorated in the religious lyrics of Israel as the great victory of God for the salvation of His people (Ex. 15; Ps. 78:12-14; 106:8-10; 135:8-11; 136:10-13). In moments of crisis and adversity the psalmists list the factors and events that should move God to intervene, and among them excels the Exodus (Ps. 77:12-21). The force of the argument is not so much that God is omnipotent, that He showed this omnipotence in snatching His people from Egypt and that therefore He can again save. Rather it resides in the conviction that God has really pledged this omnipotence in a salvific design for Israel.

The wonderful deeds of the past become a pledge for the future, for they are a concrete manifestation of God's constant decision in favor of His people. The Exodus, then, contains in a nutshell all the later development of the history of salvation, and becomes the type for God's salvific interventions which must perforce carry the people to the fulfilment of sacred history (Isa. 41:18; 42:16; 43:19; 48:21; 1 Cor. 10:1, 2).

In the strict sense of the word, the Exodus is the last decisive act in a series of events that led to the liberation of Israel, and in particular the miracle of the Sea of Reeds, recounted in Exodus 13:17-15:21. With this particular event the present article deals. For connected materials *see* COVENANT, EGYPT, MOSES, PASSOVER, PLAGUES. On the event itself, the Bible contains different traditions. One is the Miriam tradition (Ex. 15:21), which is probably the most ancient and later than the event itself. This states with sobriety that "horse and chariot he has cast into the sea." The other is the canticle of Moses (Ex. 15:1-18) which is also very ancient, but in its present form it is certainly later than the entry into Canaan (15:13-18).

The narrative traditions can be read in Exodus 13-14 and belong to the Yahwist, Elohistic and Priestly traditions (JEP). The Priestly document is the easiest to isolate: 14:1-4, 8, 9, 15-18, 21, 22-23, 26, 27a, 28a, 29. The rest is Yahwist with some Elohistic elements (13:11, 17-19; 14:19-20, 25a).

The Priestly document comprises three acts divided into two scenes. In the first scene God gives Moses the pertinent instructions which in the second scene he carries out. Yahweh intends to harden the heart of the Pharaoh so that he will pursue the Israelites who were encamped in front of Pihahiroth, between Migdol and the sea. P seems to think that the mass of water obstructing the passage of the Israelites was Lake Sirbonis, east of the delta, separated from the Mediterranean by a strip of land (Ex. 14:1-9). When they noticed the presence of the Egyptians the Israelites called on the Lord. He instructed Moses on what to do. At Moses' command the waters were to divide, allowing the Israelites through and then closing over the pursuing Egyptians, drowning them (Ex. 14:15-18, 21a, 22-23, 26, 27a, 28a, 29). This version of the prodigy offered by P is undoubtedly the one that succeeded best in later tradition, especially extra-biblical tradition, but also in other lyrical presentations of the event (*see* Pss. 78:13; 105). It is however a version that is certainly not shared by Ex. 15:8-10 nor by Ex. 15:21; Ps. 114:3-4, nor, as we shall see, by J or E.

According to JE the journey was different. The people did not follow the sea road. The reason adopted, fear of the Philistines, is an anachronism, for the Philistines did not settle along the coast of Palestine until the 12th century B.C. The fleeing Israelites turned southwards towards the **yam suph**, which is not the Red Sea but the Sea of Reeds (*see* RED SEA), one of the masses of water found in the Suez isthmus, but which has not been identified.

For JE the Exodus was a typical case of a holy war (*see* Ex. 14:10-14 and Deut. 20:1-4, *see* WAR): God present in the midst of His people fights for Israel and gives them victory without their having to engage in battle. God's weapon in these cases is the panic He seeds in the enemy, rendering it incapable of defense or attack and thus making it easy prey for His people, who exterminate them (*see* Ex. 14:24 and Josh. 10:9, 10).

The miracle of the sea is presented differently in JE from its account by P: God with a hot dry wind dried up the mass of water that obstructed the passage of Israel in flight. He then sowed panic in the hearts of the Egyptians who penetrated into the zones vacated by the waters, upon which the waters returned, overwhelming the Egyptians. Here in reality, two different versions are being fused: one is the tradition of the panic put in the Egyptians' hearts by God, so that they end up in the sea, and the other uses the story of the withdrawal and return of the waters of the sea (Ex. 14:19-20, 24, 25, 27b, 28b, 30, 31).

There is a common basis to both traditions. Differences arise in the explanation of how God executed His designs. Both traditions are convinced that God alone, without the cooperation of the people, brought about their delivery. Moreover the people in their flight were moving from east of the delta towards the Sinai desert when they found themselves in imminent danger of being routed or led back into Egypt by a detachment of Egyptian chariots of the Pharaoh. This danger was eliminated by a prodigious intervention of God who caused the detachment to disappear in the sea in a mysterious manner. Even then it was probably not possible to give the event an explanation. The Israelites "saw the Egyptians lying dead on the seashore" (Ex. 14:30; 15:21).

The differences, then, arise in the attempt to explain the event, or give it more details. P tends to explanations on a grander, more miraculous scale, while the others took recourse to the classical elements of a holy war. A third explanation, perhaps relying on a historical record or on a phenomenon more or less characteristic of thé place, speaks of the return of the waters that had been driven away by the wind. On the data *see* EGYPT. On the participants *see* ISRAEL.

Exodus, Book of, The second book of the Pentateuch. In Greek the word means exit, which is the title of the Greek translation from which it carried over to other editions of the Bible. The title expresses well the contents of the book, which describe the liberation of the Israelites from the oppression of Egypt and the events connected with that liberation. In reality however the book emerged from the division into five parts of the whole Pentateuch, so for its origin and division *see* PENTATEUCH.

The book starts with a list of the people who settled with Jacob in Egypt, thus forming a link with the story of Genesis. It also mentions the extraordinary multiplication of the people in Egypt which is the fulfilment of the first part of the promise to the patriarchs (Ex. 1:1-7; *see* Gen. 15:1-5). Exodus 1:8-14 gathers some typical stories to illustrate the oppression of the Israelites in Egypt: they were forced into slave labor 'with clay and brick' in the construction of the cities Pithom and Raamses, and into all kinds of work in the fields.

The Pharaoh's order to do away with all the males born of the Jews forms the background for the story of the birth of Moses, the future savior of Israel (Ex. 2:1-10). Moses' flight from Egypt (2:11-15) leads to the introduction of the traditions on Moses' stay among the Midianites (the revelation of the name of God, 3:13-15, Ex. 6:1-13; the announcement of salvation 3:1-2, and Moses' vocation 3:16-4:1-17).

Chapters 7-12 tell of Moses' dealings with the Pharaoh, that is, the account of the ten plagues of Egypt. The threatened and fulfilled death of the first-born of Egypt brings on the proclamation of the laws concerning the feast of the passover, and those who take part in it (cc. 12-13).

Chapter 14 contains the story of the Sea of Reeds where "as the water flowed back, it covered the chariots and the charioteers of Pharaoh's whole army which had followed the Israelites into the sea," and this in turn leads to its celebration in the Canticle of Moses in c. 15.

Chapters 16-18 tell of the first stages of the journey through the desert until Sinai was reached. There is also the story of Moses' encounter with his father-in-law Jethro (c. 18). The events of Sinai extend from Exodus 19 to Numbers 10. The length of this account is better understood when it is remembered that the biblical tradition transmitted the greater part of its legislative material framed in terms of the revelation of God on Mt. Sinai.

To the book of Exodus belongs: the story of the offering (19:3-8) and of the ratification of the pact (19:9-24:11, with the Ten Commandments in Ex. 20:1-17 and the Book of the Covenant, the oldest code of laws, in Ex. 20:22-23:19).

In chapters 25-31 are contained all the dispositions which God gave to Moses concerning the construction of the Tabernacle with all its fittings, the making of the sacred vestments, and the consecration of Aaron and his sons. All of these dispositions were then carried out to the letter (Ex. 35-39). To this is united the story of the apostasy of Israel and the idolatrous cult of the golden calf (*see* CALF, GOLDEN), and the consequent renewal of the covenant (Ex. 34).

The book concludes with the erection and solemn dedication of the Tabernacle; God approves of the work by covering the Tabernacle with a cloud which expresses His taking possession of it (Ex. 40).

Exorcism, The practice of expelling evil spirits from persons and places. The only example in the Old Testament is in Tobit 6:7-18. The remedy chosen reflects the popular opinion of the times, that evil spirits who had taken possession of men could be driven out by fumigation. Thus Tobiah was instructed to take the heart and liver of the fish and lay a little of it on the burning incense so that at the smell of it the demon would flee.

The gospel tradition has conserved several instances of exorcism worked by Jesus (*see* for example Matt. 8:28-34; 9:32-34; 12:22-24; 17:14-18; Mk. 1:23-28; Lk. 13:10-17 and parallel texts). On the literary genre and the historicity of these accounts *see* MIRACLES.

The stories form an integral part of the history of Jesus and are intimately connected with his teaching on the advent of the kingdom of God (*see* Mk. 1:39; 3:7-12). In fact the first act in the establishment of the kingdom is the abolition of the reign of Satan, who has taken possession of the present world, as was symbolized and expressed in the devil's taking possession of many people (*see* Matt. 12:43-45). When Jesus was accused of exorcising in the name of Beelzebul, the prince of devils, he retorted that the accusation was absurd, seeing that "a kingdom divided against itself cannot stand" (Mk. 3:24 and parallels).

The exorcisms performed by Jesus are a sign of the coming of the kingdom of God (Matt. 12:28; Lk. 11:20). They ring the knell of the defeated kingdom of Satan (Mk. 1:24; 3:11; Lk. 4:41; 10:17-20). The 'strong one' has been bound because there has appeared on the scene one stronger than he who will destroy his house (Lk. 11:21, 22; Mk. 3:27; Matt. 12:29).

The exorcisms do not simply state a generic superiority of Jesus over the devil: Jesus, who wins this victory over Satan, is an essential part of the kingdom of God, for he is the instrument used by God to establish his kingdom. This is why Jesus exorcises in his own name while he confers on the disciples the power to exorcise in his name (*see* Matt. 10:1-8; Mk. 6:7; 9:38-40; Lk. 10:17-20).

expectation
e. of the wicked comes Prov. 10:28   *e.* of the wicked is wrath

Prov. 11:23

explained, explaining
he kept *e.* things   Mk. 4:34   *e.* to him God's new way
Peter then *e.*   Acts 11:4   Acts 18:26

Eye, In Scripture the eye is frequently mentioned, not just for the physical act of seeing, but also as expressing emotional and mental attitudes, such as sorrow when it sheds tears (Ps. 119:136; Jer. 14:17), well-being when it brightens (Ps. 13:4), arrogance when it is haughty (Prov. 6:17), despisal and mockery when it fills with scorn (Prov. 30:17).

In the New Testament the eye is stated to be the lamp of the body, through which it walks in the light: thus the spiritual light which comes from within a person gives it direction (*see* Lk. 11:34). 1 Jn. 2:16 speaks of the lustful eye, which is also referred to in the Sermon on the Mount (Matt. 5:27-30). The eyelid was painted green or black in ancient Egypt and Babylonia, but the Bible generally mentions it in connection with evil women, such as Jezebel, who "shadowed her eyes" (2 Kgs. 9:30; *see* Ezek. 23:40).

Ezekiel, Son of Buzi, third of the major prophets of the Old Testament and priest. He was deported to Babylon with King Jehoiachin during the first deportation which took place in 597 B.C. (Ezek. 1:1-3; 33:21; *see* 2 Kgs. 24:14-16). He lived with his wife, who died in the ninth year of the exile (589/588 B.C., *see* Ezek. 24:1, 15-18), at Tell-Abib beside the river Khebar, a canal of the river Euphrates near Nippur (*see* Ezek. 1:1-3; 3:15, 24). His call to be a prophet took place in a splendid vision of the glory of God during the fifth year of his captivity, that is, in 593 B.C. His last oracle dates from 571 B.C. (*see* Ezek. 29:17).

Ezekiel, Book of, The book which bears his name is a collection of his visions and discourses, brought together by his disciples, who used writings and notes belonging to Ezekiel. This explains a certain incoherence in the disposition of the material of the book even though a unity of style and mentality pervades the whole writing. The book follows an order that is at the same time both thematic and chronological. First comes the inaugural vision and the call of the prophet. Then follows: a. cc. 3:22-24:27 contain oracles and visions against Jerusalem before the siege of the city. During this period Ezekiel's actions and preaching were similar in content and intent to those of his contemporary, Jeremiah, at Jerusalem. Indeed some authors believe that the whole tenor of this part demands that Ezekiel should have exercised his ministry at Jerusalem, so that his deportation would have taken place a decade later, in 587. Against this hypothesis lies the argument, first, that it is unnecessary, since for the most part it is a question of visions, and secondly, the explicit testimony of the book itself which places all of Ezekiel's ministry in Babylonia. Moreover the silence of the book of Jeremiah argues against it. On the other hand the moral and spiritual situation of the exiled was not totally different from that of those who remained, as is evidenced by the letters written by Jeremiah to those in exile (*see* Jer. 29:1-32).

b. The oracle against the nations is contained in cc. 25:1-32:2. It is directed especially against those who were accómplices in the ruin of Judah and who took advantage of her disaster: Ammon (25:1-7), Moab (25:8-11), Edom (25:12-14), Philistea (25:15-17), Tyre and Sidon (26-28) and Egypt (29-32).

c. Cc. 33-39 are oracles during and after the siege of Jerusalem. It is a collection of promises of the future restoration of Israel. Outstanding are the discourse against the evil shepherds of Israel who were responsible for the ruin of the nation and the following one on the promised good shepherd who would gather the flock, care for it and lead it to pasture. This was an allusion to the return from exile. The flock is then entrusted to "my servant David," that is, to the Messiah (c. 34). Chapter 37 contains the famous vision of the dry bones which joined together, were covered with sinews, flesh and skin, and came to life again in an immense army. This is the announcement of a restoration which reaches beyond the traditional scheme of hope and promises, and is the work of the Spirit of God (37:14). This will include the remission of sins, the interior transformation of man, who will be made capable of hearing the voice of God and following with docility and freedom the lead of the law (Ezek. 36:15-32).

d. Cc. 40-48 contain a description of the ideal Israel in the future restoration. The prophet is carried in a vision to Palestine where from the top of a mountain he contemplates the new Temple (40-42). Then follows a description of the return of the glory of the Lord (*see* Ezek. 10:18-19; 11:17-21) who came to inhabit the new Temple, and the laws which regulate the cult of the new Temple and its priesthood (43-46). A spring of water emerges from the Temple and washes the land of Palestine bringing life and fruitfulness to the whole land (47:1-12). Finally Ezekiel assists at the distribution of the land to the twelve tribes of Israel (47:13-48:35).

These chapters are obviously not a practical project for national renewal. Rather are they a concrete and imaginative description of an ideal. Ezekiel often translates theological theses into practical and concrete terms. One example of this is the plan for the restoration of the Temple which could not be realized as it did not fit in to the local topography of Jerusalem and Israel; however the prophet teaches symbolically the function which the Temple and the cult must have in the restored Israel.

Here and there however there are concrete measures that are nearer reality, and are meant to be put into practice after the return to Israel. All in all, chapters 40-48 show a firm decision eventually to renew the national religious life of Israel after the maturing process of the sobering inactivity of exile.

Ezekiel's prophetic ministry is not a little different in its visions, symbolic actions and allegories from the classical pre-exilic prophets. Many of these visions undoubtedly reflect ecstatic and visionary experiences which the prophet had. In other cases however (40-48) they can be reliably stated to be literary forms deliberately chosen by the author, or an elaboration of ecstatic experiences that were originally not so complex (cc. 1-3). This predominance of visionary experiences, as also occurs in Zechariah 1-8 and Daniel, presages the transformation of prophecy into the apocalyptic. The apocalyptic tradition was aware of its origins and of the spiritual affinity it had with Ezekiel. It borrowed from him much symbolic material and some central themes such as Gog and Magog (Ezek. 38 and 39 and Rev. 20:7-10). Numerous also are the symbolic actions (4:1-12; 5:1-4; 12:7) among which must be included the dumbness of the prophet, referred to more than once (3:26; 24:27; 33:22). This should be interpreted as a voluntary silence, symbol of God's silence, rather than as an affectation or a physical or psychical want (*see* 3:26, 27).

Ezekiel's symbolic actions, in contrast to those of his predecessors, are too contrived and laborious. Through too much use of the imagination and tortuous artificiality they lose much of their incision, and in this are distinguished from authentic poetry. The allegories suffer in the same way (cc. 16, 23, 27, 29): they are overdeveloped and too packed with allusion, and they project the lesson so obviously that they become superfluous. From the literary point of view, Ezekiel is nearer to baroque apocalyptic than he is to the classic style of Isaiah.

Ezer, Name of several Old Testament men (Gen. 36:21; 1 Chron. 1:38; 4:4; 7:21; 12:10; Neh. 3:19; 12:42).

Ezion-geber (ee′-zi-on-gee′-ber), A city in the northern corner of the Gulf of Aqaba, today known as Tell-el-Kheleifeh, two miles west of the modern city of Aqaba. It was one of the encampments of the Israelites on their journey towards Canaan (Num. 33:35; Deut. 2:8). It was a seaport and a center of commerce with Arabia (Ophir) at the time of Solomon (1 Kgs. 9:26; 2 Chron. 8:17). Jehoshaphat of Judah tried to revitalize this commercial artery during his reign (873-849 B.C.) but the fleet prepared for the project was destroyed by a storm in the Gulf (1 Kgs. 22:49; 2

Chron. 20:36). According to 1 Kgs. 9:26 Ezion-geber is near Elath on the Red Sea. Excavations carried out in the area from 1938-1940 show that Ezion-geber and Elath are nothing more than two successive names for the same place which suffered up to four destructions and reconstructions. The name was changed between the reigns of Jehoshaphat and Amaziah (800-783 B.C.). Elath-Ezion-geber was retaken by Uzziah (783-742; 2 Kgs. 14:22), probably from Edomite dominion, to which it fell again soon after at the time of Ahaz (735-715 B.C., 2 Kgs. 16:6). The excavations uncovered the ruins of metal foundries stemming from the time of Solomon.

Ezra, Son of Seraiah, a Zadokite priest, "a scribe versed in the laws of Moses"—a term probably referring to his position in the Persian court as functionary in charge of Jewish affairs, but translating it into an expression more consonant with his later mission at Jerusalem (*see* Ezra 7:1-6). In the 7th year of King Artaxerxes of Persia, Ezra returned from Babylonia to Jerusalem with a caravan of repatriates and letters from the king empowering him to resettle all the Jews of Babylonia who wished to return to Jerusalem. He was further commissioned to bring from the king and the Babylonian Jewish community various offerings for the Temple at Jerusalem. He was also empowered to draw from the king's treasury what monies were necessary for the refurbishing of the Temple (7:15-24). If he saw that it was necessary, Ezra was given the task of instructing the Jews in the law of God which henceforth was to be the law of the empire for the Jews (7:14, 25-26). Ezra 8 recounts how he carried out the repatriation and supplied resources for the Temple. Ezra 9-10 narrates an episode that has a parallel in the Memories of Nehemiah (Neh. 13:23-30): all those who had married foreign women were obliged to repudiate their wives, if they were other than Jewish, or forfeit their possessions and be excommunicated.

The solemn proclamation of the law is recorded in Nehemiah 8: in front of the people gathered together to the southeast of the Temple Ezra read the law of Moses, explaining and clarifying it so that they could understand what was being read (Neh. 8:8). After the reading followed the feast of the Tabernacles (Neh. 8:13-18) and then came a penance assembly (Neh. 9).

The book of the law which was read to them was the Pentateuch, in the form that it had at that time evolved into, or perhaps some of the law collections that were contained in it.

Although the account of Ezra's mission obviously reflects the Jewish point of view, it is solidly historical and fits perfectly into the framework of the policy of tolerance introduced by Cyrus and continued by his successors in regard to the religious customs and worship of the peoples of the empire.

The promulgation of the law by Ezra is a central event in the history of the Jews. From then on, besides the Temple and the cult, the law became the axis on which Jewish life revolved and a center of cohesion which saved the Jews as an ethnic and religious community even in the most adverse circumstances. Later tradition exalted Ezra almost to the height of Moses. Apocalyptic literature made him one of its perferred personages to whom it attributed the visions of the celestial world and future history. To him was attributed the redaction of all the sacred books of Israel which had been lost during the time of exile. *See* ESDRAS.

The books of Ezra-Nehemiah, which are the only source for the work of these two personages, create a difficult chronological problem over which the exegetes are divided. The mission of Ezra took place during the 7th year of Artaxerxes (7:1). Was this Artaxerxes I (465-425 B.C.) or Artaxerxes II (404-359 B.C.)? Nehemiah's mission took place in the twentieth year of Artaxerxes I (445 B.C.). In the first case Ezra's mission would have preceded that of Nehemiah, while in the second case it would have succeeded it. A third hypothesis corrects the text of Ezra 7:1 and reads "in the 27th year of Artaxerxes (i.e. the First, 432 B.C.) and places Ezra's work between the first and second journey of Nehemiah to Jerusalem.

Ezra and Nehemiah, Books of, These are among the historical books of the Old Testament. In the Hebrew Old Testament they are given the title Ezra-Nehemiah and treated as if they were one book, which in fact was the clear intention of the arranger-editor of the documents and memoirs of the two men. The Vulgate calls the first book of Esdras, Ezrah, and the second book of Esdras, Nehemiah. In the Septuagint 1 Esdras is an apocryphal work, a summary of the canonical books of Ezra and Nehemiah, while 2 Esdras (or 2 and 3 Esdras) are the canonical books of Ezra and Nehemiah. The uncertainties concerning the title show that the book, which was originally one work, was later divided at a time unknown so as to distinguish the works of its two principal characters, and in imitation of a similar division that was introduced in Kings and Chronicles.

The books treat of the return of the exiled from Babylonia to Jerusalem after the edict of Cyrus (539 B.C.) and the settlement of the repatriated on the land of Palestine. It treats moreover of the restoration of the national and religious life of the people, and of the reconstruction of the Temple and of the city, up to the end of the fifth century B.C.

Except for the scant facts one can gather from the contemporary prophets Haggai and Zechariah 1-8, these books form the only source available for this period in which were planted the foundations for the religious and political life of the post-exilic Jewish community. The account makes use of official documents of the period, which are also quoted, and this gives to the work a recognized historical value. Over and above this, it is an account often overloaded with concrete details and dates, through which nevertheless there shines the spirit that sustained the work of restoration and formed post-exilic Judaism. This spirit had matured in the bitter years of exile, and led the Jews to renounce their unrealistic political dreams of a restoration of the pre-exilic monarchy. They came to terms with their position as part of the Persian empire and learned to take advantage of the tolerant policies of the Persian kings while remaining zealously attached to the sacred traditions of Israel that were incorporated into their worship and laws.

On the content of the books and their chronology *see* EZRA, NEHEMIAH. In all probability the books of Ezra-Nehemiah formed the last part of the work of the Chronicler (1-2 Chronicles), the last of the great historical works of Israel (*see* 2 Chron. 36:22 and Ezra 1:1-4). The date of final composition is placed around 300 B.C. (*see* Chronicles 1 and 2). For this part of history the Chronicler used not only official documents of the Persian chancellory (*see* Ezra 4:6-6:18, written in Aramaic) but also two contemporary descriptions of the facts: **The Memories of Ezra** (Ezra 7-10; Neh. 8:9) and **The Memories of Nehemiah,** the latter of which are penned in the first person (Neh. 1-7, 10-13).

F

Fable, A didactic narrative style in which animals, and even plants think and behave like humans. It was much in use in the ancient east and especially in Greece and Rome (e.g. Aesop's Fables). Usually the intention was to illustrate or inculcate some doctrine, and ordinarily this had a moral to it. The Old Testament has only two examples of fables: in Judges

9:8-15 Jotham told a fable of trees who went out to anoint a king to rule over them, to dissuade the people from accepting Abimelech as their king. In 2 Kings 14:9 (which is the same as 2 Chron. 25:18) Jehoash, king of Israel, (801-786 B.C.) answered the ambassadors of Amaziah of Judah (800-783 B.C.) with a fable of the thistle and the cedar in an attempt to dissuade him from war. He failed.

Face, In Bible language sentiments and interior dispositions of people, and even of God, are not directly described, but instead their manifestation on the face is recounted. For this reason there are many figurative expressions whose sense is often difficult to uncover or which for us remain ambiguous. To avert or hide the face from someone occurs a sign of disgust (Isa. 53:3), aversion or indignation. This often occurs in descriptions of God in the Psalms: Pss. 13:2; 27:9; 102:3; Isa. 54:8; Jer. 33:5. To harden the face is an expression of decisiveness, of impudence or even of stubbornness (Isa. 50:7; Jer. 5:3; Ezek. 3:8). Happiness, joy and benevolence for others make the face shine (Job 29:24; often used of God, Num. 6:25; Pss. 4:7; 31:17; 44:4; 67:2; 80:4, 20), while, on the other hand, anger makes the face fall (Gen. 4:5; Jer. 5:3). To placate someone's anger, or God's, is to sweeten his face. To lift someone's face is an ambiguous expression which could mean to show favor and benevolence towards someone (Deut. 10:17; Job 34:19; Gen. 19:21; 1 Sam. 25:35) but can also mean to act in an arbitrary manner showing partiality to someone (Prov. 18:5; Ps. 82:2; Lev. 19:15). To see the face of the king was to be received into his presence and have one's requests listened to (2 Sam. 3:13; 14:24, 28, 32). To see the face of God or appear before his face was to share in the cult of the sanctuary (Ex. 23:15; 34:20) on the annual feast-days. To see God face to face meant to experience him in intimacy and immediacy (Gen. 32:31; Ex. 33:11; Deut. 34:10; 1 Cor. 13:12).

face

sweat of your *f.*	Gen. 3:19	My *f.* is inflamed	Job 16:16
spit in his *f.*	Deut. 25:9	lift up your *f.*	Job 22:26

fail

he *f.* you or forsake you		promise *f.* for all	Ps. 77:9
	Deut. 31:6	The vintage will *f.*	Isa. 32:10
with you and will never *f.*			
	Deut. 31:8		

Fair Havens, A port in southern Crete not far from Lasea (Acts 27:8). On Paul's journey to Rome his ship ran into strong headwinds off Crete, but succeeded in struggling along the coast until it came to Fair Havens.

Faith, Faith and to believe translate the Greek **pistis** and **pisteuein** and various forms of the Hebrew verb '**aman**. Its etymology gives a first insight into the Biblical meaning of the word. The root '**mn** expresses the notion of firmness, solidity, constancy. The form of the verb '**aman** which is translated **to believe** is a causative form which could be rendered 'to make oneself firm, secure' and in this case to have one's firmness, one's security based on God.

In the first mention of faith in the Bible, Gen. 15:6, faith on the one hand is the sure adherence of the mind to the truth of the words uttered by God which contained his promise to Abraham; but on the other is also not less emphasized the confident and full surrender of Abraham to God who promises and saves. Abraham commits himself unreservedly to God.

Faith then means that man is docile, that he holds himself at God's disposal, open to God in the totality of his person. It is then a supremely free act in which man confesses his radical insufficiency, and the same time his

183

total confidence that he will receive all from God. By faith man abdicates his self-sufficiency and his reliance on others outside God, he ceases to count on his own resources, and launches himself into the saving advances of God. In abandoning his self-reliance and totally committing himself to God, man makes the "just" response to God's initiative, and the only one that is adequate to God's offer which is a gracious and gratuitous promise of salvation: "Abraham believed God, and it was credited to him as justice" (Rom. 4:3). The nexus between faith and justice or justification was later developed by Paul.

The biblical tradition will at one time underline one aspect and later another depending on the turn of the history of revelation; its structure however will stay constant throughout the whole biblical tradition, and as such remains the first and fundamental demand of the God of the covenant (Ex. 14:31; 19:9; Josh. 24). Isa. 7:9 contains one of the most solemn calls to faith: here it is no generic acceptance of the truth of the existence of God and his omnipotence, but the demand to have complete confidence in Yahweh, to rely on him because of his promises and election expressed in the covenant. This faith is the pledge of salvation (Isa. 28:16) and excludes the empty search for security in alliances with neighboring peoples, relying on human resources and on others' gods (Isa. 30:15; Jer. 17:5; Ps. 52:9).

In the New Testament, faith is above all faith in Jesus. He demands faith (Matt. 9:28; Mk. 4:36; Lk 8:25) and makes it a condition for salvation (Matt. 9:22; Lk. 8:48). The faith Christ asks of those who seek his help is not confidence in him as a miracle worker, but faith in his mission as the preacher and founder of the eschatological kingdom of God, the signs of which are the miracles and exorcisms (Matt. 11:1-5; Matt. 12:27, 28). Faith is blocked not only by pride (Matt. 18:1-7) but can also be put to the test by the disconcerting humility of the divine decision to choose the economy of the enfleshment of Christ and the contradiction of salvation through a gibbet (Matt. 11:6; 26:31-35; 26:69-75). Even the disciples were incredulous, even after the resurrection (*see* Matt. 8:26; 14:31; 16:8; Matt. 28:17; Lk. 24:11, 25, 41) for the redemption event seemed incredible.

St. John has it that the Son was life-filled and became man to come into this world so that all could share this life (Jn. 5:26; 6:57; 10:10).

Faith is to believe that Jesus really came from God, whose Son he is (Jn. 16:30; 6:69; 20:31). The believer possesses eternal life and has passed over from death to life (Jn. 11). While faith is man's free decision, it is at the same time God's free gift (Jn. 6:37, 44, 65). Disbelief is freely separating oneself from the light which is Christ: this carries with it its own sentence; but at the same time it is the genuine fruit of a perverse heart, on account of which man becomes morally incapable of belief (Jn. 3:19).

In his dispute with the Judaizers on justification Paul calls on the example of Abraham, who was the very type of those who are justified by faith and not by works (*see* Gen. 15:6; Rom. 4:1 ff.; Eph. 2:8-10; Gal. 2:16). This doctrine opposes the Jewish position that justification is through good works and not the gracious and gratuitous gift of God. These wanted to claim justification from God for perfectly fulfilling the law. Paul rebuts this doctrine by pointing up the impotence of the law to justify one, a forcelessness that is explained by man's enslavement to sin (Rom. 7:7 ff.; 8:1-4).

Man is justified through believing in the death and resurrection of Christ. Faith opens a person to a new life that springs from the Spirit and is sustained by him, and which makes of this person in his turn a part of the new humanity, Spirit-filled, whose fruits are love, peace, patience, joy (*see* Rom. 8; Gal. 5:5). Paul then is not in contradiction to James 2:14, where the latter speaks of a dead faith which is certainly not the justifying faith of which Paul writes (2:19). Paul denies the worth of the works performed before justification, but justifying faith bursts forth in a newness of life and is unfolded in the exercise of love (Gal. 5:6; Rom. 8:4; 13:8-10; Gal. 5:14).

For the author of the epistle to the Hebrews, faith means holding firm to the things believed and being convinced of their invisible reality (Heb. 11:1). Addressing a community that was experiencing difficulty and distress in confessing the faith, and suffering persecution, the author proposes for their comfort a whole gallery of examples in this faith who figured in the Old Testament, to show that such a faith will never be disappointed.

falcon
various species of *f.*   Lev. 11:14   various kites and *f.*   Deut. 14:13

Fall, The, The story of the first sin is found in Gen. 2-3. This belongs to the Yahwist source of the Pentateuch. It belongs to the first scene of primitive history which reaches up to the call of Abraham. Although the story carries us back to the beginning of time, it is intended to be history in the human sense. At the center of the story is a free decision of man, which, on account of his continuance in his children, influences the whole course of history. Through the first man's transgression sin came into the world: from this point it made its way into his descendants to bring them to death (Gen. 4:6-9, 11; *see* Rom. 5:12 ff.).

Gen. 2-3 is history not only in the symbolic sense that this event was a concrete expression of what happens in every man, who upon reflection, must feel himself a sinner before God. The author did not merely intend to picture an ideal primitive time and Everyman, who gathered into himself what is common experience. To reconstruct the first moments of history the author did reflect on what was universal religious experience to sketch a man in whom everybody could recognize himself. He inserted this however in a historical context and showed his conviction that the evil of sin had its absolute and historical beginning, which in turn conditioned the flow of history: this beginning he wishes to portray.

It is not however history based on oral or written traditions. The most moderate estimates of the palaeantologists (600,000 years?) quite obviously exclude a tradition that would carry the author back to the beginnings. The similitude of form and content of several elements in the story with other eastern religious texts, together with the presence in the Bible of other variants of the same theme (*see* Ezek. 28:12-15) suggest that psychological and reflective processes were at work analogous to those which among other people led to the elaboration of myths. In the case of the Hebrews however it was reflection on the religious and human condition of man in the light of the Yahwistic faith.

While such an event cannot be reconstructed in an external way, that is, through witnesses and documents, it can be reached through the internal channels based on the experience of sin and divine action as it is presented in revelation. Many scholars rightly point out that the author's contact with the past is like the prophet's contact with the future. The prophet does not grasp the future in its external phenomena, but rather the sense or signification of the future in the totality of sacred history. The future is seen through the present divine action, not in itself. Likewise the author of Gen. 2-3 starts off with reflection that is the fruit of a divine charism, discovers the sense of sin and of the more remote past in the totality of sacred history. In a paradoxical manner of speaking, Gen. 2-3 is a "prophecy of the past."

An attempt can be made to reconstruct the process by which the author arrived at the conclusion that the first sin took place at the origins of the human race. Although it remains hypothesis, it is not without foundation for it is based on elements that are clear in the account. Moreover it helps to place the event in its full global context. For the individual points of the story *see* ADAM, DEMONOLOGY, KNOWLEDGE OF GOOD AND EVIL, LIFE'S TREE, MAN, SERPENT, SIN, PROTOEVANGELIUM, WOMAN.

According to many scholars, the beginning of reflection was the tension between faith in Yahweh who is infinitely good, all-wise and all-powerful, all of whose works could not but be good and perfect, and the actual tragic situation of man. The author of Genesis 2-3 gathered the most stunning elements of this tragedy into the sentence of God which concludes the narrative (3:14-19). What the story came to was where the reflection started. The author was, however, selective and so took those elements which seemed to him more rooted in human nature and therefore more universal. The facts taken are typical of man: a thumbnail sketch which in a few strokes suggests a whole environment.

The incompatibility between the good God and the bad world evidences a rupture between God and man: the bad could only be the fruits of sin. But how and when? Sin was not selective. It was a common experience both as guilt and as impulse, rising up from the very intimacy of his person and ineluctably bound up with his being. The inborn spontaneous reaction of shame was the stigma of sin on his very body. Disharmony marked his deeper relationships with woman and the world (Gen. 3:16-19). The profound and universal experience of sin led spontaneously to common historical sources, especially where social cohesion and human solidarity were so deeply ingrained.

The nomadic and tribal origins of Israel and the structure of society that came from it served to intensify the sense of a common destiny and a common inheritance. This awareness is expressed in the genealogies they cherished (*see* GENEALOGY); at this point it is important to recall that Israel elaborated one for the whole of humanity (*see* Gen. 10; 1 Chron. 1:1-23; *see* TABLE OF NATIONS).

The experience of God's revealing himself in history in saving interventions sent reflection in search not of extra-temporal laws, but of human decisions in the past to explain the actual human situation.

In fact other biblical texts besides Gen. 2-3 point up a similar process that we are here attempting to reconstruct, not to explain the anomalous situation of the whole of mankind, but the constant rebellion of Israel against the voice of God (*see* Hos. 9:9; 12:1-3). Thus the story of the golden calf is introduced immediately after the alliance (Ex. 32), and in fact it burdened and conditioned the whole subsequent history. Moreover expressions such as "we have sinned with our fathers" (Ps. 106:6) can only arise from a consciousness of the existence of a link between generations in sin. Later generations "walk in the ways of their fathers" not simply because they do the things their fathers did, but because in so doing they show themselves true sons of their fathers and that what they spontaneously carry out in them is inborn.

From what has been said some conclusions can be drawn:

a. The account of the first sin arose from a reflection on the wrong condition of mankind. This is intimately connected with the tragic beginning of its history in which everyone is involved. God's word unveils the depth and sweep of the tragedy and invites man to accept the sentence, not in order to despair but so that he might learn that where sin abounded grace would also abound (Rom. 5:12-19).

b. The original state of man is not described except in dependence and in contrast to the present sorry state. It served to highlight how free and dramatic was the decision of the first man. When closely examined, the account turns out to be vague and provides no clear basis for direct information of the pre-sin man.

What least appears and is yet most fundamental is the structure of the event. Briefly, God creates Adam and Eve, establishes them in Eden, gives them an apodictic command with a threatened punishment. They don't obey, and after a brief questioning, God imposes the punishment. God does not however abandon man. The history of man with God continues, but in a minor key: benefits, law, sin, punishment, reconciliation. But this is the plan in which the age-old experience of Israel's relationship with God falls. It is very frequently repeated in the historical books, Joshua-2 Kings, and is put down as a thesis in Judges 2. This plan which sums up and presents Israel's life with God is used by the author to construct the story of paradise, filling out the spaces in ways that were adapted to the historical moment to which it was applied.

On connected subjects *see* DEATH, PENTATEUCH, ECCLESIASTICUS, WISDOM, BOOK OF.

false

not repeat a *f.* report	Ex. 23:1	*F.* scales are an abomination	
f. to the fellowship	Ps. 73:15		Prov. 11:1
	by *f.* brothers	2 Cor. 11:26	

falter

Why did you *f.*	Matt. 14:31	trust and do not *f.*	Matt. 21:21

fame

his *f.* spread throughout		David's *f.* was spread	
	Josh. 6:27		1 Chron. 14:17
	never heard my *f.*	Isa. 66:19	

Family, The Israelite family was patriarchal, which is evident even in the name used to designate it: bet 'ab, the house of the father. This is also seen in the genealogies in common use in Israel which were drawn through the paternal line. The father, lord (or ba'al) of his wife, had full authority over all members of the family. The Jewish family, besides wife and children, included the children's families if they were in the paternal home, outsiders who habitually resided there, and persons confided to the protection of the head of the family. The principle of paternal authority as the center of cohesion is again reflected in the juridic dispositions of Ex. 20:5 and Deut. 5:9, that God punishes the sin of the father in his sons and even to the fourth generation. More than solidarity in sin, this disposition must be seen rather as a case of so-called ruler's punishment: the chief is also punished in what is his, and the fourth generation was about the greatest extension of his family that could be expected in his life.

Among the members of the family was an active and conscious solidarity in which the whole group closed ranks to protect, defend or even punish the individual members: this was regulated by the juridic institution of go'el (*see* AVENGER).

family

against that man and his *f.*		married out of his *f.*	Lev. 21:4
	Lev. 20:5	of an immigrant *f.*	Lev. 25:47
	When his *f.* heard	Mk. 3:21	

Famine, Famine is often spoken of in the Bible. It could be due to the lack of rain (1 Kgs. 18:3) or plagues of locusts, blight or mildew (Joel 2). Or it could be caused in time of war by the length of a siege (e.g. Samaria: 2 Kgs. 6:25; 7:4; Jerusalem: 2 Kgs. 25:3). During periods of prolonged famine the people of Syria and Canaan would often make for Egypt where the Nile assured irrigation waters and crops even in severe drought. This practice was so common that the Egyptian authorities made laws to regulate it. This theme appears in some patriarchal traditions (Gen. 12:10; 26:1; 47:4). Famine was also considered to be God's punishment on a certain people and region (Jer. 14:13-18; Amos 4:6). Acts 11:28 recalls the famine that took place under the emperor Claudius, which is placed by Latin historians in Claudius' second year. On that occasion Paul and Barnabas were commissioned to bring help to the Jerusalem Christians.

famine

f. in the land	Gen. 12:10; 26:1	David's reign there was a *f*.
severity of the *f*.	Gen. 47:13	2 Sam. 21:1
	great *f*. broke out	Lk. 15:14

far

F. be it from you	Gen. 18:25	hostile land, *f*. or near	1 Kgs. 8:46
his name is too *f*.	Deut. 12:21	The night is *f*. spent	Rom. 13:12

fare

paid the *f*.   Jonah 1:3

farewell

avoid these things. *F*.   Acts 15:29

fashion

Did not the same One *f*. us
                          Job 31:15

Fast, Abstention from food was practiced always and in the most diverse religions as a penance and a means of self-humiliation. It was prescribed and used together with prayer and other forms of penance in times of distress and calamity (Joel 1:14; 2:15; 1 Sam. 7:6; Jer. 14:12) and as a sign of mourning (1 Sam. 31:13; 2 Sam. 1:12; 3:35). The law mentions only the fast of the Great Day of Atonement (Lev. 16:29) but at times fasts were ordered as a part of the public penitential celebrations (Jgs. 20:26; Joel 1:14; 2:15; 1 Kgs. 21:9; Jer. 36:6, 9). The prophets take exception to the cultic formalism that infected even fasting, which then becomes an empty rite, void of any internal conversion which alone is true penance (Isa. 58:1; Jer. 14:12; Zech. 7:5). Jesus condemned the exhibitionism of the fasting Pharisees (Matt. 6:16). He however fasted for forty days and nights before setting out on his public ministry (Matt. 4:2). Contrary to the practice of John's followers, Jesus' disciples did not fast. When questioned on this point, Jesus replied that it was unthinkable that one should fast while the bridegroom was with them: it would steal from the joy of the occasion. When however the bridegroom is taken, then fasting will ensue (Mk. 2:18; Matt. 9:14; Lk. 5:33). Fasting accompanied prayer in particular circumstances (Acts 13:2; 14:23).

Fat, The fat of animals offered in sacrifice was burnt on the altar. It was the most prized part of the animal and so was consecrated to God (Lev. 3:7-11).

fat

seven handsome, *f*. cows	seven *f*., healthy ears	Gen. 41:7
	Gen. 41:4 All the *f*. that covers	Ex. 29:13
	f. of the sin offering Lev. 16:25	

Father, In the patriarchal type of Israelite family the father was the center of cohesion and held absolute authority over its members. *See* FAMILY. This authority, with its attendant paternal responsibilities for the whole family, was severely protected by the law (Ex. 21:15, 17; Lev. 20:9) and by the Decalogue (Ex. 20:12; Deut. 5:16) which prescribed the death sentence for verbal or personal offenses against father or mother.

The fatherhood of God is a frequent theme in the Bible, though less so in the Old than in the New Testament. God is Father because he is creator (Deut. 32:6; Mal. 2:10) and for that reason he has a concern and care for his creatures (Ps. 103:13). Besides this generic fatherhood however, God is said to be Father of Israel in an altogether particular way because he chose it as his own people. The relationship that arose in history between God and his people and sanctioned in the covenant shows it to be a Father-son relationship (Hos. 11:3-8; Jer. 31:9, 20). This fatherhood born of the covenant, though often offended by the sins of the people (Jer. 3:4, 19; Mal. 1:6) remains nevertheless the source of hope for the future (Isa. 63:15; 64:8). The king is considered a son of God in a particular way. This concept however is not derived directly from the idea of the divine affiliation of kings so prevalent among many of the peoples of antiquity, and especially Egypt; it centers rather the sonship of the people of Israel on the king as head and representative. It is based on the historical election of David as king (2 Sam. 5) which was also a covenant (2 Sam. 23:1; Pss. 132:11; 89:4) in which God pledged particular benevolence and protection to the king, who in turn was especially bound in obedience and submission (Ps. 89).

So Jesus is the son of God in this sense because he is the Messiah and David's descendant. His resurrection and enthronement in his messianic kingdom is the act by which he has been constituted Son of God in power (Rom. 1:4; Acts 13:32 ff.). The fatherhood of God which Jesus revealed far outstripped all the expectations of the Old Testament. The relationship of father to son in the case of God and Jesus is ineffable (Lk. 10:21; Matt. 11:25-27) and cannot be put on an equal basis with God's fatherhood in relation to the rest of men, even those who are disciples of Jesus (Matt. 15:13; 16:17; 18:10; 20:23; 26:39-43). Jesus is in reality the natural son of God (Jn. 1:14, 18), the Father is his life source (Jn. 6:57) and he makes one reality with the Father (Jn. 10:30).

Because he is Son he is the perfect revelation of the Father (Jn. 14:7-9; 1:18; 6:46; 10:15) and he came into the world to communicate to us divine life (John 6:57). Jesus reveals himself as the love of the Father for those who love him and believe in him (Jn. 14:21). He taught men to address God with the word **Abba! Father!** which is what a child calls his father. This is an invitation to intimacy and confidence in God's goodness and to the good things that he has in store for all (Matt. 6:5-8; 7:11; 10:29-31). It is moreover a pledge of forgiveness and a title of hope in his mercy (Matt. 6:14; 18:35; Mk. 11:25; Lk. 15:11-32).

The fatherhood revealed in the New Testament is governed by the natural sonship of Christ, from which it is derived and in which it shares. God sent his son to communicate by adoption the sonship that was natural to him (Gal. 4:6; Rom. 8:15). The Christian is immersed into Christ by baptism, and lives from the vital source who is the risen Christ by the power of the Spirit of the Son who also is given in baptism and cries out in man's flesh Abba! Father! (*See* also 2 Cor. 1:3; Col. 1:3).

Fathom, A measure of depth, theoretically computed as the distance between the tips of the fingers of a man's outstretched arms (Acts 27:28), now fixed as 6 feet.

fault

you who are at *f*	Ex. 5:16	point out his *f.*	Matt. 18:15
no *f.* to find	1 Sam. 29:3	does he find *f.*	Rom. 9:19

favor

she won his *f.*	Esth. 2:17	given Daniel the *f.*	Dan. 1:9
	not regarded as a *f.*	Rom. 4:4	

fear

Dread *f.* of you	Gen. 9:2	*f.* you as long	1 Kgs. 8:40
begin to put a *f.*	Deut. 2:25	My *f.* is that	2 Cor. 11:3

feast

Abraham held a great *f.*	Gen. 21:8	seven days of the *f.*	Jgs. 14:12
Isaac then made a *f.*	Gen. 26:30	Let us celebrate the *f.*	1 Cor. 5:8

feathers

f. shall be removed	Lev. 1:16

feel, feels

Suppose my father *f.* me?		that I may *f.* you .	Gen. 27:21
	Gen. 27:12		

feet

his *f.* into the bed	Gen. 49:33	*f.* on the necks	Josh. 10:24
sandals from your *f.*	Ex. 3:5	place at his *f.*	Ruth 3:7

Felix, Marcus Antonius Felix was Roman procurator of Judea from 52 to 59 A.D. His second wife was Drusilla, sister of Agrippa II, who abandoned her legitimate husband, Azizus, king of Emesa. Felix was cruel and intolerant, hated by the Jews, and to his intemperate rule is attributed the discontent that finally exploded in the revolt of 66-70 A.D. Paul, a prisoner in Jerusalem and Caesarea, was brought to trial before Felix and Drusilla (Acts 23:24-24:27). Festus succeeded Felix as governor while Paul remained a prisoner.

fell

trance *f.* upon Abram	Gen. 15:12	*f.* upon the young people	Job 1:19
	f. into enemy hands	Lam. 1:7	

fellow

This *f.*, they sneered	Gen. 19:9	*f.* come into my house	
striking your *f.* Hebrew	Ex. 2:13		1 Sam. 21:16
	said to his *f.* disciples	Jn. 11:16	

Festus, Porcius Festus was Roman procurator of Judea from 59 to 61 A.D. He intervened in Paul's trial at Caesarea to propose to Paul that he should agree to be tried in Jerusalem. Paul, however, appealed to Caesar. Afterwards Festus presented the case to King Agrippa who with his sister-mistress Bernice had come to Caesarea, and before whom Paul offered his defense (Acts 25-26). Festus died after barely two years of governorship.

field

the *f.* and the cave in it		the fragrance of a *f.*	Gen. 27:27
	Gen. 23:11	glean in anyone else's *f.*	Ruth 2:8
	Buy for yourself my *f.*	Jer. 32:7	

Field of Blood, English translation of Akeldama. *See* AKELDAMA.

fierce

be their fury so *f.*	Gen. 49:7	carry out his *f.* anger	1 Sam. 28:18

fifteen

rising *f.* cubits higher	Gen. 7:20	*f.* shekels for a man	Lev. 27:7
extent of *f.* cubits	Ex. 27:14	found it to be *f.*	Acts 27:28

Fig Tree, One of the most common trees in Palestine (Deut. 8:8) often planted among the vines (1 Kgs. 5:5; Mic. 4:4; Zech. 3:10). The figs can be eaten fresh, or dried for conservation and pressed into cakes (1 Sam. 25:18; 30:12; 1 Chron. 12:41). Blossoms on the fig tree are a sign that spring has arrived (Matt. 24:32; Mk. 13:28; Lk. 21:29-31). In the sayings of Jesus we hear that figs cannot be gathered from thistles (Matt. 7:16). There is also the parable of the barren fig tree (Lk. 13:6-9). As a symbolic action Jesus cursed a fig tree that was all leaves and no fruit to warn the unfaithful of the judgment that would befall them (Matt. 21:18-22; Mk. 11:12-25).

Fire, Fire for its qualities and varied uses becomes an obvious symbol for religious purposes. Besides its cultic use in the sacrifice ritual (Lev. 6:1-6) fire is often used in describing the divinity. It constantly figures in visions of God (Ex. 19:18; 24:17; Deut. 4:11-36; 5:4-26). God is described as a consuming fire, an expression that can refer to his sanctity and zeal (Deut. 4:24; Ps. 79:5; Ezek. 36:5) or to his anger which does not permit sin to go unpunished (Pss. 79:5; 89:47; Jer. 4:4; 21:12; Ezek. 21:36; 22:21; Zeph. 1:18).

In a figurative sense, fire stands for tribulation or calamity (1 Kgs. 8:51; Jer. 11:4). The purification of the just is through fire, and use of the furnace for smelting and purifying metals is frequently recalled (Ps. 66:12; Isa. 43:2; Zech. 13:9; Jer. 6:29; Ezek. 22:20; 24:12). Most of all, however, fire comes up in expressions of the judgment and the punishment of the perverse, often in an eschatological context (Gen. 19:24; Amos 1:4; 2:5; Jer. 5:14; 11:16; 17:27; 21:14; Ezek. 24:9; Isa. 66:15; Ezek. 38:22; 39:6; Mal. 3:19). This theme which was developed in apocalyptic literature (Dan. 7:11) is frequent in the New Testament, where the torments of the damned are said to be eternal fire in **gehenna** (Matt. 3:10; 5:22; 7:19; 13:40; 18:8-9; 25:41; Mk. 9:43-48; Lk. 17:29). Especially in Revelation does it occur (8:7; 9:18; 11:5). On the purifying fires of purgatory *see* 1 Cor. 3:13-15 and also, perhaps Mk. 9:49; Lk. 12:49.

Firmament, Translation of the Hebrew **raqia'** which, according to oriental cosmology, was the sky, and was thought of by peoples of the Near East as an inverted bowl which served as ceiling to the earth and divided the waters above from the waters below, leaving a free space between for the earth, air and whatever peoples it (*see* Gen. 1:6; Pss. 104:4; 19:2; Ezek. 1:22-25).

First-born, In the Israelite home the first-born occupied a place of privilege (Deut 21:15-17; Gen. 27:29-36). According to Israelite law the first-born of men and of animals belonged to God (Ex. 22:28-29; 34:19-20). The first-born of animals were sacrificed to God if they were pure animals. If however the animal had a blemish, or was lame or blind or had any serious defect, it was not sacrificed. An impure animal was either killed or redeemed for a price (*see* Deut. 15:19, 20; Lev. 27:26, 27; Ex. 13:13; 34:20; Num. 18:15). The first-born children were redeemed as a sign that the Lord had brought the Israelites out of the bondage of Egypt with a mighty hand (*see* Ex. 13:11 ff.; 34:19-20; Num. 3:46, 47). The price of redemption for the first-born was five shekels (Num. 18:15-17). According to Numbers 3:11-13 the Levites were especially consecrated as the price of redemption of the first-born (*see* Num. 3:40-51; 8:16-18). "First-born" did not necessarily imply that there were more children (Lk. 2:7).

Jesus is the first-born of the Father (Jn. 1:18). Paul calls him the first-born from the dead (Col. 1:18; *see* Rev. 1:5) and also the first-born among many brothers. This means that he is the first of many Christians who through him share in the sonship of God (Rom. 8:29). Colossians 1:15

191

also names him the first-born in all creation, that is, at one and the same time transcending all creation and nevertheless sharing intimately and vitally in the whole creative work of the Father who through him made all that there is (Col. 1:15-17; *see* Jn. 1:3).

first-born

You, Reuben my *f.*	Gen. 49:3	*f.* of many brothers	Rom. 8:29
birth to her *f.*	Lk. 2:7	*f.* of all creatures	Col. 1:15

First Fruits, As was the case with the first-born, so too for the Jews the first fruits of the field (Ex. 23:19; 34:26), be it corn, wine or oil, and the first fruits of fruit-bearing trees (Lev. 19:24) all belonged to God. The first fruits were offered especially at the Feast of Weeks, which was originally the Harvest Festival (Ex. 23:16), the Feast of Unleavened Bread and the Feast of Tabernacles. The offering was a practical acknowledgement of the gift of the promised land which Yahweh had made to his people (Deut. 26:1-11). Paul declares that Christ in being raised from the dead is the first fruits of all who have fallen asleep (in death) (1 Cor. 15:20). Paul means that Christ is the first to enjoy the resurrection which is the future of all the faithful. These have received the first fruits of the Spirit as an earnest of the eschatological glory that is to be theirs (Rom. 8:23).

Fish, Fishing, Ritual law distinguished for the Jews between pure and impure fish. They could eat anything that had fins and scales: all other water creatures were considered impure (Lev. 11:9-12). Fishing was practiced in Palestine in Old Testament times, especially in the Sea of Galilee which was rich in different kinds of fish. To judge however from the rare mention given in the Old Testament to fishing and fish as food, it does not seem to have been very common (*see* Isa. 19:8; Amos 4:2; Hab. 1:15; Job 40:25; Neh. 13:16; Num. 11:5, 22). Several of Jesus' apostles were Galilean fishermen (Mk. 1:16-20; Jn. 21:1-8). The gospel story has two accounts of fish miracles (Lk. 5:1-11; Jn. 21:1-8) and the story of the miraculous multiplication of the loaves and fishes (Matt. 14:17 ff.; 15:36; Mk. 6:38; Jn. 6:1 ff.). The disciples' mission is to be fishers of men (Matt. 4:19; Mk. 1:17; Lk. 5:10), and the kingdom of God is compared to the sorting out of the good from the bad fish that follows net-fishing (Matt. 13:47).

fish

the *f.* of the sea	Gen. 1:26	killed their *f.*	Ps. 105:29
f. in the river shall die	Ex. 7:18	first *f.* you catch	Matt. 17:27

flax

f. and the barley were ruined		around his arms became as *f.*	
	Ex. 9:31		Jgs. 15:14
stalks of *f.* spread out	Josh. 2:6	She obtains wool and *f.*	
			Prov. 31:13

Flesh, The Hebrew **basar** strictly means flesh, that is, the soft parts of the living body of a man (Gen. 2:21; Ex. 4:7; 1 Sam. 17:44) or of animals (Lev. 4:11; 6:20, etc.). It was extended to mean the body itself (Ex. 30:32; 1 Kgs. 21:27; Num. 8:7). "All flesh" is a common way of expressing "every living thing" (Gen. 6:17, 19; 7:16, 21; Lev. 17:11, 14), "of all mankind" (Gen. 6:12; Isa. 40:6; 49:26; Jer. 12:12). Man is often called "flesh" to underline the weakness, fragility and transience of human nature, especially when contrasted with God and his Spirit which is strength (Ps. 78:39; Isa. 40:5-8; 2 Chron. 32:8; Isa. 31:3; etc.).

The New Testament inherited and developed these concepts. Flesh, in Greek **sarx**, is man in his weakness (Rom. 6:19; Gal. 4:13 ff.) in opposition to the eternity and power of God which is the spirit. So "flesh" and "flesh and blood" designate the natural condition of man as distinct from God's transforming grace (Matt. 16:17; 1 Cor. 15:50; Gal. 1:16; Rom. 9:8; Gal. 3:3; Jn. 3:6; 6:63, etc.).

For Paul there is a particular alliance between flesh and sin: sin is a personified power which has taken possession of the flesh, inseminating into it all its concupiscences (Rom. 7:5-25; 13:14; 2 Cor. 7:1; Gal. 5:13, 19; Eph. 2:3; Col. 2:13-23).

For this reason flesh is committed to corruption and death, which is sin's wages (1 Cor. 15:50; Gal. 6:8; Rom. 8:6, 13; 2 Cor. 4:11). Christ took on flesh similar to ours, that is, the human condition without sin, and in his own flesh triumphed over sin (Rom. 8:1-4; Eph. 2:14-16; Col. 1:22). By their baptism Christians are immersed in Christ's death and resurrection, so that they are no longer in the sin-infested flesh, but in the life-bestowing Spirit (Rom. 7:5; 8:9; Gal. 5:24; Col. 2:11). They have not yet reached the fulness of glory and incorruption, for they are still "in the flesh," that is, in their earthly condition, but this is no longer the possession of sin (Phil. 1:22-24).

Flint, A very hard stone, a variety of quartz which breaks up into shell-shaped pieces and so was used in prehistory to make knives, axes, sickles, etc. In Israel a flint knife was used in the rite of circumcision (Ex. 4:25; Josh. 5:2-3).

Flood, The, The account of the flood is found in Gen. 6-9. The text is a fusion of two different versions of the same event, the one belonging to the Yahwist tradition (Gen. 6:5-8; 7:1-5, 7-10, 12, 16b, 17b, 22-23; 8:2b, 3, 6-12, 13b, 20-22) the other to the Priestly document (6:9-22; 7:6, 11, 13, 16a, 17a, 18-21, 24; 8:1-2a, 4, 5, 13a, 14-19; 9:1-7). The cause of the flood is different in each. For the Yahwist (J) the flood was the result of a downpour lasting 40 continuous days and nights. The Priestly document (P) however attributes it to a cosmic cataclysm during which the division of the waters described in the creation story of Genesis 1 was suspended, so that abysmal waters were loosed on the earth. P even disagrees on the duration of the flood which for J was 40 days, but for P 1 year and 11 days (7:11-8:14). J states that one couple each of the impure animals and seven each of the pure animals were saved, but P has it that one couple only of each animal was saved (7:2-3; 7:8-9).

Both agree that the flood was a divine judgment which was intended to punish man and do away with corrupt humanity. This judgment however is mitigated in the case of Noah and his family who will give birth to post-flood humanity. In both traditions God solemnly pledges to send no more floods on the earth and to keep intact the rhythm of the seasons of the year (J: Gen. 8:21-22). P develops this epilogue (9:1 ff), impregnating it as usual with his theology: just as the flood temporarily suspended God's creative action, the epilogue shows God making a new gift of the earth to man in a scene parallel to that of the creation story in Genesis 1:23-28. Special dispositions are made to contain the spilling of blood within certain limits. Man may eat the flesh of animals but not the blood, which must be poured out on the earth. Blood was considered to be where life resided (Lev. 17, 14), and so pouring it out was a symbolic confession of the absolute and exclusive dominion of God over every living thing. In apodictic and absolute terms God bans murder, which must be paid for with the death of the killer. Finally God makes a pact with Noah in the form of a solemn oath never again to send a deluge on the earth. The rainbow will be a reminder of this pact, and a sign and pledge of God's given word. There are allusions to the flood story in Isa. 54:9; Wis. 10:4; 14:6; Sir. 44:17-18; Matt. 24:37-39; Heb. 11:7; 1 Pet. 3:20; 2 Pet. 2:5.

The problem of the historicity of the deluge story is not confined to the Bible, for the account in Gen. 6-9 clearly depends on Mesopotamian traditions of much greater antiquity, of which some examples are extant in the epic of Gilgamesh, the legend of Atrahasis and the Sumerian Ziusudra. There is mention of the flood in the list of the kings of Mesopotamia until the end of the Isin dynasty: there too the flood divides two periods of history as it does for Genesis. It seems likely that the memory of a flood disaster in that region was carried along in epic tradition until it acquired the proportions in which it is now described. Perhaps the narration is that of a typical fact that reflected flooding phenomena that occurred in the region and which are attested to by archeological excavation. The Israelites probably adopted the tradition in Canaan, interpreted it in the light of its own Yahwist faith to make of it a central event in the reconstructed prehistory of salvation.

Flower, Flowers abound in Palestine in the spring-time but quickly fade as hot summer arrives (S. of S. 2:12), and so are often used to symbolize the transitoriness of man and of his works: "Man blossoms, and he withers like a flower, fleeting as a shadow, transient" (Job 14:2; *see* Ps. 103:15; Neh. 1:4; Isa. 5:24; 40:6-8). Isaiah refers to "the fading blooms of his glorious beauty" (Isa. 28:1, 4). Flowers are, in the New Testament, signs of God's provident care of all his creatures (Matt. 6:28; Lk. 12:27).

Fly, The Bible mentions several species of flies but it is not easy to identify them Ecclesiastes 9:18 seems to refer to the domestic fly, but more aggressive gadflies or horseflies played their part in the fourth plague of Egypt (Ex. 8:21-29; Ps. 78:45), while mosquitoes are a figure of Assyria in Isaiah's prophecy against Judah in 7:18.

Folly, Fool, Folly and fool are typical terms in the Wisdom tradition and can best be understood when contrasted with their opposites, wisdom and the wise man. The wise man is docile to wisdom which not only instructs, but makes him prudent, respectful, cautious, fearful of God; while the fool holds himself to be wise. But only in his own eyes is he so (Prov. 12:15); he is imprudent and improvident in the conduct of his life and his affairs (Eccles. 4:5; Prov. 12:11; 24:30-31). The fool is brash, intolerant of the advice and warnings of his parents and of the wise (Prov. 12:16; 15:5; 18:13; 10:14; 13:16; Sir. 20:13; 21:16; 27:13). Nothing good is to be expected from him (Prov. 24:7; 27:22). He is only constant in his errors and sins, he lacks the fear of God that is the beginning of wisdom, and indeed he places no credence in the truth of a God who judges and punishes (Prov. 10:23; 13:19; Ps. 14:1; 53:2; Job 42:8; 2:10).

In Matthew 5:22 Jesus condemns the man who would call his fellow man a fool: what Jesus is aiming at here however is the gravity even of interior dispositions of hate or malevolence, against those who would say that the fifth commandment bans only the external act of murder. The disciples are called foolish by Jesus in Luke 24:25 (*see* Matt. 15:16; Mk. 7:18), but in a mild sense, upbraiding them for their spiritual insensibility and lack of understanding. Paul declares that to be wise one must learn to be a fool (1 Cor. 3:18): he is using a Greek notion of wisdom and ignorance. The wise of the world would account the gibbet of the cross foolish, but God used it to confound that wisdom.

Foot, Foot, besides its usual physical sense, is often used in metaphor and symbol by the Bible. It stands for the whole person in such phrases as "He will guard the footsteps of his faithful ones" (1 Sam. 2:9). "To set things under one's feet" is to be their lord (Ps. 8:7) or victorious over them (Josh. 10:24). Many of the metaphors are self-explanatory, such as the slipping of the foot to signify weakening of faith (Ps. 73:2), the stumbling foot for disaster (Ps. 38:17), planting one's foot on the land for possession (Josh. 1:3). Even the Lord is described as having feet, with the ark his footstool (1 Chron. 28:2). Journeys were made barefoot or in sandals along dusty roads, and washing the feet of the guest was a courtesy, performed by the sinful woman for Jesus while it was omitted by his host Simon (Lk. 7:36-50) and performed by Jesus for his disciples at the Last Supper (Jn. 13:1-16). Thus Jesus summed up in symbol what the Christian must do for his fellow man: he must give himself totally. Some see in this symbolic action an allusion to Baptism and/or the Eucharist which John does not recount in his narration of the Last Supper.

Fortifications, "Fortifications," as the military general-archaeologist Yigael Yadin writes, "are basically an artificial barrier, whether or not they are built around naturally defensive terrain, whose purpose is to deny the enemy the two important advantages in assault—mobility and firepower—and to provide a foundation of security for the defender." A simple barrier would not serve: fortifications had to be designed to provide freedom of movement and firepower to the defenders themselves. Furthermore a passive barrier, as Yadin points out, could only hold up an attacker temporarily: the walls could be scaled with ladders or portable towers, or breached by battering rams. "Walls had therefore to be so built as to enable the defenders to fire their weapons from the top, and so frustrate the enemy design. The wall and its fortifications comprised three principal components: the wall itself—the barrier; its upper structures, to enable the defenders to fire their weapons and to give them protection while doing so—the firing platform and defensive cover; forward obstacles and traps, set up in front of the wall to keep the enemy archers as far away as possible and to prevent battering rams from being brought into action. To make scaling difficult the wall had to be high. To prevent breaching it had to be thick. And to withstand undermining or tunneling below it, its foundations needed to be deep and broadly based. A wall both high and thick . . . requires additional strengthening by a series of regularly spaced buttresses of considerable thickness, protruding from the wall's outer face." Defenders inside these buttresses could direct flanking fire on enemy personnel attempting to scale or breach a wall. "The city gate posed a special problem . . . inevitably the weakest part in the system of fortifications." One answer was to build an approach path to the gate that exposed attackers to a maximum degree. The second was to plate the doors with metal to prevent their being burned, and the use of massive beams as bolts to prevent breaking in the double doors by ramming. Finally, means were designed whereby defenders could fire directly into the recessed entryway from the sides and from above, at minimum risks to themselves. For capturing a superbly sited and fortified city like Jerusalem, either penetration by ruse (David-Joab) or siege (Nebuchadnezzar) had to be resorted to.

Fortunatus, A Christian from Corinth who visited Paul at Ephesus, together with Stephanas and Achaicus (1 Cor. 16:17). He was probably one of Chloe's people (1 Cor. 1:11) who brought news of the Corinthian church and its problems to Paul.

Forum of Appius, Mentioned with the Three Taverns in Acts 28:15 as the place to which the Roman Christians came to meet Paul as he was being led a prisoner from Puteoli, the port of disembarkation, to Rome. It is on the Appian way, 43 miles south of the city (*see* Acts 28:15).

Foundation Gate, One of the gates of Jerusalem where Jehoiada planted a third of his men in the revolt which led to Athaliah's overthrow and Joash's accession to the throne. It is also called the Gate Sur (835 B.C.; *see* 2 Chron. 23:5; 2 Kgs 11:6).

Fowl, Domestic fowl were known in Palestine before the Persian period, but do not seem to have been common. By New Testament times however they were well-known enough to be used by Jesus to express his care and love of his people (Lk 11:12; 13:34) and the cock plays a significant part in the history of the passion. Cock-crow marked the beginning of one of the night-watches, and as Jesus had predicted, marked the time of Peter's repeated denial (Matt. 26:34, 74; Mk. 14:20, 72; Lk. 22:34, 60; Jn. 13:38; 18:37).

Fox, The Hebrew word for fox probably includes the jackal as well. Samson caught 300 foxes, tied them tail to tail and attached torches to them and ran them through the lands of the Philistines to destroy their corn, vines and olive-trees (Jgs. 15:4-5). They were noted for the damage they caused to the crops (S. of S. 2:15; Ezek. 13:4; Lam. 5:18). Jesus called Herod Antipas a fox, for his animal cunning (Lk. 13:32; *see* Neh. 3:35). In Matt. 8:20 Jesus' words are: "The foxes have lairs" (*see* Lk. 9:58).

Frankincense, *See* INCENSE.

Freedmen, Synagogue of Roman, One of the several synagogues in Jerusalem mentioned in Acts 6:9, catering to Greek-speaking Jews. They were liberated slaves, or the children of liberated slaves who had returned to Jerusalem. Just as freed Jewish slaves, according to Tacitus, caused trouble to the government, so did the Greek converts at Jerusalem agitate the infant church, which in turn led to the ordaining of Stephen and his companions as the first deacons (*see* Acts 6:1 ff.). Some interpreters have conjectured that, in the Greek, for "freedmen" one should read "Lybians" (that is, **libystinion** for **libertinion**).

Freedom, *See* LIBERTY.

Fringes, In Numbers 15:37-39 and Deuteronomy 22:12 Yahweh told the Jews to wear hems on their clothes and tassels with a violet cord on the four corners of the cloak in which they wrapped themselves to remind themselves to keep the Lord's commandments. Jesus wore such a cloak, the fringe of which was touched by the woman with the hemorrhage (Matt. 9:20, *see* 14:36; Mk. 6:56; Lk. 8:44). He condemned however the hypocrisy of the Pharisees who wore enlarged tassels to assert their loyalty to the law while not observing it (Matt. 23:5).

Frog, The frog is mentioned only in the account of the second plague with which Yahweh afflicted Egypt to convince them that it was better to let the Jews go. The rivers swarmed with frogs which made their way into the houses and very beds of the people. Reference to this episode is made in Psalms 78:45; 105:30; Wisdom 19:10. Revelation 16:13 describes a vision of three foul spirits which looked like frogs.

Funeral, *See* BURIAL.

Furlong, A measure of length, in Greek **stadion,** equal to about 220 yards. The road to Emmaus, along which the disciples met the risen Christ was said to be 60 furlongs in length, or about 7 miles (Lk. 24:13; *see* 2 Mac. 12:9, 10; Jn. 6:19; 11:18; Rev. 14:20; 21:16).

G

Gaal (gayʹ-al), Son of Obed, of the city of Shechem. Together with his brothers he tried to rouse the city against King Abimelech, son of Gideon, and against its governor Zebul. He was defeated by Abimelech but succeeded in fleeing to the city from which he was expelled by Zebul (Jgs. 9:26-41).

Gaash (gay′-ash), A peak of the hill country of Ephraim near the tomb of Joshua (Josh. 24:30).

Gaba, *See* GEBA.

Gabael (gab′-a-el), Son of Gabrias who had in deposit some money of Tobit. Tobit sent his son, Tobiah, to collect it (Tob. 1:4; 4:20; 9:2-6; 10:2).

Gabaon, *See* GIBEON.

Gabbatha (gab′-ba-tha), An Aramaic word which probably means height. In John 19:13 it is stated that it is the Aramaic equivalent of the Stone Pavement, where the trial of Jesus before Pilate was carried out. There is still a discussion about where exactly it was. It depends on where the **pretorium** or Roman governor's residence was. There are two hypotheses: it was either the palace of Herod or the fortress Antonia. In the excavations at the convent of Notre Dame of Sion, which is on the site of the fortress Antonia, an extensive flagstone pavement has been found, which is indeed a **lithostroton,** but whether it is the one mentioned in John 19:13 is uncertain for the reason given.

Gabrias (gay′-bri-as), The father (Tob. 4:20) or brother (Tob. 1:14) of Gabael, to whom the young Tobiah was sent to get back the money of his father Tobit.

Gabriel, "God is strong," the angel who interpreted for Daniel some visions (Dan. 8:16-26; 9:21-27) and was also entrusted with the announcement to Zechariah of the birth of John the Baptizer, and to Mary of the birth of Jesus (*see* Lk. 1:11-20; 1:26-38). In apocalyptic literature Gabriel is one of the seven archangels who stand before the Lord.

Gad, 1. The seventh son of Jacob, born from Zilpah, Leah's slave (Gen. 30:11) and the founding father of the Israelite tribe of the same name. This tribe is praised for its courage and warrior spirit in the blessings of Jacob (Gen. 49:19) and of Moses (Deut. 33:20-21). The territory of Gad extended north from the river Arnon in Transjordan to the southern edge of the Sea of Galilee (Josh. 13:24-28), and therefore was exposed to the incursions of the Moabites to the south and the Aramaeans to the north (2 Kgs. 10:33). Its geographical position explains, too, how this tribe lived on the margins of the tribal cohesion on the near side of the Jordan, as the episode of Joshua 22 seems to insinuate. The tribe of Gad tried to liberate itself from some of the demands of the tribal confederation. A dispute arose, but peace was made (Josh. 22:30-34). After the exile, Gad passed over to the Ammonites (Jer. 49:1).

2. A prophet at the time of David. He stuck by David during the dispute with Saul (1 Sam. 22:3-5) and rebuked the king in God's name for carrying out the census of the people. He gave dispositions for bringing to an end the plague sent as a punishment (2 Sam. 24; 1 Chron 21). He compiled a chronicle which was one of the sources used by the Chronicler for his history (1 Chron. 29:29).

Gadara (gad′-a-ra), A Greek city of the Decapolis in Transjordan, about five miles southeast of the Sea of Galilee in the place of the modern Umm Qeis. Matthew 8:28 places the cure of the possessed person in Gadara, while according to Mark 5:1 and Luke 8:26 it took place in Gerasa.

Gaham (gay′-am), A son of Nahor, Abraham's brother, by his concubine Reumah (Gen. 22:24).

gain

who hate dishonest *g.*	Ex. 18:21	unlawful *g.* takes away	Prov. 1:19
is it a *g.* to him	Job 22:3	of them to his own *g*	Isa. 1:19
	to *g.* the whole world	Matt. 16:26	

Gaius (gay´-us), 1. A Christian of Corinth, in whose house Paul stayed when he wrote to the Romans (Rom. 16:23). He was one of the two Christians at Corinth whom Paul baptized personally (1 Cor. 1:14).

2. A Christian of Macedonia, with Aristarchus, a companion of Paul, when they found themselves in the midst of a riot provoked against them by the silversmith Demetrius at Ephesus (Acts 19:29).

3. A Christian in Derbe, a companion of Paul in the journey from Ephesus to Macedonia (Acts 20:4).

4. The person to whom John wrote his third epistle.

Galaad, *See* GILEAD.

Galatia, The region occupied by the Galatians, an Indo-European people who came out of Gaul to invade central Asia Minor from 279 B.C. on and settled there. The territory was situated around the city of Ankara, between the regions of Bithynia, Pontus and Lycaonia. From 24 B.C. it was a Roman province called Galatia which comprised, over and above the territories of the ancient kingdom of Galatia, the southern regions of Pisidia and Pamphylia, with the cities of Antiochia and Pisidia, Derbe and Lystra, which were visited by Paul during his first missionary journey. From this arises the question about the people to whom the letter to the Galatians was addressed. *See* GALATIANS, EPISTLE TO THE.

According to Acts 16:6 and 18:23 Paul visited the region of Galatia on the second and third apostolic journeys. Seeing that Luke generally uses the ancient names for the region and not the political denomination, the texts quoted should be taken to mean the ethnic region of the Galatians. When Paul was writing 2 Timothy, Crescens had gone to Galatia (*see* 4:10). 1 Peter is also addressed to the churches of the region.

Galatians, Epistle to the, Paul wrote to the churches of Galatia (1:2) to cope with the danger of defections from the faith as a result of some Judaizing preachers who had come to the region after Paul's second visit there (Gal. 1:7; 4:13, 17). These preachers held that converts from paganism must submit to the Jewish rite of circumcision and to the observance of the law in order to be saved (Gal. 5:1-5; 3:1-5). Paul demanded only faith and baptism, and held them exempt from the practice of the law.

In the pursuit of their aim it seems that these preachers carried out a denigrating campaign in regard to Paul, trying to show how he was in contrast to the Apostles in Jerusalem, that he was no true apostle and that he was a religious opportunist.

The letter for these reasons is intensely polemic. It deals with the personal attacks and defends his doctrinal positions. It is divided thus: a. Introduction: 1:1-10; b. a defense of his own person: his association with the other Apostles of Jerusalem, dealings on a level of equality and accord precisely on the question of circumcision, which became evident in a meeting with Peter, John and James which was held in Jerusalem (probably that narrated in Acts 15), 1:18-2:10, in a meeting with Peter in Antioch, 2:11-14; the discourse continues without transition with a presentation in synthesis of Paul's thought in the matter, 2:15-21; c. the doctrinal part: justification through faith without the works of the law, 3:1-5; the example of Abraham, 3:6-9; the law and the curse, 3:10-14; the law and the promise,

3:15-18; the role of the law, 3:19-29; the spirit and sonship, 4:1-10; Paul's dealings with the Galatians, 4:11-20; the concluding allegory on Hagar and Sarah, 4:21-31; d. the exhortatory part: Christians are called to freedom, 5:1-12; and to love, 5:13-6:10. The conclusion is in his own hand-writing (6:11-18).

There is no unanimous opinion on when it was written or to whom. *See* GALATIA. Tradition and the greater part of today's scholars believe that Paul was writing to the churches of the region occupied by the Galatians, not to the churches which were then in the Roman province of Galatia, but were in reality in Pisidia. The principal reason is the acclamation: "O mad Galatians," where the word is obviously meant in the ethnic sense. Paul visited this region on the second and third journey (Acts 16:6; 18:23) and from Galatians 4:13 one can deduce that there were other visits also before Paul wrote this letter. Thus the letter was probably written during his third missionary journey (54-57 A.D.). Those however who hold that the letter was written to the Christian communities of Pisidia, Lystra, Derbe, and Iconium, which he had already visited on the first missionary journey (Acts 13:13-14), date its composition during the second journey while the apostle was at Corinth (around 50 A.D.).

Galaunitis, A region in Transjordan from Mt. Hermon to the river Jarmuk but the southern limits which separate it from Batania and Traconitis are not certain. Its name is derived from the Greek form of the city of Galan. It was part of the kingdom of Herod I the Great, afterwards of the tetrarchy of Philip (4 B.C.-34 A.D.) until it became a part of the Roman province of Syria (34-37 A.D.). Caligula assigned it to the kingdom of Herod Agrippa (37-44 A.D.) but after his death it returned to Roman jurisdiction.

Galbanum (gal′-ba-num), A resinous aromatic gum employed as an ingredient for the incense used in the Tabernacle cult (Ex. 30:34; *see* Sir. 24:15).

Galeed (gal′-i-ed), The name given to a heap of stones erected by Jacob and Laban to memorialize the covenant made by the two and to mark the boundary for their respective countries (Gen. 31:46-54).

Galgala, *See* GILGAL.

Galilee, A region in northern Palestine with the Mediterranean to the west and the Jordan to the east, the plain of Esdraelon to the south and the Nahr-el-Qasimiyeh to the north. It was occupied in the time of Joshua (Josh. 11) with the tribes of Zebulun, Naphtali, Asher and Issachar settling there (Josh. 19:10-39). Solomon gave Hiram of Tyre twenty Galilean cities in payment for the materials with which Solomon built the Temple and a palace for himself in Jerusalem (1 Kgs. 9:10-13). Hiram was not satisfied with the gift.

Galilee was conquered by Tiglath-pileser III at the time of King Pekah of Israel (737-732 B.C.; 2 Kgs. 15:29) and there he settled a mixed non-Israelite population. Isaiah 9:1 calls it Galilee of the Gentiles (*see* Matt. 4:15). At the time of the Maccabees it did have a Jewish population (1 Mac. 5:14-23). After the conquest by Pompey, Galilee was united to the kingdom of John Hyrcanus. It became part of the kingdom of Herod I the Great, and later, together with Perea, was assigned to the tetrarch of Herod Antipas (Lk. 3:1; 13:31).

Galilee is the scene of most of the synoptic tradition about Jesus who carried out a great part of his public ministry there. The principal cities mentioned in the Gospels are Capernaum, Cana, Tiberias, Nazareth. The people of Galilee were not very highly esteemed by the sophisticated Jews of Jerusalem and Judea (Jn. 1:46; 7:52), probably on account of the strong Hellenization of the region and the mixed population it held.

Galilee, Sea of, *See* GENNESARET, LAKE OF.

gall

my g. upon the ground	Job 16:13	wine flavored with g.	Matt. 27:34
put g. in my food	Ps. 69:22	poisoned with g.	Acts 8:23

Gallim, The home of Palti to whom King Saul gave his daughter Michal as wife (1 Sam. 25:44).

Gallio, Lucius Junius Annaeus Gallio, son of the rhetorician Marcus Annaeus Seneca and brother of the philosopher Seneca. He was born in Spain and adopted by Lucius Junius Gallio whose name he took; previously he had been Marcus Annaeus Novatus. He was Roman proconsul of the province of Achaia with residence at Corinth, and before him Paul was put on trial on a charge of propagating a cult contrary to the law. Gallio showed disinterest in the case as he considered it an internal affair of the Jews (Acts 18:12-16). This episode is important for establishing the chronology of Paul's life. According to Roman sources, Gallio was proconsul of Achaia in the twenty-sixth acclamation of Claudius, that is, in 52 A.D. Paul's arrival in Corinth where he remained eighteen months must then be placed at the end of the year 50 A.D.

Gamaliel (ga-may'-li-el), Rabban Gamaliel I, so called to distinguish him from his grandson Gamaliel II who lived around 100 A.D., also called "the Great." He was a Pharisee and a member of the Sanhedrin which judged Peter and John. Gamaliel intervened in favor of the apostles with prudent reasons: if the Christian movement were merely human it would of itself break up; if it were from God then it would endure, and should not be opposed (Acts 5:34-39). In his address to the Jews in Jerusalem Paul claimed that he had studied under Gamaliel (Acts 22:3).

game

he was fond of g.	Gen. 25:28	some g. for me	Gen. 27:3
	'Bring me some g.	Gen. 27:7	

Garden, The gardens mentioned in the Bible are more like orchards (Jer. 29:5, 28; Amos 9:14), often well irrigated by springs and cisterns (S. of S. 4:15; Isa. 58:11; Jer. 31:12) and prized not just for their products but also as places of ease and recreation (Dan. 13:17). In the Old Testament there is mention of a royal garden beside the palace in Jerusalem (2 Kgs. 25:4; Jer. 39:4; 52:7), of the garden of Uzzah where King Manasseh (2 Kgs. 21:18) and Amon of Judah (2 Kgs. 21:2-6) were buried. In the New Testament there is mention of the garden of Gethsemani where Jesus was accustomed to retire to pray and where he was arrested (Jn. 18:1-26), and the garden beside Calvary where Jesus was buried (Jn. 19:41; 20:15). On the garden of Eden, *see* EDEN.

garden

the g. of Eden	Gen. 2:15	and beyond his g.	Job 8:16
banished him from the g.		an enclosed g.	S. of S. 4:12
	Gen. 3:23	g. of the Lord	Isa. 51:3
	There was a g. there	Jn. 18:1	

Gareb, One of the Thirty warriors among David's soldiers (2 Sam. 23:38; 1 Chron. 11:40).

garrison

where there is a g.	1 Sam. 10:5	Saul had overcome the g.	
overcame the Philistine g.			1 Sam. 13:4
	1 Sam. 13:3	the Philistine g. was	
			1 Chron. 11:16

Gaspar, One of the three Wise Men or Magi; the name is given only in late Christian tradition.

Gate, According to 2 Samuel 18:24 ff., the city gate was surmounted by a roofed room. From the roof the lookout kept watch, and in this case, shouted, to the waiting King David below, the news of who was coming. Marketing was carried on at the city gate (2 Kgs. 7:18). There too the elders sat in judgment (Deut. 21:19; Amos 5:12, 15).

gate

from g.to g.	Ex. 32:27	leading to the g.	2 Sam. 15:2
g. of his home city	Deut. 21:19	went forth to the g.	Job 29:7
	at his g. lay a beggar	Lk. 16:20	

Gath, One of the five cities of the Philistine Pentapolis (Josh. 13:3; 1 Sam. 5:7-10), first inhabited by the Anakim (Josh. 11:22; 2 Sam. 2:22; 1 Chron. 20:8), a gigantic people of whom Goliath was one. While fleeing from Saul, David served with his troops as mercenaries to Achis king of Gath (1 Sam. 21:11; 27:2). The city was later taken by David (2 Sam. 21:20; 1 Chron. 18:1). It was fortified by Rehoboam (2 Chron. 11:8), taken by Hazael of Damascus (2 Kgs. 12:18) and was Philistine property at the time of Amos (Amos 6:2; *see* 2 Chron. 26:6). In 711 B.C. it was conquered by Sargon II of Assyria. Gath guarded the southeast border of Philistia.

gather

g. herbs	2 Kgs. 4:39	g. them in her shadow	Isa. 34:15
g. in the yield	Job 39:12	g. his grain	Matt. 3:12
	they g. nothing	Matt. 6:26	

Gath-hepher, A city on the borders of the territory of Zebulun (Josh. 19:13), home of the prophet Jonah, a contemporary of Jeroboam II, king of Israel (786-746 B.C.; 2 Kgs. 14:25) who is distinct from the Jonah of the book called Jonah.

Gath-rimmon, A Levitical town in the territory allotted to the tribe of Dan (Josh. 19:45; 21:24).

Gaza (gay′-za or gah′-za), A very ancient Canaanite city on the principal road between Egypt and Syria and Mesopotamia. It turned its attention to the great caravan routes to the east rather than to shipping (as did Ashdod) and it became the greatest trade center of biblical Palestine. It was inhabited by the Avvim (Deut. 2:23) and later became one of the cities of the Philistine Pentapolis (Josh. 13:3; Jgs. 16:1-2, 21; 1 Sam. 6:17). It is necessary to place the conquest of Gaza at the hands of Judah (Jgs. 1:18; Josh. 15:47) in the monarchic period (*see* the story of Samson in Jgs. 16:1). It is mentioned as the southern limit of the kingdom of Solomon (1 Kgs. 5:4) but was later captured from the Israelites (Amos 1:6) to be retaken for a brief period by Hezekiah (715-687; 2 Kgs. 18:8). The possession of Gaza was disputed again in succeeding centuries, by the Egyptians under Neco (Jer. 47:1, 5), later taken by Cambyses (529) and by Alexander (322) and once more passing into the hands of the Jews in the Maccabean period (1 Mac. 11:61, 62). The modern city has the same name and location as the old one.

Gazelle, A proverbially swift and graceful member of the antelope group, ranging from fawn to brown in color and from 21 to 25 inches in height. Gazelles were food for Solomon's table, according to 1 Kings 5:3. They frequently occur in love poetry, representing the beloved, roaming like a gazelle on the mountains (S. of S. 2:17) with breasts like twin fawns, the young of the gazelle (S. of S. 4:5; 7:14).

gazing

g. through the windows S. of S. 2:9　*g.* up into the heavens　　Acts 1:10

Geba (ge′-ba), A Levitical city (Josh. 21:17; 1 Chron. 6:45) of the land of Benjamin (Josh. 18:24; 1 Chron. 8:6) about 8 miles northeast of Jerusalem. It played a significant part in the wars with the Philistines during the time of Saul (1 Sam. 13:14) and of David (2 Sam. 5:25, although perhaps here Gibeon is meant). It was fortified by Asa of Juda (913-873 B.C.; 1 Kgs. 15:22; 2 Chron. 16:6) on account of its strategic position on the northern border of the land of Judah (2 Kgs. 23:8). It was re-populated after the exile (Neh. 11:31). In the predicted restoration Zechariah sees the entire country 'from Geba to Rimmon' renewed (Zech. 14:10).

Gebim (ge′-bim), A city of Benjamin (Isa. 10:31).

Gedaliah (ged′-a-ly′ah), 1. Son of Ahikam, named by Nebuchadnezzar governor of Judah after the conquest of Jerusalem (587 B.C.; 2 Kgs. 25:22). Gedaliah's father had intervened in favor of Jeremiah (Jer. 26:24), and it seems that the son was a friend of the prophet (Jer. 39:11-14). Gedaliah was treacherously killed by Ishmael, son of Nethaniah (Jer. 40:13; 41:2; 2 Kgs. 25:25). The people of Judah, high and low, and the commanders of the troops fled into Egypt for fear of the anger of the Babylonians over the murder of Gedaliah (2 Kgs. 25:26); in this they disregarded the advice of Jeremiah, who was taken with them into exile (Jer. 42:1-43:7).

2. Son of Pashur, one of the leading men at court who asked for the death of Jeremiah (Jer. 38:1-6).

3. Grandfather of the prophet Zephaniah (Zeph. 1:1).

Gedeon, *See* GIDEON.

Gederah (ge-deer′-ah), 1. A city of Judah, according to Joshua 15:36; but the list there is based on an enlarged "greater Judah" district of the time of King Soloman. Gederah was a town in the traditional territory of Dan, at the northern end of the plain of Shephelah.

2. A city of Benjamin (1 Chron. 12:5).

Gederoth (ge-deer′-oth), A town in the plain of Shephelah (Josh. 15:41), exact site unknown, probably near Soco, conquered by the Philistines in the time of Ahaz (2 Chron. 28:18).

Gehazi (ge-hay′-zy), A servant of Elisha (2 Kgs. 4:13; 8:4). When Elisha cured the Aramaean general, Naaman, of leprosy, he refused to accept anything for his services. Gehazi went after Naaman and with a fraudulent story extracted two talents from him. Elisha met Gehazi on his return, and struck him and his descendants with leprosy for his misdeed (2 Kgs. 5:19-27).

Gehenna, From the Greek **geenna** which translates the Hebrew **ge-hinnom,** the Valley of the son of Hinnom, south of Jerusalem where an idolatrous cult with human sacrifices was at times carried out (2 Kgs. 23:10; 2 Chron. 28:3; 33:6) and for this reason cursed by the prophet Jeremiah (Jer. 7:32; 19:6; *see* Isa. 66:24). The name passed into apocalyptic literature to designate the place of eternal torment through fire reserved for the impious after their death. This is the sense in which it is used several times in the New Testament (Matt. 5:22; 5:29; 10:28; Mk. 9:43, 45, 47; Lk. 12:15; James 3:6).

Gelboe, *See* GILBOA.

Gemariah, An officer of King Zedekiah of Judah sent as legate to Nebuchadnezzar; Gemariah carried with him on this occasion a letter from the prophet Jeremiah to the exiles in Babylon (Jer. 29:3).

Genealogy, In the Bible long genealogical lists continually appear, especially in Genesis, Numbers, 1 Chronicles, Nehemiah and Ezra. In general it can be said that these are no mere artificial confections, but they are difficult to interpret and use because, for one thing, there is no way of evaluating them, and for another it is not always clear what real relationships they intend to express. The origins of this type of writing must be sought in the social organization, which was tribal. The tribe is an autonomous group of families who hold themselves to be descended from one common father. What keeps this group together is the awareness of common blood. The genealogies then trace the limits within which the principle of cohesion and tribal solidarity holds.

To the importance attached to blood relationship goes the responsibility for creating a common founding father, in a fictional way, who was held to have borne the actual name of the group of people now forming in fact a tribe. Thus there were geographical names (Judah, Ephraim, etc.) or trade names (Cain, probably) which were in turn given to the fictional founding father. Moreover it was necessary to transpose the historical relationships of alliance, function or living together into links ascending to and descending from common ancestors. These common ancestors were made brothers or blood relations, whether or not this corresponded to fact. The genealogies then, especially in the story of the patriarchs, have a true historical value, but must be interpreted with great skill.

Jesus' genealogies in Matthew 1:17 and Luke 3:23 are in part confected from Bible sources. In the last part however, from David to Joseph, the genealogies have found only two names in common, a problem that up to the present has found no satisfactory solution. The traditional interpretation would make Matthew's the genealogy through Joseph, and Luke's the genealogy through Mary, while others hold that both are Joseph's genealogy, with Matthew giving his natural genealogy and Luke tracing it through Heli, Joseph's father in virtue of the levirate law.

generation
and that whole *g.* died	Ex. 1:6	preserve us always from this *g.*
and kept in every *g.*	Esth. 9:28	Ps. 12:8
		for God is with the just *g.* Ps. 14:5
	so that this *g.* will have to Lk. 11:50	

generosity
have produced an abundant *g.*	your *g.* in sharing with them
2 Cor. 8:2	2 Cor. 9:13
the fruit of the Spirit is *g.* Gal. 5:22	

Genesis, The first book of the Bible and the first of the five books which form the Pentateuch. The name Genesis, in Greek meaning origin, is read in the Greek translation of the Seventy (LXX) and from this passed into other translations. In Hebrew it is designated with the two words **b're'sit** meaning "in the beginning." The Greek title expresses well the theme of the book, which recounts the origin of the world, the beginning of humanity and the people of Israel. For its composition and origin *see* PENTATEUCH.

There are two main divisions in the book: 1. Primitive history, an artificial reconstruction and religious interpretation of the history of the world and of man up to the time of Abraham—creation (1:1-2:4a); the creation of man and woman and the first sin (2:4b-3:24); the history of the progress and diffusion of mankind and of sin and the accompanying divine judgment, the story of Cain and Abel (c. 4); the genealogy of Adam (c. 5); the story of the flood (cc. 6-9); the diffusion of humanity after the flood and the sons of Noah (c. 10); and the episode of the tower of Babel with the genealogy of Abraham (c. 11).

2. The history of the patriarchs and of the origins of Israel. It is dominated by the theme of the promise of descendants and the possession of the land of Canaan, which God made to Abraham and repeated to his descendants, and by the theme of God's fidelity to the promises he had made. This guides the patriarchs and brings their sufferings to an end by secretly controlling the events. There are three tradition cycles: on Abraham (cc. 12-15), Isaac (26, 27), and Jacob and his children (cc. 28-50). This third cycle contains the story of Joseph which is meant to explain by what vicissitudes Jacob and his family were brought into Egypt where the first part of the promise was fulfilled in the multiplication of the people (*see* Ex. 1).

Gennesaret, Lake of (ge-ness′-a-ret), The Hellenistic Greek of the Hebrew Chinneroth (*see* CHINNERETH) which was the name of a city and plain near the northwest corner of the Galilean Sea (Josh. 11:2; 19:35; 1 Kgs. 15:20). Jesus reached the plain of Gennesaret by crossing the Sea of Galilee from the place where he had multiplied the bread (Matt. 14:34; Mk. 6:53). The name then spread to include the nearby lake (Num. 34:11; Deut. 3:17; Josh. 13:27; Lk. 5:1) which is more commonly called the Sea of Galilee (Matt. 4:18; 15:29; Mk. 1:16; 7:31) or the Lake of Tiberias from the city of Tiberias on the northern edge of the lake (*see* Jn. 6:1; 21:1).

The Lake of Gennesaret is fed by the river Jordan in a depression of volcanic origin between the hills of Galilee to the west and the highlands of Haman to the east. It is eight miles wide and thirteen miles long. Its surface lies 690 feet beneath sea level and it has a depth of 160 to 230 feet. Around the shores of the lake are several towns, Capernaum (Matt. 4:13; Mk. 2:1), Bethsaida (Mk. 6:45; 8:22), Magdala, and Tiberias. This neighborhood was the scene of a great part of Christ's public ministry. Some of the gospel episodes took place on the lake: the two miraculous catches of fish in Luke 5:1-11 and John 21:1; the calming of the storm (Matt. 5:23-27; Mk. 4:35-41; Lk. 8:22-25) and the vision of Jesus walking on the waters (Matt. 14:21-33; Mk. 6:45-52).

Gentile, Gentiles, that is non-Jews (in the Old Testament they are simply called "the peoples," **goyim**) is a term that has at one and the same time an ethnic and religious connotation. This of course derives from the eminently nationalistic character of the religion of the Old Testament, which centered on the notion of God's choice of Israel as his people. In Jewish usage the term acquired a definitely pejorative sense which is reflected in some passages of the New Testament (Matt. 5:47; 6:7, 32; Lk. 12:30; 1 Cor. 5:1; 1 Thess. 4:5). It is linked with the term "publican" or tax-collector to denote a segment of humanity excluded and despised.

In spite of these racialist remnants the attitude of the New Testament to the Gentiles is radically different from that of contemporary Judaism. It is true that from the third century B.C. the Jews had carried on missionary activity among the Gentiles. (*See* PROSELYTE.) This however was no universalism in which the privileges of the chosen were now offered to all. On the contrary, the basic conviction was that the privileges of the Jews were Jewish and one could share in them only in so far as one became a Jew. In contrast, the missionary activity of the Church is centrifugal. Once the question of the obligation of the law of Moses for the Gentiles had been resolved (Gal. 1-2; Acts 15), the Christian message reached out to all without distinction of race or condition (Gal. 3:27, 28). The new spirit of Christian universalism has its best representative and asserter in Paul, who was called to be the "apostle of the Gentiles" (Rom. 11:13), that is, chosen by Christ to announce him among all the Gentiles (Gal. 1:15, 16).

Gentiles, Court of, The outermost courtyard of the Temple of Herod in Jerusalem, to which there was access even for non-Jews (Mk. 11:15), but beyond which they might not go.

Gera (gee′-ra), 1. A Benjaminite clan (Gen. 46:21; 1 Chron 8:3, 5) and the name of the father of Ehud, judge over Israel (Jgs. 3:15).

2. Father of Shimei who cursed David while he was fleeing from Jerusalem during the revolt of Absalom (2 Sam. 16:5; 19:6, 18; 1 Kgs. 2:8).

Gerar (gee′-rar), A Palestinian city in the south, probably what is today Tell Jemmeh, south of Gaza. Abimelech, king of Gerar, had dealings with Abraham (Gen. 20:2) and with Isaac (Gen. 26:6). It was in Philistine hands for some time (Gen. 26:1). The city was taken by Asa of Judah (913-873 B.C.; 2 Chron. 14:12).

Gerasa (gur′-a-sa), A Greek city in Transjordan, part of the Decapolis or confederation of the ten cities. (*See* DECAPOLIS.) Today it is Jerash. According to Mark 5:1 and Luke 8:26 Jesus cured a possessed person in the region of the Gerasenes. Matthew 8:28 places the same episode in the region of the Gadarenes. (*See* GADARA.)

Gergesenes, A variant reading for Gadarenes and Gerasenes in some manuscripts of Matthew 8:28; Mark 5:1; Luke 8:26.

Gerizim, A mountain south of mount Ebal, and opposite it; between the two mountains is the city of Nablus, at the entrance to the valley is Shechem. The mountain is 2900 feet high. Here was carried out the ceremony of the renewal of the covenant (Josh. 8:30-35) according to what Moses had laid down (Deut. 27). On the meaning of this ceremony *see* EBAL. After the exile, and probably already in the time of Nehemiah, the Samaritans who had cut themselves off from the Jews built there a temple, which was later profaned by Antiochus IV Epiphanes (2 Mac. 6:2) and destroyed by John Hyrcanus (128 B.C.). The place was the center of Samaritan cult during the time of Jesus (Jn. 4:20, 21) and remains so today.

Gershom, 1. The first-born of Moses and Zipporah, born during the stay of Moses in Midian (Ex. 2:22; 18:3). From him descended the priests of Dan (Jgs. 18:30) and a Levite family (1 Chron. 23:15; 26:24).

2. A descendant of Pinehas, grandson of Aaron (Ezra 8:2).

3. The same as Gershon. *See* GERSHON.

Gershon, The first-born of Levi and brother of Kohath and Merari (Ex. 6:16; Num. 3:17; 1 Chron. 6:1; 23:6). He was born in Canaan (Gen. 46:11) and was father of Libni and Shimei (Ex. 6:17; Num. 3:18; 1 Chron. 6:17, 20), and the ancestral founder of a Levitical clan (Josh. 21:27; 1 Chron. 6:56-61).

Geshem, An Arab who, together with Sanballat and Tobiah, opposed Nehemiah's plans to rebuild the walls of Jerusalem (Neh. 6).

Geshur, A kingdom in northern Transjordan east of the Sea of Galilee, a territory never fully absorbed by the Hebrews (Deut. 3:14; Josh. 12:5). David maintained friendship with Geshur and married the daughter of King Talmai, from whom Absalom was born (2 Sam. 3:3; 1 Chron. 3:2).

Absalom took refuge in Geshur when he had killed his half-brother Amnon to vindicate the outrage committed against his full sister Tamar (2 Sam. 13:37-14:24).

Joshua 13:2 and 1 Sam 27:8 speak of another region by the same name in the desert south of Judah.

Gestas (guest´-as), The name of the unrepentant thief who was crucified with the Lord (*see* Lk. 23:39-43). The name is given only in late Christian tradition. *See* DYSMAS.

get

"*G.* me this girl for a wife"	A degrading beating will he *g.*
Gen. 34:4	Prov. 6:33
G. wisdom, *g.* understanding	his disciples *g.* into the boat
Prov. 4:5	Matt. 14:22

Gether, An Aramean kingdom listed among the sons of Aram and Shem in the Table of Nations (Gen. 10:23).

Gethsemani, The place where Jesus retired with his disciples after the Last Supper, and where he was arrested (Matt. 26:36; Mk. 14:32). Luke does not mention Gethsemani but states that these events took place on the Mount of Olives (Lk. 22:39). John adds that there was a garden there where Jesus used to retire to pray (Jn. 18:1).

Gezer (ge´-zer), A very ancient Canaanite city, today Tell Jezer, 18 miles northwest of Jerusalem on a Shephalah hill above the maritime plain. With four other cities of western Palestine it opposed the advance of Joshua (Josh. 10:33; 12:12). It was involved in the wars between the Philistines and the Israelites at the time of David (2 Sam. 5:25; 1 Chron.14:16; 20:4) and appeared among the Levitical cities of Ephraim (1 Chron. 6:52; 7:28). At the time of Solomon it was seized from the Canaanites by an Egyptian Pharaoh and given to Solomon as a dowry for his daughter (1 Kgs. 9:15). Solomon transformed Gezer into one of his chariot cities, strategically located military centers. After the exile until the time of Maccabeans it was not occupied by the Jews (1 Mac. 4:15; 9:50; 13:43-48; 14:7, 34; 15:28; 2 Mac. 10:32-38).

Ghost, Holy, *See* SPIRIT.

Giant, *See* ANAKIM.

gibbet

Have a *g.* set up	Esth. 5:14	be hanged on the *g.*	Esth. 6:4
and he had a *g.* erected	Esth. 5:14	on the *g.*	Esth. 7:10

Gibbethon (gib´-a-thon), A Philistine city, in the primitive territory of Dan (Josh. 19:44) besieged in vain by some kings of Israel (Nadab, 1 Kgs. 15:27; Zimri and Omri in 1 Kgs. 16:15-17).

Gibeah (gib´-e-ah), A city of Benjamin (Josh. 18:28; in Josh. 15:57 it is numbered among the cities of Judah), 4 miles north of Jerusalem (Jgs. 19:12). At the time of the Judges the citizens of Gibeah were guilty of a terrible outrage against the concubine of a passing Levite who was a guest in the city (Jgs. 19-21). Gibeah was Saul's birthplace (1 Sam. 10:10-26; 11:4; 15:34; Isa. 10:29) and was his residence as king of Israel (1 Sam 22:6; 23:19; 26:1). In 1 Samuel 13-14 there is some confusion between Geba, Gibea and Gibeon, which is often corrected thus: Geba in 1 Sam. 13:2, 5; 14:2, 16; Gibeah in 13:3. Today it is Tell-el-Ful, 4 miles north of Jerusalem.

Gibeon, A Horite city originally, it allied itself with Joshua (Josh. 9:3, 17) and was defended by him against the five Canaanite kings from central Palestine who opposed this alliance with the Israelites (Josh. 10). It was assigned to the territory of Benjamin (Josh. 18:25; 1 Chron. 8:29; 9:35) and is mentioned among the Levitical cities (Josh. 21:17). David defeated the Philistines near Gibeon (1 Chron. 14:16). In revenge for the Gibeonites Saul had put to death, David handed over to them seven of his sons who were impaled on the mountain before Yahweh (2 Sam. 21:1-14). Near the pool of Gibeon took place the battle between the supporters of Abner cousin of Saul and Saul's general, and Joab who was faithful to David (*see* 2 Sam. 2:12 ff). At Gibeon also Ishmael was killed. He had treacherously killed Gedaliah, governor of Judah after the destruction of Jerusalem (587 B.C.; Jer. 41:12, 16). King Solomon offered a thousand holocausts on the altar in the high place there, and during the night in a vision asked God for "a heart to understand" (1 Kgs. 3:4-15). Gibeon was again occupied by the Jews after the exile (Neh. 3:7; 7:25). Today it is called El-Jib, 8 miles northwest of Jerusalem.

Gideon, Son of Joash, of the family of Abiezer, of the city of Ephrah, of the tribe of Manasseh (Jgs. 6:11). He was a judge over Israel (cc. 6-8). He was also called Jerubbaal (7:1; 8:29-35; 9:1; 2 Sam. 11:21) for having destroyed an altar of Baal which had belonged to his father (Jgs. 6:25-32). Gideon freed Israel from the oppression of the Midianites, who would steal into the land and destroy crops whenever the Israelites sowed them (6:1-10). Gideon's call is narrated in 6:33-40. Gideon took with him three hundred strong men and by night broke into the Midianite camp, provoking such confusion that the enemy was forced into wildly confused flight (7:15-23). The Ephraimites were tipped off by Gideon and took possession of the fords of the Jordan to block the escape of the Midianites. This move was unsuccessful but they did succeed in taking two of the chieftains, Oreb and Zeeb (7:24-25). Gideon pursued the Midianites beyond the Jordan, caught up with them and defeated them east of Nobah and Jogbehah, killing their kings Zebah and Zalmunna (Jgs. 8:1-21). During the campaign the towns of Succoth and Penuel had refused food for the army, so on his return Gideon took revenge on them, slaughtering the townsmen and destroying the tower of Penuel (8:4-9, 14-17). For his defeat of the Midianites, the Israelites wished to make Gideon king, but he refused (8:22-27). The history of this attempted establishment of the monarchy continued with Abimelech, the son of Gideon (Jgs. 9). Gideon's victory is recalled in several later books (Ps. 83:10; Isa. 9:3; 10:26; Heb. 11:32 f).

gift

has brought me a precious *g.*	A secret *g.* allays anger
Gen. 30:20	Prov. 21:14
A man's *g.* clears the way for	If you bring your *g.* to the altar
Prov. 18:16	Matt. 5:23

Gihon, 1. One of the four rivers of Paradise (Gen. 2:13, *see* EDEN).

2. A spring on the eastern slope of the hill of Zion in Jerusalem, today called the Fountain of the Virgin, in the Valley of Kidron. At Gihon Solomon was anointed king (1 Kgs. 1:38). In order to keep this main water supply to the city abundant even in time of siege, Hezekiah cut a conduit, 1777 feet long, through the rock to the western slope of the hill to the valley of Tyropoeon (2 Kgs. 20:20; 2 Chron. 32:30; Sir. 48:17). In 1880 an inscription was found commemorating the opening of the conduit in the time of Hezekiah.

Gilboa, A range of hills on the eastern side of the plain of Jezreel, today called Jebel Fuqu'ah, where the Hebrews were badly defeated by the Philistines in a battle that saw the death of Saul and Jonathan (1 Sam. 28:4; 2 Sam. 1:6; 21:12; 1 Chron. 10:1).

Gilead, A region in Transjordan whose limits are given differently by different texts. Originally it was probably the name of a mountain or locality south of the river Jabbok, between Mahanaim and Mizpah (Gen. 31:23-32, where a popular etymology is given for the name). It was the native place of the judge Jephthah (Jgs. 10:17, 18; 11:29; 12:4). The name also designated the whole territory of the tribe of Manasseh in Transjordan. Gilead is also considered to be the founding father of the tribe of the territory, son of Machin, and grandson of Manasseh (Num. 32:39, 40; 1 Chron. 2:21, 23; 7:17; Josh. 13:11; 17:1, 3). Jephthah is said to be son of Gilead and of a prostitute (Jgs. 11:1). Gilead is taken to mean all the region of Transjordan occupied by the Israelites, where the tribes of Gad, Reuben and half the tribe of Manesseh settled (Deut. 3:12, 13; Josh. 13:31; Num. 32:1, 26; 1 Chron. 5:9-15). The region is celebrated for its fertility, its wood and its flocks (Jer. 8:22; 22:6; 46:11; Num. 32:1; S. of S. 6:5), and also for its medicinal balm (Jer. 8:22; 46:11). It was the occasion of rivalry between the Israelites and the Aramaeans of Damascus (2 Kgs. 10:32; Amos 1:3). It was conquered by Tiglath-pileser III, who made it an Assyrian province (2 Kgs. 15:29). After an unsuccessful attempt to take the region, Judas Maccabeus withdrew his troops to the near side of the Jordan (1 Mac. 5:9-54).

Gilgal, 1. A place and Israelite sanctuary along the Jordan near Jericho marked by twelve pillars in a circle, erected to commemorate the passage across the Jordan under Joshua (Josh. 4:19). Here the Israelites who had come from the desert underwent the rite of circumcision and celebrated the first Pasch in the land of Canaan (Josh. 4-5). The sanctuary of Gilgal was still in use in the time of Samuel (1 Sam. 7:16) and Saul (1 Sam. 10:8; 11:14; 15:33) and in this neighborhood Saul fought the Philistines and the Amalekites (1 Sam. 13:4; 15:12). The prophets Hosea and Amos speak of Gilgal as an important sanctuary of the kingdom of Israel in their time (Hos. 9:15; 12:12; Amos 4:4; 5:5).

2. A place in the mountains of Ephraim mentioned in the story of Elijah and Elisha (2 Kgs. 2:1; 4:38) which is identified by some authors with the previous Gilgal.

Gimel, The third letter of the Hebrew alphabet (g).

Ginath (gy′-nath), The father of Tibni, who disputed with Omri the usurpation of the Israelite throne (1 Kgs. 16:21, 22).

gird
Let everyone g. on his sword   G. up your loins now   Job 38:3
                1 Sam. 25:13   G. your sword upon your thigh
g. yourselves with sack cloth   Ps. 45:4
              2 Sam. 3:31

Girgashite, One of the peoples who lived in Canaan before the arrival of the Israelites (Gen. 15:21; Deut. 7:1; Josh. 3:10; 24:11; Neh. 9:8), descendants from Canaan in the genealogy of Gen. 10:16.

girl
Let the g. stay with us   Gen. 24:55   Let us call the g.   Gen. 34:57
              and given to the g.   Matt. 14:11

Girzites, A Bedouin tribe living south of Judah, mentioned in the campaigns of David when he lived at Ziklag (1 Sam. 27:8).

glad

his heart will be *g*.	Ex. 4:15	The just man is *g*.	Ps. 64:11
are *g*. when they reach the grave		A wise son makes his father *g*.	
	Job 3:22		Prov. 10:1

Glass, There is no evidence of a glass-making industry in Palestine of biblical times. Glass like the clear Roman glass of later times was rare, and therefore precious. Job states that wisdom is unequalled by gold or crystal (Job 28:17).

Gleaning, According to the Israelite law, one was forbidden to harvest to the end of the field, or to gather the gleanings of the harvest. One should not strip the vine bare nor gather up the fruit that had fallen. These gleanings were for the poor and the stranger (Lev. 19:9-10; 23:22; Deut. 24:19-22; Ruth 2).

glorify

you shall *g*. me	Ps. 50:15	Father, *g*. your name	Jn. 12:28
and *g*. your name	Ps. 86:12	*g*. him in himself	Jn. 13:32

Glory, Glory (in Hebrew **kabod,** in Greek **doxa**) is one of the fundamental theological concepts in biblical language. Difficulties frequently occur in understanding this term because it is so different from today's usage. Everybody knows what it is "to give glory to God" (Pss. 29:1; 96:7; 115:1; 1 Col. 6:20; 10:31), that is, acknowledge God for what he is, confess and proclaim his divinity with one's words and life. More difficult however are such expressions as "the glory of God appeared" or "the glory of God filled the Temple" (1 Kgs. 8:11).

One could say that the "glory of God" is the sensible manifestation of his presence, what he reveals of himself to man when he appears to him (Ex. 33:18-22). In some texts this manifestation is conceived of in very concrete terms, such as the pillar of cloud and fire that accompanied the Israelites during the Exodus (Ex. 13:21, 22; 16:10), or the cloud that rested on the Tabernacle in the desert (Ex. 40:34) or the cloud that filled the Temple at Jerusalem on the day of its consecration (1 Kgs. 8:11) or the smoke that filled the sanctuary where Isaiah had his vision which sealed his prophetic mission (Isa. 6:3, 4). In other texts the glory of God is something apart from these material manifestations and is associated with the saving events themselves which give unambiguous witness to the goodness, omnipotence and sanctity of their author (Isa. 40:5; 68:18). The glory of God which fills the earth is the manifestation of the majesty of God in creation (Isa. 6:3). The heavens recount the glory of God without words or noise. Their mute praise is transmitted from day to day and night to night without interruption (Pss. 19:2, 3; 96:3).

The concept is enriched in the New Testament when it is seen in relationship to the work of salvation realized in Christ. In the signs (*see* SIGN) which Jesus works, his disciples see his glory, for they reveal his divinity (Jn. 2:11). These signs however only begin the revelation, for the glorification of Jesus takes place in his death and exaltation (Jn. 12:23; 17:1-5). It is the hour when Jesus departs from this world to the Father (Jn. 13:1) who will glorify him with the glory that he had with the Father before the world began (17:5). For Paul too Christ's resurrection is his glorification. It is then that his humanity, after the freely willed humiliation of the incarnation, will reflect the divine glory that belongs to Jesus as Lord (Phil. 2:6-11). Christians who share in the passion of the Lord will also share in his glory (Rom. 8:17; *see* Rom. 5:2). "He will give a new form to this lowly body of ours and remake it according to the pattern of his glorified body, by his power to subject everything to himself" (Phil. 3:21).

glory

array yourself with *g*.	Job 40:10	Who is this king of *g*.?	Ps. 24:10
that the king of *g*. may come in		with his Father's *g*.	Matt. 16:27
	Ps. 24:7		

Glossolalia, *See* TONGUE.

glutton

he is a *g*. and a drunkard		and the *g*. come to poverty
	Deut. 21:20	Prov. 23:21
one is a *g*. and a drunkard	Matt. 11:19	

Gnosticism, Gnostics, (noss′-ti-cism), The Gnostics were heretics, consisting of various sects, that began to appear as early as the days of the Apostles, and that sought, agreeably to the philosophic opinions which they severally embraced, to extract an esoteric meaning out of the letter of Scripture, and the facts especially of Christianity, such as those only of superior speculative insight could appreciate. They set a higher value on knowledge (Greek **gnosis,** whence their name) than faith. Thus their understanding of Christianity was speculative and not spiritual, and their knowledge of it the result of thinking and not of life. The Gnostics elaborated strange systems of the unseen universe, peopling the vast interval between the infinite God and the finite material creation with emanating and descending series of existences. They made much of these celestial genealogies (Tit. 3:9) and doctrines of "angels" (Col. 2:18). There is an implied reference to the Gnostic heretics in the writings of John and the later epistles of Paul. As far as can be gathered from his epistles, the Gnostics of St. Paul's time betray no acquaintance with the more elaborate systems which appeared only in the second century. They are rather to be associated with Jewish mystical speculations, and may be in reaction to apocalyptic Judaism, which led to national disasters in 70 A.D. and again in 135 A.D. It may be against Gnosticism that the first two chapters of 1 John are directed. Simon Magus (Acts 8:9ff) was thought by the Church Fathers to have proclaimed a system of Gnostic doctrine. Paul declared that the true knowledge was that which came with Christ (Col. 1:9f; 2:2f).

Goad, The goad was a wooden stick sometimes tipped with iron, used for driving the oxen when plowing (1 Sam. 13:21), and occasionally used as a weapon (Jgs. 3:31) as, for instance, in the case of Shamgar who routed six hundred Philistines with an ox-goad. It is also used in figurative language: the word of the wise man can goad a person to good works (Sir. 12:21), and on the road to Damascus Saul heard a voice saying to him: "It is hard for you, kicking like this against the goad" (Acts 26:14).

Goah, A section of Jerusalem (Jer. 31:39).

Goat, The goat was one of the first animals to be domesticated by man. In Israel goats provided milk (Deut. 32:14), meat (Deut. 14:4) and material for canvas and cloth (Ex. 25:4; 26:7). The skin of the goat made a skin bottle (Gen. 21:14; Josh. 9:4).

The legislation on the sacrifice of goats is found in Leviticus (1:10; 22:19, 26) and Numbers (7:16, 17, etc.). Goats are figuratively used to denote the wicked as opposed to the good sheep in Matthew's description of the last judgment (25:31-46).

goat

a three year old she-*g*.	Gen. 15:9	shall offer a he-*g*.	Ezek. 43:25
If he presents a *g*.	Lev. 3:12	The he-*g*. became very powerful	
and the he-*g*.	Prov. 30:31		Dan. 8:8

Gob, A town near Gezer, which is on the northern border of Philistine country. At Gob David won two battles over the Philistines (2 Sam. 21:18).

God, The Hebrew terms for God or the gods in general are 'el, 'eloah, and the plural 'elohim. These terms serve to designate both the gods of other nations "other gods" (Ex. 20:3; Deut. 5:7) and the God of Israel (Ex. 20:2; Deut. 5:6). El is furthermore the proper name for the supreme god of the Canaanite pantheon. (*See* BAAL; UGARIT.) It appears in titles such as El-Shaddai, El-Olam, El Bethel, El-Elyon. These titles were applied to the God of the patriarchs, who is identical with the God of Israel. (*See* PATRIARCHS, RELIGION OF THE.)

Elohim is a plural form which is used both in a plural sense to mean a plurality of gods (*see* Ex. 12:12; 18:11; Deut. 10:17) and in a singular sense for one definite god (Jgs. 11:24). It is also used to denote Yahweh, the true God and God of Israel (Gen. 1:1, etc.).

From the semantic point of view this plural can be explained as the plural of abstraction (the divinity) or the plural of intensity to show that the subject gathers into himself in intensity all the characteristics of his category. The biblical use of the term has no trace of polytheism.

The proper name however of Israel's God is Yahweh. Biblical tradition (Ex. 3:13, 14; 6:2-7) has it that this name for God was unknown to the patriarchs and revealed to Moses. The revelation of his own name means that God wishes to make himself more directly accessible to man, with whom he also wishes to enter into interpersonal relationship. (*See* NAME; YAHWEH.)

This tradition confronts us with the most salient characteristic of the biblical doctrine on God: it is something God himself reveals. What the Bible hands down is no fruit of merely human speculation or reflection. It is God's own word to man, in which he reveals himself and his saving designs for man.

Biblical tradition was aware that the fathers of Israel had adored false gods in Mesopotamia (Josh. 24:2) until God himself had come to them, made himself known, and established a relationship aimed in the long run at making himself equally known to all men (*see* Gen. 12:1-3).

God's self-revelation does not take place at the margins of the religious and cultic forms of humanity at that time. God does however make use of these forms to accommodate himself to man's understanding, without however running the risk of having his genuine voice confused, misunderstood or misinterpreted (*see* PATRIARCHS, RELIGION OF THE; YAHWEH). The Old Testament does not disdain what the language and cultural environment had to offer in this regard. The unmistakable countenance of the true God however emerges. Here some of his features will be pointed out.

The first two precepts of the Decalogue (Ex. 20:2, 3; Deut. 5:7, 8) contain a profession of faith in the unicity and transcendence of God, which had been revealed to Israel during the Exodus. The first commandment obliges men to a total and exclusive service of Yahweh. "You shall not have other gods besides me." This commandment was not immediately understood in a purely monotheistic sense. It did however give unambiguous expression to God's intolerance of any other god being revered by the Israelites. (*See* JEALOUSY.) This intolerance does not have analogies in the history of religions and already suggests what ultimately emerged as the only adequate explanation, namely that Yahweh alone was God. The author of Exodus 15:11, 12, astonished at the prodigies worked by God during the Exodus, placed Yahweh incomparably above any other god:

"Who is like to you among the gods, O Lord? Who is like to you, magnificent in holiness?" Deuteronomy 32:39, having denounced empty hopes in other gods, states: "Learn then that I, I alone, am God, and there is no god besides me. It is I who bring both death and life, I who inflict wounds and heal them, and from my hand there is no rescue." Eventually their monotheistic faith was to inspire the prophets to a sarcastic polemic against idolatry, especially during the Exile when the people fell prey to the powerful influence of the splendid Babylonian cult. (*See* IDOLATRY.)

The second commandment states: "You shall not carve idols (of Yahweh) for yourselves." Through it shines God's transcendence. To get to the genuine meaning of the commandment it is necessary to understand how ancient peoples treated idols. These were not identified with the gods themselves, nor were they even adequate representations of the divinity. They were, however, the privileged place where God and man met, in a universe in which there was real continuity with the world of the gods. While ancient religions were not formally pantheistic, they had not yet unshackled themselves from the world of nature gods. The one was an epiphany of the divine, the other a transfiguration of nature. Between the two there was a real ontological continuity, difficult to express in conceptual terms, but nevertheless seen and expressed in the symbolic language of myth. (*See* MYTH.)

The prohibition of idols or images presupposes a concept of the relationship between God and nature that is radically opposite. God is nature's absolute Lord and Master, without being enveloped in it. Nature stands before God in total obedience and full dependence (*see* Ps. 104; CREATION). Belief in the unicity and transcendence of God allowed Israel to oppose her own strict notion of creation to the cosmologies of other religions.

Yahweh is a moral God. The demand for exclusive service contained in the first commandment is unfolded in the concrete stipulations of Israelite legislation. (*See* COVENANT; LAW.) It must be underlined that the most ancient collections of apodictic law, expressing Yahweh's fundamental demands, have a formally ethical content (*see* DECALOGUE and Ex. 20; Deut. 5; Deut. 27:15-26). These very ancient collections refute the thesis rather commonly held some years ago, which would have it that the prophets from Amos on were the inventors of Israel's monotheism.

Yahweh is a moral God because he is just. (*See* JUSTICE.) The Old Testament pictures Yahweh totally devoid of the capriciousness and arbitrariness that mark the gods' relationships with men in other religions. The ways of God, that is, his concrete dealings with man, are "mercy and truth," that is, goodness and fidelity. (*See* MERCY; TRUTH.) When the just man Job holds himself unjustly smitten by God's anger, he is carried along in an implacable process that concludes in unconditioned surrender to God who is Lord and Judge, but whose ways of goodness and justice are too high and mysterious for man in his mediocrity to judge: "I know that you can do all things, and that no purpose of yours can be hindered. I have dealt with great things that I do not understand; things too wonderful for me, which I cannot know. I had heard of you by word of mouth, but now my eye has seen you. Therefore I disown what I have said, and repent in dust and ashes" (Job 42:2-6; *see* JOB, BOOK OF).

Yahweh is Lord of the world and of history. This he proves himself to be in the mighty deeds of the Exodus, which originated the history of Israel as a people and as God's people. During the Exodus Yahweh revealed himself capable of enacting his own plans and bringing to naught the projects even of the most powerful empires on earth. This is sung in epic tones in Ex. 15:9-18. There too even creation itself faithfully served its

Creator: at God's appearance the heavens and the earth stand in awe (Jgs. 5:4 ff; *see* THEOPHANY). They become God's instruments for the fulfilment of his plans (Jgs. 5:20) in accordance with the principle expressed in Wisdom 5:17 in reference to the last judgment: "He (God) shall take his zeal for armor and he shall arm creation to requite the enemy."

Not only is Yahweh stronger than any empire on earth, but it is he who directs history: "Rather, it is he who gives to all life and breath and everything else. From one stock he made every nation of mankind to dwell on the face of the earth" (Acts 17:25, 26). The choice of Israel was deliberate and it has sense only against the horizon of God's unlimited control over peoples and history, as is asserted in Exodus 19:5, 6. For Deuteronomy 32:8-10, the election of Israel as the people of God was made "when the Most High assigned the nations their heritage, when he parceled out the descendants of Adam, he set up the boundaries of the people, after the number of the sons of God."

These themes were developed with vigor by the prophetic tradition, which envisions the various peoples carrying out the roles assigned to them by God. Assyria is the rod and fury of God (Isa. 10:5). God however will snap the rod when it has served its function. God raises up a nation (Amos 6:14) to punish the infidelity of his people, or unleashes the victorious career of Cyrus of Persia to bring about the liberation on his people from the exile of Babylonia (Isa. 45:1-6).

In history God realizes his plan to have all humanity return to him from their sins, and so come to salvation. (*See* SALVATION HISTORY.) In bringing this plan to completion God shows himself Savior and Judge. His saving action is addressed to man, inviting him to total surrender and self-opening, to the abandonment of false security. His security and salvation thus come with absolute certainty from God. (*See* FAITH.)

In the New Testament God reveals himself in the concreteness and immediacy of the incarnation. Because Jesus is the Son of God, he is the perfect and full revelation of God, that is, he is the Truth. (*See* TRUTH.) To see Jesus is to see the Father, because the Father is in him and he in the Father. (*See* WORK.)

In the New Testament, the Greek Theos with the article (The God) means the Father of Our Lord Jesus Christ (*see* Rom. 1:7; 1 Cor. 1:3; 2 Cor. 1:2, etc.). Thus God is almost the name of the first person of the blessed Trinity. Without the article, God designates the divinity, and so is applicable to the pre-existing Word (Jn. 1:3). The term God is applied to Jesus in only a few texts, and even their interpretation is under dispute (Jn. 20:28; Rom. 9:5; Tit. 2:13; 2 Pet. 1:1). It is to be noted that here we are speaking of the New Testament usage of the word **theos**, God. From the fact that the term is almost exclusively used for the first person of the Trinity, it does not follow that the divinity of Jesus or the Spirit is uncertain. This certitude however is expressed by other means. *See* LORD; SPIRIT.

Gog, A sovereign prince of the Meshech and Tubal of the land of Magog, which in some future time would attempt an invasion of Israel only to be annihilated by God (Ezek. 38-39). Meshech and Tubal are countries in Asia Minor on the coast of the Black Sea. Magog must be sought in the same region. Some scholars wished to identify Gog with King Gyges of Lydia (7th century B.C.) but it is a conjecture without any evidence to support it other than a phonetic similarity in the names. Ezekiel prophesies in eschatological tones, and his geography and history take on a symbolic character which is maintained even more obviously in Rev. 20:3.

Golan, A city in the territory of Manasseh, in the region of Bashan in Transjordan. It was a Levitical city and a city of refuge (Deut. 4:43; Josh. 20:8; 21:27; 1 Chron. 6:71).

Gold, Known in Palestine from very ancient times, recognized as precious, but non-existent as a mineral in Palestine. Instead it was imported, especially from Ophir (1 Kgs. 9:28; 10:11), Sheba (Isa. 60:6; Ezek. 27:22) and Havilah (Gen. 2:11). It was used for jewelry, to adorn buildings (1 Kgs. 6:15) and clothes, (Ex. 28:5) and for the sacred utensils of Tabernacle and Temple (Ex. 25-29; 1 Kgs. 6:20; 1 Kgs. 10:16-21).

Golgotha (gol′-goth-a), A defective transcription of the Aramaic **gulgulta'** which is translated "place of the skull," where Jesus was crucified (Matt. 27:33; Mk. 15:22; Lk. 23:33; Jn. 19:17). The name Calvary comes from the latin translation **"calvariae locus."** The place was not far from Jerusalem, outside the walls of the city (Matt. 27:32; Mk. 15:21; Heb. 13:12) and near the place of Jesus' burial (Jn. 19:20). The basilica of the Holy Sepulcher which encloses the traditional place of crucifixion and the tomb, was constructed by the Crusaders in 1149 on the site of the ancient Constantinian basilica. This traditional identification of the site goes back to the fourth century (Eusebius of Caesarea).

Goliath, The Philistine champion, of gigantic stature, killed in single combat by David, according to 1 Samuel 17. Goliath belonged to the Rephaim who lived in the Philistine city of Gath (2 Sam. 21:22; 1 Chron. 20:8). According to 2 Samuel 21:19 Goliath was killed by Elhanan, son of Jair, one of the warriors of David, to whom 1 Chronicles 20:5 attributes the killing of Lahmi, Goliath's brother. On the question *see* DAVID, ELHANAN.

Gomer, 1. The first-born of Japheth father of an ancient people, the Cimmerians, an Indo-European people who settled in Asia Minor in the 7th century B.C. and are also known to us from classical Greek sources.

2. Daughter of Diblaim and wife of Hosea (Hos. 1:2-9) whom he took to wife and from her had three children, Jezreel, "Unloved," and "No-people-of-mine." Gomer's prostitution was a symbol of the infidelity of the people of God, Israel's spouse. *See* HOSEA.

Gomorrah, One of the cities of the Pentapolis probably located around the southern end of the Dead Sea, south of the Lisan Peninsula (Gen. 14:2, 8; Wisdom 10:16), destroyed by fire in punishment for the perversion of its inhabitants, according to Genesis 19. The punishment of Gomorrah and of other cities stayed on in tradition as a type of divine judgment and it is often recalled in other books of the Bible (*see* Deut. 29:23; Isa. 1:9, 10; 13:19; Jer. 23:14; 49:18; 50:40; Amos 4:11; Zeph. 2:9; Matt. 20:15; Rom. 9:29; 2 Pet. 2:6; Jgs. 7). *See* LOT; SODOM.

Gorgias (gor′-jus), One of the Seleucid generals sent to quash the Maccabean revolt. He was defeated by Judas Maccabeus near Emmaus (1 Mac. 4:1-22) but prevailed over Joseph and Azariah who, against the orders of Judas, imprudently marched on Jamnia (1 Mac. 5:61). He became governor of Idumea (2 Mac. 10:14) but did not succeed in subjugating Judas Maccabeus (2 Mac. 12:32-37).

Gortyna (gor-tie′-na), A city of Crete beside the river Letheus, mentioned among those to whom a letter was sent by the Roman senate in favor of the Jews in the time of the Maccabees (around 139 B.C.; 1 Mac. 15:23).

Goshen, 1. A region in the eastern part of the Nile delta, where the Israelites settled at the time of Joseph (Gen. 46:28; 47:1, 4, 6, 27; 50:8; Ex. 8:18; 9:26).

2. A city in the mountainous region of Judah, occupied at the time of Joshua (Josh. 10:41; 11:16; 15:51).

Gospel, Gospel translates the Greek **euaggelion,** which literally means "good tidings." The New Testament never uses the word as it is today used, to mean Matthew, Mark, Luke and John. (*See* JOHN, GOSPEL OF; LUKE, GOSPEL OF; MARK, GOSPEL OF; MATTHEW, GOSPEL OF.) Gospel refers to the happy announcement of the coming of the kingdom of God (Matt. 4:23; Lk. 4:43; 8:1; 16:16; Mk. 1:15), or the happy announcement of the salvation brought about through the death and resurrection of Jesus (Acts 5:42; 11:20; 14:7; Rom. 15:20; 1 Cor. 15:1, 2, etc.). Paul often speaks of "my gospel" (Rom. 2:16; 1 Cor. 15:1; 2 Cor. 4:3; Gal. 1:11; 2:2, etc.). Here he certainly does not wish to contrast his own personal gospel with what the other apostles announce (*see* Gal. 1:7), but only to underline his own personal commission as apostle of the Gentiles (Gal. 2:7-10) in the whole missionary work of the Church.

The change of meaning in the word "gospel" tells us that the books we call gospels are no more than the written form which at a certain point in history the preached gospel took on. Our gospels have behind them a long history, part of which was already in writing (*see* SYNOPTIC QUESTION) and part of which was still oral (*see* TRADITION). Form criticism seeks to study the period of the oral transmission of the gospel. It will help briefly to outline the principles of this method of study, worked out contemporaneously by two German authors, R. Bultmann and M. Dibelius, around 1920, and today used in all gospel exegesis.

The method starts off from the premise that our gospels, and especially the Synoptics, are mostly collections of accounts and words of Jesus that were independent of one another. These were handed down as isolated accounts and sayings in the ambit of the primitive Christian communities. All this heritage of traditions about Jesus was not handed on in a mechanical way. Rather they lived with the same life of the primitive community. Each one of the narrations or sayings—or more accurately, each one of the types or genres according to which they could be classified— responded to a particular life-situation in its multiple manifestations such as liturgy, catechesis, the instruction of neophytes, the anti-Jewish polemic, etc. As an example, the eucharistic institution was handed down in the liturgical commemoration of the last supper, which formed the center of the primitive Christian communities. To put it in the technical terms of this method, each gospel tradition had its sociological dimension, its setting in the life of the apostolic churches. This insertion of the gospel tradition in the life of the community has an important consequence, namely, that the tradition is understood and reinterpreted in the light of the problems of the Church. This is an undeniable fact. It does not however amount to saying that the Church obscured or indeed betrayed the tradition of the words and deeds of Jesus. A serene and objective consideration of the life of the primitive churches excludes the scepticism of those who want to deny any link of continuity between the community of disciples around Jesus and the church of the apostles after the resurrection. (This point is carefully taken up in the article on TRADITION.) The Church then carried the gospel with fidelity to living generations, giving the tradition itself life without corrupting it, and making it actual without dislodging it from its roots in its ultimate normative source, Jesus himself.

From this heritage of oral tradition came the first written collections, and from these came our gospels. (*See* SYNOPTIC QUESTION.) One must however correct the judgment of Bultmann and Dibelius on the evangelists. These were much more than simple, unskilled collectors. They showed them selves very faithful to the tradition they had received without however being mere passive collectors. They were real authors who gave shape to the materials they gathered. By the use of simple techniques, such as the choice of material, its lay-out, the geographical setting, the chronology of Jesus' ministry, they succeeded in throwing light on a particular facet of the rich figure of the Savior. At the same time they are faithful to their sources and witnesses to the continual development or deepening of insight into them. This stage of the composition of the gospels is called **Redaktionsgeschichte** or the history of redaction.

Gourd, Probably to be identified with the castor bean, a plant with very large leaves. God caused the plant to grow as shelter to Jonah from the torrid sun (Jonah 4:6-9).

governor

as *g.* of the country	Gen. 42:6	while Quirinus was *g.* of Syria
g. of West-of-Euphrates	Ezra 5:3	Lk. 2:2

Gozan, A city and region in northern Mesopotamia, conquered by the Assyrians (2 Kgs. 19:12; Isa. 37:12) to which some of the Israelites were deported from the kingdom of Israel by Tiglath-pileser III (745-727) (*see* 2 Kgs. 17:6; 18:11).

Grace, In Christian language today, both theological and common, the word grace above all refers to the **gift** of grace, in the objective sense, by the power of which we are internally sanctified, and which is given us in the sacraments. This gift is like the created reflection of the divine benevolence or grace (i.e. subjective sense), that which God's love produces in us. In biblical language (Hebrew **'hen,** Greek **charis**) grace is above all taken in the subjective sense, even though it always evokes the concrete and objective manifestation of this grace. God shows his grace or favor by forgiving sins (Isa. 27:11; Ps. 51:3), by saving his people from their enemies (Isa. 30:18; 33:2), or the individual from adversity (frequent in the psalms of lamentation and thanksgiving; *see* Pss. 4:2; 6:3; 31:10; 102:14).

In the New Testament the term acquires all the fulness of salvation brought about by Christ. Two categories of meaning above all can be distinguished in the use of the term. In an adverbial sense it denotes the way in which salvation has been accomplished and given to us, that is, gratis, without any merit on our part. The whole initiative was God's, who in this way wished to show forth his goodness (*see* Rom. 3:24; Eph. 1:6; Tit. 2:17). Then again grace encompasses the content of salvation, the love and favor of God shown forth in Christ to those who believe. Christians live in the grace of God (Rom. 5:2), which has proved itself more powerful and more abundant than the killing power of sin (Rom. 5:12-21).

In the dispute between Paul and the Judaizers (Romans and Galatians) grace and law are opposed like two incompatible systems of justification. The first system, that of grace, accepts in faith the gift of salvation, unmerited, while the second attempts to win salvation from God on one's own merits (Gal. 5:4; Rom. 4:4; 6:14). Paul thus asserts that those who intend to justify themselves through their own works make grace an empty thing (Gal. 2:21; *see* JUSTIFICATION; FAITH; WORK). *See* also CHARISMA.

gracious

"May God be *g.* to you, my		you are a *g.* and merciful God
	Gen. 43:29	Jonah 4:2
He will be *g.* to you	Isa. 30:19	Let your speech be always *g.*
		Col. 4:6

grapes

and its clusters ripened into *g.*		looked for the crop of *g.*	Isa. 5:2
	Gen. 40:10	what it yielded was wild *g.*	Isa. 5:2
so I took the *g.*	Gen. 40:11	Like *g.* in the desert	Hos. 9:10
his robe in the blood of *g.*		ever pick *g.* from thornbushes	
	Gen. 49:11		Matt. 7:16

Grave, *See* BURIAL.

Great Sea, The Mediterranean Sea (Num. 34:6; Josh. 1:4; Ezek. 47:10).

greedy

This is the fate of everyone *g.*		The *g.* man stirs up disputes
	Prov. 1:19	Prov. 28:25
He who is *g.* of gain	Prov. 15:27	

Greek, In the New Testament the term Greek (**hellen**) is taken in the sense it had in the first century. It meant not only citizens of Greece, but all who spoke Greek and had been brought up in Greek culture. Since the time of Alexander the Great, Greek culture had spread over the whole eastern Mediterranean region. So the Acts of the Apostles can state that Paul preached to the Greeks of Asia Minor and Macedonia (11:20; 14:1).

A person who was not Greek was native, that is, unversed in the Greek language and culture (Rom. 1:14; 1 Cor. 14:11; Col. 3:11; Acts 28:2, 4). From the religious point of view however Paul distinguishes between Jews and Greeks (Rom. 1:16). The Jews had a privilege of priority: because to them the promise had been made, to them its fulfilment was first preached (Acts 13:46). This was a privilege that Paul respected both in theory (Rom. 1:15) and in practice (Acts 13:45-48). This was however without detriment to the universality of Christian salvation, which made no distinction, but was equally meant for Greeks and barbarians. Jews and Greeks (Gal. 3:28; Col. 3:11).

groan

From the dust the dying *g.*		How the beasts *g.*	Joel 1:18
	Job 24:12	*g.* inwardly while we await	
the wounded will *g.*	Jer. 51:52		Rom. 8:23

ground

the *g.* and blew	Gen. 2:7	does trouble spring out of the *g.*	
formed out of the *g.*	Gen. 2:19		Job 5:6
Part of it fell on rocky *g.*		Matt. 13:5	

growth

when the late *g.* began	Amos 7:1

grudgingly

not *g.*, for God loves	2 Cor. 9:7

grumble, grumbling

you should *g.* against us	Ex. 16:7	set the whole community *g.*
as he heeds the *g.*	Ex. 16:8	Num. 14:36
Your *g.* is not against us	Ex. 16:8	

guard

to *g.* the way to the tree	Gen. 3:24	*g.* your heart	Prov. 4:23
the officers of the *g.*	1 Kings 14:27	was assigned to keep *g.*	Acts 28:16

guests

all the *g.* were with him		the nether world are her *g.*	
	1 Kgs. 1:41		Prov. 9:18
All the *g.* of Adonijah	1 Kgs. 1:49	the king came in to meet the *g.*	
			Matt. 22:11

guide, guides

or *g.* the Bear with its train   Then the Lord will *g.* you
                     Job 38:32   Isa. 58:11
and *g.* them beside springs   to *g.* our feet into the way
                     Isa. 49:10   Lk. 1:79
She has no one to *g.* her Isa. 51:18

Gum, A product obtained from the resin of some plants and a commercial commodity much prized in antiquity (Gen. 37:25; 43:11).

Gur, "The ascent of Gur" near Ibleam (about 20 miles north of Shechem), where King Ahaziah of Judah was fatally wounded by the soldiers of Jehu (2 Kgs. 9:27).

H

Habakkuk (ha-bak′-uk), The eighth of the minor prophets in the Hebrew canon of the Old Testament. All that is known about him is his name and what little can be inferred from his book. From Daniel 14:33-39 one might deduce that Habakkuk was Daniel's contemporary, but the allusion there is pure legend.

Following the title there are two complaints of the prophet (1:2-4, 12-17) to which God responds with two oracles (1:5-11; 2:1-4). Then follow five imprecations against the oppressors (after the introduction 2:5, 6, they continue in vv. 2:6; 2:9; 2:13; 2:15; 2:19). The third chapter is a victory song showing God coming from his dwelling-place, accompanied by his army (3:3, 5) to save his people with a powerful intervention. This song is equipped with liturgical and musical annotations which are characteristic of the psalter (*see* 3:1, 3, 9, 13, 19); many authors doubt their authenticity, an opinion confirmed by their absence in a commentary on Habakkuk found at Qumran.

Scholars are divided on the occasion on which the book was composed. Some see cc. 1-2 as a liturgy and consider Habakkuk a cultic prophet (*see* PROPHETS). Others hold that Habakkuk merely copies the liturgical style. The date of composition depends on the interpretation of 1:6, where the Chaldeans are mentioned. Chaldean in the Bible is the common name of the neo-Babylonian empire, and so the majority of scholars put the book between 605 B.C., when the battle of Carchemish took place establishing Babylon in the Near East as the dominant power, or 597, the year of the first conquest of Jerusalem.

Habiru, Hapiru (hah′-bi-roo), Numerous Middle Eastern documents from the 12th to the 20th centuries B.C., and stemming from Egypt across to Mesopotamia, speak of a people called Hapiru, Habiru, and also, in Egypt, 'apiru. The etymology of the name is not clear. The Habiru sometimes figure as mercenaries in the king's pay—such as in Mesopotamia at the time of Hammurabi—and then again as roving bandit gangs who prey on the settled regions—this is their image in the Mari texts. *See* MARI. Sometimes they appear as strangers, people of a different ethnic origin, who hire themselves out as slaves—this they are in the Nuzi texts. *See* NUZI. Finally they sometimes are just foreign slaves, and probably war slaves, in Egypt. The Tell-Amarna letters show the Habiru creating difficulties for the Egyptians in their domination of Canaan by conspiring with the Canaanite kings against Egypt. *See* TELL-AMARNA.

The name itself, Hapiru, does not seem to refer to racial or ethnic origin, but rather to a social status. Despite the difference in time and place, what linked the Hapiru in a common bond was their misfortune: they were the disinherited who lived on the fringes of society. They also lived off society in their own very specialized brand of banditry, especially when the political conditions allowed for this, and they were always ready to offer their professional services to others.

From the biblical point of view a problem that presents itself is the relationship between these Habiru and the Hebrews of the Bible. It seems that the names at least are linked. Hebrew (ibri) is the same as Hapiru. Today "Hebrew" has become synonymous with Jew or Israelite, but this was not so in the Old Testament, where it was rarely used and moreover was not the name the Israelites gave to themselves. It was used by the Israelites when speaking with foreigners, or when these wished to identify the Israelites. (*See* HEBREW.) In the Bible however the term "Hebrew" was understood as the name of a people, and it only fitted the Israelites, nor did the Israelites believe, it seems, that there were other "Hebrews" besides themselves. It is necessary therefore to admit an evolution in the meaning of the term to the point where it was no longer understood in the sense of the Hapiru of the older, extra-biblical documents.

To the question whether the Habiru are the Hebrews of the Bible, that is, the Israelites, in anything more than name, one must answer by making some distinctions. It is certainly impossible to make a perfect equation between the Habiru and the Israelites, for the first Habiru appear in lands where the Israelites never were, and at a time when they did not even exist as a separate people. When however this extreme has been avoided, there still remain several possibilities on which scholars are quite divided. One can exclude the opinion that the Habiru who operated in Canaan at the time of Tell-Amarna were Israelites, or the ancestors of those who under Joshua invaded Palestine. The Israelite conquest took place in the twelfth century B.C., later than Tell-Amarna. However, one cannot exclude the possibility that Israel's patriarchal ancestors who wandered through Palestine as nomads were in some way connected with the Habiru. In this regard it is curious to note that in the only military exploit recorded for the whole patriarchal epoch, when Abraham by night struck the encampment of the kings from the east to liberate Lot, Abraham is called "the Hebrew" (Gen. 14:13). One must not however overlook the fact that this battle account is out of harmony with the traditions concerning the patriarchs, who are always pictured as semi-nomadic, peace-loving shepherds. Genesis 14 is in fact an enigma in the whole book.

All indications point to a link, if any, between Habiru and Hebrew that occurred in Egypt. Exodus 1 continually calls the Israelites by the name Hebrew (*see* Ex. 1:15-19; 2:6, 7, 9, 11, 13; 3:18, etc.). The Hebrews found themselves in a social condition not unlike that of the Habiru: they were employed as state slaves and subjected to forced labor in the Pharaoh's construction projects. Further possibilities flow from this: the Israelites were either a group of Habiru, or were in fact reduced to the same condition as the Habiru without however belonging, in the strict sense of the word, to them.

Habor (hay′-bor), A major tributary of the Euphrates, today called Khabur. Some of the Israelites deported from the kingdom of the north were brought to its banks by the Assyrians (2 Kgs. 17:6; 18:11; 1 Chron. 5:26).

Hacaliah (hak′-a-ly′-ah), Father of Nehemiah (Neh. 1:1; 10:1).

Hachilah, The hill of Hachilah, near Ziph, where David took refuge when pursued by Saul (1 Sam. 23:19; 26:1).

had

who *h.* charge	Gen. 24:2	*H.* not the men of my tent
H. I rejoiced at the destruction		Job 31:31
	Job 31:29	And I say, "*H.* I but wings
		Ps. 55·7

Hadad (hay′-dad), 1. The god of storms and fertility of the earth in Canaanite and Akkadic mythology. *See* BAAL.

2. The name of the two kings of Edom in the list of the kings who ruled there before the Israelite monarchy was established (Gen. 36:35-36, 39; 1 Chron. 1:46, 47, 50-51).

3. An Edomite prince who fled into Egypt when David annexed Edom. He was the instigator of the revolt against Solomon (1 Kgs. 11:14-25).

Hadadezer (had′-a-dee′-zer), An Aramaean king of Zobah. He came to the aid of the Ammonites against the Israelites, but was defeated by Joab at the head of David's army (2 Sam. 10:6-18). 2 Samuel 8:3-8 records yet another victory of David over Hadadezer (*see* 1 Chron. 18:3-10; 19:16-19).

Hadadrimmon, A Canaanite divinity (*see* HADAD, BAAL) who was worshipped in Megiddo with a cult containing lamentations (Zech. 12:11) probably analogous to those used in fertility cults.

Hadassah, According to Esther 2:7, the Hebrew name of Esther.

Hades, *See* SHEOL.

Hadramaweth (hay′-dra-may′-weth), A region in southeastern Arabia, today Hadramaut, whose inhabitants, according to Gen. 10:26; 1 Chron. 1:20 descended from Shem. The New American Bible spells it Hazarmaveth.

Hagar (hay′-gar), An Egyptian slave belonging to Sarah, Abraham's wife (Gen. 16:1). As Sarah was sterile, she suggested to Abraham that he take Hagar and have children from her (Gen. 16:2). Ishmael was the fruit of this relationship. This kind of relationship was regulated by ancient Mesopotamian law (e.g. code of Hammurabi and the laws of Nuzi). Hagar however despised Sarah for her sterility, taunted her, and was sent away by Abraham with her son Ishmael on Sarah's complaint (16:3-6). To a vision of God given to Hagar in the desert in favor of Ishmael is attributed the origin of the sanctuary of El-roi (God who sees) in the desert beside the oasis of Kadesh (16:7-15). Genesis 21 contributes a somewhat different version of the same events: there the theophany takes place in the desert of Beer-sheba (Gen. 21:14).

The rivalry between Hagar and Sarah and their children Ishmael and Isaac is given an allegorical explanation by Paul in Gal. 4:21-31: Hagar symbolizes the old economy of servitude in the Old Testament while Sarah represents Christian liberty.

Haggadah (hag-gah′-dah), A non-juridical biblical commentary which was typical of the Judaic post-biblical tradition. *See* MIDRASH.

Haggai (hag′-eye), The tenth of the minor prophets in the Hebrew canon of the Old Testament. He carried out his prophetic ministry in the years following the return from exile (537 B.C.) and played a decisive part in the restoration of the nation under Zerubbabel. He was a contemporary of the prophet Zechariah (Hag. 1:1; Zech. 1:1).

The first oracle (1:1-13) dated in August of 520 B.C. is addressed to Zerubbabel and Joshua the High Priest. It exhorts them to undertake the restoration of the Temple of Jerusalem, which lay in ruins. A little later the restoration was started (1:14-15).

The second oracle (2:1-9) was given in the month of September of the same year, addressed to the same people. It was a prophecy of the future glory of the Temple which would cancel out the modesty of the work that had hitherto been done.

The third oracle (2:10-14) came in December of the same year, on the occasion of a consultation that took place with the priests on questions of ritual purity. Haggai denounces the impurity of the people and announces the blessings of the Lord for having undertaken anew the Temple restoration.

The last oracle, December 520 (2:20-23), is again addressed to Zerubbabel, David's descendant, to whom is renewed the Messianic promise.

Haggi (hag′-eye), A son of Gad (Gen. 46:16; Num. 26:15).

Haggith, A wife of David, mother of Adonijah, who backed the dynastic ambitions of her son (2 Sam. 3:4; 1 Kgs. 1:5, 11; 2:13; 1 Chron. 3:2).

Hagiographa (hag′-i-og′-ra-fa), The third part (after the law and the prophets) of the Hebrew canon of the Old Testament, also called "The Writings." It comprises Psalms, Proverbs, Job, Song of Songs, Ruth, 1-2 Samuel, Ecclesiastes, Esther, Daniel, Ezra, Nehemiah, 1-2 Chronicles (*see* Sirach prologue, v. 10).

Hagrites, A nomadic tribe in Transjordan (Ps. 83:6) whose territory was occupied in Saul's time by the tribes of Reuben, Gad and Manasseh (1 Chron. 5:10, 19-22). A Hagrite by the name of Jaziz was head of David's shepherds (1 Chron. 27:31).

Hail, Violent hail storms were not uncommon in Palestine, given its climate. These could wreak havoc on the crops and even injure animals and men (Ex. 9:18-34; Hag. 2:17). It frequently accompanied visions of God (Isa. 28:2, 17; Pss. 18:12-13; 148:8) and in the battle between Joshua and the Amorite kings, "the Lord hurled great stones from the sky above on them all the way to Azekah, killing many" (Josh. 10:11; *see* Ezek. 38:22).

Hair, From the description of Absalom's beauty in 2 Sam. 14:26 it may be gathered that hair in abundance was a mark of beauty. Absalom would let it grow until it became too heavy for him, and cut it once a year. Perhaps his long hair was his undoing when he was trapped in the branches of an oak and left suspended for Joab and his armor-bearers to kill. Or, as many hold, his neck was caught in the fork of a branch of a tree, as his horse charged beneath it, causing the rider a violently painful wound and leaving him helpless. In the Nazirite vow (*see* NAZIRITE) the vower was not to touch his head with a razor, but to allow his hair to go free until the vow was completed and then, at the entrance to the Tent of Meeting, he was to shave off his consecrated hair and burn its locks in the fire of the communion sacrifice (Num. 6:1-21; Jgs. 13:5; 16:17; 1 Sam. 1:11). The hair was cut as a sign of sorrow and mourning by both men and women (Isa. 15:2; Jer. 41:5; 7:29; Mic. 1:16). By New Testament times long hair for men was out of style; indeed Paul states that nature itself tells us that long hair on a man was nothing to be admired, while to a woman her long hair was her glory (1 Cor. 11:7-15).

"Not a hair on his head will fall" was a frequent expression in the Old Testament to denote that a person would be completely protected (e.g. 1 Sam. 14:45; 1 Kgs. 1:52). Christ assures his listeners that such is the Father's care for his own that the very hairs of the head are numbered (Matt. 10:30; Lk. 12:7; *see* Lk. 21:18). That sinners were attracted to Jesus is illustrated in the story of the sinful woman who at supper washed his feet with tears and wiped them with her hair (Lk. 7:38, 44). John narrates that Mary, sister of Lazarus and Martha, anointed Jesus' feet with precious ointment and wiped them with her hair (Jn 11:2; 12:3).

Halah (hay′-lah), A city or region of Mesopotamia to which the Assyrians brought part of the Israelites who were deported from the northern kingdom (2 Kgs. 17:6; 18:11; 1 Chron. 5:26).

Halakah (hah′-lah-kah′), A juridical commentary on Scripture, typical of post-biblical Judaism. *See* MIDRASH.

half

Moses took *h*. of the blood	*h*. that amount, that is,	Ex. 30:23
Ex. 24:6	two years and a *h*.-year	Dan. 12:7
	leaving him *h*.-dead	Lk. 10:30

Half-Shekel, The amount of Temple tax required of every Jew. It was equal to two Greek drachmas (Matt. 17:24).

Halicarnassus, A Greek city on the southwest coast of Asia Minor to whose citizens, among others, was addressed the letter from the Roman senate supporting the Jews in the time of the Maccabeans (1 Mac. 15:23).

hall

The porch of the columned *h*.	the width of the columned *h*.	
1 Kgs. 7:6		1 Kgs. 7:6
	led Jesus away into the *h*.	Mk. 15:16

Hallel, From the Hebrew for "to praise," it was the designation for a group of psalms (Pss. 113-118) whose recitation was ordered on some solemn feasts such as the paschal supper (*see* Matt. 26:30). The so-called Grand Hallel comprised Pss. 120-136.

Hallelujah, From the Hebrew **halleluyah,** "Praise the Lord," a liturgical exclamation intended to encourage the congregation to praise God. It is read at the beginning and the end of several psalms (Pss. 104-106; 111-113; 115-117; 135; 146-150). It was adopted by the Christian liturgy especially where it occurs during the paschal season.

Ham, 1. The second of Noah's three sons (Gen. 5:32; 6:10; 1 Chron. 1:4). He was guilty of grave disrespect for his father, but for some unexplained reason Noah's wrath and curse fell not on Ham but on his son Canaan. This transformation is obviously a reflection on Israel's hostility against the Canaanites (Gen. 9:18-27). In the genealogy of Genesis 10 Ham is the father of the peoples of Egypt, Cush, Mizraim, Put and Canaan (10:6). The division of peoples does not take place on linguistic grounds but on a geographical-historical basis. In some texts (Pss. 78:5; 105:23, 27; 106:22) Ham means Egypt, the most important region of the Hamites.

2. A city of Transjordan, where the Zuzim were defeated in the time of Abraham (Gen. 14:5).

Haman (hay′-man), In the book of Esther he is the prime minister of King Ahasuerus (Xerxes) of Persia (3:1). Esther's uncle Mordecai refused to give the homage that Haman exacted from his subjects, so Haman offered 10,000 talents to the king in exchange for a decree to have all the Jews of the empire eliminated. Ahasuerus told him to keep the money but also offered him the people. Esther, Ahasuerus' wife, told the king of Haman's plans. Moreover the king suspected Haman of designs upon his wife so he ordered that he be hanged on the gibbet he had prepared for Mordecai. *See* ESTHER.

Hamath (hay′-math), A Syrian city on the river Orontes, today Hama. It was first occupied by the Hittites and later by the Aramaeans (2 Sam. 8, 9). It was one of the city-states which resisted the Assyrian advance under Shalmaneser III in the battle of Qarqar (853 B.C.) but it was later taken by

Tiglath-pileser III (745-727 B.C.; 2 Kgs. 17:24, 30; 18:34; Isa. 36:19; 2 Kgs. 19:13; Isa. 37:13; Isa. 10:9). **Lebo-Hamath,** or "Hamath's Entrance" is the ideal northern limit of Canaan and Israel (Num. 34:8; Ezek. 47:15, 20), but it was a political reality only in the time of David and Solomon (1 Kgs. 8:65; 2 Chron. 7:8) and of Jeroboam II of Israel (786-746 B.C.; 2 Kgs. 14:25; Amos 6:14). What the expression means is not quite clear. Some believe it to designate the entry to the valley between Lebanon and Anti-Lebanon, while others would identify it with a city, not the Hamath (Homs) of the upper Orontes, but with Lebo-Hamath (means "the entering of Hamath") as the site of modern Lebweh, farther down the valley on the river Orontes.

Hammedatha (ham′-ma-day′-tha), The son of Haman who was made prime minister by Ahasuerus (Xerxes) according to Esther 3:1.

hammer
so that no *h.*, axe,   1 Kgs. 6:7   like a *h.* shattering rocks Jer. 23:29
                    the *h.* of the whole earth   Jer. 50:23

Hammurabi (ham′-mur-ah′-be), The sixth king of the first Babylonian dynasty (1728-1686 B.C.) and the creator of the Babylonian empire which reached from the Persian gulf to the Mediterranean. He is known above all for the code of laws inscribed on a pillar which was found in 1902 at Susa, whither it had been brought as a war trophy by Elamite invaders in the 12th century B.C. It is a code along ancient Middle East lines, a common patrimony on which several codes including that of Israel depend. On Hammurabi-Amraphel *see* AMRAPHEL.

Hamonah (ha-moe′-nah), The place where Gog's army will be destroyed according to the prophecy of Ezekiel 39:11-16.

Hamon-Gog, "The multitude of Gog," the symbolic name of a valley in Transjordan where the army of Gog was to be buried after the eschatological battle with the people of God (Ezek. 39:11, 15). *See* GOG.

Hamor (hay′-mor), Father of Shechem, killed by Simeon and Levi in revenge for the violation of their sister Dinah (Gen. 34). This episode mirrors a failed attempt at a coalition between the clans of Jacob and the Canaanite population in the center of Palestine. *See* DINAH.

Another tradition has it that Jacob bought from Hamor a tract of land for one hundred pieces of silver, upon which he pitched his tent and erected an altar (Gen. 33:18-20). Here Joseph was buried (Josh. 24:32). Acts 7:16 confuses this with Genesis 23 where the cave of Machpelah, which Abraham bought for the burial of Sarah, is mentioned.

Hamul (hay′-mul), Son of Perez and grandson of Judah (Gen. 46:12; Num. 26:21; 1 Chron. 2:5).

Hamutal (ha-mue′-tal), Wife of King Josiah of Judah (640-609) and mother of kings Jehoahaz II (Shallum) (609) and Zedekiah (598-587; *see* 2 Kgs. 23:21; 24:18) but not of another ruling son, Jehoiakim (609-598), whose mother was Zebudah (2 Kgs. 23:36).

Hanamel (han′-a-mel), A cousin of the prophet Jeremiah, from whom the prophet bought the field in Anathoth during the siege of Jerusalem, a symbolic action to predict the restoration of the kingdom after the imminent destruction of Judah (Jer. 32).

Hanan (hay′-nan), Personal name (1 Chron. 8:23; 11:43; Ezra 2:46; Neh. 10:11; 13:13; Jer. 35:4).

Hananel, Tower of, (han′-a-nel), A wall turret on the walls of Jerusalem to the north at the time of Jeremiah (Jer. 31:38). It was reconstructed under Nehemiah (Neh. 3:1; 12:39; Zech. 14:10). Its place was taken by the fortress Antonia, built by Herod I the Great.

Hanani (ha-nay′-ni), 1. The father of the prophet Jehu (1 Kgs. 16:1).

2. The name of several other men (1 Chron. 25:4; Ezra 10:20; Neh. 7:2; 12:36).

Hananiah (han′-a-ny′-ah), 1. A false prophet, a contemporary of Jeremiah. Jeremiah prophesied the defeat of the alliance which King Zedekiah prepared against the Babylonians. Hananiah opposed by predicting the imminent end of Nebuchadnezzar and the return of the Jews who had been deported to Babylonia in 597. Hananiah died soon after, as Jeremiah predicted (Jer. 27-28).

2. Son of Zerubbabel, a descendant of David and head of the Jews returned from exile (1 Chron. 3:19, 21).

3. One of the three youths who accompanied Daniel, and whose name was changed to Shadrach (Dan. 1:6-7, 11, 19).

Hananiel, Grandfather of Tobit (Tob. 1:1).

Hand, Hand is a frequently used word in the Bible, mostly referring to that part of the body, or in phrases that are self-evident or have even become part of today's languages. To hand over is to give into one's power (e.g. Gen. 9:2 in some versions), while the word of one's hands is what one has accomplished (Deut. 27:15; 28:8, 12, etc.). A strong hand is a strong man (Josh. 1:14) and to have a person's hand with one is to have him on one's side (1 Chron. 4:10). John the Baptizer predicts the coming of the Messiah with a fan in hand (Matt. 3:12), while the same hand of Jesus was that through which he healed the leper and thus showed his saving power (Mk. 1:41).

Hands, Imposition of, This rite was used in the Old and New Testaments with different meanings. Leviticus 1:4 prescribes that a person bringing an animal for holocaust should lay his hands on the victim's head, not as a transference of guilt, but signifying that it was his. (*See* SACRIFICE.) Hands were imposed in the act of blessing by Jacob (Gen. 48:14) and by Jesus (Matt. 19:15; Mk. 10:13, 16). Moses appointed Joshua as his successor, giving him his orders publicly and a share in his authority by the laying on of hands (Num. 27:18-21). In the New Testament the seven deacons were ordained by the laying on of hands with prayer. Peter and John imparted the Holy Spirit on the Samaritans by the imposition of hands, and Paul reminds Timothy of the spiritual gift he received when the body of elders laid their hands upon him (1 Tim. 4:14; 2 Tim. 1:6).

Hanes, A city of Upper Egypt, named by the Greeks Heracleopolis, "the City of Hercules" (Isa. 30:4).

Hanging, Death by hanging (or crucifixion) is unknown in Israelite penal law. The Persians used it, and later the Greeks, while among the Romans it was in common use. Deuteronomy 21:22-23 prescribes that if the body of the executed person is suspended from a tree, it must not remain there overnight, but must be buried the same day. In this sense must be interpreted Joshua 8:29, 10:27 and 2 Samuel 4:12 concerning the body of Saul and his sons who died in battle. There is some obscurity about Numbers 25:4 and 2 Samuel 21:9.

Hannah, 1. The wife of Elkanah and mother of Samuel (1 Sam. 1). The so-called Canticle of Hannah belongs to a later date (*see* 2 Sam. 2:1-10) but is well adapted to the context (*see* 2:5). It served as a model to the Magnificat that Luke records of Mary in 1:46-55.

2. *See* ANNA.

Hanoch (hay'-nok), Founding father of a Midianite clan. He was a descendant of Abraham through his second wife Keturah (Gen. 25:4; 1 Chron. 1:33).

Hanukkah (hah'-nu-kah), The Hebrew name for the Feast of the Dedication of the Temple which commemorated the purification of the Temple under Judas Maccabeus (165 B.C.). *See* DEDICATION, FEAST OF.

Hanun (hay'-nun), King of the Amorites, son and successor of Nahash, a contemporary and friend of David. At the death of Nahash, David sent envoys to convey his condolences but these were rejected by Hanun, whose counselors suggested that the envoys were on a spying mission. David sent Joab with an army to wage war on the Amorites. He laid siege to Rabbah the capital, defeated the Aramaean allies of the Amorites, occupied the city and made Shobi, Hanun's brother, a tributary king (2 Sam. 10:1-14; 11:1; 12:26-31; 17:27).

happened

the harvesters *h.* to be   Ruth 2:3   his wife told him what had *h.*
but that an accident *h.* to us   1 Sam. 25:37
                          1 Sam. 6:9

happy

H. is the man   Job 5:17   *H.* are you who fear   Ps. 128:1
H. the man whose quiver is filled   and he is *h.* who holds   Prov. 3:18
                          Ps. 127:5
                   h. is he who is kind to   Prov. 14:21

Hara (har'-a), A region in Mesopotamia to which the Israelites of the Transjordan tribes (Reuben, Gad and half of Manasseh) were deported by the Assyrians (1 Chron. 5:26).

Haradah (ha-ray'-dah), An encampment of the Israelites in the journey to Canaan (Num. 33:24, 25).

Haran (har'-an), 1. Son of Terah, brother of Abraham and father of Lot (Gen. 11:26-31).

2. A city of northern Mesopotamia, on the river Bialik, today Harran, the place of origin of the patriarchs (Gen, 11:31, 32; 12:4-5), where some of the relatives remained, such as Bethuel, Rebekah's father (Gen. 24) and Laban, father of Rachel and Leah (Gen. 28:29). Haran was situated on the road between Mesopotamia and Syria. From ancient times it was an important commercial center, often caught up in wars because of its strategic importance (2 Kgs. 19:12; Isa. 37:12).

harass

Saul began to *h.* the church
                          Acts 8:3

Harbona, One of the seven eunuchs who served king Ahasuerus as chamberlains (Esth. 1:10).

hardened

became stiff-necked and *h.*   no one grows *h.* by the deceit
                          2 Chron. 36:13   Heb. 3:13
his spirit *h.* by insolence   Dan. 5:20

Hare, An impure animal according to the cultic laws (*see* Lev. 11:6; Deut. 14:7).

Harim, The name of several Old Testament men (1 Chron. 24:8; Ezra 2:32, 39; 10:21, 31; Neh. 3:11; 7:35, 42; 10:6, 28; 12:15).

Harlot, *See* PROSTITUTION.

harm

did not let him do me any *h.*   not to threaten Jacob any *h.*
Gen. 31:7   Gen. 31:24
David is trying to *h.* you   1 Sam. 24:10

Harosheth (ha-roe′-sheth), The home of Sisera, head of the army of Jabin, the Canaanite king of Hazor (Jgs. 4:2, 13, 16), who was defeated by Barak.

Harp, *See* MUSIC.

Hart, The Hebrew word 'ayyal means deer, hind, buck or stag. It is uncertain whether this refers to the red deer or to the smaller fallow deer. Harts are no longer found in Palestine. Venison graced Solomon's table (1 Kgs. 4:23). The animal is often used in figurative and poetic language (e.g. Gen. 49:21), celebrated for its swiftness (2 Sam. 22:34; Pss. 18:34; 42:1) and the way in which it leaps (Isa. 35:6). The Song of Songs sings, in the mouth of the bride, of the groom as a gazelle, a young stag (2:9) and the image of the hart is again and again evoked by the poet (2:7; 2:17; 3:5; 8:14).

Haruz (har′-uz), Grandfather of King Amon of Judah (2 Kgs. 21:19).

Harvest, In the oldest liturgical calendars of the Israelites, the harvest marked the beginning and not the end of the year. This held true until after the death of Josiah in 609 B.C. when due to subsequent vassalage to Nebuchadnezzar, the Babylonian calendar was adopted, with spring beginning the year.

According to a tenth century B.C. text inscribed on a limestone tablet, and found at Gezer, the year begins with the two months of the Ingathering. Then follow four months of seedtime, succeeded by one month of flax gathering, a month for the barley harvest, a month for the wheat, and then two months for pruning, followed by a month for summer fruits, making twelve months in all.

The times of the year then were noted by the harvest that was gathered during them, or the other agricultural activities that took place. At the time of the wheat harvest, according to Judges 15:1, Samson went back to see his wife, and the broken-hearted Rizpah spread sackcloth for herself on the rock from the beginning of the barley harvest until the rain fell from the sky on them (1 Sam. 21:10).

The Harvest Festival, or Feast of Weeks was the second great feast of the Israelite year, although strictly speaking it was the feast of the wheat harvest (*see* Ex. 34:22; Gen. 30:14; Jgs. 15:1; 1 Sam. 6:13; 12:17). The Greek name for the feast was Pentecost, which was the day after the seventh sabbath after the first sheaf was presented to Yahweh, thus reaching the fiftieth day, or Pentecost.

The feast was the farmers' feast, and adopted by the Israelites after they too settled on the land. Orthodox Jews considered it of secondary importance and so it is not found in the calendar of Ezekiel 45:18-25 nor does it merit notice in the complete treatment of annual feasts of the Mishnah. *See* FEAST OF WEEKS, PENTECOST.

harvest

seedtime and *h.*   Gen. 8:22   the appointed weeks of *h.*
during the wheat *h.*   Gen. 30:14   Jer. 5:24
they rejoice before you as at the *h.*   The *h.* is good   Matt. 9:37
Isa. 9:2

Hasadiah (has'-a-dy'-ah), Son of Zerubbabel (1 Chron. 3:20).

Hashabiah (hash'-a-by'-ah), Name of several Old Testament men (1 Chron. 9:14; 25:3; 26:30; 27:17; 2 Chron. 35:9; Ezra 8:19, 24; 10:25; Neh. 3:17; 11:22; 12:21).

Hashmonah, A stopping place of the Israelites in the journey to Canaan (Num. 33:29, 30).

Hashubah (ha-shoo'-bah), One of Zerubbabel's sons (1 Chron. 3:20).

Hasideans (has'-i-dee'-ans), Probably from the Hebrew **hasidim,** "the devout or pious ones," the name of a group of Jews at the time of the Maccabees, who were distinguished for their fidelity to the law. They supported the Maccabean cause and for this suffered the revenge of the high priest Alcimus who was on the side of the Seleucids. He slew 60 of them in one day (1 Mac. 2:42; 7:13; 2 Mac. 14:6). The faction of the Pharisees was probably formed from the Hasidean group.

Hasmonean (haz'-moe-nee'-ans), The name of the Maccabean dynasty which governed Judea from the time of the Maccabean revolt until the Roman conquest in 63 B.C. According to Josephus Flavius Asmonaeus was the great-grandfather of Mattathias, the father of the Maccabeans. Although the name pertains to the whole dynasty, it is restricted to the heads of the people from 135 to 63 B.C. while the name Maccabees is reserved for Judas, Jonathan and Simeon, sons of Mattathias. The history of the entire period is better known from the works of Josephus Flavius than from 1 and 2 Maccabees.

The three brothers were succeeded by:

1. John Hyrcanus: third son of Simeon Maccabeus, who ruled as ethnarch of Judea from 135 to 105 B.C. (*see* 1 Mac. 16:19-24). When the aggression of Antiochus VII Sidetes came to nothing, Hyrcanus tried to increase his power by subjugating the Samaritans, whose temple on Gerizim he destroyed, and the Idumeans on whom he imposed circumcision. The Pharisees accused him of personal ambition, so he abandoned their support for that of the aristocratic Sadducean party.

2. Aristobulus I, son of John Hyrcanus, assumed power and governed as king from 105 to 104 B.C. He tried to keep the throne by ignoring the dispositions of his father and eliminating the members of his family to the point where he even allowed his mother to die of hunger in prison.

3. Alexander Jannaeus (104-76 B.C.) was the brother of Aristobulus. He waged long and not always successful campaigns against Egypt, the Nabateans and the Seleucids, but eventually succeeded in spreading his dominions almost to the limits of David's kingdom.

4. Salome (75-67 B.C.) was the widow of Alexander Jannaeus. She sought to reconcile the Hasmoneans with the Pharisees. After her death a civil war broke out between her sons Hyrcanus II and Aristobulus II. Both called in Pompey who took the city, exiled Aristobulus II and made Hyrcanus II high priest in 63 B.C. Judea was reduced to its pre-Maccabean dimensions and placed under the supervision of the Roman province of Syria.

haste
Yet not in fearful *h.*   Isa. 52:12 They went in *h.*   Lk. 2:16
proceeding in *h.* into the hill
                        Lk. 1:39

Hate, In biblical anthropomorphic language hatred, like anger, is attributed to God to show the incompatibility between him and sin (Num. 10:35; Deut. 7:15; 33:11; Ps. 5:6; Hos. 9:15; Sir. 27:24), injustice (Isa. 61:8), the idolatry of other nations (Deut. 12:31; 16:22; Jer. 44:4) and even the cult of Israel when it became an empty formalism void of interior dedication (Isa. 1:14; Hos. 9:15; Amos 5:21; Mal. 2:13-16). The root sn', translated by "hate" was a more forceful term in Hebrew than it is in modern languages. Not only does it signify true enmity and loathing (Lev. 19:17; Deut. 19:11) but as the opposite of love it can be lack of esteem, negligence, antipathy or simply the fall-off of love (Jgs. 11:7; Deut. 21:15; 22:13; 24:3). Hate can also be what is not chosen in preference: thus Yahweh loved Jacob and hated Esau (Mal. 1:2-3; Rom. 9:13) meaning that he chose Jacob. The person who wants to follow Jesus must prefer him to any other person or thing (Matt. 10:37; Lk. 14:26). In the New Testament hate is opposed to Christian love, and therefore acquires a connotation that is absent in the Old Testament; as is evident in 1 John which is largely composed of a description of contrasts between hate and love. Besides the command to love enemies, "those who hate you" (Lk. 6:27), Jesus predicts that his disciples will be hated by the world, thus sharing the lot of the Master (Jn. 7:7; 15:18; Matt. 10:22; Mk. 13:13; Lk. 21:17). This hate by the world is however a sign of the incompatibility between the sin-infested world and grace-endowed Christians.

Hathach (hay'-thak), A eunuch of King Ahasuerus who was appointed to attend Queen Esther; through him Esther knew about Haman's plan to exterminate the Jews of the Persian Empire (Esther 4:5-9).

Hauran, A region in Transjordan north of the river Yarmuk, also called Bashan. *See* BASHAN. The name Hauran occurs only in Ezek. 47:16, 18. It is the northeastern limit of the ideal land of Israel to be restored after the exile. During New Testament times it was included in the tetrarchy of Herod Philip (Lk. 3:1) and then became part of the kingdom of Herod Agrippa I (37-44 A.D.).

Havilah (hav'-i-lah), A region mentioned in the legendary geography of Gen. 2:11-12, which is said to have been very rich in gold. Havilah also appears in the Table of Nations, the first of the descendants of Ham (Gen. 10:7) and later counted among those of Shem (Gen. 10:29) and in the tradition of Ishmael (Gen. 25:18 *see* 1 Sam. 15:7). It is thought to have been in Arabia.

Havvoth-jair, 1. "The villages of Jair," a clan of the tribe of Manasseh, who settled in the region of Bashan in Transjordan (Deut. 3:4; Num. 32:41, 42). *See* JAIR.

2. Descendants of Jair the Galaadite, a judge in Israel for 22 years (Jgs. 10:4).

hawk, hawks

various species of *h.*	the *h.* soars	Job 39:26
Lev. 11:16; Deut. 14:15		

Hazael (hay'-za-el), An Aramaean king of Damascus, a contemporary of Jehoram (849-842 B.C.), Jehu (842-815 B.C.) and Jehoahaz of Israel (815-801 B.C.). According to 1 Kgs. 19:15-17 Elijah was commanded by God on Mt. Horeb to anoint Hazael king of Damascus. This was carried out by Elisha (2 Kgs. 8:7-15). Hazael killed Ben-hadad I, usurped his throne and began to enlarge his territories at Israel's expense by occupying zones in Transjordan (2 Kgs. 8:28; 9:14; 10:32; 13:3-22) and eventually penetrating as far as Judah until he threatened Jerusalem itself. Jehoash king of Judah (837-800) bought him off by handing over all the sacred offerings, made by himself and his ancestors, together with all the Temple and palace gold (2 Kgs. 12:19). Hazael was defeated by Shalmanasar III king of Assyria (841-833 B.C.), but succeeded in saving the capital. His son Benhadad succeeded him (2 Kgs. 13:24).

Hazarmaveth, *See* HADRAMAWETH.

Hazazon-tamar (haz′-a-zon-tay′-mar), An Amorite city conquered by the kings of the east at the time of Abraham, during their punitive expedition against the Pentapolis (Gen. 14:7), identified with En-gedi by 2 Chron. 20:2.

Hazeroth (ha-zer′-oth), An encampment of the Israelites on their journey through the desert towards Canaan where Miriam and Aaron revolted against Moses (Num. 13:17, 18; 11:35-12:16; Deut. 1:1).

Hazo, A son of Nahor, Abraham's brother (Gen. 22:22).

Hazor (hay′-zor), 1. A Canaanite city in northern Palestine, today Tell el-Qedah, 10 miles north of Lake Gennesaret. The Canaanite king of the city, Jabin, organized a coalition of the kings of the north against the Israelites, but was defeated by Joshua (Josh. 11:1-15). A similar situation is narrated in Judges 4-5 where Jabin is defeated by Deborah and Barak. Hazor was assigned to the possession of Naphtali (Josh. 19:36), was fortified by Solomon (1 Kgs. 9:15) and eventually captured by Tiglath-pileser III of Assyria (745-727 B.C.; 2 Kgs. 15:29). The city is mentioned in the Maccabean wars (1 Mac. 11:67-74).

2. A town of Judah somewhere in the Negeb near Ziph (Josh. 15:23).

He, the fifth letter of the Hebrew alphabet (h).

Head, In biblical language "head" in metaphorical usage is limited to those first in order, authority, dignity, etc. Thus, for example, Exodus 6:14 speaks of "heads of the ancestral houses" to indicate those holding authority. This metaphorical sense has importance in the understanding of Paul's reference to Christ as the head. This title is his above all because he has been exalted in glory to hold dominion over the world, the church and the angels. Christ is the head of every principality and power (Col. 2:10). Paul sums up the whole content of the "mystery" in the phrase: "bring all things . . . under Christ's headship" (Eph. 1:10), which should be understood in the sense of making Christ head over all things by submitting them to divine and regal dominion. This is the sense given to the phrase a little later: "This you can tell from the strength of his work in Christ, when he used it to raise him from the dead and make him sit at his right hand, in heaven, far above every Sovereignty, Authority, Power, or Domination or any other name that can be named, not only in this age but also in the age to come" (Eph. 1:20, 21; *see* also 1 Cor. 11:2-4). When Christ is spoken of as head of the Church, the sense of dominion or primacy is always present. This is so, for instance, in Ephesians 1:22 and Colossians 1:18 where the metaphor is immediately explained by the words: he " is the beginning, the first-born from the dead, so that primacy may be his in everything." It is already clear in these texts that his primacy is also one of causality: he is the effective source of salvation for all. This aspect of the mystery emerges into prime importance when the metaphor of Christ the head is enriched by the Hellenistic notion of the head as vital principle to the whole body, whence flows all its energy and drive.

This enrichment was evoked by the other typical Pauline expression of the church as Christ's body (*see* BODY). Christ is then head of the Church because "by him the whole body is fitted and joined together, every joint adding its own strength, for each separate part to work according to its function. So the body grows until it has built itself up, in love" (Eph.

4:16). Paul for this reason underscores the importance of remaining united to the head who is Christ, for "it is the head that adds strength and holds the whole body together, with all its joints and sinews—and this is the only way in which it can reach its full growth in God" (Col. 2:19). To pass from one application of the metaphor to the other was an easy matter: both elements coexist and one or the other emerges into relief according to the context. When Paul establishes a parallelism between Christ and the Church and the husband and his wife, he exhorts the wife to be subject to her husband, because the husband is the head of the woman just as Christ is head of the Church, and just as the Church is subject to Christ, so also wives should be subject in all things to their husbands (Eph. 5:23-24). Christ however is also savior of the body of which he is head. Thus Paul continues: "Husbands, love your wives, as Christ loved the church. He gave himself up for her to make her holy. . . . Husbands should love their wives as they do their own bodies" (Eph. 5:25, 26).

head

He will strike at your *h.*	Gen. 3:15	do not swear by your *h.*	Matt. 5:36
holding the Philistine's *h.*		the *h.* of John the Baptizer	
	1 Sam. 17:57		Mk. 6:25

health

thriving and still in good *h.*		man's whole being they are *h.*	
	Gen. 43:28		Prov. 4:22
This will mean *h.*	Prov. 3:8	faith has given him perfect *h.*	
			Acts 3:16

hear

nor did I ever *h.* of it	Gen. 21:26	*H.*, O heavens, and listen	Isa. 1:2
when the people *h.* me speaking		to John what you *h.* and see	
	Ex. 19:9		Matt. 11:4

heard

he *h.* their groaning	Ex. 2:24	Have you not *h.*	Isa. 40:1
as your servant has *h.*		your prayer has been *h.*	Lk. 1:13
	1 Sam. 23:11		

hearken

H., Laishah	Isa. 10:30

Heart, In biblical language the heart is the vital center of life that is specifically human: sense life, the life of the will and intellectual life. For this reason the figurative use of the word is vaster in the Bible than in modern languages. The Bible speaks for instance of thoughts that arise from the heart (Jer. 7:31; 19:5; 1 Cor. 2:9), of the perverse designs that proceed from the heart (Mk. 7:21-23; Lk. 6:45), to open the heart of someone to understanding (Acts 16:14), or to apply the heart, that is, attention and will, to something (Lk. 21:14). God scrutinizes the heart, that is, he knows the most intimate movements of a person and his most secret intentions (Ps. 17:3; Jer. 12:3; Lk. 16:15; Rom. 8:27).

Seeing that the heart of man is bent on evil (Jer. 17:9), the salvation promised by God will be a purification of the heart, that is, the radical transformation of the very intimate core of personhood which will make him adhere fully to God's saving will: God will write this law right into his heart (Jer. 31:33, 34) and even give man a new heart (Jer. 32:39) made to know God (Jer. 24:7; *see* Jer. 4:4). God will take out the heart of stone, that is, the hardened insensible core, and replace it with a heart of flesh that is saturated in the Spirit (Ezek. 36:24-26; Ps. 51:12). The same language is used in the New Testament to explain the saving action of God deep within every person, with special reference to Jeremiah's prediction in 31:31 (Rom. 2:15; 2 Cor. 3:3; Heb. 8:8-13). God pours his Spirit into the heart of every man (Gal. 4:6) who suffuses him with charity (Rom. 5:5) and gives him wisdom and understanding of Christ who enlightens the heart's eyes (Eph. 1:17). 1 John 5:20 repeats the same message in other words: God has given us a mind to know him.

heat

cold and *h*.	Gen. 8:22	Like the glowing *h*. of sunshine	
the *h*. scorches my very frame			Isa. 18:4
	Job 30:30	a full day in the scorching *h*.	
shade from the parching *h*.	Isa. 4:6		Matt. 20:12

Heathen, *See* GENTILE.

Heaven, The cosmology of the Bible has no scientific pretensions. It transcribes reality with ingenuity, as its author saw it, and so the sky was a fixed transparent vault, an inverted bowl, covering the disc of the earth (Gen. 1:6 ff.), like an immense tent spread over it by God (Ps. 104:2; Isa. 40:22). In this vault, or hanging under it, were the sun, the moon and the stars "to divide the day from the night, and to indicate festivals, days and years" (Gen. 1:14-18). This inverted bowl, the firmament or heaven, separated the waters above the vault from the waters under the vault, thus leaving a space in between in which the earth exists (Gen. 1:6-8). The waters above the firmament poured down on the earth through sluices or windows set there, and through these opened sluices poured the waters that caused the flood (*see* Gen. 7:11; *see* FLOOD, THE). Rain, snow and hail are stored in the heavens and from there they are poured down on the earth (Job. 37:9; 38:22, 37). The sun has its own tent from which "it comes forth like the groom from his bridal chamber and, like a giant, joyful runs its course. At one end of the heavens it comes forth, and its course is to their other end" (Ps. 19:6-7). The heavens are the work of the hands of God (Ps. 8:4) and show forth his glory. The heavens are a wordless and noiseless hymn of praise, and yet "through all the earth their voice resounds and to the ends of the world, their message" (Ps. 19:2-5).

"The heavens and the earth" is a very common expression for the whole universe (Gen. 1:1). Often however the heavens seem to transcend the earth, for God's dwelling is there (Deut. 10:14; Pss. 11:4; 148:4, etc.). It is there he has built his palace (Ps. 104:2, 3) and from there he hears prayers (1 Kgs. 8:30). This sense of transcendence is further underlined in the phrase "the heavens and the highest heavens" (1 Kgs. 8:27; Ps. 148:4). Heaven is used to denote God's habitation not so much as a topographical area as to express figuratively the divine transcendence. In this way the "heavens" became in Jewish usage a veiled expression for God himself when they began to omit calling God by his own name lest they should profane it. Traces of this can be seen in the New Testament. Matthew always speaks of the "reign of heaven" where the other evangelists call it God's reign. (*See* KINGDOM OF GOD. *See* also Mark 11:30; Luke 15:18, 21.) 'Heavenly' then is more a qualitative than a place expression. It is, for instance, the quality of the body of the second Adam, the risen Christ, in contrast with the first Adam who was earthly and from the earth (1 Cor. 15:45-49).

Through his resurrection Jesus has been exalted to "the right hand of God in the heavens." This expression occurs often in the New Testament (Mk. 16:19; Acts 2:34; 7:56; Rom. 8:34; Col. 3:1; Heb. 8:1; 1 Pet. 3:22; Rev 3:21), and is an echo of Jesus' answer to Caiaphas before the Sanhedrin (Matt. 26:54; Mk. 14:62; Lk. 22:69). Jesus' response is a fusion of Daniel 7:3 and Psalm 110:1 and was understood by the Jews as a blasphemy, for it presupposed equality with God and the exercise of universal domination which God alone can claim.

Jesus has been assumed into heaven (Acts 1:9-11) and from there he will come on the last day for the judgment of the living and the dead (Matt. 24:30; 1 Thess. 1:10). Christians will then be taken up with the Lord in the heavens to be always with him (1 Thess. 4:16-18). Heaven is then the Christians' fatherland, to which their pilgrimage tends, and where God has already prepared for them their home (Matt. 5:12; 6:20; 2 Cor. 5:1-5; 1 Pet. 1:4). While Jesus' departure is sad for the disciples, they must console themselves by being mindful that he is gone before them to prepare for them a mansion, and that he will return to take them with him (Jn. 14:1-3).

Heave Offering, *See* SACRIFICE.

Heber (hee′-ber), 1. A Kenite who lived in Galilee, husband of Jael, the woman who enticed Sisera, the general of the army of Jabin, king of Hazor, into her tent and killed him, after his defeat by Deborah and Barak (Jgs. 4:11, 17; 5:24).

2. A clan of the tribe of Asher (Gen. 46:17; Num. 26:45; 1 Chron. 7:31-32).

Hebrew, In the Bible the term has a somewhat different meaning from today's indiscriminate use of the word to signify an Israelite or a Jew. The Hebrew 'ibri is used to designate the Israelites in a very precise context, that is, when speaking with foreigners (Gen. 40:15; Ex. 2:7; 3:18; 5:3; 7:16; 9:1, 13; Jonah 1:9) or by foreigners to designate the Israelites (Gen. 39:14; 41:12; Ex. 1:16-19; 2:6, 9; 1 Sam. 13:19; 14·11; 29:3). In other texts the context of foreigners is implicit (Gen. 14:13; Ex. 1:15; 2:11; 1 Sam. 13:3; 14:21). In the New Testament it means a Jew who speaks Aramaic, as distinguished from the Greek-speaking Jews (Acts 6:1; 2 Cor. 11:22; Phil. 3:5). The Table of Nations makes the Hebrews descend from a founding father by the name of Eber, a descendant of Shem, and also father of other peoples (Gen. 10: 21-23). On the origin and history of the people of Israel *see* HABIRU, ISRAEL, PATRIARCHS.

Hebrew Language, The language spoken by the people of Israel, and in which most of the books of the Old Testament were composed. It was never called the Hebrew language in the Bible. It was known instead as the language of Canaan (Isa. 19:18) or of Judah (2 Kgs. 18:26; Isa. 36:11: these texts speak of a time later than the kingdom of the north when Judah was the last bulwark of the Israelites in Palestine). When the New Testament speaks of the Hebrew language or of something called, or written in, Hebrew (Acts 21:40; 22:2; 26:14; Jn. 5:2; 19:13, 17, 20; 20:16), it refers to the Aramaic which was then the spoken language of the Jews. An exception to this is Revelation 9:11. (*See* also Sirach, prologue.)

The Hebrew language used in the Bible is a western Semitic language. The western Semitic languages are divided into two great families: Aramaic and Canaanite. Among the Canaanite languages were Ugaritic (*see* UGARIT), Phoenician (from which was developed the Punic language of the Carthaginians), Moabite and Hebrew. Hebrew then was the particular form of the Canaanite family of languages which the Hebrews adopted when they came into Palestine. From Judges 12:6 we learn that Hebrew was not a rigid unity, but admitted of variations in dialect or at least in pronunciation (*see* SHIBBOLETH). Hebrew remained the living language of the Israelites up to the end of the exile (6th century B.C.). Then Aramaic began to gain ground. It was adopted by the Jews in Babylonia, and was in fact the **lingua franca** of the whole Middle East. Hebrew gradually disappeared as an ordinary spoken language but it remained a sacred and literary language up to New Testament times. Many of the Qumran writings, from the 2nd and 1st centuries B.C. are in Hebrew. As a literary and scholastic language Hebrew remained on in the rabbinical schools well into the Christian centuries. It was a Hebrew, however, strongly influenced by Aramaic and more developed than the Bible language. This modified Hebrew is the language in which the Mishna and a great part of the Talmud, together with other rabbinical writings, are written (*see* MISHNA, TALMUD).

The books of the Old Testament are written in Hebrew with the exception of Daniel 2:4-7:28, Ezra. 2:8-6:18, 7:12-26, and Jeremiah 10:11, all of which were penned in Aramaic; Wisdom, 2 Maccabees and the deuterocanonical parts of Daniel and Esther, which were composed in Greek; 1 Maccabees and Judith, of which the original Hebrew or Aramaic have been lost, so that they are available only in Greek translation; Sirach, of which the complete version is preserved only in the Greek, although four fifths of the original Hebrew have been found; Tobit, which is preserved in Greek although some Aramaic fragments have been discovered.

Examples of extra-biblical Hebrew are rare. These have been uncovered in excavations. They are the calendar of Gezer (*see* MONTH) from the eleventh or tenth century B.C., the commemorative inscription for the opening of the Siloam canal by Hezekiah (2 Kgs. 20:20; 2 Chron. 32:30; *see* SILOAM) and the ostraka of Lachish from the sixth century B.C. (*see* LACHISH).

Hebrew words as a rule are formed of three fixed consonants. The different noun and verb forms are built on this triliteral root through a change in the vowels and the addition of prefixes and suffixes. In ancient times Hebrew had only consonants. Later on commenced the practice of using some consonantal signs which were phonetically near the opportune vowel sounds to help in reading. Thus for example the letter **yod** was used for the vowel sound **i**, the **waw** for the **u** and **o** sound, some weak gutturals for **a** and **e**, and so on. The different systematic attempts to supply the language with a vowel apparatus date from the early middle ages, and were made by the Masoretic schools of Palestine and Babylonia. (*See* TEXT, OLD TESTAMENT.) The pronunciation, however, that they indicate in their manuscripts is in large part artificial. It does not represent the Hebrew pronunciation of Isaiah's time, but the contemporary pronunciation of the sacred text, and so there are differences from school to school. Today's Hebrew grammars are in reality grammars of the Masoretic Hebrew, which was inductively elaborated from the biblical text prepared by the Masoretes and printed in today's editions.

Hebrews, Epistle to, A deuterocanonical book of the New Testament that is traditionally numbered among the letters of St. Paul. One scholar has humorously remarked that there are three problems in Paul's letter to the Hebrews: the first is whether it is Paul's, the second is whether it is a letter, and the third is whether it is to the Hebrews. We will treat in order its literary genre, its author, and those to whom it was written.

a. Literary genre: The epistle to the Hebrews and 1 John are the only letters in the New Testament which do not have a typical epistolary introduction, that is, the name of the sender, the name or names of the people it is sent to, and the initial greeting. (*See* LETTER.) Hebrews however does have an epistolary conclusion (13:22-25) with information on a common friend Timothy and an exchange of greetings. From the first verse of chapter 1 to 13:22, however, there is no indication that this is a letter, and it reads like a theological and exhortatory tract. The epistolary conclusion calls it "words of advice" or "exhortatory discourse," and this undoubtedly is its best description. In fact the "letter" is a homily put together with care: this emerges from a study of the way in which the subject is developed and of the style, which is the most elaborate of all the New Testament. The discourse concludes with the doxology of 13:21. Then an epistolary note was added and the homily sent in this way to another community. Thus it became a letter, without in the least affecting its content and style, which is more rhetorical than expository.

b. The author: The epistle belongs to the deuterocanonical writings of the New Testament due to the fact that some regions of the ancient church had doubts about its inspiration, and thus its canonicity was not universally recognized until the fourth century. The cause for this uncertainty was in great part the uncertainty about the author. The epistle was known and esteemed in the early western church, as can be gathered from the letter of Clement to the Corinthians, 35:12-36:5, but did not succeed in being accepted as canonical until towards the end of the fourth century. In the east there was a stronger tradition affirming Pauline authority for the letter. Nevertheless it was clear to many that Hebrews could not be called Paul's in the same way as such definitely Pauline writings as Romans, 1 and 2 Corinthians and Galatians. Hebrews was too different in style. Clement of Alexandria (150-215 A.D.) thought that Paul wrote it in Hebrew and that Luke translated it into Greek. Origen praised the beauty of language and style, so far removed from the other writings of Paul; so he proposed that the thoughts were Paul's and that these were put on paper by one of Paul's disciples. Origen added that only God knew who had penned it, but that some had mentioned Clement or Luke.

A person going from a reading of the letter to the Romans to that of the Hebrews immediately sees the difference that Clement and Origen sought to explain by invoking a second author or translator. The differences however are too great to be explained simply by translation. It is not just a question of a different vocabulary, or a more correct Greek. Here the personalities of the authors that emerge from their writings are as different as their writings. Hebrews' author has a decided rhetorical formation, and takes pleasure in searching out the most apt and refined expression. All this is notably absent from the more direct and incisive Pauline style which flowed from his passionate nature and reflects it.

The author of the Hebrews, moreover, shows familiarity with the Hellenistic Jewish mentality of Alexandria. He follows in the footsteps of Philo of Alexandria, who does not influence Paul's other writings. Obviously Hebrews does not contradict Paul's doctrine, but here too it is clear that the development of the same themes is quite different from that of Paul's letters. The central subject of Hebrews is the more perfect expiation carried out by Jesus who was the mediator of the New Covenant (cc. 8-9). This is also one of Paul's themes, but Hebrews' development of it does not evoke Paul's treatment of the same subject, e.g. in Romans 3:25 and 1 Corinthians 5:7, and Ephesians 5:2. The relationship between the law and the newness of the Christian reality is developed by Hebrews on the basis of how what was imperfect in the Old Testament prefigured and gave way to what was made perfect in the New Testament. The specific Pauline theme of the opposition between law and grace is absent. *See* LAW, LIBERTY.

All exegetes of every school hold in common today that Paul did not write the epistle to the Hebrews. Who then was the author? Origen's answer holds also today: only God knows. Different scholars have tried to be more precise and have proposed names with no great backing, however, from the evidence. The least gratuitous of these hypotheses would make

Apollos the possible author of the letter. Apollos was in fact a Jew, a native of Alexandria, an eloquent man and well-versed in the Scriptures, according to the witness of Acts 18:24. *See* APOLLOS.

c. To whom was the letter addressed? The inscription "to the Hebrews" is not original, even though it is very ancient, dating back to the second century. In the New Testament the Hebrews are those who speak Aramaic, not Greek. (*See* HEBREWS.) In the letter, however, perhaps the name is synonymous for Jews who had been converted to Christianity. The inscription probably does not depend on any precise historical information. It merely expresses what would occur to a person reading the letter, since it continually appeals to the Old Testament and the sacred institutions of Israel, and would therefore have in mind a group of readers who were not only familiar with the Old Testament but for whom it remained a sacred patrimony. It is impossible to say more precisely who these Hebrews were. The author does not seem to have any particular group in mind. The sections that might seem to allude to definite churches or circumstances are too generic (e.g. 6:10; 10:32) and are applicable to several churches. They probably sketch a general picture of the movement of the Church which would then fit each particular church in its own environment. One must not forget that Hebrews is more a homily than a letter, and that only occasionally does it read like a letter. The conclusion of 13:22-25 is too vague. One can only conclude from these words that the letter was sent, maybe by the author, from a church in Italy. Because Timothy is mentioned, one deduces that the church was served directly or indirectly by Paul.

Although Paul did not write the letter, it was sent and received on Pauline authority. This is a fact that demands an explanation. Many possibilities present themselves. The apostle could have directly and expressly approved of the epistle. This would mean that the letter should have been written before 67/68 A.D. which is the latest possible date for Paul's martyrdom. In this case some would hold that the epistolary conclusion stemmed from Paul himself. Other scholars think the letter was not written before 80 A.D., or at the earliest, before 70 A.D. It would in this case have been written by one of Paul's disciples or by a person belonging to Paul's circle, who then published his writing in the name and on the authority of his master.

The central theme of the letter is Jesus' priesthood. This is developed with rigor and logic. This logical development must be seen by the reader if he is to understand the letter. Often it escaped the commentators, who were too bent on finding in the letter the so-called binary scheme—dogmatic exposition and moral application or exhortation—which was so typical of Paul's letters. More recently the epistle has been the object of a brilliant study by A. Vanhoye: his conclusions we will summarize here.

The epistle is divided into five parts, which in turn have several sections. There is a consistent alternation between dogmatic exposition and exhortation. At the end of the solemn introduction (1:1-4) the theme of the first part is announced (1:5-2:18): the name of Christ is above that of the angels. This superior condition is summed up in his sonship with God, and his sonship enfleshed, that is, in his likeness to man in all things except sin. These Christological considerations pave the way for the priestly theme: "He had to become like his brothers in every way, that he might be a merciful and faithful high priest before God on their behalf, to expiate the sins of the people" (2:17).

The second part (3:1-5:10) portrays Jesus as our high priest, who has proved himself faithful (3:1-4:14) and merciful (4:15-5:10). At the conclusion of this second part the author solemnly announces the subject of the third and central part of the whole epistle: ". . . and when perfected, he became the source of eternal salvation for all who obey him, designed by God as high priest according to the order of Melchizedek" (5:9, 10). The themes are listed: his becoming perfect, his being the cause or source of eternal life, and his being proclaimed high priest of the order of Melchizedek. These are the themes of the three doctrinal sections of the third part. But this is put into relief by being framed in two other sections, the first, an introduction aimed at gaining the attention of the audience (5:11-6:20) and the final peroration (10:19-39) in the form of an invitation: "let us draw near in utter sincerity and absolute confidence, our hearts sprinkled clean from the evil which lay on our conscience and our bodies washed in pure water" (10:22).

The first doctrinal section develops the last of the three announced themes: Jesus, a priest according to the order of Melchizedek. This is a priesthood superior to the Levitical priesthood of the Old Testament, because Jesus was holy, innocent and uncontaminated, beyond the influence of sinners, and raised up above the heavens: "It was fitting that we should have such a high priest; holy, innocent, undefiled, separated from sinners, higher than the heavens. Unlike the other high priests, he has no need to offer sacrifice day after day, first for his own sins and then for those of the people; he did that once for all when he offered himself" (7:26, 27).

The second section speaks of the consecration of the priesthood of Christ, that is, of his sacrifice. The theme is developed by a consistent comparison between the rite of the Day of Atonement and the perfect atonement accomplished by Christ. This underlines the similarities and calls into relief the perfect and definitive character of the salvation achieved by Jesus (cc. 8 and 9).

The third section presents Jesus as the cause or source of eternal salvation for all by virtue of the sacrificial consummation of his priesthood (c. 10).

The fourth part (11:1-12:13) comprises two sections, and is built on the second part which dealt with Jesus the high priest who was faithful and patient. The first section recalls the examples of perseverance in the faith that the Old Testament affords us (11:1-40), while the second section exhorts to patience which is necessary for Christians (12:1-13).

The fifth part (12:14-13:19) is an exhortation to an authentic Christian life which is lived in charity and holiness, and proposes peace as the fruit of this life. The homily or letter concludes with a doxology.

Hebron (hee′-bron), A city in the land of Judah, about 20 miles south of Jerusalem, first called Kiriath-arba (Gen. 23:2; 35:27; Josh. 14:15; 15:13, 54; 20:7; 21:11; Jgs. 1:10; Neh. 11:25). According to Numbers 13:22 it was founded seven years before Tanis (Zoan), the Egyptian capital of the Hyksos. Near it lay Mamre, a place associated with the Patriarchs Abraham (Gen. 13:18; 14:13, etc.) and Jacob (Gen. 35:27; 37:14), and with Machpelah where Abraham bought a tract of land with a cave for the burial of Sarah (Gen. 23). There are divergent traditions on the people who lived there before the Israelites came. Genesis 14:3 says they were Amorites; 23:3 asserts Hittites; Numbers 13:22 calls them Anakim, while Judges 1:10 holds they were Canaaneans.

The city was taken by the Calebites (Josh. 14:13; Jgs. 1:20) who were later integrated into the tribe of Judah (Josh. 15:54; Jgs. 1:10). It occurs in the list of the cities of refuge (Josh. 20:7) and among the priestly cities (Josh. 21:11-13).

In Hebron David was made king of Judah (2 Sam. 2:4) and the city remained the capital of the kingdom for seven years and seven months (2 Sam. 5:5). There the elders of Israel went to meet him, in order to offer him the kingship of the northern tribes (2 Sam. 5:1-3). Hebron too was where Absalom started his revolt and proclaimed himself king (2 Sam. 15:7-12). It was fortified by Rehoboam (2 Chron. 11:5-12) and rebuilt and repopulated after the Exile (Neh. 11:25). Hebron figures again in the history of the Maccabees, where the siege of the city, then in the hands of the Idumaeans, is re-recorded (1 Mac. 5:65).

heel
you strike at his *h.* Gen. 3:15   raised his *h.* against
A trap seizes him by the *h.*   Ps. 41:10; Jn. 13:18
                        Job 18:9

Hegai, King Ahasuerus' eunuch who was in charge of the women (Esth. 2:3).

Hegemonides, Governor of the region between Ptolemais and Gerar under Antiochus V Eupator (164-161 B.C.).

height, heights
in the *h.* of the heavens   Job 22:12   the breadth and length and *h.*
neither *h.* nor depth   Rom. 8:39   Eph. 3:18

Heir, *See* INHERITANCE.

Helam (hee'-lam), A city in Transjordan where David defeated the Aramaean army of Hadadezer who had come to the help of the Ammonites (2 Sam. 10:16, 17).

Heled (hee'-led), One of the group of David's warriors known as the Thirty (2 Sam. 23:29).

Heli, *See* ELI.

Heliodorus (hee'-li-o-dor'-us), Minister of King Seleucus IV Philopator (187-175 B.C.) who was commissioned to despoil the Temple treasury in Jerusalem (2 Mac. 3:7). He was foiled in his attempt by the mysterious appearance of a gilt-clad horseman and two magnificent youths who belabored him until he was senseless. His health was restored by the prayers of the high priest Onias. The same mysterious persons appeared once more to tell him the cause of his curse. On his return Heliodorus dissuaded the king from repeating the attempt.

Heliopolis (hee'-li-op'-o-lis), A Greek name ("sun city") for the Egyptian city On, the center of the cult of the sun god Atum-re (Jer. 43:13; Isa. 19:18). Joseph, son of Jacob, married Asenath the daughter of Potiphera who was priest of On (Gen. 41:45, 50; 46:20).

Helkath-hazzurim (hazh'-oo-rim), A place near Gibeon, the scene of a duel fought between 12 warriors of Joab, David's supporter, and 12 warriors of Abner who was defending the dynastic rights of Saul's house (*see* 2 Sam. 2:14-16).

Hell, *See* GEHENNA.

Hellenism, Hellenists, The Greeks were Aryans, and in early times they occupied the country in the southeast of Europe still known as Greece, and composed partly of islands and partly of a continent indented by bays in innumerable shapes. The "Isles" of Greece appear to have been vaguely known in the times of the Israelite kingdom. Joel tells us that the Syrians sold children of Judah as slaves to the Greeks (3:6). In the book of Daniel Greece appears on the stage of the great world-empires (e.g. 8:21), a reference to the Macedonian empire of Alexander and his successors, which included Palestine and the Jews in its sweep of conquest. The odious Syro-Grecian dominion that called out the patriotic heroism of the Maccabees was the outcome of this conquest of the East by Greece. It succeeded the Persian supremacy; it fell in turn before the onslaught of the iron legions of Rome. The political relation of the Greeks to the Jews resulting from their conquest of the East was less important than the intellectual consequences of the contact of Greek culture with Hebrew life and thought. All over western Asia Greek civilization spread among the educated classes. In the time of Jesus everyday **koine** Greek was the language of the Near East. This is why the New Testament, though written on the whole by Jews, was nevertheless composed in Greek.

The term Hellenist is applied to two different classes of people. It denotes either a Greek proselyte to Judaism, or a Christian of Greek as distinct from one of Jewish descent (Acts 6:1; 9:29); but it also denotes a Jew who has become Grecianized by contact with Greek civilization, and has learned to employ the Greek language to the exclusion of Aramaic. At first a Hellenist in this sense was a Jew who came to prefer having Jewish thought and life more or less transformed, in spirit as well as fashion, after a Greek pattern. But when that idea was no longer to be entertained, in consequence of the expressed stern refusal of the Jewish people in the Maccabean struggle to sink their nationality in the presence of any other, the term came to denote a Jew who was open to learning as much from the civilization of the Greek as was consistent with the maintenance of the principles of his own religion in their integrity.

The great center in which this tendency, giving rise to a new phase of Jewish character and faith, began to develop was Alexandria, and the fruits of a Grecian quality which it produced were more pronounced in this city than in perhaps any other center of the Dispersion. For not only were the Jewish Scriptures here translated into Greek, but the Jewish mind here began to acquire a new expressiveness and learned to assimilate forms of thought and action to which it was presumed to be alien. Here it was that Hellenism took its rise, and that the Jew proved, notwithstanding his professed exclusiveness, how wide an affinity the religion of his fathers had with those other forms of life which the Greek had developed for the good of humanity. It was the merit of the Hellenist that he recognized this affinity, and that he became the medium of broadening the Jewish faith and preparing the way for the Christian religion which was to baptize all nations.

Philo the Jew was Greek in thought: he made it his business to convert the Hebrew Scriptures into allegories of Greek philosophy. Apollos was trained in this school of teaching, and the Gospel of St. John and the Epistles to the Colossians and the Hebrews bear traces of its influence. At Athens and Corinth in particular St. Paul came into contact with popular Greek philosophy. Greek thought was essentially naturalistic. It discerned the beauty of nature, but except in the case of the great tragic writers, Aeschylus and Sophocles, it was strangely blind to moral evil. Keen in intellect, the Greeks were scornfully skeptical of the spiritual truth which is the life of the Hebrew faith. And yet the searching questions of Socrates and the soaring speculations of Plato, as well as the lofty ethics of the Stoics, were like the law among the Jews—schoolmasters to bring men to Christ.

Helmet, There is little reference to armor in the Old Testament, and even though one can infer that a helmet was used for protection of the head, its shape is not known. At the time of Paul's writing, the Roman helmet could not be but well-known. In early times it was a leather protection, but metal was later used and the helmet developed protective pieces for the face and a visor. In 1 Thessalonians 5:8 Paul exhorts Christians to have the hope of salvation for a helmet, while in Ephesians 6:17 he tells them to accept salvation from God as their helmet.

help, helps

God of your father, who *h.* you		I will come to *h.* you 2 Sam. 10:12
	Gen. 49:25	to Egypt whose *h.* is futile
h. him, rather, to raise it up		Isa. 30:7
	Ex. 23:5	who go down to Egypt for *h.*
you shall *h.* me 2 Sam. 10:11		Isa. 31:1

Heman (hee′-man), 1. A legendary figure, one of the sons of Mahol, mentioned with Chalcol and Darda whose wisdom that of Solomon exceeded according to 1 Kings 4:11. 1 Chronicles 2:6 calls him a member of the tribe of Judah.

2. The son of Joel, and probably to be identified with the Heman above. He was of the Levitical clan of Kohath, head of one of the choirs in the worship at Jerusalem during the time of David and Solomon (1 Chron. 6:18-32; 15:17; 25:1; 2 Chron. 5:12). Psalm 88 is attributed to him.

hemmed

whom God has *h.* in   Job 3:23

Hen, *See* FOWL.

Hena, A town in Syria (so indicated by the context of references to it), conquered by the Assyrians before they laid siege to Jerusalem under Sennacherib (2 Kgs. 18:34; 19:13; Isa. 37:13). We know nothing further of the locality nor of the time or occasion of the event.

Hepher (hee′-fur), 1. A town northwest of Samaria, near the Mediterranean coast and south of Mt. Carmel.

2. A clan in the tribe of Manasseh (Num. 26:32).

3. The name of several Old Testament men (Num. 27:1; 1 Chron. 4:6; 1 Chron. 11:36).

Hephzibah, Wife of King Hezekiah of Judah (715-687), and mother of Manasseh, his successor (687-642 B.C.; *see* 2 Kgs. 21:1).

Heresy, From the Greek *hairesis*, a choice. In the New Testament it does not have the technical sense it later acquired in theology, that is, the knowing denial of a dogma defined by the Church as divinely revealed. In the New Testament it is used in the larger sense of party, sect or faction in religious matters. Thus the "sect" of the Sadducees and Pharisees is mentioned in Acts 15:5; 5:17; 26:5. The Christian church was called by the others the sect of the Nazarenes (Acts 24:5; 24:14). In Paul's letters heresy acquires a pejorative sense, related to sins such as envy, rivalry, etc. (*see* 1 Cor. 11:19; Gal. 5:20). In 2 Peter 2:1 heresy is related to doctrinal errors.

Hermes, 1. A Greek God, son of Zeus, the herald and messenger of the gods. At Lystra Paul healed a cripple. The excited people shouted that the gods had visited them, calling Paul's companion, Barnabas, Zeus, and addressing Paul, who was the principal speaker, as Hermes (Acts 14:12).

2. A Christian in Rome to whom Paul sends greetings (Rom. 16:14).

Hermogenes (her-moj′-e-nees), A Christian who with Phygelus and all the others in the province of Asia refused to have anything to do with Paul (2 Tim. 1:15).

Hermon, The most southerly mountain of the Anti-Lebanon range, 9232 feet high. It was also called Sirion (Deut. 3:9; Ps. 29:6) and Senir (Deut. 3:9; 1 Chron. 5:23; Ezek. 27:5; S. of S. 4:8). Mount Hermon formed the northern limit of the Amorite kingdom of Og (Deut. 3:8; 4:48; Josh. 12:5; 13:11), of Joshua's conquests (Josh. 11:17; 12:1; 13:5), and of the land of Manasseh (1 Chron. 5:23). The source of the Jordan is in the vicinity, fed by the melting snows which constantly cover Mt. Hermon. There are poetic allusions to Hermon in Pss. 29:6; 42:7; 89:13; 133:3; S. of S. 4:8).

Herod Agrippa, *See* AGRIPPA I.

Herod Antipas (ant′-i-pas), Son of Herod I the Great and Malthace, who was also mother to Archelaus. By his father's will he became tetrarch of Galilee and Peraea (Lk. 3:1; 4 B.C.-39 A.D.). He married the daughter of the Nabataean King Aretas IV (9-40 A.D.) but later repudiated her to live with Herodias, daughter of Aristobulus, son of Herod I the Great and of the first woman named Mariamme whom he married. Herodias was therefore the niece of Antipas. Furthermore, she was the former wife of Herod Philip, son of Herod I the Great and of the second Mariamme whom he took to wife. The repudiated daughter of Aretas IV returned to her father, and relationships between Herod Antipas and that king worsened. In 36 A.D. on account of a frontier dispute Aretas IV declared war on Herod Antipas who suffered a heavy defeat. When Agrippa was nominated king of Judea, Herod Antipas, at the instigation of Herodias, went to Rome to ask for himself the same honor from Caligula the emperor (37-41 A.D.). The emperor however listened to Agrippa's accusations against Antipas and instead of making him king, stripped him of his tetrarchship and banished him to Lyons, France, to which Herodias accompanied him.

Herod was tetrarch of Galilee during the public ministry of Jesus (Lk. 3:1; 13:31). John the Baptizer publicly denounced the irregularity of Herod's union with Herodias, and for this was imprisoned by the tetrarch. Herod however was afraid to put him to death as the people considered him a prophet (Matt. 14:3-5; Lk. 3:18-20). Later however he found himself cornered into doing it through an imprudent oath that he swore in front of his guests to Salome, Herodias' daughter, when she had danced, to the company's great pleasure, to celebrate his birthday (Matt. 14:6-12; Mk. 6:14-30). When later he heard about Jesus and the works he performed he believed that this was John the Baptizer alive again to haunt him (Matt. 14:1-2; Mk. 6:14-15; Lk. 9:7-9). His fear was at the same time superstitious and political. His friendship with the Romans was the guarantee of the stability of his position, and so could be threatened or compromised by the popular enthusiasm that surrounded Jesus' ministry. Luke recounts how some Pharisees came to Jesus to advise him to leave Herod's territory, Galilee, as Herod wished to do away with him (Lk. 13:31-33). This was probably a maneuver of Herod's to get rid of Jesus without having to intervene in a way that would arouse the people and so disturb the Romans, who in reality only tolerated Herod's rule. Perhaps in allusion to these sly maneuvers Jesus called Herod 'that fox' in his answer, announcing that he would go ahead with his mission until his work was done.

Luke also recounts the personal meeting of Jesus with Herod in Jerusalem during the Passion. Pilate discovered from the interrogation that Jesus came from Galilee, and to avoid a difficult decision in the case of Jesus, and to ingratiate himself with Herod who was then in Jerusalem for the feast of the Pasch, he sent Jesus to him. This meeting had no other result than the further humiliation of Jesus and the reconciliation of Herod and Pilate, who hitherto had been hostile to each other (Lk. 23:7-12). The ill-feeling between Herod and Pilate was due to Herod's politics. Herod's favor with the emperor Tiberius was won by reporting back to him on the

Roman authorities in Palestine and Syria. This would also explain why Pilate wanted Herod involved in a decision involving the capital punishment of a Jew, despite the profound contempt in which he held him.

Herod I The Great, King of Judea (37-4 B.C.), born in 73 B.C., son of the Idumean Antipater and of Cypris, an Arabian princess. Antipater was appointed procurator of Judea alongside of the high priest and ethnarch Hyrcanus II by Caesar. He nominated his sons Phasael and Herod governors of Jerusalem and Galilee (47 B.C.). Soon after this Herod received from Sixtus Caesar, the Roman governor of Syria, the governorship of Coelesyria. He took advantage of the civil wars that were being waged for power in Rome and changed with the wind so that he succeeded always in winning favor with the victor. In the meantime Antigonus, brother to Hyrcanus II, had succeeded in having himself named king of the Jews. Herod fled to Rome where he got from the senate the same honor and with the help of the Romans conquered Jerusalem after three years of war. Thus he became in effect king of Judah (37 B.C.). He then set about enlarging his kingdom. A mixture of cunning and adulation towards the Romans helped him in the end to the possession of Judea, Samaria, Galilee, Idumea and Transjordan.

He repudiated his first wife, the Idumean Doris, to marry Mariamme, granddaughter to Hyrcanus II of the Hasmonaean dynasty. He was tyrannical and suspicious, and made a profession of political crime until under the accusation of real or presumed conspiracy, he succeeded in eliminating all possible rivals, and, consequently, all the survivors of the Hasmonaean house. Aristobulus, Mariamme's brother, his wife's grandfather Hyrcanus II, Mariamme herself and several members of Herod's own family such as his brother Joseph, the husbands of his sister Salome, these were all victims of his treachery.

He supported the Greek culture while he intensely despised the Jewish customs and traditions, but was astute enough to please Rome and not to offend openly the religious factions of the Israelites. He founded numerous new cities on Greek lines (Sebaste, the ancient Samaria, Caesarea, Antipatris, Jericho, Phasael). He also satisfied the religious zeal and national pride of the people by undertaking a splendid reconstruction of the Temple in Jerusalem (19 B.C. and only finished in 64 A.D., a few years before its destruction). He dotted the land with new or reconstructed military fortresses. Jerusalem had the Antonia at the corner of the Temple, then there was Machaerus, where John the Baptizer died, Masada, Hesbon, Gadara, Alexandreion, etc.

All these works and the astute ways that he employed to cultivate the affection of the people failed in their intent. He was hated by the people, and continually threatened by the intrigues and rivalries of his own family. The formula to make his work endure escaped him, so that it fatally collapsed after his death. He divided his kingdom among his sons. Archelaus, son of Herod's fourth wife Malthace, was named king of Judea; Herod Antipas, Archelaus' brother, was named tetrarch of Galilee; while Philip, son of Herod's fifth wife Cleopatra, was made tetrarch of Trachonitis and other Transjordanian regions.

It was during his reign that Jesus was born (Matt. 2:1; Lk. 1:5). According to Matt. 2:1-18 Herod, on hearing of the birth of a "king of the Jews," ordered the slaughter of all the male babies of Bethlehem under two years of age.

Herodians, These men appear twice in the New Testament alongside of the Pharisees (Mk. 3:6 and 12:13-17; *see* Matt. 22:16-22). Who exactly they were is a disputed question. It seems that without doubt they were not a religious faction. The most probable opinion holds them to be supporters of Herod's dynasty or simply members of his retinue.

Herodias (he-roe′-di-as), Daughter of Aristobulus (son of Herod I, the Great) and of Bernice (daughter of Salome, Herod's sister). She was given as wife to Philip, a half-brother of her father (Mk. 6:17) who became tetrarch of Peraea. She left her husband to become wife to Herod Antipas (son of Herod I and Malthace). The scandalous union was publicly condemned by John the Baptizer for which he was imprisoned in the fortress of Machaerus. On Antipas' birthday, Salome, daughter to Herodias and Philip, danced for the guests assembled for dinner, and under the instigation of her mother, asked for the head of John the Baptizer on a plate as a reward (Mk. 6:17-29; Matt. 14:3-12; Lk. 3:19-20). When Herod Agrippa I was made king of Judea by the emperor Caligula (37 A.D.), Herodias persuaded Antipas to go to Rome to ask for this position for himself in the place of Agrippa. Caligula however would hear nothing of it and exiled Antipas. Herodias followed him into exile.

Herodion (he-roe′-di-on), A Jewish convert in Rome, greeted by Paul (Rom. 16:11).

Herodium, The fortress and funeral monument of Herod I the Great, four miles southeast of Bethlehem.

Heshbon, The capital city of the Amorite King Sihon, captured by the Israelites under Moses (Num. 21:25; Deut. 1:4; 2:26; Jgs. 11:9) and afterwards a Levitical city and a city of refuge in the land of Reuben (Josh. 13:17, 26; 21:37; 1 Chron. 6:66), and later again certainly a Moabite possession (Isa. 15:4; 16:8-9; Jer. 48:2). It is today Hesban, about sixteen miles east of the Jordan.

Heth, Founding father of the Hittites (Gen. 10:15; 1 Chron. 1:13). *See* HITTITES.

Heth, The 8th letter of the Hebrew alphabet (emphatic h).

Hexateuch, The first six books of the Bible taken together, from Genesis to Joshua inclusive. Some critics prefer to speak of the Hexateuch instead of the Pentateuch (first five books, to the exclusion of Joshua) as the story did not originally end with the death of Moses but with the conquest of Canaan (Josh.). *See* PENTATEUCH.

Hezekiah, King of Judah (715-687 B.C.), son and successor of Ahaz (2 Kgs. 18:2). Hezekiah undertook a religious reform in the shape of a centralized cult in Jerusalem. 2 Kings 18:4 speaks of the destruction of high places (*see* HIGH PLACES) and of the sacred poles, and even of the serpent that Moses had made and to which the Israelites had offered sacrifice. (*See* SERPENT, NEHUSHTAN.) The over-all judgment of the historical compiler is more than favorable: "He put his trust in the Lord, and neither before him nor after him was there anyone like him among all the kings of Judah" (2 Kgs. 18:5). The parallel account in 2 Chron. 29:30 is much richer in detail, but it probably attributes by anticipation to Hezekiah's reign the reforms that actually only took place under Josiah (640-609 B.C.; 2 Kgs. 22).

Hezekiah's policy in external affairs seems to have been above all directed towards putting an end to vassalage to Assyria, which he had inherited from his father Ahaz (2 Kgs. 16:7) and which had had its resonance in the internal affairs of the country and even in the religious sphere. There is some uncertainty about the course and chronology of the events narrated in 2 Kings 18:13-20:19 and Isa. 38-39. The difficulty arises from the fact that 18:13-16 and 18:17 ff. seem to be speaking of two different occasions.

Both of these sieges of Jerusalem are attributed to Sennacherib (705-681 B.C.), and so some are of the opinion that Sennacherib carried out two campaigns in Judah (e.g. W. F. Albright). One of these would have taken place in 701 B.C., and this is also recorded in Assyrian annals. The other would have taken place after 689 B.C.: beyond this year and up to 681 B.C. there is no information on Sennacherib.

While the chronology of John Bright, following Albright, is widely accepted in the U.S., a radically different chronology contends that Hezekiah's reign should be dated 728-699 B.C. Following this line, it has been thought that 2 Kings 18:13-16 attributes to Sennacherib a campaign that really took place under his predecessor Sargon II, who, in fact, around 714-711 B.C. did carry out an expedition into the west and captured the Philistine city of Ashdod. To these years, too, belongs Hezekiah's illness (2 Kgs. 20) after which Merodach-baladan, king of Babylon, sent him letters and a gift which so delighted him that he took the messengers on a tour of his treasurehouse, showing them all his riches (Isa. 39). Merodach-baladan was also the chief instigator of the anti-Assyrian revolt in the eastern region of the empire. Since Ahaz's time however Isaiah had advised neutrality as the only avenue to survival for a small nation like Judah. For this reason he reproved Hezekiah for his anti-Assyrian alliances (Isa. 39:5-8; Isa. 31:1-7). Sargon II, then, made an "expedition against all the fortified cities of Judah and captured them." Hezekiah succeeded in saving Jerusalem at the price of a huge tribute in gold and silver, for which he found it necessary to strip the Temple (2 Kgs. 18:13-16).

The second invasion would then take place during the first years of Sennacherib's reign (701 B.C.). A series of revolts all over the empire came in the wake of his accession to power. He settled things in the east, and then turned westwards to settle accounts there too. He took Lachish (2 Kgs. 18:17) and then put Jerusalem under siege. The dramatic account of this siege (2 Kgs. 18:17-19, 36) underlines the important part played by Isaiah in sustaining the king. The city was saved *in extremis*. According to Isaiah's oracle in 2 Kings 19:7 Sennacherib put an end to the siege on account of an unexpected need to return to Assyria: "I (God) am about to put in him such a spirit that, when he hears a certain report, he will return to his own land, and there I will cause him to fall by the sword." 2 Kings 19:35 however has a miraculous explanation for the fact: "That night the angel of the Lord went forth and struck down one hundred and eighty-five thousand men in the Assyrian camp. . . . So Sennacherib, the king of Assyria, broke camp, and went back home to Nineveh." The author is describing in terms of a divine intervention what was probably an epidemic that broke out among the soldiers. Herodotus, the Greek historian, describes a campaign of Sennacherib in Egypt which he was forced to abandon on account of a plague of rats that ate the army supplies, and one cannot exclude from 2 Kings 19:35 an echo of what Herodotus tells us about the Egyptian campaign.

When Hezekiah foresaw the inevitable siege of the city he undertook the project of fortifying Jerusalem: "he rebuilt the wall where it was broken down, raised towers on it, and built another wall outside" (2 Chron. 32:5). He prepared supplies and organized the army (2 Chron. 32:6-8) while he closed up all the springs of water around the city to cut off the besieging army's water supply. Then he constructed an underground aqueduct in the rock to carry the water from the well of Gihon right into the city of David. This notable work of engineering is still preserved (2 Chron. 31:30; 2 Kgs. 20:20).

hid

The man and his wife *h.*   Gen 3:8 I was naked, so I *h.* myself
                                                                  Gen. 3:10

Hiddekel (hid′-de-kel), The Hebrew name for the river Tigris (Gen. 2:14; Dan. 10:4).

hidden

for it rather than for *h.* treasures	these things you have *h.* Job 10:13
Job 3:21	nothing *h.* that will not
Men whose path is *h.* from them	Matt. 10:26
Job 3:23	

Hiel (hie′-el), A man of Bethel who, during the kingdom of Ahab of Israel (869-850 B.C.), dared to undertake the reconstruction of Jericho despite the curse pronounced by Joshua against anybody who should try such a thing in the future (Josh. 6:26). Hiel's sons Abiram and Segub died, which was interpreted as fulfilment of Joshua's curse. The formula of the curse is possibly derived from the story of Hiel (1 Kgs. 16:34).

Hierapolis (hie′-a-rap′-o-lis), A city of Phrygia in Asia Minor in the valley of the river Lycus, opposite Colossae and Laodicea. It had a Christian community probably founded by Epaphras (*see* Col. 4:12-14).

Hierarchy, The word hierarchy comes from the Greek **hieros** meaning sacred, and **arche** meaning primacy or authority. It means then, literally, sacred authority. The New Testament never uses the term with the specific meaning it was later to acquire in ecclesiastical use, that is, signifying that group of people who held the power of orders and jurisdiction in the Church. For the sake of convenience and clarity however, under this word we examine the notion of priesthood, or presbyterate, and episcopacy in the New Testament.

The following problem arises: how did the apostolic authority pass to the post-apostolic Church? From the witness of St. Ignatius, who died a martyr under Trajan (90-117 A.D.) and of St. Irenaeus, who died around 202 A.D. one concludes that already in the second century the hierarchical structure of the local churches was practically identical with what appears in succeeding centuries and remains today. At the head of the community there is a bishop, one for each community, who is assisted by presbyters with priestly functions and by deacons. It is also clear however that even though in the New Testament the terms bishop (episcopos, overseer) and presbyter [priest] are used, they are not taken in exactly the same sense. Paul, for example, addresses his letter to the church at Philippi "with their bishops (plural) and deacons" (1:1) without any mention of priests, while in Acts 20:17, 18 and Titus 1:5, 7 the terms bishop and priest are practically interchangeable.

Moreover it is necessary to note that the concrete manner in which the apostolic authority was distributed was not necessarily the same in all places. Nor can we exclude the possibility that the Church imitated or at least was influenced by similar Jewish or Hellenistic organizations. This influence is clear even in the very names adopted to denote the functions of authority in the Church.

The Greek **presbyteros** means elder. Among the Greeks and Jews the more important members of the community were called elders. These were people who enjoyed a natural and spontaneous authority that all recognized, either on account of their age, or dignity, or riches or lineage. This system of government was collegial, and it supervised the administrative and judicial life of the community with different powers according to the place or time. (*See* ELDER.) It was very common in the Palestinian Jewish world and in that of the Diaspora

The Greek **episcopos** is a term for an overseer or superintendent whose task it is to take charge of a certain order or class of things. In the Hellenistic world this is a functionary with personal power and responsibility for a specific office or direction or supervision.

The "colleges" of presbyters seem to have been the most ancient form of authority that emerged in the Church below that of the apostles. To the presbyters was entrusted the care of the Church in Jerusalem (Acts 11:30), and with the apostles they form a kind of senate to take into consideration common problems. This was the case, for example, at the Council of Jerusalem (Acts 15). Later they form a group around James who is the head of the presbyterial senate and the center of the Christian community in Jerusalem (Acts 2:18). Acts 14:22 states that Paul and Barnabas appointed presbyters in the churches they founded in Asia Minor during their first missionary journey.

One may then legitimately conclude that the Church at the beginning adopted the age-long Jewish tradition of colleges of ancients to govern the local churches. This was true first of all for the church in Palestine, but later the practice spread, by imitation, also to other churches. The elders were selected by the apostles and their task was to govern the local church in the absence of the apostles. For this purpose they were given authority fitted to their office. There were variations however from community to community. The church at Jerusalem under James and his elders seems to have achieved an internal autonomy not enjoyed, for example, by the church of Antioch (Acts 11:23; 31:1) or by the churches of Asia Minor which were even more bound to the personal authority of the apostles or their delegates, who filled the supreme role exercised by James in Jerusalem.

With the exception of the pastoral epistles, that is, 1 and 2 Timothy and Titus, Paul never speaks of elders in his letters. Paul prefers the word **episcopoi**, bishops, or more literally, overseers, but he is not consistent in the use of this terminology. Paul adopts different words to designate the people who have been chosen among the members of the community to care for its government. 1 Thessalonians exhorts the Christians of the city to be considerate "to those who are working amongst you and are above you in the Lord as your teachers." These words sufficiently designate their authority and the pastoral function entrusted to them. Romans 12:8 lists the gifts and functions distributed among the members for the good of the community: those in charge Paul exhorts to be diligent. These are called "pastors" in Ephesians 4:11 and "bishops" in Philippians" 1:1.

Besides the local hierarchy Paul speaks of his own immediate collaborators whom he calls apostles (*see* APOSTLE), and also fellow workers (**synergos**) and fellow ministers or servants (**syndoulos**). These are Silas, Timothy, Titus and others (*see* Rom. 16:3; Philem. 1; Col. 1:7; 4:7; 4:11; Philem. 24, etc.). These texts reveal an important aspect of Paul's apostolic tactics: around him moved a certain number of personages, his collaborators, who shared intimately in his apostolic plans and projects, and also shared his authority. They are sent by him with specific functions, at times quite concrete, and temporary tasks, such as the mission of Timothy to Thessalonica (1 Thess. 3:2) and that of Timothy (1 Cor. 16:10) and Titus to Corinth (2 Cor. 8:23). Paul then retains direct and immediate authority over all the communities that were born of his apostolic labors, and even over some that were not directly founded by him, e.g. Colossae. Paul enumerates among his trials "daily tension pressing on me, my anxiety for all the churches" (2 Cor. 11:28). Paul exercises this authority through his collaborators and at the level of the local churches, through the bishops or overseers who watch over the ordinary life of the community, preside at the Lord's Supper, instruct the Christians and so on.

Towards the end of Paul's life, as can be gathered from the pastoral epistles, Paul's collaborators came more into relief and achieved more autonomy. Titus and Timothy received from Paul the mandate to found other communities and to provide for their organization. Titus was left by Paul at Crete "that you might accomplish what had been left undone, especially the appointment of presbyters in every town" (Tit. 1:5). Timothy was sent to Ephesus with a similar task (1 Tim. 1:3; 3:1-13). In Paul's instructions to Timothy and Titus emerge the clearest picture of the duties of the presbyters who were also called bishops: they must teach others (1 Tim. 3:3) and govern the church of God (1 Tim. 3:5). They are God's representatives (Tit. 1:7) and thus should have the moral and human endowments that such an office requires: prudence, sobriety, patience, firmness of character and of faith, and so on. It is not possible to determine whether among the bishops one is placed above the others or not. The tone of the exhortation seems however to suggest this. The authority of Titus and Timothy is unquestioned in all their territories.

This system which was typical of the Pauline churches was maintained after his death at least until the end of the first century. In Clement's letter, written in the name of the Roman church to the Corinthian church around 98 A.D. the local hierarchy is composed of presbyters and bishops and deacons who were inducted by the apostles or by other men of rank (44:3). Eusebius of Caesarea is more explicit: he traces the transition from the apostolic age to the post-apostolic age, in the following terms: "Many others were well known at the time, belonging to the first stage in the apostolic succession . . . leaving their homes behind, they carried out the work of the evangelists, ambitious to preach to those who had never yet heard the message of the faith . . . staying only to lay the foundations of the faith in one foreign place or another, appointing others as pastors, and entrusting to them the tending of those newly brought in, they set off again for other places and peoples" (III, 37).

Behind these generic outlines it is easy to perceive the continuance of the Pauline apostolic system even after his death. With time this system developed to the point where these itinerant apostles settled in one place, and thus arose the system that was in vigor in the Jerusalem church from the beginning and was also found elsewhere, that is, in John's churches.

Revelation 1-3 supplies sufficient information on these churches to be able to discern a monarchical episcopate which is not different from that described and theologically defended by the martyr Ignatius of Antioch. In these chapters the Spirit through John sends seven letters to the seven churches of Asia Minor. These letters are addressed to the "angels" of these churches. Here we cannot go into detail, but it should be noted that in the most common exegesis given to the texts today, the "angels" are not celestial beings, nor even ideal figures representing the churches themselves, but those who have charge of the community, and should therefore look after its orthodoxy and fervor. These, then, would be the bishops. Perhaps they were called angels after texts like Malachi 2:7 and Haggai 1:3 (*see* also Dan. 12:3). The organization of a monarchical episcopate took its inspiration from a precise concept of the ministry in the Church and of its unity. The bishops are the instruments of Christ, appointed like angels to the various churches to watch over their purity of faith and fervor in charity. On the other hand they are the symbol and bond holding together the different communities, whose spirit they embody.

This then was the way in which the hierarchy, by the second century, became more highly organized. The distinction between bishops and presbyters among the ministers of a church reflects a distinction of degree that existed in diverse forms right from the beginning, where there were not only apostles, but their collaborators or local bishops (James in Jerusalem, for example) and the presbyters and bishops who as a college acted in his absence as the true head of the churches.

High Places, The usual translation for the Hebrew **bamoth.** In the cultic sense, the **bamoth** were open-air sanctuaries or places of worship, often situated in the highlands (1 Kgs. 11:7; 2 Kgs. 16:4; 17:9-10) but not necessarily so (Jer. 7:31; 32:35). They consisted of an elevated platform, approached by a series of steps, on which there was an altar (2 Kgs. 21:3; 2 Chron. 14:2; Ezek. 6:6). The high places are often spoken of together with the **massebot** and **aseroth** which were typical of but not exclusive to the Canaanaean cult. The former consisted of dressed stone pillars, the latter of wooden stakes driven into the ground (*see* ASHERA; 1 Kgs. 13:23; 2 Kgs. 18:4; 23:13). The high places are mentioned in the story of Samuel (1 Sam. 9:13, 14, 19, 25) and of Solomon (the high place of Gibeon, 1 Kgs. 3:1) without being condemned.

In other places, however, in 1-2 Kings and often in the Prophets (Hos. 10:8; Amos 7:9; Jer. 7:31), the kings are rebuked for not having destroyed or explicitly condemned the worship carried out there. This poses the question of their legitimacy. It is clear that the negative judgments of 1-2 Kings depend largely on the rigid centralization of cult according to Deuteronomy 12, which was put into practice by Josiah (2 Kgs. 23), and already attempted in some way by Hezekiah (2 Kgs. 18:4). On the other hand the judgment of the more ancient prophets such as Hosea and Amos, who came before the centralizing movement, was by no means favorable. If in fact the places were, and they were, legitimate places of worship of Yahweh, they were also open to syncretism, that is, they were prone to assimilate Canaanite cultic traditions in fertility and funeral rites. Against this perversion of the true cult the prophets cried out, as did later those who inspired the centralizing law.

High Priest, *See* PRIEST.

Highwayman
come upon you like a *h.*   poverty come upon you like a *h.*
                      Prov. 6:11   Prov. 24:34

Hilkiah, 1. High priest at the time of King Josiah of Judah (640-609 B.C.) who found a book of the law in the Temple. By order of the king he went to consult with the prophetess Huldah over the discovery (2 Kgs. 22:3-20; 2 Chron. 34:8-28).

2. Father of the prophet Jeremiah (Jer. 1:1).

Hillel, A doctor of the law who lived during the reign of Herod, and was noted for his rather liberal interpretation of the law in contrast with the school founded by his famous contemporary Shammai.

hind, hinds
Naphtali is a *h.* let loose   my feet swift as those of *h.*
                      Gen. 49:21   2 Sam. 22:34
                   even the *h.* in the field   Jer. 14:5

Hinnom, *See* GEHENNA.

Hippopotamus, The Hebrew **behemoth** in Job 40:15-24 is usually identified as the hippopotamus even though the description is not perfectly correct. Perhaps the author even was writing from hearsay.

Hiram, 1. King of Tyre (969-935 B.C.), a contemporary of David and Solomon with whom he had commercial dealings. Hiram was the purveyor of materials for the building programs of the two kings of Israel, and especially for the king's palace and the Temple of Jerusalem (2 Sam. 5:11; 1 Kgs. 5:15). Solomon paid for Hiram's services by making over to him some cities in Galilee (1 Kgs. 9:10; *see* 2 Chron. 8:2). Hiram also collaborated with Solomon, providing expert crews for the fleet at Eziongeber, in the gulf of Aqaba, to sail the gold and spice-laden ships from Ophir in Arabia (1 Kgs. 9:26; 10:11, 12; 2 Chron. 8:17; 9:10).

2. A highly skilled bronzeworker from Tyre, the son of a widow of the tribe of Naphtali, who worked for Solomon in fitting out the Temple (1 Kgs. 7:13-47; 2 Chron. 2:12-15). In 2 Chron. 2:12 he is called Huramabi, the son of a woman of the tribe of Dan.

hire, hired

The well-fed *h*. themselves out	No one has *h*. us	Matt. 20:7
1 Sam. 2:5	When those *h*. late	Matt. 20:9
the razor *h*. from across the river		
Isa. 7:20		

History of Salvation, *See* SALVATION HISTORY.

Hittites, An Indo-European people who settled in Asia Minor around 2000 B.C. and created a great empire which flourished especially from the 15th to the 13th century B.C. with Hattush (today Baghazhöy in northeast Turkey) its capital. Under Suppiluliuma, around 1380 B.C. they were in control of Syria and northern Mesopotamia. Its expansion southwards was brought to a halt by Ramses II of Egypt in a battle near Kadesh on the Orontes. The battle was indecisive but it led to a pact determining the different areas of influence. The decomposition of the Hittite empire in the 13th century B.C. saw the rise of small states in Cilicia and northern Syria, which finally fell to the Assyrian empire in the 9th century.

According to Genesis 10:15, 1 Chronicles 1:13, Heth, the founding father of the Hittites, appears among the descendants of Shem together with Canaan. The genealogy is describing a situation of fact, that is, the presence of Hittites in Canaan. Abraham bought the cave at Machpelah from Ephron, a Hittite at Hebron (Gen. 23:10; 25:9; 49:29-30; 50:13), while Esau took to wife one of the daughters of Heth (Gen. 26:34; 27:46; 36:2). The Hittites are listed in the stereotyped groupings of the pre-Israelite inhabitants of Palestine (Ex. 3:8, 17; 13:5; 23:23, 28; Deut. 7:1; 20:17; Josh. 3:10, etc.) and they seem to have been concentrated especially in the central mountain region (Num. 13:29).

David had Hittites in his army, among them Ahimelech and Uriah (1 Sam. 26:6; 2 Sam. 11:3). Solomon had commercial dealings with the Hittite kingdoms of the north (1 Kgs. 10:29), and Hittite women were included among his numerous wives and concubines (1 Kgs. 11:1).

Hivites, *See* HORITES.

Hobab, Father-in-law of Moses (Num. 10:29; Jgs. 4:11) called Jethro in Ex. 3:1, 18:1 and also Reuel in Ex. 2:18. He is a Midianite in Numbers 10:29 but a Kenite in Judges 4:11. The uncertainty of his origins does not undermine the fact that Moses was related to the nomad tribes of the Sinai desert and to the priest of Midian (Ex. 2:18; 3:1; 18:1), who in the beginning perhaps was nameless and later identified with various personages.

Hobah, A region in Syria north of Damascus (Gen. 14:15).

Hodaviah (hod′-a-vy′-ah), Personal name (1 Chron. 3:24; 5:24; 9:7; Ezra 2:40; Neh. 7:43).

Hoglah, One of the five daughters of Zelophehad (Num. 26:33; 27:1; 36:11; Josh. 17:3). *See* INHERITANCE; ZELOPHEHAD.

Hoham (ho′-ham), King of Hebron who allied himself with the other kings of central Palestine against Joshua and the Gibeonites (Josh. 10:3).

Holiness Code, The code of laws in Leviticus 17-26. *See* LAW, PENTATEUCH.

Holofernes (hol′-o-fer′-nees), In the book of Judith he is the general of Nebuchadnezzar's army which invaded Palestine. He was beheaded by Judith who in this way saved her people and land. *See* JUDITH.

Holy, Holy and holiness (in Hebrew qadosh and qodesh) designates one of the fundamental and primary religious categories. It permits only an approximative translation and not an exhaustive translation in conceptual terms. Holy describes what is divine and pertains to God. Sanctity then is more than a divine attribute. It is his most intimate essence in which he radically transcends all that is created. To say then that God is holy and that only he is holy (Isa. 6:3) is almost repetitious, but on man's lips it makes sense, for it is his way of expressing the radical otherness of God who reveals himself as creator and savior. "I am God and not man, the Holy One present among you" (Hos. 11:9). The experience of the divine sanctity excites man at once to fascination and terror, attraction and flight, which sentiments in the Bible are expressed in the conventional gestures which are man's reaction to a theophany or manifestation of the divine (*see* Gen. 28:16, 17; Ex. 3:1-6; 20:18-21; and above all Isa. 6:1-6. *See* THEOPHANY).

Holiness extends to whatever is in relationship with the divine and is therefore one of the principal cultic categories. In this application "holy" expresses, negatively, the idea of separation and opposition to what is profane and common. Positively it expresses the idea of belonging to or being possessed by God, of consecration. The place where God appears is holy (Gen. 28:16; Ex. 3:4) and so also is the place where God has decided to fix his dwelling among men, that is, the Tabernacle in the desert (Ex. 28:43), with its two chambers, one "the Holy" and the other the "Holy of Holies" or "The Most Holy" (Ex. 26:33, 34). The Temple is holy (1 Chron. 29:3; Isa. 64:10), as is the mountain (Isa. 11:9; 56:7) and the holy city, Jerusalem (Isa. 48:2; 52:1). The cult objects, especially the altar, and the ministers of the cult are holy. Special consecration rites consign them to God (Ex. 40; Lev. 8 and 9). Holiness further extends to the gifts and victims offered to God (Lev. 22:10-16; 1 Sam. 21:5-7) and to the times reserved for worship (Neh. 10:32, *see* SABBATH). Holiness in worship places is demanded of all those who draw near to the service and take part in it. Its victims must be clean animals, and the people participating must also be in a state of ritual purity. (*See* CLEAN.) To share in the cult or in any manifestation of the divine one must pass through a ritual preparation that signifies the transition from the earthly and profane to the sacred (Ex. 19:10-11; Jgs. 7:13). God watches over the sanctity of his cult and will not leave unpunished any assault against it or against any person or thing that is consecrated to him (Lev. 10:1-7; Num. 16-17).

The notions of holy and holiness however extend in the Bible beyond the field of ritual. They are also used to express the election of Israel as the people of God (*see* ELECTION). By reason of God's choice, Israel has been consecrated to God and thus has become his special possession, a kingdom of priests and a holy people, that is, a people made over and bound to God (Ex. 19:6; Deut. 7:1-6). God watches over Israel so that no assault on this people sacred to him will go unpunished: "Sacred to the Lord was

Israel, the first fruits of his harvest; should anyone presume to partake of them, evil would befall him" (Jer. 2:3). Being God's possession, however, also places on the people certain demands which are spelled out in the Law. The Law unfolds in its multiple ritual and moral dispositions what in practice it means to belong to God and be a people consecrated to him: "Be holy, for I, the Lord, your God, am holy" (Lev. 17-26). The notion of sanctity carries with it here a sense of moral demand not formally present in its ritual or cultic use. Sanctity however does not become synonymous with morality. The demands of the one and of the other coincide materially, but sanctity is what is demanded by reason of belonging to God and being consecrated to him.

The title 'Holy One of Israel' was coined by Isaiah. In it reechoes the experience of divine sanctity that the prophet had (Isa. 6:1-6) and with it he wishes to express the paradoxical fact of a holy and transcendent God who deigns to join to himself a people, Israel. The title is at the same time a pledge of salvation and a threat of judgment. It pledges salvation, for God never abandons what belongs to him: "Shout with exultation, O City of Sion, for great in your midst is the Holy One of Israel" (Isa. 12:6; *see* 10:20). It is also a threat of judgment, for God who is holy does not tolerate anything impure around him: "For they have spurned the Law of the Lord of hosts, and scorned the word of the Holy One of Israel. Therefore the wrath of the Lord blazes against his people, he raises his hand to strike them" (Isa. 5:24, 25). The Lord brings judgment: "the Light of Israel will become a fire, Israel's Holy One a flame that burns and consumes" (Isa. 10:17). A remnant however shall be saved, the first fruits of salvation (Isa. 10:20-22).

At times one reads in the Bible that God "sanctifies himself" or "sanctifies his name." The meaning of this expression is that God manifests his holiness, that is, he reveals himself for what he is in the splendor of his transcendence. God's holiness is revealed in creation, judgment and salvation. "The Lord of hosts," writes Isaiah, "shall be exalted by his judgment and God the holy shall be shown holy by his justice" (Isa. 5:16). Deutero-Isaiah announces the title Holy One of Israel in the work of God's creation: "To whom can you liken me as an equal, says the Holy One. Lift up your eyes on high and see who has created these" (Isa. 40:25, 26). Again in the work of salvation and in concrete at the return of the Israelites from exile he is declared holy (Isa. 41:13-16). The return from exile was also for Ezekiel a revelation of God's holiness: "I will prove the holiness of my great name, profaned among the nations, in whose midst you have profaned it. Thus the nations shall know that I am the Lord, . . . when in their sight I prove my holiness through you" (Ezek. 36:23; *see* Ezek. 20:41; 39:27). To this revelation of his holiness on God's part corresponds an acknowledgement of it on man's side, that is, the sanctification of God's name. When God will have accomplished what he has announced, then the Israelites will know that he is the Lord (Ezek. 20:42) and will never again profane his holy name with idols and idolatrous cult (20:39).

The work of definitive salvation, that is, the establishment of God's kingdom, will then be the supreme sanctification of the name of God. This is the first petition of the Our Father (Matt. 6:9; Lk. 11:2; *see* LORD'S PRAYER). In the New Testament, holy, holiness and sanctification are transferred to the Christian realities as the fulfilment of what was begun in the Old Testament. Christians are holy ones, or saints, because they are members of God's new people (1 Pet. 2:9, which applies to Christians the text of Ex. 19:5). This is the title they give to themselves: God's saints (Acts 9:13; Col. 1:13), saints through vocation, that is through being called by God to be his own (Rom. 1:7; 1 Cor. 1:2; 2 Cor. 1:1; Col. 3:12).

They are holy because they have been sanctified, that is, they have been transferred from the dominion of sin and death which is inimical to God, to the kingdom of life and justice. God has the initiative in this sanctification, and through Christ he extends it to men (1 Cor. 1:30; 1 Thess. 4:5; 5:23). In each individual, sanctification takes place through faith and baptism (Rom. 15:16; 1 Cor. 6:11) which makes one belong to God (Rom. 6:19, 22). The Spirit is holy because he is divine and is the agent of our holiness. By living in us, he makes us into holy temples of God (1 Cor. 3:17; Eph. 2:21). This nearness and belonging to God, which is the Christian's holiness, demands from him a life that expresses his status as a person consecrated to God (1 Pet. 1:15; Eph. 5:3; Rom. 16:2).

Holy is also a title belonging to Christ. It is a messianic title and expresses the fact that he is the chosen one and consecrated to God (Acts 3:14; Mk. 1:24). As happens in the New Testament, one and the same title serves to designate Christians and Christ, but when applied to Christ it denotes a way of belonging to God that is over and above what can be said of Christians and eventually implies Christ's divinity.

Holy of Holies, The innermost room of the Tabernacle in the desert and of the Temple in Jerusalem (*see* TEMPLE, TABERNACLE).

home
as they were leaving for *h.*   my serving boy is at *h.*   Matt. 8:6
        1 Sam. 2:20   as you enter his *h.* bless it
Saul also went *h.* to Gibeah   Matt. 10:12
        1 Sam. 10:26

Homer, A dry measure equal to ten ephahs (Ezek. 45:11) about 450 quarts.

Honey, In Exodus 3:8 Yahweh told Moses: "Therefore I have come down to rescue them from the hands of the Egyptians and lead them out of that land into a good and spacious land, a land flowing with milk and honey." This was to become a common description of the promised land (Ex. 3:17; 13:5; 33:3; Deut. 6:3; 8:8; 27:3; Josh. 5:6, etc.). Honey can sometimes mean a thick grape or fig syrup. Besides that there was wild honey (Deut. 32:13; Ps. 81:16) and honey that was produced and counted among the fruits of the field (2 Chron. 31:5). Honey was not used in sacrifice, because, like the leaven which was also prohibited, it fermented easily (Lev. 2:11). John the Baptizer's food was locusts and wild honey (Matt. 3:4; Mk. 1:6) and his disciples offered the risen Christ at his request some grilled fish and a honey comb, which he ate before their eyes, sharing the leftovers with them (Lk. 24:43).

honor
H. your father and   for I will *h.* those who *h.* me
    Ex. 20:12; Deut. 5:6   1 Sam. 2:30
    No prophet is without *h.*   Matt. 13:57

hoofs, hooves
any animal that has *h.*   Lev. 11:3   with horns and divided *h.*
but does not have *h.*   Lev. 11:4   Ps. 69:32
    The *h.* of their horses   Isa. 5:28

Hope, Several words in the Hebrew Old Testament express the notion of expectation, hope, security. Principal among these are **batah** and **qawah.** The former describes a person being at ease, safe and secure, even complacent in that security; Isaiah warns idle women against this overconfidence and self-sufficiency (Isa. 32:9-10; *see* Jgs. 18:7, 9-10; Zeph. 2:15). The latter word reaches into the future for the reasons for that security:

Proverbs 23:17-19 tells those tempted to envy the seeming good fortune of sinners that there is a morrow, and one's hope will not be nullified. The New Testament uses **elpis**, hope, and **elpizein**, to hope. The noun expresses not only hope, but expectation or prospect (*see* Rom. 8:24; 2 Cor. 1:7) and also the one hoped in (*see* 1 Thess. 2:19; 1 Tim. 1:1; Col. 1:27), or the thing hoped for, the object of one's expectation (*see* Col. 1:5; Tit. 2:13; Rom. 8:24). The verb also can be used with an indication of what is hoped for (Lk. 6:24; Phil. 2:19; 1 Tim. 3:14; 2 Jn. 12:3) or of the person or thing that is the basis of hope (Matt. 12:21; 1 Cor. 5:19; 1 Tim. 5:5).

The Old and New Testament are promise and fulfilment respectively. The Old Testament is the history of God's promise to Abraham (Gen. 12) and his continued fidelity to that promise despite the frequent disloyalty of the people. It is understood then not simply in terms of what happened in the past, but in terms of what the past augured for the future. To Abraham God promised: "All the tribes of the earth shall bless themselves by you" (Gen. 12:3; *see* 22:18). Through the prophet Nathan, God repeated to David: "I will give you fame as great as the fame of the greatest on the earth. Your House and your sovereignty will always stand secure before me and your throne be established for ever" (2 Sam. 7:9, 16). God's word of promise was not withdrawn, even when the people sinned. Even when tragedy beset the nation in 922 B.C. and it divided into the kingdoms of Israel and Judah, hope was sustained by the prophets Elijah, Elisha, Amos, Hosea, and Isaiah. At a time when danger threatened and eventually the people were deported to Babylon (597 B.C., 587 B.C.), Jeremiah's prophecy stood in clear contrast to what seemed to be the end of Israel: "Deep within them I will plant my Law, writing it on their hearts. Then I will be their God and they shall be my people" (Jer. 31:33). God's word stood firm for their hope when they were subjugated by the Lagids (323-203 B.C.), the Seleucids (until 145 B.C.) and finally found themselves under Roman domination.

The Epistle to the Hebrews starts out thus: "In times past, God spoke in fragmentary and varied ways to our fathers through the prophets; and in this, the final age, he has spoken to us through his Son, whom he has made heir of all things and through whom he first created the universe" (Heb. 1:1). Jesus claimed himself to be the fulfilment of the prophecy of Isaiah 61:1-2: "The spirit of the Lord God has been given to me, for God has anointed me" (*see* Lk. 4:16-22; *see* Matt. 3:16; Zeph. 2:3). Jesus states that Abraham, to whom had been made the promise, "rejoiced to think he would see my Day; he saw it and was glad," and then Jesus added: "Before Abraham was, I am" (Jn. 8:56-58). Jesus then, in a way that far outstripped even the prophets' most vivid expectation, was the fulfilment of all their hopes for Israel.

Christ in his own humanity has achieved redemption for all mankind. Paul states that he wants everybody to be saved (1 Tim. 2:4). Christ surrendered himself for all mankind (1 Tim. 2:5-6). In his own flesh the full fruits of redemption are present, where now, as man, he shares with the Father the life that was his as God, and in human flesh now glorified, has become the pleader of our cause with the Father (Rom. 8:34; Heb. 7:25). His resurrection and glorification is the pledge of ours (*see* 1 Cor. 15:20; Rom. 8:11; Col. 1:18; 1 Thess. 4:14).

Baptism inserts the Christian into the life-giving mystery of his death and resurrection (Rom. 6:1-11; Col. 2:11-13). The Holy Spirit cries out in the baptized person the Abba of Christ, his plea to the Father, and with that plea lays a claim on the inheritance of Christ: "The Spirit himself gives witness with our spirit that we are children of God. But if we are children, we are heirs as well; heirs of God, heirs with Christ, if only we suffer with him so as to be glorified with him" (Rom. 8:14-17; Gal. 4:4-7). The immortal life pledged by Christ in the promise of the eucharist has already begun at baptism (Jn. 6:51-54).

The Holy Spirit lives on in Christians the life of Christ (Jn. 3:24), so that "You were sealed with the Holy Spirit who had been promised" (Eph. 1:13-14). The continuation of the life of Christ in Christians through the Holy Spirit becomes their "hope of glory" (Col. 1:27; 3:4; Eph. 2:12). His life within them is however still hidden (Col. 3:3; 1 John 3:2) but faith gives entrance to the invisible realities which are the substance of what the Christian hopes for (Heb. 11:1).

Christ has brought about the redemption of the world "once for all" (Heb. 9:12); through baptism the Christian becomes a sharer in that redemption. The decision of Christ to bring all to definitive salvation is irrevocable: salvation however can only happen between people with freedom, the freedom of God in self-gift and the freedom of the Christian in the continued reception of that gift. Paul warns the baptized Corinthians of their past, lest they should once more return to it, away from the saving Christ (1 Cor. 6:9-11). There is, then, the tension of walking through this pilgrimage keeping eyes on horizons that are only visible to faith, and only fully attainable through hope: "In hope we were saved. But hope is not hope if its object is seen; how is it possible for one to hope for what he sees? And hoping for what we cannot see means awaiting it with patient endurance" (Rom. 8:24-25).

The writings of Paul, especially 1 and 2 Thessalonians mirror a vivid awareness in the first Christians that this life will give way to another, and that we must be on our way to meet Christ at his second coming (1 Thess. 4:13-18; 5:1-11). That they were under the impression that the second coming was imminent is reflected in 1 Thess. 4:13 ff., where Paul speaks of those "of us who are still alive" when that takes place (*see* v. 16). 2 Thessalonians attempts to correct some false impressions, and offers some signs by which the second coming can be foreseen (2 Thess. 2:1-11).

Too much emphasis on the future one hopes for could lead to the abandonment of the present world's problems. The present life is not just the theater of one's trials while one awaits Christ (1 Pet. 1:6). The world itself, of which man is the crown, is caught up in one great act of giving birth (Rom. 8:22). What we are waiting for, according to 2 Peter 3:12-13, is the new heavens and the new earth, the place where righteousness abounds. The present world is the garden given by God to man to subdue and bring to perfection (Gen. 1:28-31). In obedience to this command of God man opened himself to receive, through Christ, the enriching Spirit. Just as everything was made in the Word (Jn. 1:3) so everything was made new, redeemed in the Word made flesh (Col. 1:19-20). The Christian's hope, then, is of a piece with the "longing of all creation" (Rom. 8:18-25): to this longing man gives a conscious voice. Through Christ all is renewed, and it is through his mystical body, the faithful, that Christ continues to envelop the whole world in his once-for-all redemptive act.

With faith, which admits one to the unseen realities of Christ, and love which is faith in action, hope comes to sustain the Christian through the life of pilgrimage (1 Cor. 13:13). In this pilgrimage, one's very sufferings can become one's boast, for "sufferings bring patience, patience brings perseverance, and perseverance brings hope, and this hope is not deceptive, because the love of God has been poured into our hearts by the Holy Spirit which has been given us" (Rom. 5:4-5). The Holy Spirit prompts Christians to look to faith for those rewards that righteousness hopes for (Gal. 5:5). Hope then is not just natural longing; like faith, it can only come as God's gift, an aspect of the gift of salvation that has already been set in the Christian through baptism, and, through hope, is growing to fulfilment.

The Holy Spirit is the well-spring of hope; through hope the Christian is convinced of the irrevocability of God's self-offering: "God's gifts and his call are irrevocable" (Rom. 11:29). His self-gift through Christ has so changed the world that everything, even seeming adversity, works for the Christian's good (*see* Rom. 8:28). God wants an unshaken hope to correspond to his unwithdrawn gift. So Abraham "hoped against hope," that is, even when it seemed that his hope could not be fulfilled, he hoped, and through doing so allowed God to make him the father of many nations (Rom. 4:18-19). Corresponding to God's steadfastness is the Christian's perseverance (1 Thess. 1:3). The extravagance of God's gift prompts the Christian to a hope that is audacious (2 Cor. 3:12) and free (Rom. 8:21; Gal. 5:5; 2 Cor. 3:17), for it carries him from the entanglement of the present and its pressures to the unlimited but guaranteed horizons of the future. So Paul, having reviewed the theology of hope in Romans 8:18-25, breaks out into a hymn in v. 31: "If God is for us, who can be against us?" Sufferings become, through Christ, the "trials through which we triumph" (Rom. 8:37).

Hophni (hoph′-nee), Son of Eli, priest of Shiloh, and brother of Phinehas (1 Sam. 1:3). Eli's two sons, priests like him, committed abuses in the exercise of the ministry (1 Sam. 2:12-17). Even when rebuked by their father, they refused to amend (1 Sam. 2:22-25). The young prophet Samuel announced to Eli that his house and family would be eliminated on account of the sins of his sons (2 Sam. 3). This prophecy is by an anonymous prophet in 2 Sam. 2:27-36. Both sons died in the defeat of the Israelites by the Philistines at Aphek, and the ark of the Lord which they had brought to the battle was taken by the enemy (2 Sam. 4:4, 10, 11). Eli died when he heard the news (1 Sam. 4:12-22).

Hophra, A Pharaoh in Egypt of the 26th dynasty (588-568 B.C.), son and successor of Psammetichus. Jeremiah predicted that he would have the same end as Zedekiah of Judah (Jer. 44:30). Hophra made a briefly successful attempt to back Zedekiah against Nebuchadnezzar. The latter was obliged to lift the siege of Jerusalem, but he returned as soon as Hophra departed (Jer. 37:5-11). Hophra died at the hands of a usurper, Amasis, who was general of the army.

Hor, 1. An Israelite encampment on their journey through the desert towards Canaan, between Kadesh and Edom, where Aaron died and was buried (Num. 20:22; 21:4; 33:37; Deut. 32:50; although Deut. 10:6 has it that Aaron died at Moserah).

2. A mountain in the extreme north of Israel (Num. 34:7, 8).

Horeb, *See* SINAI.

Horem, The Canaanite king of Gezer defeated and killed by Joshua (Josh. 19:38).

Horesh, A place in the desert of Ziph where David took refuge when pursued by Saul. At Horesh David met Jonathan (1 Sam. 23:15-19).

Horites, According to Deuteronomy 2:12, 22 the Horites occupied the region of Seir before the Edomites settled in the region. The Horites again appeared in the genealogy of Esau-Edom (Gen. 36:20-22; 29:30; 1 Chron. 1:39; *see* Gen. 14:6). Scholars believe that Horite should be read in the Hebrew text where Hivite is found. The name appears in the lists of pre-Israelitic people in Palestine (*see* Ex. 23:23). The Horites (Hivites) lived in central Palestine (Shechem, Gen. 34:2; Josh. 9:7; 11:19) and in northern Transjordan (Josh. 11:3; Jgs. 3:3). There is mention of them again in the time of David and Solomon (1 Sam. 24:7; 1 Kgs. 9:20).

Scholars identify the Horites with the Hurrians who are known from extra-biblical sources. Some however limit this identification to the Horites-Hivites. The Seir Horites would then be a people about whom nothing more is known. The Hurrians were an Armenoid people who settled in the Middle East from the end of the third millenium, first in Mesopotamia, then in Syria and Canaan. They took advantage of the temporary weakness of the Hittite, Egyptian and Assyrian empires to establish numerous small kingdoms in Mesopotamia and Syria, among which the kingdom of Mitanni in the region of Subartu in northern Mesopotamia gained renown in the 16th and 15th centuries B.C.

Hormah, A city in the south of Palestine in the territory of Simeon (Josh. 19:4) and of Judah (Josh. 15:30; 1 Sam. 30:30). Different traditions are connected with the name of the city which means "complete destruction." According to Numbers 14:15; Deuteronomy 1:44 the Israelites' first attempt to invade Palestine from the south failed and they were beaten back as far as Hormah. According to Numbers 21:1-3 the name of Hormah was given to the place because of the victory the Israelites won there over the king of Arad, putting the place under ban, while Judges 1:17 recounts that the city was conquered by the tribe of Simeon and Levi who changed its name from Zephat to Hormah (*see* Josh. 12:14; 1 Sam. 30:30).

Horn, The horn frequently appears in the Bible as a symbol of force or power, whether saving or destructive. In a usage that has today lost its impact, God can be called by the psalmist "my horn," or "the horn of salvation" (*see* Ps. 18:3; Lk. 1:69; 2 Sam. 22:3). Similar sayings were applied to Joseph's tribe (Deut. 33:17), to the Messiah descending from David (Ps. 132:17; Ezek. 29:21), and otherwise frequently in the Psalter (Pss. 75:5; 92:11; 112:9; 148:14). In apocalyptic literature kings are frequently symbolized by horns (*see* Dan. 7:8, 20; 8; Rev. 12:3; 13:1; 17:3, 12).

horn

the ram's *h.*	Josh. 6:5	my name shall his *h.* be exalted
the *h.* of my salvation	Ps. 18:3	Ps. 89:25
and by your favor our *h.*	Ps. 89:18	raised a *h.*	Lk. 1:69

Horonaim (hor′-o-nay′-im), A Moabite city in Transjordan (Isa. 15:5; Jer. 48:3, 34).

horror
before are struck with *h.* Job 18:20   and *h.* overwhelms me   Ps. 55:6

Horse, The horse was introduced into the Middle East by people of Indo-European origins who streamed into the region as early as the third millenium before Christ and during the second millenium. The horse was used by them to draw chariots of war. The Hyksos brought this practice to Egypt. Israel's army adopted war-chariots during the time of David and especially Solomon, who distributed chariot divisions throughout the land (*see* 2 Sam. 8:4; 1 Kgs. 5:6; 10:26; *see* CHARIOT). Horseback riding was in practice as early as the 9th century B.C. but cavalry divisions in war did not become common until the Persian and Greek period. The Bible mentions horseback riding on few occasions (*see* Esth. 6:8; perhaps in 2 Kgs. 9:17). Comparisons and figures of speech involving the horse are not infrequent in poetic texts (Isa. 63:13; Jer. 5:8; 12:5; 50:11; Amos 6:12; Hab. 3:8, 15) where, for instance, the prophesied invading army has the appearance "of horses; like steeds they run" (Joel 2:4). Job has an exhilarating description of the fearless horse: "frenzied and trembling he devours the ground" (*see* Job 39:19-25). In apocalyptic literature the horse often appears in complicated visions, and as a symbol (*see* Zech. 6:2-36; Rev. 6:2-8; 19:11, 14, 19, 21).

Hosanna, From the Hebrew **hosi'ah-nna** which means "save, we beseech," a liturgical invocation (Ps. 118:25) adopted by the crowd who received Jesus on his triumphal entry into Jerusalem (Matt. 21:9, 15; Mk. 11:9, 10; Jn. 12:13).

Hosea (hoe-zay'-a), The first of the twelve minor prophets according to the Hebrew canon of the Old Testament. The inscription to the book states that Hosea was a contemporary of Uzziah (783-742 B.C.), Jotham (742-735), Ahaz (735-715) and Hezekiah (715-687), all kings of Judah, and of Jeroboam II (786-746) king of Israel. He was a native of the north, for a while a contemporary of Amos, and exercised his prophetic ministry during the final years of the kingdom of Israel, that is, from the last years of Jeroboam and during the reigns of Menahem (745-738), Pekahiah (738-737), Pekah (737-732) and also perhaps during the reign of Hosea, his namesake (732-724). It does not seem that he lived to see the last siege of Samaria.

Of his life we know only what is narrated in cc. 1-3, which are autobiographical. God commanded him to marry a whore and Hosea had from her three children, Jezreel, "Unloved" and "No-people-of-mine." This very well-known episode has analogies in the symbolic actions of other prophets, but not on the same level. For here the very life of Hosea and the tragedy of his marriage and unfaithful wife become the vehicle of revelation: to express the despised and rejected love of a faithful God for his faithless people.

Scholars disagree on the reconstruction of the facts. A few scholars refuse to consider the story true: they would hold that here is a parable. There is however a greater discussion on whether it is a question of one or two women (1:2; 3:1), whether two episodes are recounted of the same woman, or two different versions of the same episode, one biographical (c. 2), the other autobiographical (c. 3).

The book gathers together several oracles without any apparent order. The very grave situation of the time was the context in which Hosea cast his judgment of reproof and his prediction of punishment on account of the immorality and infidelity of the people (4:4-10; 5:1-7; 7:3-7), with frequent reference to the preceding story, to the traditions of the Patriarchs and Judges where the perversity of the people first appeared (9:10-17; 10:9, 10; 11:1-6). The repeated announcement of inevitable ruin in cc. 4-13 does not however stifle the hope of a restoration that will follow after punishment (Hos. 11:7-11; 14).

The book of Hosea had a profound influence on the succeeding prophetic tradition, and especially on Jeremiah. The theme of the relationships between God and his people in the image of conjugal love inspired pages in other prophets such as Jeremiah, Ezekiel, Isaiah and perhaps also the Song of Songs. His denunciation of a cult devoid of interior content (4:11-14) and his insistence on a religion of the heart was inherited by Jeremiah and became, thanks to him, a common theme of the whole prophetic tradition.

Hoshea (hoe-she'-a), 1. Son of Nun, afterwards called Joshua by Moses (Num. 13:8, 16).

2. Son of Elah, the last king of Israel (732-724 B.C.). He usurped the throne by assassinating his predecessor Pekah (737-732), with the support of the Assyrians (1 Kgs. 15:30; 17:1). He remained a faithful vassal of the

Assyrians for some years, and then struck up a coalition with the Egyptians (1 Kgs. 17:3, 4). In retaliation the Assyrian king deposed and imprisoned him (724), laid siege to his capital Samaria, took it in 722 and deported the inhabitants (1 Kgs. 17:6-7).

Hospitality, In the desert no man can live alone, so that not only did this fact lead to very close family and tribal bonds, but it also made hospitality a necessity. The guest was received with honor and wined and dined, and a sacredness surrounded his person, so that he was immune from attack on his person for three days and for as long as the food he had eaten was still in his stomach. With some tribes this immunity reached out to a radius of many miles.

The sacredness of the guest is seen in the stories of the Patriarchs. On encountering the three men at the Terebinth of Mamre, Abraham bowed to the ground and begged the privilege of being allowed to afford them hospitality, assuring them of water to wash and bread to eat, and then slaughtered a fine calf to feed them (Gen. 18:1-8). Lot beseeched the perverse men of Sodom to spare his guests, "for they have come under the shadow of my roof." To save them, he went so far as to offer his own virgin daughter to satisfy their lust (Gen. 19:6-11; *see also* Jgs. 19:16-24).

Jesus' public work is set in the framework of hospitality, for he himself had "no where to lay his head" (Matt. 8:20; Lk. 9:58) and so is often a guest in others' homes (Lk. 7:36; 9:51 ff.; 10:38 ff.; 14:1 ff.; Mk. 1:29 ff.; etc.). Paul's long journeys were also made possible through the hospitality of the Jews and the Gentiles (Acts 14:28; 15:33; 16:15; 17:1; 18:3, 27; 21:16). Paul exhorts Christians to practice hospitality (Rom. 12:13; *see* Heb. 13:2) and Peter adds that it should be shown without murmuring (1 Pet. 4:9). Jesus likens himself to a guest knocking at the door. If it is opened to him he will come in and enjoy the hospitality.

Once more the eastern attitude returns: it is not the guest who is honored by the hospitality, but the host: "Anyone who loves me will be true to my word, and my Father will love him, he will come to him and make our dwelling place with him" (Jn. 14:23).

Hosts, Lord of, This is the customary translation of the name **Yahweh Sebaoth**. This translation directly depends on the Greek and Latin translations of the Old Testament, which translate it as **Kyrios dynameon, the Lord of the armies.** Lord is translated from the Hebrew **Adonai,** the name that with time began to replace the name Yahweh in the reading of Scripture, and later was used in the translations of the sacred text (*see* LORD). At times the Greek version of the Septuagint translates **Kyrios Pantokrator,** the Lord Almighty. It conveys the meaning while also capturing the solemnity which surrounded this name of God.

The original meaning of the term is not clear. In the most ancient texts the name is linked with God's invisible presence in the Ark of the Covenant. 1 Samuel 4:4 calls it the "Ark of the Lord of hosts, who is enthroned upon the cherubim." The title is associated with power and majesty in the Philistines' exclamation at the news that the Ark had arrived at the Hebrew camp: "Woe to us! Who can deliver us from the power of these mighty gods" (1 Sam. 4:8). This same idea of majesty and universal lordship accompanies the use of the title in Isaiah's vision of God's throne, recounted in Isa. 6:1-6: the seraphim sing out in choir before the throne of God: "Holy, holy, holy is the Lord of hosts; all the earth is filled with his glory." In Psalm 24:7-10 the title Lord of hosts seems to comprise and even exceed the titles King of glory, Lord strong and mighty, and Lord mighty in battle.

The Septuagint translation does convey the sense of the use of the term in the Hebrew. The .translation **Pantokrator** should be interpreted in the sense of **panton kraton**, that is Lord of all powers, and so comes very near to the original sense of the term.

The singular form of **sebaoth** is **saba'**, which in fact means army, especially when drawn up for war (*see* Gen. 21:22; Josh. 4:13; Jgs. 4:7; 8:6, etc.). It is not clear however to which armies reference is made. The Bible also uses the term, always in the singular, for the heavenly army (Gen. 2:1), that is, for the total of heavenly bodies who populate the heavens. Josh. 5:20 speaks of a mysterious prince of Yahweh's army, and seems to refer to the angelic hosts. On the other hand in Ex. 7:14 and 12:41 "the hosts of my people" or "the hosts of the Lord" are the Israelites. Perhaps at the beginning Yahweh **sebaoth** was the title of God who marched at the head of his people to assure them victory (*see* Ps. 68:8-11; *see* WAR). In later prophetic texts however the plural form of the term is not specific and seems to comprise the sum total of powers to underline the universal dominion of Yahweh. This is how the Greek translators understood it and translated it.

Hour, As a regular division of time, the hour was unknown in the Old Testament. The day was divided in an imprecise manner according to the position of the sun: the dawn (Josh. 6:15; 1 Sam. 30:17), the morning (Ex. 18:13), midday (1 Kgs. 18:29), the hour of heat (1 Sam. 11:11; Gen. 18:1), the sunset (Gen. 15:12, 17, etc.). The night was divided into watches. In New Testament times the Roman practice of dividing the night into four watches had been adopted (Mk. 13:35; Matt. 14:25) as had their division of the day into 12 hours of differing length according to the season (Matt. 27:45; Mk. 15:33; Lk. 23:44; Acts 3:1).

2 Kings 20:9-11 speaks of the "steps of Ahaz": as a sign from Yahweh, Isaiah had the shadow of the sundial go back ten steps for Hezekiah. Perhaps there was a system of marking the hours by the sun's shadow cast on a graduated pattern.

In the New Testament the hour is often mentioned, not as a measure of time, but to indicate a given moment, a time destined for a determined action or event. The "hour of Jesus" is a characteristic saying of John and obviously refers to Jesus' glorification which coincides with his exaltation on the cross (Jn. 12:23; 13:1; 17:1). The mention of this hour again and again in John's gospel shows clearly that it is governed by a divine plan which Jesus has come to enact (Jn. 2:4; 7:30; 8:20). This Johannine theme has very close parallels in the synoptic tradition (Mk. 14:35, 41; Lk. 22:35; Matt. 26:45).

hour

did only one *h's.* work	Matt. 20:12	Yet an *h.* is coming	Jn. 4:23
with me for even an *h.*	Matt. 26:40	It was at that very *h.*	Jn. 4:53
My *h.* has not yet come	Jn. 2:4	his *h.* had not yet come	Jn. 7:30
an *h.* is coming	Jn. 4:21	Father, the *h.* has come!	Jn. 17:1

House, Although the word for house or dwelling is used innumerable times throughout the Bible, very little is known about the construction due to the lack of ruins, which in turn suggests that the houses of the Israelites in general were not very robustly built. The word for house is **beth** but its etymology is uncertain, possibly coming from a root meaning to enter, or pass the night.

Solomon's palace at Jerusalem described in 1 Kings 7 was undoubtedly a magnificent structure, but the dwellings of the ordinary folk were unpretentious small mud or stone buildings with little wood used. The house consisted of a central room with smaller adjacent rooms for storage, and, in the case of larger dwellings, for sleeping. In the poorer houses, most of the furniture was rush matting on which the inhabitants slept and rested, and from which they ate. There were few or no windows, and the roof was made of a layer of marl and straw laid on beams and branches. It was sometimes equipped with a shelter, and the roof could be easily removed, as it was by the men carrying the paralytic in the hope of a cure from Jesus (Mk. 2:4).

Houses were clustered together both for defensive purposes and for convenience. In New Testament times, especially in urban areas, buildings were constructed to a height of several stories. From a third story window casement a young man fell to his death while attending the Lord's Supper in Troas. Paul however raised him to life (Acts 20:7-12).

House in Hebrew and Greek could refer to a family or dynasty. Yahweh promised David: "Your house and your kingdom shall endure forever before me; your throne shall stand firm forever" (2 Sam. 7:16). Exodus 1:21 recounts that because the midwives feared God he "built them (the Israelites) houses," meaning that he granted them descendants.

howl
H., for the day of the Lord   *H.*, O gate; cry out   Isa. 14:31
    Isa. 13:6   and *h.* for anguish of spirit
         Isa. 65:14

Hul, An Aramean group or kingdom listed among the sons of Shem in the Table of Nations (Gen. 10:23).

Huldah, A prophetess of Jerusalem, wife of Shallum who was wardrobe keeper for King Josiah (640-609 B.C.). She was consulted by Hilkiah the priest about the discovery in the Temple of a book of the law (2 Kgs. 22:15-20). Huldah's oracle threatened disaster to the city because of its not having observed the Lord's law, but she had comforting words for Josiah.

humble
He guides the *h.* to justice   Ps. 25:9   I am gentle and *h.* of heart
         Matt. 11:29

humbled
h. themselves and prayed   *h.* yourself before God
    2 Chron. 7:14   2 Chron. 34:27

hundred
Shem was one *h.* years old   a *h.* Philistine foreskins
    Gen. 11:10   2 Sam. 3:14
    laden with two *h.* loaves   2 Sam. 16:1

Hunting, Nimrod, whose name became proverbial (Gen. 10:9), was a mighty hunter in the eyes of Yahweh. Jacob's son Esau became a skilled hunter, a man of the open country (Gen. 25:27). When Isaac was old and near to death, he asked Esau to go with bow and arrow and hunt some game for him so that he might give him his blessing before he died. Jacob however with the cooperation of Rebekah his mother obtained the blessing by trickery (Gen. 27).

When the Israelites had settled, they did not depend on hunting for food, but game is listed among Solomon's daily provisions: deer and gazelles, roebucks and the cuckoo. Deuteronomy 14:3 lists, among game animals that it was licit to eat, the deer, gazelle, roebuck, ibex, antelope, oryx, and perhaps wild mountain sheep, while the hare and the hyrax were forbidden. When game was caught that was lawful to eat, its blood had to be poured out and covered with earth, for the life of all flesh is its blood (Lev. 17:14).

There are references in the Bible to hunting for the protection of flocks or for defense. As proof of his ability to tackle Goliath, David boasted that if a lion or a bear came and took a sheep from the flock, he would follow him and strike him down and rescue the sheep from his mouth, and if the wild beast turned on him, David would seize him by the hair of his jaw and strike him down and kill him (1 Sam. 17:34-37). Judges 14:6 recounts that Samson tore a lion to pieces with his bare hands.

Jeremiah in 16:16 predicts punishment in terms of "huntsmen who will hunt them out of every mountain, every hill, out of the holes in the rocks." The fall of Egypt is foretold by Ezekiel in hunting terms: the hunters themselves will go down with the slaughtered in spite of the terror they inspired, they too will go down into the pit (Ezek. 32:30).

Hur, 1. In the traditions of Ex. 17:10-12 and 24:14, Hur and Aaron are Moses' closest collaborators. They both supported Moses' arms on the mountain while the Israelites fought the Amalekites (Ex. 17:10-12). They cared for the people while Moses was alone on Mt. Sinai to receive the decalogue from God (Ex. 24:14).

2. Probably not the same person as above, Hur is named founding father of some clans of Judah in several genealogies (1 Chron. 2:19, 50; 4:1, 4).

3. One of the Midianite kings defeated by Moses (Num. 31:8; Josh. 13:21).

hurry
H., escape there	Gen. 19:22
	H. back, then, to my father
	Gen. 45:9

husband
and the second *h.*, too, comes	her *h.'s* brother shall go to her
Deut. 24:3	Deut. 25:5
former *h.*, who dismissed her	For my *h.* is not at home
Deut. 24:4	Prov. 7:19
Yes, all will be taken, *h.* and wife	Jer. 6:11

Hushai (hoosh′-eye), One of David's counselors, who remained faithful to the king during Absalom's revolt. He stayed on in Jerusalem, when David had to flee, in order to feign friendship with Absalom, gather information and keep David informed of Absalom's intentions so as to foil the latter's plans (2 Sam. 15:32-37; 16:15-19). On Hushai's advice Absalom delayed the pursuit of David, which afforded the latter time to prepare for battle (2 Sam. 17:23).

Husham, A king of Edom Gen. 36:34, 35; 1 Chron. 1:45, 46).

Hyksos (hik′-sos), The name given by the Egyptians to the people who towards the end of the eighteenth century B.C. invaded the region of the Nile delta from Asia. The name means foreign rulers. They succeeded in winning power in Egypt around 1670 B.C. and retained it for a century. They made the city of Avaris, later called Tanis, in the eastern region of the delta, their capital. They were expelled from Egypt in 1570 B.C. by the Pharaohs of the eighteenth dynasty.

The ethnic origin of the Hyksos is not known with any precision. Their invasion of Egypt was probably due to pressure exercised from the north by non-Semite peoples who in those centuries were pushing into northern Mesopotamia and Syria. Some scholars think that the settlement of the Israelites in Egypt was part of this wave of movement of peoples southwards. Moreover these authors would find in a regime of foreigners like that of the Hyksos a better explanation for the remarkable political success of a Joseph, himself too a foreigner.

Hymenaeus (hie′-me-nee′-us), A Christian who lost his faith and was consigned by Paul to Satan, that is, he was excommunicated (1 Tim. 1:29). In all probability he is the same person who is mentioned with Philetus in 2 Timothy 2:17, 18, rebuked for the "corrosive gangrene" of their assertions that the resurrection had already taken place.

Hymn, A lyrical literary style very common to the Bible from earliest times, as is exemplified by Miriam's canticle (Ex. 15:1-21) and Deborah's song (Jgs. 5). The Psalter abounds with hymns (e.g. Pss. 8, 19, 29, 33, 65, 67, 100, 103, 104, 105, 111, 113, 114, 135, 136, 145, 146, 147, 148, 149, 150) and they are present too in other Old Testament books, and in the New Testament, which contains the celebrated **Magnificat** (Lk. 1:46-55), the **Benedictus,** or Zechariah's canticle (Lk. 1:68-79) and Simeon's song (Lk. 2:29-32). Paul's letters contain traces or fragments of Christological hymns (*see* Phil 2:5-11; Col. 1:13-20; 1 Tim. 3:16).

The hymn is a song of praise and generally takes this shape: a. The introduction as an invitation to praise God, directed to others or spoken to oneself; this introduction can be prolix, as it is itself praise of God, as for example Ps. 150 which consists completely of an invitation to praise God. b. The body of the hymn sings the reasons for praising God, his attributes or better, his works in nature or history. c. The conclusion often returns to the introduction theme, or in some cases, this invitation is repeated throughout the hymn at intervals to separate the verses (e.g:, Pss. 98:4, 8; 147:1, 7, 12).

hypocricy
while *h.* fills   Matt. 23:28

hypocrite, hypocrites
You *h.!* Remove the plant   O you *h.!*   Lk. 13:15
                    Matt. 7:5

Hyrcanus, 1. *See* HASMONEAN.

2. 2 Mac. 3:11 speaks of a certain Hyrcanus who had a large amount of money deposited in the Temple treasury.

Hyssop, A small plant with branches and dense leaves which grew on walls (1 Kgs. 5:13) and was used in rituals to sprinkle blood and water (Ex. 12:22; Lev. 14:4-6; 14:49-52; Num. 19:18; Heb. 9:19; *see* Ps. 51:9). According to John 19:29 the soldiers offered Jesus on the cross a vinegar-soaked sponge on a hyssop stick. Since this was hardly a convenient way to do it, some authors have changed the reading in favor of a similar Greek word which means lance (**hysso** for **hyssopo**), while others guess that John, in his own style, was making a symbolic allusion to the paschal rite.

I

Ibhar, Son of David born in Jerusalem (2 Sam. 5:15; 2 Chron. 3:6; 14:5).

Ibleam (ib′-le-am), A city in the land of Issachar, and later in that of Manasseh (Josh. 17:11-12). It probably did not become Israelite until the time of the monarchy (Jgs. 1:27). It was a Levitical city of Manasseh (1 Chron. 6:55).

Ibzan, One of the minor judges born at Bethlehem, according to Judges 12:8-10. He had thirty sons and as many daughters whom he gave in marriage outside his clan, while he brought in thirty brides for his sons. He ruled as judge for seven years and when he died was buried in Bethlehem.

ice
Though they may be black with *i*.   Out of whose womb comes the *i*.
                    Job 6:16   Job 38:29

Ichabod, Son of Phinehas and nephew of Eli, the priest of Shiloh. His mother gave birth to him when she heard the news of the death of Phinehas, which took place in the battle of Aphek against the Philistines. In this battle the Israelites were defeated and the Ark captured (1 Sam. 4:21). His name is again read in the genealogy of Ahijah, who was priest during Saul's reign (1 Sam. 14:3).

Iconium, The capital city of Lycaonia in Asia Minor, in the Roman province of Galatia after 25 B.C. It was visited by Paul during his first apostolic journey with Barnabas (Acts 13:51-14:6) and also probably during his second journey, even though Acts 16:1 only mentions the nearby cities of Derbe and Lystra.

Iddo, Seer and prophet whose writings are cited as sources for the Chronicler for the reigns of Rehoboam and Abijah (2 Chron. 12:15; 2 Chron. 13:22).

identify
He failed to *i*. him   Gen. 27:23

idle
you been standing here *i*.
                    Matt. 20:6

idleness
eats not her food in *i*.   Prov. 31:27

Idol, Idolatry, From the Greek **eidolon,** which means "image." The term idol received a more precise meaning as a sacred image, the cultic representation of a divinity. Idolatry in itself would be the worship offered to the material representation of a divinity, but the term also involves a negative judgment on any such religion. This negative judgment is presupposed in the biblical polemics against idolatrous cults. This polemic however arises from a rigorous monotheistic concept which already has taken a definite stand on the question of idols as these were understood in other religions. Several questions then can be distinguished.

a. The idols of the non-biblical religions: To give a fair judgment on the use and function of the idol in the context of non-biblical religions, one must beware of two extremes. In the first place the idols were not identified with the gods they represented. While biblical polemics took it that they *were* identified with the gods they represented, it must be remembered that the Bible attacks from a firm monotheistic position which other religions did not share. On the other hand it would be mistaken to think that the idols were simply representations of the god, with no other relationship than a merely intentional one between them and the divinity. The idol was the privileged place of the god's active presence. It was therefore the place of contact between the god and the worshipper. The idol then was framed in a concept of nature as the epiphany of the god and of the divine world as the transfiguration of nature. Between them was a real bond of communication that was difficult to conceptualize but nevertheless clearly expressed in the symbolic language of the myth. This is why the destruction, loss or capture of an idol was an immense tragedy, for it deprived the group of the center on which their religious life converged, and at which the divinity with his power was in contact with them. This obviously lent itself to a magical concept and veneration of the idol. The god in the idol became something man could manipulate. Moreover man could become so attached to the representation that for him his god was really there, and eventually reduced to the dimensions of the created image, until eventually the image itself was no longer considered the god's representation but the god himself.

b. The anti-idolatry polemic. The Bible pronounces judgment on idolatry in two different contexts: in the anti-idolatry polemic and in the absolute prohibition of images. The first is found above all in the prophets of the exile (Isa. 40:18-20; 44:9-20) and of a short time previous to it (Jer. 10:1-16), as well as in some psalms that stemmed from the same era (Ps. 115:3-8) and Jeremiah's letter added to the book of Baruch (Bar. 6:3-8). The date is important, for only then has Israel added to its practical monotheism (the demand for the exclusive worship of Yahweh, prescribed in the Decalogue—Ex. 20:2) a theoretical monotheism, that is, the negation of the very existence of other gods besides Yahweh. It is no longer a question of not worshipping other gods: they simply do not exist. This point of view was obviously not shared by those who took part in idolatrous worship, but from it the prophets launched their attack. They did not interest themselves in what the idol might stand for or represent for the worshipper, as already explained. With implacable sarcasm they pour ridicule on those who worship a piece of wood or metal as if it were god, while to it no transcendent reality corresponded. The prophets were justified in this over-simplification of the facts in that their concern was not the sincere worshipper of another religion, but the Israelite who in a strange land might be fascinated into worshipping an idol. The prophets gravely warn them and give an objective judgment on such worship from the theological position of Yahwist monotheism.

c. In the light of these considerations we can attempt an explanation of the meaning of the prohibition of images (Ex. 20:4; Lev. 19:4; Deut. 4:15-20; 5:8). According to the unanimous opinion of scholars, this prohibition is one of the most ancient and genuine pieces of Mosaic legislation in the Hebrew religion. In the Decalogue the prohibition is intended to prevent images or representations of Yahweh himself, but already a very ancient addition (Ex. 20:4b-5) extends the prohibition to every figure or representation in the Israelite worship. This then covered not only images of Yahweh but also those of other gods. With this addition the second precept repeats once more the exclusion of other gods from the Israelite cult, which had been stated in the first precept. This also seems to be the interpretation proposed by Deuteronomy 4:15-20, which, to justify the precept, calls on the normative character of the Sinai revelation, where the people heard the voice of God and saw no image.

The second commandment does not exclude the cherubim above the ark, because they in no way represent God, but the throne on which he invisibly reigns. (*See* ARK OF THE COVENANT, CHERUB.) Nor does it exclude the two golden calves that Jeroboam of Israel (922-901) made for the temples of Bethel and Dan, as they too were rather the pedestals on which God was invisibly present. (*See* CALF, GOLDEN.) These however could easily lend themselves to the adoration of the faithful who might venerate them as true idols. Thus Hosea and the deuteronomic tradition condemned them. The prohibition of images of Yahweh is without parallel in ancient religious life. This prohibition obviously is intended to announce something about God, namely his transcendence. This is not simply in the sense that no image is capable of truly representing him because it is inferior to him. Rather, in contrast with religions that indulged in idols, the Israelite revelation insisted on the radical otherness of God: he was utter-ly distinct from his creation. He is in no way enveloped in nature, but stands over against it as its creator. There is then neither real nor mythical continuity between God and nature, and so the idol becomes superfluous. To admit it would be radically to change the countenance and concept of the God Yahweh. *See* MYTH.

Idumaea (id′-you-me′-a), The Greek name for the region of Edom. *See* EDOM.

if

I. you do well, you can hold   And *i.* they will not believe
           Gen. 4:7   Ex. 4:9
I. Cain is avenged sevenfold   *I.* you refuse to let him go
           Gen. 4:24   Ex. 4:23
I. they will not believe you Ex. 4:8 *I.* you fear the Lord 1 Sam. 12:14

Igal, 1. Son of Joseph (Num. 13:7).

2. Son of Nathan (2 Sam. 23:36).

3. Son of Shecaniah (1 Chron. 3:22).

Igdaliah (ig′-da-lie′-ah), A prophet of Jerusalem (Jer. 35:4).

ignominy
Filled with *i.*   Job 10:15

ignorance
that you acted out of *i.*   Acts 3:17 I do not want to leave you in *i.*
you are thus worshiping in *i.*   1 Cor. 12:1
        Acts 17:23 because of their *i.*   Eph. 4:18
        shaped you in your *i.* 1 Peter 1:14

ignorant
I do not want you to be *i.*
        Rom. 11:25

Ijon, An Israelite town south of Mount Hermon captured by King Ben-hadad of Damascus during the reign of Baasha of Israel (1 Kgs. 15:20; 2 Chron. 16:4).

Ilai (eye′-lie), One of the Thirty warriors of David (1 Chron. 11:29).

ill
Moses fared *i.* on their account   your *i.* repute cease not
        Ps. 106:32   Prov. 25:10
        All goes *i.*, with the work Isa. 3:11

illegitimate
We are no *i.* breed   Jn. 8:41

ill-formed
scrawny, most *i.* and gaunt
        Gen. 41:19

illicit
by having *i.* relations   Num. 25:1

illumine
His lightnings *i.* the world Ps. 97:4

Illyria, The region on the east coast of the Adriatic, which became a Ro-man province around 9 A.D. In Romans 15:19 Paul boasts of having fulfilled his ministry from Jerusalem to Illyria. He probably does not in-tend to say that he preached in the region, but it is quoted as being the boundary of Macedonia, which was in fact evangelized by Paul, and was the most westerly point to which, at that time, the Apostle had reached.

Image of God, Besides the prohibition in the Decalogue against making images of God, and the polemics against idolatry, the biblical expression "image of God" did have its applications and developments in anthropology and christology.

a. Man, God's image: The most important, and almost the only text dealing with man's creation is the Priestly account in Gen. 1:26, 27. This text speaks of the species of man, and therefore in a collective sense. Man is said to be created "in the image and likeness of God." God deliberated: "Let us make man in our own image" (v. 26). The same is repeated after the deluge in Genesis 9:6. It is never explained however in what sense exactly is man made to God's image. This surprising silence prompts the search for the exact meaning of being God's image. It has been noted that in Egypt, among the titles attributed to the Pharaoh was the following: "The Pharaoh is the living image of the god Ra," and yet more explicitly "the Pharaoh is the splendid image of the Lord of the universe. . . . Ra (the god) begot him in order to have his own progeny on earth, for the salvation of men, his own living image." From this and other texts it seems clear that to be the image means to represent: to be God's image means to be God's representative. Through his image God appears on earth. It is not then a case of searching out some likeness between God and man which would justify the phrase "God's image." Rather it is a question of function: man is in God's stead on earth, he is God's representative. Man, in God's place and as God's representative, exercises dominion over all that is in the universe. Man is there, in God's place and name, to fill the earth and "conquer it" (1:28). This interpretation is confirmed by Psalm 8, which has an equivalent phrase: man is not said to be God's image, but to be made "a little less than God," and this is explained in the sense of a universal vicarious dominion which man, in God's place, holds. Sirach 17:3 explicitly poses the problem of man's likeness to God and answers the question similarly. Man is God's image because he dominates creation. So that he might exercise this dominion God has vested man with God's power and inspired every living thing with fear of him. Man then has been created king of the created order, God's vicar on earth, endowed with God's strength so that the animal kingdom stands in awe of him.

The question is proposed and resolved in a slightly different manner in Wisdom 2:23, and this already announces the christological application. The author considers the origin of death and of the creative plan of God and so teaches that "God made man imperishable, and created him to the image of his own nature, and of his own eternity"—that is, God created man to make him a sharer in God's incorruptibility and eternity.

b. Christ, God's image: "[Christ] is the image of the invisible God" (Col. 1:15). This declaration of Paul recalls Wisdom 7:26. In fact the hymns of Wisdom (*see* WISDOM) were the principal sources from which Paul and John drew inspiration when they formulated the relationships between Christ-God and God the Father. This however is more than a consideration of the relationships within the Trinity. For the relationships between Father and Son were never considered by the New Testament except in so far as they had to do with the order and economy of salvation. Moreover the theme of Christ, the image of God, with its background in biblical anthropology, evoked the theme of Christ as the second Adam, the head and author of redeemed humanity. Christ is in truth God's image (*see* Heb. 2:5-9 where to Christ is applied Ps. 8, referred to above). His resurrection invested him with glory and power (2 Cor. 4:4). He is the new creation which involves all the believers (2 Cor. 5:17; Col. 3:10) and to which all the faithful must be likened, being more and more transformed to his image (2 Cor. 3:18; Rom. 8:29). Christ is God's image, for in his glorified humanity he is the first fruits of the new creation. Through him all will be transformed to become truly as he is, God's image.

Imalkue (i-mal′-cue-a), An Arabian prince who had charge of the young Antiochus VI, son of the Seleucid king Alexander Balas (1 Mac. 11:39).

imitate
and *i*. their faith   Heb. 13:7

Imlah, The father of the prophet Micaiah (1 Kgs. 22:8, 9).

Immanuel, *See* EMMANUEL.

immediately
Go up *i*., for you should not   *I*. the man's leprosy disappeared
       Sam. 9:13   Matt. 8:3
and *i*. they abandoned boat   and *i*. they could see   Matt. 20:34
       Matt. 4:22

immigrant
came here as an *i*.   Gen. 19:9

immoral
if he is *i*., covetous   1 Cor. 5:11

immortal
To the King of ages, the *i*.
       1 Tim. 1:17

immortality
and *i*. by patiently doing right   and the mortal *i*.   1 Cor. 15:54
       Rom. 2:7   brought life and *i*. into clear
this mortal body with *i*.   2 Tim. 1:10
       1 Cor. 15:53

impaled
to be lifted up and *i*. on it
       Ezra 6:11

Impalement, An ancient method of execution in which the condemned person was fixed on a pointed stake stuck in the ground or in a wall. The edict of Darius discovered at Ecbatana authorizing the building of the Temple carried with it the sanction that anyone disobeying the emperor's orders "should be pilloried upright on a beam torn from his house" (Ezra 6:11). Impalement is probably referred to several times in the Old Testament (Num. 25:4; Deut. 21:22-23; Josh. 8:29; 2 Sam. 21:6, 9; Esth. 9:14). *See* HANGING.

impartial
you must be *i*.   Deut. 16:19

impartiality
act with complete *i*.   1 Tim. 5:21

impatient
you are *i*.   Job 4:5   And why should I not be *i*.
       Job 21:4

impediment
who had a speech *i*.   Mk. 7:32

impenitent
your hard and *i*. heart   Rom. 2:5

imperishable
but we a crown that is *i*.
1 Cor. 9:25

implore
I *i*. you in God's name   Mk. 5:7

impose
it is not permitted to *i*.   Ezra 7:24

Imposition of Hands, *See* HANDS, IMPOSITION OF.

impossible
Nothing would be *i*. for you   Things that are *i*.   Lk. 18:27
                     Matt. 17:20   it is *i*. to make them repent
it is *i*.   Heb. 6:6
   Matt. 19:26; Mk. 10:27; Lk. 1:37

imprisoned
that I *i*. those who believed
                     Acts 22:19

imprisonment
or a fine on his goods, or *i*.   scourging, even chains and *i*.
                     Ezra 7:26   Heb. 11:36

impudent
and with an *i*. look says to him
                     Prov. 7:13

imputes
is the man to whom the Lord *i*.
                     Rom. 4:8

Incense, A mixture of aromatic gums and resins. The burning of incense
had an important place in Israelite worship. According to Exodus 30:1-6
an altar was set up before the veil that was in front of the ark of Testimony, on which morning and evening the priest burned fresh incense. A
similar altar figures in the description of the furnishings of Solomon's
Temple (1 Kgs. 6:20-21; 7:48). There are probable allusions to other altars of incense (Lev. 26:30; 2 Chron. 14:4; 34:4, 7; Isa. 17:8; 27:9; Ezra
6:4-6). The offering of incense had particular importance on the Day of
Atonement (Lev. 16:12-13). Particular directions were given for the composition of the incense for worship: storax. onycha, galbanun, sweet
spices and pure frankincense were blended together in equal parts to
make a "salted, pure, holy" incense. This then was ground into a fine
powder. It was forbidden to use this mixture for profane use under pain of
being outlawed from the people (Ex. 30:34-37). These and other aromatic
substances were imported from Arabia (1 Kgs. 10:2-10; 2 Chron. 9:19;
Isa. 60:6; Jer. 6:20). Incense was one of the gifts the Magi offered the
infant Jesus (Matt. 2:11). In figurative use, the prayers of the just ascend
like incense to the throne of God (Ps. 141:2; Rev. 5:8; 8:3-4).

Incest, The general norm on incest is laid down in Leviticus 18:6; "None
of you shall approach a close relative to have sexual intercourse with her."
Then follows a list of specific prohibitions, spelling out the norm. Nobody
may have intercourse with father or mother, father's wife, sister or half-
sister, granddaughter, aunt on father's or mother's side, uncle's wife,
daughter-in-law, sister-in-law, or with a mother and daughter, or two sisters. The patriarchs however were broader in practice than was the Leviticus law. Reuben had intercourse with Bilhah, his father's concubine
(Gen. 35:22), which however Jacob decried. Lot's two daughters got their

father drunk and by him mothered, one the Moabites and the other the Sons of Ammon (Gen. 19:30-38). When Tamar lost her husbands, Er and Onan, Judah's sons, he refused her his third son Shelah, whereupon by a trick she had intercourse with Judah and conceived a son (Gen. 38).

The punishment for incest (Lev. 20:21) is childlessness, but for the more serious crimes such as having intercourse with one's father's wife or daughter-in-law the penalty was death for both. If a man has intercourse with a woman and her mother, all three should be burned to death.

St. Paul upbraids the Corinthian church for tolerating in its midst a man living with his father's wife: he should be expelled from the community. Paul said that "united in spirit with you and empowered by our Lord Jesus, I hand him over to Satan for the destruction of his flesh, so that his spirit may be saved on the day of the Lord" (1 Cor. 5:1-5).

incline
i. your ears to the words   Ps. 78:1   Let not my heart *i.* to the evil
I. my heart to your decrees   Ps. 141:4
                   Ps. 119:36

incorruptibility
corruptible frame takes on *i.*   1 Cor. 15:54

incorruptible
what rises is *i.*   1 Cor. 15:42   the dead will be raised *i.*
                                                            1 Cor. 15:52

increase, increases
He must *i.* while I must decrease   And may the Lord *i.* you
                   Jn. 3:30   1 Thess. 3:12
in order to *i.* offenses   Rom. 5:20   speech *i.* his persuasiveness
and *i.* your generous yield   Prov. 16:21
                2 Cor. 9:10   and *i.* the faithless among men
                                                            Prov. 23:28

incurable
him with an *i.* disease   pain continuous, my wound *i.*
            2 Chron. 21:18   Jer. 15:18
            I. is your wound   Jer. 30:12

indescribable
Thanks be to God for his *i.* gift   2 Cor. 9:15

India, The name of the country that formed the eastern boundary of the empire of Ahasuerus (Esth. 1:1; 8:9). Not the present-day sub-continent is meant, but the territory through which the Indus River flows, a region conquered by Darius. Caravans from "India" brought luxury goods to Palestine (Ezek. 27:15, 19, 24).

indictment
For the Lord has an *i.* against   Jer. 25:31

indignant
became *i.* at the two brothers   Jesus became *i.* when he
                   Matt. 20:24   Mark 10:14
the scribes became *i.* when   on hearing this, became *i.*
                   Matt. 21:15   Mark 10:41
            i. that Jesus should have   Lk. 13:14

indignation
shocked and seethed with *i.*   *i.* slays the simpleton   Job 5:2
                   Gen. 34:7

industrious
he was also an *i.* young man
                    1 Kgs. 11:28

Inerrancy, Inerrancy, for the Bible, not only means that no errors are
found there, but also that no errors are possible there. Inerrancy is no
more than a logical conclusion of inspiration. If God is the principal author of Scripture, it cannot contain errors. One must however understand
inerrancy correctly. While inerrancy extends to the whole Bible, it refers
only to what the sacred author intends to affirm and with that degree of
certitude with which it is affirmed. It is obvious that no author commits his
whole authority and responsbility to each and every material assertion in
his work. Any writer at work makes use of a whole panorama of opinions,
concepts and mental categories which go to make up the cultural background. No author intends to pronounce himself personally on how well
founded or established this whole background is. These opinions, concepts, mental categories are, as it were, vehicles of thought, an extension
of the language in which we formulate our concepts. It is to our own
concepts or thought that we commit ourselves.

During the last century and at the beginning of this one the question of
inerrancy was vehemently discussed. Today there is a greater understanding of the mechanism of language and human thought, and a better comprehension of literary genres and of the ways in which ancient Middle
Eastern literatures expressed themselves. All this has contributed to a better understanding of the terms of the problem. In this new climate Vatican
II has taken up the traditional thought of the Church on the inerrancy of
Scripture and has given it a more positive and richer expression. This is
contained in the Constitution **Dei Verbum** on Sacred Revelation: "Since
everything asserted by the inspired authors or sacred writers must be held
to be asserted by the Holy Spirit, it follows that the books of Scripture
must be acknowledged as teaching firmly, faithfully, and without error
that truth which God wanted put into the sacred writings for the sake of
our salvation" (**Dei Verbum** III, 11). These words clearly establish the
ambit of the teaching which the Bible wants to transmit, what then it
offers, and what can be expected from it.

The object of biblical teaching is the saving plan of God as it unfolds until
it is brought to its fulfilment in Christ. The Bible documents the **progressive** revelation of salvation. It does not hide, then, the still imperfect beginnings, which however must be viewed in the light of the perfect end to
which they tend. On the other hand the decisive and perfect stage of the
work of Christ should not be detached from its age-long preparation in
which it is rooted. This double movement, towards the beginnings and
towards the end, shows forth the coherence of the same saving design and
the profound unity of biblical revelation despite the multiplicity of voices
and human authors. (*See* DEI VERBUM IV, V.)

inexcusable
who judges another is *i.*   Rom. 2:1

infancy
from your *i.* you have known
                    2 Tim. 3:15

infant, infants
an *i.* who lives but a few days   and women, children and *i.*
                    Isa. 65:20   1 Sam. 15:3
          men of flesh, as *i.* in Christ   1 Cor. 3:1

inferior
take your place, *i.* to yours   In what way are you *i.* to the
                    Dan. 2:39   2 Cor. 12:13

infirmities
It was our *i.* he bore   Matt. 8:17

inflames
while wine *i.* them   Isa. 5:11

informed
You have been *i.* that you teach
                    Acts 21:21

inhabitants
making me loathsome to the *i.*   I will sling away the *i.*   Jer. 10:18
                    Gen. 34:30   against the *i.* of the land
drove out the *i.* of the land   Hosea 4:1
                    2 Chron. 20:7   Let the *i.* of Sela exult   Isa. 42:11

inherit
and his descendants *i.* the land   no slanderers or robbers will *i.*
                    Ps. 25:13   1 Cor. 6:10
and *i.* everlasting life   Matt. 19:29 flesh and blood cannot *i.*
I. the kingdom prepared for   1 Cor. 15:50
                    Matt. 25:34

Inheritance, The legislative texts referring to the rights of inheritance are
very scarce. Deuteronomy 21:15-17 is only concerned with protecting the
rights of the first-born. To him went a double share of whatever his father
owned, even if the father had another son by a second and better-loved
wife, for this (true) first-born is the first fruit of his strength, and the right
of the first-born is his (vv. 16, 17). Numbers 27:1-11 tackles the case of a
man who dies without male issue. In this case, Yahweh decided through
Moses that the property should pass to his daughter; if there is none, to
his brothers; if there is none, to his father's brothers; if there is none, to
the member of his clan who is most nearly related (vv. 8-11). Verses 1-4
recount the circumstances and tell the purpose of this ordinance: Zelophehad son of Hepher of the tribe of Manasseh had five daughters and no
son. The daughters pleaded with Moses, Eleazar the priest and the community leaders to provide for his name to be continued in the clan, since it
was through no fault of his own that he had no sons. Numbers 36:6-9
adds some dispositions concerning the marriage of daughters who are
heirs: "every daughter who inherits property in any of the Israelite tribes
shall marry someone belonging to a clan of her own ancestral tribe, in
order that all the Israelites may remain in possession of their own ancestral heritage. Thus no heritage can pass from one tribe to another, but all
the Israelite tribes will retain their own ancestral heritage" (Num. 36:8,
9).

The adopted sons of slave girls were treated like the sons of free wives and
so had their share in the inheritance. The sons of Bilhah, Rachel's slave
girl, and of Zilpah, Leah's slave girl are treated in the same way as the
sons of the free wives. This norm was not observed by Abraham and
Sarah, who sent away from home Ishmael and his slave mother Hagar, so
that he might not have a share in Isaac's inheritance (Gen. 21:9, 10).
Widows are excluded from the inheritance. They remain with the oldest
son, and if they have no sons they return to the house of their father
(Gen. 38:11; Lev. 22:13; Ruth 1:8). They can however pass over to the
household of the deceased husband through a levirate marriage (*see* LEVI-

RATE; *see* Ruth 2-4). At least in the early days of the monarchy, the king's harem passed to his successor (2 Sam. 12:8; 16:21-22).

To the sons of Aaron came no inheritance in the land. God himself was to be their portion and their inheritance among the sons of Israel (Num. 18:20) while the Psalmist (Ps. 16:5) sings of "The Lord, my heritage, my cup." Joel's prayer for deliverance is that Yahweh should not make his heritage a thing of shame. The Lord in answer pledges to call to judgment those who have dealt badly with "Israel, my people and my heritage" (Joel 3:2).

In the definitive salvation brought about by Christ, those who believe and are baptized become coheirs to his inheritance (Rom. 8:17; Gal. 4:4-6). The seal of the Holy Spirit, stamped on the Christian, becomes the pledge of that inheritance (Eph. 1:14), God's assurance to us that what has been begun in us will come to full fruit (2 Cor. 1:22).

inheritance

mountain of your *i*.	Ex. 15:17	and my *i*., Israel	Isa. 19:25
have no share in the Lord's *i*.		and then we shall have his *i*.	
	1 Sam. 26:19		Matt. 21:38

iniquities

For my *i*. have overwhelmed me	Blest are they whose *i*. are
Ps. 38:5	Rom. 4:7

Ink, A chemical analysis of the remains of ancient ink reveals that it was made of burned remains of ivory, wood or other material which were then suspended in a gum solution. The natural product of the sepia was also used. Metallic ink was a relatively more recent product. Ink is mentioned in Jeremiah 36:18; 2 Corinthians 3:3; 3 John 13. Other colored substances or dyes were also used in writing, such as red lead, purple, and in the Christian centuries even liquified gold and silver.

ink

I wrote them down with *i*.	a letter written not with *i*.
Jer. 36:18	2 Cor. 3:3

Inn, Survival alone was impossible in the desert and so hospitality was a necessity for the traveler, out of which nomads made a virtue, vying with one another for the honor of receiving the guest. (*See* HOSPITALITY.) The virtue of hospitality stayed with the Israelites even after they settled down. The Hebrew word for lodging place embraced many kinds of shelter or places in which to spend the night, be it for individuals (Jer. 9:2; Exod. 4:24; Gen. 42:27) or for whole armies or nations (2 Kgs. 19:23; Josh. 4:3, 8). Kahn Kimham, where the people under Johanan made a halt on their flight to Egypt, was either the habitation or the inn of Kimham, near Bethlehem. Some have thought to identify it with the inn of Luke 2:7, but it is unlikely, as this was in Bethlehem. The Greek word used here, **kataluma,** could mean a special room for guests or for eating, as is its meaning in Mark 14:14; Luke 22:11, the place where Jesus and his disciples ate the Last Supper. The Good Samaritan left the wounded traveler at a **pandocheion** on the road between Jerusalem and Jericho, and paid the innkeeper, so perhaps here is something more in the line of a modern boarding house, pension or hotel. Tradition has identified this inn of the gospel with Khan el-Ahmar or Kahn Hathrur on the way from Jerusalem to Jericho.

inn

and brought him to an *i*. Lk. 10:34

innocence
I wash my hands in *i.*   Ps. 26:6

innocent
even though he is *i.*   Gen. 20:4   the guilt of shedding *i.* blood
The *i.* and the just you shall not   Deut. 21:8
                        Ex. 23:7   *i.* blood by killing David
i. blood will not be shed   1 Sam. 19:5
               Deut. 19:10   what *i.* person perishes   Job 4:7
       wrong to deliver up an *i.* man   Matt. 27:4

Innocents, The Holy, The title under which in Christian tradition are venerated the children of Bethlehem who were killed on Herod's orders, in his vain attempt to eliminate Jesus, whose birth the Magi had announced by asking "Where is the newborn king of the Jews" (Matt. 2:2; *see* 2:16-18). This episode is not recorded in any extra-biblical source on the reign of Herod. Authors however are agreed that it was only too much in keeping with the suspicious and superstitious cruelty of Herod during the latter portion of his reign. He even had his own sons slain on a suspicion that they were plotting against him. Matthew 2:16-18 links this episode with the prophecy of Jeremiah 31:15, but the connection is not very binding: it is not really a question of the fulfilment of a prophecy but more an illustration of a midrashic nature. *See* MIDRASH.

inscribed
I even discovered an altar *i.*
                        Acts 17:23

inscription
head is this, and whose *i.*   The *i.* proclaiming his offense
                        Matt. 22:20   Mk. 15:26
and whose *i.* is it?   Mk. 12:16   It bears this *i.*   2 Tim. 2:19

inscrutable
How *i.* his judgments,   Rom. 11:33

insects
various winged *i.* that walk   winged *i.* that have four legs
                        Lev. 11:21   Lev. 11:23

insignificant
I am poor and *i.*   1 Sam. 18:23

insolent
slanderers, they hate God, are *i.*
                        Rom. 1:30

Inspiration, Inspiration means God's action in the composition of the books of Sacred Scripture. In 2 Timothy 3:16 Paul exhorts Timothy to remain faithful to the true doctrine imparted by Sacred Scripture, which can be profitably used for teaching, for refuting error, for guiding people's lives and teaching them to be holy. The reason for this is that "all scripture is **theopneustos**," that is, inspired by God through the action of his Spirit. 2 Peter 1:20 explains this doctrine more fully: no scriptural prophecy is the fruit of human conjecture: "It is rather that men impelled by the Holy Spirit have spoken under God's influence" (v. 21). The Fathers have illustrated the relationship between the human author's part and that of God by comparing the human authors to musical instruments played by God. Like every comparison however this one also limps, for it gives the impression that the sacred author was a dead thing in the hands of God which idea would completely falsify the reality. The same must be said of the notion of inspiration as mere dictation.

Inspiration does not take away from the human author the full use of his responsibilities and human faculties. What comes from them however has also God as author. On the other hand God's intervention is more than a vague moral influence on the human author. The first Vatican Council took a stand against certain insufficient and exaggerated concepts of inspiration by defining that "the Church holds as sacred and canonical the books of Sacred Scripture, not because they were written by human industry and later approved by God's authority, nor because they contain revelation without error, but because, through the inspiration of the Holy Ghost, they have God as their author." This definition established the limits of the Catholic concept of inspiration: on the one hand it demands full participation by the human author, who is a true author of the book, while on the other it postulates direct action by God on the human author, not just a later approbation, so that in truth, God is also the author of the book.

The magisterium of the Church adopts from tradition and correctly interprets the concept of instrumentality in order to explain inspiration. God is the principal author, the sacred human writer his instrument. God's action does not neutralize or suppress the human author's own action, but makes use of it, respects it while elevating it. God's action does not contradict human action but works through the actuation of the human author's own faculties, that is, his intellect, will and so on. Leo XIII puts this clearly and precisely in his Encyclical *Providentissimus Deus*. Having quoted Vatican I, he goes on to state: "Wherefore it is of no great consequence that the Holy Spirit took men for his instruments in writing, as though anything false could slip out, not indeed from the principal author but from the inspired writers. For by his supernatural power he so excited and moved them to write, he so assisted them while they were writing, as to make them rightly conceive in their mind, and wish to write faithfully, and express fitly and with infallible truth all those things and only those things which he himself should command; otherwise he would not himself be the author of the whole Sacred Scripture."

Benedict XV in his encyclical **Spiritus Paraclitus**, written to commemorate the centenary of St. Jerome, once more expounds the Catholic doctrine on inspiration, following Jerome's teaching, by insisting clearly on the activity of the human author without detriment to the divine authority; "He (Jerome) asserts that the Books of Holy Scripture were written by the inspiration of the Holy Spirit. . . . Wherefore he has no doubt that the individual writers placed themselves freely at the service of the divine dictation according to their several natures and gifts, for he speaks not only always of what is common to all the sacred writers—that in writing they allowed themselves to be led by the Spirit of God, so that God is to be regarded as the first cause of every thought and every sentence of Scripture—but he also accurately distinguishes the special characteristics of each one of them individually" (*The Teaching of the Church*, Alba House: New York, 1965, pp. 68, 73 and 74).

Inspiration then is framed in the mystery of collaboration between God and man in the order of grace. This must not be sought for in the human author at the level of his psychological consciousness. Indeed there is clear evidence of the fact that the authors were not even aware of the fact that they were being inspired by God (*see* e.g. Luke 1:1-2; 2 Mac. 2:23-31). Inspiration then does not relieve the human author of the work that every author must do: collection, study and judgment of the material, editing it according to his stylistic and linguistic resources, writing it into the manuscript. Yet he places all these acts under the interior influence of God.

This doctrine on inspiration has important consequences for the interpretation of Scripture. a. All the books are equally inspired, and received with equal reverence by the Church. The distinction between protocanonical and deutero-canonical books does not refer to the character of their inspiration, which is equal for all, but only to the date at which they were universally accepted by the Church as inspired. (*See* CANON, DEUTERO-CANONICAL BOOKS.) b. The books in their entirety come from God and from the human author. Inspiration then extends to the whole book and may not be restricted to what deals with faith and morals. This is more than evident, but there have been attempts to restrict inspiration to one or other category in order to explain difficulties that have arisen in regard to the inerrancy of Scripture. They would have it that in matters of profane history or science the human author would have been left to his own devices and thus suject to error. Leo XIII in **Providentissimus Deus** rejected this explanation. c. The inspired book, because it is God's work, cannot be deceiving nor deceive us, and is absolutely free from error. The Church has not defined this formally, but it pertains to the unanimous faith of tradition and of the Church and is therefore an undefined dogma of faith. On the meaning of this assertion however *see* TRUTH OF THE BIBLE. d. By virtue of inspiration the Bible is the written word of God and is provided with that salvific power that faith attributes to the word of God. The authors speak of the sacramentality of the word of Scripture, that is, they see in it a power to save that is analogous to the saving power of the sacraments. In 2 Timothy 3:16 Paul recalls the fact that the Scriptures are inspired in order to explain their power to instruct, refute error, guide people's lives and teach them to be holy. This is not just an efficacy that might attach to any written or spoken word. The Bible is an agent of revelation, a means through which God speaks, and therefore pregnant with his saving power, just as the preaching of the Gospel, for the same reasons, is God's word to bring salvation to men (1 Thess. 2:13; Heb 4:12).

inspired
of them named Agabus was *i.*   All Scripture is *i.* of God
         Acts 11:28   2 Tim. 3:16

instant
suddenly, in an *i.*, you shall be   suddenly, in an *i.*
         Isa. 29:5   Isa. 30:13

instruction
Receive *i.* from his mouth   the training and *i.* befitting
         Job 22:22   Eph. 6:4

instrument
strikes another with an iron *i.*   with ten-stringed *i.* and lyre
         Num. 35:16   Ps. 92:4
     This man is the *i.* I have chosen   Acts 9:15

insubordinate
are known not to be wild and *i.*
         Tit. 1:6

insult
shrewd man passes over an *i.*   they ostracize you and *i.* you
         Prov. 12:16   Lk. 6:22
     in speaking this way you *i.* us   Lk. 11:45

insurrection
been thrown in prison for *i.*
         Lk. 23:25

integrity
When a man walks in *i.*
> Prov. 20:17

intercede
they would *i.* with the Lord
> Jer. 27:18

intercession, intercessions
petitions, prayers, *i.* and   he forever lives to make *i.*
> 1 Tim. 2:1   Heb. 7:25

interest
who increases his wealth by *i.*   could have had it back with *i.*
> Prov. 28:8   Matt. 25:27
> I could get it back with *i.* Lk. 19:23

interpret
no one could *i.* his dreams   If you know how to *i.* the look
> Gen. 41:8   Matt. 16:3
you are told a dream you can *i.*   unless the speaker can also *i.*
> Gen. 41:15   1 Cor. 14:5
> with another to *i.* what   1 Cor. 14:27

Interpretation, The principles of biblical hermeneutics (from the Greek **hermeneuein,** to interpret) are logically deduced from the doctrine of inspiration (*see* INSPIRATION). The sacred books were composed by human authors who lived in a definite epoch and place and belonged to a particular people and civilization. To study and understand the sacred books one must use the same methods and means that are necessary for the study and interpretation of an ancient book: textual criticism, study of the original language, study of ancient history, comparison with related works of other cultures, especially those neighboring Israel and so on.

The Bible however has also God as author. The Holy Spirit is the primary author. He made use of human writers to communicate in writing the divine revelation. It is therefore clear that the authentic interpretation, namely one that is both true and imposed with authority, is the prerogative of the Church which God has appointed infallible custodian of revelation. The Church propounds this authentic interpretation in different ways. The most solemn one is dogmatic definition of the meaning of a biblical text, even when this merely excludes wrong interpretations. Very few however have been the texts on which the Church has deliberated in this way.

For the most part the Church uses her power to interpret Scripture through her ordinary magisterium, that is, her day to day teaching. Rather than giving the full weight of her authority to the interpretation of a single text, the ordinary magisterium creates the spiritual environment in which Scripture finds its true interpretation. The authority of the Fathers of the Church should be esteemed in an analogous manner, for they are qualified witnesses to the Christian tradition, and when they agree unanimously in their teaching, they document the genuine Christian tradition. Similarly the Fathers have their value in expressing the spirit in which the sacred books are to be read and understood. There are some few texts on which the Church has concentrated with all the vigor of her power, such as Romans 5:12 in establishing the universal need for salvation on account of the universal grip of sin.

interpretation
had given this favorable *i.*   you can also give its correct *i.*
> Gen. 40:16   Dan. 2:9

interpretation (cont.)

he might give him the *i*.	Dan. 2:16
I will tell him the *i*. of the dream	
	Dan. 2:24

who can give the *i*. to the king	
	Dan. 2:25
pray for the gift of *i*.	1 Cor. 14:13

invade, invades

did not allow Israel to *i*.	
	2 Chron. 20:10

Decay *i*. my bones	Hab. 3:16

investigation

if after a thorough *i*.   Deut. 19:18

Ionian Sea, The Adriatic Sea between Italy, Yugoslavia and Greece (Acts 27:27).

Iota, The name of the letter **i** in the Greek alphabet. In Matthew 5:18, the reference is to **yod,** the corresponding letter of the Hebrew alphabet. The letter yod was the smallest one in the so-called square writing which was borrowed from the Aramaic after the exile and in common use during Jesus' time.

Ira, 1. David's priest (2 Sam. 20:26).

2. Two of the Thirty warriors of David (2 Sam. 23:26, 38; 1 Chron. 11:28, 40).

Irad, According to the Yahwist genealogy of Genesis 4:18 he was son of Enoch and father of Mehujael. He was a descendant of Cain. The name is transcribed as Jared in the Priestly genealogy of Genesis 5:18, 19 and he is numbered among the descendants of Seth.

Irijah (eye-rye′-jah), A sentry at the Benjamin Gate of Jerusalem, whose suspicions were aroused when, just after the Chaldeans had been forced to raise the siege of Jerusalem, Jeremiah began to leave the city. Irijah accused Jeremiah of deserting to the Chaldeans and would not listen to his plea of innocence. He had him arrested and handed over to the officials who threw him into the dungeon (Jer. 37:13, 14).

Iron, According to Gen. 4:19, 22, Zillah, Lamech's wife, presented him with a son called Tubalcain, the "ancestor of all metalworkers in bronze and iron" (*see* Gen. 10:2). "Cain" in other semitic languages means smith.

The existence of iron in Palestine at the time of Joshua's invasion is referred to (Josh. 6:24): all the iron and bronze objects in Rahab's house were to be consecrated to Yahweh. Iron is among the spoils mentioned in Joshua 22:8 (*see* Num. 31:29). The Philistines are believed to have introduced iron into Palestine, but they refused to allow the Israelites to develop their own iron industry, lest they should produce their own swords and spears, so that in the whole army no one except Saul and his son Jonathan possessed a sword or a spear. This placed the Israelites at a military disadvantage. Jabin with his nine hundred iron-plated chariots had cruelly oppressed the Israelites for twenty years. Nevertheless the latter routed Sisera's army with its chariots. The situation was remedied by David who provided for himself, perhaps as war booty, great quantities of iron (1 Chron. 22:3; *see* 29:7).

Ezion-geber (*see* EZION-GEBER) was an iron-smelting center and a sea port (1 Kgs. 9:26-28; 2 Chron. 8:17; 1 Kgs. 22:48; 2 Chron 30:35 ff). The frequent hostilities between Edom and Judah were probably over the control of this important industrial center, in which was smeltered and refined copper and iron, from which iron implements were produced.

Iron is frequently used in metaphor as in modern languages. Judah's sin is written with a pen of iron (Jer. 17:1) while the Psalmist sings of the Messiah ruling the earth with a sceptre of iron (Ps. 2:9; *see* Mic. 4:13; Dan. 7:7; etc.)

Isaac, The second of the great patriarchs of Israel, son of Abraham and Sarah and father of Jacob and Esau. Isaac is the abbreviated form of **Yishaq-el,** "God smiles," or "be propitius." The birth accounts handed down about Isaac contain allusions to the etymology of the abbreviated name (**sahaq,** to laugh or play). Sarah laughs in incredulity when Abraham receives the announcement of the birth of a son to his wife (Gen. 18:11-15). Afterwards, when the happy event took place, Sarah exclaimed, almost in justification of the name of the baby: "God has given me cause to laugh, and all who hear of it will laugh with me" (Gen. 21:6). Later Sarah watched the son that Hagar the slave girl had borne to Abraham playing with Isaac, which provoked her to demand from Abraham that he drive away the slave girl and her son so that he should not share in Isaac's inheritance (Gen. 21:9-10). Paul gives to this episode an allegorical interpretation in Galatians 4:21-32: Hagar and Sarah are figures of the Old and New Testament. One is that of Sinai, which gives birth to slaves; Sarah, on the other hand, is a figure of the celestial Jerusalem, which is free, and she is the mother of the children of promise. Paul interpreted the "play" of Hagar's son as persecution, and saw in it a prefiguring of the persecution of the Christians by the Jews.

In the Jewish traditions about Abraham, Isaac is the son of promise (Gen. 15:1-4), born to Abraham and the sterile Sarah through the omnipotence of God (Gen. 18:10-15) so that he might have an heir (Gen. 21:9-10). God was to test the faith of Abraham by ordering him to sacrifice his son, but once Abraham had proved the promptitude of his obedience, God stayed his hand (Gen. 22). The author then gives a long account of the marriage of Isaac and Rebekah: this story still belongs to the cycle of Abraham (Gen. 24).

The Genesis traditions about Isaac are few and of little importance (Gen. 26). One is parallel to the account of the stratagem that Abraham twice used to save himself from men who would want to get rid of him to have his wife: he passed her off as his sister (Gen. 12:12-20; 20). In Isaac's case, his rival is still Abimelech of Gerar (26:1-11) who already had had an encounter in similar circumstances with Abraham (20:1-18). The other traditions concern the ownership and use of water-wells in the desert of the south (26:12-33) and these too have parallels in the Abraham traditions (Gen. 21:22-34).

Isaac makes yet another appearance in the traditions about Jacob (Jacob's blessing, Gen. 27). According to Genesis 35:27-29 Isaac died at Mamre assisted by his two sons Esau and Jacob. On very few occasions is Isaac mentioned elsewhere in the Bible (Amos 7:18; Sir. 44:22; Rom. 9:7), but often with Abraham and Jacob with whom he constituted the great patriarchal triad, and whose names accompany that of God who revealed himself to them: "The Lord, the God of your fathers, the God of Abraham, Isaac and Jacob" (Ex. 3:16).

The scarcity of details handed down about the person of Isaac is accounted for by the role he played in the patriarchal story: he is important because he was son and heir to Abraham and the link between him and Jacob, who was father of the twelve tribes of Israel.

Isaiah, Book of, According to the inscription to the book (1:1) the activity of the prophet Isaiah extended from the reign of Azariah (Uzziah) (783-742 B.C.) to that of Hezekiah (715-687 B.C.). His prophetic vocation was received during a vision he had in the Temple "in the year that king Azariah died," that is 742 B.C. (Isa. 6:1-6). He was married and had two sons who had the symbolic names of Shear-jashub, meaning "a remnant will return" (Isa. 7:3), and Maher-shalal-hash-baz, meaning "speedy-spoil-quick-booty." The first alludes to the mitigation of the divine judgment on Israel which will make possible the continuity of sacred history (*see* Isa. 6:11-13), while the second name was suggested by God to the prophet at the birth of the son to indicate "that before the child knows how to call his father or mother by name, the wealth of Damascus and the spoils of Samaria shall be carried off by the king of Assyria" (Isa. 8:1-4).

Isaiah lived in a very turbulent era. In 722 B.C. Samaria fell to the Assyrians as the prophet had foretold (Isa. 28:1-6). Isaiah had a role of prime importance in the religious and political life of Judah, especially during the reign of Hezekiah, whom he supported during the most serious crisis of the siege of Jerusalem by Sennacherib (701 B.C.; *see* Isa. 36-38; 2 Kgs. 18:13-20:19), brought about by the pro-Babylonian and pro-Egyptian policies of the king, which the prophet severely censured (Isa. 30:1-7; 31:1-3; 39:1-8). Already during the reign of Ahaz (735-715 B.C.) Isaiah had lived through a crisis in the form of a threat from Pekah of Israel and Rezin of Damascus who had invaded Judah in order to oblige Ahaz to join their anti-Assyrian coalition, or else supplant him with a more cooperative sovereign. This was known as the Syro-Ephraimite war, and was the occasion of the prophet's most celebrated oracles, such as the one that speaks of the birth of Emmanuel (*see* EMMANUEL, Isa. 7:9). At that time, too, Isaiah counselled a policy of neutrality: calmly resist, because the Assyrian king, for his own interests, would not delay to put an end to the aggression of Israel and Damascus. Ahaz instead declared himself vassal to the Assyrian king Tiglath-pileser III, and suffered the grave consequences of this step (*see* 2 Kgs. 16).

The book of Isaiah is a classic of the Hebrew language, and together with the author of the book of Job, Isaiah is perhaps the greatest poet of the Bible. He is far from the studied fantasy of Ezekiel and from the sentimental and passionate outbursts of Jeremiah. For the conciseness of his style, the effectiveness of his imagery, the equilibrium of his form and content, Isaiah represents that type of poetry that is defined as classical. From the theological point of view Isaiah moves in the religious traditions associated with David's dynasty and the election of Sion, and he contributed in a determining manner to the shape and expression of the messianic hopes (Isa. 7; 9:11).

In the book that bears his name have been gathered oracles of various authors. After many years of study and discussion, all today agree that cc. 40-66 are not from Isaiah's pen. It is not easy to find the reasons that led to the introduction of these and other chapters to the collection of Isaiah's oracles, but this difficulty does not shake the conclusion that they belong to a different author. The authentic oracles of Isaiah are found in the first part of the book (Isa. 1-36; cc. 37-39 and an historical appendix which is also read in 2 Kgs. 18:13-20:19), but even here not everything is Isaiah's.

The oldest collection is found in Isaiah 6-12. This contains the account of the vocation and mission of the prophet (Isa. 6), the oracles referring to the Syro-Ephraimite war (Book of Emmanuel cc. 7-9), oracles concerning the crisis of 701 B.C. (Isa. 10) and other salvation oracles (Isa. 11). The collection concludes with a thanksgiving song (Isa. 12). Isaiah 13-23 has oracles against the nations, among which are some fragments that are not Isaiah's. 28-33 contains in general the last part of Isaiah's activity, during the reign of Hezekiah.

Chapters 2-5 collect the oracles of the first part of the prophet's ministry.

The first chapter is by way of introduction to the whole work, and offers some typical oracles that set the tone for the themes of the rest of the book.

Isaiah certainly did not originate chapters 24-27 and 34-35, the so-called "Great" and "Little Apocalypse." They are clearly post-exilic.

The second part of the book (Isa. 40-66) is clearly distinguished from the Isaian texts both in its style, which is rhetorical and occasionally prolix, its vibrant note of universal monotheism, and above all in his historical background. The prophet is addressing the exiled in Babylonia, to whom he brings a message of joy: exile time is finished and the time of the return to Palestine has come (Isa. 40:1-5). The prophet speaks of Cyrus as the instrument chosen by God to bring about the liberation of his people (Isa. 44:28; 45:1-3; *see* CYRUS). The prophet expends himself in trying to reanimate the people and shake them from their lethargy and defeatism. He takes issue with idolatry (44:6-23) which had by its splendor attracted the exiles, and in contrast to the apathy of his co-nationals he exalts the figure of Yahweh, the creator and father of nature and history, who is able to do what he promises. This is borne out by the past history of Israel (Isa. 48:1-11) and will once more be demonstrated when the power of Babylon is broken (Isa. 47).

These are the themes that return again and again with infinite variations in cc. 40-45. The author of these chapters cannot have been Isaiah. He is called Deutero- or Second Isaiah, who carries out his mission during the astonishing political and imperial ascent of Cyrus, before Babylon was taken (539 B.C.). It was his message and the scope of his ministry that is summed up in the first words of his book, which is called the "Book of Consolation": "Comfort, give comfort to my people, says your God . . ." (Isa. 40:1, 2).

Chapters 55-66 are, in all probability, the work of a third author, who is also anonymous, and for convenience sake is referred to as Trito-Isaiah, or the Third Isaiah. The chief proof for a different author is again in the diversity of historical circumstances that is reflected in the oracles. No longer is there talk about the return from exile to Palestine, but about the restoration of Jerusalem and the Temple. One notes that the prophet's audience is feeling somewhat deluded by the failure to realize the happy outcome predicted by Deutero-Isaiah. To their complaints the prophet responds by recounting their sins and injustices (56:10; 57:1; 58:2-6; 64:5, 6).

Very probably cc. 55-66 were composed during the first years of the post-exilic community in Palestine. The altar of holocausts has been erected (66:3) but the Temple as yet has not been rebuilt. This would place the author between 537 and 520 B.C. The prophet has also a message of consolation. He foresees the future glory of the city on which the nations will converge bringing in homage their riches. God will dwell there (Isa. 58:12; 60:10; 61:14) and the splendor of the future Temple will outshine the one that is gone (60:7-17). Here the prophet sings the same theme that was to be Haggai's message a little later (Hag. 2:1-9).

Ishbaal, Literally, "the man of the Master." Baal however is also the name of a Canaanite god. Ishbaal was one of Saul's sons (1 Chron. 8:33) who is also called Ishvi in 1 Sam. 14:49 and Ishbosheth in 2 Sam. 2:8. *See* ISHVI, ISHBOSHETH.

Ishbak, The fifth son of Abraham and Keturah (Gen. 25:2).

Ishbosheth (ish-bo′-sheth), Son of Saul. The name Ishbosheth is a deformation of his true name Ishbaal (bosheth in Hebrew means "shameful thing"). Baal meant "master" or "lord" and could be used legitimately for Yahweh. It was however the most noted name of the most popular of the Canaanite gods. (*See* BAAL.) After Saul's death in the battle of the Mountains of Gilboa, Abner, the general of the army, brought Ishbaal to Mahanaim in Transjordania where he made him king of Gilead, the Ashurites, Jezreel, Ephraim, Benjamin and all Israel (2 Sam. 2:8-11). Soon there was war with David who had been made king of Judah at Hebron (2 Sam. 2:12-13:1). Ishbaal lost the support of Abner (2 Sam. 3:6-11) who began to negotiate with David about giving over to him the control of the tribes of the North (2 Sam. 3:12-21). These negotiations were interrupted when Abner was treacherously killed by Joab in revenge for the death of his brother Asahel (2 Sam. 3:22-39). Without the military support of Abner, Ishbosheth was practically defenseless. Intrigue, however, once more hastened the end. Ishbosheth was assassinated by two of his officers, Baanah and Rechab, who thought they were doing a favor to David. He however had them executed for having killed an honest man in his house, and on his bed (2 Sam. 4). Finally the elders of the tribes of the North came to offer David the kingdom of the North (2 Sam. 5:1-3), thereby united the tribes under one monarch.

Ishmael, 1. Son of Abraham and Hagar, Sarah's slave. As Sarah was sterile she suggested to Abraham that he take Hagar her slave and beget a son from her. (*See* HAGAR.) When Hagar became pregnant, she began to taunt the sterile Sarah, who thereupon treated her so badly that she ran away from the home (Gen. 16). An angel of Yahweh met her on the road and told her to return. A similar story is told of Hagar, but after the child was born, in Genesis 21. Both accounts culminate in the appearance of an angel (Gen. 16:7-16; 21:17-21), in which is announced the glorious future of Ishmael. Ishmael is, in fact, the founding father of several tribes in Arabia (Gen. 25:12-18) of which the Bible further speaks in the account of the merchants who brought Joseph to Egypt, who were Ishmaelites (Gen. 37:25-28; 39:1), as was one of the wives of Esau through whom were related the Edomites and the Ishmaelites (Gen. 28:9; 36:3). The variations in the traditions that sometimes attribute the same fact to the Midianites and sometimes to the Ishmaelites show that there was a close relationship between these nomad tribes of the Arabian desert (Jgs. 8:24; Gen. 37:28). The territory of the Ishmaelite tribe stretched from Havilah to Shur in Arabia (Gen. 25:12-18).

2. Son of Nethaniah, of royal lineage (2 Kgs. 25:25) who, after the capture of Jerusalem by Nebuchadnezzar, went over to the Ammonites. They sent him to assassinate Gedaliah, whom the king of Babylon had made governor of Judea. He slaughtered his retinue and guests, and many others, filling a large cistern at Mizpah with corpses, and led the remnant of the people away as prisoners, together with the royal princesses. Johanan son of Kareah heard of this, mustered his followers and friends and set out in hot pursuit. Ishmael with eight of his men succeeded in escaping to the Ammonites, while Johanan led the remnant of the people into Egypt (Jer. 40:7-41).

Ishvi, Literally, "the man of Yahweh." He was Saul's son, who is also called Ishbaal (1 Chron. 8:33) and Ishbosheth (2 Sam. 2:8). *See* ISHBAAL, ISHBOSHETH.

Israel, According to Genesis 32:29 Israel is the name that Jacob received at Penuel while returning from the house of Laban. He had wrestled all night with a mysterious personage, during which his hip was dislocated, and in the morning Jacob was told: "Your name shall not longer be spoken of as Jacob, but as Israel, because you have contended (from the Hebrew *sarah*) with divine and human beings and have prevailed." The change of name is again recorded in 35:10 without any explanation. The explanation offered in 32:29 is a popular etymology. The name probably means: El rules, or let El rule. The Old Testament uses Israel as the personal name for Jacob, but much more often it refers to the people. The expression "sons of Israel" retains some of the resonance of the personal name of the individual, but in practice all it meant was "members of the people of Israel."

This people appears in history in diverse forms and therefore Israel, as the name of a people, did not always mean the same thing. Before Saul's time, Israel was the name of the confederation of twelve tribes. These held themselves to be the descendants of Jacob's twelve sons, and were therefore Israel. From Exodus times this scheme was rigorously observed in the Bible. All scholars however are in agreement that this scheme is partly artificial and partly an anachronism. It is artificial because the formation of the people of Israel as it is organized at the time of the Judges was the result of a much more complex process than mere linear descent from the twelve fathers. The genealogy however does mirror a factual solidarity at a certain point in time, that is, after the arrival in Canaan. A consciousness of their solidarity was translated into the simple terms of linear descent and thus blood links. (*See* GENEALOGY; NOMADISM.) It is an anachronism because the confederation of twelve tribes did not exist until the Canaan period. The previous history of the group who went to make up this confederation is to a great extent unknown. Something of it can be gleaned from the blessings of Moses and Jacob (Gen. 39; Deut. 33). It is certain that not all were in Egypt, nor did all then escape with Moses. The most northern tribes can be excluded (Naphtali and Zebulun), while one can hold for certain to the presence of the tribe of Benjamin and the "house of Joseph," that is, Ephraim and Manasseh. These are the tribes most directly involved in the traditions concerning the conquest contained in Joshua. Judah and Simeon were in all probability in Egypt, but it is equally probable that they did not go out with Moses and did not penetrate into Palestine with Joshua from the east but from the south.

The historical and religious traditions of one group of tribes became the common patrimony of the whole confederation, which is then projected into the past as if all that happened, happened to all the twelve tribes. The confederation was built on a religious basis, namely, the exclusive service of Yahweh and the sharing in a common worship at a central sanctuary where the ark was preserved. The tribes also had in common the sacred law, which was in all probability the collection now contained in Exodus 20-23, the Book of the Covenant (*see* Josh. 24).

Outside of this link, however, the tribes led their own autonomous and independent life, each taken up with better establishing itself in its own territory. The confederation was put into a state of alarm only when danger threatened its existence or the existence of one of its constituent parts, but even then not every tribe rallied around the common banner to support the confederation (*see* Jgs. 5:14-18; 19-21).

It was precisely this type of common danger that made Israel tighten its structures. The Philistines had established themselves along the coastal region and had formed a confederation of five cities which were strong from a technical and military point of view (1 Sam. 13:1-21). Moreover they were moving dangerously towards the central mountainous region. Israel's setback at Aphek, in which the Ark of the Covenant was captured (1 Sam. 4) brought home to them that they could only survive this massive threat to their existence by effectively uniting all their forces. The people asked for a king: "There must be a king over us. We too must be like other nations, with a king to rule us and to lead us in warfare and fight our battles" (1 Sam. 8:20). Thus Saul became king of Israel. On the pro-monarchy and anti-monarchy tendencies in 1 Sam. *see* SAMUEL, BOOKS OF.

Saul's monarchy ended tragically. His first mistake was to tamper with the sacred traditions of Israel, which alienated support from him (1 Sam. 15). Then he succumbed to the attack of the Philistines on the mountains of Gilboa (1 Sam. 31). In the meantime however was emerging a person who was to arouse in Israel a national consciousness and give to the monarchy a permanent place among the people. This was David, who was first elected king of Judah (2 Sam. 2:1-4) and then of "Israel," that is, of the tribes of the North (2 Sam. 5:1-5). Here Israel is taken in a narrower sense, as opposed to Judah, and signifying the people of central and northern Palestine, which centered on Shechem and the mountains of Ephraim. The two regions were united in the person of David, who became king of both. The same state of affairs held during the reign of Solomon, but his son Rehoboam was not accepted in Israel. In this way started the schism between Judah and Israel which perdured until the end of both kingdoms (1 Kgs. 12). *See* KING; JEROBOAM; REHOBOAM.

The kingdom of Israel, as different from that of Judah, had its own very turbulent history. The monarchy there did not have the sanction of dynastic continuity such as Judah had from the oracle of Nathan (2 Sam. 7). Massacres of the royal house were not infrequent. This was the end of the house of Jeroboam (1 Kgs. 8-14) and of the house of Omri-Ahab (2 Kgs. 9:1-10:31). Dynastic changes followed one another with extraordinary rapidity in the years that preceded the ruin of the kingdom (2 Kgs. 14:17-17:6). The kingdom of Israel fell a victim to the imperial expansion of Assyria. Tiglath-pileser III made short shrift of an attempted Israelite-Aramaean coalition by capturing Damascus and a large part of the territory of the north. He deported the population (2 Kgs. 15:29, 30). There remained only the capital Samaria and a small piece of land. That this was saved was due to the death of King Pekah at the hands of the philo-Assyrian Hoshea son of Elah and his political group (732-724 B.C.; 2 Kgs. 15:29, 30). Hoshea however did not remain loyal, for at the death of Tiglath-pileser III (727 B.C.) he tried to shake off the Assyrian yoke with the help of the Egyptians. In 724 B.C. Shalmaneser V, the new king of Assyria, occupied the rest of the land and laid siege to the capital, which held out until 722 B.C. when it fell into the hands of Sargon II. He ordered the massive deportation of the population to Assyria while he settled in their place other peoples (2 Kgs. 17).

The kingdom of Israel thus disappeared from history, but not the name. Judah inherited this, but with a new content. Israel was no longer the name of a political and geographical entity, but the name of an ethnic and religious entity, the people of God, chosen by him and the depository of his promises. Israel then becomes an evocative title: it calls up from the past an ever more idealized picture of the twelve tribes under the immediate dominion of God, while at the same time it becomes a word pregnant with the future in which promise will become reality. From the past to this future move the Jewish people, carrying the glorious title of Israel as a pledge of election and future magnificence, even though at present they were but exiles in Babylon, future subjects of the Persian and Seleucid empires, and after a brief glorious period of freedom subjects again of the Romans.

"The Jews" and "The Israelites" became contrasting aspects of the same people. The Christian Church, which Paul held to be the heir to the promises of the Old Testament, is the true "Israel of God" (Gal. 6:6) as distinct from "Israel according to the flesh" (1 Cor. 10:18). Paul devotes a long discussion to the tragic lot of this people who missed what they were tending towards: "Israel as a whole did not find what it was seeking" (Rom. 11:7; *see* cc. 9-11). One portion believed, but the rest became hardened. So not all who belong to the race of Israelites are Israel, nor are all

Abraham's blood descendants his true sons (Rom. 9:6). The criterion for true sonship to Abraham is to have believed as he believed (Rom. 4).

Issachar (iss′-a-kar), The ninth son of Jacob, born from Leah (Gen. 30: 18) and founding father of the tribe of the same name. Issachar settled on the eastern side of the plain of Esdraelon (Deut. 33:18-19; Josh. 19:17-23; Josh. 21:28; 1 Chron. 6:57) which belonged to Canaanite patrimony (Josh. 17:11-13; Gen. 49:14-15). The tribe does not play an important part in Bible history. It was among the tribes that fought with Deborah and Barak against the Canaanites of Hazor (Jgs. 5:15). Two important personages come from this line: Tola, son of Puah, one of the minor judges (Jgs. 10:1) and Baasha, king of Israel (1 Kgs. 15:27) and, quite probably, Omri (1 Kgs. 21:1-4).

Isshiah (i-shy′-ah), Personal name (1 Chron. 7:3; 12:7; 23:20; 24:25).

Italica Cohort, The cohort stationed in Caesarea in which Cornelius was one of the centurions. Cornelius was the first pagan received into the Christian church (Acts 10:1).

Italy, The name Italy is read in Acts 18:2 and 27:1, 6.

itch
eczema and the *i.*   Deut. 28:27

Ithamar (ith′-a-mar), The fourth of Aaron's sons (Ex. 6:23; Num. 26:60; 1 Chron. 6:3; 24:1). To him eight of the twenty-four priestly classes lay claim (1 Chron. 24:4) while the others link themselves with Eleazar. Ithamar and Eleazar did not take part in the irregular worship of Nadab and Abihu (Lev. 10; Num. 3). To Ithamar was entrusted the direction of the work in the construction of the Sanctuary (Ex. 38:21) and its transferral along the journey through the desert (Num. 4:28, 33; 7:8).

Ithra, The father of Amasa (2 Sam. 17:25). *See* AMASA.

Ithream (ith′-re-am), Son of David and Eglah, born at Hebron (2 Sam. 3:5; 1 Chron. 3:3).

Ittai (it′-tie), 1. A Philistine of Gath, captain of David's mercenary troops. When Absalom revolted, Ittai remained loyal to the king. He accompanied David and his followers when they abandoned Jerusalem. Later, together with Joab and Abishai, he commanded the troops that defeated the rebels in the battle of the mountains of Ephraim, in which Absalom died (2 Sam. 15:19-22; 2 Sam. 18:2, 5, 12).

2. A Benjaminite from Gibeah, one of the Thirty warriors of David (2 Sam. 23:29; 1 Chron. 11:21).

Ituraea (it′-your-ee′-a), The Greek name of a region in Bashan (Lk. 3:1). *See* BASHAN.

Ivory, In the ancient Middle East ivory was considered, as it is everywhere today, a precious material and was carved especially in the production of objects of ornament. It was imported to Palestine from Egypt, Mesopotamia and Arabia (1 Kgs. 10:22). Tyre was an active commercial center trading in ivory (Ezek. 27:15). Ivory is often spoken of in the Bible to highlight luxury and riches. Solomon's throne, for instance, was of ivory (1 Kgs. 10:28; 2 Chron. 9:12). Amos declaims against the self-indulgent lying on their ivory beds and sprawled on their divans (Amos 6:4). 1 Kings 22:39 tells of the ivory house of Ahab (*see* Amos 3:15; Ps. 45:8), and Ezekiel tells that the ships of Tyre were ornamented with ivory (Ezek. 27:6) A house or bed of ivory was one decorated artistically with ivory pieces, not something entirely manufactured from the precious material.

Iye-abarim (eye′-ya-ab′-a-rim), An encampment on the last leg of the journey of the Israelites through the desert to Canaan. It is south of Moab (Num. 21:11, 12).

Iyyar (ee′-ar), Second month of the Hebrew calendar, corresponding to our April-May.

J, The letter by which is denoted the Yahwistic document, or oldest stratum of tradition in the Pentateuch. *See* PENTATEUCH.

Jaar (jay′-ar), A place mentioned in the poetic description of the transferral of the Ark of the Covenant to Jerusalem, contained in Ps. 132:6. It is identified with Kiriath-jearim. *See* KIRIATH-JEARIM.

Jaasiel (jay-ay′-zi-el), Son of Abner and a commander of troops of Benjamin (1 Chron. 27:21).

Jaazaniah (jay-az′-a-nie′-ah), 1. A Jew of Maacha who, with several others, joined forces with Gedaliah when he was appointed governor of Judah by Nebuchadnezzar in 587 B.C. (2 Kgs. 25:23).

2. Jaazaniah son of Shaphan, whom Ezekiel saw among the seventy elders of Israel, each with a censer in his hand, in the act of idolatry (Ezek. 8:7-13).

3. Jaazaniah son of Azzur, accused by Ezekiel with twenty-four others of having filled the city with corpses and adopted the manners of the neighboring nations while disobeying the law of Yahweh and refusing to keep his observances. Ezekiel, in Yahweh's name, threatens them with dire judgment (Ezek. 11:1-12).

Jabal (jay′-bal), Son of Lamech and Ada in the Yahwist genealogy for the tribe of Cain. According to Genesis 4:20 he was the ancestor of tent-dwellers and owners of livestock.

Jabbok, A river of Transjordan, tributary to the Jordan, today called the Nahr-ez-Zerqa. It rises in the neighborhood of Amman and flows into the Jordan fifteen miles north of the Dead Sea, near the ford of ed-Damieh. The lower course of the river has cut a deep valley which shaped the natural boundary between the Amorite kingdom of Sihon and the Ammonites (Josh. 12:2) and later between Israel and the Amorites (Jgs. 11:22).

At Jabbok (Gen. 32:23-32) Jacob wrestled with God all night, and survived, except for a dislocated hip. He received this blessing, that as he had been strong against God, so he should prevail against men; and he received the name Israel. The Genesis story remarks that Jacob's injury was the reason why the Israelites do not eat the sciatic nerve of animals, which was in the socket of the hip, even though this food-law is not mentioned elsewhere in the Bible.

Jabesh (jay′-besh), The father of King Shallum of Israel (2 Kgs. 15:10).

Jabesh-gilead, A town in the land of Gilead in the Jordan valley beside the present wadi-Yabis, about twenty miles south of the Sea of Galilee. The inhabitants of Jabesh-gilead did not turn up at the Assembly of Mizpah which at first decided to be relentless in the punishment of the Benjaminites for their hideous crime (Jgs. 19:11-30) but then decided to soften the blow. They had sworn a solemn oath threatening death on whomsoever would not come into the presence of Yahweh at Mizpah. Twelve thousand men were accordingly dispatched to carry out the threat on Jabesh. Nobody except four hundred virgins were spared, and these were handed over to the Benjaminites to help them rebuild their depleted tribe (Jgs. 21).

1 Samuel tells that the inhabitants of Jabesh, in memory of the kindness they had received from Saul, recovered his body and those of his sons from the walls of Bethshan where the Philistines had suspended them. They were given decent burial under the tamarisk of Jabesh, and the people fasted for seven days (1 Sam. 31:10, 13). When David heard of their goodness, he called Yahweh's blessing on the men of Jabesh and he promised to treat them well because of it (2 Sam. 2:4-7).

Jabin (jay′-bin), A Canaanite king of Hazor who promoted a coalition of the Canaanite kings of the north against the Israelites. He was defeated by Joshua (Josh. 11:1-12). Another victory over Jabin king of Hazor is reported of Deborah and Barak in Judges 4:2, 24.

Jabneel, 1. A town on the northern boundary of Judah (Josh. 15:11) four miles from the Mediterranean coast and twelve miles south of Joppa. Today it is called Yibna. It was in Philistine hands and reconquered by Uzziah of Judah (783-742, 2 Chron. 26:6). Under the name of Jamnia it played an important part in the history of the Maccabees as a basis of operations for the Seleucid armies of Gorgias (1 Mac. 4:15; 5:58), Apollonius (1 Mac. 10:69) and Cendebeus (1 Mac. 15:40) until it fell to Judas Maccabeus, who set fire to it (2 Mac. 12:8). After the destruction of Jerusalem (70 A.D.) Jamnia was one of the most active centers of Judaism and the seat of the Council of Jamnia around 100 A.D., to which Talmudic tradition attributes the determining of the Hebrew Canon of the Old Testament.

2. A city of Naphtali (Josh. 19:33), southwest of the Sea of Galilee.

Jachin and Boaz (jay′-kin and boe′-az), Two bronze pillars, eighteen cubits high and twelve cubits in girth, topped by capitals in cast bronze and elaborately decorated, which Solomon had erected in front of the vestibule of the sanctuary. He named the pillar on the right Jachin and the one on the left Boaz (1 Kgs. 7:15-22). The interpretation of the names is disputed. The first one could mean "he will establish" or "well founded," and the second could mean "strength." Some authors consider them a phrase in which God is addressed, an invocation asking his blessing on the Temple. Others hold that they are the names given them by Hiram of Tyre, their artisan, on account of their dimensions. The function of the pillars remains obscure, even though there are parallels in Phoenician and Canaanaean religious architecture (*see* 2 Chron. 3:15-17; Jer. 27:19; 2 Kgs. 25:13).

Jacinth, Hyacinth, A precious stone nearly pure orange in color (Ex. 28:19; 39:12; Rev. 21:20).

Jackal, A carnivorous mammal, akin to the wolf but smaller, which will live on poultry, fruit or even carrion. It is mentioned in descriptions of abandoned or ruined cities in several prophetic oracles: Isa. 13:22, 34:13, Jer. 9:11, 10:22, 51:37, Lam. 5:18, Mal. 1:3.

Jacob, The third of the three great patriarchs of Israel. He was son of Isaac and Rebekah and twin brother of Esau. The name is probably theophoric, meaning "May (God) protect." The Bible however explains the name from the fact that at birth Jacob was grasping his twin brother's heel (heel—'aqeb) (Gen. 25:26), while in 27:36 and Hosea 12:4 the name is made to derive from the fact that Jacob supplanted ('aqab) Esau, depriving him of the right of first-born (Gen. 25:29-34) and especially of the blessing of Isaac which he deceitfully took from his brother (Gen. 27:36).

285

For fear of Esau's anger and on the advice of his mother Rebekah, Jacob set out for Haran to stay with his uncle Laban, Rebekah's brother (Gen. 27:41-45; there is another version of the journey in Gen. 27:46-28:5).

During the night at Bethel Jacob had a vision. A ladder appeared to him, based on the earth but reaching up to heaven, and on it the angels of God ascended and descended. At the top was the Lord who confirmed to Jacob the promises he had made to Abraham. When Jacob awakened he took his pillow-stone and erected it into a monument, pouring oil over it, and changed the name of the place from Luz to Bethel, which means the house of God (Gen. 28:10-22).

Jacob worked at Haran for his uncle Laban so as to have his daughter Rachel to wife. When however he had paid his price of seven years work, Jacob received as bride Leah instead of Rachel. Upon Jacob's protest over the deception Laban gave him Rachel, too, in exchange for another seven years of labor (Gen. 29). The Bible continues with the account of the birth of the children by Leah and the slave girls Bilhah and Zilpah. By Leah he had Reuben, Simeon, Levi and Judah. By Rachel's slave Bilhah he had Dan and Naphtali and by Zilpah, Leah's slave, he had Gad and Asher. Then by Leah again he had Issachar, Zebulun and a daughter Dinah. And finally to Rachel he gave a son, Joseph (*see* Gen. 29:31-30:24). Later, Benjamin was born to Rachel near Ephrath (Gen. 35:16 ff.).

Jacob decided to return to Canaan with his wives and children. Laban agreed that his wages for all the years of labor he had given should be "every dark animal among the sheep and every spotted or speckled one among the goats" (Gen. 30:32). The Bible then has a popular and picturesque account of how Jacob artfully mated the animals that were his, thus increasing his store, and eventually coming into the possession of the sturdy animals while Laban was left the feeble. Jacob became exceedingly rich with large flocks, slaves, camels and donkeys. Laban was enraged. On Yahweh's orders, Jacob took flight to the land of his fathers with all that he had (Gen. 31:1-16). Rachel stole the teraphim, the household idols which could establish a claim to inheritance.

When Laban heard that Jacob had taken flight he gathered his relatives and servants and gave chase, overtaking Jacob at Mount Gilead. He upbraided Jacob for having left without bidding farewell, and for having stolen the teraphim. Jacob invited him to search through the baggage, but Laban failed to find the idols. Rachel had hidden them in the camel's litter on which she was sitting, protesting that she was unwell and could not move (Gen. 31:17-42). Jacob and Laban however were reconciled, and erected a cairn of stones as a monument to their treaty (Gen. 31:45-54).

On the return journey, at a place called Penuel, "some man wrestled with him (Jacob) until the break of dawn" (Gen. 32:25). This mysterious personage changed the name of Jacob to Israel "because you (Jacob) have contended with divine and human beings and have prevailed." Jacob named the place Peniel "because I have seen God face to face . . . yet my life has been spared" (Gen. 32:29-31).

Then follows the account of the meeting and reconciliation of Jacob and Esau (Gen. 33). On the episode of the kidnapping and outrage of Dinah, *see* DINAH. On his way to Bethel Jacob ordered his people to get rid of all the foreign gods, and when he arrived there, God repeated to him the promises (c. 35:11, 12) and confirmed him in his new name Israel (35:10).

He departed from Bethel, but while they still had some distance to go on the way to Ephrath, Rachel brought forth Benjamin in a difficult birth, and then she died and was buried there on the road to Ephrath. Jacob erected a monument to her memory (35:16-20).

The rest of the story of Jacob belongs to the story of Joseph. (*See* JOSEPH.) Jacob died in Egypt, was embalmed and later buried in the cave in the field of Machpelah where Abraham had buried Sarah (Gen. 50:1-14).

Outside of Genesis the name Jacob means not just the person of the patriarch but the people of Israel in general. On the interpretation of the patriarchal traditions on Jacob, *see* PATRIARCHS. Here we must confine ourselves to some particular points.

The traditions of nomadic peoples often attach to the ancestor of the group episodes and events in which the whole group took part over the years. (*See* GENEALOGY, NOMADISM.) In the form in which these traditions are found in the book of Genesis, it is not always easy to discover what was the original meaning and intent of the various events and episodes recounted. The narrative interest often took over and transformed the original story. One can hardly doubt however that the two principle cycles, that of the relationship between Jacob and Esau and between Jacob and Laban reflect conflicts that arose between the Aramaeans of Jacob (Deut. 26:5) and those of Laban, and differences that arose with the Edomites of Esau. This can be considered the fertile field out of which the traditions later developed with a certain independence.

According to the scheme of the origin of the people of Israel in Exodus 1:1-7, Israel is made up of the descendants of the twelve tribes of Jacob. Scholars are today agreed that the real origins of Israel were much more complex and not at all so linear. This genealogy sanctioned the effective composition of Israel in Canaan in a confederation of twelve tribes, which however were not always the same twelve. Although in a certain sense they had ethnic and historical affinity, the groups that went to make up the Israelite confederation had a different past. (*See* ISRAEL.) In all probability the connection between the groups of Jacob and Israel in the premonarchic period were established through the "house of Joseph" (Ephraim and Manasseh). *See* JOSEPH. The same genealogy of Gen. 29: 31-30:24, which distinguishes between the sons of Leah, Rachel, Zilpah and Bilhah, sufficiently documents the same type of origins one must seek for those who entered into the Israelite confederation.

Not less artificial seems the link of descent between Abraham, Isaac and Jacob. This too rather mirrors the historical relationships of coalition and fusion between groups which carried the name of Abraham, Isaac and Jacob. It is not known however whether this fusion coincides with the constitution of Israel or if it belongs to a more ancient period.

Jacob, Blessings of, The traditional title for the words of Jacob recorded in Genesis 49, which he pronounced on his sons before he died. They are not properly speaking blessings, as c. 49 expressly states, but rather prophecies about the future of his sons. In reality however the oracles do not deal with the sons as individuals, but refer to the characteristics of the historical tribes of Israel. There is no certainty about the date of composition of the different sayings. The greater part can be dated in the premonarchic era, but that of Judah (49:8-12) seems to be a clear reflection of David's monarchy.

Jacob's Well, According, to John 4:5, 6 the meeting between Jesus and the Samaritan woman took place at the well which Jacob had dug (Jn. 4:12). The Old Testament gives no indication about the well nor does it contain any tradition that might go back to patriarchal times in its regard. John is almost certainly referring to the one hundred foot deep **Bir Ya'qub** at the foot of Mt. Gerizim. There is an unfinished church on the site, inside of which is the above mentioned well.

Jael, Wife of Heber the Kenite. He had cut himself off from the tribe of Lain and had pitched his tent near the Terebinth of Zaanannim, not far from Kedesh. Sisera, who was general of the army of Jabin, king of Hazor, had his nine hundred iron-plated chariots drawn up in battle formation together with all his men, but Barak with his ten thousand rushed down from Mount Tabor and routed him. Sisera leapt from his chariot and fled on foot. He took refuge in Heber's tent at Jael's invitation. She covered him with a rug, and when he had fallen fast asleep from exhaustion she took a peg and drove it through his right temple into the ground, killing him. When Barak appeared, she showed him the body (Jgs. 4:17-22). In the song of Deborah and Barak, Jael is celebrated for this deed (5:24-27).

Jahaz (jay'-haz), A town in Transjordan, which was captured by the Amorite king Sihon (Num. 21:23; Deut. 2:32), given to Reuben (Josh. 13:18) and was later a Moabite possession (Isa. 15:4; Jer. 48:21).

Jahaziel (ja-hay'-zi-el), 1. An early warrior for David (1 Chron. 12:5).

2. A Levite priest (1 Chron. 16:6).

3. Son of Zechariah (2 Chron. 20:14).

Jahveh, *See* YAHWEH.

Jair, 1. One of the minor judges, who was judge over Israel for twenty-two years. He had thirty sons who rode on thirty asses and possessed thirty towns which were known as the villages of Jair in Gilead. Jair was buried at Kamon (Jgs. 10:3, 4).

2. The villages of Jair are mentioned again in Joshua 13:30 where their number is sixty, and in 1 Chronicles 2:22 where they total twenty-three. They are said to have been in Gilead (Num. 32:41; 1 Kgs. 4:13). The name of Jair then seems to be the name of a clan and not that of a person, which belonged to the tribe of Manasseh (Deut. 3:14).

3. Father of Elhanan, a warrior of David who killed Goliath according to 2 Sam. 21:19, but Goliath's brother according to 1 Chron. 20:5. On the problem of who killed Goliath, *see* GOLIATH.

Jairus (jay-eye'-rus), One of the synagogue officials at Capernaum whose daughter Jesus raised to life (Mk. 5:21-43; Lk. 8:40-56; Matt. 9:18-26).

Jakeh (jay'-ka), Father of Agur, the author of the collection of proverbs contained in Proverbs 30:1-14.

Jalam (jay'-lam), A son of Esau by his second wife Oholibamah (Gen. 36:5).

Jambres, *See* JAMNES.

James, 1. One of the apostles, son of Zebedee, brother of John the Apostle and evangelist (Matt. 10:2; Mk. 3:17; Lk. 6:14; Acts 1:13). He was a fisherman. He was called by Jesus with his brother John while they were repairing the nets beside their father's boat (Mk. 1:19; Matt. 4:21). With Peter and John he was the privileged witness of some episodes in the life of Christ, such as the raising to life of Jairus' daughter (Mk. 5:37; 8:51), the Transfiguration (Matt. 17:1; Mk. 9:2) and the agony in the garden at Gethsemani (Matt. 26:37; Mk. 14:33). With John his brother he received from Jesus the name "Sons of Thunder" (Mk. 3:17), probably because of his impetuous zeal (Lk. 9:54).

Their mother had ambitions for her sons, and asked that they might be seated at the right and the left of the Lord when he should establish his kingdom. In reply Jesus promised them that they should drink his cup, that is, share his lot, whereas the seats at his right and his left were not his to give, since they belonged to those to whom they had been assigned by the Father (Matt. 20:20-28; Mk. 10:35-45). James's death is recounted in Acts 12:2: he was beheaded by order of Herod Agrippa (42 A.D.).

A tradition with little foundation holds that he preached in Spain where his relics are venerated today, in Santiago de Compostela.

2. The lists of the Twelve speak of another James, son of Alphaeus, called James the Less in tradition (Matt. 10:3; Mk 3:18; Lk. 6:15; Acts 1:13). Tradition tends to identify James the Less with James the brother of the Lord.

Today however exegesis leans towards distinguishing these two. James, the brother of Joseph, Simon and Jude of Nazareth (Matt. 13:55; Mk. 6:3) who was the brother of the Lord (*see* BRETHREN OF THE LORD) was head of the Church at Jerusalem (Acts 12:17; 21:18; Gal. 2:9), and played a very important part in the so-called Council of Jerusalem (Acts 15:13-23). This James was a faithful observer of the law and even venerated by the Jews, according to the tradition handed down by Hegesippus (2nd century). After the death of the Roman governor Festus (62 A.D.) and before the installation of his successor, Albinus, he was taken at the instigation of the high priest before the Sanhedrin and killed. James "the brother of the Lord" is never called apostle. Galatians 1:19 seems to include him among the apostles, but it can be understood in an exceptive sense: "I did not meet any other apostles; except James, the brother of the Lord."

James, Epistle of, The first of the so-called catholic epistles of the New Testament. The letter is entitled: "James, a servant of God and of the Lord Jesus Christ" (1:1), and according to tradition, this James is the brother of the Lord and head of the Church at Jerusalem. On the relationship between James, the brother of the Lord, and James the Apostle *see* JAMES. The letter quite obviously stems from the Judaeo-Christian environment of the primitive Church, but it does not seem to have come from a Palestinian background. The Greek language used is correct and beautiful, and is laced with certain devices that characterized the moral preaching of the Stoics, such as the diatribe. This leads one to search for its origins in Judaeo-Christian surroundings of a Hellenistic stamp. The author must be searched for among those ideal twelve tribes of the Dispersion to whom the letter is addressed (1:1).

Attributing a writing to a well-known name was an accepted practice and very frequent in classical literature, and it is not without parallel even in the New Testament where, for example, the second letter of Peter is attributed to the Apostle Peter. The whole letter of James is a mosaic of small exhortatory pieces, on different subjects, which takes advantage of the long wisdom tradition that lay behind it, as well as using some apocryphal writings of the Old Testament and Judaeo-Hellenistic literature. Thus there is in 1:2-18 a discourse on the usefulness of trials, which should be considered a privilege; 1:19-27 deals with true religion, "Looking after orphans and widows in their distress and keeping oneself unspotted," while 2:1-13 demands respect for the poor. Chapter 2:14-26 teaches the uselessness of a faith that is not expressed in good works, c. 3:1-12 deals with the sins of the tongue and c. 3:13-18 discourses on real wisdom and its opposite. Chapter 4:1-12 treats of the sins of discord, c. 4:13-5:6 is on the dangers of riches and 5:7-20 concludes the letter with a final exhortation.

Some authors have thought to see in c. 2:14-26 a barely disguised disagreement with Paul's doctrine that justification is had through faith without good works. And perhaps James had in mind some exaggerated and false interpretations of the Pauline doctrine, against which Paul himself had had to take a position (*see* Rom. 6:1; Cor. 6:12). James and Paul however are not in contradiction. Paul is speaking of the act of justification: what justifies a man is not obedience to the Law but faith in Jesus Christ (Gal. 2:16; *see* Rom. 3:20, 28), while James is dealing with a person who is already justified, that is, who has already come to the knowledge of Christ and has been baptized into the true faith. If this person's faith is not expressed in works of charity and mercy, then it is an empty and dead faith. "So it is with the faith that does nothing in practice. It is thoroughly lifeless" (James 2:17). Paul's writings bear this out: "What matters is keeping God's commandments" (1 Cor. 7:19). Charity for Paul is the life of faith, without which all else counts for nothing (1 Cor. 13:1-13).

There is no indication which permits the scholars to give to the letter an exact date: however they do lean towards a date later than 70 A.D.

Jamnia, *See* JABNEEL.

Jannai (jan'-eye), An ancestor of Jesus (Lk. 3:24).

Jannes and Mambres (jan'-ez and mam'-brez), The magicians or sages and sorcerers with whom Moses and Aaron had to contend before Pharaoh (*see* Ex. 7:11-22). Their names are found in 2 Timothy 3:8 which depends on extra-biblical, Jewish traditions. The second magician is also called Jambres.

Janneus (ja-nee'-us), Alexander Janneus, king of Judea (103-76 B.C.), son of John Hyrcanus. *See* HASMONEAN.

Japheth (jay'-feth), The third son of Noah (Gen. 5:32; 6:10; 7:13; 9:18). When Noah had taken some wine and was lying naked in his tent, Shem and Japheth went in with a cloak and covered him, for which Japheth merited his blessing (Gen. 9:27). In the Table of Nations Japheth is the father of nonsemitic peoples north and west of Palestine, in the regions of Asia Minor, the Black Sea and the Caspian Sea.

Japhia (ja-fie'-a), 1. An Amorite king of Lachish who in alliance with other Amorite kings formed an unsuccessful coalition against Joshua (Josh. 10:3).

2. Son of David born in Jerusalem (2 Sam. 5:15; 1 Chron. 3:7; 14:6).

jar, jars
six stone water *j.*   Jn. 2:6 Fill those *j.* with water   Jn. 2:7
                     There was a *j.* there   Jn. 19:29

Jared, A pre-deluge patriarch in the Priestly genealogy for Adam (Gen. 5:15-20; 1 Chron. 1:2) also mentioned in the genealogy of Jesus according to Luke 3:37. *See* IRAD.

Jarmuth, A Canaanite town in the land of Judah a few miles north of Adullam. (Josh. 15:35) which was part of the Canaanite coalition defeated by Joshua (Josh. 10:3).

Jashar (jay'-shur), **Book of,** "The Book of the Just" or "The Book of the Valiant," a most ancient collection of what were probably epic songs, two of which found their way into the Old Testament. One celebrates Joshua's victory at Gideon over the coalition of Canaanite cities (Josh. 10:12, 13). The other is the elegy of David for the death of Saul and Jonathan (2 Sam. 1:17-27). The Greek translation of the Bible known as the Septuagint

(LXX) cites as a source for 1 Kings 8:12, 13 the "Book of Songs" (ysr) which is probably a confusion with the "Book of the Just" (ysr).

Jason, 1. Jason I, high priest of the Jews from 174 to 171 B.C., brother of the high priest Onias III. He obtained the high priesthood illegally from Antiochus IV Epiphanes with promises of money, and he took measures to introduce Hellenistic customs in Jerusalem (2 Mac. 4:7-17), even to the point of countenancing idolatry (2 Mac. 4:18-20). He was dispossessed of the high priesthood by Menelaus who got the office by using the same means. Jason had to flee to Ammonite country (2 Mac. 4:23-26). He returned with an army of a thousand and captured Jerusalem but was not able to hold it. He again took refuge with the Ammonites. He was kept under restraint by the Nabataean king Aretas, and had to run from town to town until finally he fled to Sparta where he died (2 Mac. 5:5-10).

2. Jason of Cyrene was the author of a history of the Maccabees in five volumes which was used as a source for 2 Mac. (2 Mac. 2:19-23).

3. Jason, king of Eleazar was legate of Judas Maccabeus to Rome and Sparta (1 Mac. 8:17; 12:16-17; 14:22).

4. A Christian of Thessalonica who gave Paul hospitality and found himself involved in the riot that was fomented against Paul (Acts 17:5-9).

5. A Christian at Corinth who sends greetings (Rom. 16:21).

jasper
an onyx and a *j*.
　　Ex. 28:20; 39:13; Ezek. 28:13

Javan (jay′-van), Son of Japhet (Gen. 10:2, 4; 1 Chron. 1:5, 7). As a geographical name it designates the Greek colonies of the west coast of Asia Minor (Isa. 66:19; Ezek. 27:13), continental Greece (Joel 4:6; Zech. 9:13) and the Greco-Macedonian kingdom (Dan. 8:21; 10:20; 11:12).

javelin

j. was like a weaver's	1 Sam. 17:7	heel of his *j*.
	nor the dart, nor the *j*.	Job 41:18

2 Sam. 2:23

jawbone

the *j*. of an ass	Jgs. 15:16	he threw the *j*. from him

Jgs. 15:17

jaws

j. of the wicked men	Job 29:17	bridle on the *j*.	Isa. 30:28
tongue cleaves to my *j*.	Ps. 22:16	hooks in your *j*.	Ezek. 29:4

Jealousy, In the anthropomorphic language and imagery in which the Bible is accustomed to speak of God, God's "jealousy" is perhaps one of the most original elements. In its usage can be distinguished diverse instances.

A stereotyped description of God is that of being a "jealous God" (Ex. 20:5; 34:14; Deut. 4:24; 5:9; 6:15; Josh. 24:19; Nah. 1:2). The phrase expresses the typical intolerance of the God Yahweh, who demands from his people an exclusive service which he will share with no other god: "I, the Lord, am your God . . . you shall not have other gods besides me" (Ex. 20:2). This jealous God is said to be a "consuming fire" (Deut. 4:24) who will not leave his people unpunished should they forget his covenant with his people and go in search of other gods. This "jealousy" of God is at the root of biblical monotheism, for it made explicit the unicity of God. God's intolerance was not just jealous of attention paid to other gods: it was a metaphysical jealousy, which excluded even their existence.

God's jealousy is also an essential component of the bond of love which he wished to establish with the people he claimed as his "special possession" (Ex. 19:5; *see* ELECTION). In this case God's "jealousy" is his passionate attachment to the people which by free choice he has made his own. It will move God to defend his possession against encroachment. His zeal for his people (Isa. 26:11) prompts him to fight the enemies of his threatened people and defend them (Isa. 9:6; 37:32; 42:13; 63:15). The Lord is exceedingly jealous for Jerusalem and Sion and angry with the nations who brought Jerusalem to ruin (Zech. 1:14; 8:2). In their moments of distress the people prayed to God to rouse his zeal or jealousy so as to ensure their salvation: "Where is your zealous care and your might, your surge of pity and your mercy? O Lord, hold not back, for you are our father" (Isa. 63:15).

God's jealousy, however, can also be inflamed like a raging fire against his own people when they prove disloyal: "The Lord's wrath and jealousy will flare up" against the transgressors of the covenant (Deut. 29:19). Judah provoked the jealousy of the Lord with its idolatrous cults (1 Kgs. 14:22). "The statue of jealousy which stirs up jealousy" (Ezek. 8:3) was probably the statue of the goddess Ashera erected by King Manasseh in the Temple (2 Kgs. 2:17).

Jebusite, A pre-Israelitic population in Palestine often referred to in the Bible (*see* e.g. Gen. 15:21; Ex. 3:8, 17; 23:23; 34:11; Deut. 7:1). They resided in the central mountain range (Josh. 11:3) and especially in Jerusalem (Josh. 15:8, 63; Jgs. 1:21), which was for that reason known as Jebus (Jgs. 19:10 ff.; 1 Chron. 11:4, 5). Jerusalem remained in Jebusite hands until the time of David who conquered it and made it the capital of his kingdom (2 Sam. 5:6-8; 1 Chron. 11:4-7). *See* JERUSALEM.

Jecholiah (jek′-o-ly′-ah), The wife of King Amaziah of Judah (2 Kgs. 15:2) and mother of King Azariah ("Uzziah") of Judah (2 Chron. 26:3).

Jeconiah, *See* JEHOIACHIN.

Jedaiah (je-day′-yah), Personal name (1 Chron. 4:37; 24:7; Ezra 2:36; Neh. 11:10; 12:6, 7; 12:19, 21; Zech. 6:10, 14).

Jedidah (je-die′-dah), Mother of Josiah king of Judah (2 Kgs. 22:1; 640-609 B.C.).

Jedidiah (jed′-i-die′-ah), The symbolic name given by Nathan to Solomon when he announced to David that Bathsheba had conceived him. The name was given, narrates 2 Sam. 12:25, in accordance with the word of Yahweh. It means "beloved of Yahweh."

Jeduthun (je-doo′-thún), A Levite, chief of one of the classes of singers in the cult at Jerusalem during the reign of David and Solomon (1 Chron. 16:41, 42; 25:1-6; 2 Chron. 5:12), identified by some authors with Ethan. *See* ETHAN. To Jeduthun are attributed Psalms 39, 77 and 62.

jeer, jeered, jeering

came out of the city and *j*.	would *j*. at him	Lk. 14:29
2 Kgs. 2:23	leaders kept *j*. at him	Lk. 23:35
elders also joined in the *j*.		
Matt. 27:41		

Jehiel (je-hie′-el), 1. A Levite, descendant of Gershon, who was guardian of the Temple treasury in the time of David (1 Chron. 23:8; 29:8).

2. A counsellor of the sons of David (2 Chron. 21:2).

3. Son of Jehoshaphat, king of Judah (871-848 B.C., 2 Chron. 21:2).

Jehoahaz (je-hoe′-a-haz), 1. King of Judah (842 B.C.), son and successor of Jehoram. *See* AHAZIAH.

2. King of Israel (850-849 B.C.), son and successor of Ahab. *See* AHAZIAH.

3. King of Israel (815-801 B.C.), son and successor of Jehu (2 Kgs. 10:35) who had to submit for a great part of his reign to the dominion of the Aramaeans of Damascus (Hazael and Ben-hadad), who had reduced Israel to a miserable military condition. The author of 2 Kings reproved the king for not having destroyed the Canaanite sanctuary of Samaria (2 Kgs. 13:1-9).

4. King of Judah (609 B.C.), also called Shallum (Jer. 22:11), who was deposed, after barely three months of rule, by the Pharaoh Neco, who made him prisoner and brought him to Egypt where he died (2 Kgs. 23:30-35).

Jehoash (je-hoe′-ash), 1. Father of the judge Gideon of the tribe of Manasseh. He had constructed an altar to Baal and a sacred post at the side of it. His son Gideon was ordered by Yahweh to destroy the altar, offer a fatted calf as a holocaust on the wood of the post, and build there instead an altar to Yahweh (Jgs.6:9-31).

2. Son of Ahab king of Israel (869-850 B.C.) who kept the prophet Micaiah in protective custody, feeding him bread and water until Ahab should return successful from the war against the Aramaeans, which Micaiah had predicted would be unsuccessful. Ahab was killed in the war at Ramoth-gilead (1 Kgs. 22:26; 2 Chron. 18:28-34).

3. King of Judah (837-800 B.C.), son of Ahaziah also known by the shorter form of the name, Joash. When Ahaziah died in the revolt of Jehu, his wife Athalia had all the sons of the king killed. Jehoash alone was saved thanks to the intervention of Jehosheba who hid him in the nurses quarters and then in the Temple where Jehoiada was high priest. When the boy was eleven years old Jehoiada presented him to the people, whereupon he was proclaimed king and Athalia was slain by the Temple guards (2 Kgs 11:1-20). Under the direction of Jehoiada, Jehoash undertook the repair of the Temple (2 Kgs. 12:1-17). Hazael king of Syria took the city of Gath and prepared to march on Jerusalem, but he was bought off by some of the treasures taken from the treasury of the Temple and the palace (2 Kgs. 12:18-19). Jehoash was assassinated in a conspiracy of his officers (2 Kgs. 12:20-22).

4. King of Israel (801-786), son and successor of Jehoahaz. Three victories of his over Ben-hadad, king of Damascus, are recorded (2 Kgs. 13:24, 25) as Elisha had predicted (2 Kgs. 13:14-19). Under provocation from Amaziah king of Judah (800-783) Jehoash marched on Jerusalem, destroyed part of the walls of the city and made off with a rich booty (2 Kgs. 14:8-14).

Jehoiachin (je-hoy′-a-kin), King of Judah (598 B.C.), son and successor of Jehoiakim. His name is also written Joiachin, Jeconiah and (Jer. 22:24) Coniah. After a three-month reign he surrendered without resistance to Nebuchadnezzar who deported him with his family and ten thousand of his subjects to Babylon (2 Kgs. 24:6-16; 2 Chron. 36:9, 10; Jer. 22:24-30). After the death of Nebuchadnezzar his successor Evil-merodach (561-560) ended the imprisonment of Jehoiachin, gave him a place at the royal table and permitted him to live with the other captive kings who were at Babylon (2 Kgs. 25:27-30; Jer. 52:31-34).

Jehoiada (je-hoy′-a-da), 1. The father of Benaiah, head of the mercenary troups of David (2 Sam. 8:18; 20:23; 23:20; 1 Kgs. 1:8).

2. A priest of Jerusalem, who successfully organized the **coup d'etat** against Queen Athaliah (849-842 B.C.) and proclaimed Jehoash, son and legitimate successor of Jehoahaz-Ahaziah, king (2 Kgs. 11). He acted as regent during the first part of the reign of Jehoash, who was only eleven years old when he ascended the throne (2 Kgs. 12:1-17).

Jehoiakim (je-hoy'-a-kim), King of Judah (609-598 B.C.), son of Josiah and successor and brother of Jehoahaz. After deposing his brother, Neco of Egypt made Eliakim king of Judah and imposed on him the name of Jehoiakim to show that he was vassal. For the privilege of being vassal king he had to tax the country to raise the amount of silver and gold that Neco demanded (2 Kgs. 23:34-35). He was an implacable enemy to Jeremiah, who severely criticized his conduct (Jer. 22:13-19). He accused him of nothing but self-interest, a shoddy broken pot, who made a failure of his life. Twice Jehoiakim tried to do away with his embarrassing critic, for having foretold the imminent ruin of the city (Jer. 26:19) and for the oracles he dictated to Baruch, and which were read to the king by Jehudi. As Jehudi read off the columns Jehoiakim cut them from the scroll and pitched them into the fire (Jer. 36:1-27). For three years Jehoiakim submitted himself to Nebuchadnezzar (604-601) but then he rebelled hoping to find support from the Egyptians (2 Kgs. 21:1). Egypt however was defeated and Nebuchadnezzar invaded Judah and came to Jerusalem a few months after the death of Jehoiakim (2 Kgs. 24:2-7).

Jehonadab, (je-hoe'-na-dab), 1. Nephew of David, son of his brother Shemei. A shrewd man, according to 2 Samuel 13:3-5, he advised Amnon who was love-sick for Tamar, Absalom's sister, to feign sickness, and ask David the king to send her so that she might prepare something for him with her own hands, for only from her would he take anything. The ruse led to the rape of Tamar (vv. 6-14).

2. Chief of the Rechabites who sustained Jehu in his revolt against Jehoram (2 Kgs. 10:15-17). *See* RECHABITES.

Jehoram, 1. King of Israel. *See* JORAM.

2. King of Judah (849-842 B.C.), son and successor of Jehoshaphat (1 Kgs. 22:5) husband of Athalia, daughter of Ahab and Jezebel (2 Kgs. 8:18). An attempt to subjugate Edom once more to Judah failed completely and Edom was never again subject to it (2 Kgs. 8:16-23). Episodes of dubious historicity are narrated about this reign in 2 Chronicles 21.

Jehoshaphat, 1. King of Judah (873-849 B.C.), son and successor of Asa (1 Kgs. 15:24). He maintained friendly relationships with Israel and was allied with Ahab against the Aramaeans (1 Kgs. 22) and with Jehoram against Moab (2 Kgs. 3). He made an attempt to start commerce across the Red Sea with Ophir, fitting out a ship to go there for gold, but his ship was wrecked near Ezion-geber and nothing came of the attempt. When Ahaziah invited him into a commercial alliance, Jehoshaphat refused. In general (according to 1 Kgs. 22:41-51), he did what was right in the eyes of Yahweh. He drove from the country the "male sacred prostitutes of those who had lived in the time of his father Asa," but he failed to abolish the high places where illegal worship was offered. He died and was buried in the citadel of David (*see* 2 Chron. 9:4-11).

2. Son of Ahilud, and royal recorder during the reigns of David and Solomon (2 Sam. 8:16; 20:24; 1 Kgs. 4:3; 1 Chron. 18:15).

Jehoshaphat, Valley of, A symbolic name ('Yahweh judges'), with no corresponding geographical site, which will be the scene of the divine judgment of those nations hostile to Israel according to the prophecy of Joel 4.

Jehosheba (je-hosh′-e-ba), The daughter of Jehoram king of Judah and sister of Ahaziah. When Athaliah decided to do away with all the royal stock, Jehosheba spirited Jehoash, her brother's son, away from among those who were being murdered and hid him with his nurse in the sleeping quarters. While Athaliah governed the country Jehoash was hidden away in the Temple where Jehoiada was high priest (2 Kgs. 11:2; 2 Chron. 22:11).

Jehovah, An artificial form of the name Yahweh which is obtained by using the consonants of the word Yahweh with the vowels of Adonai, which means "My Lord." Due to reverence for the Bible text the Jews would not make a correction even where there was an obvious error. Since to read the error as written would itself sound ridiculous they distinguished between **kethibh,** the text as written, and **qere,** what was to be read. The divine name was considered too sacred to be pronounced so the written consonants (kethibh) were given the vowels to be read (qerê), thereby producing what is an impossible word to pronounce if read aloud. It was always understood however that the reader should not pronounce Yahweh but Adonai. This became known as the permanent **qere,** or what must always be read instead of what is written.

Jehozabad (je-hoe′-za-bad), Son of Shomer, an officer in the army of Jehoash (Joash) king of Judah, who with other officers rebelled and hatched a plot against the king. Jehozabad and Jozacar struck the king down at Beth-millo (2 Kgs. 12:21; 2 Chron. 24:26).

Jehu, 1. King of Israel (842-815) son of Nimshi, an officer in the army of Jehoram. With the help of the prophets, especially of Elisha (2 Kgs. 9:1-10) and of the Rechabites (2 Kgs. 10:15-27) he succeeded in overthrowing King Jehoram and putting an end to the dynasty of Omri. Jehoram was killed at Jezreel (2 Kgs. 9:11-30) and thrown into the field of Naboth which Ahab his father had treacherously taken for himself. Ahaziah king of Israel tried to flee but was wounded in his chariot and took refuge in Megiddo where he died. Jehu then went to Beth-eked of the Shepherds where he slaughtered forty-two members of the royal family, not sparing a single one (2 Kgs. 10:12-14). Jehu's **coupe d'etat** was motivated by politico-religious reasons, and aimed at reestablishing the Yahwist tradition against the alarming increase of the Canaanean cult of Baal, thanks to the undertakings of Jezebel, Ahab's wife, and his condescension to her (2 Kgs. 10:15-27).

With Jehu's action the prophecy of Elijah against the house of Ahab came to fulfilment (2 Kgs. 9:11+30). We know from Assyrian sources that Jehu was obliged to pay tribute to Shalmaneser III of Assyria in 841 B.C.

2. Son of Hanani, a prophet during the reign of Baasha, king of Israel (900-877 B.C., 1 Kgs. 16:1-12) and of Jehoshaphat of Judah (873-849 B.C., 2 Chron. 19:2). His "book of Jehu" was a source used by the Chronicler (*see* 2 Chron. 20:34). Jehu the prophet predicted the end of the house of Baasha for the evil he had done in the sight of Yahweh, and for having destroyed the house of Jeroboam. Jehoshaphat, on the other hand, he chided for being friendly with God's enemies, but praised him for having removed the sacred poles and having set about seeking God (2 Chron. 19:2).

Jehudi (je-hue′-die), Son of Nethaniah, a dignitary of the court of Jehoiakim (609-598 B.C.) who read to the king the oracles of Jeremiah, which the latter had dictated to Baruch. As Jehudi read the columns the king cut them from the scroll and threw them into the fire, and then he ordered the arrest of Baruch and Jeremiah for having predicted the Babylonian conquest. So Jeremiah predicted to the king the end of his own house (Jer. 36:11-31).

Jeiel (je-eye′-el), 1. Brother of Beerah, prince of the Reubenites (1 Chron. 5:7).

2. The founder of Gibeon (1 Chron. 9:35).

3. Personal name (1 Chron. 11:44; 15:18; 2 Chron. 20:14; 26:11; 35:9; Ezra 10:43).

Jekamiah (jek′-a-my′-ah), A son of king Jehoiachin of Judah exiled with the royal family to Babylon (1 Chron. 3:18).

Jemimah, The first of the three daughters born to Job after Yahweh had restored his fortunes. The name means 'Turtledove' (*see* Job 42:14).

Jephthah, Judge over Israel, the son of a prostitute in Gilead. The legitimate sons banished him from the paternal home, so he became a bandit chieftain (Jgs. 11:1-3). When the Ammonites attacked Israel, the elders of Gilead sent for Jephthah who was hiding away in the land of Tob. On condition that the people of Gilead should accept him as their leader, Jephthah agreed to return and fight the Ammonites (Jgs. 11:4-11). When the king of the Ammonites refused to negotiate or to acknowledge Israel's rights to the land of Gilead (11:12-28), Jephthah went to war with them. He vowed to offer in sacrifice the first person he should meet if he returned victoriously. He beat the Ammonites back from Aroer through twenty towns almost to Minnith and to Abel-keramim, inflicting on them a severe defeat.

Upon his return his only child, a daughter, ran out to meet him. He was grief-stricken. His daughter asked for two months' reprieve to retire to the mountains with female friends and bewail her virginity. On her return, Jephthah fulfilled his vow. Judges 11:39-40 tells that this was the origin of the Israelite custom in which the daughters of Israel leave home yearly to lament Jephthah's daughter for four days in the mountains.

Judges 12:1-7 records another victory of Jephthah over the Ephraimites, who were offended for not having been invited to take part in the campaign against the Ammonites. After 7 years of rule, Jephthah died and was buried at Mizpah in Gilead.

Jephunneh (je-fun′-neh), The father of Caleb (Num. 13:6; 14:6). *See* CALEB.

Jerahmeel (je-rah′-me-el), A tribe in the southern desert of Palestine (1 Sam. 27:10; 30:29) which was later absorbed into the tribe of Judah (1 Chron. 2:9, 25-27, 33, 42).

Jeremiah, The second of the major prophets of the Old Testament. Jeremiah was born at Anathoth in the land of Benjamin around 650-645 B.C., the son of a priest called Hilkiah (Jer. 1:1). The account of his call as a prophet (Jer. 1:2-10) calls him a "youth" and it is dated in the thirteenth year of Josiah (640-609 B.C.), that is in c. 627 B.C. We know little of the life of the prophet during the reign of Josiah. The oracles from this period are gathered in cc. 1-6. Nor is it known what part he played in the religious reform undertaken by the king around 621 B.C. (2 Kgs. 22). 2 Chronicles 35:25 informs us that Jeremiah composed a lamentation on the death of Josiah, "which is recited to this day by all the male and female singers in their lamentations over Josiah. They have been made obligatory for Israel, and can be found written in the Lamentations." This notice is at the origin of the traditional attribution of the Book of Lamentations to the pen of Jeremiah. He however certainly is not its author. (*See* LAMENTATIONS, BOOK OF.)

With Josiah's death also ended the king's work of national and religious reconstruction. His son and successor Jehoiakim was a creature of the Pharaoh Neco (2 Kgs. 23:34-35). He reduced the country once more to the sad state it suffered under Amon and Manasseh, but he had in Jeremiah an implacable censor and critic, for which however Jeremiah suffered. The accusation of Jeremiah in 22:13-19 probably dates from the first years of the reign; in it he predicts to the king that to him "the burial of an ass shall be given, dragged forth and cast out beyond the gates of Jerusalem"(22:19).

In 605 B.C. Nebuchadnezzar who was not yet on the throne, defeated Egypt at Carchemish. Jeremiah saw in the victory the instrument that the Lord was preparing with which to strike his people. In a last attempt to move the people to penance the prophet received from the Lord the order to commit to writing "all the words I (God) have spoken to you (Jeremiah) against Israel, Judah and all the nations, from the day I first spoke to you in the days of Josiah, until today. Perhaps . . . they will turn back each from his evil ways" (Jer. 36:2, 3).

Jeremiah summoned Baruch, son of Neriah, who wrote down on a scroll, as Jeremiah dictated. The volume was read by Baruch before the people in the Temple. The king heard of it and ordered Jehudi to bring him the book and read it in his presence. "Each time Jehudi finished reading three or four columns, the king would cut off the piece with a scribe's knife and cast it into the fire in the brazier, until the entire roll was consumed in the fire" (Jer. 36:23). Finally he ordered Jerahmeel, a royal prince, together with others, to arrest Baruch, the prophet's secretary. Both however were in hiding on the advice of princes of Judah who had foreseen what the reaction of the king would be (Jer. 36:19, 26). Jeremiah again dictated the volume, "adding many other words of the same kind in addition" (Jer. 36:32), which Baruch took down, in writing. In it he repeated his prophecy on the violent death of the king and on the decision of the Lord to deliver the city and the inhabitants of Judah over to destruction.

This was not the only attempt that the king made on Jeremiah's life. In fact, "in the beginning of the reign of Jehoiakim" (609 B.C.; *see* Jer. 26:1), after a discourse of Jeremiah on the certainty and imminence of the destruction of the Temple if the people failed to repent (Jer. 26:1-6), the priests and prophets laid hold of him and threatened him with death (Jer. 26:1-10). Another prophet, Uriah son of Shemaiah, prophesied the same fate as Jeremiah. Jehoiakim tried to kill him but Uriah fled to Egypt. Jehoiakim however had him return and had him put to death and his corpse put into a common grave. Ahikam however protected Jeremiah, and in this way he escaped death.

In 601 B.C. Jehoiakim, for several years a vassal to Nebuchadnezzar, sought once more the support of Egypt (2 Kgs. 21:1). Jehoiakim died three months before the arrival of Nebuchadnezzar. Jehoiachin, his successor, surrendered the city without resistance. He was deported to Babylonia with the royal family and ten thousand Jews. Nebuchadnezzar put King Zedekiah on the throne in his stead (598-587 B.C.)

Zedekiah's attitude to Jeremiah was not as hostile as had been that of Jehoiakim. He consulted him more than once during the siege of the city (Jer. 21:1; 37:17; 38:14). From 38:24-28 the king appears as the weak instrument of the blind political nationalism of most of the princes of Judah. Jeremiah's advice was: "Submit your necks to the yoke of the king of Babylon; serve him and his people, so that you may live" (Jer. 27:12). This is what he openly told the ambassadors of the small neighboring kingdoms who had come to Jerusalem to form with Zedekiah a coalition against Nebuchadnezzar (Jer. 27). The king, however, succumbed to the rash policy of independence, which brought him to his end.

This decision was however received with approval and sustained with
promises of triumph by the prophet Hananiah, with whom Jeremiah had a
violent confrontation (Jer. 28). Jeremiah was now convinced of the imminent end of Judah, so he turned his attention to those who had been
exiled with Jehoiakim. In these Jeremiah foresees the basis for a future
restoration, but at the same time he warns them against the seductions of
those prophets who blindly forecast for them a glorious imminent return
to Palestine. They must submit themselves and attend to the task of the
moment while awaiting deliverance (Jer. 29).

Nebuchadnezzar did not delay in rising to the challenge of Zedekiah.
From the city of Riblah in Phoenicia he directed an army to strike at
Judah and Jerusalem, which he put under a siege that lasted until 587 B.C.
During a brief interruption of the siege due to the threat to Nebuchadnezzar of an army of the Pharaoh Hophra, Jeremiah left the city to go to
Anathoth, to take part with his family in the division of an inheritance. At
the Benjamin gate however he was arrested by the captain of the guard
and accused of desertion. He was beaten and thrown into prison. Zedekiah had him freed, but confined him to the guard quarters (Jer. 37). This
measure however did not assuage the prophet. He continued his implacable prediction that the end of the city was at hand. The chiefs decided to
liquidate him for being a demoralizing influence on the soldiers and on
the citizens.

So Jeremiah was "thrown in the cistern of Malchiah, which was in the
quarters of the guard, letting him down with ropes. There was no water in
the cistern, only mud, and Jeremiah sank into the mud." Through the
intercession of Ebed-melech, a Cushite, Zedekiah ordered Jeremiah to be
freed from the cistern, but still confined him to the guards' quarters (Jer.
38:1-13). There Zedekiah sent for him and asked him for his message.
Jeremiah's word was the same. As a last resort, to spare what was possible
of the city, Jeremiah advised the king to surrender without resistance. His
advice was not taken (Jer. 38:14-28). When the city was finally taken by
Nebuchadnezzar, Jeremiah was still confined to the quarters of the guard
(Jer. 38:28). Nebuchadnezzar ordered that he be freed, well treated, and
that his requests should be granted. And so he remained on in Judah
under the governor Gedaliah, who was named by Nebuchadnezzar (Jer.
39:11-14). When Gedaliah was assassinated, the people who had remained on in Judah, for fear of Nebuchadnezzar's revenge, decided to
flee to Egypt. Jeremiah was opposed to this decision; but fear in the people overcame his reasons; so they fled, taking him along with them by
force (Jer. 40:13-43:13). Jeremiah's last discourse, given while he was in
Egypt, can be read in c. 44.

According to tradition he was murdered in Egypt by some of his fellow
countrymen.

Jeremiah is the prophet about whose life we know the most. Besides the
prophetic oracles, his book also contains numerous biographical and autobiographical accounts. The book also however admits us to the interior
drama of the prophet who lived through the deepest tragedy of the history
of Israel. In his so-called "confession" (Jer. 11:18-12:6; 15:10-21; 17:14-
18; 18:18-23; 29:7-18) the prophet opens his soul to God with a liberty
and boldness of expression that often remind one of Job's most daring
pronouncements. In the style of psalms of lamentation Jeremiah complains of the superhuman burden that his ministry imposes on him, of the
contrasts to which he is abandoned, of the failure of his preaching, of the
solitude and isolation to which his mission has reduced him. These passages are also of great interest for the study of the psychology of the
prophet. He often speaks of an internal force that obliges him to speak

and overcomes all his resolutions to take flight or to stay quiet: "I say to myself, I will not mention him, I will speak in his name no more. But then it becomes like fire burning in my heart, imprisoned in my bones: I grow weary holding it in, I cannot endure it" (Jer. 20:9).

Jeremiah's is the longest book of the Bible. The Greek version of the Septuagint presents a different order for it. The last sections of the Hebrew text—that is, the oracles against the nations (Jer. 46-51)—are read in the Septuagint after c. 25:13, and they follow a different order from that of the Hebrew.

The nucleus of the book of Jeremiah is the collection of oracles "against Jerusalem, Judah, and the nations" which Jeremiah pronounced up to 605 B.C., and which Baruch wrote under dictation (Jer. 36:2, 29, 32). This volume coincides more or less with cc. 1-25, and the oracles against the nations in Jer. 46-51. Chapter 25 is a transition between these two parts. C. 25:1-13 is the conclusion of the words against Jerusalem and Judah while c. 25:15-29 introduces the oracles against the Gentiles. The Septuagint version, then, preserves the order that is nearest the original.

To this volume Baruch added biographical notes on the prophet, with precise dates referring to the reigns of Jehoiakim and Zedekiah, and to the flight into Egypt after the capture of the city. The chronological order is today changed: 19:2-20:6; 26:36; 45:28-29; 51:59-64; 34:8-22; 37-44. There were also gathered into the book other minor collections such as the Book of Consolation (cc. 30-33) and others with the same theme (oracles on the kings of Judah, Jer. 21:11-23:8; Jeremiah and the Jerusalem prophets, 23:9-40 and others). Finally a historical appendix was added (c. 52), which was culled for the greater part from the Book of Kings (2 Kgs. 24:18-25, 34).

Jeremoth, Personal name (1 Chron. 7:8; 8:14; 23:23; 25:22; 27:19; Ezra 10:26, 27, 29).

Jericho, The city lies near the southern end of the Jordan valley, 6 miles from the Dead Sea and 5 miles from the Jordan, in a most fertile oasis irrigated by the spring of Elijah (2 Kgs. 2:19-22). The Old Testament city, also called the City of the Palms (Deut. 34:3; Jgs. 3:13; 2 Chron. 28:15) was situated on today's Tell-es-Sultan, south of the modern er-Riha, which occupies the place of the New Testament Jericho (Matt. 20:29, the cure of the two blind men at the entrance to the town).

Jericho is the most ancient example of urban civilization that has yet come to light. Excavations carried out by Miss Kathleen Kenyon (1952-58) have uncovered the ruins of a walled town which goes back to the seventh millenium B.C. According to Joshua 2 and 6, the city was captured by Joshua. The account of the capture of the city with its obvious liturgical display cannot be taken as a faithful history of the events as they happened.

It was assigned to the tribe of Benjamin (Josh. 6:1, 7; 18:12, 21). Despite the prohibition of Joshua contained in 6:26, 27 it does seem that Jericho was occupied at the time of David (2 Sam. 10:5) and afterwards (2 Kgs. 2:4-18). 1 Kings 16:34 tells that Hiel of Bethel rebuilt Jericho, obviously alluding to the curse pronounced by Joshua on anyone who should in future do so. The passage must not be interpreted as if Hiel started rebuilding an abandoned city

It was colonized after the return from exile (Neh. 3:2) and fortified by Bacchides, general of the Seleucid army (1 Mac. 9:50). There too Simon Maccabeus was treacherously killed (1 Mac. 16:11).

Zacchaeus the publican lived at Jericho. He gave Jesus hospitality (Lk. 19:1-3) and there the Lord cured the blind man Bartimaeus (Matt. 20:29-31; Mk. 10:46-48; Lk. 18:35-37). The road from Jerusalem to Jericho is the scene of the story of the Good Samaritan (Lk. 10:29-37).

Jeroboam (jer′-o-boe′am), 1. Son of Nebat and first king of the northern kingdom, or Israel (922-901 B.C.). Solomon noticed his skill in the building of the Millo and closing the breach in the Citadel of David, so he put him in charge of all forced labor. One day, according to 1 Kings 11:27-39, the prophet Ahijah accosted Jeroboam on a road outside Jerusalem, and tearing the new cloak he was wearing into twelve pieces, he predicted the downfall of the united kingdom and that Jeroboam should have ten parts of it after Solomon's death. Jeroboam, however, had to flee for his life to Egypt until after Solomon died.

Then he returned to Israel where he took part in the assembly of Shechem which was to have confirmed Rehoboam as king of the tribes of the north. They sought some respite from the hardship imposed by Solomon, but Rehoboam imprudently listened to the advice of inexperienced young men and threatened even greater hardship on them. This led to the break-up of the kingdom and Jeroboam was chosen as king of the north (1 Kgs. 12:1-24). Jeroboam was aware of the political consequences of so many of his subjects going to Jerusalem for worship at the Temple; to offset it he established two national sanctuaries, one at Bethel and the other in Dan. Thus he restored long-standing cultic traditions (1 Kgs. 12:25-33). *See* CALF, GOLDEN. For the authors of 1 and 2 Kings this setting up of independent sanctuaries was an unforgivable sin, for which Jeroboam and his successors are constantly reproved. The premature death of Jeroboam's son Abijah was interpreted as punishment for this sin (1 Kgs. 14:1-18).

2. Jeroboam II, king of Israel (786-746 B.C.) son and successor of Jehoash (2 Kgs. 13:13) who extended his dominions until they almost reached the limits set by David and Solomon, following his victories over the Syrians of Damascus (2 Kgs. 14:23-28). During his reign Hosea the prophet exercised his ministry (Hos. 1:1), as did Amos (Amos 7:9-11). After his long, prosperous and relatively quiet reign there began a steady disintegration in the kingdom until it fell, in a mere thirty years, into the hand of the Assyrians (722 B.C.).

Jeroham (je-roe′-ham), 1. Father of Elkanah (1 Sam. 1:1).

2. Father of Zebadiah (1 Chron. 12:8).

3. Father of Azarel, head of the tribe of Dan (1 Chron. 27:22).

Jerubbaal, The name given to Gideon for having destroyed the altar of Baal that had been erected by his father (Jgs. 6:32). *See* GIDEON.

Jerusalem, Jerusalem is situated on two hills of the central mountain range of Palestine, whose average height is 2300 feet above sea level. The hills join the mountain range only from the north, and are flanked by deep valleys on the other sides. To the east is the Valley of Kidron which divides the city from the Mount of Olives. West and south is the Valley of Hinnom. (*See* GEHENNA.)

The ancient city was built on the two hills with the dividing valley in between. Today that valley has almost been filled in with debris so as to form more of a depression than a valley. Josephus Flavius names it Tyropoeon. The eastern hill was the first to be occupied (*See* JEBUSITES.) This reaches towards the south and on it, coming from south to north, are found the citadel of David, or Zion (2 Sam. 5:7; 1 Kgs. 8:1), the palace erected by David and completed by Solomon, and the Temple of Solomon. Both the city of David and the inhabited quarter of the western hill are today outside the southern walls of the city, which is a short distance to the north.

Jerusalem appears in Egyptian documents as early as the second millenium B.C. A patriarchal tradition links the city with Melchizedek, king of Salem (Jerusalem) and priest of El-Elyon. Melchizedek was a contemporary of Abraham (Gen. 14:17-24; *see* Heb. 5-7). At the time of the conquest of Canaan, Jerusalem was in the hands of the Jebusites (*see* JEBUSITES) and did not become an Israelite possession until the time of David, who captured it and made it the capital of his kingdom (2 Sam. 5:6-9). This was a stroke of political (as well as military) genius, for the city, never before occupied by the Hebrews, was on the border between David's Judah and the northern tribes from which Saul had drawn his strength. So Jerusalem had no ties to either faction in the united kingdom.

David constructed the house of the king on the hill of Zion and thought of building the Temple there (2 Sam. 7) but this project was completed by Solomon (1 Kgs. 6:8). Solomon probably enclosed the western hill as well with walls. Throughout the monarchy the city suffered all the vicissitudes of internal and external politics that affected Israel. Soon after Solomon's death the Pharaoh Shishak (935-914) plundered the Temple and made off with an immense booty (1 Kgs. 14:25-27), as did Jehoash of Israel (801-786) at the time of Amaziah of Judah (800-783). Sennacherib (704-681) laid siege to the city without being able, however, to take it, during Hezekiah's reign (715-687, Isa. 36-37; 2 Kgs. 18:13-19). The city failed to withstand Nebuchadnezzar (604-562). It surrendered at the outset without resistance at the time of Jehoiachin (598) who was deported with his family and 10,000 others to Babylon.

Later Zedekiah (598-587), ignored the advice of Jeremiah and revolted against Nebuchadnezzar. The Babylonian king-general laid siege to the city and after 18 months captured it and destroyed it, ordering the population to be deported en masse (587 B.C.; 2 Kgs. 25; 2 Chron. 36:11 ff.).

The decree of Cyrus in 537 repatriating the Jews also authorized the reconstruction of the Temple and of the walls of the city (Ezra 1-7; Neh. 1-4).

In 169 B.C. the city was captured by Antiochus IV Epiphanes who profaned the Temple. Judas Maccabeus succeeded in retaking the city (165 B.C.) but not the fortress of Akra which had been built by the Seleucids, and which resisted until 145 B.C. when it fell to Simon Maccabeus.

Pompey's conquest did not damage the city (63 B.C.), and Herod the Great began a new period of splendor for the city. He undertook the building of a new Temple, which was completed only in 64 A.D. He constructed the fortress Antonia at the northern corner of the Temple and a royal palace on the western hill of the city. During the revolt that broke out in 66 A.D. the city was captured and the Temple set on fire (70 A.D.) by Titus and Vespasian. After the suppression of the second revolt (132-135 A.D.) the Emperor Hadrian made of Jerusalem a Roman colony with the name of Aelia Capitolina.

Jeshua, *See* JOSHUA.

Jesse, Son of Obed, grandson of Boaz and Ruth (Ruth 4:17-22), father of David. He came from Bethlehem in Judah and had eight sons, of whom the youngest was David (1 Sam. 16:1-13; 17:3; Isa. 11:1, 10). When David had to flee from Saul he moved his family to Moab (1 Sam. 22:3, 4).

Jesus Ben Sira, *See* ECCLESIASTICUS.

Jesus Christ, Jesus Christ is taken, both words together, as a proper name, and as such it is used in the New Testament. It is easy to see the origin of this fusion and the meaning of the two elements. Jesus is the name that Mary's son received at birth. It stems from the Hebrew Yeshua, a short form of Yehoshua, Yahweh saves, "for it is he who will save his people from their sins" (Matt. 1:21). Christ comes from the Greek Christos, which translates the Hebrew name Messiah. When therefore in the New Testament Greek the word is used with the article as Jesus **ho (the) Christos** it should be translated, not Jesus Christ, but Jesus the Messiah, which is the original sense of the title and name. Jesus the Messiah mirrors one of the most ancient confessions of faith: Jesus who was killed on the cross, was exalted by God to his right hand and established as Lord and Messiah (Acts. 2:36), that is, he has initiated his reign. *See* MESSIAH.

The union of both names, Jesus and Christ, in one is already an answer to the most important problem that is today discussed about Jesus, and to which this article is directed. In the present discussion of the problem the terms have a more precise meaning: Jesus designates the man Jesus from Nazareth who lived, preached and worked in Palestine in the first century, that is, the historical Jesus who emerges from the historical research carried out on the documents that refer to him. Christ is the Christ of faith, that is, the image of Christ afforded by the faith of the apostolic church, as this is witnessed in the New Testament. The problem can be framed in the following terms: Is the one to be identified with the other, or, at least, is there continuity between the one and the other? Or must we conclude that there is an unbridgeable gap between the different ideas and images, and, in this case, which of the two should prevail as a norm for Christianity?

The problem of Jesus posed in these terms is of recent times. It arose at the time of critical illuminism in the eighteenth century and since then has remained at the center of the critical-historical study of the Gospels. The position of Catholic exegetes and of the majority of Protestant exegetes, especially of the English language, has remained coherent in itself, even though their line of argument has developed and progressed with the progress of biblical studies themselves. It has not however digressed from adherence to the first of the alternatives proposed above: there is identity between both terms in the problem, or to put it better, there is real continuity. This continuity is to be understood in the sense that the resurrection did introduce a radical change in the condition of Jesus; the change in condition however took its place without rupture with the past in the consciousness that Jesus himself had of his person and of his mission.

In one part of Protestant theology, especially German-speaking where the debate has always been much more inflamed, there has been a profound change between the last century and this century. This profound change has also had repercussions in the contrasting positions in the debate. Nineteenth-century liberal theology, to distinguish it from rigid Lutheran orthodoxy, systematically applied the techniques of historical investigation to the Gospels. The scope of the investigation was to recapture from the past of theological speculation and faith the authentic genuine image of Jesus of Nazareth. For, they held, the primitive church, through its faith and theology, had deformed the face of Christ. As a norm for Christianity it was necessary to have a sort of chemically pure Jesus of Nazareth. In reality however the fruits of their work were more than disappointing, for as many historical Jesuses emerged as there were authors to describe Him. All however ended up by portraying Jesus as an exemplary moralist with a message of peace among men and trust in God.

The author who gave to this search for the historical Jesus the coup de grace was Albert Schweitzer in his famous book, **The Quest of the His-**

torical Jesus, 1913. With a brilliant style and incisive criticism he denounced the arbitrariness of the studies that had hitherto been done in this field. The change in the study of the problem however was the fruit of a more profound research into the origins of the Gospels carried out in accordance with the principles of Formgeschichte or Form-criticism. (*See* GOSPELS.) The Gospels were collections of independent oral traditions circulating in the primitive Christian community. These traditions had arisen in great part to meet the needs of the community itself in its many manifestations. The Gospels then were, above all, witness to the faith of the living Christian community which was the Church, and only indirectly, and to a much smaller measure, could they give us a glimpse of Jesus as he really existed. The form-criticism method is well worked out, but when it was applied by its inventors and by others who followed them, this application necessarily followed their principles. Catholic exegesis also uses form-criticism without however reaching through it the same conclusions. *See* TRADITION.

One of the most immediate consequences of the new vision of the origin and nature of the Gospels which emerged under the searchlights of form-criticism was the conviction that it was impossible to write a biography of Jesus. This conviction is common today to all scripture scholars, both Catholic and Protestant. It should however be well understood. It does not mean that nothing can be historically known of Jesus. It states that the only sources that we have for Jesus do not, as historical sources, allow one to reconstruct chronology or topography for his life. Nor can one attempt such a story, taking into account the internal development of his personality and of his activity, and so there can be no biography of Jesus in the sense that is usually given to that term. In the words of a great Catholic exegete, M. J. Lagrange, the only life of Jesus that it is possible to write are the Gospels themselves.

One must however immediately add that while it is impossible to write a strict biography of Jesus or to reconstruct an objective chronological sequence for the different events of the Gospel, this does not exclude the possibility of describing, at least in broad outline, the development of his ministry. No author calls into doubt the synchronization of the Gospel story with contemporary history that Luke makes in 3:1. The most probable computation of the fifteenth year of Tiberius Caesar places the beginnings of John the Baptizer's ministry in 27/28 A.D. One can also give credence to the general outline of the Gospel story which is confirmed by ancient texts in the Acts of the Apostles (*see* Acts 10:34-43; 13:23-31). Two principal stages in the development of Jesus' activity are distinguished. After the baptism of John comes the ministry in Galilee which began with an enthusiastic reception by the people and ended with almost total apostasy. There followed a shorter period when Jesus withdrew with his disciples.

The duration of the ministry is very unclear. What the Synoptics tell could be pushed into one year. John on the other hand speaks of two Paschs besides the one in which Jesus was crucified, which therefore demand at least two complete years. One must moreover except the story of the Passion from the general difficulty in reconstructing a minute history of the facts. For the Passion story has different scenes which follow one another with a strict connection between them, and each is meaningful only as a part of the whole. *See* PASSION.

One must also insist that the difficulty in situating with chronological exactness the time, place and order of the single events of the Gospel does not mean that their historicity is being denied. Each event must be examined in itself. The individual views of the authors are often in contrast. In many cases, where the event narrated is adjudged non-historical, this judgment is based on the actual form of a definite word or fact, which however may well have been itself culled from a still more ancient form, on which then the judgment would be quite the opposite.

The present discussion on the problem of the historical Jesus revolves around the work of one of the most important figures in the exegesis of our time: Rudolf Bultmann. He was one of the initiators of form-criticism. His application of it to the Gospels led him to a fairly sceptical position in regard to the historicity of a great part of the Gospel tradition. What however will surprise even more the Catholic reader is that his exaggerated critical scepticism in no way affects his adherence to the Christ of faith. For a summary exposition of this problem *see* DEMYTHOLOGIZING.

The position of Bultmann and of other radical exegetes has had its repercussions on the form in which the problem is today posed by Catholic exegesis. In the past the central point of apologetics was to establish the truth of all that Jesus had said about himself by calling on the miracles he performed as confirmation of the truth of his words. Since only God could work a miracle, these were taken to be his seal on the words of Jesus and therefore sufficient criteria for credibility. God could in no wise put his seal on error or lies.

Today however the relationship between the historical Jesus and the Jesus of faith is called into question. So the first problem is to determine what Jesus said of himself: what did he declare his mission to be? What was the mission with which he felt he was invested? Here we outline the road to be followed when constructing such a demonstration. Many of the individual points touched on are treated in other entries, which can be referred to.

The question we are faced with can be stated in the following terms: for the Church's faith the event of Christ, that is, of his incarnation, death and resurrection as Son of God, is the culminating point of the history of salvation, the final decisive intervention or eschatological event brought about by God for the salvation of the world. To this culminating event the whole past tended and in it is contained the whole future. The Gospels and in general the New Testament identify this eschatological event with the life of a man, Jesus of Nazareth. He was born of Mary and died on the cross. He arose after three days and is now seated at the right hand of the Father. The problem is not to prove rationally the truth of the faith of the Church, but to examine the validity, the soundness of this identification proposed by the Gospels. In the last analysis this means examining if Jesus of Nazareth really claimed for himself in the history of salvation the position that the Church attributed to him.

Perhaps one might ask whether there would still be room for faith if this problem were to be resolved in a positive manner. The answer is of course in the affirmative. In fact, in the measure granted us by the Gospel sources, it is possible to hear the very voice of Christ telling us that in him the kingdom of God is present and inviting us to receive his message. If we are to follow him in fact, then for us as for his disciples of old, it is always a question of faith. Even when we have completed our investigation, we do not arrive at conclusions so certain that they dispense us from faith. Rather we end up with a question that Jesus himself puts to us. It is this same question that is addressed to us by the preaching of the Church. In this way can be seen the continuity between the historical Jesus and the Christ of faith.

It is necessary to begin with what is admitted by all authors without exception, namely, that Jesus presented himself as the herald of the coming of the eschatological kingdom of God. The evangelists have been able to gather with extreme exactness what was the center of this message: it is summed up in the words placed at the beginning of the public ministry of Jesus: "This is the time of fulfillment. The reign of God is at hand! Reform your lives and believe in the gospel" (Mk. 1:14; Matt. 4:17). This means: "The time of definitive salvation has arrived, change your conduct and your spirit so that you can share in this salvation." The establishment of God's kingdom is not an instantanous event however, for it has a beginning and a completion, so that it is already here, and yet has a future still to be unfolded. *See* KINGDOM OF GOD.

At this point it is necessary to ask: What connection did Jesus see between his own person and mission and the event of the kingdom of God, that is, the realization of definitive salvation? What was the relationship between his person and his message? Did he believe himself to be, as did the prophets of the Old Testament, the carrier of a message, outside the content of which he was to remain? Or did he believe himself to be the person in whom and through whom the kingdom of God was to come about?

This is a question that involves not just the initial stage of the kingdom's establishment but also its perfect accomplishment. The answer can only be had from those words of Jesus whose authenticity can be established by positive reasons.

A first important indication is found in Matthew 11:12, 13; Luke 16:16: "From John the Baptizer's time until now the kingdom of God has suffered violence, and the violent take it by force. All the prophets as well as the law spoke prophetically until John." With these words Jesus clearly establishes the line that divides the period of preparation for the kingdom from the time of its realization. The first reaches as far as John the Baptizer, but to the second belongs the ministry of Jesus (*see* also Matt. 12:41 ff.; Lk. 11:31 ff.). This is even more clear in a beatitude Jesus addressed to the disciples: "But blest are your eyes because they see and blest are your ears because they hear. I assure you, many a prophet and many a saint longed to see what you see but did not see it, to hear what you hear but did not hear it" (Matt. 13:16, 17; Lk. 10:23, 24). The beatitudes proclaim, they do not augur, the blessedness of those who are and will be sharers in definitive salvation (*see* Matt. 5:3-12; Lk. 6:20-23). It is spoken of as being present and offered to those who are with Jesus and become his followers. It is what they see and hear, and what the prophets of old desired to see and hear, namely the words and works of Jesus. Thus he insinuates with sufficient clarity that definitive salvation, at least in its initial stage, has come with his words and works.

This too was the meaning that Jesus gave to the miracles he performed and to the exorcisms he commanded. Often in apologetical theology the miracles are used as arguments confirming the truth of Jesus' words, God's seal on his mission. This is legitimate and based on Scripture itself (*see* Acts 2:22). On the other hand however it is also certain that when the evangelists recount for us the miracles performed by Jesus, they do not intend them merely as external criteria guaranteeing the authenticity of Jesus' mission. The miracles are an integral part of that mission. It is necessary to see in which sense this is true.

In the parable of Mark 3:27 (Matt. 12:29; Lk. 11:21, 22) Jesus expresses himself on his exorcisms in the following terms: "No man can make his way into a strong man's house and burgle his property unless he has tied up the strong man first. Only then can he burgle his house." The exorcisms do not just point up a generic superiority of Jesus over Satan: they also prove that Satan's reign is at an end. This world has been subjected to the devil's domination, and so the first act in the establishment of the kingdom is the abolition of the devil's domination and his definitive defeat (*see* Rev. 20:2, 3). The parable is moreover suffiiciently clear on the identity of that "stronger person" (Lk. 11:22; *see* Lk. 3:16) who binds Satan and breaks his dominion. It is Jesus: "But if it is by the Spirit of God that I expel demons, then the reign of God has overtaken you" (Matt. 12:28; Lk. 11:20). Jesus is the person in whom and through whom the kingdom of God has already arrived and is present, at least in its initial stage (*see* also Lk. 10:17-20). *See* EXORCISM.

The significance of the cures worked by Jesus is no different. While they are certainly manifestations of God's omnipotence, they also show Jesus' mercy and compassion. They are more, however, than this. When John, in prison, sent his disciples to ask Jesus if he was the "one who was to come," Jesus answered by drawing attention to his works: "Go back and report to John what you hear and see; the blind recover their sight, cripples walk, lepers are cured, the deaf hear, dead men are raised to life, and the poor have the good news preached to them" (Matt. 11:1-5; Lk. 7:18-23). This answer is apparently nothing more than a summary of Jesus' work, such as is found elsewhere too in the Gospels (*see* Mk. 3:7 ff). In reality however it is quite different, for the answer is constructed from prophetic texts, knit together from statements about the eschatological salvation which are read in Isaiah 28:18-19 and 61:1-2. The question about his person is answered by Jesus with an invitation to look at his works as the realization, in its initial stage at least, of definitive salvation. Jesus is conscious of bringing, in his own person, the kingdom of God. This is why he concludes: "Happy the person who is not scandalized in me." The beatitude has the same function and meaning as that already explained: the condition for sharing in the eschatological salvation is "not to be scandalized in him," that is, to keep faith in him through whom God is already bringing about the eschatological salvation. The negative form employed, "Happy those not scandalized," is a warning not to allow oneself to be confused and misdirected by the humble appearance of the Savior or by preconceived ideas which his hearers might have formed in this regard.

We have seen how Jesus' works immediately posed the question of his identity: when John heard of these works, he immediately sent his disciples to ask: "Are you he who is to come?" (Matt. 11:3). The same question is asked by the disciples who witnessed the calming of the storm by Jesus: "Who can this be that the wind and the sea obey him?" (Mk. 4:41). The same question forms on the lips of those who saw the exorcisms (Mk. 1:27; Lk. 4:36) and heard his words. "The people were spellbound by his teaching because he taught with authority, and not like the scribes" (Mk. 1:22; Matt. 7:28, 29; Lk. 4:32; Jn. 7:46). What "teaching with authority" means can be seen from the antitheses of the Sermon on the Mount where Jesus opposes to the word of the Law and of Moses his own word: "I, however, say to you . . ." (Matt. 5:21, 22; 5:27, 28; 5:31, 32).

The question "Who is Jesus?" was not always asked with admiration and internal adherence. It is often inspired by scandal and disapproval. Upon hearing Jesus say to the paralytic: "Your sins are forgiven you," some scribes exclaimed: "Who is this who speaks blasphemy?" (Lk. 5:21; Mk. 2:6; Matt. 9:3). Jesus became an enigma. He finds himself confronted by a perplexed crowd whose question is: "Who is he?" They do not ask to which category or profession does he belong, because he is evidently outside of any category. He is unique, and the question arises as to what is his place and function in the whole history of salvation. The crowd, too, attempted their own answers. In a very curious text of the Gospels Jesus asks his disciples: "Whom do men say I am?" Their answer was: "Some say John the Baptizer, others Elijah, and others Jeremiah or one of the

prophets" (Matt. 16:13-14; Mk. 8:27-28; Lk. 9:18, 19). Herod thought he
was John the Baptizer arisen from the dead (Matt. 14:1-2; *see* Mk. 6:14-
16; Lk. 9:7). Then Jesus poses the same problem to the disciples and Peter
answers: "You are the Messiah, the Son of the living God" (Matt. 16:16-
18) or "The Messiah" (Mk. 8:29) or "The Messiah of God" (Lk. 9:20).
Jesus however ordered them not to say anything about him to anyone
(Mk. 8:30; Lk. 9:21; Matt. 16:20). This surprising attitude of Jesus who
does not reject the title, but rather accepts it without reserve while imposing silence on the disciples is called the Messianic secret. *See* MESSIANIC
SECRET.

With this command to keep silence one would seem to have reached a
stalemate. The title Messiah was not rejected by Jesus, and certainly corresponds to Jesus' awareness of himself and his role. On the other hand
he has reservations on the meaning and mission sometimes attributed to
the title. For this reason he directs attention to another figure, that of the
Son of Man. On the figure of the Son of Man in the biblical and apocalyptic tradition *see* SON OF MAN.

Jesus often spoke of the Son of Man. Indeed, according to the New Testament only Jesus spoke of this figure. The New Testament itself never gives
Jesus this title, the only exception being in Acts 7:56, which is, however,
almost a quotation of Jesus' response given in Acts 26:54. Jesus makes
contrasting affirmations about the Son of Man. After Peter's confession
and the command of silence, Jesus continues: "It is necessary that the
Son of Man suffer much and be condemned by the elders" (Mk. 8:31; Lk.
9:22). On the other hand, in the trial before Caiphas, he sidestepped the
High Priest's question as to whether he was the Messiah, and added:
"You will see the Son of Man seated at the right hand of the Power (God)
and coming in the clouds of heaven" (Matt. 26:64; Mk. 14:62; Lk.
22:69).

These words on the future glory of the Son of Man approach most nearly
what is read in the Jewish tradition about him, and so from here it is
necessary to begin: the Son of Man is the judge and eschatological Savior
who is to be revealed at the end of time to inaugurate the kingdom of
God. In Mark 8:38, (*see* Lk. 9:26; 12:8, 9; Matt. 16:27; 10:33) Jesus
states: "If anyone in this faithless and corrupt age is ashamed of me and
my doctrine, the Son of Man will be ashamed of him when he comes with
the holy angels in his Father's glory." Jesus wishes to underline the decisive importance of the present moment and of one's decision for or
against Jesus in relation to eschatological salvation. The importance of
this decision lies in the fact that it anticipates the eschatological judgment
of the Son of Man (*see* Jn. 3:18-21 and JUDGMENT). What then is the
relationship between the present time and that eschatological judgment;
should the latter infallibly ratify the former? Radical exegesis maintains
that here Jesus was distinguishing between himself and the Son of Man,
whose coming he awaited. The Son of Man, according to these authors,
will ratify with his judgment the decision now taken for or against Jesus.

At first glance this interpretation would seem to be the most obvious;
Jesus is speaking of the Son of Man in the third person. With this exception however, every other consideration excludes such an interpretation.
In fact the words of Jesus in Mark 8:38 clearly imply that the person,
authority and mission of Jesus anticipate the eschatological judgment of
God. This is, remember, the essential function of the Son of Man. The
relationship, then, between the present time and the future does not lie in
the fact that a third personage will ratify at that time the decision now
taken, but that the future, that is, the last judgment, will be the exact
inversion of the present in that he (Jesus) who now appears to be judged,

will himself appear as the judge, the Son of Man. The opposing interpretation is confronted with an insurmountable difficulty: what can be historically established about Jesus leaves no room for any third personality who would intervene between Jesus and his Father, God. There is no trace in Jesus of any awareness that he was the precursor of another.

This interpretation is also confirmed by Jesus' answer to Caiphas during the trial (Matt. 26:64; Mk. 14:62; Lk. 22:69) where any possible reference to another is excluded. Indeed, Jesus was accused of blasphemy for having asserted that they should see the Son of Man seated at the right hand of Power (God) "and coming in the clouds of heaven." If he was accused of blasphemy it was because these words pretended to equality with God. In fact, several times in John's Gospel Jesus is accused of making himself "equal to God" (Jn. 5:18; 10:33), which sound like an echo of the trial scene.

Jesus' response is a fusion of two biblical texts: Psalm 110:1 and Daniel 7:13. Psalm 110 states: "The Lord said to my Lord, sit at my right hand," and was interpreted in a messianic sense (*see* Matt. 22:43). In itself, however, it only indicated a vicarious or delegated sharing in the royal authority of God, for the Messiah was to be the king of God's people. When however the text was fused with that of Daniel 7:13, it places the Messiah in the heavens, in a state of perfect equality with God. Here too Jesus foresees a reversal of the situation: now he is judged and condemned, but he proclaims that the hour is coming and about to arrive in which he will appear in his condition as God's equal, exercising the dominion and judgment of God.

Jesus then was aware that he had a central role to play in the establishment of God's reign, indeed his was the central role.

Between these two stages however Jesus inserted a third moment: "It is necessary that the son of man suffer much, and be rejected by the elders, the chief priests and the scribes, and be put to death" (Mk. 8:31; Matt. 16:21; Lk. 9:22; Mk. 9:31; Matt. 17:22; Lk. 9:43; Mk. 10:32; Matt. 20:17; Lk. 18:31; Mk. 10:45; Matt. 20:28; Mk. 9:12; 14:21, 41). On the authenticity of these texts *see* DEATH OF JESUS.

Here is one of the most original and most disconcerting elements in Jesus' message. The newness does not consist in the fact that Jesus foresees his own tragic end, but in that the glory and domination that will belong to the figure of Son of Man will be the fruit of his humiliation and passion. "It is necessary" means "It is written," that is, it is part of the plan, it is the way chosen by God to bring about salvation, and this is how it has been stated in Scripture. Jesus does not just foretell his own death in these words, but he reveals the meaning of this death in the whole picture of his work and mission. This was to be the way to his glorious exaltation in the future, and thus also the instrument of salvation for all (Mk. 10:45). In the view of Jesus his death and his subsequent exaltation are the very center of his work and mission. From the word quoted, Jesus is seen to have been conscious that his lot was the lot of the kingdom of God, and his triumph the triumph of that kingdom, the establishment of his reign and his coming.

Jesus suffered, was crucified and died. On the third day after his death the apostles proclaimed his resurrection, of which they had been appointed witnesses: "Therefore let the whole house of Israel know beyond any doubt that God has made both Lord and Messiah this Jesus whom you crucified" (Acts 2:36). It might surprise one to hear Peter now attribute to Jesus the title Messiah, about which Jesus himself had entertained such reservations. The only explanation for this was that times had changed.

And not just in the banal sense of the term, that fashions or modes had taken a turn. Times really had changed because Jesus himself had changed, as is expressly stated in Acts 2:36: God had made Jesus Messiah and Lord. The humble condition of his incarnation had been absorbed into divine glory which he had donned, so that the Person who had appeared as a slave was now Lord in full divinity (Phil. 2:5-11). *See* LORD.

It was in view of this that we could assert a real continuity between the Jesus of history and the Jesus of faith, without in the least diminishing the decisive part that the resurrection had to play. Jesus' resurrection introduced a transformation, the importance of which can hardly be exaggerated. It was not, however, a rupture with the past, for it was part and parcel of the consciousness Jesus himself had of his mission and work.

There are also other reasons for the different attitudes of Jesus and of the Church in regard to the title Messiah. We find in Jesus a certain reluctance to allow himself to be framed, or as it were, trapped in a given scheme or category. This reluctance was due in part to the fact that no preconceived scheme or category could ever capture the radical newness and uniqueness that was Jesus. A second reason followed from the first, for that very newness and uniqueness demanded from Jesus' followers a genuine faith which would be threatened at its very roots if Jesus were to be caught up in prejudice and preformed concepts in regard to his mission and work. This state of affairs could be compared with Jesus' attitude to the Law. (*See* LAW.) Jesus was accused of acting irreligiously towards the Law: "he did not observe the sabbath" (Jn. 5:18; 9:16). On the other hand he could with justice say of himself that he had not come to abolish the Law (Matt. 5:17). In Jesus himself was found the reconciliation of these seemingly contradictory terms, for his mission was not to "observe" the Law, but to fulfill it. For the Law's sake it was to be a vehicle of God's will for the people. The Law however could have and did have a contrary effect. Instead of giving rise to a perfect surrender and attitude of docility to God's will, it could and did bring about the suffocation of that willing docility in that it gave the observant man the feeling that he was all right with God, and so had his own justice in which he could, as it were, stand in self-sufficiency born of observance before God.

So, to frame Jesus in a pre-made concept was like having created him for oneself, or having knowledge already, on one's own score, of all that was to be known about him. This was tantamount to closing oneself from the start to whatever he had new to offer, and of blocking out from oneself his uniqueness and what was essential to the concept he had of his person and mission. The man who imprisoned Jesus in his own pre-made concepts could superficially delude himself into believing that he really believed in Jesus. In reality however he did not believe, he did not surrender fully to him, but simply judged him. In other words, he went to see if Jesus measured up to his own preconceived personal ideas of what the Messiah should be like.

Jesus, on the other hand, by the very superabundance of his person and the density with which he packed the interpretation of the messianic prophecies, overflowed the "messianic" pattern, and could not allow himself to be identified with it. This was the reason why Jesus refused to give to the Pharisees a sign confirming his messiahship. Such a sign would not have brought them to belive: it would merely have confirmed them in their unbelief.

It was only possible to give Jesus the title of Messiah when the danger of these equivocations was excluded. Then Messiah was no longer a closed pattern into which Jesus fitted. Jesus' own reality had given the messiahship its form and content. The title Messiah meant continuity with the promise, that is, with the history of salvation. No longer however was the title that which had previously been understood of it: Jesus' own reality had enlightened what really the Messiah was. This was the reason why the Old Testament was avidly read. There the first Christians searched out in the old prophecies traces of the unexpected newness that was Christ. The concrete reality of Christ ended up being the name itself of the Savior, Jesus Christ, or Jesus the Christ, which means the Messiah. On the theological developments of Christology in the New Testament *see* BODY OF CHRIST; DEATH OF JESUS; MESSIAH; MESSIANIC SECRET; PASSION; SON OF GOD; SON OF MAN; *see* also MIRACLES; TEMPTATIONS OF JESUS; EXORCISM; RESURRECTION OF CHRIST.

Jether (jee′-ther), 1. Son of Gideon (Jgs. 8:20-21).

2. An Ishmaelite, father of Amasa who was chief of Absalom's army (2 Sam. 17:25; 1 Kgs. 2:5, 32).

Jethro (jeth′-roe), A priest of Midian, father-in-law of Moses who married his daughter Zipporah. Moses' wife and sons Gershom and Eliezer remained with Jethro when Moses returned to Egypt, and he took them with him when he returned with the Israelites who had come out of Egypt. Jethro offered sacrifices to Yahweh with Moses on Sinai, and he advised Moses to nominate judges who should have competence in judging lesser matters, "You cannot do it alone," Jethro advised him, "Appoint leaders of thousands, hundreds, fifties and tens, to be at the service of the people to administer justice at all times" (Ex. 18:13-23). Moses took his advice. Then Jethro made his way back to his own country. Moses' father-in-law is also called Reuel and Hobab. *See* REUEL, HOBAB.

Jew, The name comes from the Hebrew **yehudi,** a term which has different meanings in the course of biblical history. Of itself the term means "belonging to the tribe of Judah," and after the separation of the tribes of the north, it meant membership in the kingdom of Judah. This last sense is however very rare (2 Kgs. 25:25; Jer. 38:19; 52:28-30). After the exile it became a more common term to designate the inhabitants of the province of Judah during its domination by the Babylonians, Persians and Seleucids, and, later, a subject of the Hasmonean kingdom. The ethnico-political sense of the term is dominant however at least in Palestine, even though it is not exclusively so. The Jews who passed over to Christianity are simply called Jews (Acts 21:39; Gal. 2:13). For John the term Jew acquired a special connotation: it meant those who opposed Jesus, refusing to believe in him and rejecting him. For John they become almost the type of the incredulous who remain undecided for Jesus (Jn. 7:13; *see* 9:22; 19:38; 20:19). John's use of the term mirrors the separation and indeed the opposition that arose in apostolic times between the church and the synagogue.

jewels
your neck in *j.*　　　S. of S. 1:10　thighs are like *j.*　　　S. of S. 7:2
　　like a bride bedecked with her *j.*　Isa. 61:10

Jezaniah, (jez′-a-ny′-ah), One of the Jewish leaders who remained at Mizpah with Gedaliah, the governor of Judah appointed by Nebuchadnezzar after the capture of Jerusalem (587 B.C., Jer. 40:8; 42:1).

Jezebel, 1. Daughter of Ethbaal king of Sidon, and wife of Ahab king of Israel. Upon marrying her, the Bible remarks, he proceeded to serve Baal and worship him (869-850 B.C., 1 Kgs. 16:31). When Jezebel set about butchering the prophets of Yahweh, Obadiah the master of the palace spirited away one hundred of them, fifty at a time, and hid them in a cave where he provided them with food and water (1 Kgs. 18:3, 4). Elijah presented himself to Ahab and accused him and his household of being the cause of the terrible drought that had afflicted Israel for having deserted Yahweh and gone after the Baals. Then he issued a challenge to the four hundred prophets of Baal who ate at Jezebel's table (1 Kgs. 18:16-19). All Israel was gathered together on Mt. Carmel to witness the challenge which reduced the prophets of Baal to ludicrousness. Elijah took them down to the Kishon and slaughtered them there (1 Kgs. 18:20-40).

Upon hearing the fate of her prophets from Ahab, Jezebel swore vengeance on Elijah. He took flight to the wilderness, where, the Bible says, he sat under a furze bush and wished he were dead (19:1-8). Jezebel next arranged for the death of Naboth so as to have his vineyard to enlarge the palace gardens. Elijah went down at Yahweh's command to announce to Ahab the end of his house, and that dogs would devour Jezebel in the field of Jezreel (21:1-26). This prophecy was verified during the revolt of Jehu. When she heard that he was coming to seize her, she adorned herself and appeared at an upstairs window. Jehu ordered the palace eunuchs to throw her down headlong. She was trampled by horses and the dogs devoured her (2 Kgs. 9:30-37). The daughter of Ahab and Jezebel, Athalia, became the wife of Ahaziah of Judah (842 B.C.; 2 Kgs. 8:18, 26).

2. A symbolic name for a self-proclaimed prophetess of Thyatira who introduced pagan customs into Christian worship as did Ahab's Jezebel with the worship of Yahweh (Rev. 2:18-23).

Jezreel (jez'-re-el), 1. A city in the land of Issachar (Josh. 19:18) on the eastern flank of the plain of the same name (also called Esdraelon) at the foot of Mt. Gilboa. Today it is Zer'in. Jezreel was the royal residence of Ahab, king of Israel (869-850 B.C.). It was the scene of the story of Naboth (1 Kgs. 21). Thither was carried Jehoram of Israel when he had been wounded in the battle against the Syrians (2 Kgs. 8:29) and there too a great part of the royal family was massacred by Jehu (2 Kgs. 9:10).

2. The city of Jezreel gave its name to the triangular plain which cuts across the central mountain range from the Jordan to the Mediterranean, separating the mountains of Galilee from the district of Samaria. The mountain range of Carmel closes it off from the south, and the mountains of Nazareth and Tabor from the north, while Mt. Gilboa lies to its east. The valley is well irrigated and very fertile. The Kishon river runs through it from Mt. Gilboa to the Mediterranean, while the Harod flows into the Jordan, cutting a passage for itself from the plain of Jezreel towards that of Beth-shan and the Valley of the Jordan. On the southern border of the plain at the foot of the Carmel range are numerous important cities. From west to east are situated Jokneam, Megiddo (where a strategic pass, much used by conquerors and traders, pierces the Carmel ridge southwards toward the coastal road), Taanach, Ibleam and Dothan.

This area was the locale for important events in Bible history. The plain is very suitable as a battlefield. Here took place the battle between Jabin, king of Hazor, and his allies and the Israelites of Deborah and Barak. The Israelites owed their victory in no small part to the swampy nature of the terrain which hindered the maneuvers of the Canaanite chariots of war (Jgs. 4:5). Later it saw the victory of Gideon over the Midianites. At the springs of the Harod, Gideon selected the three hundred men who should accompany him (Jgs. 6:7). Saul and Jonathan were afraid to meet the Philistines on the plain and so took up their positions on Mt. Gilboa, but the Israelites were totally defeated. Jonathan and Saul died there (1 Sam. 31). In the region of the Kishon river Elijah ordered the massacre of the prophets of Baal after their confrontation on Mt. Carmel (1 Kgs. 18). Josiah king of Judah wished to bring Neco to a halt when he was coming to the help of the Assyrians via the coastal road and the pass guarded by Megiddo. He offered him battle on the plain but was killed in the battle and brought to Megiddo (2 Kgs. 23:29). The story of Judith also took place in an unidentified place called Bethulia, on the plain of Jezreel (4:6).

During the Hellenistic period the valley was called Esdraelon, which is a corruption of the Hebrew name Jezreel. According to Revelation 16:16 Esdraelon will be the battlefield during the eschatological events. *See* AR-MAGEDDON.

3. The first-born of the prophet Hosea, born of Gomer, his wife. The name, like those of his other two children, is symbolic: "Give him the name Jezreel, for in a little while I will punish the house [dynasty] of Jehu for the bloodshed at Jezreel" (Hos. 1:4). "The bloodshed at Jezreel" is the massacre of the dynasty of Ahab perpetrated at Jezreel by the usurper Jehu (2 Kgs. 9:10).

Joab, Son of Zeruiah, David's sister; brother of Abishai and Asahel, and general of David's army (2 Sam. 8:16; 20:23; 1 Chron. 2:16). 1 Chronicles 11:6 attributes to him the decisive step that led to the conquest of Jerusalem. He is at the head of the army in all the principal campaigns of David against Ishbaal, Saul's son (2 Sam. 2:13-3:1); against Absalom, the rebellious son of David (2 Sam. 18); against the Aramaeans and the Ammonites (2 Sam. 10:7-19; 11:1-27). He was a great warrior and most loyal to the king, but at times his zeal carried him to excesses for which David reproved him. While Abner was being chased by Joab's brother Asahel, he struck him in the abdomen with the butt of his spear and killed him. David allowed Abner, who had been general in Saul's army, to go free, but Joab called him back, took him aside and stabbed him to death in revenge for Asahel's death (2 Sam. 2:18-23; 3:24-27). David was much grieved by Abner's death (2 Sam. 3:28-37).

In the battle of the mountains of Ephraim against Absalom, Joab came upon him as he was caught by the head in the branches of a terebinth. Joab took three lances and stabbed him through the heart, against the expressed wishes of David (2 Sam. 18).

Joab was not entrusted with the command of the army in the war against the rebellious Sheba. He however suspected Amasa, the designated leader, of indecisiveness, so Joab took him aside, and in the act of greeting him with a kiss, stabbed him to death (*see* 2 Sam. 20). Joab took Adonijah's side against Solomon in the struggle for succession (1 Kgs. 1:7). Before he died David summoned Solomon to him and listed the crimes of Joab, concluding that "it would be wise not to let his grey head go down to Sheol in peace." Solomon sent Benaiah son of Jehoiada to Joab who had fled for sanctuary to the altar in the Tent of Yahweh. There Joab was killed (1 Kgs. 2:5, 6, 28-35).

Joah, Personal name (2 Kgs. 18:18; 1 Chron. 26:4; 2 Chron. 29:12; 34:8; Isa. 36:3).

Joakim (joe′-a-kim), The husband of Susanna (Dan. 13:1, 4). *See* SUSANNA.

Joanna, One of the pious women who provided for Jesus from their possessions. She was the wife of Herod's steward (Lk. 8:3). According to Luke 24:10 Joanna was among the women who discovered the Lord's tomb empty on Easter Sunday.

Joarib (joe′-a-rib), Ancestor of the priestly family from whom the Maccabees descended (1 Mac. 2:1).

Joash (joe′-ash), *See* JEHOASH.

Job, Book of, A wisdom book of the Old Testament which gets its title from the chief actor in the story, Job, who became a quasi-legendary personage for his sufferings and just dealings (Ezek. 14:14, 20). The action takes place outside Palestine in the land of Uz (Job 1:1) which probably was a region of Arabia close to Edom (*see* Gen. 36:28; Lam. 4:21) from which also come Job's three friends to console him. These were Eliphaz of Teman, Bildad of Shuah and Zophar of Naamath (Job 2:11).

The author seems to have used an older tradition, a prose folk-tale (*see* cc. 1, 2, 42:7-17), which he freely used as the framework for a long poetic discourse on the problem of pain, which is typically represented in the case of Job.

The poetical part starts with a lamentation of Job because of his lot (c. 3). Then the dialogue is introduced and developed in three cycles, in each of which the three friends in turn present their point of view, and to each Job makes answer (4:14; 15-21; 22-27). The dialogue is quite different from the dialogues of other literary traditions. It is not a question of searching for the truth through the dialectic of question and answer. Each speaker expounds at great length his own opinion without being in the least concerned with what the others have to offer. There is in reality no progress in the discussion and the argument ends about where it started.

The friends' thesis is simple: if Job suffers, it is because he has sinned. Let him then acknowledge his sin, do penance, and submit to God who can change his miserable lot. Job's answer is no less decided and insistent: he holds to his conscience which pronounces him innocent, but he does have recourse to God without however begging his pardon.

His recourse to God evolves in two stages. First he beseeches him to defend his innocence against his friends. As the discourse develops however, Job challenges God on the subject of his innocence, of which he is more than certain, in order to see what response God has to offer (cc. 29-31). God's answer awaits the introduction, which was probably later, of a new personality called Elihu, who up to this is not mentioned in the story (cc. 32-37).

The whole solution lies in God's two discourses (cc. 38-41), of which the second seems to have been added later (38:1; 40:6; 40:3-5; 42:1-6). When God is called to judgment by Job he offers no doctrinal dissertation on the meaning of the pains of the just nor on the motives that led him to test Job. God answers Job by manifesting himself to Job's eyes (42:3). The discourse then, according to the author, is a faltering attempt to describe the experience of the vision of God. The image of God seen by Job is translated into a long enumeration of the wonderful works of God in nature. The author's problem of the just man's pain receives no doctrinal answer. Rather it is answered in the actual order of existence.

The author does not expound to the reader the reasons that might clarify the necessity or suitability of putting the just man to the test, but invites him instead to cling by faith to the God whom Job sees. God appeared to him as creator and governor of the universe, but the author chose those works which could more strikingly bring home the sense of mystery in the ways of the Lord. Job thus submits, not in fear of an arbitrary God, but confounded in the presence of a God whose omnipotence, wisdom and providence are superior to any human reckoning.

The discourses of Elihu (cc. 32-37) seem to have been added later by an author who considered that the solution contained in God's discourse was insufficient from a doctrinal point of view. He takes up the theory of Job's friends and takes account of the criticism levelled against them by Job. He insists for example on the merciful pedagogy of God who can also make use of misfortune to correct or prevent the deviation of the just (37:21-24).

The question of the historicity of Job is impossible to answer. Whether such a person as Job, celebrated for his almost legendary virtuousness, existed or not is impossible to say. The dialogue is obviously a poetic composition which is interesting not for the personal details it gives but for the typical case it represents, and for its attack upon the stereotyped view about suffering.

The book contains no evidences that might help to date it accurately. Internal reasons of language and doctrine argue for a post-exilic origin.

Jochebed, A Levite woman, aunt of Amram whom she married to become mother of Moses, Aaron and Miriam (Ex. 2:1; 6:20; Num. 26:59).

Joel, The second of the minor prophets in the Hebrew canon of the Old Testament. Nothing is known of his person. Internal indications, such as mention of the exile and of Greeks, and the emphasis on temple sacrifices, along with late elements in the language, suggest a date of composition late in the Persian period, perhaps 400-350 B.C. The Book of Joel consists of two long poems, each on a different theme.

a. Chapters 1 and 2 describe a plague of locusts that invades Judea like a powerful army. There are liturgical penances and a divine oracle on the end of the plague and the restoration of the land. Although perhaps at the beginning the plague referred to a historical event, in the context of the book it is a sign of the approach of the Day of the Lord (1:15; 2:1, 10) which is the theme of the second part.

b. Chapters 3 and 4 predict the outpouring of the prophetic spirit on Israel, and the judgment of the nations in the valley of judgment. (*See* JEHOSHAPHAT, VALLEY OF.) Then comes the description of the final restoration when "the mountains will drip new wine, and the hills shall flow with milk, and the channels of Judah shall flow with water" (4:18).

In Acts 2:16-21 Peter interprets the event of Pentecost as the fulfilment of the prophecy of Joel 3:1-5 concerning the outpouring of the Holy Spirit.

Johanan, 1. Son of Josiah (1 Chron. 3:15).

2. Son of Kareah and one of the military heads of the Jews who remained with Gedaliah, the governor of Judah appointed by Nebuchadnezzar after the conquest of Jerusalem (587 B.C., Jer. 40:8; 2 Kgs. 25:23). Johanan informed Gedaliah of the conspiracy of Ishmael to assassinate him, but Gedaliah would not listen (Jer. 40:13-16). *See* GEDALIAH, ISHMAEL.

John, 1. John the Baptizer, son of Zechariah, priest of the section of Abijah (Lk. 1:5) and of Elizabeth, who was a descendant of Aaron (Lk. 1:5). Elizabeth was related to Mary the mother of Jesus (Lk. 1:36).

In the announcement of the birth of John appear the elements later to be developed in the Gospel tradition on John's ministry. There is asceticism, the prophetic mission, the preaching of penance and the Messiah, and his being compared to Elijah (Lk. 1:15-17).

His first days John passed in the desert until the day of his manifestation in Israel (Lk. 1:80). This information and other elements in his preaching and ministry have raised the question of the relationship between John and the apocalyptic sect that had its center in the monastery of Qumran. Some authors hold that John lived among these Qumran monks. While this assertion remains at the level of hypothesis it is certain that there are several points of contact with the doctrine and cultic practices of Qumran. Some examples are the baptism of penance, the exegesis of Isaiah 40, some of the eschatological elements, etc.

It is also possible, however, to imagine a much broader influence, for Qumran's way of life and doctrine went beyond the walls of the monastery.

The three synoptics begin their account of the mission of Jesus with a brief presentation of the way of life and preaching of the Baptizer (Mk. 1:2-8; Matt. 3:1-12; Lk. 3:3-17). All three describe more or less the same elements: his external appearance and his way of life make one think of Elijah; his preaching is a provocation to penance in view of the imminent judgment. Luke adds a sample of his moral preaching (3:10-14). The imminent judgment will be brought about by one stronger than John and exercised through fire and spirit. John pronounces himself as one called to prepare a people well disposed to the Lord. The baptism he administers is an external expression of penance. Tradition is unanimous on the fact that Jesus presented himself to be baptized by John (Matt. 3:13-17; Mk. 1:9-11; Lk. 3:21).

John's gospel is almost alone in being interested in the messianic preaching of John the Baptizer and in his witness in favor of Jesus (Jn. 1:19-36; 3:25-30; *see* 1:6).

The Baptizer's life had a tragic end. He was imprisoned by Herod Antipas for having reproved him on account of taking Herodias, his brother Philip's wife, as his own. When Herodias' daughter danced for the guests on Herod's birthday, he was so delighted that he pledged under oath to give her anything she might ask. Under Herodias' instigation she asked for the head of John the Baptizer, whereupon he was beheaded, and his head delivered to the girl on a dish, who handed it to her mother (Matt. 14:1-2; Mk. 6:14-28; Lk. 3:19, 20; 9:7-9).

The synoptic tradition has conserved some of Jesus' words on the Baptizer. Jesus acknowledged the validity of his mission and recognized in him realization of the expected return of Elijah (Matt. 11:7-19; Lk. 7:24-35; Matt. 7:13; Mk. 9:13; Matt. 21:25-27; Mk. 11:30-33; Lk. 20:4-8). Jesus is also careful however to draw the line between the time of the promise and the time of eschatological fulfilment: "The law and the prophets lasted until John" (Matt. 11:12, 13; Lk. 16:16; Matt. 9:14-16; Mk. 2:18-20; Lk. 5:33-35). The apostolic preaching took, as its starting point for the proclamation of the good news, the baptism of John (Acts 13:24, 25; *see* 1:22; 10:37).

John gathered around himself disciples some of whom he directed to Christ (Jn. 1:19-36). These are again mentioned in John 3:25-30, Matthew 11:2-6 and Luke 7:18-23. They were still active even in places far from Palestine long after John's death (e.g. in Ephesus, Acts 18:25; 19:3).

2. John, one of the Twelve, son of Zebedee and brother of James (Matt. 10:2; Mk. 3:17; Lk. 6:14; Acts 1:13), a fisherman from Bethsaida, who was called by Jesus while he repaired the nets with his brother and father (Matt. 4:21, 22; Mk. 1:19, 20). With Peter and his brother James he belonged to the more intimate circle of Jesus' friends, and was the privileged witness of some events in Jesus' life such as the raising of the daughter of Jairus to life (Mk. 5:27; Lk. 8:51), the Transfiguration (Mk. 9:2; Matt. 17:1; Lk. 9:28), and the agony in the garden at Gethsemani (Mk. 14:33; Matt. 26:37).

Both brothers were called "Sons of Thunder" by Jesus probably because of their impetuous zeal (Lk. 9:54; Mk. 9:38; Lk. 9:49). When their mother, who was ambitious for them, asked that they might receive seats at the right and the left of the Lord in his kingdom, he responded by offering them a share in the cup he was to drink, that is, in his lot (Matt. 20:20-28; Mk. 10:35-45). They accepted his offer.

In the Acts of the Apostles John often appears in the company of Peter (Acts 3:1-11; 4:13, 19; 8:14) as already he had appeared with him in the preparation of the Last Supper (Lk. 22:8), probably in the story about the identification of the traitor at the Last Supper (Jn. 13:21-30), and in the story of the empty tomb (Jn. 20:3-10). Paul met him at Jerusalem when he came there to discuss with the other apostles the question of the obligation of the Mosaic law on the Gentile converts (Gal. 2:9). Tradition has it that he died at Ephesus at a very advanced age. On his writings *see* JOHN, GOSPEL OF; JOHN, EPISTLES OF; REVELATION.

John, Epistles of, The epistolary literature of the New Testament contains three letters which tradition attributes to the apostle John. None of them however bear his name. The second and third letters have proper epistolary inscription and content. Both are sent by a person who calls himself "the elder" or "presbyter." John's second letter is sent to "a lady who is elect and to her children" (v.1). This should be understood as a metaphorical expression for a local Christian community (*see* v. 13). The purpose of the letter is to exhort its destinataries to remain stable in the commandments received (vv. 4-6) and to put them on their guard against those "antichrists" who are going around spreading false doctrines, and especially denying the reality of the Incarnation (vv. 7-11). The author in the end promises to visit his people soon and concludes with the customary greetings.

The third letter of John is addressed to a Christian by the name of Gaius whose virtue, loyalty and hospitality the author praises (vv. 2-8, 11, 12). He then reproves a certain Diotrephes, an ambitious and obstinate Christian. The latter refuses to receive the brothers who come to him, nor does he wish to receive the letter sent to him by the author, the "presbyter" (vv. 9-10). He promises to visit soon, and says his farewell (vv. 13-15).

Some churches did doubt the canonicity of the two letters, both in the East and in the West. This sporadic doubt endured until the fourth century and was perhaps due to the scanty use that was made of these letters on account of their brevity and subject.

The first letter of John is different in form and content. This has neither inscription nor conclusion that is epistolary. The writer launches into the argument straightaway with phrases that recall the solemn introduction to the fourth gospel (1 Jn. 1:1-4). Nor does the content remind one of a letter, but rather a didactic writing addressed in general to all the faithful without having any particular church or individual in mind.

The subject is not developed logically. The exhortations and instructions follow one another like variations on the same theme: communion of life with God in Jesus, God's Son, and its moral demands. The author's words acquire an urgency and gravity on account of the continual condemnatory references to heretics who are insinuating themselves with their false doctrines: they deny that Jesus has come in flesh (1 Jn. 4:2; *see* 2 John 7) and refuse to accord him the title of Christ and Son of God (2:22; 4:15; 5:5). On the other hand they boast of a superior knowledge and communion with God which places them on a plane above the common Christian (1:6; 4:6, 9; 4:8, 20). The author shows the falsity of these positions by proving their incompatibility with the demands of a true communion with God.

In the errors that the author combats are seen elements that were to emerge with clarity in the Gnostic and Docetist heresies. These were to be attacked within a few years by Ignatius of Antioch, who died a martyr under Trajan, i.e. between 97 and 117 A.D. Other writings of the New Testament such as Jude, Revelation 1-3 and 2 Peter refer to errors that developed along the same lines.

The question of authorship is debated. The similarities of style and theology are undeniable and oblige one to put 1 John in the same tradition from which comes the gospel of John. So what has been said of the Johannine authority for the gospel also holds true here, in a broad sense. The second and third letters have with more insistence and better reason been attributed to John the Presbyter of whom Papias, bishop of Hierapolis, speaks. (*See* JOHN, GOSPEL OF.) In these letters the author identifies himself as the presbyter. The title however is not so univocal as to impose this solution. For Papias the "presbyters" are the disciples of the apostles, that is, the second generation of Christians, which was already dying off at the time of Papias. In the epistle then it can be understood in its obvious sense of "elder," alluding perhaps to the venerableness and longevity of the apostle, who, according to Irenaeus, lived to a ripe old age. This expression would be more obvious if one were to admit that the second and third letter were written in his name, and in the first person, but by another who spontaneously used the title by which the apostle was commonly known.

In 1 John 5:7, 8 the original text of the epistle is: "There are three who give witness: the Spirit, the water and the blood, etc." The words: . . . "in heaven: the Father, the Word and the Holy Spirit, and these three are one. And there are three who give witness on earth" are only read in the Latin version; from there they passed into some Greek manuscripts. The added words form the so-called Johannine comma. They contain an allegorical exegesis of the three witnesses, which later passed into the text as a gloss on the Latin and finally found its way into the scripture text itself. The words probably originated in Spain or Africa in the fourth or fifth centuries, but they are not found in the manuscripts until the ninth century.

John, Gospel of, The fourth of the canonical gospels is attributed by tradition to John the Apostle, brother of James. (*See* JOHN.) The most ancient and important witness to this tradition is Irenaeus, a native of Asia Minor and bishop of Lyons in France. He died around 202 A.D. According to Irenaeus, John lived in Ephesus until the time of the emperor Trajan (98-117 A.D.) and there wrote his gospel. Irenaeus' testimony is very important as he was a disciple of Polycarp who had personally known the apostle John, who had appointed him bishop of Smyrna.

This solid chain of tradition was called into doubt in the last century on account of a celebrated text of Papias, bishop of Hierapolis in Phrygia, Asia Minor. According to Irenaeus, Papias was also a disciple of John. In a text however that has been conserved by the historian Eusebius of Caesarea, Papias expresses himself somewhat differently. This is the disputed text: "Wherever anyone came who had been a follower of the presbyters, I (Papias) inquired into the words of the presbyters, what Andrew or Peter had said, or Philip or Thomas, or James or John or Matthew, or any other disciple of the Lord, and what Aristion and the presbyter **John**, disciples of the Lord, were still saying." After citing the text Eusebius comments: "Here it should be observed that he (Papias) twice included the name of John. The first John he puts in the same list as Peter, James, Matthew, and the rest of the apostles, obviously with the evangelist in mind; the second, with a changed form of expression, he places in a second group outside the number of the apostles, giving precedence to Aristion and clearly calling John a presbyter" (Hist. Eccl. 3:39).

Eusebius was making his point for another reason: he wishes to deprive Revelation, which the millenarists were quoting in their own favor, of the authority of John. To this purpose he attributes Revelation to the presbyter John. Even prescinding however from this hypothesis of Eusebius, it must be acknowledged that his interpretation is the most obvious. Very few scholars today hold that Papias, while making two mentions in the same passage of a John was in reality referring to the same person.

Neither Eusebius nor Papias ever doubted the apostolic origin of the gospel. When however in the last century the traditions concerning the origins of the gospels were subjected to critical analysis, some wished to extend to the gospel what Eusebius had proposed for Revelation. Their argument ran thus: Just as Irenaeus was mistaken in making Papias a disciple of John the Apostle, so too he could have been mistaken when he made Polycarp a disciple of John the Apostle. Both references were in reality to John the Presbyter. So too, while Eusebius held that it was John the Presbyter and not John the Apostle who was the author of Revelation, so it could be that the gospel was attributed to the apostle through the confusion that arose between him and his namesake, the presbyter.

Little by little however this type of argumentation appeared gratuitous. In fact, the attribution of the gospel to the apostle did not depend solely on Irenaeus. At the same time in other churches of the East and West the gospel was taken as John's. Clement of Alexandria (150-211 A.D.), Origen and Tertullian (160-222 A.D.) speak in this vein. The Muratorian canon (*see* MURATORIANUM, CANON) has a polemic thrust against those who would deny John's authorship to the gospel, even though this was being done to combat more decisively the Montanist heresy, which claimed the authority of that gospel. On the other hand, even if Irenaeus could have erred in the case of Papias, whom he did not personally know, the same could hardly be asserted of Polycarp, whose disciple Irenaeus had actually been.

While the connection between John the Apostle and the fourth gospel rests on sound foundations, one must immediately add that he is not its author in the sense, say, that Paul is the author of the Epistle to the Galatians. John is at the source of the tradition that is gathered in the gospel. The work itself however is the fruit of a long process of composition, the details of which are not perfectly clear. This is the conclusion one draws from some characteristics of the writing.

The argument before all others that has served to settle in a decisive manner the question of authorship, and which is based on the identification of the "disciple whom Jesus loved," points in the direction of a long and complex process of composition. The gospel has two conclusions, one in John 20:30 and the other in John 21:24, 25. Chapter 21 then is an appendix to a first redaction of the work, which was in all probability added after the death of the "disciple whom Jesus loved," (*see* Jn. 21:20-23) and whose witness is collected in the gospel (Jn. 21:24). This is the same disciple who reposed on the breast of the Lord at the Last Supper (Jn. 13:23), who stood at the foot of the cross (Jn 19:26) and accompanied Peter to the empty tomb (Jn. 20:2). Some author's think that the same disciple is referred to in two other texts that refer to an anonymous disciple (Jn. 1:40; 18:15) but, at least in the case of 18:15, this identification does not seem the most probable interpretation.

Tradition has always seen in this disciple whom Jesus loved the apostle John, and with every reason. For he was certainly one of the twelve and one of the three intimates, Peter, James and John. It cannot have been Peter because he is referred to in context by name (*see* 13:6), nor James who died a martyr in Jerusalem around 42 A.D. (*see* Acts 12:1, 2), and about whom we could not have the information supplied in John 21:20-23. It cannot therefore have been anyone but John.

Only with difficulty, however, can we imagine that John would have chosen for himself that designation. On the other hand, the 'disciple whom Jesus loved' appears, without dissolving into an ideal figure, to be the type of the true disciple. All this would seem to express the veneration of the disciples of John for their master, whose testimony they gathered into this book.

To come then to the question of composition. First and foremost must be excluded from the text, as being non-authentic, two passages: a. John 5:4 is an explanatory gloss, neither canonical nor inspired and b. John 7:53-8:11, on the woman taken in adultery: the text is canonical and inspired, but did not originally belong to John and is in fact missing from the better manuscripts in all the recensions or found at other points in the gospel (e.g. after Jn. 21, or Jn. 7:35 or even after Lk. 21:38).

For the question of composition other factors are also important. First, it is difficult to say where the discourse with Nicodemus finishes. From John 3:14 it seems that it is no longer the Lord but John that is speaking. The same occurs in John 3:31-35, which do not seem to be the words of John the Baptist, but once more the reflections of the evangelist.

Secondly, for some time now some incoherence has been noticed in the order of chapters 5-7 in the gospel. In 7:15-24 Jesus refers to the miracle of c. 5: "one work have I done," but in the altered order of cc. 5 and 7 a whole year should have intervened as c. 6 speaks of a Pasch. Then in 5:54 Jesus is in Galilee, in 5:1 in Jerusalem, and in 6:4 he is going across the Sea of Galilee. In chapter 7:1 however it states that "after these things, Jesus went through Galilee, not being able as yet to go through Judaea, for the Jews wished to kill him," which alludes to c. 5:18. The most logical order would seem to be c. 4, c. 6, 5:47 ff., c. 7:15-24, c. 7:1 ff.

Finally chapter 21 is clearly an appendix as we have already stated.

It is not possible here to outline all the explanations that have been offered. Some scholars have thought to explain the second and third points above through a chance disturbance of the pages of the apostle's manuscript. Others have attempted a reconstruction of the sources or documents from the fusion of which the gospel would have come. The most satisfying results have come from the distinction between the "Booklet of Signs" (*see* Jn. 20:30) which contained a selection of miraculous cures or "signs" worked by Jesus (*see* SIGNS) and another collection of the principal discourses of Jesus, those, that is, that revolve around his solemn declarations: "I am" the light, the shepherd, the life and so on.

Any explanation of the origin of the fourth gospel cannot limit itself to the written stage but should also reach back to the time when the gospel was first preached.

The fourth gospel, like the Synoptics, has its roots in the catechesis, preaching, cult and life in general of the communities of one or other definite environment of the apostolic church. This common origin is above all clear in the account of the Passion and in the narrative material of chapters 2 to 12. It is not so clear however when one refers to the discourses of Jesus. Any person reading the gospel is struck by the differences between the discourses of Jesus in Matthew, Mark and Luke and the long monologues that Jesus holds in John.

At one time scholars hoped to explain this difference by the fact that John was reporting what Jesus said in his ministry in Jerusalem while the Synoptics dealt with his mission in Galilee. The fact remains however that the author of 1 John speaks exactly the same way as does Jesus in the gospel of John.

A more leisurely and minute examination of the discourses of Jesus as reported by John reveal that they are developed from or converge in words of Jesus that are not absent from parallel statements in the synoptic tradition. A recent author, C. H. Dodd, has noted that "in examining parallels to Synoptic sayings we found ourselves several times brought directly to the heart of Johannine theology." In the Johannine tradition the words of Jesus have undergone a peculiar treatment. On the one hand they have adopted characteristic literary forms, as for instance in the revelation discourses, "I am," allegorical forms and so on. On the other hand they spread by means of a repetition that is concentric and reveal ever more clearly and profoundly their implications in the light of the paschal faith.

A typical example of this method is the last part of the discourse on the bread of life (Jn. 6; *see* LORD'S SUPPER), which is constructed on the words of Jesus that were pronounced at the Last Supper. The conversation with Nicodemus (Jn. 3) is constructed on the baptismal instruction (Mk. 16:16; 1 Pet. 1:3, 23; Matt. 18:3). The theme of the mutual knowledge of Father and Son which is central to John has a clear parallel in Matthew 11:27 and Luke 10:22.

The Johannine tradition developed first as an oral tradition and later crystallized in writing around a narrative nucleus which was made up of the "Book of Signs." Other authors think that the fusion between discourse and narrative had already taken place in the oral stage. In either case, the attempts to put the tradition in writing had to make a definitive choice and take a definite order with a well-defined scope and direction in mind. Even after its first redaction in writing, however, the writing continued to increase and assimilate new material, bringing about the unbalance which we have noticed. This process ended after the death of the apostle (*see* 21).

If we admit this long process of composition, then the classical problem of the relationship between John and the Synoptics appears in a new light. The opinion of the fathers that John wrote to complement and in part bring more precision to what the Synoptics had put down no longer holds. The gospel of John is clearly an independent work. Although one cannot exclude the possibility that John knew our gospels of Mark and Luke, today scholars are more inclined to think that the contacts between the different writings took place at the level of the traditions they contained and that the influence was mutual. The most interesting similarities are noticed between John and Luke, particularly in the account of the Passion.

The Gospel of John creates in the reader the impression of unity and coordination of parts such as he doesn't find in the Synoptics. The Synoptics are more obviously collections of single, independent incidents or sayings. It is on account of this unity that John's Gospel is often compared to the seamless garment of Jesus referred to in John 19:23.

In John 20:31 the author tells us what was the point of the writing: "that you may believe that Jesus is the Christ and that believing you may have life in him." These words are a re-echo of the reflections of the evangelist on the outcome of Jesus' ministry in 12:37-43: "Though they had been present when he gave so many signs, they did not believe in him. . . ." This unbelievable incredulity is then explained by a quotation of Isaiah 6:8, 10 about their hardness of heart. There follows a résumé of the principal themes of the gospel (Jn. 12:44-50). The first part then comprises cc.

1-12 and, following the author's own words (v. 37), can be called the "Book of Signs." The second part begins with 13:1: "Before the Feast of the Pasch, when Jesus knew that his hour had come to pass from this world to the Father, . . ." The second part can then be entitled "The Hour of Jesus," that is, the hour of his exaltation and glorification, which includes the cross and resurrection (*see* 12:23). This hour is the point towards which the whole preceding narrative tends (*see* 2:4; 7:30; 8:20; *see* HOUR).

The theme of the "Book of Signs" is the progressive and inchoate revelation of the glory of Jesus. This is presented as a selection of episodes which involve a narrative and a discourse. The discourse attempts to highlight the revelation contained in the sign. (*See* SIGN.) Jesus heals the paralytic but this shows that he is the life-giver (c. 5). He feeds the crowds to proclaim the bread of life that has come down from heaven (c. 6). He raises Lazarus to life to announce himself "resurrection and life" (c. 11). These episodes for the most part take place in Jerusalem and in a context that is not unrelated to the great Jewish festivals. On the Feast of Tabernacles Jesus states that he is the light of the world and the source of living water. (*See* TABERNACLES, FEAST OF.) The Eucharistic discourse was given "when the Pasch was near" (Jn. 6:4). Other discourses are evidently saturated with liturgical-sacramental doctrine and reference, such as the baptismal one in c. 3 and the Eucharistic one in c. 6.

The themes that are listed are so many centers of interest that in themselves they suggested the episodes narrated. They are however worked into a dynamic and dramatic structure. The progressive revelation that Jesus makes of himself provokes and demands from men a reaction. It brings about judgment (Jn. 3:18): the apostles respond with faith (Jn. 2:11) while others become hardened with an incredulity that culminates in the decision to kill Jesus. The drama unfolds to the eyes of the reader, not simply as a story told of the past with no reference to him, but with all the urgency of an option that he too must make.

The prologue is probably an adaptation of a Christological hymn (Jn 1:1-18). The author then follows a catechetical plan. He begins with the tradition on John the Baptizer, of which the witness in favor of Christ is alone retained. (*See* JOHN; LAMB.) There follows an account of the beginnings of the ministry which culminate in the faith of the disciples (Jn 2:11). The first part of the ministry of Jesus comprises the first Pasch in Jerusalem with the promise from the new Temple (2:12-24), the dialogue with Nicodemus on birth from the Spirit (Jn. 3) and the revelation of Jesus' messiahship to the Samaritan woman. This part finishes with Cana where Jesus cures the son of the dignitary of Herod's court (Jn. 4:43-54).

From chapter 5 on, everything converges on the mystery of the person of Jesus. On the occasion of the cure of the paralytic Jesus presents himself as a Person with divine power received from the Father to vivify and judge. The reaction of incredulity sharpens. In chapter 6 Jesus tells that he is the bread of life come down from heaven. A great part of his followers abandon him but the disciples' faith is reaffirmed on the lips of Peter. Chapters 7 and 8 tell of Jesus revealing himself openly as the light of the world on the occasion of the Feast of Tabernacles. The debate that develops around his person becomes more inflamed. The Jews (*see* JEWS) attempt to draw the hesitant crowds to their side, and Jesus is obliged to hide himself from them when they attempt to stone him. Chapters 9 and 10 take up themes from Ezekiel 36: Jesus repudiates and denounces the shepherds of Israel and reveals himself as the Good Shepherd who gives life. Jesus in chapter 11 goes up towards Jerusalem to raise Lazarus from the grave and announce himself as the resurrection and life. This is also

Jesus' deliberate surrender into the hands of those who sought to kill him and had laid snares for his life. From chapter 12 John takes up the thread of the synoptic tradition.

join

may *j.* our enemies	Ex. 1:10	*j.* the two sticks Ezek. 37:17
He *j.* with him	2 Chron. 20:36	foreigners who *j.* themselves
Woe to you who *j.*	Isa. 5:8	Isa. 56:6
	j. ourselves to the Lord Jer. 50:5	

joined
latter kings *j.* forces   Gen. 14:3

joints

Israel between the *j.*		his hip *j.* shook Dan. 5:6
1 Kgs. 22:34; 2 Chron. 18:33	upheld by *j.* and sinews Col. 2:19	
	j. and marrow Heb. 4:12	

joking
sons-in-law thought he was *j.*
     Gen. 19:14

Jokneam (jok′-ne-am), A Levitical town in the land of Zebulun, (Josh. 19:11; 21:34) at the foot of Mount Carmel towards the plain of Jezreel, northwest of Megiddo. Today it is Tell Qeimun. It was conquered by Joshua (Josh. 12:22), and was situated in the fifth of Solomon's districts (1 Kgs. 4:12).

Jokshan, Son of Abraham and Keturah, and father of Sheba and Dedan (Gen. 25:2, 3; 1 Chron. 1:32).

Joktan, In the Table of Nations, the son of Eber (Gen. 10:25-30).

Joktheel (jok′-the-el), The name given by Amaziah king of Judah (800-783 B.C.) to the Edomite city of Sela when he captured it (2 Kgs. 14:7).

Jonadab, *See* JEHONADAB.

Jonah, Son of Amittai, of the tribe of Zebulun, a native of Gath-hepher, a prophet who was probably a contemporary of King Jeroboam II of Israel (786-746 B.C.). According to 2 Kings 14:25 Jonah prophesied the recovery of the territory of Israel from the pass of Hamath to the sea of Arabah, that is, the Dead Sea. Jonah is the central figure in the book of Jonah. *See* JONAH, BOOK OF.

Jonah, Book of, The fifth of the minor prophets in the order of the Hebrew canon of the Old Testament. In contrast to the other prophetic books, Jonah is not a collection of oracles pronounced by the prophet who then gave his name to the book. The Book of Jonah belongs to the narrative literary genre and recounts some surprising episodes in which Jonah is the central character. These episodes pose particular historical problems which must be resolved in the light of the literary genre of the book and taking into account the didactic intent of its author.

Jonah, the son of Amittai, receives from the Lord the order to go to Nineveh to preach against its wickedness. The reluctant Jonah, however, disobeys the Lord and embarks at Joppa on a ship bound for Tarshish. The Lord however sends down a storm that brings the ship close to shipwreck. The sailors suspect the other-worldly origin of this storm and draw lots to identify the person on whose account they have met with this misfortune. The lot falls to Jonah who confesses that he is at fault and proposes that they throw him into the sea so that the storm may cease. The sailors pray to God to have pity on the man and then carry out his proposal. The Lord however sends a great fish which swallows Jonah. There in the belly of the fish Jonah remains for three days and three nights. From the fish's belly Jonah prays a prayer of thanksgiving. Then the Lord commands the fish to spew Jonah upon the shore (cc. 1-2).

In c. 3:1 the Lord repeats his command to Jonah, who this time obeys him. He arrives at Nineveh, "an enormously great city; it took three days to go through it" (3:3). He preaches his message of repentance and obtains an unexpected success with his preaching: "they (the Ninevites) proclaimed a fast and all of them, great and small, put on sackcloth" (3:5). The description of these manifestations of penance have something of the grotesque. The king not only arose "from his throne, laid aside his robe, covered himself with sackcloth and sat in the ashes" (3:6) but he proclaimed a fast that had to be observed by both men and animals! These too should be covered with sackcloth and call loudly to God (3:7-9). When God saw their repentance he repented of the evil that he had threatened them with.

The book has a last surprise in store for the reader: Jonah was indignant and fell into a rage at the way in which the Ninevites had converted and avoided the evil destined for them. He reproves God for being "a gracious and merciful God, slow to anger, rich in clemency, loathe to punish" (4:2). Jonah retires from the city and waits from afar to see what would happen. The Lord provided a gourd plant that grew up over Jonah's head, giving shade that relieved him of any discomfort, but the next morning God sent a worm which attacked the plant, so that it withered.

Jonah was again enraged and protested to God. God however had caused all this to silence Jonah's protests: "You are concerned over the plant which cost you no labor . . . and should I not be concerned over Nineveh, the great city, in which there are more than 120,000 persons who cannot distinguish their right hand from their left, not to mention the many cattle" (4:11).

This is the way the book ends. Jonah has been called the reluctant prophet. The author of the book however is not so much interested in recording the personal adventures of the prophet as in demonstrating a thesis. His doctrinal position is in fact found in the verses that conclude the book. The God of Israel is too great to be exclusively absorbed in the nationalistic interests of the Hebrews. This is proposed with strong polemic accents. Israel for the author personifies the closed mentality which wishes to stigmatize others. To pillory and denounce this mentality the author rallied a not insignificant force of humor and irony. To make his point cuttingly the author chose, as Israel's rival in being the object of God's attention and mercy, the Assyrian people and the city of Nineveh, both of them associated with some of the worst disasters in Jewish history.

The city however is seen and described for the polemic purposes of the book, without any claim to historical accuracy. The city is so great that it takes three days to walk through it! The people promptly respond to the call for penance, and the animals share in this response! The number of citizens can be guessed from the fact that there were 120,000 infants! All this was to bring home to the Jews how small a nation they were and how reluctant in carrying out the will of God. Like Jonah himself, they only respond when God forces them. The book then wishes the Jews to come to a more realistic self-awareness and to view other peoples too with the eyes of Yahweh.

If chapters 3 and 4 cannot be taken as an account of an episode in Assyrian history that really took place, then neither should more be asked of chapters 1 and 2, which speak of Jonah in the belly of the fish. Any explanation that attempts to comprise all aspects of the narrative runs into insurmountable difficulties. Moreover one must consider the imbalance that exists between the prose account of chapter 1 and the psalm recited by Jonah in chapter 2. This psalm belongs to the type of thanksgiving hymns one reads in the psalter. In this type of psalm, the psalmist recounts the grace received, and therefore the difficulty or calamity from which he has been snatched. This calamity which often placed his life in jeopardy, is described in almost epic tones, with conventional style and phrases. *See* LAMENTATIONS.

The psalmist was already on the point of entering the region of the dead (Jonah 2:3) when God heard his voice and freed him. The danger of death is sometimes described with the image of a rushing river or a swirling sea (*see* e.g. Pss. 18:5, 17; 42:8; 69:2, 3, 16). In this class must be placed the psalm of Jonah (2:4-7). In fact he doesn't speak of finding himself in the fish's belly. Instead he speaks of having been freed, while the liberation does not really take place until after the hymn. One is tempted to state that the prose version is nothing more than a too literal interpretation of what the psalm poetically sings, with the addition of new elements drawn from the author's imagination. The psalm sings in epic tones of a danger of death from which God releases the author: the prose makes the poetic elements too material. Like Jonah the people are reluctant, and like Jonah they still cannot believe that God can spread his mercy also to others, whom he finds more disposed to his advances than they are. And in this way the author of Jonah makes his doctrinal point.

The New Testament makes allusion to Jonah in the words of Jesus in the answer he makes to the Pharisees who ask for a sign. In Mark 8:11, 12 Jesus categorically refuses to grant the request of the Pharisees for a sign, for theirs was an incredulity that no sign could have overcome. Matthew 16:1-4 however refers to the sign of Jonah, which is explained in the same gospel in 12:38-40. The sign of Jonah is the resurrection of Jesus. This however was not a concession to the incredulity of the Pharisees, for this takes nothing away from the absolute demand for faith. Jesus just used the sign of Jonah as an allusion to his definitive victory, which will be salvation for the believer and judgment for those who still hold themselves in obstinacy.

In Matthew 12:41 Jesus condemns the incredulity of his generation by comparing it with the prompt response of the Ninevites to Jonah's call to repentance. Theirs will be a judgment ever so much heavier, seeing who it is that invites them to conversion. Luke 11:32 repeats Matthew 12:41, but in Luke 11:29-30 there is a somewhat different version of the sign of Jonah: Jesus does not expressly refer to the permanence of Jonah in the belly of the fish, but only to his preaching repentance to the men of Nineveh. Jonah's stay in the fish's belly is probably included, in that, for Luke, Jonah was a person redeemed from death to bring to men a message of repentance and conversion. With this interpretation the version of Luke 11:29-30 and Matthew 12:38-40 coincide in substance.

The fact that the New Testament uses the Jonah story as a type for Christ does not oblige us to affirm its historicity. All that the typical sense demands is the literary reality of the type in Sacred Scripture, not the historical reality. *See* TYPICAL SENSE.

Jonam (joe´-nam), An ancestor of Jesus in the genealogy given by Luke 3:30.

Jonathan, 1. Jonathan, son of Gershom, son of Moses, and his descendants were priests in the tribe of the Danites in the city of Dan (the ancient Laish) until the time of the captivity of the land. The story of the sanctuary of Dan and of the emigration of the tribe to this territory is one of the appendices to the book of Judges (Jgs. 17-18).

2. Jonathan, the eldest son of King Saul. Helped only by his armor-bearer, Jonathan attacked an outpost of the Philistines in the pass of Michmash, killing about twenty men. Panic seized the whole encampment of the Philistines. Saul's lookouts in Geba of Benjamin told the king of the confusion that reigned among the Philistines. The Israelites decided to exploit the situation, in which they won a great victory (1 Sam. 14). While the battle was in progress Saul made the following vow: "Cursed be the man who takes food before evening, before I am able to avenge myself on my enemies." Without being aware of the vow, Jonathan "thrust the end of the stick he was holding into the honeycomb and put his hand to his mouth, then his eyes brightened." When told of his father's curse, Jonathan took issue with it, stating that had the people been allowed to eat their fill of the booty, the victory would even have been greater (1 Sam. 14:27-30). Saul decided to pursue the Philistines into the night and on this the priest consulted the Lord. When no answer was forthcoming this was interpreted to mean that somebody had transgressed the ban pronounced by Saul. Jonathan was found guilty and Saul wished to punish him with the death he had threatened to any transgressor. The soldiers, however, interceded for Jonathan, showing the victory had been made possible because God was with him (1 Sam. 14:45, 46). Jonathan and David became fast friends in the court of Saul (1 Sam 18:1-4). When Jonathan heard that Saul had decided to do away with David, he warned him and assured David that he would speak with the king on his behalf. Jonathan succeeded in assuaging the king's anger and David returned to court (1 Sam. 19:1-7). The peace was short-lived. There was another attempt at reconciliation by Jonathan and then the friends separated (1 Sam. 20). They met again at Horesh in the desert of Ziph (1 Sam. 23:14-18). Jonathan died in the battle of Mt. Gilboa against the Philistines. In the same battle his brother Abinadab and Malchishua and his father Saul were also killed (1 Sam. 31). At Ziklag David got the news of their death (2 Sam. 1:1-10) and composed an elegy on the two (2 Sam. 1:19-27).

Jonathan had a son Meribbaal, whose feet were crippled. Later David was to provide for his welfare (2 Sam. 9:1-13; *see* MERRIBBAAL).

3. Jonathan, son of the priest Abiathar. When David had to abandon Jerusalem due to Absalom's revolt, Jonathan and Ahimaaz, son of Zadok, remained on at En-rogel, in the neighborhood of the city, to be a link between David and those who remained loyal to him in Jerusalem (2 Sam. 15:24-37; 17:17). Later they were discovered and forced to flee. They went first to Bahurim, where they hid in a cistern, and later they reached David (17:18-22). Jonathan and his father Abiathar took the part of Adonijah against Solomon in the scramble for the succession to the throne of David (1 Kgs. 1:42-43).

4. Jonathan, a scribe in Jerusalem, a contemporary of Zedekiah, king of Judah (598-587 B.C.). Jeremiah was confined to his house when he was accused of having tried to pass over to the Babylonian camp during the siege of the city (Jer. 38:26).

5. Jonathan, son of Mattathias, brother of Judas and Simeon and one of the chieftains of the Maccabees. Jonathan succeeded his brother Judas when he was killed in the battle against Bacchides (1 Mac. 9:28-31). Jonathan retreated with his men to the desert of Tekoa. Then he sent his brother John with a convoy to ask permission of his friends the Nabataeans to deposit with them their great quantity of baggage. John was attacked and killed and lost everything. Jonathan carried out an expedition of reprisal as an example to others and then took refuge in the mar-

shes of the Jordan (1 Mac. 9:35-42). In another encounter with Bacchides, Jonathan and his men saved their lives by swimming to the other
bank of the Jordan (1 Mac. 9:43-49).

After the death of the High Priest Alcimus (159 B.C.) Bacchides returned
to Syria. After a truce of two years he returned but was defeated in his
attempt to take Bathbasi, where Jonathan and his brother Simon had fortified themselves. Terms of peace were settled on and Jonathan became
undisputed head in Judea. He took advantage of the internal conflicts of
the Seleucid regime to consolidate his own position and secure his reign.

First he gave his support to Demetrius who promised to gather an army as
his ally. Jonathan made use of him to establish himself in Jerusalem and
fortify the city (1 Mac. 10:1-14). Then came Demetrius' rival Alexander,
who, to draw Jonathan's support from him, made him High Priest on the
Feast of the Tabernacles, 152 B.C. (1 Mac. 10:15-21). Demetrius' response
was to increase his offers, but Jonathan did not trust such an intimate
friendship and decided to remain on the side of Alexander (1 Mac. 10:22-
47). Alexander conquered Demetrius, who died in the battle (1 Mac.
10:48-50).

Demetrius' son, Demetrius II Nicator, started his offensive against Alexander in 147 B.C. His general, Apollonius, decided to wipe out Jonathan's
position, but after various skirmishes in the region of Philistea, Jonathan
emerged victorious and won for himself new favors from Alexander (1
Mac. 10:67-89).

Demetrius II succeeded in installing himself as king, but having experienced Jonathan's strength, he decided it was better to have him as an
ally than as an enemy, so he confirmed him as High Priest (1 Mac. 11:20-
37). Jonathan in fact helped him against his rival Trypho (1 Mac. 11:38-
51). When however Demetrius had secured for himself his throne, he
broke all his promises and estranged himself from Jonathan. Jonathan
thus went over to Trypho and his brother Antiochus VI, son of Alexander
Balas, and defeated the army that Demetrius had sent against him (1 Mac.
11:54-74). Jonathan renewed the alliance with Rome and Sparta which
his brother Judas had made (1 Mac. 12:1-23).

Trypho was determined to become king and do away with king Antiochus, but was afraid that Jonathan would not permit him. So he decided to
do battle with him. When however he saw the superiority of Jonathan's
forces, he decided to get rid of him by treachery. He persuaded Jonathan
to leave his army and come with him to Ptolemais with a small band. As
soon however as they entered the city, its gates were closed, and Jonathan
was taken and killed (1 Mac. 12:39-53). His brother Simon succeeded
him.

Joppa, Today called Jaffa, a city on the Mediterranean coast of Palestine
south of modern Tel-Aviv, with which today it forms one city. Joppa was
assigned to the territory of Dan (Josh. 19:46). There were unloaded the
cedars of Lebanon for the Temple of Solomon (2 Chron. 2:16) and for the
post-exilic Temple (Ezra 3:7). It was the nearest seaport to Jerusalem.
Jonah embarked at Joppa for Tarshish (Jonah 1:3). During the Maccabean wars Joppa fell successively to different masters, and was lost at
least four times by the Jews (1 Mac. 10:75; 12:33; 13:11; 14:5). At Joppa
Peter raised Tabitha to life (Acts 9:36-47). It was while he was in the
house of Simon the Tanner at Joppa that Peter had the vision that moved
him to admit the first Gentiles to the church (Acts 10).

Joram, 1. King of Israel (849-842 B.C.) brother and successor of Ahaziah
and son of Ahab (2 Kgs. 1:17; 3:1-3). Mesha king of Moab refused to pay

the tribute fixed by Joram, and so with the help of Jehoshaphat of Judah (873-849 B.C.) and the king of Edom, he organized a punitive expedition against Moab. During the journey Elisha miraculously provided water for the army and predicted the victory of Israel. However, in the siege of Kir-hareseth, the last refuge of Mesha, it seems that Israel suffered a severe setback, for they had to withdraw (2 Kgs. 3:4-27). 2 Kings 3:27 attributes this withdrawal to the bitter indignation of the Jews at the act of Mesha, who took his eldest son and offered him as a sacrifice on the city wall.

Joram set out with Ahaziah of Judah (842 B.C.) to do battle against Hazael king of Aram at Ramoth-gilead, but he was wounded in the battle. He returned to Jezreel to recover from the wounds, and there Ahaziah went to visit him. In the meantime Jehu was plotting against him. They met in the field of Naboth, and when Joram sensed what was happening he turned and fled, but Jehu drove an arrow between his shoulder-blades and into his heart. His body was tossed into Naboth's field in fulfilment of the prophecy against his house (2 Kgs. 9).

2. King of Judah. *See* JEHORAM.

Jordan, The largest river of Palestine. It is formed from the fusion of four streams which collect the waters of Anti-Lebanon. After a 7-mile run the river spreads to form Lake Huleh which is today drained and cultivated. From this point the river descends rapidly for a distance of ten miles until it reaches the very low level of 696 feet below sea level at Lake Gennesaret (or the Sea of Tiberias, or of Galilee). A little further south it is joined by the River Yarmuk which brings to it the waters of the Bashan highlands. Later comes, from the western side, the river Jalud, which rises in the plain of Jezreel. To the south again it is joined from the east by the Jabbok. Between Gennesaret and the Dead Sea the river descends to a still lower level until it is 1286 feet below sea level.

Despite the abundance of its waters the river is exploited very little. While the immediate banks of the river, richly irrigated, are very fertile, the rest of the valley, which is higher, is arid and its climate suffocating. The valley spreads south of Jabbok reaching a breadth of fourteen miles around Jericho. As the crow flies the distance covered by the river is 80 miles, but in reality it is 200 miles long, so tortuous, so snakelike, is its course.

Joseph, 1. Son of Jacob and Rachel (Gen. 30:24; 35:24). Unlike the other brothers, Joseph is presented as the founding father of two tribes, Ephraim and Manasseh, who are often called "sons of Joseph" (Josh. 17:14; 18:11; 24:32), or "the house of Joseph" (Jgs. 1:22; Amos 5:6). This is the group that brought Joshua to Canaan and which went with Moses out of Egypt (*see* ISRAEL; JOSHUA), and was later to become the center of cohesion in the confederation of the twelve tribes in Palestine. After the schism between the two kingdoms, this group formed the principal part of the kingdom of the north (Amos 5:6, 15; Zech. 10:6; Ps. 77:16).

There is, besides, a long account in Genesis 37-50 of the life of the patriarch. He was sold out of jealousy by his brothers to merchants who brought him with them to Egypt (Gen. 37:28), and in turn sold him to Potiphar, a courtier of Pharaoh (Gen. 37:36). When Potiphar's wife was repulsed by Joseph, she falsely accused him, upon which he was thrown into prison (Gen. 39). Here he came to know the chief cupbearer and chief baker of the Pharaoh, who had fallen into disgrace with their master. Joseph interpreted the dreams of both of them in a way that turned out to be true (Gen. 40).

Later the Pharaoh had a dream, and his cupbearer, who in accordance with Joseph's intrepretation had been restored to his position, informed the Pharaoh of it. Joseph was called and predicted for Egypt seven years of abundance followed by seven years of famine. The Pharaoh gladly put Joseph in charge of the whole land of Egypt and gave him the name of Zaphenath-paneah, "God speaks and he lives." Joseph married Asenath, the daughter of Potiphera, priest of Heliopolis (Gen. 41).

When the seven years of famine came, the granaries in Egypt were filled. So the sons of Jacob, Joseph's brothers, repaired to Egypt for food. Joseph recognized his brothers but they did not recognize him. When eventually he made himself known to them, he established them and his father Jacob in the region of Goshen. Jacob died in Egypt, not however before blessing Joseph's two sons, Ephraim and Manasseh (Gen. 42-48). Joseph also died in Egypt but was embalmed (Gen. 50:24-26) and brought back by the Israelites when they were led by Moses to Palestine, where they buried him at Shechem (Ex. 13:19).

The story of Joseph offers an explanation of how Jacob's family settled in Egypt, and thus joins up the story of the patriarchs with the account of the book of Exodus. From the religious point of view the story of Joseph is one of the most effective in showing how God secretly operates in the course of history. Without obvious intrusion in the play of human passions and emotions, God nevertheless works through them to achieve his designs. In this story God's design is not just to protect Joseph, but through him God solders a new link to the chain of providence by which he brings to accomplishment the salvific design expressed in the promises to Abraham.

The sacred author gives clear expression to this idea on Joseph's lips, when he made his identity known to his brothers: "Do not be distressed and do not reproach yourselves for having sold me. God sent me on ahead of you to ensure for you a remnant on earth and to save your lives in an extraordinary deliverance. So it was not really you but God who had me come here" (Gen. 45:5-8). Again he states in the conclusion: "Even though you meant harm to me, God meant it for good, to achieve his present end, the survival of many people" (Gen. 50:20).

From the historical point of view the story of Joseph poses many difficult problems. The discussion chiefly revolves around the meaning of the whole piece rather than the historicity of the details. One can exclude without further discussion the thesis that this is collective history, involving the whole group or various tribes. It is not to be denied that the intervention of certain of the brothers, such as Judah and Reuben, mirrors the environment (the tribe of Judah, etc.) in which the tradition could have been handed down and elaborated. To give the whole account however such an interpretation is to force it against the evident sense of the story.

From the historical point of view there is no difficulty in accepting the tradition as it is read in Genesis, that the settlement of the ancestors of Israel in Egypt was motivated and facilitated by the surprisingly successful political career of one of their members. Some scholars have with good probability dated the account to the period of the Hyksos domination in Egypt. The Hyksos were foreigners, which makes it easier to understand how another foreigner like Joseph could have occupied an important administrative post.

When however we have acknowledged this historical nucleus to the story, the question remains: what precisely was the aim of the author of the story of Joseph which was later adopted into Genesis? Some scholars suggest that it was put in for biographical interest. Some Egyptologists state that the author is well informed about Egyptian customs and life. Others note that the Egyptian environment described therein belongs to the eleventh and tenth centuries, and not to the time in which Joseph would have lived. More recently another interpretation has been proposed with some success: the Joseph tradition was elaborated from the wisdom tradition which wished to make of him a live, concrete model of the human ideal to be proposed to the formation of youth for public office. This elaborated tradition was then adopted into Genesis, due emphasis being placed on his importance in the whole salvific design of God for Israel.

2. In Luke's genealogy for Jesus there are two unidentified persons called Joseph (Lk. 3:24, 30).

3. Joseph, the husband of Mary, of whom Jesus was born (Matt. 1:16). In the genealogy of Matthew 1, Joseph is the son of Jacob, but in Luke 3:23 he is called the son of Heli. The differences between the two genealogies extend to all the names between Joseph and King David. Up to the present this problem has found no satisfactory solution. The traditional interpretation would make Matthew's genealogy through Joseph and Luke's the genealogy of Jesus through Mary, while others hold that both are Joseph's genealogy, with Matthew giving his natural genealogy and Luke tracing it through Heli, Joseph's father only in virtue of the levirate law.

In the tradition on the public ministry of Jesus the name of Joseph appears only to designate Jesus as "the son of Joseph." He was called this by his fellow townsmen of Nazareth (Lk. 4:22), by Philip of Bethsaida (Jn. 1:45), and by the men of Capernaum (Jn. 6:42). In Matthew 13:55, and its parallels Luke 4:22 and Mark 6:3, Jesus is called the son of the carpenter. This silence about Joseph is traditionally interpreted to mean that Joseph had died when Jesus began his public ministry.

On the other hand Joseph is a figure of prime importance in the Infancy narratives, and especially in Matthew 1-2. While Mary was betrothed to Joseph, he learned through the revelation of an angel during sleep of the virginal conception of Mary (Matt. 1:18-25). Later, acting on a warning from the angel, he fled with Mary and the child into Egypt to save their lives (2:13-25). When news came of the death of Herod, Joseph was told to return to Palestine, but when he heard that Archelaus was reigning in Judea he feared to go there. Again came the advice in a dream, and so he left for Galilee and settled down at Nazareth (2:19-23). Luke informs us that before the birth of Jesus, Joseph and Mary had lived at Nazareth (Luke 1:26, 27). They had transferred to Bethlehem for the census ordered by Quirinius (Lk. 2:1-5), since Joseph was a descendant of David.

4. One of the "brothers" of Jesus (Matt. 27:56). In Mark 6:3 and 15:40 he is called Joses.

5. Joseph, a rich man of Arimathea, who was a disciple of Jesus, "but secretly for fear of the Jews" (Jn. 19:38). He was a member of the council, a "good and righteous man" (Lk. 23:50). After the death of Jesus he asked Pilate for Jesus' body, and with his permission took it down from the cross and wrapped it in a linen shroud, and laid it in a rock-hewn tomb on his own property, where no one else had previously been buried (Matt. 27:57-60; Mk. 15:43-46; Lk. 23:50-54; Jn. 19:38-42).

6. Joseph, called Barsabbas, who was surnamed Justus, was a candidate with Matthias for the place in the Twelve left vacant by the betrayal and death of Judas Iscariot (Acts 1:23). Matthias was chosen by lots.

7. Joseph, surnamed by the apostles Barnabas (Acts 4:36). *See* BARNABAS.

Josephus Flavius, A Jewish historian (37-100? A.D.) who stemmed from a priestly family and had a Pharisaic upbringing. He wrote **a History of the Jewish War against Rome** in which he played a part, first on the side of the Jews and later in the service of Vespasian and Titus. He also penned a history of the Jews known as **Jewish Antiquities**, in twenty-two books, covering the period from creation up to the time of Nero. His books are an important source on the Jewish background of early Christian history.

Joses, One of the "brothers" of Jesus (Mk. 6:3; 15:40) called Joseph in Matthew 13:55; 27:56.

Joshua, 1. Son of Nun, of the tribe of Ephraim (Num. 13:8), designated by Moses as his successor to lead the people (Num. 27:18-23; 34:17; Deut. 31:3; 14:23) and accomplish their establishment in Canaan. *See* JOSHUA, BOOK OF

2. Son of Jozadak, High Priest of Jerusalem, a contemporary of Zerubbabel, with whom he returned from Babylonia to Palestine when Cyrus II decreed the repatriation of the exiled Jews (Ezra 2:2). He undertook the reconstruction of the Temple (Ezek. 3:8; 5:2). Joshua appears in a vision of Zechariah (3:1-10) "standing before the angel of the Lord, while Satan stood at his right hand to accuse him." Joshua, who wore filthy garments, received festal garments and a clean mitre for his head. The vision indicates the rehabilitation of the priesthood which had been guilty of so many crimes during the period of exile, and it ends with a promise of the Lord where the increasing importance of the priesthood after the exile is insinuated. On the substitution of the name Zerubbabel for that of Joshua in Zechariah 6:11 *see* ZERUBBABEL.

3. Governor of the city of Jerusalem at the time of Josiah (640-609 B.C.; 2 Kgs. 23:8).

Joshua, Book of, A historical book of the Old Testament which recounts the conquest of Canaan under the command of Joshua, and the distribution of the territory among the twelve tribes. In the Hebrew canon the book of Joshua is the first of the early prophets, and its composition is attributed to Samuel.

The central character of the book makes his first appearance in some passages of the Pentateuch. This is Joshua, son of Nun of the tribe of Ephraim (Num. 13:8). His original name, Hoshea, was changed by Moses to Joshua (Num. 13:16). He figures as a military head of Israel against the Amalekites (Ex. 17:9-14), and was later chosen with eleven men from the other tribes to scout the land of Canaan. Ten of these scouts brought back negative reports and thought the invasion of the land ill-advised, but they were decisively opposed by Joshua and Caleb. For this reason these two were spared the punishment decreed by the Lord on the Israelites (Num. 13:14). Joshua was named by Moses to succeed him as head of the people (Num. 27:18-23).

As in the book of Judges, so too in the book of Joshua one must distinguish the individual traditions gathered there and the framework in which they are placed. This plan or framework gives unity to the account. Joshua, commander-in-chief of all Israel, that is, of the twelve tribes, in a series of lightning campaigns took over first the central portion, then the south, and finally the north of the country (Josh. 1-12). With the military campaigns behind him, Joshua received the command from God to proceed to the distribution of the land among the nine and one-half tribes who had not as yet come into the possession of any. Reuben, Gad and half of Manesseh had already established themselves beyond (east) the Jordan at the time of Moses. When the distribution was complete (Josh. 13-21) and some divergences between the Transjordanian and the other tribes settled (Josh. 22), Joshua called the whole of Israel together and gave them a farewell discourse which is his testament. Joshua 24 sums up the acts of the tribal confederation between them and God.

This account of a mass penetration of the land of Canaan by the Israelites through lightning military campaigns is at variance with the concrete information on the invasion that comes from the traditions of the separate tribes and is gathered into Judges 1. On the other hand if the book of Joshua is attentively read it becomes obvious that the whole story revolves around the occupation of Jericho, Ai-Bethel up to Shechem, and an alliance with the pre-Israelite inhabitants of Gibeon, the consequences of which were to call into doubt the security of other neighboring cities (Josh. 10). The campaign to the north against Jabin, king of Hazor, and his allies seems to be an anticipation of what Deborah and Barak achieved against the same king. The traditions, then, that form the central part of the book are limited to the tribes of Benjamin and Ephraim who occupied the center of Palestine.

Even here, however, one should not imagine that Joshua's campaign was a blitzkrieg in which the land was taken over. The episodes narrated are in reality isolated and should be thought of as incidents of violence in what was in reality a less rapid and more peaceful process of penetration and establishment. The incoming Israelites aimed at the areas that had less urban concentration. One can state that with few exceptions the cities of the bronze age did not pass over to the Israelites. Up to the time of the monarchy the population of Palestine remained a mixed one. Only then, with the advent of central government, did the Israelites succeed in taking the cities that had remained on as Canaanite islands in the country (*see* Josh. 13:2-6).

On the other hand it must not be forgotten that the scheme involving the twelve tribes was also spread back to the times of the Exodus and the journey through the desert, while it is clear that not all the twelve tribes were under Moses there. The "house of Joseph," that is, Ephraim and Manasseh, represent the most important group that came with Moses from Egypt and came across the Jordan into Canaan with Joshua. The confederation of twelve tribes was established in Canaan, as is clearly suggested by Joshua 24, when other related tribes accepted the exclusive sovereignty of Yahweh. In this way all the tribes became heirs to a common patrimony, but not all were equally creators of this inheritance.

Cc. 13-21 contain different lists. On the list of the Levitical tribes *see* LEVITICAL CITIES (Josh. 21:1-42). On the cities of refuge *see* MURDER; REFUGE, CITIES OF (Josh. 20:1-9). The other two lists are: a. the limits of the territories of the different tribes (15:1-12); 16:1-8; 17:7-10; 18:11-20, etc.); b. a list of the cities in the territories of the individual tribes (*see* e.g. 13:10-21; 13:25-27; 15:20-62, etc.). While these lists are certainly no invention, neither can they be dated to the time of Joshua. Scholars are not agreed on how they originated or what was their original meaning. The territorial limits described for each tribe are probably what each tribe claimed, even though they were not their effective limits. These probably date from pre-monarchic times. During the period of the monarchy, tribal organization was absorbed into the unity of the kingdom. The listing of cities dates perhaps to the first period of the monarchy (David-Solomon) and was drawn up for administrative purposes, the exact scope of which it is not possible today to say.

The book of Joshua belongs to the historiographical synthesis that draws on Deuteronomic inspiration and extends as far as 2 Kings. Some authors think that it should be made one with the Pentateuch at its conclusion, for otherwise, in their opinion, the Pentateuch would remain incomplete without its logical conclusion in the conquest of Canaan. Whatever can be said for this opinion, it is clear that Joshua is linked by literary and theological bonds with the books that follow it rather than with Genesis-Numbers. Deuteronomy is the source of its theological inspiration, and was probably the Introduction to the history of Israel as it is laid out in Joshua-2 Kings. *See* DEUTERONOMY.

Josiah, King of Judah (640-609 B.C.), son and successor of Amon (2 Kgs. 22:1,2). Amon died as the result of a conspiracy, but the people slew all who had conspired against King Amon, and proclaimed his son Josiah as king. At that time he was only eight years old (2 Kgs. 21:23, 24). The favorable judgment given on his reign by the author of 2 Kings refers above all to the reform he undertook in the eighteenth year of his reign (621 B.C.). The author records the work of restoration carried out in the Temple (2 Kgs. 22:3-7) during which was discovered the "book of the law," that is, in all probability, the core of the "Book of Deuteronomy." (*See* DEUTERONOMY.) The "book of the law" thus became the program of reform. The king commanded the high priest Hilkiah to remove from the Temple of the Lord all the objects that had been made for Baal and other gods, and he had these burned outside Jerusalem (2 Kgs. 23:4). His zeal then turned against the priests who were guilty of having taken part in worship forbidden by the Law of the Lord (2 Kgs. 23:5-7). The reform took the direction of centralization of cult in Jerusalem, which was imposed by Deuteronomy 12. In this way were execrated all the "high places" of the land as well as all the illegitimate cults that were exercised at Jerusalem (2 Kgs. 8-27). He renewed the Covenant with God in the name of the people (2 Kgs. 23:1-3) and ordered the celebration of the Passover according to the prescriptions of the Law (2 Kgs. 23:21-23; *see* PASSOVER).

This religious reform also had its political aspect, just as the religious syncretism that preceded it under his predecessors Manasseh and Amon was the consequence of vassalage to Assyria. The reform was made possible by the collapse of the Assyrian empire under the impetus of the neo-Babylonians. So the religious reform of Josiah was a national re-affirmation which also attempted to re-assert itself politically in the recovery of their territory of the kingdom of the north that had by now disappeared (2 Kgs. 23:15-19).

Josiah died in the battle of Megiddo against the Pharaoh Neco of Egypt, who was marching to the north to help the last Assyrian king. Josiah wished to block this and so marched out against Neco (2 Kgs. 23:29; 2 Chron. 35:20-27). The prophet Jeremiah composed a lamentation for the death of Josiah, which is distinct however from the Book of Lamentations which goes under his name (2 Chron. 35:25; *see* LAMENTATIONS, BOOK OF).

Jot, In some versions of Matthew 5:18 this translates the Greek **iota,** the name of a letter in the Greek alphabet, corresponding to the English letter "i". It expressed the equivalent of the Hebrew **yod,** the smallest letter of the Hebrew-Aramaic alphabet.

Jotbathah (jot′-ba-tha), A stopping place on the journey of the Israelites through the desert between Mt. Hor and Ezion-geber on the Gulf of Aqaba (Num. 33:33-34). According to Deuteronomy 10:7 it is situated in "a region where there is water in the wadies."

Jotham (joe′-tham), 1. The youngest of the sons of the judge Gideon. He saved himself by hiding from the massacre of his brothers perpetrated by Abimelech. Later, when Abimelech was made king of Shechem, Jotham addressed the men of the city from the mountain of Gerizim, telling them the fable of the trees that wished to have themselves a king. Through this story he wished to bring home to them the injustice of their conduct towards Gideon, who had previously been their savior. Now, not only did they tolerate the massacre of his family, but they elected as king the assassin. Jotham fled to Beer to escape the revenge of Abimelech (Jgs. 9:5-21).

2. King of Judah (742-735 B.C.), son and successor of Uzziah-Azariah. When his father contracted leprosy, Jotham acted as master of the palace and regent for about 8 years (2 Kgs. 15:5). Rezin of Damascus and Pekah of Israel invaded the territory of Judah to try to force Jotham to enter a coalition against the Assyrian king Tiglath-pileser III, but Jotham died before the invaders could reach Jerusalem. His son Ahaz succeeded him (2 Kgs. 15:37, 38). In 2 Chronicles 27:1-9 there is a mention of a victory of Jotham over the Ammonites, from whom he exacted tribute.

journey

Have you not come from a *j.*		he has gone on a long *j.*
	2 Sam. 11:10	Prov. 7:19
or may be on a *j.*	1 Kgs. 18:27	Jesus, tired from his *j.* Jn. 4:6

joy

the Lord with *j.*	1 Chron. 15:25	That is my *j.* Jn. 3:29
this house of God with *j.*		my *j.* may be yours and your *j.*
	Ezra. 6:16	Jn. 15:11
	make my *j.* complete Phil. 2:2	

Jozabad (joe′-za-bad), 1. An early warrior for David who later deserted (1 Chron. 12:5, 20).

2. Personal name (2 Chron. 31:13; 35:9; Neh. 11:16).

Jozacar (joe′-za-kar), Son of Shimeath and an official of King Jehoash of Judah. With Jehozabad, son of Shomer, he killed the king at Beth-millo (2 Kgs. 12:21, 22).

Jozadak (joe′-za-dak), The father of the High Priest Joshua, a contemporary of Zerubbabel (Hag. 1:1, 12; Zech. 6:11).

Jubal (joo′-bal), In the genealogy of Cain, he was son of Lamech and Ada, "the ancestor of all who play the lyre and the flute" (Gen. 4:21).

Jubilee, Year of, According to the law of Leviticus 25:8-17, 23-55 every fiftieth year, that is, after seven cycles of seven years, or after seven sabbatical years (*see* SABBATICAL YEAR) the Israelites should free their slaves, the landed property should return to its original owner, the land itself should rest without seeding or harvesting. Seeing that the 49th year was a sabbatical year, and therefore subject to similar prescriptions, some have thought that the Jubilee Year was the 49th and not the 50th. Otherwise there would have to be an unlikely two years without seeding or harvest.

However, this solution is not really necessary, for the law of the Jubilee Year is rather an ideal, not an applicable law. There is no trace in the entire Bible of any observance of the Jubilee Year, and the law itself belongs to the more recent legislation of the Pentateuch. The same dispositions are repeated also in Leviticus 27:16-25; and Numbers 36:4 but these texts depend on Leviticus 25: The law intends to give concrete expression to a theological principle expressed in 25:23: "The land is mine (Yahweh's) and you are aliens who have become my tenants." From this principle was drawn the conclusion that all had the same right to the land, and that therefore inequalities should be periodically ironed out by annulling the changes that had been introduced in one's economic condition through inheritance, good or bad fortune, etc.

The name Jubilee comes from the Hebrew **yobel** "ram's horn" which was blown on this occasion (*see* Lev. 25:9).

Judah, The fourth son of Jacob, born of Leah (Gen. 29:35; 35:23; 46:12; Ex. 1:2). Judah diverted the murder of Joseph by suggesting that instead he be sold to the merchants (Gen. 37:26, 27). Later when Joseph in Egypt demanded that Benjamin, who had remained in Canaan with Jacob, should come to him, Judah guaranteed his safe return to Jacob with his own life. When through Joseph's stratagem Benjamin seemed responsible for stealing Joseph's cup, Judah offered himself in substitute for his brother (Gen. 42:8, 9; 44:18, 32-34).

Judah had three sons, Er, Onan and Shelah. Er married Tamar and died before he had any children from her. Onan refused to fulfill his duty to Tamar, his sister-in-law, who had now by virtue of the levirate law become his wife, and for this was punished with death by God. Judah then feared for the life of his remaining son, Shelah, and delayed in giving him to Tamar as husband. Tamar outwitted Judah by dressing as a harlot and drawing him into intercourse from which she became pregnant. When Judah was told that Tamar was pregnant he was angry, but when Tamar sent to him the objects he had left her in pledge of payment of her services he acknowledged that he was the father. Tamar brought twins into the world, Perez and Zerah (Gen. 39).

The tribe of Judah settled in the south of Palestine (Josh. 15:1-12; 15:20-62). They probably penetrated into Palestine from the south together with Kenite and Calebite groups (Jgs. 1:1-15; 1:17-20) before Joshua invaded it from the east. Though perhaps the tribe of Judah had been in Egypt, it certainly did not come out with Moses, but on some other occasion. It shared but little in the common life of the confederation before the monarchy, if one can judge from the silence in its regard in the book of Joshua. During the first years of the monarchy however the situation changed. David was a Judahite from Bethlehem. He served Saul and then the Philistines before being anointed king of Judah at Hebron (2 Sam. 2:1-4). After the ephemeral reign of Ishbosheth, Saul's son, David also became king of Israel (2 Sam 5:1-5). The blessing of Jacob on Judah probably refers to this prodigious career of David (Gen. 49:8-12). In the persons of their common kings, David and Solomon, Judah and Israel remained united. When however Solomon died in 922 B.C. his son Rehoboam king of Judah was not confirmed king of Israel at Shechem, and thus took place the schism which was to last until the end of the two kingdoms (1 Kgs. 12).

In Judah there was dynastic continuity, and so the kingdom was spared the frequent and deleterious assassinations and massacres of the kingdom of the north.

The kingdom of Judah perished at the hands of Nebuchadnezzar. In 597 Jehoiachin surrendered without resistance. He, together with the royal family and ten thousand Jews, was deported to Babylonia. Nebuchadnezzar established on the throne Zedekiah, son of Josiah and uncle of the deported Jehoiachin. He was but a vassal to Nebuchadnezzar. Nevertheless he foolishly revolted and then offered opposition to the forces that laid siege to his city. Jerusalem as a result was set on fire and destroyed. Zedekiah was captured, taken to Riblah where Nebuchadnezzar had him blinded, and carried off to Babylon where he died. The Babylonian king ordered another, larger deportation in 587 B.C. (2 Kgs. 24:25).

Judah, Desert of, The desert region between the hill country of Judah and the west bank of the Dead Sea. It extended briefly north of the Dead Sea to take in a part of the deep valley of the Jordan. John the Baptizer started his ministry in the desert of Judah (Matt. 3:1; Mk. 1:4; Lk. 3:2).

Judas, The Latin form of the Hebrew Judah.

1. Third son of Mattathias, the priest of Modein who began the revolt against the Hellenization of the Jews that had been decreed by Antiochus IV Epiphanes. Judas received the name Maccabeus, that is, "hammer." He was appointed by his father to head the armed revolt against the Seleucids (1 Mac. 2:66). He was an insuperable master of the art of guerrilla warfare, and with a numerically small force and enthusiasm succeeded in stemming the impetus of the Seleucid army. His most noted victories were those against Apollonius who had penetrated from Samaria into Judea. Apollonius died in the battle. Judas seized Apollonius' sword "and fought with it the rest of his life" (1 Mac. 3:10-12). At Beth-horon the Seleucid army under the command of Seron was defeated (1 Mac. 3:13-26). Then at Emmaus he routed Gorgias and at Beth-zur he overcame Lysias (1 Mac. 3:38-4:35).

With the Seleucid danger out of the way Judas set about the purification of the Temple which had been profaned by order of Antiochus IV Epiphanes. The solemn dedication of the Temple took place on the 25th day of the ninth month of the year 165/164 B.C. This was then celebrated annually on the feast of the Dedication or Hanukkah: *See* DEDICATION, FEAST OF. Judas also sought to consolidate his position by eliminating possible allies of the Seleucids among the neighboring peoples, thus also taking revenge for what had been suffered from them.

Lysias, now regent of Antiochus V Eupator, launched a campaign against Judas, this time with more success. He defeated him at Beth-zur (1 Mac. 6:28-54) but he had to retreat to Antioch as his position began to be endangered (1 Mac. 6:55-63). Demetrius, the new king (1 Mac. 7:1-4) sent Bacchides, one of his generals, to install Alcimus as High Priest (1 Mac. 7:8-20), and later sent Nicanor, "a bitter enemy of Israel with orders to destroy the people" (1 Mac. 7:26). Nicanor however was defeated and killed in battle (1 Mac. 7:39-50). Judas made a pact with Rome (1 Mac. 8:1-32). After the defeat and death of Nicanor, Demetrius sent Bacchides on the same mission. In the ensuing battle Judas was killed. Jonathan and Simon took their brother and buried him in the tomb of their fathers at Modein. He was succeeded by his brother Jonathan (1 Mac. 9:11-22).

2. Son of Chalphi, one of the commanders of the army of Jonathan Maccabeus (1 Mac. 11:70).

3. Son of Simon Maccabeus. To Judas and his brother John, Simon confided the command of the army which was to oppose Cendebeus. Judas was injured in the battle (1 Mac. 16:1-10). Judas and his brother Mattathias were treacherously killed with their father Simon in the fortress of Dok during a banquet given them by Ptolemy, governor of the plain of Jericho (1 Mac. 16:11-17).

4. Judas the Galilean who headed a revolt against the Roman dominion at the time of the census of Quirinius. Gamaliel cited him as an example of a false messianism, of man's invention and not from God, and for that very reason doomed to failure (Acts 5:37).

5. Judas, "the brother of Jesus" (Mk. 6:3). *See* JUDE, EPISTLE OF.

6. Judas Iscariot, one of the Twelve chosen by Jesus, who later betrayed him (Matt. 10:4; Mk. 3:19; Lk. 6:16). Numerous attempts have been made to comprehend and explain the motivation of Judas, by both scholars and creative writers. Did he believe that Jesus was about to, or could, usher in an earthly, political kingdom? To a man with such ideas Jesus' words to the disciples after the Transfiguration would be not only disap-

pointing but almost intolerable. Did Judas want to force a crisis, make Jesus perform another and this time unmistakable sign, or make him claim the throne of David? Did he feel that if Jesus were the Messiah, nothing could happen to him; and if something did happen to him, why then he was not the Messiah and therefore deserved it? Had Satan entered into him, as Luke (22:3) explains it? Was Judas a part of God's foreordained plan?

However interesting these speculations, tradition is almost unanimous in giving avarice as the motivation for his betrayal. John explains his intervention against Mary of Bethany who had anointed Jesus with precious ointment: "He did not say this out of concern for the poor, but because he was a thief. He held the purse, and used to help himself to what was deposited there" (Jn. 12:6). When Jesus' death was already decided upon, Judas came up with a solution for his arrest that would avoid an uproar, and received for his pains a recompense in money (Matt. 26:14-16; Mk. 14:10-11; Lk. 22:3-6). Judas led those commissioned to arrest Jesus to Gethsemani and identified Jesus for them by saluting him with a kiss (Matt. 27:47-56; Mk. 14:43-52; Lk. 22:47-52). That Judas was to betray him was not unknown to Jesus as is evident from the episode of the Last Supper, even though it is told slightly differently by all four evangelists (Matt. 26:20-25; Mk. 14:17-21; Lk. 22:21-23; Jn. 13·21-26).

There are different traditions on the death of Judas. According to Matthew, Judas was stricken with remorse when he saw Jesus condemned, so he took the thirty shekels of silver back to the priests, who however were unwilling to take them. Judas therefore threw them down in the Temple and then went and hanged himself. With the money, the priests bought the potter's field for the burial of strangers. According to Acts 1:18-19, with the money he had got for the betrayal, Judas bought a field. The text does not say that he hanged himself, but it notes that "That individual bought a piece of land with his unjust gains, and fell headlong upon it. His body burst wide open, all his entrails spilling out." The remembrance of the facts has been adorned with some Old Testament texts which speak of the tragic end of the impious (Wisdom 4:19) and of the death of the traitor Ahitophel (2 Sam. 17:23).

"Iscariot" is an appellative often added to his name. The meaning of the word is uncertain: possibly "of Kerioth," a town; perhaps from Gk. **sikarios**, Latin **sicarius**, a daggerman or assassin, in which case the word might have either patriotic overtones or opprobrious ones.

7. A Christian of Damascus to whose house Paul was taken after his conversion and where Ananias baptized him (Acts 9:11).

Jude, Epistle of, A deuterocanonical work of the New Testament. The author presents himself as "Jude, the brother of James" (v. 1). This James is obviously the "brother of the Lord" who headed the Christian community of Jerusalem (Gal. 1:19; 2:9; 1 Cor. 15:7) and in all probability distinct from the two apostles of the same name. (*See* JAMES.) Jude, "brother of the Lord," is also mentioned in Matthew 13:55; Mark 6:3 and he is also distinct from the two apostles of the same name.

The writing is very probably under a pseudonym as is the letter of James. (*See* JAMES, EPISTLE OF.) Like James's letter, this one too draws on the Judeo-Christian homiletic tradition, but its aim is more precise. Jude wishes to warn his destinataries about doctrinal heterodoxy (v. 11) and caution them about licentious conduct (vv. 8, 10, 12, 16, etc.).

To justify their position they appeal to grace they say they received from God (v. 4). This makes one think of people who exploit Paul's doctrine on liberty and grace and transform it into libertinage, even though references to Pauline themes are not so clear as in James. Some have tried to identify these errors with the gnosis that developed in the second century, but it is not necessary to delay the composition of the letter for so long. For the errors denounced have similarities with what is decried also in Revelation (2, 6, 14, 20). They have principally to do with moral deviations, and there is no trace of the complex gnostic speculations of the second century.

The letter of Jude emerged from the environment of the Jewish-Christian churches, as can be seen from the abundant use he makes of the Jewish apocryphal writings (Book I of Enoch, The Assumption of Moses, vv. 4, 6, 9, 14). The inscription has a very vague reference to destinataries. On the other hand the homiletic character of the book leaves nothing to be desired. Jude was used by 2 Peter 2:1-22. The date of composition is uncertain, but was probably not before 70/80 A.D.

judge

and *j.* over us	Ex. 2:14	set apart by God as the *j.*
or to the *j.*, shall die	Deut. 17:12	Acts 10:42
I *j.* as I hear	Jn. 5:30	

Judges, Book of, A historical book of the Old Testament which tells the story of the Israelite tribes in Palestine from the death of Joshua until Samuel and the beginning of the monarchy. In the Hebrew canon of the Old Testament it is placed among the so-called early prophets, and its authorship attributed to Samuel.

As we have it today the book belongs to the great historiographical synthesis that we owe to Deuteronomic inspiration, and which extends from Joshua to 2 Kings. It is necessary to distinguish the ancient traditions of the pre-monarchic period of Israel that are gathered there and the theological and historical framework in which these traditions are inserted. There is a certain tension between these two elements, as we shall see.

The central part of the book comprises the adventures of the twelve judges of Israel (Judges 3:7-16:31). There are long accounts of the deeds of prowess in favor of Israel in the case of six of them: Othniel, Ehud, Deborah, Gideon, Jephthah and Samson. Of the other six the book gives only the place of birth, the duration of "judgeship" and the place of burial. These are Shamgar, Tola, Jair, Ibzan, Elon and Abdon (*see* 10:1-5; 12:8-15; and 3:31).

For this reason a distinction is usually made between the major and the minor judges. However, they are not only distinguished because of the length or brevity of their accounts, but also because of the nature of their mission.

The major judges (and Shamgar, 3:31) were charismatic leaders who took up arms against the neighboring peoples to save Israel from oppression. There are differences too among them. Deborah was a prophetess "who used to sit under Deborah's palm-tree, situated between Ramah and Bethel . . . and there the Israelites came to her for judgment" (Jgs. 4:5). She entrusted to Barak the command of the tribesmen in the struggle against Jabin king of Hazor. Samson on the other hand is described for his personal adventures: what he achieved against the Philistines was carried out at the level of personal revenge (Jgs. 14-16). Jephthah fled from home because of altercations with his brothers, to become the head of a gang of bandits who roamed the countryside living off the people. The elders of Gilead invited him in to put an end to the Ammonite incursions. Othniel, Ehud and Gideon are also leaders that emerged in moments of great danger to save the people. They were called "judges of Israel," not in the obvious sense of the word in today's language, for with the exception of Deborah, such an activity was foreign to them. They were judges in the sense of "liberators" or "saviors of Israel." The word **saphat,** to judge, does not mean explicitly to pass sentence but to restore to order or repair, with a just solution, something gone awry.

The chronology of this period of Israelite history is drawn substantially from the information given on the six minor judges. They are presented as people in office stably for a certain period of time, and they succeed one another. They belong to diverse tribes, and their activity is summed up with the words: "he judges Israel" (*see* 10:2, 3). There is nothing to warrant interpreting their activity in the military sense of the major judges. There is no information available that would permit a reconstruction in detail of what precisely their office entailed.

A plan is presented as a thesis in 2:6-3:6. The Israelites do evil by forgetting the Lord and the prodigious works he has accomplished for the benefit of his people, and by going after the strange gods of neighboring peoples. For this God delivers them over to the hands of their enemies who oppress them and prey on them. Under the burden of this oppression the people return to the Lord, who, to save them, raises up "judges," or saviors, who bring them to victory. When a judge dies the people forget the Lord once more and the whole scheme repeats itself. This plan or scheme is not exclusive to the Book of Judges. It can be seen also in Exodus 32:33, Numbers 13:14, 2 Kings 17:7-23, Psalm 106. The plan of sin, punishment, penance (or intercession) and grace is a theology very Deuteronomic in tone, but in the last analysis it originates in the experience of the history of relationships between Yahweh and his people.

Told from this point of view the scheme becomes a song to the mercy and loyalty of God (Ps. 106). It strengthens the hope of the people when they find themselves oppressed and defeated. God's faithfulness comes home to them written into their very history, and it remains their only hope of restoration. We should not forget that the history of the Jews is told from the point of view of a people who are awaiting that intervention of God which will put an end to the disaster of the exile (2 Kgs. 25:27-30).

The stories of the judges were also completed with the use of other traditions that stemmed from the pre-monarchic period. Judges 1:1-36 contain the traditions of the individual tribes as they established themselves in Canaan. They serve to complete and balance the account of the conquest that is contained in the book of Joshua. (*See* JOSHUA, BOOK OF.) Cc. 17-21 contain two episodes, one relating the transfer of the tribe of Dan from south to north, and the second a case of one tribe being punished by the rest of the tribes of the confederation.

Judgment, Judgment ordinarily translates the Hebrew **mishpat,** which is the substantive of the verb **shaphat,** "to judge." The Greek translates it **krino, krisis, krima. Mishpat** is the sentence of the judge, the result of his intervention as judge. Once a sentence was passed, it easily created a precedent for deciding similar cases in the same way for the future. **Mishpat,** for this reason, also meant a legal norm or law. This is the sense in which it is used in the introduction to the "Book of the Covenant" in Exodus 21:1, in the alliance at Shechem in Joshua 24:25 and frequently elsewhere. In these places the word is translated "rules," "ordinances" and other synonymous expressions. The word also spreads out to cover any constant and habitual way of acting, be this established by law or by custom (*see* Jgs. 13:12; 1 Sam. 27:11; 30:24-25; 2 Kgs. 1:7).

Among ancient peoples, including Israel, justice was administered in a single undivided process, and not distributed as in later ages into judicial, executive, legislative and other powers. The administration of justice was one of the fundamental attributes of the king (1 Sam. 8:5; 2 Sam. 8:15; 12:1-6; 15:4; 1 Kgs. 3:9; 7:7). Justice was administered not just in the proclamation of the sentence, but also in the effective restoration of the injured order of things, that is the effective safeguarding of the rights of the individual. Mishpat then included, and often as its first task, authoritative intervention in favor of the injured party so as to restore social harmony or justice. Psalm 72:1-4 gives very concrete expression to this essential function of the king: "He shall govern your people with justice and your afflicted ones with judgment. . . . He shall defend the afflicted among the people, save the children of the poor, and crush the oppressor." Mishpat can then indicate in concrete the right that demands to be safeguarded.

God is the supreme judge over all the earth and over all peoples (Gen. 18:25; Pss. 7:7; 96:13; 110:6). He is the protector of the abused rights of the poor, of the widows and orphans, and of people who are in any way oppressed (Pss. 76:10; 82:3; 140:13). They make their appeal at his tribunal, asking for his intervention. In the lamentation psalms, the psalmist frequently sets out to move God to intervene by expounding his cause, proclaiming his innocence and the injustice that he is suffering (Ps. 18:21-31). These protests of innocence might surprise a person reading or reciting the Psalms unless he remembers the judicial context in which the divine help is invoked.

God's judgment, then, is above all his efficacious intervention in which he protects rights. This judgment is not only exercised between individuals but also between peoples in the course of history. It can constitute an episode in the course of history or coincide with God's definitive and irreversible intervention at the end of time when he will establish an order that can no longer collapse. The Lord will judge those peoples who have contributed to the ruin of his nation. Through the mouth of Ezekiel is announced the punishment of Ammon, Moab, Edom, etc. (Ezek. 25). In Joel 4:2 God announces: "I will assemble all the nations and bring them down to the Valley of Jehoshaphat (a symbolic name which means "Valley of the Judgment of God") and will enter into judgment with them there on behalf of my people and my inheritance, Israel; because they have scattered them among the nations, and divided my land." Here, as frequently in other places, judgment is understood as condemnation, or God's punitive intervention. Even the people of Israel itself are not immune to this judgment. The prophets tried to shake the people of Israel from their false sense of security: they too were open to judgment and condemnation for their sins. (Jer. 1:16; 4:12; Ezek. 5:7; 7:3). The judgment however will be mitigated by the fidelity of God who will preserve a remnant in whom to continue his initiative of salvation (*see* REMNANT), just as previously he saved Noah and his family from the flood (Gen. 6-9).

The idea of God's judgment acquires some new dimensions in the apocalyptic tradition, while others are more clearly expressed. Daniel 7:9-11 speaks of a judgment which will embrace all nations and inaugurate the establishment of the kingdom of God. Without minimizing the notion of judgment as an efficacious intervention, it clothes it with solemn juridical apparatus: God sits on his throne, the nations appear before him to undergo just judgment, while to the just is given power, glory and domination.

This notion of judgment is clearly eschatological and opens the doors to the world of the future. As such it frequently occurs in the New Testament (*see* Rev. 17-20). Above all in Matthew 25:31-45, Jesus as Son of Man is proclaimed Judge. (*See* SON OF MAN.) His judgment will be shaped by the attitude and conduct of people towards one another (Matt. 7:1; Lk. 6:37). It will take into account the opportunities of conversion that were neglected (Matt. 10:15), and will demand an account of words spoken in vain (Matt. 12:36). Here too judgment is often taken in the sense of condemnation (Matt. 23:33; Mk. 12:40; Lk. 20:47). The Lord will seat the Twelve as judges of the twelve tribes of Israel (Matt. 19:28; Lk. 27:30; *see* 1 Cor. 6:20). Through his resurrection and exaltation to the right hand of the Father in glory Jesus has been constituted judge of the living and the dead (Acts 10:42; 17:31). He will execute this judgment when he returns in glory (2 Tim. 4:1), and his judgment will be in accordance with the works of each one (Rom. 2:5-11; 2 Cor. 5:10).

The notion of judgment as the victorious intervention of God, without however assuming juridical apparatus, is sometimes used to illustrate the saving efficacy of the death and resurrection of Christ. Thus Jesus through his death and resurrection "condemned" sin in the flesh, that is, he abolished it (Rom. 8:3; *see* Col. 2:15). According to John 12:31 the moment of the exaltation of Jesus was also the moment of the judgment of this world, and the prince of this world has been thrown out (*see* Jn. 16:11; *see* PARACLETE).

In John's gospel, judgment is one of the all-pervading themes, and it is elaborated along lines that are in part original. The judgment in a certain sense is anticipated by, and linked with, the first coming of Jesus. The most important text in this regard is John 3:16-21: God has sent his only Son not to judge, that is, condemn the world, but to save it. Nevertheless his coming does unleash a judgment on the world. The person who does not believe is already judged, that is, he has placed himself in a condition in which he is inevitably doomed to be deprived of salvation. His judgment consists in the fact that "the light has come into the world, and men have preferred darkness to the light." Judgment is thus anticipated, and moreover it is internalized, that is, it takes place in the very heart of man without any external juridical apparatus or solemnity, for his incredulity puts roadblocks between him and the only possible way to salvation.

John finds the reason for this perverse decision of incredulity in the fact that "their works were evil." He often returns to this theme: incredulity, like faith, cannot simply be explained as a freely made decision for or against Jesus arising from the arbitrariness of the moment. While faith is obviously a free decision on the part of man (Jn. 6:66-70), it is also a free gift of God (Jn. 6:37, 44, 65). Incredulity too is nourished by perversion in the heart of man (Jn. 5:39-47; 8:23, 24; 8:43-47; 10:25, 26; 13:37-43).

The ultimate roots of these two attitudes toward Jesus, faith and incredulity, are illustrated by John in the figure of the person who sins by night so that his works might not appear. This is in reality a little allegory, in which Christ is the light, hatred for the light is born of the moral impossibility to believe, and the spontaneous coming to the light, or belief, is born of an intimate affinity with the light which carries him along to Christ. For John, to come to the light is to believe (*see* 5:40; 6:35, 37, 44, 45). Judgment moreover is not confined to the historical apparition of Jesus, to his earthly ministry, but is exercised throughout history and is realized wherever the word is preached (Jn. 20:31).

This original way of treating the theme of judgment is not without its parallels in John's writings. The great eschatological themes of the New Testament such as life, resurrection, the coming of the Son of Man and judgment are linked up by John in strict relationship with Jesus' first apparition, without however eliminating the tension towards the full realization of these same realities in the future (*see* Jn. 6:39, 40, 44, 54; 12:48). It must however be acknowledged that the center of gravity is shifted to the first coming of Jesus. This tendency in the case of the judgment, which is here under consideration, is due to two factors: first, it draws the ultimate consequences from the fact that the coming of the Son of God, his death and resurrection is the eschatological event that saves, and the consummation that has once and for all been achieved by Christ. Secondly the decisive importance of faith as the only way to salvation and its counterpart, incredulity, as the certain way to inevitable perdition, is brought to the fore. John's concern is to underline this. He does not in any way wish to affirm that man's salvation or condemnation is brought about in one single act of man himself, so that he who does not now believe can never believe. Jesus' own ministry offers a continuing possibility for belief (Jn. 12:35-37). Nevertheless it remains true that the attitude that man freely assumes towards Jesus is what determines his future lot.

This judgment will then be ultimately sanctioned on the last day. John speaks of one resurrection for life, and the other for judgment (Jn. 5:24), and with incisive expression announces that it will be the word of Jesus that is today rejected that will judge and condemn the incredulous "on the last day" (Jn. 12:48).

Judith, A deuterocanonical narrative book of the Old Testament. The subject of the book is the bold undertaking of a Jewish woman called Judith, who brought about the salvation of her people when this was threatened by the army of Holofernes.

This episode is an incident in a political and military conflict that involved the whole Middle East. "Nebuchadnezzar, king of the Assyrians in the great city of Nineveh" launched a military campaign against Arphaxad "who ruled over the Medes in Ecbatana" (1:1). Nebuchadnezzar invited all the peoples who dwelt in the west from Cilicia to Ethiopia to unite with him in fighting the Medes. His ambassadors were sent back to him, however, empty-handed and in disgrace. Without their help Nebuchadnezzar fought and won, and then decided on his revenge (1:1-2:1).

Holofernes was chief of staff of Nebuchadnezzar's forces. He took his orders from his king, and in a few brief campaigns he had moved as far as Palestine where he camped on the plain of Esdraelon (Judith 2:2-3:10). The Jews had only recently returned from exile, and "only recently had all the people of Judea been gathered together" (4:3). They felt secure even from the imposing forces that Holofernes was leading against them. The High Priest Joakim wrote from Jerusalem to the inhabitants of Bethulia, "which is on the way to Esdraelon, facing the plain of Dothan," and instructed them to keep firm hold of the mountain passes, since these offered access to Judea (4:6, 7). Holofernes was surprised by this insane resistance offered to his advance. He asked an explanation for it, whereupon Achior, the leader of the Ammonites, explained to him, with a brief summary of Israelite history, that "if these people (the Jews) are at fault, and are sinning against their God . . . then we shall be able to go up and conquer them. But if they are not a guilty nation, then your Lordship should keep his distance; otherwise their Lord and God will shield them, and we shall become the laughing stock of the whole world" (5:20, 21). The author of the Book of Judith has put into the mouth of Achior the message of his whole work. The rest of the story is the minute description of the way God chose to show the truth of that thesis.

Holofernes put Bethulia under siege. Soon it was reduced to extremities. The people pleaded with Uzziah and with the other rulers of the city to deliver it over to Holofernes. Uzziah asked for a stay of five days more "for the Lord our God to show his mercy towards us" (7:30).

At this point Judith, a widow of three or four months, presents herself.

She reproves the people and their leaders for their cowardice and offers to go down personally to the enemy camp and bring about the salvation of the city before the five days are out (c. 8). The rest of the story is well known. With her slave girl, Judith appeared in front of the enemy camp. She was taken to Holofernes who fell in love with her. On the third day he threw a banquet, at the end of which he was well drunk. He asked that Judith be brought along, and as the night wore on, the others left and Judith and Holofernes remained alone. He was completely drunk by this time, and collapsed on his bed. Judith took him by the hair of his head and decapitated him with his own sword. She gave the head to her servant who was waiting outside, and then the two left the camp together, climbed back to the gates of the city and ordered them opened to admit her. When the Assyrians discovered the death of their leader they took to flight. The book concludes with a hymn of thanksgiving sung by Judith and all the people (16:1-17).

There is no other information on the historicity of the adventure of Judith than that provided by the book itself. The didactic intent of the author is all too clear, summed up as we have seen in the words of Achior (c. 5), and repeated again at the end of the book (16:1-17). The name of the heroine is **Yehudith**, i.e. "Jewess," and seems to be symbolic. Even the location of Bethulia, where the event took place, is unknown. All this points in the direction of a "historical novel" such as we find in Esther.

More discussion has arisen about the historical background against which the episode is cast. At first sight the author would seem to be in total ignorance of the political history of the last half of the sixth century B.C. when the story takes place. Nebuchadnezzar was not the king of the Assyrians, but of the Babylonians. He did not reign at Nineveh, which had been razed, and never rebuilt, in 612 B.C., while he reigned from 604 to 562 B.C. The Babylonian empire passed definitively to the hands of the Persians under Cyrus in 539 B.C.

It seems difficult, however, to accept that the author created this historic background from his own imagination simply to put the story of Judith there. He describes the background in detail for three chapters. This is why many authors do not rest satisfied with simply asserting his ignorance of the period. They therefore manipulate the scene a little in an effort to bring it into a historical focus. The most successful of these attempts is based on the inscription that Darius had etched on a rock at Behistun (521-486 B.C.) telling his deeds. There it is read (49): "The Babylonians separated from me for a second time, an Armenian by name Araka . . . rebelled in Babylonia. He deceived the people saying: 'I Nebuchadnezzar, son of Nabonidus.' In this way the Babylonian people divided itself from me and passed over to Araka who became its king." It is not possible here to examine all the historical details. Suffice it here to note that this Nebuchadnezzar, who was still alive and still with imperial ambitions, is not to be confused necessarily with Nebuchadnezzar II who conquered Jerusalem in 587 B.C.

The historical background of the book of Judith is the struggle for power which broke out in the Persian empire at the death of Cambyses. The inscription of Behistun makes no reference to a campaign of Araka-Nebuchadnezzar in the West, but such an expedition would logically fit into his imperial ambitions. This would especially hold if Assyria, of which Judith 1:1 speaks, is not to be taken to be the classical Assyria of the empire of Tiglath-pileser III, but Syria, in accord with the usage of the documents of the epoch.

The book of Judith was written in Hebrew or Aramaic, but the original is lost and only the Greek version is extant. Even this has different forms.

The book was certainly written after the exile but it is difficult to give for it a more precise date. For the purpose of dating the work scholars appeal above all to the message of the book which points one's attention to a historical situation similar to the one that Judith by her bravery resolved. It would then have been written to sustain the faith and hope of the people in a situation in which they were bowed down under foreign oppression. In this hypothesis the most apt time would be during the revolt of the Maccabees, but perhaps this seems so because that period is particularly well known.

jug
lowered the *j.*   Gen. 24:46 and the water *j.*
                                                    1 Sam. 26:11; 26:12

juice
and pomegranate *j.*   S. of S. 8:2

Julia, A Christian woman at Rome, greeted by Paul in Romans 16:15.

Julius, The Roman centurion of the Augustan cohort in whose custody Paul was placed on the journey from Caesarea to Rome (Acts 27:1-3). He was kind to Paul and in fact saved his life when the soldiers wished to kill him lest he escape in the confusion of the shipwreck off the coast of Malta (Acts 27:42-44).

Junias, A Christian of Rome, kinsman and fellow prisoner of Paul, greeted by the Apostle (Rom. 16:7).

jurisdiction
under Herod's *j.*   Lk. 23:7

just
how *j.* and upright he is   the *j.*, the perfect man   Job 12:4
                                    Deut. 32:4 *j.* in the sight of God   Rom. 2:13
you have been *j.*   Neh. 9:33

Justice, Justification, Justice, righteousness and their derivatives translate a group of words which have the Hebrew root SDQ: **sedeq, sedaqa,** justice, **saddiq,** just, **hisdiq,** to justify. The original sense of the root is that of adherence or conformity to a norm. Those things are just which are as they should be, or are as one would expect them to be (Lev. 19:36; Deut. 25:15; Ezek. 45:10: just scales and weights; Deut 33:19; Ps. 51:21: just sacrifices, that is, performed in the right way, etc.).

When this fundamental meaning is applied to human and religious relationships it develops in different directions. The principal distinction one can draw is between the forensic and non-forensic use of the terms. By forensics is meant the usage that mirrors or is derived from the use of the term in judicial processes and tribunals.

In its non-forensic sense justice applies to the objective condition of a society or human group. It is its prosperity, harmony and social concord, which it is the king's preeminent task to protect. The just king is the one who bends himself to the conservation and renewal of this social condition. Doubtless one of the means to this end is the right exercise of judgment (Isa. 11:3, 4), but it also involves the protection of rights, good government and so on.

Justice such as this will be one of the remarkable characteristics of the messianic king: "Justice shall be the band around his waist" (Isa. 11:5; *see* Jer. 23:5; Ps. 72:1).

In human relationships justice designates the comportment of one person with another in conformity with the relationship that binds them, be this a relationship freely entered into by pact, or one derived from the nature of things, such as blood link. A person is just to another when he relates to him in a way that the bonds linking them dictate (*see* Job. 31). It is this idea of justice that is most frequently transferred to the sphere of religion, that is, to the relationship between God and man.

These relationships are defined and sanctioned in the alliance. Man's justice will be his conformity with the demands of the alliance, that is, the observance of the law (Ezek. 18:15-17), faultless moral conduct. God is also called just because he fully clings to the demands of his relationship, the alliance. He freely determines to enter into an alliance with his people and will not disappoint the expectations of those whom, on his own initative, he has invited into the covenant. The primacy of the promise (*see* PROMISE) as God's gratuitous, absolute and unwithdrawn pledge, is conserved also in the alliance (*see* COVENENT) so that his justice is not measured by man's response to the covenant, that is, his observance of the law, but by God's pledge to bring to reality his promised designs of salvation. God's justice itself becomes his gratuitous salvific activity in that it corresponds to his freely taken pledge to bring about salvation.

When Israel experienced humiliation at the hands of her adversaries, she claimed this justice for herself (Pss. 5:8; 143:1). When individuals are persecuted and oppressed, they take refuge in this justice (Pss. 31:1; 36; 71:2; 88:12; 143:11). Deutero-Isaiah presents God as the "just one and Savior" (Isa. 45:21) and parallels God's justice with salvation, which in this case was to be the return from exile and the restoration of Israel to its own land (Isa. 46:13; 51:1; 56:1; *see* Ps. 97:2). The 'just deeds of God' are the concrete manifestations of this justice, that is, the individual saving events that reveal him as just (1 Sam. 12:7; Judges 5:11).

In the forensic sense, that is, in legal processes, the just person is the one who is proved right, or who wins the case, whether this is the accused who clears himself, thus showing his innocence, or the accuser, who vindicates his cause (Ex. 23:7; Deut. 25:1). In this context "to justify" means to declare innocent, to render justice (2 Sam. 15:4). The just judge is the one who "justifies" the just person, that is, the innocent party, and condemns the guilty party (*see* Deut. 25:1; Ex. 23:7; Isa. 5:23; Prov. 17:15).

This forensic context is also mirrored in the use of the terms "justice" and "just" in the religious relationship with God. God is just as judge (Job 8:3; 34:17; Pss. 7:10; 11:7) and as king, in his function as moderator of the universe, and supreme guardian of the rights of the poor and the oppressed (Ps. 72:1; Deut. 32:4; Job 36:3). He is also just however in his treatment of his people. This is declared in the confession of sins which contrasts God's justice with the guilt of Israel's infidelity. God is irreprehensible above all in his adherence to the commitments he has undertaken in regard to Israel. And here we arrive at the previous notion of justice: God cannot be accused of having failed in fidelity: "In all that has come upon us you have been just, **for you kept faith,** while we have done evil" (Neh. 9:33; *see* Ps. 51:7; Dan. 9:14; Baruch 2:9).

In the New Testament the notions of justice and justification are at the center of Paul's polemic against the Judaizers in Galatians and Romans. Paul's usage of the term should be understood in the light of the Old Testament context. It was, however, provoked in the concrete by the theses of the Judaizers, and, in the last analysis, by the Pharisaic position. Paul contrasts justification by faith to justification by works, which was the position of the Jews who rejected Christ. The point in question was on which basis should man establish himself in the just relationship to God in order to achieve salvation. In Paul's mind the position of the Jews was this: fulfilment of the works prescribed by the law, and its observance, made a man just, and thus did justified man present himself to God. The connection between justice and salvation is one of merit. Paul holds that this tenet is in conflict with what the Scriptures themselves teach. The law cannot justify, not solely because it finds in man a resistance that cannot be overcome because he is possessed by sin (Rom. 7:7-25), but also because such a principle inverts the relationships with God. God's graciousness and gratuitous self-giving is substituted by the affirmation of man's self-sufficiency before God, a self-glorification that is inane.

To the works of the law Paul opposes faith, and to the notion of merit or salary due Paul opposes the notion of grace and favor, freely bestowed by God. To the forensic or legal justification by God, who acknowledges the present human work, he opposes the "justification of the unholy," that is, the effective interior transformation of man, who becomes a new creature, enlivened by the Spirit of God who is poured into the flesh to bring about in it as its fruit what the law itself proclaimed just (Rom. 8:5-11; *see* FAITH, LAW, LIBERTY).

Justus, 1. The surname of Joseph Barsabbas, nominated to stand with Matthias for the place in the Twelve vacated by the betrayal and suicide of Judas. He was one of those who were with the Lord all the time from John's baptism to the day of Christ's ascension. When the lots were drawn after prayer, Matthias was chosen in preference to Joseph (Acts 1:21-26).

2. When Paul was insulted in the synagogue at Corinth he continued to preach in the house of Titus or Titus Justus (Acts 18:7).

K

Kab, A measure of volume, Babylonian in origin, equal to a little less than four pints (*see* 2 Kgs. 6:25).

Kabzeel (kab′-ze-el), A city in Judah (Josh. 15:21; 2 Sam. 23:20; 1 Chron. 11:22).

Kadesh, Kadesh Barnea, (kay′-desh-bar′-ne-a), A three-spring oasis in the arid wastes south of Palestine, situated at the northern limit of the Sinai region (Num. 20:1; 33:35). Today it is identified with Ain Qudeirat. After an unsuccessful attempt to invade Palestine from the south, Kadesh became the center of the desert existence of Israel for 38 years (Deut. 1:46; 2:14; Jgs. 11:18). There Miriam died (Num. 20:1) and there the people wearied of the wait and murmured against Moses that he had led them out of Egypt only to let them die in the desert (Num. 20:2-5). To placate the people, Moses struck the rock at Yahweh's command, and water gushed forth in abundance (20:11). Moses however was punished for his impatience, and was refused admittance to the promised land (Num. 20:12). Kadesh was allotted to the tribe of Judah (Josh. 15:3).

Kadmiel, (kad′-mi-el), A Levite (Ezra 2:40; Neh. 7:43; 9:4; 5; 10:10; 12:8, 24).

Kain, *See* CAIN.

Kamon, (kay′-mon), A city in Gilead (Jgs. 10:5).

Kanah (kay′-nah), A city in the territory of Asher (Josh. 19:28).

Kareah (ka-ree′-ah), The father of Johanan (2 Kgs. 25:23; Jer. 40:8; 41:11; 42:1).

Karkor, A place in Gilead (Jgs. 8:10)

Karnaim (kar-nay′-im), *See* ASHTEROTH-KARNAIM.

Kartah, A town in the territory of Zebulun (Josh. 21:34).

Kedar (kee′-dar), A nomadic tribe of Arabia belonging to the Ishmaelite group (Gen. 25:13; 1 Chron. 1:29), renowned as bowmen (Isa. 21:16, 17). They were shepherds (Isa. 60:7) and Ashurbanipal records that they were governed by a king.

Kedemah (ked′-e-mah), A son of Ishmael (Gen. 25:15; 1 Chron. 1:31).

Kedemoth (ked′-e-moth), A city of Transjordan, from the neighborhood of which Moses sent envoys to King Sihon of Heshbon, asking permission to lead the people through his territories. Sihon refused, so his territories were invaded and taken by force (Deut. 2:26 ff.). Later Kedemoth was a priestly city of the tribe of Reuben (Josh. 13:18; 21:37).

Kedesh (kee′-desh), 1. A city of northern Galilee, in the land of Naphtali, on the site of the modern Qades. It is listed in Josh. 12:22 among Joshua's conquests. According to 20:7 it was designated as a city of refuge, while 21:32 apportioned it to the Levitical clan of Gershon. During the reign of Pekah, king of Israel (737-732 B.C.), Tiglath-pileser, king of Assyria, captured Kedesh and deported the population to Assyria (2 Kgs. 15:29, 30). It was in the vicinity of Kedesh that Jonathan Maccabeus defeated the Seleucid army of Demetrius (1 Mac. 11:63-73).

2. A city of Issachar (1 Chron. 2:72; *see* Josh. 21:28).

Kedron, (kee′-dron), A town in Judah (1 Mac. 15:39-41; 16:9).

keep
and his posterity to *k.*	Gen. 18:19	*K.* your tongue from evil	Ps. 34:14
k. it until the fourteenth	Ex. 12:6	never let her go, *k.* her,	Prov. 4:13

keeper
Abel became a *k.* of flocks		*k.* of the wardrobe	2 Kgs. 22:14
	Gen. 4:2	*k.* of the east gate	Neh. 3:29
to the *k.* of the baggage			
	1 Sam. 17:22		

Kehelathah (kee′-he-lay′-thah), A stopping-place in the desert (Num. 33:22, 23).

Keilah (kee-eye′-lah), A town of Judah (Josh. 15:44), today Khirbet Qila, in the Shephelah. It was won by David against the Philistines, but later he was obliged to abandon it for fear of Saul (1 Sam. 23:1-13).

Kelaiah (ke-lay′-yah), A Levite (Ezra 10:23).

Kelita (ke-lie′-ta), A Levite (Ezra 10:23; Neh. 8:7; 10:11).

Kemuel (kem′-you-el), 1. A son of Nahor (Gen. 22:21).

2. A Levite (1 Chron. 27:17).

3. A chief of the tribe of Ephraim (Num. 34:24).

Kenan (kee′-nan), Son of Enosh (Gen. 5:9-14). *See* CAIN.

Kenaz (kee′-naz), An Edomite clan according to Genesis 36:11-15. They were related by blood and marriage to the Calebites (Josh. 15:17; Jgs. 1:13; 3:9) and are numbered among the clans of Judah in 1 Chronicles 4:13. Together with the Calebites they occupied Hebron, and Caleb gave his daughter in marriage to Othniel, Kenaz's son when he captured Kiriath-sepher (Josh. 14:14-16; Jgs. 1:13).

Kenites (ken′-ites or kee′-nites), A nomadic tribe of southern Palestine. At times it appeared among the Amalekites: Saul warned them to withdraw lest they too should be killed in the rout of the latter (1 Sam. 15:6). They were also, however, associated with the tribe of Judah into which eventually they were absorbed (Jgs. 1:16; 1 Sam. 30:29). Their dealings with the Israelites date from before the conquest of Canaan. According to Judges 4:11 Hoab, father-in-law to Moses, was a Kenite. Jael, wife of Heber, was also a Kenite. She won notoriety when she received the fleeing Sisera into her tent and slew him while he slept by driving a peg through his head (Jgs. 4:11 ff.). Some Kenite traditions were freely adopted by the Israelites and thus made their way into the Israelite heritage. Some can be found in Genesis 4. *See* CAIN.

Kerioth (ker′-i-oth), A city of Moab (Jer. 48:24; Amos 2:2).

Kerioth-hezron (ker′-i-oth-hez′-ron), A town in Judah (Josh. 15:25).

Keros (ker′-os), The ancestor of a family of temple servants (Ezra 2:44).

Kerygma, Kerygma is a Greek word meaning "preaching" or "the proclamation made by a herald." In the apostolic church and in the New Testament the kerygma is the message of salvation brought about by God in crucified and risen Jesus. In the New Testament the word also designates the proclamation of the advent of the kingdom, as it came from Jesus' lips (Mk. 1:14). In the apostolic church the kerygma is addressed to those who have not yet heard of Christ. The content and progress of this primary message can easily be reconstructed by the examples gathered by Luke in the Acts of the Apostles: the discourses of Peter (Acts 2:14-36; 3:12-26; 5:29-32; 10:34-43) and of Paul (13:16-41; 14:15-17; 17:22-31) are concrete examples of the most ancient preaching of the apostolic church.

There are two principal types of kerygma, depending on whether the audience is Gentile or Jewish. In the latter case, the kerygma proclaims the salvation brought about by Jesus as the fulfilment of the promises of the Old Testament (Acts 2:16-21; 3:18,24; 10:43). In the former case, the kerygma takes advantage of some of the themes used by Jewish propaganda against idolatry, and starts by inviting the pagans to convert to the living and true God, creator of heaven and earth (Acts 14:15; 1 Thess. 1:9). The best example of this type of introduction is found in Paul's discourse on the Areopagus of Athens (Acts 17:24). The import of the kerygma in both cases is that God has glorified Jesus and made him Lord and Judge, who now dispenses the eschatological gift of salvation which is the Spirit. The kerygma culminates in an invitation to conversion with the promise of forgiveness of sins and salvation to those who will believe and be baptized.

The instruction of those who had become believers and belonged to the Church was "doctrine" or teaching. This aimed at deepening the message of salvation and included instruction on how to live out the Christian life. The clearest examples of this are found in the epistles of the New Testament, and especially in Paul's letters to the churches.

kettle
basin, *k.*, cauldron or pot	The city is the *k.*	Ezek. 11:3
	1 Sam. 2:14 and the city is the *k.*	Ezek. 11:7
	shall not be a *k.* for you Ezek. 11:11	

Keturah (ke-toor′-ah), After Sarah's death, Keturah was Abraham's wife (Gen. 25:1-4; 1 Chron. 1:32-33). She bore him 5 sons.

Key, The metaphorical use of keys to designate the supreme power in a group or society is frequent in the Bible, e.g. "I will place the key of the

347

House of David on his shoulder; when he opens, no one shall shut, when he shuts, no one shall open" (Isa. 22:22). The most celebrated text is that in Matthew 16:19 where Christ addressed Peter: "I will entrust to you the keys of the kingdom of heaven ..." This text does not refer directly to the church, but rather to the definitive gift of salvation, and very probably to its full realization in the future. Thus in Matthew 23:13 Jesus upbraids the Pharisees for slamming the door of the kingdom of heaven in men's faces. The parallel text in Luke 11:52 blames the Pharisees for taking away the key of knowledge, not entering themselves, and barring others from entry. By comparing these texts, Christ's promise to Peter in Matthew 16:19 emerges as the power to lead the church efficaciously to its final fulfilment which is salvation in the kingdom of heaven. Jesus won salvation by his surrender and resurrection: it is through this redemptive act that the Church exists, and through the Church Christ permeates humanity to save it. To Peter as head of the community he committed the power to carry forward Christ's work.

Other uses of the metaphor are found in Revelation 1:18; 2:1; 20:1.

Keziah (ke-zy′-ah), A daughter of Job (Job 42:14).

Khirbeth Qumran, *See* QUMRAN.

Kibroth-hataavah (kib′-roth-ha-tay′-a-vah), One of the encampments of the Israelites on their way from Egypt through the desert to the promised land. It was there that a wind blew quails in from the sea and down upon the camp. Some of the Israelites gorged themselves, and while the meat was still between their teeth, Yahweh struck them down. The people who died because of their greed were buried there, hence the name, which means The Graves of Desire (Num. 11:31-35; 33:16, 17; Deut. 9:22).

Kibzaim (kib-zay′-im), A city in Ephraim (Josh. 21:22).

kick
hard for you to *k.* against
Acts 26:14

Kid, The goat's young, used as a victim in sacrifices at the Passover (*see* Ex. 12:5; Num. 15:11-16). It was also much valued as meat. Isaac asked for it before he gave his blessing (Gen. 27:9), while the prodigal son's priggish brother complained to his father that he had never even been offered a kid to celebrate with his friends (Lk. 15:27). The command not to cook the flesh of the kid in the milk of the mother (Ex. 23:19; 34:26; Deut. 14:21) was a polemic antidote to a magic rite in use among the Canaanites.

kid

I will send you a *k.*	Gen. 38:17	prepared a *k.*	Jgs. 6:19
You shall not boil a *k.*	Ex. 23:19	bringing a *k.*	Jgs. 15:1

Kidneys, The kidneys, like the heart, often figure in Bible language in some versions as the seat of man's internal life, the core of his desires and violent passions (Ps. 73:21; Job 16:13; 19:27), the place of his conscience and intention where God scrutinizes him even to the very center of his being (Ps. 26:2; Jer. 11:20; 17:70; 20:12). In the sacrificial rites of the Israelites the kidneys and their covering fat were among the prized parts of the victim, and therefore burnt in offering on the altar (Ex. 29:13; Lev. 3:4, 10, 15, etc.).

kidneys

its two *k.*	Ex. 29:13	as well as the two *k.*	Lev. 3:4
	the fat of rams' *k.*	Isa. 34:6	

Kidron, The Valley of Kidron lies east of Jerusalem between the city and the Mount of Olives (2 Sam. 23:15; Jn. 18:1). It is also called the Valley of the King (2 Sam. 18:18). It was often the location of idolatrous rites. These were suppressed by Asa (1 Kgs. 15:13), Hezekiah (2 Chron. 29:10) and Josiah (2 Kgs. 23:4, 6, 12). The valley was also used as a cemetery (2 Sam. 18:18).

kill

anyone may *k*. me at sight	and to *k*. my son	1 Kgs. 17:18
	Gen. 4:14 a chance to *k*. him	Jn. 7:1
was resolved to *k*. David		
1 Sam. 20:33		

kin

one of our next of *k*.   Ruth 2:21

Kinah (ky′-nah), A city in Judah (Josh. 15:22).

kind, kinds

and every *k*. of fruit tree	This *k*. does not leave	Matt. 17:21
	Gen. 1:11	Men have one *k*. of body,
and all *k*. of winged birds		1 Cor. 15:39
	Gen. 1:21	

kindled

he *k*. coals into flame	2 Sam. 22:9	that *k* coals into flame Ps. 18:9
	For a fire has been *k*. Jer. 17:4	

kindness

presume on his *k*.	Rom. 2:4	meekness and *k*. of Christ
know that God's *k*.	Rom. 2:4	2 Cor. 10:1

kindred

and to my *k*.   Gen. 24:4   my own *k*.   Gen. 24:41

King, After some attempts at local monarchy that either failed (Jgs. 8:22, 23) or were ephemeral (Jgs. 8:31; 9), a national monarchy emerged in Israel to counter the ever-growing Philistine threat, which by now hung over the very existence of all Israel. Saul was the first king over Israel, but the monarchy was still in evolution, and he carried on many of the functions of the classical judges. Saul was a charismatic king (1 Sam. 10:6, 10; 11:5). His role was primarily and perhaps exclusively military, and this was more due to the political circumstances of the time than to his limited competence. Saul selected from the mass of the people, who up to this formed the basis of the army, some career soldiers, while he also employed some non-Israelite mercenaries (1 Sam. 13:2, 15; 14:2, 52; 21:8; 22:18).

The trend toward monarchy, however, was not a straight line. Exegetes have noticed a combination of two trends or traditions in the history of the origins of the Israelite monarchy. One is favorable (1 Sam. 9:1-10, 15; 11:1-11) while the other is contrary (1 Sam. 8:1-22; 10:18-25) to the monarchy. For while advantages were to be reaped from it, it was also seen as an unjustified assimilation of non-Israel usages (1 Sam. 8:7; 12:12) which could call into question the exclusive regality of God over Israel. The monarchy, then, was a governing factor in the alliance which welded the diverse tribes of Israel, without however being comfortably integrated into it. The anti-monarchic tradition endured for centuries, especially among the northern tribes, from whom Saul came, but who could not share in the kingly tradition stemming from David (*see* 1 Sam. 8:11-17; Deut. 17:4-20; Hos. 8:4; 10:13, 14; 13:11).

Some texts exaggerate the similarities between the kingships of David and

Saul (1 Sam. 16:1-13). David however was first chosen as king of Judah by the elders of Judah (2 Sam. 2:4), and after a civil war with Saul's heirs, he was also recognized by the elders of the northern tribes who came to him at Hebron. The two kingdoms however did not fuse: they remained united only in the person of two kings: David, who was anointed a second time as Israel's king (2 Sam. 5:1-4), and Solomon, David's successor. When Solomon died, the elders of Israel met at Shechem and refused to accept as their king Rehoboam, who had been designated king of Judah in succession to Solomon. Thus commenced the schism which soon was to lead to the ruin of both kingdoms. The charismatic aspect of Saul's kingship stayed alive in the separated northern kingdom (1 Kgs. 11:31, 37; 19:15) where the hereditary system never fully established itself, which helps explain the many dynastic turnovers.

The southern kingdom of Judah stayed loyal to the Davidic monarchy, which had been sanctioned by the prophet Nathan's oracle: "I will preserve the offspring of your body and make his sovereignty secure" (2 Sam. 7:12). Nathan's prophecy sparked off the whole messianic hope in the Davidic line. The monarchy is tied into the covenant. David and his family become God's instrument in bringing to flower the seeds sown in the promise: through them God enacts his designs, and David's family becomes the seat of the blessings (and the curses) contained in the covenant (Ps. 89:19-37). The choice of Zion to which David transferred the ark and the choice of David's family from now on became the center of the religious traditions of Jerusalem, while the north cradled and kept alive the pre-monarchic tribal traditions.

The crowning involved a solemn rite in which crown and armlets were put on, the anointing took place, the king was enthroned, the people acclaimed him, and to him was given the "testimony," which probably was a document of divine ratification (*see* 2 Kgs. 11:12; 1 Kgs. 1:46; 2 Kgs. 11:19).

This divine ratification was very likely similar to texts in Pss. 2:7-9; 110:2; 89:20-38; 132:11-12, e.g. "Let me proclaim the Lord's decree: . . . You are my son, today I have become your father." This divine affiliation did not confer a divine dignity on the king as it did, for example, in Egypt: rather it highlighted the special relationship that now existed between God and his elect, just as the whole people is called Son of God on the basis of the alliance. *See* FATHER, SON OF GOD.

king

Melchizedek, *k.* of Salem,	no *k.* in Israel	Jgs. 17:6
Gen. 14:18	a *k.* over you	1 Sam. 12:1
	speak to the *k.* for you	1 Kgs. 2:18

Kingdom of God, Reign of God, The central theme of Jesus' teaching is the coming of God's kingdom (Matt. 6:10; Mk. 1:14). Matthew prefers the expression "kingdom of heaven," but the meaning is the same: the form is the result of Jewish scrupulosity at the time about using the name of God. The use of the form "kingdom of God" is also due to a scruple of similar nature, namely the care to avoid any direct reference to the person of God as subject or complement of an action. So, for instance, instead of saying "God speaks," "the word of God" is used; instead of "God inhabits," "the habitation of God," and instead of "God reigns," there is talk of the "kingdom of God," which appears or is manifested. Thus Mark's expression in 1:14 "The kingdom of God has come" means "God reigns." In what sense? Of themselves the words could refer to God's universal rule over all creatures, man included, on account of being their creator. That God is king in this sense is coherent biblical doctrine (*see*

Pss. 93; 104; Matt. 5:34; 11:25; Lk. 10:21). Jesus, however, speaks of an event which comprises God's becoming king, or establishing his dominion.

The meaning of the expression is derived from the Old Testament, and indirectly from the king as Savior which was prevalent in oriental tradition: the king brought about salvation above all by a just government of his territory, which led to the well-being and happiness of his people. A savior-king was concerned above all with the happiness of those he ruled. This is the sense of the kingdom of God in Exodus 15:18. A group of psalms (47, 93, 96-99) make this sense even clearer: "God is king of the whole world, of the nations, he reigns on his holy throne, he reigns supreme. . . ." These and similar phrases mean that God has become king, he has acquired possession of his kingdom and established his rule in it.

The event leading up to his establishment of himself as king is a powerful intervention aimed at salvation, through which God overcomes his enemies and those of his people, whose immediate care he takes upon himself, to lead them victorious to full salvation.

Such powerful interventions in the Old Testament were the Exodus (Ex. 15), the conquest of Canaan (Ps. 47) and the return from exile (Isa. 51:52). The Israelites upon reflection became aware that creation too was just such a powerful event (Ps. 93; *see* CREATION). Last of all, the future intervention which will bring about definitive salvation, and which is called eschatological, can also be expressed in the same categories.

The notion of the eschatological kingdom of God was above all developed in apocalyptic literature, which reaches beyond the national boundaries to embrace the whole world and all peoples, leading to the fulfillment and end of history.

This literature also emphasizes that this end is transcendental, that is, it will see the dissolution of the present cosmic order to make place for "new heavens and a new earth."

Jesus proclaims that the eschatological saving intervention of God is imminent, and in a certain sense already present: "Reform your lives! The kingdom of heaven is at hand" (Matt. 4:17). "The law and the prophets were in force until John. From his time on, the good news of God's kingdom has been proclaimed" (Lk. 16:16; Matt. 11:12). It is the hour of salvation (Lk. 4:17-21; *see* 2 Cor. 6:2). There is then an unmistakable note of urgency in Jesus' message. The time factor in it is essential. His preaching exacts from the men who hear him a response that will suffer no delay (Lk. 12:54-59). One must hold oneself always prepared, always alert like the faithful servant awaiting his master (Lk. 12:35-40). There is no excuse for the indolent (*see* Parable of the ten virgins, Matt. 25:1-13; Lk. 14:15-24; Matt. 22:2-10).

The urgency in Christ's message is all the more felt in that he demands from man a decision involving his whole existence. Whoever searches for the kingdom must be prepared to give over in exchange for this treasure all that he has and all that he is (Matt. 13:44-46), and to renounce whatever might compromise his complete response to the call of Christ (Lk. 9:57-62; Matt. 8:18-22; 18:8-9; Mk. 9:43-47).

The kingdom of God is the gift of salvation (Matt. 25:34), life (Mk. 9:43) and eternal life (Mk. 10:17). Jesus makes use of the classical images of the Old Testament tradition (Matt. 8:11; Lk. 14:16-24) especially in the parables. In a world however that was slave to Satan and sin, the gift of salvation is presented above all as the radical overthrow of the demon empire (of which Jesus' exorcisms are a sign *see* Mk. 3:27; Matt. 12:29; Lk.

11:21, 22; Matt. 12:28; Lk. 10:17-20; 11:20; *see* EXORCISM) and the universal offer of pardon (*see* the mercy parables in Lk. 15), which if accepted will rejoice the heart of God.

The offer of pardon immediately encountered the insurmountable obstacle of human pride to become one of the strongest affirmations of the gospel. It is interesting to keep in mind that the mercy parables were directed precisely to the Pharisees and scribes who murmured that Jesus received sinners and ate with them (Lk. 15:2). Jesus indeed did not disdain to meet with sinners and publicans (Matt. 9:10 and ff.; 11:19), and the way in which he lived with them is not just a practical demonstration of God's mercy but is intended as a practical reassurance of the part they share in the kingdom Jesus establishes (Matt. 21:31, 32; Lk. 18:9-14; 7:29-30). This behavior of Jesus provoked the scandal and indignation of those "just" who held themselves not in need of mercy (Lk. 15:7; 18:10-13). Jesus' action for them took away from the demands of divine justice. Jesus thus proclaims that he is sent to call not the just but sinners (Matt. 9:13; Mk. 2:17; Lk. 5:32).

The offer of pardon and salvation must however be taken seriously: it is accompanied by a pressing invitation to conversion (Mk. 1:15) along with the threat of judgment on those who would allow grace to pass them by (Matt. 11:20-24; Lk. 10:13-15; Matt. 12:41, 42; Lk. 11:31, 32; 13:1-9).

The conversion Jesus asks for is described in concrete terms in the parables (Lk. 15:11-32; 18:10-14) and gospel episodes (Lk. 7:36-50). It is transformed into the search for the greater justice (Matt. 5:20) and for perfection that is modeled on that of the Father in heaven (Matt. 5:48) described in the sermon on the mount (Matt. 5-7). It is the unconditional following of the Christ (Matt. 8:19-22; Lk. 9:57-62; Mk. 10:21, 28, etc.).

When, however, will the kingdom of God come? This question was asked of Jesus (Lk. 17:20) and touched on one of the most controverted points of interpretation in his whole message. The problem emerges from the existence in the gospels of two series of texts which at first glance seem contradictory. The one series highlights the actual presence of the kingdom (*see* e.g. Lk. 11:20; 16:16; 7:28; 17:21; Matt. 12:28; 11:11-13) while the other underscores its future reality (Matt. 5:20; 6:10; 22:12; 25:10; Mk. 14:25; Lk. 22:30, etc.). So one group of authors takes the first series as fundamental (realized eschatology) while another makes the second series its own (consequent eschatology).

Both these positions are too radical and do not respect the whole tradition which shies away from an either/or opinion and sees eschatology as a tension that arises between something of which the seeds have been sown, but which has not yet come to full flower. The kingdom is present and operative in the person of Jesus and through him its forces have been let loose on the world. (*See* EXORCISM, MIRACLES.) Its full and perfect realization is still in the future and therefore an object of hope and prayer: "your kingdom come" (Matt. 6:10). They are not then two events, but two stages, the initial and the final stage of the same eschatological event. Jesus invites men not to be deceived by its meagre beginnings (seed, mustard grain, grain of corn) for these beginnings carry within themselves the pledge of harvest (Mk. 4:3-9; 4:26-29; Lk. 13:18-21 and parallel texts).

The coming of the kingdom of God is intimately connected with the person of Jesus. Jesus does not merely announce the coming of the kingdom as did the prophets of the Old Testament. He is the person through whom God establishes his reign (Mk. 3:27; Matt. 12:28; Lk. 11:20; Matt. 11:1-5). Faith in this reality is what Jesus seeks from those who follow him (Matt. 11:6). The progress of the kingdom coincides with the destiny of

Jesus, whose triumph is the kingdom's triumph, and thereby its establishment (Mk. 9:1; Matt. 16:28; Mk. 8:38; 14:62; Lk. 22:16-18, 29-30). This is why the notion of the kingdom quickly vanishes from the apostolic preaching (*see* Acts 8:12; 14:22; 19:8; 20:25; 28:23), and its place is taken by "Jesus the Lord" who has been raised and enthroned at the right hand of the Father (Acts 2:32-36; 5:31; 13:33; Rom. 1:4).

Kings, Books of, 1 and 2 Kings, like 1 and 2 Samuel, formed originally one, and appear as one in the Hebrew canon. The division into two was the work of the Septuagint, in which, as in the Vulgate, they are designated severally as the "Third and Fourth Books of Kings" the books of Samuel being called the First and Second. They contain, as the title implies, the history of the nation under the kings, and the narrative covers a period from its establishment under David to the fall of the kingdom of Judah. It commences with the death of David and the accession of Solomon, and extends to the Babylonian exile. During this time the kingdom falls into two, named respectively Israel and Judah. For their sins both kingdoms go into captivity, first Israel and then Judah, more than a hundred and thirty years after. It is less a history of the kings themselves than of the theocracy, in which the prophets play a conspicuous and important role, since it is according as their words are listened to or disregarded that the national fortunes are determined. The author appears to have belonged to this class, but who he was is unknown. He writes after the commencement of the captivity, and from the place of it, but he draws from documents of an earlier date, and incorporates in his account narratives many of which look as if they proceeded from contemporaries. His object, which is didactic, is to show how Israel, on the one hand, because of her apostasy and persistent disregard of the prophet's word, fell into deeper and deeper guilt, till she became hopelessly demoralized, and had to be driven from her land; and how Judah, on the other hand, though she too must go into captivity, might, if she repented and returned to the Lord, yet recover all her forfeited privileges.

The history is divided into three parts and gives an account (1) of the reign of Solomon; (2) of the kingdoms of Israel and Judah until the fall of the former; and (3) of the kingdom of Judah after the dispersion of Israel until the captivity at Babylon.

kinsfolk
the land of your *k.*   Gen. 12:1 Leave your country and your *k.*
                                                                    Acts 7:3

Kir, An unidentified region or town in Mesopotamia. When Tiglath-pileser, king of Assyria, captured Damascus in 732 B.C. he deported the population to Kir (2 Kgs. 16:9) which, according to Amos 9:7 was the place of origin of the Aramaeans.

Kir Hareseth (cur-har′-a-seth), The capital city of Moab, on the site of the present Kerak where Mesha took refuge when his territory was invaded by Jehoram of Israel (849-842 B.C.), Jehoshaphat of Judah (873-849 B.C.), and the king of Edom. Though this alliance besieged the city, they were unable to take it. Mesha took his eldest son and heir and offered him in sacrifice on the city wall, which caused such bitter indignation among the Israelites that they withdrew (2 Kgs. 3:24-27). Kir Hareseth is often cited in anti-Moab oracles (Isa. 15:1; 16:7, 11; Jer. 48:31-36).

Kiriathaim (cur′-i-a-thay′-im), A city of Transjordan, in the kingdom of Sihon (Josh. 13:19) consigned to the tribe of Reuben (Num. 32:37) and was later in the kingdom of Moab (Jer. 48:1-23).

Kiriath-arba, The ancient name for Hebron (Josh. 14:15). *See* HEBRON.

Kiriath-huzoth, A city in Moab (Num. 22:39).

Kiriath-jearim (cur′-i-ath-jee′-a-rim), A Gibeonite city which allied with Joshua (Josh. 9:17) and numbered in Josh. 15:60 among the towns of Judah. It was formerly Kiriath-baal. The ark of the covenant rested there for 20 years after its recovery from the Philistines, until David had it transferred to Jerusalem (1 Sam. 6:21; 7:1, 2). Another name for the city was Baalah (Josh. 15:9).

Kiriath-sepher (see′-fer), The old name for Debir (Jgs. 1:11, 12). *See* DEBIR.

Kish, A Benjaminite of Gibeon, father of Saul (1 Sam. 9:1; 10:21; 2 Sam. 21:14; Acts 13:21).

Kishion, A city in Issachar (Josh. 19:20; 21:28).

Kishon (ky′-shon or kish′-on), A rivulet which flows into the Mediterranean north of Mt. Carmel. The song of Deborah and Barak states that the torrent of Kishon swept away the kings of Canaan. The site of the battle is placed in the valley of Jezreel where in June the Kishon can reach a width of thirty feet and a depth of three or four (*see* Jgs. 5:19, 21). At the Kishon, Elijah slaughtered the prophets of Baal (1 Kgs. 18:40).

Kiss, As in modern times, the kiss was a usual form of greeting. The Song of Songs starts with the bride singing: "Let him kiss me with kisses of his mouth" (1:1), but the kiss was a familiar form of greeting between father and son (Gen. 27:27; 29:11), brothers (Ex. 4:27) and in general between people (Prov. 24:26, etc.). In the New Testament the woman who was a sinner continued to kiss Jesus' feet even though his host privately thought it a scandal (Lk. 7:38, 45). The kiss was a greeting among early Christians and referred to frequently in Scripture (Acts 20:37; 1 Cor. 16:20; 2 Cor. 13:12). The kiss could also be treacherous. Joab took Amasa by the beard with his right hand to kiss him in greeting while his left hand plunged the sword into his entrails, killing him (2 Sam. 20:9, 10). Judas' betrayal of Jesus has made the traitor's kiss or embrace proverbial (Matt. 26:48, 49; Lk. 22:47; Mk. 14:44, 45).

kiss
and *k*. me	Gen. 27:26	the Son of Man with a *k*.
as if to *k*. him	2 Sam. 20:9	Lk. 22:48
	one another with a holy *k*. 2 Cor. 13:12	

kite
the *k*.	Lev. 11:14 the various *k*.	Deut. 14:13

Kitron, A city in the territory of Zebulun (Jgs. 1:30).

Kittim, According to Genesis 10:4 the Kittim were descendants of Japheth. The Kittim referred to in Isa. 23:1, 12 and Ezek. 27:6 are a commercial colony in Cyprus. For 1 Maccabees 1:1; 8:6 the Kittim are the Macedonians while for Daniel 11:30 they are the Romans.

knead, kneaded, kneading
K, it and make rolls	Gen. 18:6 Taking dough and *k*. it	
she *k*. it and baked	1 Sam. 28:24	2 Sam. 13:8
	once the dough is *k*. Hos. 7:4	

Knee, Kneel, In Hebrew the word has the same root as the word for blessing, which leads one to suppose that blessings were received kneeling. Kneeling was a posture of adoration and prayer (Isa. 45:23; 1 Kgs. 8:54). The knees or lap was where Delilah lulled Samson to sleep (Jgs. 16:19; *see* 2 Kgs. 4:20), while children were fondled (Isa. 66:12) and blessed while they were on or between the knees (*see* Gen. 48:12). In the New Testament, as in the Old, bowing the knee was an expression of reverence to a ranking person, and so used by the soldiers to mock Jesus (Matt. 27:29; Mk. 15:19).

knee, kneel

he made the camels *k*.	Gen. 24:11	strengthened his faltering *k*.	
from his father's *k*.	Gen. 48:12		Job 4:4
born on Joseph's *k*.	Gen. 50:23	*k*. before the Lord	Ps. 95:6
his head between his *k*.		with a request, *k*. down	Mk. 1:40
	1 Kgs. 19:42	*k*. down before him	Mk. 10:17
Wherefore did the *k*. receive me		then he *k*. down	Acts 9:40
	Job. 3:12	I *k*. before the Father	Eph. 3:14
	your weak *k*.	Heb. 12:12	

knew, know, knows

the Lord *k*. face to face		Beer-sheba came to *k*.	1 Sam. 3:20
	Deut. 34:10	No one *k*. the Son	Matt. 11:27
	the world did not *k*.	Jn. 1:10	

knife

the fire and the *k*.	Gen. 22:6	And put a *k*. to your throat	
he took a *k*. to the body	Jgs. 19:29		Prov. 23:2

knock, knocking

K., and it will be opened	Matt. 7:7	*k*., and it shall be opened	Lk. 11:9
	you stand outside *k*.	Lk. 13:25	

Know, Knowledge, The Hebrew verb **yada'** which is normally translated by **to know** expressed for the Hebrews an activity of heart and mind, more than something drily intellectual. Knowing involved experience, familiarity, a willing adhesion of the person knowing and what is known, an immersion in the reality that is absent from the more abstract knowledge of the Greeks and western civilizations in general. So true is this of the Bible that the word 'to know' is used to express the sexual intimacy of a man and woman (Gen. 4:1, 17, 25; 1 Kgs. 1:4, etc.).

In religious parlance, knowing God is much more than accepting his existence on an intellectual level. To know God is to open oneself to him in personal surrender with all that it involves: acknowledging him for what he is, adoring him, thanking him, praising him, and the continuance of this in one's life (*see* Jer. 2:8; 9:2-5; Pss. 9:11; 36:11; 87:4; Deut. 4:39; 8:5; 29:5). For Hosea, knowing God comprised practically the whole religious life of the Hebrews, all that God evokes from man (Hos. 4:1; 6:6). Even in the Bible texts that were composed in Greek, such as Wisdom and the New Testament, where popular Greek philosophy played its part in Jewish apologetics, to the theoretical "knowledge" of the Greeks was added the duty to give glory to God (Rom. 1:21). In the last times, the earth will be filled with the knowledge of God (Isa. 11:9), the law of the new Covenant foreseen by Jeremiah 31:33 will be written into man's heart, and all will know God.

This fundamental sense is maintained throughout the New Testament (Rom. 2:18; 10:19; 1 Cor. 2:14; 4:6; 2 Cor. 8:9; Col. 1:6, etc.).

In the gospel and letters of John, the term acquires particular importance from a theological point of view. It can comprise the object of Christ's mission (Jn. 17:2, 3), the relationship existing between Christ and his Father (Jn. 7:29; 8:55) and between Christ and his disciples (Jn. 10:14-15). This intrinsic knowledge of faith and love is practically identified with it, and flowers into mutual immanence (Jn. 17:21-26). The person who knows God keeps his commandments (1 Jn. 2:3-5) which are summed up in love, seeing that God himself is love, so that he who does not love has not come to know God (1 Jn. 4:7-10). The person who knows Jesus also knows the Father (Jn. 14:7), seeing that the Father is in Jesus and Jesus in the Father (Jn. 10:37, 38). The Jews think they know God (Jn. 8:41-45) but they reject Jesus and for that reason they show that they do not know the Father nor him whom the Father has sanctified and sent into the world (Jn. 8:19; 10:34-38).

In the Pauline letters, besides the typical meaning for it in the Old Testament, there is also a knowledge (epignosis, gnosis) which is a charism (1 Cor. 12:8; 14:6), a gift of God which the Apostle often asks for the churches to which he writes (*see* 1 Cor. 1:5; 2 Cor. 8:7; Eph. 1:8; 1:17, 18). This knowledge is built up on faith, and love (Eph. 3:17, 18) and is the fruit of a particular enlightenment of the eyes of the spirit (Eph. 1:18) which renders them capable of appreciating, tasting and penetrating more deeply the saving mystery of God (Eph. 1:8, 9) which is revealed in Christ. The object of this epignosis is the hope to which the Christian is called, the riches and glory to which he is heir, the power of God shown forth in Christ (Eph. 1:18, 19) and the love of Christ which surpasses all understanding (Eph. 3:18, 19).

This interior enlightenment starts with baptism (2 Cor. 4:6; 1:22) but is called to increase and intensify under the influence of the Spirit (Col. 1:9). Christian gnosis has nothing in common with the empty speculations of human wisdom which does not know God (1 Cor. 1:17-25; 2:6-9), a wisdom which puffs up but does not build up, because it is devoid of charity (1 Cor. 8:1; 13:8).

Knowledge of Good and Evil, Tree of, The story of the first sin is centered in Genesis 2-3 around two trees of the Garden of Eden which the author calls the tree of life and the tree of knowledge of good and evil. The interpretation of the first tree is not so difficult both on account of the obvious symbol used and on account of other extant non-Biblical parallels. About the second tree, however, opinions differ. The question is important for, from its answer, depends the answer to the problem of the first sin. It is not a matter of saying in what exactly the first sin consisted from a historical point of view. Rather it is an enquiry into which sin the sacred author wished to suggest as the root of all the other sins by placing it at the historical origin of all sin (*see* FALL, THE).

A few exegetes insist on the circumstances such as nudity, shame, the serpent which was an animal much associated with fertility cults (*see* SERPENT) to suggest that the author intended a sexual sin. It is difficult however to imagine in what sense the author could have considered a sexual relationship sinful. The expression "knowledge of good and evil" seems void of any sexual connotation. The fact remains that a couple sinned: there is a certain irony, touching on the tragic, in the way the author shows how the "help like unto himself" sought after in 2:18-25 to shape the primordial community of destiny turns out to be a contradiction in terms, keeping only the memory and some traces of the ideal.

Others believe that the word-couple "good and evil" expresses a totality, "everything" or "all knowledge," without a direct moral connotation. It was then the aspiration to omniscience that led man to sin. This however does not seem well framed in the context. In fact the only truly parallel text is Sirach 17:6 where knowledge of good and evil is nothing other than wisdom itself. This has led to an agreement among authors that Genesis 2-3 must be studied in the light of the wisdom tradition, to which its author belonged. It is more than logical to be persuaded that central to the paradise story should be the theme that was the foundation of the whole wisdom tradition (*see* WISDOM).

Wisdom gives life and teaches one to avoid death (Prov. 8:35, 36) because it confers a practical discernment between good and evil. Good and evil here mean moral good and evil, but not in the sense of conforming to an extrinsic and absolute law, but rather meaning that man's true good is that which brings him to life, and man's true evil is that which entices him away from it.

Biblical wisdom tradition came to identify wisdom with the Law (*see* Sir. 24:2). The Law is a doctrine of life, it is true wisdom. The perfect integration of Law and wisdom is the end of the process, the solution of a conflict.

Emphatic assertions such as those of Deuteronomy 4:5-7; 30:15-17 make one suppose that there was a period in which a certain form of wisdom became a dangerous competitor to the conception of human life as something that finds the true way of life in the word of God.

In fact wisdom is by no means an Israelite development but is a cultural phenomenon common to the whole East. It seems that wisdom cultivated by a specialized class of people was introduced into Israel principally from Egypt in the time of Solomon, when most probably the Yahwist also lived, and when international trade and cultural intercourse was at its freest. The author then had before his eyes a problem much discussed in his time, that is, the conflict between different concepts of human life. One held that listening to God's word was the way to life. The other challenged this and claimed that life was not had from listening to God's word, and indeed opposed it to the point that God himself was cast in a bad light (Gen. 3:1-5). It is this conflict of decision that faced Adam and Eve in the garden, according to the author. He suggests that this is the problem of Everyman. Living however without giving heed to the word of God carries within it the seeds of death, and therefore it is false wisdom. The true wisdom, that is, the true art of life is God's word (Deut. 4:5-7).

Kohath (koe'-hath), Son of Levi (Gen. 46:11; Ex. 6:16), father of Amram (Ex. 6:18; Num. 3:19) and grandfather of Moses and Aaron (Ex. 6:20; Num. 26:59). The Levitical clans who descended from Kohath received various cities of Judah and Ephraim (Josh. 21:4-26; 1 Chron. 6:54-70).

Koheleth, *See* QOHELETH.

Kolaiah (ko-lay'-yah), The father of the prophet Ahab (Jer. 29:21).

Korah, 1. An Edomite clan, stemming from Esau (Gen. 36:5, 14, 15, 18).

2. A Levite who descended from Kohath (Ex. 6:21-24) and headed the revolt of those Levites who challenged the cultic privileges of the priestly family of Aaron (Num. 16). The account of this revolt was later combined with the analogous narration of the revolt of Dathan and Abiram against Moses, to form one story. The Levites of Korah's family appear together with the Kohathites as singers in the Temple during the reign of Jehosphaphat (2 Chron. 20:19). Korah's name figures again in the titles of several of the Psalms (Pss. 42; 44-49; 84; 85; 87; 88), probably because they belonged to this choir's repertory.

Kore, *See* KORAH; also the name of two Levites (1 Chron. 9:19).

Kushaiah (koo-shay'-yah), A Levite, singer in the Temple during the reign of David (1 Chron. 15:17).

L

Laadah (lay´-a-dah), A Judahite (1 Chron. 4:21).

Laban (lay´-ban), Son of Bethuel, brother of Rebekah (Gen. 24:29; 25:20; 28:5), father of Rachel and Leah, Jacob's wives (Gen. 29:16). Gen. 25:20; 31:24 calls him the Aramaean. He lived in the city of Nahor (Gen. 29:5) or Haran (27:43; 29:4) in the region of Paddan-aram or Aram Naharaim (Gen. 28:2) in northwest Mesopotamia. Abraham's servant had to treat with him when he went to look for a wife (Rebekah) for his master's son, Isaac. He again appears in the history of Jacob's stay in Haran (Gen. 29-31). *See* JACOB.

labor
began to be in *l.*   Gen. 35:16   enduring *l.*, hardships,
superintendent of the forced *l.*   2 Cor. 11:27
                              1 Kgs. 4:6

Lachish (lay´-kish), A city of southern Palestine about 25 miles southwest of Jerusalem. Today it is Tell-ed-Duweir. It was captured by Joshua (Josh. 10:3-35), given over to Judah (Josh. 15:39) and fortified by Rehoboam (2 Chron. 11:9). Amaziah of Judah (800-783 B.C.) was assassinated in this city to which he had fled from a plot hatched against him in Jerusalem (2 Kgs. 14:19; 2 Chron. 25:27). During the siege of Jerusalem Lachish was the basis of operations for Sennacherib (2 Kgs. 18:14-17), and Nebuchadnezzar took it before he marched on Jerusalem (Jer. 34:7). During the excavations carried out there from 1933 on, various inscriptions and 21 ostraka were found, of which eighteen were letters written to the head of the garrison of the city during the last years of Zedekiah (597-586 B.C.) when the conquest at the hands of Nebuchadnezzar's neo-Babylonians was already imminent.

lack, lacking
perishes for *l.* of prey   Job 4:11   through your *l.* of self-control
for nought is *l.* to those   Ps. 34:10   1 Cor. 7:5
                he who gathered little had no *l.*   2 Cor. 8:15

Ladan (lay´-dan), 1. An Ephraimite, ancestor of Joshua (1 Chron. 7:26).
2. A Levite of the family of Gershon (1 Chron. 23·7-9; 26:21).

laden
our oxen be well *l.*   Ps. 144:14   people *l.* with wickedness   Isa. 1:4

ladies
Persian and Median *l.*   Esth. 1:18

Lahad (lay´-had), A Judahite (1 Chron. 4:2).

Lahmam (lah´-mam), A town in Judah (Josh. 15:40).

Lahmi (lah´-my), Brother of the giant Goliath (1 Chron. 20:5). *See* ELHA-NAN; GOLIATH.

laid
and *l.* it on   Gen. 22:6   The foundations . . . were *l.*
and *l.* it on the head of Ephraim   1 Kgs. 6:37
                              Gen. 48:14   *l.* them on cots and mattresses
                                                                        Acts 5:15

lain
I should have *l.* down   Job 3:13   where Jesus' body had *l.*   Jn. 20:12

Laish (lay´-ish), The ancient name of the city of Dan, before it was occupied by the Israelites of the tribe of Dan (Jgs. 18:7, 14, 27, 29). *See* DAN.

Laishah (lay'-i-shah), A city of Benjamin (Isa. 10:30).

lake

L. of Gennesaret	Lk. 5:1 A windstorm descended on the *l.*
by the side of the *l.*	Lk. 5:2 Lk. 8:23
	down the bluff into the *l.* Lk. 8:33

Lake of Gennesaret, *See* GENNESARET.

lama, lema
Eli, Eli, *l.* sabachthani Matt. 27:46 Eloi, Eloi, *l.* sabachthani
Mk. 15:34

Lamb, The lamb is one of the most frequently sacrificed victims in the Israelite ritual. It is prescribed for the paschal liturgy (Ex. 12:3 ff.), for the Feast of Weeks (Num. 28:26, 27) and for the Feast of Tabernacles (Num. 29:13-15). It is also ordered for the Day of Atonement (Num 29:7-8) and for the daily sacrifices (Ex. 29:38-42) and at other times.

This sacrificial context, with its special reference to the Pasch, is the reason for applying to Jesus the title "Lamb of God" in the Johannine version of the Baptizer's testimony (Jn. 1:29-36), which also re-echoes the song of the Servant of the Lord of Isa. 53; (*see* especially 53:7 and Acts 8:32; 1 Peter 18, 19). In Revelation "Lamb" is a frequent title for Christ, not only in his condition of sacrificial victim (c. 5:6; 7:14; 12:11; 13:8) but also in his present glorified condition (5:12-13; 7:9, 10; 27:1, 3), and in his role as future judge of the universe (13:8; 17:14; 21:27).

lame

he who is blind, or *l.*	Lev. 21:18 Then will the *l.* leap Isa. 35:6
For your servant, who is *l.*	and the crippled, the *l.* Lk. 14:13
2 Sam. 19:27	

Lamech (lay'-mek), In the Yahwist genealogy for Cain, Lamech is the son of Methusael (Gen. 4:18-24). The author rebukes his fierce spirit of vindictiveness and his polygamy. The traits are outlined in a song of Lamech to his wife quoted in vv. 23-24, an ancient piece of Kenite tradition (*see* CAIN). In the Priestly genealogy for Adam, Lamech is the son of Methuselah and father of Noah (Gen. 5:25, 28, 30).

Lamed (lah'-med), The 12th letter of the Hebrew alphabet (l).

Lamentation, A lyrical literary genre that occurs frequently in the Psalms. In fact about one third of the Psalms are composed in this style. The lamentation Psalms are prayers poured out to God in particular public calamities (*see* Joel 1:2 and esp. 2:17), or even private disasters. With slight variation they follow this pattern: a. invocation of God, b. the lamentation properly so-called, that is, the disaster or calamity that afflicts the person in prayer is expounded, and very often this description is lively and vehement. Then follows c. the prayer for divine intervention, often accompanied by imprecations or accusations against the enemies of the psalmist, asking that God deal with them in accordance with their deserts. The next portion d. outlines the motives that should draw God to give the help implored. Quite often the basis of these motives is the fact of God's saving intervention in the history of his people. Sometimes this part takes the shape of a protestation of innocence to move God to act and show himself the protector of the oppressed. The conclusion e. can have several forms.

Not a few lamentations finish up with a proclamation of certainty that one has been heard or with a hymn of thanksgiving. These elements are explained by the cultic context of this literary style. In fact they were almost formulas of prayer for the use of the faithful. After the lamentation there followed an oracle or promise of salvation given by a prophet or priest. The response to this oracle, or promise, was a hymn of thanksgiving. The oracle is obviously missing in the Psalms, which were chanted by the faithful, but traces of it are to be found in Pss. 5:4; 22:22 ff. Moreover it is to be found in the lamentations of the prophetic books (e.g. Jer. 15:18). The Psalter contains no lamentation for the dead. The Psalter was known and used in Israel (e.g. 2 Sam. 1:17; 3:33) but it does not seem to have passed into cultic use. However it does find its echo in some prophetic oracles dealing with the destiny of peoples or cities (Isa. 14:4-21; Jer. 9:16, 22; Ezek. 26:17; 27:32; 28:12-19; 32:19, 20).

Lamentations, Book of, A collection of five lamentations on the ruin of Jerusalem and the lot of Judah after the city had been conquered and the people deported in 587 B.C. at the hands of Nebuchadnezzar. The first four lamentations are alphabetic acrostics. Tradition attributes the book to Jeremiah. This is probably based on the information contained in 2 Chronicles 35:25 about Jeremiah composing lamentations for the death of King Josiah. Today Jeremiah is no longer considered their author. The lamentator must be sought for among the Jews who remained in Judah after the deportation, as the composition of the lamentations seems not to be long after the events they commemorate and lament. Very probably these were composed for, and used in, the liturgy. It is known from Zechariah 7:3 that during and after the exile the Jews commemorated the destruction of Jerusalem with special penitential rites (*see* also Jer. 41:5). The Lamentations would then have been composed, or at least used, during these ceremonies, as were some Psalms such as Pss. 74 and 79.

Lamp, Lamps dating as far back as the third millenium B.C. have been unearthed. At the beginning they were simply clay saucers with the rim pinched into one or more corners to support the wick that drew on the oil fuel. With time the lamps became more sophisticated, with the pinched corners eventually developing into a spout, while the lamp itself acquired a base. In the fifth century B.C. metal lamps made their appearance. The lamp was always kept burning in the home because of the lack of natural illumination and because lighting it was a problem.

The lamp and lampstand are used frequently in metaphor and symbol in the Bible. David's men urged him not to go again into battle "lest he put out the lamp of Israel" (2 Sam. 21:17; 1 Kgs. 11:36; 15:4). The Psalmist sings of the Lord: "You yourself are my lamp, my God lights up my darkness" (Ps. 18:29) while his word is a lamp to the Psalmist's feet, a light on his path (Ps. 119:105).

In the New Testament, Jesus declared that John the Baptizer was a "lamp alight and shining" (Jn. 5:35). In the Sermon on the Mount Jesus tells his listeners to let their good works shine before them like a lamp on a lampstand which shines on everyone in the house (Matt. 5:15-16). The bridegroom was met by ten virgins with lamps, but the foolish virgins took no oil for theirs (Matt. 25:1-13). The servants awaiting their master's return are dressed ready for action, with their lamps lit (Lk. 12:35). In both cases, we have a reference to the coming of the kingdom, or of the Son of Man, which may be at any time, and which is compared to a wedding feast for those ready.

Again, the seven lamps on the golden lampstand of the vision are interpreted by the angel as the eyes of Yahweh that cover the whole world (Zech. 4:1-4). Jesus states that the lamp of the body is the eye, referring by metaphor to the inner lamp of man's spirit, which if impaired, will lead to great darkness (*see* Prov. 20:27; Lk. 11:34-35).

Latin

lamp

keep the *l* burning   Ex. 27:20

The *l.* of God was not yet

         1 Sam. 3:3

You are my *l.*, O Lord!

         2 Sam. 22:29

their *l.* he specified   1 Chron. 28:15

lampstand and its *l.*

         1 Chron. 28:15

The eye is the body's *l.*   Matt. 6:22

lampstand

a *l.* of pure beaten gold   Ex. 25:31

place the table and the *l.*

         Ex. 26:35

toward the front of the *l.*

         Num. 8:2

lamps of the golden *l.* burn

         2 Chron. 13:11

land

my *l.* lies at your disposal

         Gen. 20:15

the surface of the whole *l.*

         Ex. 10:15

a *l.* which the Lord, your God,

         Deut. 11:12

The *l.* then was at rest   Jgs. 3:11

language

each with its own *l.*   Gen. 10:5

spoke the same *l.*   Gen. 11:1

people in its own *l.*   Esth. 1:22

people whose *l.* you   Jer. 5:15

languish, languishes

the world *l.* and fades   Isa. 24:4

never again shall they *l.*   Jer. 31:12

everything that dwells in it *l.*

         Hos. 4:3

Laodicea (lay'-od-i-see'-a), A city in Phrygia, Asia Minor, in the valley of the river Lycus, near Colossae and Hierapolis (Col. 2:1; 4:13, 15). In Paul's time there was a Christian church in Laodicea, but it was not founded by Paul. Paul nevertheless wrote a letter to the church of Laodicea (*see* Col. 4:16). Some authors think that the letter referred to is the letter to the Ephesians, which was, in reality, an encyclical letter, addressed to different communities. The church at Laodicea is among those to whom the seven letters of Revelation are addressed (Rev. 3:14-22). Nothing now remains of the city but ruins.

lap

sleep on her *l.*   Jgs. 16:19   fondled in her *l.*   Isa. 66:12

Lappidoth (lap'-pi-doth), Husband of the prophetess Deborah in the book of Judges (Jgs. 4:4).

large

in my own *l.* handwriting

         Gal. 6:11

Lasea (la-see'-a), A town on the southern coast of Crete, mentioned in the journey of Paul to Rome as a prisoner (Acts 27:8).

Lasha (lay'-sha), A town near the southern end of the Dead Sea, exact site unknown (Gen. 10:19).

last

L. night it was I   Gen. 19:34

the *l.* of the divisions   Num. 2:31

    the *l.* one of all   Mk. 9:35

the *l.* state of that man

         Matt. 12:45

Lasthenes, The Seleucid governor of Coelesyria at the time of Jonathan Maccabeus (1 Mac. 11:32).

Last Supper, *See* LORD'S SUPPER.

Latin, John 19:20 records that the sign appended to the cross was written in Aramaic, Greek and Latin. Latin does not however seem to have been used in Palestine except in official documents. The latinisms in the New Testament Greek are for the most part names of coins (**denarius**) or of officials (**kenturion, spekulator**).

laugh

Why did Sarah *l.*	Gen. 18:13	you shall *l.*	Job 5:22
God has given me cause to *l.*		you shall *l.*	Lk. 6:21
	Gen. 21:6		

laughter

our mouth was filled with *l.*		Of *l.* I said: "Mad!"	Eccl. 2:2
	Ps. 126:2	Sorrow is better than *l.*	Eccl. 7:3
in *l.* the heart may be sad			
	Prov. 14:13		

Law, In Hebrew **Torah,** translated by the Greek version of the Septuagint as **nomos,** law, which from Deuteronomy on became the favorite term to designate the whole collection of divine dispositions which should regulate the life of Israel in the context of the Covenant (Deut. 32:46). **Torah** also means instruction or teaching (Prov. 1:8). It was technically the decision (or perhaps oracles) given by the priests in the name of God on concrete questions of morality or cult which had been proposed to them (*see* Hag. 2:11, 12; Amos 2:4; Deut. 33:10; Isa. 8:20; Jer. 2:8; 8:8).

The choice of this term to signify the whole Israelite legislation is perhaps due to the fact that this name put into relief its divine origin and its character of instruction or warning so much insisted upon in Deuteronomy. The term was then spread to include the whole Pentateuch (Sirach, prologue, v. 2; 1 Mac. 12:9) and the economy of the Old Testament as opposed to the New (Rom. 8:1-3; Gal. 2:21; 3:2).

Almost the whole of Israelite legislation, moral, civil, penal and cultic is contained in the Pentateuch and is handed down against the background of the Covenant of Sinai (Ex. 19-Num. 10; Deut. 12-26). The principal legislative codes or collections of laws are:

a. The Decalogue (Ex. 20; Deut. 5) *see* DECALOGUE.

b. The so-called cultic Decalogue (Ex. 34:17-27) handed down in the J document and exclusively religious in content.

c. The Covenant code (Ex. 20:22-23, 33; *see* Ex. 24:7), which is the most ancient collection after the Decalogue. A study of the social and economic conditions that it mirrors leads one to date this code in pre-monarchic times but after the occupation of Canaan. It was the common law of the Israelite confederation at the time of the Judges.

d. The Deuteronomic code (Deut. 12:26) *see* DEUTERONOMY.

e. The Holiness code (Lev. 17:26) so called because of the insistent repetition of formulae such as that of Lev. 19:2: "Be holy, for I, the Lord, your God, am holy." It is cultic and moral in content and comprises the traditions of the priestly circles at Jerusalem, and was first drawn up before Ezekiel, but its present form dates from the exile or thereafter.

Attributing all this legislation to a direct revelation of God to Moses is more of a theological judgment than a solution to the problem of its historic origins. Israel's law from a historical point of view is the result of a long process of assimilation, not simply in a passive or servile manner, but actively and critically, of the juridic patrimony of the ancient East. Study of ancient Assyrian, Hittite, Hurrite and other codes that have come to light in excavations shows that Biblical law fitted easily into this common heritage. Authors distinguish two types of laws. The first is casuistic which in the last analysis consists of a conditional sentence (or paragraph) in which the protasis describes minutely a case, and the apodosis gives it a solution (*see* e.g. Ex. 21:33-34; 22:6-7; 21:28-32). These laws would ordinarily have been handed down by tribunals and usually solved disputes between contending parties. The solutions were notably equitable. This type of law is more common in extra-biblical legislation.

Apodictic laws are so called because of their categorical style. They do not take time to distinguish case from case: they simply state the crime. They do not dally over circumstances, nor think of compromises inspired by principles of equity. They are the undisputed decisions imposed by a will that is acknowledged as superior. It was thought that this categorical type of law was exclusive to Israel, and that it owed its origin to the proclamation of God's will in cult. Today cult is still acknowledged as one of the contexts in which apodictic law was proclaimed, but the origins of it are sought for in the social-usage laws of nomadic and semi-nomadic clans.

In the context of the Covenant, especially in its Deuteronomic version, the law has a two-fold relationship, with the history related in the historical prologue and with the blessings and curses attached to fulfilment or non-fulfilment of the law. (*See* COVENANT.) The dispositions of the law are the concrete ways in which God demands to be served exclusively by the people to whom he had granted salvation and which he has made his very own.

The relationship between future blessing and present fulfilment of the law must not be understood as an exchange contract between God and his people. Fulfilment nevertheless is a condition without which the blessings will not be enjoyed. The law then establishes how the people must live as God's people in order to have from him the salvation which he has freely decided to give to Israel in the future.

In the post-exilic period there is a partially new emphasis. The law becomes progressively more absolute in the sense that the historical context which governed its interpretation and gave it its sense is lost sight of and the prescriptions of the law become the absolute norm almost supplanting direct relationships with God. How this development came about is not quite clear. One possible influence was that of the wisdom tradition which identified the law with true wisdom, which was in turn a help to living and to obtain life. The recompense aspect was emphasized somewhat unilaterally (Sir. 24; 32:1-11). The Pharisaic tradition brought this glorification and absolutizing of the law to exasperating lengths in the period between the Old and New Testaments. This tradition started the oral law which aimed at interpreting, applying and preserving the law by creating new, minute and exact precepts.

Jesus' dispute with the Pharisees was to a great extent directed at these excesses and the arbitrariness of the oral law which at times found ways around the real meaning of the law or succeeded in annulling the divine will under the weight of human traditions (Mk. 7; Matt. 15). Jesus' outlook on the law, properly so-called is different. The law's prescriptions are gathered into the law of the love of God and one's neighbor (Matt. 22:34-40; Mk. 12:28-34; Lk. 10:25-28). Jesus declared that he had come not to do away with the law and the prophets but to bring them to fulfilment (Matt. 5:17-20).

Jesus wished to revive the idea of the law as the revelation and channel of God's will. For this reason Jesus proclaims himself superior to the letter of the law in order to show the real implications of the will of God (Matt. 5:20-48; 9:1-10; Mk. 10:11, 12; Lk. 16:18).

The law is no longer that supreme and absolute norm behind which God disappears. Jesus, however, has restored to it its true value as a vehicle or channel through which God makes known his will and through which people give themselves to God. Man is still called to a complete surrender to this will. Man can no longer take refuge in a false independence in which he measures himself for his own comfort against a list of works to be performed.

Paul's dispute with the law was also developed along these principles, but in different ways. At first reading it seems that Paul's declarations on the law are inconsistent. While the law is holy, good and spiritual (Rom. 7:12) it was nevertheless introduced to multiply transgressions (Gal. 3:19; Rom. 5:20) and is the work of anger (Rom. 4:15). This apparent contradiction can be resolved by distinguishing with Paul between the law as a manifestation of the will of God, which is holy and spiritual, and the law as a means of justification and salvation. In the present economy of salvation, the law is quite incapable of giving life (Gal. 3:21). This incapability was not so much the fault of the law, but due to man who had become a slave to sin (Rom. 7:14). He was deprived of that interior power that could make him rise above the works of the flesh (Rom. 8:5).

A person seeking to work out his own salvation by the works of the law is merely affirming himself. Paul ironically remarks that such a person has something to boast about, but not something of God's he can boast about (Rom. 4:2). For Paul this is the radical perversion of the relationship between God and man. It excludes God from giving to man what man could never achieve for himself, that is, salvation in Christ Jesus.

Christ overcame man's sin in his own flesh (Rom. 8:3) and has sent his spirit to become in man that interior force to fulfil what the law had prescribed, that is, to fulfil the will of God that was revealed in it. So Paul could reply, to those who accused him of trying to destroy the law, that justification by faith is the law's fulfilment (Rom. 3:31).

Lawyer, A translation of the Greek **nomikos,** the term chosen by Luke to designate the group called scribes (Lk. 7:30; 11:45-46; 14:3; 10:25; and Matt. 22:35). In Titus 3:13 one Zenas is called lawyer, this time probably in the general sense of one knowledgeable in the law.

lawyer
and one of them, a *l.*   Matt. 22:35   The Pharisees and the *l.*   Lk. 7:30
                          a *l.* stood   Lk. 10:25

Lazarus, 1. The poor man who sat at the gate of the rich man in the parable of Luke 16:19-31. He is the only person in all the parables who is given a name by Jesus. Perhaps the choice of the name was for symbolic purposes: Lazarus is the Greek transcription of the name Eleazar, God helps.

2. Lazarus of Bethany, brother of Martha and Mary, whose resurrection from the tomb is the theme of John 11. The original event was edited by John to stress the fact that Jesus is the life. In the raising of Lazarus to life there is revealed, in an initial way, the divine power of Jesus who is God's victory over death. The raising of Lazarus does not immediately or directly bear on the future glorious resurrection of the just; it is a sign of the divine power that brings life where there had been death to the man who hears the call of the Son of God and believes. The event of Lazarus is intimately connected with the passion of Jesus, for it hastened those conspiring against Jesus in their plans (Jn. 11:45-54; 12:9-11, 17). Even the disciples had forseen that going up to Jerusalem at this point was risky (Jn. 11:7, 8, 16). John wished in this way to underline the truth that the

granting of eternal life was to come through the death and resurrection of Jesus, and the raising of Lazarus anticipated this in sign. The journey to Jerusalem was undertaken to raise Lazarus to life and at the same time to surrender freely into the hands of those who wished death on Jesus.

Lazarus was at table at the supper offered for Jesus six days before the Pasch. At this supper there occurred the episode of the anointing of Jesus which he interpreted as an anticipatory anointing for his burial (Jn. 12:1-11).

lazy
They are *l*.   Ex. 5:8   because you are *l*.   Ex. 5:17

Lead, Lead was scarce in Palestine which had to import it (Ezek. 27:12). It does not seem to have been much in use. The Bible records the use of lead in the purification of silver (Jer. 6:29), and also perhaps for weighting the nets so that they would sink when used for fishing (Ex. 15:10). Lead is also mentioned for its use in the plummet in building (Amos 7:7-8).

lead
like *l*. they sank   Ex. 15:10   the *l*. is consumed by the fire
                                               Jer. 6:29

lead
and *l*. me on   Ps. 27:11   they shall *l*. me on   Ps. 43:3

leaf, leaves
a plucked-off olive *l*.   Gen. 8:11   and whose *l*. never fade   Ps. 1:3
a wind-driven *l*.   Job 13:25   As the *l*. wilts   Isa. 34:4

Leah (lee′-ah), Sister of Rachel and daughter of Laban, who was deceitfully given in marriage to Jacob instead of her sister Rachel who was the expected bride, and for whose hand Jacob had served Laban for seven years. Though given Rachel also after a week, Jacob had to serve yet another seven years in recompense. (Gen. 29:15-30). Leah's sons were Reuben, Simeon, Levi, Judah (Gen. 29:32-35), Issachar, Zebulun and her daughter, Dinah (Gen. 30:14-21). From Leah's slave, Zilpah, Jacob had Gad and Asher (Gen. 30:9-13). Leah accompanied Jacob to Cannan and died there. She was buried in the cave of Machpelah which had been bought by Abraham for the burial of Sarah (Gen. 49:29-31). The tribes of Leah probably constituted a tribal confederacy before the Israelite confederation of tribes, which comprised also the tribes of Rachel, was formed. *See* GENEALOGY.

leaks
the house *l*.   Eccl. 10:18

learn
waiting to *l*.   Gen. 24:21   that I may *l*. your statutes
l. to fear me   Deut. 4:10   Ps. 119:71
            and *l*. from me, for I am   Matt. 11:29

least
the *l*. servants of my lord   whoever breaks the *l*.   Matt. 5:19
              2 Kgs. 18:24   for the *l*. one among you   Lk. 9:48
l. among the princes   Matt. 2:6

Leather, One word in Hebrew, **'or,** is used for skin, pelt, hide, leather. Similarly the Greek **dermatinos** comes from the word **derma,** a generic term for skin or leather. The skins out of which God made clothes for the man and his wife in Genesis 3:21 were probably, in the author's mind, tanned skins, or leather.

Simon the Tanner owned the house by the sea in which Peter lodged at Joppa. But the process of tanning is not mentioned in the Bible. Leather however (or hide) was used in garments, girdles, footwear (Lev. 13:48; 2 Kgs. 1:8; Ezek. 16:10), as a covering for the tabernacle (Ex. 26:14) and for various other objects referred to in general (e.g. Lev. 13:48-49). Wineskins and waterskins, as well as milk containers, were made out of animal hide (Gen. 21:14; Jgs. 4:19; Sam. 1:24; Matt. 9:17) while leather was also used for writing materials.

leave

a man *l.* his father and mother	they will *l.* you no grain
Gen. 2:24	Deut. 28:51
may eat what the poor *l.* Ex. 23:11	does not *l.* the ninety-nine
	Lk. 15:4

Leaven, The word is usually applied to a piece of leavened (i.e. yeasted) dough which was preserved from a previous preparation of bread in order to ferment the next batch, and so on. The fermentation or leavening is generally considered a degenerate process, so that it was excluded from sacrifices (Ex. 23:18; 34:25). During the Passover season the Jew was forbidden to keep leavened bread in his house.

In the New Testament St. Paul warns the Corinthians that even a small amount of yeast can leaven all the dough. He is referring to how even a small amount of evil can work insidiously for the ruin of an entire community. Jesus however in Matthew 13:33 uses leaven metaphorically to signify the unseen, silent, steady growth of the kingdom of heaven (*see* Luke 13:21).

Lebanah (le-bay´-nah), The ancestor of a family of temple servants (Ezra 2:45).

Lebanon, A mountain range along the coast of Syria and north of Galilee. It is about 100 miles long and reaches a height of over 10,000 feet. It is separated from the parallel range of the Anti-Lebanon mountains by the valley of **el-Beqaa,** which is five to eight miles wide. Lebanon was renowned in ancient times for its cedars (Ps. 29:5; Isa. 2:13; Ezek. 17:3) and cypresses (Isa. 14:8) which were used in the construction of the Temple and the royal palace at Jerusalem (1 Kgs. 5:13; 7:2). In poetic texts Lebanon occurs as a symbol of majesty and beauty (Ps. 29:6; Isa. 29:17; 33:9, etc.)

Lebbaeus (le-bee´-us), A variant (Matt. 10:3) of the name of the disciple Judas "the son of James" (Lk. 6:16), also called Thaddaeus in some manuscripts (Matt. 10:3 and Mk. 3:18). "Lebbaeus" is dropped in the NAB and RSV translations in favor of simply Thaddaeus.

Legion, The principal division in the Roman army, which at the time of the empire consisted theoretically of six thousand men. In the New Testament the word is used to designate a large number of the angelic (Matt. 26:53) or demoniac hordes (Mk. 5:9; Lk. 8:30).

Lehabim (le-hay´-bim), An unknown people, son of Egypt in the Table of Nations (Gen. 10:13; 1 Chron. 1:11).

Lehi (lee´-hy), In Hebrew, jawbone; the name of a place in Judah mentioned in the traditions about Samson (Jgs. 15:9-15).

Lemuel, The name of a king of Massa who was author of a collection of Proverbs (31:1-9). The sayings were taught him by his mother.

Lentils, An annual plant of the pea family, abundant in Palestine. Esau sold his rights as first-born for a plate of lentils (Gen. 25:34). They were brought as a gift to David (2 Sam. 17:28), and were included in Ezekiel's emergency bread recipe (Ezek. 4:9).

Leopard, A ferocious carnivorous mammal of the feline family. Jeremiah speaks of his stealth and ferocity (Jer. 5:6), while Habakkuk speaks of his agility (1:8). He is known for the characteristic markings on his skin (Jer. 13:23). He frequently appears in apocalyptic visions, (e.g. Dan. 7:6: a beast like a leopard, with four bird's wings on its flanks, and four heads, to whom power had been given; *see* Rev. 13:2). Leopards were not common to ancient Palestine but were familiar further north, in Lebanon and Hermon (S. of S. 4:8).

Leprosy, The Hebrew **sara'at** which was translated by the Septuagint into the Greek **lepra,** leprosy. It is not however the leprosy of modern medicine (called Hanson's disease) as is evident from the symptoms described in Leviticus 13. The word is applied to a variety of eruptive and today easily curable skin infections. The same term is used for damp stains on the walls of houses (Lev. 14:33-53). "Leprosy" in the Bible could affect woolen or linen clothing, or leatherwork, which would show itself in reddish or greenish color spreading on the article (*see* Lev. 15:17-59; 14:33-53).

"Leprosy" rendered people or things impure: it was the function of the priest to ascertain its existence or to pronounce it cured, basing his judgment on precisely dictated symptoms described in Leviticus 13-14. Here there is a whole list of swellings, scabs, discolorations, rash, loss of hair, etc., directions about isolating the sick person for a time to see if the disease recedes or spreads before coming to a diagnosis. The cured leper had to present himself to the priest so that the cure could be officially declared (Lk. 17:11-19; Matt. 8:1-4; Mk. 1:40-45; Lk. 5:12-16). He was also obliged to offer the prescribed sacrifices for his purification.

There are few cases of leprosy reported in the Old Testament: Naaman (2 Kgs. 5), King Uzziah (2 Kgs. 15:5), and the four lepers in Samaria (2 Kgs. 7:3). The leprosy mark that appeared and disappeared on the hand of Moses was taken as a sign of his mission (Ex. 4:6). Moses' sister Miriam and Elisha's servant Gehazi were punished by God with leprosy (Num. 12:10; 2 Kgs. 5).

Jesus refers in general to the cure of lepers when he lists the miracles he performed as signs of his mission (Matt. 11:5; Lk. 7:22). He conferred this power on the apostles (Matt. 10:8). Moreover the gospels contain two accounts of miraculous cures of lepers (Matt. 8:1-4; Mk. 1:40-45; Lk. 5:12-16, and the ten lepers in Lk. 17:11-19).

Letter, Of the inspired books of the New Testament, twenty-one are letters or epistles of which thirteen carry Paul's name, one (Hebrews) is attributed to him even though it is anonymous, two are in Peter's name, one is Jude's and three are given John's name by tradition, while one is in James's name.

In general the New Testament letters follow the epistolary pattern of antiquity. This meant introducing the letter with the name of the sender and the person to whom the letter was addressed, together with a formal greeting. An example is 2 Timothy 1:1, 2: "Paul, by the will of God an apostle of Christ Jesus . . . to Timothy, my child whom I love. May grace, mercy, and peace from God the Father and from Christ Jesus our Lord be with you" (*see* Acts 15:23; 23:26; James 1:1, etc.). Then followed the body of the letter and the conclusion, which was usually brief and written by the sender and not by the scribe or amanuensis who was often used for writing the rest of the letter. Thus Romans 16:22 reads: "I, Tertius, who have written this letter, send you my greetings in the Lord," while 1 Corinthians 16:21 has: "It is I, Paul, who send you this greeting in my own hand."

In their introductions most of the letters of the New Testament follow the pattern of oriental letters derived from the chancellory style of the Persian empire. The style had two points: the first comprised the name and titles of the sender and the person or group addressed, to which was added then a salutation in the form of good wishes (1 Thess. 1 and 2 Thess. 1). From this formal pattern could be deduced the official and solemn character which the authors wished to give their letters. Paul developed this part to a great extent (1-2 Cor., Gal., Rom.) until it becomes itself an introduction to the theme of the letter.

The composition of the letter was very much the work of scribes or amanuenses, who wrote under dictation (Rom. 16:22). The conclusion written in the author's hand served as authentication (Gal. 6:11). Sometimes the literary composition of the letter itself was confided to a secretary to whom the subject matter and the questions had been expounded (1 Pet. 5:12).

Scholars attempt to distinguish between true letters and epistles. Epistles are really tracts or dissertations addressed to the public and presented in epistolary form. Such was for instance the letter from Seneca to Lucilius. Letters were communications between specific persons on subjects of common interest. These letters could be either public or private. Most of the letters of the New Testament are of this type—public letters—while more epistolary in form are James, Hebrews, 1 John, 1 and 2 Peter, and Jude. Even these however, with their almost homiletic form and theological development, are nevertheless addressed to a definite category of readers and have determined circumstances in mind, even though they are more generic in application.

On the other hand some of the Pauline "letters" such as Romans and Ephesians read like a theological tract or dogmatic exposition. Thus the attempt to distinguish between letters and epistles seems a dubious exercise.

Levi (lee′-vie), 1. The third son of Jacob born of his first wife Leah (Gen. 29:34; 35:23) and founding father of the Israelite tribe that bears his name. (*See* LEVITES.) With Simeon his brother he vindicated the honor of his sister Dinah, who had been raped by Shechem, the son of Hamor the Hivite during a visit to the women of that region. Hamor, Shechem's father, went to Jacob to try to arrange a marriage beween Dinah and Shechem. Jacob's sons answered that it would not be right to give their sister to an uncircumcised man, so that if they wished to have her, then all the males of the town should undergo circumcision. This was agreed to, but on the third day, while the men were still in pain, Simeon and Levi marched into the town with swords drawn and killed all the males, pillaged the town and took Dinah away with them. Jacob was not pleased with this, as he was afraid the people of the region would unite against him, so he decided to change residence (Gen. 34). This story must be interpreted as an unsuccessful attempt on the part of Jacob (or Levi and Simeon) to settle on the central plain of Shechem. (*See* DINAH.) There is an allusion to this in the blessing of Jacob (Gen. 49:5-7), and it can be concluded that the episode had negative repercussions on the reputation of the two tribes.

The sons and tribes of Levi appear in the history of Israel as the priestly tribe (Deut. 33:8-11, Moses' blessing), which had no territory of its own. *See* LEVITES.

2. In Luke's genealogy for Jesus the name of Levi is read twice (3:24; 3:29).

3. Another name of the disciple Matthew in Mark 2:14; Luke 5:27, 29. *See* MATTHEW.

Leviathan, The biblical name for the Ugaritic Lothan, a mythological sea-monster which personifies the forces of chaos. He engages in a struggle with the god Baal from whom he suffers defeat. (*See* BAAL.) Residues of this myth can be traced in Israel's tradition: Scripture uses it to express faith in the creation of the world by Yahweh. (*See* CREATION.) Thus, for example, Isaiah 27:1 states "In that day the Lord with his hard and great and strong sword will punish Leviathan the fleeing servant, Leviathan the twisting serpent, and he will slay the dragon that is in the sea." Psalm 74:14 adds that God crushed the head of the monster and gave it as food to the beasts. In Psalm 104:26 Leviathan's character is different: he is no longer a monster wreaking havoc on creation and threatening the dominion of God, but rather a great fish, probably the dolphin, created by God "to sport with." In Job 40:25 it is the crocodile described in terrifying terms.

Levirate Law (lee′-vi-rate or lev′-i-rate), From the Latin **levir** meaning "relative." It is the law found in Deuteronomy 25:5-10 according to which if brothers dwell together and one of them should die leaving no son, the wife of the dead man should not marry outside the family to a stranger: "her husband's brother shall go in to her, and take her as his wife, and perform the duty of a husband's brother to her." The first son whom she bears should then bear the name of the brother who is dead, that his name might not be blotted out of Israel. Should the live brother refuse to accept her on these conditions, then she was entitled to denounce him publicly to the elders of the city. If not even these can convince him, then his brother's widow should go up to him in the presence of the elders, pull his sandal off his foot and spit in his face, publicly insulting him, so that the bad name should go down with his family in Israel.

The cases of levirate marriage noted in the Bible are very few. The case posed by the Sadducees to Jesus was purely academic, and was aimed at the doctrine of the resurrection of the dead which the Sadducees did not hold (Matt. 22:23-33; Mk. 12:18-27; Lk. 20:27-40). Genesis 38 relates the case of Tamar, widow of Er, son of Judah. His brother Onan refused to have children by Tamar and was punished by God with death. Judah did not then want to give to Tamar his other son Shelah. Tamar disguised herself as a whore, and invited Judah himself to have intercourse with her. In pledge of payment Judah left her his signet, cord and stick. These she kept, and when later she was condemned to death by Judah for harlotry, she produced the incriminating evidence, upon which Judah confessed that he was more guilty than she for refusing to give her his son Shelah for a husband.

A different case occurs in the book of Ruth. In this case the buying of land also brought with it the right to "the widow of the dead, in order to restore the name of the dead to his inheritance"; this would keep the property in the name and in the hands of the family circle (Ruth 4:5; *see* AVENGER). Moreover the right to acquire property and the marriage that was annexed to it was extended beyond the brothers to less intimate degrees of relationship. In order to marry Ruth, Boaz had to get Naomi, a nearer relative of Ruth's, to renounce her rights (Ruth 4:7 ff.).

Levites, In the later sources of the Old Testament, such as the Priestly source of the Pentateuch and the Chronicler's work, there is a sufficiently coherent account of the rank, origin and functions of the Levites. They were descended from Levi, a son of Jacob, and formed a priestly tribe which God reserved to himself to carry out the cult and exercise the other priestly functions (Num. 1:50; 3:6-7). They were chosen, according to Num. 3:12, "in place of the first-born, those who open the mother's womb among the Israelites. The Levites therefore are mine" (*see* Num. 8:16; FIRST-BORN). The Levites as a tribe did not have their own lands (Job 13:14) but were to live off the cult offerings and from other contributions which the people were to make in their favor (Num. 18:21-24). They lived in cities distributed throughout the territories of the other tribes (Num. 35:1-8; *see* LEVITICAL CITIES). Levi's children were divided into two categories: the priests, who were Aaron's descendants (Ex. 29:9, 44; 40:15) and the Levites properly so-called who have minor functions in the cult (Num. 3:6-9; 18:1-7).

The question of the Levites is very complex and to it no adequate solution or clarification has yet been offered. This note will be limited to a presentation of the elements of the problem and to hint at some of the proposed solutions to the question.

Whatever the solution proposed, one must retain the certain fact that there existed a tribe of Levi. Genesis 34 and 49:5-7 point to the traditions about this tribe in which there is no allusion to their priestly function. On the other hand it is certain that at the time of the judges and of the monarchy there existed non-Levite priests, that is, priests not descended from Levi, even though later they were given a fictitious genealogy so that Levi would appear as an ancestor. Examples of this are the son of Micah (Jgs. 17:5), Samuel (1 Sam. 1:1; 2:18), Eleazar, son of Abinadab (1 Sam 7:1), and Jeroboam who established non-Levite priests at Bethel (1 Kgs. 12:31; 13:33).

During this time there was a tendency wherever possible to prefer Levites for the functions of the cult (*see* Jgs. 17:13). This state of affairs is confirmed indirectly by Exodus 32:25-29 and Deuteronomy 33:8-11. These texts affirm that the exercise of the priesthood devolved on the tribe of Levi because of its loyalty to the Lord in circumstances where the rest of the people almost totally apostatized. At the same time however a polemical note can be noticed which aims at justifying and defending a monopoly on the priesthood which was not yet perfectly in possession.

By the time of Deuteronomy 10:8, however, this monopoly had been secured (8th c. B.C.). In this book one notices the two categories of priests and Levites, a division clearly sanctioned for the first time in the program of restoration of Ezek. 44:6-31. This distinction was the fruit of long maturation. With the centralization of cult in Jerusalem the Levites of the other sanctuaries throughout the land were left without function, for they were deprived of their places of worship while the central sanctuary in Jerusalem was in the hands of the priests there and jealously guarded by them.

We have here then the post-exilic situation which however, by anticipation, is placed at the beginning of the history of Israel.

It remains to be explained how the tribe of Levi came to be associated with the priesthood. The Old Testament gives an explanation which is both theological (Num. 3:12; *see* FIRST-BORN) and historical (Ex. 32:25-29; Deut. 33:8-11), but somewhat contradictory. Thus we seem to have a theological explanation of a **de facto** situation.

One must above all beware of transferring to antiquity the modern Christian concept of the priesthood. In antiquity, including ancient Israel, the priesthood was a profession or trade rather than a vocation. It was at that time hereditary, a speciality that passed from father to son. The idea then of a tribe specialized in the priesthood is perfectly in accord with the situation of the times, and was not any detriment to society, the dignity of the priestly function or the cult.

How did the tribe of Levi come to specialize in the priesthood? Some authors hold that this was due to the breakup of the tribe of Levi in the Israelite confederation. This would follow the traditions of Gen. 34 and 49:5-7 where, in his blessing, Jacob forsees the descendants of his sons Levi and Simeon scattered throughout Israel. When they were reduced to a minority, their only chance of survival lay in specialization which would also serve as an instrument of cohesion. Otherwise they would end up being absorbed by the other tribes.

Other authors believe that the tribe of Levi that really existed at one time had only one thing in common with the Levites, the name "Lewy," which meant "given," "devoted to," or "attached to" (the divinity) (*see* Gen. 29:34). This would then have been a common name for those who exercised the cult. They formed a group which was not linked by blood but by function, which however was later framed in a tribal genealogical scheme.

Levitical Cities, According to Joshua 21:1-42, when Canaan was distributed among the tribes of Israel, Levi did not receive its own territory but got instead forty-eight cities, four for each of the tribes, with the surrounding lands (*see* also 1 Chron. 6:39-66). This was done in obedience to the dispositions left by Moses (Num. 35:1-8). Scholars are agreed that this record certainly does not go back to the time of Joshua, even though it is not purely fictional. It is certain that the Levites did not have their own territory like the other tribes. It is also certain that at the time of Deuteronomy (8th c. B.C.) they were scattered throughout the land, with no great financial assets, so that they are insistently recommended to the goodness and charity of the Israelites (Deut. 12:12, 18-19; 26:12-13). The cities attributed to the Levites were not Israelite until the time of David and Solomon. So some authors have concluded that the allotment of cities to the Levites was a project of one of these kings, which however was not reduced to practice or did not last long, as is evident from the Levites' condition in Deuteronomy. Other scholars think that at the beginning no cities were given to the Levites, but groups of Levites in fact lived there outside the great cultic centers of Jerusalem and Bethel. Despite these attempted explanations, the question of the Levitical cities is still an enigma.

Leviticus, The third book of the Torah or Pentateuch. The name **levitikos** is read in the Greek translation, and refers to the content which is almost exclusively of a cultic or ritual character, and therefore related above all to the priestly tribe of Levi. On its origin and composition *see* PENTATEUCH. This book belongs to the Priestly source (P) of the Pentateuch.

The content of the book is almost exclusively legislative. Cc. 1-7 are laws concerning sacrifices. Cc. 8-9 deal with the investiture of Aaron and his sons as priests. C. 10 recounts some anecdotes relating to other cultic customs. Cc. 11-15 contain the rules that distinguish between the ritual purity and impurity of persons, animals and things. C. 16 has the ritual of the Great Day of Atonement (*see* ATONEMENT, DAY OF). Cc. 17-26 are the so-called Holiness Code, one of the major collections of legislation that have found their way into the Pentateuch (*see* LAW). C. 27 is an appendix with various dispositions regarding offerings and taxes.

Liberty, The notions of slavery (*see* SLAVERY) and liberty are used in the New Testament and especially by Paul to illustrate the radical change that the salvation won for us by Christ introduces into the religious condition of man. In John's view (8:31-36) man, and even "the sons of Abraham" who claim that they are free, do not enjoy liberty, for the man who sins becomes a slave to sin. Only Jesus who brings the truth can truly free man. This declaration should be understood in the light of John's concept of truth. (*See* TRUTH.) Truth, which is the revelation which Jesus brings with him, becomes, for the person who receives it with faith, an internal dynamism to instruct, guide and sustain him as he walks in the way of the precepts of Jesus, that is, in love. Truth understood in this way, brings about freedom in man.

The same doctrine appears in Paul's writings. His terminology however is a little different. Moreover his concept of freedom becomes a little more complex because it was the center of those polemics with the Judaizers that occupied a great part of Paul's missionary effort, and lay at the origin of his letters to the Galatians and the Romans.

Man is born a slave of sin and death. Through faith and baptism he is sacramentally inserted into the death and resurrection of Jesus, that is, into the act by which Christ passed from death to life, which was his victory over sin and death (Rom. 6). Paul also speaks of freedom from the law (Rom. 7:1-7; 8:2; Gal. 3:23-29; 4:1-7). In order to understand this correctly one must recall that "law" here means the proposing and imposing from without of a moral obligation, the observance of which merits salvation. The "law" is a system of salvation or a way of understanding the relationship between God and man that differed radically from the faith: "It should be obvious that no one is justified in God's sight by the law, for 'the just man shall live by faith' " (Gal. 3:11).

The "law" understood in this way cannot bring salvation (Gal. 3:21, 22). Sin in the flesh radically vitiates this system, for it renders man's efforts at observance vain, and so the "law" instead of saving man, becomes his accuser. Liberty from the law then becomes another aspect of the liberation from sin. The gift of the Spirit brings to nothing the old regime of the law, which could only bring death. Paul calls it "the law of sin and of death" (Rom. 8:2). The Spirit inaugurates the regime of liberty. Man is spontaneously moved from within by the dynamism of the Spirit and he is brought to fulfil, in fact, what the law declares to be just (Rom. 8:1-4). Paul thus can speak of the law of the Spirit of life (Rom. 8:2), that is, of the internal law which is the Holy Spirit in us, bringing us to life. The life of a Christian that emerges from this internal dynamism is described in Romans 8.

While Christians are living in this world, their freedom should grow and become more and more firmly established. It is not perfect from the beginning. The Christian will find himself in an internal struggle between the Spirit and the flesh (Gal. 5:16-25). This contrast is not the one described in Romans 7:7-25 between the interior man and the flesh that is still enslaved to sin. While in his struggle the Christian is not certain that he will avoid defeat, he knows that he has the strength necessary for victory.

The Christian then finds himself in a peculiar situation which might be summed up in the exhortation to become that which he is: he must bring about in his life that victory over sin which he has already radically won in Christ. All that Paul has to write on the transformation that takes place in the Christian through his being incorporated into Christ is accompanied by the exhortation, and indeed the demand, to make it an actuality in his whole life. He has overcome sin: he must perpetuate this victory. He has become a new creature: he must live out his life in this newness. Freedom is his: he must make it his constant possession (Rom. 6:1-19).

Even in Paul's own lifetime his doctrine on liberty was subject to misunderstanding. Some used it as a charter to licentiousness and freedom from all moral demands. Paul himself was not unaware of possible misrepresentation. In Romans 6:15 he rhetorically asks: "What does all this lead to? Just because we are not under the law but under grace, are we free to sin?" His answer follows, "By no means."

Paul tried to clear up misunderstandings by underlining the commitments that Christian liberty brings with it. Paradoxically, these can be called slavery, service, a service of God and of Christ who has ransomed us for himself (Rom. 6:22; 14:18; 16:18; 1 Cor. 6:19; 3:23). The Christian also has his law, which is love, inspiring him and imposing on him uncondi-tioned self-giving to others (Gal. 5:13; 1 Cor. 10: 23-33; Rom. 14).

Libnah, 1. An encampment on the journey of the Israelites through the desert towards Canaan (Num. 33:20-21).

2. A city of Judah (Josh. 15:42), conquered by Joshua (Josh. 10:29; 12:15), a Levitical city (Josh. 21:13; 1 Chron. 6:42). When Jehoram was king of Judah (849-842 B.C.) Libnah revolted against his rule (2 Chron. 21:10). Later, during the reign of Hezekiah (715-687 B.C.), it was besieged by Sennacherib (2 Kgs. 19:8; Isa. 37:8). The city's site is probably under the present Tell-es-Safi, southwest of Jerusalem.

Libni (lib′-nie), The first-born son of Gershon, son of Levi (Ex. 6:17; Num. 3:18, 21; 1 Chron. 6:17, 20).

Libya, A coastal region of north Africa, west of Egypt on the Mediter-ranean coast. During the second millenium B.C. there were several at-tempts on the part of the Libyan tribes to penetrate into Egypt. During the millenium before Christ, a Libyan occupied the Egyptian throne. He was the Pharaoh Shishak, a contemporary of Solomon and a protector of Jeroboam I. After Solomon's death Shishak invaded Judah and sacked the Temple. In Egypt he founded a dynasty with its capital at Bubastis; this dynasty held power for two centuries (950-730 B.C. approximately). There were also Libyan soldiers in the army of Shishak which invaded Palestine (2 Chron. 12:3; *see* 2 Chron. 16:8; Nah. 3:9). These are the only times the Libyans are mentioned in the Old Testament. On the feast of Pentecost there were Jews from Libya present in Jerusalem, according to Acts 2:10.

Life, Life and to live (**hayyim** and **hay** in Hebrew) are used in the Bible as in all other languages with a wide range of meanings and applications. It can simply and neutrally indicate the duration of existence, as for exam-ple, the genealogies of Genesis 5 count out the ages of each person. It can also, however, reach out to the ideal of human existence, or designate the vitality of the organism together with its functions. Then it can refer to the bare fact of existence as a radical good, and so on.

The value of life and its ideals depend in a very determined manner on the prospects that open up to the individual after his death. The people of Israel, like their cultural neighbors, were profoundly convinced of a sur-vival after death. Until this conviction eventually drove them to think of a resurrection, almost at the end of the pre-Christian era, life-after-death was hardly life: it was survival deprived of any element that might make it attractive or something to be desired. (*See* RESURRECTION; SHEOL.) For this reason the Israelite was deeply attached to this life, while at the same time he showed a great sensitivity to the inexorable way in which life was flee-ing from his grasp and the inconsistency of it all (*see* Isa. 40:6, 7; Pss. 39:6; 103:15, 16; Job 7:7, 16; 8:9; 14:2 and so on).

The ideal of life that is proposed re-echoes the experienced inexorability of a survival without hope. This ideal is extremely modest in its aspira-tions, an ideal worked out and formulated by the wisdom tradition. Wis-dom (*see* WISDOM) is the art of living. Wisdom praises itself for the gifts it gives to those who receive it: "Long life is in her right hand, in her left are riches and honor" (Prov. 3:16; *see* Prov. 8:18). Wisdom's good life consisted then in a long life, peace, family concord, the love of friends, a good name, moderate affluence. To call this hedonistic is to be in ignorance of the moderation of these aspirations, and of the internal religious dimension that they held for the Israelite.

In the Bible the most characteristic and insisted-on element of life was its total and absolute dependence on God: he is its absolute lord who gives and takes as he pleases (Ps. 104:29; Job 4:9; 34:14-15, etc.; *see* SPIRIT). Since life is God's to give or take, he tolerates no intrusion into his rights over it, and has even placed similar limits on doing violence to animals (Gen. 9; Ex. 20:13; Deut. 5:17).

From him too come the gifts that help realize life's ideal: indeed these gifts would be without meaning or consistency if they were not part and parcel of a life of obedience to God's voice. Wisdom, which is the key to life, is itself the gift of God (Prov. 2:6). Personified wisdom which invites man to follow its counsels is God himself seen under a new facet (*see* WISDOM), a new language which God addresses to man to invite him to adhere to his will and thus enjoy life (Prov. 1:20-23). God's law is wisdom: to follow God's law is to have life (Sir. 24:22-23; *see* Prov. 3:1-10).

The same link between life and obedience to his law is proclaimed even more peremptorily in the context of the Covenant. The long list of blessings and curses that conclude the text of the Covenant (*see* COVENANT; Deut. 28) are summed up thus: "Here, then, I have today set before you life and prosperity, death and doom. If you obey the commandments of the Lord . . . you will live and grow numerous, and the Lord your God will bless you in the land you are entering to occupy. . . . I have set before you life and death, the blessing and the curse. Choose life, then, that you and your descendants may live, by loving the Lord your God, heeding his voice and holding fast to him. For that will mean life for you, a long life for you to live on the land which the Lord swore he would give to your fathers" (Deut. 30:15-20).

The prospect of a life after death in the full sense only emerges with clarity in Daniel 12:1-3. (*See* RESURRECTION.) The hope of resurrection obviously had profound repercussions on the biblical notion of life. Above all, life in the fullest sense of the word, as the highest good and as salvation, is transferred to the beyond. Many of this life's enigmas are now seen in a new light. Premature death of the just man, the prosperity of the wicked at the expense of the just, and other problems which had shaken the established doctrine of the just remuneration of man in this life (*see* JOB) are now taken up again by Wisdom and receive a new solution.

The prosperity of the wicked is vain: it is destined to death, and is already dead (Wis. 2). With the just however it is different: "For if before men, indeed, they be punished, yet is their hope full of immortality" (Wis. 3:4). Their present sufferings are a test by God, "but they shall be greatly blessed, because God tried them and found them worthy of himself" (3:5-7). Even the premature death of the just finds its explanation: "He who pleased God was loved . . . snatched away lest wickedness pervert his mind or deceit beguile his soul" (4:11). The wicked who mock the life of the just do not know the mysteries of God (2:21-24); they will be dismayed and confused when they see the triumph of the just on the judgment day (c. 5).

In the New Testament the words "life" and "eternal life" are practically interchangeable with the terms "kingdom (or reign) of God" (*see* Mk. 9:43, 45) and salvation. The adjective "eternal" which so often accompanies the word "life" points up its endless duration and the radical difference between it and the present life. In this is mirrored the doctrine of the "two ages" which characterized Judaism between the Old and New Testaments. This is also the basic scheme of New Testament eschatology. In this framework, "age" (Hebrew 'olam, Greek aion) indicates at the same time a definite period of time and a definite order or condition of things. The present "age" extends from creation, or better still, from sin, right up to the "close of the age" (*see* Matt. 28:20).

The "future" or "coming" age will be inaugurated with the dissolution of the present age (*see* Gal. 1:4; Rom. 3:26; Eph. 1:21). The difference between the two ages is not just chronological: it is above all qualitative. The first is subject to corruption, sin and death, but the second is born with the glorious resurrection of the dead and is filled with the goodness of God.

Between the Jewish and Christian concept of the two ages there is a fundamental difference that is underscored especially by John and Paul. For the Jews the future age follows the dissolution of the present one, but for Christians the future age with its goods is already present. In both concepts the future age is inaugurated with the resurrection. For the Jews this is an event yet to occur, while for Christians it is something that has already radically happened with the resurrection of Christ (Rom. 1:4). Christ's death and resurrection carry with them the abolition of the present age (*see* Matt. 27:51 ff.). After Christ's resurrection the two ages co-exist, but the first age is already doomed to an abolition that has already begun, while the second age is destined to grow and come to full flowering. In a certain sense Christians belong both to one and the other. Through faith and baptism they already live a life that derives from the risen Christ (Gal. 2:20), they are already enjoying the goods of the future life, they are possessed by the Spirit who raised up Jesus from the dead and will also raise up their mortal bodies (Rom. 8:10-11). At the moment they hold their life hidden away, but it will be revealed in all its splendor when Christ manifests himself in his glory (Col. 3:3-4). On the other hand, they will walk in the flesh, that is, in the condition of corruption which, however, will be absorbed by the full victory of life over death (1 Cor. 15:42-49; Phil 3:20-21).

In John's gospel the concept of life or eternal life is cast particularly into relief, for it comprises all that, in other places of Scripture, is designated with different words such as kingdom of God, salvation, redemption, etc. Life is the sum total of all the goods present or future that a Christian possesses. In the first epilogue to his gospel John expresses the intent of his work:"But these have been recorded to help you believe that Jesus is the Messiah, the Son of God, so that through this faith you may have life in his name" (Jn. 20:31). The gift of life is the purpose of Jesus' mission (Jn. 10:10) which he is able to accomplish because "in him is life" (Jn. 1:4; 5:26), indeed he is "the life" (Jn. 14:6) or "the resurrection and the life" (Jn. 11:25).

It was on the occasion of the raising of Lazarus to life that Jesus revealed himself as "the resurrection and the life" (Jn. 11). Jesus took this opportunity to reveal in an inchoate way his life-giving power. This power is shown as victory over death: "I am the resurrection." This saying refers first of all to the passage from death to life that takes place when man hears the voice of the Son of God and receives his words with faith (Jn. 11:25, 26). Thus man passes from a corrupt and perverse life, which in reality is death, to the possession of an indestructible life, so that even "though he should die, will come to life and whoever is alive and believes in me will never die" (Jn. 11:26).

The account of the raising of Lazarus to life is expressly associated with the free handing over of himself into the hands of the enemy on his last journey to Jerusalem (Jn. 11:7, 8, 16). At the end, there once more appears the decision of the Sanhedrin to do away with Jesus, and Caiphas' words are recorded: "It is better for you to have one man die [for the people]" (Jn. 11:45-53), words that recall in a different tone and with a different intent Jesus' discourse on the good shepherd who gives his life for his sheep (Jn. 10). It is clear then that John wished to highlight the truth that the gift of life which Jesus came to offer was to be the fruit of his own death and resurrection.

Finally, John insists on the divine character of the life Jesus gives. This is doctrine common to the rest of the New Testament, and especially clear in Paul. Through his resurrection Jesus becomes a "life-giving spirit" (1 Cor. 15:45) and receives "a name above every other name" (Phil. 2:9). This means that Jesus in his humanity enters into the glory that was his as son, and thus that humanity shines forth with the glory of which Jesus stripped himself to become man. The Christian life shares in the life of the risen Christ, and so shares in the divine life. John insists on the same doctrine but proceeds, in his development, in an inverse way: he starts out with the preexistence of the Word. The Son of God has in himself the divine life because he is the Son (Jn. 5:26). He was sent by the Father so that with his life he might defeat death and confer this life on men (Jn. 10:10).

The bestowal of life takes place in two stages: first it is inchoate, through signs (*see* SIGN), but later it is given in all its fulness when Jesus' humanity will perfectly manifest his divine glory, that is, after his exaltation which takes place in his death and resurrection (Jn. 17:5, 24). Thus John who wrote in 1:14: "The Word became flesh," can say in 1 Jn. 1:2: "This life became visible."

Light and Darkness, The combination light-darkness is very widely used in religious symbolism. In the Bible it occupies a preeminent position. This is especially true of John's gospel, where it is employed to present Jesus' own mission. This light-darkness combination is principally used, not in its intellectual sense to express knowledge and ignorance, but in a sense that can be called soteriological. This sense is already evident in the account of creation (Gen. 1). God's first creative action is, in fact, his overcoming darkness through light (1:3; *see* also Job 12:22). In flooding the primordial chaos of darkness with light, God accomplished the first and fundamental work towards the creation of the cosmos where life would be possible.

Already on the first page of the Bible, light-darkness appear destined to be symbols respectively of life-salvation and death-damnation. Perhaps symbolism is too weak a word to express the relationship that arose between the two notions, for both light and darkness seem to have a real consistency in the mind of the author and to have a real operative continuity with life and death. So one encounters in the Bible phrases like "the light of life" or "of the living" (Ps. 56:14; Job 33:30), and of the "shade" or "darkness of the dead" (Ps. 88:7; *see* Ps. 88:11-13; Job 38:17). The mention of light then evokes the concept of the gift of life (Ps. 49:19), the well-being and pleasures of life (Amos 5:18, 20; Isa. 60:19-20; Ps. 97:11), salvation (Mic. 7:8-9), just as darkness is associated with death and the habitation of the dead (Isa. 45:19; Job 10:22), and with sin.

This general description acquires a more specific religious value when it is placed expressly in relationship with God. God is the one author of life, and so is proclaimed the one true source of light (Pss. 36:10; 27:1; Mic. 7:9) and its creator (Gen. 1:3). There is also however an evident connection between light and the glory of God (*see* GLORY), or the sensible light-filled manifestation of God's presence especially in his definitive self-revelation at the end of time in the days of the definitive eschatological salvatión (Isa. 60:1-3, 19). This theme is taken up again in Revelation 21:23, 24.

Life is a path to walk, and the law, wisdom and God's word are the light that can rightly guide the steps of man so that he will not trip up on his way to eternal life and salvation (*see* Jn. 9:4-5; 12:35). Wisdom and the law are the gifts of God which bring man safely to life. In this application of the metaphor, the intellectual aspect is more marked, but it is not primary, for it is not a question of intellectual enlightenment as such but a true schooling for salvation. The law and wisdom appear as true mediators of salvation (*see* Baruch 3:37-4:3; Prov. 6:23; Ps. 119:105).

In the period between the two Testaments, i.e. in the apocryphal books of the Old Testament and in the Dead Sea scrolls, all these elements are presented in the form of an irreconcilable dualism between light and darkness. This paved the way for the use John was to make of these themes. Like a reflection of the separation of light and darkness and the tension between the two that is described in Genesis 1, they now appear as two kingdoms that are radically different and incurably opposed. The difference between the two is at the same time ethical-moral and soteriological, and the discourse moves easily from one aspect to the other. This division transcends the world of men and is first and foremost positioned in the world of the spirits. What is effected there, however, is powerfully experienced in the human sphere. God himself is light as John states in 1:5 of his gospel, an expression aimed at evoking the riches of light and salvation present in him, and his moral and ontological sanctity. The kingdom of light through the spirits of light pervades the world of men with its beneficial action, and leads them along the right way to salvation. The kingdom of darkness however, that is, the kingdom of sin, death and perdition, is also operative in the world through the spirits of darkness who try to lead men along the ways of death to damnation.

In the New Testament it is John who especially develops these themes, but they are also to be found here and there in the other writings. Light is associated with God in 1 Timothy 6:16 and James 1:17, and with his gifts and particularly the gift of Christian salvation (Eph. 5:14; Col. 1:12; 1 Pet. 2:9). Christians have been transferred from darkness to light and are the children of light (1 Thess. 5:5; Eph. 5:9). The appearance of Jesus is the manifestation of the light of salvation for those who stood in the shadow of death (Matt. 4:16; Lk. 2:32; *see* Isa. 42:6). In the transfiguration the intimate divine being of Jesus is revealed as a splendid light (Mk. 9:2-8; Matt. 17:1-8; Lk. 9:28-36; *see* TRANSFIGURATION).

In John 8:12; 9:5 Jesus solemnly declares that he is the light of the world. The cure of the man born blind is a sign of Jesus' being the light of the world (Jn. 9:5, 39-41; *see* SIGN). The first aim of these declarations is to express Jesus' salvific mission.

John explains this by comparing Jesus to the light of day which is necessary so that a man may not trip up on his way (*see* 11:9, 10; 12:35, 36). When we recall what has already been said about the law and wisdom being the light, perhaps we could conclude that John is here deliberately replacing the law and wisdom with Jesus, whom he proclaims to be the one and only Savior of men, that is, he alone can free them from the kingdom of death and bring them to the light which is life (8:12; 12:46). In this sense the "light of the world" would be a soteriological title proclaiming Jesus as the only true Savior.

With this, however, the content of these declarations is not exhausted. Light and death do not remain in the realm of metaphor. Darkness is the kingdom of death, which through the incredulity of men, is attempting to destroy the very light (3:19). "I am the light of the world" (8:12) is, in the last analysis, simply a claim to be God. It is not then a title that refers merely to his messianic function: it is a confession of the intimate reality of Jesus, which explains his mission. It is parallel then to the notion of life (*see* LIFE). Light and life are, for John, different aspects of the same gift of salvation. Now Jesus is life (14:6) not just in the sense that he came to give life; he is in himself life, he has in himself divine life from the Father (5:26). For this reason Jesus can enlighten, that is, he can snatch people from the darkness and bring them to the light (12:46). Jesus is light, that is, he possesses in himself the fulness of divine light which is the riches of life and salvation (Jn. 1:5, 9).

John 3:18-21 puts more into relief the ethical-moral aspect of the light-darkness symbolism, and ties it up with Jesus' function as judge. God's point in sending his son was not to condemn the world, but that through him the world might be saved. Whoever does not believe in the son is already condemned, that is, he has established himself in the condition of one who has entered into irreparable eschatological condemnation. This judgment, in the sense of condemnation, consists in this: the light came into the world, and men preferred the darkness to the light. Man's incredulity closes him off from the only way by which he can pass from the kingdom of darkness to the kingdom of light.

The reason for this perverse choice on the part of man was that his works were evil. John often insists on the moral roots of incredulity (8:23, 24; 8:43-46; 5:39-47; 10:25, 26).

John presents the life of Jesus like a judicial process in which it seems that Jesus himself is being judged. On it center the contrasting positions of faith, hesitation and incredulity on the part of man (c. 7). In reality however it is Christ who judges: he, the light, adjudges salvation to those who accept him and believe, so that they share the light, while those who refuse already stand condemned.

The soteriological and judgmental role of Christ is combined in the sign of the man born blind whom Christ healed. There Jesus condemns the Pharisees, who remain blind, while he enlightens the eyes of the person who approaches him with faith (c. 9).

Lightning, Thunder and lightning storms take place in Palestine especially in spring and autumn. They were frequently taken as visible manifestations of God's power and formed a regular part of the scenario of the theophany. Lightning is often used in poetic imagery in the Bible. The Psalmist calls on the Lord to flash his lightning and shoot his arrows to scatter his enemies (Ps. 144:6). The Song of Moses in the Hebrew text refers to the lightning of Yahweh's sword with which he will take vengeance on those who hate him (Deut. 32:41). *See* THUNDER, THEOPHANY.

Lilith, A demon or evil spirit who haunts ruins and desolate places (Isa. 34:14). This demon comes from the popular Canaanite religion, and has only a marginal importance in the context of the biblical revelation. Its one mention is more a concession to popular folklore than something to be taken seriously.

Lily, This is the common translation of the Hebrew **sosan,** a flower of uncertain botanical classification. The Arabic word of similar root, **schoschanna,** is a generic word including all spring flowers. This would seem to be the meaning of **sosan** in some texts of the Song of Songs (2:1; 2:16; 4:5; 6:3, etc.). In Hosea 14:6, and Matthew 6:28 (Lk. 12:27) it seems to be a generic name for the little colored flowers that adorn the fields after the spring rains. In Hosea 14:5 the abundant blossoming of these flowers is a symbol of the future restoration of Israel. In Matthew 6:28 Jesus pointed to these flowers as an example of the providence of the Father which cares even for such humble things. In Psalms 45, 69, 80 the inscription has the words: "upon lilies," which probably alludes to the melody to be used in the singing of these psalms: "lilies" would be a well-known song. Other scholars think that this refers to a musical instrument (*see* also Ps. 60:1).

Linen, Egypt was the principal producer of linen in antiquity. The fiber for the cloth was obtained from the stalk of the linen plant. Once ripe, it was collected and spread in the sun to dry. (Joshua 2:1 ff tells how Rahab the harlot hid the spies under the linen stalks she had on the roof, probably for the purpose of drying out.) Then the stalks were beaten to separate the fibers which, when they were clean and dry, were given to the weavers.

Palestine also had its linen crop (*see* Josh. 2:6). The agrarian calendar of Gezer (*see* MONTH, YEAR) makes provision for a month to collect the linen. In the Old Testament there is mention of different types, which however are impossible to identify today. Linen was used to make the priestly vestments (Lev. 16:4, 23, 32; Ex. 28:42; 39:28). The ephod **bad,** or ephod of linen was a type of short tunic and apron that the priests and those active in the cult used (*see* 1 Sam. 2:18; 22:18; 2 Sam. 6:14; *see* EPHOD). Linen was also the material used for the clothes of the rich and important (Gen. 41:42; Lk. 16:19). Jesus' body was wrapped in a linen cloth (Matt. 27:59; Mk. 15:46; Lk. 23:53) and the face covered with a linen napkin (Jn. 20:5-7).

lintel
sprinkel the *l.*   Ex. 12:22 Seeing the blood on the *l.*
                                                                    Ex. 12:23

Linus (lie′-nus), A Christian at Rome who sends greetings to Timothy (2 Tim. 4:21). According to Irenaeus (**Adversus Haereses,** 3, 3, 3), Linus was Peter's first successor as bishop of Rome.

Lion, Lions were a fairly common animal in Palestine during biblical times as one must deduce from the numerous references that are made to the animal in Scripture. They have disappeared completely, however, since the XIII-XIV centuries after Christ. The Palestinian lion was found also in Asia and Persia, though somewhat smaller than the African lion. The lion dwelt in the forests (Amos 3:4; Jer. 49:19; 50:44) and the less inhabited regions (2 Kgs. 17:25). He was a threat to the flocks on which he preyed (Amos 3:12), so that shepherds had to be on their guard against him. Samson, David and Benaiah were said to have killed lions with their bare hands (Jgs. 14:5; 1 Sam. 17:34; 2 Sam. 23:30). Lions were captured by the use of snares, pits, nets and hooks (Ezek. 19:4-9). In general the lion appears as a fierce and audacious animal whose roar can spread terror. Isaiah foresees the last times when, in a sign of eschatological peace, the lion will live in harmony with the lamb, the calf, and the kid (Isa. 11:6-7).

Just as in modern language, so too in the Bible the lion is used metaphorically to express the strength or courage of a person (Gen. 49:9; Prov. 19:2; 1 Mac. 3:4), the implacable aggressiveness of an enemy (Isa. 5:29; Jer. 2:15; 4:7; Ezek. 32:2; Pss. 17:2; 22:4) or divine punishment (Amos 1:2; 11:10; 13:7 ff; Isa. 31:4; Jer. 49:19).

The lion is a decorative element of many religious and profane constructions of the ancient East, including Israel (*see* 1 Kgs. 7:29, 36). Solomon's throne had two carved lions as arm rests, while on each of the six steps leading up to it on either side stood another lion, amounting to twelve in all (1 Kgs. 10:19, 20).

lip, lips

though her *l.* were moving	strike their lying *l.*	Ps. 31:19
1 Sam. 1:13	This people pays me *l.* service	
with smooth *l.* they speak Ps. 12:3		Matt. 15:8

listen

l. to the message 1 Sam. 15:1	*l.* to the reproof from my lips	
still they would not *l.* Neh. 9:30		Job 13:6
l., O distant peoples Isa. 49:1		

live

and *l.* forever Gen. 3:22	But your dead shall *l.*	Isa. 26:19
May he *l.* to be given Ps. 72:15	he shall surely *l.*	Ezek. 3:21
I cannot *l.* forever Job 7:16		

liver

the lobe of its *l.* Ex. 29:13	the lobe of the *l.*	Lev. 3:4
an arrow pierces its *l.* Prov. 7:23		

lizards

the various kinds of *l.* Lev. 11:29

Lo-ammi, The second son and third child that Gomer bore Hosea the prophet. At God's word Hosea named him Lo-ammi, which means "not-my-people," to express symbolically that God would no longer recognize Israel as his own (Hos. 1:9). However in 2:25 God predicts the day when he will say: "I will say to Lo-ammi, 'You are my people;' and he shall say, 'My God.'"

Loan, Bankers and bondsmen in the commercial sense were unknown in the early centuries of the Hebrew commonwealth. The law (Deut. 23:20) prohibited the taking of interest from fellow-Israelites on personal loans, but not from foreigners. Other passages (Ex. 22:24ff; Ps. 15:5; Prov. 28:8; Ezek. 18:13, 17; 22:12) commend lending without interest as an obligation or ideal. On the other hand the prevailing attitude of the Old Testament is probably reflected in Deuteronomy 28:12 and 44: it is good (a blessing) to be a creditor, bad to be a debtor. This has led some scholars to the view that pledges on the part of the debtor—of a cloak (Ex. 22:25), other garments (Amos 2:8); of the ox and the ass (Job 24:3); and of children (Job 24:9)—reflect the grim realities of debt among the poorer people. It then follows that the laws mitigating the taking up of the debtor's pledge by the creditor (Deut. 24:6, 10; Ex. 22:24; Ezek. 18:16) were laws of social necessity rather than social idealism. Thus laws were laid down saying that a millstone could not be pledged (Deut. 24:6) and houses could not be entered to seize a pledge (Deut. 24:10) because millstones were being pledged and houses entered to seize pledges, and this was impoverishing the poor to the point where they could not grind their own chief food-reliance and stay warm at night with their clothing over them. That the intellectual leaders of the nation and the prophets saw the problem is clearly reflected in the Jubilee-year laws (Ex. 21:2; Lev. 25:39; Deut. 15:9), the Writings (Prov. 6:1,4; 10:15; 17:18; 20:16; 22:26; Pss. 15:5; 27:13) and the Prophets (Jer. 15:10; Ezek. 18:13; 22:12). Systematic breaching of the lending laws was attacked by Nehemiah after the return from the exile (Neh. 5:1, 13). With the advent of the Greeks (c. 323 B.C.) banks were introduced and rates of interest became stabilized at about ten percent. In earlier centuries both loans and interest were much more apt to be in kind (materials, animals, etc.) than in money.

Locust, Locusts are numbered among the pure animals in Leviticus 11:22, and therefore could be eaten. Locusts were the food on which John the Baptizer lived (Matt. 3:4 and Mk. 1:6). They are still eaten today by the Bedouins of the desert. In the Bible, locusts are noted above all for the catastrophic effects they could have on crops. One of the plagues of Egypt was that of the locusts "who ate all the plants in the land and all the fruit of the trees which the hail had left; not a green thing remained, neither tree nor plant of the field through all the land of Egypt" (Ex. 10:15; *see* Pss. 78:46; 105:34). God threatens locusts on the land of Israel should the people fail to observe his law (Deut. 28:38). The most powerful description of the plague of locusts is read in Joel 1:4-19; 2:2-11: "what the cutting locust left, the swarming locust has eaten, what the swarming locust has left, the hopping locust has eaten, what the hopping locust has left, the destroying locust has eaten," etc. They are compared to an immense army advancing (*see* 2:4 ff.) (*see* also Jgs. 6:5; 7:12; Jer. 46:23; Nah. 3:15, 17).

Lod, See LYDDA.

Lodebar (lo-dee′-bar), A city of Transjordan, in the land of Gad, near Mahanaim. There resided Machir, son of Ammiel, a friend of David who had given hospitality to Meribbaal, Jonathan's lame son (2 Sam. 9:4; 2 Sam. 17:27).

Logos (log′-os), A Greek word meaning "word" as opposed to **ergon**, "deed." Its exact meaning however depends on context. It can mean "question" (Matt. 21:24; Lk. 20:3), "prayer" (Matt. 26:44), "preaching" (1 Tim. 5:17), "prophecy" (Jn. 2:22), "command" (Lk. 4:36), and such other meanings as assertion, declaration, speech, revelation, computation, settlement of an account, reason or motive. Most importantly however, John's gospel has as its central theme that the Word became flesh (Jn. 1:14). On the background and meaning of this, *see* WORD.

Loins, The word in Hebrew and Greek (**osphus**) indicates the waist, the place where a belt or girdle was tied. "Let your loins be girded" means "let you be dressed for action." Normally loose clothing was tied in preparation for a journey or for other activity.

The loins, or middle part of the body, are also the source of human reproduction. Thus God told Jacob: "Kings shall issue from your loins" (Gen. 35:11), meaning that his descendants would be kings. Nahum urges Judah to "gird your loins" (Nah. 2:2), while Isaiah (in some texts) predicts the victory of Cyrus over kings whose loins Yahweh will strip (45:1), probably meaning that with the belt will go the weapons.

Lois, Mother of Eunice and grandmother of Timothy, praised for her sincere faith (2 Tim. 1:5).

loneliness, lonely

my *l.* from the grip	Ps. 22:21	How *l.* she is now	Lam. 1:1
	he went off to a *l.* place	Mk. 1:35	

long

for a *l.* time	Gen. 26:8	*l.* in mourning	2 Sam. 14:2
we stayed a *l.* time	Num. 20:15	without food for a *l.* time	Acts 27:21

longed, longing

satisfied the *l.* soul	Ps. 107:9	He *l.* to fill his belly	Lk. 15:16
consumed with *l.*	Ps. 119:20	for he reported your *l.*	2 Cor. 7:7

look, looking

L. about you	Gen. 13:14	*L.* up to the skies	Job 35:5
l. toward the propitiatory		Why *l.* you jealously	Ps. 68:17
	Ex. 25:20		

loose, loosed

Naphtali is a hind let *l.*   Gen. 49:21   they have *l.* their bonds   Job 30:11
whatever you declare *l.*   Matt. 18:18

loot

took for *l.*   Gen. 34:29

lops

l. off the boughs   Isa. 10:33

Lord, Lord is the translation of two Hebrew words: **baal** and **adon.** The first expresses, above all, property and possession, while the second gives the idea of superiority and dominion. Both words are applied to the divinity in Israel and also in other parts of the semitic world.

In the Canaanite religion (*see* the Ugaritic texts in UGARIT), Baal became the proper name for its most popular god, and thus also the name of the principal rival to the Lord in the struggle between the Canaanite and the Israelite religions (*see* BAAL). For this reason in Israel, long before the exile, the name Baal as an appellation for God was avoided and its synonym, **Adon,** used instead.

At the time of the judges, however, and during the first years of the monarchy the name **Baal** was used for the Lord. This is clear in several theophoric names, that is, names compounded with the name of God such as Jerubbaal (Jgs. 6:32), the second name of the judge Gideon; Ishbaal, the son of Saul whose name was later changed into Ishbosheth for the reasons given (**bosheth** means shameful thing, *see* ISHBAAL); and Meribbaal, another son of Saul (1 Chron. 8:34; 9:40), whose name was also deformed into Mephibosheth (2 Sam. 9:1-13). There are several other instances.

The title **adon,** Lord, applied to God, appears under the form Adonai, which is in appearance a plural form with the possessive suffix of the first person, which would therefore literally mean, my Lords. It is in reality a deliberate deformation to distinguish its religious use from its ordinary use in the language.

The form Adonai eventually became, for other reasons, the proper name of the God of Israel. Excessive reverence for the name of the God of Israel gave rise to the evermore common habit after the exile of avoiding the pronunciation of his name to exclude any possibility of even an involuntary profanation. This scruple is noticed, for example, in the later books of the Old Testament (1-2 Chronicles, Ecclesiastes, Daniel). These books prefer and constantly use the common name **Elohim,** God. Adonai however became the preferred substitute, above all in the reading of the sacred books. Where the reader found Yahweh written, he read Adonai.

When the text of the Old Testament was equipped with vowel signs (*see* TEXT OF OLD TESTAMENT), the consonants YHWH of Yahweh, God's name, were given the vowel sounds of Adonai. From this came the word Yehowah, which however was never used, for the vowel signs only served to indicate that Adonai should be read out loud.

The Greek translators of the Old Testament (*see* SEPTUAGINT) accommodated themselves to this usage. Where they found YHWH written in

the Hebrew text they translated it **Lord,** which is in reality a Greek translation of Adonai, Lord. This is how in Hellenistic Judaism the name **Kyrios** practically became the proper name for the God of Israel. This was to have important repercussions on New Testament christology.

The title **Kyrios,** Lord, is most often used in the New Testament to designate Jesus. In its most ancient usage it proclaimed the royal dignity of Jesus who had been raised from the dead and exalted to the right hand of God in heaven. In practice it was the same as the title Messiah, which is also a royal title: "Therefore let the whole house of Israel know beyond any doubt that God has made both Lord and Messiah this Jesus whom you crucified" (Acts 2:36; *see* MESSIAH).

The title Lord, especially in its Aramaic form with the first person plural suffix, i.e. **maran** or **marana,** "Our Lord," was used in the oriental courts to designate the king. 1 Corinthians 16:22 and Revelation 22:20 have preserved in Aramaic the invocation **marana tha,** addressed to Jesus. With this invocation the Christians called on Jesus to return gloriously as King and Messiah (*see* MARANATHA).

Jesus is granted this same honor in one of the most ancient and briefest confessions of faith of the Christian church: **Kyrios Iesous,** that is, Jesus is Lord (*see* Rom. 10:9; 1 Cor. 12:3). This confession is based on the resurrection and glorification of Jesus (Rom. 4:24; 1 Cor. 9:1; 2 Cor. 4:14; *see* also the words of the dying Stephen in Acts 7:59).

The use of the title Lord, as applied to Jesus, underwent two principal developments. In the gospels of Luke and John the title Lord is given to Jesus even during his public life. This is a legitimate and logical extension of the use of the term. The evangelists recount the words and deeds of the Person who is actually their Lord. They anticipate in his terrestrial life the title that he now possesses, even though it is a title that he acquired for his humanity when it was glorified through the resurrection from the dead (Rom. 1:4).

The title Lord, applied to Jesus, was further enriched when it was related to the divine name **Kyrios.** Nor was it by chance or arbitrarily that the relationship was instituted, simply because the two names happened to be identical. On the contrary it was the legitimate and logical conclusion one drew from the divine character of the kingship of Jesus as expressed in the title Kyrios.

In answer to the question to him by the High Priest before the Sanhedrin, Jesus passed over the title of Messiah to proclaim the regal and universal dominion to which in a short time he would be exalted, thus claiming for himself equality with God (Matt. 26:63-65; Mk. 14:61-62; Lk. 22:67-70). The title **Kyrios** was applied to Jesus to denote precisely his exalted position at the right hand of God. As a royal title then, it also had a divine content that outstripped all previous meanings.

"Lord" is used by Paul in some trinitarian formulas to indicate the second Person of the Blessed Trinity incarnate (*see* 1 Cor. 12:4-6). It comes up frequently in the formula: "God, the father of our Lord Jesus Christ" (Rom. 15:6; 2 Cor. 1:3; Eph. 1:3 and in the initial salutation of the epistles). The divine kingship of Jesus, acknowledged in the title **Kyrios,** is discovered in texts of the Old Testament which speak of the salvation effected by God, of his coming to save, of the invocation of his name as the only means of salvation (*see* Joel 3:5; Isa. 28:16; Isa. 57:19).

The two currents that converge in the title **Kyrios** enrich and clarify each other. First, because **Kyrios** is God's name, it clarifies, without possibility of ambiguity, the divine condition of Jesus. Secondly, because the name is associated with the hopes for salvation, it highlights Jesus' salvific role. The coming of the kingdom becomes a reality in the person of the Lord Jesus.

This is why one must not wonder that the theme of the kingdom of God, which lies at the center of Jesus' preaching, disappears in the preaching of the Christian church to make place for the preaching the Lord Jesus and his dominion in the church and in the world.

The richest synthesis of all the elements that are here expounded can be found in the christological hymn of Philippians 2:6-11. The emptying of self of which 2:7 speaks is not simply the fact of the incarnation, but enfleshment in a condition that is bereft of the glory that was his while he was "in the form of God." He became man to share the whole mortal human condition to the exclusion, however, of sin. Because of his surrender even to the death of the cross, God exalted him and gave him the name above all names, that is, the divine name **Kyrios.** It is not as if only then did Jesus become God; such an interpretation would be absurd. Jesus, in his exaltation, acquired in his **humanity** that glory and dominion that was his and that as eternal God, he fundamentally possessed.

Lord's Prayer, The Lord's prayer is found in the gospels in two slightly different versions. One is Matthew 6:9-13 and the other in Luke 11:2-4. Matthew has inserted it into the Sermon on the Mount together with other instructions on the right way to pray (6:5-15). Luke presents it to us in another context which reproduces more faithfully the circumstances in which Jesus taught it to his disciples: Jesus was praying, and when he had finished his prayer, one of the disciples asked him: "Lord, teach us to pray, just as John (the Baptizer) taught his disciples." In answer to this request Jesus taught them the Our Father.

It is not easy to determine whether the Lord's Prayer was originally proposed as an instruction on the method and object of the prayer the disciples should say, or itself a formula of prayer. One thing however is certain: at the time the evangelists wrote, the Lord's Prayer was used as a formula of prayer.

Matthew's version contains seven petitions besides the initial invocation. Luke however has only five; his formula lacks the third ("May your will be done") and the seventh ("Deliver us from evil"). Some manuscripts add: "for yours is the kingdom, and the power and the glory." This comes from liturgical use, not from the gospel text.

Luke has preserved more faithfully the tenor of the initial invocation, that is, "Father," without any qualification. This is typical of Jesus and had no parallels in contemporary Judaism. To his listeners this seemed a great and audacious innovation. Perhaps this explains why it went over, in its Aramaic form, Abba, to the Greek-speaking churches (*see* Gal. 4:6; Rom. 8:15). Abba was the term children used in calling their father. It was chosen by Jesus to express the intimacy of relationship that existed between him and his father, and the intimacy of the relationship into which, through himself, God wished to draw men. It is an invitation to trust in the goodness of God which embraces everybody (Matt. 6:5-8; 7:11; 10:29-31), a pledge of pardon and a title to hope in his mercy (Matt. 6:14; 18:35; Lk. 15:11-33). Matthew's formula, "Our Father in heaven" follows the Jewish usage in prayer, but clearly the concept of Father has the same resonance as in Luke 11:2.

The first three petitions of Matthew and the first two of Luke (Matthew's third is not found in Luke) express under different aspects the same aspiration, which coincides with the central object of Jesus' message and work: "The kingdom of heaven is at hand" (Matt. 4:17; Mk. 1:15; *see* KINGDOM OF GOD). Jesus announces the advent of God's kingdom, that is, the coming of that eschatological intervention by God which will be the definitive salvation of man. This he wishes to be the center of every disciple's prayers and aspirations. In exchange for this a person should be willing to give all that he has (Matt. 13:44-46) and to renounce whatever could compromise one's total response to the call of Jesus (Lk. 9:57-62; Matt. 8:18-22; 18:8, 9; Mk. 9:43-47).

The coming of the Kingdom of God is the supreme sanctification of the name of God. God sanctifies his name in the different manifestations of his omnipotence in the creation and salvation order. In them he reveals himself for what he is. In Ezekiel 36:22, 23 God announces his decision to save his scattered people in the following terms: "Not for your sakes do I act, house of Israel, but for the sake of my holy name, which you profaned among the nations to which you came. I will prove the holiness of my great name, profaned among the nations, in whose midst you have profaned it. Thus the nations shall know that I am the Lord, says the Lord God, when in their sight I prove my holiness through you. For I will take you away from among the nations, gather you from all the foreign lands, and bring you back to your own land" (*see* Ezek. 20:41; 39:27). Definitive salvation then will be the perfect sanctification of his name (*see* Jn. 12:28; 13:31; 17:1-6). This however implies the demand on man to recognize God for what he is, that is, that man himself must sanctify God's name. Coming from man's lips then, the Lord's Prayer, and in particular this petition, has meaning only if it is accompanied by that dedication to God which Jesus demands from those who would inherit the kingdom.

The third petition asks for the fulfilment of God's will. This is not to be taken in a sense of resignation to the inevitable. The will of God does not refer in the first place to events in the world and in the individual's life, even though faith teaches that all is in God's hand and that his will extends also to this sphere. However the will of God in the third petition is, in its most genuine sense, his salvific designs, which have been partly accomplished in Christ and in part are the object of Christian hope. The third petition then resounds with the same aspiration that we have seen in the two previous ones (*see* Mk. 4:11-12; Matt. 11:25; Lk. 10:21; Jn. 6:37-40). Paul expounds the stages of this saving design in Ephesians 1:3-12.

Of the remaining petitions, difficulties of interpretation might be encountered in the last two of Matthew (the last one is absent from Luke): "Subject us not to the trial but deliver us from the evil one" (Matt. 6:13). The expression "from the evil one" is ambiguous, as in the Greek text it can be taken to mean "from evil" or "from the evil one," that is, Satan. Many commentators today prefer the latter interpretation, though the Revised Standard Bible and New English Bible translate "from evil," with a note offering the alternative. It is in fact more in line with one of the fundamental aspects of the gospel story. Jesus' mission is unfolded at two levels: on one Jesus finds himself in conflict with the Jewish religious authorities, while on the other Jesus struggles with Satan. In fact Jesus' mission is to destroy Satan's reign (Mk. 3:27; Matt. 12:28-29; Lk. 11:20-22). Jesus foiled Satan's attempt to have him deviate from his authentic mission (*see* TEMPTATION OF JESUS), and in the passion he suffered Satan's most powerful assault (Lk. 22:53) from which however Jesus emerged completely victorious (Jn. 12:31). Satan however continues to prey on Jesus' disciples (Lk. 22:31) and on those who believe in Jesus (Matt. 13:19; 13:28; 1 Tim. 5:14; 1 Pet. 5:8-9). From them he wishes to snatch the gift of salvation. These considerations help to clarify the sense of the preceding petition: in it one asks God to be spared temptation. This is not a request to be freed from every difficulty and misfortune: it asks to be spared that test or temptation in which salvation itself might be called into question (*see* Mk. 14:38 and Jn. 17:15).

Lord's Supper, Tradition and Christian theology have given the name "eucharist" (from the Greek **eucharistein,** to give thanks) to the celebration of the central rite of the Christian community which Paul called "the supper of the Lord" (1 Cor. 11:20). This name, "eucharist," underlines one of the fundamental characteristics of the whole celebration, and is based on the frequent mention of "thanksgiving" as part of the rite of the Lord's supper (*see* Matt. 26:27; Mk. 14:23; Lk. 22:17; 1 Cor. 11:24 and also Matt. 15:36; Mk. 8:6; Jn. 6:11). The biblical terminology is more apt because it immediately suggests the real historical context of the celebration, its origin and its essence, which is to be a commemoration (**anamnesis,** Lk. 22:19; 1 Cor. 11:25) of the Last Supper celebrated by the Lord with his disciples before he died.

The New Testament contains many texts referring to the eucharist. Here we will briefly analyze the principal ones to attempt a faithful synthesis of the biblical teaching on this sacrament.

The logical and chronological beginnings of the rite are to be found in the Last Supper which is described in two different versions. Matthew 26:26-29 and Mark 14:22-25 give the same account of Jesus' words; Luke 22:19, 20 and 1 Corinthians 11:23-25 differ a little from Matthew-Mark in the words pronounced over the chalice and they add the explicit command of Jesus to repeat the rite "in memory of me." These differences are due to varied environments through which the tradition of the Lord's Supper passed in the apostolic church.

Jesus instituted the eucharist during the celebration of the paschal supper; this is explicitly mentioned by Luke 22:15, but it is indirectly confirmed by Matthew 26:17-19 and Mark 14:12-17. John has no account of the institution of the eucharist and follows a different chronology for the Passion (*see* PASSION), placing the death of Christ on the parasceve of the Pasch while Matthew, Mark and Luke date it on the day of the Pasch itself. A totally satisfying explanation to this problem has not yet been found; this does not however affect the paschal character of the Lord's Supper. If John's chronology be adopted, it would then affect the way in which the eucharist was first celebrated.

The Jewish Pasch celebrated and commemorated the liberation of the Jewish people from Egypt. The Christian Pasch is the sacramental commemoration of the definitive salvation brought about by Jesus. In the Jewish paschal rite the lamb suggested the means used by the Lord to free the people from the plague of the slaughter of the firstborn. Although it is not explicitly pointed out in the text, Jesus took the place of the paschal lamb (*see* 1 Cor. 5:7). His function however is to be understood in the light of the prophetic figure of the suffering servant of the Lord (*see* SERVANT OF THE LORD): his was to be a sacrifice of expiation of sins. This aspect is sufficiently implied by the insistence on the beneficiaries of the "handing over" of his body and the "out-pouring" of his blood, which evokes the prophecy of Isa. 53: Jesus, the new paschal lamb, saves us by immolating himself. For John 13:1 Jesus' immolation is his Pasch, that is, his passing over from this world to the Father through the full expression of his love on the cross (Jn. 19:30). The disciples who share in the Lord's Supper and the Christians of all times who take their places at the table of the Lord also reap the fruits of this immolation. They are caught up in the Passover of Jesus from death to life: they re-enact what has radically happened to them in Baptism, according to the explanation of Paul in Romans 6:1-11.

The words pronounced over the chalice are an evident allusion to the rite of the Covenant of Sinai (Ex. 24:8). Jesus' immolation sanctions the new Covenant, which is explicitly mentioned in the consecration words: "This is my blood, the blood of the covenant, to be poured out in behalf of many for the forgiveness of sins" (Matt. 26:28; Mk. 14:24), and in the parallel tradition of Luke-Paul: "This cup is the new covenant in my blood which will be shed for you" (Lk. 22:20; 1 Cor. 11:25).

On Sinai Moses sealed with a visible rite God's adhesion to his people, expressed in the Covenant document: "Then he took the blood and sprinkled it on the people, 'This,' he said, 'is the blood of the covenant which the Lord has made with you, in accordance with all these words of his' " (Ex. 24:8). The new alliance is the effective return of man to God. This return is not just stipulated in a written document: it is a law written in man's heart, so that all might know God (Jer. 31:33; Heb. 8:8-13; 2 Cor. 3:2-5). This return bears the remission, or better, the victory over sin in man (Jer. 31:34). The blood of Christ, then, is no mere extrinsic sanction of an alliance: his blood brings about the return of man to God. The Lord's Supper is the sacramental commemoration of this act. Those who share in it through communing in the body of the Lord, make that alliance effective in themselves.

The celebration of the Lord's Supper, "the breaking of bread," was at the center of the life of the Christian community of Jerusalem. According to the account of Luke in Acts 2:42, 46, the primitive community, all alive in the Spirit, devoted themselves to the Apostles' teaching and to fellowship, to the breaking of bread and the prayers. The same is reported of Troas in Acts 20:7, 11: "On the first day of the week, i.e. Sunday, when we gathered for the breaking of bread." The same was true of the communities founded by Paul. Paul rebuked the Corinthians for some abuses that had crept into the celebration, and recalls the people to the respect due to the body of Christ. In this text Paul points up the reality, and not just the metaphorical sense, of the eucharist: "This means that whoever eats the bread or drinks the cup of the Lord unworthily sins against the body and blood of the Lord. A man should examine himself first; only then should he eat of the bread and drink of the cup. He who eats and drinks without recognizing the body eats and drinks a judgment on himself" (1 Cor. 11:27-29).

The custom of the agape or love-feast underlines the symbolism that is inherent in the eucharist which is the supper of the Lord. The Lord's Supper nourishes the Church from within. All share in the common bread which draws Christians together in Christ: "Because the loaf of bread is one, we, many though we are, are one body, for we all partake of the one loaf" (1 Cor. 10:17). *See* BODY OF CHRIST.

In another celebrated passage of the first letter to the Corinthians, Paul answers in the negative a question about the liceity of eating food sacrificed to idols. He draws on the doctrine of the eucharist for his reasons. Those who eat food sacrificed to idols enter into communion with Satan, for while the idols are empty in themselves, Satan hides himself in them. Then Paul parallels the pagan sacrifices and the celebration of the eucharist to show their radical incompatibility: "You cannot drink the cup of the Lord and also the cup of demons. You cannot partake of the table of the Lord and likewise the table of demons" (1 Cor. 10:21). Paul alludes to the eucharistic celebration: "The cup of blessing which we bless, is it not a participation in the blood of Christ? The bread which we break, is it not a participation in the body of Christ?" Paul's line of argument mirrors the conviction of the first Christians that the eucharist had a truly sacrificial character.

John has no account of the institution of the eucharist during the last supper. His doctrine on the eucharist is found in a long discourse on the bread of life which Jesus gave in the synagogue at Capernaum (Jn. 6:48 ff.) after the miracle of the multiplication of breads (Jn. 6:1-13).

The immediate occasion of the discourse is the anxious search for Jesus by those who have 'eaten the bread and had been filled" (Jn. 6:26). Jesus takes the occasion to raise them from the search for ordinary bread by inviting them to reach for "food that remains unto life eternal, food which the Son of Man will give you" (Jn. 6:27).

The discourse then develops in three parts. The first part (6:28-34) to some degree unveils the mystery of this bread of life by comparing it with the manna, "the bread from heaven" given by Moses. Jesus however tells his listeners that this was not the true bread from heaven: "it is my Father who gives you the real heavenly bread. God's bread comes down from heaven and gives life to the world" (6:32, 33). Their fathers ate manna in the desert, only to die, but this bread is given that man may not die (6:49, 50).

The second part (6:35-50) clarifies the ambiguities in this last statement. Jesus is the one who comes down from heaven and gives life to the world: he is the bread of life. This bread's vivifying function is developed in the verses following (6:36-40).

When Jesus however declares that he is the bread which came down from heaven, his statement was received with scepticism and scandal (Jn. 6:42). Instead of proffering them a direct answer, Jesus tells the people not to murmur: only the internal attraction by the Father can bring people to Christ, that is, only the internal action of God's self-giving can bring people to believe in Christ and see the truth and foundation of his declaration that he is of a divine origin.

The third part of the discourse begins by repeating v. 41: his listeners murmured at the hardness of the saying (*see* v. 61). Jesus however insists on the radical truth of his words. He is the bread of life because he truly gives his flesh to be the food for the life of the world. Verse 51 contains the formula of the consecration of the bread in substance: "the bread which I shall give for the life of the world is my flesh" (*see* 1 Cor. 11:24). It is shaped, however, to the sequence of the discourse as a whole, which is a promise and pledge of the Bread to be given.

Lo-ruhama (lo′-roo-hay′-ma), A symbolic name which Hosea gave to his second child, the daughter of Gomer. The word means "unpitied" or "unloved," and symbolized the Lord's decision not to pity or love Israel any more (Hos. 1:6). In 2:25 however the Lord does pledge mercy and love: "I will love Unloved."

lost
As for the asses you *l.*   1 Sam. 9:20   The children whom you had *l.*
(like a *l.* sheep)   Ps. 119:176   Isa. 49:20
                             save what was *l.*   Lk. 19:10

Lot, According to the genealogy of Genesis 11:27, Lot was the son of Haran, one of Abraham's brothers. Haran died before his father in the Ur of the Chaldeans, and Lot came with Terah, his grandfather, and Abraham his uncle, from Ur to Haran, and with Abraham from Haran to Canaan (12:5). The patriarchal traditions tell us about Lot: a. That he settled in the region of Sodom and Gomorrah (Gen. 13:1-13); to avoid disputes and rivalry between his shepherds and those of Abraham he separated from Abraham and chose for himself the region of the five cities south of the Dead Sea. b. That Lot was made prisoner during the punitive expedition of the four eastern kings against the five kings of the Pentapolis, but he was freed by Abraham (Gen. 14). c. That Lot and his family were spared, through a divine intervention, the calamity that fell on Sodom and Gomorrah on account of the vice of the inhabitants (Gen. 19:1-29), but that Lot's wife was turned into a pillar of salt for having, against God's command, turned back to look. d. That Ammon and Moab, the founding fathers of the peoples of those names, were born of Lot's daughters through relationships they had with him after they had plied him with wine (Gen. 19:30-38).

These traditions are not all of the same origin, nor for that matter, of the same value. The genealogy of 11:27 probably does not mirror blood links between individuals, but, as is often the case with nomadic peoples (*see* GENEALOGY, NOMADISM), is rather a reflection of alliance or historical relationships between peoples who claimed descent, respectively, from Abraham and Lot, sanctioned by a basic but very broad blood link.

Of the Genesis traditions, it can be held as historically established that Lot's groups lived in Transjordan, south of the Dead Sea. No clear idea, however, can be had of the part played by Lot in the destruction of the cities of the Pentapolis. The southern half of the Dead Sea is of recent formation but it does not seem possible to date it from the time of Abraham (*see* SODOM). The episode about the death of Lot's wife is an etiology which seeks, in the past of legend, an explanation for a rocky formation in the shape of a woman to be found on the shores of the Dead Sea. This is also true of the explanation given of the origin of the peoples of Ammon and Moab: they are etymological etiologies, that is, there is an attempt to explain the present name in terms of a legendary past. From the linguistic point of view, however, the etymologies are false, but they express the consciousness of a blood relationship between Ammon, Moab and Israel.

Lotan, A son of Seir (Gen. 36:20; 22:29; 1 Chron. 1:39).

Lots, The custom of deciding questions by casting or drawing lots was common in antiquity and Israel was no exception. Israel did not just think it luck that such or such a lot was drawn. They used lots as a concrete way in which to leave the decision in a discussion up to the Lord, or, to put it another way, to free the decision from every human will or manipulation in a disposition of surrender to whatever the Lord might decide, or make known, through the lots cast. Proverbs states categorically: "When the lot is cast into the lap, its decision depends entirely on the Lord" (16:33). In certain cases the drawing of lots was minutely regulated and was a priestly function, so that its use became a way of obtaining oracles. *See* EPHOD, URIM AND THUMMIM, DIVINATION.

In the Old Testament the territory of Canaan was distributed to the tribes by lot, according to the idealized version of Numbers 26:55; Joshua 14:2; 18:6. The sacrificial victim for the rite of the Great Day of Expiation was chosen by lot (Lev. 16:7-10; *see* ATONEMENT, DAY OF). Lots also determined the guilt of a person (Josh. 7:14), God's election of a person for a specific mission (e.g. Saul as king of Israel; 1 Sam. 10:20-21), the distribution of war booty (Joel 4:2, 3), decisions in particular problems (Neh. 10:35), and the solution in the case of disputed rights.

An easily explained evolution of meaning led to the same word in Hebrew (goral—lot) being used for the portion or thing that fell to a person, and hence to mean the inheritance, one's destiny or lot in life (*see* Ps. 16:5, 6; Jer. 13:25).

In the New Testament lots were employed to discover the divine choice of the person who was to succeed the traitor Judas in the Twelve (Acts 1:26). Soldiers who carried out an execution could divide among themselves whatever the condemned man brought with him to the gibbet. So they divided up Jesus' clothes among them and cast lots for the seamless tunic that he had worn (Matt. 27:35; Mk. 15:24; Lk. 23:34; Jn. 19:24; see Ps. 22:19).

Lotus, The sacred plant of Egypt. It is mentioned only once in the Old Testament, in Job 40:21-22. There Behemoth (the hippopotamus?) is said to lie beneath the lotus among the reeds in the swamp. It is not, then, the Zizyphus lotus which grows in dry areas, but the sacred water lily of Egypt.

Love, The Old Testament uses a large variety of words to express love in its many faces. Chief among these is the word 'ahab, which can in Hebrew stand for human and divine love. In human love sex is frequently implied. God said to Hosea: "Give your love to a woman beloved of a paramour, an adulteress;" (Hos. 3:1). The Song of Songs sings: "He brings me into the banquet hall and his emblem over me is love" (2:4).

Love in the Old Testament is an all-embracing relationship between people reaching from the depths of the psyche and including loyalty, dedicatedness, intimate knowledge, mutuality, responsiveness and responsibility, and of course, sexual love, already alluded to.

Human love is at its most elemental in the faculty and use of sex. According to the Yahwist tradition of Genesis, Adam was lonely until God made him a helpmate like unto himself (Gen. 2:18), whereupon he sang a song in praise of Eve. Then follows the sealing word on the summit of human love: "That is why a man leaves his father and mother and clings to his wife, and the two of them become one body" (Gen. 2:24).

The same word, "knowledge," is used for man's intimate relationship with his wife and for his relationship with God. Indeed the one evokes the other. Adam "knew" his wife Eve, and she conceived, and gave birth to Cain, whereupon she said: "I have acquired a man with the help of the Lord." The diversity of the sexes had been blessed by God in the act of creation, who told them "be fertile and multiply; fill the earth and subdue it" (Gen. 1:28).

Given the original nomadic character of the Israelites, the bond between members of the same family and the same tribe ran very deep. These relationships were based on a real or presumed blood-link, but the love that flourished on it welded the members tightly together. The story of God's command to Abraham to sacrifice Isaac, his only son, brings out the depth of love between them (Gen. 22). The book of Ruth illustrates the love that can bind together a mother-in-law and daughter-in-law: to Naomi the women said: "for his mother is the daughter-in-law who loves you. She is worth more to you than seven sons" (4:15). The deep family ties of love brought with them co–responsibility, loyalty, and a concern for the good standing of the family or tribe that had its own legislation in Israel. *See* AVENGER, GO'EL.

While the love of God for man is manifested in creation (Gen. 1-2), and above all in election (Gen. 12), Israel's attitude at the beginning was one of fear and reverence. With Deuteronomy however, all that was involved in God's creation and election, and man's reception of these gifts, matured into love. The great commandment, even in the Old Testament, is: "You shall love the Lord your God with all your heart, and with all your soul, and with all your strength" (Deut. 6:4; see Deut. 11:13, 22; 19:9; 30:16; Josh. 22:5; 23:11).

In the history of Israel God's love was to remain unwithdrawn, even though the Israelites were to prove unfaithful. The Lord remains true to his words to Moses: "The Lord, the Lord, a merciful and gracious God, slow to anger and rich in kindness and fidelity, continuing his kindness for a thousand generations and forgiving wickedness and crime and sin" (Ex. 34:6-7). Again, through Nathan the prophet, God spoke to David: "If he does wrong . . . but I will not withdraw my favor from him. . . . Your house and your kingdom shall endure forever before me; your throne shall stand firm forever" (2 Sam. 7:14-16).

Hosea speaks of God's relationship to his people in terms of the love of a husband for a wife (*see* Hos. 2). God's love is such that even though the wife should prove adulterous, God will not withdraw his love. Instead "I will allure her; I will lead her into the desert and speak to her heart. She shall respond there as in the days of her youth when she came up from the land of Egypt" (2:16-17). God will then betroth her to himself with integrity and justice, with tenderness and love, with faithfulness, and Israel will come to know the Lord (Hos. 2:21-22).

On occasions when Israel's response to the Lord was an empty facade of multiplied sacrifices, God spoke: "I am sick of holocausts of rams, the blood of bulls and of goats revolts me." What then is the response God wants from his people? "For it is love that I desire, not sacrifice, and knowledge of God rather than holocausts" (Hos. 6:6).

The most important New Testament verb for 'to love' is **agapan**, and its noun **agape**, while the adjective **agapetos**, loved, also figures largely. The verb, **agapan**, to love, occurs 141 times, the noun **agape**, love, 117 times, and the adjective, **agapetos** (beloved), 61 times. Another word, **philein**, to love, is less frequent and less important: it occurs 18 times in the gospels and twice in St. Paul. The adjective **philos** occurs 29 times within the gospels, Acts and Epistles. Closely related to love is the word **epipothein** and **epipothetos**, which involve a longing or yearning for something or someone. Love, then, is one of the most important themes of the whole New Testament, and in it can be summed up the whole Christian reality.

John sums it up by stating: "God is love" (1 Jn. 4:8). God's love is made evident to man in the flesh of his Son, whom he sent into the world, that we might have life through him (1 Jn. 4:9). The proof that this life is in us consists in the love that we manifest to one another: "No one has ever seen God. Yet if we love one another, God dwells in us and his love is brought to perfection in us" (1 Jn. 4:12; *see* Jn. 13:34-35). Christ, the evidence of God's love for us, lives on in us through the Holy Spirit that is given us (1 Jn. 3:24) in accordance with Christ's own promise (Jn. 14:16; 16:7). "The way we know we remain in him and he in us is that he has given us of his Spirit" (1 Jn. 4:13). If God is love, the Christian reality is a share in that love, through which the Spirit transmits to us Christ's life, by which we become God's children.

In the love relationship between God and man, what is paramount is the initiative on the part of God. Man had nothing that might attract the love of God. On the contrary, sin had made man very unlovable, so that it was not as if we had loved God, but "Love, then, consists in this; not that we have loved God but that he has loved us and has sent his Son as an offering for our sins" (1 Jn. 4:10). This initiative is evidenced in that "The Son of Man has come to search out and save what was lost" (Lk. 19:10; Matt. 10:6; 15:24). The sign of the coming of God's saving love is that he fulfils Isaiah's prophecy in coming to evangelize the poor, to heal the contrite of heart, to preach liberation to the captives, and bring sight to the blind and healing to those who are broken and downhearted (Luke 4:18; Isa. 61:1 ff.). To John's messengers Jesus gave the following account of his mission: "Go and report to John what you have seen and heard. The blind recover their sight, cripples walk, lepers are cured, the deaf hear, dead men are raised to life and the poor have the good news preached to them" (Lk. 7:22).

The sweep of this initiative is even more astonishing when we realize that it is the beloved Son, in whom the Father takes delight (Lk. 3:22), who is sent into the world to win men. This is God's only-begotten Son (Jn. 1:14; Rom. 8:31, 32), whom the Father loves (Jn. 3:35; 10:17; 15:9; 17:24, 26). Into the Son's hands as a mark of love are consigned all things (Jn. 5:20; 17-23). The Son on his part reciprocates this love: he is not alone (Jn. 8:16) but speaks only those things that his Father committed to him (Jn. 8:26), and carries into effect only those things told him by his Father (Jn. 14:31). The Father was abidingly present to the Son, and the Son lived in intimacy with him by always doing the things that pleased him (Jn. 8:29). In the concluding hymn of Romans 8, Paul sings: "What shall we say after that? If God is for us, who can be against us? Is it possible that he who did not spare his own Son but handed him over for the sake of us all will not grant us all things besides?" (Rom. 8:31, 32).

Christ at the Last Supper prayed that his followers would be caught up in a communion and intimacy in the Trinity such as exists between him and his Father: "That all may be one as you, Father, are in me, and I in you; I pray that they may be (one) in us, that the world may believe that you sent me. I have given them the glory you gave me that they may be one, as we are one. I living in them, you living in me—that their unity may be complete. So shall the world know that you sent me, and that you loved them as you loved me" (Jn. 17:21-23). Such a union would be quite impossible for man had not Christ pleaded (Jn. 16:7 ff.) and sent (Acts 2) the Holy Spirit, among whose first fruits in the just is love (Rom. 5:5; Gal. 5:22), through which we are gathered up into the priestly surrender of Christ on the cross (Rom. 6:1-11).

When through baptism the Holy Spirit comes into a person, he carries on in them Christ's Father-directed life: on account of the Spirit's presence the Christian can cry out to the **Abba,** Father, of Christ, laying a claim to a share in Christ's inheritance (Gal. 4:4-6; Rom. 8:14-17). This is no mere metaphor. John exhorts Christians to "See what love the Father has bestowed on us in letting us be called children of God! Yet that is what we are" (1 Jn. 3:1).

The perfect prayed-for communion is still in the achieving. "We are God's children now; what we shall later be has not yet come to light. We know that when it comes to light we shall be like him for we shall see him as he is" (1 Jn. 3:2).

In the meantime, the life of pilgrimage through which Christians must walk to future fulfilment is summed up by Christ in the two great commandments of love (Matt. 22:40). When Paul had summed up the Christian mystery as being merged in Christ's surrender through the Spirit (Rom. 6 and 8), the living out of this mystery he summed up as follows: "Offer your bodies as a living sacrifice holy and acceptable to God, your spiritual worship. Owe no debt to anyone except the debt that binds us to love one another. He who loves his neighbor has fulfilled the law" (Rom. 12:1; 13:8-10).

The love of which Paul and John speak as summing up the whole Christian life is not just the natural adherence of the will and affection: it is natural love suffused by the Spirit and rendered capable of truly Christ-derived acts. While the Spirit gives the liberty of love (Rom. 5:5; 8:15; Gal. 5:13, 22; 2 Cor. 3:17), it does not prompt self-indulgence, but rather urges Christians to serve one another in works of love (Gal. 5:13).

While gifts differ, each person belongs to the other in the body of Christ (Rom. 12:3-8; 1 Cor. 12:12 ff.). Love then is not an effort to bridge the gap between people; it is rather what emerges from the indwelling Spirit who makes all cohere in the one Christ (1 Cor. 12:12). To speak divisive words and do anything to impair that unity would be to grieve the Holy Spirit of God who has marked Christians with his seal "to be set free when the day comes" (Eph. 4:29-32). We must then aim at imitating God, who is love, as his children whom he loves. We must follow Christ by loving as he loved us (Eph. 5:1, 2).

The beginning of the Church was especially marked with an abundance of out-of-the-ordinary spiritual gifts, such as the gift of preaching, faith, healing, working miracles, prophecy, discretion of spirit, glossolaly, interpretation. All of these derived from the same Holy Spirit (1 Cor. 12:4-11) and were meant for the building up of the Church. Paul however reminds his readers that there is a gift higher than all these extraordinary manifestations of the Spirit: "Now I will show you the way which surpasses all the others" (1 Cor. 13:1). Thereupon Paul launches into the famous hymn on love, the Spirit's first gift to all Christians.

Without love to animate it, even the most eye-catching and impressive deeds are dead, even though they might have the outer semblance of virtue (1 Cor. 13:1-3). It is only the Spirit who can give rise to a love that runs through the Sermon on the Mount (Matt. 5-7), a love always patient and kind, never jealous, never conceited, never rude or selfish, that is always ready to excuse, to trust, to hope, and to endure whatever comes (1 Cor. 13:4).

The movement of love is centripetal: when it arises from the Spirit within and is expressed in life, it intensifies the Christ-life in men. John argues that a person who hates his brother whom he sees cannot love God whom he does not see: anyone who loves God must also love his brother (1 Jn. 4:20-21). For the love of brother is the measure of one's love of Christ, who identifies himself in his brethren (Matt. 25:31-46; *see* Jn. 15:1-11).

The perfect communion prayed for by Christ (Jn. 17) will not be achieved before his second coming. Nevertheless Christians are on their way to meet him. The steps they take are those of love, or, in Paul's words, "love upbuilds" (1 Cor. 8:1). When faith, through which we now lay hold of a hidden reality (Heb. 11:1), will brighten into the vision of God, when we shall see face to face (1 Cor. 13:12; 1 Jn. 3;2), and hope will become possession, then love will abide forever (1 Cor. 13:8) to cement the communion that is also the consummation.

Low Country, *See* SHEPHELAH.

Lubim (loo'-bim), *See* LYBIA.

Lucas, Another form of Luke. *See* LUKE; LUKE, GOSPEL OF.

Lucifer, The name of the prince of demons. The name comes from the Latin translation of Isaiah 14:12 which means "morning star" or "day star" and is addressed in satire to the king of Babylon. The fathers of the church, however, interpreted it as a description of the defeat of the rebellious angels, the name Lucifer being given to the presumed chief of the rebellion.

Lucius, 1. A Roman consul who was contemporary with the Maccabees. He was a signatory to a letter from the Senate in favor of the Jews (1 Mac. 15:16-21).

2. Lucius of Cyrene was a prophet and teacher in the church at Antioch (Acts 13:1).

3. A Christian and fellow countryman of Paul (Rom. 16:21).

Lud, In the Table of Nations Lud is son of Shem (Gen. 10:22; 1 Chron. 1:17), and is identified with the people of the region of Lydia in Asia Minor (Isa. 66:19), whose king was defeated by Cyrus of Persia in 546 B.C. Among the sons of Ham appears a people with the same name (Gen. 10:13; 1 Chron. 1:11) about whom no more is known: they were probably African (Jer. 46:9; Ezek. 30:5).

Luhith (loo′-hith), A city in Moab (Isa. 15:5; Jer. 48:5).

Luke, According to tradition the author of the third gospel and of the Acts of the Apostles. (*See* LUKE, GOSPEL OF; ACTS OF THE APOSTLES.) His name occurs only three times in the New Testament. Some authors identify him with Lucius of Cyrene, one of the prophets of the church of Antioch (Acts 13:1) and with "Lucius, my kinsman," mentioned in Romans 16:21, but such an identification is purely conjectural. Philemon 24 calls Luke Paul's fellow worker while in Colossians 4:14 he is called "the beloved physician." 2 Timothy 4:11 tells us that Luke was with Paul during his second Roman imprisonment. Tradition has it that Luke was a Syrian from Antioch. Perhaps this explains how Luke shows a great awareness of the affairs of the church of Antioch.

In the Acts of the Apostles some passages are written in the first person plural (16:10-17; 20:5-16; 27:1-28). The most common interpretation of this is that Luke was Paul's companion in the events described in these passages. Some however believe that it is a question of a diary of the journey made by another person and used by Luke. In the former case Luke would have met Paul at Troas and accompanied him as far as Philippi, where during the third journey they again joined up and were together as far as Jerusalem. Luke would have remained on with Paul during his confrontation with Peter, and would thereafter have accompanied him to Rome.

Tradition adds that Luke, who never married, composed his gospel at Achaia and died at the age of eighty-four in Boeotia in Greece.

Luke, Gospel of, Tradition attributed the authorship of the third canonical gospel to Luke, a companion of Paul (*see* LUKE). The most ancient witnesses to this come from the second half of the second century. The Muratorian Canon, dating from after 155 A.D., is the oldest of all (*see* MURATORIANUM, CANON). Its evidence is indirectly confirmed by Marcion's conduct. (*See* MARCION.) Marcion, living in the first half of the second century, was one of the first heretics of the church. He proposed his own canon of the New Testament to which he admitted only ten of Paul's epistles and one gospel. This gospel is an elaboration of our gospel according to Luke. Marcion was deeply devoted to Paul, so that his reasons for choosing Luke above the others should be sought in the fact that Luke was Paul's companion. From around the same date as the Muratorian Canon appears the Latin prologue to the gospel according to Luke, composed at Rome between 160 and 180 A.D., which takes Marcion to task and also provides other information. From it we gather that Luke was a Syrian from Antioch who lived with Paul until Paul's martyrdom. He never married, and died at the age of eighty-four in Boeotia in Greece. He wrote his gospel in Achaia after Matthew and Mark had penned theirs, and his gospel was addressed to the Greeks. No further information is provided by later writers such as Irenaeus, Tertullian, Origen, Clement of Alexandria; they merely insist on the link between Paul and Luke, just as there was a relationship between Mark and Peter. In fact, tradition attempted in this way to enhance the value of Luke's gospel, since he was not an eyewitness to the events he described.

The third gospel is the only one which has a prologue. In it the author tells us of his work of research and of the reasons that induced him to compose his gospel (Luke 1:1-4). This is a very common type of prologue in Hellenistic writings and manifests Luke's intention of composing a literary work. With Luke we are at the beginnings of Christian literature properly so called. Luke speaks of the work of his predecessors: "many have undertaken to compile a narrative . . . " (v. 1), and of the sources used, those who from the beginning were "original eyewitnesses and ministers of the word" (1:2). While Luke, even as a literary author, does not depart from the Christian context, and explicitly proposes to offer a "history," it would be a mistake to expect from his pen a scientific history. While Luke's is a new account coming after Mark and Matthew, he too is first and foremost a witness to the tradition of the Church.

When, then, Luke speaks of "writing in order," one must not expect an exact unfolding of the individual events, and, although he states that he has investigated all from the beginning, it would be vain to hope from him a critical-scientific research. Undoubtedly Luke evaluated the written and oral traditions about Jesus, but Luke too is writing as a member of the church, and is not calling its unquestioned authority into doubt. The historical-critical problem of Jesus did not occur to Luke: it first made its appearance only in the eighteenth century (*see* JESUS CHRIST).

Luke dedicates his gospel to Theophilus, probably a well-known Christian who had converted from paganism. Theophilus could also however be a symbolic name for all Christians, for in the Greek it comes from **theos** and **philos**, loved by God.

In Acts 1:1, 2, in dedicating the work to the same Theophilus, Luke refers to the gospel. This, taken together with other internal indications, shows that Luke considered his gospel and the Acts as one work in two volumes. In this way Luke reached beyond the canonical limits of the kerygma (from the baptism of John . . . until the day on which he [Jesus] was assumed [Acts 1:22]) by including the infancy narrative (cc. 1-2) but also into the future by inserting the story of the witness of the apostles [Acts 1:8] as the fruit and unfolding of the central event of salvation, namely, the coming of Jesus (*see* ACTS OF THE APOSTLES).

That Luke intended to write history is seen above all in his attempt to synchronize events with profane history. This occurs for the birth of Jesus (Lk. 2:1-3), the beginning of the Baptist's ministry (3:1), Jesus' age at the beginning of his public ministry and the introduction of the genealogy of Jesus which ends with "Adam, son of God" (3:38). These datings by Luke afford to posterity the basis of a chronology of the New Testament, but they also show an express and conscious opening of the Christian message to the pagan world. The salvation events belong in truth, though not exclusively, to human history. Here, however, they are presented in a breath-taking audacity as the axis and determining event on which the whole of history revolves. The universal vision, which in no way compromises the 'judaic' realism of the Christian event, is one of Luke's most incisive characteristics, which is unfolded from the gospel story on to the story of its realization in the wide world of Acts.

Critical study of Luke's gospel, especially by comparing it with the other two synoptics (*see* SYNOPTIC QUESTION) has revealed Luke's method of work and the way in which he used his sources. It seems certain that he knew and used the gospel of Mark: in fact he made it the basis of his own gospel. He kept its general order but inserted into his own writing, in two great blocks of material, the traditions he had known and which were absent from Mark (6:20-8:3 and 9:51-18:14). To Mark's general plan he prefixes an important new passage: the Infancy Gospel (cc. 1-2).

The first block of non-Marcan material (6:20-8:3) is made up of a long discourse of Jesus "at a level stretch" (6:17) which is very similar to but shorter than Matthew's Sermon on the Mount (Matt. 5-7). Luke begins with four beatitudes and four imprecations (6:20-26) and finishes, like Matthew, with a parable (6:47-49). Then follow two miracles, the servant of the centurion (*see* Matt. 8:5-13) and the son of the widow of Nain, which is proper to Luke. There follows another discourse of Jesus on John the Baptizer (7:18-35) which is also reported by Matt. 11. Luke alone has the final scene of the sinful woman who approached Jesus in the house of Simon (7:36-50). Chapter 8:3 takes up again Mark's material, avoiding repetition of the same episodes, or similar episodes, such as the second multiplication of bread and connected events reported in Mark 6:45-8:26.

In cc. 9:51-18:14 we have the "great insertion" which is cleverly presented by Luke in the context of Jesus' journey from Galilee to Jerusalem, where he was to be "received up" (*see* 9:51; 13:22; 17:11). This section revolves around traditions that are found only in Luke or, in some cases, in Matthew. It is however charged with dramatic tension, for it is shot through with the free and conscious decision of Jesus to bring to fulfilment his mission and work through his death: "Today and tomorrow I cast out devils and perform cures, and on the third day my purpose is accomplished. For all that, I must proceed on course today, tomorrow, and the day after, since no prophet can be allowed to die anywhere except in Jerusalem" (13:32, 33).

In 18:15 he once more takes up Mark's narrative, which he then continues with only slight variations. A comparison with Mark shows that Luke respected the sources he used. He keeps to the order that he finds and describes the events in a new style which is not always the best Greek, since he is intent on copying the sacred language of the Greek version of the Bible (*see* SEPTUAGINT). It has been noticed that when Luke departs from Mark, he coincides with Matthew, but the coincidence is of such a nature that it excludes Luke's having seen Matthew, or Matthew's having seen Luke. Both seem to depend, but independently of each other, on a common tradition. This common tradition is thought to be a document of the life and work of Christ which is referred to as Q, from the German **Quelle**, source. Many scholars think that this Q was an actual collection of the sayings of Jesus which is lost, but was in the hands of Luke and of Matthew.

According to the witness of tradition, cited at the beginning of this article, Luke wrote in Achaia and wished with his gospel to serve, above all, the needs of the ethnic Christians. It is difficult to establish the date of writing. Luke certainly writes after Mark and before he composed the Acts of the Apostles. (*See* ACTS OF APOSTLES.) The years 70-80 A.D. are very probably the time of composition. but it is not possible to be more precise.

lunatics
possessed, the *l.*, the paralyzed
Matt. 4:24

lust, lustfully

L. not in your heart	Prov. 6:25	burned with *l.* for one another	
who looks *l.* at a woman			Rom. 1:27
	Matt. 5:28	that *l.* which is idolatry	Col. 3:5

Lute, A stringed instrument with a sound box in the shape of a pear, played by strumming or plucking the strings.

luxuriously, luxury

| someone dressed *l.* | Lk. 7:25 | those who dress in *l.* | Lk. 7:25 |

Luz, The ancient name of the city which was later called Bethel by Jacob in memory of the vision of God that he had there (Gen. 28:19; 35:6; Josh. 18:13; Jgs. 1:23). *See* BETHEL.

Lycaonia (lik′-a-oh′-ni-a; also lie′-ka-oh′-ni-a), A region in the southern central area of Asia Minor which took its name from the tribe of Lycaonians, who at the time of Paul still held on to their own language (Acts 14:11). Paul and Barnabas visited the region during their first apostolic journey and preached in the cities of Derbe, Lystra and Iconium (Acts 14:6). Paul returned there on his second apostolic journey (Acts 16:1-7) and on the third (Acts 18:23), provided that Galatia here means the Roman province and not the geographic region. On this problem *see* GALATIA.

Lycia (lish′-i-a), A region occupying the southwestern corner of Asia Minor. Paul stopped at Myra, the principal port of the region during his journey to Rome as a prisoner (Acts 27:5).

Lydda (lid′-a), The Greek name for the ancient Lod, a city of Benjamin (1 Chron. 8:12) which was occupied after the exile (Ezra 2:33; Neh. 7:37). Jonathan Maccabeus got from Demetrius Nicator the annexation to Judea of the Lydda district together with two other Galilean regions (1 Mac. 11:34; *see* 10:30, 38; 11:28, 57). It was the seat of one of the first Christian communities in Palestine, and was visited by Peter who there cured a paralytic by the name of Aeneas (Acts 9:32-35). The town was later called Diospolis, and today it is Ludd, twelve miles southeast of Jaffa.

Lydia, A woman, a dealer in purple (dye), native of Thyatira in Lydia (Asia Minor) whom Paul met and converted in Philippi (Acts 16:14, 15, 40). *See* also LUD.

Lyre, A stringed instrument similar to a harp, used for the accompaniment of song in the ancient world.

lyre

l. for the chanters	1 Kgs. 10:12	music of cymbals, harps and *l.*	
and music on *l.*	1 Chron. 13:8		Neh. 12:27
	the *l.* Ps. 81:3		

Lysanias (li-say′-ni-as), Tetrarch of Abilene, the region of the city of Abila, northwest of Damascus at the time of Jesus' public ministry (Lk. 3:1).

Lysias (lis′-i-as), A nobleman belonging to the royal family, to whom Antiochus IV Epiphanes (175-164 B.C.) entrusted the government of his kingdom from the Euphrates to the Egyptian border while he set out on an expedition into Persia. Lysias was also appointed regent of the heir Antiochus V and was ordered to execute the latter's plans against the Maccabees (1 Mac. 3:32-37). Lysias first sent an army under the command of Ptolemy, Nicanor, and Gorgias which was defeated by Judas Maccabeus (3:38-4:25). Later he came with Antiochus and was again defeated at Beth-zur (4:26-35). After the death of Antiochus IV Epiphanes, he usurped from Philip the regency of Antioch V Eupator (1 Mac. 6:14-17) and organized a new expedition against Judas. This time he was successful and Judas died in the battle of Bethzechariah. Lysias put the citadel at Jerusalem under seige (6:28-54), but upon hearing the news of Philip's arrival with the army that had accompanied Antiochus IV to Persia, he came to terms with the Jews and returned to Syria (6:55-53). Lysias was made prisoner and killed by Demetrius, son of Seleucus who took power in 162 B.C. (1 Mac. 7:1-4).

Lysimachus (lie-sim′-a-kus), Brother of the high priest Menelaus who substituted for a time for his brother when the latter was called to the presence of the Seleucid king (2 Mac. 4:29). He was hated by the people because of his sacrilegious thievery. He was killed in Jerusalem during a revolt of the mob provoked by his excesses (2 Mac. 4:39-42).

Lystra, A city in Lycaonia in Asia Minor, evangelized by Paul during his first (Acts 14:6-21; 2 Tim. 16:2) and second apostolic journeys (Acts 16:1). It was the native place of Timothy, one of Paul's disciples (Acts 16:2). The site of the city is known but nothing remains of it today.

M

Maacah (may′-a-kah), 1. Daughter of Talmai, king of Geshur. From her marriage with King David was born Absalom (2 Sam. 3:3; 1 Chron. 3:2) and Tamar, raped by Amnon (2 Sam. 13:1-22).

2. Daughter of Abishalom (son of David?) and mother of Abijam, king of Judah (915-913 B.C.; 1 Kgs. 15:2) and grandmother of Asa, king of Judah (913-873 B.C.; 1 Kgs. 15:10). Asa deposed his grandmother Maacah from her position as queen mother because she had made an idol for Asherah, a Canaanite goddess. Asa cut down this idol and burned it in the Kidron Valley (1 Kgs. 15:13-15).

3. The name of one of Caleb's concubines (1 Chron. 2:48).

4. A small Aramaean kingdom south of Mt. Hermon, near the headwaters of the Jordan, whose capital was Abel-beth-maacah (Josh. 12:5; 13:11). Maacah allied with the Ammonites against David, sending one thousand men to help in the first Ammonite campaign. When the battle opened, the men of Maacah kept their distance in the open country. David's general Joab routed the Aramaean wing, which caused the Ammonites to flee, and the victory was David's. The territory was incorporated into the United Kingdom.

Maadiah (may′-a-dy′-ah), A priest among those who returned from Babylon (Neh. 12:5).

Maarath (may′-a-rath), A town in Judah (Josh. 15:59).

Maasai (may′-a-sie), A priest who returned from the exile (1 Chron. 9:12).

Maaseiah (may′-a-see′-yah), 1. One of the heads of the army who took part in the coup d'etat of Jehoiada the priest against Athalia (837 B.C.; 2 Chron. 23:1).

2. Father of the prophet Zedekiah, a contemporary and adversary of Jeremiah (Jer. 21:1; 29:25; 37:3).

Maath (may′-ath), An ancestor of Jesus in Luke's genealogy (3:26).

Maaziah, (may′-a-zie′-ah), The ancestor of a priestly family (1 Chron. 24:18).

Maccabees, Books of, The deuterocanonical historical books of the Old Testament which tell the story of the wars of the Jews under the leadership of the Maccabees against the Seleucid kings. These wars were aimed at securing the religious patrimony of the Jews and at gaining liberty and political independence. The two books are independent of each other even though their names suggest a continuity of actions and unity of style.

1 Maccabees starts by analyzing the circumstances that led to the revolt and presents the contenders (cc. 1 and 2). Then follows a narration of the principal exploits of the great Maccabean leaders: Judas (3:1-9:22; 166-160 B.C.), Jonathan (9:23-12:53; 160-142 B.C.) and Simon (13:1-16:24; 142-134 B.C.)

The book was originally composed in Hebrew as is attested to by St. Jerome, who states that he saw in his own time a copy of the Hebrew text. Moreover, this is borne out by the language of the book which bears the traces of having being translated from a semitic original. It was written in Palestine, where the author imitated the style of Palestinian history writing (1-2 Samuel and 1-2 Kings). He accepts the religious concept of history that was imposed by these books: God directs and intervenes in history, bringing about judgment or salvation according to his plan by making use of chosen instruments, in this case, the three great heroes of the Maccabean house.

The book was certainly written after 134 B.C., when Simon died, and probably during the reign of his son, John Hyrcanus (134-104 B.C.). 16:24 imitates the usual formula of 1-2 Kings, but this is not sufficient reason for dating the book after the death of Hyrcanus. It is our best source for Jewish history in the period 175-135 B.C.

2 Maccabees is not the continuation of 1 Maccabees, but an independent account of the events narrated in 1 Maccabees 1-7. The introduction contains two letters from the Jews of Palestine to those of Egypt inviting them to celebrate the Feast of the Dedication of the Temple, which took place thanks to the initiative of Judas Maccabeus (164 B.C.), followed by the author's prologue (cc. 1-2).

The first episode, the punishment of Heliodorus, took place during the reign of Seleucus IV (187-175 B.C., c. 3). The Hellenization program of Antiochus IV Epiphanes and the internal rivalry to gain the high priesthood were the circumstances which provoked the Maccabean insurrection (cc. 4-7). Only the work of Judas, culminating in the dedication of the Temple, is recorded (cc. 8:1-10:8). The rest of the book records other victories of Judas against neighboring peoples and against the Seleucids of Lysias and Nicanor (10:9-15:37).

The author wrote in Greek. He tells us that his is a summary of a five-volume history of the Maccabees composed by Jason of Cyrene (2:19-31). The use of Greek and the interests of the author point towards Alexandria as the book's place of origin.

The book has the avowed purpose, clear from the two letters at the start (cc. 1 and 2), of interesting the Jews of Alexandria in the religious and political events in Palestine, and above all in the Temple, which was the center and symbol of unity for the whole Jewish family.

This aim dictated the style and the choice of events for narration so that they would center on the dedication of the Temple. There is also, however, a marked leaning towards the awe-inspiring and supernatural as a means of boosting the sanctity of the Temple and interesting people in it. The book, then, has a broader range than 1 Maccabees. Its purpose is to edify, and so it takes advantage of the liberties that are usual to this type of historical narrative. Rhetoric plays a great part in it.

The date of composition is after 124 B.C., during which the first letter was written. The book was probably written about 80 B.C.

Maccabeus, From the Hebrew **maqqebet,** hammer, the name by which Judas was known. He was the son of Mattathias, head of the Jewish revolt against the measures towards Hellenization imposed by Antiochus IV Epiphanes (165-161 B.C.; 2 Mac. 2:4). This name later passed on to his brothers Jonathan and Simon.

Macedonia, A region to the north of Achaia which became well-known in ancient history thanks to the prowess of Philip, the conqueror of Greece, and his son, Alexander the Great, who conquered the Orient (1 Mac. 1:1). Macedonia became a Roman province in 148 B.C. Paul visited Macedonia on his second (Acts 16:9) and third (Acts 20:1) apostolic journeys, during which he founded the churches at Thessalonica and Philippi.

Machaerus (ma-kee'-rus), A place in Transjordan east of the Dead Sea where Alexander Jannaeus erected a fortress which was later demolished by the Romans (57 B.C.) and reconstructed by Herod I the Great. According to the history of Flavius Josephus, it was here that John the Baptizer was imprisoned and beheaded.

Machbannai (mak-ban'-eye), An officer of David's army (1 Chron. 12:14).

Machbenah (mak-bee'-nah), A town in Judah (1 Chron. 2:49).

Machir (may'-kir), 1. The name of an ancient tribe or clan of the Israelite confederacy, related to the tribe of Manasseh, which settled on the west side of the Jordan north of Ephraim (Jgs. 5:14) but later emigrated across the Jordan to Gilead (Josh. 13:31; 17:1) to be intermingled with the tribe of Manasseh. This complex and partially hypothetical reconstruction of the vicissitudes of the tribe of Machir has left traces in the genealogies. Machir appears as son of Manasseh (Gen. 50:23; Num. 26:29; 27:1; 32:39; 36:1) and father of Gilead (Num. 26:29; 1 Chron. 7:14-17).

2. Son of Ammiel of Lodebar in whose house Meribbaal, Jonathan's crippled son, stayed (2 Sam. 9:4, 5). He later assisted David with provisions while the latter took refuge at Manahaim during the revolt of Absalom (2 Sam. 17:27-29).

Machpelah (mak-pee'-lah), The name of the cave and the surrounding field near Hebron which was bought by Abraham from Ephron the Hittite in order to bury his wife Sarah there (Gen. 23). Later Abraham was buried there (Gen. 25:9), as were Isaac, Leah and Jacob (Gen. 49:30; 50:13). A tradition which comes from the fourth century identifies this place with the present mosque of Hebron.

Macron (may'-cron), Ptolemy Macron was the Egyptian governor of Cyprus under Ptolemy VI Philometer (181-145 B.C.) who abandoned his position to pass over to Antiochus IV Ephiphanes. He was a protector of the Jews, and was accused of this to Antiochus V (164-161 B.C.). On hearing himself denounced on every side as a traitor, he committed suicide by poisoning himself (2 Mac. 10:12-13).

mad

until you are driven *m*.		Of laughter I said "*M.!*"	Eccl. 2:2
	Deut. 28:34	they have become *m*.	Jer. 51:7
the man is *m*.	1 Sam. 21:15	the man of the spirit is *m*.	Hos. 9:7

made

God *m*. the dome	Gen. 1:7	God *m*. all kinds of wild animals	
God *m*. the two great lights			Gen. 1:25
	Gen. 1:16	for I have *m*. him . . . obdurate	
			Ex. 10:1

madman

acted like a *m*.	1 Sam. 21:14	Why did that *m*. come	2 Kgs. 9:11

Madmannah, A city in Judah (Josh. 15:31; 1 Chron. 2:49).

Madmenah (mad-me′-nah), A town north of Jerusalem (Isa. 10:31).

Madon (may′-don), A Canaanite city in Galilee, allied with Jabin king of Hazor against Joshua (Josh. 11:1; 12:19).

Magadan (mag′-a-dan), According to Matthew 15:39, the name of the region to which Jesus retired with his disciples after the second miracle of the loaves. He reached it by boat, suggesting that it was situated on the coast of the lake of Gennesaret. However the reference is uncertain and the place unidentified. Mark 8:10 refers to Dalmanutha at this point, which is also unidentified.

Magbish, A place in Judah (Ezra 2:30).

Magdala (mag′-da-la), A town on the western coast of the lake of Gennesaret, today Mejdel, the home of Mary Magdalene (Matt. 27:56, 61; Mk. 15:40; 16:1; Lk. 8:2; 24:10; Jn. 19:21; 20:1, 8). Magdala stood on a major route to lower Galilee.

Magdalene, *See* MARY.

Magdiel (mag′-di-el), A clan of Esau-Edom (Gen. 36:43). *See* ESAU.

Magi (may′-jie), The personages who came from the east guided by a star to adore the king of the Jews, according to the account of Matthew 2:1-12. The account does not specify their number nor tell their names. Tradition however has filled this lacuna. Neither does the account refer to their royal status, even though this is insinuated from the Old Testament context which inspired the gospel story (Ps. 72:10-15; Isa. 49:23; 60:6). What the story obviously intends is to present Jesus being accepted by the Gentiles while rejected by his own people. It has the strong coloring of Old Testament texts that were held to be messianic (besides those already cited, *see* Gen. 49:10; Num. 24:17 on the star of Jacob). This strong Old Testament influence in the story makes it very difficult to judge its historicity. The wise men are said to be from the east, and were possibly astrologers from Arabia or Babylon.

Magic, Magic in the Old Testament is categorically forbidden under the pain of death (Ex. 22:17; Lev. 19:31; 20:27; Deut. 18:10). Yahweh is superior to every magical power, whether in rites or words, and magic is incompatible with worship of him. This superiority and incompatibility is inculcated in the story of the plagues of Egypt, where Moses proved more resourceful than the magicians of Egypt (Ex. 7:10-23; 8:1-7; 8:8-12), and in the story of Balaam, who had been called to curse Israel but was ineluctably forced to bless instead (Num. 22-24).

The historical books nevertheless do not hide the fact that magic was in favor at certain periods. Israel lived, after all, in an environment that was saturated with magical practices. The accounts of religious reforms allude to the measures taken to eradicate the abuse (2 Kgs. 21:6; 23:24). The prophets are strong in their condemnation of magical practices (Isa. 57:3; Jer. 27:9; Ezek. 13:18, 19; 2 Kgs. 9:22; 17:17). Even in the New Testament there is the account of the victorious encounter of Peter and Paul with the magicians (Acts 8:9-24; 13:6-11; 19:13-19).

magicians

So he summoned all the *m.*		Egyptian *m.* did the same	
	Gen. 41:8		Ex. 7:22
I have spoken to the *m.*		The *m.* could not stand	Ex. 9:11
	Gen. 41:24	the wise men, enchanters, *m.*	
the *m.* of Egypt	Ex. 7:11		Dan. 2:27

magistrate

appoint *m*.	Ezra 7:25	the *m*. stripped them Acts 16:22
to appear before a *m*.	Lk. 12:58	the *m*. dispatched officers
turned them over to the *m*.		Acts 16:35
	Acts 16:20	officers reported this to the *m*.
		Acts 16:38

Magnificat, The first word of the Latin version of Mary's canticle in Luke 1:46-65, from which word it gets its name. The song is freely inspired by that of Hannah, Samuel's mother (1 Sam. 2:1-10), and like that song it is with all probability anterior to and independent of the context in which it is found today in Luke 1:46-55.

Magog (may´-gog), The country of King Gog in Ezekiel 38:2; 39:6 (*see* GOG) mentioned among the sons of Japhet (Gen. 10:2; 1 Chron. 1:5) and thought to be in the region of the Black Sea. The name is that of a person, together with Gog, in Revelation 20:8.

Magpiash (mag´-pi-ash), One of the Jews who set their seal on the covenant proclaimed by Nehemiah (Neh. 10:21).

Mahalab, (may´-a-lab), A town in the territory of Asher (Josh. 19:29).

Mahalalel (ma-hal´-a-lel), Son of Kenan, father of Jared (Gen. 5:12-17; 1 Chron. 1:2), listed among Jesus' ancestors in the genealogy of Luke 3:37.

Mahanaim (may´-a-nay´-im), A town in Transjordan near the meeting of the Jabbok and the Jordan (Gen. 32) in the land of Gad (Josh. 13:26, 30). It was a Levitical city (Josh. 21:36), residence of Ishbaal son of Saul (2 Sam. 8:12) and David's refuge during Absalom's revolt (2 Sam. 17:24-27). The name means "two encampments" and is derived from the meeting of Jacob with Esau on the former's return to Canaan: he prepared for the meeting by dividing the people, the flocks and the cattle into two separate groups (Gen. 32:3).

Mahaneh-dan (may´-a-neh-dan´), "The camp of Dan," where the tribe of Dan camped when seeking a new homeland (Jgs. 13:25; 18:12).

Maharai (may´-a-rie), One of the warriors of David known as The Thirty (2 Sam. 23:28; 1 Chron. 11:30; 27:13).

Mahath, A Levite who was active in the reforms of King Hezekiah (2 Chron. 29:12; 31:13).

Mahazioth (ma-hay´-zi-oth), A son of Heman, singer in the temple of Jerusalem (1 Chron. 25:4, 30).

Maher-shalal-hash-baz (may´-er-shal´-al-hash´-baz), "Speeds the spoils, hurries the prey," the symbolic name Isaiah gave his son. It signified the imminent ruin of Syria and Samaria, whose kings had invaded Judah to force King Ahaz into an alliance against Assyria (Isa. 8:1-4).

Mahlah (mah´-lah), One of the five daughters of Zelophehad (Num. 26:33; 27:1; 36:11). *See* INHERITANCE; ZELOPHEHAD.

Mahli (mah´-lie), Ancestor of a priestly family (Ex. 6:19; Num. 3:20; 26:58; Ezra 8:18).

Mahlon (mah´-lon), Son of Elimelech and Naomi, husband of Ruth (Ruth 1:2, 5; 4:9, 10).

Mahseiah (mah-see′-yah), The grandfather of Baruch (Jer. 32:12; Bar. 1:1). *See* BARUCH.

maid, maids

intercourse, then, with my *m*.		Your *m*. is in your power	
	Gen. 16:2		Gen. 16:6
Sarai took her *m*.	Gen. 16:3	her *m*. walked along the river	
gave my *m*. to your embrace			Ex. 2:5
	Gen. 16:5		

mail
arming him with a coat of *m*.   1 Sam. 17:38

maimed
blind or crippled or *m*.   Lev. 22:22   Better to enter life *m*.   Matt. 18:8
to enter life *m*.   Mk. 9:43

majesty

m., splendor, and glory		with grandeur and *m*.	Job 40:10.
	1 Chron. 29:11	*m*. and splendor you conferred	
God's awesome *m*.	Job 37:22		Ps. 21:6
	the splendor of his *m*. Isa. 2:19		

majority
inflicted by the *m*.   2 Cor. 2:6

make

Let us *m*. man in our image		*M*. yourself an ark	Gen. 6:14
	Gen. 1:26	*M*. an opening for daylight	
I will *m*. a suitable partner			Gen. 6:16
	Gen. 2:18	incense you shall *m*.	Ex. 30:1

Maked, A city in Gilead (1 Mac. 5:26, 36).

Makheloth (mak-he′-loth), A stage on the journey of the Israelites through the desert to Canaan (Num. 33:25-26).

Makkedah (mak-kee′-dah), A Canaanite city. The kings who had formed an alliance against Joshua took refuge there but they were captured and executed (Josh. 10:16-39). It was afterwards a city of Judah (Josh. 15:41).

Malachi (mal′-a-kie), The last of the minor prophets in the Hebrew canon of the Old Testament. The book is probably anonymous. Malachi is not a person's name, but has been taken from 3:1 which means "my messenger." The content of the book determines the epoch of the writer: it is later than the rebuilding of the Temple after the exile (516 B.C.; 1:10; 3:1, 10) and before the religious reforms of Ezra and Nehemiah, especially in regard to the problem of mixed marriage (2:10-16). It was, then, during the Persian period (1:8) at a time of depression and decadence which followed the enthusiasm inspired by Haggai and Zechariah. Now the Jewish community was in danger of losing its very identity.

The book consists of six discourses constructed in a similar manner, almost a dialogue. The prophet makes a statement which is challenged by the audience, priests and people, and finishes with a declaration of judgment or salvation. C. 1:2-5 is on the love of Yahweh and Israel; 1:6-2:9 reproves the priests; 2:10-16 condemns mixed marriages and divorces; 2:17-35 is about the Day of Yahweh; 3:6-12 of the offering of tithes; 3:12-21 deals with the triumph of the virtuous and the punishment of the ungodly; while 3:22-24 contains the conclusions.

The Day of Yahweh in 3:1-5 is the day of his coming to the Temple to judge and purify the priests. His coming will be anticipated by the arrival of his messenger, which 3:23 and the Jewish tradition identify with Elijah. Jesus declared that this hope was fulfilled in John the Baptizer (Matt. 11:10-14; *see* JOHN THE BAPTIZER, ELIJAH).

Malachi describes in 1:11 what the worship of Yahweh in messianic times will be like in contrast to the misdeeds of the contemporary priests. This prophecy, according to the Christian tradition and the Council of Trent, was fulfilled in the institution and celebration of the eucharist.

Malchijah (mal-kie′-jah), "The Lord is king," a common personal name in the Old Testament (1 Chron. 24:9; Ezra 10:25; Neh. 3:11, 14; 31; 8:4; 10:3; 12:42; Jer. 38:6).

Malchiram (mal-kie′-ram), A son of King Jehoiachin (1 Chron. 3:18).

Malchishua (mal′-ki-shoo′-a), A son of King Saul by his wife Ahinoam (1 Sam. 14:49; 31:2; 1 Chron. 10:2).

Malchus (mal′-kus), A servant of the high priest Caiaphas. At the arrest of Jesus, Peter drew his sword and cut off the man's right ear, but Jesus told Peter to desist, and touching the ear, healed the wound (Lk. 22:47-53).

male, males

m. and female he created	seven pairs, a *m.* and its mate
Gen. 1:27	Gen. 7:2
he created them *m.* and female	and all the *m.* Gen. 34:24
Gen. 5:2	every *m.* in it to the sword
	Deut. 20:13

mallet
took a *m.* in her hand   Jgs. 4:21

Mallothi (mal′-o-thie′), A son of Heman, singer in the temple of Jerusalem (1 Chron. 25:4).

Malluch (mal′-uk), Personal name (1 Chron. 6:29; Ezra 10:29, 32; Neh. 10:5, 28).

Mallus, A city in Cilicia (Asia Minor), which revolted against Antiochus IV Epiphanes (2 Mac. 4:30).

Malta, An island in the Mediterranean, south of Sicily, where the ship carrying Paul a prisoner to Rome ran aground and broke apart (Acts 27:39-28:1). They were received well by the local inhabitants and by the governor, Publius, whose sick father Paul cured. They remained there for three months (Acts 28:2-11). The point traditionally identified with Paul's landing is Paul's Bay on the northern coast of the island.

Mammon, An Aramaic word, used in some translations, meaning property, wealth. It is read in some statements of Jesus, with negative connotations, to condemn the almost idolatrous attachment to riches which is incompatible with the honor due to God (Matt. 6:24; Lk. 16:13). He calls it the "mammon of iniquity," or filthy lucre, to condemn the injustices that too often accompany riches (Luke 16:9-11).

Mamre (mam′-ri), A place near Hebron opposite the cave of Machpelah (Gen. 23:17; 25:9; 49:30; 50:13) where Abraham (Gen. 13:18; 18:1) and Isaac stayed (Gen. 35:27). A tradition going back to the 1st century identifies the place with today's Ramet-el-Khabil, two miles north of Hebron.

Man, The Bible views man more in an existentialist than in an essentialist way, that is, man is considered in the concrete, with his multiple relationships to the world, to his fellow man and to God, rather than in his essence. No attempt is made to define him or his various components, such as his nature, his body, soul or spirit. Biblical anthropology, then, is a series of factual assertions about man which are never subjected to philosophical analysis or reflection. For this reason one must not search in the Bible for a fixed and precise terminology: it is not there. (*See* SOUL, SPIRIT.) One must note first of all that the Bible sees man as a unity of body-soul without conceiving of any possible separation or opposition in concrete existence between the embodied soul or the animated body. From this arise the difficulties in translating such terms as **nephes**, "soul," and **basar**, "flesh," which for the Jew did not mean the different components of man, but rather as different aspects of the same individual. *See* FLESH, SOUL.

The first page of the Bible offers an insight that in fact conditions the whole biblical concept of man: he is created by God, and humanity is created as man and woman (*see* MARRIAGE; WOMAN), and as God's image Man is God's image because he is king of creation, that is, God's viceroy on earth and therefore lord of all inferior creatures. (*See* IMAGE OF GOD.) This "image," however, has also an aspect that is God-directed, for as God's vicar on earth, man is responsible to God, and can be involved in conversation with God in a dialogue that is the most profound dimension of his history.

The second account of creation (Gen. 2:4b-3) contains texts that are packed with biblical doctrine on man. In 2:7 the author uses the relationship between the word 'adam (man) and 'adamah (earth), a kind of pun, to give a profile of man's place in creation. Man is made from the dust of the earth. On the form thus shaped from the dust God breathed a breath of life, and thus we had a living person. All authors are agreed that one must not search in this text for the basis of a doctrine unforeseen by the author and outside his ken. The Bible neither favors nor contradicts the theory of evolution, for it is dealing with man on a different plane. The idea of man being formed from the earth is something also found among other ancient peoples. The conviction comes from elementary observation: after his death, man returns to dust. It also, however, shows a value judgment on man, that is, it shows the basis of man's fragility and inconsistency and so his absolute dependence on God who shaped him as a potter shapes his wares from clay : "Why are dust and ashes proud? Even during life man's body decays" (Sir. 10:9); "Like clay in the hands of a potter, to be molded according to his pleasure, so are men in the hands of their Creator, to be assigned by him their function" (Sir. 33:13; *see* also Isa. 29:15, 16; 45:9; 64:7; Jer. 18:1-12; Rom. 9:20-24). In speaking of his conception, Job addresses God: "Remember that you fashioned me from clay" (Job 10:9-12; 33:6). Man is dust; he is also tied with parental links to the 'adamah, the earth, which is his natural environment on which he depends. He is a "man of the earth from the earth."

On this "man," shaped from the dust of the earth, God breathes a breath of life, and thus man becomes a living person. This second step in man's formation has its deeper dimension. God is the unique and exclusive dispenser of life. God freely breathes the breath of life, and can withdraw it whenever he pleases (Job 34:14, 15; Ps. 104:27-30). God's breath animates everything that is alive, both men and animals (Job 27:3; 33:4; Isa. 42:5; 2 Kgs. 5:7).

Man is free and responsible, but not autonomous. Man's actual condition is one of trouble and sorrow, even burdened with pain when he carries out his essential functions of work in the earth and when woman fulfils her call to motherhood. The relationship between the sexes has been distorted (Gen. 3:15-19). All this however must not be blamed on the Creator. Man refused to obey, that is, to surrender himself to God's will for him. This will of God was not something that arose from caprice, nor a jealous retention of rights and privileges, but a design or plan inspired by God's goodness. If man had opened himself to God's design, then he would have enjoyed it. He detached himself from God, thus giving rise to death, for the only source of life is God. Man, in his fragility, carries around with him the seeds of his own destruction. *See* FALL, THE.

Man, moreover, is seen by the Bible, not in the abstract, but as part of a history and of a social group or community which in turn conditions his existence. Israel's nomadic past made the people particularly sensitive to this conditioning that took place through history and through the group. This self-awareness in the group, and its cohesion were the fruit of a common patrimony and a common destiny. It found its expression in particular literary genres, in genealogies and etiologies. These took on the particular form that their nomadic character dictated, but through them is had a permanently valid insight, something that today is called man's historicity. This means that the individual finds himself the heir to a past that is greater than he, and in which he is brother to his fellow man. This typical dimension of human existence is also taken account of in the divine saving initiative. Salvation is presented and actuated in history, and so it becomes something inherited. What is inherited, however, is the promise made to the forefathers, which points man to the future salvation pledged by God (Gen. 12:1-3).

The problem of man is taken up, without the typical historical framework of the author of Genesis 2-3, in Sirach 17. Here, too, the seer has universal horizons in that he speaks of man, of everyman. Man is earth, and therefore his days are numbered (*see* ECCLESIASTICUS), but he is also God's image, lord of creation, endowed with power so that other living creatures view him with awe: "God gave man authority over everything on earth" (2:4). Man has received from God wisdom to distinguish good from evil, to contemplate the works of God and praise him for them (17:5-9), but he also gave man a command which is summed up: "Avoid evil." Man's ways are clear and open to God, who is judge and rewarder (17:15-18). To every people God has given a ruler (the angels? *see* Deut. 32:8), but he has reserved Israel for himself (17:4).

This description of man is too empirical and without historical perspective. It is in contrast with Wisdom 1-5 which takes up the themes of Genesis 2-3. God made man for immortality: "the image of his own nature he made him," by making him to share in the immortal life of God. Death, then, is no work of God. Man himself brought death by allowing himself to be seduced by the devil. The doctrine of the resurrection (*see* RESURRECTION) opened up horizons that had remained hidden from the view of the Old Testament writers up till then. Thrown against these horizons, a new insight is gained into the actual condition of man. He is now enslaved to sin, mortality and corruptibility, but in him still there burns a longing for a better life, an afterlife with God. The passage from the one to the other is through the resurrection, which will take place when the eschatological events occur. This is the background against which the New Testament doctrine on man is understood.

The risen Christ is the new man, created in accordance with God's designs in justice and the holiness of truth (Eph. 4:24; 2:15). Every Christian at baptism takes on not only the likeness of Christ, but also the newness of his humanity (2 Cor. 5:17; Gal. 3:27). The risen Christ is thus the beginning of a new humanity, he is the new Adam (1 Cor. 15:49) to whose image we must allow ourselves to be shaped (1 Cor. 15:50) while ridding ourselves of the old humanity.

</>

The Christian is still living in the flesh, and belongs to this world, and is still subject to its corruptibility, but has "tasted the heavenly gift and become sharers in the Holy Spirit" (Heb. 6:4), and lives from the same vital source that animates the glorious humanity of Christ (Gal. 2:19-20). This life is a real thing, even if at the moment it remains hidden with Christ in God (Col. 3:3). It is not however something that grows automatically without involving the man himself. Here is at play the principle that governs the whole Pauline doctrine on the Christian reality, which might be summed up: become that which you are. Paul asserts that the baptized man already is a new creature, but this reality must reach out to involve the whole man until he is perfected.

"You form a building which rises on the foundation of the apostles and prophets, with Christ Jesus himself as a capstone. Through him the whole structure is fitted together and takes shape as a holy temple in the Lord; in him you are being built into this temple, to become a dwelling place for God in the Spirit" (Eph. 2:20-22).

Romans 7:22 and 2 Corinthians 4:16 speak of Paul's distinction between the "inner man" and the "outer man," that is, man's reasoning self and the vulnerable and mortal part of man. In Ephesians 3:16 and 2 Corinthians 4:16 the "inner man" is the man made new in the Christian sense.

Manaen (man'-a-en), One of the prophets and teachers in the church of Antioch, who had been brought up (or was an intimate friend, or courtier, depending on the meaning given the Greek **syntrophos**) by Herod Antipas (Acts 13:1). Some authors identify him with the son of Herod's employee who had been cured by Jesus (Jn. 4:46-54).

Manasseh (ma-nass'-eh), 1. First-born of Joseph, son of Jacob, brother of Ephraim, with whom he was adopted and blessed by Jacob. Jacob preferred Ephraim however to the first-born (Gen. 41:51; 46:20, 48). Manasseh is the founding father of the tribe of Manasseh. While Moses was still living, half of the tribe of Manasseh settled in Transjordan in the land of the kingdom of Og in Bashan (Num. 32:33-40; Deut. 3:13-14; Josh. 13:29-31). The other half established itself to the west of the Jordan, north of Ephraim (Josh. 17:7-13).

2. King of Judah (687-642 B.C.), son and successor of Hezekiah (2 Kgs. 20:21; 2 Chron. 32:33). He pursued a policy of friendship with the Assyrians which won him a precarious peace at the time of his accession. It had a very negative influence however on the cult of Yahweh, for vassalage to Assyria also obligated one to the official introduction of Assyrian cult into one's country. Manasseh introduced it to Jerusalem for which he merited a most severe reprimand (2 Kgs. 21:1-7 and 2 Chron. 33:1-10). 2 Chronicles 33:11-20 tells of Manasseh's imprisonment in Assyria and of his conversion and penance. This information is legendary, and gave rise to the "Prayer of Manasseh," an apocryphal writing which was often printed in the Vulgate editions of the Bible.

Mandrake, The botanist's **Mandragora officinarum** which is an herb with large green leaves and a small berry like a plum. It is very common in Syria and of old was considered an aphrodisiac. This is reflected in the story of Rachel and Leah in Genesis 30:14-16, while the Song of Songs sings of the fragrance of the mandrakes (7:14), though the smell would not be considered sweet in the West.

Manger, The new-born Jesus was placed in a manger (Lk. 2:7) from which animals were wont to eat (*see* Lk. 13:15). The tradition about Jesus being born in a cave dates from at least the second century. It was not unusual for people to take advantage of a natural covering, such as a cave, in which to house and feed the animals. The dwelling would then be built on top of the cave. It is possible that the stable was the lower part of a built structure, in which people inhabited the raised portion. Remains of mangers found at Megiddo (*see* MEGIDDO) show them to be carved out of stone, three feet long, eighteen inches wide and two feet deep. They could also be carved out of the walls of the cave, or could be built with masonry. The wooden relics of the manger preserved in the Basilica of St. Mary Major in Rome are from a later epoch.

manger

the nights by your *m*.	Job 39:9	in a *m*. you will find	Lk. 2:12
laid him in a *m*.	Lk. 2:7	baby lying in the *m*.	Lk. 2:16

Manna, A resinous substance which exudes from the **Tamarix mannifera,** a bush that is very common in the southern desert, and which is used even today for food purposes. The Bible tradition records the use of this food, which was hitherto unknown, as a particular sign of the providence of God towards his pilgrim people on their desert journey to Canaan.

Tradition has added particulars that underline the supernatural and providential character of the event. According to Exodus 16:31-35 the manna was like coriander seed, white in color and sweet to the taste. It fell each day of the week with the exception of the Sabbath The Israelites lived off this food during their forty years in the desert (*see* also Num. 11:7-8; Deut. 8:3-16; Ps. 78:24).

In John 6:32-34, 49-51 manna is a type of the eucharist. What the Jews called bread from heaven was not the true bread from heaven. This bread is Jesus himself, the gift of God for the life of the world (Jn. 6:35). The discourse becomes more precisely eucharistic as it continues on (Jn. 6:49-53).

Hebrews 9:4 and Revelation 2:17 allude to a tradition of dubious historical value, which is also mentioned in Exodus 16:33, namely, that a container filled with manna was preserved in the ark of the covenant.

Manoah (ma-no′-ah), Father of the judge Samson. He was "a man of Zorah of the tribe of Dan" (Jgs. 13:2). The angel of the Lord appeared to his barren wife to tell her she was to conceive a boy who would be a nazirite from his mother's womb. When Manoah heard this, he pleaded with the Lord for instructions on how to bring up this boy. Another apparition occurred in which Manoah was told to keep the boy from wine and strong drink and anything unclean. When Manoah wished to offer hospitality to his divinely sent guest, the latter suggested that a sacrifice be offered instead, and when Manoah asked his name, he answered that it was a mystery. As the flame of the holocaust ascended to Yahweh, the angel ascended in the flame. So a child was born to Manoah and his wife, and they called him Samson (Jgs. 13).

mantle

a beautiful Babylonian *m*.		a loose end of his *m*.	1 Sam. 15:27
	Josh. 7:21	Elijah took his *m*.	2 Kgs. 2:8

Manuscripts, *See* TEXT, OLD TESTAMENT AND NEW TESTAMENT.

many

m. of them will be struck		you have instructed *m*.	Job. 4:3
	Ex. 19:21	how *m*. are my adversaries	Ps. 3:2
has given me *m*. sons		Behold, my enemies are *m*.	
	1 Chron. 28:5		Ps. 25:19
among the *m*. nations	Neh. 13:26		
		downfall and the rise of *m*.	Lk. 2:34

Maoch (may′-ok), The father of Achish, king of the Philistine city of Gath (1 Sam. 27:2).

Maon (may′ on), A city of Judah (Josh. 15:55), the home of Nabal, who refused to help David and his men while they were avoiding Saul. His wife Abigail cleverly and graciously succeeded in averting David's revenge. Nabal died soon, and David married Abigail (1 Sam. 25).

Marah (mar′-ah), A stage on the journey of the Israelites from Egypt to Sinai. The bitter waters of the local springs (from which it gets the name Marah, which means bitter) were sweetened by Moses through a divine intervention (Ex. 15:23-26; Num. 33:8).

Maranatha (mar′-a-nath′-a), An Aramaic expression that can mean, depending on the division of the words one chooses, either "The Lord comes" (maran 'atha') or "Come! Lord!" (marana' tha'). The latter is the preferable translation according to Revelation 22:20. (It is also read at the end of 1 Cor. 16:22). It was therefore a liturgical exclamation that passed also into the Greek churches, probably in the rite of celebration of the eucharist (*see* 1 Cor. 11:26) The exclamation **marana' tha'** expresses the pent-up yearning of the community for the glorious return of Christ, of which the eucharistic celebration is a pledge and a beginning.

marble

quantities of *m*.	1 Chron. 29:2	His legs are columns of *m*.
rings on *m*. pillars	Est. 1:6	S. of S. 5:15

Marcion (mar′-shon), A heretic of the second century (died around 160 A.D.), son of the bishop of Sinope in Pontus (Asia Minor). Marcion began with an erroneous interpretation of Luke 6:43 and 5:36-38 to conclude that the Old and the New Testament were inalterably opposed to one another. The Old Testament for Marcion was the work of God the Just, but not of God the Good and Father of Jesus Christ. According to Marcion only Paul has preserved the true doctrine of Jesus. The other Apostles have recast the gospel in Judaic terms. The authentic gospel is found in Luke and ten of Paul's epistles. Marcion's heresy was important in that it accelerated the formulation of the canon of the New Testament, even though he was not its creator. Indeed his doctrinal position cannot be explained if it is not supposed that he had at hand a collection of apostolic writings which were looked upon as having divine authority and origin.

Marduk, A deity of the city of Babylon who became chief in the Mesopotamian pantheon when Babylon became capital and center of the empire of Hammurabi. Marduk at that time inherited the functions, titles and attributes of the Creator-God Enlil. The poem **Enuma-Elish**, the so-called poem of creation, is in reality the mythical account of the enthroning of Marduk as head of all the gods of the universe following his victory over Tiamat and Apsu, who were the gods of the abysses. *See* CREATION.

Mareal (mar′-e-al), A city in the territory of Zebulun (Josh. 19:11).

Maresha (ma-ree′-sha), 1. Caleb's first-born (1 Chron. 2:42).

2. A town of Judah (Josh. 15:44) fortified by Rehoboam (2 Chron. 11:8). Here Asa of Judah (912-871 B.C.) blocked the army of the Ethiopian Zerah of Gerar (2 Chron. 14:9-14). Maresha figures again in the story of the Maccabees when it was under the dominion of the Seleucids of Gorgias (2 Mac. 12:35). Today it is Tell-Sandahannah.

Mari, A city of Mesopotamia on the western bank of the Euphrates, today Tell-Hariri. It is not mentioned in the Bible. Excavations carried out since 1933 have uncovered ruins of the royal palace of Zimrilin, king of the city and contemporary of Hammurabi of Babylon. Around 20,000 tablets from the royal archives have also come to light, giving a new insight into the the history of the Middle East in the second millenium B.C.

mariners
to be your *m.*   Ezek. 27:8

Mark, John Mark, cousin of Barnabas and son of Mary, in whose house the Christian community in Jerusalem used to gather (Acts 12:12; Col. 4:10). Mark accompanied Paul and Barnabas on their first apostolic journey, but he abandoned them at Perga in Pamphylia (Acts 12:25-13:13). After the council of Jerusalem Barnabas wished once more to take his cousin Mark along, but Paul opposed this on account of Mark's previous conduct. The outcome was that Paul started out with Silas and Mark accompanied Barnabas to Cyprus (Acts 15:37). Mark was nevertheless with Paul in Rome when the latter wrote the letters to Philemon and to the Colossians (Philem. 24; Col. 4:10). In 2 Timothy 4:11 Paul requests that Mark come to him, for he found him a useful helper in his work. According to 1 Peter 5:13 Mark was with Peter in Rome. Peter calls him "my son Mark." Tradition has it that after Peter's martyrdom Mark departed for Alexandria where he founded a church of which he was the first bishop. Tradition also attributes to him the composition of the second gospel. *See* MARK, GOSPEL OF.

Mark, Gospel of, The ancient tradition of the Church is unanimous in attributing the second of the canonical gospels to John Mark. The most ancient evidence is from the beginning of the second century: Papias, bishop of Hierapolis in Phrygis, who lived at the time of the Emperor Hadrian (117-138 A.D.), hands down with a comment the words of John the Elder, according to whom "Mark, Peter's interpreter, carefully wrote down whatever he recalled of the things said and done by the Lord, but without order." Papias attributes this "disorder" in reporting to the fact that Mark never saw or heard the Lord but depended on Peter's preaching for what he wrote down. The same tradition is read in other witnesses of the second century (Irenaeus, Muratorian Canon, and probably also in the "Memories of Peter," quoted by Justin Martyr, Dial. 106, 3, which seem to refer to Mark), and of the third century (Clement of Alexandria and Origen, of whom the former asserted that the gospel was read and approved by Peter).

This tradition is commonly accepted by the critics and no internal reason weakens it. The connection with Peter's preaching is not to be taken in too exclusive or direct a sense. Even if some internal indications seem to confirm a dependence on Peter's preaching, it is also obvious that Mark did not limit himself simply to what Peter preached.

Mark's gospel is addressed to the Christians of the Hellenistic churches, as can be deduced from his care to translate the most typically Jewish terms, which would not be at all familiar to non-Jews, or to render Aramaic words into Greek (*see* 2:26; 3:17; 5:41; 7:34; etc.).

The most ancient tradition, that of Irenaeus and Clement of Alexandria, add that Mark wrote in Rome or Italy. A later tradition of John Chrysostom has it that Mark wrote at Alexandria, but this is explained from a confusion that arose between this and the tradition that Mark was the founder and first bishop of the church in that city.

Except for Clement of Alexandria, the other witnesses seem to insinuate that Mark wrote after Peter's death. The sobriety of details in which Mark cites Jesus' prophecy on the destruction of Jerusalem and the Temple would seem to suggest that the book was written before that event (70

A.D.; Mark 13), though some scholars prefer a slightly later date. It was, however, written before the other synoptics, Matthew and Luke, took their present shape.

Mark's gospel, in contrast with the other three, confines itself to the apostolic kerygma (*see* Acts 1:22; 20:37-42) and begins with the ministry of John the Baptizer, the theophany that took place at Jesus' baptism and his solemn messianic investiture, together with a brief reference to his temptations in the desert (1:1-13). The first part of the gospel contains three cycles which begin with general and summary accounts of Jesus' activities, followed by the accounts of the vocation or mission of the disciples (1:14-20; 3:7-19; 6:6-13).

The first cycle, which begins with 1:21-39, could be titled "The Day at Capernaum." It knits together in a perfect chronological and topographical sequence the different episodes. It begins with the preaching in the synagogue at Capernaum (1:21-28), then follows the cure of Peter's mother-in-law (1:29-31), the confluence of sick at the door after sundown, and Jesus' departure for other destinations (1:32-39). The cure of the leper is told apart (1:40-45).

The second section is an account of five controversies that illustrate the points of contrast and friction between Jesus and various Jewish groups. These are arrayed in a mounting tension that climaxes with the Pharisees' decision to do away with Jesus (3:6). This section seems to be a previous collection, drawn on by Mark, composed precisely to show the way in which the contrast between Jesus and the religious heads of the Jews reached such incurable proportions that they decided to condemn Jesus. In the second section, 3:19-35 is very much like 2:1-3:6. It gathers together "the accusations brought against Jesus" (*see* 3:21; 3:22), fitted in between the presence of Jesus' mother and his relatives at the beginning and the end (3:21, 31).

There follows the discourse in parables (4:1-33) and the section 4:35-5:43, which for its unity makes one think of 1:21-39. There is a series of incidents, even though they are not related to one another: the storm at sea (4:35-41), the cure of the demoniac at Gerasa (5:1-20), of the woman with the hemorrhage and of the daughter of Jairus (5:21-43). The second cycle concludes with the rejection of Jesus by the people of his own village (6:1-6a).

There is an interlude to recount the death of John the Baptizer (6:14-29) and then the third cycle begins. This contains two passages that parallel one another, following the same plan: 1. The multiplication of bread (6:30-44; 8:1-9). 2. The return journey by sea (6:45-52; 8:10). 3. The discourse with the Pharisees (7:1-23; 8:11-13). 4. Journeys (7:24-30; 8:14-21). 5. Two very similar miracles (7:31-37; 8:22-26). It is a question of the same scheme of things filled out with analogous material. The center of cohesion is the miracle of the multiplication of bread (and the subsequent journeys on the lake). This is again recorded in 8:14-21, which might explain why it is recorded on two different occasions as if there were two different incidents.

The second part of the ministry of Jesus (8:27-9:52) is of a different character. Jesus almost always appears alone with his disciples, who follow him. Jesus is no longer the itinerant preacher wandering through Galilee: now he is on his way from Galilee, through Peraea and Judea, up to Jerusalem. And the tenor of the journey is given in the three announcements of his forthcoming passion which he gives along the way; 8:31-33; 9:30-32; 10:32-34. The first is at Caesarea Philippi, the second in Galilee, and the third as they go up to Jerusalem.

Jerusalem is the scene of the third part. In 11:1-25 is described Jesus' solemn entry into the city and the subsequent events, his teachings, the five controversies, which form a group like those of 2:1-3:6. Then comes the apocalyptic discourse to the disciples alone (c. 13).

The fourth part is taken up with the account of the Passion, the climax to the whole gospel, and towards which the gospel since 3:6 has been pointing. This climax of course includes the discovery of the empty tomb together with its angelic interpretation: Jesus is risen.

A problem surrounds the conclusion of the gospel, for in some manuscripts it finishes with 16:8, while other manuscripts contain the ending we find today in it. The present conclusion is inspired and canonical, but there is no certainty that it is Mark's work. All the indications are that Mark brought his book to a close in v. 8 and that later this conclusion seemed too abrupt and a more fitting ending was added. The actual conclusion is nothing more than a summary of the apparitions of Jesus recounted in the other gospels.

marketplace
standing around the *m*.   Matt. 20:3

Maroth, A city of Judah (Mic. 1:12).

Marriage, The story of creation in Genesis 2 tells us that God did not make man to be alone. In the popular imagery of the Yahwist account, God said: "It is not good for the man to be alone" (2:18). God paraded all living creatures before Adam so that he could exercise his dominion over them by giving them their names, and thus, too, their places in the created order of things. (*See* NAME.) There was found, however, no one like to himself (2:19, 20). God therefore induced a deep sleep in Adam, and from his ribs shaped for him a woman, whom he presented to Adam's delighted, waking eyes (vv. 22, 23).

The epilogue to the story is: "That is why a man leaves his father and mother and clings to his wife, and the two of them become one body" (v. 24). This is not a continuation of the first man's speech, but rather a conclusion interpolated by the narrator. The conclusion gives an inkling of why the story was told. It offers an explanation in terms of the original facts, for the strength of love (*see* S. of S. 8:6), the drive of sex and the meaning of marriage.

Marriage is clearly monogamous in this account. Christ referred back to this original design of God for marriage in Matthew when he spoke against divorce. He asserts that Moses, on account of their hardness of heart, allowed the Jews to divorce their wives "but it was not so from the beginning." Paul reiterates this doctrine (1 Cor. 7:10-11).

Despite this ideal from the very beginning, polygamy soon appeared in Cain's family: one of his descendants, Lamech, took to wife Adah and Zillah. Abraham, the father of the faith, had Sarah to wife, but also had a son from Sarah's slave, Hagar, with Sarah's consent (Gen. 16:1-2). Genesis 25:6 speaks of the sons of Abraham's concubines.

Jacob had two sisters, Leah and Rachel, to wife (Gen. 29:15-30). When Rachel proved barren, she gave Jacob Bilhah, her maid, so that through her he could present Rachel with a child (Gen. 30:1-8). When Leah passed child-bearing age, she too gave Jacob her maid Zillah from whom to have children (Gen. 30:9-13). Judges 8:30 tells us that Gideon had seventy sons, his own offspring, for he had many wives, and a concubine in Shechem (8:31). Deuteronomy even has legislation that envisages the rivalries that could arise between different wives and their offspring (Deut. 21:15-17).

Among the kings, Saul had wives (2 Sam. 12:8) and a concubine (2 Sam. 3:7). David had six wives in Hebron (2 Sam. 3:2-5) and many more in Jerusalem (2 Sam. 5:13; 2 Sam. 19:6). Absalom, to assert his partial victory in putting David to flight from the Holy City, and on Ahithophel's advice, publicly took his father's ten concubines, whom David had left in the city to look after the palace (2 Sam. 15:16; 16:21-23). Rehoboam had eighteen wives and sixty concubines, from whom he had twenty-eight sons and sixty daughters (2 Chron. 11:21). 2 Chron. 13:21 states that Abijah grew powerful and took fourteen wives, from whom he had twenty-two sons and sixteen daughters. The number of wives and concubines was a sign of power and glory.

Solomon's love became proverbial. He loved many women, according to 1 Kings 11:1-13, not only Pharaoh's daughter, but Moabites, Edomites, Sidonians, and Hittites. He had a reported seven hundred wives of royal rank and three hundred concubines. However exaggerated these reports, his multiple wives, from many cultures, were also his undoing when he grew old, for they perverted his heart to worship Astarte and Milcom, the Sidonian and Ammonite divinities respectively.

At first sight it seems surprising that David, the ideal king and inspiration of the many messianic hopes, and Abraham himself, should in their lives have contradicted the clearly taught monogamism of Genesis 2:24. At the beginning the barrenness of the wife is given as the reason for taking the maid (Abraham and Hagar, Gen. 23:1-2; Jacob, Rachel and Bilhah 30:1-9), but these did not become wives. The Code of Hammurabi (around 1700 B.C.) and the region of Kirkuk (1500 B.C.) only entitled the husband to a second wife when the first proved barren, but in Hammurabi's Code he could not do so if the wife provided him with a slave as a concubine. The moral practice of the semi-bedouin patriarchs was considerably looser than in these regions,

One must not, however, expect the revelation of God to bring about a violent rupture with the ethical and cultural environment in which it is received. God's word is like rain and snow that comes down from the heavens and does not return without watering the earth. It works away in a hidden fashion until eventually the fields yield seed and wheat (Isa. 55:10). God's word is a promise and guarantee of a future and strength, to those who receive it, to walk towards that future, and eventually enjoy it fully. Paul is at great pains to point out that Abraham, for instance, had no merits to fall back on, for reliance. His great lesson to mankind was that of faith, or self-opening, so that God could lead him out and make him the father of the nations (*see* Rom. 4). One must not then search for today's morality in all its details from these heroes of the past: they taught the succeeding generations by putting their hope in the future of God's promise.

In ancient Bible times it was possible to have a love-marriage. When Saul did not fulfil his promise to give his daughter Merab to David as a wife, the story states: "Now Saul's daughter Michal loved David" (1 Sam. 18:20). Saul tried to use this love as a lever to get David to endanger himself at the hand of the Philistines, hoping David would be killed. David however defeated his hopes by coming back victorious and so married Michal (1 Sam. 18:27). As it turned out, this marriage was an unhappy one (*see* 2 Sam. 6:22). As a rule however marriages were arranged, which is understandable when it is borne in mind that, as far as can be deduced through careful calculation, children married while they were still in their early teens. Ishmael's mother arranged her son's wedding by choosing a wife for him (Gen. 21:21), as did Judah for Er, his first-born (Gen. 38:6), and Hamor for his son Shechem (Gen. 34:4-6).

When a marriage was arranged, the amount of the **mohar** was discussed. The **mohar** was the dowry, or alternatively, as in the case of Jacob (Gen. 29:15-30) the service given by the fiancé to the financée's father (*see* Gen. 34:12; Ex. 22:16; 1 Sam. 18:25). If the marriage was a compulsory one after a virgin had been violated, "the man who had relations with her shall pay the girl's father fifty silver shekels and take her as his wife, because he had deflowered her. Moreover, he may not divorce her as long as he lives" (Deut. 22:29). Since this was a fine as well as a **mohar**, the ordinary one must have been less. Although the husband is the **ba'al** or lord or proprietor of the wife, (Ex. 21:3, 22; 2 Sam. 11:26; Gen. 20:3; Deut. 22:22, etc.), the wife was not common chattel bought on the level of a concubine (Ex. 21:7-11), and the **mohar** was probably returned to the daughter when her father or her husband died.

Close relations could and did marry, but marriages also took place between different families, and with non-Israelite women, although this often led to conflict as when Moses married Zipporah the Midianite (Ex. 2:21) and occasioned the rancor of Miriam and Aaron (Num. 12:1) while Solomon's foreign wives are the cause of his religious downfall (1 Kgs. 11:1 ff.). This too was the fate of Ahab (869-850 B.C.) who married Jezebel, daughter of Ethbaal king of the Sidonians, and then proceeded to serve Baal and worship him (1 Kgs. 16:31). Ezra, concerned for the religious purity of those recently returned from exile, dissolved the marriages with foreigners and ordered that they should not take place any more (Ezra 9:1, 11).

An engagement took place, during which the boy and girl were promised to one another, and the **mohar** was paid in money or in kind. Deuteronomy 20:7 and 22:23-27 has special legislation for the betrothed. For the betrothed to engage in carnal commerce with another man was a crime punishable by death (Deut. 22:23, 24), and the reason is given that she is another man's wife (v. 24). Unchastity between betrothed couples was not fornication in the full and flagrant sense of the term, since the parties were already pledged to one another.

Although no mention of it has come down in the Bible, other evidence leads one to the conclusion that a formal marriage contract was drawn. From the Jewish colony at Elephantine in the fifth century B.C. there are several contracts, in which the formula, in the husband's name is: "She is my wife and I am her husband, from this day forever," while the bride made no statement.

The marriage was carried out with great ceremony. The bridegroom went with his friends and a band to the house of the bride where she, veiled, waited for him. Richly bedecked, she set out with her companions to the house of the bridegroom (S. of S. 3:11; 4:1, 3; 6:7; Ps. 45; Isa. 61:10). Songs in praise of the pair were sung. The feast might go on for seven days (Gen. 29:27; Jgs. 14:12) or even for two weeks (Tob. 8:20; 10:7). The marriage was consummated that first night (Gen. 29:23; Tob. 8:1) and the evidence of the bride's virginity preserved against slander (Deut. 22:13-21).

A man could divorce his wife by writing her a declaration: "for she is not my wife, and I am not her husband" (Hos. 2:4), or "I hate (i.e. do not love any more) my wife." Few were the women whose marriage was protected by the law: the woman whose husband had accused her of not being a virgin on the night of the marriage (Deut. 22:13-19) and the woman who, as a virgin, has been raped, and her attacker forced to marry her (Deut. 22:29). A woman could not divorce her husband.

Marriage itself was protected by the death penalty against adulterers (Lev. 20:10; Deut. 22:22), and as we have seen, this held even if the girl was only engaged when she betrayed her husband-to-be (Deut. 22:23 ff.). The penalty was by stoning or burning alive (Gen. 38:24; Deut. 22:23 f.; Ezek. 16:40; Jn. 8:5). Commentators think it doubtful whether in later times this law was enforced with rigor. It is to be noted that the husband was punished only when he infringed another man's rights by having relations with the latter's wife or fiancée, but otherwise he was much less harshly treated than the wife (Prov. 5:15-19).

In the Sermon on the Mount Jesus recalls marriage to its pristine ideal: "everyone who divorces his wife—lewd conduct is a separate case—forces her to commit adultery. The man who marries a divorced woman likewise commits adultery" (Matt. 5:31, 32). At the beginning of the fifth section of Matthew's gospel, the question on marriage is again introduced when the Pharisees asked Jesus to resolve the discussion between the rabbinical school of Hillel, which would permit divorce for any reason whatsoever, and that of Shammai, which would permit it only for adultery (Matt. 19:1 ff.). Jesus once more answers that to break up a marriage sealed by God, except in the case of fornication, would be tantamount to adultery. This exception about 'lewd conduct' does not appear in Mark's text (Mark 10:2-12). The word, **porneia**, means prostitution, unchastity, fornication, or any kind of unlawful sexual intercourse, even adultery in Sirach 23:23. Jesus seems to be saying that a man can dismiss a woman with whom he is living in concubinage. Yet Jesus is quite clearly undercutting the discussion between the rabbinical schools of interpretation to reinstate the original marriage ideal, so he cannot be interpreted as conceding that Shammai is correct. The Church has interpreted this to mean the exclusion of divorce from every marriage that is a sacrament and as such consummated. When this is the case, even should the marriage break up so that the husband and wife no longer live together, they are still bound not to marry.

Paul too interprets Christ's doctrine (*see* 1 Cor. 7:10, 12) to the exclusion of remarriage even if a husband and wife must depart from one another. Divorce therefore, in the full sense of leaving the parties free to enter another marriage, is excluded on the Lord's authority. Paul however does make an exception in favor of the faith, which is the higher good, in the famous Pauline privilege. He states that in the case of a marriage between an unbeliever and a Christian, should the parties be content to live together peacefully, then they should continue to do so, and thus the Christian member becomes a means of sanctification for the non-Christian party, and for the children of the union (1 Cor. 7:12, 14). Should the unbeliever however not consent to this, then they should separate, and the Christian party is not any longer tied to the marriage, but is free to remarry for "God has called you to live in peace" (1 Cor. 7:15).

Many have taxed Paul with a very poor image of marriage, and certainly there are more glowing pages to be found on it as an institution in non-Christian writers of the era such as Musonius Rufus than here in 1 Corinthians. However this passage is in answer to specific questions placed to him by the Corinthians: "Now for the matters you wrote about" (1 Cor. 7:1) and the answers are given from a definite point of view, namely that of the coming Parousia. To what Paul here writes (which, to be noted, gives to wives equal rights in marriage with the husband, and protects these rights) must be added what is found in Ephesians 5:25. There marriage is seen in the beauty of creative love to be an image of the much deeper mystery in which it shares, that of Christ's creative intimacy with the Church. The beauty of marital love evokes for Paul the wonder of Christ's espoused love for the Church, and he exhorts husbands to "love their wives as they do their own bodies. He who loves his wife loves himself. Observe that no one ever hates his own flesh; no, he nourishes it and takes care of it as Christ cares for the church—for we are members of his body" (Eph. 5:28-29).

Paul was here re-echoing an image dear to the prophets. Hosea the prophet got a command from the Lord to marry a whore and have children by her (Hosea 1:2). In this way God wanted to bring home by shattering symbolism what his spouse, Israel, had done to him. Even though God bitterly denounces, through Hosea, the people's unfaithfulness, the prophecy is not realized; God's faithfulness and loyalty overcome his anger and he states: "So I will allure her, I will lead her into the desert and speak to her heart. . . . I will espouse you to me forever; I will espouse you in right and in justice, in love and in mercy; I will espouse you in fidelity and you shall know the Lord" (Hos. 2:16, 21, 22; Jer. 31).

Marriage in the new Covenant is a sacrament instituted by Christ, to maintain, in the living evidence of the flesh, the evidence of his love for the Church. One interpretation of Matthew 19:22, sees in the "some . . . who have freely renounced sex for the sake of God's reign," those who, through no fault of their own, are in broken marriages, but who, nevertheless, for the sake of the kingdom, and to symbolize God's unshakable loyalty even to a disloyal people, refuse to remarry.

Marsena (mar-see′-na), A prince of Media and Persia during the reign of Ahasuerus (Esth. 1:14).

Mars' Hill, This is how the King James Version translates **Areios pagos**, the Areopagus, the hill south of the Agora in Athens, which also became the name of the Athenian city council which sat there. Paul was brought there to explain his doctrine, either to the council or in that place. Luke comments that the chief amusement around Athens was discussing the latest ideas and listening to lectures about them (Acts 17:19-21).

Martha, Sister of Mary and Lazarus, of Bethany. While she was busy with the serving, her sister sat at the Lord's feet listening. When Martha complained that she was left alone to do the serving, she received the celebrated reply contained in Luke 10:41, 42. (*See* Jn. 11:1-12.)

Martyr, A transcription from the Greek **martus** which means witness. In the New Testament the term does not yet have the meaning it was later to acquire, and that it retains today, namely, one who sheds his blood in witness to the faith. Nevertheless this meaning was foreshadowed in such texts as Acts 22:20 and Revelation 2:13; 17:6. *See* WITNESS.

Mary, From the Greek **Mariam,** the Latin **Maria,** a transcription from the Hebrew **Miryam.**

1. *See* MIRIAM.

2. Mary, the mother of Jesus. According to Luke 1:26, Mary was from Nazareth and a cousin of Elizabeth, Zechariah's wife and mother of John the Baptizer (Lk. 1:40), and, like her, also perhaps of priestly lineage (Lk. 1:5). In this case the Davidic descent of Jesus would be adoptive, through Joseph (Matt. 1:20). In the story of the Annunciation Luke underscores Mary's faith (Lk. 1:26-28) which stands in bold contrast to the incredulity of Zechariah, who for this was punished by the angel with the loss of his speech (Lk. 1:20). Mary became the fiancée of Joseph, but before they lived together, Mary conceived through the overshadowing of the Holy Spirit (Matt. 1:18-25). Jesus was born at Bethlehem, where Mary and Joseph had gone to fulfil the requirements of the census ordered by Augustus (Lk. 2:1-7). In the infancy narrative of Matthew, Mary has a

secondary place compared to Joseph, except in the visit of the Magi where the presence of Joseph is passed over in silence (*see* Matt. 1:18; 2:13, 14; 2:21; 2:11). With Luke however Joseph is of secondary importance. Mary's words in Luke's account, besides her conversation with the angel Gabriel, include the Magnificat, the hymn of thanksgiving which draws liberally on Anna's hymn of thanksgiving in 1 Samuel 2:1-10 (*see* MAGNIFICAT), and the words she addressed to Jesus when he remained behind in the Temple (Lk. 2:49). Otherwise Mary is pictured by Luke in silent reflection mingled with wonderment at the mystery of Jesus unfolding before her very eyes (Luke 2:19; 2:33; 2:48; 2:51).

The references to Mary in the rest of the New Testament are very few. Jesus is called "the son of Mary" (Mark 6:3; Matt. 13:55; *see* BROTHERS OF THE LORD). Mark 3:31 (Matt. 12:46-50; Lk. 8:19-21) recounts the only meeting between Jesus and his mother during the public ministry that is recorded in the synoptic tradition. Jesus' answer on this occasion could cause wonder: he underlines on what level are the relationships with him that count, that is, on the level of obedience to God. This answer is an echo of the answer that he gave to Joseph and Mary in Luke 2:49 which expressed an uncompromising detachment when it was a question of his mission. The same principle inspires the answer Jesus gave to Mary at the wedding feast of Cana in Galilee (Jn. 2:1-11). This account has two seemingly contrasting sections: the refusal to take Mary's request into consideration is followed by the miracle of the changing of the water into wine, to an extent that went beyond the request. The first refusal however is qualified with the words: "My hour has not yet come." Jesus' hour is that of his death and exaltation. Does his refusal, thus qualified, mean that Mary would have a part in his work when the hour came? It is significant that John is the only evangelist that speaks of Mary's presence at the foot of the cross (Jn. 19:25) where she received from the dying Jesus the mandate to treat his beloved disciple as a son, while to John was confided Mary as a mother. It is obvious that John here intends more than a mere testamentary disposition on the part of Jesus so that his mother might be cared for. At this moment Jesus established between Mary and the "disciple whom he loved" a relationship of motherhood and sonship that was somehow involved in his redemptive work. Tradition has rightly seen in this the biblical foundation for the parallelism between Eve and Mary, often dwelt on by the Fathers. Mary is the new Eve, that is, "the mother of the living," that is, of the new humanity created by Christ's redemptive act. Mary is with the Apostles in the upper room (Acts 1:14) during the days that followed Jesus' ascension. Paul's only allusion to Mary, without naming her, is in Galatians 4:4 where the Apostle wishes to underline the reality of the incarnation. In Revelation 12:1-6, the "woman clothed with the sun, with the moon under her feet and on her head a crown of twelve stars" is traditionally thought to be Mary. Another tradition that is not very secure tells us that Mary finished her earthly journey in Ephesus.

3. **Mary Magdalene,** that is from Magdala, a village on the west coast of the Lake of Gennesaret. According to Mark 16:9 and Luke 8:2 Jesus had driven out of Mary Magdalene seven demons. Mary Magdalene is among the women who accompanied Jesus to provide for his needs (Lk. 8:2) and later she is among the women who assisted from afar at his crucifixion (Matt. 27:56; Mk. 15:40; Jn. 19:25), and at his burial (Matt. 27:61; Mk. 15:47). On the morning of the third day she was among those who discovered the tomb open and empty (Matt. 28:1-10; Mk. 16:1; Lk. 24:10). Matthew 28:9-10 speaks of a vision the women saw while they were returning from the tomb. The discovery of the empty tomb is described in detail by John 20:1-18 (*see* Mk. 16:9). In this account Mary Magdalene plays a part of prime importance. She went to the tomb alone and found

that the stone which had closed the tomb had been rolled away. Then she ran to announce this to Simon Peter and the disciple whom Jesus loved, and all together they went to the tomb to verify it. Mary stayed on at the tomb weeping when a person, whom she took for the gardner, addressed her. When she offered to take the body away, the person addressed her: "Mary," whereupon she recognized him. Jesus told her not to cling to him but to announce his resurrection to the brethren.

Mary Magdalene is frequenty identified but without any reason with the woman who was a sinner in the city and who came to weep at Jesus' feet during the banquet offered by Simon (Lk. 7:36-50). Neither is Mary Magdalene to be identified with Mary of Bethany, sister of Martha and Lazarus (Jn. 12:3-8).

4. Mary of Bethany, sister of Martha and of Lazarus. Jesus stayed at their house. While Martha was busy serving, Mary sat at the Lord's feet listening to his words. Martha complained that she was being left to do the serving by herelf while her sister sat around. Jesus gave the surprising and celebrated answer: "Martha, Martha, you are anxious and upset about many things; one thing only is required. Mary has chosen the better portion and she shall not be deprived of it" (Lk. 10:38-42). The two sisters sent a message to Jesus that Lazarus was ill, and gently reproved Jesus for not arriving in time (Jn. 11). Mary anointed Jesus with very costly ointment, drawing the criticism of the disciples (Matt. 26:8, 9) and particularly of Judas (Jn. 12:4, 5) who thought that the ointment should have been sold and the money given to the poor. Jesus again defended her and immortalized her name by proclaiming that what she had done for him would be announced wherever the gospel was preached in remembrance of her (Matt. 26:13). Mary's name does not appear in the account in Matthew 26:6-13 and Mark 14:3-9, but the parallel story of John 12:3-8 identifies the woman. On the customary identification with Mary Madalene *see* MARY 3.

5. Mary the wife of Clopas; she stood at the foot of the cross with the mother of Jesus (Jn. 19:25) and is probably to be identified with Mary the mother of James and of Joses, mentioned in the parallel passage of Mark 15:40, 47 and in the discovery of the empty tomb in Luke 24:10; Mark 16:1.

6. Mary, mother of John Mark the Evangelist (Acts 12:12). In the house of Mary the Christians of Jerusalem congregated, and there they were gathered in prayer when Peter arrived after his miraculous liberation from prison through the intervention of an angel (Acts 12:12-17).

7. Mary, a Christian in Rome, greeted by Paul in Romans 16:6.

Mash, A son of Aram in the Table of Nations (Gen. 10:23).

masons
carpenters and *m.*   2 Sam. 5:11 along with *m.*   1 Chron. 14:1
            hired *m.* and carpenters 2 Chron. 24:12

Masrekah (mas´-re-kah), A place in Edom, the home of King Samlah (Gen. 36:36; 1 Chron. 1:47).

Massa, A son of Ishmael and ancestor of an Arabian people (Gen. 25:14).

Massah, An encampment of the Israelites on their journey through the desert from Egypt to Sinai. Exodus 17:1-7 tells of the murmurings of the people for the want of water and of the miracle of the rock that spurted water on being struck by Moses. This story is similar to what is narrated in Numbers 20:1-13. Both attempt to explain the name of the place: the first Massah (temptation, Ex. 17:7), the second Meribah (challenge, confrontation, Num. 20:13). At times these are recalled as one episode only (Ex. 17:7; Deut. 33:8; Ps. 95:8) and it is very probable that both traditions refer to the same event, which however was situated in different places and received therefore corresponding popular etymologies. *See* MERIBAH.

Massoretes (mas′-o-reets), The original Hebrew Bible did not have vowel signs; it was written in consonants only, and, while still a living language, the reader knew which vowels to fit to which consonants. From the second to the tenth centuries A.D. however, while the consonant text was kept immune from all correction, an effort was made to devise a system of vowels or vowel signs so that not only the written text, but also its pronunciation could be handed down. The work of inventing a vowel sign system was carried out by specialized scribes in a systematic manner from the sixth century on. These specialized scribes were called Massoretes, and the fruit of their work is called the Massoretic text. There were different schools of Massoretes. The Massoretes of the sixth century in Palestine had worked out a very simple method of signs placed above the consonants to indicate the vowel sounds. At the same time, the flourishing schools of Babylonia had their own system of signs over the consonants. From the ninth and tenth centuries two families of Tiberias in Palestine, that of Ben Asher and that of Ben Naphtali, brought to completion a very accurate vowel sign system, in which the signs were placed underneath the consonants. Through this system the traditional pronunciation could be handed down to the last detail. The critical edition of the Hebrew Bible by Kittel is based on the Massoretic text of the manuscripts worked on by the family of Ben Asher.

mast
to make you a *m.*   Ezek. 27:5

master
of his Egyptian *m.*   Gen. 39:2   to greet our *m.*   1 Sam. 25:14
When his *m.* saw   Gen. 39:3   went back to their *m.*   2 Kgs. 6:23
                    the slave like his *m.*   Matt. 10:25

Mattan, A priest of Baal who was killed in the revolt of the priest Jehoiada against Athalia (2 Kgs. 11:18).

Mattanah (mat′-a-nah), A stage on the journey of the Israelites towards Canaan. It lay between the river Arnon and the frontier of the Amorite kingdom of Sihon in Transjordan (Num. 21:18-19).

Mattaniah (mat′-a-ny′-ah), The name given at birth to King Zedekiah of Judah (598-587 B.C.). When Jehoiachin, king of Judah (598 B.C.) surrendered to Nebuchadnezzar and was deported to Babylonia, Nebuchadnezzar placed on the throne Mattaniah, a son of Josiah and uncle of Jehoiachin, and changed his name to Zedekiah (2 Kgs. 24:17).

Mattatha (mat′-a-tha), Son of Nathan and grandson of David, listed among Jesus' ancestors in the genealogy of Luke 3:31.

Mattathias (mat′-a-thy′-as), 1. Son of John, a priest of the family of Joarib. During the days of the persecution of the Jews faithful to the law ordered by Antiochus IV Epiphanes (175-174 B.C.; 1 Mac. 1), Mattathias left Jerusalem and settled in Modein, a village twenty miles northwest of Jerusalem, with his five sons, John, Simon, Judas, Jonathan and Eleazar (1 Mac. 2:1-5). When the officers of King Antiochus went to the village of Modein to enforce the apostasy from the law, Mattathias and his sons refused to obey. When a certain Jew came forward in the sight of all to offer sacrifice on the altar of idols in accordance with the king's orders,

Mattathias "filled with zeal" killed him there on the altar. Then he also killed the officer of the king and tore down the altar. Then Mattathias ran through the town shouting at the top of his voice, inviting all those who were unwilling to submit to the king's command to follow him to the mountains, leaving behind him all his possessions. Many went out into the desert to settle there and live according to the Jewish customs. These however, out of zeal for the Sabbath rest, were unwilling to take up arms even to defend their own skin when they were attacked by the soldiers, and thus they died.

When Mattathias and his friends heard of it, they decided to offer armed resistance. The Hasideans united with them and together they gathered an army and began to destroy the pagan altars and to punish the apostates. This was the beginning of the Maccabean revolt, which was continued when Mattathias died, with his sons Judas, Jonathan and Simon by his side, in 166 B.C. and was buried in the tomb of his father in Modein (1 Mac. 2).

2. Son of Simon Maccabeus who was treacherously killed with his father in the fortress of Dok at the dinner offered there by Ptolemy, who was military commissioner for the plain of Jericho (1 Mac. 16:11-16).

Mattenai (mat′-e-nie), Personal name (Ezra 10:33, 37; Neh. 12:19).

Matthat (math′-at), The name of two ancestors of Jesus in the Lukan genealogy (3:24, 29).

Matthew, One of the Twelve chosen by Jesus (Matt. 10:3; Mk. 3:18; Lk. 6:15; Acts 1:13). In Matthew 10:3 he is called the tax-collector to identify him with the publican or tax-collector of the same name whose vocation is narrated in 9:9-13. The parallel text in Mark 2:14 calls him Levi, son of Alphaeus, and Luke 5:27 names him Levi. In all probability it is the same person who had two names, a frequent occurrence in the Judaism of the first century. Tradition attributes to Matthew the composition of the original Aramaic of the first gospel. *See* MATTHEW, GOSPEL OF.

Matthew, Gospel of, Tradition attributes the composition of the first gospel to Matthew the publican, called by Our Lord to be one of the Twelve. (*See* MATTHEW.) The most ancient testimony to his authorship is found in Eusebius of Caesarea (**Ecclesiastical History** III, 39, 16), and this is taken from a writing, now lost, of Papias, bishop of Hierapolis. His book was **"The Sayings of the Lord Explained,"** in which he tells us that Matthew compiled the **logia** (sayings) in the Hebrew (i.e. Aramaic, *see* Acts 21:40; 26:14) language, and that everyone interpreted as well as he could. Because of its brevity the testimony is obscure. The discussion is over the words **logia** and **interpreted. Logia** certainly means sayings. Does this mean that Matthew's work contained only the words of Jesus? This is the theory of those who see in this Aramaic collection of Jesus' sayings the postulated Q source in the synoptic hypothesis of the Two Sources. (*See* SYNOPTIC QUESTION.) From this source the authors of the Greek gospel attributed to Matthew and Luke would have drawn material for their own uses. This thesis is very improbable, for Papias is obviously thinking of the Greek gospel of Matthew such as we have it today, and he states that this is a translation from the Aramaic original of Matthew. Can then **logia** mean both the sayings and deeds of Jesus? This is an improbable solution that contradicts what we know of the use of the word **logia**, which always and only means "sayings." The most probable view is the following: Papias is definitely referring to our present Greek gospel. Papias himself is writing an interpretation of the sayings of Jesus and is therefore primarily interested in this part of Matthew. He criticizes Mark for his haphazard collection while he praised Matthew for having compiled with **order** (this is the exact translation of the word Papias uses) the words of the Lord. The "interpretations" of which Papias speaks are not, then, translations from the Aramaic original of Matthew, but commentaries on the words of the Lord, of the type that Papias himself has written on them.

Later tradition above all was to confirm the information on an Aramaic version of Matthew, now translated into Greek. There was not the slightest suspicion that this translator went further and even composed a new work that used as a source the original of Matthew. Irenaeus in the second century repeats the same information and adds that Matthew wrote for the Jewish Christians, while Peter and Paul founded the church of Rome. This synchronism is not to be taken in a strict chronological sense. Irenaeus wishes to point out the simultaneous diffusion of the same doctrine in diverse and distant regions. Pantaenus, a martyr in Alexandria around 200 A.D., states that he found in India a copy of the Aramaic gospel of St. Matthew. In all probability this was not the gospel according to Matthew, but an apocryphal work called the Gospel according to the Hebrews. This confusion between the Aramaic Matthew and the gospel according to the Hebrews is repeated in St. Jerome's writings.

Papias rightly praised the gospel according to Matthew for the orderly disposition of the words of the Lord. These are gathered into five great discourses; at the end of each the evangelist repeats the same phrase to underline the importance of these five booklets in the structure of the whole work: "When Jesus had finished these discourses . . ." (*see* Matt. 7:28, 29; 11:1; 13:53; 19:1; 26:1). The first is the most noted of all: The Sermon on the Mount (Matt. 5-7). There is the unmistakable intention to recall to the mind of the readers the scene of the proclamation of the law on Sinai. The Sermon on the Mount is the "more perfect justice" (Matt. 5:20), while reference is frequently made to the dispositions "of the fathers" with which are contrasted the more radical moral demands of Jesus (Matt. 5:17-48). Immediately after the Sermon on the Mount is a narrative section where the evangelist has the accounts of ten miracles, broken into three groups by the account of the calling of the disciples. After the cure of the leper (8:2-4), the son of the centurion at Capernaum (8:5-13), and of the mother-in-law of Peter (8:14-17) the evangelist inserts the call of the first disciples (8:18-22). Then another three miracles, the calming of the storm (8:23-27), the cure of the demoniac at Gadara (8:28-34) and of a paralytic (9:1-8), followed by the call of Levi (9:9-13). Then come the stories of four more miracles, the woman with the hemorrhage, the daughter of Jairus, the two blind men and the dumb demoniac (Matt. 9:18-34).

Cc. 5-9 are constructed by Matthew in form of a diptych, in which the author intends to summarize at the beginning the account of the public ministry: "Jesus toured all of Galilee. He taught in their synagogues, proclaimed the good news of the kingdom, and cured the people of every disease and illness" (Matt. 4:23). This part, then, could be entitled: Jesus powerful in work and doctrine (Lk. 24:19).

Cc. 9:35-10:4 contain the introduction to the following discourse: Jesus chooses twelve of his followers to send them to preach. The discourse then sums up Jesus' instructions given for the mission, now seen and realized however in the mission activity of the apostolic church (Matt. 10:5-11:1). Matthew has gathered here all that pertained to the theme. The first part of the discourse (10:5-16) is well adapted to the mission of the disciples in Galilee, and is, in fact, what is also given in Mark 6:6 ff. and Luke 9:1-5 (and Lk. 10:1-2 for the 72 disciples) in parallel passages. From Matthew 10:17, however, the horizon changes and the situation of the Church becomes more evident. There is talk of kings, rulers, pagans, and so one has passed the narrow confines of Palestine. So interested is Matthew in handling of the Lord's words, and thus emphasizing their importance, that he forgets to tell us how the mission fared and when the disciples returned, information which is however supplied by Mark 6:30 and Luke 9:10 and 10:17.

The second narrative section is contained in cc. 11:2 to 12:50. The structure of the piece is less clear than in cc. 8-9. The episodes narrated, however, do have one thing in common: the incomprehension and hostility encountered by Jesus which stands in bold contrast to the buoyancy and hopefulness that characterized cc. 5-9. So Matthew includes at this point some of the controversies that arose between Jesus and the Pharisees (12:1; 12:9) and mentions a conspiracy against the life of Christ which, in Mark, is found almost at the beginning of his gospel (Mark 2:1-3, 8). Here too crop up the accusations of acting by virtue of the prince of demons (12:22-37) and the petition for a sign, which in reality is a proclamation of incredulity (12:38). Jesus hides himself, something Matthew underlines by quoting in its regard Isa. 42:1-4, the first song of the Servant of Yahweh (Matt. 12:15-21).

At this point Matthew inserts the Third Discourse: the parables. The context would seem to suggest that by adopting this style Jesus wants to teach something hidden, to which he explicitly alludes in Matthew 13:12, 13: "To the man who has, more will be given until he grows rich; the man who has not, will lose what little he has. I use parables when I speak to them because they look but do not see, they listen but do not hear or understand." Matthew has collected seven parables. The first four are pronounced at the lakeside: the sower (13:3), the weeds (13:24), the mustard seed (13:31) and the leaven (13:33). The last three, that is, the treasure, the pearl and the net (Matt. 13:44-50) are reserved for the disciples alone, once the crowds have been dismissed and Jesus having returned to the house (13:36).

From c. 13:54 Matthew practically follows the same order that Mark has in his gospel from c. 6:61 on, leaving out, of course, the material that he had already anticipated. This part covers Jesus' journeys through the north of Palestine (13:54-16:20). From 16:21 on, the tone of the story changes. For the first time Jesus speaks to his disciples of his death as part of the mission of the Son of Man. This is an unexpected sequel to Peter's confession of Jesus' messiahship (16:16-20).

The fourth discourse of Matthew is read in c. 18:1-19 and is called the Rule of the Community. The occasion is the dispute among the disciples about who should be greatest in the kingdom of heaven (Matt. 18:1-5). Matthew has added other words of Jesus on the mutual relationships between the disciples and on the responsibilities of those who preside over the community. This includes the discourse on scandal (18:6-9), fraternal correction with the parable on the lost sheep (18:10-20), and the obligation to forgive as the Father forgives us (18:21-35). Then Matthew continues with the account of Jesus' journey from Galilee to Jerusalem (cc. 19-20), following Mark's order of events. Jesus' ministry at Jerusalem is narrated in cc. 21-23 and the last discourse, the "Eschatological Discourse," followed by the warnings and parables on the necessity of watchfulness are found in cc. 24-25.

With the usual formula (26:1) Matthew goes on to the description of the Last Supper, the Passion and Resurrection, keeping close to Mark's account of the same events. Matthew's principal additions to the history are: Pilate's wife's intervention (27:19), the request of the Pharisees to Pilate to place a guard on Jesus' sepulcher (Matt. 27:62-66), Jesus' apparition to the women while returning from the sepulcher (28:9, 10), buying off the sepulcher guards to falsify the resurrection account (28:11-16). The only apparition of Jesus to the disciples contains the missionary mandate and the formula of baptism (28:16-20; *see* RESURRECTION OF JESUS).

Matthew's gospel, like that of Luke, has broadened the scheme of the most ancient preaching ("from the baptism of John . . ." *see* Acts 1:22; 10:37). At the beginning of his gospel he inserts an account of the baptism and infancy of Jesus. After the genealogy, different from that of Luke (*see* GENEALOGY, Lk. 3:23-38), the infancy narrative has five scenes with as many quotations from the Old Testament, the last one unidentifiable: Matt. 1:23—Isa. 7:14; Matt. 2:6—Mic. 5:1; Matt. 2:15—Hos. 11:1; Matt. 2:18—Jer. 31:15; Matt. 2:23. *See* NAZARENE.

The infancy narrative answers two questions connected with the account of Jesus' work: Who is he? What is his origin? The answer is: he is the savior (1:21) promised by the prophets, conceived by Mary through the work of the Holy Spirit (1:20), son of David (1:18; 2:1-6), born at Bethlehem according to the prophecies (Matt. 2:6), received by the nations (2:10, 11) but persecuted and repulsed by his own people (2:13-17). Already at his birth the destiny to which he is called is marked out.

According to tradition the first gospel is a translation from the Aramaic original of Matthew the apostle. The gospel as it stands, however, does not seem to be a mere translation from the Aramaic. It is written in correct Greek and contains fewer semitisms than Mark or Luke. The quotations from the Old Testament found in Matthew are not translations from the original Hebrew. More than half of them that Matthew has in common with Mark and Luke are taken from the Septuagint. The other half do not coincide either with the Septuagint or with the original Hebrew, but they are nearer to the former than to the latter. For these reasons one must conclude that Matthew's gospel was not thought out in Hebrew or Aramaic but in Greek, and that it depends on the common tradition from which Mark and Luke also drew. The common opinion that the Greek writer Matthew knew of, and used, Mark's gospel has some reasons in its favor from the analysis just made.

On the other hand, only with difficulty can one deny the existence of a "gospel" in Aramaic belonging to Matthew. Where however is it to be sought? The principle solutions offered to this difficulty are two: Aramaic Matthew is nothing other than the Q source of the Two Source theory (*see* SYNOPTIC QUESTION), or that Aramaic Matthew is the most ancient attempt at a gospel, and used in the general structure common to all three gospels.

The data of tradition, then, do not perfectly coincide with what the study of the gospels reveals. The existence of an ancient Aramaic gospel of Matthew is not denied, but on the other hand it must be admitted that tradition has oversimplified the connection between our Matthew and this Aramaic writing. Tradition speaks of a simple translation whereas there must have been a much longer and more complex process leading to the present Matthew. What this process was is far from clear. This simplification by tradition however is understandable: it wished to put the clear stamp of apostolicity on the Greek Matthew, just as tradition has insisted on the close relationship between Mark and Peter so that the second gospel might enjoy the aura of Peter's apostolic authority.

There is no agreement on the exact date of composition. Matthew was written after Mark which makes it impossible to take Irenaeus literally when he states that it was penned while Peter and Paul founded the church of Rome. The most likely date is between 70 and 80 A.D. The author wrote for a Jewish-Christian reading public, probably in Syria or Palestine.

Matthias (ma-thie′-as), A disciple of Jesus who was chosen by lot to fill the place of Judas the traitor among the Twelve (Acts 1:15-26).

Mattithiah (mat′-i-thie′-ah), Personal name (1 Chron. 15:18; 16:5; 25:3; Ezra 10:43; Neh. 8:4).

mature
among the spiritually *m.*
1 Cor. 2:6

Meals, The Israelites had two meals a day, the Romans four. The first meal was eaten late in the morning. Ecclesiastes condemns early morning eating as childish (Eccl. 10:16). The rule in Exodus states: "At twilight you shall eat meat, and in the morning you shall be filled with bread" (9:12). The heavy meal was held, then, in the evening, according to the Roman custom. Peter, however became hungry around the sixth hour, or at noon (Acts 10:9-10).

A festive meal or banquet was held by the Israelites in the evening, by the Babylonians at noon. This was not just for eating, but for friendship, hospitality (Gen. 19:1-3; Job 1:13-14), and, unfortunately, sometimes for treachery (Jer. 41:1-3; 1 Mac. 16:15, 16). Guests at a banquet honored their host by coming in festive dress (Isa. 61:3; Matt. 22:11-12) garlanded with flowers (Isa. 63:1; Wis. 2:7-8). The host honored the guests by giving them a welcoming kiss (Lk. 7:45), washing their feet (Gen. 18:4; 24:32; Jgs. 19:21; 1 Sam. 25:41; Lk. 7:44) and having them anointed head and feet with oil (Jn. 12:3; Matt. 26:7; Lk. 7:38; Ps. 23:5; Eccl. 9:8; Amos 6:6).

Music and dance could accompany the feast, as is evident from the tragic story of John the Baptizer's death (Mk. 6:21-29; Matt. 14:3-12; Lk. 3:19-20). Music at a banquet was very much appreciated (Eccl. 32:5-6).

Meals were taken from a mat, the diners squatting on the floor, but by Roman times, they were taken reclining, which explains the scene of the Last Supper in which the beloved disciple leaned back on Jesus' breast (Jn. 13:22-23). This scene also tells us that cutlery was not used: the food was drawn from the common dish by hand (Prov. 26:15; Jn. 13:27).

The meal began with a blessing invoked by the one presiding, whereupon the head of the house broke and distributed the bread. He was the first to put his portion in his mouth. At the end of the meal the head of the house or the most honored guest, at the former's request, took a cup of wine, "the cup of benediction," lifted it up and said a blessing over it. All replied "Amen" and then drank from the cup. These rites were not only for the solemn paschal meal or the bigger feasts, such as marriages and circumcisions, but also whenever there was an organized meal, or a meal with guests.

In New Testament times, good Jews often formed brotherhood groups, or clubs in which the members met periodically to eat. At these meals the sanctification of the bread and wine took place. These confraternities were called **haberot** and their meal was the **haberot** meal.

The Paschal meal was taken in haste, with loins girt, sandals on, staff in hand, all set for the journey (Ex. 12:11), but after the Jews had entered into the possession of the land and were free, the meal was taken with solemnity and festivity, and reclining. A double blessing began the meal. This was pronounced over the meal and the wine. Then followed the washing of the right hand, the food hand. The first course was bitter herbs dipped in savory sauce and well chewed: it reminded them of the years in slavery. Then followed the various dishes, the father of the family taking the occasion to explain their meaning. There was the unleavened bread, unleavened because of the haste in leaving Egypt; the lamb, to remind them of the lamb through whose blood on their door jambs the Jews had been spared the death-dealing angel; the wine of joy and gratitude. Then followed the first part of the Hallel and a second glass of wine. The dishes thus explained were then eaten, with the usual blessing over the bread, and the final blessing of the wine that was passed around. The second part of the Hallel was then said (Pss. 114-118).

On the link between the eucharist and the Paschal meal *see* EUCHARIST. On the meaning of the meals eaten in the sacrifice, and the various attempts to explain their significance *see* SACRIFICE.

mean, means

This is what it *m*.	Gen. 40:12	What do you *m*. by crushing
what these stones *m*. to you		Isa. 3:15
	Josh. 4:6	understand what this *m*.
		Ezek. 17:12

meaning

dream with its own *m*.	Gen. 40:5	could tell me its *m*.	Dan. 4:5
the *m*. of this proverb	Ezek. 18:2	the *m*. of the vision	Acts 10:17

Measures, *See* WEIGHTS AND MEASURES.

Medad (mee´-dad), One of the seventy elders on whom the Lord bestowed some of that spirit which was in Moses to share with him the burden of governing the people. When they were congregated in front of the Tent of Meeting, Medad and Eldad were absent from the camp. Nevertheless they received the spirit and began to prophesy. Joshua asked Moses to put a stop to it, but Moses answered: "Are you jealous for my sake? Would that all the people of the Lord were prophets! Would that the Lord might bestow his spirit on them all" (Num. 11:16-30). The prophecy of which the sacred text speaks is a state of mystic exaltation of which 1 Sam. 10:10; 19:20 also speaks. It is commonly held that the account of Num. 11:16-30 wishes to attribute a Mosaic origin and therefore unconditional approval to these manifestations of 1 Sam. 10:10, etc. *See* PROPHECY; PROPHET.

Medan (mee´-dan), The third-born of Abraham and Keturah, the wife Abraham took at the death of Sarah (Gen. 25:1, 2; 1 Chron. 1:32).

Medeba (med´-e-ba), A city of Transjordania, today Madeba, 25 miles south of Amman, capital of the Kingdom of Jordan. Medeba was captured from the Moabites by Sihon, king of the Amorites of Heshbon (Num. 21:30). It was captured with the whole kingdom of Sihon by the Israelites and consigned to the tribe of Reuben (Josh. 13:9, 16), but at the time of Isaiah it was again Moabite (Isa. 15:2). John, son of Mattathias and brother of the Maccabees, was taken by surprise and killed by the sons of Jambri from Medeba. The Maccabees waited down under cover of the mountain for a bridal procession in which the sons of Jambri were escorting the bride with a great caravan of possessions to meet the groom. When they met, the Jews ambushed them and carried out a great slaughter while the survivors took flight to the mountains, leaving the caravan of possessions as booty (1 Mac. 9:36-42). Medeba was conquered by John Hyrcanus, son of Simon Maccabeus. On the pavement of a Christian church of the sixth century at Medeba is a mosaic representing Palestine at the time. This is an important source for the study of the topography of ancient Palestine.

Media (mee´-di-a), A region northwest of Iran, peopled during the second millenium B.C. by Indo-Europeans (*see* Gen. 10:2; 1 Chron. 1:5). King Deioces (eighth c. B.C.) succeeded in uniting the Median tribes, forming the basis of the Median empire with its capital at Ecbatana. The empire's most splendid period was under Cyaxares (625-585 B.C.), an ally of Nebuchadnezzar against Assyria. His successor Astyages (585-550 B.C.) was defeated by Cyrus II, king of the Persians, and thereafter the fortunes of the Medes were tied to those of the Persians (*see* Jer. 51:11-18).

Medicine, The practice of medicine is not frequently referred to in the Bible. Disease is above all seen from the religious point of view: it is a test (Job 2:7, 8) or punishment sent by God (Deut. 28:21, 22), and to God therefore must the sick man turn for a cure (Isa. 38:9-20; Ps. 38). When King Asa of Judah (913-873 B.C.) contracted what was, perhaps euphemistically, described as a serious disease in his feet, he was reproved (2 Chron. 16:12) in that "he did not seek the Lord, but only the physicians." Ahaziah of Israel (850-849) on the other hand was wounded when he fell through the lattice of his roof terrace at Samaria; and he was reproved by Elijah for having had recourse to Baalzebub, the god of Ekron; "Is it because there is no God in Israel that you are going to inquire of Baalzebub, the god of Ekron?" were Elijah's words (2 Kgs. 1:3).

The king died in punishment for his sin. Sirach however is more favorably disposed to doctors: "Hold the physician in honor, for he is essential to you, and God it was who established his profession" (Sir. 38:1-15). It is God who gives him the wisdom, just as it is God who gives the healing herbs with which the druggist prepares his medicines. Sirach sees in this divine providence the continuation of God's creative work. Therefore he exhorts: "When you are ill, delay not, but pray to God, who will heal you," but then place was to be given to the doctor lest he leave, for all need him, too. The doctor also must beseech God that his diagnosis be correct and his treatment bring about a cure. He, however, "who is a sinner toward his Maker will be defiant toward the doctor." This wise and religious attitude is reechoed in the important admonition of Jesus not to consider every disease the fruit of sin, even though sin and disease are not always separable (Jn. 9:3; Matt. 9:2; Mk. 2:5; Lk. 5:20).

The medical and hygienic instructions found in Leviticus (Lev. 12; 13; 15; 21:1-3) contain excellent information about practice, but they are proposed not from the medical but the ritual point of view. It is the priest's task to diagnose certain diseases such as leprosy (*see* LEPER) in order to determine the state of ritual purity or impurity of the patient. *See* CLEAN.

Some therapeutic methods are referred to incidentally. Wounds, bruises and open sores were "drained, bandaged, eased with salve" (Isa. 1:6). Isaiah had a boiling poultice of figs applied to the boil which tormented King Hezekiah (2 Kgs. 20:7). Some of the miracles attributed to Elisha were probably due to his expertise. Thus for instance, in 2 Kings 2:20-21, Elisha purifies the waters of the fountain of Jericho by throwing salt into it, and in 2 Kings 4:38-41 he renders innocuous a pot of poisonous vegetables by throwing flour into it. The therapeutic use of oil was well-known in antiquity (Mk. 6:13) and it remained on in Christian tradition as the matter for the sacrament of the sick (James 5:14). Wine mixed with myrrh (and gall?) was a pain-killing potion for those condemned to crucifixion (Mk. 15:23). According to Mark 5:25 the woman with the issue of blood for twelve years had spent all her money on doctors searching for a cure only to find herself worse. Paul recommends to Timothy (1 Tim. 5:23) a little wine for his stomach's sake. "People who are healthy do not need a doctor; sick people do. I have come to call sinners, not the self-righteous" (Mk. 2:17) and "Physician, heal yourself" (Lk. 4:23) are proverbs used by Jesus in his preaching. According to Col. 4:14 Luke was a doctor, and some have thought to see this mirrored in many expressions of a technical nature that he uses in his writings, such as "severe fever" (4:38), "paralysis" (5:18), "perfect health" (7:10), "hemorrhage" (8:43), etc. Others however see no special medical significance in these terms.

Mediation, Mediation and Mediator are not words that are found frequently in the Bible. In fact, the first is entirely absent and the second is read only in the New Testament with reference to Moses (Gal. 3:19-20) and to Christ (1 Tim. 2:5). The concept of mediation and the role of mediator is, however, essential to biblical religion. Biblical religion is a positive religion, that is, it originates in revelation, a divine initiative that began with the call of Abraham (Gen. 12:1-3) and culminated in Christ. In accomplishing the design of salvation God made use of certain persons to whom He gave specific roles and functions: prophets, priests and kings, all of whom are "mediators" of God's plans. For these three types of mediators, *see* KING, PRIEST, PROPHET. Here we will simply underline the characteristics of mediation carried out by them.

The priest is mediator, in the terms of Hebrews 5:1, "taken from among men and made their representative before God, to offer gifts and sacrifices for sins." In early Israel great stress was placed on the oracular function of the priest, exercised by means of the Urim and Thummim and Ephod. This is the priestly function that takes first place in Deut. 33:10—taking precedence even over the task of promulgating God's decisions to Jacob and his laws to Israel, and of offering sacrifice. In each case the function of the priest as mediator is institutional, static. The priests are members of the priestly tribe, heirs to a tradition, and their mediating role is exercised always in the context of recurring situations.

The mediating role of the prophets, on the other hand, is dynamic and quite unpredictable, as can be seen in the prophet-writers from the eighth century on especially. Their vocation is to be spokesmen for the God of Israel, not just in the sense of being mechanical mouthpieces, but in the much more burdensome task of being God's ambassadors to a people for the most part no longer capable of hearing the voice of the Lord. The prophet's interventions, however, are dynamic, for the word they transmit is the divine word, that is, the word of the God who spoke and the world sprang into being (note above all, Isa. 44:25, 26; 55:6-11). God is not judged by the power of the people who adore Him, but by His ability to give direction to the events of history. This ability is actuated and demonstrated by the prophetic word (Isa. 41:1-5; 41:21-29; 43:8-15; 44:6-8; 45:20-25). The prophet has also another mediating function that frequently fails to be sufficiently emphasized, namely, his mediation as intercessor: God pleads with Jeremiah not to intercede for the people, as if the prophet's prayer were capable of disarming God in His anger towards His unfaithful people. Through the mouths of Jeremiah and Ezekiel God condemns those prophets who failed to fulfil this function and so are guilty by neglect of the disasters that occurred, even though the disasters were a just punishment for the sins of the people (Jer. 7:16; 14:11; 15:1; 18:20; Ezek. 9:8, 13; 13:4, 5; for Moses, Ex. 32:11-14; for Abraham, as prophet, Gen. 20:7, 17). The prophet's mediation is then also one of reconciliation which equals and indeed surpasses that of the priest who carries out the liturgical rites.

The king, too, has a mediating function. He has priestly functions (Ps. 110:4; 1 Kgs. 8, etc.), but above all, in the Davidic monarchy, the king is irrevocably chosen by God as the person appointed to be "prince over my people Israel" (2 Sam 7:8. and *see* MESSIAH, MESSIANISM).

The Old Testament mediator above all others is Moses. His mediating role, however, is so fundamental and rich that it is impossible to contain it in any one category. He is at once prophet, king (in the sense of being chief and savior) and priest (Ps. 99:6). He is at the normative source of

Israelite religion. Biblical tradition could find no better way of proclaiming the unique and incomparable mediatorship of Moses between God and Israel than by handing down the Pentateuch under his name.

These three roles of mediation-reconciliation in the Old Testament point to the future of eschatological salvation. The hope of a messiah, that is, of a savior emerges from the mediating role of the king. As God's instrument the future savior will bring about the definitive salvation of Israel and of the just (*see* MESSIAH, MESSIANISM). From the mediating role of the prophet is born the hope of the prophet of the last times (Deut. 18:15-17, and for the New Testament, Jn. 1:29, 45; 6:14; 7:10) who will accomplish reconciliation and the remission of sins through a new type of intercession, namely, that of offering his own life as sin's expiation (Isa. 53 and *see* SERVANT OF THE LORD). The mediating role of the priest provided the author of the epistle to the Hebrews with an Old Testament background and source in the light of which to present the work of Christ: He is the mediator of the new covenant "since his death has taken place for deliverance from transgressions committed under the first covenant, those who are called may receive the promised eternal inheritance" (Heb. 9:15).

The three forms of mediation fuse in the work of the "one Mediator between God and men, the man Christ Jesus" (1 Tim. 2:5) through whom God reconciled man with Himself (2 Cor. 5:18, 19). Jesus won a kingdom which he will present to the Father on the last day (1 Cor. 15:24) and, in the meantime of pilgrimage, he is always living to make intercession for us (Heb. 9:24).

meet

m. a band of prophets	1 Sam. 10:5	moved to *m.* David	1 Sam. 17:48
he went to *m.* Saul	1 Sam. 15:12	came out to *m.* Jesus	Matt. 8:34

Megiddo (me-gid′-oh), A ciy at the southern limits of the plain of Jezreel, on the slopes of the Carmel range between Jokneam and Jezreel. The city dominates the plain of Jezreel and is near the principal way through the Carmel range, that is, the Wadi 'Arah, which cuts through the mountains and opens a way from the coast and from Egypt to the plain of Jezreel and the north. The ruins of the city are today called Tell el Mutesellim. The place was first occupied in the fourth millenium B.C. It was later taken by Tuthmose III (1502-1448 B.C.) who made it the principal bulwark in the Egyptian domination of Palestine. According to Joshua 12:21 it was occupied by Joshua, but Joshua 17:11, 12 admits that the tribe of Manasseh failed to capture it. It was probably not an Israelite possession until the time of David. Solomon fortified it and made it the capital of the fifth administrative district (1 Kgs. 4:12; *see* 1 Kgs. 9:15; 1 Chron. 7:29). The Oriental Institute of the University of Chicago has uncovered, from Solomon's works, splendid walls and the gate of the city, the latter being the principal monument of its kind discovered in Palestine. Also unearthed were the remains of large stables for the chariot division, probably capable of housing five hundred horses (*see* 1 Kgs. 9:19), which probably belong to the time of Ahab of Israel (869-850 B.C.). When Ahaziah of Judah was wounded in Jehu's revolt he took refuge in Megiddo where he died (2 Kgs. 9:27). There too Josiah died after he had been defeated by Neco, Pharaoh of Egypt (2 Kgs. 23:29 ff.; 2 Chron. 35:22-24). In the vision of Revelation 16:16 the kings of all the earth will be gathered for the battle of the great day of God Almighty at Armageddon, which, in Hebrew, is the plain of Megiddo, the scene of several battles in Israelite history (*see* Jgs. 5:19; 2 Kgs. 23:29).

The "waters of Megiddo" were where Barak and Deborah were victorious over Sisera's Canaanites: they are the sources of the Kishon in the vicinity of Megiddo.

Megiddo, Plain of, Also known as the Plain of Jezreel (Zech. 12:11). *See* JEZREEL.

Megilloth (mi-gill′-oth), The plural form of Megillah, scroll or volume. The "Five Megilloth" are the Song of Songs, Ruth, Lamentations, Ecclesiastes, and Esther. They were read in the synagogue worship on the five principal feasts of the Jewish year, that is on Passover, Pentecost, the ninth day of the month of Ab (July-August, the date of the destruction of the city and the Temple in 587 B.C.; *see* Zech. 7:3), Tabernacles and Purim. *See* ESTHER.

Mehetabel (me-het′-a-bel), The wife of Hadar, king of Edom (Gen. 36:39; 1 Chron. 1:50).

Mehida (mi-hie′-da), Ancestor of a family of temple servants (Ezra 2:52; Neh. 7:54).

Meholathite (me-hoe′-la-thite), Adriel the Meholathite (that is, from Abel-Meholah) was the husband of Merab, a daughter of King Saul (1 Sam. 18:19; 2 Sam. 21:8).

Mehujael (me-hue′-ja-el), Son of Irad in the genealogy of Cain (Gen. 4:18).

Me-jarkon, "The waters of Jarkon," a stream which flows into the Mediterranean in the territory of the tribe of Dan (Josh. 19:46).

Melchi (mel′-kie), Ancestor of Jesus according to Luke 3:24, 28.

Melchiel (mel′-ki-el), A man of Bethulia, whose son Charmis was among the magistrates of the city (Judith 6:15).

Melchior (mel′-ki-or), The name given by tradition to one of the anonymous Magi who came to pay homage to the infant Jesus (Matt. 2:1-12). Tradition also numbers the Magi as three, because three gifts were offered, but in reality the number is not specified by Matthew. The names of the other two in tradition are Gaspar and Balthasar. All have been made kings in tradition: Melchior king of Persia, Gaspar king of India and Balthasar king of Arabia. The cathedral of Cologne holds the relics of these legendary figures. *See* MAGI.

Melchizedek (mel-kiz′-e-dek), King of Salem (Jerusalem), a contemporary of Abraham. When Abraham returned from the attack in which he liberated Lot, who had been made prisoner of the kings of the East when they came to fight the kings of the 5 Dead Sea city-states, Melchizedek king of Salem brought out bread and wine, and being a priest of God the Most High, that is of El Elyon (*see* PATRIARCHS, RELIGION OF THE), he blessed Abraham with the words: "Blessed be Abram by God the Most High, the creator of heaven and earth; and blessed be God Most High, who delivered your foes into your hands." Then Abraham gave him a tenth of the booty taken from the vanquished (Gen. 14:18-20).

To Christian readers the mention of bread and wine suggests the eucharist, and in fact some Fathers have attempted to find in Melchizedek's bread and wine a prefiguration of the eucharist. This however is not suggested in the New Testament, nor indeed is it supported in the text. For the offering of bread and wine to Abraham was not a sacrifice, but hospitality. As a priest Melchizedek only blesses Abraham.

Interest in the account arises from the fact that only here in the history of the patriarchs are they linked with the city of Salem, that is, Jerusalem, which was to become the capital city of the kingdom of David. It is also clear that the story was interpreted in the light of this fact. It seems to give sanction to the link between David and the king-priest of Jerusalem who at the beginning of Israel had ties with the most authoritative of the patriarchs. On the other hand David inherited the sacred traditions of the city and brought together in a single personage the kingship and priesthood. This would seem to be the meaning of the "priesthood according to the order of Melchizedek" which is attributed to the king in Psalm 110:4.

In the Epistle to the Hebrews (5:6; 6:20; 7:1, 10-11; 7:15, 17) Jesus is called a priest according to the order of Melchizedek. Rather than emphasize the convergence of kingship and priesthood in the same person, the author points out the way in which Melchizedek appeared on the scene in Genesis 14:18-20, that is as a non-levitical priest, a unique and isolated phenomenon in that no information is given on his ancestry or posterity, and therefore with a priesthood not just inherited but conferred personally by God, and therefore superior to Abraham and to Levi, who was "from Abraham's loins." Abraham, in fact, paid him the homage of the tithes. All these, in the author's mind, are characteristics which make Jesus a priest according to the order of Melchizedek, and make Melchizedek a type and figure of Christ who was to come.

Melea (mee'-le-a), An ancestor of Jesus according to the genealogy of Luke 3:31.

Mem, The 13th letter of the Hebrew alphabet (m).

members

offer the *m.* of your body	in my body's *m.* another law
Rom. 6:13	Rom. 7:23
the law worked in our *m.*	has one body with many *m.*
Rom. 7:5	Rom. 12:4
your bodies are *m.* of Christ 1 Cor. 6:15	

Memmius Quintus, The Roman legate, who with his fellow legate Titus Manius, wrote to Judas Maccabeus (12 March 164 B.C.) after peace had been made with Lysias (2 Mac. 11:34-38).

memory

banish the *m.* of these Ps. 109:15	wiped out all *m.* of them
The *m.* of the just Prov. 10:7	Isa. 26:14
be told in her *m.* Mk. 14:9	

Memphis, The principal city of Lower Egypt and capital of united Egypt from the third dynasty until the sixth, with some interruptions however. This was during the second half of the third millenium before Christ. Memphis retrieved some of its ancient importance for a short time during the reign of the Hyksos (*see* HYKSOS). It underwent the lot of the other great cities during the Assyrian and Persian invasion. Some of the Jews who fled Jerusalem after the assassination of the governor Gedaliah settled in Memphis (587 B.C.; Jer. 44:1). Memphis is sometimes mentioned by the prophets (*see* Hos. 9:6; Isa. 19:13; Jer. 2:16; 46:19; Ezek. 30:13, 16). The few remains of the city are found thirteen miles south of Cairo on the west bank of the Nile.

Memucan (me-moo'-kan), A prince of Persia and Media during the reign of King Ahasuerus (Esth. 1:14, 16, 21). *See* AHASUERUS; ESTHER; XERXES.

men

At that time *m.* began Gen. 4:26	he saw three *m.* standing
When *m.* began to multiply	Gen. 18:2
Gen. 6:1	estimation of the Lord and *m.*
Yet like *m.* shall you die Ps. 82:7	1 Sam. 2:26
as *m.* entrusted with the good tidings 1 Thess. 2:4	

Mene, Tekel, Peres

Menahem (men′-a-hem), Son of Gadi and king of Israel (745-738 B.C.). He assassinated his predecessor Shallum and usurped the throne (2 Kgs. 15:13). Menahem implacably suppressed all resistance. He sacked Tappuah, killing all who were in it, ripping open the pregnant women because it had not supported him (2 Kgs. 15:16). Tiglath-pileser III of Assyria invaded Menahem's territory. Menahem submitted and succeeded in holding on to his kingdom and his position through the payment of 1,000 talents of silver. Menahem gathered the tribute by exacting it from all the men of substance in the country, fifty silver shekels from each. At his death his son Pekahiah succeeded him to the throne (1 Kgs. 15:17-22).

Menelaus (men′-e-lay′-us), The High Priest of the Jews (172-162 B.C.) appointed by Antiochus IV Epiphanes in the place of Jason. Jason, Onias' brother, had obtained the dignity of the high priesthood through paying a high sum of money to the Seleucid king (2 Mac. 4:7-9). Three years after his nomination he sent Menelaus to deliver the money to the king, but Menelaus got the high priesthood for himself by outbidding Jason by three hundred talents of silver. Menelaus then returned to Palestine with the new dignity while Jason fled to the Ammonites (2 Mac. 4:23-26). When Menelaus deferred the payment of the promised sum he was summoned before the king in Antiochia. He left his brother Lysimachus as his substitute in Palestine (2 Mac. 4:27-29). In the meantime Antiochus had to set out to put down a revolt of the poeple of Tarsus, while he left Andronicus, one of his dignitaries, in charge. Menelaus took advantage of the king's absence and offered Andronicus some gold vessels from the Temple. At the suggestion of Menelaus, Andronicus treacherously killed Onias, the legitimate high priest, who had been deposed when Jason was nominated to the office. Onias had taken refuge in the sanctuary at Daphne but was lured out by a false oath of Andronicus, and immediately put to death (*see* ONIAS). The king at his return punished Andronicus, but Menelaus, the real culprit, managed to escape by buying the favor of Ptolemy, who then spoke to Antiochus in Menelaus' favor. In this way he was able to hold on to his office (2 Mac. 4:30-50). When a false rumor circulated that King Antiochus was dead, Jason, the high priest whom Menelaus had outbidden, gathered an army and attacked Jerusalem. Menelaus was besieged in the citadel and resisted until Antiochus himself arrived to stamp out the revolt with great cruelty. Antiochus dared enter the Temple, where Menelaus served as his guide, handing over to him whatever of value was there. Menelaus was confirmed in the high priesthood (2 Mac. 5:5-26). Menelaus was practically put out of office when Judas Maccabeus succeeded in taking Jerusalem and the Temple and ordered its purification and consecration (2 Mac. 10:1-8). In 163-162 B.C., Lysias, the chancellor of King Antiochus V Eupator led an army to put an end to the agitation in Judea. Menelaus was with him and did his best to turn to his advantage the military campaign of the Seleucids. Lysias however informed the king that Menelaus was really the cause of the situation now holding in Judea. Antiochus ordered that he be taken to Beroea and executed there "in the customary local method. There is at that place a tower 75 feet high, full of ashes, with a circular rim sloping down steeply on all sides towards the ashes. A man guilty of sacrilege or notorious for certain other crimes was brought up there and then hurled down to destruction. In such a manner was Menelaus, the transgressor of the law, fated to die" (2 Mac. 13:1-7).

Mene, Tekel, Peres (mee′-ne, tek′-el, per′-eez), According to Daniel 5:5, while Belshazzar and his noblemen, his wives and women singers were quaffing their wine from the sacred vessels looted from the Temple at Jerusalem, the fingers of a human hand appeared and began to write on the plaster of the wall behind the lamp stand, to the terror of the king. He shouted for his enchanters, Chaldaeans and wizards, but they were unable to explain it. At the queen's suggestion Daniel was summoned. He refused the gifts that were offered and explained the writing as follows: "**Mene,** God has numbered (**menah,** to number) your kingdom and put an end to it; **Tekel,** you have been weighed (**tekal,** to weigh) on the scales and found wanting; **Peres,** your kingdom has been divided (**peras,** to divide) and given to the Medes and Persians" (5:27, 28). The prediction was fulfilled, for, reports Daniel 5:30, that very night Belshazzar was murdered and Darius the Mede took the kingdom.

Meni (me-nie′), Meni and Gad, translated by Isa. 65:11 as Destiny and Fortune, are in all probability divinities, objects of idolatrous worship on the part of the Jews who had returned to Jerusalem from exile. The text records, as part of the worship, sacred banquets: "You who spread a table for Fortune and fill cups of blended wine for Destiny."

Menna, An ancestor of Jesus in the genealogy of Luke 3:31.

Menorah, The Hebrew word for lampstand, and, par excellence, for the seven-branched lampstand in the Tabernacle of the Temple (*see* Ex. 37:17-24). It was made of pure gold, three branches reaching from either side, in which the cups, calyx and petal were of one piece with it. The lamps had their snuffers and trays of pure gold. A talent of gold was used in the making. The Menorah of Herod's Temple was among the trophies taken from Jerusalem by the Romans, as can be seen in the bas-relief on the Arch of Titus in Rome.

Mephaath (mef′-a-ath), A city of Transjordania, in the land of Reuben (Josh. 13:18), a Levitical city of the Levite clan of Merari (Josh. 21:37). At the time of Jeremiah, Mephaath was in Moabite territory (Jer. 48:21).

Mephibosheth (me-fib′-o-sheth), A changed form of Meribbaal (*see* MERIBBAAL). The name was changed to get rid of the name Baal, which in itself means Master or Lord, and thus could be applied to Yahweh, but had become the proper name of Canaan's most popular god (*see* BAAL). For Baal was substituted **Bosheth,** which means shameful thing. *See* LORD.

Merab (mir′-ab), The elder daughter of Saul (1 Sam. 14:49). She was promised in marriage to David, "if you become my champion and fight the battles of the Lord." Saul in reality hoped David would be killed in the war against the Philistines. Saul did not keep his promise, and Merab was given in marriage to Adriel of Meholah, while David married Michal, the younger daughter of Saul (1 Sam. 17:17-20). Merab's five sons, together with Saul's two sons by Rizpah, Meribbaal and Armoni, were handed over to the inhabitants of Gibeon by David, so that they might avenge themselves for the cruelties the city had suffered under Saul (2 Sam. 21:1-9).

Meraioth (me-ray′-yoth), 1. An Aaronite priest (1 Chron. 5:32, 33; 9:11).

2. Ancestor of Ezra (Ezra 7:3).

Merari (me-rar′-eye), The third son of Levi, brother of Gershon and Kohath (Gen. 46:11; Ex. 6:16) and ancestor of the Levite Merarites (Josh. 21:7, 34-40; 1 Chron. 6:14, 29-32). The sons of Merari were Mahli and Mushi (Num. 3:33-37).

Merathaim (mer′-a-thay′-im), A region in Babylonia (Jer. 50:21).

merchants
from the traffic of *m.*   1 Kgs. 10:15 temple slaves and the *m.*
                                                        Neh. 10:31
        you *m.* of Sidon Isa. 23:2

Mercurius, The Latin name for Hermes, a Greek Olympic God. Paul and Barnabas, while preaching at Lystra, were taken by the inhabitants for Zeus (Barnabas) and Hermes-Mercurius (Paul). Paul was identified as Hermes because he was the chief speaker. Hermes was the messenger of the gods (Acts 14:12).

Mercy, Mercy translates the Hebrew term **hesed.** In a certain sense, the translation is conventional, because authors are agreed that the Hebrew **hesed** is much more ample and nuanced than the English word mercy. **Hesed** evokes the idea of goodness, not in a generic sense, nor even a disposition or spirit of goodness, but a goodness with someone in view. It could be described as the goodness, help and benevolence that is born as it is demanded of a relationship between people such as the members of the same family, friends, guests, and so on, and finally between God and his people on the basis of the Covenant. It is, then, the manifestation of solidarity between people, and it is the link that keeps this solidarity alive and active, and gives to solidarity its content. **Hesed** then is no mere vague goodness of soul or character: it is the concrete realization and actualization of what binds people together to make solidarity a real and true thing. Mercy is often allied with faithfulness (*see* TRUTH) of which it is the content, just as faithfulness is mercy made constant and enduring in time. Mercy is also however justice and judgment (*see* JUDGMENT), piety, compassion, help and salvation.

God freely pledged himself to Abraham, and therefore his attitude and relationship to Abraham is all goodness. Abraham's slave who was sent to look for a wife for Abraham's son, reminded God of this "moral" duty: "Lord, God of my master Abraham, let it turn favorably for me today and thus deal graciously with my master Abraham" (Gen. 24:12). And when he found what he sought he blessed God: "who has not let his constant kindness towards my master fail" (Gen. 24:27).

This goodness (**hesed**) also comprises the pledge God gave to Israel in the Covenant. At this point however the "goodness" of God is enriched with a quality that never abandons it throughout history. His "goodness" will be his concern for all who observe his Covenant, and this goodness will endure a thousand generations (Ex. 20:6; 34:6; Deut. 5:10). It is also this "goodness" which moves God to maintain his pledge to his people even when they have proved disloyal. God's **hesed** is manifested precisely in forgiving sin and restoring Israel. When Israel disobeyed and refused to enter Palestine from the south God decided to "strike them with pestilence and wipe them out" (Num. 14:12). Moses interceded for them with the same formula, already quoted (Ex. 20:6): "The Lord is slow to anger and rich in kindness . . . Pardon, then, the wickedness of this people in keeping with your great kindness" (Num. 14:18, 19). God's "goodness" is not bound by a conditioned alliance or reciprocity in **hesed:** God's presence and action in his people is gratuitous, in no way founded on man's rights or merits. It is as gratuitous as is God's choice of Israel as his own, and as is the promise (*see* ELECTION, PROMISE). God's goodness is not just the content of what he does for man: it is what drives God to make a covenant with man, and it is the only power that maintains the covenant when the people have been unfaithful in it. In the concrete, then, **hesed** is God's will to save man, arising out of pure goodness on the part of a God, who while he does not leave sin unpunished, nevertheless knows how to overcome sin and render it inoperative through his own goodness.

God's goodness is manifested in the individual (Ps. 13:6) and in all creation. It saves Israel from all enemies (Pss. 25:6; 40:11; 79:8; Jer. 42:12). It is the force that makes God put an end to the exile and bring back his people to the land to restore it (Ezek. 39:25; Isa. 54:10; 63:7). His goodness prompts him to forgive infidelity and sin (Deut. 13:17; Isa. 54:8; 55:7; Hos. 1:6-7; Micah 7:19). Psalm 136 attributes all the work of God in history to his goodness, which knows no end: "Give thanks to the Lord, for he is good, for his mercy endures for ever" (Ps. 136:1). Here the Psalmist extends to the whole of creation that goodness that up to this we have seen operative in God's relationships with his people. Creation too sets up a relationship between the creature and God, in which goodness is the most stable quality and content of God's whole attitude toward his creatures: "Of the kindness of the Lord the earth is full" (Ps. 33:5). "He is good to all and compassionate toward all his works" (Pss. 145:9; 119:64). "He gives food to all flesh, for his mercy endures forever" (Ps. 136:25). Creation itself, like the Covenant, is a work of his goodness (Ps. 136:4-9).

Greek tradition and the New Testament translate **hesed** as **eleos**, mercy. This captures the predominant aspect of God's **hesed** which is his will to save those who not only stand in need of it, but are unworthy of it. The will to save is made manifest in Jesus who came "not to save the just but sinners" and who invited the Pharisees who were implacably censorious of Jesus' goodness to sinners, to learn the meaning of the saying: "It is mercy I desire and not sacrifice" (Matt. 9:13; 12:7; 23:23; *see* Hos. 6:6). Jesus' familiarity with publicans and sinners was not just a show of God's generic love for them, but the pledge of their sharing in the kingdom, that is, in salvation. Jesus reserved special kindness for sinners to show that the mercy of God does not look to man's merits or rights, but asks from him submission and humility, self-opening to receive what can only be received as gift, namely, salvation. Salvation can never reach the "just," that is, those who hold themselves justified and have raised up between themselves and God's goodness the barrier of their presumed merits.

The God who offers man his mercy in and through Jesus, also wishes man to show mercy to his fellowman (Matt. 18:33). The merciful will receive God's mercy (Matt. 5:7), like the Samaritan who "showed mercy" to the man he found half-dead on the road from Jerusalem to Jericho (Luke 10:37). On the other hand severe judgment, "making them pay the whole debt," is reserved for those who, like the servant of the parable, forget the forgiveness they have received and refuse to show mercy to their fellow man in trouble (Matt. 18:23-28).

Mercy Seat, *See* ARK OF THE COVENANT.

Meremoth (mer′-e-moth), A priest among those who signed the covenant proclaimed by Nehemiah (Ezra 8:33; Neh. 3:4; 10:5).

Meres (mir′-eez), A prince of Media and Persia during the reign of King Ahasuerus (Esth. 1:14). *See* AHASUERUS; ESTHER; XERXES.

Meribah (mer′-i-bah), According to Exodus 17:7 Massah and Meribah, that is, "testing and quarrelling," was the name of the place between the desert of Sin and the Sinai where the Israelites murmured against Moses because they had no water. Moses provided water by striking a rock with his staff (Ex. 17:1-7). Numbers 20:1-13 narrates a very similar story. Meribah, or the "waters of bitterness" is located in the desert of Zin near Kadesh. On this occasion Moses showed little faith and for this was reproved by the Lord, who punished him by depriving him of the future pleasure of entering the land of Canaan (Num. 20:12). In all probability both are variations of the same episode; in fact both names are often mentioned together (Ps. 95:8; Deut. 33:8 and in Ex. 17:7.). Deuteronomy 33:8 links the episode of the "testing" at Massah and the "quarrelling" at Meribah with the origins of the priestly functions of the tribe of Levi. On this occasion the tribe of Levi showed itself faithful. This fact records, not the traditions on Massah and Meribah, but rather the punishment of the idolatrous Israelites at Sinai, which was carried out by the Levites who took the part of Moses (Ex. 32:25-29). As can easily be seen, the traditions are confused. Massah and Meribah should be looked for in Kadesh, which was also called the "Spring of Justice." This name suggests a place where the "testing" and "quarrelling" were resolved through a sacred judgment in the form of an oracle. The names were later explained as "testing" God, and "quarrelling" with Moses, and therefore related to the traditions about the murmurings of the Israelites on their journey through the desert. Levi himself was "tested" and "quarrelled" with (Deut. 33:8) but he proved himself faithful and thus received the priesthood. *See* MASSAH.

Meribbaal (mer′-i-bale), 1. Son of Saul, born from his concubine Rizpah, daughter of Aiah. David decided to revenge the injustice committed by Saul against the inhabitants of Gibeon and so asked the Gibeonites what he might do to regain their loyalty to the crown. They demanded to have handed over to them seven descendants of Saul that they might "dismember (or impale) them before the Lord in Gibeon." David spared Meribbaal son of Jonathan, but he gave over to them Saul's two sons by Rizpah, Armoni and Meribbaal, and five grandsons by Merab, Saul's daughter; these seven were executed together. Rizpah mercifully kept the birds by day and the beasts by night from the bodies, until David took the bones of Saul, Jonathan and those who had been executed and buried them all fittingly in the tomb of Saul's father Kish (2 Sam. 21:1-9).

2. Meribbaal, the crippled son of Jonathan, and grandson of Saul (2 Sam. 4:4). He lived in the house of Machir in Lodebar. David wanted to show kindness to the sole survivor of Saul's house for the sake of his intimate friendship with Jonathan, so he summoned him and restored to him all the lands of his grandfather Saul, and had him live at court and eat at the king's table. Meribbaal took with him his slave Ziba to whom David gave the task of working Saul's land and providing food for the family (2 Sam. 9:1-13). When Absalom forced David to abandon Jerusalem, Ziba went to him with provisions. Moreover he accused Meribbaal of betraying David, stating that he did not accompany the king in the hope that the kingdom would come back into the hands of Saul's family. David then gave to Ziba all Meribbaal's property. When however David returned to power, Meribbaal accused Ziba of deception and slander, and pleaded his lameness as an excuse for not having gone out to David. Nonplussed, David decreed the division of the properties between Ziba and Meribbaal, but the latter responded: "Let him have it all, now that my lord the king has returned safely to his palace" (2 Sam. 19:25-31).

Merneptah (mer′-nep-tah), A Pharaoh of Egypt of the XIX dynasty (1234-1220 B.C.), successor of Ramses II. His name is not found in the Bible. A stele discovered at Thebes in the funeral monument of the Pharaoh contains a hymn that celebrates his triumphs. There Israel is mentioned as already living in Canaan. It is however difficult to determine if the Israel mentioned is the confederation of the twelve tribes of the Bible, or another group, not better identified, from which the name would have been inherited.

Merodach, The Hebrew transcription of Marduk, the name of the national god of Babylonia (*see* Jer. 50:2). *See* MARDUK.

Merodach-baladan (mer′-o-dak-bal′-a-dan), King of Babylonia, a contemporary of Hezekiah of Judah (715-687 B.C.), called Marduk-apal-iddina in Assyrian documents. Merodach-baladan was an Aramaean chieftain of the tribe of Bit-Yakin, who in a particularly critical moment in the Assyrian empire, during the reign of Sargon (720-711), succeeded in making himself king and achieving independence in Lower Mesopotamia. This revolt was only the first symptom of restlessness that marked the empire under Sargon II. Hezekiah of Judah, who had inherited vassalage to Assyria from his father Ahaz (2 Kgs. 16:7-9) tried, with the support of Egypt, for independence (Isa. 20:1-6). When Hezekiah recovered from his illness (2 Kgs. 20:12-19; Isa. 39:1-8) Merodach-baladan sent him ambassadors bearing felicitations, whereupon Hezekiah showed them all his treasures and armaments. It was obvious that under the guise of a friendly visit were hidden political maneuvers and alliances against the common enemy Sargon II, king of Assyria. Sargon, however, made short shrift of his subjects' hopes for independence. Merodach-baladan was forced to flee to Elam, and Hezekiah saved himself only by paying a large tribute (2 Kgs. 18:13-16; *see* HEZEKIAH). Merodach appeared again during the first years of Sennacherib's reign (705-681 B.C.), and succeeded once more in occupying Babylonia. The city however fell to Sennacherib in 702 B.C. and Merodach-baladan again took flight. Sennacherib established in his place Bel-ibni, who was loyal to the Assyrians (702-700 B.C.). He too however allowed himself to be persuaded by hopes of independence and attempted a revolt that proved unsuccessful. In 699 Sennacherib established as king of Babylon his son Ashshur-nadin-shumi (699-694 B.C.).

Merom (mer′-om), The "waters of Merom," a wadi or stream in Upper Galilee where Joshua defeated the coalition of the Canaanite kings of the north, whose chief was Jabin, king of Hazor (Josh. 11:5, 7). Today it is Wadi Meiron, beside the village of the same name. The Wadi Meiron pours into the lake of Gennesaret from the west.

Meroz (mer′-oz), The inhabitants of Meroz are cursed in the Song of Deborah, "for they came not to my help, as warriors to the help of the Lord," against Jabin and Sisera (Jgs. 5:23). It has not been identified, but is thought to have been in the northern boundaries of the region occupied by the Israelites, around Lake Huleh.

merry

made *m.* with him	Gen. 43:34	When Ammon is *m.*	2 Sam. 13:28
Nabal was *m.*	1 Sam. 25:36	when the king was *m.*	Esth. 1:10

Mesha (mee′-sha), King of Moab, and contemporary of Ahab (869-850 B.C.) and Joram (849-842 B.C.), kings of Israel. According to 2 Kings 3:4-27, Mesha, who raised sheep, used to pay the king of Israel as tribute a hundred thousand lambs and the wool of a hundred thousand rams, but when Ahab died, Mesha rebelled. Joram with the kings of Judah and Edom organized a military campaign against Moab, at which Elisha the prophet was present. According to the biblical version, the Israelite armies defeated and slaughtered the Moabites, who with their king took refuge in the capital Kir-haresheth. When Mesha saw he was losing all, he took seven hundred swordsmen to break through to the king of Aram, but he failed. So he took his first-born, as heir apparent, and offered him as a holocaust upon the wall. "The wrath against Israel was so great that they gave up the siege and returned to their own land" (2 Kgs. 3:27). These words, however, gloss over a defeat that the Israelites suffered. The wrath against Israel, in all probability, should be interpreted as the anger of Chemosh, the national god of the Moabites, against Israel. Information on Mesha is also available from the stele he had erected at Dibon, which was found in 1868 and is today preserved in the Louvre. On this Mesha recounts his conquests in Israelite territory across the Jordan (Ataroth, Nebo, Mediba, etc.) and the works of fortification he undertook.

Meshach (mee′-shak), The Babylonian name which the chief chamberlain of Nebuchadnezzar imposed on Mishael, one of Daniel's three companions at the court of Babylon (Dan. 1:7).

Meshech (mee′-shek), In the Table of Nations, son of Japheth (Gen. 10:2; 1 Chron. 1:5). Meshech was one of the lands ruled by Gog (Ezek. 38:2). It is often mentioned with Tubal and Javan (Ezek. 32:26; 39:1; 38:2). It is to be identified with the Mushki, known from Assyrian and Greek documents. They lived between the Caspian Sea and the Black Sea, northwest of Armenia. The Mushki were defeated by Tiglath-pileser III (745-727 B.C.) and their King Mita later became a vassal to Sargon II (721-705 B.C.).

Meshullam (me-shool′-am), A common personal name in the Old Testament (2 Kgs. 22:3; 1 Chron. 3:19, 20; 5:13; 8:17; 9:7, 8, 11, 12; 2 Chron. 34:12; Neh. 3:6; 6:18; 8:4; 10:8, 21; 12:13, 16, 25, 33).

Meshullemeth (me-shool′-e-muth), The wife of King Manasseh of Judah (2 Kgs. 21:19).

Mesopotamia, The land between the river Tigris and Euphrates (from the Greek **mesos** and **potamos,** river). Here were cradled the most ancient civilizations of human history. On the history of the region *see* AKKAD, ASSYRIA, BABYLON, SUMERIANS.

messenger

Lo, I am sending my *m*.	Mal. 3:1	I send my *m*. before you	Mk. 1:2
I send my *m*. ahead of you		I send my *m*. ahead of you	
	Matt. 11:10		Lk. 7:27

Messiah, Messianism, Messiah is the transcription of the Hebrew word **Mashiah** which means "anointed." In the New Testament and in the post-biblical Jewish writings it designates the king, son of David, who will bring about the definitive salvation of his people at the end of time. It is, however, never used in this sense in the Old Testament. In the Old Testament "the anointed one," or "the anointed of the Lord," means the king or any king, and it alludes to the rite of anointing with which the king was enthroned in his kingly dignity, in virtue of which he became a sacred and untouchable person. The historical books of the Old Testament explicitly mention the anointing of Saul (1 Sam. 10:1-3), David (1 Sam. 16:13), Solomon (1 Kgs. 1:39), Jehu (2 Kgs. 9:6-8), Jehoash (2 Kgs. 11:12) and Jehoahaz (2 Kgs. 23:30). The sacred character of the person of the king is well expressed by David, who though he had Saul in his power did not dare touch his person: "I will not raise a hand against my Lord, for he is the Lord's anointed and a father to me" (1 Sam. 24:11). For the same reason David punished with death Saul's servant who at Saul's wish had killed him on the mountains of Gilboa: "You are responsible for your own death, for you testified against yourself when you said. 'I dispatched the Lord's anointed' " (2 Sam. 1:16).

Messianism is the hope of a future salvation to be accomplished by an anointed king of the family of David. We pass over the other soteriological figures of the Old Testament that do not have this explicit regal and Davidic character, such as the Servant of Yahweh and the Son of Man (*see* SERVANT OF THE LORD, SON OF MAN). In defining messianism we have spoken of the future to embrace the diverse forms that the messianic hope took down through the history of Israel. The term eschatological will be reserved to what appertains to the end of time, when history reaches its terminus. Eschatology supposes a universal point of view that takes up the question of the history of all peoples. It is a common opinion that such an eschatology is only present in the Bible after the exile and develops its most decisive forms only with the apocalyptic writings. Messianism is certainly eschatological at this time, but to begin to distinguish messianism and eschatology would involve us in profitless difficulties when the point of the examination is messianism at its birth and first development. It is certain that the messianic hope, such as we find it in the New Testament writings, did not come about all at once at a certain moment in time. It underwent transformations and adjustments in the light of the course of salvation history itself. When the most ancient messianic oracles of the Old Testament are subjected to analysis in the light of the New Testament, the difficulty arises of how to determine the sense in which these speak of Christ. This poses the dilemma: either choose a direct, literal messianic interpretation, or a typical one. In the first case, the text would speak directly of the future eschatological messiah. The second however seems to be eluding the problem, that is, account is taken of the fact that the New Testament quotes the texts of the Old Testament and applies them to Christ, but the exegete finds himself in difficulties. On the other hand the direct literal interpretation seems to have to ignore the historical situation in which these oracles were pronounced and their only too clear reference to a historical king. Perhaps this difficulty can find a solution in the development of the messianic hope itself.

The messianic hope has its ultimate roots in the soteriological function played by the king in the eyes of the ancient peoples of the East. What shines out in the king is not his majesty, dignity and power. These qualities follow on and are justified in the fact that the king is the person who guarantees the well-being and social harmony of the people by just and equitable government. (*See* JUSTICE.) It is the king who leads the people to victory in battle, saves it from what might injure it, and takes immediate care of it for the benefit of his subjects. When the people ask Samuel for a king, what they really want is a savior: "There must be a king over us. We too must be like other nations, with a king to rule us and to lead us in warfare and fight our battles." What does "to rule us" mean in practice? This is expressed in concrete terms in Psalm 72:1-4: "O God, with your judgment endow the king . . . he shall govern your people with justice and your afflicted ones with judgment, the mountains shall yield place for the people, and the hills justice. He shall defend the afflicted among the people, save the children of the poor, and crush the oppressor." This text is moreover interesting because exegetes consider it to be messianic. The messianic hope then, at first reading, appears to be nourished by what people expected of a king, but to these expectations is added a divine pledge and guarantee.

This divine pledge to make promise a reality is contained in the oracle transmitted by Nathan to David (2 Sam. 7; 1 Chron. 17). David had shortly before transferred the ark of the covenant to Jerusalem, and had decided to build for the Lord a house (Heb. bayth). Nathan communicates to David an oracle on the point. In the first part he dissuades David from his project: "Should you build me a house to dwell in?" (2 Sam. 7:5). But he goes on: "The Lord also reveals to you that he will establish a house (bayth) for you" (2 Sam. 7:11). In this second part the word "house" is not used in the sense of building, but in the sense of descent or lineage, of continuity in the family and therefore of dynasty. It is not a question of a strict biological continuity, but of a dynasty in which the hopes that surround every kingly figure will be kept alive and made into a reality (2 Sam. 7:14-16). The first part of God's discourse might seem to be a reproof, but in reality God accepts and is pleased with what Psalm 132 calls David's "anxious care" for the ark of the Lord (Ps. 132:1-10). In this psalm too Nathan's oracle in favor of David is an answer by God to his piety (Ps. 132:11-13). God then freely pledges himself with an oath, a promise (Ps. 132:11) and a covenant (2 Sam. 23:5) to David and his dynasty: "Your house and your kingdom shall endure forever before me;

your throne shall stand firm forever" (2 Sam. 7:16). This pledge is given by God not only in favor of David, but above all in favor of the people to whom David is king. God chooses David and his dynasty to bring into effect his designs for the salvation of Israel: "I will make you famous like the great ones of the earth. I will fix a place for my people Israel. I will plant them so that they may dwell in their place without further disturbance" (2 Sam. 7:10, 11). In a certain sense it could be said that the saving designs of Sinai were concentrated in the person of the king, whom God wished to associate with his saving will for Israel in the future. Just as the Covenant of Sinai demanded reciprocation, so also did the promise to the king. His personal conduct and attitude can not only condition the response of the people, but he can also draw on himself and his people the curses that the covenant itself held over the heads of transgressors. He could then put obstacles in the way of the immediate realization of God's plan of salvation, but not even his sins would force God to revoke the pledge he had taken towards David's monarchy: "If his (David's) sons forsake my law ... I will punish their crime with a rod and their guilt with stripes. Yet my kindness I will not take from him, nor will I belie my faithfulness" (Ps. 89:33-34). Through Nathan's oracle, then, God chose David and his successors forever as the instrument for the realization of his design for salvation. The messianic hope is as open to the future as is God's plan itself. As history unfolded, the vague outline of this plan became less and less vague. We will briefly outline this development in the consciousness of Israel throughout its history.

It is obvious that the messianic promise had a message of good news and hope for each individual king. Before it looked to the distant future, messianism integrated the institution of the monarchy in the institution of the Covenant. The initial antagonism between the two, that God through Samuel's mouth indicated to the Jews who were demanding a king, was overcome: "It is not you they reject, they are rejecting me as their king" (1 Sam. 8:7; *see* KING), God himself put his seal on the monarchy as the means through which he would bring about salvation. The promise made to David finds its resonance in the hymns that accompany the enthronement of every king (Pss. 2 and 110; *see* also Ps. 72). In their immediate and more ancient sense, these were enthronement hymns (*see* 1 Kgs. 1:32-48; 2 Kgs. 11:12-20). The king was enthroned in the Temple. The priest consigned to him the insignia of his office, the diadem and a document called the "Solemn Statute" or "Pact," whose content, as is evidenced in Psalm 89:40, was nothing other than the promise of which 2 Samuel 7 speaks. This was a writing in which to the king was given divine affiliation in the sense that this has in the Old Testament (*see* SON OF GOD), together with the promise of divine assistance in what Psalm 2:7 calls the "decree of the king": "I will proclaim the decree of the Lord:/The Lord said to me: 'You are my son;/this day I have begotten you./Ask of me and I will give you/the nations for an inheritance/and the ends of the earth for your possession'." Psalm 110 puts it more poetically: "Rule in the midst of your enemies. Yours is princely power in the day of your birth, in holy splendor; before the day star like the dew I have begotten you" (Ps. 110:2, 3). Then he is given the sceptre (Ps. 110:2). After the anointing the king is acclaimed (1 Sam. 10:24; 2 Sam. 16:16; 2 Kgs. 9:13). Then he proceeds from the Temple to the place where, seated on his throne, he recieved the homage of his subjects (Ps. 110:1; 1 Kgs. 1:46). Psalms 2 and 110 are messianic because they give expression to the oracle of Nathan in 2 Samuel 7 and proclaim it for every king.

While it was applied to every king, however, the messianic promise itself remained open to the future, just as did the plan of salvation for Israel. The history of salvation did not just have a past, from the patriarchs to the entry into the land of Canaan (*see* Deut. 26:5-10; Ps. 136). The history of salvation was future-directed. The Jews experienced a real tension between the glorious promises of the past and their but limited realization in the present. So they awaited an intervention by God in the future, the "Day of the Lord," in which would be fully realized all that was promised. This hope in a certain sense was already eschatological, for it was to be the decisive and concluding act to the drama started with the promise. On the other hand, it was not fully eschatological because it is not seen in the context of a universal plan of God embracing all peoples and all history.

The messianic hope is caught up in an opening to the future. The promises made to David are made concrete in the king of the future who will be God's instrument in the realization of salvation. This will be the new David, not just because he will be David's son, but because in him will return the piety, justice and power that David enjoyed. The ideal will have been achieved. The chief singer of this king is Isaiah.

The circumstances in which Isaiah exercised his ministry are well known (Isa. 7). The continuity of the house of David was now in danger. Rezin of Damascus and Pekah of Israel have invaded Judah and have threatened to depose Ahaz if the latter does not fight with them against Tiglath-pileser of Assyria. Isaiah exhorts the king to faith and calm, for his enemies will not see success. Despite the refusal of Ahaz to ask for a sign as warranty of the truth of the oracle, Isaiah offers one, that of Emmanuel: "The virgin shall be with child and bear a son, and shall name him Immanuel ... Before the child learns to reject the bad and choose the good, the land of those two kings who you (Ahaz) dread shall be deserted". (Isa. 7:14-16). In the article on Emmanuel we have pointed out the reasons why Isaiah was directly referring to the future King Hezekiah. *See* EMMANUEL. The two messianic oracles of 9:1-6 and 11:1-9 seem also to have been applied to King Hezekiah, and refer in all probability to his birth. The personage described by Isaiah however is not in the same line or on the same level as the kings hitherto, even the holy ones among them. Before the prophetic eyes arises a perfect and ideal figure, not just a model to imitate or a program to follow (*see* e.g. Ps. 101) but a person whose reality is postulated and therefore guaranteed by the promise made to David.

It is true that Isaiah sees him already born in Hezekiah, but what is important and what was well understood by those who gathered his oracles is the taking shape, on the horizons of the future of messianic promise, the reality of a savior, son of David, who will bring to fruition the hopes that had hitherto eluded the empirical monarchy. Did Isaiah err then when he thought of Hezekiah? When the question is asked like this it does not make sense. Isaiah had his own tragic part to play, like every precursor, just as had John the Baptizer, when through his disciples he asked Jesus: "Are you 'He who is to come' or do we look for another?" (Matt. 11:3). There could be confusion in the identification of those signs which are meant to reveal the event of which they are heralds. Isaiah did not apply to Hezekiah the ideal image of the messianic king which was well known and awaited. Rather, the political turn of events and other circumstances that preceded and accompanied the birth of the king opened the eyes of the prophet to the meaning of the messianic promise to be realized in a perfect and ideal king.

From then on the empirical monarchy, that is, the effective succession of kings, remained in a sense outside the messianic promise, except as a link with the future king, who was to be son of David. However this was a prelude, an antecedent condition for the realization of the promise. This is why there was profound disturbance when the dynastic continuity was irreparably interrupted by the exile. One can notice an echo of this tragic sense in Psalm 89:39-52: it seemed to make void the whole promise. Even this however was overcome in the prospects opened up by the prophets who foresee the restoration of the kingdom at the end of the exile. Then the messiah, the new David, will take his place at the head of his people (Jer. 23:5, 6; Ezek. 34:23; 37:24). Zerubbabel, the head of the Jewish community that returned from exile in Babylonia becomes the center on whom converge the messianic hopes (Hag. 2:20; Zech. 6:9). Deutero-Isaiah purifies the image of the King-Savior from the excessive external splendor so often associated with him, and presents him as a "just savior, meek and riding on an ass, on a colt, the foal of an ass" (Zech. 9:9-13).

In the Jewish literature between the two testaments an intense messianic fervor is noticeable. Here a few points should be underlined. The more popular messianism, nurtured under the harsh experience of the Roman oppression, aspired to the overthrow of this dominion and so it automatically took on a political color with all its intolerance for the oppressor. This sparked the revolt of the Zealots. (*See* ZEALOTS.) There were not a few false messiahs in New Testament times (*see* Acts 5:35-39). Messianic movements were then naturally held in suspicion by the Romans. With this messianic idea as a foundation, a great variety of eschatological speculation was carried on, with computations and minute descriptions of the different phases of the last times, in the center of which appeared the different figures of a savior, who often gathered into himself elements from different traditions: he was to be a Davidic messiah and the Son of Man. The Targum identifies the Servant of Yahweh of Isaiah 42:1 with the messiah, while the aprocryphal works, the Fourth Book of Esdras and the Apocalypse of Baruch, adorn the Davidic messiah with elements taken from the Son of Man.

On the messianic consciousness of Jesus *see* JESUS CHRIST, MESSIANIC SECRET. Here must suffice a few words on the interpretation given to some of the messianic texts by the New Testament. First of all it must be kept in mind that the point of departure in reading the New Testament is the reality of Christ, who clarifies the meaning of Scripture. This was no novelty. It was the final unfolding of the meaning of the oracles and promises as they were seen through the developing history of Israel. The oracle of Nathan remained open to the future just as much as did the salvific plan of God of which it was a promise and a part. What was a thumb-nail sketch in Nathan was fiilled in through the action of God in history. The oracles of Isaiah were a rereading of 2 Samuel 7. Ezekiel 21:32 took up the blessing of Jacob on Judah (Gen. 49:10), while the Greek version of the Bible, the Septuagint, discovered in the Proto-evangelium itself (Gen. 3:15) the figure of the messiah (*see* PROTOEVANGELIUM). With the resurrection of Christ, however, the vague lines were clarified and brought to convergence, and the messianic oracles were seen in their most profound significance. Psalms 2:7 and 110, which are often quoted in the New Testament, are gradually interpreted as applying to the eternal generation of the Word. The "Today" of Psalm 2:7 becomes the crowning moment of Christ's mission, when, arisen from the dead, as man he takes possession of his rightful glory at the right hand of God in the heavens (Heb. 1:5; 5:5; 6:20; Acts 13:34; Rom. 1:4). When Psalm 110:1 is linked up with Daniel 7:13, it refers to the same moment: Christ's enthronement at the right hand of God. Christ's resurrection and exaltation to the right hand of God is the solemn enthronement of the messiah king of whom the Psalm sang. But all is not yet brought to completion. 1 Corinthians 15:27 and Hebrews 10:13 still await the perfect fulfilment of Psalm 110:1, 2. What the Old Testament says of the messianic kingdom is unfolding to its full flowering in the time between Christ's own exaltation and his second coming. This is the era of the Church. Already in the flesh of Christ have the messianic oracles found their fulfilment, but they still await their full and perfect realization when the kingdom of Christ and God will be manifested in all its fulness.

Messianic Secret, "The Messianic Secret in the Gospels" is the celebrated title of a study by W. Wrede, who for the first time subjected to systematic study a rather surprising aspect of Jesus' preaching in regard to his messiahship. This surprising aspect is that, especially according to Mark, Jesus goes to great pains to hide his messiahship. For this reason he imposes silence on the demoniacs who recognize him (Mk. 1:22-25; 5:3-5), while he warns the cured to remain silent about the miracle (Mk. 1:40-45; 5:21-43; 7:31-37; 8:22-26). Later he imposes silence on Peter, when, speaking for all, he confesses Jesus' messiahship (Mark 8:30).

Wrede's explanation for this was the following: the messianic secret was Mark's own invention. His intention was to reconcile the faith of the Church of his time, which proclaimed Jesus Messiah, with the more ancient tradition on Jesus and with the historical reality, in which nothing had been said about the messiahship of Jesus. Instead of changing the ancient tradition to meet the faith of the Church of his day, Mark explained the silence by attributing to Jesus the clear intention of keeping his messiahship hidden until it should be revealed with his resurrection. Although Wrede's theory is ingenious and arbitrary, it had the merit of focusing attention on a real problem, on which up to this no fully satisfying solution has been established.

If it is true that the messianic secret is put into particular relief by Mark, it is equally true that Mark is not its inventor. In fact the secret mirrors a historical attitude of Jesus. It is also planted as a thesis at the beginning of the discourse in parables, when Jesus turned to his disciples and said: "To you the mystery of the reign of God has been confided. To the others outside it is all presented in parables" (Mark 4:11) The parables are not self-evident explanations of the mystery of the kingdom of God for the non-initiated. Several of them more than need an explanation. They are rather the vehicles of a revelation in mystery, in veiled allusion, demanding an explanation that Jesus reserves for the few. This procedure has a parallel in the apocalyptic tradition, and precisely in regard to the Son of Man. (*See* SON OF MAN.) In fact, according to this tradition, the Son of Man already exists and is hidden with God. His glorious manifestation will take place at the end of time. Before this comes, however, his existence and the other eschatological mysteries have been revealed to a chosen few, that is, to those who by special privilege have been admitted for a time behind the veil to receive the vision. These privileged people are the ancient personages to whom the apocalyptic books have falsely been attributed. These in turn reveal what they have seen to a select group of pious and just men, who then are encouraged and established in their hopes by this revelation. In the same way Jesus enveloped in mystery his self-revelation and that of the mysteries of the kingdom of God, which in the final analysis are one and the same thing: In him and through him the kingdom of God becomes a present reality.

What is the intention and scope of this conduct of Jesus? Different explanations have been offered, which do not exclude one another but are rather complementary, and move at different levels of profoundity. From the first centuries of the Christian era, the silence that Jesus imposed was explained as a measure of prudence so that his mission might not be compromised by an equivocation that could prove fatal. Popular messianism had taken on a political and seditious character, so that the mere name of Messiah was enough to move the people to an erroneous enthusiasm about the real mission of Jesus, and at the same time provoke the suspicions of the constituted authority in the land.

As time went on, however, it was not just a measure of prudence, seeing the deformation that the concept of Messiah had undergone. The secret was an indispensable condition for faith in him. By means of the secret Jesus showed his reluctance to allow himself to be framed and, as it were, trapped within the confines of an already shaped title. It was possible to give to Jesus openly the title of Messiah without these equivocations and without these dangers to the faith, when the title itself was no longer a box into which to close Jesus, but the reality of Jesus himself dictated to the title its contents. Messiahship means continuity with the promise, that is, with the whole history of salvation. The idea of Messiah that had formed during the times of promise was however inadequate to the reality of Christ: in the light of his coming the promises could really be understood. This is why the Old Testament was avidly read in the light of its fulfilment in the New. The old prophecies were searched for traces of the unexpected newness that was Christ. Since it was the reality of Christ that gave to the title Messiah its content, the messiahship itself finished up by being contained in the name of the savior, Jesus Christ.

In the final analysis however the messianic secret does not rest on the plane of Jesus' attitude. For this attitude signals something much more profound: the great and radical hiddenness of Christ is his incarnation that redeemed, an enfleshment totally similar to ours except that he made no concession to sin. While he was God, he came in the form of a slave by emptying himself (Phil. 2:5 ff.). The mystery of the enfleshed Word then could not become transparent in all its splendor except when the risen and exalted Christ took possession also as man of his universal saving dominion, the fruit of his death. This is why he is called Christ without danger of ambiguity, a mystery he had hidden while he still walked in the form of a slave.

Methusael (me-thoo′-sa-el), In the genealogy of Cain, he is son of Mahujael and father of Lamech (Gen. 4:19). In all probability this is a variant version of the Priestly genealogy of Adam in Gen. 5:21-27.

Methuselah, Son of Enoch and father of Lamech. Methusaleh lived 969 years (Gen. 5:21-27). *See* METHUSAEL.

Meunites, (me-oo′-nites), An Arab tribe of the south of Palestine. With the Ammonites and the Moabites, the Meunites invaded the territory of Judah from the south up to En-gedi at the time of Jehoshaphat, king of Judah (873-849 B.C.). He succeeded in checking and driving them back. He fought a battle with them in the desert of Tekoa (2 Chron. 20:1-23). 2 Chronicles 26:7 speaks of another victory over them by Uzziah of Judah (783-742 B.C.). Among the Nethinim (*see* NETHINIM) who returned from exile there were also Meunites, probably descendants from slaves of the wars during the monarchy (Ezra 2:50; Neh. 7:52).

Mibsam, A son of Ishmael and ancestor of an Arabian tribe (Gen. 25:13; 1 Chron. 1:29).

Mica (my′-ka), Son of Meribbaal and grandson of Jonathan, friend of David (2 Sam. 9:12; *see* also 1 Chron 8:34-35).

Micah, 1. An Ephraimite who lived at the time of the judges. Micah had carved for himself an idol which he overlaid with silver. He also had an ephod and **teraphim** (household gods) made, and he consecrated one of his sons as priest of his domestic sanctuary. When a Levite of Bethlehem came to his house, he engaged him as priest. When the Danites were unable to secure attractive holdings in the land "allotted" them because of the aggressiveness of the Philistines, they went in search of new territory. Five of them were sent to explore the region, and when they had come to Micah's house they asked him to consult God on their undertaking. The Danites settled to the north at Laish. The five explorers reported what they had seen in Micah's house and returned with 600 armed men to rob the sacred objects which they brought to Dan in their new territory. This was the origin of the sanctuary of Dan. Micah's idol remained at Dan throughout the whole pre-monarchic period (Jgs. 17-18).

2. Micah, the sixth minor prophet in the Hebrew Canon of the Old Testament. *See* MICAH, BOOK OF.

Micah, Book of, A prophetic book of the Old Testament, the sixth of the minor prophets in the Hebrew Canon of the Old Testament. The inscription reads: "Micah of Moresheth," that is from Moresheth of Gath or Moresheth-gath, a village of Judah (Mic. 1:14) near the Philistine city of Gath, which today is probably Tell el-Judeideh. Micah ministered under King Jotham, 750-742 B.C.), Ahaz (735-715 B.C.) and Hezekiah (715-687 B.C.), all of Judah (Mic. 1:1). He was then a contemporary of Hosea, Amos and Isaiah. Nothing more is known of him. He is not to be confused with Micaiah son of Imlah, prophet at the time of Ahab of Israel (*see* MICAIAH, 1 Kgs. 22; 2 Chron. 18).

The inscription also describes the theme of the book: "The vision Micah received concerning Samaria and Jerusalem" (1:1). With strains like those of Amos, Micah censures the crimes of the Israelites of the northern kingdom, especially those of the ruling class (1:5; 3:9-11) and predicts without ambiguity the imminent ending of the kingdom of the north and of its capital Samaria, which in fact took place in 722 B.C. (2 Kgs. 17). He was no less implacable in denouncing the sins of Judah, and announces the future destruction of Jerusalem (Mic. 3:12). Jeremiah quotes this oracle, giving Micah's name to it (Jer. 26:18). Jeremiah also informs us that Micah's preaching provoked Hezekiah to repentance, so that "the Lord repented of the evil with which he had threatened them" (Jer. 26:19). Another characteristic of Micah also found in Jeremiah's preaching is the polemic with false prophets who predict a false peace, "who, when their teeth having something to bite announce peace, but when one fails to put something in their mouth, proclaim war against him" (Mic. 3:5-8). In contrast to them Micah knows he is filled with the Spirit of the Lord "to declare to Jacob his crimes and to Israel his sins" (3:8).

Micah's oracles on salvation are his most noted ones. In 4:1-5 is described the glory of the future Zion, to which will come all nations seeking the word of the Lord, and from which the Lord will judge and make peace among the nations. This oracle is also read, to the letter, in Isaiah 2:2 ff, and it is not possible to determine which of the two contemporary prophets was its originator. Micah in 5:1-4 speaks of the birth of the messiah-king in an oracle quoted in Matthew's gospel in the account of the magi in Jerusalem (Matt. 2:6). This portrait of the messiah is much like that of the famous oracles of his contemporary, Isaiah (cc. 9 and 11) (*see* MESSIAH, MESSIANISM), and should probably be related to the birth of King Hezekiah.

Micah 7:6 is quoted in Matthew 10:35. Among the Dead Sea scrolls was found fragments of a Midrash or commentary on Micah.

Micaiah (mi-kay′-yah), 1. Micaiah, son of Imlah, a prophet who exercised his ministry under Ahab of Israel (869-850 B.C.) and Jehoshaphat of Judah (873-849 B.C.). All that is known about him is the episode recounted in 1 Kings 22 (2 Chron. 18). Before setting out to war against the Aramaeans, Ahab and Jehoshaphat consulted the prophets, "about four hundred of them" (1 Kgs. 22:6), on the outcome of the campaign. The answer was favorable. Jehoshaphat however wanted to consult yet another prophet, so Ahab called Micaiah, son of Imlah, who, according to Ahab, "prophesies not good but evil about me." Micaiah ironically repeats the favorable word of the other prophets, but at the insistence of the king, told the truth: "I see all Israel scattered on the mountains like sheep without a shepherd." And he adds that the prophets who predicted otherwise were deceived by God himself, who sent into them a spirit "who became a lying spirit in the mouth of all his (Ahab's) prophets." One of these, Zedekiah, son of Chenaanah, came up and struck Micaiah on the jaw. The king ordered Micaiah arrested and handed over to Amon, governor of the city, to be held in prison and fed on bread and water until the king should come back safe and sound from the war (vv. 24-28). The prophecy was fulfilled, however, and Ahab died, hit by a random arrow which penetrated between the joints of the scale-armor of his breastplate (vv. 34-38).

2. Micaiah, one of the officers of King Jehoshaphat of Judah (873-849 B.C.) who was commissioned by the king to go through the land teaching the law of the Lord (2 Chron. 17:7-9).

Michael, 1. In the angelology of the apocalyptic tradition Michael is the angel entrusted by God with the task of watching over the people of Israel (Dan. 10:13, 21; 12:1). Jude 9 speaks of Michael's struggle with the devil over Moses' body: this legend is taken from the apocryphal work, The Assumption of Moses. In Revelation 12:7 Michael leads the angelic armies in their fight against the dragon and his angels. This then is the basis of the whole ecclesiastical tradition on Michael the Archangel. The struggle (Rev. 12:7) is transferred to the beginning of time, and Michael is made the chief of the army of angels who defeat the rebellious spirits. Later he appears also as the protector of the Church, the new people of God, whose departed members Michael leads to paradise.

2. Son of King Jehoshaphat of Judah (873-849 B.C.), killed, with his brothers, by Jehoram, still another brother, who in this way secured his hold on his father's kingdom (2 Chron. 21:2-4).

3. Also a personal name (Num. 13:13; 1 Chron. 5:13, 14; 7:3; 8:16; 12:21; 27:18; 2 Chron. 21:2; Ezra 8:8).

Michal (myʹ-kal), The younger daughter of Saul (1 Sam. 14:49). Saul had promised David his elder daughter Merab on condition that David "fight the battles of the Lord." Saul's intention was to see that David was killed in battle. Then he gave Merab to another. Michal the younger daughter loved David, and Saul decided to take advantage of the situation once more. He offered David his daughter in marriage in exchange for 100 foreskins of the Philistines, comparable to 100 scalps for an American Indian brave (1 Sam. 18:17-19). David however rose to the challenge and set out with his men, killing two hundred Philistines, whose foreskins he counted out before Saul. So the marriage took place. When Saul, jealous of David's growing popularity and power, decided to kill him, Michal informed David of her father's plans, thus enabling him to escape. Michal then took the household idol and laid it in the bed, putting a tress of goat's hair at its head, and covering it with a bedspread. When Saul's servants came, Michal told them he was ill. Saul nevertheless ordered that he be brought to him on his bed, whereupon the trick was discovered. Michal excused herself on the grounds that David had threatened to kill her if she refused to say David was ill (1 Sam. 19:11-17). Saul then gave Michal, David's wife, to Palti son of Laish from Gallim (1 Sam. 25:43). When Abner, the general of the army of Saul and of his son Ishbaal, was negotiating the reconciliation of the tribes of the north with David, the latter made it a condition that Michal, his rightful wife, should be restored to him. Ishbaal sent for her and took her away from her second husband Palti, "who followed her weeping as far as Bahurim," where Abner ordered him to go back (2 Sam. 3:14-16).

When the ark was brought to Jerusalem, David, girt with a linen apron, came "dancing before the Lord with abandon." Michal was watching the show from a window and "despised him in her heart." On his return, she rebuked him for playing the buffoon in front of the servant-maids, but David retorted that he danced for Yahweh and not for them, and while in Michal's eyes he might be base, in the maid's eyes he would be held in honor. And as a result, Michal had no more children to the day of her death (2 Sam. 6:14-16, 22-23).

Michmash (mik′-mash), A city in the land of Benjamin (Neh. 11:31), about 10 miles north of Jerusalem (Isa. 10:28), today Mukhmas. It was the scene of Jonathan's exploits and of his attack on an advance outpost of the Philistines (1 Sam. 13-14). It was the residence of Jonathan Maccabeus (1 Mac. 9:73).

Middin, A town in Judah a few miles inland from the northwest corner of the Dead Sea (Josh. 15:61).

Midianites, A nomadic people whose founding ancestor Midian appears as Abraham's son by Keturah, his second wife (Gen. 25:2-4). At this period the Midianites wandered in the desert around the Gulf of Aqaba, both eastwards and westwards, that is, in the Sinai desert. When Moses fled from Egypt he took refuge with the Midianites, and with them he lived as **ger,** benefiting from the hospitality of the tribe. Moses was particularly close to the "priest of the Midianites," sometimes called Reuel, sometimes Jethro, whose daughter Zipporah he married (Ex. 2:15-23; 4:18-23). These relationships continued after the Exodus. Jethro went out to meet Moses and offered a holocaust and other sacrifices to God. From him Moses received the sound advice to appoint minor judges to take care of ordinary questions, reserving to himself only those that were more serious (Ex. 18). According to Numbers 10:29-32, Hobab, son of Reuel and brother-in-law of Moses, became guide to the Israelites when they set out from Sinai.

Numbers 22:4-7 reports that the elders of Midian consulted with King Balak of Moab on how to check the advance of the Israelites. They decided to call on Balaam to help them. Again they are mentioned in the Book of Judges. By now the Midianites occupied territory on the edge of the desert east of Moab and Edom. When life became desperately hard for them they would raid the Israelites (and no doubt Moabites and Edomites) on their camels, filch grain from their fields and steal from their flocks. Gideon was the savior of Israel. He slew the two Midianite chieftains Zebah and Zalmunna (Jgs. 6-8). This victory is recorded several times in the Bible: it was the "Day of Midian" (Isa. 9:3 and 10:26; *see* also Ps. 83:10). The Midianites and Edomites are closely related in 1 Kings 11:18.

Midrash, The word **Midrash** is an exact transcription from the Hebrew. **Midrash** is the substantive of the verb **darash,** which means to search, to investigate, to study and, also, to expound the fruits of this research. The term has been preserved in English and in other languages instead of attempting a translation because this research has its own field, its own methods and precise aims. The field of research is Scripture, and thus Midrash is related to exegesis and biblical interpretation. The modern exegete, however, attempts to find the genuine meaning of the ancient texts in their particular historical and literary context. This he does through modern scientific methods. Midrash's aim, on the other hand, is to draw from Scripture a lesson for the present.

Midrash could be defined as "a reflection on Scripture in the light of the actual situation of God's people and of the developments of God's action on its history." This takes place in two directions at once, for while it draws from Scripture a lesson for the moment, it also seeks a deeper understanding of the sense of Scripture itself. Midrash was developed when the Scriptures acquired the character of authoritative and normative witness. At the base of the concept was the conviction that God's word remains forever, that is, it contains a lesson that is not exhausted by its literal meaning, nor even by the historical circumstances in which it was written or pronounced. This prophetic dimension was not limited to oracles but was present in every episode or law. From this point of view Midrash was not unaware of what Christian hermeneutics puts under the heading of the fuller and typical sense of Scripture. *See* INTERPRETATION; TYPICAL SENSE.

New problems that involve God's people in history are examined in the light of the text to find insights for the present. Thus for example, a problem of the practical order, which was not explicitly foreseen in the letter of Scripture, is resolved with a norm of conduct, which however was not seen as a novelty, but rather as an extension of the letter of Scripture. This is the Midrash **halakah**, from **halak**, to walk, to behave. It must be admitted that today it is difficult to see how such an exegesis could have satisfied the rabbis. It is difficult, for example, to see how Paul could have upheld the right of the gospel workers to live from their work from the text of Deuteronomy 25:4: "You shall not muzzle an ox when it is treading out grain" (1 Cor. 9:8; 1 Tim. 5:18). One must however immediately add that the mentality that gave rise to Midrash was not only convinced of the permanent value of God's word, but also deeply aware of the continuity in the history of salvation and of the completeness and perpetuity of God's will for Israel expressed in the law. For these reasons, rather than being the deduction of a norm from Scripture, Midrash was the sincere effort of the Jew to hook up to the letter of Scripture the concrete solutions he worked out to new problems that arose.

Midrash haggada comes from **higgid**, to announce, proclaim, narrate. This Midrash proposed to explain the meaning of a new event in the whole design for salvation traced out in Scripture, or to elucidate the meaning of Scripture in the light of the later historical experience of God's people. This kind of interpretation often opened the door to embellishments of the sacred accounts, anachronisms, and a freedom in handling and maneuvering the data of tradition that was at times a little too candid and certainly very imaginative. However, one must not generalize nor despise, just as one cannot afford to despise the heritage of patristic homiletics, which has so much in common with Midrashic methods, simply because they do not comment scientifically on the sacred text.

Midrash (plural Midrashim) is also called the exposition of this reflection on the word of God. Here there is a great variety of methods of exposition, of which we offer a few samples.

In the category of Midrash can be placed the more or less extended reelaboration of the sacred text in the light of the fuller sense that later tradition discovered in it. This touching up of the text is very frequent in the prophetic tradition, but there is a little of it in the whole of Scripture. The books of Chronicles, for example, are a Midrash of the history of God's people as it is known to us from 1-2 Kings. The authors rethink the history, underlining the decisive role played in it by David, the Temple and the priesthood. These then become a presage of the future. The various sources and strata of the Pentateuch take up, in a different age and in the midst of different preoccupations and interests, the central facts of the faith of Israel. Here too is mirrored the same penchant for making Scripture pertinent and actual that characterizes Midrash. When the Old Testament is quoted in the New, it is not only to show that the prophecies were fulfilled in Jesus, but also to reveal the deeper and at times hitherto hidden meaning of these prophecies in the light of their fulfilment in Christ.

Midrash however can also take the opposite direction. Instead of elaborating the texts in the light of the present reality, the present history is recounted in terms, expressions and allusions to the texts of the Old Testament which reveal the meaning of the present. History is seen through the framework set up for it by the Old Testament. Thus, for example, the story of the infancy of Jesus in Matthew and Luke is seen in the light of the prophecies of the Old Testament which announced the origin of the Messiah. This is what renders the interpretation of these documents as history such a delicate affair.

Finally Midrash can take on the form of a commentary on the sacred text. The **halakah** or the **haggadah** worked out on the individual texts are collected according to the order of chapters in the sacred text or simply in a continuing commentary on the sacred text. To this literary genre belongs, for instance, the commentary on the book of Habbakuk found at Qumran (*see* DEAD SEA SCROLLS) in which the book is interpreted in the light of the history of the sect. (*See* QUMRAN.) Another example are the Midrashim of post-biblical Jewish history, of which the most ancient are the Halachic Midrashim from the second and third centuries A.D., which include the Mekhilta (on Exodus), Sifra (on Leviticus), Sifre (on Numbers and Deuteronomy) and the Midrash Rabbah on Genesis (haggadic) from the third century on.

Midrashic utilization of Scripture, that is halakah and haggadah, in particular texts is also found in the Mishna, Targums and Talmuds. *See* TARGUM, TALMUD.

midrash

the *m.* of the prophet Iddo	a written account in the *m.*
2 Chron. 13:22	2 Chron. 24:27

Migdal-el, A place in Naphtali (Josh. 19:38), unidentifiable otherwise.

Migdalgad, A town in Judah (Josh. 15:37), possibly a location near Bozkath.

Migdol, A place in lower Egypt. The references in the Bible are probably to three different places, as the name in itself means "tower" or "fortress," and was applied as a proper name to more than one fortress erected from the time of Seti I onwards along the Egyptian frontier to the east of the delta. Exodus 14:2 speaks of Pi-hahiroth, between Migdol and the sea. The sea is probably the Mediterranean which would then place Migdol along the coastal road from Egypt to Palestine. (*See* EXODUS.) According to Jeremiah 44:1 and 44:6 the Jews who fled to Egypt after the destruction of Jerusalem in 587 B.C. settled down in Migdol, Tahpanhes, Noph and the land of Pathros. Noph is an old, incorrect translation of what is Memphis. In Ezekiel 29:10 and 30:6 Migdol and Syene represent the extreme north and south of the land of Egypt.

mighty

He was a *m.* hunter	Gen. 10:9	power of these *m.* gods 1 Sam. 4:8
	m. in strength Job 9:4	

Migron (mig′-ron), A city of Benjamin north of Jerusalem (Isa. 10:28) near Gibeah (1 Sam. 14:2). In Samuel the text is often corrected to **goren,** which means a threshing-floor.

Mijamin (mij′-a-min), Name of three priests and a layman (1 Chron. 24:9; Ezra 10:25; Neh. 10:8; 12:5).

Miktam, The term is read in the inscription of Psalms 16 and 56-60. The sense is obscure. Once scholars thought it derived from **ketem,** a species of gold, and that it referred to the psalm as a golden song. Today it is thought to derive from **katam,** expiate, and to refer to the psalm as one of expiation. This however, does not seem to fit the content of these Psalms.

Milcah, Milkah, 1. The name of Nahor's wife, and sister-in-law to Abraham (Gen. 11:29). She mothered eight children (Gen. 22:20-23), among whom was Bethuel the father of Rebekah, Isaac's wife (Gen. 24:15).

2. One of the daughters of Zelophehad, who died without male issue. The daughters appeared before Moses, Eleazar the priest and the elders of the whole community, and claimed for themselves some way in which to continue their father's name, since he had died blameless but without a son. So the Lord through Moses legislated that in this case the property should pass to the daughters (Num. 26:33; 27:1; 36:11; Josh. 17:3; *see* INHERITANCE).

Milcom, The national god of the Ammonites, which was also worshipped in the high place built under Solomon in Jerusalem (1 Kgs. 11:5, 33) and destroyed by Josiah king of Judah (640-609 B.C.; 2 Kgs. 23:13). When David captured Rabbah, the capital of Ammon, he took as booty the crown that sat on the idol of Milcom. It weighed a talent of gold and contained precious stones. It was placed on David's head (2 Sam. 12:30; 1 Chron. 20:2). Milcom's name is again read in the oracle of Jeremiah against the Ammonites (Jer. 49:1, 3) and in Zephaniah 1:5.

Mile, A measure of length. The Roman mile had eight **stadia,** or furlongs, each measuring about 220 yards but varying according to place (Matt. 5:41). The Roman mile was a little less than the present mile.

Miletus (my-lee′-tus), A city and seaport on the western coast of Asia Minor, south of Ephesus, at the mouth of the river Meander. While returning from his third missionary journey Paul met the elders of the church of Ephesus at Miletus, and addressed to them a farewell discourse which moved them to tears: "throwing their arms around him and kissing him" (Acts 20:15-38). According to 2 Timothy 4:20 Trophimus, a companion of Paul, was detained at Miletus through illness.

Milk, Goat and sheep's milk was and is one of the principal elements in the alimentary diet of nomads and shepherds in Palestine. Camel's milk could also be drunk by humans. Milk was preserved in skins (Jgs. 4:19), or a kind of soft cheese or yoghurt was made of it (Gen. 18:8; Jgs. 5:25). "A land flowing with milk and honey" is the stereotyped expression for the fertility and abundance of Canaan, especially Numbers 14:8 and in Deuteronomy (*see* Ex. 3:8; Deut. 6:3; Sir. 46:8, etc.). The abundance of milk is also frequently brought forward to suggest the prosperity and happiness of the last times (Isa. 55:1). Joel takes Deuteronomy's description and applies it literally to the last times: "On that day, the mountains shall drip new wine, and the hills shall flow with milk." The teeth of the bridegroom of the Song of Songs are milk-white: "His teeth would seem bathed in milk and are set like jewels" (S. of S. 5:12) while of the bride he sings: "Your lips, my promised one, distill wild honey. Honey and milk are under your tongue" (S. of S. 4:11). Milk, the typical food of infants, is used figuratively by Paul to indicate the rudiments of doctrine. Paul justifies the way in which he preached on his first visit to Corinth by pointing out the inability of new Christians to take anything more solid: "I fed you with milk and did not give you solid food because you were not ready for it. You are not ready for it even now" (1 Cor. 3:2; *see* Heb. 5:12-13). In 1 Peter 2:2 the "pure milk of the spirit" is the genuine Christian doctrine which comes with the newness of life received at baptism.

Mill, The oldest type of mill was the hand-mill consisting of a lower stone on which the grain was placed and an upper stone which was rubbed along the lower stone to grind the corn. Later, millstones powered by water, animals or humans came into use. It is probably to this, by hyperbole, that Christ refers when he states (Matt. 18:6) that it would be better to be drowned in the depths of the sea with a great millstone tied about one's neck than to scandalize one of the little ones (*see* Mk. 9:42). The smaller mill was and is still used by the poor. Millstones were usually of basalt. Other references to milling abound (e.g. Ex. 11:5; Matt. 24:41; Prov. 31:15, etc.).

million

a *m.* talents of silver	a force of one *m.* men
1 Chron. 22:14	2 Chron. 14:8

Millo, Millo is a form of the verb **mala'** which means to fill. The word millo, literally "filling," is the name of the works of fortification on the walls at the north of the "city of David," that is, the most ancient part of Jerusalem. (*See* JERUSALEM.) Before establishing his residence in the city David "built up the area from Millo to the palace" (2 Sam. 5:9). Millo would then seem to have been already in existence. Millo is again mentioned in the list of the works of Solomon for which he levied forced labor (1 Kgs 9:15 ff.). Hezekiah repaired Millo before the invasion by Sennacherib (2 Chron. 32:5). These bits of information, however, are not sufficient to form a clear, idea of what Millo was. Some think it was an artificial earthwork or raised platform of stamped earth to fill in a natural depression in the terrain which would naturally be a weak point in the defense of the city. 1 Kings 11:27 says in fact that Solomon built Millo to close up "the breach of his father's City of David."

Miniamin (min'-ya-min), Name of two men (2 Chron. 31:15; Neh. 12:17).

Minister, *See* DEACON, HIERARCHY.

Minni, A people and a state at the time of the Assyrian empire, south of Mount Ararat, and perhaps immediately south of Lake Urmia (Jer. 51:27).

Minnith, A city of the Ammonites conquered by Jephthah (Jgs. 11:33).

Mint, In upbraiding the scribes and Pharisees Jesus pilloried their hypocrisy in attending to insignificant details while passing over the substance of the law, justice, mercy and good faith. Thus they tithed the most insignificant of plants, such as mint, a plant that grew on the banks of streams and rivers and moist places and was used for seasoning food and in medicine (Matt. 23:23; Luke 11:42).

Miracles of Jesus, The "works of power" and the "signs and portents" that Jesus worked are an important part of his mission, and in fact, alongside his words, occupy a not insignificant portion of the evangelical tradition. The question to be examined here is what were their meaning and significance in Jesus' own consciousness of his mission. First however a brief note on two points: the way in which the miracles appertain to tradition and their historicity.

"Formgeschichte," or the study of literary genres in the formation of the gospel tradition, has subjected the portion on miracles to accurate analysis, identifying the form and the characteristics of this type of narration. The accounts of miracles and exorcisms unfold in three stages: a) The case is presented, be it the sick person or the demoniac. The whole build-up is to show the reader the extraordinary character of the cure that is to follow. Mention is made, for instance, of the duration of the disease (Mk. 5:25; 9:21; Lk. 13:11), or its gravity (Mk. 5:3-5; 9:18, 20) and of the unsuccessful attempts to regain health that previously had been made (Mk. 5:26), etc.

b) A description of the miracle. All the authors underline the almost total absence of manipulations and grotesque remedies to work the cure. The only exceptions to this are Mark 7:33; 8:33, while in contrast this is most frequent in Hellenistic accounts of miracles. Jesus works miracles with simple gestures. He takes the hand of the sick person (Mk. 1:31; 1:41; 5:41; 8:22), or he expresses his will (Mk. 1:41; 2:11; 3:5; 10:52) with perfectly intelligible words, without a trace of magical incantation, which so often occurs outside the gospel accounts. Jesus acts in his own name and power, while the disciples act "in the name of Jesus" (Mk. 9:38; Acts 3:6; 9:34).

c) The success of the cure or the exorcism is indicated, e.g. when the miraculously cured person is dismissed (Mark 7:29; 10:52) or by pointing out something that reveals unambiguously the cure (Mark 1:31; 1:44; 2:11). At times the account concludes with the so-called "final choir," that is, the narration includes an account of the astonishment that the miracle has provoked in the people who witness it: there is admiration, surprise, praise of God, etc. (Matt. 8:27; 9:33; Mk. 2:12).

We have alluded in passing to the non-evangelical accounts of miracles which can be read in Hellenistic literature. There is a surprising likeness between these accounts and the gospel narrative in so far as the form or so-called *ternary schema* described above is concerned. Some scholars have not resisted the temptation to postulate a dependence of the gospel miracle stories on the Hellenistic ones. In reality, this is most improbable, first because this likeness is also found in the narrations of miracles of other places and times in which any dependence would be quite out of the question. Indeed, as some authors have noted with humor, the same schema is used in publicity campaigns for patent medicines. It would seem, then, that the material itself demands this type of account. Secondly, as we have noted, the gospels lack that artificial and studied search after the prodigious and marvelous which is so typical of the Hellenistic accounts, and which in them plays an essential part. The gospel miracles however are subordinated to quite different premises and aims.

There can be no doubt about the fact that Jesus worked surprising cures and brought about astonishing exorcisms. Some of the words of Jesus that even the most radical of critics acknowledge as authentic speak unambiguously of miracles and prodigies (Matt. 11:4; 11:20-24; 12:25-29; Mk. 3:22-30; Lk. 11:14-22; 13:32). On the other hand this should not cause wonder, seeing that all authors agree in acknowledging Paul's witness in which he affirms that he himself has worked "mighty signs and marvels" (Rom. 15:18; 1 Cor. 12:9, 10; 2 Cor. 12:12). The evangelical testimony can be confirmed from without by the witness of rabbinical tradition. In the gospels it is stated that Jesus' adversaries did not deny the works Jesus performed, but they attributed them to Beelzebul, the prince of devils

(Mk. 3:20-30). The same interpretation is perpetuated in the Jewish tradition. It states that Jesus was put to death because he had seduced Israel to apostasy and had exercised magic. The Christian apologetes of the second and third centuries, Justin, Tertullian, Origen, still recount this interpretation. We probably have here an echo of the same controversy that Jesus had with his adversaries. This again convinces us that the real question was not a question of facts, which were admitted, but a question of interpretation. Were they, or were they not, works of God? Could they be attributed to magic? Jesus' adversaries, as we have seen, made their choice.

Somewhat different is the question of the historicity of the individual episodes as they are found in the gospel. The miracle tradition and its use in the preaching of the gospel is very ancient (*see* Acts 2:22; 10:38). One cannot, however, on that account exclude the possibility that some accounts may have undergone transformations or may have arisen outright in imitation of authentic miracles. Each individual case should be examined. Some of the accounts present, even at first reading, unmistakable signs of authenticity. Some for example have precise information on places, occasions and persons. This is almost an invitation to check the story out by calling on the witnesses who can verify it. Other accounts are so saturated with the historical situation of Jesus, as distinct from the historical situation in which the Church lived, that the possibility of the stories being confected at a date later than that asserted is practically excluded. These would be the miracles that had a polemic thrust against the Pharisees, such as cures worked on the Sabbath, the cure of lepers, etc. (*see* e.g. Mk. 3:1-6). Moreover by comparing the different accounts of the same miracle that are offered by the different evangelists it is possible to identify in the miracle the elements that belong more strictly to the original content, and in this way to go back to a more ancient stage of the transmission, and thus also to get nearer to the facts themselves.

If now we ask for the meaning and significance of the miracles and exorcisms in the life and mission of Jesus, we find a first answer in the term that was used to denote them. They were **dynameis**, "powers," or "works of power." This "power" must not be understood in an impersonal sense, but rather as Paul understood it when he defined the gospel as "the power of God for salvation" (Rom. 1:16). Through the works that Jesus accomplishes God establishes his kingdom. (*See* KINGDOM OF GOD.) The exorcisms and the miracles illustrate two aspects of the same kingdom of God.

When the Pharisees accused Jesus of exorcising in the name of Beelzebul, he refuted them by reducing their accusation to the absurd (Mk. 3:22-26). He adds another argument to reduce them to silence, pointing out that the disciples of the Pharisees also exorcise (Matt. 12:27; Lk. 11:19). Jesus pronounces on the scope and meaning of his exorcisms in the parable of the "strong man" whose house is plundered (Mk. 3:27; Matt. 12:29; Lk. 11:21, 22), which seems to be using a popular saying of which traces are found in Isaiah 19:24. The exorcisms clearly show Jesus' superiority over Satan, but in the parable Jesus wishes to specify more clearly this superiority. The exorcisms appertain to the definitive victory over Satan, which is an essential part of the coming of the kingdom of God. From this point of view, the exorcisms worked by Jesus are essentially different from those carried out by the disciples of the Pharisees. This difference however is not something that can be established merely from an external view of the events themselves. It is precisely to this that Jesus wishes to attract the faith of his listeners, a faith that, in the last analysis, believes that in Jesus the kingdom of God is present. The connection between the exorcisms and the kingdom of God is still more explicit in Matthew 12:28 and Luke 11:20: "If I in the Holy Spirit (Matthew) or in the finger of God (Luke) expel the demons, then the kingdom of God has come." Luke's expression "the finger of God" seems to be inspired by Exodus 8:15 where it clearly designates the omnipotence of God bringing about the salvation of Israel. According to Acts 10:38, Jesus was anointed with the Holy Spirit and with power, and "of the way God anointed him with the Holy Spirit and power. He went about doing good works and healing all who were in the grip of the devil." To this victory over Satan, which was part of the coming of God's kingdom brought about through Jesus and in Jesus, he alludes in Luke 10:18-20: "I watched Satan fall from the sky like lightning. See what I have done; I have given you power to tread on snakes and scorpions and all the forces of the enemy, and nothing shall ever injure you. Nevertheless, do not rejoice so much in the fact that the devils are subject to you as that your names are inscribed in heaven." These words are often badly interpreted to refer to the sin of the angels.

The cures worked by Jesus are the fruit of his compassion, mercy and love for whoever suffers (*see* Mk. 8:2). One must not rest here however at the surface. These cures are manifestations of the omnipotence of God who is bringing about definitive salvation, and establishing his kingdom. John the Baptizer sent his messengers asking: "Are you 'He who is to come' or do we look for another?" Jesus answer was a simple narration of the facts as they stood: "Go and report to John what you have seen and heard. The blind recover their sight, cripples walk, lepers are cured, the deaf hear, dead men are raised to life and the poor have the good news preached to them" (Lk. 7:22-23; *see* Matt. 11:1-6). The significance of this text is immediately caught if one adverts to the fact that it quotes two texts of Isaiah (Isa. 28:18-29; 61:1-2) in which the prophet describes the last times and definitive salvation. This answer is an invitation to faith that can overcome the first astonishment at the humble appearance of the Savior, so much in contrast with the image of the Messiah which the people had formed for themselves. This is also the faith that Jesus demands, and so often requests, from those coming to him to seek help (*see* Mk. 5:34, 36; 9:23, etc.). This is no vague trust in the superhuman powers of a wonder-worker but a faith in Jesus in whom and through whom God is now establishing his kingdom.

The miracles have also a message in themselves. Each one, in the concrete, reveals one or other specific characteristic of the Savior and of the salvation he brings. This aspect of the miracles has been elaborated with profound insight by John. *See* SIGNS.

Miriam, Daughter of Amram and Jochebed, and sister to Moses and Aaron (Ex. 6:20). In the story of Moses' birth, however, she is spoken of without being given a name (Ex. 2:4, 7, 8). Miriam is presented as a prophetess and directress of song and dance of the women after the passage through the Red Sea (Ex. 15:20, 21). The song of Miriam is one of the most ancient examples of Israelite poetry: "Sing to the Lord, for he is gloriously triumphant; horse and chariot he has cast into the sea" (Ex. 15:21). Once more Miriam appears with Moses, contesting his leadership on the basis that through Aaron and herself God also spoke to the people. God however gave to Moses a position above every prophet. Miriam was stricken with leprosy but cured, through Moses' intercession, after seven days, during which she was shut outside the camp (Num. 12:1-16). Miriam died and was buried at Kadesh (Num. 20:1). She is alluded to in Deuteronomy 24:9 and Micah 6:4.

Mirror, Mirrors were made of polished metal (Ex. 38:8; Sir. 12:11). Glass mirrors appear only in the Roman epoch. In 1 Corinthians 13:12 Paul contrasts the obscure vision had through "the mirror" of faith with the future face-to-face vision of God (*see* also James 1:23).

Mishael (mish′-a-el), One of the three friends of Daniel who were brought to the court of Nebuchadnezzar in Babylon. He received the Babylonian name of Meshach (Dan. 1:6-7).

Mishal (my′-shal), A city in the territory of Asher (Josh. 19:26; 21:30).

Mishma, 1. The name of a son of Ishmael (Gen. 25:14).

2. A descendant of Simeon (1 Chron. 4:25).

Mishmannah (mish′-man-ah), One of the men of Gad who joined David at Ziklag (1 Chron. 12:11).

Mishnah, Mishnah is a Hebrew word meaning repetition, and therefore oral tradition. It is a collection of the oral traditions of the most ancient teachers of Judaism who were called the **Tannaim,** the 'repeaters' from the Aramaic Tenah, to repeat. The Mishnah was compiled during the third century A.D. by Judah ha Nasi. This compilation is almost entirely of a juridical nature (*see* MIDRASH; HALAKAH) and is a compendium of the so-called oral law or tradition of which there is some mention in the gospels (e.g. Mk. 7:5). The Mishnah is divided into "orders" or parts, which are called **seder,** and these into tracts (**masseket**), sixty-three in all. The Talmud is a commentary on the Mishnah. *See* TALMUD.

Misrephoth-Maim (miz′-re-foth-may′-im), A place near Sidon mentioned in the account of Joshua's victory against the Canaanite kings of N. Palestine (Josh. 11:8; 13:6).

Mitanni, A kingdom in upper Mesopotamia founded by the Hurrians (1500-1370 B.C.) and afterwards absorbed into the Hittite empire. *See* HURRIANS, HITTITES.

miter
a *m.* and a sash   Ex. 28:4   tied over the *m.*   Ex. 28:37
                        Put the *m.* on his head   Ex. 29:6

Mithkah, A stopping-place of the Israelites en route to Canaan (Num. 33:28, 29).

Mithredath (mith′-re-dath), Treasurer of King Cyrus II of Persia, who ordered him to give back to Sheshbazzar, prince of Judah, the sacred vessels taken from the Temple in Jerusalem to Babylon by Nebuchadnezzar (Ezra 1:8-11).

Mitylene (mit′-e-lee′-ne), A city and seaport on the island of Lesbos in the Aegean Sea, where Paul stopped while returning from Achaia to Jerusalem at the conclusion of his third missionary journey (Acts 20:14).

Mizar (mie′-zar), A mountain apparently near Mt. Hermon and the sources of the Jordan river (Ps. 42:7), but otherwise unknown.

Mizpah, Mizpeh, This is the substantive of the verb **saphah** which means "to look out," "to walk over," hence Mizpah is a "look-out point." It is then a suitable name for many places, and in fact in the Old Testament it designates several cities or towns:

1. Mizpah, in Gilead, the residence of the judge Jephthah (Jgs. 11:11, 29, 34), probably identical with Ramath-mizpeh which is also in Gilead (Josh. 13:25) and with the place of the same name mentioned in the pact between Jacob and Laban (Gen. 31:49).

2. Mizpeh in northern Palestine. Having defeated Jabin king of Hazor and his allies, Joshua "pursued them to Greater Sidon . . . and eastward to

the valley of Mizpeh" (Josh. 11:8). It is probably to be identified with the "land of Mizpeh" at the foot of Hermon, where the Hivites settled. (*See* HORITES.)

3. Mizpeh, a city of Judah (Josh. 15:38) in the lowlands.

4. Mizpeh of Moab, where David met the king of Moab to whom he entrusted his parents while he was on the run from Saul (1 Sam. 22:3-4).

5: Mizpeh in the land of Benjamin (Josh. 18:26), today Tell en-Nasbeh, eight miles north of Jerusalem. In the premonarchic period Mizpeh was a place where the tribes met to judge together the crime that Benjamin had committed at Gibeah against a Levite and his concubine (Jgs. 20:1-4; 21:1). Thither too Samuel called the tribes during the war against the Philistines (1 Sam. 7:5-6; 7:11-12) and later Saul was there acknowledged as king of the tribes (1 Sam. 10:17). After the destruction of Jerusalem (587 B.C.) it was the residence of Gedaliah, the governor of Judah appointed by Nebuchadnezzar (2 Kgs. 25:23-25; Jer. 40:10) and there he was assassinated by Ishmael (Jer. 41). After the exile it was occupied by repatriates (Neh. 3:7-15). At Mizpeh Judas Maccabeus organized armed resistance to the Seleucids (1 Mac. 3:46-56).

Mizraim (miz´-ra-im), A Hebrew name for Egypt.

Mnason (nay´-son), A Christian of Jerusalem who received Paul into his home during the latter's last visit to the holy city (Acts 21:16).

Moab, Moabites, A semitic people related to the Israelites (Deut. 2:9) and with the Ammonites (Gen. 19:37) who settled in Transjordan in the thirteenth century B.C., before the Israelites established themselves in Canaan. Moab territory comprises the highlands east of the Dead Sea, between the river Arnon to the north and the Zered to the south. The northern boundary of the kingdom of Moab often changed. Before the Israelites arrived, Moab had occupied the region north of the river Arnon, but they had been defeated and pushed south of the river by Sihon, king of the Amorites from Heshbon (Num. 21:26-30). When the Israelites defeated Sihon, they took all the land as far as the Arnon (Num. 21:24). The Israelites camped on the "steppes of Moab," that is, on the plain east of the river Jordan opposite Jericho, before crossing the river into Canaan. This is the scene of the discourse of Moses in Deuteronomy (Deut. 1:1-4) and of the last episodes of the Book of Numbers. While they were camped there, Balak king of Moab had Balaam come to curse Israel (Num. 22-24). The Israelites allowed themselves to be seduced by the Moabite women and to embrace the cult of the god Baal of Peor. Phinehas started the reaction against idolatry by making an example of an Israelite who took to himself a Midianite woman: he followed them into the alcove and ran them through with a lance (Num. 25). Moses died on Mt. Nebo (Deut. 34; *see* 32:49).

In the Book of Judges the Moabites intervene in the episode of Ehud. Eglon, king of Moab, in alliance with the Ammonites and the Amalekites attacked and defeated Israel, taking possession of Jericho. Ehud, a Benjaminite son of Gera, went to Eglon with the tribute, but on the pretext of having a secret to tell the king, got a private audience with him during which he stabbed him to death. Then he gathered the men of the mountains of Ephraim, occupied the fords of the Jordan leading to Moab, and permitted no one to cross. The Bible states that on that occasion they slew ten thousand Moabites (*see* Jgs. 3:12-30). Ruth, Naomi's daughter-in-law, was a Moabite (Ruth 1:1-5). David was a descendant of Ruth and Boaz. He left his family with the king of Moab at Mizpeh when he was a fugitive from Saul (1 Sam. 22:3, 4).

During the monarchy the relationships between Israel-Judah and Moab were always tense. Saul (1 Sam. 14:47), and afterwards David, fought with success against Moab. David made Moab a vassal to Israel (2 Sam. 8:2). Moab rebelled at the time of Jehoram king of Israel (849-842 B.C.). Mesha king of Moab used to pay the king of Israel as tribute "a hundred thousand lambs and the wool of a hundred thousand rams," but rebelled when Ahab died. Jehoram, with the king of Judah and the king of Edom, invaded Moabite territory and put the capital, Kir-hareseth, under siege. Elisha the prophet accompanied the king on this campaign. (*See* ELISHA.) It was not a successful campaign. According to 2 Kings 3:27 the king of Moab, seeing himself defeated, "took his first-born, his heir apparent, and offered him as a holocaust upon the wall. The wrath against Israel was so great that they gave up the siege and returned to their land." This is a veiled way of confessing defeat. There is also a Moabite account of his campaign on the stele erected by Mesha to record this victory. (*See* ME-SHA.) During the following centuries there is reference to warlike action on the part of Moab against Israel (2 Kgs. 3:10) and against Judah (2 Chron. 20; 2 Kgs. 24:2; Zeph. 2:8; Ezek. 25:8). After the affair of Judah there is no more reference to Moab. Later the Nabataeans appear in their land, as well as in Edom.

The prophets have various oracles and threats against Moab (Isa. 15-16; Jer. 9:25; 25:1; 27:3). Amos censured the Moabites for the treatment meted out to the Edomites in a war that is not identified. Among the traditions dealing with Lot is one that treats of the origins of Moab and Ammon. This has to do with the popular etymologies of the names. Both peoples would have come from Lot's relations with his daughters. Moab is thus interpreted "from my father" in Hebrew **meabi**, and Ammon is "the son of my kin" in Hebrew **ben ammi.**

mock

you can *m*.	Job 21:3	I will *m*. when terror	Prov. 1:26
	who will *m*. him	Mk. 10:34	

Modein (moe′-deen), A village of Judea, twenty miles northwest of Jerusalem, to which Mattathias and his sons, the Maccabees, retired during the persecution ordered by Antiochus IV Epiphanes against the Jews who were faithful to the law. At Modein Mattathias refused to obey the king's officials who asked him to apostatize, and he slew a Jew who dared to sacrifice in front of all. Then Matthathias, his sons, and all who did not wish to submit themselves to the king fled to the mountains (1 Mac. 2). Mattathias was buried at Modein at the tomb of his fathers (1 Mac. 2:70), where also were buried Judas (1 Mac. 9:18-21) and Jonathan Maccabeus (1 Mac. 13:25, 26). Simon erected over the tomb of his father and his brothers a monument of stones, raised high enough to be seen at a distance. The monument is described in 1 Maccabees 13:27-30.

moisture

withered through lack of *m*.

Lk. 8:6

Moladah (mol′-a-dah), A city in the territory of Simeon (Josh. 15:26; 19:2; Neh. 11:26).

Molech, Moloch (moe′-lek, moe′-lok), A non-Israelite god. The name is more of a title meaning king (in Hebrew **melek**). The title also appears in Adrammelech and Arammelech, gods venerated by the people of Sepharvaim who were settled in Samaria by the Assyrians. The names are translated as "King Hadad and his consort Anath" (2 Kgs. 17:31). Milcom, the national god of Ammon, is the same name (1 Kgs. 11:7). Molech was venerated especially with human sacrifices (Lev. 20:2-5) by making one's children pass through fire (Lev. 18:21; 2 Kgs. 23:10; Jer. 32:35); one of the chief places for these sacrifices was Tophet in the Valley of Hinnom, near Jerusalem.

moment
That very *m*.
Matt. 9:22; 15:28; 17:18

Money, The first coins were minted c. seven hundred B.C. and consisted of a piece of metal with its exact weight and value impressed on it, together with the authority that guaranteed it. Before this, commercial exchange and payment were made in kind, by barter (1 Kgs. 5:25; 2 Kgs 3:4) or precious metal chosen for the occasion (Gen. 42:25; 2 Sam. 24:24; Jer. 32:9). The metals used in minting coins were gold, silver, bronze and brass. The first coins mentioned in the Bible are gold darics (Ezra 8:27; 1 Chron. 29:7), weighing 8.41 grams. Other Persian coins are silver shekels weighing around five grams (Neh. 5:15). After the conquest of Alexander the Great, Greek coins became widespread. The basis of the Greek system was the drachma of silver, weighing about 3.6 grams. The shekel was equal to the tetradrachma, that is, four drachmas, and therefore about 14 grams. The didrachma, or two drachmas, was half a shekel, and was the annual tribute to be paid to the Temple. Jesus paid it for himself and for Peter with a stater, which was equal to a tetradrachma or half-shekel (Matt. 17:24-27). When the Pharisees to test Jesus asked him whether it was licit to pay tribute to Caesar or not, he asked them to show him the coin of the tribute. What they showed him was a Roman denarius, with the effigy and inscription of Augustus (Matt. 22:15-22; Mk. 12:13-17; Lk. 20:20-25). The denarius was the laborer's daily wage (Matt. 20:1-12). The talent and the "mina" or pound was a weight rather than a value measure. The talent corresponded to 6,000 drachmas and the "mina" to 100 drachmas (Matt. 25:14-30; Lk. 19:12-27). The widow's offering at the Temple treasury was two bronze coins (**lepton**) equal to one **quadrans,** a bronze Roman coin of 3.1 grams, quarter of an **as**. Four **as** made a sesterce.

Coining money was reserved to the supreme authority which could make certain concessions in this matter to the provinces of the empire or to free cities, but almost always to the exclusion of minting gold or silver. In 138 B.C. Antiochus VII Sidetis allowed Simon Maccabeus to mint his own money (1 Mac. 15:6) but this was probably not used until the time of John Hyrcanus (135-105 B.C.). From this minting have come down bronze coins. During the Jewish revolt, to show their independence, the Jews minted coins in bronze and silver in 66-70 A.D. and 132-135 A.D.

money changers
overturned the *m*. table   Matt. 21:12; Mk. 11:15

Monotheism, Monotheism is the doctrine that professes the existence of but one God. It may come as a surprise to find that the Bible contains discussions on monotheism. The word first calls for clarification. Monotheism holds to the existence of one God only, while monolatry admits the worship of only one God, to the exclusion of others, whose existence, however, is by no means denied. The monotheistic question, then, is not so much a religious one as a doctrinal tenet, that is, a theoretical enunciation on the existence of one or more personal divinities. Moreover, it should be noted that there is no doubt about Israel's monotheism once the people had reached maturity, especially through the doctrinal enrichment and purification that resulted from the prophetic movement (*see* PROPHETS). The question, then, is about the genesis of Israel's monotheistic faith. When and how did the people come to an explicit profession of monotheism?

The most explicit profession of monotheism is found in the polemic of the prophets of Israel against idolatry. Examples of this can be found in Isa. 40:18-20; 44:9-20, and still earlier in Jer. 10:1-9 (*see* also the polemic of Wis. 13–15 and 1 Thess. 1:9). Here we have so self-assured a monotheism that it adopts the weapons of sarcasm and ridicule against its enemies. Perhaps less obvious, but for that very reason even deeper, is the monotheistic faith of a prophet like Amos, whose God is the God of the universe and its peoples, who everywhere punishes the injustice of the Gentiles, even when Israel is not the victim (Amos 1:2–2:3).

One will also discover, however, more ancient texts of the Bible (e.g. Ex. 15:11; 18:11) where Israel's God is declared superior to the gods of other nations. These texts, then, admit the existence of other gods, who however have no competency over Israel. Here the question arises: Is Israel's confession of the one God, as it is found, e.g. in the first commandment (Ex. 20:3; 22:19; 23:13) monotheistic? The answer must be that the existence of other gods for other nations is not excluded. From Israel, however, is demanded a total and exclusive worship of its God, the Savior of the people. In other words, the first precept of the Decalogue is not the enunciation of a doctrine on the deity but a demand for a response from the whole person. The reason behind such a demand, besides the fact that God has been Savior to Israel (Ex. 20:2), is that God is a jealous God (Ex. 20:5-6; Deut. 5:9-10). God's jealousy does not tolerate any sharing of Israel's worship with any other god. This exclusiveness on the part of the God of Israel is without parallel in the history of religions, and constitutes an emotive, though not as yet conceptualized, monotheism. The point of this exclusiveness emerged with time in the conscience of Israel. God's "jealousy" was not just an intolerance of attention paid to other gods: it amounted to an intolerance of their very eixstence (Deut. 32:37-39). Eventually Israel came to the conviction of theoretical monotheism. In the meantime the people lived in a climate of what can best be termed practical monotheism. In this atmosphere the glory of the one God was respected and eventually translated into theoretical or conceptual monotheism.

monster, monsters

the great sea *m.*	Gen. 1:21　you sea *m.*	Ps. 148:7
or a *m.* of the deep	Job 7:12　*m.* amidst your Niles	Ezek. 29:3

Month, The Israelites, like the orientals in general, followed the lunar month, beginning with the new moon. In Hebrew month is **yerah,** which means moon, and **hodes,** which means new moon. The months had alternatively 29 or 30 days. To distinguish the different months the Canaanaean names, which are related to the seasons of the year, were used.

In the Bible occur the months Abib, which means green ears of corn, and stood for March-April (Ex. 13:14; Deut. 21:1); Ziv, meaning flower, equivalent of April-May (1 Kgs. 6:1, 37); Ethanim, meaning constant waters, for September-October (1 Kgs. 8:2) and Bul, which means rain, for October-November (1 Kgs. 6:38).

A similar system found on a tablet of the ninth century which was discovered at Gezer distributes the months according to the work in the fields. To the harvest is allotted a period of two months, to the sowing two months, to late sowing two months and so on. Traces of this system can be seen in the calendar of religious feasts (*see* Ex. 23:16; 34:22; 1 Sam. 12:17; 21:9, 10).

The method of counting the months with the ordinal numbers starting with March-April probably commenced under Josiah (640-609 B.C.) (*see* e.g. Jer. 36:9, 22; 28:17, etc.).

During and after the exile the Babylonian names were adopted beginning with March-April, as follows: Nisam, Iyyar, Sivan, Tammuz, Ab, Elul, Tishri, Marheshvan, Chislev, Tebeth, Shebat, Adar. Some of the official documents of 2 Maccabees are dated with the names of the Macedonian calendar, such as Xanthicus for April (2 Mac. 11:30; *see* 11:21, 33, 38) while Tobit 2:12 has Dystros for March.

Moon, Genesis 1:14, 15 with a certain insistence affirms that God made the moon and the stars to "mark the fixed times, the days and years, and sure as luminaries in the dome of the sky, to shed light upon the earth." He repeats the same concepts in 1:16-18. This reveals a polemic thrust against the cult of the stars which was widespread in Babylonia, the cradle of astrology. The Babylonian moon-god was venerated at Ur and Harran. In the Hebrew calendar the months were lunar. (*See* MONTH.) The new moon was announced with the sound of trumpets (Ps. 81:3), and particular sacrifices were offered on that day (Num. 28:9-15) which was a day of rest like the Sabbath (Amos 8:5). A special solemnity surrounded the new moon of the seventh month (Tishri, September-October) which coincided with the beginning of the year in the pre-exilic Hebrew calendar (Lev. 23:34; Neh. 8:2). Despite its eclipses and its changing face throughout the cycle, the moon is a symbol of faithfulness and constancy (Pss. 72:7; 89:38), perhaps because of the regularity of its movements and appearances. Like the rest of creation in general, the moon is involved in the upheaval of nature that accompanies God's interventions in history (Josh. 10:12; Hab. 3:11), and especially God's eschatological interventions: the moon shall give no more light (Joel 3:15; Matt. 24:29; Mk. 13:34) and shall be changed to blood (Acts 2:20; Rev. 6:12), that is, to red. In the heavenly Jerusalem the light of the sun by day and the moon by night will be superfluous, because "the glory of God gave it light and its light was the Lamb" (Rev. 21:23). In this way will the moon terminate the mission confided to it in creation (Gen. 1:14-18). Psalm 121:6 and Matthew 4:24 and 17:15 show traces of the universal belief that the phases of the moon somehow affect mentally disturbed people, whence the name "lunatics."

Mordecai, (mor′-de-kie), The cousin and foster-father of Esther. The Lord made known to him in a dream that the king's eunuchs were plotting against the life of the sovereign. Mordecai informed the king of this and so saved his life. The king had these things recorded and appointed Mordecai to serve at court, rewarding him for his actions (Esth. 2:19-23). Shortly afterwards King Ahasuerus raised Haman to high rank and ordered all the king's servants to kneel and bow down to Haman. Mordecai however refused, and this was reported to Haman, who angrily decided to exterminate all the Jews of the empire on a certain day, the fourteenth day of the twelfth month, Adar. Mordecai came to know of his plans and informed Esther of them. She presented herself to the king, even though it endangered her life to do so unsummoned, and invited the king and Haman to a dinner she was preparing. In the meantime Haman had erected the gibbet on which he was to hang Mordecai. On the night before the banquet the king was unable to sleep and so started reading the chronicles of the kingdom in which he found recounted the favor Mordecai had done to him, by informing on the eunuchs and thus saving his life. He then asked what recompense had been made to Mordecai for the great good he had bestowed on the king and kingdom. The reply was that none had been made. So he asked Haman's counsel, without mentioning Mordecai's name and when he had done this, he ordered him to take the honors he had listed and bestow them on Mordecai.

During the banquet Esther revealed to the king Haman's plan to exterminate her people. Moved by the news the king withdrew to the garden. Haman knew that he was in danger so he stayed behind to beg Esther for his life. When the king returned he found Haman had thrown himself down on the couch on which Esther was reclining. Suspecting that Haman was attempting violence on the queen he ordered him to be hanged on the gibbet he had prepared for Mordecai, while the latter was given the post thus vacated by Haman. At last the king issued a decree which authorized the Jews in each and every city "to group together and defend their lives, and to kill, destroy, wipe out ... every armed group of any nation or province which should attack them and to seize their goods as spoil." This decree was to go into effect on the same day throughout the provinces of Ahasuerus, the thirteenth day of the twelfth month, Adar. On the historicity of Esther *see* ESTHER, BOOK OF; PURIM.

more

and he loved her *m.* than Leah		hated him all the *m.*	Gen. 37:8
	Gen. 29:30	*m.* so than we ourselves	Ex. 1:9
circumstances are *m.* favorable	1 Cor. 16:12		

Moreh, The "terebinth of Moreh," a sacred tree in the vicinity of Shechem. There Abraham encamped, built an altar and invoked the name of God (Gen. 12:6-18). There too Jacob buried all the foreign gods of the people (Gen. 35:4). It is probably to be identified with the Diviner's Oak, near Shechem, which figures in the story of Abimelech (Jgs. 9:37; *see* also Josh. 24:26). *See* OAK.

Moresheth (mor′-e-sheth), Birthplace of the prophet Micah (Mic. 1:1) in Judah, probably Tell el Judeideh, east of the city of Gath.

Moriah, (mo-rie′-ah), "The land of Moriah," the site of the sacrifice of Isaac, three days journey from Beer-sheba (Gen. 22:1-4). Tradition identifies Moriah with the hill of Jerusalem on which the Temple of Solomon was built (2 Chron. 3:1).

morning

and *m.* followed	Gen. 1:8; 1:13	but in the *m.*	Matt. 16:3
rose in the *m.*	2 Sam. 24:11	Early next *m.*	Mk. 11:20

Mortar, The, A section of Jerusalem (Zeph. 1:11).

mortify

shall *m.* himself	Lev. 16:29

Moserah, Moseroth (moe′-ze-rah), An encampment of the Israelites on their journey through the desert to Canaan. In Deuteronomy 10:6 where it is called Moserah, it is stated that here Aaron died and Eleazar succeeded him to the high priesthood. In Numbers 33:30-31 it is called Moseroth. According to Numbers 33:38 Aaron died on Mt. Hor.

Moses, Moses is the central figure, not only of the Pentateuch, but of the Old Testament. He is the central figure because he stands at the source that became the norm for the whole religion of Israel. This central importance however has not served to keep a clear picture of his person and work. Rather, it has obscured him in history. This seems to be a paradox: under his name, authority and personal achievement is placed the whole later development of the religious institutions of Israel, the law and the cult; but, from the strictly historical point of view one must frankly acknowledge that Moses is not the author of the Pentateuch (*see* PENTATEUCH), nor can the law as we today find it in the Bible be traced back to him (*see* LAW), nor to him can we directly attribute the cult as it is ordered and described in Exodus and Leviticus (*see* SACRIFICE). Some authors have been tempted in the past to deny the historical existence of Moses. Even today some would limit the personal role of Moses to the founding of Israel, asserting that the most we know about him is his death and burial at Mt. Nebo. This scepticism however leads to an historical absurdity. For at the origin of the religious phenomenon called Yahwism, which possesses such vigor and originality, one must place a personality that was as vigorous and original. The Bible names Moses in this role. The scepticism of these authors however does warn us from falling into an anachronism. We must, in a certain sense, renounce the effort to reconstruct the Mosaic Israel as it was at that time, and search rather for those original impulses that set the whole religion of Israel in movement, impulses which in turn cannot be divorced from the work and religious experience of Moses.

Moses is the decisive figure in the period that saw the start of the religious heritage of Israel. One can distinguish the revelation of Yahweh, the Exodus, the Covenant, the law, and the journey through the desert.

From an etymological point of view, Moses is an Egyptian name. The same name appears in Pharaohs such as Tuth-mose and Ramses, and it means "born." With Moses the name of the god (Tot, Ra) is absent. A popular etymology for this name is offered by Exodus 2: Moses would be the participle of the verb **masha**, "to draw." The etymology, however, does not completely fit the account, for **Moshe** is an active participle while the story demands a passive participle: "drawn" from the historical point of view, and in fact it exploits certain connected themes from various infancy stories of great heroes, such as the dangers that threaten his existence and survival, his surprising rescue, his being born hidden from the eyes of those he was to conquer and so on (Ex. 2:1 ff.). Then, in more concrete terms, the episode of his being placed in a basket at the river's edge is also told of Sargon, the founder of the Akkadic dynasty in Mesopotamia (2350-2150 B.C.). According to Exodus 2:1 and the genealogy of Exodus 6:16-27, Moses was of the tribe of Levi, of the family of Kohath, and was born to Amram and Jochebed. His brother was Aaron and his sister Miriam.

The traditions that speak of Moses in the land of Midian (Ex. 2:11-4:20) have a more solid historical basis. The central point of this tradition is the account of the meeting with Yahweh on Horeb, the mountain of God. The preceding story of his flight from Egypt served to link up the account of his birth with that of his presence in Midian (Ex. 2:11-16). It is a source of wonder, and at the same time a guarantee of the antiquity of the stories, that Moses had fairly close links with a people who at the time of the judges were the irreconcilable enemy of the now settled Israel (Jgs. 6:1). This nomadic tribe moved in the region around the Gulf of Aqaba towards the east, but also towards the west and Mt. Sinai. Moses lived with them as a ger, a foreigner enjoying the hospitality and protection of the clan. So his son by Zipporah is called Gershom, "a stranger in a foreign land" (Ex. 2:22). Of great importance is the relationship between Moses and the priest of Midian, who has been given various names in tradition: Jethro (Ex. 3:1; 4:18; 18:1), Reuel (Ex. 2:18) and Hobab, called Reuel's son in Numbers 10:29. Zipporah, Moses' wife, was Reuel's daughter, and besides Gershom (Ex. 2:21, 22), Moses also had from her Eliezer (Ex. 18:4).

According to the narrative of 3:1-4 the mountain of God, Horeb, was a sacred place before Moses arrived there. Who was the god venerated there? Many authors say it was Yahweh (*see* YAHWEH). In this case one would have to conclude that the worship of Yahweh was known and practiced before Moses. Indeed this is the opinion gathered from 4:26. This however does not detract anything from the religious experience of Moses. God's revelation never takes place in a vacuum, that is, in terms unconnected with the concrete forms of religion of the times and of men to whom the revelation is addressed. However, it is none the less true that through these forms God really speaks and reveals himself. The true countenance of Yahweh was what Moses and later the Israelites experienced, and not the figure that the God of Sinai hitherto might have had.

Moses received from Yahweh the mission to free his people who were enslaved in Egypt (Ex. 3:7). With this mission and message Moses returned to Egypt. The tradition of the vocation and mission of Moses is shaped in the literary genre of vocations of men of God, as is evident also in Jeremiah 1:4-8; Judges 6:12-17. The details of the story are not to be taken as historical details. In the final analysis the story of Moses' vocation is retrieved from the past on the basis of the experience of personages in biblical history who were the object of an analogous choice on the part of God.

The story of the liberation is contained in the "Booklet on the Plagues" (Ex. 7-13) and in the account of the miracle of the sea (Ex. 14-15). On the interpretation of these accounts *see* PLAGUES OF EGYPT, EXODUS.

After the exodus from Egypt, Moses' name is linked with the Covenant of Sinai and the journey through the desert. The traditions on the Covenant of Sinai (Ex. 19-24) cannot be taken as a direct and immediate chronicle of events as they happened. They immediately reflect the periodic commemorative rites of the Covenant in the Israelite cult. (*See* TABERNACLES, FEAST OF.) An attentive reading of the text reveals liturgical and ritualistic indications that are incompatible with the historical circumstances and indeed with what precedes and what follows the account (e.g. Ex. 19:21 speaks of the priests of the Lord, whose institution is narrated in Lev. 8). While these traditions do not allow us to reconstruct events as they happened on Sinai, they do serve as vehicles of transmission for the significance and inner meaning of those events. Moses led the people he had liberated to the place of his first encounter with God, where he had received his revelation and his mission. There he obliged the people to accept the cult and exclusive service of this God, together with the observance of some of his fundamental demands. This people, whom Moses had led out of Egypt and who had experienced the power of Moses' God, Yahweh, in their regard, thus became the people of God, and Yahweh became the God of Israel. This link was sanctioned by rites that it was customary to use to seal pacts between men, and thus became the Covenant of which Moses was the mediator, and with which his name is inseparably involved. (*See* COVENANT.) Thus out of the heterogeneous rabble that fled from Egypt was born a people. Moses, in his function as mediator in the meeting with God, soldered that link which was to prove stronger than, and survive, every historical vicissitude, be it schism, exile or dispersal among the nations.

The Decalogue is traditionally associated with the Sinai Covenant (Ex. 20; Deut. 5). The text of the Decalogue does not in itself contain anything incompatible with the time of Moses. Whatever the judgment on the Mosaic origin of the Decalogue (*see* DECALOGUE), typically Mosaic and genuine formulations of the revelation Moses received and transmitted are the following: a. The practical monotheism announced in the first commandment, together with the exclusive service of Yahweh and intolerance of any other deity on the same level as Yahweh: all this contains in a nutshell the explicit and speculative monotheism of the prophetic tradition. (*See* GOD, JEALOUSY.) b. The prohibition of images of the Lord, in the second commandment, which is equivalent to a confession of his transcendence and radical otherness to his creation. (*See* IDOL, IDOLATRY.) c. From Moses also comes the interpretation of the Exodus and the miracle of the sea, in which God revealed himself as the Savior and Lord of history and nature. The Exodus was the inspiration of Israel's hopes and faith, and through it Moses reached down through sacred history into the New Testament and the salvation wrought by Jesus. (*See* EXODUS, REDEMPTION.) d. Moses also placed first importance on the moral demands of the God whose prophet he was. The Decalogue was a compendium of these moral demands, which are reflected on the countenance of the God who imposes them. So from them is absent all arbitrariness or caprice so often found in the too human temperament of the gods of neighboring peoples.

The Exodus however and the settlement in Canaan was the work of a generation, which the Bible calculates at forty years. The books of Exodus and Numbers have conserved many traditions of this period, with which other articles deal. After failing to penetrate Canaan from the south (Num. 13:14), Israel returned to a nomadic existence in the desert around the oasis of Kadesh and the surrounding countryside (Num. 13:26). Different groups contest Moses' authority and leadership. Dathan and Abiram criticize him for failing to find a definitive settlement for the people (Num. 16:14-16). Korah rebelled against Moses' position as religious head of the people (Num. 16:3). Both accounts are in Numbers 16. (*See* ABIRAM, DATHAN, KORAH.) Even his own family, Aaron and Miriam reprove him for the marriage he had contracted with a Kushite woman. But in reality they were contesting Moses' prophetic charism: "Is it through Moses alone that the Lord speaks? Does he not speak through us also?" *See* AMALEK, MANNA, QUAILS.

The name of Moses is also associated with the **Torah,** the law. **Torah,** in its most ancient meaning, signifies instruction, and instruction in the form of an answer, often in oracular form, to a specific question (*see* Deut. 33:8-11; Num. 27:1-11). In the last analysis this is legislative activity, for the decisions handed down in this way become normative for the future. Moses exercised his legislative function principally at Kadesh during the years in which the links that had made Israel a people were being solidified. It was probably this activity of Moses to which Miram and Aaron objected (*see* Num. 12:2).

With the exception of Deuteronomy, which is an undated edition of the law, the Pentateuch inserts the legislation as a whole into the Sinai story. This is more a judgment of value than a historical fact. Its intent is to underline the function of the actual law in the context of the Covenant which was struck at Sinai. (*See* LAW.) Moreover it represents the further development of the tradition that was initiated for Israel by Moses at Kadesh. On the cultic institutions *see* ARK OF THE COVENANT, SACRIFICE, TABERNACLE.

A new attempt was made to invade Canaan by circling around the territory of Edom, crossing through Moab and thus coming to the east bank of the Jordan north of the Dead Sea (Num. 20-36). Moses was still at the head of the people. To him is attributed the conquest of the territories of Transjordania belonging to Kings Og of Bashan and Sihon of Heshbon. On these lands were settled Reuben, Gad and half of Manasseh. Moses however was unable to see the work through. He died on Mount Nebo, but his burial place was unknown when Deuteronomy 34 was written. The premature death of Moses, in that he did not enter the promised land, is explained by an obscure incident that had taken place in Kadesh (Num. 20:7-13). It is not likely that tradition created such an unimportant incident merely to explain Moses' questionably premature death, unless there had been something more important that was hard to eradicate from the tradition. It is difficult however to establish what exactly it was or how it came about that such an accusation was brought against Moses. Kadesh was the scene of factions and rivalry among the people, and it may be that Moses' own memory suffered as a result.

The figure and work of Moses is so rich that it could hardly be encapsulated under one title. The various titles given him illustrate the aspects under which his work was viewed in the succeeding centuries and aspects of which were underlined in the different epochs.

In the Pentateuch Moses is called the "Servant of God," not simply in the sense of being a loyal adorer of Yahweh, but above all because he was a chosen instrument of God for the realization of his design for salvation. Numbers 12:6-8 underscores the more direct link that God wished to create with Moses and which is not seen in other personages who might have the same title: "My servant Moses, throughout my house he bears my trust, face to face I speak to him" (Num. 12:7, 8). In this too lies the distinction between Moses and the other prophets through whom the word of God comes. Moses is numbered among the prophets as the first and greatest of them all (Deut. 18:15-20). Because of his constant intercession on behalf of the people Moses is also listed in the category of priests (Pss. 99:6-8; 106:23; Jer. 15:1). Finally as legislator he appears above all in the post-exilic books with evident reference to the Pentateuch, whose author he is held to be. *See* PENTATEUCH.

In the New Testament Moses is seen in the light of Christ. He prefigured Christ, but because of the debates that arose with the Jews who claimed Moses as the intangible and insuperable foundation of their existence, Christ is compared with Moses very often to underline the difference between them, which in turn leads to a re-evaluation of his importance. Moses, representing the law, gave witness to Christ in the Transfiguration (Matt. 17:1-8; Mk. 9:2-8; Lk. 9:28-36). In fact, Moses predicted Christ's coming (Jn. 1:45; 5:46; Acts 26:22). Moses however is inferior to Christ. Hebrews 3:2-6 underscores the differences between them: "Moses, too, 'was faithful in all God's household,' but Jesus is more worthy of honor than he. . . ." The Christian realities then have their counterpart in the Old Testament traditions on Moses and the Exodus, but they achieve their effective realization on the level of God's free self-giving and divine life: law and grace (Jn. 1:17), the bronze serpent and Jesus raised on the cross (Jn. 3:14), the manna and the eucharist (Jn. 6:32), Exodus through the water and baptism (1 Cor. 10:2), the Old and the New Testament (Heb. 8-9). This correspondence attests to the unity of God's design throughout history. This design was but sketchily foreseen in the beginning, but its full realization in Christ throws light on these beginnings, permitting us to see God's finger already tracing his plan.

Most High, God the Most High is the usual translation of El-Elyon. *See* PATRIARCHS, RELIGION OF THE.

Moth, The destructive character of this insect is used exclusively to illustrate the precariousness and corruptibility of human life (Isa. 50:9; Hos. 5:12) or the instability of riches (Matt. 6:19, 20; Lk. 12:33).

mother
m. of all the living   Gen. 3:20 Her brother and *m.* replied
presents to her brother and *m.*   Gen. 24:55
                  Gen. 24:53 sister of Joab's *m.*   2 Sam. 17:25
                  Seeing his *m.* there   Jn. 19:26

Mourning, After the death of a relative there followed an official period of mourning that could last for seven (1 Sam. 31:13; 1 Chron. 10:12; Sir. 22:2) to thirty days in special cases (Num. 20:30; Deut. 34:8). Mourning imposed the use of customary gestures that accompanied or expressed grief, such as tearing one's clothes (Gen. 37:29-34), putting on sackcloth (Gen. 37:34; 2 Sam. 3:31), spreading ashes on one's head (2 Sam. 1:2), fasting (1 Sam. 31:13; 2 Sam. 1:12; 3:35; 12:16), weeping accompanied with the striking of one's breast or sides (Jer. 31:9). A person in mourning neglected the care of his own body (2 Sam. 14:2; 15:30). All these gestures also went into penitential practices. *See* LAMENTATION and BURIAL.

Mouth, The word is used in its obvious meaning of orifice for eating and drinking (Jgs. 7:6; 1 Sam. 14:26-27), and the organ of speech (Deut. 13:15; 23:23). It was spoken anthropomorphically of God (Deut. 8:3), from whose mouth fire comes forth (Ps. 18:8). The opening of a well was its mouth (Gen. 29:2; 29:8).

Moza, 1. The name of a descendant of Judah (1 Chron. 2:46).

2. The name of a descendant of King Saul (1 Chron. 8:36).

Mozah, A city of Benjamin (Josh. 18:26).

Mulberry, A bush grown in ancient Palestine, as it is today, for its fruit. According to 1 Maccabees 6:34, before battle the soldiers showed the army elephants the juice of grapes and mulberries to provoke them to battle.

Mule, A cross between horse and donkey, an animal prized for its strength, solidity and prudence, and used for riding by the king (2 Sam. 13:29; 18:9; 1 Kgs. 1:33). It was also used as a beast of burden (2 Kgs. 5:17; 1 Chron. 12:40; Isa. 66:20). Leviticus 19:19 forbids the breeding of mules, but they were imported (*see* 2 Chron. 9:24; Ezek. 27:14).

Muratorianum, Canon (myoor′-a-tor′-i-an′-um), A list of the inspired and canonical books of the New Testament composed in Rome during the second half of the second century. It was not an official list but did indicate what was held in the churches of the region. It is called the Muratorianum from the name of its discoverer, Lorenzo A. Muratori, who found it in 1740. The beginning is missing, and undoubtedly spoke of the gospels of Matthew and Mark. The catalogue lists all the books of the canon defined in the Council of Trent, with the exception of Hebrews, James and 2 Peter. It also permits the private reading, but not the public reading in church, of the "Pastor Hermes," of which it is said that its author was the brother of Pope Pius, who was Supreme Pontiff between 140-155 A.D., and that he had composed it somewhat earlier than the Muratorianum Canon. It is from this indication that the Muratorianum Canon can be dated in the second half of the second century, perhaps before 180 A.D.

Murder, Murder is forbidden by the fifth commandment of the Decalogue (Ex. 20:13; Deut. 5:17) and this prohibition is repeated elsewhere in the Old Testament (Jer. 7:9; Hos. 4:2) and in the New Testament (Matt. 15:19; 19:18; Mk. 7:21; 10:19; Lk. 18:20; Rom. 13:9; James 2:11).

The law of the Decalogue is apodictic (*see* LAW) to which is attached the penalty of death. It does not distinguish at least at first between murder and involuntary manslaughter (as does neither Ex. 21:12 nor Gen. 9:4-6) but includes under the one heading all killing with the exception of what happens in war or capital punishment (Ex. 21:12).

The distinction between voluntary and involuntary homicide, a distinction established on the existence or non-existence of a previous enmity (Deut. 19:1-13; Num. 35:10-34) seems to belong to a second stage when to the apodictic law of Exodus 21:12 was added by way of explanation verse 13 and 14. These made provision for cities of refuge for those who had caused involuntary homicide. Then Exodus 20:15 and Deuteronomy 5:18 were only understood of willful killing. This later stage appears in Deuteronomy 19:1-13 and Numbers 35:10-34. The judicial process for murder and the very notion of the crime in the Old Testament seems tied also to the tribal institution of blood-revenge. *See* REFUGE, CITIES OF.

In Matthew 5:21, 22 Jesus interprets the Decalogue in a radical, soul-searching way by including in the prohibition anger for, or interior aversion from, another person. Its opposite is incumbent on every Christian, namely the forgiveness and love of enemies.

murmur, murmuring

the Jews started to *m*.	Jn. 6:41	Stop your *m*.	Jn. 6:43
		were *m*.	Jn. 6:61

Music, Music played an important part in many aspects of Israelite life. It is practically impossible to retrieve from the past this music as it really sounded. There are only generic allusions to songs and dances, the mention of musical instruments, and some difficult-to-interpret indications in the titles of the psalms. (*See* PSALMS.) Like other peoples of the east and west, Israel paid homage to the legendary inventor of music: "Jubal, who was the ancestor of all who play the lyre and the flute" (Gen. 4:21). His name is derived from **yobel**, a ram's horn (Ex. 19:13), a wind instrument made from the horn of the animal. Israelite music, like all ancient music, was unaware of the principles of harmony. The instrumental accompaniment to song maintained its melodic tone and beat out its rhythm. Dance and song accompanied different festivities and celebrations. At the vintage feast in Shiloh the girls danced through the vineyards (Jgs. 21:21). Dance and song welcomed the warriors from war (Jgs. 11:34-35; 1 Sam. 18:6-7), and thus too were guests sent on their way (Gen. 31:27). Victories were danced and sung to (Ex. 15:20, 21) as was the coronation of the king (1 Kgs. 1:39-40; 2 Kgs. 11:14).

Music also marked the rites of lamentation and sorrow (2 Sam. 1:17-18; 2 Chron. 35:25; Matt. 9:23; *see* MOURNING).

Above all, however, music adorned the cult. 1 Chronicles tells how David organized down to the last detail the people who had a part in liturgical worship. Although this exaggeration does not withstand the test of history, nevertheless it reflects the real situation at a later date. Besides the inscriptions, the Psalms contain many allusions to singing, and also to accompanied singing (Pss. 96:1, 2; 108:2-3; 137:2-4; 149:1-3; 150). David was himself a poet, a singer and a harpist (1 Sam. 16:16-23; 2 Sam. 6:14-15). He undoubtedly contributed to the lyrical religious heritage of Israel, even though it is not possible to identify in the concrete what this contribution was. (*See* PSALMS.) The largest orchestra known of, besides that of Psalm 150, is that of Nebuchadnezzar, king of Babylonia (Dan. 3:5-15).

The principal instruments mentioned in the Bible are as follows:

Wind instruments: the flute (Hebrew **'ugab**: Ps. 105:4), the pipe or oboe (**halil**: 1 Sam. 10:5; Isa. 30:29; Jer. 48:36), the horn (**qeren**: Josh. 6:5; 1 Chron. 25:5), the trumpet (**sopar**), which was in reality a barely elaborated horn of an animal, without the possibility of giving off more than two different tones, and was more an instrument for giving signals than accompanying song. It accompanied the immolation in sacrifice (2 Sam. 6:13, 15), and was also used in the charge in battle (2 Sam. 2:28). It is still used in the synagogue. There was also the metal trumpet (**soserah**: *see* Num. 10:1; Hos. 5:8).

Stringed instruments: the lyre (**kinnor**: 1 Sam. 16:16-23), the harp (**nebel**: Ps. 150:3) which could have up to twenty-three strings. The 'ashor and the shalishim seem to have been varieties of lyre with 10 strings in the first and 3 strings in the second.

Percussion instruments: the hand tambourine (**top**: Ex. 15:20; Jer. 31:4), and various types of cymbals (**selselim, mesilsayim**: 1 Chron. 16:5, 42; Ps. 150:5).

Mustard, Twice Jesus refers to the proverbial smallness of the mustard seed (Matt. 13:31; Mk. 4:31; Lk. 13:19 and Matt. 17:20; Lk. 17:6). It is called the "smallest of all seeds," not, obviously, in the absolute sense of the term, but relative to the size of the plant which can rise to eight or ten feet. Some difficulties are seen in making it a place where birds can nest, as it is an annual plant and unsuitable for nests at the time of nesting.

Muzzle, According to Deuteronomy 25:4, "You shall not muzzle an ox when it is treading out grain." From this verse St. Paul argues that a laborer has the right to live on the fruits of his labor, and so too have the "gospel workers" (1 Cor. 9:9; 1 Tim. 5:18). This is a typical case of hala-kah, that is, a Jewish type of exegesis which draws from scripture a norm of conduct, or rather which links to scripture a norm that is not found there and is based quite obviously on other considerations. Paul adds (1 Tim. 5:18) the principle that Jesus had already enunciated: "The laborer is worth his wage" (Lk. 10:7).

Myndos (min′-dos), A port-city of southern Turkey, mentioned among those to which the Roman Senate addressed the letter in favor of the Jews in 139 B.C. (1 Mac. 15:23).

Myra, A city and port in southern Turkey, 100 miles east of Rhodes, mentioned in Paul's journey as a prisoner to Rome (Acts 27:5).

Myrrh, An aromatic and resinous substance used in the confection of perfumes (Esth. 2:12; Ps. 45:8; Prov. 7:17) and oil for anointing (Ex. 30:23). Wine with myrrh was given to criminals condemned to the cross to ease the pain (Mk. 15:23). The body of Jesus was dressed with myrrh and aloes in preparation for the burial (Jn. 19:39). Tradition has seen in the gift of myrrh to the child Jesus a presage of his passion (*see* Matt. 2:11) but obviously it means merely a precious gift.

Mysia (mish′-ia), A region in the northwest corner of modern Turkey. From the year 133 B.C. Mysia formed part of the Roman province of Asia. Its principal cities were Pergamum and Troas. Troas was visited by Paul on his second journey. This was the scene of the long sermon at night during which a young man fell asleep and tumbled out the window (Acts 20:7-12). Here too Paul had the vision of the young Macedonian inviting him to Macedonia (Acts 16:6-11; *see* 2 Cor. 2:12).

mysterious
not too *m.*   Deut. 30:11

Mystery, During the first centuries of the Christian era the mysteries of the Hellenistic religions were esoteric and secret cults. At the center of the typical mystery was a myth, almost without exception referring to the death and resurrection of a god. Typically, too, it.was a myth of nature based on the periodic renewal of life in nature. (*See* MYTH.) These cultic myths are distinguished from the myths common to ancient religions in general by two traits: the first trait was their secrecy. Not all could participate. Before arriving at this celebration one had to submit to rites of purification that progressed through various grades. The person who wanted to penetrate into the mystery was led little by little from one grade to the next until he came to the top grade, or inner sanctum which was the **epopteia**. This was the full contemplation of the mystery. This was the **mimesis** of the rite, in which the initiate was made a sharer in the mystery by being inserted into the death and life that it expressed. This insertion could be signified in different gestures such as the vision and contact with the sacred symbols, drink, bathing and so on. The second trait was the accentuated individualistic character of the cult. It sought to satisfy the aspirations of the individual: social interests and the common good took second place to make room for the single man who felt himself caught in a universe that was hostile and decadent. The initiates believed themselves rejuvenated by this contact with the rebirth of life that was evoked in the myth.

Some mysteries such as the Eleusinian, Dionysian and Orphic mysteries, had a long tradition in Greek religion. They received however a totally new position in the Hellenistic and Roman periods when the oriental religions spread across the Mediterranean and occupied the place left vacant in the religious life of the individual by the official religion of the city.

When at the beginning of this century Hellenistic religions were studied systematically for the first time, some scholars thought they had discovered a very significant influence of mystery religions on the New Testament, especially in the Pauline doctrine of baptism (Rom. 6). As time and study progressed, however, this influence was seen to be much more limited: Hellenistic religions and mysteries in general had very little influence on Christianity, and there was no link between Christian worship and the Greek mysteries.

It is interesting that in Romans 6, where these scholars thought to find the greatest affinity with the mystery initiations, the word "mystery" is completely missing.

In reality the New Testament notion, and particularly that of Paul on mystery, has its roots in Judaism, and, in particular, in the apocalyptic tradition. In this tradition the notion of mystery has nothing to do with rite or worship, but refers to the secrets of God yet to be revealed. According to the apocalyptic way of seeing things, the future eschatological realities already exist in heaven. The Son of Man, the glory of the saints, the future Jerusalem are all awaiting the moment of their revelation. However, before this eschatological panorama breaks on human eyes, it is made known to a few privileged souls, who are admitted to contemplate it in heaven (1 Enoch) or have been informed of it in vision (Dan. 2:18, 19; 2:27-30; 4:6). The mysteries of God are summed up in his salvific design to be realized in the future **eschaton**, even though this also means judgment. It also means, paradoxically, its anticipated revelation to some, and its definitive revelation to all, through its realization in the future.

In Wisdom 2:22 the mysteries of God are his designs for the immortality of the just, which are hidden from the impious who blaspheme God's providence. In the Dead Sea Scrolls (*see* DEAD SEA SCROLLS) the term mystery (in Hebrew **raz**) often occurs with the same meaning: it is the plan of God for the last times, as it has been revealed to the Master of Righteousness, the sect's founder. The revelation of these mysteries has been made not through visions, but by opening the heart to the understanding of the sacred books.

The mysteries of the kingdom have been revealed to the disciples, but to others only in parables (Matt. 13:11; Mk. 4:11; Lk. 8:10; *see* PARABLES).

The mysteries of the kingdom are God's plans for the definitive realization of the kingdom in the words and work of Jesus. *See* JESUS CHRIST.

Paul holds to the basic meaning of the word mystery which, however, in his writings has different applications. In 1 Corinthians 2:6-16 Paul contrasts the mysterious and hidden wisdom of God to the wisdom of this world: God's saving design which is now revealed through the Spirit to the saints leaves worldly wisdom wordless. The content of the mystery is unfolded in christological terms in Ephesians and Colossians: everything must be gathered up into Christ (Eph. 1:9, 10), the salvation both of Jews and Gentiles who are now reconciled in him (Eph. 2:11-23; *see* Rom. 11:25 ff.). The mystery then is, in the concrete, Christ (1:26; 2:2) or the Church (5:32) because in him has been brought to realization God's design. The mystery's revelation coincides with its realization. This mystery, then, that was hidden in times past from angels and men (Eph 3:5) is now proclaimed by the apostles, who have been made the dispensers of the mysteries of God (Eph. 3:6-13). "The mystery of our religion" (1 Tim. 3:16) is also Christ, above all the enfleshed Word, now elevated to glory. The "mystery of evil" is also related to the eschatological events, in that it will be the last extravagant display of the force of the Evil One and an assertion of his power, which, however will only prove futile, for it will be brought to nothing by the coming of Christ (2 Thess. 2:7).

Myth, According to the definition that is given by scholars, only to be immediately challenged or criticized by them, myths are narratives or stories about gods or super-human beings. This definition touches only the most superficial aspect of the myths, which remains even when the myths have lost their content and become mere literature. Since today we no longer give credence to myths, this is what they have become for us.

In reality, however, myths are more than the fruit of some poet's fancy or gratuitous religious speculation. They are above all religious interpretations of nature, her power and her phenomena which are seen as the manifestations of a sacred reality. They are also an interpretation of man himself, in the midst of nature and conditioned by it. The divine events that are told in myth are not told for their own sake, nor are they thought out according to some inner logic of their own. They exist as normative events or archetypes of the world of nature and of man. For instance man notices the yearly cycle of nature with its verdant spring, summer maturity, its fruition and universal death. Man finds in this not just a unifying link between the various stages, but also something transcendent and sacred which the cycles themselves reveal. This insight man gathers up and expresses in a myth, for example, of a god that dies and rises again. Obviously the god does not die and rise each year; this happened once, outside our time and outside space, but it is annually expressed in the cycle of nature.

The concept of the archetype seems the best adapted to convey the meaning of the mythical mentality which is so diverse from ours. An archetypal event is first of all a representative event, a typical event, in that this event gathers into a relatively simple and animated scheme of things the multiple experiences and circumstances that periodically re-occur in the world of man. In this way multiplicity is reduced to unity, and it is explained by being projected into a remote past which has become normative. From this point of view there is an analogy between myth and the eternal types of world literature. World literature also collects in one personage or one event a multiplicity of experiences. Each of us can identify with these experiences, or at least recognize in them something perennially human. Today there is much insistence on giving the creative faculty from which myths proceed an autonomous place alongside the other cognitive faculties of man, and to acknowledge in him the power to catch through symbols a truly sacred or numinous dimension of things which has perdured and survives even the desacralization of the world brought about by science.

The immortal types of literature—Othello, Hamlet, Don Giovanni, Faustus—can again and again be read and experienced without ever being exhausted. They are so rich that they cannot be given full expression in just one work. So too with the myths and the divine event that is described therein: each year it returns to be re-enacted in the cycle of nature. The mechanisms of this repetition, however, are different. In fact, for the man who lives them, the mythical events are not fictitious, but real. Indeed they are the reality. In them we have the origin (arche) of all reality that man experiences. This origin should not be understood exclusively or primarily in a temporal sense. While it is true that the mythical events are placed "at the beginning," or "once upon a time," it is not a question of the beginning of historical time nor of chronological continuity with the time that measures man's life. To point out the difference between this "time" and historical time, scholars have coined the term "meta-time" (and meta-space) in which primordial events happen. This expression also wishes to insinuate that the priority of mythical events is of the "ontological" order rather than chronological. In the myth, however, the narration sends them back to the beginning of time to assert their priority in the order of being.

The mythical events are called archetypal because between them and their divine world and the world of man there is a real continuity. In this regard some have spoken of the "Platonic structure of primitive ontology." The divine and human sphere are intimately involved in the same events. The world of myth is, to put it one way, a "transfiguration" of nature, for through the myths the density of natural events becomes transparent, as well as their sacred and divine dimension. Nature on the other hand is the epiphany or revelation of the sacred. Between the two there is a continuity in the order of reality. The gods who are the heroes of the myths are not just personifications of the forces of nature, which would then reduce them to simple literary or poetic fictions. Under the forms and gestures that are borrowed from the world of man, they are the primary forces that move and shape this world. From this point of view one can see how modern science, and indeed the biblical notion of creation, banishes the ancient gods from their traditional seats of power.

Finally the myth as a literary composition does not primarily intend to afford knowledge about the beginning of things. Its first purpose is to be the apodictical and unspoken word, re-evoking through recitation the primordial event and thus regenerative through contact with its origins, the world and time. This is why the myth is essentially recitation and repetition. The myth accompanies the rite, which becomes then the mimed repetition of the primordial event. These two elements, myth and ritual, constitute the cultic event. The most noted example of this is the **Enuma Elish**, the Babylonian poem recounting the creation, which was solemnly recited and acted out on the Feast of the New Year in Babylonia. The celebrations, then, that marked the New Year everywhere did not arise by chance nor were they arbitrary or just entertaining. They had a function of capital importance. In the words of a recent author (T. H. Gaster), these celebrations were the ritual mechanism through which society sought periodically to renew itself and thus secure its own continuity.

Are there myths in the Bible? The answer depends on what one means by myth. If the explanation for myth is taken for what is explained in this article, then the answer cannot but be negative. The reason is that the concept of the divine world contained in the myths is absolutely incompatible with the idea of God which is the soul of the Bible. The God of the Bible reveals himself as unique and transcendent. While Israel's monotheism was, at the beginning, more practical than theoretical (*see* GOD), the fact is that for Israel there could be no other God but the Lord: "You shall not have other god besides me" (Ex. 20:2). Besides this the God of the Bible is transcendent. This transcendence is the typical note of the God Yahweh and the deepest reason why the making of idols was prohibited. (*See* IDOL, IDOLATRY.) Even though in antiquity the idols in the ancient religions were not identified with the gods themselves, nor were they taken to be adequate representations of the gods themselves, nevertheless they were the privileged seat of the gods' presence and efficacy, and therefore the point of contact with their faithful in a world of gods and men, divinity and nature, without there being an adequate line drawn between these two dimensions.

The prohibition to make idols supposes a different concept of the relationships between God and nature, from which God is radically distinguished. While God is the absolute Lord of nature, he does not become a part of it. The world and nature are other than God and contrasted to him as is one who serves to one who commands. On God everything depends. The modern theology of secularization is right at least in this: that it underlines in the biblical theology of creation the definitive step towards the secularization of nature. The theology of creation has put the nature gods to flight.

On the other hand, the terrain in which God's revelation is primarily unfolded in the Bible is not nature but history. The Letter to the Romans states: "Since the creation of the world, invisible realities, God's eternal power and divinity, have become visible, recognized through the things he has made" (Rom. 1:20). This is, however, not a question of myth but of reason. In the Bible the creation is not the primordial event but the first event. The beginning in which God creates (Gen. 1:1) is not the mythical origin, but the first moment of our time, to which is linked a precise chronology. Creation is an irreversible event (Gen. 2:1-4). The fertility of the fields and the continuity of life are not something to be had through the re-enactment of the primordial event, but through the gift of God (Deut. 28:1-14). The Bible shows a tendency to "historify" myths which it finds in the literature of other peoples. It fits the myth into history and substitutes its cyclic repetition with the linearity and irreversibility of historical time.

Nevertheless the Bible does contain mythical elements. This should not cause surprise nor does it go back on what we have said about there being no true myths in the Bible. For myth, as we have seen, is a complex operation in which diverse faculties have their different functions. One of these functions is symbolic and representative. This is always valid and remains active in the poetry of all time. From this point of view the account of creation in Genesis 2-3 could be called mythical. It is in fact an insight and symbolic representation of the religious situation of every man. It is a typical story in which every man can see something of himself. It is not however a myth, for the author intends to give things not a mythical explanation but a historical one. Genesis 2-3 is not an exposition of a generic and timeless truth, but an event in history that has shaped history itself. On the presence of myth in the biblical presentation of creation *see* CREATION. On the problem of myth in the New Testament *see* DEMYTHOLOGIZING.

N

Naam (nay'-am), A Judahite, descendant of Caleb (1 Chron. 4:15).

Naamah (nay'-a-mah), An Ammonite wife of Solomon who gave birth to Rehoboam, his successor (1 Kgs. 14:21; 2 Chron. 12:13).

Naaman (nay'-a-man), General of the army of the Aramaean king of Damascus, who was cured of leprosy by Elisha (2 Kgs. 5). Jesus refers to this episode in Luke 4:27.

Naarah (nay'-a-rah), A city in the territory of Ephraim (Josh. 16:7).

Naarai (nay'-a-rie), One of the warriors of king David (1 Chron. 11:37).

Nabal (nay'-bal), A rich owner living in Maon in Judah, who was married to Abigail. Nabal refused to help David and his men. David swore to take vengeance, but the opportune and astute intervention of Abigail dissuaded him. After Nabal's death David took Abigail to wife (1 Sam. 25; 27:3; 30:5; 2 Sam. 2:2; 3:3).

Nabataeans (nab'-a-tee'-anz), A people of the Arabian desert who from the fourth century B.C. on settled in the ancient territory of Edom and Moab and there established an important commercial center around Petra, south of the Dead Sea and east of the Arabah. This center controlled the caravan routes linking the regions of the Persian Gulf, Arabia, Egypt and Syria. The Nabataeans appear as allies and friends to the Maccabeans Judas and Jonathan (1 Mac. 5:25; 9:35; *see* 2 Mac. 5:8), probably because of the common Seleucid enemy. There ensued, however, some rivalry between them for territorial and commercial reasons. They had more problems with Herod Antipas, who repudiated the daughter of King Aretas IV after their marriage, in order to marry Herodias. The outcome of these wars was favorable to the Nabataeans who extended their influence more to the north. From 85 B.C. until 65 B.C. and from 37 A.D. on, the Nabataeans controlled the territory of Damascus. Paul was converted on the road to Damascus and had to escape the city by being let down the walls in a hamper (2 Cor. 11:32). The independent kingdom of the Nabataeans came to an end in 105 A.D. when Trajan annexed the land to the Roman province of Arabia.

Nabopolassar (nab'-o-po-lass'-ar), King of Babylon (625-605 B.C.), the conqueror of Nineveh (*see* NINEVEH); his son and successor was Nebuchadnezzar II.

Naboth (nay'-both), A citizen of Jezreel and owner of a vineyard near the palace of Ahab, king of Israel (869-850 B.C.). Ahab wished to buy the vineyard in order to augment his garden but Naboth did not wish to sell. So Jezebel wrote conspiratory letters in Ahab's name and sealed them with his seal, and then arranged for two scoundrels to denounce Naboth for cursing God and the king. Naboth was taken outside the town and stoned to death, whereupon Ahab took possession of his vineyard. Elijah condemned the crime and took the occasion to announce to the king the tragic end of his dynasty, which was exterminated by Jehu (1 Kgs. 21; 2 Kgs. 9:21-26).

Nabuchodonosor, *See* NEBUCHADNEZZAR.

Nadab (nay'-dab), 1. First-born son of Aaron (Ex. 6:23; Num. 3:2), consecrated priest together with his brothers (Ex. 28:1). Nadab and his brother brought unlawful fire before the Lord, and for their crime a flame leapt out from the Lord's presence and consumed them (Lev. 10:1-7; Num. 26:61).

2. King of Israel (901-900), son and successor of Jeroboam. He did what

was displeasing to the Lord. Baasha, son of Ahijah, of the house of Issachar, plotted against him and killed him at the siege of the Philistine town of Gibbethon. He butchered the whole family of Nadab and reigned in his place (1 Kgs. 15:25-31).

Naggi (nag'-eye), An ancestor of Jesus in Luke's genealogy (Lk. 3:25).

Nahalal (nay'-ha-lal), A Levitical town in the territory of Zebulun (Josh. 19:15; 21:35; Jgs. 1:30).

Nahaliel (na-hay'-li-el), A stopping-place in the journey of the Israelites to Canaan (Num. 21:19).

Naharai (nay'-a-rie), The armor-bearer of Joab and one of the Thirty warriors of King David (2 Sam. 23:37; 1 Chron. 11:39).

Nahash (nay'-hash), King of the Ammonites, a contemporary of Saul and David (2 Sam. 10:2), defeated by the former while besieging the city of Jabesh-gilead (1 Sam. 11:1-11).

Nahath (nay'-hath), Personal name (Gen. 36:17; 2 Chron. 31:13).

Nahor (nah'-hor), 1. A city of northern Mesopotamia, near Haran (Gen. 24:10).

2. Father of Terah and therefore grandfather of Abraham (Gen. 11:22-25; Lk. 3:34).

3. Son of Terah, brother of Abraham (Gen. 11:26; Josh. 24:2), father of Bethuel (Gen. 22:22, 23; 25:15) and grandfather of Rebekah and Laban (Gen. 29:5).

Nahshon (nah'-shon), Son of Aminadab; husband of Elisheba, daughter of Aaron; head of the tribe of Judah in the priestly narrative of the journey of the Israelites through the desert (Num. 1:7; 2:3; 7:12; 10:14). His name occurs in the genealogy of David (Ruth 4:20-22) and of Jesus (Matt. 1:4; Lk. 3:32).

Nahum (nay'-um), The seventh of the minor prophets in the Hebrew canon of the Old Testament. The title of the book is "An Oracle against Nineveh" (1:1) and its theme is the destruction of the Assyrian capital which took place at the hands of the Babylonians in 612 B.C. In epic accents the prophet describes the destruction of the hated city, which was a symbol of Assyrian oppression, in the oracles of 2:2-13 and 3:1-19. The incomplete alphabetic poem in 1:2-8 is a description of a vision of God who prepares himself to execute his sentence. The terms are generic, but even if originally they did not refer to the central theme of the book, they were interpreted by the compiler as a solemn introduction to the divine intervention described in cc. 2-3. 1:9-2:1 contains various oracles against Assyria and Nineveh (1:11, 14) and various promises of salvation to Judah (1:9, 10, 12, 13). The oracles must be dated after 663, the date of the sack of Thebes of which 3:8 ("No-amon"=Thebes) speaks, and before 612 which saw the destruction of Nineveh. A later date would be incompatible with the succeeding history. Perhaps between 615 and 613 fits best. In fact the ruin of the Assyrian empire did not bring independence to Judah, but only left them the prey of other overlords, who in 610 began to threaten Judah and finally brought about its ruin in 587 B.C. The title tells that Nahum was from Elkosh, the location of which is unknown.

nailing
n. it to the cross   Col. 2:14

nails

pare her *n*.	Deut. 21:12	The weight of the *n*.	2 Chron. 3:9
to make *n*. for the doors		With *n*. and hammers	Jer. 10:4
	1 Chron. 22:3	without probing the *n*. prints	
			Jn. 20:25

Nain, A city of Galilee, in some manuscripts Naim, and probably the same as the modern Nein about five miles southeast of Nazareth. Here Jesus raised to life a widow's only son who was being brought to burial, and restored him to her (Lk. 7:11-16).

Naioth (nay′-yoth), A place a few miles north of Jerusalem, near Ramah, occupied by a group of prophets at the time of Samuel, where David took refuge from Saul's anger (1 Sam. 19:18-24; 20:1).

naked

were both *n*.	Gen. 2:25	he lay *n*.	1 Sam. 19:24
they were *n*.	Gen. 3:7	*N*. I came forth	Job 1:21
because I was *n*.	Gen. 3:10	passed the night *n*.	Job 24:7

Name, In the Bible and especially in the Old Testament one often finds importance attached to the names and the naming of persons and places (*see* Gen. 2:23; 4:1; 4:25; 5:29; 11:9, etc.). Traditions purporting to explain the choice of a particular name are preserved in the sacred writings (Gen. 16:14; 19:30-38; 26:15-33, etc.). Particular importance is attached to the imposition or the change of a name (*see* Gen. 17:5-15; Matt. 16:18, etc.).

All this is evidence to the importance in which names were held among ancient peoples. This was in part due to a naive and simple concept of language, which was not, for them, a mere system of conventional signs or tags for people and things to be changed at will. The particular combination of sounds that go to make up a word has its own sense. Naming a thing is not a simple matter of imposing from without one or another combination of sounds, but something much more serious.

In the case of God, who also named his works (Gen. 1), the naming itself was an act of power and dominion by which he asserted his creatorship. Giving a name to a thing was, in this case, tantamount to assigning to it its own determinant function or role in creation, and this role was contained in the very name. In the case of Adam who named all the animals (Gen. 2:19-20), the meaning is somewhat different. It was not a question of creating a name and a language for the animals, but of finding the most suitable name, the right word to fit each. This then was a sign of Adam's great wisdom, and through it Adam proved himself one of the great wise men. *See* WISDOM.

The author gives us an insight into his concept of the importance of the name in his account of the formation of the woman (Gen. 2:22, 23). The name is intended to embrace the reality of the woman as being of the same condition and of like nature, which Adam to his delight saw in this good work of God.

The names of people, which for us are even more conventional than the names of things, were nevertheless for the ancients subject to the same rules of language. They are more like what today would be called nicknames in that they attempted to catch in a word some notable characteristic of the person (Esau was hairy, Gen. 25:25), or of his personality (Jacob was the supplanter, Gen. 27:36), or some incident concerning his birth (such as the story of the Moabites in Gen. 19:30-38; *see* 21:1-7; 29:31-35, etc.).

More important are the cases in which the name a person receives is intended to signify his destiny. Then its imposition by God also becomes a promise, and indeed a pledge or guarantee of fulfilment. In this way God changed the name of Abram to Abraham, for he was to be the father of a multitude of nations (Gen. 17:5). Sarai's name was likewise changed to Sarah (Gen. 17:15), Jacob's to Israel (Gen. 35:9-10), and Simon's to Peter (Matt. 16:18).

A variation of this is found in Isaish 8:1-4 and 10:20-21. The latter text explains the name of Isaiah's elder son Shear-jashub in terms of the destiny of the whole people, and not of the person himself (*see* Hos. 1:6-9; 2:15). In Matthew 1:21 the name of Jesus is explained as signifying his work as Savior of the people.

It is clear that these meanings do not always correspond to the etymological derivations of the names, nor indeed do they always reflect the historical facts. Often the derivations are explained long after the facts, and an attempt is made to explain in the name all that is known about that person or place. And so infrequently can be found contrasting explanations of the same name (Gen. 21:22 and 26:28; 18:12; 21:9 and 26:8).

This fascination with names on the part of the ancients was not merely aesthetic, nor has it a purely semantic explanation. Names, like words in general and even writing, hold a special place in the use of magic. Israel's religion peremptorily banned the magical use, or rather abuse, of the name of God (*see* Ex. 20:7 and MAGIC). There exists a rich Israelite theology concerning God's name. According to Exodus 6:3 the two decisive turning points of Hebrew history revolved around the revelation of the names of God. The first name by which God revealed himself to the patriarchs was El Shaddai. The second was revealed to Moses: "I am the Lord. I will free you from the burdens which the Egyptians lay on you." It was the announcement of the Exodus.

The revelation of the name of God at this point takes on an importance analogous to that of the imposition of names, as we have seen. The revelation of the name responds to the need to identify oneself. In a world infested with superhuman powers as was that of ancient man, it was necessary to determine irrefutably the origin of the "divine" manifestations to which man was witness. This is why we find Jacob pleading with God: "What is your name?" (Gen. 32:28), and the spontaneous self-identification by God at the beginning of every theophany (*see* Gen. 17:2; Ex. 3:6).

If then the name is conceived of as a compendium or definition of the thing it signifies, the revelation of the name is the revelation of the thing, and, in the case of God, it is revelation of the divinity, a true theophany. Moreover, in making his name known, a person makes himself over in the sense that he creates the possibility of a direct and personal relationship with him. God becomes accessible, he puts himself at man's disposition. Man on his part finds that he can invoke, praise and beseech God for help. On God's part, revealing his name shows his wish to enter into a relationship with man, he becomes God for us. For Israel the name of God took the place of the idol in other religions (*see* IDOLATRY), creating that link through which God gave himself and made himself available to man.

In expressions of Israelite piety the name of God, since it stood for God himself, and was in fact God for us, was the object of praise (Ps. 135:1), a saving power (Ps. 9:16), that in which hope is placed (Pss. 33:21; 124:8). The name of God is glorious (Ps. 72:19), and its invocation is the pledge

of salvation (Joel 3:5). In some later texts, such as those of the deuteronomic tradition, the name of God acquires the dimensions of the person
of God, or as it were, his double, for it resides in the Temple, and God
himself causes his name to reside in Zion (Deut. 12:11; 16:11; 1 Kgs.
8:16). These texts are readily interpreted in the light of what has been said
about the name of God being God for us.

From these considerations an attempt can be made at explaining the
meaning of the two stages of self-revelation proposed in Exodus 6:3. It is
not easy to determine what difference existed between the first and the
second stages; nor to ascertain how the two names, for the author, differed. (*See* GOD.) On the other hand it was not a question of speculation
but an attempt to explain a historical fact that cannot be denied, namely,
that Israel only commenced invoking God with the name of Yahweh in
the time of Moses, and that the patriarchs only spoke of God with the
name El Shaddai. (On the question of the Yahwist *see* PENTATEUCH.) The
author however was convinced that both names referred to one and the
same God.

The revelation of the name of Yahweh brought with it a greater and more
open accessibility to God, while God by this self-revelation allied himself
more closely with man and became more available to him. How exactly
did this greater access to God operate? Perhaps for the priestly author the
answer was in the cult of Israel. In fact for the author Sinai is above all the
place of the institution of the cult of Israel, where the Tabernacle was
constructed and the glory of God became visibly present (Ex. 40). Here it
was that Moses spoke face to face with God (Ex. 33:11). From this point
of view the epoch of the patriarchs was clearly inferior and preparatory.

In the New Testament the name of God is expressed in categories similar
to those of the Old Testament (*see* Matt. 6:9; Lk. 11:2; Jn. 10:25; 17:11,
etc.). The name of Jesus however is given supreme importance and the
same functions and power that in the Old Testament are assigned to the
name of God. It is one of the several cases of a christological reading of
the Old Testament, that is, the transposition of biblical themes referring
to God, and applying them to Jesus. In this way is expressed the faith of
the Church in the divinity of Christ.

The glorification of Jesus, which is likened with his resurrection, is for
Paul the act in which God confers on Jesus the name which is above all
names, that is the divine name of Lord (Kyrios). In other words, this is
the moment in which Jesus in his humanity is invested with the glory and
power that is his as God (*see* Heb. 4:1-14). Jesus then is Lord and Savior,
the only name that is given in which we can be saved (Acts 4:12). In his
name are sins forgiven (Acts 10:43), miracles performed (Mark 16:17;
Acts 3:6), baptism conferred (Acts 2:38).

The whole work of salvation, the preaching of the gospel (Acts 5:40;
8:12; 9:28), the faith of believers (Jn. 3:18), the prayer of the Church (Jn.
14:13) can be expressed in relationship to the name of Jesus. In all these
activities the name of Jesus calls to mind his condition as Savior and Lord
and therefore sums up his reality as God enfleshed for us. So the name of
the name of God in the Old Testament finds its fulfilment, not just in a
figurative or metaphorical sense, but in the real Word of God incarnate.

Nanaea (na-nee′-a), A Syrian goddess, equivalent of Artemis of the
Ephesians, whose temple in Elymais Antiochus IV Epiphanes proposed to
plunder. He was enticed inside with a small retinue. Once inside, the
priests closed the temple, opened the secret door in the ceiling and struck
down the leader and his party by hurling stones. They then dismembered
them (*see* 1 Mac. 6:2; 2 Mac. 1:13-18). Extra-biblical sources, such as

Josephus and Polybius, state that it was in the Temple of Artemis that this happened.

Naomi (nay-oh′-mi), Wife of Elimelech, mother of Mahlon and Chilion, mother-in-law of Orpah and Ruth. After the death of her husband and sons, she returned to Bethlehem with Ruth and got her to marry Boaz, a rich relative of her husband. From this marriage was born Obed, David's grandfather (Ruth 1-4).

Naphish (nay′-fish), A son of Ishmael (Gen. 25:15; 1 Chron. 5:19).

Naphtali (naf′-ta-lie), Son of Jacob and Bilhah, Rachel's slave (Gen. 30:8), the founding father of the Israelite tribe of the same name (Gen. 49:21; Deut. 33:23) which settled in the northern part of the country on the western side of the Jordan and Lake Gennesaret. (Josh. 19:32-39). The tribe took part in the battle against Jabin, king of Hazor, and his Canaanite allies from the north. At Kishon, under the command of Barak of the tribe of Naphtali he was defeated (Jgs. 4:6-10; 5:18). Naphtali also campaigned victoriously with Gideon against the Midianites (Jgs. 6:35; 7:23). The land of Naphtali was occupied by Ben-hadad of Damascus at the time of King Baasha of Israel (900-877; 1 Kgs. 15:20) and later became part of the growing Assyrian empire, in 734 B.C. (2 Kgs. 15:29; 2 Chron. 16:4; Isa. 8:23, a text cited by Matt. 4:13, 15).

Naphtuhim (naf′-tu-him), An unknown people listed in the Table of Nations among the sons of Ham (Gen. 10:13; 1 Chron. 1:11).

Narcissus, The head of a household in Rome (some of whose members were Christians) greeted by Paul in Romans 16:11.

Nard, A perfume extracted from the plant of the same name of great worth which the woman at Bethany poured over Jesus' head while he was at dinner. Jesus defended the woman saying that she had anointed him beforehand for his burial (*see* Mk. 14:3-9; Jn. 12:3; S. of S. 1:12; 4:13, 14).

narrow

a passage so *n.*	Num. 22:26	the *n.* gate	Matt. 7:13
Ephraim are so *n.*	Josh. 17:15	But how *n.*	Matt. 7:14
is a *n.* pit	Prov. 23:27	through the *n.* door	Lk. 13:24

Nathan, 1. A prophet who was a contemporary of David. He predicted to David that his dynasty would be secure for ever: "Your house and your sovereignty will always stand secure before me, and your throne be established for ever" (2 Sam. 7; 1 Chron. 17). This prophecy stands at the origin of the whole biblical messianism. Later he rebuked David for his adulterous affair with Bathsheba and for having sent her husband Uriah to his death; he also predicted the death of the infant to be born from this adulterous union (2 Sam. 12). In the fight for succession Nathan supported, with Bathsheba, the cause of Solomon (1 Kgs. 1:5-48). According to 1 Chronicles 29:29 and 2 Chronicles 9:29 Nathan wrote a chronicle of the kingdoms of David and Solomon.

2. Son of David, born in Jerusalem (2 Sam. 5:14; 1 Chron. 14:4) and recorded in the genealogy of Jesus (Lk. 3:31).

Nathanael (na-than′-i-el), A native of Cana in Galilee who was presented to Jesus by Philip. His first moment of scepticism was overcome by Jesus' remarks: "This man is a true Israelite. There is no guile in him" (*see* Jn. 1:45-51; 21:1) and by his superhuman knowledge. This story seems to indicate that Nathanael was called to be one of the twelve; his name however does not appear in the lists. For this reason some authors identify him with Bartholomew whose name always follows that of Philip in the list (*see* Mk. 3:18).

Nathan-melech (mel'-ek), The chamberlain of King Josiah of Judah (2 Kgs. 23:11).

nation

judgment on the *n*.	Gen. 15:14	a holy *n*.	Ex. 19:6
make a great *n*.	Gen. 21:13	subverting our *n*.	Lk. 23:2
assembly of *n*.	Gen. 35:11	our sanctuary and our *n*.	Jn. 11:48

Nations, *See* GENTILES.

native

in his *n*. land	Gen. 11:28	*n*. of Chaldea	Ezek. 23:15
		in his *n*. tongue Acts 2:8	

natural

n. intercourse	Rom. 1:26	the *n*. wild olive	Rom. 11:24
the *n*. branches	Rom. 11:21	A *n*. body is put down	
			1 Cor. 15:44

Nazarene, Matthew recounts that on the return from the flight into Egypt Joseph took the child and his mother to Nazareth in order "that what was spoken by the prophets might be fulfilled, 'He shall be called a Nazarene'." This prophecy cannot be identified in the Old Testament. There are two forms of the word in the Greek text, "Nazarenos" (Mk. 1:24) and "Nazoraios" (Matt. 2:23; Lk. 1:26). The evangelists understood this to mean the person who came from Nazareth (Matt. 21:11; Mk. 1:9; Jn. 1:45; Acts 10:37). It would however be difficult, though not impossible, to derive "Nazoraios" from the word meaning Nazareth. Some therefore would claim that the word derives from the sect of the Nazarenes, or Observants, which was a term later used of the Christians themselves. The undiscovered prophecy cited by Matthew in 2:23 is possibly Isaiah 11:1: "But a shoot shall sprout from the stump of Jesse, and from his roots a bud shall blossom." There is an assonance between the Hebrew word for branch (nsr) and Nazarene.

Nazarenes, Gospel of the, An Aramaic version of the canonical Gospel of St. Matthew, which was in use in northern Syria in the second century. The author(s) not only translates Matthew but very often changes and embellishes the original text.

Nazareth, The village in Galilee where Jesus lived until he began his public ministry (Lk. 2:39; 2:51; Matt. 2:23; Mk. 6:1). Luke narrates that Mary and Joseph lived in Nazareth and that the birth of Jesus took place in Bethlehem on account of the census of Quirinus (Lk. 1:26; 2:1). Matthew, however, seems not to have any knowledge of the previous Nazareth residence of Mary and Joseph, so the question arises as to how they came to settle there afterwards (Matt. 2:23). Mark does not allude to the birth, but implies that Nazareth was Jesus' home town "his own part of the country" (6:1). Without doubt Jesus did live at Nazareth up to the time of his public ministry: he is often identified as Jesus of Nazareth (Matt. 21:11; Mk. 1:9; Jn. 1:45; Acts 10:38). The adjective Nazarene (Greek Nazarenos or Nazoraios) is interpreted in its obvious sense in tradition to mean "from the town of Nazareth," where Jesus came from (Matt. 2:23). On account of the difficulty of deriving the word **Nazoraios** from the name Nazareth, some authors have sought another origin and meaning for the adjective, which was only later, in their opinion, attached to the town. In Acts 24:5 the word is used to designate Christians, and probably meant the observant or devout (from the Hebrew **nasar**) by analogy with a similar Jewish sect of the same name which is presumed to have been there.

Jesus returned to his home town at least once during his ministry, but was received with hostility by his townsmen (Matt. 13:54-55; Mk. 6:1-6; Lk. 4:16-30; *see* Jn. 1:45, 46). The old Nazareth is identified today with the town called En-Nasira by the Arabs, and is situated in the Galilean hills, 15 miles west of Lake Gennesaret.

Nazarite, The man or woman who has freely taken a vow of special consecration, regulated by Numbers 6:1-21. The external signs of this consecration are abstention from wine and fermented drinks, allowing the hair to grow long, and avoiding contact with corpses. When the time of the vow had lapsed, the Nazarite had to offer sacrifices specified by the law. The most noted example of a Nazarite is Samson (Jgs. 13-16). Other references to this practice can be read in Amos 2:11 and 1 Mac. 3:49-51. The vows of Acts 18:18 and Acts 21:23, 24 are considered to be Nazarite vows.

Neah, A city in the territory of Zebulun (Josh. 19:13).

Neapolis, The port city of Philippi in Macedonia, where Paul disembarked when going from Asia Minor to Europe on his second journey (Acts 16:11).

near

town ahead is *n.*	Gen. 19:20	You, O Lord, are *n.*	Ps. 119:151
be *n.*	Ps. 22:12	neighbor *n.* at hand	Prov. 27:10
		you who are *n.* Isa. 33:13	

Nebaioth (ne-bay′-yoth), Ishmael's first-born, son of Abraham and Hagar (Gen. 25:13; 28:9; 36:3), the founding father of Arab tribes which according to some authors are related to the later Nabateans. *See* NABATEANS.

Nebat (nee′-bat), The father of Jeroboam I, king of Israel (1 Kgs. 11:26).

Nebo (nee′-bo), 1. A deity venerated at Borsippa in Mesopotamia, son of Marduk, patron of scribes (Isa. 46:1).

2. A city of Moab in the land of Reuben (Num. 32:3, 38) which was captured by Mesha king of Moab and was still in Moabite hands at the time of Isaiah (*see* Isa. 15:2 and Jer. 48:1, 22).

3. A mountain in Transjordan rising from the plains of Moab from which Moses contemplated the promised land of Canaan (Deut. 32:49) and where later he died (Deut. 34:1). According to one tradition which is certainly legendary, before the destruction of the Temple Jeremiah hid the ark and the tabernacle in a cave on Mt. Nebo (2 Mac. 2:1-8).

Nebuchadnezzar (neb′-u-kad-nez′-zar), King of Babylon (605-562 B.C.), son and successor of Nabopolassar. While the father was still living, Nebuchadnezzar scored an important victory over Neco, Pharaoh of Egypt, at Carchemish and secured Babylonian control in the western region. After this victory Jehoiakim became a vassal of Babylon. The Egyptians however, under Hophrah, fared better in a battle in 601. Against the opinion of Jeremiah, Judah, after three years submission to Nebuchadnezzar, aligned itself on the side of the Egyptians (2 Kgs. 24:1). Soon after, Nebuchadnezzar once more campaigned against Egypt and her allies. In 598 Nebuchadnezzar's marauders captured Jerusalem without a struggle, Jehoiakim was killed in battle, and was succeeded by his son, Jehoiachin (2 Kgs. 24). The latter reigned only 3 months before Nebuchadnezzar deported the royal family and ten thousand Jews to Babylon and despoiled the Temple. In place of Jehoiachin he made his uncle Matthaniah king, and he changed his name to Zedekiah (2 Kgs. 24:10-17). Zedekiah's submission however did not last, so after two years of siege Nebuchadnezzar took and burned the city and Temple, imprisoned the king and his family, and deported large numbers of the population to Babylon. Judah became a province of the empire under the administration of a Jewish governor named Gedaliah (2 Kgs. 25; 587 B.C.).

Nebushazban (neb′-u-shaz′-ban), An officer of Nebuchadnezzar who took part in the conquest of Jerusalem (Jer. 39:13).

Nebuzaradan (neb′-u-za-ray′-dan), An officer of Nebuchadnezzar who took part in the conquest of Jerusalem in 587 B.C. To him is attributed the burning of the Temple, the palace and the city, and the destruction of the walls. Then he decided on the deportation of the people, freed Jeremiah, and installed Gedaliah as governor of Judah (2 Kgs. 25:8-20; Jer. 39:9-14; 40:1-5; 41:10; 43:6; 52:12-30).

Necho, *See* NECO.

Neco (nee′-ko), A Pharaoh of Egypt (609-594) of the 26th dynasty. Josiah of Judah tried to stop Neco from advancing against the Babylonians, but he was defeated and killed at the battle of Megiddo, 609 B.C. After a 3-month reign by Shallum (also called Jehoahaz II), Neco replaced him with another son of Josiah, Eliakim, and changed his name to Jehoiakim to denote his position as a vassal (2 Kgs. 23:29-35; 2 Chron. 35:20-24). Neco was later defeated at Carchemish (605) by Nebuchadnezzar.

Nedabiah (ned′-a-bie-ah), A son of King Jehoiachin ("Jeconiah") of Judah (1 Chron. 3:18).

Negeb (neg′-eb), A desert region south of Palestine. Its northern limit ran from the Mediterranean to the southern corner of the Dead Sea, in the area of Beer-sheba. Its southern limit was from Kadesh to the gulf of Aqaba. Some of the traditions concerning Abraham and Isaac are centered in the oasis and territory around Beer-sheba. (Gen. 12:9; 20:1; 24:62). The region was populated by various semi-nomadic groups who gave their names to its different parts: Caleb, Cain, Jerahmeel, Amalek. The Negeb of Kereth was the most western tract, under Philistine control. On the east, around Beer-sheba, lay the Negeb of Judah. During the Seleucid and Hellenistic period the Negeb was part of the Nabataean kingdom. A system of colonization and irrigation during this period gave the Negeb a new look until it became one of the most fertile areas in Palestine. The science of water use the Nabataeans developed was not understood by their Arab successors in the region.

Nehemiah, Son of Hacaliah, a Jew in the service of Artaxerxes I, king of Persia (465-425 B.C.; Neh. 1:1; 2:1) living in Susa (1:1). When he heard of the sad situation in Jerusalem and of the Jewish population in Palestine (1:2-11), he took advantage of his position as royal cupbearer to ask and obtain permission to go to Palestine and undertake the reconstruction of the walls of the city (2:1-10). This first mission took place in the year 445/444 B.C. The re-building of the walls was viciously opposed by the neighboring peoples, but despite the threat of armed attack, the work was brought to completion in 52 days (Neh. 3:1-4, 17; 6:1-19). As governor of the country of the Jews he brought to an efficient and prompt end the woes of a great part of the people who were weighed down with debts and had fallen into slavery to pay them (Neh. 5). He infused new life into the city by settling there one tenth of the rural population of the land (11:1-36). In 432 Nehemiah returned to Susa (Neh. 13:6) but came back to Judea some time later. He set about helping the Levites (13:10-14), seeing to the worship in the Temple and to the observance of the Sabbath (13:15-22). He had seen the danger of being absorbed by the neighboring peoples, and so banned mixed marriages and ordered that alien women married by the Jews should be repudiated (13:23-30). Sirach 49:13 praises Nehemiah, and 2 Maccabees 2:13 speaks of his preserving the sacred books of the Jews. *See* EZRA AND NEHEMIAH, BOOKS OF.

Nehushta (ne-hoosh′-ta), The wife of King Jehoiakim of Judah, taken with her son Jehoiachin to exile in Babylon (2 Kgs. 24:8).

Nehushtan (ne-hoosh′-tan), A bronze serpent which was worshipped in the Temple of Jerusalem. It was destroyed during Hezekiah's reform (715-687). It was identified with the bronze serpent made by Moses in the desert (Num. 21:8, 9) but it was probably an image of a deity connected with the Canaanite god of fertility (2 Kgs. 18:4). *See* SERPENT.

neighbor, neighbors

ask her *n.*	Ex. 3:22	*n.* and friends	Jer. 6:21
given it to a *n.*	1 Sam. 15:28	Gomorrah, and their *n.*	Jer. 49:18
Better is a *n.*	Prov. 27:10	who is my *n.*	Lk. 10:29

Nekoda (ne-koe′-da), Personal name (Ezra 2:48, 60; Neh. 7:50, 62).

Nepheg (nee′-feg), Son of David, born in Jerusalem (2 Sam. 5:15; 1 Chron. 3:7; 14:6).

Nephilim (nef′-i-lim), A quasi-legendary people who inhabited Canaan before the arrival of the Israelites (Num. 13:32, 33) finding a place in the world of myth (Gen. 6:1-8). Here the "sons of God" found the daughters of men attractive and married them. This story was gathered by the Yahwist author and placed at the introduction of the story of the flood to explain the origin of this people who were identified with the heroes of antiquity, as the product of the union between sons of God and daughters of men.

Ner, The father of Abner who was chief of the army under King Saul (1 Sam. 26:5).

Nereus (ner′-oos or ner′-e-us), A Christian of Rome greeted by Paul in Romans 16:15.

Nergal, A Mesopotamian deity venerated at Cutha, whose cult was introduced into Samaria by the colonists from Cutha who were settled there by the Assyrians after the conquest of Samaria in 722 B.C. (2 Kgs. 17:30).

Nergal-sharezer (sha-ree′-zer), An officer of Nebuchadnezzar who took part in the siege of Jerusalem in 587 B.C. (Jer. 39:3, 13) with other princes of the king of Babylon.

Neri (ner′-eye), An ancestor of Jesus in Luke's genealogy (Lk. 3:27).

Neriah (ne-rye′-ah), Father of Baruch, Jeremiah's scribe (Jer. 32:12) and of Seraiah who brought Jeremiah's oracles to Babylon (Jer. 51:59-63).

Nero, Nero Claudius Caesar was emperor of Rome from 54-68 A.D. Paul appealed to him at his trial at Caesarea (Acts 25:11), and tradition has it that during Nero's reign both Paul and Peter suffered martyrdom, around 68 A.D. John (Rev. 13:18) remarks that there is need for shrewdness to identify the beast with the number 666 (though some mss. read 616). There have nevertheless been many attempts to do so. The likeliest solution to the problem is to be found through gematria, adding the numerical equivalent of the letters in a person's name. **Neron Caesar,** nrwn qsr in Hebrew adds up this way: 50+200+6+50+100+60+200=666.

nest

your *n.* is set	Num. 24:21	to build his *n.*	Job 39:27
a bird's *n.*	Deut. 22:6	the swallow a *n.*	Ps. 84:4
In my own *n.*	Job 29:18	his *n.* on high	Hab. 2:9

net, nets

headlong into a *n.*	Job 18:8	Andrew, casting a *n.*	Matt. 4:18
with his *n.*	Job 19:6	casting their *n.*	Mk. 1:16
in his *n.*	Ps. 10:9	and lower your *n.*	Lk. 5:4
a *n.* for my feet	Ps. 57:7	the *n.* loaded	Jn. 21:11

Nethanel (ne-than′-el), A common personal name in the Old Testament (1 Chron. 2:14 [a brother of King David]; Num. 1:8; 2:5; 10:15; 1 Chron. 15:24; 24:6; 2 Chron. 17:7; Ezra 10:22; Neh. 12:21, 36).

Nethaniah (neth′-a-ny′-ah), Personal name (2 Kgs. 25:23; 1 Chron. 25:2; 2 Chron. 17:8; Jer. 36:14).

Nethinim (neth′-i-nim), Etymologically the word means "given," and it designated personnel of inferior rank who served in the Temple (Ezra 2:43-54; Neh. 7:46-60). Groups of these Temple servants returned from the exile with Zerubbabel (1 Chron. 9:2) and with Ezra (Ezra 7:7; 8:17-20). They were probably state slaves at the time of the monarchy (Ezra 8:20; Ezra 2:43-58), whose function it was to serve at the cult (*see* Josh. 9:23-27; Deut. 29:10). Perhaps they were the descendants of prisoners of war which would explain Ezekiel's denunciation of admitting uncircumcised aliens to perform duties in the Temple (Ezek. 44:7-9).

Netophah (ne-toe′-fah), A village in Judah near Bethlehem (2 Sam. 23:28-29; 1 Chron. 2:54; Ezra 2:21-22; Neh. 7:26).

nettles

under the *n.*	Job 30:7	covered with *n.*	Prov. 24:31
	A field of *n.*	Zeph. 2:9	

never

n. tasted happiness	Job 21:25	to eat and *n.* die	Jn. 6:50
he *n.* sees	Ps. 10:11	*N.* have we been slaves	Jn. 8:33
shall *n.* be disturbed	Ps. 15:5	*n.* wash my feet	Jn. 13:8
n. be put to shame	Ps. 71:1	*n.* eaten anything unclean	
			Acts 10:14

new

Then a *n.* king	Ex. 1:8	built a *n.* house	Deut. 20:5
the *n.* cereal offering	Lev. 23:16	*n.* song into my mouth	Ps. 40:3
make room for the *n.*	Lev. 26:10	I drink it *n.*	Matt. 26:29
	n. wine into old	Mk. 2:22	

New Moon, The new moon or neomenia marked the beginning of the month in the Israelite lunar calendar. Numbers 28:11-15 prescribes for that day special sacrifices. Moreover it was a day of rest as was the sabbath (Amos 8:5). The observance of the new moon is very ancient (1 Sam. 20:5-27); Isa. 1:13-14; Hos. 2:13; 2 Kgs. 4:23) and was maintained also after the exile even to New Testament times (Ezra 3:5; Neh. 10:34; Col. 2:16). Of especial importance was the new moon of the month of Tishri, which marked the beginning of the year (Lev. 23:24, 25; Num. 29:1-6). *See* NEW YEAR.

news

they related the *n.*	1 Sam. 11:4	must bring good *n.*	1 Kgs.1:42
the *n.* about Saul	2 Sam. 4:4	proclaim good *n.*	Lk. 2:10
to bring the *n.* today	2 Sam. 18:20	proclaiming the good *n.*	Lk. 8:1
	believe in the good *n.*	Acts 8:12	

New Year, Almost to the end of the monarchy of Judah the year began with the autumnal equinox (i.e. in September). When however the Babylonian names of the months were adopted, the year began with the spring equinox, and Nisan (corresponding to our March-April) was the first month of the year. This new computation appears, for example, in Ezekiel 40:1 and in Exodus 12:2. Nevertheless the first day of the seventh month, which corresponded to the beginning of the year in the old computation, retained a certain solemnity, as is evidenced in Leviticus 23:24-25 and Numbers 29:1-6.

Post-biblical Judaism attaches great solemnity to Rosh Hashanah, the beginning of the New Year in September. On the other hand it is known that in ancient middle eastern civilizations the beginning of the year was celebrated with particular solemnity and was one of the principal festivals. It inaugurated the yearly cycle of life and was the mythical actuation of the mythical origins of the universe. This poses the question whether or not in Israel too there existed in pre-exilic monarchic times a feast of the New Year. Scholars hold widely differing opinions.

The most radical opinion is held by the "Myth and Ritual" school, whose tenets are that a single cultural cloak covered the middle east, including Israel. This cult pattern is a sacred drama of rites and myths. This drama had a salvific value in that it efficaciously evoked the primordial mythical event of universal creation and the divine sovereignty.

The principal parts of this rite were: a. The stylized dramatic representation of the death and resurrection of God, represented by the king. b. The recitation of the myth of the creation of the world with its epic struggle between the monsters of the abyss and the creating god (in Babylon the **Enuma Elis** was recited, *see* CREATION). c. The **hieros gamos** or sacred wedding celebration aimed at increasing the fruitfulness of the earth and its inhabitants for the coming year. d. The solemn enthroning of the god-king at the conclusion of a ritual procession.

Scholars admit that there is no explicit description of such a festival in the Bible; thus their theory is based on elements and indications which are gathered above all in the Psalter, and which are in their opinion nothing more than the residue of such a feast. They insist first and foremost on the so-called psalms of the kingdom of God (Pss. 47; 93; 96-99) which are distinguished by the inscription "malak Yahweh" — "God has been constituted king." *See* KINGDOM OF GOD.

Other scholars point out that there is no explicit reference to such a festival, and on this absence of any explicit indication to the contrary, they deny this whole hypothesis.

More interesting than these two extreme positions is the attempt of moderates to take all the evidence into account. They concede to the "Myth and Ritual" school that they have indeed gathered elements that demand explanation, but they reject the system built of these elements and the "Myth and Ritual" interpretation. The so-called cult-pattern would seem to be a deduction that is ill-founded since it is based on hints and indications gathered here and there over a wide area, and certainly not a universal type that is vigorously pursued and verified universally. These scholars take issue with the way in which the altogether special religious character of the Bible and of the Jewish traditions are neglected.

These moderates then address themselves to the question of the significance of the Feast of the Tabernacles in ancient Israel. At the beginning this was an agrarian feast borrowed from the Canaanites. Through it, rain and fecundity were sought for the new annual cycle. Just like the other feasts in Israel, such as the Feast of the Unleavened Bread and Pentecost, this became a celebration commemorating the glorious works of God in favor of his people Israel—accounts which were handed down in tradition.

This aspect however is not so evident in the texts. It is affirmed in a general way, but no specific details are given. These authors try to take account of the justified observations of the "Myth and Ritual" school while not betraying the Israelite heritage: this they do by interpreting them in the context of the Feast of Tabernacles.

Some hold that the Feast of Tabernacles derived in the beginning from the theophany on Sinai and the proclamation of the law. This interpretation is based on Deuteronomy 31:10-13 which prescribes the reading of the deuteronomic law every seven years on the Feast of Tabernacles. Moreover this opinion calls to its support the fact of the renovation of the Covenant carried out by Ezra precisely at the beginning of the seventh month where the Feast of Tabernacles is explicitly mentioned (Neh. 7:72-8:18).

In this context the theme of God's sovereignty is present but is not its prime emphasis. Thus other authors insist more on this theme and suggest that the Feast of Tabernacles, at least in Judah, commemorated David's election, and that of the city of Zion (the Temple) as the dwelling place of God, "King of all the earth" (Ps. 48). The psalms known as the songs of Zion are connected with the Feast of Tabernacles, and in fact celebrate this election. Psalm 137 seems to commemorate annually the transfer of the ark to Jerusalem, which sanctioned that election. In Judah this became the typical form of the feast, while the kingdom of the north remained more faithful to the older significance of the feast, which was to commemorate and renew the Sinai covenant. *See* also TABERNACLES, FEAST OF.

Neziah (ne-zie′-ah), Ancestor of a family of temple servants (Ezra 2:54).

Nezib (nee′-zib), A village in Judah (Josh. 15:43).

Nibhaz, A deity venerated by the colonists of Avva who were settled by the Assyrians in Samaria after 722 B.C. (2 Kgs. 17:31).

Nibshan, A town of Judah (Josh. 15:62).

Nicanor (ny-kay′-nor), 1. General of the Seleucid army of Antioch IV Epiphanes (175-164 B.C.) and of Demetrius I (161-150 B.C.). With Ptolemy and Gorgias he was commissioned by Lysias to quell the Maccabean revolt. He was defeated however by Judas near Emmaus (1 Mac. 3:38-4:25; 2 Mac. 8:9-34). Once more he returned under Demetrius to be again defeated at Beth-horon, 13th of Adar of the year 160 B.C. This became a day of celebration for Judah's victory (1 Mac. 7:26-50; 2 Mac. 14:11-15, 36).

2. One of the seven Hellenistic Jewish Christians who were chosen by the apostles to attend to the needs of the poor in the Christian community in Jerusalem (Acts 6:1-6).

Nicodemus, A Jew, a member of the Sanhedrin and follower of Jesus. A discussion held by night with Jesus is reported with comment by John in c. 3 of his gospel. He intervened in favor of Jesus, pleading that he should not be condemned without a hearing in a meeting of the Pharisees reported in Jn. 7:45-52. Nicodemus brought myrrh and aloes and helped prepare the body of Jesus for burial (Jn. 19:38-39).

Nicolaitans (nik′-o-lay′-i-tanz), The followers of a certain Nicolaus of whom we know only that he taught an unorthodox doctrine which was repudiated by John in a letter to the churches of Ephesus and Pergamum (Rev. 2:6, 15). Authors assume that the Nicolaitans were a gnostic sect.

Nicolaus (nik′-o-lay′-us), One of the seven Hellenistic Jews chosen by the apostles to attend to the needs of the poor in Jerusalem (Acts 6:1-6).

Nicopolis (ni-kop′-o-lis), A city in Epirus in Greece. Paul invites Titus to come and pass the winter with him there in Tit. 3:12.

Niger (nie′-jer), Simon Niger, one of the prophets and teachers in the church at Antioch (*see* Acts 13:1).

Night, Like the Mesopotamians the Hebrews divided the night into three watches (Lam. 2:19; Jgs. 7:19; Ex. 14:24; 1 Sam. 11:11). By New Testament times the Roman custom of dividing the night into four watches had been adopted (Matt. 6:48; 14:24; Mk. 13:35). On the symbolic use of night as the time of darkness *see* LIGHT AND DARKNESS

night.

darkness he called "*n.*"	Gen. 1:5	all *n.* long	Jgs. 16:2
separate day from *n.*	Gen. 1:14	to the Lord all *n.*	1 Sam. 15:11
govern the *n.*	Gen. 1:16	It was *n.*	Jn. 13:30
That *n.* God came	Num. 22:20	The *n.* is far spent	Rom. 13:12

Nile, This immensely long river makes its way over 4000 miles from East Central Africa to the Mediterranean. The origin of the name is obscure. In ancient Egypt is was **h'py** and in Hebrew **haye'or**, a loan word meaning stream. The river played then as now a vital role in the Egyptian economy and production. The Egyptians worshiped the river-god Hapi, but Osiris became lord of the rains to outdo Hapi in importance. The Lord promised the Israelites a "land watered by the rain from heaven, unlike Egypt where you sowed your seed and watered it by tread," which probably refers to a waterwheel system of irrigation, of which there are still examples in Egypt (*see* Deut. 11:10-11). Moses was found by Pharoah's daughter in the reeds at the river's edge where his mother had hidden him (Ex. 2:1-10). In his prophecy against Egypt, Ezekiel quotes the Lord as threatening to dry up the arms of the Nile (Ezek. 30:12; *see* Isa. 19:5-8).

Nimrod, In the genealogy of Genesis 10:8-12 Nimrod, son of Cush, was a great hunter in the eyes of Yahweh and became first king of Babel, Erech, and Accad. This is certainly legendary, but the origins of the story are not clear. Some authors would identify him with the god Ninurta, while others look for him among the legendary heroes of the world of myth, such as the Nephilim (Gen. 6:4) or among the personages of the epic of Gilgamesh.

Nimshi (nim′-shy), The father of King Jehu of Israel (1 Kgs. 19:16; 2 Kgs. 9:20; 2 Chron. 22:7).

Nineveh (nin′-e-veh), A city in Mesopotamia on the left bank of the Tigris opposite the modern Mosul. It was the residence of the Assyrian kings, especially of those from Sennacherib on (705-681 B.C.). He embellished it with splendid palaces and public buildings, as did his successors, Esarhaddon and Ashurbanipal. The ruins of these, together with Ashurbanipal's magnificent library, have been uncovered in excavations. The Bible shows Jonah preaching in Nineveh (Jonah 3; Matt. 12:41), and there too, according to Tobit 1:11, Tobit lived. An overjoyed Nahum predicted Nineveh's complete destruction at the hands of the Medes and the Neo-Babylonians (612 B.C.); he was joined in his prophecy by Zephaniah (*see* Nah. 2:3; Zeph. 2:13-15). After this destruction it was never again occupied.

Nisan (nie′-zan), First month of the Babylonian calendar, corresponding to March-April, and to the month of Abib in the Canaanean calendar. *See* MONTH.

Nisroch, An Assyrian deity venerated in Nineveh, in whose temple according to 2 Kings 19:37, Isaiah 37:38, Sennacherib was assassinated.

No, *See* THEBES.

Noadiah (noe′-a-dy′-ah), 1. A Levite (Ezra 8:33).

2. A prophetess (Neh. 6:14).

Noah, Son of Lamech, the hero of the biblical deluge (Gen. 5:29), father of Shem, Ham and Japheth, from whom sprang post-flood humanity (Gen. 6-9; *see* FLOOD, THE). Noah appears again (Gen. 9:20-27) as the first farmer, and especially the first to plant the vine. This tradition links him with the genealogy of Cain given in 4:16-24, and so with the founders of other trades and arts such as "tent-dwellers and owners of livestock, all who play the lyre and the flute, all metalworkers in bronze and iron" (*see* Gen. 4:16-24), Noah is again recalled in Ezekiel 14:14, 20 as a man of integrity (*see* 2 Pet. 2:5). Hebrews 11:7 numbers him among the men of faith of the Old Testament.

2. One of the five daughters of Zelophehad (Num. 26:33; 27:1-11; 36:11; Josh. 17:3). *See* INHERITANCE; ZELOPHEHAD.

No-amon (noe-am′-on), The Hebrew name of Thebes (Nah. 3:8). *See* THEBES.

Nob, A town in Benjamin territory near Jerusalem (Isa. 10:32; Neh. 11:32), residence of Ahimelech and of the other priests who were killed by Saul for having helped David and his men (1 Sam. 21:1-11; 22:6-23).

Nobah, 1. The name of a town in Gilead, southeast of Damascus, and also its Israelite conqueror (Num. 32:42).

2. Another town of the same name also in Gilead (Jgs. 8:10, 11), site unknown.

Nod, A region that is probably imaginary, to the east of Eden, where Cain took refuge after the killing of Abel.

Nodan (noe′-dan), The owner of the threshing-floor near which Uzzah died during the transfer of the Ark of the Covenant to Jerusalem by King David (2 Sam. 6:6). Also Nachon (KJV) and Nacon (RSV). *See* UZZAH.

Nogah (noe′-gah), Son of David, born in Jerusalem (1 Chron. 3:7).

Nohah (noe′-hah), A son of Benjamin (1 Chron. 8:2).

Nomadism, The nomadic tribes of the Syrian and Arabian desert played a role of the first importance in the political, cultural and religious history of the ancient Middle East. Not a few of the great stages of this history, as is evidenced from the documents, coincide with the massive migration of these tribes to the zones of urban, sedentary culture. At the beginning this mass migration arrested progress in the sedentary culture, which was much superior to that of the newly arrived and settled nomads. Soon however the sedentary culture, nourished by the new influx of nomads, found itself making new forward thrusts. The Akkadians, Amorites, proto-Aramaeans and the Aramaeans themselves, and down into the Hellenistic period with the Nabataeans and still later the Arabians—these were the creators of empires, kingdoms and cultures which gave its characteristic countenance to middle-eastern history from the third millenium B.C.

This penetration by the nomads could be unexpected and violent, but generally speaking it was prepared for by a long, slow process of settlement and undisturbed penetration into the unpopulated areas of the sedentary zone. It is true however that the definitive coming to political power was always accompanied by violence and destruction. This process was repeated a thousand times over in small or greater proportions, and is also the explanation of the settlement of the Israelite tribes in Canaan. This was idealized and brought back to its prime origins in the episode of the tower of Babel in Genesis 11. (*See* BABEL, TOWER OF.) The author of this tradition knew how to gather into an effective story the transformations that mark the passage from nomadic existence to an urban and sedentary culture. From being an obscure people without history or progress, if not without aim, the nomadic peoples were caught up in an irresistible movement of ascent and human conquest, which made them a part of history.

The study of nomadism holds great importance for the knowledge of the Bible, for the patriarchs and the tribes who settled in Canaan and joined together to form the Israelite confederation were nomads. The residue of their nomadic existence can be discovered in more advanced stages of their sedentary history and in some of their religious institutions. Here follows a brief note on 1. the social structure of nomadism and 2. the nomadic type of life.

1. Sedentary society is linked together by the land it lives on. Nomadic society, by its very name, has no land to call its own. It is essentially itinerant and mobile, and so its principle of cohesion was not land, but blood. Nomadic society is structured on ever-widening circles of consanguinity, while these circles are centered, for their part, on the common ancestor of all the members. The families with a common ancestor form a clan, while clans following the same process converge in a tribe, while several tribes together can form a people. The individual members are then designated according to their descent from a common ancestor as the son or sons of N. (**ben** or **bene** N.)

Because of this blood-link there arose between the members a strict solidarity which was nourished by an awareness of a common heritage and a common destiny. This solidarity was transformed into a powerful defense organism against any agent, external or internal, who should threaten or offend the life of the community. An offense committed by one member of the tribe was vindicated by the tribe itself, and failure to observe the apodictic laws that guarded the life of the tribe brought with it exclusion from the clan, tribe or people. This was equivalent to liquidation, as nomadic existence was not possible in isolation. *See* AVENGER, MURDER.

This social structure is mirrored in some typical literary genres of which we have numerous examples in the Bible: the genealogies and the etiologies. Genealogy determined in blood links of descendance who belonged to what tribe or group, and therefore the limits within which the forces of cohesion and the "immunilogical" defense system worked. (*See* GENEALOGY.) In the etiologies a group's virtues and vices, its manner of life and characteristics are explained on the basis of presumed personal characteristics or exploits on the part of the individual who originated the genealogical scheme. This person, who also gives his name to the tribe or people, becomes the type or representative in whom the individual members recognize one another. As an example of this *see* CAIN.

The awareness of the blood link is so deep that the historical relationships that arose between different groups were later translated into genealogical terms. Ancestors, real or presumed, of individual groups, were made brothers or relatives. Thus arises a fictitious genealogy, which however, if rightly interpreted, gives an insight into the historical vicissitudes of a particular people. On the other hand, while the actual name of a given tribe may have been derived from its geographical situation or its trade, it is given to a fictitious ancestor created by the genealogy as founder of the tribe.

The mentality and understanding of existence that is manifested in these literary genres evokes the idea of a living organism. For this reason it has suggested the term "corporate personality" to designate it. "Corporate personality" means that one individual incorporates or reassumes in himself the whole group and its destiny. The use and indiscriminate application of this term to biblical theology and especially to christology has been contested in recent years. *See* SON OF MAN.

2. The sedentary life developed in regions that could be cultivated, while nomadic life belonged to near-desert and steppe areas, and to the desert itself. This distinction of climatic zones suggests that there were different types of nomadic existence. Nomadic life in the desert became possible with the domestication of the camel. The date for this is disputed, but the camel seems to have been in use already at the beginning of the second millenium B.C. even though it did not become very common until the fourteenth or thirteenth century B.C. This nomadism, typical of the Bedouins, was characterized by hostility and contempt for the sedentary life. It is clear that the nomadic life practiced by the ancestors of Israel is not this. They were nomads of the steppe regions, shepherds of flocks of sheep and goats, and even of cattle. They were mainly a peaceful people.

With their flocks they roamed the steppes at the margins of the cultivated land, following the grass that the seasons and scarce rains of the region produced. With the sedentary peoples they maintained cordial relationships, asking their permission to penetrate into their lands to feed their flocks during the arid periods of the year. They followed fixed itineraries along the course of the wells for water, over which there was a rigorous right of property and use. They looked on the sedentary peoples with envy, and many groups settled down to the cultivation of the land, without however altogether abandoning the wanderings of the tribes in search of pasture for the flocks. Eventually however they end up settling down in a stable manner, once they have found favorable circumstances.

Israel's nomadic past left her with profound traces that even marked her religious ideals. The period of the so-called journey through the desert from Egypt to Canaan, during which the Lord revealed himself to Israel on Sinai, was to remain for later Jews, and especially for the prophets, a time characterized by genuine Yahwism as opposed to the corruption and syncretism of sedentary and urban religion. This held true despite the recorded sins and unfaithfulness of the discontented people in the desert. The prophets looked back with yearning on a time when God took his people by the hand, and entered into direct and intimate contact with them, as a father to his children, or a husband to his wife (Hos. 13:5; Amos 2:10; Jer. 2:2). Hosea goes so far as to describe the future salvation to be worked by God as a return to the desert where he will once more purify and convert as once he had already done in Israel (Hos. 2:16-17; 12:10). This ideal was the norm of life for a rigorous and intransigent Israelite group called the Rechabites, whom Jeremiah praised (*see* Jer. 35). *See* RECHABITES.

noon ·

dine with me at *n.*	Gen. 43:16	They marched out at *n.*	
Joseph's arrival at *n.*	Gen. 43:25		1 Kgs. 20:16
from morning to *n.*	1 Kgs. 18:26	with her until *n.*	2 Kgs. 4:20
		The hour was about *n.*	Jn. 4:6

North, On the west, Israel was washed by the Mediterranean while to the east lay the Syro-Arabian desert. In the Hebrew mentality then, the only way to come or go was north or south. To the south lay Egypt and Ethiopia; to the north Assyria, Babylonia, the Syrians, Media, Persia and Elam, and in general, the other great powers. For the Canaanites the gods inhabited the north. Isaiah satirizes the king of Babylon who wished to challenge God saying to himself: "I will sit on the Mount of Assembly in the recesses of the North" (Isa. 14:13). The north was the region from which the threats of the great nations arose for Israel (Jer. 46:10; Zeph. 2:13). To the Israelites exiled in the north comes the word of God urging them to repentance (Jer. 3:11-13).

nose

hook in your *n.*	2 Kgs. 19:28	the *n.* rings	Isa. 3:21
or pierce his *n.*	Job 40:24	a ring in your *n.*	Ezek. 16:12
n. is like the tower	S. of S. 7:5	cutting off your *n.*	Ezek. 23:25

nostril, nostrils

blew into his *n.*	Gen. 2:7	Smoke rose from his *n.*	
in its *n.*	Gen. 7:22		2 Sam. 22:9
out of your very *n.*	Num. 11:20	is in my *n.*	Job 27:3

nothing

the earth over *n.*	Job 26:7	have *n.* to eat	Matt. 15:32
knows *n.*	Prov. 9:13	*N.* would be impossible	
profit *n.*	Prov. 10:2		Matt. 17:20
	take *n.* on the journey	Mk. 6:8	

nought

my argument to *n.*	Job 24:25	profits a man *n.*	Job 34:9

now

n. he dares	Gen. 19:9	time until *n.*	Matt. 11:12
I know *n.*	Gen. 22:12	Sleep on *n.*	Matt. 26:45
that I may *n.* die	Gen. 27:2	man you are living with *n.*	
			Jn. 4:18

Numbers, The fourth book of the Pentateuch. The title comes from the Greek translation known as the Septuagint (LXX), where it is called **arithmoi**. It gets this name from the accurate census drawn up in cc. 1:1-4:49 and 26. On its origin and composition *see* PENTATEUCH. The book consists of greatly varied material. Beside the already-quoted census there are other lists and catalogues drawn up with precision, whose origin is much discussed. Clearly they do not reflect the historic circumstances of the journey through the desert, nor are they pure fantasy. Examples of these lists are: Numbers 33, the encampments on the journey through the desert; 7, the offerings of the delegates of the tribes at the sanctuary; 10:11-28, the order of the clans when marching; and the supervisors of the allotment of the land (Num. 34:16-29).

The narrative material comprises the journey from Sinai (10:33) to the plains of Moab (36:13). The most salient events are: the murmuring of Miriam and Aaron against Moses for having taken a Cushite woman to wife (Num. 12); the mission of the spies and the defeat of the Israelites by the Amalekites and Canaanites who harried them as far as Hormah (13, 14); the revolt and punishment of Korah, Dathan and Abiram, who were swallowed up by the earth (16, 17); while 20:1-13 tells of the mysterious incident of the water at Meribah and Moses' incredulity, on account of which he died before entering the promised land. 20:14-21:35 tells of the events, the dealings and the wars with the peoples of Edom, Negeb, and Transjordan.

Cc. 22-24 have the account of the episode of Balaam, the seer called on by Balak, king of Moab, to curse the Israelites. The story ends with the distribution of territories in Transjordan between the tribes of Gad, Reuben and half of Manasseh (Num. 32). This whole story is studded with legislative dispositions, especially of a cultic nature (*see* Num. 15:18, 19; 28-30; 35-36).

Numenius (noo-mee′-ni-us), Son of Antiochus and one of the legates sent by Simon to Rome (1 Mac. 15:15).

Nun, Joshua's father (Ex. 33:11; Num. 11:28, etc.).

Nun, The 14th letter of the Hebrew alphabet (n).

Nunc Dimittis (di-mit′-is), The first words of the Latin version of the canticle Simeon sang on receiving the Child Jesus into his arms, recorded in Luke 2:29-32.

Nuzi, Nuzu (noo′-zi, noo′-zu), A Mesopotamian city east of Ashhur in modern Iraq, occupied by the Hurrites of Mitanni towards the middle of the 2nd millenium. Excavations carried out from 1925 to 1931 brought to light many tables written in Akkadic which help tell the history of the period and describe the social and economic life of the people. A comparison with some elements of the history of the patriarchs revealed many interesting similarities and points of contact, such as adoption, matrimonial contracts and others, which confirm the Mesopotamian origin of the patriarchs and helped reassess the antiquity and historic value of this part of the Bible tradition.

Nymphas, A Christian of Colossae in whose house the Christians met (Col. 4:15).

O

Oak, In the whole of the ancient Near East a sacred character was attributed very often to large trees, such as the oak and the terebinth, whether they had grown in isolation or in small groups. They were taken as special manifestations of the fertility gods. They are often associated with places of cult or with what one can suppose were such. Genesis 13:18 speaks of the terebinth of Mamre at Hebron where Abraham built an altar to Yahweh (*see* Gen. 18:4, 8). Shechem's holy place was the Oak of Moreh where Yahweh appeared to Abraham (Gen. 12:6 ff.). This context underlies the several references found in the Bible to cult offered "on high mountains, on hills, under any spreading tree" (Isa. 1:29; 57:5; Hos. 4:13, 14; Deut. 12:2; 1 Kgs. 14:23; 2 Kgs. 15:4, etc.)

oak
takes a holm or an *o*.　　Isa. 44:14　highest *o*. of Bashan　　Ezek. 27:6

oar
they made your *o*.　　Ezek. 27:6　all who ply the *o*.　　Ezek. 27:29

Oath, The purpose of an oath was to call on God to back one's word. It was taken to the accompaniment of holy words or acts and usually in connection with some shrine and the priesthood. Among the Israelites, as among the surrounding peoples, it was in frequent use to solemnize contracts or consecrate a pledge of loyalty, and in other circumstances that demanded sacred ratification or confirmation.

Hebrew has two words for swearing, **saba'** and **alah,** the first deriving from a word meaning seven, the second meaning to curse Genesis 21:27-31 tells of the seven lambs Abraham offered as evidence to Abimelech that he had dug the well, over which a dispute had arisen. The story concludes that the place was called Beer-sheba because there the two of them swore an oath. The curse was pronounced by the priest in the case of an accused adulteress, in order to extract the truth (Num. 5:21).

The full oath was accompanied by a curse the speaker threatens on himself or others if the words sworn to do not turn out to be true. Ruth swore her loyalty to Naomi saying: "May the Lord do so and so to me, and more besides, if aught but death separates me from you!" (Ruth 1:17; *see* 1 Sam. 3:17; 14:44). Ezekiel cites the Lord swearing by his own life (Ezek. 17:16; *see* Zeph. 2:9). A very full example of the curse is found in Job 31.

Eventually the fully outspoken curse was dropped and the oath became simply an "if" clause with the curse-filled apodosis presumed or understood; not spoken.

Jesus preached simple speech in which a man was as good as his word. "What I tell you is, do not swear at all. Do not swear by heaven (it is God's throne), nor by the earth (it is his footstool), nor by Jerusalem (it is the city of the great King); do not swear by your head (you cannot make a single hair white or black). Say 'Yes' when you mean 'Yes' and 'No' when you mean 'No'." (*see* Matt. 5:33-37). When however at his trial he was invoked under oath, he did answer (*see* Matt. 26:63).

Paul swears to the truth of what he pronounces on several occasions, using Old Testament forms (2 Cor. 1:23; Gal. 1:20; Phil. 1:8).

Obadiah, 1. The Master of the Palace during the reign of Ahab, king of Israel (869-850 B.C.), the protector of Yahweh's prophets during the persecution launched by Jezebel, Ahab's wife (1 Kgs. 18:3-18).

2. The fourth of the minor prophets in the Hebrew canon of the Old Testament. There is nothing known of him. His prophecy, a mere 21 verses, is the shortest in the Old Testament and called simply "Vision of Obadiah about Edom" (v. 1). It is divided into two parts: a sentence is passed on Edom (2-7, 10, 14, 15b) and the day of Yahweh is heralded with the triumph of Israel (8, 9, 15a, 16-21). The first part, which belongs to the common prophetic tradition of oracles pronounced against the nations, is found also in Jeremiah 29:7-22. The book is difficult to date. It was certainly composed before the fourth century B.C. when the Nabataeans settled in Edom. The prophet does not seem to be denouncing Edom's conflicts at the time of the monarchy (*see* 2 Kgs. 8:22), but rather Edom's conduct towards the Jews who remained in Palestine during the exile (*see* Lam. 4:21 ff.; Ps. 137:7; *see* v. 20), that is, from 587 B.C. on.

3. Obadiah, meaning "Servant of the Lord," is a common personal name in the Old Testament (1 Chron. 3:21; 7:3; 8:38; 9:16; 12:10; 27:19; 2 Chron. 17:7; 34:12; Ezra 8:9; Neh. 12:25).

Obal, An Arabian people listed among the sons of Shem in the Table of Nations (Gen. 10:28).

obdurate
he became *o.*   Ex. 8:11   Pharaoh became *o.*   Ex. 8:28

Obed, Son of Boaz and Ruth, father of Jesse and grandfather of David (Ruth 4:17-22; 1 Chron. 2:12) whose name is listed in Jesus' genealogy by Matthew and Luke (Matt. 1:5; Lk. 3:32).

Obed-edom (oh′-bed-ee′-dom), A native of Gath living in Kiriath-jearim: the ark of the covenant stayed at his residence for three months when, on account of the sudden death of Uzzah, David was struck with terror and decided to postpone its transferral to Jerusalem (2 Sam. 6:10-12; 1 Chron. 13:13-14; 15:24, 25).

obedience, obedient

o. to them	Lk. 2:51	Gentiles to *o.*	Rom. 15:18
bring to *o.* faith	Rom. 1:5	he recalls the *o.*	2 Cor. 7:15

obey

a curse if you do not *o.* the		if they *o.* not, they perish	
	Deut. 11:28		Job 36:12
If they *o.* and serve him	Job 36:11	the winds and the sea *o.* him	
			Matt. 8:27

Obil, An Ishmaelite who was in charge of the camels of King David (1 Chron. 27:30).

Oboth, An encampment of the Israelites on their journey to Canaan, situated in Moab between Punon and Iye-Abarim (Num. 21:10, 11; 33:43, 44).

observe

be careful to *o.*	Deut. 13:1	*o.* my statutes	Ezek. 20:19
Do not *o.* the statutes	Ezek. 20:18	not *o.* my statutes	Ezek. 20:21

obstinate

So Pharaoh remained *o.*	Ex. 7:22	Yet Pharaoh remained *o.*	Ex. 8:15
	the Lord made Pharaoh *o.*	Ex. 9:12	

Ochran, The father of Pagiel of the tribe of Asher (Num. 1:13; 2:27; 7:72; 10:26).

Ocina (oh-sy´-na). A place on the Mediterranean coast S. of Tyre (Judith 2:28).

Oded, A prophet during the reign of Ahaz, king of Judah (2 Chron. 28:9).

Odomera (od´-o-mer´-a). An Arabian sheik defeated by Jonathan Maccabeus (1 Mac. 9:66).

offense

crime or *o.* have I committed	
	Gen. 31:36

offering, *See* SACRIFICE.

not delay the *o.*	Ex. 22:28	princes brought *o.*	Num. 7:10
animal *o.* to the Lord	Lev. 1:2	Levites bring the *o.*	Neh. 10:40

officers

police *o.* in the house	Jer. 29:26

officials

give them to his *o.*	1 Sam. 8:14	*o.* he had in his service	1 Kgs. 4:1

often

How *o.* is the lamp	Job 21:17	How *o.* they rebelled	Ps. 78:40
	How *o.* have I yearned	Matt. 23:37	

Og, King of Bashan defeated by Moses at the battle of Edrei. The kingdom of Bashan was wiped out and its lands assigned to Reuben, Gad and Manasseh (Num. 21:33-35; 32; Josh. 13). Other books of the Bible recall this victory (Deut. 3:1-13; 4:47; Josh. 9:10; Pss. 135; 136:20; Neh. 9:22). In the Bible tradition, Og assumed legendary proportions (Deut. 3:11).

Ohad, A son of Simeon (Gen 46:10; Ex. 6:15).

Ohel, A descendant of David (1 Chron. 3:20)

Oholah, Oholibah (oh-hoe'-lah, oh-hoe'-li-bah), The names of the two sisters who symbolically represent Samaria and Jerusalem in the allegorical account of the history and sins of the two kingdoms in Ezekiel 23. What exactly the words refer to has never been quite clear, though they do derive from the Hebrew root 'ohol meaning tent, and so perhaps referring to the sanctuaries of the two cities.

Oholibamah (oh-hoe'-li-bam'-ah), One of the wives of Esau (Gen. 36:2).

Oil, Olive oil was one of Palestine's principal products (Deut. 11:14; Jer. 31:12; Joel 2:19), a commercial commodity (Ezek. 27:17; Hos. 12:2; Rev. 18:12-13), and much prized for its many uses: medicinal (Lk. 10:34), cosmetic (Ps. 104:15; Matt. 6:17), culinary (Deut. 32:13; Jgs. 9:9), as fuel for oil lamps (Ex. 27:20; Lev. 24:2), and as a basis for ointments like myrrh and nard. It also occurs in figures of speech such as "words smoother than oil" (Ps. 55:22).

Ointment, *See* ANOINTING.

old

eighty-seven years *o.*	Gen. 5:25	the wicked survive, grow *o.*
years *o.*	Gen. 5:28, 32	Job 21:7
ninety-eight years *o.*	1 Sam. 4:15	two years *o.* and under Matt. 2:16

Old Testament, *See* BIBLE; TEXT, OLD TESTAMENT.

Olive, An evergreen, the most common tree in Palestine, and the most honored of them (*see* Jgs. 9:8). Hosea predicts the day when the restored Israel will have the beauty of an olive (Hos. 14:7). The olives were gathered in October by beating them from the trees, but the law prescribed that the trees must not be gone over twice, so that something would remain for the stranger, the orphan and the widow (Deut. 24:20). Paul speaks of the wild olive grafted onto the cultivated one to explain God's providence in regard to the Gentiles (Rom. 11:14 ff.). The olive was invaluable for its olive oil for cooking and use in lamps. *See* OIL.

Olives, Mount of, A hill to the east of Jerusalem. The river Kidron flows between it and the city (2 Sam. 15:30; Zech. 14:4). On its western slope lay the garden of Gethsemane (Matt. 26:30; Mk. 14:26; Lk. 22:39) while the villages of Bethany and Bethphage were on its eastern incline. On the Mount of Olives Jesus pronounced the eschatological discourse while spread before his eyes was the panorama of the city and the Temple (Matt. 24:3; Mk. 13:3). The Mount of Olives was also the scene of the Ascension (Acts 1:52).

Olympas, A Roman Christian greeted by Paul in Romans 16:15.

Omar, A clan of Edom (Gen. 36:11, 15; 1 Chron. 1:36).

Omega (oh-meg'-a, oh-mee'-ga), According to Revelation 21:6, the enthroned Christ said in a vision: "I am the Alpha and the Omega, the Beginning and the End." Alpha and Omega are the first and last letters of the Greek alphabet. Christ declares himself the vital source and final fulfilment of all that is (*see* Rev. 1:8; 22:13).

Omer, A Hebrew dry measure, one tenth of an ephah, equal to about half a gallon (Ex. 16:36).

Omri (om'-rye), King of Israel from 876-869 B.C. He had been an officer in Elah's army and a rival to the usurper Zimri, who in desperation at the fall of Tirzah, burnt the palace down over his own head and died. The people then split, one half following Tibni. The factions endured for four years until Tibni died. Omri continued to reside in the royal city of Tirzah for six years before transferring his residence to the new city of Samaria, a strategic military location which he had built on a hill bought from Shemer for two talents of silver. His reign is summed up by belittling Judean historians thus: he did what is displeasing to Yahweh, and was worse than all his predecessors (1 Kgs. 16:15-28; Mic. 6:16). Nevertheless, Omri's reign was marked by a considerable commercial development of Israel and good trading relations with neighboring nations. As part of Omri's international strategy, he married his son Ahab to the Phoenician princess, Jezebel.

On, *See* HELIOPOLIS.

Onan, Son of Judah (Gen. 38:4-10; 46:12). His brother Er married Tamar, but for displeasing Yahweh died young without leaving any children. Judah told his son Onan to take Tamar and have children in his brother Er's name. Onan however did not relish the idea of fathering children who would not be considered his, so he took measures to avoid any conception. He thus broke the levirate law, for which Yahweh brought about his death. *See* LEVIRATE.

once

my sin *o.* more	Ex. 10:17	Christ, *o.* raised	Rom. 6:9
O., by my holiness	Ps. 89:36	I was stoned *o.*	2 Cor. 11:25

one

became *o.* body	Gen. 2:24	*o.* from each tribe	Deut. 1:23
forms *o.* whole	Ex. 26:6	they may be *o.*	Jn. 17:22

Onesimus (oh-nes´-i-mus), A slave belonging to Philemon who fled from his master's house to reach Paul in Rome. When he had become a Christian, Paul sent him back to his master with a letter of recommendation (the epistle to Philemon), and with Tychicus as a companion and bearer of the letter to the Colossians. Colossians 4:9 describes Onesimus as a Colossian, a dear and faithful brother. "Onesimos" in Greek means "useful," so Paul plays on the word (Phil. 11): "He has become in truth Onesimus [Useful], for he who was formerly useless to you is now useful indeed both to you and to me."

Onesiphorus (on´-e-siph´-o-rus), An Ephesian Christian who helped Paul during his imprisonment and came to him in Rome (2 Tim. 1:16-18; 4:19).

Onias (oh-nye´-as), 1. Onias I, high priest of the Jews, father of Simon I who was also high priest, and a contemporary of Arius, king of Sparta, (309-265) with whom he struck a treaty based on the presumed affinity of the two peoples (1 Mac. 12:7-23).

2. Onias II, high priest, son of Simon I, a contemporary of Ptolemy III Euergetes (264-221 B.C.), father of Simon II (Sir. 50:1).

3. Onias III, high priest, son of Simon II, a contemporary of Seleucus IV (187-175 B.C.). During his pontificate there took place the attempt of Heliodorus to despoil the temple. He was foiled by a miraculous intervention: a gold-clad horseman flanked by two other magnificent young men appeared to bar his path and reduce him and his henchmen to helplessness (2 Mac. 3). Onias was accused by Simon of being behind this affair, and had to go to Antioch to defend himself and the public cause before the king (2 Mac. 4:1-6). Menelaus however succeeded by adulation in having himself named high priest, upon which Onias looked for sanctuary in the temple of Daphne near Antioch. Menelaus persuaded Andronicus to murder Onias. By swearing friendship and offering his right hand Andronicus deceitfully enticed Onias from the temple and murdered him

on the spot. When the king returned from Cilicia, he was indignant at the crime, stripped Andronicus of the purple, paraded him through the city and executed him on the spot where he had done away with Onias (2 Mac. 4:30-38).

only

O. Noah	Gen. 7:23	*o*. do not lay a hand	Job 1:12
o. a voice	Deut. 4:12	Against you *o*.	Ps. 51:6

Ono, A town in the territory of Benjamin (Ezra 2:33; Neh. 7:37; 11:35).

onyx

o. stones	Ex. 25:7	*o*. or the sapphire	Job 28:16
a chrysolite, an *o*.	Ex. 28:20	beryl, chrysolite, *o*.	Ezek. 28:13

opens

that *o*. the womb	Ex. 13:2; 34:19	he *o*. the ears	Job 33:16
	o. not his mouth	Ps. 38:14	

Ophel, A section of Jerusalem at the northeast corner of the City of David and south of the Temple (2 Chron. 27:3; Neh. 3:27). *See* JERUSALEM.

Ophir, A region in western Arabia, noted most of all for its gold (Isa. 13:12; Ps. 45:10; Job 28:16) which some kings of Israel had imported by sea. Hiram's fleet brought Solomon four hundred and twenty talents of gold while the queen of Sheba brought him one hundred and twenty. Ezion-geber, at the head of the gulf of Aqaba, was the port used (1 Kgs. 9:26-28; 10:10). Ophir is probably opposite the present Somaliland.

Ophni (off′-nye), 1. A city of Benjamin (Josh. 18:24).

2. With Phinehas, his brother, was a son of Eli and a priest of Yahweh in Shiloh (1 Sam. 1:3). He was guilty of abuses in the exercise of the priesthood. With Phinehas he accompanied the ark to the battle of Aphek, but the Israelites were defeated by the Philistines, the ark captured and Phinehas and Ophni were killed (1 Sam. 4:1-11).

Ophrah (off′-rah), 1. A city of Benjamin (Josh. 18:23), the scene of the wars with the Philistines during Saul's reign (1 Sam. 13:17-18), probably to be identified with Ephron in 2 Chronicles 13:19 and Ephraim in 2 Samuel 13:23, John 11:54. Today it is et-Taiyibeh, northeast of Bethel (Beitin).

2. A city of Manasseh, birthplace of Gideon near today's Beisan (Jgs. 6:11, 14).

opportunity

looking for an *o*.	Lk. 22:6	most of the present *o*.	Eph. 5:16
While we have the *o*.	Gal. 6:10	lacked the *o*.	Phil. 4:10

oppressor

o. receives	Job 27:13	leave me not to my *o*.	Ps. 119:121
crush the *o*.	Ps. 72:4	*o*. has reached his end	Isa. 14:4

oracles

received the *o*. of life	Acts 7:38

Ordeal, An ancient form of referring judgment to God by submitting the accused to a trial by water, lot, fire, etc. Numbers 5:11-31 contains legislation for a trial by ordeal by making a woman accused of adultery drink "the water of bitterness and cursing," which should leave her unscathed if innocent, but would swell her belly and shrivel her thighs if guilty, so that she would become an outcast among her people.

Oreb and Zeeb, The Midianite chieftains who oppressed the Israelites at the time of Gideon. They were captured and put to death, the one at Oreb's rock and the other at Zeeb's winepress. Their heads were brought to Gideon. This victory is recalled several times in the Bible (Jgs. 7:24-8:3; Ps. 83:11; Isa. 9:4; 10:26).

Orion (oh-ry′-on), A constellation of stars (Job 38:31; Amos 5:8).

ornaments
no one wore his *o*.   Ex. 33:4   Take off your *o*.   Ex. 33:5

Orpah, A Moabite woman, married to one of the sons of Elimelech and Naomi. After the death of Elimelech and her husband, Orpah returned to her father's house, while Naomi and Ruth returned to Bethlehem (Ruth 1).

orphaned
not leave you *o*.   Jn. 14:18

Osnappar, The Assyrian king who settled foreign colonies in Samaria (Ezra 4:10). The name is probably a corruption of Ashurbanipal (668-621 B.C.).

osprey
the vulture, the *o*.
          Lev. 11:13; Deut. 14:12

Ostrakon, Ostraka (os′-tra-kon, ka), A potsherd, or piece of crockery or tile, much used in ancient times for official documents such as contracts, and for private writings such as letters, lists, etc. Ostraka (plural form) were very durable, and much writing that has endured the ages is preserved on them. One wrote on an ostrakon with ink.

Ostrich, An impure bird, according to the law (Lev. 11:16; Deut. 14:15), which lived in the desert and in uninhabited regions (Isa. 34:13; 43:20; Jer. 50:39; 30:29). Job has a meditation on the ostrich in 39:13-18, an unwise, uncaring and cruel bird, yet, if she bestirs herself to her height, she can make fools of horse and rider too.

Othniel (oth′-ni-el), Son of Kenaz, Caleb's younger brother (Jgs. 1:13; 3:9), founding father of the clan of his name (1 Chron. 27:15). Upon his conquering Kiriath-sepher, Caleb gave him, as he had promised, his daughter Achsah as wife. Othniel figures again as the first of the minor judges of Israel, who defeated Cushan-rishathaim, king of Edom, under whom the Israelites had been enslaved for eight years (Jgs. 3:7-11).

our
in *o*. image   Gen. 1:26   *o*. ears have heard   Ps. 44:1
the Lord, *o*. God   Ex. 3:18   *O*. Father in heaven   Matt. 6:9

outstretched
by my *o*. arm   Ex. 6:6   with *o*. hand   Jer. 21:5
o. arm   Deut. 4:34   by my *o*. arm   Jer. 27:5

Oven, Ovens for the baking of bread consisted of a cylindrical or conical structure of burnt clay. There is an opening at the bottom to introduce the fuel, which among the poor included dry grass, thorny bushes or even dung mixed with straw. At the top was an aperture to let the smoke out. When the furnace was sufficiently hot, the burning fuel was withdrawn and the cake to be baked was inserted, either deposited on the floor of the oven or stuck to its walls.

overcame, overcome
Now Jonathan *o*.   1 Sam. 13:3 I have *o*. him   Ps. 13:5
                                    did not *o*.   Jn. 1:5

overlaid

Solomon *o.*	1 Kgs 6:21	entire temple was *o.*	1 Kgs 6:22
o. it with gold	1 Kgs. 6:21	*o.* with gold	1 Kgs. 6:28

overseers

their *o.*	2 Chron. 34:12	to the *o.*	2 Chron. 34:17

overshadow

bright cloud *o.*	Matt. 17:5	Most High will *o*	Lk. 1:35
A cloud came, *o.*	Mk. 9:7	and *o.* them	Lk. 9:34

overtake,

disaster from *o.*	Gen. 19:19	pursue and *o.* them	Ex. 15:9
When Laban *o.* Jacob	Gen. 31:25	and *o.* him	2 Kgs. 25:5

overthrow

not *o.* the town	Gen. 19:21	for its *o.*	1 Chron. 19:3
God *o.* the cities	Gen. 19:29	Shall be *o.* by God	Isa. 13:19

overwhelm

they *o.* the land	Job 12:15	threaten *o.* them	Ps. 140:10
	wrath *o.* Prov. 27:4		

owe

who *o.* him	Matt. 18:24	do you *o.* my master	Lk. 16:5
a fellow servant who *o.*		*O.* no debt	Rom. 13:8
	Matt. 18:28		

owl

the *o.*, the cormorant, the screech		like a desert *o.*	Ps. 102:7
o., the barn *o.*, the desert *o.*		become like an *o.*	Ps. 102:7
	Lev. 11:17,18	the hoot *o.* shall nest	Isa. 34:15

own

flesh of your *o.* sons	Deut. 28:53	make their *o.* gods	2 Kgs. 17:29
his *o.* children	Deut. 33:9	his *o.* wife	1 Cor. 7:2

owner

The *o.* of the ox	Ex. 21:28	An ox knows its *o.*	Isa. 1:3
the former *o.*	1 Kgs. 16:24	say to the *o.*	Mk. 14:14

Ox, The domestic ox was one of the most valuable animals in the Middle East for its many uses as a draft animal (2 Sam. 6:6), its work in the fields drawing a plow, and its function at the threshing floor (*see* Deut. 22:10; 25:4). The Bible has legislation about ownership and responsibility for the animal (Ex. 21:28-22:18) and lays down rules for its human treatment, ordering for it a day's rest in the week (Ex. 23:12; Deut. 5:14) and adequate feeding (Deut. 25:4). It was listed among the pure animals (Deut. 14:4). and was one of the most frequently prescribed sacrificial victims in the Israelite ritual (Ex. 20:24; Lev. 3:1, etc). *See* BULL.

oxen

wagons and *o.*	Num. 7:6	yoke of *o.*	1 Sam. 11:7
wagons and eight *o.*	Num. 7:8	five yoke of *o.*	Lk. 14:19

Ozem, Son of Jesse and David's brother (1 Chron. 2:15).

Oziel (oh′-zi-el), An ancestor of Judith (Judith 8:1).

Ozni (oz′-nye), A man of the tribe of Gad (Num. 26:16).

P

P, The letter indicating the Priestly codex, the latest of the four basic documents or sources that can be analyzed in the Pentateuch. *See* PENTATEUCH.

Paarai (pay'-a-rye), One of the warriors of David known as The Thirty (2 Sam. 23:35).

Paddan-aram, "The plain of Aram" (Hos. 12:13), a region in northern Mesopotamia, also called Aram-naharaim where the Priestly document of Genesis places the origin of the patriarchs and the residence of Laban (Gen. 25:20; 28:2-7; 31:18; 33:18; 35:9-26).

Padon (pay'-don), Ancestor of a family of temple servants (Ezra 2:44; Neh. 7:47).

Pagans, *See* GENTILES.

Pagiel (pay'-gi-el), Son of Ochran of the tribe of Asher (Num. 1:13; 2:27; 7:72; 10:26).

Pahath-moab (pay'-hath-moe'-ab), Ancestor of a family of exiled Jews who returned to Palestine with Zerubbabel (Ezra 2:6; 10:30; Neh. 10:15).

pain

in *p*. shall you	Gen. 3:16	your *p*. is without relief	Jer. 30:15
bore him with *p*.	1 Chron. 4:9	Writhe in *p*., grow faint	Mic. 4:10

palace

citadel of the royal *p*.	1 Kgs. 16:18	killed him within the *p*.	2 Kgs. 15:25
servants in the *p*.	2 Kgs. 20:18		

Palestine, The land in which the Israelites under Joshua established themselves is called in the Bible the "Land of Canaan," and also by the name of different peoples who lived there (*see* Gen. 15:18-21; Deut. 7:1). Later it was called Israel (1 Sam. 13:19) or Judah and Israel. Palestine means Philistine land, and became its designation during the Greek period. The complete name was Palestinian Syria, to distinguish it from Coelesyria and Upper Syria. *See* SYRIA.

Palestine is a segment of the fertile land that reaches from the mouth of the Nile in Egypt to the mouth of the combined Tigris and Euphrates rivers in Mesopotamia. This stretch of land is known as the "fertile crescent" and is bordered on the concave side by the Syro-Arabian desert, while the convex side is closed off by the Mediterranean and the mountains of Armenia, together with the Elam highlands. Its two extremities, Egypt and Mesopotamia, were the cradles of two of the most ancient and prosperous civilizations in antiquity. Their peoples were rooted in an imperial culture. The central portion had no geographical cohesion and so failed to affirm itself as an autonomous unity. It became the logical area of imperial expansion from both extremities. Whenever it did have a political unity, this was something imposed on it from without. When the threat from without disappeared, fragmentation followed.

The natural limits of Palestine are the following: to the north is the river Litani, which flows south from the east side of the mountains of Lebanon, and then westward to the Mediterranean north of Tyre. To the east of the Litani as it flows to the Sea is Mt. Hermon, whose peaks are the southern most of the Anti-Lebanon range. To the west is the Mediterranean, to the east the steppes and the desert, and to the south the desert that reaches beyond an imaginary line drawn from the upper extremity of the Dead Sea to the Oasis of Beer-sheba, and on to the Mediterranean coast at the Wadi-Aris, the "Brook of Egypt" of the Bible (*see* BROOK OF EGYPT). In the Bible these limits are indicated with expressions such as "from Dan to Beer-sheba," or "to the Brook of Egypt" (*see* e.g. Judges 20:1; 1 Sam.

3:20), and beyond the Jordan, from the river Arnon, to the south, to Mt. Hermon (Josh. 12:1).

The land thus framed can be divided into five parallel zones from west to east (the zones running north and south) as follows: the coastal zone, the hill territory, the central mountain range, the Jordan valley region and the Transjordanian highlands.

The coastal zone lies in a straight line that is only interrupted in any considerable way by Mt. Carmel, which reaches to the sea. North of Carmel is the plain of Acco with a mediocre natural port, Haifa, which was named Ptolemais by the Egyptians and S. Joanne of Arc by the Crusaders. South of Carmel as far as modern Tell-Aviv/Jaffa (Joppa in biblical times) extends the fertile plain of Sharon (Song of Songs 2:1). From Joppa to Gaza stretched the land of the Philistine pentapolis. There are no natural ports in this zone south of Carmel. Herod I the Great constructed one at Caesarea in Palestine by clever use of artificial means of protection against storms. Joppa was used as a port (2 Chron. 2:15; Ezra 3:7), but it was barely suitable for this function. On account of the geographical make-up of the coast line and control by non-Hebrew peoples, the sea and navigation had but a peripheral part to play in Bible history. *See* SAILING.

Between the coastal plain and the central mountain range is the so-called Shephelah or "hill country" (Jgs. 1:9) (*see* SHEPHELAH) which was fought over by the Philistines and the Israelites.

The central mountain range runs from north to south of Palestine like a backbone. Running down the mountain range from north to south, there are first the high mountains of Galilee, with their fertile valleys in Upper Galilee and then gradually descending to form the fertile hills in Lower Galilee. From west to east they are now interrupted by the plain of Jezreel (also called later Esdraelon), a triangle with its sharpest angle towards the Mediterranean. The plain is closed in by the hills of Nazareth and Tabor to the north, the mountains of Gilboa to the east, and the Carmel range to the southwest. The plain is very fertile and abounds in water: the river Kishon runs towards the Mediterranean and the Harod pours into the Jordan. The plain of Jezreel was the scene of important military actions. Judges 4-5 tells of Deborah; Judges 7 of Gideon; 1 Samuel 31 of the battle of the mountains of Gilboa in which Saul died; 2 Kings 23:29-30 of the confrontation between the Pharaoh Neco and King Josiah. Important cities are on its borders: Jokneam, Megiddo, Taanash, Jezreel. *See* JEZREEL, PLAIN OF.

The mountains of Samaria emerge south of the plain of Jezreel. Their natural center is the plain of Shechem, closed from the north by Mt. Ebal and Gerizim. Between these lies the road that brings one to the city of Samaria and the north. Between the mountains of Samaria and those of Judah is the narrow plain of Benjamin, providing another east-west crossing of the land. The mountains of Judah reach their greatest height around Jerusalem and again at Hebron, from which they slope down until they are lost in the desert. The mountain range of Judah pushes somewhat westward until it flanks the Dead Sea. The region between it and the Dead Sea, which slopes abruptly down, is the desert of Judah, one of the most arid and inhospitable regions of the world.

The Jordan bed is part of the deep geological cleft which extends from Lebanon and Anti-Lebanon down to the Gulf of Aqaba and the Red Sea. The Jordan rises in Mt. Hermon beside the city of Banias (Caesarea Philippi), it widens in the marshy flats of Lake Huleh (drained to a large extent for agricultural purposes by modern Israel) from which it rapidly descends 696 feet, spreading out to form the Lake of Gennesaret or the Sea of Galilee. After Galilee the river continues its frantic descent to a valley where it meanders in snake-like convolutions, until it reaches 1286 feet below sea level at the Dead Sea into which it pours. The deep valley between the Sea of Galilee and the Dead Sea is virtually closed to the east by the Transjordanian highlands and to the west by the mountain range of Samaria and Judah. The region is torrid and arid, and the river water affords almost no relief to the land around it. Agriculture is possible only in fertile oases of Bethshan to the north and Jericho to the south. *See* JORDAN; DEAD SEA.

Transjordan is steppe. From north to south in succession are Bashan; the river Yarmuk which flows into the Jordan a little below the Lake of Gennesaret; Gilead, between the river Yarmuk and the Jabbok; the ancient Ammonite kingdom between the Jabbok and the Arnon; Moab, between the Arnon and the Wadi-Zeree at the southern corner of the Dead Sea. Edom reaches farther to the south. *See* AMMON; BASHAN; EDOM; GILEAD; MOAB.

There are two seasons, generally speaking, in Palestine: summer and winter (Gen. 8:22). On the rainy period *see* RAIN. The seasons, however, are irregularly distributed over the land. The humid air comes from the west and rarely passes over the central mountain region without condensation. For this reason the lands bordering the Jordan valley are arid and the waters of the river cannot make up for this, engulfed as they are in their cleft. The Transjordanian highlands receive some rain (16 inches per year). Here too the rivers prove to be of little use agriculturally as they run through deep-cut valleys. On the other hand the coast line and the central mountain range have rains comparable to those of the European continent.

The system of roads, which gave importance to the cities that were on them, was itself conditioned by the nature of the land. The main route within Judah-Israel follows the central mountain range from north to south. It is periodically cut across by horizontal lines that follow the natural valleys of the rivers. They ensure passage from the coastal plain to the central mountain range and from there to the Jordan and beyond. This central south-north route begins at Beer-sheba, the most southerly limit of the land (Jgs. 20:1) and moves to Hebron, continuing via Bethlehem to Jerusalem. After Jerusalem it passes Ramah to come to Bethel (Jgs. 19:11-13) where Jeroboam I erected two golden calves (1 Kgs. 12:26). Beside Bethel is Shiloh (Jgs. 21:19), the sanctuary of the ark during the period of the judges.

From Bethel it continues north as far as Shechem (Gen. 33:18 and 35:1). The route continues through Mt. Ebal and Gerizim (Deut. 11:29; 27:12; Josh. 8:33), and then turns a little to the west to come to Samaria, capital of the kingdom of Israel (1 Kgs. 15:24). After Samaria the road turns north through Dothan to the plain of Jezreel or Esdraelon. The plain of Esdraelon is opened to the east toward Beth-shan in the Jordan valley. Following the course of the river northwards one comes to Gennesaret. The route then proceeds around either side of the lake, and then north to Hazor where it crosses the river to go on to Damascus.

Parallel to this road as far as the plain of Esdraelon ran the more famous, heavily traveled, so-called "Sea Road" or Trunk Road, from Egypt to Damascus. It led from Egypt to Gaza and from there followed the coastline as far as Carmel. Here it turned east to cross the mountain through the Wadi Arar which pours into the plain of Jezreel at Megiddo (1 Kgs. 9:15; 2 Kgs. 23:29).

The horizontal lines that go from the sea to the central highland follow the valleys of Shephelah, known above all on account of the wars between the Philistines and the Israelites. (*See* SHEPHELAH.) The principal ways from the center eastward to the Jordan were the following: from Jerusalem to Jericho, spoken of in the parable of the Good Samaritan (Lk. 10:30-37) and in the account of the flight of David from Jerusalem (2 Sam. 15:23-32), and through the ford of Adamah (Jgs. 12:5). From Shechem northeastwards Wadi Farah was reached. This brought one as far as the Jordan opposite Succoth and the mouth of the Jabbok. Jacob followed this route on his return journey from Aram (Gen. 32).

A third major north-south route lay in Transjordan and followed the eastern edge of the Transjordanian plateau. It ran from Ezion-geber in the south, at the tip of the arm of the Red Sea, northward through Edom, Moab and Ammon, on to Damascus.

Pallu, A son of Reuben (Gen. 46:9; Num. 26:5, 8; 1 Chron. 5:3).

Palm, The date palm, or **phoenix dactylifera** was very common in the Middle East from Mesopotamia to Egypt. In Palestine it grows on the plains near the coast and in the valley of the Jordan, around Jericho (Jgs. 1:16; 3:13) and in the oases of the southern desert (Ex. 15:27; Num. 33:9).

Palti (pal´-tie). A Benjaminite to whom Saul gave his daughter Michal, David's wife (1 Sam. 25:43; 2 Sam. 3:15).

Paltiel (pal´-ti-el), Son of Azzan, of the tribe of Issachar (Num. 34:26).

Pamphylia (pam-fil´-i-a), A region on the central southern coast of Asia Minor, west of Cilicia. Paul evangelized Perga, a city in Pamphylia during his first missionary journey (Acts 13:13; 14:24).

pangs
the *p.* of your childbearing   *p.* and sorrows take hold   Isa. 13:8
                         Gen. 3:16   stages of the birth *p.*   Matt. 24:8

Paphos (pay´-fos), A city and port on the west coast of Cyprus. It was the residence of the Roman proconsul Sergius Paulus. The city was evangelized by Paul and Barnabas during their first apostolic journey (Acts 13:6).

Papias (pay´-pi-as), Bishop of Hierapolis in Phrygia, Asia Minor, at the time of the emperor Hadrian (117-138 A.D.). He was the author of a five-volume work called the "Interpretation of the Lord's Oracles," in which he contributes information on the authors of the gospels. His work has been lost, but the relevant texts have been preserved for posterity in the ecclesiastical history of Eusebius of Caeserea (III, 39).

Papyrus, Papyrus is an Egyptian word ("river plant") which designates a kind of reed plant found in abundance in the region of the Nile delta. It could reach a height of twenty feet. It was the symbol of Lower Egypt. Today papyrus is but rarely found. It grows in Italy (Sicily and Lake Trasimeno) and in Palestine beside Lake Huleh. In ancient times papyrus was the material most used in the production of paper for writing, which was, in fact, called papyrus. Paper was prepared by cutting into very fine strips the soft inner core of the plant. These were placed side by side on a damp table. Then other strips were placed across these. The flat pages thus constructed were glued, pressed and beaten, smoothed out and dried in the sun. One wrote on the side in which the fibers ran horizontally. In the case of a lengthy writing, several sheets were gummed together and then rolled on a wooden staff or spool. Papyrus for writing was invented by the Egyptians and was already in use in the third millenium B.C. It was in common use by Greeks and Romans. The Arab invasion put an end to the flourishing Egyptian papyrus industry (640 A.D.), which had, however, already in large part been replaced by the use of parchment.

Parable, The word parable comes from the Greek **parabole,** which, from the etymological point of view, means putting two things side by side, to confront or compare them. The etymological meaning of the word already affords us some elements for the correct definition of a parable. In a parable two realities or situations are compared or contrasted to illustrate one by the other. Both terms of the comparison are kept well distinct. The author of the parable however brings them forward together to invite his audience to reflection so as to discover the point in which they coincide. The parable then is a developed simile.

A parable is distinguished from an allegory. An allegory is a developed metaphor. In a metaphor two terms are not paralleled or confronted; rather there is a fusion or identification between the two. Since the two things are in reality diverse, identification is had by taking one of the terms in a transferred or metaphorical sense. When for instance Jesus asserted he was the 'light of the world' (Jn. 8:12), "light" cannot be taken in the physical sense of the term, but in a metaphorical sense. Jesus states that he is the source of the light of the Spirit and the one fountain of life and source of salvation. On the other hand, when he states that the kingdom of heaven is like a man who went out to sow his seed (Mk. 4:3-9), Jesus draws a picture of the work of every farmer, thus bringing before the eyes of his hearers an everyday scene, inviting them to discover in this picture by comparison what also happens with the coming of the kingdom of heaven.

The interpretation of the parables sets out to discover the point in which the two situations coincide, that is, the kingdom of heaven and the story sketched in the parable account. One must not accede to the temptation of giving metaphorical interpretation to every single element, for this would be to confound the parable with an allegory. The allegorical interpretation of the parables was cultivated for a long time, and especially in the preaching of the Fathers of the church. They were not so much intent on interpreting the parables as taking the occasion of a parable to teach a body of doctrine, drawing on the parable for all possible meanings and applications.

For the most part the gospel parables are to be taken in the sense just explained. For the most part, for it is undeniable that among the parables there are also some allegorical elements. The presence of these allegorical elements does not however destroy the structure of the parable. Rather they help the reader towards the meaning of the parable. Thus for example the king who celebrates the marriage of his son (Matt. 22:2) and the lord who calls the workers to his vineyard (Matt. 21:33) are figures of God the Father. The only son which the father sends to get the fruits from the vine-workers who ill-treated the servants (Matt. 21:37) designates Jesus himself, etc.

The parable is an ancient oriental literary genre. Jesus often made use of it and with supreme art. There is however a discussion over why precisely Jesus made use of this type of discourse to announce the gospel of the kingdom. The parable has an obvious pedagogical aim. For centuries it had been one of the preferred ways of teaching in the wisdom schools. One must not, however, misunderstand its pedagogic function. Pedagogy must accommodate itself not only to the demands of the audience, but also to the exigencies of what is being taught. The object of Jesus' parables was to bring faith alive in his hearers, and they were used so as not to betray the mystery of the kingdom of heaven, to present it in a form that would show it was not of man's making, nor could he use it at his pleasure, just as he was not its judge. Through the parables revelation took place, but it was a veiled revelation, inviting man to reflect and provoking him not to take the kingdom of heaven as something of this earth. Rather he must give himself to it, surrendering to it through faith.

Now, not all were open to the faith, nor did all listen to the voice of God. This docility to the voice of God is the moral context in which faith germinates, for it is nothing other than the meeting of human freedom and divine grace. For this reason the parable, which handed down in a veiled manner God's invitation, could and did become a stumbling block for many who found in Jesus' word a kind of challenge to which they responded, not with faith, but with rejection and despisement. The parable instead of enlightening them became a blinding force and something which hardened them against Jesus. Preaching in parables put the seal on their lack of comprehension (Mk. 4:11-12; Matt. 13:10-17; Lk. 8:9-10; *see* Isa. 6:9-10; Jn. 12:40).

Jesus preached many parables (Mk. 4:34). If one is to include the many parabolic sayings and expressions, they then amount to more than 70. The longer parables appear in block-sections of the gospels. Jesus however did not give them out one after the other as they now appear in the gospels. The block-sections gather together parables pronounced by Jesus on different occasions, in different places and at different times. The following is a list of the parables that are strictly so:

The sower: Matthew 13:3-8; Mark 4:3-8; Luke 8:5-8.

The wheat and weeds: Matthew 13:24-30.

The wheat that grows alone: Mark 4:26-29.

The yeast: Matt. 13:33; Luke 13:20, 21.

The mustard seed: Matthew 13:31, 32; Mark 4:30-32; Luke 13:18, 19.

The net: Matthew 13:47, 48.

The precious pearl: Matthew 13:45, 46.

The treasure hidden in a field: Matthew 13:44.

The lost sheep: Matthew 18:12-14; Luke 15:4-7.

The unmerciful servant: Matthew 18:22-35.

The two sons: Matthew 21:28-32.

The wedding banquet: Matthew 22:1-14; Luke 14:16-24.

The talents: Matthew 25:14-30; Luke 19:12-27.

The murderous vine-workers: Matthew 21:33-44; Mark 12:1-11; Luke 20:9-18.

The ten virgins: Matthew 25:1-13.

The children who play: Matthew 11:16-19; Luke 7:31-35.

The faithful servants: Matthew 24:45-51; Luke 12:42-46.

The two debtors: Luke 7:41-43.

The good Samaritan: Luke 10:25-37.

The importunate friend: Luke 11:5-8.

The rich fool: Luke 12:16-21.

The sterile fig tree: Luke 13:6-9.

The last place at banquets: Luke 14:7-11.

The tower and war: Luke 14:28-32.

The lost drachma: Luke 15:8-10.

The prodigal son: Luke 15:11-32.

The unfaithful steward: Luke 16:1-8.

The rich man and Lazarus: Luke 16:19-31.

The unjust judge: Luke 18:1-8.

The Pharisee and the publican: Luke 18:9-14.

Paraclete, In John's gospel the Holy Spirit is also called the Paraclete (Jn. 14:26). The word comes from the Greek **parakletos** and is often incorrectly translated "consoler." The word has a juridical connotation, meaning the advocate who defends the accused at a trial. In its general religious usage it designates the person or persons, above all the angels, who intervene and intercede in favor of the good, while Satan, which means "accuser," would plead against them. In Judaism these paracletes were the people's defenders, not only in a juridical context, but actively concerned for the good of the faithful, fighting off adversaries and guiding them along the way of salvation. In the manuscripts of the desert of Judah (*see* DEAD SEA SCROLL), paraclete is the name given the prince or angel of light and truth, who breathes into the sons of light the spirit of truth, just as Belial inspires the spirit of perdition. This dualistic context is the background for understanding the figure of the Paraclete, which John employed to bring out some precise functions of the work of the Holy Spirit.

For John the first Paraclete is Christ himself (Jn. 14:16). During his life he cared for his disciples, prayed for them, and through his death and resurrection conquered the powers of sin and death, thus liberating them from slavery to the demon (1 Jn. 2:1; for Christ's prayer *see* Jn. 17). In his exaltation Jesus returned to the Father, having completed his mission. Then, in accordance with his promises, he sent down "another Paraclete" whose function it would be to bring to fulfilment Christ's own work (Jn. 14:16, 17). When Jesus promised to send the Paraclete, he spoke more specifically of his work in John 14:25, 26; 16:13, 14; 15:26, 27 and 16:8, 9. The Paraclete is regularly called the Spirit of Truth, which suggests that the object of his mission will be the truth, that is, the revelation brought by Jesus. (*See* TRUTH.) This truth the Spirit would make live in the hearts of the faithful, rendering it perfectly active and efficacious and vindicating it in the world.

The Paraclete-Spirit will teach the whole truth, not of his own accord, but, like Jesus himself, having heard it (14:25, 26; 16:35). His task it would be to bring back to mind all that Jesus had taught, not simply as it had come home to the apostles during Christ's mortal existence, but in the light of the consummation of sacred history through the exaltation of Jesus (*see* e.g. Jn. 2:22). He will show the true sense, not immediately evident, of future things, that is, of the definitive plan of salvation realized by Jesus.

In the midst of the opposition the disciples were to find in the world the Spirit will witness to Jesus in their hearts, and thus strengthened, they will proclaim Jesus to the world (Jn. 15:26, 27; *see* Matt. 10:19, 20; Mk. 13:11; Lk. 12:11, 12). In this context of opposition on the part of the world to Jesus and his message must be understood the obscure passage of John 16:8, 9, which can be paraphrased thus: The disciples find themselves hated by the world, but within their hearts the Spirit will witness to Jesus. How will this come about? He will clarify for them the outcome of the conflict which had seen Jesus himself opposed to the world, in which conflict they now find themselves sharing. They will by this experience come to know the world for what it really is, and see where sin lay, where justice (in the sense of victory), and where judgment (in the sense of defeat) in that conflict.

Paradise, *See* EDEN.

Parah, A village in Benjamin (Josh. 18:23).

Paralipomenon (par′-a-li-pom′-e-non), *See* CHRONICLES, BOOKS OF.

Paran (par′-an), A desert region south of Palestine inhabited by the Ishmaelite tribes (Gen. 21:21). The Israelites passed through it on their journey towards Canaan from Sinai (Num. 10:11, 12; 13:3, 26; Deut. 1:1). In the blessing Moses pronounced before he died he sang of Paran as the mountain from behind which the Lord shone forth (*see* Deut. 33:2 and Hab. 3:3; Jgs. 5:4-5).

parapet
the *p.* of the temple   Matt. 4:5; Lk. 4:9

Parchment, The skins of certain animals, such as sheep, goats, cattle, pigs, antelopes, and so on, naturally tanned, were used from earliest times to write on (*see* Isa. 34:4; Jer. 36). Parchment was used for manuscripts recently discovered at Qumran. According to an ancient tradition that is probably legendary, Ptolemy V Epiphanes (205-181 B.C.), out of jealousy for the library at Pergamum, forbade the exportation of papyrus from Egypt. It was then that Eumene II (or Attalus) king of Pergamum, to save his library, invented a new material by curing skins of animals in a different way from that normally used for leather. The skin was steeped in a lime solution to soften it, then it was scraped with a knife to take the hair from it and finally cleaned with pumice stone. The parchment or membrane only took the form of a codex or book, since it was too rigid to be rolled into scrolls.

parents
turn against *p.*   when the *p.* brought   Lk. 2:27
       Matt. 10:21; Mk. 13:12   *p.* used to go   Lk. 2:41
              When his *p.* saw him   Lk. 2:48

Parmashta, A son of Haman, the vizier of King Ahasuerus (Esth. 9:9). *See* HAMAN.

Parmenas (par′-me-nas), The sixth of the seven people, filled with the Spirit, who were deputed by the apostles to serve the needs of the poor, when, according to Acts 6:1-6, the Hellenists complained that their widows were being overlooked in the daily distribution of food.

Parosh, Personal name (Ezra 2:3; 8:3; 10:25; Neh. 3:25; 10:15).

Parousia (pa-roos′-zhia), Parousia is a Greek word signifying "presence," and by extension, the act of being present, and so the advent or arrival. In the New Testament the parousia is the second coming of Christ at the end of time (1 Cor. 15:23; 1 Thess. 2:19; 3:13). In contrast to his first coming which was in the humility and hiddenness of mortal flesh, Christ's second coming will be in glory and power. He will appear with the angels and saints (1 Thess. 3:13). This will take place at the end of time when Jesus will come as Lord and Judge of the living and the dead. The second coming will coincide with the resurrection of the dead (1

Thess. 4:13; 1 Cor. 15:23) and the manifestation of the future world. The scenario for the parousia is taken from the biblical tradition on the coming of God at the end of time, especially as this has been developed by apocalyptic tradition (*see* Dan. 7). Jesus spoke of his second coming as the glorious Son of Man (*see* SON OF MAN), taking his inspiration from Daniel 7 (*see* Mk. 8:38; Lk. 9:26). Then the Son of Man will take his seat on his throne and will bring all before him for judgment (Matt. 24:27; Mk. 13; Lk. 21).

In Matthew 24:3 the disciples ask Jesus about time and signs of his second coming. We know from 1-2 Thessalonians that the apostolic community lived in expectation of the parousia of the Lord, not as a distant event, but as salvation to take place within their own generation. The imminence of the parousia was not just a thesis they supported with arguments but a vivid hope that was nourished by some not too clear statements of Jesus himself. In truth however Jesus had unequivocally affirmed that the day of the parousia was something unknown to everybody except the Father (Mk. 13:32; Matt. 24:36). On the other hand he also spoke of its imminence, so that Christians must hold themselves in waiting and prepared (Matt. 25:1-30). It would come when least expected, like lightning or a thief in the night (Matt. 24:27; Lk. 17:24; 1 Thess. 5:24). In other places Jesus speaks of the end of the world and the coming of the kingdom as if they would arrive within his generation (Matt. 10:23; 24:34; Mk. 13:30; Lk. 21:32).

The question of the imminence of the parousia is one of the most complex and discussed in the whole New Testament. Two aspects can be distinguished. What importance had this expectation of an imminent parousia in the primitive Christian community, and why were the consequences of this expectation being foiled? There have been many exaggerated responses to these questions. The epistles of Saint Paul, which are the best witness we have to the apostolic church, certainly do not show us a group of visionaries living already by anticipation in the next world. The live expectation of the parousia forms the horizons, with more or less intensity according to place and time, within which the activity of the apostolic church moved. Against this background is cast the missionary effort, the Christian life and its serious moral and social commitment. Awaiting the parousia had led astray some of the believers considerably (e.g. 1-2 Thess.), only to provoke Paul's reaction in affirming the uncertainty of the future and asserting the commitment of the Christian to the present as well.

One should not, then, speak outright of delusion when the parousia did not come. Rather there was a gradual relaxation of tension towards the future according as the task of the present emerged with greater clarity. This relaxation of eschatological tension permitted the community to realize with greater clarity its pilgrim function. To think that the church emerged as a result of the great disappointment at Christ's failure to appear is to close one's mind to the witness of the New Testament, or to take one aspect and exaggerate it until all the rest is neglected or passed over. The second aspect refers to Jesus' preaching. Here we must limit ourselves to some general considerations, for brevity's sake. An exhaustive exegesis of the texts is in fact fraught with difficulties as we are no longer able to reconstruct with exactitude the historical circumstance in which this or that word was pronounced. Today, for instance, it is commonly admitted that the so-called "eschatological discourse" (Mk. 13; Matt 24; Lk. 21) was not originally all of a piece, but made up, as were the other long discourses of the synoptics, of isolated sayings of Jesus. In gathering them together there also seems to have been some reinterpretation on the part of the apostolic church and the evangelists.

With this assertion in mind, it is undeniable that on the one hand Jesus declares that the "day" of his coming is known alone to the Father, while on the other, one cannot escape the impression that Jesus spoke as if it was about to happen. Jesus however is not in this matter making an innovation. He is following the prophetic and apocalyptic tradition which views the present in the light of the final consummation, and the final consummation as the counterpart of the present. The question to be asked then is not: when, according to Jesus, should the end of the world take place? Rather, one must enquire why Jesus, and before him the apocalyptic tradition, expressed themselves in this way? There is only one answer to this question: Jesus had no preoccupation with computing the time of his second coming in days and years—this was absent from his mind, *see* Mark 13:32; Matthew 24:36. Therefore one must not speak of the end of the world except in the terms which Jesus himself used as a frame of reference, namely, in terms of imminence that is more qualitative than temporal. The end, towards which the whole historical-salvific process tends, is that end, in view of which the present must be lived. All Jesus' discourses about the end are aimed at getting Christians prepared, making them live in view of what is to come.

Parshandatha (par-shan/-da-tha), A son of Haman, the vizier of King Ahasuerus (Esth. 9:7). *See* HAMAN.

Parthians, An Iranian tribal group, present in Jerusalem on the day of Pentecost when the Holy Spirit descended on the apostles (Acts 2:9-11).

Parvaim (par-vay/-im), A region, probably in Arabia, from which gold was imported for the Temple of Solomon (2 Chron. 3:7).

Pasach (pay/-sak), A son of Japhlet of the tribe of Asher (1 Chron. 7:33).

Paseah (pa-see/-ah), "The lame one," personal name (1 Chron. 4:12; Ezra 2:49; Neh. 3:6).

Pashur (pash/-ur), 1. Son of Immer, police superintendent in the Temple. Because of Jeremiah's continued prophecies against the city and Temple, he had him beaten and put in stocks at the Temple gate of Benjamin. When Pashur released him next day, Jeremiah frightened him with a dismal prophecy on Jerusalem and Judah and the population, who would be taken, Pashur and his family included, into exile to Babylon (Jer. 20:1-6).

2. Son of Malchiah, sent by King Zedekiah to consult Jeremiah on the outcome of the war with Nebuchadnezzar. Jeremiah's answer was discouraging, to say the least (Jer. 21:1-11; 38:1).

Passion, In the gospel tradition as a whole the account of the Passion of Jesus constitutes an exception. The Passion history is not told as a series of scenes that are independent, nor can the order of events as they are there set down be changed around without doing considerable damage to the whole. Even though, in a certain sense, the scenes are complete in themselves, nevertheless they are put down in a logical, chronological and topographical order with a precision that gives coherence and meaning to the whole story and to its individual parts. All admit that the Passion account is the most ancient part of the written gospel, and even before it was put on paper, it had been developed as a serious and well-ordered history. It was necessary to elaborate such an account to explain from the theological and apologetic point of view the death of the Person who was being proclaimed by the church as the Messiah. The antiquity and unity of the Passion story is confirmed by the unusual way in which not only the three synoptics but even John coincide. It is also obvious that the primitive account was later elaborated and enriched by other traditions in the

different gospels, but even today it is possible to discover a common structure at the origin of all four.

The Passion story moreover served as a point of crystallization for the
whole gospel tradition. The Passion was in fact the conclusion of a process that had its roots in the public ministry of Jesus. This took place
under two aspects. On the one hand the passion and death was not a
catastrophic and unforeseen event, but belonged to the very mission of
the Messiah as Jesus understood it. On the other hand it was the conclusion of a conflict with the Jewish religious authorities which had arisen
much earlier. From this point of view it has been said that the gospels are
nothing other than the account of the Passion with a prologue. This is
above all true of the second part of the gospel account of Jesus' ministry,
from Matthew 16:21 and parallel texts in Mark and Luke. This account
unfolds under the shadow of the triple prediction of the Passion and is
directed towards Jerusalem, where Jesus was to die. This holds above all
for Luke (*see* Lk. 9:51) where it is told that Jesus freely set himself for
Jerusalem for the completion of his mission (Lk. 13:31-33).

The account of the Passion starts with the history of the Jewish plot
against Jesus (Matt. 26:1-3; Mk. 14:1-2; Lk. 22:1-2). In John this account
is more intimately connected with the narrative of the resurrection of
Lazarus (Jn. 11:47-53; *see* LAZARUS). In all probability the original Passion story ended with the discovery of the empty tomb and the announcement by the angels to the women that Jesus had arisen (Matt. 28:1-8; Mk.
16:1-8; Lk. 24:1-10). Here too John follows a somewhat different course
(Jn. 20:1-11). There are various reasons for this. First it was unthinkable
that the account of the Passion, presented as it is as an ample development of the announcement of salvation (*see* 1 Cor. 15:1-5) should make
no reference to the resurrection. Secondly, the gospel accounts coincide
up to this point, while they vary on the apparitions of Jesus after his resurrection. Finally it is strictly connected with what precedes it, as can be
seen from the insistence on mentioning that the women were present at
the moment of burial (Matt. 27:56-61; Mk. 15:42-47; Lk. 23:50-56; Jn.
19:31-38). It was the same women who discovered the empty tomb. On
the importance of this fact for the study of the resurrection accounts, *see*
RESURRECTION OF JESUS.

What strikes the reader of the Passion account is its utter sobriety which
confers on it a solemnity that is lost if one tries to complete it with detailed
descriptions or considerations of the torments and sufferings of the Savior. The account aims at relating the facts without comment. However, it
is not on that account a theologically neutral narrative of events: it is a
witness to faith and contains an interpretation of the events that unfolds
itself to the reader. This interpretation, however, is inserted into the text
with extreme discretion. As could have been expected the story recounts
and evaluates the events in the light of the Old Testament. Only in a few
cases, and in John (*see* 19:24; 19:28; 19:36, 37) is the reference to the Old
Testament explicit. In the other evangelists and elsewhere in John, Scripture reference is built right into the description of the facts by way of a
carefully studied choice of terms aimed at calling to the reader's mind a
certain Old Testament context in the light of which the history is told.

The Old Testament contexts that are recalled are, in particular, Isaiah 53
and the psalms of individual lamentation in the Psalter. Isaiah 53 had
already given substance to the Passion prophecies and to the account of
the Last Supper. (*See* DEATH OF JESUS; LORD'S SUPPER; SERVANT OF THE
LORD.) The second context is present in the account of the plot against
Jesus' life (Matt. 26:1-5 and Pss. 2:2; 31:14; 71:10), Judas' betrayal
(Matt. 26:21; Mk. 14:18; Jn. 13:18), the crucifixion (Mk. 15:23; Matt.

27:35 and parallels and Ps. 22:19), and the attitude of those present at the crucifixion (Mk. 15:29-32; Lk. 23:35-37; Matt. 27:39-44 and Ps. 22:8, 9). With arms extended on the cross Jesus himself prayed to the Father in the words of Psalm 22 (Matt. 27:46; Mk. 15:34) and according to Luke 23:46, in the words of Psalm 31:6. Through these clear allusions to the Old Testament the evangelists propose an unequivocal interpretation of the Passion event. In Jesus has been verified what the Psalmist prophetically foretold: the Person who was just and innocent was nevertheless persecuted and put to death by the impious, only to be brought to life and saved by God.

All four accounts of the passion are in general agreement on the order of episodes, but each has elements peculiar to itself, while at times there are contrasting accounts of the same fact. Some of these contrasts in the telling are among the most celebrated "interpreters' crosses" in the whole New Testament. The most noted of these is perhaps the discussion on the date of the Passion. All four agree that Jesus died on Friday, lay in the tomb during the sabbath, Saturday, and that on Sunday morning, the first day of the week (*see* Matt. 28:1; Mk. 16:1; Lk. 23:1; Jn. 20:1) the tomb was found empty. There is disagreement however over which day of the month. According to Matthew, Mark and Luke Jesus celebrated the Pasch on its eve with his disciples (Matt. 26:17-20; Mk. 14:12-17; Lk. 22:7-14), was arrested during the night, and died at the ninth hour of the day of the Pasch, the fifteenth day of Nisan, corresponding to March-April (Matt. 27:45; Mk. 15:33; Lk. 23:44). According to John, Jesus died on the day before the Pasch, that is, while preparations were going ahead for its celebration (Jn. 18:28; 19:14; 19:42). This would then be the 14th Nisan.

A solution has been sought to this problem by going back over the calendar. In the years 30 and 33 A.D. the 14th Nisan fell on a Friday. In the year 34 the 15th Nisan fell on a Friday. The year 34, however, seems too late and so John's date would seem to be the correct one. But it must be remembered that the beginning of the month depended on the appearance of the new moon, and so it is not possible to make calculations on the date with the precision that we use today.

Another way to resolve the difficulty is to take one account as the correct one and try to explain why the other account differs. Those who back John assert that the others wished to underline the Paschal nature of the eucharist by placing its institution during the Paschal banquet. Those on the other hand who prefer the chronology of Matthew, Mark and Luke reply that John saw Jesus as the Lamb and so wished to have him die at the moment at which the Paschal lambs were killed in the Temple.

A third attempt at solution affirms that John and the Synoptics were using different calendars. John was following the calendar used in the liturgy of the Temple, and according to this Jesus died on the day before the Pasch. According to Matthew, Mark and Luke, however, the death of Jesus was dated in accordance with a calendar that he and others such as the monks of Qumran had followed. These groups made use of a solar calendar which made the Pasch and other festivities always fall on a Wednesday. Jesus would thus have celebrated the Pasch with his disciples. Then the whole account was compressed within the space of a night, while in reality it took more than one day.

Another famous difficulty arises from the account of the trial before the Sanhedrin. According to Matthew and Mark there were two sessions before the Sanhedrin, one during the night in which Jesus was condemned (Matt. 26:57-66; Mk. 14:53-65), another in the morning during which the sentence was ratified and Jesus was sent to Pilate (Matt. 27:1,

2; Mk. 15:1, 2). Luke however has only one morning session during which all that Matthew and Mark placed in the first nocturnal session occurred (Lk. 22:66-71). According to John, Jesus was first brought before Annas, who carried out a preliminary interrogation (Jn. 18:19-23), and then was sent on to Caiaphas. He does not, however, report what happened there (Jn. 19:24). Early next morning he was taken before Pilate (Jn. 18:28). Numerous solutions are proposed to this difficulty. Some would have it that Luke gives the more faithful version of the facts: there was only one morning session during which the sentence was handed down and a decision was reached to take the case before the Roman prefect. The double account of Matthew and Mark is explained by the confusion over the interrogation before Annas.

Jesus was condemned for blasphemy (Matt. 26:65, 66 and parallel texts and Jn. 5:18; 10:33), that is, for having claimed for himself equality with God, appealing to Psalm 110:1 and Daniel 7:13. (*See* JESUS CHRIST.) He was not, then, condemned for having claimed to be the Messiah, but for having claimed to be a Messiah who had the kind of universal dominion in the order of judgment and salvation that belonged to God alone. The messianic claim of Jesus was astutely brought out, in a political light, in the trial before Pilate (Matt. 27:11; Mk. 15:2; Lk. 23:2). At this point John inserts a dialogue between Jesus and Pilate that was aimed at clarifying the nature and origin of this claim (Jn. 18:29-38). Luke alone adds yet another appearance of Jesus, this time before Herod (Lk. 23:6-16).

Finally, what can be said of the justice of the trial of Jesus? Today, after so many studies have been made of the gospel accounts, it is possible to give a more even-headed evaluation than was possible in the past. Two things must be kept in mind. First, the evangelists were no mere spectators describing an event in which they had no real involvement. Not only are they convinced of the innocence of Jesus, they believe in him. They see in his passion and death the realization of the design for salvation. The Person who is repudiated, condemned and killed is in reality the Messiah, not just somebody who said he was the Messiah. In Acts 3:17 Luke himself puts these words on Peter's lips: "Yet, I know, my brothers, that you acted out of ignorance, just as your leaders did. God has brought to fulfillment by this means what he announced long ago through all the prophets." In this way he approached the point of view of the judges who condemned Jesus.

Secondly, from the historical point of view, two questions must be clearly distinguished: the guilt of the judges and the legitimacy of the trial. In regard to the first point, the evangelists cannot be accused of calumny when they state that the religious authorities in Jerusalem arranged the trial, not to examine the case, but "legitimately" to suppress Jesus. In other words the decision had been reached before the trial began. What motives had urged them to this course? Were they politically inspired, as John 11:47-50 suggests? Or were they sincerely convinced that Jesus did not come from God (Jn. 9:16), scandalized, as they professed to be, by his disconcerting freedom when treating of the law and by his unheard of pretensions? Or were they motivated by personal interests which were threatened or revealed by Jesus? It is impossible to give an answer from the historical point of view.

To the second question, on the legitimacy of the trial, it seems that the answer must be affirmative: due process was had. It is true that the gospel account does not satisfy the demands of a capital trial as these are laid down in the Mishna (*see* MISHNA), but the Mishna, the written redaction of which is a third century A.D. product, is not itself in this case above suspicion. As it is there described, it is so complicated that instead of being a practical norm, it seems to be a construction drawn up in defense against Christian accusations. It is as if they wished to prove that despite the possibilities that due process offered Jesus so that he could prove his innocence, he failed to do so, and so the Jews could not be, in this case, accused of fixing the trial or dealing illegally.

Passover, One of the principal feasts in the Israelite religious calendar. The legislation governing the feast is inserted in the story of the Exodus, at the point of the tenth plague of Egypt, the slaying of the first-born (Ex. 12). The foundations for the feast are the means God revealed to the Israelites to escape the plague. And so it should be continued as a rite to perpetuate the memory of God's saving power and its enduring efficacy. The name of the feast, **Pesah,** is held to be derived from the verb **pasah,** to pass over or spare, for on that night God spared the Israelite homes when he struck the Egyptians (Ex. 12:12, 13, 23, 27). Exodus 12:23 states that the plague was brought about by the Destroyer, or destroying angel, **mashut,** the messenger to whom was committed the work of God's vengeance.

The Passover lamb was killed and the blood spilled into a basin. Then with a spray of hyssop the blood was brushed on the lintel and two door-posts, to mark the Israelite homes so that the Destroyer would pass over them. The lamb had to be eaten hastily, with their waists girt, sandals on the feet and a staff in hand, all ready for the journey. The unleavened bread, the bitter herbs are explained by the historical circumstances in which the first Pasch took place, in view of the imminent Exodus journey.

To be noted is the exclusively domestic character of the feast, with no intervention of the official ministers of cult and with no relationship to the Temple. This is clear in the Exodus ritual of c. 12, but in the Deuteronomic reform, which aimed at centralizing the cult in Jerusalem, the exclusively domestic character disappeared (Deut. 12). Thus it becomes a pilgrim feast, and although the lamb is eaten at home, the priests of the Temple kill the lamb (Deut. 16:1-7). On the fusion of this feast with the feast of unleavened bread, *see* UNLEAVENED BREAD.

The connection between the Pasch and the events of Egypt is certainly very ancient, as is borne out by the Yahwist tradition of Exodus 12:23-27, 39. However the feast was not established there and then by the Exodus events. The Pasch is a typically nomad feast. It was celebrated in the spring, and its probable scope was to ensure prosperity and fertility in the flocks. Spreading blood on the tent-poles was aimed at frightening away hostile powers, that is, the destroyer mentioned in Exodus 12:23. Later the rites of the feast were reinterpreted in terms of the history of the Exodus. Perhaps there was a chronological coincidence between the feast of which the plague tradition speaks so insistently (Ex. 5:1, etc.) and the paschal feast. When later Israel became a settled people, and the original meaning of the Pasch was somewhat lost, it was reinterpreted in terms of the events of the Exodus.

According to John, Jesus celebrated at least two Paschs in Jerusalem (2:13; 13:1). The Synoptics agree with John in placing the passion of Jesus during the Pasch, even though there is disagreement on the exact chronological course of events. Matthew 26:17-19; Mark 14:12-17 and Luke 22:7-14 tell that Jesus ate the Pasch with his disciples. John 18:28; 19:14 states that Jesus died on the day before the Pasch. *See* PASSION. On the relationship between the Pasch and the Lord's Supper, *see* LORD'S SUPPER. On Jesus, the Paschal Lamb, *see* LAMB.

Pastoral Epistles, Both letters to Timothy and the letter to Titus are grouped under the common title of Pastoral Epistles because their principal scope is to instruct on how one must exercise one's pastoral ministry in the churches. On those to whom they were written *see* TIMOTHY, TITUS. All three bear the name of Paul, and until the past century this point had never been disputed. For some time a rather heated discussion arose over the authorship of the letters. On the 12th of June 1913 the Pontifical Biblical Commission intervened in the dispute with a decree backing the traditional position. Nevertheless further developments in the debate have drawn many more Catholic authors to the opinion that Paul was not the author of the letters. Here we first will deal briefly with the subject and circumstances of the composition of the letters, as these are reflected in them, and then we will summarily treat of the debate on authorship.

1 Timothy: Before departing for Macedonia Paul left Timothy at Ephesus with the mandate to root out of the community the 'false doctrines' that were packed with "interminable myths and genealogies" (1:3-6; 1:18-20). After some autobiographical outpouring, Paul goes on to give concrete instructions, not however on how to combat the heresy, but on questions of ordinary good government, such as prayer (2:8-10), the conduct of the women in the assemblies (2:9-15), the qualities with which bishops should be endowed (3:1-7) and what deacons should be like (3:8-13). Paul adds that he has hopes of going to Ephesus, but in the case of delay he wishes to send on ahead these instructions on how one must behave in the church of God (3:14, 15). In the fourth chapter he returns to the errors to be fought. To avoid repetition we can here anticipate what is also said in the other letters on these heretical doctrines. On the one hand they are certainly of Jewish origins. In 1 Timothy 1:7 the teachers of these doctrines are said to believe themselves "masters of the Law" and in Titus 1:14 their teachings are called "Jewish myths or rules invented by men who have swerved from the truth" (*see* also Tit. 1:10). Chapter 3:9 calls them foolish investigations, genealogies, questions and struggles over the law. On the other hand there are also some tendencies that were later, in the second century, to appear, systematically elaborated in gnostic circles. Such are the insistence on knowledge, **gnosis**, of secret heavenly events as the key to salvation. 1 Timothy 6:20 stigmatizes those who teach "what is falsely called knowledge" while in Titus 1:16 Paul states that they claim to know God but this assertion is refuted by the facts. They lean towards denying the reality of Jesus' incarnation, which draws from Paul his insistence on the humanity of the Savior (1 Tim. 2:5). This docetist tendency is born of a dualism denying the goodness of matter, which leads them to abstain from marriage and from foods which God created so as to be pure in giving thanks (1 Tim. 4:3). Paul, however, responds that to the pure all things are pure (Tit. 1:15), and that everything created by God is good, so that nothing should be rejected (1 Tim. 4:4, 5).

In 1 Timothy 5-6 Paul once more takes up his pastoral concerns, giving instructions on how to treat the widows and assist them in the Christian community (1 Tim. 5:1-16). He has instructions for the presbyters (5:17-25), the slaves (6:1-2), on handling false teachers (6:3-10). He concludes with a general exhortation on the practice of virtues and a severe warning on fidelity in protecting the deposit of faith, which was being threatened by false doctrines (6:11-21). The letter to Titus is very similar to that of 1 Timothy. Paul had left Titus at Crete with the task of completing the work there and appointing elders in each city (Tit. 1:5). To this purpose he gives Titus counsel on the best way to proceed in carrying out his delicate mission. He lists the qualities of the people to be appointed and their duties (Tit. 1:6-16). He then turns to the other members of the Christian community, men and women, the youth and the slaves, giving them opportune instructions on how they should live their life (2:1-15). He recalls to them the duty to submit themselves to the magistrates and the authorities (3:1). He then goes on to general considerations on the motives that should inspire them to do good and the dangers attending heretodox doctries already referred to in 1 Timothy. The letter concludes with some notices and recommendations (1 Tit. 3:12-15).

In 2 Timothy Paul's situation is changed. Paul is a prisoner in Rome (1:16, 17). Hopes of liberation are almost gone, and Paul already feels that the moment of his departure is near (4:6). He is abandoned by some (4:10) and has only Luke with him (4:11). He asks Timothy to come to him in haste (4:9), bringing with him a cloak he had left with Carpus at Troas and some books, especially the parchments (4:13). He refers to a first defense in which nobody took his part (4:16). Given his critical situation, Paul's exhortations to Timothy assume greater gravity and urgency than in his other letters (*see* 4:1-5). He insists on the trials that await the Christian (2:8-13) and the sufferings that are linked to the battle of the faith (2 Tim. 1:6-12), as well as on the necessity of maintaining oneself faithful to the deposit of doctrine that has been confided to him (2 Tim. 1:13, 14). He should take care to resist false teachers (2 Tim. 3:1-9).

Such are the letters. Are they Paul's? It must be admitted that they present some disconcerting characteristics. On the one hand the author is so much at home with Paul's, Titus' and Timothy's movements, as well as those others that move in Paul's world, that at first one is spontaneously prompted to give him credence and say he is Paul (*see* 2 Tim. 4:9-22). The author even uses some of Paul's phrases and his style, and starts and ends his letters like Paul: the introduction, greetings, thanksgiving at the beginning and the final good wishes. On the other hand, however, there is a surprising divergence in style and vocabulary, and above all a new way in which Paul confronts a crisis in his churches. Instead of writing to the churches, he writes to Titus and Timothy. He does not take up time examining the errors and unmasking them to refute them with his usual genius. Beyond a denunciation he goes no further than to offer severe warnings about staying loyal to what was handed down in faith. The churches that are seen reflected between the lines of the letters are no longer the churches Paul lived with, linked personally to him. They are more autonomous communities which no longer draw their life and inspiration directly from Paul, but from the elders and bishops who exercise their ministry there in a more stable surveillance and direction. The local church has become more mature, more solidly inserted into its world with its tradition behind it, worthy of respect and capable of being proposed as a norm for life and belief. The errors being fought have to do with gnosticism and the deformation of Christianity it caused. This would take us towards the end of the first century.

These are in brief the reasons that have moved many scholars to consider the pastoral letters not the work of Paul, but of some unknown author towards the end of the first century. This author was rooted in the Pauline tradition, and had perhaps been a disciple or companion of the apostle. Nor should one wonder that he took the name of Paul. Such a practice was not thought of in terms that one would today attach to it. It was considered a legitimate means of bringing to life and applying to present circumstances the teaching and spirit of a preeminent figure of the past. The same occurs with 2 Peter, James, and Jude in the New Testament, and it probably holds true of Revelation of John. It would then seem that the generation following that of the apostles spontaneously chose pseudonymnous authorship to develop and complete the apostolic doctrines for the needs of their own day, considering themselves in this way as merely spokesmen of the work and as teachers true to the "pillars" on which the church had been built once and for all.

513

This however poses a delicate historical problem: what historical value can be attached to the biographical information about Paul's life contained in these letters? It is certain that the movements of Paul in 1-2 Timothy and Titus do not fit into the picture of his life given us in the genuine epistles and in Acts 13-28. Timothy accompanied Paul to Ephesus on the third apostolic journey, but he did not stay on there, but accompanied the apostle and took part in the crisis of the church at Corinth. (*See* CORINTHIANS.) Paul visited Crete only as a prisoner on his way to Rome (Acts 27:7-17). If, then, the information in the pastoral letters is to be taken as authentic it should be placed after the end of Acts (62-63 A.D.) and the martyrdom that tradition states Paul suffered in Rome under Nero towards 67-68 A.D. Had the author been a companion of Paul, or had he had access to an authentic correspondence between Paul, Timothy and Titus, there should be no objection to the truth of what he hands down in Timothy and Titus. About this, however, we have no certainty. In practice biographies make use of this information to describe what happened in Paul's life after his trial in Rome. (*See* PAUL.) One must not forget the problematic character of this information nor should one lightly treat of Paul's own self-professed plans to go west, and not return towards the former field of his apostolate (Rom. 15:22-24). It is true that Paul could have changed plans and that the visit to Spain remains in doubt. (*See* SPAIN.) In Acts 20:25 it seems that Paul was not to see his disciples at Ephesus any more. This was the prophecy of Agabus. Luke would hardly have included this if the facts had later proved the prophecy wrong. Reconstructing the last years of the apostle, then, have proved a complex question. In the absence of other elements however, it is legitimate to give credence to the information contained in the pastoral letters.

Patara (pat′-a-ra), A city and port of Lycia on the southern coast of Asia Minor. Paul passed through there on his way to Caesarea, on his return from his third missionary journey (Acts 21:1).

path, paths
watch all my *p.*	Job 13:27 abide not in its *p.*	Job 24:13
has veiled my *p.*	Job 19:8 steadfast in your *p.*	Ps. 17:5

Pathros, Pathrusim (path′-ros, pa-throo′-zim), A transcription from the Egyptian which means "land of the south," given to Egypt south of the Delta in Isa. 11:11; Jer. 44:1, 15; Ezek. 30:14 (*see* Gen. 10:14; 1 Chron. 1:12).

patient
be *p.* with me	Matt. 18:26 By *p.* endurance	Lk. 21:19
	with *p.* endurance Rom. 8:25	

Patmos, A small craggy island in the Aegean in the archipelago west of Miletus. John (Rev. 1:9) recounts that he was on the island of Patmos for having preached God's word and witnessed to Jesus. It was the Lord's day when the Spirit possessed him and he had the visions recounted in Revelation.

Patriarchs, Acts 7:8, 9 gives the title of patriarch to the twelve sons of Jacob, from whom originated the twelve tribes of Israel. The title, however, belongs above all to Abraham, Isaac and Jacob, to whom was given the promise in which the whole history of salvation finds meaning and consistency (Heb. 7:4).

The history of the patriarchs is found in Genesis 12-50. This contains three tradition cycles, on Abraham (Gen. 12-25); Isaac (25-27); and Jacob and his sons, particularly Joseph (28-50). The whole story is told in the framework of the promise of land and descendants made to Abraham by God (Gen. 12:1-3), and later repeated to Isaac (Gen. 26:1-6) and Jacob (Gen. 35:11-13). It is a story of God's fidelity. He shapes and guides events even when they seem to be opposed to his designs, so that through them is realized his plan of salvation which was announced at the beginning in the form of a totally gratuitous and absolute promise (*see* Gen. 45:7-8; 50:18-21).

The story of the patriarchs is drawn up on the basis of independent traditions which at the beginning had different functions and interests. There has been a great diversity of opinion on the antiquity and historicity of these traditioms. Some scholars wished to defend the absolute historicity of the stories, while at the other extreme were those who held them to be a later reconstruction, stemming from around the ninth century B.C., and therefore void of any historical value. Increased knowledge of the political, cultural, social and religious history of the second millenium B.C. today enable one to offer a better founded judgment on the patriarch traditions. It cannot be doubted that by means of these traditions we are able to reach back through history to those groups of nomads who claimed for themselves Abraham, Isaac and Jacob. The patriarchal traditions above all reflect customs that had to do with family rights, which were, however, unknown in later Israel. We have knowledge of them during the first half of the second millenium from law codes discovered in Mesopotamia. (*See* NUZI.) On the other hand it must be acknowledged that these same traditions do contain elements and points of view that belong to later periods. This should cause no wonder: the traditions on the patriarchs have come down through Israel after a long period of oral transmission. While oral tradition did have inbuilt tenacity and fixedness among ancient peoples, it was nevertheless kept alive and updated to keep contact with the life and times of the people among whom it was handed down. So one can give a cautious historical assent to the patriarchal traditions taken as a whole, without dispensing one from a serious historical criticism of the individual accounts so as to interpret them in accordance with the demands of the literary genre of the text.

The groups who were said to be descended from Abraham, Isaac and Jacob were semi-nomadic peoples, shepherds who wandered on the fringes of settled areas. With the settled peoples they had peaceful and frequent contacts. With these they stayed during the summer periods. Search for pastures for their flocks imposed on them constant traveling along fixed itineraries between wells and oases. *See* NOMADISM.

The Bible tradition has conserved the information that the patriarchs were not native to Palestine. They had come from northern Mesopotamia (Gen. 12:4). Genesis 11:27-31 goes back further, to Ur, a city of southern Mesopotamia. One should place the migration of the patriarchs towards the south among the displacements of western-semitic peoples which mark the history of the second millenium B.C. According to Deuteronomy 26:5 the patriarchs were "wandering Aramaeans," and their place of origin Paddan-aram, that is, the plain or steppe of Haran (Gen. 25:2; 31:18; 24:10), where dwelt Laban "the Aramaean," a relative of the ancestors of the Israelites (Gen. 25:20; 28:5; 31:20, 24).

There has been much discussion over this tradition that makes the patriarchs descend from the Aramaeans of Haran. The reason for this is that in the extra-biblical sources the Aramaeans are only spoken of in the thirteenth century B.C., that is, practically at the time of Moses. At that time the Aramaeans were organized into city-states in the region of Syria and northern Mesopotamia. Later, new documents discovered at Mari (*see* MARI) speak of Aram as a region and a people already in the eighteenth century. These belong to the same root as the Aramaeans of the thirteenth century, but they constitute a more ancient ethnic wave of nomadic tribes who came in from the desert to city life. So the biblical traditions appear to be well founded and exact.

Biblical tradition places the three patriarchs in relationship of father to son. For some time this genealogy has been suspect. In fact ancient genealogies often translate historical relationships of alliance or fusion between groups and peoples into family relationships that claim a common ancestor. (*See* GENEALOGY.) The traditions on Abraham seem to be anchored around the south of Palestine for the most part, in the neighborhood of Shechem and Bethel. The Isaac traditions, which are also the least numerous, also veer to the south. Thus there are different groups who are ethnically and historically related to one another, established in different regions and later associated with one another in ways that can no longer be reconstructed. From this association was formed a patrimony common to both, then to all three, sanctioned by a genealogy that placed them in the relationship of father to son. On the religion of the patriarchs *see* PATRIARCHS, RELIGION OF THE; PROMISE; FAITH.

It is very difficult to determine the chronological limits of the patriarchal story. For a long time Abraham was considered a contemporary of Hammurabi (1728-1686 B.C.; *see* HAMMURABI). This chronology however was based on a false identification between Amraphel (Gen. 14:1) and Hammurabi. (*See* AMRAPHEL.) Very probably one can be no more precise than to state that the patriarchs belong to the first half of the second millenium B.C. On the individual patriarchs *see* ABRAHAM; ISAAC; JACOB.

Patriarchs, Religion of the, According to the Genesis account the religion of the patriarchs expressed itself in acts of extreme simplicity. This simplicity reflected the nomadic condition of the patriarchs. It stands however in vivid contrast with the complexity of the cultic legislation of Israel. Genesis only speaks of the offering of sacrifices and the invocation of the name of God (Gen. 12:7-9), of the transmission and interpretation of oracles (Gen. 15), and of the erection of commemorative stelae (Gen. 28:18; 31:13; 35:14). There was nobody especially designated for the carrying out of the cult. The head of the family as chief and representative of the group spontaneously took on the priestly functions. *See* PRIEST.

The central problem however with the religion of the patriarchs is the identification of God who is at the center of their worship. The problem arises from the historical and not from the theological point of view. According to the witness of the Bible the one and true God, who manifested himself to Israel at Sinai, had also made himself known to their fathers, to whom he had pledged himself with promises to the benefit of their children. The question arises, under what particular form did God make himself known to Abraham? In other words, when God wished to come out from his silence to enter into contact with man, under what forms was his voice heard? Revelation does not lie at the margins of the forms of religion elaborated by man, but is rather incarnate in them. Our task, then, is to seek to determine what precisely were these forms.

In answer to this question we can state: the religion of the patriarchs was addressed to the God El as their personal God. How is this assertion explained?

In patriarchal traditions God is often designated by titles such as El-Shaddai, that is, names composed of the word El, which in semitic languages means God. El had become the proper name for the god who was chief god in the Canaanite pantheon. (*See* UGARIT.) The second word, Shaddai, is of obscure meaning (Ex. 3:3); other appellations in use were Elyon (the Most High, Gen. 14:18), Berith (of the Alliances, Gen. 33:18-20), Olam (eternal, Gen. 21:33), Roi (the seer, Gen. 16:7-14) and others. These names do not designate different gods, but rather the same God El who is adored and called upon in different localities, El-Berith in Shechem, El-Olam in Hebron, El-Roi in Beersheba and so on.

On the other hand the God who made himself known to the patriarchs is also called the "God of the Fathers," that is God of Abraham, Isaac and Jacob (*see* Gen. 26:24 ff.; 28:11 ff.; 31:5, 29, 42, 53). These names are typical of a type of religion of the time, which is known as the "religion of the personal God." In it is expressed the tendency to associate oneself with a definite God to whom one is dedicated and from whom one awaits guidance and protection. As in the case of the patriarchs, this dedication can take on an exclusive note, which in the last analysis is the equivalent of a practical monotheism. The personal God of the patriarchs is El. In the framework of the religion of this personal God the theme of the promise finds its place. The promise is the central theme of the patriarchal traditions of Genesis. In fact different religious documents of Mesopotamia attest to promises made by one's personal god. It seems that it was precisely these manifestations of benevolence on the part of God that moved his worshipper to dedicate himself fully to him.

Patrobas (pat'-ro-bas), A Christian of Rome greeted by Paul in Romans 16:14.

Patroclus (pa-troe'-clus), The father of Nicanor, a chief of the Seleucid army (2 Mac. 8:9). *See* NICANOR.

Pau (paw or pay'-oo), A city in Edom, the home of King Hadar (Gen. 36:39).

Paul, Saul, who is also called Paul (Acts 13:9) was born at Tarsus in Cilicia, Asia Minor, around 10 A.D. He came from an Aramaic-speaking Jewish family (2 Cor. 11:22) of the tribe of Benjamin (Rom. 11:1; Phil. 3:5) which had Roman citizenship (Acts 22:24-29). He was circumcised on the eighth day after birth (Phil. 3:6) and received, besides the Hebrew name Saul, the Latin one Paul. Paul's native city, Tarsus, was the Athens of Asia Minor, and so Paul grew up in the midst of Greek language and culture, which was not lost on him (*see* Acts 17:28; 1 Cor. 15:33; Tit. 1:12). Despite his education, he was a most zealous follower of Jewish traditions. When he was about eighteen years old he came to Jerusalem where he sat as a disciple at Gamaliel's feet to learn the doctrine of the Pharisees (Acts 22:3; 23:6; Phil 3:6). He thus became a passionate defender of the Jewish traditions and surpassed all his fellows in his attachment to the Jewish patrimony and in protecting them against Christian deviations (Gal. 1:14). Paul also learned the trade of tent-maker (Acts 18:3) which provided his livelihood, as he never wished to be a burden to the churches (Phil. 4:10-20; 2 Cor. 11:9; 1 Cor. 9:4-23). Paul was present at Stephen's stoning and took an active part in the persecution of the nascent church that followed in Palestine (Acts 7:58-60) and Damascus (9:1-2).

His conversion took place on the road to Damascus. Of this event there are three versions in the Acts. One is Luke's account (Acts 9:1-19), the other two in Paul's own words (22:5-16; 26:12-18). His conversion was also his mission and investiture as apostle, for it made him a witness of Christ and charged him with spreading this witness to the Gentiles (Acts 26:16; Gal. 1:15, 16; Phil. 3:12; 1 Cor. 9:1; 15:5-9). After his conversion Paul preached for some days at Damascus (Acts 9:19-22), and then retired to Arabia, that is, to the region near Damascus which was part of the Nabataean kingdom (Gal. 1:16-18). He returned once more to Damascus (Acts 9:23-25) from which however he was forced to flee becauŝe he was brought before King Aretas of Damascus (2 Cor. 11:23 ff.). He went to Jerusalem where he stayed fifteen days with Peter and James (Gal. 1:18, 19; Acts 9:26-28). There, however, some Jewish Christians remembered his period as persecutor of the Church, so he returned to Tarsus (Acts 9:29, 30; *see* Gal. 1:23).

After some time Barnabas came to him there and brought him to Antioch to work in the church (Acts 11:25, 26). With Barnabas he brought to Jerusalem the alms that had been collected to alleviate the famine that struck the region during the reign of Claudius (Acts 11:25). From that point on, Antioch was to become for Paul the center of the mission to the Gentiles. Although Paul is the "Apostle of the Gentiles" he always respected the privilege of the Jews (Rom. 1:16; 2:9, 10; 3:1, 2, 29; 9:4-6; 11). He chose the great cities of the Hellenistic world to serve as centers of irradiation for the Christian message. First of all he went to the Jews and proselytes in the synagogues (Acts 13:5; 14:1; 16:13), or if this were not possible, he preached in the open air (Acts 17:2).

Not infrequently his preaching aroused the opposition of the larger part of the Jewish community, obliging him to abandon the city (14:2-6, 18; 17:5, 13; 18:12) or to break with the Jewish community and turn to the pagans (18:6, 7; 19:8, 9). It was Paul's custom to visit again the churches he had founded in the preceding journey to confirm them in the faith (14:21; 16:36, 41; 15:13) and to install the elders (14:22).

Paul's apostolic work was accomplished in three great missionary journeys that brought the faith to Cyprus, Asia Minor, Macedonia and Achaia. His first journey (46-49 A.D.) was undertaken with Barnabas and Mark to Cyprus, where in Salamis and Paphos the word of God was proclaimed. At Paphos Paul met the proconsul Sergius Paulus. From there they went on to Asia Minor. At Perga Mark abandoned them, while they went on to Antioch of Pisidia, Iconium, Lystra and Derbe. On their way back they visited the same cities in Asia Minor, and boarded a ship at Attalia for Antioch (Acts 13-14). On their arrival they discovered that Jewish-Christian converts were exaggerating the obligation of the observance of the law and circumcision by the Hellenist Christians, and so a decision was reached to bring the question to the apostles at Jerusalem (Acts 15; Gal. 2).

The second journey was from 50 to 53 A.D. Paul had a disagreement with Barnabas over Mark, and so took with him instead Silas-Silvanus. He returned to the churches of Asia Minor, and at Lystra took Timothy into the band (Acts 16:1-3; 2 Tim. 1:5). Later he stayed at Phrygia and Galatia, and then reached Troas where he met Luke. From Troas he passed on to Macedonia, making stops at Philippi, Thessalonica and Beroea. Paul set out alone for Athens where he made a speech on the Areopagus, and then, with Timothy, reached Corinth. Here he met Aquila and Priscilla. He remained there for eighteen months. He was brought by the Jews before Gallio the proconsul on an accusation of breaking the law, but Gallio eased himself out of the case, claiming it was outside his competence. From Corinth Paul returned to Antioch. It was from Corinth that 1 and 2 Thessalonians were written (Acts 15:36-18:22).

Paul's third journey (54-58 A.D.) was through Galatia and Phrygia to Ephesus, where for three months he preached in the synagogue and for two years in the school of a man called Tyrannus. He was expelled because of a commotion caused by the silversmiths of the city. He went from there to Macedonia and stopped at Corinth. After three months he returned by the same way to Troas and then to Miletus whither he had summoned the elders of Ephesus. He went by sea to Caesarea where a prophet called Agabus foretold the tribulations that awaited him in

Jerusalem (Acts 18:25-21:19). During this journey he wrote Galatians (from Ephesus), Romans (from Corinth), Philippians (from Ephesus), and 1-2 Corinthians (from Ephesus and Macedonia).

There is a detailed description of what happened in Jerusalem and the journey to Rome in Acts 21:17 ff. Notwithstanding his efforts to win over the Jews, he was arrested by them, and got away with his life only through the strategy of the Roman tribune. Twice he was taken before the Sanhedrin (22:30-23:10) and, when the conspiracy against him was discovered, he was sent by night to Caesarea, to the Roman procurator Felix (24:1-21). There Paul spent two years in jail (24:22-27). When the new procurator Festus came along, Paul appealed to Caesar (25:1-12) and later appeared before Agrippa and Bernice (25:13-26:32). Then he was put on board ship for Rome, where he arrived after an exciting journey during which he was shipwrecked on Malta and forced to stay there for a brief period (27:1-28:16). He stayed in Rome for two years, in custody, preaching the gospel, before being taken to trial (Acts 27:17-31). During his Roman captivity Paul composed the letters to Philemon, to the Colossians and to the Ephesians. The information about Paul after this first captivity is taken from the pastoral letters about whose authenticity there is much discussion. In Romans 15:24-28 he expresses his plans for going to Spain, but it is not known if he completed this journey. According to the pastoral letters he visited Crete (Tit. 1:5), Ephesus (1 Tim. 1:3) and the adjacent cities (2 Tim. 4:20), Macedonia and Epirus (from Nicopolis he wrote Titus and 1 Timothy).

The reasons for his second imprisonment are unknown, nor do we know where he was imprisoned. According to 2 Timothy 1:8, 16, 17; 2:9 he is a prisoner in Rome and is awaiting death. Tradition places his martyrdom in Rome on the Ostian Way, during the persecution of Nero (67 or 68 A.D.).

Paulus, Sergius, Proconsul of Cyprus, who was converted by Paul to Christianity after he had unmasked and punished the magic of a Jew named Bar-Jesus, also known as Elymas, who was a companion to the proconsul (Acts 13:7-12).

pavement

set it on a stone *p*.	2 Kgs. 16:17	chambers and a *p*.	Ezek. 40:17
down upon the *p*.	2 Chron. 7:3	The *p*. lay alongside	Ezek. 40:18
		called the Stone *P*.	Jn. 19:13

paws

those what walk on *p*.   Lev. 11:27

Pe, The 17th letter of the Hebrew alphabet (p).

Peace Offering, *See* SACRIFICE.

pearls

it surpasses *p*.	Job 28:18	search for fine *p*.	Matt. 13:45
toss your *p*.	Matt. 7:6	gold ornaments, *p*.	1 Tim. 2:9

Pedahel (ped′-a-hel), A leader of the tribe of Naphtali (Num. 34:28).

Pedahzur (pe-dah′-zur), The father of Gamaliel, a leader of the tribe of Manasseh (Num. 1:10; 2:20; 7:54; 10:23).

Pedaiah (pe-day′-ah), 1. "The Lord has redeemed," personal name (1 Chron. 27:20; Neh. 3:25; 8:4; 11:7; 13:13).

2. The father of Zerubbabel (1 Chron. 3:18, 19). *See* ZERUBBABEL.

Pekah (pee′-kah), Son of Remaliah and king of Israel (737-732 B.C.) after the assassination of his predecessor Pekahiah (2 Kgs. 15:25-27). With Rezin, king of Damascus, he invaded the land of Judah to force Ahaz to enter into a coalition against the Assyrians, or if he refused, to depose him. Ahaz called Tiglath-pileser III to his help. The latter quickly conquered Galilee and Gilead and reduced the kingdom of Israel almost to the environs of its capital (Isa. 7; 2 Kgs. 16:5-9; 15:29). Pekah died in the conspiracy organized by Hoshea, who then proclaimed himself king.

Pekahiah (pek′-a-hy′-ah), King of Israel (738-737 B.C.), son and successor of Menahem; he was killed by Pekah, an officer of the army, who proclaimed himself king (2 Kgs. 15:23-26).

Pekod (pee′-kod), An Aramaean tribe, residents of Mesopotamia, who were subjugated by the Assyrians at the time of Tiglath-pileser III (746-727 B.C.). *See* Jer. 50:21; Ezek. 23:23.

Pelaiah (pe-lay′-yah), Personal name (1 Chron. 3:24; Neh. 8:7; 10:10).

Pelatiah (pel′-a-tie′-ah), A proper name borne by four men in the Old Testament (1 Chron. 3:21; 4:42; Neh. 10:23; Ez. 11:1, 13).

Peleg (pee′-leg), The son of Eber and Shem (Gen. 10:25; 11:16-19; 1 Chron. 1:19, 25).

Pelethites (pel′-e-thites), Foreign mercenaries who, with the Cherethites (both related to the Philistines), formed the personal guard of David under the command of Benaiah (2 Sam. 8:18; 15:18; 20:7; 1 Kgs. 38:44; 1 Chron 18:17). *See* CHERETHITES.

Pella, A Transjordanian city to which the Christian community of Jerusalem moved during the Jewish war with the Romans (66-70 A.D.), before the destruction of the Holy City.

Pelusium (pe-loo′-shi-um), A fortress on the northeast border of Egypt (Ezek. 30:15).

Pen, The writing instrument most used in antiquity was the metal, bone, or ivory stylus, or one made of some other material. This was used to write on wax tablets, or even to scrape words on harder surfaces. To etch words in monuments a hard metal chisel was used (Job 19:24; Jer. 17:1). The pen or "calamus" was used to write on softer materials: it was a small reed with a point divided in two (Jer. 36:23; 3 Jn. 13). The quill came much later, around the sixth century A.D.

Penance, By sin man turns away from God (*see* SIN) and by penance he turns back to receive God's forgiveness. In the Old Testament the most common term for repentance is *sub, to turn back* (Jer. 8:4; Ezek. 33:19) and the equivalent term of the Septuagint and the New Testament is *apostrepho* or *epistrepho*, I turn back on the road I have been travelling, *metamelomai*, I change my mind, and *metanoeo*, I repent, I change my attitude and decision, in this case from sin which divides me from grace, back to God.

The importance of *penance* or *conversion* in the New Testament can be gathered from the number of times it occurs: *metanoeo* appears thirty-two times, (Matt. 3:2; 4:17 etc.), *metanoia*, repentance, twenty-two times (Matt. 3:8; Mk. 1:4 etc.), *metamelomai* six times.

In the Old Testament the prophets continually called the people to repentance so that they might remove the barriers between them and God's attendant blessings. Days of national repentance were called (Neh. 9), liturgies of repentance proclaimed (Isa. 63:7-64; Dan. 9:4-19). Grief in penance was expressed in the rending of one's clothes, fasting, sackcloth and ashes (Jonah 3:5, 8; Matt. 11:21; Lk. 10:13).

The prophets of old, however, exhorted the people of Israel not just to the externals of penance but to a real interior conversion of the heart to God (Ezek. 18:31; Hos. 6:6; Amos 5:21–24). When the last of the prophets, John the Baptist, prepared the way for the coming of the Lord, he called for worthy penance, laying the axe at the root of the tree (Matt 3:8, 10). Jesus, the fulfilment of the prophecies, called for a cleansing of the inside of the cup (Matt. 23:26; Mk. 7:15). There is to be no compromise with what divides one from God (Matt. 5:29; 6:19; 17:13; Mk 3:31–35; 10:21). One must not just change one's external behavior, but one's whole life (Matt 18:3). This change reaches out from the roots of one's being, right from the new heart placed there by God (Ezek. 36:24–28; Jer 31:31–34).

While John and Paul do not use the vocabulary of repentance, the doctrine is there presented in new depth. The call of Christ in their writings is to communion in the Spirit, who gathers the Christian from his sins into Christ (Rom. 6:1–11; 8:15; Gal. 4:4–8). Indeed, it is God who begins in the sinner the good work of which he is, on his own power alone, incapable (Acts 3:26; 5:31; 11:18; Rom. 2:4; 2 Cor. 7:9; 2 Tim. 2:25; Rev. 2:21).

Sin enslaves man in such a way that he is incapable of liberating himself. God in his mercy draws man from his sins back into the communion of life (Matt. 11:27–31; Jn. 6:44). The movement to repentance is initiated by God, and the joy caused by the returning sinner reverberates in heaven (Lk. 15). Christ continues His forgiving presence in the community through the sacrament of penance, the open door left to the repentant sinner through which he can return to the communion of life in Christ. *See* SIN; FORGIVENESS.

Peninnah, The second wife of Elkanah, Hannah's husband (1 Sam. 1:2, 4). *See* ELKANAH; HANNAH.

Penknife, A knife used by scribes to sharpen the points of their pens (Jer. 36:23).

Pentateuch (pen′-ta-te-ook, tuke), The first part of the Old Testament Canon of the Jews is called the **Torah,** which the Greeks translated **ho nomos,** the law. This comprised five volumes. Although this division into five volumes is not original, it is very ancient. Even before the Greek translation of the Septuagint it was the Greek custom, at least from the second century B.C., to call this group of books **he pentateuchos** (penta=5, teuchos=roll, volume) biblos (=book). The division substantially corresponds to the different stages of history that are recounted there. The titles given by the Greeks to the individual parts also succeed, almost always, in conveying the essential content of the books. **Genesis,** or origin, describes the beginnings of the earth, humanity and the people of Israel, that is, the patriarchs. **Exodus** describes the exit from Egypt and the constitution of the people through the Covenant. **Leviticus,** given the ritual character of most of the laws that are contained there, is taken up with the priestly tribe of Levi. **Numbers,** however, only designates a part of that work, cc. 1-4 and 26, which cover the census of the people, while the rest treats of the journey from Sinai to the Jordan. **Deuteronomy,** or the second law, is a title taken from Deuteronomy 17:18, understood as a law given by Moses on the plain of Moab to bring to completion the revelation at Sinai.

In non-biblical Jewish tradition Moses is not only the mediator of the revelation of the law, but also the true literary author of the Pentateuch. This tradition has certainly left its traces in the New Testament (*see* Mk.

12:26; Lk. 24:44; Matt. 19:8; Jn. 5:45-47) and passed into the tradition of
the ancient Church. The Bible itself is much less explicit on this point. It
only appears in the post-exilic books, when the Pentateuch reached the
actual form it today enjoys (*see* Ezra 6:18; 10:3; Neh. 8:3; 13:1; 2 Chron.
25:4; 30:16). Even if the Pentateuch does contain many exploits and sayings of Moses, it owes little to his literary activity (*see* Ex. 17:24; Ex. 24:4;
34:27; Num. 33:2 and Deut. 31:9, 24). Attributing the authorship of the
whole Pentateuch to Moses must then be understood somewhat like the
attribution of the Psalter to David, or the attribution of the Wisdom books
to Solomon. Thus to Moses is attributed the definitive stage of the work in
legislation that he certainly initiated. Moreover the books contain all that
took its origin in his personal activity, and what was built on the foundations he laid and in fidelity to his spirit throughout the history of Israel.

The Pentateuch can be attributed to Moses then in two ways. First, he was
the founder of Yahwism, or the specific religion of Israel, the mediator of
the Covenant, and the chief hero in the history of the normative and
constitutive period of the sacred history of the Old Testament. Secondly it
can be understood in the sense that Moses was the literary author of the
books. The first assertion is of the utmost importance and intimately connected with the altogether particular character of the religion of Israel.
The second assertion, however, is far less founded, and is concerned with
the literary order. It has for many centuries served to express in a clear
and concrete fashion what is stated in the first assertion, even though the
content of this is independent and distinct, and in fact the second assertion is today untenable.

A close look at the books reveal that they cannot be assigned as a whole
to the Mosaic area. As they now stand, they are the result of a centuries-
long process of composition. The theory that most scholars today hold,
and which is the fruit of two centuries of research, is the so-called documentary theory. Here it is presented in general outline, without going into
the history of its formation or into the details on which authors vary.

The documentary theory today seems the most obvious response to some
characteristics of the work, which themselves are not the result of any
theory, but objective data which any theory must take into account. The
narrative in the Pentateuch is often brusquely interrupted, or, contrari-
wise, an account takes off without the necessary introduction one would
expect for the sake of adequately understanding the passage. It would,
however, be a mistake to think that the whole work consisted of detached
episodes. The continuation of an interrupted narrative is found later on
without any effort at shaping a continuing story (H. Cazelles). These interrupted episodes, when linked together, form a longer logical and
chronological series of coherent episodes, qualities lost by the manner in
which they are fitted into the Pentateuch. For instance, if after the creation account in Gen. cc. 1-2:4a one skips the following creation account
and reads on from c. 5:1; 11:10, 27; 25:12; 26:1, one finds a logical continuation of episodes told in the same form and style. This permits one to
reconstruct a very developed account of sacred history, presented with
accurately drawn up genealogies.

In the Pentateuch there are accounts so similar, even down to the details,
that they sound like true repetitions. For example there are two accounts
of the creation (Gen. 1-2:4a; 2:4b-3:21); two genealogies for Adam
(Gen. 4 and 5), two accounts of the flood, fused together in Gen. 6-9; two
covenants of God with Abraham (Gen. 15 and 17); two expulsions of
Hagar (Gen. 16 and 21); three times, twice for Abraham and once for
Isaac is the wife (or wives) of the patriarch or patriarchs put in danger and
saved through the same stratagem (Gen. 12:20, 26); twice is there a mira-

cle of quails and manna, with the same reaction on the part of the people (Ex. 16 and Num. 11). At other times there are contrasting versions of the same fact (Gen. 21:31 and 26:34; Gen. 28:19 and 35:14; Gen. 32:28 and 35:10).

In the legislative section there are also frequent repetitions, such as laws about the same thing (e.g. Ex. 20:24 and Deut. 12:14; Ex. 28:1 and Deut. 18:7, etc). Here the laws are often at variance on the same subject, and make one suppose that they were issued in the different social, economic and cultural circumstances of a people recently settled (Ex. 20-22: Book of the Covenant) and of a well settled and centralized society. There is, then, a true historical evolution in the laws. When however we think of a possible Mosaic origin, the question arises: how could Moses legislate for conditions that only became a reality several centuries later?

The Pentateuch as a whole can also be divided into series that are parallel in style and vocabulary. These series, which are already distinguished by the subjects they treat, also show forth unvarying characteristics that are exclusive to them. The convergence of form and content makes the theory more solid. The most celebrated case is the usage of the name for God in Genesis. One series of texts in Genesis speaks of Yahweh, another of Elohim. The reason for this diversity is found in Exodus 3:14 and 6:3, that is, God did not reveal himself with the name of Yahweh to the patriarchs. The author who wrote this is consistent with the principle in the way in which the patriarchal story is told, while another author has extended to this period the later title Yahweh, seeing that both are names for the same God. There are also other indications in the vocabulary used. As regards style, there are three easily distinguishable: first, the abundant, slow heavy oratorical style of Deuteronomy, a book which is isolated and forms a compact unity in the whole of the Pentateuch (*see* DEUTERONOMY). The second is the precise, accurate, coherent use of technical terms and expressions which remind one of the long passages of cultic legislation. This has been named the Priestly codex, and is denoted by P. In contrast to this precision of terminology and composition is a third series of texts among which there are two masterpieces of the narrative genre. Here is a different spiritual and religious environment that is more spontaneous and immediate. God's action is described without the solemn cultic literary apparatus which is underlined in other texts. Instead he intervenes more gently and yet more decisively in common human vicissitudes. In this series of largely narrative passages must be distinguished, from the use of the name for God, Yahweh, the Yahwist (J); and another document which uses in Genesis the name Elohim, the Elohist (E).

The Pentateuch then, as it is today has come from four different strata or cycles of tradition, J E D P. It is now necessary to see how these four fused in time, to try to reconstruct the process that led to this result. One must from the beginning exclude any simplistic solution such as has in the past led to many misunderstandings. These four documents J E D P are not new works written by individual authors, but are themselves what was written down after a long process of oral tradition. Therefore merely dating the writing does not automatically resolve the problem of dating the individual documents or traditions contained in that writing. So, even if a chronological order is established between the documents, that is, J E D P, this is not to conclude that P, for example, is posterior in all its details to J. Here we are dealing with parallel series, even in time, transmitted contemporaneously in different environments of the people of Israel and put down in writing in a definitive manner in different epochs.

The most ancient documents, according to the unanimous opinion of the scholars, is J. In the case of J it is also necessary to suppose an author with a definite character and ability, who knew how to give the different traditions he gathered in writing a unity of form and thought. This author is thought to have lived towards the end of the reign of David and the beginning of that of Solomon. Some scholars also attribute to him the so-called history of the succession of David (2 Sam; *see* SAMUEL, BOOKS OF), which perhaps formed the conclusion of J's work. This then is the most ancient organized synthesis of the oral traditions, some of them very old, which circulated in the south of Palestine.

Not much later a similar synthesis was attempted in the northern kingdom. This was the Elohist, dated certainly before 722 B.C. when Samaria was conquered and the northern kingdom brought to ruin. It is not possible to establish with certainty when J and E were fused, but this probably took place in Judah later than 722 when those fleeing from the ruined northern kingdom took refuge in the south. This was probably during the reign of Hezekiah (715-687 B.C.). At least in its most ancient form Deuteronomy (*see* DEUTERONOMY) is the book of the law found in the Temple of Jerusalem in 621 B.C. during Josiah's reign (640-609 B.C.) and which inspired the religious reform brought about by this king (2 Kgs. 22:3-23:27). This book was also brought from the northern kingdom, and was probably known during the reign of Hezekiah, but it remained hidden in the Temple only to be rediscovered there during some repairs.

P gathers the theological, narrative, legislative and cultic traditions of the priests of the Temple at Jerusalem. Even though it is the most recent, all authors agree that it contains some very ancient material. It was definitively shaped during or after the exile and in part coincided with the programs of national and religious resurgence that were worked out before the return to Palestine. Of these programs there is an example in cc. 40-44 of Ezekiel, which shows surprising similarities in mentality and content to P. Ezekiel was himself a priest.

The final fusion of all this material of J E D P perhaps took place through the work of Ezra (around 444 B.C.), or even more recently, but not after the Samaritan schism (*see* SAMARITANS), because the Samaritans took as sacred and canonical only the Pentateuch.

Pentecost, One of the feasts of pilgrimage (**hag**) in the Israelite religious calendar. It is called the Harvest Festival (Ex. 23:16; 34:22) or the Feast of Weeks (Deut. 16:9-10), seeing that it was celebrated seven weeks after the Feast of Unleavened Bread (Num. 28:26; Lev. 23:15-21), that is, fifty days after the Pasch when the Feast of Unleavened Bread and the Pasch were one festival. From this computation comes the Greek name **Pentecoste,** which means the fiftieth (day). As is evident from the most ancient religious calendars (Ex. 34:22; 23:16), this was a typical agricultural religious festival to celebrate the end of the harvest, and was therefore adopted by the Israelites after they settled down in Canaan. Like the other agricultural festivals (Unleavened Bread, Tabernacles), it was not long before this too became associated with Israel's sacred history, and, it seems, it became a commemoration of the conclusion of the Covenant and the revelation of the law on Sinai. This interpretation, however, has left little or no trace in the Old Testament, except perhaps in 2 Chronicles 15:10. It is sufficiently witnessed to in the aprocryphal works of the Old Testament. The Christian Feast of Pentecost commemorates the outpouring of the Holy Spirit, the unexcelled eschatological gift, on the apostles and on the Church, which took place on the Jewish Feast of Pentecost (Acts 2).

Penuel (pe-noo′-el, pen′-yoo-el), A place in Transjordan at the point where the river Jabbok meets the Jordan. Here took place a theophany to Jacob. From this fact the site got its name ("Face of God," Gen. 32:24-32). The inhabitants of Penuel refused to aid Gideon when he was pursuing the Midianites. When he then returned victorious, Gideon took his revenge by slaying the male inhabitants of the town (Jgs. 8:8-17). In 1 Kings 12:25 Penuel is one of the cities fortified by Jeroboam I (922-901 B.C.).

people

the *p.* of Israel	Gen. 48:20	a stiff-necked *p.* Ex. 33:3
as my own *p.*	Ex. 6:7	a *p.* sacred to the Lord Deut. 7:6
	redeeming it as his *p.* 2 Sam. 7:23	

People of God, *See* CHURCH.

Peor, *See* BAAL-PEOR.

Perazim, *See* BAAL-PERAZIM.

Perea (pe-ree′-a), A district on the east side of the Jordan along its bank just north of the Dead Sea. After the death of Herod I the Great, Perea and Galilee were assigned to his son Herod Antipas with the title of tetrarch. Although the name is not read in the New Testament, it is implicit in John 1:28; Matthew 19:1 and Mark 10:1.

Peresh (per′-esh), A son of Machir of the tribe of Manasseh (1 Chron. 7:16).

Perez (per′-ez), One of the twins born to Judah and Tamar (Gen. 38:29; 1 Chron. 2:4; 4:1).

Perez-uzzah, "Breach of Uzzah," the name given to the place where Uzzah was struck dead for having touched the ark of the covenant while it was being transferred to Jerusalem in the time of David (2 Sam. 6:8; 1 Chron. 13:11).

perfection

vie with the *p.*	Job 11:7	the seal of *p.* Ezek. 28:12
	If, then, *p.* Heb. 7:11	

perfume

P. and incense	Prov. 27:9	Instead of *p.* Isa. 3:24
with the *p.*	S. of S. 3:6	alabaster jar of *p.* Mk. 14:3
	a pound of costly *p.* Jn. 12:3	

Perga, A city of Pamphylia in Asia Minor on the southern coast of Asia Minor near the port of Attalia. It was visited by Paul and Barnabas twice on their first apostolic journey (Acts 13:13, 14; 14:25). At Perga John Mark abandoned his travelling companions and returned to Jerusalem (Acts 13:13; 15:38)

Pergamum (per′-ga-mum), A city of Asia Minor, near the west coast and north of Smyrna. It had a Christian community to which one of the seven letters of Revelation was addressed (2:12-16). *See* PARCHMENT.

Perizzites (per′-i-zites), One of the pre-Israelite peoples of Canaan, in all probability of Hittite origin (Ex. 3:8-17; 23:23; 34:11, etc.). They occupied the wooded central region of Palestine (Josh. 17:15).

persecute

we *p.* him	Job 19:28	insult you and *p.* you Matt. 5:11
they *p.* me wrongfully	Ps. 119:86	they *p.* you in one Matt. 10:23
	mishandle and *p.* you Lk. 21:12	

Persepolis (per-sep′-o-lis), The ancient capital of Persia which was conquered and destroyed by Alexander the Great. Persepolis (city of the Persians) in 2 Maccabees 9:2 is to be interpreted in the generic sense of capital city of Persia.

Perseus, The last king of Macedonia, son and successor of Philip III, who was defeated by the Romans at Pydna (168 B.C.; 1 Mac. 8:5). Macedonia then became a Roman province.

Persians, An Asian people of Indo-Germanic roots, related to the Medes, who established themselves on the highlands south of Elam and east of the Persian Gulf in the modern Iran. Under Cyrus II (559-529 B.C.) they created for themselves one of the greatest empires of antiquity. Cyrus II conquered the Babylonians in 539 B.C. and pushed the limits of the empire as far as Asia Minor and the frontiers of Egypt, which fell into the hands of his successor Cambyses II (528-522 B.C.). The empire was organized into twenty satrapies by Darius I (521-486 B.C.). It endured through various vicissitudes until 333 B.C. when it fell into the hands of Alexander the Great. On the history of the Persian Empire *see* CYRUS, DARIUS, ARTAXERXES, AHASUERUS, ALEXANDER THE GREAT. On the relationships between it and Judah *see* EXILE, EZRA, NEHEMIAH.

Persis, A Christian woman whom Paul greets in Romans 16:12.

Peruda (pe-roo′-da), Ancestor of a family of Solomon's servants (Ezra 2:55).

Peshitta (pe-shee′-ta), A Syriac version of the Bible. *See* SYRIAC VERSIONS OF THE HOLY SCRIPTURES.

Peter, Simon or Simeon, which is the Greek form of the name, was son of Jonah (Matt. 16:18), or John, and one of the Twelve chosen by Jesus (Matt. 10:2; Mk. 3:16; 21:15-17; Acts 1:13). From Jesus he received the additional name of **Kepha**, an Aramaic common name which means rock, translated into Greek by the word **Petros** (Gal. 2:7, 8). He was from Bethsaida and a fisherman (Matt. 4:18-22; Jn. 1:40-42), married, and resident of Capernaum (Matt. 8:14; Mk. 1:29; 1 Cor. 9:5). He was a brother to Andrew and a disciple of John the Baptizer (Jn. 1:40-42). He was called to the apostolate by Jesus beside the Lake of Gennesaret (Matt. 4:18-22; Mk. 1:16-20; Lk. 5:1-11). The gospel tradition gives Peter a certain preeminence among the Twelve even during the life of the Master. With the sons of Zebedee, James and John, Peter is one of the intimates of Jesus among the Twelve (Mk. 1:15; Matt. 4:18; 5:37; 9:2), and even among these intimates he holds the first position (Lk. 5:1; Matt. 14:28; Mk. 8:29; 9:5) and was spokesman for the Twelve with the Master (Matt. 16:16; 18:21; Lk. 12:41; Mk. 10:28). When the Passion was imminent Peter more than the others protested his loyalty, which however he soon betrayed by denying Jesus three times as Jesus himself had predicted (Matt. 26:33-35; Mk. 14:29-31; Lk. 22:33, 34; Jn. 13:36-38).

After the resurrection, it is for Peter that the women receive the message from the angel (Mk. 16:7) and to him the Lord appeared (1 Cor. 15:5; Lk. 24:34). John's gospel gives a certain importance to the disciple whom Jesus loved, without however hiding the preeminence of Peter, which was also pointed out by the Synoptics (Jn. 13:24; 18:15). This position is sanctioned and acknowledged by the lists of the Twelve which always have Peter in the first place (Mk. 3:16; Lk. 6:14; Acts 1:13 and Matt. 10:2 expressly underline the fact).

The name given by Jesus to Simon is explained in Matthew 16:18, which is inserted here as Jesus' response to Peter's confession of Christ's messiahship. Though it may have been pronounced on another occasion, perhaps during the Last Supper (*see* Lk. 23:31-34), its authenticity is on sound foundations. The interpretation of the text is a delicate matter since it is composed of three very common metaphors of biblical tradition, the meaning of which does not become immediately apparent. The name given by Jesus is in direct relationship with his function as foundation which should secure for the eschatological messianic community of the saved consistency and durability (*see* the use of the expression in Jer. 12:16; 24:6; 31:4; Zech. 3:9; 4:7 and Matt. 7:24, 25). On the metaphor of the keys *see* KEYS.

The power entrusted to Peter is further specified as the power to tie and loose, which, in accordance with the use of the expression in the Jewish tradition, comprises the power to declare something prohibited or licit, or to impose, or dispense from, an obligation. This power must be in the context of the power that Peter received, namely authority in the service of the community as it tended towards its eschatological end as expressed in the previous metaphor.

In Luke 23:31-34, immediately after having predicted Peter's denial, Jesus addresses him with words that are an echo of Matthew 16:18. The tribulation that is to be Jesus' lot will also strike the disciples. In fact the passion is first and foremost the supreme conflict between Jesus and Satan who will try to bring the disciples too to ruin (Lk. 4:31), just as he succeeded in the case of Judas the traitor (22:21-23; 22:53). Jesus however pledges to intercede for Peter with the Father so that his faith will not fail. In his turn Peter must confirm his brothers. It can be said that Luke 23:31-34 proposes one of the fundamental components of the service that Peter is to give the Church to assure its consistency and endurance to the end. John 21 reports how Jesus, with evident reference to the triple denial, now confers on him the care of his flock, the people who have been saved through Jesus' work. To this purpose Jesus makes use of one of the most common biblical images to express the relationship between God and his people. *See* SHEPHERD.

Acts 1-12 shows Peter in the effective direction of the nascent church. He proposes that the group of the Twelve be completed again after the defection of Judas (Acts 1:15-26). It is he who speaks for the group (Acts 2:2, 4, 5, 29). Even when he appears in the company of John, Peter is obviously the leader and representative of the Twelve and of all the faithful (5:15).

The authority of Peter however is not isolated from the group of the Twelve. Together they have responsibility for the church and the diffusion of the gospel. So Peter and John are sent to Samaria (Acts 8:14) and later Peter alone visits the communities of western Palestine, and makes the definitive step for admitting the first Gentile to the church (Acts 10). He was imprisoned in the persecution in which James perished, and after his miraculous liberation, he left Jerusalem for some other unnamed destination (Acts 12:14).

After this episode there is no trace of Peter until we find him again at Jerusalem around 49-50 A.D. for the Council of Jerusalem (Gal.2; Acts 15) and later at Antioch (Gal. 2: 11-14) where between himself and Paul an outspoken confrontation took place in which Paul reproved him for his equivocal behavior in regard to the Gentile converts and their observance of the Jewish Law.

1 Corinthians 1:12; 3:22 leads one to believe that there was a "Peter's group" at Corinth, and that therefore Peter preached at Corinth. The inscription of 1 Peter 1:1 suggests that Peter exercised the ministry in differ-

ent regions of Asia Minor. 1 Peter 5:13 sufficiently indicates his presence at Rome where he suffered martyrdom during Nero's persecution (67/68 A.D.). A well-founded tradition places Peter's martyrdom and burial on the Vatican hill, under the altar of the Confession in St. Peter's Basilica.

Peter, Letters of, The New Testament contains two letters which are attributed to the pen of Peter. The first letter is addressed to the inhabitants of the diaspora of Pontus, Galatia, Cappadocia, Asia and Bithynia (1:1), all regions in Asia Minor. The author has particularly in mind the Christians converted from paganism (1:18-19; 2:9-10; 4:3-4). The body of the letter contains no concrete references to the particular circumstances of the destinataries. So the letter is more an encyclical or circular letter with an exposition of some points of Christian doctrine that could be addressed to a large and widespread group of readers. The letter abounds in exhortation, especially to faithfulness in the midst of tribulation and persecution, which however is not further specified (2:12; 3:16; 4:15-16). The author is inspired in his exhortation by the themes connected with baptism (1:3, 23; 2:2; 9:18-22). For this reason authors are more than justified in seeing in 1 Peter a reflective commentary on baptismal catechesis.

The author claims to be "Simeon Peter, servant and apostle of Jesus Christ" (1:1 and *see* 5:1, 13). This assertion however does not seem to hold against considerations of language and style. Moreover the theology is remarkably Pauline in tone. A sufficient explanation for this can be had in 5:12 where the author states that he wrote through Silvanus, Paul's companion. Silvanus was not just secretary or scribe, but editor if not author of the letter.

Again some insist that the reference to persecutions threatening the church suppose a date much later than Peter's death—around 90 A.D. under Domitian. However the text does not oblige one to suppose that it refers only to the great official and systematic persecutions that are known from the history of the church. They refer to the first anti-Christian movements that were destined to gather momentum and break loose in the imperial persecutions. The objections to Petrine authorship, with Silvanus' cooperation, are not sufficient to bear the day, and so the letter should be dated at Rome between 64 and 67 A.D. (5:13). On 3:19-4:6 *see* DESCENT INTO HELL.

The second letter does not identify those to whom it was written besides the generic fact that they were Christian (1:1-2). The only theme of the letter is the **parousia** or second coming of Christ. It exhorts the recipients to a standard of life that is in keeping with their expectation of the Lord's return (1:3-21) and warns against the false teachers who cast doubt on his future glorious reappearance (8:1-16). The central part (2:1-22) coincides so well in content, language and vocabulary with the letter of Jude that it seems impossible to deny literary relationship of one to the other. Which came first is however disputed, but more authors take it that 2 Peter depends on Jude.

The author claims to be Peter (1:1) who witnessed the transfiguration of the Lord (1:16-18) and who authored another letter (1 Pet.; 2 Pet. 3:1). It refers to the "Paul our beloved" (2 Pet. 3:15). This insistence however does not deceive the critics who hold that the letter's claim to authorship by Peter is fictitious. Not a few indications in the letter persuade one to date it towards the end of the first century. Its probable dependence on Jude would place it after 70 A.D. The author speaks in 3:2 of the "fathers," that is, the first Christian generation, and of the "apostles" in a way that makes one think of them as personages of the past. The parousia problem reflects the situation that developed acutely after the destruction of Jerusalem.

The canonicity of Peter was not universally accepted until the end of the fourth century. It is listed among the deuterocanonical works of the New Testament.

Pethahiah (peth′-a-hie′-ah), Personal name (1 Chron. 24:16; Ezra 10:23; Neh. 9:5; 11:24).

Pethor, A Mesopotamian city, place of origin of Balaam, who was called on by Balak to curse Israel (Num. 22:5; 23:7; Deut. 23:4).

Pethuel (pe-thoo′-el or peth′-yoo-el), Father of Joel the prophet (Joel 1:1).

Petra (pee′-tra), The capital city of the Nabataean kingdom.

Phanuel, (fa-noo′-el or fan′-yoo-el), The father of Anna (Luke 2:36).

Pharaoh (fair′-oh), An Egyptian term meaning "Great House," the title of the kings of Egypt from the eighteenth dynasty (around 1500 B.C.). *See* EGYPT.

Pharisees, From the Hebrew **perusim,** the separated ones, or the ones apart, a religious sect among the Jews, obscure in origin, but probably stemming from the Hasidean group, which had allied itself with the Maccabees. *See* HASIDEANS. The Pharisees recruited their members especially among the scribes and lay people. They were noted for their zeal for the Law of Moses. However, over and above the five books of the Torah, they subscribed to the whole chain of oral tradition that had come down uninterruptedly from Moses (*see* Matt. 15:2; Mk. 7:5). The oral tradition was taken as an interpretation or elucidation of the law, in order to unfold the whole substance of the law and moreover to safeguard that substance against any possibility of infraction. In doctrinal Judaism the Pharisees held an avant garde position. While the Sadducees kept rigidly to the letter of the Law of the Pentateuch, the Pharisees were able to assimilate more recent doctrines such as the resurrection from the dead, the judgment, and the existence of spirits and angels, which do not appear in the old books, but were nevertheless sought there by the Pharisees through a complicated and arduous exegesis.

The Pharisees were probably the most influential religious group in Judaism at the time of the New Testament. Their authority was acknowledged by the mass of the people, who felt more akin to this group, which stemmed from the middle classes, than to the more aristocratic priests and Sadducees. This however in no way prevented the Pharisees from openly despising the "people of the earth," ignorant of the law, incapable of its observance and therefore destined to perdition (Matt. 9:9-13; Mk. 2:13-17; Lk. 5:27-32; Jn. 7:19; 9:24-34).

Politically, the Pharisees were realists. While it is true that their intransigent attitude to the politico-religious pretensions of the Hasmonaeans earned them persecutions, this also prompted them to a cautious external behavior, even while treating with the Romans. Inwardly they nurtured a hearty despisal and aversion for anyone who dared subjugate God's people.

It seems that at the beginning the Pharisees had apocalyptic tendencies and their own messianic patrimony. The bitter experience of history, however, and especially the Jewish wars of 66-70 A.D. made them neglect if not forget altogether this typical element of biblical tradition.

It cannot be doubted but that Pharisaism was sustained by a sincere and zealous personal commitment—even though Christ did justly condemn the hypocrisy that infected some of the pharisaic zeal (*see* Matt. 15:1; Mk. 7:1; Lk. 18:9-14; Matt. 5:20; 23:1-39 and parallel texts), and substituted the law's absolutes for God's will.

The conflict that arose between Jesus and the Pharisees was predictable. First and foremost they found intolerable the claims to doctrinal authority which Jesus made so clearly in the Sermon on the Mount (Matt. 5:20 ff.). Equally unbearable to them was the apparent ease and nonchalance with which Jesus interpreted some of the precepts such as that of the sabbath (Matt. 12:2; Mk. 2:24; Lk. 6:2; Jn. 5:9) and the ritual purifications (Matt. 15:1; Mk. 7:1). Such interpretations put Jesus, for them, at the level of the publicans and sinners, whose company, in fact, Jesus preferred (Matt. 9:9-13; Mk. 2:13-17).

Jesus' message was aimed at confronting man with God and making the law a vehicle of God's will, but to the Pharisees it seemed to dismantle the whole of Moses' Torah and to reek of apostasy.

The gospel tradition passes a decidedly condemnatory judgment on the Pharisees, though the justice of this is disputed by some scholars. It is true that the evangelists are writing from a Christian point of view after years of conflict between church and synagogue, which was the Pharisees' stronghold. However the evangelists did not deform the substance of the conflict. The Pharisees were among Jesus' most bitter opponents (Matt. 22:15; Mk. 12:13; Lk. 20:20) and had a major part to play in the plots which eventually took Jesus to his death on the cross (Matt. 12:14; Mk. 3:6; Jn. 11:46-57).

Pharpar (far'-par), One of the rivers of Damascus (2 Kgs. 5:12). *See* ABANA.

Phaselis (fa-see'-lis), A city and sea port of Lycia in Asia Minor. It is mentioned among those to whom was addressed a letter of the Roman senate in favor of the Jews (138 B.C.; 1 Mac. 15:23).

Phicol (fie'-kol), Head of the army of Abimelech, king of Gerah, a contemporary of Abraham (Gen. 21:22-32) and Isaac (Gen. 26:26-31).

Philadelphia, 1. A city of Lydia in Asia Minor which had a Christian community in the early church. One of the letters of Revelation is addressed to Philadelphia. The community there is praised because, though not very strong, it had kept the commandments and had not disowned Christ's name (Rev. 1:11; 3:7-13).

2. The Greek name for Rabbah, capital of Ammon.

Philemon, Letter to (fi-lee'-mon), The shortest of Paul's letters, having a mere 25 verses. Philemon, to whom it was written, was a well-off Christian at Colossae (Col. 4:9, 17), who had been converted by Paul (Philem. 19) probably at Ephesus. A slave of his, named Onesimus, had fled the home of his master and sought asylum with Paul while he was a prisoner, probably at Rome (62-63 A.D.). He converted to Christianity and was sent back by Paul with this note asking Philemon to receive the fugitive with kindness as a brother in the faith. Nobody contests the Pauline origin of the letter. Despite its brevity the letter has its importance because it shows in a concrete case what the Christian attitude of the day towards slavery was. Christianity did not set out to overthrow this social organization in which it was born, even though slavery was in fact incompatible with Christian principles. A general belief in the imminence of the parousia (*see* PAROUSIA) was probably the reason the church at this time was reluctant to attempt whosesale changes for the betterment of society. The letter merely aims at changing the master-slave relationship into one of brotherhood, which radically opposes the old relationship of subjection and domination (*see* Col. 3:22; 4:1).

Philetus (fi-lee′-tus), A heretic, probably of gnostic bent, who denied the genuine Christian concept of the resurrection of the body (2 Tim. 2:17). *See* HYMENAEUS.

Philip, 1. One of the twelve disciples (Matt. 10:3; Mk. 3:18; Luke 6:14; Acts 1:13). He was a native of Bethsaida in Galilee. After John, Andrew and Peter, Philip was the fourth to be called. He was a friend of Nathanael (Jn. 1:43-46). He is especially mentioned in three scenes of John's gospel. Jesus asked him what should be done with the large crowd of followers who were now hungry (Jn. 6:1-15). In Jerusalem some Greeks who wished to have an interview with Jesus came to Philip to arrange it, and he with Andrew came to Jesus (Jn. 12:21, 22). Finally, during the Last Supper Philip addressed Jesus with the words: "Lord, show us the Father, and that will be enough for us" (Jn. 14:8).

2. Philip II, king of Macedonia (359-336 B.C.), and father of Alexander the Great.

3. Philip V, king of Macedonia (220-179 B.C.) who was defeated by the Romans at Cynocephalae in 197 B.C. (1 Mac. 8:5).

4. Philip, a friend of Antiochus IV Epiphanes (175-164 B.C.), who named him regent and tutor of his son and successor Antiochus V Eupator (164-161 B.C.). Philip, however, was ousted by Lysias (1 Mac. 6:14-18; 2 Mac. 9:29).

5. Philip, son of Herod I and Cleopatra of Jerusalem. He was husband of Salome, Herodias' daughter, tetrarch of the Transjordanian territories of Ituraea, Batanaea, Trachonitis, Araunitis, Gaulanitis and Panias (*see* Lk. 3:1) from 4 B.C.-34 A.D. He built the city of Caesarea Philippi (Matt. 15:13) and transformed Bethsaida, re-naming it Julia.

6. Philip also called Herod Philip, son of Herod I and of Mariamne the daughter of Simon the high priest. He was the first husband of Herodias (Mk. 6:17; Matt. 14:3), and father of Salome.

7. One of the seven Hellenist Jewish Christians chosen by the apostles to look after the feeding of the poor of the community at Jerusalem (Acts 6:1-6). He preached in Samaria (Acts 8:5-13) and converted the treasurer of the queen of Ethiopia (Acts 8:26-40). He continued preaching along the Mediterranean coast as far as Caesarea (Acts 8:40). Paul met him at Caesarea where the latter lived with his four virgin daughters who had the gift of prophecy (Acts 21:8, 3).

Philippi, A city of Macedonia founded by Philip II of Macedonia (359-336 B.C.). It was conquered by the Romans in 167 B.C. Paul and Silas visited it during the second apostolic journey (Acts 16:12) and received hospitality from Lydia of Thyatira, one of Paul's converts (Acts 16:13-15).

Paul cured a girl who had a divining spirit, to the great chagrin of her masters who saw their source of earning destroyed. They had Paul and Silas imprisoned. During the night an earthquake opened the prison doors, but Paul and Silas deliberately refused to escape (Acts 16:25-34). The amazed guard, with his family, converted to the faith. After their liberation Paul and Silas took leave of the brethren and set out for Thessalonica (Acts 16:16-17:1). Once more during the third missionary journey Paul visited Philippi (Acts 20:8). To the church at Philippi Paul addressed one of his letters. *See* PHILIPPIANS, EPISTLE TO THE.

Philippians, Epistle to the, With the epistles to the Ephesians, the Colossians, and Philemon, the letter to the Ephesians is known as one of the letters of the captivity, so called because it was written by Paul during one of his imprisonments. According to Philippians 1:13, 14 Paul was "in prison for the gospel." Some people had taken advantage of his confinement to preach the gospel with intentions inimical to Paul "thinking that it will make my imprisonment even harsher" (1:17). Paul then takes into consideration what the future holds for him, death, or liberty and a consequent renewal of his apostolic work: he inclines towards this second possibility (1:19-26). In 1:26 and 2:24 Paul hopes soon to be in a position to visit the church of Philippi. In conclusion Paul thanks the Philippians for their gifts: in accepting them Paul made an exception to his general policy in this regard (4:10-20).

It was traditionally held that Paul wrote the letter to the Philippians, as well as Colossians and Ephesians, during the same period, namely that of his imprisonment in Rome (Acts 28:30-31). Now however it seems that the letter to the Philippians belongs to another period of his life. In fact what Paul states in 1:12-26 about his confinement does not seem to be in keeping with what Acts 28:30, 31 tells of his imprisonment in Rome. More and more authors today hold to the opinion that Philippians was written by Paul at Ephesus during an imprisonment not recorded in Acts, which was the result of a commotion organized against him during the third apostolic journey (54-57 A.D.; Acts 19:8-20:1). This would explain how Paul could hope soon to visit Philippi (1:26) which in fact he did (Acts 20:1-2), something that would have proved difficult had Paul been writing from Rome. This, too, would explain the visit of Epaphroditus who came from Philippi to help Paul (4:18, 19). 3:2-4 evidently refers to the Judaizers and is better placed in Ephesus a little after Galatians and a little before Romans, which was written at Corinth at a later stage of the same journey.

Against this opinion has been advanced the mention of the "praetorium" (1:13), and of the Christians of "Caesar's household," which would seem to indicate Rome. One is not bound, however, to identify the praetorium with the praetorian guard of the emperor in Rome. "Praetorium" in general was the name given to the residence of the Roman governor of a given locality (*see* e.g. Pilate's "praetorium" in Jerusalem in Matt. 27:27; Mk. 15:16; Jn. 18:28, 33; 19:9). The "household of Caesar" not only included those in service in his residence but also all those in general who were in the service of the Roman emperor, in Rome or elsewhere.

As it stands today the letter to the Philippians is probably made up of at least three brief notes by Paul. This intense correspondence also suggests some place near Philippi, such as Ephesus, and not Rome. The reason for this division is the absence of unity and coherent development of any one theme. Scholars however are not agreed on the points of division. On some points there is accord: 4:10-23 would be a letter of thanks for help sent through Epaphroditus; a second letter seeks to reassure them about Epaphroditus, who had been sick but now was cured and was not returning. Paul also announces a mission for Timothy, to take place soon. The main intent of the letter, however, seems to have been to bring back peace and order to the disturbed community (2:19-30). This letter would then conclude in 4:2-7. A third letter, longer than the other two, takes up the crisis with more forthrightness. First it speaks of Paul's situation (1:1-31), then exhorts the people to peace, humility and concord (2:1-18) and finally upbraids the Judaizers who were causing the crisis, while driving home once more Paul's principles on justification and salvation (3:1-4:1). The principal uncertainties about this letter are the following: the chronological order of the last two and the way in which the doctrinal chapters are distributed (2:1-18 and 3:1-4:1).

Philippians 2:6-11 proposes as a theological foundation for the exhortation to humility and abnegation the example of Christ. In all probability the text is a christological hymn, being quoted by Paul. In this are described the phases of the mystery of Christ in accordance with a scheme similar to that of 1 Timothy 3:16; Colossians 1:15-20; Ephesians 1:3-14. The self-emptying of which 2:7 speaks is not just incarnation in the abstract, but the enfleshment of a Person who thus disrobed himself of the glory that properly belonged to him, given his divine nature (2:6). His humanity was totally akin to ours except that no sin marked him. He took on the condition of slavery. For his obedience to the death, God exalted him and gave him a name above all names, that is, conferred on him the divine name of Lord. It would of course be absurd to conclude that therefore Jesus then "became" God. The text affirms that at that moment Jesus acquired also for his humanity that glory and dominion that was his as God.

Philistines (fi-lis′-tinz, teenz, tines), In the Table of Nations the Philistines sprang from the Caphtorim who in turn are listed among the sons of Egypt (Gen. 10:13, 14). In other places, too, the Philistines are held to come from Caphtor (Amos 9:7; Jer. 47:4). Caphtor is in all probability Crete, or at least is to be sought in the Aegean basin. The connection with Egypt is by no means arbitrary, for the Philistines are part of the "sea peoples" who were driven by the Doric invasions towards the south, and attempted to penetrate into Egypt from the Sea. They were however repulsed by Ramses III (1196-1165 B.C.) and settled along the southern coastal region of Canaan where they established a confederation of five cities, from south to north along the coast, Gaza, Ashkelon, Ashdod, and inland, from south to north, Gath and Ekron. The Philistines were, from a military and cultural point of view, superior to the Canaanite and Israelite inhabitants of the land, and soon made their presence felt to effect. They brought to Palestine the use of iron. According to 1 Samuel 13:19-22 they exercised an oppressive monopoly in this field, through it reaping an undeniable military superiority and great economic advantages. In all of Saul's army there were only two swords, that of Jonathan and that of Saul.

With time the relationships between Israelites and Philistines became worse. In the Samson traditions the Philistines are "the rulers" (Jgs. 15:11), and to them the men of Judah and Dan were subject in a way that made any attempt at revolt foolish. The one case of intransigent defense of rights was that of Samson, who on that account became a national hero, even though his exploits had a merely private character. Closer scrutiny however of the accounts reveal the possibility of easier coexistence and even familiar relationships between the Philistines and the Israelites. (*See* SAMSON.) The increasing power and numbers of the Philistines, however, forced the tribe of Dan to travel northwards from its original territory in search of more hospitable territory (Jgs. 18). In 1 Samuel the Philistines and the Israelites are already at war. The severe defeat that Israel suffered at Aphek also cost them the ark and caused a crisis among the people (1 Sam. 4). The tribal league had hitherto sufficed to fight off invaders from without. Now, however, it proved inadequate against the pretensions and oppression of the Philistines. The people demanded a king, Saul, "to rule us and lead us in warfare and fight our battles" (1 Sam. 8:20). With the king came the formation of an army of professional soldiers (1 Sam. 14:52). The Philistines had made their way right into the central mountain range (1 Sam. 13:15-18) but they were driven back and harshly punished by the Israelites at Michmash (1 Sam. 14:1-23) and at Elah, where according to tradition David distinguished himself in single combat against Goliath (1 Sam. 17; *see* DAVID; ELHANAN). There are also a few passages on partial conflicts (*see* 1 Sam. 18:17-30; 27:25-28). These glorious beginnings were darkened by the king's melancholy. In contrast to Samuel, Saul held David suspect and so alienated from himself the very support that could have helped command the situation. David went over to the Philistines as vassal though he did not take their part against Israel (1 Sam. 27; 29). The Philistines decided to give battle and advanced on the plain of Jezreel while Saul and his men took up position on the mountains of Gilboa (2 Sam. 28:1-7). The battle turned against Israel, and Saul and Jonathan died (1 Sam. 31). In the meantime David had strengthened his position. He became king of Judah (2 Sam. 2:1-5) and of Israel (2 Sam. 5:1-5), and gave first priority to the solution of the Philistine question. The course of his maneuvers is not described in detail (2 Sam. 5:17-25; 21:15-22; 23:9-17), but success was complete. The Philistines returned to their own lands, and with the exception of sporadic and limited incursions (1 Kgs. 15:27; 16:15; 2 Kgs. 18:18; 2 Chron. 21:16; 26:6), they no longer constituted a danger to the existence of the two kingdoms of the Israelites.

They did continue to exist as an enclave of cities at the edge of Judah and suffered the same vicissitudes as Judah at the hands of the Assyrians. The prophetic books contain numerous oracles against the Philistine cities (Isa. 14:18-31; Jer. 47:1-7; Ezek. 16:27, 57; 25:15, 16) which are still re-echoed in the second century B.C. in Sirach 50:26.

Philologus (fi-lol′-o-gus), A Christian in Rome greeted by Paul in Romans 16:15.

Phinehas (fin′e-as), 1. Son of Eleazar and nephew of Aaron (Ex. 6:25; 1 Chron. 5:30) who is recorded in the biblical tradition because of the zeal he showed against the Canaanite cult of Baal which had seduced Israel on the plains of Moab (Num. 25:6-13; 31:6; Ps. 106:30, 31; Sir. 45:23-25; 1 Mac. 2:26). For this loyalty he received the promise of an enduring priesthood. Phinehas was sent to rebuke the Transjordan tribes of Reuben, Gad and the half-tribe of Manasseh for having built an immense altar near the circle of stones in Canaanite territory. When the Transjordan tribes cleared their name, Phinehas brought back their answer to the land of Canaan and the Israelites (Josh. 22:11-34).

2. Son of Eli, priest of Shiloh and brother of Hophni (1 Sam. 1:3). The sons were priests like their father, but were guilty of grave abuses in their priestly ministry by filching meat from the sacrifice, and even taking it while it was still raw. Thus they treated with contempt the offering made to Yahweh (1 Sam. 2:12-17). Through Samuel God predicted an end to Eli's house for the sins of his sons. Phinehas and Hophni went into the battle of Aphek with the ark of the covenant, but they were killed and the ark was captured (1 Sam. 4:2-11). Phinehas' wife was pregnant at the time, and at the news of the tragedy she went into labor and brought forth a boy whom she called Ichabod, who continued the priestly line as far as Abiathar, a priest of David who was deposed by Solomon in favor of Zadok (1 Sam. 2:12-36; 4; 1 Kgs. 2:26-27).

Phlegon, A Christian in Rome, greeted among others by Paul in Romans 16:14.

Phoebe, A deaconess of the church of Cenchreae, port of Corinth. Paul asks the Roman Christians to give her a worthy welcome (*see* Romans 16:1,2).

Phoenicia, A strip of coast land along the Mediterranean from the River Eleutherus (today Nahr-el-Kebir) to the north and to Mt. Carmel to the south. In ancient times it was inhabited by a semitic people of the Canaanite group, organized in city-states which often were rivals one to the other. Principal among these were Tyre, Sidon, Byblos and Ugarit. On account of the mountains to the east, the region is small, but it is fertile. The Phoenicians however did not win their name for agriculture but for their sea-going exploits. In fact the territory has many natural harbors, and being closed in by the mountains from behind, it was geographically apt for maritime undertakings. The Phoenicians were the undisputed lords of maritime commerce between 1500 and 700 B.C. when first they became rivals and later subjects of the Greeks. On the relationships between the Israelites and the Phoenicians *see* HIRAM, SIDON, TYRE. The chief sources for information on the Canaanite religion come from Phoenicia. *See* BAAL, UGARIT.

Phoenix, A port on the southern coast of Crete mentioned in the itinerary of Paul on his way to Rome (Acts 27:12).

Phrygia, A region in the western half of Asia Minor south of Bithynia. Paul went through it on his second (Acts 16:6) and third apostolic journeys (Acts 18:23). Among the cities of the region are Colossae, Hierapolis and Laodicaea, in each of which there was a Christian community (Col. 2:1; 4:13; Rev. 3:14).

Phygelus (fie´-je-lus), A Christian of Asia Minor who, with Hermogenes and others, abandoned Paul (2 Tim. 1:15).

Phylacteries, A literal interpretation of texts such as Exodus 13:9, 16 and Deuteronomy 6:18; 11:8 brought about among the Jews the habit of carrying biblical texts in capsules on the forehead and on the left arm at the height of the heart (Ex. 13:1-16; Deut. 6:4-9; 11:13-21). They were appended to head or arm by strips of cloth (*see* Matt. 23:5). The phylactery had to be worn by every male Jew during his morning prayer

Physician, *See* MEDICINE.

Pibeseth (pie-bee´-zeth), A city of Egypt in the Nile Delta (Ezek. 30:17).

Pi-hahiroth (pie´-ha-hie´-roth), The first encampment of the Israelites after the crossing of the Red Sea (Ex. 14:2, 9; Num. 33:8). *See* EXODUS.

Pilate, Pontius Pilate was Roman prefect of Judea 26-36 A.D. In extra-biblical sources of Josephus and Philo, Pilate is portrayed as a cruel and insensitive person who delighted in offending the religious sentiments of his Jewish subjects whenever he suspected anti-Roman sentiments or movements towards revolt. This should be discounted to some extent, for Philo at least was prejudiced and unreliable as a reporter of events in Palestine. In Pilate's defense it may be said that the Jews, in truth, were a difficult people to govern—proud, resentful of the Roman yoke, certain of their national resurrection at some longed-for moment in history, quick to protest. It was Rome's policy to allow the Jews control over their religion except for the appointment of the high priest. In practice it was difficult, if not impossible, to draw a line between religion and politics: the categories of Greco-Roman thought cannot be applied to Judaism. The Jews of the first century were constantly vexing their Roman governors by their missions to Rome to appeal over the heads of the prefects to the emperor, or by seemingly stepping over the line between religious activity and political, not to say rebellious, activity. To the Jews it looked quite the opposite: that Roman prefects were constantly defiling their Temple and insulting their religious traditions, and thereby not carrying out the emperor's orders. Little wonder that the Roman governors chose to live in Caesarea rather than in the national capital.

To Pilate's credit is the building of an aqueduct from Bethlehem to Jerusalem which provided the capital and the Temple with an ample water supply for all contingencies for the first time, and was an example of Rome's engineering capabilities. Pilate is often accused of weakness of character (Matt. 27:11-26; Mk. 15: 1-15; Lk. 23:1-25; Jn. 18:29-19:17). Perhaps his action is better explained by the two motifs of his rule: on the one hand his complete inability to understand the Jews and everything Jewish, and on the other the determination not to compromise his position as prefect which was already endangered by repeated complaints of the Jews (*see* Jn. 19:12). His shaky standing in Rome probably explains why Herod Antipas wanted no part of a decision Pilate had to make (Lk. 23:12).

A few years after the trial of Jesus, Pilate was suspended from office by Vitellius, the superior-ranking provincial legate to Syria, and ordered to Rome to account to Emperor Tiberius, charged by Samaritans with having suppressed a religious manifestation on their holy mountain, Gerizim. This event, again, was not without political overtones, for the Samaritans involved were all bearing arms. Subsequent events within Samaria make Pilate's apparently harsh conduct in this episode seem almost lenient, for Vespasian's general, Cerealis, according to Josephus, slaughtered 11,600 Samaritans on Mt. Gerizim. Before Pilate arrived in Rome, Tiberius died. Though a Jewish mission appeared to bring charges against Pilate for the Samaritan incident, the new emperor, Caligula, gave Pilate a friendly verdict and retired him without other penalty. Legends about Pilate's ultimate fate are but legends; he slips out of history.

That Pilate's title was "prefect" and not "procurator" has recently been proven by the inscription on a stone found in the city of Caesarea, which while incomplete can clearly be reconstructed as a tribute to Tiberius from Pontius Pilatus, *praefectus Iudaeae*—a stone originally used in the Tiberium, a building Pilate had erected in honor of the emperor. The traditional title "procurator" is based on anachronisms in the writings of Josephus: during the reigns of Augustus and Tiberius governors of Judea were "prefects." Not until the time of Claudius (41-54 A.D.) was the position called "procurator." In the Greek Mss. of the New Testament Pilate is called simply "governor."

Pildash, A son of Nahor, Abraham's brother (Gen. 22:22).

pillar
into a *p.* of salt	Gen. 19:26	The *p.* which he named	
memorial *p.* in Shechem	Jgs. 9:6		2 Sam. 18:18
p. and erected it	2 Sam. 18:18		

Pinon (pie′-non), One of the chiefs of Esau-Edom (Gen. 36:41; 1 Chron. 1:52). *See* ESAU.

Piram (pie′-ram), King of Jarmuth, a Canaanite city south of Jerusalem; he allied himself with the king of Jerusalem against Joshua.

Pirathon (pir′-a-thon), A town in the land of Ephraim, birthplace of Abdon, who was one of the minor judges (Jgs. 12:13-15) and of Benaiah, one of the thirty warriors of David (2 Sam. 23:30).

Pisgah, A range of mountains in Transjordan rising from the plain of Moab, opposite Jericho (Num. 21:20; 23:14; Deut. 3:17; 4:49). From here Moses contemplated the promised land (Deut. 3:27). According to Deuteronomy 32:48 Moses climbed Mt. Nebo which is one of the peaks of the Pisgah (Deut. 34:1).

Pishon, One of the four rivers of Eden according to the legendary geography of Genesis 2:11. *See* EDEN.

Pisidia (pi-sid′-i-a), A region in the central southern part of Asia Minor, between Galatia to the north and Pamphylia to the south. The capital of the area was Pisidian Antioch, which was evangelized by Paul on his first apostolic journey (Acts 13:14-51; 14:21).

Pispa, Son of Jether of the tribe of Asher (1 Chron. 7:38).

pit

p. he has made	Ps. 7:16	down into the *p.*	Ps. 30:4
sunk in the *p.*	Ps. 9:16	adulteress is a deep *p.*	Prov. 22:14
	Terror, *p.* Isa. 24:17		

Pitch, Pitch was used of old to seal ships. It was spread inside and outside the hull (*see* Gen. 6:14; Ex. 2:3).

Pithom (pie′-thom), A city of Egypt, in the construction of which the Israelites labored before the Exodus (Ex. 1:11). It lay in northeastern Egypt, east of the Nile delta, in Goshen; but its exact site has not been determined.

Pithon (pie′-thon), A descendant of King Saul, of the tribe of Benjamin (1 Chron. 8:35; 9:41).

Plagues of Egypt, Plague is the translation for **maggephah,** which strictly speaking is the mark left by a blow, and is used metaphorically to designate a misfortune sent by God in punishment. Above all, however, the name has come to mean the pestilences which God inflicted on the Pharaoh of Egypt in order to force the release of the chosen people from their bondage. The account of these plagues is read in Exodus 7-13. The law of the Pasch is inserted into the account of the last plague, the death of the first-born of Egypt. The reader of these accounts today finds himself puzzled on many points, which call for comment on three levels: a. the text in the actual form in which today we have it; b. the sources used; and c. the beginnings of the tradition.

a. The account is given in accordance with a carefully drawn up plan, which immediately reveals its artificiality. The introduction already presents the master themes that are woven through the whole story. Moses is to exercise his prophetic office before Pharaoh, handing on to him God's message: "Let my people go." God himself had made it known to Moses that his request should not be honored, but that God should then multiply his prodigies to bring home to the Egyptians that it was Yahweh who spoke. These prodigies, the plagues, are then above all to be understood as God's way of revealing himself to the Egyptians. Only secondarily (Ex. 10:2) is the revelation also addressed to the Israelites. (*See* also Deut. 6:20; 29:1-3, 28 S.) Here then is the key to the solution of one of the enigmas of the story. the prolonged contrast between the Pharaoh and God is no indication of weakness on God's part. The very reluctance on the part of the Pharaoh and his persistence in disobedience took place because God willed it so as to give God an occasion to show himself for what he is, Yahweh, the Lord, who reveals himself in power and prodigy. God then makes the heart of the Pharaoh obstinate (7:13, 22; 8:11, 15, 28; 9:7, 35). While interpreting this "hardening of the heart of the Pharaoh" two errors must be avoided. First, this is not a psychological presentation of the facts, but a theological one, as is frequently the case with the Bible. On the other hand the text, like Romans 9:14 which refers to it, is not dealing with the personal predestination of the Pharaoh, that is, the grace of conversion or final reprobation. The Bible is exclusively interested in the role God makes him play in the history of salvation and the realization of his salvific plan. God employs two persons to bring about the saving of his people: Moses and the Pharaoh. With different functions, under God's control, they cooperate towards the same end of glorifying the name of God. Moreover the whole description by the author is aftersight, a reflection on what happened in the past, as well as being apologetic in purpose, that is, the author is bent on safeguarding the incontestable omnipotence of God. The event is described in such a way that the negative answer of the Pharaoh could not be interpreted as opposing the omnipotence of God. The Pharaoh's reluctance had already been counted on by God, not simply foreseen, but willed. God willed the Pharaoh's reluctance, and made use of it to bring Moses to docility. The story of the plagues follows a coherent rhythm. The number ten shows in itself a certain completeness. In a series of ten, number three and number seven are outstanding numbers. Logical it was then that with the third and seventh plague there is an increasing intensity.

After the opening skirmishes with the Pharaoh's magicians the water turns to blood and frogs swarm over the land. These prodigies however are also effected by the magicians (Ex. 7:8-14; 7:22, 25; 8:3). With the third plague however a decisive victory is won for Moses, for the magicians failed to bring forth gnats by their magic arts (8:14). At this the magicians themselves told the Pharaoh: "This is the finger of God" (8:15). With the fourth plague yet a new element makes its appearance: the Egyptians, but not the Israelites, are victims. This further dissipates any ambiguity that might have arisen (the flies: 8:16-20; the pestilence and death of the Egyptians' livestock, 9:1-7; the boils, 9:8-12). On the other hand the Pharaoh's obstinacy begins to soften, and concessions are made (8:21). As was to be expected, the seventh plague has particular importance. The new introduction indicates another decisive step. God threatens to send "all his blows" upon Egypt (9:14) and hurled down a hail storm on those who had refused to believe and take refuge (9:20). At this evidence the Pharaoh exclaims: "The Lord is just, it is I and my subjects who are at fault" (9:27). In accordance with what God had foretold through Moses, however, the Pharaoh once more becomes obdurate (Moses 9:35). With the eighth plague of locusts (10:1) and the ninth of darkness (10:21), new concessions are made. With the tenth however, the death of the first-born, not only does he permit, he commands the chosen people to go: "Take your flocks, too, and your herds, as you demanded, and begone; and you will be doing me a favor" (12:32). God's victory is complete.

b. The redactor of these chapters ably fused the accounts he found in the Yahwist and Priestly documents into a neat ten plagues. (*See* PENTATEUCH.) The Yahwist source contains only seven plagues, while the Priestly source certainly contains five, the first, second, third, sixth and tenth. An examination of the artful fusion shows that what are described as different plagues are in reality different versions of the same episode, e.g. the third of gnats in P is the fourth of flies in J, which also holds for the fifth of pestilence in J and the sixth of boils in P. This distinction in the sources is remarkably confirmed by Psalm 78:43-51 which enumerates only seven plagues, the Yahwist ones, and in the following order: 1st, 4th, 2nd, 8th, 7th, 5th, 10th. Psalm 105 has eight plagues, listed thus: 9th, 1st, 2nd, 4th, 3rd, 7th, 8th, 10th.

c. Is it possible to reach beyond these sources to what happened? It must be kept in mind that Exodus 7-13 and Psalm 78:105 are not the only texts, nor do they represent the only way, in which Scripture speaks of the plagues of Egypt. When the Exodus is mentioned, a form that is frequently used and undoubtedly enjoys great antiquity and value is the following:

"The Lord then brought us out of Egypt with his strong hand and wrought before our eyes **signs and wonders**, great and dire, against Egypt and against Pharaoh and his whole house" (Deut. 6:22; *see* Deut. 4:34; 7:19; 26:8; Josh. 24:5, etc.). These signs and wonders are nothing other than the plagues. As historical documents these have more value than Exodus 7-13 even though the amount of information transmitted in these texts is minimal. However it is possible to determine important elements from the terminology used: signs and wonders. "Wonder" in Hebrew is **mopheth**, a portent or prodigy, which is not only used of miraculous events but also of episodes that presage something else, or have meaning, or are instructive and teach a lesson (*see* Isa. 8:19). "Sign," **oth**, in its concrete use in these cases, means a sign that reveals the active presence of God in the exercise of his work of judgment and salvation. A very similar use of both terms is found in Deuteronomy 28:46 at the conclusion of the list of curses on the transgressors of the Covenant. These curses are natural calamities that will fall on whoever disobeys God. In both cases (the plagues of Egypt and Deut. 28:46) the text deals with events that are considered to be arranged by God and the result of his intervention as Judge. In this sense they are signs and prodigies, that is, in them is revealed the presence of God as judge and savior: "This is the finger of God" (Ex. 8:15). The epic account of 7-13 does not oblige us to catalogue these events in the theological category of miracle. *See* SIGNS.

The account of the Exodus is always tied to the memory of a certain number of calamities that hit Egypt, or rather, the region where the Israelites had been living, and which were interpreted by the prophetic word (*see* SALVATION HISTORY) as **oth** and **mopheth**, signs and wonders, the concrete expression of the divine judgment on the oppression and the anticipation therefore of his saving action in favor of his elect.

What value then have the facts narrated in Exodus 7-13? One could think of them as concrete examples of the type of event that was usually interpreted as sign and prodigy, without their containing any real link with what actually happened. It is interesting however to note that the greater part of the events narrated are typical for Egypt—locusts, flies, darkness, i.e. sand-storms, or episodes which because of their infrequency, would constitute a prodigy, such as hail. The most curious one is the water turned into blood, which is nothing other than the color of the Nile waters at its mouth, and could therefore only with difficulty be considered a plague or a prodigy by those acquainted with the phenomenon. In the Exodus presentation of the event, theological interpretation pervades the account. What was the fruit of a prophetic interpretation and an object of faith became an account of what really happened. Here are present and active the resources of epic style and popular story-telling.

plant

p. that bears seed	Gen. 1:11, 12	you *p.* a vineyard	Deut. 28:30
not *p.* a sacred pole	Deut. 16:21	like a young *p.*	Job 14:9

pleasant

how *p.* the country	Gen. 49:15	the *p.* harp	Ps. 81:3
fallen on *p.* sites	Ps. 16:6	and how *p.*	Ps. 133:1

Pledges, *See* LOANS.

Pleiades (plee′-a-deaz), A constellation of stars (Job 38:31; Amos 5:8).

Pleroma (ple-roe′-ma), A Greek word often used by Paul to denote the sum total or superabundance of God or Christ, or his blessing (Rom. 15:29; Eph. 3:19) or the fulness of time (Gal. 4:4; Eph. 1:10). *See* BODY.

plot

| in the *p.* of ground | Josh. 24:32 | middle of the *p.* | 2 Sam. 23:12 |
| a *p.* of land | 2 Sam. 23:11 | that very *p.* of ground | 2 Kgs. 9:26 |

plowshares

| beat their swords into *p.* | | Beat your *p.* into swords | Joel 4:10 |
| | Isa. 2:4; Mic. 4:3. | | |

plummet

| and with the *p.* | 2 Kgs. 21:13 | *p.* in hand | Amos 7:7 |
| | I answered, "A *p.*" | Amos 7:8 | |

Poetry, One of the forms in which the joys and sorrows, aspirations and concerns of a primitive people first begin to be expressed. Prose, on the other hand, seems more like an aftergrowth. Poetry is rhythmical and free-flowing in form, like the naturalistic motions of the primitive dance which it so frequently accompanied in ancient times (Ex. 15:20-21). Here we can deal only with the peculiarities that distinguish Hebrew poetry.

The semitic nations have nothing approaching an epic poem, in contrast to non-semitic neighbors. In the case of the Hebrews this lack may be due to the fact that Israel proclaimed but one God and not a collection of unruly, jealous and competing gods, demi-gods and titans. As for dramatic poetry, the Hebrew character seemed to have no faculty for it; at least we have no example, for the Book of Job is neither truly a dramatic poem nor Hebrew, containing nothing specifically Hebraic and much (especially its pessimism) foreign to Israel, so that most critics view it as a basically Edomitic work. What the Hebrews did produce, and even excel in, was lyric and gnomic poetry.

The lyric element goes back to pre-Mosaic times: a snatch is preserved in Lamech's sword speech (Gen. 4:23f). Five fragments from the Exodus experience survived the editorial development of the Pentateuch: the Song of Miriam (Ex. 15:21), the Blessing of Moses (Num. 10:35f), the Lord's Leadership (Num. 21:14f), the Song of the Well (Num. 21:17f), and a Victory Song of Israel (Num. 21:27-30). Lyric poetry flourished in rude vigor during the heroic age of the judges (notably in Joshua's Victory Shout [Josh. 10:12b-13a], the Song of Deborah [Jgs. 5], and Samson's Riddle [Jgs. 14:14, 18]). (Happily all these and others are now printed in verse form in all modern versions of Scripture.) It reached perhaps its highest excellence in David, the warrior-poet, notably in his lament over Saul and Jonathan, and over Absalom. Laments and dirges of great beauty are frequent in Scripture (Pss. 22, 79, 83; Amos 5:1f; Micah 1:10-14; Jer. 9:17-21; the Book of Lamentations). Lyrics were composed to celebrate a marriage (Ps. 45), a birth (1 Sam. 4:20), a victory (Gen. 4:23), the digging of a well (Num. 21:17f), and many other secular occasions. They were preserved no doubt because they were poetry and easier to commit to memory and pass on in unaltered form. (*See* also, of course, PSALMS.)

Gnomic poetry is the product of a more advanced culture. It arises from the desire felt by the poet to express the results of the accumulated experiences of life in a beautiful and memorable form. It gives expression not like the lyric to the impassioned feelings of the moment, but to poised philosophic reflection. This class of poems is peculiarly semitic, and it represents the nearest approaches made by the people of that race to anything like philosophic thought. It is not reasoning in the Greek manner, but offers a distillation, or perhaps the results only—results which are the product of observation and reflection rather than of induction and argumentation. *See* WISDOM.

Hebrew poetry does not rhyme. Assonance, alliteration and rhyme, so common in occidental poetry, only occasionally occur in Hebrew poetry, not being in any way essential. Nor is there a regular recurrence of long or short syllables or feet, but the rhythmical tendency was strongly felt, and unconsciously led to producing lines of the same number of main accents, including at times a secondary accent. The line was made to end at a break in the sense, except in rare cases.

But the one overwhelmingly essential and noticeable characteristic of Hebrew poetry is parallelism. By this is meant that the sentiment of one line is echoed or built upon in the next. This parallelism is of various kinds: 1. Synonymous, when the thought of the first line is repeated in slightly different words in the second line: "And now, O kings, give heed;/ take warning, you rulers of the earth."

2. Progressive parallelism, in which the second line expresses a new idea more or less closely related to the first, as in Job 3:17: "There the wicked cease from troubling,/ there the weary are at rest."

3. Synthetic or constructive parallelism, in which there is parallelism of structure only, while the thought of one line serves as the foundation upon which to build a new thought: "The precepts of the LORD are right, rejoicing the heart;/ The command of the LORD is clear, enlightening the eye." (Ps. 19:9)

4. Climactic parallelism, in which the characteristic words are repeated and form the ladder on which the thought climbs to completion or to emphatic reiteration: "The LORD will guard you from all evil;/ he will guard your life./ The LORD will guard your coming and going,/ both now and forever." (Ps. 121:7-8)

5. Antithetic parallelism, in which the thought is made more clear by contrast: "The wicked man flees although no one pursues him;/ but the just man, like a lion, feels sure of himself." (Prov. 28:1)

6. Comparative, in which the thought is explained by comparison with something else that is familiar: "As the shepherd snatches from the mouth of the lion/ a pair of legs or the tip of an ear of his sheep,/ So the Israelites who dwell in Samaria shall escape/ with the corner of a couch or a piece of a cot." (Amos 3:12)

The New Testament contains little poetry except quotation from the Old and four songs that found their way into the liturgy of the early Church: the Magnificat (Lk. 1:46-55), the Benedictus (Lk. 1:68-79), the Gloria in Excelsis (Lk. 2:14) and the Nunc Dimittis (Lk. 2:29-32).

Polytheism, Asserting or holding to the plurality of gods, and thereby denying the one true God. Israel's history is marked by an enduring war against polytheism. *See* IDOLATRY, MONOTHEISM.

Pontius Pilate, *See* PILATE.

Pontus, A mountainous region in Asia Minor lying on the south shore of the Black Sea, east of Bithynia. There were Jewish (Acts 2:9) and Christian communities there (1 Pet. 1:1). Part of it became a Roman province after Pompey's conquest of the area.

pool

at the *p.* of Gibeon	2 Sam. 2:13	at the *p.* of Samaria	1 Kgs. 22:38
near the *p.* in Hebron	2 Sam. 4:12	wash in the *p.* of Siloam	Jn. 9:7

poor

the *p.* among you	Ex. 23:11 If a man is *p.*	Lev. 14:21
the *p.* give less	Ex. 30:15 hand to your *p*	Deut. 15:11
	blest are the *p.* Matt. 5:3	

Porathai (poe-ray′-tha-i), A son of Haman, the vizier of King Ahasuerus (Esth. 9:8). *See* HAMAN.

Posidonius, One of the three legates of the Seleucid Nicanor sent to propose a truce to Judas Maccabeus (2 Mac. 14:19).

Possession, Diabolical, *See* DEMONIAC.

Potiphar (pot′-i-far), An official of the Pharaoh of Egypt who bought Joseph as a slave. Potiphar's wife tried to seduce Joseph and when she failed she accused him of attempting carnal violence and showed the tunic she had pulled from him as evidence. Joseph was thrown into prison on this account (Gen. 37:36; 39).

Potiphera (po-tif′-e-ra), An Egyptian priest of On, father of Aseneth who became Joseph's wife (Gen. 41:45, 50; 46:20).

Potter's Field, Matthew recounts that Judas was struck to his heart with remorse at having betrayed innocent blood. He took the blood-money back to the priests and elders who refused it, so he flung it down in the sanctuary. The priests who had engineered Christ's condemnation were caught in a scruple about what to do with the price of their crime. They bought with it the potter's field for the burial of strangers, which thereafter was called **Akeldama,** the "Field of Blood." Acts 1:19 states that Judas himself bought the field. It was probably situated in the Valley of Gehinnon. *See* JUDAS.

Pottery, Pottery is man's most ancient product. The origins of the art and industry are placed in Jericho in neolithic times. In Palestine during Bible times, the raw material was fine red clay mixed with water. The clay was graded, washed and weathered and then mixed with water into a putty-like ball. In very early times this was then shaped by hand, but the potter's wheel was in use during most of the biblical period. The soft ball of wet clay was put on the center of the wheel which was then spun, either by an assistant or by the potter, while the latter shaped the vessel. The potter's wheel evolved into a foot-driven machine by the time Sirach 38:30 was written: "With his hands he molds the clay and with his feet softens it." The text describes the production: he bends alert to his work, flicking it with his finger, pummeling with his arm, softening it with his feet, and setting his heart on perfecting the glaze. The shaped clay was fired in a kiln. Israelite pottery was not remarkable for its decorative art.

Humble pottery, nevertheless, has provided biblical archaeology with an invaluable tool for dating. As Nelson Glueck has written: "Each era, from the pottery Neolithic period on, evolved its own styles, decorations and forms of pottery. Through empirical evidence it is possible to recognize the variations from one age to another and thus to establish the date of a period of occupation from pottery discoveries alone."

There are thirty-four different Hebrew and Aramaic terms for earthenware or pottery vessels, all of which are difficult to identify with exactitude. They included bowls, cups, cooking utensils, lamps, jars, pitchers, jugs, storage vessels, and even ornaments and toys.

The ease of production, the malleability of the materials, its brittleness when finished, all suggested figurative applications which the Bible authors used.

Isaiah upbraids those who think their evil designs are hidden from God:

"Is the potter no better than the clay? Can something that was made say of its maker, 'He did not make me'" (Isa. 29:16; *see* 41:45). The Psalmist threatens that the Lord will shatter his enemies like potter's ware (Ps. 2:9; Rev. 2:27-28). Ecclesiasticus says a man's conversation is his test, just as the kiln tests the potter's work (Sir. 27:5, 6). Paul invokes the figure of the potter and the vessel to refute the argument that God seems unjust in his designs (Rom. 9:21). *See* POTTER'S FIELD.

poured

and *p*. oil on	Gen. 28:18	who *p*. water	2 Kgs. 3:11
p. out oil	Gen. 35:14	spirit from on high is *p*. out	
p. some of the anointing oil			Isa. 32:15
	Lev. 8:12		

power

the *p*. of God		*p*. of God leading everyone	
	Matt. 22:29; Mk. 12:24		Rom. 1:16
the *P*. of God	Lk. 22:69		

Praetorium, The name given to the residence of the governor of a province or other territory of the Roman empire (Matt. 27:27; Mk. 15:16; Jn. 18:28, 33; 19:9). On the question of Pilate's praetorium in Jerusalem *see* GABBATHA. The palace built in Caesarea by Herod the Great was used afterwards as an habitual residence of the Roman governors of Judea (Acts 27:35).

praise

your brothers *p*.	Gen. 49:8	I will sing *p*.	Ps. 9:3
high in *p*.	Deut. 26:19	*p*. to my God	Ps. 104:33

Prayer, In Scripture prayer envelops the whole range of human attitudes and aspirations towards God and his wonderful works. There is petition, thanksgiving, narration and praise, astonishment, distress, contrition, adoration, meditation.

The patriarchs conversed with God in ways both surprising and frank, according to the traditions preserved in Genesis. When Cain, who murdered his brother, complained about the gravity of the punishment, God mitigated it for him (Gen. 3:9–16). The same conversational tone marks Abram's dealings with God (Gen. 15:2–3): "My Lord Yahweh, what do you intend to give me? I go childless. . . ." Jacob wrestles with God the whole night long, to receive the following compliment: "You shall no longer be spoken of as Jacob, but as Israel, because you have contended with divine and human beings and have prevailed" (Gen. 32:26–29). Moses tells God to relent in his wrath (Ex. 32:11–13).

In the Song of Moses, however, can be found the various expressions of Old Testament prayer. There is praise and confession to the whole world of the goodness and greatness of God (Deut. 32:1–3). The events of mercy God has brought about are called to mind as surety for his further faithfulness and protection (vv. 4–11). The whole of mankind is invited to join in the joy of God's praise, adoring him, proclaiming his goodness, with the total assurance that God will stand by his people (v. 43). In Moses' blessings on the tribes (c. 33) are spelled out his prayerful wishes, the granting of which will depend on Yahweh's loyalty (cf. e.g. Deut. 33:7).

In Job is illustrated the enigma of a good life beset with misfortune, calling into question the mercy of God, who promises good things to those who subject themselves to him. While Job expostulates with God because of his tragedy (Job 10:18ff.), his prayerful solution nevertheless is: "I know that you can do all things, and that no purpose of yours can be hindered. I have dealt with great things that I do not understand; things too wonderful for me, which I cannot know" (42:2, 3).

The Psalter was the liturgical prayerbook of the Old Testament, which was also assumed into the new convenant. Here can be found the whole range of human experience translated into prayer to God. Man's options in life, for or against God, are contrasted and decision is made (Ps. 1); the promised Messiah is called to mind in anticipation (Ps. 2); the wonder of the gift of creation breaks into song (Ps. 8); there is a cry for delivery from suffering and persecution (Ps. 7). Sins are lamented with the assurance of the joy of forgiveness (Ps. 51); God is relied upon even in the midst of one's worst enemies (Pss. 56, 57). The law of the Lord is constantly meditated (Ps. 119), while there is a song for the return from exile (Ps. 126). Praise, petition, thanksgiving and victory are all worked into the psalms (Pss. 145, 146, 147), while the book culminates in a cosmic hymn of praise (Ps. 148), a paean of triumph (Ps. 149), and an Alleluia chorus (Ps. 150).

The expected Messiah of the New Testament is a man of prayer. He prayed alone on the mountain (Matt. 14:23; cf. Lk. 9:18; Mk. 1:37). Christ was in prayer at his baptism (Lk. 3:21), spent the night in prayer before choosing his apostles (Lk. 6:12), was transformed in prayer at the transfiguration (Lk. 9:29). Christ broke into a prayer of exultation in Matthew 11:27-31, and Luke 9:18 records that he was "praying alone in the presence of his disciples." Eventually the disciples, seeing him pray, asked him to teach them too, whereupon he taught them the *Our Father*.

Christ culminated the last discourse with the priestly prayer of John 17. This is a prayer of glorification and petition. Christ asks that his redemptive work be brought to its fulfilment, and that its fruits be shared by the apostles and by those who should come through their word to him (vv. 1, 16, 17, 21ff.). Finally Christ poured out his anguished soul in the prayer of the garden (Lk. 22:39-46; cf. Matt. 26:36-46; Mk. 14:32-42), and on the cross with the words from Psalm 22.

Christ left to the community the word to pray always (Lk. 18:1), and guaranteed that the prayer of the Christian would not go unheard (Lk. 11:5-13; Matt. 18:19-20). Christ will perform whatever is asked in his name (Jn. 14:13, 14). In fact, the Father will grant whatever is needed, because he loves those who love Christ (Jn. 16:23, 26, 27).

How the Church from the beginning carried out Christ's command to pray can be gathered from Acts 2:42; 4:31. Paul's letters continually exhort the community to persevere in prayer (Col. 4:2; Eph. 6:18-20) and are themselves redolent with prayer (e.g. 1 Cor. 11:4-5; 11:13; 2 Cor. 1:11; Rom. 8:26; Phil. 1:4; 1 Tim. 2:1).

Christian prayer however is no mere pious meditation or human elevation of the soul to God. What makes the Christian prayer a part of the whole Christian mystery is that the Holy Spirit cries out in the Christian the very prayer of Christ: Abba, Father (Rom. 8:15; Gal. 4:4-8). Baptism welds the Christian, by the fires of the Spirit, into the surrender of Christ (Rom. 6:1-11) and from then on becomes the life source promised by Jesus (Jn. 4:14; 7:39) which enacts in the Christian Christ's own life (1 Jn. 3:24).

This prayer of the Christian takes place *par excellence* in the liturgy, when the Spirit in the community reenacts Christ's surrender and resurrection and gathers the people up into it ever more fully. While the liturgy climaxes the Spirit's prayerful activity, his presence permeates the rest of the Christian's day, making of it a continual oblation (Rom. 13:1). By the love which the Spirit infuses (Rom. 5:5; Gal. 5:22) it manifests the abiding presence of Christ (Jn. 13:34) and becomes the guarantee in the Christian that prayer will be granted (Eph. 1:13; 2 Cor. 1:22; 5:5).

Prayer, even particular prayer for particular objects, has God's own guarantee of being heard and granted (John 14.13). If then some particular request goes seemingly unheard, it is because its granting would run counter to the greater and immortal gifts that God will grant the Spirit asking in man.

prayer

make this *p.* to you	2 Sam. 7:27	Look kindly on the *p.*	
Look kindly on the *p.*	1 Kgs. 8:28		2 Chron. 6:19
offering this entire *p.*	1 Kgs. 8:54	a house of *p.*	Lk. 19:46

Prayer of Manasseh, A prayer attributed to Manasseh on his conversion. Both the attribution and the conversion are unsupported in history. *See* MANASSEH, 2.

Presbyter, From the Greek, meaning the older of two people, or the men of old, or an official in the synagogue. It can also mean the elder of a community. On its use *see* ELDERS, HIERARCHY.

Priest, In patriarchal society the function of the priest in offering sacrifice was exercised by the head of the family without any intervention of a constituted priest. Abraham (Gen. 22) and Jacob (Gen. 31:54) offer sacrifices, erect altars and call on the name of God (Gen. 12:8). The Israelite priesthood appears, already constituted, with every detail, in the Priestly source of the Pentateuch and the books of Chronicles. The priests are the sons of Aaron, Moses' brother. Aaron and his sons Nadab, Abihu, Eleazar and Ithamar are consecrated priests with a special rite on Sinai (Lev. 8:1-10:20). When Nadab and Abihu proved unfaithful in the ministry they were struck by God in his anger and died (Lev. 10:1-5) so that the priestly families claimed descent only from Ithamar or Eleazar (2 Chron. 5:27-41). On the Levites *see* LEVITES. There is no doubt about the artificial construction of this account which reflects the point of view of the post-exilic priesthood which was then projected back to the beginning of Israelite history to have its validity sealed.

The information afforded by the more ancient historical books paints a picture of greater complexity. The scantiness of detail, however, does not permit one to form a coherent and complete account of the evolution of the priesthood before the exile. The Bible authors are above all interested in the Jerusalem priesthood, since this was the most important sanctuary, even though it certainly was not the only one. The centralization of cult in Jerusalem that took place in the time of Josiah (Deut. 12; 1 Kgs. 22) had important repercussions on the history of the priesthood, especially on that of the Levites. From the pre-monarchic period there is information on different sanctuaries cared for by a hereditary priesthood, by Dan, for instance (Jgs. 17-18), and by Eli and his sons at Shiloh where the Ark of the Lord was kept (1 Sam. 1:3). Abiathar, a descendant of Eli, was the only survivor of the massacre of the priests of Nob carried out by Saul in revenge on them for having helped David (1 Sam. 22:20-23). Abiathar became "the priest of David" (1 Sam. 23:6, 9; 30:7). After the conquest of Jerusalem Abiathar shared his position with Zadok (2 Sam. 8:17; 15:24-29; 17:15; 20:25). Abiathar was a supporter of Adonijah, Solomon's rival for the throne, and was sent into exile by the new monarch (1 Kgs. 2:26-27) while Zadok alone became chief priest of the Temple in Jerusalem (1 Kgs. 2:35).

Zadok is presented as a descendant of Aaron (1 Chron. 5:27-34; 6:35-38). These genealogies, however, which place all the priests of the pre-exilic period in the line of Aaron, are very suspect. Some have contended, with reason, that Zadok was the priest at Jerusalem before David conquered it, and that there he remained in the service of the sanctuary of the city. He then would have been a "priest according to the order of Melchizedech"

(Ps. 110:2, 3; Gen. 14:17). The house of Zadok remained at the head of the priests of Jerusalem until the exile (1 Chron. 5:34-41) and again at the time of Ezekiel; the priests were simply called "sons of Zadok" (Ezek. 44:15; 48:11). When the cult was centralized in Jerusalem the family of Zadok got a monopoly over the whole territory of Judah while the priests of the sanctuaries of the countryside went to swell the ranks of the Levites. *See* LEVITES.

Zadok's preeminence does not seem to have been uncontested, however. The books of Samuel and Kings justify with a divine oracle what happened to Abiathar and Eli (*see* 1 Sam. 2:27-36; 3:11-14; 1 Kgs. 2:27). This is obviously polemical and directed against the just recriminations of the descendants of Abiathar, who linked themselves up through Eli to the beginnings of Israel and the sons of Levi (1 Sam. 2:27-36). During the exile this discord was settled, and in all probability the fruit of this was the new priestly genealogy brought about by P and 1 Chronicles. Aaron, Moses' brother, is at the beginnings of the Israelite priesthood. The two rival lines attached themselves to his two surviving sons, Eleazar (Zadok) and Ithamar (Abiathar), with a certain preeminence of the first over the second (1 Chron. 5:27-29; 6:34-38). The high priesthood by right belonged to the first.

The high priesthood is a typical figure of post-exilic Judaism. Even in the time of the monarchy there was certainly some kind of hierarchy among the priests in Jerusalem. Among them there is one who is head over all and is numbered among the ministers of the king with the title "The Priest" (*see* 1 Kgs. 4:2; 2 Kgs. 11:9; 16:10; Isa. 8:2). In 2 Kings 25:18 there is a distinction between "Seraiah the high priest" and "Zephaniah the second priest." His authority however does not reach beyond the Temple and the clergy for whom he was responsible to the king (*see* 2 Kgs. 12:15-17). The high priest of Judaism on the other hand is the spiritual and civil head of the nation, presiding over the Sanhedrin (*see* COUNCIL) and representing the people before the imperial Persian, Seleucid and Roman powers. Upon the return from exile the priest Joshua occupied, together with Zerubbabel who was of Davidic lineage, a more preeminent position than had the priests before the exile (*see* Hag. 1:1, 12-14; 2:4; Zech. 3:1-9; 4:1-14). Little by little his successors were to succeed in bringing to completion the evolution of the high priesthood such as it is known from the praises of Simon as they are sung by Sirach (Sir. 50). The investiture and accoutrements of the high priest were to be elements inherited from a kingship that no longer existed, such as anointment (*see* ANOINTMENT), the crown and the turban (Zech. 6:9-14).

Onias III was the last legitimate high priest of Zadokite lineage. He was put out of office through the intrigues of his brother Jason (2 Mac. 4:7-20), who in his turn was expelled by Menelaus (2 Mac. 4:23-26). His successor was Alcimus, a descendant of Aaron, but not of Zadok (1 Mac. 7:14). From Jonathan Maccabeus up to the Hasmonaean Antigonus, the high priesthood remained effectively united to the political, military and, later, the royal power (1 Mac. 10:17-20; 1 Mac. 13:42). Under the Romans the high priest was elected at will by the Roman authorities from a restricted number of families whose members in the New Testament are called high priests (Acts 5:24), even though the office was only being exercised by one of them at a time. The New Testament mentions Annas and Caiaphas by name. They were related as father-in-law and son-in-law, and the latter held office at the time of the ministry and trial of Jesus (*see* Lk. 3:1; Matt. 26:64) and during the first years of the church (Acts 5:17-41).

The priestly functions also underwent partial evolution through history.

In the most ancient texts great stress was placed on the oracular functions of the priest, exercised by means of the Urim and Thummim (see URIM): "To Levi belong your Thummim, to the man of your favor your Urim" (Deut. 33:8, in the blessing of Moses on Levi). The sacred lots and the ephod (see EPHOD) were part of the priestly vestments. Abiathar carried the Ephod with him when he followed David, and used it at the request of the king (1 Sam. 23:9-12). After David's time, however, this specific function of the priest disappeared, even though the relics of this ancient usage remained on the priestly vestments (Ex. 28:6-30; 39:2-21). After the oracular function the priests' chief function is "to promulgate your (God's) decisions to Jacob and your laws (torah) to Israel" (Deut. 33:10). In Jeremiah 18:18 and Ezekiel 7:26 the torah is the distinctive function of the priest. The priestly torah is instruction of a practical order or conduct on a certain point. The priests are presented in the exercise of this function in texts such as Haggai 2:11-13; Zechariah 7:3. Examples of priestly 'laws' are found in the legislation of Leviticus on purity and impurity (see Lev. 11-15). The priest's task also was to apply these dispositions to individual cases. This function was still in power during New Testament times. Jesus told the cured lepers to show themselves to the priest (Lk. 17:4; see Lk. 5:14; Matt. 8:14; Mk. 1:44). Priestly teaching however reached beyond the ritual field. During the festivities, especially when the sanctuaries drew the crowds, the priests gave moral and religious teaching and inculcated the traditions of the Israelite people of which they were the guardians (see Hos. 4:6; Jer. 2:8). Some scholars see in Deuteronomy an echo of the typical preaching of the Levites of the sanctuaries of the northern kingdom.

In Deuteronomy 33:10 the offering of sacrifice is mentioned last: "They bring the smoke of sacrifice to your nostrils and burnt offerings to your altars." In itself it was not the function of the priests to kill the victim: theirs it was to present it on the altar and carry out the rites prescribed in connection with its blood. See SACRIFICE.

Priesthood in the Old Testament is indissolubly bound up with the place of cult. They are its custodians and ministers. For this reason the priesthood perished with the Temple of Jerusalem (70 A.D.). From that time on Judaism has had no temples or effective priesthood.

The ministers of the church are never called priests in the New Testament. Both the gospels and Paul speak without ambiguity of the sacrificial nature of Christ's death. (See SACRIFICE, SERVANT OF THE LORD.) The theology of Christ the priest is developed however only in the letter to the Hebrews. Jesus is priest by divine designation. Moreover he is not a priest of the line of Levi or Aaron, but according to the order of Melchizedek. (See MELCHIZEDEK.) Jesus exercised his priesthood by offering himself once and for all. The expiation he brought about was not, like the Levitical priests' offerings, an extrinsic purification rite. He purifies consciences from dead works so as to serve the living God (Heb. 9:11-13). The author of the letter to the Hebrews sets up a series of contrasts between the rites of the Day of Expiation which were repeated annually because they were incapable of radically expiating sin, and the expiation of Jesus who once and for all went into the Holy of Holies—that is, into the true sanctuary of God, which is heaven—thus winning an eternal redemption (Heb. 7:26-28; 9). The expiation and priesthood of Christ brought to its completion, and thus too to its abolishment, the ritual and priesthood of the Old Testament. These were radically incapable of bringing man back to God or of founding a true alliance with him, which Jesus "the High Priest of future goods" achieved in his self-sacrifice.

Prisca, Priscilla, See AQUILA.

Prison, As known today prisons did not exist in ancient biblical times, nor indeed was there provision for them in Roman law. Imprisonment was for those arrested awaiting trial which led to their release, fine, corporal punishment, mutilation, forced labor, enslavement or execution. Jails did not exist, so a person awaiting his fate was confined in whatever prevented his escape. Joseph was confined in a cistern until he was sold to the Ishmaelites who took him to Egypt (Gen. 37:21-26). Jeremiah was confined to the Court of the Guard while Jucal and Pashhur tried to arrange his death (Jer. 37:20-21; 38:1-4). Into their hands the king gave Jeremiah, whom they threw down a well in the hope that he would perish (Jer. 38:4-6). John the Baptizer was imprisoned by Herod because he was a public embarrassment to Herod's household. When the opportunity arose, John was beheaded (Matt. 14:3, 10; Mk. 6:17, 28). The apostles were imprisoned while they awaited trial (Acts 5:18 ff.) as was Peter (Acts 12:5). In Philippi Paul and Silas were thrown into the inner prison, the more secure part of the place of arrest, and also the more airless, uncomfortable and inaccessible part (Acts 16:19-24). People awaiting trial could also be placed under house or personal arrest with a military guard. Paul in Rome lived in his own rented lodging for two years, welcoming all who came to visit him. Two years was the legal time during which the trial should have taken place, so presumably at the end of that period Paul was released (Acts 28).

Prochorus (prok′-o-rus), One of the seven Hellenistic Jewish Christians chosen by the apostles to attend to alms for the poor and their distribution in the first Christian community in Jerusalem (Acts 6:1-6).

proclaim

in Jerusalem to *p.*	Neh. 6:7	Jesus began to *p.*	Matt. 4:17
To *p.* liberty	Isa. 61:1	*p.* from the housetops	Matt. 10:27

Proconsul, The governor of a Roman senatorial province, that is, a province that directly depended on the senate. In the New Testament the proconsul Gallio of Achaia sat in judgment over Paul at Corinth (Acts 18:12-17), and one of Paul's converts was the proconsul Sergius Paulus of Cyprus (Acts 13:6-12).

profane, profaned, profaning

p. the name of your God		Do not *p.* the sacred gifts	
	Lev. 18:21		Num. 18:32
thus *p.*	Lev. 19:12	*p.* the sabbath day	Neh. 13:17
p. my holy name	Lev. 20:3	*p.* the name of my God	Prov. 30:9

profit

nor food at a *p.*	Lev. 25:37	treasures *p.* nothing	Prov. 10:2
neither *p.* nor save	1 Sam. 12:21	there is *p.*	Prov. 14:23
	What *p.* has a man	Eccl. 1:3	

Promise, Even though the Hebrew language has no word that can properly be translated promise, it nevertheless is one of the fundamental categories of biblical revelation. The real beginning of salvation history is the word addressed by God to Abraham (Gen. 12:1-3). It is simply called the word or oath or even covenant (Ps. 105:8-10), and translated by Paul by the Greek **epaggelia** meaning promise (Gal. 3:16-18). The promise made to Abraham is absolute and unconditioned and is therefore an expression of pure and gratuitous benevolence on the part of God to man. It draws its whole existence from God's goodness, and nothing from man. Of it one can affirm what Deuteronomy 7:6, 7 states of the election of Israel. The promise solemnly pledges God's fidelity, and it was sanctioned with rites which men customarily used to express a pact or mutual obligation (Gen. 15). God's fidelity or "truth" becomes, then, the force that carries to accomplishment his saving designs that were revealed in the promise. This fidelity is often celebrated and honored, as for example, in the lyrical accounts of sacred history (Ps. 105). It manifests itself all the more clearly and all the more gratuitously in overcoming sin, the obstacle that man places in the way of God's salvific initiative to prevent its accomplishments (Ps. 106; Jgs. 2).

The promise creates a tension in history, for it continues to be affirmed in the face of circumstances which discountenance it. God promises numerous descendants to the sterile couple, Abraham and Sarah (Gen. 15:1-6). It pledges to the people the possession of the land in which they are but vagrants (Gen. 15:7-21). This tension is resolved when the promises are fulfilled. Fulfilment, however, does not take place in a lineal, logical and, as it were, mechanical process. The realization of what was promised has a history of its own in which each achievement which might have seemed the end became itself another point of departure and a further tension towards the future. This tension between promise and fulfilment, beginnings and consummation governs the whole of salvation history. Every partial realization throws new light on the promise itself and on the course of events which took their origin there. This is why sacred history was and must always be subjected to a continual reinterpretation, and why the promise itself is only understood fully in the light of its realization. From this comes all the difficulty of biblical eschatology, especially in the New Testament. This too explains how the realization itself can be so disconcerting that the people fail to recognize it as such. This was the paradox which surrounded the coming of Christ in whom the promises were fulfilled (*see* Gal. 3:15-18).

From man the promise asks faith (Gen. 15:6; Gal. 3:6 ff.; Rom. 4) which is a firm assent to what God says and a full surrender and self-opening of man to God who will save him. Because faith is a free act in which man formally acknowledges his insufficiency, it is the right and adequate answer to a promise that is gratuitous and absolute.

When God pledges to Abraham a numerous progeny and the possession of the land of Canaan, both are proposed like so many other manifestations of the divine blessing which, through Abraham, were destined to reach all the nations of the earth (Gen. 12:1-3). The promise thus outreaches the limits of the Old Testament and finds its fulfilment in Christ (Acts 13:32 ff.; Rom. 15:8). For God's promises to Abraham went beyond the numerous descendants and the possession of the land of Canaan to comprise the gift of salvation (Heb. 4:1, 3, 11) and the formation of a new people (Rom. 4:1, 12), the body of the faithful whose father Abraham would be.

Prophet, Prophecy, The terms prophet and prophecy are today associated with the idea of predicting the future. This however does not exactly correspond with the original notion as expressed by these terms both in Greek and Hebrew (**nabi'**). The prophet is the authorized spokesman of the divinity. In religious phenomenology the following were the marks of the prophet: a consciousness of having been chosen and called by God; awareness of having a message from God, and with this message a mission to make it known in the name of God and as his word.

This description fits many personages, even outside the Bible, and in Christian and non-Christian religions such as the Muslims and Zarathustrians. The originality of biblical prophetism then should be studied against the background of a common basis of forms and attitudes which went to make up the phenomenon of prophecy. It should be studied from the point of view of the history of religions.

The Bible prophets of whom the Old Testament prophetic books speak were not the only ones in Israel. They undoubtedly were exceptional figures as is demonstrated by the fact that a need was felt to commit their message to writing. They appeared however in a world that was saturated with charismatic personages, people inspired from above. The activities and interventions of these inspired people very often differed quite a bit from the great prophetic writers. Nevertheless on these too is conferred the name nabi' or its equivalent, which was what the great prophets were known by.

What we know about the ancient history of prophetism is gleaned from 1 Samuel-2 Kings The information afforded there is scarce and fragmentary, and the sketchy picture that emerges is curious and uncertain on many points. At least it reveals the variety and complexity of the prophetic phenomenon in Israel. There is, for instance, group prophetism. This occurs in places of cult in what might be described as a religiously inspired phrenetic exaltation that was very contagious and probably provoked by music and dance (1 Sam. 10:5-12; 19:20-24). In 1 Kings 18:22-29 we see the prophets of Baal. They too are in a state of religious exaltation, cutting themselves until blood flowed. 1 Kings 22 on the other hand shows us the prophets of Yahweh at work. They are consulted by Ahab on the outcome of a military campaign against the Aramaeans. Their prediction is favorable, expressed with symbolic actions. Another dissident prophet however makes his appearance to predict disaster in the forthcoming battle. This conflict between the prophets of calamity and the prophets of peace is the first stage of the major conflict that would set the classical prophets up against their contemporaries. This is especially documented by the book of Jeremiah (*see* Jer. 5:31; 6:13; 8:10; 23:9-40).

In group prophecy the most curious phenomenon is formed by the "sons of prophets," to be understood in the sense of "disciples of the prophets" or better still as the individuals or members in a well defined category. These seem to have been organized with greater coherence than the groups we have just seen. As a general rule the "sons of prophets" live in common (2 Kgs. 4:38; 6:1; *see* also however 4:1), at places such as Bethel, Jericho, Gilgal (2 Kgs. 2:3, 5; 4:38), that is, where there were well-known centers of worship. They probably exercised part of their ministry around these shrines, perhaps even with manifestations of collective ecstasy. Elisha was the inspirer and "father" of these prophetic communities (2 Kgs. 4:38; 6:1; *see* ELISHA). He had inherited the spirit of the prophet Elijah (2 Kgs. 2). In a period of crass religious syncretism the "sons of prophets" were stout upholders of pure worship of the one true God, even when spurious forms of worship enjoyed the protection of the reigning dynasty of Omri. Perhaps they came to the defense of the religious heritage of Israel with a definitive program of religious activism. Even though they lived a little at the margin of society their intervention was decisive in the revolt of Jehu (842-815 B.C.; *see* JEHU) against the dynasty of Omri. The existence of dissident groups such as the "sons of prophets" is not only documented in later Judaism (Qumran) but also in monarchic times. (*See* RECHABITES.) 1 Samuel-2 Kings tells of still others who are bearers of the "word of God," but they lived apart or on the fringes of the group. They are designated by different names such as "man of God" (1 Sam. 2:27; 1 Kgs. 12:22), "seer" (1 Sam. 9:9; 2 Sam. 24:11), and also nabi'. The variety of names employed itself witnesses the extreme complexity of the prophetic movement and of its numerous modalities, and is also a warning against any attempt to reduce it to simplified schemes.

The "seer," for instance, of whom 1 Samuel 9:9 speaks (Samuel) is held to be capable of knowing things hidden from others, perhaps through revelation (9:15) or also through natural means or gifts. Gifts are given when information is asked (9:8; *see* also 1 Kgs. 14:3). Other isolated figures of whatever type have this in common: they are spokesmen for God in the most diverse circumstances. Among these might be mentioned the man of God who announced to Eli the end of his family (1 Sam. 2:27), the prophet Ahijah of Shiloh who announced the schism to Jeroboam (1 Kgs. 11:29; 14:1-18), the anonymous man of God who announced the destruction of the altar of Bethel (1 Kgs. 13:1-10), Jehu (1 Kgs. 16:1-4), and Jonah (2 Kgs. 14:25). Gad and Nathan make many appearances and seem to have a stable office and function in David's court as seers and prophets. *See* GAD; NATHAN.

The author of 1 Samuel-2 Kings tells only of their intervention and message and leaves us completely in the dark concerning their prophetic office and their concrete position in the social context of the people. Nevertheless the information afforded us does show the long tradition that lay behind the classical prophets. On two prophets of the ninth century B.C., however, tradition has been quite clear. In Elijah and Elisha are traced the essential lines of the prophetic office as it was lived out and understood a century later by Amos, Hosea, Isaiah and Micah. *See* ELIJAH; ELISHA.

On the great prophetic writers *see* AMOS, BARUCH, DANIEL, EZEKIEL, HABAKKUK, HAGGAI, HOSEA, ISAIAH, JEREMIAH, JOEL, JONAH, MALACHI, MICAH, NAHUM, OBADIAH, ZECHARIAH, ZEPHANIAH.

In the prophetic books there is mention of other prophets besides those under whose name the book was written. The principal source for these is the book of Jeremiah. The prophet is one of the spiritual guides of the people (Jer. 18:18) and one of those responsible for its well-being (Jer. 2:26; 4:9; 8:1; 13:13; Ezek. 22:25-28). There is great esteem and veneration for the prophets of the past (Amos 2:11, 12; 3:17; Hos. 12:10, 14) who were sent by God to warn and exhort the people (Jer. 5:13; 7:25; 25:4; 26:5; 29:19; Deut. 18:9-20). On the other hand the judgment on contemporary prophets is particularly severe and negative. When Jeremiah castigates the prophets he probably has in mind the prophets of the Temple of Jerusalem (Jer. 5:31; 23:11; 26:7; Lam. 2:20). These were not the only prophets (*see* 2 Kgs. 22:14) but they were certainly the best known, and the group enjoying most authority because of their association with the Temple. These prophets elaborated a message of peace (Jer. 23:17) based on an unshakeable confidence in the inviolability of the Temple (Jer. 7:4). According to Jeremiah, God was not behind their message nor their mission. What they gave off as God's word was but their own heart's dream (Jer. 14:13, 14; 23:16-32; 27; 28; Ezek. 13:2-15).

What function had the prophets in the Temple? Jeremiah gives no answer to this question. The book of Psalms however very probably supplies the information. There are among the psalms texts that are much like the prophetic oracles in form (*see* e.g. Pss. 5:4; 6:10; 12:5; 22:22; 27:14, and also Jer. 15:15-27). Nor should it be forgotten that one of the essential functions of the prophets was intercession. It would seem legitimate then to give to this prayer of intercession the official form used in cult. Other psalms (Pss. 50; 81; 85; 90) suggest that the prophets took part in the more substantial and solemn of the Temple rites in the guise of authorized proclaimers of the will of God for the people.

The Temple prophets were not necessarily false prophets (*see* e.g. Ps. 50). It is not right to extend the judgment of Jeremiah to all the Temple prophets of all time. Given the nature of these prophets' function, their intervention was not always or necessarily spontaneous or inspired. It should rather be thought of as variations on traditional themes that were imposed by the ritual itself, and in conformity with the theological traditions of the group. After the exile the Temple prophets became "schools of cantors" or choirs (*see* 1 Chron. 25:1; 2 Kgs. 23:2, compared with 2 Chron. 35:18; 2 Chron. 20:14).

The discovery of Temple or cult prophets poses two questions. Are there some parts of their prophecies preserved among the prophetic books of the Old Testament? This possibility arises for the books of Nahum, Joel and Habakkuk, which have a strong liturgical coloring. Were the prophet writers Temple prophets? There is nothing against this in principle, but it should be remembered that the Temple prophets were but one of the forms of prophetism. The majority of scholars hold that the prophet writers did not belong to the Temple groups.

While keeping to the classical prophets, something should be said of the process of revelation which they in turn handed on. The following remarks are from a psychological, not a theological, point of view: what is sought is the echo in the psychic make-up of the prophet of the word spoken by God.

The prophet "hears" and also "sees" the word of God. The revelation event is often indicated with the phrase: "The word of God came on (e.g.) Jeremiah." Such expressions do not oblige us to conclude that the revelation was auricular: what is intended is a generic expression to indicate that God had contact with the prophet. The "word" of God, in the language of the prophets, was the typical expression to designate the experience of revelation. This probably was due to the fact that the word was also the vehicle of proclamation employed by the prophet for his audience. The prophet, in relationship to God, was like the people in relationship to the prophet, listening to the word of God.

Characteristic of biblical prophetism is the total absence of any awareness of being possessed by the divinity, which is the case with Greek manticism. The prophet knows that he keeps his own personality. It is God who manifests some truth to him, who speaks to him and causes him to act. Revelation is through inspiration. From the psychological point of view, inspiration is experienced by the prophet when in his interior world he becomes aware of a whole ensemble of ideas, things seen or heard, impulses and sensations had with such force and spontaneity that he knows they are not his own, nor the fruit of his own labor or reflection, but must come from elsewhere.

The prophet's concentration of these phenomena can vary in intensity, but it always brings with it a suspension of the normal psychic life, that is, of his ability to respond to external stimuli. Inspiration can be had, with obvious marginal differences, either while awake or asleep. Dreams were always considered a way in which God could communicate, and this is also true of the Bible (*see* Gen. 20:3-7; Matt. 1:20; 2:13, 19). Numbers 12:6 contrasts the dream with a more perfect way of divine communication, that used with Moses. Jeremiah is not opposed to it in principle even though he is aware of the abuses that can be made of it (Jer. 23:25). On revelation through vision *see* VISION.

Both in the event of the revelation and in its transmission the prophet's own personality plays its part. His culture and temperament are the material in which the word is received and transmitted. He speaks and acts in the full use of his faculties and abilities. Inspiration takes place in the intimacy of the prophet's person, but then it makes its way to the people through his imagination and literary qualities.

Another mark of the psychology of the prophet is his awareness that he had a mission and a mandate from God that he is not free to resist. This awareness does not only arise from the obligation or moral commitment assumed by the prophet at his call, but also from the very impulse of the revelation itself. Jeremiah has given unsurpassed expression to this aspect of the prophetic personality in 20:7-13.

According to different texts of the Acts and the Pauline epistles there were prophets in the apostolic church. These are mentioned in reference to the charisms and functions which God placed in his church (*see* Rom. 12:6; 1 Cor. 12:10; Eph. 4:11). This would seem to suggest that they exercised a regular and official function in the life of the community (Acts 11:27; 13:1-13). It is not possible however to determine what precisely was the nature of this function. It is probably necessary to think of them, with the suitable distinctions, as taking after the Temple prophets in the type of service they gave the community. They were, then, inspired people with a function and a role, particularly in the liturgical life of the community, during which they intervened with inspired prayer, exhortation and admonition.

Proselyte, The dispersal of the Jews outside the limits of Palestine, especially in the Hellenistic world, and the re-awakening of missionary activity among the non-Jews (*see* Matt. 23:15) gave rise to the category of proselytes, non-Jews who accepted Jewish practices and doctrine and were integrated into the Jewish community. The acceptance of Jewish doctrine and customs, and hence integration into the Jewish community, could take place at several levels. There were proselytes properly so-called or "proselytes of justice" who accepted the whole of Judaism. Initiation into the community took place through circumcision, a bath of ritual purification and the offering of particular sacrifices (*see* Acts 2:11; 6:5; 13:43). Others, called "the God-fearing," (*see* Acts 10:2, 22) were rather sympathizers with the Jews and accepted their moral doctrine and their monotheism, as well as the "commandments of Noah" which made possible a relationship with the Jews; they also attended the synagogue. They did not, however, take the definitive step of circumcision. This class of people was much more numerous than the other, and played an important role in the diffusion of Christianity in the Hellenistic world. They were more prepared to understand and accept the Christian message and at the same time more disposed to overcome the typical exclusiveness of the Judaism of the time (*see* Acts 13:16; 16:14; 17:4, 12, 17; 18:4, 7).

Prostitution, Prostitution is severely reproved by the Old and the New Testament (*see* Deut. 23:18; Jer. 5:7; Hos. 4:14; Prov. 7:6-27; Rom. 1:24 f.; 1 Cor. 5:9-12; 6:15-20; Gal. 5:19, 20; Eph. 5:3, 5; Col. 3:5). From what can be gathered from other sources this insistence was not unjustified or in any way excessive (*see* Gen. 38:15, 16; Josh. 2; Jgs. 11:1; 16:1; 1 Kgs. 3:16). In a separate category was ritual prostitution of men and women which was practiced in the Canaanite sanctuaries as part of the worship of their fertility gods, and this practice also contaminated the Israelites (Deut. 23:18; 1 Kgs. 15:12; 22:47; 2 Kgs. 23:7).

A logical development of the image of marriage to express God's intimacy with his people was the image of prostitution to show the people's disloyalty to God (Hos. 1-3; Isa. 57:7-13; Jer. 3:1-4; Ezek. 16 and 23). The nations hostile to Israel are often compared to prostitutes (Nah. 3:1-7; Isa. 23:15-18). This usage of the figure was borrowed from the apocalyptic tradition which used it to damn undertakings that seduced God's people (Rev. 17:1-6; 19:2).

proud

p. waves be stilled	Job 38:11	Though the p. scoff	Ps. 119:51
deserts to the p.	Ps. 94:2	Though the p. forge	Ps. 119:69
rebuke the accursed p.	Ps. 119:21	p. have dug pits	Ps. 119:85

proudly
who act *p*.   **Ps. 31:24**

Proverbs, Book of, A wisdom book of the Old Testament. It gathers together collections of proverbs of different origin and author.

a. Prov. 1-9: this first part is distinct in form from the rest of the book. It is not in fact a collection of proverbs, but rather discourses with advice to seek and accept the teaching of wisdom. These discourses are placed on the lips of wisdom personified (1:20-23 and cc. 8 and 9), as in Job 28 and Sirach 24. This is the most recent part of the writing and does not go back further than the fourth or third century B.C.

b. Prov. 10-22:15: "The Proverbs of Solomon" (10:1), according to its title. It gathers together 375 proverbs in no particular order that can be seen. C. 16:12-15 has the same theme and 11:9-12 the same form, as is also found in 15:13-17. The book is an infinite variation on the same fundamental theme: the differing behavior and end of the wise man and of the unwise. Their diverse lot is often spelled out in the two parts of the same proverb (cc. 10-15).

c. Prov. 22:17-24:22: "The Words of the Wise," according to its title in 22:17. It follows very closely an Egyptian wisdom writing: "The Wisdom of Amenemophis."

d. Prov. 24:23-34: "Solomon's proverbs gathered by the men of Hezekiah" (25:1) king of Judah (715-687 B.C.).

f. Prov. 30:1-14: "Agur's words." Agur was an Israelite wise man.

g. Prov. 31: "Lemuel's words." He was non-Israelite. Both this and the previous collection are attributed to Arabian wise men of Ishmaelite origins.

h. Prov. 30:15-35: a collection of numerical proverbs, a type also found in Sirach 25:1-2 and Proverbs 6:16-19.

i. Prov. 31:10-31: an alphabetic poem in praise of the perfect wife and mother who is busy and concerned for the good of her husband and home.

The title of the work attributes it to Solomon, son of David and king of Israel (1:1). From what we have seen this cannot be taken in the sense that Solomon was the literary author of the book. Solomon is rather the great initiator of the Israelite wisdom tradition and the great patron of its further development (1 Kgs. 5). It is said of him that he pronounced three thousand proverbs and wrote one thousand and five songs (1 Kgs. 5:2). While the numbers may be exaggerated, nothing prevents us from attributing to Solomon this role in the wisdom tradition. Perhaps some of his works really figure in the collections that bear his name, but it is impossible to identify them or even to assert how many.

provide

God himself will *p*.	Gen. 22:8	*P*. yourselves with neither	
widow there to *p*.	1 Kgs. 17:9		Matt. 10:9
p. meat for his people	Ps. 78:20	Also *p*. horses	Acts 23:24

provision

p. given them	Gen. 42:25	*p*. for a journey	Josh. 9:4
he supplied them with *p*.		as *p*.	Josh. 9:12
	Gen. 45:21	abundant *p*.	Ps. 132:15
	make no *p*.	Rom. 13:14	

provoke, provoked

you so *p.* the Lord	Deut. 9:8	Since they have *p.* me	Deut. 32:21
you *p.* the Lord	Deut. 9:22	by which he *p.*	1 Kgs. 15:30
They *p.* him	Deut. 32:16	because our fathers *p.*	Ezra 5:12
	Why do they *p.* me	Jer. 8:19	

prudent

but the *p.* man	Prov. 14:17	understanding of its *p.* men	
but *p.* is he	Prov. 15:5		Isa. 29:14
a *p.* wife	Prov. 19:14	perished from the *p.*	Jer. 49:7
	him who is *p.*	Hos. 14:10	

prune, pruned

for six years *p.*	Lev. 25:3	it shall not be *p.*	Isa. 5:6
nor *p.* your vineyard	Lev. 25:4	He *p.* away	John 15:2

Psalms, Book of, The Book of Psalms or Psalter is a collection of 150 religious poems which stem from different origins and authors. The Hebrew canon of the Old Testament places it in the third group of books, among the so-called "writings" or hagiographa. In the editions of the Hebrew text and in the translations, the psalms are numbered progressively but there are differences between the Hebrew text and the Septuagint and Vulgate which give a different division for some psalms according to the following scheme:

Massoretic Text: 1-8/9, 10/11-113/114.115/116/117-146/147/148-150.

Septuagint: 1-8/9/10-112/113/114.115/116-145/146.147/148.150.

The Psalter is divided into five parts or books. The end of each is indicated by a doxology that does not pertain to the text of the Psalms: 1-41; 42-72; 73-89; 90-106; 107-150. Psalm 150 is the final doxology to the whole Psalter. This division seems to wish to imitate the division of the Torah into five books, but it also conserves traces of older collections from which the present Psalter has been formed. (Ps. 72:20, after the final doxology of the second book in Ps. 72:19).

Several psalms have at the beginning an inscription, that is, a brief introduction which tells about the "author," the literary genre, the musical mode, the liturgical use and the composition. The Hebrew and Septuagint texts are not in agreement on the number, nor in regard to the information given in the inscriptions. They would, then, be later additions, not belonging to the inspired text. Examples are:

a. The liturgical rubric: Pss. 120-134, songs of ascents, that is, in the traditional interpretation, songs for pilgrimages that were on their way to Jerusalem; Ps. 92 for the sabbath; Ps. 38:70 for the sacrifice prescribed in Lev. 2; Ps. 100 for the sacrifice of which Lev. 7:12 speaks.

b. Musical notes: these are difficult to interpret. An example is Ps. 4:6, 54 which speaks of the instruments to be used in accompaniment, while Ps. 22:56, 57, 59 gives the first words of a song whose tune the Psalm should follow. So, at least, some scholars think.

c. Notes on the occasion of composition: e.g. Pss. 51,60. These notes have little or no historical value.

d. Often the Psalms are inscribed with the name of a person with the preposition l, by which customarily the author is signified. This was the interpretation given in the past to these names, but today one can see that this is not its true sense. Fifty-five psalms are "for the choir-master," which is the name of an office, not an author. Seventy-three carry the name of David, twelve are from the sons of Asaph, twelve from the sons of Korah, two have Solomon's name, and one (Ps. 90) is from Moses.

These inscriptions can be compared to the use of giving the different parts of a poem the name of the cycle to which they refer. Thus these inscriptions also indicate the collections from which the different psalms have been taken: Asaph, Korah, Ethan, Heman are known from the historical books as names under which various schools of singers went in the cult (*see* e.g. 1 Chron. 6:16-32; 15:14-24; 2 Chron. 5:11-14; 29:13; Ezra 2:41; 3:10). The psalms bearing the name of David are taken from a collection that went by his name, and the same holds for those of Solomon. That attributed to Moses supposes the interpretation of this information as an indication of the author.

The Psalter is, then, an anthology. Its origin and composition, like that of the anthologies that preceded it, comprise a long reach of time and a complex process that we can hardly put back together from the past. The Psalter certainly had canonical value towards the middle of the second century B.C. (*see* prologue of Sir., 1 Mac. 7:17). It seems to have substantially reached the form in which today we have it by the fourth or third century B.C. (*see* 2 Mac. 2:13). The opinion of some authors which would date the composition of many Psalms in the Maccabean period seems to have been definitively disproved. Such a recent date could only be discussed in reference to Pss. 44, 74, 79, and 83. The Psalter has within it indications of older collections. Pss. 3-41 is the oldest Davidic collection (*see* 2 Chron. 29:25 and Prov. 25:1). Pss. 42-89 is the so-called Elohistic collection, which gets its name from the use of the title Elohim to designate God. In this collection itself can be distinguished the Psalms taken from the repertoire of the sons of Asaph, Korah, and a smaller Davidic collection (Pss. 51-72). The last part is less homogeneous. There are two Davidic groups (Pss. 138-145 and Pss. 108,110,111-118) as well as the series of the "Songs of the Ascents" (Pss. 120-134).

Ancient Jewish and Christian tradition, as can be gathered from the New Testament (*see* Matt. 22:43; Acts 2:25; 4:25; Rom. 4:6), attributed the whole Psalter to David. As has already been stated, this attribution cannot be understood in the sense that David was literary author. From solidly established traditions we know that David was a poet and musician (1 Sam. 16:18-23; 18:10; Amos 6:5), and some of his compositions have been inserted into the historical books (2 Sam. 1:19-27; 2 Sam. 3:33; 22 [Ps. 18]; 23: 1-7). It was David too who inaugurated the cult in Jerusalem where he had the ark of the covenant brought. With reason, therefore, he was considered the beginner and great patron of the lyrical religious literary genre so intimately connected with liturgical worship. So his name is inseparably joined to the Psalter, but not in the modern sense of being its author. David did compose Psalms but it is no longer possible to ascertain which or how many of our Psalms were in fact penned by David.

Pseudepigrapha (soo'-de-pig'-ra-fa), Non-Catholics call pseudepigrapha the books which the Catholics call apocrypha. For non-Catholics the apocrypha are the so-called deuterocanonical works of the Old Testament. *See* APOCRYPHA.

Ptolemais (tol'-e-may'-is), *See* ACCO.

Ptolemy (tol'-e-mi), 1. The name of the fourteen members of the 31st dynasty of Egypt founded by Ptolemy I Soter (323-283 B.C.), who had been one of the generals of Alexander the Great, among whom the empire was divided at his death. The Ptolemies ruled over Egypt until 30 B.C. when Egypt became a Roman province. They fought with the Seleucids over the sovereignty of Palestine. For the whole third century they held sway over it, but had to renounce it after 198 B.C. There are allusions to this struggle in Daniel 11:6-17; the kings there referred to are Ptolemy II

Philadelphos, 283-246 B.C. (Dan. 11:6), Ptolemy III Euergetes, 246-221 B.C. (Dan. 11:7-9), Ptolemy IV Philopator, 221-203 (Dan. 11:11, 12) and Ptolemy V Epiphanes, 203-181 B.C. (Dan. 11:13-18).

Ptolemy VI Philometor, 181-145, decided to exploit the internal struggle for the Seleucid throne between Demetrius and Alexander Balas. He supported Alexander with the secret design of eventually dethroning him and taking over the Seleucid kingdom. The plan was uncovered, and Alexander fought a battle with Ptolemy which he lost. Ptolemy, however, died from the wounds which he had received in the battle (1 Mac. 11:1-19). 1 Maccabees 15:16-21 carries the text of the letter of Lucius the Roman consul to Ptolemy VII Euergetes (145-116) in favor of the Jews.

2. A general of the army of Antiochus IV Epiphanes, who together with Nicanor and Gorgias was defeated by Judas Maccabeus in the vicinity of Emmaus (1 Mac. 3:38). *See* MACRON.

3. Son of Abub, head of the region of Jericho, who treacherously killed Simon Maccabeus and his sons Mattathias and Judas in the fortress of Dok (1 Mac. 16:11-22).

Puah (pue′-ah), One of the midwives of the Hebrew women who did not obey the Pharaoh's command to kill all the Hebrew male babies (*see* Ex. 1:15-21).

Publicans, Among the Romans those who were commissioned to exact the taxes were called publicans. The publican would pay the state a fixed sum proportionate to the theoretical amount that should be receivable, and in this way acquired for himself the right to collect the taxes from the people. Publican was also the name given in general to minor officials involved in the collection of taxes. Publicans had a very bad name in Judea and were in fact hated both because of the unenviable profession they exercised and also because they were not infrequently guilty of extortion and injustice, and of course, were collaborators with the Roman powers. They were classified with public sinners, prostitutes and gentiles (*see* Matt. 5:46, 47; Lk. 6:32; Matt. 21:31, 32, etc.). To the great scandal of the Pharisees Jesus did not disdain to keep company with publicans (Lk. 7:34; 15:1; Matt. 9:11; Mk. 2:15, 16), for he had "come to call sinners, not the self-righteous" (Mk. 2:17).

In a parable Jesus unfolded the intimate attitudes of these "sinners" and these "self-righteous," and the divine judgment on them (Lk. 18:9-14). Zacchaeus was the chief publican of Jericho who gave hospitality to Jesus in his home (Lk. 19:1-11). Matthew-Levi received the call to become one of the Twelve while he was seated at the counting house (Matt. 9:9-13; Mk. 2:14).

Publius, The chief and most noble of the inhabitants of Malta who gave hospitality to Paul and his companions, and whose sick father was cured by the apostle (Acts 28:7,8).

Pudens (pue′-denz), A Christian in Rome who sends greetings to Timothy (2 Tim. 4:21).

Pul (pool), The name that Tiglath-pileser III of Assyria (745-727 B.C.) had as king of Babylonia (729-727 B.C.; *see* 2 Kgs. 15:19; 1 Chron. 5:26).

punishment

p. is to great	Gen. 4:13	oppressed by your *p*.	Isa. 26:16
on the day of *p*.	Isa. 10:3	their time of *p*.	Jer. 8:12; 10:15
	to eternal *p*.	Matt. 25:46	

Punon (pue′-non), A stopping-place on the journey of the Israelites to

Canaan (Num. 33:42, 43). It is today called Feinan, in the depression of
Arabah. This was an important mining center in antiquity.

Purah (pyoor′-ah), A servant of Gideon (Jgs. 7:10, 11).

pure

with *p.* gold	Ex. 25:11	on the *p.* gold lampstand	
propitiatory of *p.* gold	Ex. 25:17		Lev. 24:4
Of *p.* gold	Ex. 25:29	My teaching is *p.*	Job 11:4
	fear of the Lord is *p.*	Ps. 19:10	

purge

began to *p.* Judah	2 Chron. 34:3	may *p.* your uncleanness	
p. Jerusalem's blood	Isa. 4:4		Ezek. 22:15

purify, purifying

p. the altar	Lev. 8:15	to have himself *p.*	Num. 19:20
to *p.* them	Num. 8:21	shall *p.* yourselves	Num. 31:19
he shall *p.* himself	Num. 19:12	*p.* every article	Num. 31:20
	and *p.* themselves	Isa. 66:17	

Purim (poor′-im or pyoor′-im), A Jewish festival that was celebrated on
the fourteenth and fifteenth days of the month of Adar (February-
March); according to Esther 9:17-32 it was celebrated to commemorate
the liberation of the Jews of Persia from the slaughter planned for them by
Haman, the minister of Ahasuerus. It was through the intervention of
Esther and Mordecai that they were spared. The name **purim**, from **pur**,
"lot," "chance," is explained by the fact that Haman had chosen by lot
the fourteenth of Adar as the extermination day (9:24). From a historical
point of view the explanation offered by the book of Esther is very doubtful, and everything seems to suggest that, whatever the historical basis of
the book in question, the story was adapted to make it the basis of a
festival that had already been celebrated independently. In the beginning
the feast was eminently profane in character (Esth. 9:15-19). It would
originally have been celebrated by the Jewish communities in Persia, having been adapted from a non-Israelite New Year festival. The first notice
of its celebration in Palestine stems from the first century B.C. (2 Mac.
15:36) and it was then called the "Day of Mordecai," which shows that
the fusion had taken place between the original feast and the Esther story.

purple

violet, *p.* and scarlet	Ex. 25:4	the *p.* garments	Jgs. 8:26
woven of violet, *p.*	Ex. 26:31	fine linen and *p.*	Prov. 31:22
gold, violet, *p.*	Ex. 28:5	in royal *p.*	Mk. 15:17
a *p.* cloth over it	Num. 4:13	stripped him of the *p.*	Mk. 15:20

pursued

p. them	Gen. 14:15	they *p.* you	Deut. 11:4
he *p.* him	Gen. 31:23	they *p.* Midian	Jgs. 7:23
p. the Israelites	Ex. 14:8	and *p.* David	1 Sam. 23:25

pursuit

went in *p.*	Gen. 14:14	be off in *p.*	2 Sam. 17:1
	in *p.* of Sheba	2 Sam. 20:13	

Put (poot), Son of Ham and brother of Cush and Misraim (Egypt) in the
Table of Nations (Gen. 10:6; 1 Chron. 1:8). The Put were an African
people probably on the northern coast of Somalia. They are mentioned
with other African peoples in some prophetic oracles (Ezek. 30:5; 38:5;
Nah. 3:9).

put

I will *p.* enmity	Gen. 3:15	*P.* your hand under	Gen. 24:2

put (cont.)

and *p*. the words in	Ex. 4:15 two men *p*. ten	Deut. 32:30
p. all these things	Lev. 8:27 *P*. this man in prison	1 Kgs. 22:27
	p. down the enthroned Isa. 10:13	

Puteoli (pue-tee′-o-li), A seaport in the bay of Naples, today called Pozzuoli. Here Paul disembarked on his way to Rome (Acts 28:13).

Putiel (pue′-ti-el), Father-in-law of Eleazar, Aaron's son (Ex. 6:25).

Puvah (pue′-vah), A son of Issachar (Gen. 46:13).

pyre

p. has long been ready   Isa. 30:33

Pyrrhus, Father of Sopater, travelling companion of Paul from Macedonia to Asia Minor (Acts 20:4).

Q

Q, From the German Quelle, source. It is the usual designation for the material that is common to Matthew and Luke but absent in Mark. *See* SYNOPTIC QUESTION.

Qere (ka-ray′), In Aramaic this means "read" or "to be read." The Massoretic text of the Bible is often marked in the margin with this word, followed by the correction. Reverence for the sacred text kept the scribes from tampering with it even where there was an obvious mistake, so the correct word was read in the margin. In another case, reverence for the divine name prohibited its pronunciation, so for it another word was substituted. Thus Adonai (qere) was read for Yahweh (ketibh) which was written.

Qoheleth, Ecclesiastes (koe-hel′-eth), A wisdom book of the Old Testament. Qoheleth (also spelt Koheleth) is the author's name or title. The word itself is the active feminine participle of the Hebrew verb **kahal**, "to assemble," which is translated in Greek as **Ekklesiastes**, and Latin **Ecclesiastes**. The full title of the book is "The Words of Qoheleth, son of David, king of Jerusalem." Qoheleth is perhaps best understood as the Preacher who presides or speaks to the assembly.

Ecclesiastes 1:1 identifies the author as son of David while v. 12 also states that the author was himself king. The reference is clearly to Solomon. This however was a literary device by which the author presented his teaching under the great name of Solomon (*see* 1 Kgs. 3:10). It was a frequent practice in ancient wisdom tradition to attribute sayings and writings to the greatest sage of all, Solomon. (*See* WISDOM.) The literary fiction is abandoned after 2:26.

The book as it stands today was edited by a disciple of the author, who also added the inscription, the epilogue (12:9-14) and 7:27. The editor has placed immediately after the inscription and immediately before the epilogue the phrase by which the book is on the lips of everyman, which sums up the author's teaching, and was undoubtedly one of Qoheleth's great inspirations: "Vanity of vanities. All is vanity" (1:2; 12:8). 'Vanity' was not understood in the moral sense of later Christian ascetics. It had a more immediate meaning of the emptiness and inconsistency of things that can neither help nor save, and lead to delusion those who set their hopes on them. Qoheleth passes judgment on the values that are sometimes upheld as necessary for a good life, and therefore worth the effort to attain to them. He becomes an extreme realist, offering an implacable judgment, and not necessarily a moral one, on what life really has to offer.

His pen of judgment delineates innumerable aspects of human life. Examples are a. the search for fame, one of the forces which has always driven men to undertake grandiose works and establish themselves in history (Gen. 11; Sir. 41:11-13; 44). Qoheleth drily teaches that an inflexible law condemns all this. There is nothing new under the sun. What has happened already is merely forgotten (3:15; 9:4-6; 7:10; 4:2; 6:3-5). The search for a place in posterity, for fame, is vanity.

b. Not even the most treasured thoughts of the wisdom tradition escape the searing eye of Qoheleth. Wisdom and justice are no panacea, leading to life and happiness. Qoheleth, himself a wise man, makes concessions to his class (4:13-16; 7:11). Fundamentally, however, his judgment is negative: "The wise man has eyes in his head, but the fool walks in darkness . . . but one lot befalls both of them" (2:13-17). Death and oblivion await them both, and indeed the wise have reserved to them greater suffering, for they see and are aware of what the stupid in their ignorance are spared (7:23; 1:18; 3:11). The same is true of justice (7:15; 8:14). Not that Qoheleth pronounces himself adverse to wisdom and justice as such, but rather against those who recommend wisdom and justice as if they infallibly led to happiness. His judgment is based on experience and observation, and is limited to a comparison between what is the dry reality of these two categories.

Qoheleth on the positive side offers extreme sobriety and austerity. He acknowledges and often records what joys God has given to man, to eat and drink and be content with his work (2:24; 3:12; 8:15; 9:7; 11:9). He absolves God of any part in causing the tragedy in man's destiny (7:29). He admires and praises the wisdom of order resplendent in God's creation, even through he does not fail to observe the battering man gets from the inexorable rhythms of the universe, deluded in his hopes for stability (3:3-11; 8:16; 7:23). Finally he invites the disciple to fear God, not the fear of terror, but the submission and reverence due to an infinite majesty. "The last word, when all is heard: Fear God and keep his commandments, for this is man's all; because God will bring to judgment every work, with all its hidden qualities, whether good or bad" (12:13).

The subject and style of the book lead to the experts dating it in the third century B.C.

Qoph (koaf), The 19th letter of the Hebrew alphabet (q).

Quail, The miracle of the quails is recounted in two versions that are almost identical, except for the topography (Ex. 16:13 and Num. 11:31). A wind from Yahweh drove quails in great number in from the sea until they came down around the camp, covering the ground to a depth of three feet along a whole day's march. Even as the people chewed the food, however, they were struck with a great plague by God in his anger and many died. This story is to be seen in the context of the annual migrations of quails from Egypt towards Syria. The bird is heavy and awkward in flight, and when it allows itself to be carried along in the wind it can easily be driven to the ground.

quake
When the mountains *q.*   Isa. 5:25   anger the earth *q.*   Jer. 10:10
         mountains *q.* before him   Nah. 1:5

quarrel
When men *q.*   Ex. 21:18   check a *q.* before it begins
looking for a *q.*   2 Kgs. 5:7   Prov. 17:14
         in a *q.* not his own   Prov. 26:17

quarreling, quarreled
shepherds of Gerar *q.*   Gen. 26:20   fast ends in *q.*   Isa. 58:4

quarried
pit from which you were *q*.   Isa. 51:1

quarter
a *q*. of a silver shekel   1 Sam. 9:8   to the Second *Q*. in   2 Kgs. 22:14

Quartus, A Christian in Rome greeted by Paul in Romans 16:23.

Queen, In the first and second books of Kings, in the introductions to the reigns of the kings of Judah the name of the king's mother is almost always recorded (*see* e.g. 1 Kgs. 15:2; 15:10 where the name of the grandmother is given in place of the mother; 22:42, etc.). The importance attached to the mother's name is explained by that fact that it was the king's mother and not his wife who exercised the functions of queen. Her spheres of influence are not specified but one can glean from various allusions here and there in the Bible an idea of the high "matrocinium" she exercised in the affairs of state. Solomon had his mother Bathsheba sit beside him on the throne (1 Kgs. 2:19). According to 1 Kings 15:13 Asa king of Judah deposed from her royal dignity his grandmother Maacha. Athalia, queen mother of Ahaziah, succeeded in reigning alone from 849 to 842 B.C. after having liquidated all but one of the princes of the royal family (2 Kgs. 11).

The institution of the queen mother seems to have been peculiar to the kingdom of Judah. There is no trace of this institution in the chronicles of Israel.

queen
The *q*. of Sheba   1 Kgs. 10:1   *q*. seated beside him   Neh. 2:6
When the *q*. of Sheba heard   and made her *q*.   Esth. 2:17
                        2 Chron. 9:1

Queen of Heaven, A non-Israelite divinity who received worship in Jerusalem and afterwards from the exiles in Egypt at the time of Jeremiah (Jer. 7:18; 46:17-19, 25). In all probability she is to be identified with Ishtar. Her cult at Jerusalem was one of the consequences of the vassalage of Judah to Assyria from the time of Manasseh (687-642 B.C.).

quench, quenched
q. my remaining hope   2 Sam. 14:7   wild asses *q*.   Ps. 104:11
q. the lamp of Israel   2 Sam. 21:17   burn without being *q*.   Jer. 7:20

question
ask you a *q*.   Mk. 11:29   about this *q*.   Acts 15:2
ask him any more *q*.   Mk. 12:34   *q*. of conscience   1 Cor. 10:25

quick, quickly
Q., three seahs   Gen. 18:6   Then go *q*.   Matt. 28:7
succeed so *q*.   Gen. 27:20   Be *q*. about   Jn. 13:27

quiet
q. and trusting people   Jgs. 18:27   *q*. words of the wise   Eccl. 9:17
city was *q*.   2 Kgs. 11:20   I will be *q*.   Ezek. 16:42

Quirinius, P. Sulpicius Quirinius, Roman legate of Syria from 6 A.D. According to Luke 2:2 it was during his legateship that the census took place which obliged Mary and Joseph to make the journey to Bethlehem where Jesus was born. On the problems that arise from this *see* CENSUS.

quiver
your *q*. and bow   Gen. 27:3   the man whose *q*.   Ps. 127:5
rattles the *q*.   Job 39:23   Their *q*. are   Jer. 5:16

Qumran, Khirbet (kir′-bet koom′-ran), "The ruins of Qumran," is a locality in Palestine near the northwest corner of the Dead Sea, in the neighborhood of the caves where from 1947 on, the so-called Dead Sea Scrolls have been discovered. (*See* DEAD SEA SCROLLS.) Since the identification of the first-found scrolls as ancient, in February, 1948, great interest was shown in the ruins that lay beside the caves as the probable location of the library that was found scattered in such inaccessible places. The excavations carried out under the direction of R. de Vaux unearthed what appeared to be the ruins of a monastery, which coincided with the type of life described in the scrolls themselves, that is, the "Rule of the Community."

According to the most common opinion of scholars, the inhabitants of the place were Essenes, who up to that time had only been known from the information supplied by Pliny and Josephus Flavius. (*See* ESSENES.) There is some divergence between what these writers tell us and what is gathered from the documents discovered in the place, especially in regard to the celibate or married condition of the "monks." In the cemetery at Qumran some female skeletons have also been discovered, and the rule provides for married members. So it seems that the Essene movement could take on different shapes.

Qumran was abandoned around the year 70 A.D. on account of a fierce attack by the Roman legion during the first Jewish war. The origins of the sect are not clear. They appear to be secessionists. They withdrew to prepare in the desert the way of the Lord after certain happenings, in their view, had rendered the priesthood in Jerusalem unworthy and illegitimate. The "Master of Justice," the spiritual guide of the sect, would have much to suffer from the intemperances of the "Impious Priest." To what events these indications refer, it is not easy to determine, as is evident from the multiplicity of solutions that have been offered, ranging from the high priesthood of Onias III (195-170 B.C.) to that of Hyrcanus II (76-30 B.C.).

The sect held itself aloof from the worship in Jerusalem. At the same time, however, it was animated by a most vivid eschatological expectation and a great zeal in the observance of the Mosaic law. Among its most characteristic rites was a veritable obsession with ritual purity through ablutions. To this purpose they had constructed a complicated system of pools and baths and had provided for ample water-supplies in an area that was practically desert. The direction of the community was in the hands of the priests. Postulants had to put in a preparatory period of two years before solemnly pledging themselves. The life of the sect was divided between work and the study of the law. They did not have a ritual worship, but gathered in prayer and community assemblies.

R

Raamah (ray´-a-mah), Son of Cush and father of Sheba and Dedah in the Table of Nations (Gen. 10:7; 1 Chron. 1:9).

Raamses (ray-am´-seez), A city of Egypt in the eastern region of the Nile delta. It was the residence of the Pharaohs from the nineteenth dynasty. It was built by Ramses II (1301-1234) on the site of the ancient capital of the Hyksos. The Israelites were obliged during the sojourn in Egypt to work on the construction of Raamses (Ex. 1:11; 12:37; Num. 33:3-6).

Rabbah, 1. A city in Transjordan, also called Rabbath Ammon, capital of the Ammonite kingdom, on the site of the present-day Amman, Jordan's capital (2 Sam. 21, 22; Jer. 29:2, 3; Ezek. 21:20; 25:5; Amos 1:14).

2. A town of Judah (Josh. 15:60), site unknown.

Rabbi, A transcription from the Aramaic meaning "my master," an honorific title addressed especially to the teachers of the law (Matt. 23:7-

8), and to Jesus by the disciples (Matt. 26:25, 49; Mk. 9:5; 14:45; Jn. 1:38; 4:31) and by others (Jn. 3:2). It was also given to John the Baptizer (Jn. 3:25). At times the more emphatic Aramaic form is read: "rabboni" or "rabbouni" (Mk. 10:51; Jn. 20:16). During the Talmudic period rabbi became the title and common designation of the masters of Judaism.

Rabbith, A town in the territory of Issachar (Josh. 19:20).

Rabboni (ra-boe′-ni), *See* RABBI.

Rab-Mag, An official at the court of Babylon whose functions are not known exactly (Jer. 39:3, 13).

Rab Saris, The chief of eunuchs at the Babylonian court (2 Kgs. 18:17; Jer. 39:3, 13).

Rab-Shakeh, A title of an Assyrian administrator or official, the senior cupbearer of the king of Assyria (2 Kgs 18:17; Jer. 39:3, 13), now translated "commander" in NAB.

Raca (Rah′-ka), From the Aramaic **reka** which means "empty" and therefore used as an offensive epitaph, the equivalent of "fool" (*see* Matt. 5:22). *See* FOOL, FOLLY. It was used in the Talmud as a term of contempt to designate those ignorant of the law.

Racal (ray′kal), A village in Judah (1 Sam. 30:29).

race

a perverse and crooked *r*.	the destruction of my *r*. Esth. 8:6
Deut. 32:5 that the *r*. is not won Eccl. 9:11	
take part in the *r*. 1 Cor. 9:24	

Rachel, The younger daughter of Laban and second wife of Jacob, who had first been married by Laban's trickery to Leah (Gen. 29:1-30). Rachel gave Jacob two sons, Joseph (Gen. 30:22, 24) and Benjamin, and died after the birth of the second (Gen. 35:16-20). She was buried at Bethlehem on the road to Ephrath, where Jacob raised a monument over her grave (Gen. 35:16-20; 1 Sam. 10:2; Jer. 31:15). From her slave Bilhah, Jacob had as children Dan and Naphtali (Gen. 30:1-8; 35:25).

In the Israelite confederacy the tribes of Rachel—Manasseh, Ephraim (together comprising the house of Joseph) and Benjamin are the most directly involved in the traditions of the Exodus and in the conquest under Joshua (Josh. 8-10). They took over the central region and formed the center of cohesion in the premonarchic confederation (*see* Josh. 24).

Raddai (rad′-eye), Fifth son of Jesse and brother of king David (1 Chron. 2:14).

Ragae (ray′-jee), A city of Media, the residence of Gabelus to whom the young Tobiah went to collect the money left to Gabael in deposit by Tobiah's father (*see* Tob. 1:14; 4:1, 20; 5:5; 6:12; 9:2). Today it is Rai, five miles south of Teheran.

rage

your *r*. against me	2 Kgs. 19:28 Why did the Gentiles *r*. Acts 4:25	

Raguel (rag′-yoo-el, or ra-goo′-al), Father of Sarah, Tobiah's wife (Tob. 3:7; 6:10).

Rahab (ray′-hab), 1. A prostitute of Jericho who received and hid in the city the Israelite spies sent by Joshua to scout out their possibilities of resistance. In return for these services she asked that she and her house be spared when the city fell into the hands of the Israelites, which was granted (Josh. 2:1-21; 6:17-25). The woman's faith in God and the services she rendered merited further praise in Hebrews 11:31 and James 2:25.

2. The wife of Solomon and mother of Boaz in the genealogy of Jesus according to Matthew 1:5.

3. A mythological sea monster overcome by God in the story of creation as God's victory over the waters (Ps. 89:10, 11; Job 9:13; 26:12; *see* CREATION). Later it became a poetic designation for Egypt: the myth became history in the Exodus when God once more prevailed over the waters. Isaiah 51:9-10 sings the Lord who "crushed Rabah," dried up "the waters of the great deep" and made the seabed a road for the redeemed to cross (*see* Isa. 30:7; Ps. 87:4).

Raham (ray′-ham), Son of Shema of the tribe of Judah (1 Chron. 2:44).

Rain, In Palestine, as in the whole Near East, the year really has but two seasons, winter and summer (*see* Gen. 8:22). During the summer from the end of April to the middle of October it rarely rains (1 Sam. 12:17; Prov. 26:1). Winter is rain-time, and the rains are usually heavy and violent. From these rains depends the whole life of the country, and want of them or their delay can prove fatal to crops and harvest (1 Kgs. 17). Rain, then, in the right time is a blessing from God (Joel 2:23; Deut. 28:12), and one of the most precious advantages of the Holy Land (Deut. 11:11-13). Drought, in contrast, was one of the worst things that could happen, and formed one of the most serious curses attached to the covenant (Deut. 28:23, 24). The season of the rains comprised the **yoreh,** that is, the first rains towards the beginning of November, **gesem** or **matar,** the heavy winter rains, and **malkos,** the last rains of March (*see* Deut. 11:11-13; Joel 2:23; Ezra 19:9, 13).

Rainbow, According to Genesis 9:12-17 the rainbow is the reminder of the covenant of God with Noah, in which God pledged never to send another flood. The rainbow should keep God in mind of his pledge, but it should also keep men in mind of the divine word given. There are other biblical allusions to the rainbow (Sir. 43:11 and Rev. 4:3; 10:1).

Rakem (ray′-kem), Son of Machir and grandson of Manasseh (1 Chron. 7:16).

Rakkath, A city in the territory of Naphtali (Josh. 19:35).

Rakkon, A town in the territory of Dan (Josh. 19:46).

Ram, *See* SHEEP.

Ramah (ray′-mah), 1. A town of Benjamin (Josh. 18:25), the present er-Ram five miles north of Jerusalem on the border of the kingdom of Israel and Judah. Baasha of Israel (900-877 B.C.) attempted to fortify it, but his effort was foiled by Asa of Judah who called the Aramaeans to his help (1 Kgs. 15:17-22). While being deported with the rest of the exiled Jews to Babylon, Jeremiah was freed at Ramah by order of Nebuzaradan, commander of the guard, who was acting under instructions from Nebuchadnezzar (Jer. 40:1-4). Near Ramah was Rachel's tomb (Jer. 31:15; Matt. 2:18) although another tradition places this in Bethlehem (Gen. 35:20).

2. A city of Ephraim, the birthplace, residence and sepulcher of Samuel (1 Sam. 7:17; 8:4; 15:34; 19:18; 25:1; 28:3) and the birthplace of his father Elkanah (1 Sam. 1:1). The city is also called Ramathaim (1 Sam. 1:1), and in the Hellenistic period, Arimatha (*see* Matt. 27:57; Mk. 15:43; Lk. 23:51; Josh. 19:38).

3. A city of Asher (Josh. 19:29).

4. A city of Naphtali (Josh. 19:36).

5. *See* RAMOTH-GILEAD.

Ramathaim (ram′-a-thay′-im), 1. A region of Samaria given to Judas Maccabeus by Demetrius Nicator of Syria (1 Mac. 11:34).

2. *See* RAMAH 2.

Ramath-lehi (ray′-math-lee′-hie), *See* LEHI.

Ramoth, A Levitical town of the territory of Issachar (1 Chron. 6:65).

Ramoth-gilead, A town in the territory of Gad in Gilead (Josh. 20:8), a Levitical city and a city of refuge (Deut. 4:43; Josh. 21:38; 1 Chron. 6:65). During the period of the monarchy the possession of Ramoth in Gilead was fought over by Israelites and Aramaeans with alternating success. Today it is Tell Ramit on the frontier between Jordan and Syria (*see* 1 Kgs. 22; 2 Kgs. 8:28; 9:1-14).

rampart
grief on wall and *r.*   Lam. 2:8   with the flood for her *r.*   Neh. 3:8

Ramses, Ramses II, Pharaoh of Egypt from 1290-1224 B.C. *See* EXODUS.

ransom
he must pay in *r.*   Ex. 21:30   to give his own life as a *r.*
I have found him a *r.*   Job. 33:24   Matt. 20:28
                  to give his own life in *r.*   Mk. 10:45

Rapha, A son of Benjamin (1 Chron. 8:2).

Raphael (raph′ or rayph′-i-el), The word means "God Heals," one of the seven angels who stand ever ready to enter the presence of the glory of the Lord, according to Tobit 12:15. He was sent to Tobit to cure him and to take care of his son during his journey to Media to recover the silver left to Gabael in deposit (Tob. 5). The angel took the boy to get the gall, heart and liver of the fish he had caught in the Tigris. From the gall was made the eye ointment to cure Tobit's blindness, while the reek of the heart and gall as it burned on the censer drove the demon away from the young Sarah (Tob. 8:1-3; *see* Tob. 6-11). *See* TOBIT.

Raphon (ra′-phon), A place near Carnaim where Judas Maccabeus defeated the Seleucid army under the command of Timothy (1 Mac. 5:37-44).

Ras Shamrah, The name of the ancient city on the Syrian coast, 8 miles north of Lattaqieh, and mound containing the remains of an important Canaanite city, called Ugarit during the second millenium B.C., much fought over by Egyptians, Phoenicians and Canaanites. *See* UGARIT.

Rassis, A region of Asia devastated by the army of Holofernes (Judith 2:23).

raven
and he sent out a *r.*   Gen. 8:7   black as the *r.*   S of S. 5:11
for the *r.*   Job 38:41 and *r.* shall dwell in her   Isa. 34:11

Razis (ray′-zis), One of the elders at Jerusalem during the period of the Maccabees, who was called "Father of the People" for having put his life in danger in defense of Judaism. Nicanor thought to make an example of him, so he sent five hundred men to arrest him. When these were on the point of capturing him, Razis fell upon his own sword, preferring a noble death to falling into the clutches of the enemy (2 Mac. 14:27-46). In the confusion however he failed, so he ran up to the wall and threw himself down on the troops. They side-stepped. Injured and bleeding he took a stone and ripped out his own entrails, flinging them at the troops while calling on the Master of his life and spirit to restore them to him some day (2 Mac. 14:37-46). The account is perhaps more legendary than factual.

Razor, The practice of shaving in various purification acts (Num. 8:7; Lev. 14:8) and as a sign of mourning very probably created among the Hebrews a skilled trade of barbering. Levites, like Egyptian priests, shaved their whole bodies. An individual, on entering the Nazirite sect, was shaved but then vowed (among other things) not to shave for the duration of his vow, when he was ceremonially shaved and his hair burned in the prescribed way. Samuel and Samson took lifelong Nazirite vows (Num. 6:5; Samuel, 1 Sam. 1:11; Samson, Jgs. 13:5). Isaiah (7:20) and Ezekiel (5:1) used the razor as a figure of speech. Paul shaved his head as a result of a vow (Nazirite? Acts 18:18) as did four converts (21:23).

read

he *r*. it aloud	Ex. 24:7	priest Zephaniah *r*. this letter	
When he *r*. the letter	2 Kgs. 5:7		Jer. 29:29
one who can *r*.	Isa. 29:11	Have you not *r*. what David did	
			Matt. 12:3

ready

everything is *r*.	Matt. 22:4	and the ones who were *r*.	
The banquet is *r*.	Matt. 22:8		Matt. 25:10

Reaiah (re-ay'-ah), "The Lord has seen," a personal name (1 Chron. 4:2; 5:5; Ezra 2:47).

reap

and *r*. your harvest	Lev. 23:10	and sow trouble, *r*. the same	
in the third year sow and *r*.			Job 4:8
	2 Kgs. 19:29	They do not sow or *r*.	Matt. 6:26
	You know I *r*.	Matt. 25:26	

rear

marching in the *r*.	1 Sam. 29:2	and his *r*. toward	Joel 2:20

reason

a people devoid of *r*.	Deut. 32:28

Reba (ree'-ba), One of the five Midianite kings slaughtered with the rest of the Midianite males by the Israelites under Moses (Num. 31:8; Josh. 13:21-22).

Rebekah, Daughter of Bethuel and wife of Isaac (Gen. 22:23; 24). After a long period of sterility Rebekah gave birth to twins, Jacob and Esau. According to Genesis 25:21-29 even before birth the children struggled inside her. This was interpreted by Yahweh as an indication that the two nations that should issue from these children would turn out rivals, and the younger would have mastery over the other (Gen. 25:21-29; Mal. 1:2-5; Rom. 9:12). Genesis 27 tells the story of how Rebekah cooked the savory food for Isaac, covered the hairless Jacob with skins and dressed him in Esau's clothes so that Isaac was mislead into giving Jacob the blessing. Rebekah was buried in the cave bought by Abraham at Machpelah for a burial-place (Gen. 49-31).

rebel

do not *r*. against him	Ex. 23:21	do not *r*. against the Lord	
			Num. 14:9

rebel (cont.)
do not *r*. against   1 Sam. 12:14

rebuke
a day of distress, of *r*.   2 Kgs. 19:3   But God shall *r*. them   Isa. 17:13
A *r*. which puts me   Job 20:3   *r*. your disciples   Lk. 19:39

receive
opened its mouth to *r*.   Gen. 4:11   *R*. instruction from his mouth
Wherefore did the knees *r*. me   Job 22:22
                             Job 3:12   If anyone does not *r*. you
                                                                      Matt. 10:14

Rechabites (rek′-a-bites), An Isrealite group related to the Kenites according to 1 Chronicles 2:55; 4:12, whose founding father was Rechab, about whom no more is known. This group remained nomadic even during the monarchy for religious reasons: they wished to remain faithful to the primitive norms of Moses' Yahwism laid down during the nomadic period of Israel (Jer. 35). The inspirer of this group was Jonadab, son of Rechab, or at least a Rechabite, who backed the politico-religious revolt of Jehu against the dynasty of Ahab (2 Kgs. 10:15-24).

reconciliation
we have received *r*.   Rom. 5:11   entrusted the message of *r*.
given us the ministry of *r*.   2 Cor. 5:19
                             2 Cor. 5:18

reconnoiter
Moses sent out to *r*.   Num. 13:16   sent me from Kadesh-barnea to *r*.
In sending them to *r*.   Num. 13:17   Josh. 14:7
Joshua had sent to *r*. Jericho   to *r*. the land   Jgs. 18:2
                             Josh. 6:25

recovered
David *r*. everything   1 Sam. 30:18 the king of Edom *r*. Elath
r. the cities of Israel   2 Kgs. 13:25   2 Kgs. 16:6
                  and had *r*. from his illness   Isa. 38:9

red
some of that *r*. stuff   Gen. 25:30   Though they be crimson *r*.
as *r*. as blood   2 Kgs. 3:22   Isa. 1:18
the wine when it is *r*.   Prov. 23:31 *R*. sky at night   Matt. 16:2

Redemption, Redemption, to redeem, and to ransom are terms taken from the language of everyday life and used to illustrate an important aspect of the work of salvation carried out by Jesus through his death and resurrection. One must not however extend the analogy beyond due limits, namely, those limits indicated in the New Testament itself.

In profane language these terms are used above all to denote the manumission of a slave through the payment of a price. The New Testament usage, however, does not directly depend on this meaning of the term. It draws more from its use in the Old Testament to illustrate the salvation brought about by God in favor of his people, principally in the Exodus (Ex. 6:6, 7; Deut. 7:6-8; 13:6; 15:15; 21:8). Now, it is obvious that God liberated his people from Egypt, not however by paying a price for their redemption, but by exercising his omnipotence against the contrary stubborn will of the Pharaoh. In the Old Testament, then, to redeem is to liberate and above all it expresses the positive saving effect of God's intervention, that is, freedom from a condition of oppression and disgrace (Pss. 25:22; 130:7, 8). To God belongs the people he thus redeemed: it becomes his people, and for this purpose the redemption took place so that among all the peoples of the earth this one should be his (Ex. 19:3-5; *see* ELECTION; 2 Sam. 7:23; Esther 13:9).

The Exodus was the type of every future saving intervention, and so the prophets applied the idea of redemption to the future eschatological salvation to be effected by God. The people exiled in Babylonia were to be redeemed by God (Isa. 52:3), and God comes to them, on the lips of the prophet, as a redeemer (Isa. 41:14; 44:6; 47:4). This redemption is not just the restoration of the people as a nation but it includes the purification of the people from their sins (Isa. 44:22; *see* Ps. 130:7, 8).

Jesus came to give his life as a ransom for men (Mk. 10:45; Matt. 20:28; 1 Tim. 2:6). This means that his death was to be the instrument of liberation, for through it the sins of all would be expiated (Rom. 3:25). So Jesus is redeemer, for through his death and the resurrection, from which it is inseparable, he conquered sin and death (Col. 1:14; Eph. 1:7; Heb. 9:15) and made us his own (1 Cor. 6:20; 7:23), so that we are now the Lord's (1 Cor. 8:6) and the sons of God (Gal. 4:4-7). This redemption is not yet complete in us. We still sigh within ourselves while we await the total redemption which will be the glorification of our bodies (Rom. 8:23). The Holy Spirit who dwells in us is the pledge and the first-fruits of this full redemption in which God will take full possession of us (Eph. 1:14; 4:30; *see* Lk. 21:28). Often in the New Testament we read that we were redeemed at a dear price (1 Cor. 6:20; 7:23), not with gold or silver, but with the blood of Christ (1 Pet. 1:18). This should not be interpreted in a way that would pose the question: to whom was the price paid? Unfortunately this moderation has not always been observed in the past, and the absurd answer has been proposed that Jesus paid this price to the devil! The devil was not compensated but defeated, bound and rendered powerless. His empire came to an end through the work of Jesus. With these expressions the New Testament wishes to bring home to Christians how arduous a task the redemption was, how great a sacrifice, seeing that it cost Jesus his life, and so how great a love he had for men. His death, his blood, were the instruments of redemption, the means through which he brought about the expiation for sin and brought humanity back to life-bestowing intimacy with God.

Red Heifer, The confection of lustral water, used in removing the impurities contracted by touching dead bodies, demanded a complicated rite which is preserved in Numbers 19 and has archaic residue. A red heifer without blemish was immolated and then burned entirely, together with cedar wood, hyssop and cochineal red. The ashes were gathered into a container to which was added river or spring water. This was then sprinkled with hyssop on the impure objects or persons. Numbers 19 places this among the sacrifices for sin (19:17). This means of purification is only mentioned in Numbers 31:23, while in Leviticus 22:4-6 other measures are prescribed for the same impurities.

Red Sea, The traditional translation of **Yam-suph,** which literally means the sea of reeds. In the Exodus tradition **Yam-suph** certainly does not mean the Red Sea, but rather some of the masses of water found along the coast of Egypt in the isthmus of the Suez (*see* EXODUS; *see* Ex. 10:19; 13:18; 15:4; Num. 33:10 f.; Ps. 106:9, 22, etc.). Yam-suph, however, does mean the Red Sea including the Gulf of Aqaba, in 1 Kings 9:26; 2 Chronicles 8:17; Numbers 14:25, and in other texts not connected with the miracle of the Exodus.

Reed Sea, *See* RED SEA.

refine
and I will *r.* them as silver   Zech. 13:9

Refuge, Blood-revenge was characteristic of nomad society (*see* AVENGER) and in general of ancient eastern civilizations. It was sanctioned in Exodus 21:13-14. This law however places limits to its exercise, for in the case of involuntary homicide there are established places of inviolable sanctuary where the accused can take refuge. (*See* 1 Kgs. 1:50-53; 2:28-31.) Later legislation, probably from monarchical times, specified the cities of refuge, which were very likely chosen because of the presence of some particularly important sanctuary to which was attached the right of asylum. There were three such cities in Transjordan: Beser, Ramoth in Gilead and Golan (Deut. 4:41-43), and three on the near side of Jordan: Kedesh, Shechem and Hebron (Josh. 20:1-9; *see* Num. 35:9-34; Deut. 19:1-13).

Regemmelech (ree'-gam-mel'-ek), One of the men of Bethel sent to ask the priests and prophets of Jerusalem about the fasting of the fifth month. This fasting was held to commemorate the destruction of Jerusalem by the Babylonians (Zech. 7:2).

Rehabiah (ree'-a-bie'-ah), Son of Eliezer and grandson of Aaron (1 Chron. 23:17; 24:21; 26:25).

Rehob, The father of Hadadezer, the Aramean king of Zobah (2 Sam. 8:3, 12).

Rehoboam (ree'-o-boe'-am), King of Judah (922-915 B.C.), son and successor of Solomon (1 Kgs. 11:43) whose mother was the Ammonite Naamah (1 Kgs. 14:21). The elders of the northern tribes met at Shechem and asked Rehoboam to lighten the burden placed on them by his father. Among his consultors the elders advised him to lighten the burden, but he took the contrary advice of the young men. This gave rise to the schism, in which the northern tribes chose Jeroboam for king (1 Kgs. 12:1-25). During Rehoboam's reign Shishak Pharaoh of Egypt invaded Judah and plundered Jerusalem, taking away in booty much of the riches gathered by Rehoboam's father Solomon (1 Kgs. 14:25-28; 2 Chron. 12). Rehoboam fortified the frontier towns to the south and west to offset any further Egyptian expedition (2 Chron. 11:5-12). The Chronicler's judgment on him is that he did evil because he had not set his heart on seeking Yahweh (2 Chron. 11:14).

Rehoboth (re-hoe'-both), 1. One of the wells dug by Isaac in the Negeb, in the valley of Gerar (Gen. 26:17-22), south of Beer-sheba.

2. A city of Edom (Gen. 36:37; 1 Chron. 1:48).

3. Rehoboth-ir was a city in Mesopotamia, established by Assur according to the genealogy of Genesis 10:11.

Rehum (ree'-um), The Persian governor of Samaria who supported the Samaritans' opposition to the rebuilding of the walls of Jerusalem. To this purpose he sent a letter to Artaxerses I (465-425 B.C.) and received a reply forbidding the work to be continued. Thus the reconstruction of the Temple was suspended until it was undertaken anew during the reign of Darius (424-404 B.C., Ezra 4:6-24).

reign

The Lord shall *r.* forever		and his *r.* will be without end	
	Ex. 15:18		Lk. 1:33
The *r.* of God is at hand	Matt. 3:2		

rejoice

r. in Abimelech	Jgs. 9:19	and the earth *r.*	1 Chron. 16:31
r. O hearts that seek the		let the plains *r.*	1 Chron. 16:32
	1 Chron. 16:20	Be glad and *r.*	Matt. 5:12

Rekem (ree′-kem), A Midianite king defeated and slain by the Israelites under Moses' command (Num. 31:8; Josh. 13:21).

religion

over issues in their own *r*.	the strictest sect of our *r*. Acts 26:5
Acts 25:19	

Remaliah (rem′-a-lie′-ah), The father of King Pekah of Israel (2 Kgs. 15:25; Isa. 7:1).

remedy

there was no *r*,

  2 Chron. 36:16

remember

R. this day	Ex. 13:3	*R*. that my life is like	Job 7:7
R. to keep holy the Sabbath day		Oh, *r*. that you fashioned me	
	Ex. 20:8		Job 10:9
r. your handmaid	1 Sam. 25:31	*r*. that you were well off	Lk. 16:25

remission

penance for the *r*. of sins

  Lk. 24:47

Remnant, Remnant, in Hebrew **shear** or **she′erit** is the part of the people, often a greatly reduced part, that survives a conquest or invasion after being defeated (*see* e.g. Isa. 14:30; 15:9; 17:3; 21:17). According to Deuteronomy 7:2 the Israelites had to wage a war of total destruction on the people of Canaan, and in Joshua 10:40 it is stated that Joshua "conquered the whole country . . . and left no survivors, but fulfilled the doom on all who lived there." (*See* WAR.) The survivors of the destruction of Jerusalem and Judah by Nebuchadnezzar are called the remnant (Jer. 40:15; 587 B.C.).

The terms "remnant" and "to leave a remnant" are ambivalent. They can denote the precarious and miserable situation to which the people has been reduced—and so the phrase "to leave but a remnant"—or they can ring out with a tone of hope, with the possibility of revival and restoration —in such phrases as "to leave at least a remnant." This ambivalence is typical of the theological use the prophets make of the word. On their lips God announces his imminent and implacable judgment. The people will be doomed to destruction. Let the person who wishes to flee this judgment know what the "remnant" will be like: "As the shepherd snatches from the mouth of the lion a pair of legs or an ear of his sheep, so the Israelites who dwell in Samaria shall escape" (Amos 3:12). The concept of remnant is here decidedly negative, (in Jer. 6:9; 8:3; 24:8 God takes punitive measures even against the "remnant").

The "remnant of the people," however, appears in another light as the result of a mitigation in the severity of the judgment. This mitigation on the part of God; who, faithful to his promises, intends to make use of the remnant to carry on and bring to completion his saving design, which had been compromised by the people's infidelity. The "remnant" is, then, the subject of future hope (Isa. 4:3; 6:13). It will come out purified from the trial of judgment and turn totally to God (Isa. 10:20, 21). Even though this remnant will be scattered among the nations, God will call them, will unite them and have them return to the land of their fathers (Isa. 11:11; Mic. 2:12; Zech. 8:6-12).

Paul uses the remnant theme in Romans 11:1-10. Among the Jews only a remnant believed, and into this remnant the mass of the Gentiles has been grafted. Again in the future however the lopped-off branches will be grafted on anew (Rom. 11:16-24). There is also the remnant theme in the account of the flood. God freely chooses Noah and instructs him on survival when the rest of humanity will be destroyed. Noah and his family form the remnant. He is called to be the beginnings of a new humanity (Gen. 6-8).

render
r. to everyone according
2 Chron. 6:30

repair, repairs
needed r. in the temple
2 Kgs. 12:7
Why do you not r. the temple?
2 Kgs. 12:8

r. the house of your God
2 Chron. 24:5
to r. it
2 Chron. 24:12

repent
is not man that he should r.
1 Sam. 15:29
may they r. in the land of
1 Kgs. 8:47

and r. in dust and ashes   Job 42:6
and he will not r.   Ps. 110:4
then they would r.   Lk. 16:30

Repentance, *See* PENANCE.

Rephael (ref'-a-el), Son of Shemaiah, a family of David's servants (1 Chron. 26:7).

Rephaiah (re-fay'-yah), Personal name (1 Chron. 3:21; 4:42; 7:2; 9:43; Neh. 3:9).

Rephaim (ref'-a-im), 1. A pre-Israelitic people in Palestine (Deut. 3:13; Josh. 17:15), at times described with mythological characteristics, like the Anakim (Deut. 2:11, 20). They lived mainly in Transjordan, and to them belonged Og, king of Bashan (Deut. 3:11; Josh. 12:4; 13:12). The Emim of the land of Moab are identified with them (Deut. 2:11), as are the Zamsummim in the territory of Ammon (Deut. 2:20).

2. The term **rephaim** from an etymological point of view means "ancestors." In the Bible and Ugaritic religious poems it also means Sheol, the habitation of the dead (*see* Isa. 14:9; 26:14; Ps. 88:10; Job 26:5; Prov. 9:18).

Rephaim, Valley of, A valley near Jerusalem on the border between the territory of Judah and Benjamin (Josh. 15:8; 18:16). It was the scene of battles between the Philistines and the Israelites at the time of David (2 Sam. 5:18, 22; 23:13; 1 Chron. 11:15; 14:9).

Rephidim (ref'-i-dim), A stage on the journey of the Israelites from Egypt to Sinai, where Moses miraculously obtained water for the people and by his prayers won them victory over the Amalekites (Ex. 17).

reproach
I have removed the r. of Israel
Josh. 5:9
in great distress and under r.
Neh. 1:3

my heart does not r. me   Job 27:6
He began to r. the towns
Matt. 11:20

request
I should like to make a r. of
Jgs. 8:24
granted the r. of his servant
2 Sam. 14:22

Whatever r. you make shall
Esth. 7:2
Oh, that I might have my r.
Job 6:8

required
as was *r.* day by day   2 Chron. 8:13   your life shall be *r.* of thee
as the daily duty *r.*   2 Chron. 8:14   Lk. 12:20
                much will be *r.* of him   Lk. 12:48

requital
day of vengeance and *r.*   Deut. 32:35

Resen (ree′-zen), A city in Mesopotamia between Kalneh and Nineveh, founded by Assur according to the Table of Nations in Genesis 10:12.

Resh, The 20th letter of the Hebrew alphabet (r).

Resheph (ree′-shef), A Canaanean god of pestilence and destruction. In the Old Testament the name is used almost as a generic name for plague or pestilence. Traces of the origin of the name can be deteceted in its use (*see* Deut. 32:34; Pss. 76:4; 78:48; Job 5:7; Hab. 3:5).

rest
r. yourselves under the tree   He sent the *r.* of the people
             Gen. 18:4   1 Sam. 13:2
pasture the *r.* of Laban's flock   carried out the ban on the *r.*
            Gen. 30:36   1 Sam. 15:15
         your souls will find *r.*   Matt. 11:29

restitution
He must make full *r.*   Ex. 22:2   he need not make *r.*   Ex. 22:14
         I will make *r.* to you   1 Sam. 12:3

restore
and *r.* you to your post   Gen. 40:13   shall *r.* the ewe lamb fourfold
I will *r.* to you all the land   2 Sam. 12:6
         2 Sam. 9:7   and he will *r.* everything
                                     Matt. 17:11

Resurrection, The doctrine of the resurrection is one of the last acquisitions of the revelation of the Old Testament. Like all the peoples of their cultural world the Israelites were convinced that men survived death, but survival was a state of such weakness and inactivity that it did not merit the name of life. (*See* SHEOL.) The doctrine of resurrection postulates not just a return to the conditions of this earth's limited life but the acquisition of the fullness of life, both corporal and spiritual, that is, a truly human life which breaks through the limitations of the present condition in that it can never more be lost. When resurrection is being discussed it is something other than the miracles of raising to life that are found in the Old Testament (1 Kgs. 17:17-24; 2 Kgs. 4:18-37; 13:20, 21) and the New (Jesus raised to life the daughter of Jairus, Matt. 9:18-26; Mk. 5:21-42; Lk. 8:40-56; the son of the widow of Naim, Lk. 7:11-17, and Lazarus, Jn. 11:1-44; or miracles by the apostles in Acts 9:36-43; 20:8-12). These are reanimations rather than resurrections in the sense explained.

From the definition given, it can be seen that in the Old Testament the problem of resurrection was posed and resolved mostly for the just and not for the wicked. Thus it is known that the resurrection of the wicked for judgment is often left in silence. In many cases resurrection becomes synonymous with glorious resurrection. At times however there is a more complete vision and the destiny of all, just and unjust, after death is described.

The doctrine of resurrection is clearly expressed in Daniel 12:1-3 and in Wisdom 1-5. Other more ancient texts are not clear and the interpretation of them is not certain. They have their interest, however, for they allow us to see the paths down which the Israelites came to the doctrine of the resurrection. From these texts it appears clear that it was not philosophical or anthropological considerations that drove them to this conclusion. In other words it was not the adaptation of more developed anthropology that distinguished body from soul that facilitated this passage. The reasons were religious. Given God's omnipotence, he was capable of giving back life to dry bones—a conviction of faith expressed in a vision of Ezekiel 36:1-14 but applied to the restoration of Israel after the exile. Resurrection was first and foremost considered the continuation after death of the life of union with God which the faithful person had lived during this mortal life (Ps. 16). The psalmist in Psalm 16 is convinced that his life of communion with God, of which he is conscious and which every day he enjoys, cannot be struck out by death: God, who is more powerful than death, will know how to conquer. The psalmist does not know how this will come about, but he has no doubt of the fact and he puts his trust in it.

In Psalm 49 the problem is posed in regard to retribution. The psalmist belongs to the Wisdom tradition and in this tradition contemplates the unequal lot of the oppressed and persecuted just man, and that of the wicked person enjoying life. His solution is similar to that of Psalm 16, namely, that the end of the wicked is death, but that God, who is stronger than death, will not let the just out of his power. How exactly this is to take place is not discussed. The author seems to allude to the cases of Enoch and Elijah, and postulates that "God will take the just to himself."

Daniel 12:1-3 clearly expresses the doctrine of resurrection in an apocalyptic framework. C. 12 is the conclusion of the vision that begins in c. 10, and in which he describes the history of the Orient beginning with the Persian empire up to Antiochus IV Epiphanes (175-164 B.C.). The tribulations that take place under this emperor, who is a contemporary of the author of Daniel, is the end. Then Michael, the protector of God's people (Dan. 10:21), will save those inscribed in the book of life, that is, in practice, the living just. To those, however, will be added the dead who have arisen to share in this salvation. According to the most common interpretation in 12:1-3 there must be distinguished two groups, the just who arise from the dead for life and the impious who return to life for judgment and condemnation.

The resurrection of the just is the theme of Wisdom 1-5. The author is arguing with those apostate Jews who have been seduced by a popular form of Greek Epicurianism according to which death was inevitable and triumphant in this life, so that it was now necessary to enjoy life to the full (Wisdom 2:1-9). To this thesis the author opposes the "mysteries of God" (2:21-24). God created man for immortality (*see* IMAGE OF GOD), that is, for the possession of an eternal and glorious life with himself. Death entered the world through the envy of the devil, and they experience it who take the devil's part. At this point it should be noted that "immortality" and "incorruption" are not to be taken in the philosophical sense: that is, it is not a question of something that belongs to man as a constituent part, nor is it his soul that is being referred to. It is not, then, mere subsistence after death. The immortality here referred to is the gift of God and the fruit of justice, an eternal life of glory. Death of which Wisdom 1-5 speaks is not merely the end of biological life but the definitive passage to eternal perdition. The author carefully avoids the term **thanatos** ("death" in the full sense) when he speaks of the just. For them he has recourse to other terms, such as transit, passage, going to sleep. The just die in the popular sense of the term but not in the theological sense which the author reserves for the death of the wicked.

The New Testament inherited (and sanctioned with its authority) this hope of resurrection that arose at the end of Old Testament times. It was however made more precise in some texts. John 5:28, 29 takes up the distinction of Daniel 12:1-3 between resurrection for life and resurrection for judgment (*see* also 2 Cor. 5:10). Both will arise, the just and the unjust, but to a different destiny. This is presupposed in the texts that speak of the general judgment (*see* Matt. 25:1-46). Generally speaking, however, the New Testament is only interested in the resurrection of Christians, so that the concept of resurrection, as we have seen from the Old Testament, is the equivalent of glorious resurrection. It is not denied nor excluded that sinners too will arise to receive their merited eternal punishment, but they cannot be said to arise in the biblical sense of the term, which is synonymous with total and definitive salvation of the whole man. The great novelty that the New Testament brought to this point is that the glorious resurrection of Christians is placed in intimate relationship with the glorious resurrection of Jesus, which is the guarantee, the evidence in his glorified flesh, that his followers will like him arise. *See* RESURRECTION OF CHRIST.

Resurrection of Christ, When there is reference to the resurrection of Christ, it does not mean a mere reanimation of his body or a return by Jesus to the condition of corporal or spiritual life that he possessed before the passion and death. Resurrection means that he acquired a grace-pervaded, glorious condition of life that was truly human, that is, both spiritual and corporal. In this sense the resurrection of Jesus went far beyond the miracles of reanimation that he accomplished during life. (*See* RESURRECTION.) The resurrection of Jesus also includes his exaltation to the right hand of God in heaven (Acts 2:36). With the resurrection, in other words, Jesus acquired the effective exercise of that universal dominion, especially in the order of salvation (Rom. 1:4), not only to which he was destined, but which radically, as incarnate Son of God, he possessed. (*See* SON OF GOD.) Jesus was constituted Messiah and Lord (Acts 2:36; *see* LORD), powerful to save all who believe in him. From this point of view the resurrection cannot be proved rationally but is a supernatural mystery to be believed by faith.

The resurrection of Jesus, however, is also historical fact, a miracle, an event that took place at a certain moment of time, and so it possesses an external aspect that leaves its traces on the order of experienced reality, thereby justly falling within the competence of historical research. Jesus, who really died on the cross, was later seen alive by some people whose testimony we possess. Therefore, while the resurrection of Jesus as a salvation event transcends the temporal order and terminates in the divine order of things, and thus remains inaccessible to pure historical research, it has nevertheless left signs in so far as it was an event that also belonged to the order of time. These signs are the empty tomb and the apparitions.

The resurrection of Jesus, then, has two aspects, the one historical which can therefore be studied for the historical value of the traditions contained in the New Testament on the empty tomb and apparitions, and the other theological, which is investigated to determine what place as a saving event it occupies in the history of salvation.

The discussion on the historical aspect has progressed notably in objectivity in recent years. All explanations that cast doubt on the sincerity of the apostolic witness have been abandoned. The point of departure, then, is that the apostles were sincerely convinced that Jesus had arisen from the dead. Moreover, instead of running to plausible explanations of how the apostles came to this persuasion, drawing especially on religious psychology, there is accord that the only way seriously to discuss the question is by a critical study of the New Testament testimony as a historical document. Even within these limits the problem is very complex. The New Testament testimony contains: 1. the gospel narrative on the discovery of the empty tomb and the apparitions of Jesus, and 2. the most ancient apostolic preaching as this can be gathered from 1 Corinthians 15:3 ff. and from the discourse of the Acts of the Apostles (Acts 2:14-36; 3:11-26; 4:8-12; 10:34-43; 13:16-41).

The empty tomb is not explicitly mentioned in this second series of texts, but there are strong indications that it was known, even though it was not yet used for precise polemic purposes. In fact the proclamation of the resurrection of Jesus could not have long been sustained without an official investigation of the tomb, given the concept of resurrection that the Jews had at the time. On the other hand only with difficulty could Psalm 16 be applied to Jesus, as it was applied in Acts 2:25 ff., if it were not known to all that Jesus' tomb was in a very different condition from that of David—that is, if an authorized investigation had not discovered it empty.

There are more precise details given for the apparitions. 1 Corinthians 15:3 contains a list of people to whom the Lord appeared: Peter and the Twelve, James and all the apostles (*see* APOSTLE), to more than 500 brethren, at last to Paul himself. In the Acts of the Apostles the theme of the apparitions is included in the notion of witness. (*See* WITNESS.) On the nature of these apparitions the sources are very sober. However two things should be noticed: the absence of the usual vocabulary in describing visions and revelations, and moreover, the expressed conviction (*see* Acts 1:4) that Jesus' apparitions continued his life with his disciples that had been interrupted by the passion and death.

Even though they coincide on the substance of the facts the gospel narratives are often discordant on details. This discordance has eluded every attempt to reduce it to one logical and coherent account. The problem is more in explaining how these divergences arose than trying to eliminate them by violence from the text.

The most ancient version of the discovery of the empty tomb of Jesus is probably that of John 20:1-18, which is confirmed by Luke 24:12: Mary Magdalene, probably not alone, visits the tomb, and finding it empty, reports to the disciples, who ascertain it for themselves. The fact however remains ambiguous. Mark 16:1-8 and parallel texts confirm the substance of the account but try to dissipate the ambiguity by introducing angels who explain to the women (and thus to the readers) the meaning of the fact, and so announce that the resurrection has taken place. This transformation is all the more explainable if the account of the empty tomb was the conclusion of the passion narrative. *See* PASSION.

In the chapter on the apparitions there are also notable differences among the gospels. According to Matthew, Jesus appears to the women and then to all the disciples in Galilee. According to Luke, Jesus appears to two disciples on their way to Emmaus, to Peter, and to the disciples in Jerusalem. John's story is that Jesus appeared to Mary Magdalene, and then twice to the disciples—once without and once with Thomas—in Jerusalem. In the appendix (c. 21) Jesus appears once more to the disciples in Galilee. Mark's gospel finished in c. 16:8 (*see* MARK, GOSPEL OF); the present conclusion is a summary of the other evangelists.

A proper evaluation of these differences must keep in mind: a. In all probability there was never a continuous and coherent account of the Paschal episodes in tradition, such as existed, for example, in the case of the passion. In fact one episode alone, one apparition alone, contained the whole Paschal kerygma. Instead, then, of a single coherent narrative, many partial cycles of stories were formed in which are reflected the interests of the individual Christian communities which shaped them.

b. Our gospels show a tendency to sum up all the elements in one decisive apparition to the disciples, in which is also contained the missionary mandate. Two principal cycles can be distinguished—one centered in Jerusalem (Luke-John) and the other in Galilee (Matthew-Mark). There is no need to exclude one or the other as non-historical, but it is not possible to establish the chronological order in which the events took place.

The resurrection of Christ is seen, through the New Testament testimony, under varying but convergent aspects. Through it the Father annulled the unholy counsel of those who killed Jesus. It is then the seal of the Father on the authenticity of the mission of Jesus of Nazareth (*see* Acts 2:22-25; 3:13-15; 4:11, which cites Ps. 118). God raised him to life and had him sit at his right hand in heaven, thus constituting him Messiah and Lord (Acts 2:36). Jesus received from the Father the promise of the Holy Spirit, and it is he who gives it to those who, repentant in faith, receive the witness of the apostles (Acts 2:33).

The resurrection of Jesus has, then, a soteriological value, that is, it is the decisive act in the event of salvation (Rom. 4:25; 1 Cor. 15:12-20). Through his resurrection Jesus was constituted Son of God with power (Rom. 1:4). He received with it a name above every other name (Phil. 2:6-11) and his humanity became a "vivifying Spirit" (1 Cor. 15:45). The individual believer through faith and baptism is incorporated into Christ and so in a sacramental way takes that step from death to life in which Jesus led the way by arising from the dead (Rom. 6). Christians then live from the life of the risen Christ (Gal. 2:19-21). They have received the Spirit of him who raised Jesus from the dead; this Spirit will give life to their mortal bodies (Rom. 8:11), and will transform them to the image of Christ. At the moment the life of Christ is hidden in us. It has nevertheless worked a profound transformation in us and has introduced us into a new life which must be expressed in a life of charity. This hidden magnificence will be revealed in the future, transfiguring our mortal body and making it glorious and immortal just like that of Christ, by the power that he has as the risen Lord (Phil. 3:20, 21).

retribution
indeed will be days of *r*.　Lk. 21:22　a stumbling stone and a *r*.
　　　　　　　　　　　　　　　　　　　　　　　　Rom. 11:9

return
Until you *r*. to the ground　　　whole heart to *r*. to the Lord
　　　　　　　　Gen. 3:19　　　　　　　　　　1 Sam. 7:3
I will surely *r*.　　Gen. 18:10　Then he used to *r*.　1 Sam. 7:17

Reu (roo or re′-ue), An ancestor of Jesus according to Luke (Lk. 3:35; Gen. 11:18-21; 1 Chron. 1:25).

Reuben, First-born of Jacob, whose mother was Leah (Gen. 29:32; 35:23; 46:8, 9; Ex. 1:2). He was the founding father of the tribe of Reuben. To save Joseph's life Reuben proposed throwing him into the cistern, with the intention of returning later to rescue him, but in the meantime Joseph was sold to the Midianites (Gen. 37:21-36). Later he took the misfortunes that befell the sons of Jacob as punishment for the evil done to Joseph (Gen. 42:22). He offered his own two sons as a guarantee that Benjamin should return (Gen. 42:37, *see* also Gen. 30:14; 35:22).

The tribe of Reuben settled with the tribe of Gad and half the tribe of

Manasseh in Transjordan north of Sihon (Num. 32:33; Josh. 13:15-23; Deut. 3:12-16), east of the northeast corner of the Dead Sea. During the monarchy the land of Reuben was disputed between the Aramaeans and the Israelites (2 Kgs. 10:33) and was finally conquered by Tiglath-pileser III who deported the population (1 Chron. 5:26).

Reuel (roo**′**-el), 1. Son of Esau and the Ishmaelite Basemath (Gen. 36:4; 1 Chron. 1:35).

2. Moses' father-in-law, a priest of Midian, father of Zipporah (Ex. 2:18; Num. 10:29). The same person is also called Jethro and Hobab. *See* JETHRO, HOBAB.

Reumah (roo**′**-mah), A concubine of Nahor, Abraham's brother, from whom he had four children: Tebah, Gaham, Tahash and Maacah (Gen. 22:24).

Revelation, The New Testament apocalyptic book. The author declares himself to be John (1:1, 4) and to have received the revelation contained in the book while he was on the island of Patmos "because I proclaimed God's word" (1:9), that is, in exile on account of being Christian. Tradition, with few exceptions, has maintained that this John is no other than John the Apostle. Today many difficulties are raised against attributing the book to John the Apostle: there are radical differences in style, language and theology between this and other writings that with more reason are considered to be John's (the gospel and the 3 epistles). For these reasons, the work is now considered more likely to have been authored by an unknown first-century Christian. Perhaps the real author wished to have his writing acknowledged as stemming from John the Evangelist. Nor should this be cause for wonder, as the procedure of attaching the name of some renowned author to a work was the general rule for apocalyptic literature, to which this work obviously belongs. This would send us on our search for the real author among the Christian prophets of the Johannine church in Asia Minor; he would therefore have been a disciple of John.

The book is famous both for the difficulty in interpreting it and for the variety of interpretations which have been proposed. But first of all it is absolutely necessary to avoid that type of interpretation which believes itself capable of discovering in the symbols used by the author veiled allusions to the later history of the Church or to the total history of the universe: to the Great Western Schism, to Luther's schism, to the French revolution, etc. This type of interpretation is completely arbitrary, and would call God's word to witness fantastic calculations about the duration of the world or the imminence of its end.

The book belongs to apocalyptic literature and should be rigorously interpreted according to its rules. Above all it intends to proclaim the sense of the future in the light of the whole history of salvation. In this it coincides with the other non-canonical apocalyptic books, using, as these do, a common patrimony of symbols and literary procedures. Yet it is distinguished from these in a radical way by the event of Christianity which commands a different vision of the future and of history. For the Jewish apocalypses, the definitive eschatological event of salvation is still to come, but for the Christians it has already happened in the death and resurrection of Christ, which is at one and the same time the exaltation of Christ to the right hand of God and therefore his enthronement as Lord of creation and history. The whole future will be the coherent development of what has already been achieved by Christ. Christians are in reality living out the last epoch in history, "the final days," and already share in the goods of the future world even though they are still bound to the figure of this world, which is inevitably doomed to destruction. From all the pages of Revelation leaps the vivid expectation of an imminent end. This however is more the typical disposition of every apocalypse, the climate in which the apocalyptic message is transmitted and an efficacious way of exhorting to fidelity and patience, rather than an exact computation of the duration of history and the hour when it is to come to an end. In the symbols used by the author there are evident allusions to historical events, but these are present or past events, viewed however in a cosmic and echatological dimension with which the historian does not deal. It is not, however, that the author is deceived on the date of the end, but rather that he discovers the deep core of all history in the conflict between good and evil, between God and Satan, which takes on body and shape in the institutions of the world of man. These events are unveiled in their deep dimensions and presented as part of the paroxysm of the final conflict. Historical events are in this way easily transfigured as the religious intent of the author paints the eschaton with the external appearance of the events themselves. The Roman empire and the worship of the emperor become for the author the incarnation of the Beast, the irreconcilable enemy of the Lamb who has won the victory.

The book's theme as it develops makes use of the traditional and symbolic apparatus of this literary genre, where the principal law is not precisely the coherence and organic development of the subject. One looks in vain, therefore, for a division that would satisfy the logic of the modern reader. Indeed some scholars believe that the book as it exists today is the fusion of at least two writings on parallel themes. This would explain some of the repetitions. After the introduction there are: 1. Seven letters to the seven churches of Asia Minor (2:1-3:22). 2. The strictly eschatological part: a. Introduction: a vision of the throne of God and the heavenly liturgy (4:1-11); b. The first part of the eschatological drama (5:1-11:14); c. Second part of the eschatological drama: the persecutions of the saints and the victory of God over his enemies Babylon, the Beast and Satan, followed by the resurrection and the judgment (11:15-20:15); d. The epilogue: the revelation of the kingdom of God and of the heavenly Jerusalem (21:9-22:5); e. Conclusion (22:6-21).

Revenge, *See* AVENGER.

reverence
and *r.* my sanctuary   Lev. 19:30; 26:2

reward
I will make your *r.* very great   for your *r.* is great in heaven
              Gen. 15:1   Matt. 5:12
         receive's a prophet's *r.*   Matt. 10:41

Rezeph (ree′-zef), A city of Syria conquered by the Assyrians before 701 B.C. (2 Kgs. 19:12; Isa. 37:12).

Rezin (ree′-zin), An Aramaean king of Damascus, a contemporary of Ahaz of Judah (735-715 B.C.). With Pekah of Israel (737-732 B.C.) he invaded Judah in order to oblige Ahaz to enter the coalition against the Assyrians or else depose him from the throne. Ahaz called the Assyrian Tiglath-pileser III to his aid, becoming his vassal. Tiglath-pileser plundered the region of Damascus, deported the people and killed Rezin (*see* Isa. 7:1-8; 2 Kgs. 15:37; 16:1-9).

Rezon (ree′-zon), Son of Eliada. He fled from his master, King Hadadezer of Zobah, and took possession of Damascus, where he established himself as king. He was a contemporary of David and Solomon and hostile to Israel (1 Kgs. 11:23-25).

Rhegium (ree′-ji-um), A port city in the south of Italy, today Reggio Calabria, where the ship carrying Paul to Rome as a prisoner put in (Acts 28:13).

Rhesa (ree′-sa), One of Jesus' ancestors in Luke's genealogy (3:27).

Rhoda, A servant in the house of Mary, mother of John Mark. When Peter was miraculously freed from prison in Jerusalem and knocked at the door of the house, Rhoda heard him and came back overjoyed to announce his arrival, forgetting to open the door to let him in (Acts 12:13-16).

Rhodes, An island in the Aegean sea opposite the southwestern corner of Asia Minor. Paul stopped there in the city of Rhodes on his way to Jerusalem after the third apostolic journey (Acts 21:1).

Rhodocus (rod′-o-kus), A traitor of the Jews, discovered and imprisoned by Judas Maccabeus (2 Mac. 13:21).

Riblah, A city of Syria on the river Orontes, on the site of the modern Rableh. At Riblah the Pharaoh Neco deposed and imprisoned Jehoahaz ("Shallum") king of Judah (609 B.C., 2 Kgs. 23:33). It was the base of operations for Nebuchadnezzar against Judah. There Zedekiah of Judah was brought into his presence (597-587 B.C.) with his sons. He had Zedekiah's eyes put out and sent him in chains to Babylon. His family was destroyed (2 Kgs. 25:6-7; Jer. 39:5-7, 52:9-11). Other nobles of Judah suffered the same lot (2 Kgs. 25:20, 21; Jer. 52:26, 27).

rich

Now Abram was very *r.*	Gen. 13:2	Once there was a *r.* man	Lk. 16:19
I made Abram *r.*	Gen. 14:23	the *r.* man said	Lk. 16:27
one *r.*, the other poor	2 Sam. 12:2	than for a *r.* man	Lk. 18:25

right

what you think fit and *r.*		over his *r.* thigh	Jgs. 3:16
	Josh. 9:25	though I were *r.*	Job 9:15, 20
	I am in the *r.*	Job 13:18	

Righteousness, *See* JUSTICE.

Rimmon, 1. Father of Rechab and Baanah, the two who killed Ishbosheth, son of Saul (2 Sam. 4:1-11).

2. An Aramaean deity venerated at Damascus (2 Kgs. 5:18) identical with Hadad-Baal, the storm-god in the Canaanean pantheon.

Rimmon-perez, An encampment of the Israelites en route to Canaan under Moses (Num. 33:19, 20).

Ring, A ring on the finger denoted authority: when the Pharaoh gave Joseph power he took his ring from his finger and put it on Joseph's finger (Gen. 41:42; *see* Gen. 38:18, 25; Esth. 3:10, 12, etc.). The officers of the army brought as offerings to the Lord the earrings, signet rings, bracelets and other gold objects they had taken in booty. The signet ring held the seal, and so was a very personal object (*see* SEAL; 1 Kgs. 21:8; Esth. 3:12; 8:8; Dan. 6:18). Before Judith went to Holofernes she decked herself out with her necklaces, bracelets, rings, earrings and all her jewelry (Judith 10:4). As a sign of reconciliation and honor, the father orders a ring to be put on the prodigal son's hand. James 2:2 warns against giving honor to the rich man who comes well-dressed with a gold ring on his finger while neglecting the poor man.

Riphath (rie′-fath), A people listed among the sons of Japheth in the Table of Nations (Gen. 10:3).

rise

a staff shall *r*.	Num. 24:17	paths they *r*. up	Job 30:12
that they may not *r*.	Deut. 33:11	After three days I will *r*.	
you *r*. and take food	2 Sam. 12:21		Matt. 27:63

Rissah (riss′-ah), A stopping-place of the Israelites during the journey to Canaan (Num. 33:21, 22).

Rithmah, A stopping-place of the Israelites en route to Canaan (Num. 33:18, 19).

Rizpah, The daughter of Aiah, Saul's concubine. After Saul's death Abner, general of the army and supporter of Saul's son Ishbosheth, took her for himself. Ishbosheth rebuked him for taking his father's concubine. Abner became enraged and turned to David with the intention of handing over to him the tribes that sustained the house of Saul (2 Sam. 3:6-21). David handed over to the Gibeonites the two sons that Rizpah had borne to Saul, Armoni and Meribbaal. These were put to death by impaling. Rizpah put on sackcloth and spent her days keeping the birds by day and the beasts by night from devouring the bodies. David, upon hearing this, had the remains decently buried in the tomb of Saul's father, Kish, at Zela in Benjamin (2 Sam. 21:8-14).

roast, roasted

eat its *r*. flesh	Ex. 12:8	Give me some meat to *r*.	
but *r*. whole	Ex. 12:9		1 Sam. 2:15

rock

on the *r*. in Horeb	Ex. 17:6	you are '*R*.,' and on this *r*.	
station yourself on the *r*.	Ex. 33:21		Matt. 16:18
in the hollow of the *r*.	Ex. 33:22		

rod

withdraw his *r*.	Job 9:34	my *r*. in anger	Isa. 10:5
the *r*. of their taskmaster	Isa. 9:3	with the *r*. of his mouth	Isa. 11:4

Rodanim (roe′da-nim), Rodanim (1 Chron. 1:7) or Dodanim (Gen. 10:4) are an Indo-European people descending from Japheth through Jaran according to the Table of Nations. The inhabitants of Rhodes are probably meant.

Rogelim (roe′-ge-lim), A city in Transjordan in Gilead, the residence of Barzillai, the rich proprietor who helped David with all kinds of provisions while he was taking refuge at Manahaim during Absalom's revolt (2 Sam. 17:27-29; 19:32).

roll

to *r*. the stone	Gen. 29:8	*r*. in the dust	Mic. 1:10
R. a large stone	1 Sam. 14:33	*r*. back the stone	Mk. 16:3

Romans, Epistle to the, The epistle to the Romans is the longest of Paul's letters. It is moreover distinguished among his letters for being the nearest thing to a theological tract in the form of an epistle that he wrote. (*See* LETTER.) Some scholars see in it the purest and most genuine expression of Pauline teaching. This position however is a little partial and one-sided as it minimizes the further development of Pauline theology as this is presented in Colossians and Ephesians. However one can concede that Paul wrote the epistle to the Romans with the purpose of giving a complete and balanced theological treatment to what was the center of the debate with the Judaizers that had occupied a great part of his apostolate up to that point. *See* GALATIANS, EPISTLE TO THE.

Paul was at Corinth during the first months of 58 A.D. He had completed his third apostolic journey and considered his work in the East completed. He had finished the mission to preach the gospel from Jerusalem and the surrounding territories as far as Illyria (Rom. 15:19). He felt that he had nothing more to detain him in these parts (Rom. 15:23). He decided to move westwards even as far as Spain. The first stage on this projected journey would be Rome, whither for a long time he had wanted to go, but no occasion offered itself (Rom. 15:24). First of all, however, he wishes to return to Jerusalem to bring to the church of the Holy City the collection he had taken up in his own churches of Macedonia and Achaia (Rom. 15:26-28). Paul is afraid lest he will not be well received, and in fact he did end up the center of a polemic that made him an object of hatred to the Jews and an object of suspicion even for the Jewish Christians (Rom. 15:31). This then was Paul's situation, and, as he had feared, what happened to him in Jerusalem ruined his plans. Paul did come to Rome, but as a prisoner (Acts 27-28). In 58 A.D. however Paul intended to prepare for his visit to the Romans by writing them a letter. He is writing to a community he does not know. One sees from the introduction (Rom. 1:8-13) that Paul is feeling his way along with great caution. He does not want it to be said that he is moving into another man's territory. He is coming to Rome like any other Christian, wanting to give and to receive, to console and to be consoled in the faith that was common to him and them. Paul was also aware that too often he was the object of suspicion and controversy, and so he wished to dissipate these doubts in his regard by expounding in an orderly and calm fashion what his personal position is on the question of Christian salvation. The epistle, then, offers us no direct information on the real situation of the church at Rome. One must not conclude that the church at Rome, like that of Galatia, was divided and agitated. The letter gives us an insight into Paul's thoughts at that time and an understanding of the conclusions he had come to in the discussion with the Judaizers. Indeed one might conclude from certain details that Rome knew of no such discussion in its own ranks, as according to Paul the church at Rome was formed of Christians who had come from paganism.

After a long introduction (1:1-4) Paul expresses the desire of soon seeing the faithful of Rome and hopes that his visit will be of mutual profit, to him and to them (Rom. 1:8-13). The theme of the letter is announced in 1:16: the gospel is the power of God for the salvation of whoever believes in it. The theme is developed in different phases. First he describes in a diptych the revelation of the anger of God against every impiety and injustice, be it of pagans (1:18-32) or of Jews (2:1-3:20). The conclusion to this part is categorical: "all men have sin and are deprived of the glory of God" (3:23). At this point is inserted the revelation of the saving justice of God (*see* JUSTICE), which gratuitously justifies through grace through the redemption which is in Christ Jesus, whom God has constituted the instrument of propitiation in his own blood (Rom. 3:21-26). Man is justified by faith, not by works; and for this reason all kinds of boasting or self-sufficiency are excluded on the part of man, who in his faith confirms his radical powerlessness to save himself (Rom. 3:26-31). Paul then shows how the principle of justification through faith and not through works was already operative in Abraham who believed, " and it was credited to him as justice" (Rom. 4:1-8; Gen. 15:6). Only afterwards did he receive circumcision as the outer seal of his justice through faith. Thus, too, those who believe like Abraham are children of Abraham and therefore heirs to the promise (Rom. 4:25).

In 5:1 Paul begins to speak of the fruits of justification. These are peace with God, a sure hope, love of God poured into our hearts (Rom. 5:1-11). Christ has overcome sin even in its very roots (Rom. 5:12-21) so that Christians who through baptism are inserted into him should no longer be enslaved to sin but live out the new life which they now have received (Rom. 6:23). Christ also liberated us from the law which was associated with the still unredeemed flesh to condemn man to death (*see* LIBERTY; Rom. 7:1-25). Now there is no condemnation awaiting the person who is in Christ Jesus (Rom. 8:1). The old law which brought men to death is substituted with the new interior law which brings men to life, and is nothing other than the Holy Spirit who guides and moves men from within to carry out the works that the law proclaims good and just (Rom. 8:2-5). Paul then speaks of the life of the Christian, as it is guided by the Spirit, and of his hope of resurrection and eternal life. This is a certain hope that cannot be in vain, for God's guaranteeing love is stronger than any other thing in life or death. This love will prove powerful in bringing to completion what he has started in men (Rom. 8:6-39).

Chapters 9 to 11 take up the problem of the Jews who as a people failed in the last moment to reach the goal to which their whole history and all God's action brought them. The real problem that Paul is treating is not so much the condition of the Jews as the problem of God's fidelity. This problem had evident repercussions on the certainty of Christian hope itself (Rom. 9:6). God cannot be accused of injustice (Rom. 9:14-33) nor of infidelity. His gifts are irrevocable and the choice of Israel has not been abolished (11:1, 2). God has saved a remnant, the chosen portion. The loss of the masses will not be for ever. And from their rejection came about the salvation of the Gentiles. Israel will however return to its God, who will then once more graft them on to the genuine olive tree from which for a time they have become detached (Rom. 11:11-36).

Chapters 12-14 contain moral exhortations and instructions on the practical conduct of Christians. In chapter 15 Paul speaks of his own situation and of his plans for the future. In 15:33 the letter seems to finish up with a general greeting: "May the God of peace be with you all. Amen." However, there follows another long chapter with greetings to specific individuals (16:1-21) which is absent from some manuscripts of the letter. It has been thought that this chapter did not originally belong to the epistle but that it was taken from another letter, perhaps Ephesians. This opinion however is not very probable. It is more probable that Paul, with the fears and uncertainties on how he would be received by the Romans, wished to reawaken the sympathy of the people he had already met and who were now at Rome. Then the absence of chapter 16 from some manuscripts is understandable. The letter was considered a doctrinal synthesis and was then conceived of as a letter no longer sent just to one particular church but to all churches of all times. So some manuscripts also omitted the name of Rome from its address.

Rome, The Roman empire had created the world into which Christ and Christianity was born. Never before was there such ease of travel due to the systematic elimination of piracy on the sea lanes and banditry on the highways which linked the territories of Europe, North Africa, Asia Minor and the Middle East. Koine Greek had become a universally viable language for daily affairs, and in this language the gospels were written, as, no doubt, they had for a long time been preached.

Roman expansion proved once to be a blessing to the Jews, for it offered them hope against the oppression of Antiochus IV Epiphanes. 1 Maccabees 8 offers a eulogy of the Romans and records an alliance between them and the Jews (*see* 1 Mac. 14:40; 15:16; 2 Mac. 11:34-38). After the Romans had done away with the Seleucid empire, internal factions between Aristobulus and Hyrcanus paved the way for the Roman take-over of Palestine. Pompey went to Damascus in 63 B.C., and there Herod Antipater appealed to him on behalf of Hyrcanus. Aristobulus offered armed revolt, which gave the Romans reason to invade the country, capture Jerusalem, where Pompey went into the inner sanctuary, and establish Roman rule there. The Roman province of Syria at that time included Syria and Palestine.

In the New Testament Rome is mentioned in John 11:48 where the council of chief priests and Pharisees expressed the fear that if Jesus were allowed to continue his career, the Romans would intervene to destroy their holy place and nation. Paul was a Roman citizen, which at times spared him further legal harassment (Acts 16:21, 37 f., 22:25-29; 23:27; 25:16). It was Paul's privilege to appeal from any lower court to the Emperor, and this brought him eventually to Rome, not as he had intended in Romans 15:22 ff., but as a prisoner awaiting trial.

The destruction of Jerusalem by the Romans in 70 A.D. saw the destruction also of the Temple and the priesthood, and it had far-reaching effects not only on Judaism but also on Christianity.

The epistle to the Romans was written by Paul to a church he had not founded and of which he knew little or nothing. So one looks to it in vain for a reflection of the real state of affairs there. (*See* ROMANS, EPISTLE TO THE.) From the Roman writers Pliny, Suetonius and Tacitus one can gather that the Christian religion was considered a superstition; it is also known that after the great fire of Rome, Christians were themselves viewed with disdain and suspicion. Tradition has it that Peter and Paul suffered martyrdom in Rome between 60 and 70 A.D., yet the city was to become with time the most important center of Christianity in the developing church.

root

r. grow old	Job 14:8	the *r*. of the matter	Job 19:28
	the *r*. of the tree	Matt. 3:10	

rope, ropes

through the window with a *r*.		with cart *r*.	Isa. 5:18
	Josh. 2:15	letting him down with *r*.	Jer. 38:6
instead of the girdle a *r*.	Isa. 3:24	cut the *r*.	Acts 27:32

Rosh (rosh), A son of Benjamin (Gen. 46:21).

rotten
declare a tree *r*. and its fruit *r*.   Matt. 12:33

rubbish
accounted all else *r*.   Phil. 3:8

Rufus, 1. Son of Simon of Cyrene, the man who was constrained to carry the cross of Jesus to Calvary (Mark 15:21).

2. A Christian of Rome greeted by Paul in Romans 16:13.

ruin, ruins

heaps of *r*.	2 Kgs. 19:25	fool is imminent *r*.	Prov. 10:14
of the *r*.	Prov. 3:25	and take in hand this *r*.	Isa. 3:6
	bring to *r*. him	Rom. 14:15	

rule

who will *r*. them	1 Sam. 8:9	which shall *r*.	Dan. 2:39
you wish to *r*.	2 Sam. 3:21	and *r*. with great might	Dan. 11:3
	with his mighty *r*.	Dan. 11:4	

Rumah (roo´-mah), A town of Judah, the home of Zebidah, mother of King Jehoiakim of Judah (2 Kgs. 23:36).

rumbling
the *r.* wheels   Jer. 47:3

run
and they will *r.*	1 Sam. 8:11	their feet *r.* Prov. 1:16
I will *r.* the way	Ps. 119:32	*r.* so as to win 1 Cor. 9:24
	I do not *r.* like a man 1 Cor. 9:26	

rust
Moths and *r.* corrode   Matt. 6:19   neither moths nor *r.*   Matt. 6:20

Ruth, Book of, A historical book of the Old Testament. The Hebrew canon includes it in the third part, among the so-called "writings," while the Christian canon has it between the Book of Judges and the First Book of Samuel.

The book is a masterpiece of narrative style, and the probable fiction one of the most delicately told stories in the whole Bible. During the period of the judges, on account of a great famine that hit the land of Canaan, Elimelech, an Israelite from Bethlehem, emigrated to Moab with his wife Naomi and his sons Mahlon and Chilion. There the sons married two Moabite women, Orpah and Ruth. Later Elimelech and his two sons died. Naomi invited her two daughters-in-law to return to their fathers' homes. Orpah followed Naomi's counsel, but Ruth did not wish to abandon Naomi, and so returned with her to Bethlehem. It was harvest time. Ruth went to follow the reapers in gathering the corn in the field of a rich man named Boaz, who noticed the presence of the young widow, found out who she was, and treated her with kindness and generosity. When Ruth returned home she informed Naomi of what had happened. Naomi explained that Boaz was a relative of theirs, one of those who held levirate marriage rights over them. The next day Naomi advised Ruth to don her best clothes, go to Boaz's field, find out where he went to rest, and then to go there and lie at his feet. This contained an implicit proposal of marriage and a request to exercise his right of avenger in her favor. (*See* AVENGER.) Boaz understood what was meant, but he explained that there was a still closer relative who should first be consulted. Boaz gathered the elders of the city and before them invited the other relative to exercise his right of avenger. The man was disposed to buy the field that had belonged to Elimelech, Naomi's husband, but not to marry Ruth. Since both conditions, however, were inseparable he thereby renounced his right, and this passed to Boaz, who married Ruth. Their son Obed was the father of Jesse and therefore grandfather of David.

The story fits into the center of the Jewish juridical institution of **go'el** or avenger, the point of which was to guarantee the cohesion and continuity of a clan or family. The book of Ruth is dealing with the conservation of the family patrimony (*see* Lev. 25:25-28; Num. 36:3, 8) and of the observance of the law of the levirate (Deut. 25:6; *See* LEVIRATE). The author, however, is not so much concerned with the functioning of the juridical institution as he is with the irreprehensible conduct and ideals of Ruth and Naomi, models of family loyalty and trust in God, and of the fidelity of God who reveals himself the protector of the defenseless who place their hopes in him.

The book is of comparatively recent date. The author indirectly confirms this when he pauses to explain the meaning of the archaic gesture alluded to in Ruth 4:7. On the other hand the fact that the book was included in the third part of the Hebrew canon (The Writings) is a certain sign that the book is post-exilic. The language contains many Aramaisms, and so points us to the same period. Some scholars contend they can even be more precise: they see in Ruth a polemic work against the rigorous measures of Ezra and Nehemiah against mixed marriages, that is, of Israelites with foreign women (*see* Ezra 9-10; Neh. 13:1-27). This opinion however is less probable, as there is no polemic overtone to be found in the book.

The late date of the book poses serious questions of its historicity. The genealogy that concludes the book can be held to be solidly historical (Ruth 4:18-22). 1 Samuel 22:3-4 would seem to suggest that David had some Moabite blood in him. However, it is impossible to finally determine if the author was using ancient traditions or constructing an idyllic story with real personages culled from the genealogy of David.

S

Saba, *See* SHEBA.

Sabaoth (sab′-a-oth), *See* HOSTS, LORD OF.

Sabbath, The seventh day of the week in the Hebrew calendar. The name is derived from the root sbt, which means to cease from or rest. It evokes the most characteristic trait of the Sabbath, which is the cessation of all the activity that fills ordinary everyday life. The observance of the Sabbath as a day of rest is very ancient in Israel. Even in the most ancient codes it appears as one of the fundamental demands of the covenant. It is found in the "Book of the Covenant" (Ex. 23:12), in the "Cultic Decalogue" (Ex. 34:21) and in the two versions of the decalogue, in which it figures as the fourth precept (Ex. 20:8-10; Deut. 5:12-14). It is found again in the Sanctity Code (Lev. 19:3, 30; 23:3; 26:2) and in other priestly documents (Ex. 31:12-17; Num. 28:9, 10).

The motivation attributed to this legislation is of two types. The first is humanitarian, with a brief reference to the sufferings of the Israelites in Egypt. Deuteronomy 5:13-14 reads: "Six days you may labor and do all your work; but the seventh day is the Sabbath of the Lord, your God. No work may be done then. . . . Your male and female slaves should rest as you do. For remember that you too were once slaves in Egypt, and the Lord, your God, brought you from there . . . that is why the Lord, your God, has commanded you to observe the Sabbath day" (*see* Ex. 23:12).

The second is more "theological" and passes over the more humanitarian aspect of the command. This is read in varying forms in Exodus 20:8-10 and in 31:12-17. The first passage is in strict relationship with the Priestly account of creation (Gen. 2:1-4): "Remember to keep holy the Sabbath day." "Remember," in Hebrew **zakar,** is spoken (*see* Ex. 13:3; Esth. 9:28) of the commemoration of a day marked by a saving intervention by God in favor of his people. The event to commemorate (Ex. 20:8) is the seventh day of creation. This "remembrance" is not just a mental operation; it is a reevocation which makes present, in its saving efficacy and its need to be shared, the saving event itself. The event is made present through an imitation or re-actualization of the event itself. In the case of the Sabbath, it was "sanctified." "Sanctification" must be understood as the banishing of all profane activity; it is "set apart" from the other days of the week. This is the meaning of the cessation from work and of repose. The precept then is not "Remember the Sabbath to sanctify it," but rather the commemoration itself takes place by sanctifying it.

The saving event that should be made present is the seventh day of creation, that is, "the repose of the Lord." This surprising trait of the creation story must be understood in the light of the tradition from which it depends (*see* Gen. 2:1-4). In the Babylonian creation poem, Marduk, the creating god, reposes, once his work is complete. Through his prodigious deeds Marduk has secured for himself and for the other gods their means of sustenance. Their merited rest sums up their well-being and happiness. This trait is conserved by the Priestly author, while at the same time he eliminates from it anything that might obscure the divine transcendence. At the end of the work of creation comes the repose of the Lord, his well-being. This, however, is presented as the seventh day of the week of creation, that is, as something that pertains to the created order. Not that God depends on the created order, but he deigns to fill it with his own well-being and invites man to share in this. The observance of the Sabbath is a sharing in the happiness and well-being of God.

In Exodus 31:12-17 the context is more specifically Israelite. The creation account is recalled (31:17), but in itself the observance of the seventh day is a "sign" of the covenant between God and Israel. This text has many traits similar to the explanation that Genesis 17 offers for the meaning and function of circumcision, and points in the direction of similar historical circumstances. (*See* CIRCUMCISION.) In fact, both circumcision and the observance of the Sabbath became decisive signs of belonging to Israel during the exile (*see* Ezek. 20:13; Neh. 13:17, 18). The different motivations offered for the precept instance the attempts of different schools and epochs to justify an observance that has very ancient roots, and that, at the beginning, was the result of differing motivations and circumstances.

The meager references to the Sabbath in the historical and pre-exilic prophetic texts show that the Sabbath was already in existence, but by no means had it the importance that was later attributed to it (*see* 2 Kgs. 4:23; 11:5-8; Amos 8:5; Hos. 2:13; Isa. 1:13). The historical origins of the institution are not clear. The most ancient legislation places it as a stipulation in the Covenant and nothing prevents its going back as far as Mosaic times. This is not to say, however, that it was an exclusively Israelite institution. It is more than probable that, as in other cases, Israel inherited this from its pre-Mosaic existence and a patrimony that it held in common with other peoples. However it must be admitted that the analogies that are drawn with other peoples are themselves not very clear.

In the post-exilic community the observance of the Sabbath became one of the principal criteria of Jewish orthodoxy. The book of Nehemiah has left us an eloquent testimony of this new spirit (Neh. 13:15-22; *see* also Isa. 58:13; Jer. 17:19-27). This is mirrored in the ever-increasing rigor with which the precept to rest is interpreted. The episode of 1 Maccabees 2:32-38 is well-known: the Jews refused to defend themselves against a Seleucid attack because it was the Sabbath. This spirit of fidelity is mitigated somewhat by Mattathias and his friends, who realistically foresaw that it could only lead to the end of them all (1 Mac. 2:39-41; 9:43-49). This realism however was unknown to the enthusiastic author of 2 Maccabees 8:25-28 (*see* 2 Mac. 15:1-3).

The New Testament affords us information of the exaggerations to which rigorous interpretation of the Sabbath repose had led (*see* Matt. 12:2; Mk. 3:2; Lk. 13:14; Jn. 5:10; Acts 1:12). Jesus presented it as an evident case of a law that had been deprived of meaning by false interpretation. (*See* LAW.) While he observed its legitimate demands, he proclaimed himself Lord of the Sabbath when some protested that he worked, and in particular, healed and exorcised on the Sabbath. When the bystanders objected, Jesus argued the absurdity of their position which put into relief the incoherence of their objections (Lk. 13:10-17; Mk. 3:1 ff.). He also drew on the Old Testament (Mk. 2:23). John 5 goes deeper into this astonishing liberty of Jesus in regard to the Sabbath, and seeks its roots in the intimacy that exists between Jesus and the Father.

The observance of the Sabbath was maintained for some time in Jewish-Christian circles. Paul used the synagogue meetings to spread the gospel (*see* Acts 13:14, 42-44; 16:13; 17:2; 18:4) but clearly proclaimed its abrogation as an institution by the new Christian economy (Col. 2:16).

sabbath

complete rest, the *s*.	Ex. 16:23	on the *s*. day	Num. 15:32
most solemn *s*. for you	Lev. 16:31	seventh day is the *s*.	Deut. 5:14

Sabbath's Journey, The distance it was licit to travel on the Sabbath day according to the rigorist interpretation of the precept to repose on the Sabbath that was in use in Pharasaic Judaism (Acts 1:12). Based on Joshua 3:4, Exodus 16:29 and Numbers 35:5, this was reckoned at 2000 cubits, a cubit being the length of the arm from the elbow to the tip of the middle finger, 18 to 22 inches. Acts 1:12 states that the Mount of Olives was "a Sabbath's journey" away from Jerusalem.

Sabbatical Year, Through analogy with the institution of the Sabbath, the last of a cycle of seven years is called a Sabbatical Year. (Sabbatical Year legislation is read in Ex. 23:10-11; Deut. 15:1-3; Lev. 25:2-8.) The laws of Exodus and Deuteronomy are concerned with the repose of the land: "For six years you may sow your land and gather its produce. But the seventh year you shall let the land lie untilled and unharvested, that the poor among you may eat of it and the beast of the field may eat what the poor leave. So also you shall do in regard to your vineyard and your olive grove" (Ex. 23:10-11). The law of Deuteronomy does not prescribe the repose of the land, but orders the automatic proscription of debts in these terms: "At the end of every seven-year period you shall have a relaxation of debts . . . Every creditor shall relax his claim on what he has loaned his neighbor; he must not press his neighbor, his kinsman, because a relaxation in honor of the Lord has been proclaimed. You may press a foreigner" (Deut. 15:1-3). It is not certain whether the liberation of slaves every seven years is in connection with the Sabbatical Year or not. *See* SLAVERY, *see* Ex. 21:2-6; Deut. 15:12-14.

Allusions to this legislation in the historical books of the Bible are very scarce. The clearest one is in 1 Maccabees 6:49-53, and refers to the repose of the land. On the liberation of slaves *see* Jeremiah 34:8-22. Nehemiah 10:32 also alludes to the Sabbatical Year. The legislation as a whole is so altruistic that it awakens the suspicion that here an ideal is proposed, about whose practical application, however, the historical books offer little information. Two observations however are in order: a. the legislation about resting the land is very ancient, with decisive evidence for it in the Book of the Covenant (Ex. 23:10-11). The sobriety and realism of this piece of legislation obliges one to believe that here were practical norms. Perhaps the altruistic aspect is exaggerated when the periodic repose of the land was itself a necessity for its continued fruitfulness. b. Perhaps the Deuteronomy law represents an attempt periodically to remedy in a drastic way the spread of pauperism, and make some provision for the destitute classes. The literal enactment of the norm probably took place only at times of particular religious fervor, such as the reform of Nehemiah and the Maccabean period.

Sabeans (sa-bee′-anz), *See* SHEBA 2.

Sabtah, *See* SABTECA.

Sabteca (sab′-te-ka), In the Table of Nations he is the son of Cush (Gen. 10:7; 1 Chron. 1:9). Sabteca is also an unidentified locality in Arabia.

Sackcloth, The word comes from the Hebrew **saq**, the Greek **sakkos** and

Latin *saccus*; possibly it came originally from Egyptian. The word meant a robust cloth woven from camel or goat hair, which was worn as a garment and sewn into bags for grain (Gen. 42:25, 27, 35; Josh. 9:4). The original shape of sack clothes is disputed. Some hold they were really sack-shaped with apertures for head and arms (*see* Gen. 42:25; Josh. 9:4) while others would have it a smaller vesture worn around the waist. To support this is the abundant reference in the Bible to girding the loins with sackcloth (1 Kgs. 20:31, 32; Isa. 20:2) or simply girding oneself with the cloth (Isa. 15:2; Jer. 6:26; Joel 1:8). Sackcloth was an expression of fasting and mourning. When Elijah pronounced God's sentence on Ahab for his crimes he rent his garments and donned sackcloth next his skin, and fasted, and slept in the sackcloth (1 Kgs. 21:27; *see* 2 Kgs. 19:1). When Haman's plan to kill off the Jews became known, there was weeping and wailing and fasting, and many put on sackcloth and ashes (*see* Esth. 4:2, 3; *see* Dan. 9:3; Joel 1:8). Jonah, with comic irony, states that in Nineveh the people and animals put on sackcloth as a sign of repentance. Sackcloth as a repentance symbol is referred to in the New Testament in Matthew 11:21, Luke 10:13. There is nothing to suggest that actual discomfort was experienced in the wearing of the cloth, even though it was put on next to the skin (*see* Job 16:16). It bespoke the interior distress of fasting, mourning and repentance.

Sacrament, The sacraments of the Church are reality-filled symbols in which Christ nourishes, and eventually immortalizes, his community. There is no New Testament or Old Testament word that covers what the Church means by sacrament, but the realities are discoverable in the Scriptures, especially in the case of the eucharist and baptism. The term itself took many centuries to crystalize in its present meaning. For the New Testament spiritual realities covered by the word "sacrament," *see* BAPTISM, CONFIRMATION, EUCHARIST, PENANCE and FORGIVENESS, MARRIAGE, ANOINTING, PRIEST.

sacred

hold a *s.* assembly	Ex. 12:16	his own *s.* contributions	Num. 5:10
smash their *s.* pillars	Ex. 34:13	their *s.* poles	Deut. 12:3

Sacrifice, How important sacrifice was in the Israelite cult can immediately be seen from the amount and sweep of the legislation that surrounds it in the Pentateuch. This article must be confined to a description of the variety of sacrificial rites contained in that legislation, and a brief exposition of the function and meaning of sacrifice in the religion of Israel. This latter must however remain sketchy, for the abundance and detail of ritual available in the sacred books is in paradoxical contrast with the meager elements afforded to construct a theology of sacrifice in Israel.

The most complete law on sacrifice appears in Leviticus cc. 1-7. This mirrors the Temple ritual after the exile, but it is undoubtedly rooted in a traditon that reaches back to the pre-exilic Temple.

a) The holocaust, in Hebrew **'olah** or total sacrifice (Deut. 33:10), comprises the burning of the whole animal on the altar, with nothing at all reserved for the priest or the person sacrificing. The person offering sacrifice himself ordinarily kills the animal (there are special cases in Ezek. 44:11; 2 Chron. 29:22), after having presented it and signified that it was his by imposing hands on it. The blood was poured around the altar by the priest. It was then quartered and arranged on the altar to be burned by the priest in the fire that perpetually burned there (Lev. 1). Holocausts are demanded in certain purification ceremonies (Lev. 12:6; 14:19; 15:1-30), consecrations (Lev. 9, for priests; Num. 6:10-14), the more solemn yearly festivals (Num. 28-29) and each day, morning and evening (Ezra 3:3; Neh. 10:34).

b) Peace offerings is the approximate translation of the term **zebah sela-mim** (*salom* means peace). The precise meaning of the term is not clear. The rite is described in Leviticus 3. Leviticus 7:11 gives certain regulations for three types of peace offerings, which are distinguished according to the finality or aim of the offering: "a peace-offering in thanksgiving" (Hebrew **todah**, Lev. 7:12); "votive" (Hebrew **neder**, that is, to which the offerer is bound by vow, Lev. 7:16-17; *see* 22:18-23); and "free-will offerings" (Hebrew **nedabah**, an offering out of pure devotion, outside of any obligation or promise, Lev. 7:16-17; 22:18-23). The rite coincides with that of the holocaust in the first part: imposition of hands, the killing of the victim, and the outpouring of its blood. The victim was divided into three parts: the fat, which belonged to God, was burned on the altar (Lev. 3:9-17). The portions of the priest are determined in Leviticus 7:28-36: the right thigh, "that has been set aside," and the breast that has been offered in ceremonies described in Exodus 29:24-28. The rest was given to the person making the sacrifice, who ate it before Yahweh with his family. This banquet is what distinguishes this type of sacrifice.

c) Atonement sacrifices were of two kinds, **hatta't** or sin offering, and **'asam** or guilt offering. The distinction between the two is not clear. Some have tried to base the distinction on voluntary and involuntary faults, or the gravity of different sins, but these opinions do not hold up even under a slight scrutiny of the evidence. The distinction has probably an old history no longer available to the redactor of these chapters. The ritual for sin offerings distinguishes between the people for whom expiation should be made: priests (Lev. 4:1-12), the whole community (4:13-21), the head of the people (4:22-26) and private individuals (4:27-35). Guilt offerings have no such distinctions: here it is only a question of private individuals (5:14-26). There is only one rite with minor variations according to the case.

In the expiation for the priests and for all the people "the priest shall take some of the bullock's blood and bring it in to the meeting tent, where dipping his finger in the blood, he shall sprinkle it seven times before the Lord, towards the veil of the sanctuary" (Lev. 4:6), afterwards rubbing the blood on the horns of the altar of incense and pouring the rest at the base of the altar of holocaust. The same is prescribed for the head of the people and for private individuals with the exception of the sprinkling of the veil of the sanctuary. The fat is burned on the altar, but the rest is not given to the offerer, but to the priests, if the expiation is being made for the head of the people or for private individuals. If, on the other hand, expiation is being made for the priests or for all the people, then the victim's meat is burned in the remains of the ashes outside the sanctuary. On the rite of the Day of Atonement, *see* ATONEMENT, DAY OF.

d) Leviticus 2 speaks of cereal offerings, or **minha**, which frequently accompany other sacrifices. The offering consisted of wheaten flour on which wine was poured and incense was placed. Then the whole was burned on the altar by the priest. The remainder of the oblation went to "Aaron and his sons; a most holy portion of the burnt offerings of the Lord" (Lev. 2:3, 10).

All this legislation is placed in the framework of the revelation made to Moses on Sinai. This is not however a historical judgment but a value judgment. (*See* PENTATEUCH.) The Israelite ritual is partly anterior to Moses and partly assimilated from the Canaanite surroundings in which Israel settled. In general it may be said that the custom of burning the victim partially or wholly on the altar was of Canaanite origins, while the ritual with the blood reflected the cultic usage of the nomadic period. Nor must one search in Israel for the basis of a religious sense of sacrifice. The scarcity of information on this point in the Bible is itself a proof that Israel's cult was nourished on what spontaneously linked up with sacrifice. Israel would then have chosen from this rich and varied symbolism what best put into relief their revealed idea of the God Yahweh, who was the whole soul of their religion.

The Bible reacts polemically to the conception of sacrifice as food offered to God. This concept was present in Mesopotamian religion and left traces that are more verbal than real in some ancient texts (Gen. 8:21; Jgs. 9:9, 13). While this may have gained ground in popular ideas of religion, it is sarcastically rejected in Psalm 50:12, 13 and Deuteronomy 32:38, while Judges 6:18-22 and 13:15-20 explicitly excludes it.

Two ancient cultic terms pointed this way: **minha** (which was later restricted to vegetable offerings) and **qorban** mean gift and are used in this sense with clear reference to sacrifices in general (*see* 1 Sam. 2:17; 26:19 and Num. 7). Sacrifices, then, are gifts offered to God, an expression of homage sanctioned by the destruction of the victim as a sign of the irrevocability of the gift, and the total or partial burning which made its fragrance go up to God. The banquet which accompanied the peace offering was a pledge of communion with the divinity, just as meals among men sealed their relationships with one another (*see* Gen. 31:44-54).

Expiation sacrifices were intended to reestablish a communion that had been interrupted through offense. The particular rites of this type of sacrifice have given rise to varied interpretations. Some have thought, for instance, that with the imposition of hands, the offerer unloaded his sins on the victim, which would then be immolated in place of the sinner, taking on the punishment he deserved. This fairly common interpretation has unfortunately been extended to include the sacrifice of Christ: it does not however withstand scrutiny in the light of biblical data. In the first place, hands were imposed in all sacrifices and expressed the fact that the animal belonged to the offerer and that in his name it was being offered. The only imposition of hands with the intent of unloading the weight of sins took place on the scape-goat on the Day of Atonement, but this was not a sacrifice! Moreover it is difficult to reconcile the idea of the victim substituting for the sinner with the holiness that is constantly insisted upon in what is offered to Yahweh. The expiatory power of this type of sacrifice is connected with the use of blood. Blood is life (Lev. 17:11), and life's absolute and exclusive Lord is Yahweh. In the sacrifice the blood is poured at the foot of the altar as an explicit avowal of this absolute dominion of God over life. The blood, because it is sacred, expiates, that is, it purifies through being sprinkled on the veil of the sanctuary and rubbed on the horns of the altar, thus banishing the impurity that had erected a barrier between God and his people. *See* BLOOD, ATONEMENT.

With the coming of Christ the whole sacrificial ritual of the Old Testament, and particularly the rite of the Day of Atonement appeared to the author of the epistle to the Hebrews as something that could not possibly bring any worshipper to perfection in his inner self, and therefore intended to be in force only until it should be time to reform them. "But when Christ came as high priest of the good things which have come to be, he entered once for all into the sanctuary, passing through the greater and more perfect tabernacle not made by hands, that is, not belonging to this creation. He entered, not with the blood of goats and calves, but with his own blood and achieved eternal redemption" (Heb. 9:11-12). "How much more will the blood of Christ, who through the eternal spirit offered himself up unblemished to God, cleanse our consciences from dead works to worship the living God!" (v. 14). Paul follows out the line that was begun by the prophets and developed in the Judaism of Alexandria: this involved a "spiritualization" of the Old Testament ritual, so that Paul saw his ministry (Rom. 1:9; 2 Cor. 2:15; Rom. 15:16) and the Christian life of faith and charity (Rom. 13:1; Phil. 2:17; 4:18) as the counterpart of the sacrificial cult of the Old Testament. Jesus himself had clearly proclaimed his immolation on the cross as a sacrifice of expiation and covenant, applying to himself the words of Isaiah 53 on the Servant of Yahweh, and making clear reference to the first pact on Sinai in the institution of the eucharist. (*See* LORD'S SUPPER; SERVANT OF THE LORD.) These texts have marked the whole terminology of the New Testament on the salvific nature of Christ's death.

Historically, the sacrificial cult of the Old Testament was abolished with the destruction of the Temple in the year 70 A.D., during the Jewish Wars. The Jerusalem Christians had continued to attend the Temple worship. But by that time the Church had readied her own cultic institutions, centered on the commemoration of the Lord's Supper.

saddle, saddled

Any *s.* on which	Lev. 15:9	the ass was *s.*	1 Kgs. 13:23
S. the ass for me			
1 Kgs. 13:13; 2 Sam. 19:27			

Sadducees (sadj′-u-seez), One of the three great "factions" or "sects" in Palestinian Judaism during New Testament times. Rather than describe them as a religious sect, it would be more exact to define them as a social class. The party of the Sadducees belonged to the priestly aristocracy and its sustainers. From their ranks came the high priests. The name is given different explanations, but is undoubtedly somehow connected with Zadok, Solomon's priest, the first of the family of high priests who succeeded one another in Jerusalem up to the time of the Maccabees. The party was conservative in religious matters and opportunist in politics. They took a conservative position against the progressive theology of the Pharisees, and paraded themselves as the faithful guardians of the religious patrimony that had been received from of old. They were therefore suspicious of the increasing authority given to the oral law and the doctrinal developments not clearly expressed in the Pentateuch. For this reason they denied the existence of the angels and the resurrection (*see* Matt. 22:22; Mk. 12:18; Lk. 20:27; Acts 23:6-8).

The eschatological sense was much dimmer in them than it was among the Pharisees. The Sadducees were hostile to the fanatical intransigence of the zealots, and wished to come to terms with the Roman authorities to keep peace and avoid the ruin of the nation. They were, then, realists rather than idealists, and so open to the accusation of being servile and traitors.

The origins of the Sadducees as a conscious and coherent group are obscure. Clearly the movement centered around the increasingly important position assumed by the high priest in the post-exilic period when the monarchy was no more. Perhaps however they came together in awareness as a group when for a while during the Maccabean period they were removed from power. Under the Hasmoneans they appear as a rival group to the Pharisees in search of favors from the kings. The Sadducee caste, being a priestly family, was intimately linked with the cult of the Temple, and so perished with the destruction of the Temple in 70 A.D., not however before they had witnessed with their blood to their attachment to the Temple. Thus they left the field free for their traditional adversaries, the Pharisees.

Sade, The 18th letter of the Hebrew alphabet (emphatic s).

Sadok, *See* ZADOK.

safe

Is the youth Absalom *s.?*	Their homes are *s.* Job. 21:9
2 Sam. 18:29	the just man runs to it and is *s.*
Is young Absalom *s.?*	Prov. 18:10
2 Sam. 18:32	

saffron

Nard and *s.*   S. of S. 4:14

Sailing, Although Israel was open to the sea along its whole west coast, the Israelites never really took to the sea. The few maritime exploits recorded in Israel's history were for specific purposes, and did not last long. Moreover they took place in the gulf of Aqaba and not in the Mediterranean, which had no natural ports and whose shore-line was in Phoenician and Philistine hands. Solomon had Hiram of Tyre transport the material necessary for the construction of the Temple and palace (1 Kgs. 5:23), and fitted out a fleet of ships in the port of Ezion-geber to carry on commerce with Ophir (1 Kgs. 9:26-28). 1 Kings 10:22 states that Solomon "had a fleet of Tarshish ships at sea with Hiram's fleet. Once every three years the fleet of Tarshish ships would come with a cargo of gold, silver, ivory, apes and monkeys." Jehoshaphat of Judah (873-849 B.C.) wished to revive the fleet of his glorious predecessor to go to Ophir, "but in fact the ships did not go, because they were wrecked at Ezion-geber" (1 Kgs. 22:49, 50). Tyre was the major maritime and commercial force in the whole Syro-Palestinian area. Ezekiel magnificently described its power, "that city standing at the edge of the sea, doing business with the nations in innumerable islands." He wrote a lamentation over its fall (Ezek. 27). Genesis 49:13 states that Zebulun sailed the seas, and Judges 5:17, 18 speaks of the harbors of Asher, but it is not possible to determine how important this activity was.

The New Testament often speaks of seas and fishing on the lake of Gennesaret (Sea of Galilee) (Matt. 14:22; Mk. 1:19; Lk. 5:2; Jn. 6:19). Herod I the Great had an artificial port built at Caesarea on the Mediterranean coast, where Paul disembarked at the conclusion of his second apostolic journey (Acts 18:22) and where, as a Rome-bound prisoner he embarked (Acts 27:2). Luke has left a minute account of this adventurous journey of Paul in Acts 27:1-28:16.

Saint, *See* HOLY.

Sakkuth and Kaiwan (sak′-uth, kye′-wan), The names of two Mesopotamian deities (Amos 5:26).

Salamis (sal′-a-mis), A city and seaport on the east coast of the island of Cyprus, which was visited by Paul and Barnabas during the first apostolic journey (Acts 13:5).

Salecah (sal′-e-kah), A city of Transjordan in Bashan, the northeastern limit of the kingdom of Og, which was conquered by the Israelites and consigned to Gad (Deut. 3:10; Josh. 12:15; 13:11; 1 Chron. 5:11).

Salem, The city in which Melchizedek was king (Gen. 14:18). Tradition identifies it with Jerusalem (Ps. 76:3).

Salim, According to John 3:23: "John too was baptizing at Aenon near Salim." The traditional identification of this place is in the valley of the Jordan, 8 miles south of Beth-shan.

Sallu (sal′-oo), Personal name (1 Chron. 9:7; Neh. 11:7; 12:7).

Salman, According to Hosea 10:14: "Salman laid Beth-arbel waste." This is probably Salamanu king of Moab who is known from an inscription of Tiglath-pileser III. Others believe it to be an abbreviation of Shalmaneser V, king of Assyria.

Salmon, Salma, 1. The son of Nahshon and father of Boaz, and great-great-grandfather of David (Ruth 4:21) cited in the genealogy of Jesus in Luke 3:32 and Matthew 1:4-5.

2. Son of Hur and descendant of Caleb (1 Chron. 2:11, 50, 51).

Salmone (sal-moe′-ne), A place on the east coast of Crete which is mentioned in the account of Paul's sea journey to Rome (Acts 27:7).

Salome (sa-loe′-me), 1. The wife of Zebedee and mother of the apostles James the Great and John. She stood with the other women on Calvary beside the cross of Jesus (Mk. 15:40, 41), and on the resurrection morning went to anoint the body of the Lord (Mk. 16:1). For her sons she asked Jesus to give them the first places in the kingdom he was to establish, but Jesus turned the request into an invitation to suffer with him (Matt. 20:20; Mk. 10:35). They accepted the invitation.

2. The daughter of Herod Philip and Herodias. Herodias left her husband and went to live with Herod Antipas. John incurred Herodias' ire because he upbraided Herod for taking his brother's wife. So the stage was set: Salome, not mentioned by name in the gospel, danced for Herod and his guests at his birthday celebrations, and so pleased them that Herod pledged himself to grant any request to the girl. Prompted by her mother, Salome demanded the head of John the Baptizer, and Herod, ashamed on account of his guests to go back on his word, ordered that it be given her (Matt. 14:6; Mk. 6:22). Salome afterwards married Philip tetrarch of Trachonitis and Ituraea (Lk. 3:1), son of Herod I the Great.

Salt, Salt was available to the Israelites from abundant natural deposits in the Jordan Valley, especially around the Dead Sea. The soft face of the Jebel Usdum, a mighty six-mile-long cliff, gives rise under the buffeting of the wind to marvellously grotesque figures in ever-changing variety. The story of Lot's wife turning into a pillar of salt is a popular explanation of some such rock shapes (Gen. 19:26). Leviticus 2:13 prescribes that every oblation should be salted, and this should never be omitted. With Aaron and his descendants God struck a "covenant of salt" (Num. 18:19), an inviolable covenant possibly drawn from the notion of salt as a preservative. It was also a condiment (Job 6:6). A new-born child was rubbed with salt (Ezek. 16:4) either for medical or ritual purposes.

Salt was seeded into the ground of Shechem by Abimelech after he captured it. This was a symbolic gesture to ensure that the land should remain barren (Jgs. 9:45).

The synoptics have preserved different versions of Christ's words on salt. According to Mark he said: "Everyone will be salted with fire. Salt is excellent in its place; but if salt becomes tasteless, how can you season it? Keep salt in your hearts, and you will be at peace with one another" (Mk. 9:49, 50; *see* Lk. 14:34). Matthew has a slightly different version: "You are the salt of the earth. But what if salt goes flat? How can you restore its flavor? Then it is good for nothing but to be thrown out and trampled underfoot" (Matt. 5:13). While the general sense can be gathered from the sayings, the exact meaning is far from clear.

Salt, City of, A town in the desert of Judah, today Khirbeth Qumran (Josh. 15:62). *See* QUMRAN.

Salt Sea, The biblical name for the Dead Sea (Gen. 14:3; Num. 34:3, 12; Deut. 3:17; Josh. 3:16; 15:2; 18:19). The name alludes to the extreme saltiness of the water, which contains the highest percentage of salt of all seas.

Salt, Valley of, A place in Edom, near the Dead Sea, where the Israelites defeated the Edomites during the reign of David (2 Sam. 8:13) and then again during the reign of Amaziah (2 Kgs. 14:7).

salvation

would come the *s*.	Ps. 14:7	Rock of our *s*.	Ps. 95:1
because of his *s*.	Ps. 35:9	announce his *s*.	Ps. 96:2

Salvation History, Although the term "salvation history" is not itself found in the Scriptures it is at the center of today's biblical theologies and is also gaining ground in other theological disciplines, in catechesis and in the liturgy. Salvation history wishes to point out that the essence of the Christian message is not a system of moral and religious truths that were revealed in a certain moment of time, but which are in themselves timeless. The essence of the Christian message, for salvation history, is the proclamation and witness given to definite interventions of God in human history through which he has accomplished his saving design in man's favor. While, then, the term is not biblical, the concept of salvation history is linked up with the Pauline theology of mystery, especially as this is expounded in the epistle to the Ephesians (*see* Eph. 1:9; 3:9; *see* MYSTERY).

The Christian notion of salvation history should not be confused with the secular ideology of the ceaseless progress of humanity. Nor is it an optimistic philosophy of history. Nor again is salvation history the thesis that humanity, by force of its own immanent laws, is engaged in a process of always going from good to better. Salvation history is placed on a level that is superior to that of human history, even though human history is the scenario in which salvation history takes place. Salvation history means that the grace-given relationship with God, which is the Christian religion and the salvation of man, has become possible and in fact has been established by God himself through definite interventions which took place in history. This relationship with God in its various stages, that is, Old Testament, New Testament and eschatological consummation, depends for its existence and nature from these interventions by God, which we call saving events.

These saving events take place in a way that is analagous to human history as such, and for this reason one speaks of salvation history.

a. If we limit our consideration to the aspect of the saving events that we can call external or empirical, as distinct from their internal or salvific dimension which is only revealed to faith, these can be subjected to critical historical investigation. The science of history obviously cannot show that the death of Jesus is the salvation of the world, but it can verify the fact that Christ died, the circumstances attending that death and what Jesus himself thought of his mission and death as this is revealed in his own words and in those of his followers who knew him directly or indirectly. (*See* JESUS CHRIST.) Christian tradition has always upheld the legitimacy of a rational proof of the historicity of the events which the Bible presents and has always taught that such a proof is compatible with the most genuine faith.

b. The salvific events are marked with the three characteristics of any historical event, that is, they cannot be repeated, they are interrelated in an organized whole, and they all tend towards a definite aim. That the salvific events cannot be repeated means more than a banal assertion that attaches to any fact that happens in time, which does not turn back on itself. The salvific events cannot be repeated because they have been accomplished once and for all, each of them constitutes something irrevocably acquired. In the New Testament this is underlined with particular emphasis in regard to the decisive event of salvation, that is, the death and resurrection of Christ (Rom. 6:10; Heb. 7:27; 9:12). Analogously however it holds true for all the events of this history. Each of them place irrevocable premises which condition their consequences in history. For the exodus from Egypt *see* EXODUS, ELECTION.

c. Between the individual saving events there is interrelationship, that is, they are not the isolated manifestations of the divine goodness to Israel, but together form a whole in which all the individual events, like parts, interplay. Christian tradition has received with equal veneration the Old and the New Testament. The New Testament is the inspired witness rendered to the definitive saving event. The Old Testament is not only the prophecy of this same event, but is also the inspired testimony of the interventions of God through which he brought to accomplishment in Christ his saving design. For this reason the Church has always opposed any attempt to detach the New Testament from the Old (*see* MARCION), nor has she acceded to the temptation of exalting the newness of the revelation of the New Testament to the point where she is cut off from her roots in the history of the Old Testament.

d. From what has been said it follows that salvation history is of its very nature eschatological, that is, it tends to a term that is absolutely the end and is definitive, which excludes indefinite, temporal and qualitative progress. The decisive event of this history, what can be called with every right the eschatological event, is the death and resurrection of Christ. The rest of salvation history, which is the object of Christian hope, has already been acquired for us in that event. We await its open and full consummation in our own person.

In its whole course and extension salvation history has been accompanied by the prophetic word whose mission it is to unveil its sense, proclaim its saving dimension, provoke man to respond with faith to the invitation that through it God is addressing to him, and open the horizons for the future which the event itself contains. The prophetic word is not just an additive, something attached from without to the event already complete in itself. The word is an integral and indispensable part of the event. Paul states this with utter clarity when, speaking of the cross of Christ, he says: "All this has been done by God, who has reconciled us to himself through Christ and has given us the ministry of reconciliation. I mean that God, in Christ, was reconciling the world to himself, not counting men's transgressions against them, and that he has entrusted the message of reconciliation to us" (2 Cor. 5:18, 19). In the same way, salvation history is no automatic process into which man can be inserted without his interior participation. On the contrary it demands from man faith, which is surrender and full self-opening to God who attracts all men to himself in Christ.

The Bible is the inspired testimony of this prophetic word which accompanies salvation history. The Bible itself can be called a "salvation history" as it contains the series of saving acts. The word "Gospel" (Greek **euangelion**) meant from the beginning the "good news" of salvation that has taken place, and so passed on to denote the four writings of the New Testament in which is described the realization of salvation in the person and event of Jesus. The rest of the New Testament is just commentary and proclamation of the event of Christ which the gospels narrate before our very eyes. A similar fact can be seen in the Old Testament. Jewish and Christian tradition has reserved a special veneration for the first five books of the Bible, the Pentateuch or Law, which also contain the very codes of the laws. These however are inserted into an ample historical account which gives to them sense and significance. *See* LAW.

The Bible has also made clear what is the central axis on which the whole history of salvation revolves by putting into relief in the symbols of faith the points which hold the whole together to give it coherence. In the New Testament are the symbols or confessions of faith, the intention of which is to gather what is essential and primary in the message of the primitive apostolic church, as it is today.

Some of these confessions are very brief (*see* 1 Cor. 12:3; Phil. 2:13; Rom. 1:4; 1 Jn. 2:22), while others are more developed (1 Cor. 15:1-7). To them can be added the accounts of apostolic preaching (Acts 2:14-39; 3:13-26; 4:10-12; 5:30-32; 10:36-43; 13:17-41). These place at the center of the Christian message, not religious or doctrinal truths, but the fact that Jesus died for our sins and arose for our justification (Rom. 4:25).

It is not difficult to find texts in the Old Testament with similar characteristics and scope. On the occasion of studies carried out on the composition and origin of the Pentateuch, some texts have been pointed out which can with reason be called the "credo of Israel," that is, they too mean to collect what was considered essential and fundamental in the whole Israelite religion. These are the enumerations of the saving actions of God in favor of his people Israel, not presented as isolated manifestations of God's kindness, but as a truly organic series which move forwards towards fulfilment of what God from the beginning had promised. The links in this chain are the promise made to Abraham, the liberation from Egypt, the journey through the desert, the gift of the promised land, the election and covenant with David (*see* Deut. 6:20-24; 26:5-9; Josh. 24:2-15; Pss. 77; 78; 105; 136). These are the facts which condition the existence and nature of the relationship of Israel with God, the moral demands of which are expressed in the Covenant which defines the relationship between God and Israel that arose and are founded on the works of salvation that he has achieved for his people.

Samaria, Capital city of the kingdom of North Israel, today called Sebastiyeh. 1 Kings 16:24 recounts the story of its foundation: "Omri, king of Israel (876-869 B.C.) reigned for six years in the capital Tirzah; then he bought the hill of Samaria from Shemer for two silver talents and built upon the hill, naming the city he built Samaria after Shemer, the former owner." Ahab beautified the city (869-850 B.C.) and built there an ivory palace (1 Kgs. 22:39; *see* Amos 6:4)—i.e. trimmed with ivory. The city followed the fluctuations of the northern kingdom. It suffered different and heavy sieges during the wars with the Aramaeans (1 Kgs. 20:1-21; 2 Kgs. 6:19-23), and lived through the bloody revolt of Jehu against Ahab's dynasty, which had been friendly to the Phoenicians (2 Kgs. 10). After a two year's siege it succumbed to the Assyrian kings Shalmaneser V and Sargon II (722 B.C.; 2 Kgs. 17). Sargon deported the population and settled in the district "people brought from Babylon, Cuthah, Avva, Hamath and Sepharvaim" (2 Kgs. 17:24). These initiated an ethnic and religious syncretism (2 Kgs. 17:26-28) which explains Samaria's fortunes in the post-exilic period. *See* SAMARITANS.

Samaria was part of the Persian, Seleucid and Roman empires. Herod I the Great constructed there a magnificent city along Greek lines, which was called in Greek Sebaste, and in Latin Augusta, in honor of the Emperor Augustus, from which it gets its present name Sebastiyeh.

Jesus crossed Samaria while returning from Jerusalem at the beginning of his ministry (Jn. 4) and at its end on his way up to Jerusalem (Lk. 17:11). The diffusion of the Christian message in Samaria was occasioned by the persecution that broke out in Jerusalem after Stephen's death, and which forced many from the holy city (Acts 8:1-25; 9:31; 15:3). At Samaria took place the meeting between Peter and Simon Magus, who offered money for the power to impart the Spirit through the laying on of hands: the sin of simony takes its name from this episode (Acts 8:9-24).

Samaritans, On his way from Judea to Galilee Jesus passed through Samaria, where he came to the town of Sychar. The woman he met there at the well expressed surprise that Jesus should speak with her: "Jews have nothing to do with Samaritans," she said (Jn. 4:9). As the conversation gets under way, the reasons for this disagreement are revealed as religious. The tensions between Jews and Samaritans had a long history that is not clear in all points.

The origins of the conflict should be sought for in the ethnic-religious syncretism of the people who settled in the cities of the district of Samaria after the deportation ordered by Sargon II when Samaria fell in 722 B.C. (2 Kgs. 17). When the Jews returned from Babylon, animated with enthusiasm for a restoration of the national and religious life, they looked with diffidence on the people of Samaria and rejected every request for collaboration. The first notice of conflict is in Ezra 4, Nehemiah 4 and 6, where the Samaritans opposed, through diplomatic channels, the rebuilding of the walls of Jerusalem. To reduce the conflict to the merely religious order would be a simplification. The Samaritans had good political reasons for opposing an eventual restoration of the Jewish nation. Samaria in fact feared the establishment of a strong state that might threaten the integrity and autonomy of the small surrounding territories and arouse the suspicions of the Persian government, forcing it to make heavier a yoke that till then was rather liberal in the administration of the ethnic minorities in all that region. The definitive break between the two occurred around the fourth century B.C. The Samaritans closed themselves off from all religious influence out of Jerusalem. They acknowledged only the Pentateuch, and that written in Hebrew characters, not that in Aramaic letters adopted after the return from exile. They constructed a temple on Mt. Gerizim, which was a rival to that of Jerusalem (*see* Jn. 4:20). The resurgence of national spirit at the time of the Maccabees had disastrous consequences for the Samaritans. Their temple was destroyed by John Hyrcanus and never again rebuilt. The few Samaritans who still remain celebrate the Pasch in the ruins of the temple of Nablus.

The antagonism between Samaritans and Jews, which is expressed in John 4, is latent in other passages of the gospels. Jesus restricts the mission of the disciples to Israel and forbids them to go into the cities of the Samaritans (Matt. 10:5). This prohibition is on religious grounds, for from the religious point of view they were considered almost as Gentiles (Lk. 17:16). With this background one can appreciate how polemic the parable of the good Samaritan sounded in the ears of its hearers (*see* Lk. 10:33), and the profound despisal the Jews had for Jesus, calling him a Samaritan and a man possessed by the devil (Jn. 8:48).

Luke records in 9:52 that Jesus and the disciples, on their way from Galilee to Jerusalem, while passing through Samaria were refused hospitality in a Samaritan village. John and James wanted to call down fire from heaven to burn them up, but Jesus rebuked the immoderate zeal of the "Sons of Thunder."

Samech (sah'-mek), The 15th letter of the Hebrew alphabet (s).

Samgar-Nebo (sam′-gar-nee′-boe), A prince of the king of Babylon, Nebuchadnezzar, who participated in the siege of Jerusalem (Jer. 39:3).

Samlah, A king of Edom (Gen. 36:36; 1 Chron. 1:47, 48).

Samos (say′-mos), An island in the Ionian archipelago, in the Aegean sea, opposite the west coast of Asia Minor between Ephesus and Miletus. Samos islanders are among those to whom the Roman consul Lucius wrote in favor of the Jews (1 Mac. 15:23). It is also mentioned in the itinerary of Paul on his way to Jerusalem at the end of his third apostolic journey (Acts 20:15).

Samothrace (sam′-o-thrace), An island in the northern part of the Aegean Sea. It figures in the second apostolic journey of Paul on the course by sea between Troas in Asia Minor and Neapolis in Macedonia (Acts 16:11).

Samson, The son of Manoah, of the village of Zorah and the tribe of Dan (Jgs. 13:2), one of the judges of Israel (Jgs. 13-16). Unlike the greater judges, Gideon and Jephthah, Samson is not a national leader for Israel. His exploits are personal encounters with the Philistines in which his extraordinary physical strength is manifested. What spurs him on to his adventures are personal reasons of revenge (Jgs. 16:28) and not the oppression of the people. More than in any other section of the Book of Judges one notices here the imbalance between the religious context inspired by the deuteronomic era, which gave its final shape to the story, and the original content and tenor of the episodes that are gathered there. The original story is that of an Israelite of the tribe of Dan who possessed extraordinary physical strength and used it to resolve personal and domestic matters at a time when relationships with the neighboring Philistines alternated between friendship and enmity. His exploits have become legendary in the folklore of his people, and at the hands of the deuteronomic editor they have taken on providential and religious dimensions in which he is seen as a "savior of Israel" (Jgs. 16:31). The story of Samson's birth follows the model of the infancy stories of great heroes, and moreover offers a religious explanation of his astonishing physical endowments: the nazirite vow made by his mother at the command of the angel who announced his birth (Jgs. 13). Samson marries a Philistine woman of Timnah (Jgs. 14 and 15). Later he falls in love with a whore of Gaza (16:1-3), and finally becomes enamored with Delilah, a woman from the vale of Sorek (16:4-30). His relationships with these three women are the occasion of the exploits and revenge of Samson on the Philistines that are universally known.

Samuel, Samuel is one of the key figures of the history of the Israelites. He represents the transition from the tribal confederation to the monarchy. During the first years of this institution he played the role of guardian of the sacred traditions and institutions of the amphyctyony against the danger that Israel should indiscriminately adhere to the monarchical types of the neighboring nations. It is difficult, however, to define the sacred office occupied by Samuel and the concrete action that he took during these critical years. The documents that describe him are collected in 1 Samuel; they originate however from very different sources and mirror in part religious preoccupations of a polemic nature that did not coincide with the life of the hero. *See* SAMUEL, BOOKS OF.

Samuel was the son of Elkanah, an Ephraimite (1 Sam. 1). The story of his infancy, like nearly all the infancy stories of great personages, is somewhat suspect from the historical point of view. He is made to come to the fore in a decisive manner in the announcement of the tragic end of the priestly family of Eli, who had charge of the sanctuary of Shiloh where the ark of the covenant was kept (1 Sam. 1-3). One must acknowledge that presenting Samuel in the role of a prophet may seem somewhat exaggerated; nevertheless it is one of the most certain characteristics of Samuel's complex personality.

He figured as a seer in the pre-monarchic account of the election and elevation of Saul (1 Sam. 9-11) and 1 Samuel 29:18-24 shows him to be in close relationship with prophetic circles.

It is moreover certain that Samuel was no mere "private seer," only able to resolve domestic problems such as that of the lost asses of Saul's father (1 Sam. 9:3-13). His was a public function among the twelve tribes. Samuel 7:15-17 reads: "Samuel judged Israel as long as he lived. He made a yearly journey, passing through Bethel, Gilgal and Mizpah, and judging Israel at each of these sanctuaries. Then he would return to Ramah, for that was his home." Samuel is, then, presented as judge of Israel, but certainly not in the same sense as Gideon and Jephthah. Perhaps he should be taken to be one of the so-called "minor judges," the guardians of the sacred rights of the Israelite confederacy: this would best fit the traditions that concern him. The difficulty in giving a more precise picture of Samuel's office and function derives from the scarce information available about the sacred institutions of the pre-monarchic period. The function of judge, after the manner of Joshua in Joshua 23 and 24 (1 Sam. 7 and 12), is not too different from the ministry of Samuel as judge and seer in Israel.

It is certain that Samuel, who should not have been so anti-monarchy as 1 Samuel 8 portrays him, did in fact at one point, and for the sake of fidelity to the sacred traditions that he represented, reject Saul. There are two versions of this episode. One reproves Saul for not observing the herem or anathema (1 Sam. 15:4-31), while the other rebukes him for having dared to offer sacrifice (1 Sam. 13:2-14). The latent conflict between the newly formed monarchy and with it its needed innovations, and the sacred traditions of the confederation were not long in erupting into the open. Whatever his position was at the beginning of the monarchy, Samuel upheld uncompromisingly the demands of the sacred traditions and decisively opposed Saul once the conflict broke out. When then the prophetic circles of the north, at a later period, found themselves in conflict with the successive kings, they thought it legitimate to appeal to Samuel and transfer to him, in theory, the origins of the conflict. This was the origin, it seems, of the anti-monarchic bias, traces of which belonged to the ancient traditions. These traces however were exploited and built into theological principles, to be thrown against the actual functioning of the monarchy of the time.

Samuel as priest emerges more clearly in 1 Chronicles 6:13, 18 and 9:22, and he is called a priest for his intercession in favor of the people in Psalm 99:6 (*see* Jer. 15:1). Samuel is idealized by Ben Sira in the "Eulogy of the Fathers" in Sirach 46:13-20.

Samuel, Books of, Historical books of the Old Testament. In Hebrew Bibles it is included among the so-called early prophets, together with Joshua, Judges and 1 and 2 Kings. Jewish tradition attributed its authorship to Samuel the prophet, who is the hero of the first part of the history that is gathered there. The division into two books was first made in the Greek translation of the Septuagint and from there passed back into the Hebrew text, centuries later. In the Septuagint and the Vulgate the Books of Samuel are called the first and second Books of Kings, while the 1 and 2 Kings of the Hebrew original are called 3 and 4 Kings.

The Books of Samuel in reality form part of the great historical synthesis that drew on Deuteronomic inspiration and extended from Joshua to 2 Kings. 1 and 2 Samuel describe the passage from tribal to monarchic organization. The Deuteronomic redaction has happily only partly obscured the original tone and amplitude of the ancient sources. Events handed down by tradition are described by the redactors as if they were almost contemporaneous. The critics distinguish the following sources:

a. The so-called "history of the succession of David" excels the rest for its literary and historical value and for the compactness of its composition (2 Sam. 9-20 and 1 Kings 1:2). It was without doubt written by an author who lived during the events he described and penned his account during the first years of the reign of Solomon. He is the creator of a narrative-historical literary genre that abandons the rules of the religious and profane epic. Acknowledging an awareness of God's action in history, he knows how to highlight the interplay of human passions, emotions and ambitions through which God secretly acts to accomplish his plans. Here there are indubitable stylistic affinities of thought-relationship with the Yahwist strata of the Pentateuch, especially in Genesis. For this reason some scholars attribute the books to the same author, and see in 2 Samuel 9-20 the conclusion to that work which was begun in Genesis 2 and later given up.

The author is a court personage, with a wisdom formation, and his work was probably aimed at an accurate reconstruction of the facts to show that Solomon's succession to the throne was legitimate. So it starts with the account of the measures that David took in favor of Saul's descendants (2 Sam. 9). The story of David's adultery and the murder of Uriah serves two ends: first to chronicle the birth of Solomon (2 Sam. 12:24, 25), and secondly to give a religious and evaluative judgment on David's act which was a sin. Its position is analagous to Genesis 2 and 3, which is the beginning of the Yahwist history. This too casts a shadow on what was to follow: sin works out its dire consequences. In the case of David there followed the bitter history of Absalom's and Sheba's revolt, revenge in the very heart of the family of the king which almost brought the family itself to extinction (2 Sam. 13). The choice of Solomon as successor has all the appearances of a happy ending to all the tragedy which filled the last years of David's reign, in which the figure of the great king emerged refined through the crucible of much suffering and contradictions.

b. David is also the hero of 1 Samuel 16:14-2 Samuel 5. This could be entitled "The history of David's accession as King of Judah and Israel." The style and mentality approach in many respects that of the author of 2 Samuel 9-20. It is however more dependent on popular traditions which are often conserved in two versions with little variation. Examples of this are the meeting of David and Saul in 16:14-23 and in cc. 17-18; the twofold account of Saul's attempt to kill David in 18:10-11 and 19:9-11; twice David spares the life of Saul in cc. 24 and 26, and so on. David is pictured as the generous hero who through no fault of his own fell into disgrace with Saul, his king and master. David remains loyal to Saul even when Saul tries to do away with him. Providence here too animates the story. When events seem to contradict every hope, the secret designs of Yahweh are at work to place David as head of his united people (2 Sam. 2:1-7; 5:1-5).

c. 1 Samuel 4-6 and 2 Samuel 6-7 treat of the ark of the covenant which fell into the hands of the Philistines in Aphek (2 Sam. 4). It is held by them, but soon they begin to pay heavily for keeping it in their cities (2 Sam. 5). Of their own accord they restore it to the Israelites (1 Sam. 6) and finally it is solemnly transferred to Jerusalem through the work of David

(2 Sam. 6). Nathan's oracle is the conclusion to this account (2 Sam. 7). The same nexus is displayed in Psalm 132 which records David's "piety" towards the Ark of the Lord (Ps. 132:9) and God's response to this piety in the form of a promise of stability for the Davidic dynasty. Many scholars have reason to think that the background to 2 Samuel 6 is cultic and should be linked up with the annual celebration of the election of David and Zion, which took place on the occasion of the Feast of Tabernacles. *See* NEW YEAR; TABERNACLES, FEAST OF.

d. The first part of 1 Samuel (cc. 1-15) is the most fragmentary. There are two different versions of the origin of the Israelite monarchy, as has been noticed for some time.' One is clearly unfavorably disposed to it. It is viewed as a defection on the part of the people and an implicit refusal to acknowledge Yahweh as the only king of Israel (1 Sam. 8; 10:17-27). Samuel as prophet warns the people (1 Sam. 1-3). Saul ends up by falling into conflict with the sacred institutions of Israel, and Samuel's prophetic words announce that he has been rejected by Yahweh (1 Sam. 15). This version of the facts is motivated by the same religious reasons that provoked Elijah and Elisha against the kings of Israel of their time. These reasons were elaborated by the prophetic circles of the kingdom of the North.

The other version has no religious scruples about enthusiastically describing the accession of Saul (1 Sam. 9:1-10, 16; 11:13-14), and even cites Samuel's approval. In both of these accounts it is difficult to reconstruct what was the original tone and attitude expressed in the material gathered here. The Deuteronomic redaction is nearer in mentality to the prophetic version of the facts, but it also adopted the pro-monarchic account, thus creating tensions within the final version which elude explanation by the normal rules of history, as we understand it, but which are all too frequent in ancient history. The ancients moved paradoxically in reconciling a faithfulness to the traditions received and an extraordinary liberty in the marginal interpretation of these traditions.

Sanballat (san-bal′-at), The governor of the district of Samaria and a contemporary of Nehemiah in the Persian empire. Sanballat and other chiefs of the neighboring peoples opposed Nehemiah's initiative in rebuilding the walls of Jerusalem (Neh. 2:10-19). First of all he ridiculed Nehemiah (Neh. 3:33-38), and then, when he heard that the work was going forward, he conspired with Tobiah, the Arabs, the Ammonites and the Ashdodites to come together and attack Jerusalem (Neh. 4). When this came to nothing, they decided to get rid of Nehemiah by treachery. They proposed that a meeting be held in Caphirim, but Nehemiah suspected their intentions and found a way to excuse himself from going (Neh. 6:1-14).

sand, sands, sandy

s. of the seashore	Gen. 22:17	the s. of the sea	Ps. 78:27
like the s. of the sea	Gen. 32:13	house on s. ground	Matt. 7:26

sandal

or a s. strap	Gen. 14:23	would take off his s.	Ruth 4:7
and strip his s.	Deut. 25:9	untie his s. straps	Mk. 1:7

sang

and the Israelites s.	Ex. 15:1	(and Barak, son of Abinoam) s.	
it was that Israel s.	Num. 21:17		Jgs. 5:1
	They s. praises	2 Chron. 29:30	

Sanhedrin (san-hee′-drin, also san′-a-drin), *See* COUNCIL.

Sansannah, A town in Judah (Josh. 15:31).

Saph (saf), A giant serving with the Philistines, slain by Sibbecai, one of the Thirty warriors of David (2 Sam. 21:18).

Sapphira (sa-fie′-ra), A Christian woman of the church of Jerusalem, wife of Ananias. The couple sold a field after the example of those who had decided to hold in common all their goods; but Ananias, by previous agreement with his wife, kept back some of the money; then he took the rest and placed it at the feet of the apostles. Peter rebuked him for this hypocrisy: "You have lied not to men, but to God." Ananias fell dead on the spot, and soon after, his wife, still ignorant of his death, repeated the lie, only to fall dead in the same way. Acts comments: "Great fear came on the whole church and on all who heard of it" (Acts 5:9-11).

Sarah, 1. Wife of Abraham and mother of Isaac. She accompanied Abraham on his journey to Canaan. On two occasions Abraham passed his beautiful wife off as his sister in order to save his life: in this way Pharaoh in Egypt (Gen. 12:10-18) and Abimelech of Gerar (Gen. 20:1-18; 26:1-11) would not be tempted to do away with the husband in order to have the wife. Genesis 20-12 quotes Abraham in self-justification as saying: "Besides, she is indeed my sister, my father's daughter, though not my mother's; and she became my wife." The incident however reflects Sarah's beauty, Abraham's cleverness by the standards of the day and God's protection over the beginnings of his people, only gradually bringing them to a fuller moral standard. Sarah was sterile, and so suggested to Abraham that he take Hagar her slave and have by her a son and heir. Ishmael was the fruit of this union. Sarah now felt that she was despised by Hagar, and so for family peace Hagar and Ishmael were sent away. There are two accounts of this in the Bible (Gen. 16:1-8 and 21:1-12); the first is from the Yahwist tradition, the second from the Elohist.

When Abraham was promised a son from Sarah who would be his heir, Sarah laughed. In Genesis 18:6-17 Sarah's laugh is an expression of surprise and almost of incredulity, while in 21:6 it is the expression of joy at the birth of the baby. Both episodes together are an explanation of the name Isaac, which is, in fact, a form of the verb **sahaq**, which means to laugh. *See* NAME.

After God's alliance with Abraham, God gave to his wife the name Sarah (till then she was Sarai), but no explanation is offered for the change (Gen. 17:15). They are really two dialectic forms of the same name. Sarah died in Hebron and was buried in the cave of Machpelah, which was bought by Abraham for this purpose (Gen. 23; 25:10; 49:31).

Paul offers an allegorical explanation of the conflict between Sarah and Hagar (Gal. 4:21-30). Sarah in this allegory represents Jerusalem, the mother of the free, while Hagar stands for the Sinai covenant, "whose children are slaves" (Gal. 4:24). There are further N. T. allusions to Sarah (Rom. 4:19; 9:9; Heb. 11:11 and 1 Pet. 3:6).

2. Daughter of Raguel, who had been given to seven successive husbands only to see them die on the marriage night at the hands of the demon Asmodeus, until she was finally freed from the curse and married to Tobiah (Tob. 3:7). *See* TOBIT.

Sardis, A city of Asia Minor, capital of the kingdom of Lydia, conquered by Cyrus II king of Persia in 546 B.C. It fell to Alexander the Great in 334 B.C. and to the Romans in 189 B.C. Sepharad, mentioned in Obadiah 20, is probably the same city: there dwelt a colony of exiles from Jerusalem, whose return Obadiah predicts. One of the seven letters of Revelation is addressed to the church of Sardis. While some members of the church are praised, the community as a whole is severely rebuked and exhorted to penance: "Wake up, and strengthen what remains before it dies" (Rev. 3:1-6; *see* 1:11).

Sarepta, A city of Phoenicia (Obad. 20), south of Sidon, and called Zarephath in the Old Testament. Following a divine impulse Elijah went there to live for a while, in a widow's house, when Israel, during the reign of Ahab (869-850 B.C.), was afflicted with drought (1 Kgs. 17:8-24). This episode is recalled by Jesus in Luke 4:26.

Sargon, 1. Sargon of Akkad was the founder of the Akkadic empire towards the middle of the third millenium (2350-2150 B.C.).

2. Sargon I king of Assyria (around 1850 B.C.), who is not mentioned in the Bible.

3. Sargon II, king of Assyria (722-705 B.C.), son of Tiglath-pileser III and brother of Shalmaneser V whom he succeeded on the throne. Sargon completed the subjugation of Samaria, which had been besieged by Shalmaneser for three years. Sargon "deported the Israelites to Assyria, settling them in Halah, at the Habor, a river of Gozan, and in the cities of the Medes" (2 Kgs. 17:6) and "brought people from Babylon, Cuthah, Avva, Harnath and Sepharvaim and settled them in the towns of Samaria to replace the Israelites; they took possession of Samaria and lived in its towns" (2 Kgs. 17:24). Once more, around 711 B.C., Sargon arrived to put down a revolt of the Philistine cities (Isa. 20:1), a revolt from which Hezekiah of Judah abstained on the advice of Isaiah. He built a great palace at Dur-Sharrukin (modern Khorsabad) and started the famous collection of clay tablets carried on by his successors and recovered by archaeologists.

Sarid (sar′-id), A town in the territory of Zebulun (Josh. 19:10, 12).

Sarsechim (sar′-se-kim), The name, or more probably the title, of one of the Babylonian princes who under Nebuchadnezzar took part in the siege of Jerusalem, 588-587 B.C. (Jer. 39:3).

Satan, In Hebrew *satan* is a common name and means adversary, for instance, in war (1 Sam. 29:4). In judicial trials, the **satan** is the accuser, the person who discovers and unfolds before the judge the failings of others (Ps. 109:6, 7; *see* 1 Kgs. 17:18). In Job 1-2, the "satan" (with the article) is one of the "sons of God" who people God's royal court, in other words, an angel. In this text Satan is not a proper name, but merely the name of the function or ministry which is carried out. What this ministry is is clear from the response to God's question: "Whence do you come?" "From roaming the earth and patrolling it" (Job 1:7). The angel, that is, patrols the earth to examine the lives of men, so as to be their accuser before God. His function is certainly far from attractive, but he is not presented as a "bad angel." He is God's faithful servant whose thankless task this is. While he is not bad, he certainly shows an inquisitorial zeal in carrying out his office. He doesn't trust the outward appearances of Job's virtue, and suggests to God that he should be put to the proof to verify if his piety is sincere or just a splenid outward show. These characteristics explain how from this figure and with the same name emerged Satan, the evil spirit, hostile to God and men, whose function it is to seduce and destroy. (*See* DEMONOLOGY.) 1 Chronicles 21:1 shows this changeover completely: Satan is no longer the name of an office but the proper name of the perverse angel who "rose up against Israel and enticed David into taking a census of Israel," thus sinning against the Lord.

In the apocryphal literature of the Old Testament the figure of Satan acquires new elements. Here there is no ambiguity about his perverse character which invests all his actions and motives, and which expresses his hatred of man. Wisdom 2:24 sees in the serpent that tempted Eve the devil, who acted through spite, even though in this passage the name Satan is not given him.

In the New Testament Satan is the prince of demons and the prince of this world which is subjected to his power (Lk. 4:6; Jn. 12:31). The coming of the kingdom of God which is definitive salvation brings with it the destruction of the kingdom of Satan. This is expressed in the exorcisms ·worked by Jesus (Mk. 3:27; Matt. 12:29; Lk. 11:21; *see* EXORCISM). The mission of Jesus then is unfolded at two levels that are related to one another. On one of these Jesus is met by the incredulity of men while on the other he must sustain the attacks of Satan. These two levels are not independent, as Satan is, in the last analysis, the ultimate source of all the obstacles·to Jesus' work. Jesus was subjected to the attacks of the tempter Satan but he came from this trial victorious (Matt. 4:1-11; Mk. 1:13; Lk. 4:1-12). Satan however only left him "to await another opportunity" (Lk. 4:13). In the meantime he did not remain inactive. He searches out all means to render the preaching of Jesus sterile (Matt. 13:19; Mk. 4:15; Lk. 8:12). Even through the mouth of Peter he suggests to.Jesus that he should turn his back on the sorrowful way of the passion (Matt. 16:23; Mk. 8:33). He went so far as to put the disciples to the proof by getting them to abandon Jesus in his passion (Lk. 22:31) and put it into Judas' heart to betray Jesus (Jn. 13:2; 13:24; Lk. 22:3).

Through his passion and resurrection Jesus has acquired for himself the whole world, and for this reason, Satan, the prince of this world, has been ejected (Jn. 12:31; 16:11; *see* PARACLETE). However, just as Jesus' kingdom awaits its full consummation, so too Satan has not completely surrendered. He still seeks to place obstacles to the apostolic work of the church (1 Thess. 2:18) and goes about in the effort to seduce Christians (1 Pet. 5:8). To this purpose he often disguises himself under·attractive appearances (2 Cor. 11:14) without however changing in the least his intentions. The end of this however will take place when the kingdom of God will arrive at its fulfilment (*see* Rev. 12:12). Then Satan will gather together all his resources in one all-out try, but will have no success in it (*see* Rev. 20:7; Rom. 16:20).

Satrap, The title by which the governor of a province in the Persian empire was known (Esth. 8:9; 9:3).

Saul, 1. Saul, son of Kish, of the tribe of Benjamin, and first king of Israel during the last decades of the eleventh century B.C. His genealogy is read in 1 Samuel 9:1, 2, where he is described as "a handsome young man. There was no other Israelite handsomer than Saul; he stood head and shoulders above the people." There is more information on his family in 1 Samuel 14:49-51: He married Shinoam, from whom was born Jonathan, David's friend, and Ishbaal, who tried to restore the kingdom after his father's death (*see* ISHBAAL) and Malchishua, as well as two daughters Merob and Michal, who married David. He had Armoni and Meribbaal from the concubine Rizpah (*see* 2 Sam. 21:8). Saul's story is read in 1 Samuel 8-31, often with two versions of the same episode. *See* SAMUEL, BOOKS OF.

After the Philistine victory at Aphek, their way was open to the central highland range of Palestine, thus exposing the people to their incursions (*see* 1 Sam. 4). The only solution to this military vulnerability was the creation of the monarchy. The people asked Samuel for "a king over us. We too must be like other nations, with a king to rule us and to lead us in warfare and to fight our battles" (1 Sam. 8:19, 20). It is not easy however to determine how Saul was chosen for this role. According to 1 Samuel 9:10 Samuel received a message from God to anoint Saul as king when he came in search of some donkeys belonging to his father Kish. He was later presented to the people by Samuel and acclaimed as king. In Samuel 10:17-27, however, Samuel convoked the people at Mizpah, and there Saul was elected by lot among the tribes. Whatever the means by which he came to the throne, it is clear that he was chosen because of his previous military exploits. It is interesting to observe that this is the version of the facts that can be gathered from 1 Samuel 11, where, at the conclusion of the victory of Saul over Nahash the Ammonite, "all the people" went to Gilgal where "in the presence of the Lord, they made Saul king." This figure of Saul's kingship links him to the role of the savior judges of Israel. After his victory over the Midianites Gideon was offered the crown: "Rule over us for you rescued us from the power of Midian" (Jgs. 8:22). Gideon however refused, stating that there was no place for a king in Israel, whose true king was God (Jgs. 8:23). This detail tells a lot in a little: the same thesis is advanced in God's discourse according to the anti-monarchical version of Saul's election (1 Sam. 8:6-9), and here is already revealed a real conflict that was to prove catastrophic for Saul's reign.

One should not think of Saul's reign after the fashion of the rest of the kings of Judah. The role of his kingship was above all, if not exclusively, military, because this was what the needs of the times demanded. Saul made an innovation in that he hired a stable group of mercenary professional soldiers who were bound in personal loyalty to Saul and into whose ranks David was accepted (1 Sam. 18:1-9). David soon distinguished himself to the extent that he aroused Saul's jealousy. The actual extension of Saul's kingdom is not clear. It seems that the tribes who pledged themselves to him were those of the North and especially of the center of Palestine. He established the royal residence at Gibeah (1 Sam. 10:26; 15:34; 22:6; 23:19; 26:1; Isa. 10:29).

Even though Saul's monarchy was modest and his reign a turbulent one, he nevertheless did succeed in forging into a common concern the independent life of the various tribes on Palestinian soil. The sporadic common enterprises of the tribes during the time of the judges show many similarities to what Saul effectively carried out during his reign. He however did more in that he gave the common effort a coherence and consistency that it was never more to lose during the life of the kingdom.

Saul failed, however, to accomplish what it was left to his successor David to do, namely, to reconcile the needs of the monarchy with the sacred traditions of the tribal confederation. Saul was a victim to this contrast and was on that account a tragic figure. Despite his human limitations he attracts the sympathy and understanding of the historian. The traditions on Saul are solid concerning his break with Samuel. Tradition attributes this rupture to the failure of Saul to observe the anathema on Amalek (1 Sam. 15) or to Saul's intrusion in the exercise of the cult (1 Sam. 13:8-15). Whatever the concrete manifestations, they were but the symptoms of a deeper rift that was settled only by David. *See* DAVID; KING; MESSIAH.

Saul found himself abandoned by Samuel and deprived by his rival David of the popularity that had hitherto sustained him. He collapsed into a state of deep melancholy (1 Sam. 16:14-23) which broke out in murderous anger against his rival (1 Sam. 18:10, 11; 19:9, 10), and finally took shape in blind and implacable persecution of the only person who could have been to him the support that his situation needed, namely David (1 Sam. 19-26). His reign was initiated with a splendid victory over the Philistines in which his own son Jonathan distinguished himself (1 Sam. 13:14), and ended with the fatal defeat of Mt. Gilboa, where both he and Jonathan met their death (1 Sam. 31).

That his work did not completely perish was due to the fact that by this time David had established his position as king of Judah (2 Sam. 2:1-5) and proved to be the only person who could also guarantee safety to the tribes of the North. After the ephemeral reign of Ishbaal, son of Saul, the elders of Israel offered David the kingdom of the North (2 Sam. 5:1-5).

Saul was, in the last analysis, unequal to the difficult task of combating enemies from without and reconciling from within an ancient tradition that was as yet incapable of assimilating the novelty of a king. Saul however can hardly be blamed for this: he found himself involved in a conflict which did not prove sterile, for it established foundations on which stood the throne of David, king of Judah and Israel.

2. The Jewish name of the apostle Paul. He is called by this name in Acts 13:9. *See* PAUL.

save, saving

for the sake of *s.* lives	Gen. 45:5	He shall *s.* my people	1 Sam. 9:16
going to *s.* Israel	Jgs. 6:36	he comes to *s.* you	Isa. 35:4

scab

skin a *s.*	Lev. 13:2

scales

both fins and *s.*	Lev. 11:9	a true *s.*	Lev. 19:36
either fins or *s.*	Lev. 11:10	Balance and *s.*	Prov. 16:11

Scapegoat, The "goat for Azazel" (*see* AZAZEL) according to the ritual of the Day of Atonement. According to Leviticus 16:20-28, the high priest lays both hands on the goat, conferring on it symbolically all the sinful faults and transgressions of the Israelites "putting them on the goat's head" (16:21). The goat was later taken by an attendant to the desert and abandoned there for Azazel. The rite expressed the purification and destruction of sin that was brought about by the rite of expiation. The scapegoat however is never presented as a victim of sacrifice nor is it offered to God nor is it ever in the New Testament put in relationship to the sacrificial death of Christ. *See* ATONEMENT, DAY OF.

scatter, scattered

that he *s.* them	Gen. 11:9	The Lord will *s*	Deut. 4:27
I will *s.* them	Gen. 49:7	*s.* the peoples	Ps. 68:31

scepter

The *s.* shall never depart		the golden *s.*	Esth. 4:11
	Gen. 49:10	golden *s.*	Esth. 8:4
	your royal *s.*	Ps. 45:7	

Sceva (see′-va), A Jew from Ephesus, a "high priest," whose seven sons attempted to exorcise those who had evil spirits by calling: "I adjure you by the Jesus whom Paul preaches." The evil spirit however retorted: "Jesus I recognize, Paul I know; but who are you?" The possessed man then threw himself at them, overpowered them and mauled them so badly that they had to flee naked and wounded from the place (Acts 19:13-17).

scorn, scorned

s. their saving Rock	Deut. 32:15	the *s.* of men	Ps. 22:7
laugh you to *s.*	2 Kgs. 19:21	the *s.* of those	Ps. 44:14

scorpion

serpents and *s.*	Deut. 8:15	or hand him a *s.*	Lk. 11:12
you with *s.*			
Chron. 10:11; 1 Kgs. 12:11			

Scourge, Scourging or flogging was the punishment prescribed in Deuteronomy 22:18 for a man who defamed his bride publicly and unjustly. Deuteronomy 25:1-3 states that the judge may prescribe a flogging for other crimes too. In this case the culprit was made to lie down in front of the judge and receive the number of strokes the judge considered proportionate to his offense. These however should not exceed forty lest the brother be excessively degraded. The Talmud has an entire tract, called **makkot,** blows, prescribing how the scourging was to take place and for which crimes. The culprit received thirteen strokes on the bare chest and twenty-six on the back, thus falling one short of the prescribed maximum. This was to ensure that the law would not be broken inadvertently. A Roman citizen could be birched (**verberatio virgis**), and the symbol of this power was the **fasces,** bundles of birches tied around the axe carried by the lictors for the execution of justice. Citizens however could not be scourged (**flagellatio**); this was reserved as a terrible punishment for disobedient slaves and non-citizens, and often preceded capital punishment. Even when capital punishment was not imposed, the scourging itself often resulted in death. This was carried out with thongs or chains studded with bone, metal or spikes. Jesus was scourged in this way. There is a difference of detail in Matthew 27:26 and Mark 15:15, where the scourging is said to precede the intended execution, compared to John 19:1, where it seems to have been Pilate's effort to free him. Luke too in 23:22 has Pilate state: "I will therefore chastise him and release him."

Paul was three times beaten with rods (2 Cor. 11:25). One of these times was at Philippi (Acts 16:22). In Acts 22:24 he claimed his Roman citizenship when the tribune had him tied down to be examined under the lash. The apostles rejoiced at the honor of suffering in Christ's name, in accordance with his prediction, when the Sanhedrin had them flogged (Acts 5:40, 41; see Matt. 10:17).

Scribe, The scribe, in Hebrew **sopher,** is a typical figure of the culture and society of the ancient Middle East. The scribe is essentially the person who knows how to read and write. It should evoke no surprise that in ancient times these two qualifications could alone constitute a profession. On the one hand one must keep in mind the extreme complexity of old oriental writing, especially in Egypt and Mesopotamia, and on the other the illiterate state of the people of the time. The scribe then was a person who put his qualifications at the service of others. To know how to read and write, however, meant much more than to be able to understand what was written or to write something down. His profession put the scribe in direct contact with all the governing classes of the land and especially with the royal administration, for which the scribe's services were indispensable.

Their function was above all practical. They put documents together, kept the archives of the state, composed the annals, carried out routine administration and so on. Their direct knowledge of affairs put them in an unequalled position as counsellors, executives and administrators, and conferred on them special authority. The profession of scribe was above that of tradesman, farmer or laborer, not because of birth or riches, but because of acquired ability. This gave to the figure of the scribe a personal prestige which was the source of his acknowledged authority.

Scribes were formed in professional schools. In view of the rank in office that he was destined to hold, the aspirant was taught more than the rudiments of reading and writing. He was also given an intellectual and human formation so that he could become a proficient functionary, prudent and vigilant and able to survive in the difficult daily contact with powerful people. He was taught to know the soul and passions that move men; in brief, he was taught to be wise. The wisdom tradition is developed from the basis of the moral and human instruction of these scribes, which gathered centuries of experience into proverbs and aphorisms. *See* WISDOM.

The class of scribes appeared in Israel with the advent of the monarchy. The **sopher** is one of the principal offices in the list of officials in David's royal administration (2 Sam. 8:17; 20:25), as in that of Solomon (1 Kgs. 4:3). The scribe played an important part under Jehoash of Judah (1 Kgs. 12:11: he is entrusted with the administration of funds for the reparation of the Temple); Hezekiah (2 Kgs. 18:18, 37; 19:2: the scribe intervenes in the negotiations with the ambassadors of Sennacherib); Josiah (2 Kgs. 22:3: Shaphan, the scribe, is entrusted with the book of the law discovered in the Temple); and often under Jehoiakim and Zedekiah (*see* Jer. 36:10; 37:15, 20; 52:25). Zedekiah's scribe was among the officials of the kingdom who were executed by Nebuchadnezzar at Riblah (2 Kgs. 25:19).

During the post-exilic period the scribes no longer enjoyed the high rank they had under the kings. Nevertheless to them is owed the composition in writing and the conservation of the historical, judicial, wisdom and prophetic patrimony of Israel. The name and work of at least one of them is well known: Baruch, Jeremiah's scribe (Jer. 36:4). During and after the exile, when Israel became in reality the "people of the Book," the class of scribes also acquired a new character and function which up to that time had been less in evidence: they were the experts in the sacred Book. It is interesting to observe that Ezra, the Moses of Judaism, is presented as "a scribe well-versed in the law of Moses" (Ezra 7:6).

From here on the scribes, even more than the priests, were to be the moral guides of the people. Not only did they compile and edit the sacred books, but they were to give them an interpretative tradition which in time gained the authority of oral law alongside the written law of Moses.

This new type of scribe very often figures in the New Testament. The scribes are the doctors of the law, the rabbis for the most part with Pharasaic tendencies. In the gospel narrative the scribes and pharisees form almost the same group, especially in so far as they were hostile to Jesus (Matt. 5:20; 12:38; 15:1; 23:2, 13-29). When they are coupled with the priests, they are no other than Pharisee scribes (Matt. 16:21; 20:18; 21:15, etc.). After the destruction of Jerusalm the doctors of the law were the uncontested leaders of Judaism. To them we owe the transmission of the Hebrew text of the Old Testament (*see* TEXT, OLD TESTAMENT) and the development and final redaction of the oral tradition in the Mishna and Talmud.

Scripture, *See* BIBLE.

Scroll, An ancient form of book in which different sheets of papyrus or leather were glued together to make one long strip which was then rolled up for storage or transportation and unrolled for reading. *See* BOOK, DEAD SEA SCROLLS.

scruples
the *s.* of those   Rom. 15:1

Scythians, A nomadic Indo-European people who moved in the seventh century B.C. from the steppes of central Asia through the Caucasus to the Middle East. They became allies of the Assyrians and were later defeated by the Persians. Herodotus speaks of a lightning invasion of Scythians through Syria to Egypt. Traces of this are seen in Jeremiah 4:5-6:26 and in the book of Zephaniah. In the Table of Nations they are called Ashkenaz, and their progenitor is made son of Japheth by Gomer (Gen. 10:3; 1 Chron. 1:6; Jer. 51:27).

Scythopolis (sith-op′-o-lis), The name of Beth-shan during the Hellenistic period. *See* BETH-SHAN.

Sea, The marginal role that the sea plays in the life and history of the Israelites is in contrast with its importance in their concepts of the cosmos. (*See* SAILING.) These cosmic concepts are not their own, but inherited through Canaan from Mesopotamia. *See* CREATION, EARTH, LEVIATHAN, RAHAB.

The Hebrew **yam,** sea, is a name that is generously applied to masses of water so small that they would not merit the title in our languages. The Lake of Gennesaret is a sea, and is often called the Sea of Galilee or Tiberias. "The sea" for the Bible is the Mediterranean, which washed the western limits of the land of Canaan, and so serves to indicate the west. Israelite territory stretches "from sea to sea," that is, from the Persian Gulf to the Mediterranean (*see* Ps. 72:8; Zech. 9:10; Sir. 44:21).

Seah (see′-a), A dry measure, the third of an ephah, equivalent to about sixteen quarts (Gen. 18:6; 1 Sam. 25:18; 1 Kgs. 18:32; 2 Kgs. 7:1, 16, 18).

Seal, In ancient times, as is the use today, seals were used to authenticate documents and to ensure their remaining unopened or "sealed" (1 Kgs. 21:8; Isa. 29:11; Jer. 32:10; Rev. 5:1). It was even more important at a time when writing was not common: the seal was a very personal possession by which one pledged oneself in writing or in deed. Seals took different shapes with figures and signs in intaglio so that these could be rolled or stamped into moist clay which was then baked solid. There were cylinder, amulet, stamp, ring and other shapes to the seal. The cylinder seal was pierced lengthwise or had a loop affixed so that it could be worn around the neck. Hence Judah left Tamar as pledge of payment for her prostitution his seal and cord (Gen. 38:16). There is reference to ring-seals in 1 Kings 21:8; Daniel 14:13.

Such a personal possession served metaphor well. The Song of Songs sings: "Put me as a seal upon your heart and as a seal upon your arm" (8:6). The Father set his seal on Christ (Jn. 6:27). The Spirit (Matt. 3:16) whom Christ has given to Christians is their seal or pledge of immortality (*see* Eph. 1:13; 2 Cor. 1:22; Gal. 4:4-6; Rom. 8:14 ff.).

Sea Monster, *See* CREATION, LEVIATHAN, RAHAB.

Sea of Galilee, The Lake of Gennesaret, *see* GENNESARET.

Sea of the Arabah, The name of the Dead Sea in Deuteronomy 3:17; Joshua 3:16; 12:3. The Arabah is the geological cleft in which the Dead Sea is situated, and which continues on south from there to the Gulf of Aqaba. *See* ARABAH.

Sea of Tiberias, The Sea of Galilee or Lake of Gennesaret. It was called the Sea of Tiberias after Herod Antipas built a city on the west coast of the lake and named it Tiberias in honor of the Roman Emperor Tiberius. *See* Jn. 6:1; 21:1; GENNESARET, LAKE OF.

Secacah (si-kay′-kah), A village in the desert of Judah (Josh. 15:61).

Second Coming, *See* PAROUSIA.

secret
and sets it up in *s.*   Deut. 27:15   A *s.* gift allays anger   Prov. 21:14
                but another man's *s.*   Prov. 25:9

Secret, Messianic, *See* MESSIANIC SECRET.

Secundus, A Christian of Thessalonica who accompanied Paul on his return from the third apostolic journey (Acts 20:4).

seed

plant that bears *s.*	Gen. 1:11	sow your *s.*	Lev. 26:16
every *s.*-bearing plant	Gen. 1:29	part of the *s.* fell	Matt. 13:7

seek

let Pharaoh *s.*	Gen. 41:33	*s.* peace	Ps. 34:15
those who *s.* you	Ps. 9:11	and *s.* their food	Ps. 104:21

Seer, *See* PROPHETS.

Segub (see′-gub), The second-born son of Hiel. According to 1 Kings 16:34, Hiel from Bethel rebuilt Jericho during Ahab's reign (869-850 B.C.). "He lost his first-born son, Abiram, when he laid the foundations, and his youngest son, Segub, when he set up the gates." The text alludes to human sacrifices to propitiate the divinity towards the work undertaken. The author does not say explicitly that Hiel sacrificed his sons. Rather he sees in their death the fulfilment of the curse pronounced by Joshua on anyone who should dare in the future to rebuild Jericho (Josh. 6:26).

Seir (see′-ir), "The mountains of Seir" form the mountain range south of the Dead Sea which reaches to the Gulf of Aqaba. The Horites inhabited the surrounding region (*see* HORITES, Gen. 14:6) and there the descendants of Esau-Edom established themselves (Gen. 25:25; 32:3; 33:14-16; 36:8). The Israelites passed through it on their journey to Canaan (Deut. 2:2). God appears on the mountain of Seir (Deut. 33:2) and from there advances towards Canaan. This text has led some scholars to look in this region for Horeb, the mountain of God (Ex. 3:1-5) where God appeared to Moses. *See* SINAI.

Sela (see′-la), A city of Edom which was conquered by Amaziah of Judah (800-783 B.C.; 2 Kgs. 14:7). With the name of Petra it was capital of the Nabataean kingdom. Isaiah 16:1 also mentions a city by the name of Sela, but the context suggests Moab and not Edom. The name **Sela** means rock and it was therefore given in all probability to more than one place. Judges 1:36 mentions yet another, this time very probably in Judah.

Selah, The transliteration of a Hebrew word, meaning uncertain, that appears 71 times in 39 psalms in the Hebrew text, and in the liturgical third chapter of Habakkuk (vv. 3, 9, 13). The Greek word used in the Septuagint means "interlude." Apparently "Selah" is a word of liturgical instruction to the leader of the service, perhaps for the musicians to provide some sort of flourish or musical interruption of the chanting of the words of the psalm. Probably first written on the margin of manuscripts to catch the eye of priest or choirmaster, "Selah" apparently later became copied into the text proper. The Jerusalem Bible (1966) translates: "Pause." The New English Bible (1970) and The New American Bible (1970) omit it entirely, presumably as not being scriptural.

Seled (see′-led), A Judahite, the son of Nadab (1 Chron. 2:30). He died without sons.

Seleucia (si-loo′-sha), From the name of King Seleucus, one of the successors to Alexander the Great. It became the name of different cities in his kingdom.

1. A city and seaport along the northern coast of Syria, founded by Seleucus I Nicator. It is called Seleucia Pieria or Seleucia of Syria to distinguish it from other cities of the same name in Cilicia and Mesopotamia. In 146 B.C. it was conquered by Ptolemy VI Philomotor of Egypt (1 Mac. 11:8).

Paul embarked at Seleucia together with Barnabas and John Mark at the beginning of the first apostolic journey (Acts 13:4).

2. Seleucia in Mesopotamia, a city on the banks of the Tigris, founded by Seleucus I Nicator in 312 B.C.

3. Seleucia in Cilicia, on the river Calycadnus.

Seleucids, (si-loo′-sids), The kings of the dynasty founded by Seleucus I Nicator, one of the generals of Alexander the Great. At Alexander's death in 323 B.C. his generals divided up among themselves the vast empire he had built. Seleucus had the satrapy of Babylonia (312 B.C., which is the beginning of the Seleucid era as used for dating in 1-2 Maccabees). After the battle of Ipsus in 301 he also came into possession of Syria and part of Asia Minor. Palestine was a territory disputed between Seleucids and Ptolemies until 198 B.C. when it passed definitely into Seleucid hands in the person of Antiochus III the Great at the battle of Panion near the headwaters of the Jordan. Of the Seleucid kings the Bible has a veiled reference to Seleucus II Callinicus (246-226 B.C.), the "king of the North" of Daniel 11:10, and to Seleucus IV Pilopator (187-175 B.C.), the "other prince" of Daniel 11:20. Seleucus IV sent his minister Heliodorus to Jerusalem to take the Temple treasures, but he was violently ejected by a horse carrying a fearsome rider and two young men of beauty and strength (2 Mac. 3:7-39; *see* HELIODORUS).

The successor of Seleucus IV was Antiochus IV Epiphanes, during whose reign the Maccabees revolted. For Antiochus and his successors in the dynasty who took part in the wars of the Maccabees *see* ALEXANDER, ANTIOCHUS, DEMETRIUS.

Through defeat at the hands of Pompey, the Seleucid kingdom in 64 B.C. became a province of the Roman empire.

Seleucus, *See* SELEUCIDS.

Semein (sem′-e-in), An ancestor of Jesus (Lk. 3:26).

Semites, From an etymological point of view, the Semites are the descendants of Shem, according to the genealogy of Genesis 10. The criterion by which the people of the Middle East are distributed into sons of Shem, Ham and Japheth is geographical and historical. (*See* TABLE OF NATIONS.) The actual use of the term, however, follows linguistic and ethnic criteria. Thus are excluded from the sons of Shem the Elamites, who spoke a non-Semitic language: they were Indo-European or Japhethites. The Babylonians and Canaanites on the other hand are Semites (=Shemites), even though in Genesis 10 they appear among the sons of Ham.

The known Semitic languages are distributed, in accordance with the geographic distribution of the peoples who spoke them, into northern Semitic and southern Semitic. The latter are Ethiopian and Arabic. The former are divided into western Semitic, to include Canaanite, Phoenician, Hebrew and Aramaic languages, and eastern, Akkadic. The cradle of the Semites is to be sought for in the Syro-Arabic desert, from which they emerged in periodic waves to wander at the fringes of settled areas and eventually themselves to settle down. Many of these movements of peoples took place in historic times. The most recent one was the Arab invasion which opened the way to the west through North Africa. *See* NOMADISM.

Senaah (si-nay′-ah), Head of a family of exiles who returned from Babylon (Ezra 2:35; Neh. 7:38).

Seneh (see′-neh), A rocky summit along the Wadi es-Suweinit, commanding the pass to the city of Michmash and facing to the south towards Geba. It is mentioned with its opposite pinnacle Bozez in the account of Jonathan's attack on the Philistine outpost at Michmash (1 Sam. 14:4).

Senir (see′-nir), The Amorite name for Mount Hermon, called by the Sidonians Hermon Sirion (Deut. 3:9; Ezek. 27:5).

Sennacherib (se-nak′-er-ib), King of Assyria (705-681 B.C.), son and successor of Sargon II. Frequently in the history of the great eastern empires succession to the throne afforded to the subjugated peoples what seemed the best opportunity to shake off the imperial yoke: a rash of revolts attended Sennacherib's accession to power, obliging him to reestablish his authority. The center of revolt in the east was Lower Mesopotamia, whose ancient aspirations to power were awakened by the intriguing Merodach-baladan. Hezekiah of Judah (715-687 B.C.) was in close relationship with Merodach-baladan (2 Kgs. 20:12-19; Isa. 39:1-8), and like him, bent on revolt. Once the eastern question was settled, Sennacherib launched a campaign against Palestine, defeated Egypt, took the cities of the Philistines and of Judah, and finally put Jerusalem under siege. A divine intervention, described in 2 Kings 18:13-19:37 and in Isaiah 36-37 saved the city just in time: "The angel of the Lord went forth and struck down one hundred and eight-five thousand men in the Assyrian camp." Sennacherib struck camp and left.

This version of the divine intervention has always been understood as a 'theologized' account of an epidemic that plagued the besieging army. The episode is much like the one Herodotus recounts at the end of Sennacherib's campaign in Egypt. 2 Kings 19:7 and Isaiah 37:7 however offer an explanation with a different slant: "I am about to put in him such a spirit that, when he hears a certain report, he will return to his own land."

There is no precise information available on the last years of Sennacherib's reign. The Bible has an account of his death: "When he was worshipping in the temple of his God Nisroch, his sons Adrammelech and Sharezer slew him with the sword and fled into the land of Ararat. His son Esarhaddon reigned in his stead" (2 Kgs. 19:37; Isa. 37:38).

Seorim (se-or′-im), A priest during David's reign (1 Chron. 24:8).

Sephar (sef′-ar), A region of Arabia (Gen. 10:30), location unknown.

Sepharad (sef′-a-rad), Among the Jews of the Middle Ages Sepharad is the Hebrew name for Spain. In Obadiah 20, however, this identification does not make sense. It is thought to allude to Sardis in Asia Minor.

Sepharvaim (sef′-ar-vay′-im), A city or territory in Syria or Mesopotamia which was conquered by the Assyrians (2 Kgs. 18:34; 19:13; Isa. 36:19; 37:13). The people of Sepharvaim were settled in Samaria after it had been conquered and its people deported (2 Kgs. 17:24, 31). Deportations were a major policy in Assyrian imperialism, and were obviously aimed at dissipating the national spirit of the subjugated lands and thus securing the cohesion of the empire.

Septuagint (sep′-too-a-jint), The name given to the Greek version of the Old Testament that was made at Alexandria from the third to the first centuries B.C. The name Septuagint stems from the legendary account of the origins of this translation; this legend is read for the first time in the letter of Aristeas, a Jewish apologetic writing from the middle of the second century. According to Aristeas, Ptolemy II Philadelphos, king of Egypt (282-246 B.C.), successor of Ptolemy I, the founder of the library of Alexandria, wished to have there the sacred books of the Jews. Since these had to be translated into Greek, he requested from the High Priest of the

Jews in Jerusalem good manuscripts and men capable of translating them. The High Priest sent to Alexandria 72 Jews, six from each tribe, who completed their work, the translation of the Pentateuch, in 72 days. Despite the legendary character of the story, there is a historical nucleus also, for there did exist in Alexandria around the middle of the third century B.C. a Greek translation of the Pentateuch. This translation however was not made at the order of the king, but to supply the religious needs, both in private reading and in synagogue use, of the flourishing Jewish colonies in Egypt.

Later witnesses, such as Philo and the Fathers, supply further elements: they speak of a translation of the whole Old Testament, and have it that the 72 translators, working independently, and producing each a translation, came out with works that corresponded to the letter, each to the other. All this embellishment added authority to the text, so that one now spoke of inspiration. In reality however, the translation of the other books was made in stages, and was substantially completed by 132 B.C. This can be deduced from the words of the translator of Sirach, who in speaking of the difficulties of translating from the Hebrew, states: "That is true not only of this book but of the law itself, the prophets and the rest of the books, which differ no little when they are read in the original" (Prol. Sir. vv. 24-26).

The translation, then, is not by one author nor from one time period, but was made in stages from the third to the first centuries B.C. The Hebrew text used often differs from the massoretic text, and for this reason has great importance in textual criticism. The Septuagint text in fact, like the Dead Sea Scrolls, gives access to the biblical text as it was before the critical work carried out on the Hebrew text from the first century A.D. on. *See* TEXT, OLD TESTAMENT.

The Greek translation contains books that were held in great veneration by the Jews of the diaspora but were absent from the Palestinian biblical canon. These books were received into the canon of the Christian church which used the Septuagint, and after some uncertainty, they were universally recognized as inspired and canonical. These are the so-called deuterocanonical books of the Old Testament (Wisdom, Sirach, Judith, Tobit, Baruch, 1-2 Maccabees). The Septuagint contains also 3 Ezra and 3-4 Maccabees. which are not accepted in the canon of the Christian Church.

The Septuagint is also important in that in many places it mirrors the theological tendencies that were special to the Jews of the diaspora. To it also we owe the theological terminology in which Christianity was expressed in the Hellenistic world. The Christian church made the Septuagint its own, and this text assumed enormous importance in the disputes between Christians and Jews. This undoubtedly explains why Judaism detached itself more and more from the ancient translation and attempted new ones that would be more faithful to the canonical Hebrew text approved by the Jews of Palestine. In 128 A.D. Aquila, a Jewish proselyte, made a most literal translation of the Hebrew text. Theodotion, a Jewish proselyte from Ephesus, made a new translation, or rather a correction of the Septuagint, to accommodate it to the Hebrew text. Theodotion's translation of Daniel supplanted the ancient version of this book, and his is the translation that is today printed in editions of the Septuagint.

At the end of the second century, in the reign of Septimius Severus (193-211 A.D.) there appeared Symmachus' translation, which is freer and more elegant than that of Aquila, and for that reason was not as successful. Only some fragments of all these translations remain.

It is not possible here to treat of the transmission of the Septuagint text down through the Christian centuries. However, a word must be said about one of the most gigantic works of textual criticism undertaken in Christian antiquity. This is the Hexapla of Origen. This great work, conserved only in the library of Caesarea of Palestine, contained in parallel columns: the Hebrew text, the transliteration of the Hebrew text in Greek letters, Aquila's translation, that of Symmachus, the Septuagint and Theodotion's translation. For some books he added up to three other translations. Origen indicated with an obelus (÷) the passages present in the Septuagint but absent in the Massoretic text, and with an asterisk (*) what was present in the Massoretic text and absent in the Septuagint.

Origen chose among the variant readings of the manuscripts of the Septuagint what was supported by other versions. Origen's scope was not precisely to offer a textual criticism of the Septuagint text in the way in which today this is understood, that is, in order to restore in its purest form the original text. He was more intent on apologetic and pastoral purposes, to provide an easy way to check out the divergences between the biblical text of the Church (the Septuagint) and the biblical text of the Jews, and in this way facilitate the polemic with the Jews. He also wished to put an end to the extreme confusion that existed in the Septuagint manuscripts used by the Church by producing a uniform text that was to a great extent a compromise between the Septuagint manuscript tradition and other Greek versions. This immense work, however, did not achieve its purpose, above all because the criteria used by Origen were not very orthodox from the point of view of textual criticism, and then because the fifth column, with the Greek text of the Septuagint prepared by Origen, was often copied without his critical notes, with the result that here was a text mixed up with the residue of other versions.

St. Jerome refers to two other recensions of the Septuagint made in the third century, that of Hesychius in Alexandria of Egypt and that of Lucianus in Antioch. On the manuscripts used for these recensions *see* TEXT, NEW TESTAMENT.

The first printed edition of the Septuagint is from the **Poliglotta Complutense** (Alcalá 1514-1517) A critical edition is being prepared for publication at Göttingen. The most used critical editions are those of Swete (3 vol. Cambridge 1887) and Rahlfs (2 vol. Stuttgart 1935).

Sepulcher, *See* BURIAL.

Serah (ser′-ah), A daughter of Asher (Gen. 46:17; Num. 26:46).

Seraiah (se-ray′-yah), 1. The scribe or secretary of King David (2 Sam. 8:17). He is called Shawsha or Shavsha in 1 Chronicles 18:17 and Shisha in 1 Kings 4:3.

2. High priest during the reign of Zedekiah of Judah (598-587 B.C.). When Jerusalem was captured Seraiah was taken prisoner with other dignitaries of Temple and court and brought before Nebuchadnezzar at Riblah who ordered their execution (2 Kgs. 25:18-21; Jer. 52:24).

3. One of the army commanders of Judah under Zedekiah. When after the fall of Jerusalem Nebuchadnezzar named Gedaliah governor of Judah, Seraiah and other commanders came with their men and put themselves at Gedaliah's disposal (2 Kgs. 25:22-24; Jer. 40:8).

4. Son of Neriah, chief quartermaster of Zedekiah of Judah (598-587 B.C.). In 594 B.C. he accompanied Zedekiah on a journey to Babylon, and brought a letter from Jeremiah to the Jewish exiles. He was also commissioned by the prophet to read there all the prophet's oracles against Babylon (Jer. 51:59-64).

5. Son of Azriel, an officer of Jehoiakim of Judah (609-598 B.C.). He was given the task by the king of imprisoning Jeremiah and Baruch (Jer. 36:26).

Seraphim (ser′-a-fim), In the vision of Isaiah 6:1-7, seraphim are grouped around the throne of Yahweh and alternate in two choirs the "Holy, holy, holy." The incomplete description given there and the functions they carried out suggest that they were anthropomorphic six-winged figures. The word seraphim is derived from the root **saraph**, to burn, and might be translated as the "ones aflame," "the fiery ones," or "the burning ones." It expresses the divine sanctity which they proclaim, and which burns away all uncleanness (*see* Isa. 6:6). The picture is not greatly different from the scene of another celebrated vision of the divine throne described in 1 Kings 29:19 ff.

There are texts in which the same word **'saraph'** is used to mean a particular type of serpent. Numbers 21:6 reads: "In punishment the Lord sent among the people saraph serpents, which bit the people so that many of them died." In all probability this refers to real, poisonous serpents and for that reason called "the burning ones." Deuteronomy 8:15 refers to the same incident. Isaiah 14:29 speaks of a "flying saraph," and probably refers to some creature of fantasy in the shape of a serpent, which is suggested by the preceding line: "For out of the serpent's root shall come an adder, its fruit shall be a flying saraph" (*see* Isa. 30:6).

Some interpreters have thought to link up these texts and conclude that the seraphim of Isaiah 6 had the shape of a serpent. Numbers 21:6-8 then would not be real serpents but seraphim in the execution of a particular mission. There is no great objection to this construction except that it seems too mechanical to put together texts merely on the basis of the use of the word **saraph.**

Sered (ser′-ed), The first-born of Zebulun (Gen. 46:14; Num. 26:26).

Seron (ser′ on), Governor of Coelesyria and head of the Seleucid army that was defeated by Judas Maccabeus (1 Mac. 3:13, 23).

Serpent, The serpent occurs frequently in the mythology and symbolism of the eastern religions, often in monstrous and fantastic guise. This view is mirrored here and there in the Bible too.

The monster of the sea has·some of the serpent's traits: this sea monster however must not be thought of as a real serpent but rather as a personification of the power of the waters ever contesting Baal's dominion over the land. (*See* BAAL.) The residue of this myth has been employed in some poetic texts (*see* Isa. 27:1; Amos 9:3; Job 26:13) to express the biblical belief about creation. *See* CREATION, LEVIATHAN, RAHAB.

Much better known from the Bible is the figure of the serpent who tempted Eve in the garden of paradise (*see* Gen. 3). From this account two questions arise; a. what is the function of this personage in the whole story, and b. what made the author choose the serpent for such a function?

a. According to the author of Genesis 3, the evils of man all stem from his free decision against the will of God. This sin, however, does not arise spontaneously from man's interior, but is portrayed as the result of suggestion from without, that is, as a seduction. In this way the author is concerned about excusing not man, but God. For this reason he introduces the mysterious personage of the serpent. If one is to ask where he came by all this astuteness and clear aversion to God, he is left without an answer. The author researches the origins of evil and finds sin at its beginning. Sin itself was due to a seducer: at this point the sacred author stops. This leaves the serpent an ambiguous figure. It is not formally presented as evil, for this would contradict the whole picture of paradise. Nevertheless evil in some way attaches itself to him, otherwise his intervention in the story would be pointless. One must not then simply eliminate the ambiguity: it is one of the built-in limitations of the story and of the author's theology, which has not yet an adequately developed demonology. (*See* DEMONOLOGY, SATAN.) The author reasons from a reflection on the present state of man, who experiences the struggle with evil that is in some way personified. This he projects backwards in search of how it all started, and translates, into terms that are as far as possible consonant with the paradise scene, what is the universal experience of the struggle with evil. *See* FALL, THE.

b. One must not register surprise that the author described the tempter in the form of an animal. In all the eastern religions there is a persuasion that there are evil spirits, and these are conceived of and presented in the shape of animals that are often fantastic. (*See* LILITH.) Within the limits of his own demonology the author was able to make use of this element. Most interpreters find in the choice of the serpent a polemic intention. In religious symbolism the serpent has the double polarity of what it usually provokes: terror and fascination. Thus in the same religious tradition the serpent can be feared as the demoniacal animal **par excellence** and at the same time venerated, if not as a god, at least as a symbol of the earth's vitality. The serpent is taken as a chthonian, underworld animal, that is, an animal in contact with the gods that govern the fruitfulness of the earth.

In the Canaanite religion, which was Yahwism's chief opponent, the serpent occupied an important position as a symbol in the fertility cult and as a phallic symbol. The sacred author would then have chosen what the Canaanites considered the carrier of life and presented it as the bringer of death to the world.

Wisdom 2:24 (*see* 2 Cor. 11:3) presents the creation story in the light of a revelation that has progressed and of a demonology that has become more precise through development. In this way many of the ambiguities vanish. The serpent is now the devil, and with this identification it is not difficult to see how to him are attached many of the monstrous and fantastic characteristics of the cosmic monster at the creation of the world. The theme of the struggle with the devil, who is Satan, reappears once more, no longer in the creation context, but in that of the eschatological battle for power (*see* Rev. 12:1-7; 20:2).

Serug (ser′-ug), An ancestor of Jesus (Lk. 3:35; Gen. 11:20, 23; 1 Chron. 1:26).

Servant of the Lord, The Hebrew 'ebed, "slave," "servant," is used in very different senses in the Old Testament. (*See* SLAVERY.) In religious usage there are two different meanings. The adorers of a divinity, the faithful of a god, are called "his servants," so in Israel "servants of the Lord," the "servants of God." The name is also given to those among God's people who are especially chosen for a specific mission, such as Moses and the prophets (Amos 3:7; Jer. 25:4). In this second sense must be understood the title given to the anonymous character who is the central personality in several poems of the second part of the book of Isaiah.

These poems are scattered through chapters 42 to 53. They undoubtedly form a unity with a close link of thought and action and are easily isolated from the actual context. The first poem is read in Isaiah 42:1-4; God speaks to Israel and makes known the mission for which he has chosen and prepared his Servant. His mission will be to make known God's law. The poem underlines the meekness, and at the same time the firmness, with which the Servant will carry out his mission. The second poem (Isa. 49:1-6) portrays the Servant himself addressing the people, recounting his election and the mandate he has received from the Lord at a time when he felt that his toil was in vain. The third poem (Isa. 50:4-9a) also contains the words of the Servant. He bitterly complains about the opposition and contradictions he experienced, but nevertheless repeats his firm resolution not to give in, but to hope in the Lord who sustains him. The fourth poem, 52:13-53:12, is the longest and the most complex. At the beginning God announces how he will reverse the fortunes of the Servant to the astonishment of the people, causing him to pass from humiliation to glorification (52:13-15). Then the prophet describes in detail the lot of the Servant, his condemnation to an ignominious death despite his innocence, and finally reveals the mystery of that scandalous end: "If he gives his life as an offering for sin, he shall see his descendants in a long life and the will of the Lord shall be accomplished through him" (Isa. 53:1-10). Finally God speaks to announce the fruit of the expiatory death of his Servant (Isa. 53:11, 12).

The first three poems were later touched up to make the mission of the Servant more specific, especially in regard to Israel, who was to be appointed "as covenant of the people and light of the nations" (42:5-7). The people are exhorted to listen to the message of the Servant (Isa. 50:10).

The poems develop an intense dramatic tension. The saving mission entrusted to the Servant is opposed, but in the end that very opposition served to bring the mission to its accomplishment through the death unjustly inflicted on the Servant. The Servant acquires his glory and the salvation of others through his most profound humiliation.

The poems pose a puzzle almost as ancient as the poems themselves (*see* Acts 8:26-39): who is this anonymous Servant? There is no doubt that Jesus saw in these texts the program of his own mission (*see* below), and the New Testament is quite definite that the Servant is Jesus. When however one asks the question from the point of view of the poems' author, there is dispute. The question of prophecy and fulfilment can be discussed at the level of the literal or the typical sense.

It is not possible to list here or discuss all the proposed identifications. Here it must suffice to offer some considerations that point in the direction of a solution. The classical Jewish interpretation and identification probably did not emerge until the second century A.D. and in polemic against the Christian interpretation. This holds that the Servant of Yahweh is a personification of the people of Israel, its mission and tragic history. This interpretation is based on the undisputed fact that Israel is called Yahweh's Servant in other texts of the second part of Isaiah (*see* Isa. 41:8; 44:1, 21; 45:4; 48:20). While admitting then that confusion can easily arise from the actual context of the poems, this must not be exaggerated to the point where one ignores the mission received from God by the Servant, or the fact that the tragic lot of the Servant came about because of opposition on the part of the people themselves.

Another fairly common interpretation of the poems seeks to identify the anonymous Servant in the past history of Israel or among the author's contemporaries. The people preferred are Moses, Jeremiah, or the author of the poems himself. If this identification is confined to the past or present of the author, then the eschatological import of the texts is ignored, while the author obviously alludes to the divine initiative that will bring to fulfilment the history of salvation. Nevertheless this interpretation has suggested some figures in history who may have inspired the author. It is clear that the author does not just receive this message in a passive way: rather is it the fruit of a divine inspiration that makes him discover, in Israel's past and the experience of God's action in Israel, God's design for the future. The figure of the Servant combines many prophetic traits with the messianic character which tradition assigned to the king. Suffering is a part of the prophet's mission: here it becomes the instrument of salvation which reverses the seeming failure. The perverse power of incredulity and sin on the part of man is recognized, but only to be defeated by the Servant's expiatory obedience. The Servant's obedience is what characterizes him, and in it the prophet discovers the dimensions of salvation that take into account both the sin of man and the saving omnipotence of God.

Jesus, in denouncing the incredulity of his enemies, foretells his imminent death in terms of the prophecies of the Old Testament (*see* Lk. 13:31-32; Matt. 23:29; Matt. 21:23; Mk. 12:1 ff.; Lk. 20:9 ff.). He told his disciples that with his death he would bring to completion the mission of the Servant of Yahweh announced in Isaiah 53. These words are only spoken to the circle of disciples and are principally contained in the so called passion prophecies (Mk. 8:31; Matt. 16:21; Lk. 9:22; Mk. 9:31; Matt. 17:22; Lk. 9:43; Mk. 10:32; Matt. 20:17; Lk. 18:31) and in some separate sayings (Mk. 10:45; Matt. 20:28; Mk. 9:12; Mk. 14:21, 41), as well as in the accounts of institution of the Eucharist. The figure of the Servant of Yahweh, however, pervades the whole public life of Jesus. The very words of the Father at Jesus' baptism are, as it were, the public investiture of Jesus with his messianic role. They are taken, with slight variations, from Isaiah 42:1, where the mission of the servant is announced.

It is interesting to note, and it is a strong indication of authenticity, that there is only one explicit citation from Isaiah (ch. 53) on the lips of Jesus, Luke 23:35 quoting Isaiah 53:12; yet Isaiah 53 is present in the evangelical tradition and in general in the New Testament by constant allusion to the central elements of Isaiah 53. Phrases and characteristics of Isaiah 53 are used to describe the mission and lot of Jesus. There is, then, a perfect fusion between the Servant of the Old Testament and Jesus in the New Testament. The Old Testament is a prophecy of which the New Testament is the fulfilment.

Jesus introduces an important innovation. He did not use the title "Servant of Yahweh," but adopted all that was said about him and transferred it to himself under the name "Son of Man." (*See* SON OF MAN.) This fusion leaves deep traces on the two figures which now converge in Jesus. On the one hand the future glorious condition of the Servant of Yahweh is better defined than in Isaiah 53, while the glory and dominion of the Son of Man appear as the fruit of his obedience in love unto death.

a. The title "servant of God"(**pais theou**) did establish itself somewhat as an appellation of Jesus in the Jewish-Christian church. It seems to have been used in the genuine sense explained at the beginning, even though it is difficult to exclude all links between this and Isaiah's poems (*see* Acts 3:13; 3:26; 4:27, 30).

b. In Mark 10:45 and the account of the institution of the Eucharist in Matthew–Mark, those to benefit from the redemptive repast are called "the many" (in Greek **hoi polloi**) a term that is ambiguous in Greek and in other languages, for the plural of the adjective is restrictive—"many," but not all. This ambiguity disappears by a study of Isaiah 53. Neither Hebrew nor Aramaic has this restrictive sense. "The many" means the multitude—all, who are many.

c. The lot of Jesus is indicated by the word **"traditur"**, "he is handed over," or **"tradetur,"** "he will be handed over." The passive form of the verb is a veiled allusion to God. The terminology is taken from Isaiah 53:5 (*see* Jn. 3:16; Rom. 8:32). That God takes the initiative in the drama of salvation is expressed in other places with the phrase: "it is necessary" (Lk. 13:33). One must immediately notice, however, that it is not a question of the unalterable necessity of blind circumstances or events, but a moral necessity that arises from the will of God who has willed this plan of salvation (*see* e.g. Dan. 2:28).

d. Mark 10:45 is almost a free quotation from Isaiah 53:10, where the death of the Servant is proposed in cultic terms (**asam**) as a sacrifice for sin. The same context is suggested for passages such as Romans 3:25 and 1 Timothy 2:11.

Seth, Third son of Adam and Eve, and father of Enoch (Gen. 4:25; 5:3-8). The name is explained in popular etymology which sees it deriving from the verb **sith,** to replace. Eve stated: "God has granted me another offspring in place of Abel." Seth fathered sons and daughters and lived, according to Genesis 5:8, for nine hundred and twelve years.

Sethur, A man of the tribe of Asher sent with others to spy on the land of Canaan (Num. 13:13).

Seven, The, The name of the group of Jewish-Hellenistic Christians who were given the task of allotting food in the Jerusalem community (Acts 21:8). Their commission was occasioned by a complaint made against the Hebrews by the Hellenists, that in the daily distribution of food, their widows were being overlooked. They are not called deacons in Acts 6:1-6, although their functions included that of serving (in Greek, **diakonein** means to serve). Tradition has seen in Acts 6:1-6 the institution of the order of diaconate. As the history of Stephen and Philip show, their mission was much wider than merely serving food to the community. They also preached and baptized. While the name is absent, there is an undoubted link between the function and mission of the seven and that of deacons, as revealed in other New Testament writings. *See* DEACON.

Shaalbim (shay-al′-bim), A city of the Amorites (Jgs. 1:35) which was nominally assigned to the territory of Dan. (Josh. 19:42) but probably not occupied by the Israelites before the monarchy (1 Kgs. 4:9). Today it is Salbit, north of Amwas. It seems to be the same as Shaalbon, the birthplace of Eliahba, one of the warriors of David (2 Sam. 23:32; 1 Chron. 11:33).

Shaalbon (shay-al′-bon), *See* SHAALBIM.

Shaalim (shay′-a-lim), A region, probably in the land of Ephraim or Benjamin, which was traversed by Saul in search of his father's asses (1 Sam. 9:4).

Shaaph (shay′-af), Father of Madmannah (1 Chron. 2:47, 49).

Shaaraim (shay′-a-ray′-im), A city of Judah (Josh. 15:36) mentioned in the account of the Israelite victory over the Philistines which followed the slaying of Goliath (1 Sam. 17:52). A city of the same name in the land of Simeon (1 Chron. 4:31) is called Sharuhen in Joshua 19:6. Sharuhen today is Tell el-Far'ah.

Shaashgaz (shay-ash′-gaz), The eunuch who served King Ahasuerus as guardian of the royal harem (Esth. 2:14). Custodian of the concubines.

Shabbethai (shab′-e-thie), A Levite who supported the work of Ezra (Ezra 10:15; Neh. 8:7).

Shaddai (shad′-eye), *See* NAME; PATRIARCHS, RELIGION OF.

Shadrach, The Babylonian name given to Hananiah, one of the three youths who accompanied Daniel in the court of the king of Babylonia (Dan. 1:7; 2:49).

Shagee (shay′-gee), The father of Jonathan, one of the Thirty warriors of David (1 Chron. 11:34).

Shahazumah (shay′-a-zoo′-mah), A town in the territory of Issachar (Josh. 19:22).

Shalem, *See* SALEM.

Shalishah (shal′-i-shah), A region in central Palestine in Ephraim or Benjamin, traversed by Saul in search of his father's asses (1 Sam. 9:4). *See* SHAALIM.

Shallum, 1. Shallum, son of Jabesh, who conspired against Zechariah king of Israel (746-745 B.C.), attacked and killed him at Ibleam and succeeded him to reign, for one month only, however. "Menahem son of Gadi came up from Tirzah to Samaria, where he attacked and killed Shallum, son of Jabesh and reigned in his place" (2 Kgs. 15:10-15).

2. Son of Tikvah and husband of Huldah the prophetess, whom Josiah consulted about the book of the law discovered in the Temple (2 Kgs. 22:14; 2 Chron. 34:22).

3. Son and successor of Josiah king of Judah (609 B.C., Jer. 22:11; 1 Chron. 3:15). He is also called Jehoahaz, in 2 Kings 23:31-35 and 2 Chronicles 36:1-3. *See* JEHOAHAZ.

4. Uncle of the prophet Jeremiah, from whom, upon a command from the Lord, Jeremiah bought a piece of family property at Anathoth (Jer. 32).

Shalmaneser (shal′-ma-nee′-zer), Shalmaneser V king of Assyria (727-722 B.C.), son and successor of Tiglath-pileser III. Hoshea king of Israel (734-724 B.C.) was a vassal of the Assyrians, but later looked for Egyptian aid to throw off Shalmaneser's yoke. The Assyrian king discovered Hoshea's double game whereupon he arrested, deposed and imprisoned him. Hoshea simply disappeared from history. Shalmaneser occupied the whole land and attacked Samaria which he put under siege for three years. He died, it seems, before he was able to conquer the city, which however fell into the hands of his successor Sargon II (2 Kgs. 17:1-6).

Shama (shay′-ma), Son of Hotham. He and his brother Jeiel were members of the Thirty warriors of David (1 Chron. 11:44).

Shamgar, Although he is not named among the judges, Shamgar son of Anath is recorded among the heroes of Israel in a period of confrontation with the Philistines (Jgs. 5:6). He routed six hundred Philistines with an ox-goad, and so merited the name "deliverer of Israel" (Jgs. 3:31).

Shamhuth (sham′-huth), A chief of David's army (1 Chron. 27:8). There were twenty-four thousand men in his division.

Shamir (shay′-mir), 1. A city of Judah (Josh. 15:48) perhaps the same as today's el-Bireh.

2. A city in the mountain region of Ephraim, home of the judge Tola, son of Puah (Jgs. 10:1-2). Perhaps it is to be identified with the site of Samaria.

Shammah, Son of Jesse and brother of David (1 Sam. 16:9).

Shammai (sham′-eye), Personal name (1 Chron. 2:28, 32; 2:44, 45; 4:17).

Shammoth, One of the warriors of David known as the Thirty (1 Chron. 11:27).

Shammua (sha-mue′-a), Son of King David, born in Jerusalem (2 Sam. 5:14).

Shaphan (shay′-fan), Son of Azaliah, a scribe who was a contemporary of King Josiah of Judah (640-609 B.C.) and of the prophet Jeremiah. Shaphan was commissioned by the priest Hilkiah to bring to the king the book of the law that had been found in the Temple. Later he was charged along with others with the task of consulting the prophetess Hulda on the book that was discovered (2 Kgs. 22:3-14; 2 Chron. 34:8-20). Shaphan's family rendered precious services to the prophet Jeremiah. Ahikam, Shaphan's son, protected Jeremiah against an attempted assassination (Jer. 26:24). Another son of Shaphan, Elasah, was the carrier of a letter from Jeremiah to the exiled Israelites (Jer. 29:3; *see* also Jer. 36:10-12). Gedaliah, appointed governor of Judea by Nebuchadnezzar, was the son of Ahikam and grandson of Shaphan (Jer. 39:14; 40:5).

Shaphat (shay′-fat), Father of the prophet Elisha (1 Kgs. 19:16, 19; 2 Kgs. 3:11; 6:31).

Shaphir (shay′-fir), A town probably in Judah (Mic. 1:11). Khirbet el-Kom, west of Hebrew, is a likely site.

Sharar (shar′-ar), The father of Ahiam, one of the Thirty warriors of David (2 Sam. 23:33).

Sharezer (sha-ree′-zer), Son of Sennacherib, king of Assyria. Sharezer and Adrammelech assassinated their father while he was praying in the temple of his god Nisroch, and then fled into the land of Ararat. It was another son, Esarhaddon, however, who succeeded the slain monarch (2 Kgs. 19:37).

Sharon, The fertile plain of Sharon occupies the central region of the Mediterranean coastal strip of Palestine. It reaches from Carmel southwards as far as Joppa and varies in width from 6 to 12 miles. It is given only rare mention in the Bible, and then usually in poetic texts (Isa. 33:9; 35:2; 65:10; S. of S. 2:1; Josh. 12:18; Acts 9:35). In spring, flowers of many varieties grow profusely on it. Today it provides Israel with citrus fruit and farm crops, among numerous modern settlements.

Sharuhen (sha-roo′-en), A city in the land of Simeon (Josh. 19:6) called Shaaraim in the parallel text of 1 Chronicles 4:31.

Shaul (sholl), Shaul of Rehoboth-han-nahar was the sixth of the kings who ruled in the land of Edom before an Israelite king ruled (Gen. 36:31, 37, 38). He succeeded Samlah and was succeeded by Baalhanan.

Shaveh (shay′-veh), The name of the valley where Abraham met Melchizedek while returning victorious after liberating Lot from the four eastern kings. Melchizedek was king of Salem, which is identified in biblical tradition with Jerusalem, and the valley of Shaveh with "the King's Valley" (2 Sam. 18:18), that is, Kidron.

Shaveh-kiriathaim (kir′-i-a-thay′-im), The plain where Chedorlaomer and the kings with him defeated the Emim, a pre-Moabite people resident in Moab (Gen. 14:5).

Shawsha, Shavsha, The scribe or secretary of King David (2 Sam. 8:17; 1

Chron. 18:17; 2 Sam. 20:25), called Shisha in 1 Kings 4:3 in the list of Solomon's ministers, which includes his two sons, Elihoreph and Ahijah, as scribes.

Shealtiel (she-al′-ti-el), Son of Jeconiah (=Jehoiakim), king of Judah (1 Chron. 3:17; Matt. 1:12) and father of Zerubbabel (Ezra 3:2; Neh. 12:1; Hag. 1:1; 2:2). His name is read in Jesus' genealogy in Matthew 1:12 and Luke 3:27, but Luke 3:27 makes him the son of Neri. 1 Chronicles 3:17-19 calls him the uncle, not the father of Zerubbabel.

Shear-jashub (she′-ar-jay′-shub), "A remnant will return," the symbolic name for the first son of Isaiah (Isa. 7:3).

Sheba, 1. Sheba son of Bichri, a Benjaminite. During the period following Absalom's revolt Sheba attempted a secessionist movement of the northern tribes against the rule of David of Judah. David gave Amasa the commission of getting the army together, but he failed to do so in the three days allowed him by David for the task. So David sent Abishai and Joab. Joab met Amasa at Gibeon and killed him treacherously. Then he set out for Abel-beth-maacah where Sheba and his followers were. Joab put the city under siege, whereupon the inhabitants killed Sheba and threw his head over the wall, thus saving the city and its inhabitants (2 Sam. 20:1-22).

2. In the Table of Nations Sheba appears among the descendants of Ham (Gen. 10:7) and of Shem (10:28). Later, in Abraham's genealogy he is numbered among the sons had by Keturah (Gen. 25:3). These "genealogical" indications point in the direction of the Arab peoples of the great Arabian peninsula. Today scholars place Sheba in the southwest corner of Arabia, in modern Yemen. 1 Kings 10 records the visit of the queen of Sheba to Solomon. This state visit is recalled in the context of showing the fame of the wisdom and riches of Solomon, but it was also undoubtedly intended to implement Solomon's policy of establishing or intensifying commercial links with that region and the regions to which the Shebans had access—luxury products, spices, gold and precious stones (Isa. 60:6; Jer. 6:20; Ezek. 27:22; Job 6:19). Solomon may also have had in mind further trade (transhipping) in these products from the port of Ezion-geber (1 Kgs. 9:26-28).

Shebaniah (sheb′-a-ny′-ah), Personal name (1 Chron. 15:24; Neh. 9:4, 5; 10:12; 12:14).

Shebat (she′-bat), The eleventh month in the Hebrew calendar, corresponding to our January-February. *See* MONTH.

Shebnah, Shebna, The secretary of King Hezekiah of Judah (2 Kgs. 18:18; Isa. 36:3) and superintendent of the king's palace (Isa. 22:15).

Shebuel, Shubael (she-bue′-el; shoo′-bi-el), Son of Gershom and grandson of Moses (1 Chron. 23:16; 26:24, 32).

Shecaniah (shek′-a-ny′-ah), Proper name of persons (1 Chron. 3:21, 22; 2 Chron. 31:15; Ezra 8:5; 10:2; Neh. 3:29; 6:18; 12:3).

Shechem (shek′-em), 1. Son of Hamor. He took by force Dinah, Jacob's daughter and then fell in love with her and asked his father to ask Jacob for her hand in marriage for himself. Jacob agreed on condition that the men of Shechem undergo circumcision. While they were still convalescing from the operation, Simeon and Levi, Dinah's brothers, marched into the town with their swords and killed all the males and pillaged the town in revenge for the dishonoring of their sister (Gen. 34). The patriarchal traditions concerning Shechem are confused. Jacob (Gen. 48:22) claimed he captured it with his sword and bow. Perhaps in the Dinah story Shechem is a personification of the city of the same name. *See* DINAH.

2. A Canaanite city in the center of Palestine, at the entrance of the pass between Mts. Ebal and Gerizim, today Tell Balatah. Shechem is often mentioned in the traditions of the patriarchs, especially those of Jacob (Gen. 12:6; 33:18, 19; 34; 48:22). According to Joshua 24:32 Joseph is buried there. Shechem was a center of the first importance in the Israelite confederacy before the monarchy came to be. There is no mention of a conquest of the city by Joshua. It is intimately connected with the traditions pertaining to the Covenant (*see* Josh. 24; Josh. 8:30-35; Deut. 27). Shechem was the scene of the ephemeral monarchy of Abimelech, son of Gideon (Jgs. 9). In Joshua 17:2 it is consigned to Manasseh and numbered among the Levitical cities (Josh. 21:21; 1 Chron. 6:52) and the cities of refuge (Josh. 20:7). At Shechem the tribes of the north decided to detach themselves from Judah after Solomon's death. They refused to acknowledge Rehoboam as king and elected for themselves Jeroboam (1 Kgs. 12) who fortified the city and made it his capital (1 Kgs. 12:25).

Shedeur (shed′-e-ur), The father of Elizur, a leader of the tribe of Reuben (Num. 1:5; 2:10; 7:30; 10:18).

Sheep, The numerous references to sheep in the Bible is an indication of the important part these animals played in the economic life of the people, especially when they were nomads, and in the sacrificial ritual. (*See* e.g. Lev. 1:10; 4:32; 5:15 etc.) Riches were often valued at the number of sheep a person possessed, as these were very much prized for the number and quality of their products, such as wool, meat, milk and their derivatives. The sheep shearing was a big occasion that was celebrated in a festive atmosphere (Gen. 31:19; 38:12; 1 Sam. 25:4; 2 Sam. 13:25-27).

On account of its meekness and need for care and defense the sheep with its shepherd is a frequent figure of speech to denote the relationship between God and his people (Ps. 23; Jer. 13:20; Ezek. 34) and between the king and chieftains and their subjects. This imagery is also frequently found in the New Testament in reference to Jesus and his mission (Jn. 10; Jn. 21; Matt. 18:10-14; Lk. 15:3-6; Heb. 13:20; 1 Pet. 2:25). *See* SHEPHERD.

Sheep Gate, Pool, A gate in the northern part of the walls of Jerusalem that were repaired by Nehemiah (Neh. 3:1; 12:39). Beside this was the pool with five porticoes where Jesus cured the paralytic (Jn. 5:2). *See* BETHESDA.

Shekel, A weight unit at first, and later also a coin in common use in the whole Middle East, and varying in value from time to time and place to place. In Israel the weight was around 11.5 grams, and was one fiftieth of a mina and one three thousandth of a talent. The shekel coins minted during the Jewish revolt (67-70 A.D.) weighed about 14.5 grams.

Shelah (she′-lah), 1. Son of Arpachshad and father of Eber, descendants of Shem in the Table of Nations (Gen. 10:24) and in the genealogy of Abraham (Gen. 11:14). In the genealogy of Christ he is the son of Cainan (Lk. 3:35-36).

2. Third son of Judah and brother to Er and Onan. After the death of these two Judah did not wish to give Shelah as husband to Tamar, who had a right to have him in accordance with the levirate law (Gen. 38).

Shelemiah (shel′-e-mi′-ah), "The Lord has rewarded," proper name of persons (1 Chron. 26:14; Jer. 36:14, 26; 37:3, 13; Ezra 10:39, 41; Neh. 3:30; 13:13).

Sheleph (she′-lef), An Arabian people listed among the sons of Shem in the Table of Nations (Gen. 10:26).

Shelomith (shi-loe′-mith), Personal name (Lev. 24:10; 1 Chron. 3:19; 23:18; 2 Chron. 11:20; Ezra 8:10).

Shelomoth (shi-loe′-moth), Personal name (1 Chron. 23:9).

Shelumiel (shi-loo′-mi-el), A leader of the tribe of Simeon in the desert under Moses (Num. 1:6; 2:12; 7:36; 10:19; Judith 8:1).

Shem, Noah's eldest son (Gen. 4:32; 6:10 ff.) who was blessed by his father for the respect he showed in covering his father's nakedness when he was intoxicated (Gen. 9:18-24). His descendants are catalogued in the Table of Nations (Gen. 10:21 ff.) and they represent, more or less, the ethnic-linguistic category of the semite peoples. (*See* TABLE OF NATIONS.) His name occurs in the genealogy of Jesus in Luke 3:36.

Shema (she′-mah), A proper name of persons (Josh. 15:26;1 Chron. 2: 43, 44; 5:8; 8:13; Neh. 8:4).

Shemaiah (shi-may′-ah), 1. The prophet who transmitted to Rehoboam the Lord's prohibition for making war on the secessionist tribes of the North (1 Kgs. 12:22-24). Once more Shemaiah intervened to announce to Rehoboam that the invasion of Shishak the Pharaoh was a punishment for having abandoned Yahweh. When Rehoboam repented, Shemaiah announced that the trial would soon be over (2 Chron. 12:5-9). Shemaiah authored a chronicle on the reign of Rehoboam which was used by the Chronicler (2 Chron. 12:15).

2. Schemaiah of Nehelam who wrote from Babylonia asking that Jeremiah be punished for having written to those in exile recommending that they settle down, as the exile would last a long time. Jeremiah called him a false prophet and announced that he and his family would not live to see the salvation that the Lord was preparing for Israel (Jer. 29:24-32).

There are at least 20 other less significant men of this name in the O.T.

Shemariah (shem′-a-ry′-ah), 1. A son of King Rehoboam of Judah (2 Chron. 11:19).

2. A man of Benjamin who joined David at Ziklag (1 Chron. 12:5).

Shemeber (shem-ee′-ber), King of Zeboiim, one of the cities of the Pentapolis of Dead Sea cities attacked by the coalition of kings from the east (Gen. 14:2).

Shemer (she′-mer), The owner of the hill bought by Omri king of Israel (876-869 B.C.) on which to build his new capital. It was called Samaria after the name of the original owner of the site (1 Kgs. 16:24).

Shemiramoth (shi-mir′-a-moth), A Levite and musician who participated in the transfer of the ark of the covenant to Jerusalem (1 Chron. 15:18; 16:5).

Shenazzar, Son of Jehoiakim (Jeconiah) of Judah, brother of Shealtiel and Pedaiah, and uncle of Zerubbabel (1 Chron. 1:17-19). Some authors would identify him with Sheshbazzar of Ezra 1:1-11; 5:14-16, first governor of Judah and the initiator of the work of reconstructing the Temple after the exile. This identification however does not seem sufficiently well based. *See* SHESHBAZZAR.

Sheol (she′-ol), The doctrine of life after death and retribution after death is relatively recent in Old Testament tradition. It is only clearly outlined in

Daniel 12, Wisdom 1-5 and 2 Maccabees 12:43. (*See* RESURRECTION.)
Nevertheless Israel was always deeply convinced, like the other peoples of
similar cultural tradition, that man did survive death in a subterranean
habitation called Sheol. The picture evoked of this underworld dwelling is
not always consistent. It is subterranean (Deut. 32:22; Isa. 14:9; Pss.
63:10; 86:13; 88:7); a place of darkness and dust from which there is no
return (Job 7:9; 17:13-16). The dead there continue an existence that is
the opposite of true life, without joy or peace, strength or activity, and this
is true of the good and the bad (Ps. 89:49; Ezek. 32:17-32; Eccl. 9:10).
Isaiah 14:9-11 and Ezekiel 32:17-32 seem to suggest that in Sheol the
social differences between king and subject persisted, but one must not
overlook the satirical thrust of these two accounts: "Your magnificence
has been flung down to Sheol with the music of your harps; underneath
you a bed of maggots. . . ." In Sheol there is no praise nor even remembrance of God (Pss. 6:6; 88:13; 94:17; 115:17; Job 26:6; 28:22; Isa.
38:18) even though it is still under God's dominion (Ps. 139:8; Prov.
15:11; Job 26:6). This affirmation however merely exalts the omnipotence
of Yahweh without altering in the least the gray existence of Sheol's inhabitants.

When the doctrine of the resurrection and retribution after death became
clear the image of Sheol was transformed, even though often enough it
seems to retain its colorlessness. Now it is the place where the dead await
the judgment and resurrection. At times a distinction is made between
where the good are and where the dead already begin to anticipate the
future sentence.

The New Testament reflects this diversity that was elaborated on in Jewish tradition between the two Testaments. In Acts 2:27 there is a quotation of Psalm 16:10, which sees Sheol as a place of corruption and death.
Other texts distinguish Gehenna, which is the place of torments for the
damned (*see* GEHENNA) and Hades, whch approaches more the Sheol of
the Old Testament. Hades (in some versions) is a symbol of death (Rev.
1:18) where it is said that Jesus holds the keys of death and Hades—that
is, he holds sway over death. In the parable of Lazarus, Hades is a place of
torment like Gehenna (Lk. 16:23). In other places (such as Matt. 11:23;
Matt. 16:18; Lk. 10:15; Rev. 6:8) it expresses total and definitive destruction.

Shephatiah (shef′-a-tie′-ah), 1. Son of David and his wife Abital, born at
Hebron (2 Sam. 3:4; 1 Chron. 3:3).

2. Son of Mattan and an official of Zedekiah king of Judah (598-587 B.C.).
During the siege of Jerusalem, Shephatiah accused Jeremiah before the
king of persuading the people to surrender without a fight to Nebuchadnezzar, and asked for his death. Jeremiah was accordingly thrown
into the well in the Court of the Guard, which was without water, so
Jeremiah sank into the mud. The eunuch Ebed-melech, a Cushite, however went to the king and got permission to rescue him before Jeremiah died
(Jer. 38:1-13).

Shephelah (shi-feel′-ah), Shephelah or "lowland" is the name of the hilly
region that extends from the Mediterranean coastal plain to the central
mountains of Judea (Deut. 1:7; Josh. 10:40; 12:8; 15:33; Jgs. 1:9, etc.).
The Shephelah runs north and south, paralleling the coastal plain as far as
Aijalon. From east to west there are deep valleys that are the only gateway to the Judean range. These were the scene of many battles in the
history of Israel. The principal valleys, starting with the northern ones
and moving southwards are: The valley of Aijalon where, with the help of
a divinely sent hailstorm, Joshua defeated the king of Jerusalem and his

allies (Josh. 10:12). The valley of Sorek, birthplace of Delilah and scene of many of Samson's exploits against the Philistines (Jgs. 16:4). The Valley of Elah where the duel between David and Goliath was fought (1 Sam. 17:2). The whole region was continually contested between the Philistines, who occupied the coastal regions, and the Israelites who belonged to the central mountainous area.

Shepherd, In ancient eastern literature the image of the shepherd and his flock is frequently used for the relationship between king and people. In Israel this imagery was deeply rooted in its nomadic past. Not only is the shepherd the self-giving, dedicated figure, all care for his flock, he is also the strong hero fit to defend it from the attacks of the beasts of the field. David's best recommendation to Saul for his offer to fight Goliath was that as a shepherd he had killed both lion and bear in defense of his flock, and so he would slay this uncircumcised Philistine (1 Sam. 17:34-37). The imagery was particularly apt and consequently used to designate relationships between God and his people. Yahweh is Israel's shepherd (Gen. 49:24; Pss. 23:1; 80:2). His action in history in favor of his people is also described in pastoral terms: Yahweh led his people through the desert like a shepherd leading his flock (Pss. 78:52; 77:21). He will once more gather and unite his flock to lead it to the promised land after the exile (Isa. 40:11; 49:10; Isa. 56:8). God confided the care of his flock to shepherds (Pss. 100:3; 79:13; 74:1). David is the shepherd of the flock of the Lord (Ps. 78:70 ff.; 2 Sam. 5:2; 24:27). Psalm 23 is a song on the same theme at the level of the individual Israelite.

In some prophetic texts the announcement of the judgment and the consequent establishment of the kingdom is made in terms of the shepherd and his flock. God through Jeremiah rebukes the chiefs for having neglected to care for the flock (Jer. 2:8; 10:21; 23:1-3), and promises pastors to look after them and pasture them so that there will be no fear or terror for them any more (Jer. 23:1-6). Ezekiel 34 has the lengthiest elaboration of the theme. God denounces Israel's pastors who have lost and killed the sheep, and pledges that he himself will take over the care of the flock to unite it, cure its wounds and lead it to abundant pastures where he will give to it a shepherd according to his own heart, his servant David.

The parable of the Good Shepherd of John 10 is based, in the last analysis, on this passage of Ezekiel. The theme is also present in other parts of the evangelical tradition. The Good Shepherd parable in Luke 15:3-7 and Matthew 18:12-14 expresses the joy of God at the return of the sinner. Jesus sees the people like a flock without a shepherd (Matt. 9:36; Mk. 6:34) and takes pity on it. His mission is to seek out the lost sheep of the house of Israel (Matt. 10:6; 15:24).

Jesus confides the care of his flock to Peter in John 21:15-17. The same imagery is used to compass the responsibility of the ministers of the Church (Acts 20:28; 1 Pet. 5:2-4; Eph. 4:11) who must "Be examples to the flock, not lording it over those assigned to you, so that when the chief Shepherd appears you will win for yourselves the unfading crown of glory" (1 Pet. 5:3, 4; Heb. 13:20).

Sherebiah (sher′-e-by′-ah), A prominent Levite in Ezra's time (Ezra 8:18, 24; Neh. 8:7; 9:4; 12:8).

Sheshach (she′-shak), A cryptogram for Babel (Jer. 25:26 and 51:41). The name is obtained by an atbash writing, that is, by inverting the order of the alphabet, so that instead of A, the first letter, Taw, the last letter is written, instead of B, the second letter, Sin, the second last letter is written, and so on. Cryptograms such as these are clearly later additions to the text.

Sheshai (she'-shy), One of the legendary giants, sons of Anak; they lived in Hebron and were defeated by the Israelites (Num. 13:22; Josh. 15:14; Jgs. 1:10).

Sheshbazzar (shesh-baz'-ar), A prince of Judah (Ezra 1:8) chief of the first caravan of exiled Jews who returned to Judea after Cyrus' edict of liberation (Ezra 1:11). To him were entrusted the sacred vessels of the house of the Lord, which Nebuchadnezzar had taken away from Jerusalem (Ezra 1:7-10). He was governor of the province of Judah and began the reconstruction of the Temple (Ezra 5:14-16).

Notwithstanding the similarities between his career and that of Zerubbabel, there is not reason enough to hold that they are the same person. If Sheshbazzar is identical with Shenazzar, who is called brother to Shealtiel and uncle of Zerubbabel, then the latter would also be his successor who carried on his work. *See* ZERUBBABEL.

Shethar-bozenai (she'-thar-boz'-e-nye), An official of the Persian administration of the province "beyond the river," who intervened in the enquiry ordered by the governor Tattenai to ascertain the Jews' right to rebuild the Temple in Jerusalem. A search of the archives turned up, in the fortress of Ecbatana in the province of Media, the scroll on which Cyrus had issued the decree allowing the restoration (Ezra 5 and 6).

Shewbread, *See* SHOW BREAD.

Shibah (shy'-bah), The name of a well near Beersheba dug by Isaac's servants (Gen. 26:33).

Shibboleth (shib'-o-lith), This word means either an ear of corn or a flowing stream. The men of Jephtah chose this word by which to identify the fugitive Ephraimites. The victorious Gileadites stood guard over the fords of the Jordan, and when a person would come to cross he would be asked to pronounce "Shibboleth," which for the Ephraimites was impossible: they would say "Sibboleth," whereupon they were seized and slaughtered there by the fords. The Bible reports that forty-two thousand Ephraimites lost their lives in this way (Jgs. 12:4-6).

Shield, The Hebrews used two types of shield, a small circular one and a large rectangular one. With the larger one a defensive front could be presented. The shield was a leather-covered frame. The leather had to be oiled to keep it from cracking. Thus when Saul died, David cried that his shield was anointed, not with oil, but with his own blood (2 Sam. 1:21; *see* Isa. 21:5). Metal bucklers and shields were probably for ceremony only: Solomon had three hundred large and three hundred small shields made of beaten gold, and placed in the Hall of the Forest of Lebanon (1 Kgs. 10:16-17). In speaking to Abraham God said: "Fear not, Abram, I am your shield" (Gen. 15:1; *see* Pss. 3:3; 18:2, 30; 33:20; 115:9). Paul exhorts Christians to put on the shield of faith as a protection against the darts of the evil one (Eph. 6:16; *see* 1 Thess. 5:8).

Shihor (shy'-hor), The Egyptian name of a stream or river. In 1 Chronicles 13:5 it indicates the southern limit of David's kingdom, and therefore probably the Wadi el-Arish, the River of Egypt (in such texts as Num. 34:5; 1 Kgs. 8:65; Ezek. 47:19). In Isaiah 23:3 and Jeremiah 2:18 it probably refers to a branch of the Nile near Raamses.

Shilhi (shil'-hie), Grandfather of King Jehoshaphat of Judah (1 Kgs. 22·42; 2 Chron. 20:31).

Shillem, A son of Naphtali (Gen. 46:24; Num. 26:49).

Shiloah (shy'-lo-ah), The open-air aqueduct bringing the water from the Gihon spring to a pool within the walls of the city, called the Lower Pool (*see* Isa. 8:6; 22:8). This aqueduct did not supply the city with enough water in times of crisis such as siege. For this reason Hezekiah king of Judah (715-687 B.C.) had a tunnel 1749 feet long dug from Gihon to carry water to a reservoir on the western side of the hill of Sion, a little above the other one (2 Kgs. 20:20). With this reservoir is identified the pool of Siloam in which the man born blind washed himself hoping for a cure, and whom Jesus healed (Jn. 9:7). Near this pool also occurred the episode referred to by Jesus in Luke 13:4: a tower in construction collapsed killing eighteen people.

Shiloh (shy'-loh), A city in the mountains of Ephraim, "north of Bethel, east of the highway that goes up from Bethel to Shechem, and south of Lebonah" (Jgs. 21:19), today Seilun. It was an important center in premonarchical times, for there was the tabernacle with the ark around which the celebrations and assemblies of the people took place (Josh. 18:1-10; 21:2; 22:9). When the Benjaminites were threatened with extinction for lack of womenfolk, they were advised to lie in ambush in the vineyards on the feast of Yahweh "which is held every year in Shiloh." When the girls came in groups to dance, they were each to seize for himself a wife (Jgs. 21:15-23). Eli and his sons functioned as priests in the sanctuary at Shiloh, and there too Samuel as a youth served (1 Sam. 1). From Shiloh the ark of the covenant was brought to Aphek where the Israelites were engaged in battle with the Philistines. The Israelites were defeated and the ark fell into the hands of the Philistines (1 Sam. 4). Shiloh was destroyed, probably during the wars with the Philistines. Jeremiah recalls this to announce the same fate for the Temple in Jerusalem (Jer. 7:12, 14; 26:6, 9; *see* Ps. 78:60). Shiloh was the birthplace of Ahijah, the prophet who announced to Jeroboam I's wife the death of their sick son (1 Kgs. 14:2, 4).

Shimeah (shim'-e-ah), David's brother and father of Jonadab, who advised Ammon how he could seduce his half-sister Tamar (2 Sam. 13:3). He was also the father of Jonathan, who killed a giant, "one of the Rephaim," who had insulted Israel (2 Sam. 21:21). He is probably to be identified with Shammah (1 Sam. 16:9). *See* SHAMMAH.

Shimei (shim'-e-eye), Son of Gera, of the same clan as Saul's family. When David was forced to flee Jerusalem on account of Absalom's revolt, and was reaching Bahurim, Shimei came out and threw stones and curses at David and all his officers. The brunt of his malediction was that Saul's blood was now being revenged on David who had usurped his throne. Abishai wanted to cut the man down, but David restrained him (2 Sam. 16:5-14). When David was returning victorious to Jerusalem Shimei again came to meet him at the Jordan and ask his pardon, whereupon Abishai again wanted to kill him, but David would not permit the joy of the day of his re-entry to Jerusalem to be stained with blood. Moreover he swore not to kill him (2 Sam. 19:16-24). When he lay dying however, he told Solomon to wreak the vengeance that he was prevented from doing on account of his oath (1 Kgs. 2:8, 9). Solomon ordered Shimei not to depart from Jerusalem. After three years Shimei disobeyed the order to pursue some slaves who had fled to Gath. Solomon thereupon ordered Benaiah to execute him (1 Kgs. 2:36-46).

At least 17 other men of the same name, but of little significance, can be identified in the O.T.

Shimri (shim'-rye), A proper name (1 Chron. 4:37; 11:45; 26:10; 2 Chron. 29:13).

Shimron, A Canaanite city whose king took part in the coalition led by Jabin king of Hazor against Joshua (Josh. 11:1). It was later assigned to the territory of Zebulun (Josh. 19:15).

Shimshai (shim'-shy), A Persian official who opposed the rebuilding of Jerusalem after the exile (Ezra 4:8, 9, 17, 23).

Shin, The 21st letter of the Hebrew alphabet (sh).

Shinab, King of Admah, one of the cities of the Dead Sea Pentapolis, who was conquered by Chedorlaomer king of Elam and his allies (Gen. 14:2).

Shinar (shy'-nar), The plain of Babylonia between the courses of the lower Tigris and Euphrates where the cities of Babel, Erech and Accad were situated (Gen. 10:10). Shinar is where the incident of the Tower of Babel took place (Gen. 11:2). Its king Amraphel took part in the punitive campaign against the cities of the Dead Sea region (Gen 14:2). *See* also Isa. 11:11 and Dan. 1:2. *See* BABEL, TOWER OF; AMRAPHEL.

Ship, A large, sea-going vessel. The Hebrews were not at all sea-minded, for the simple reason that the Phoenicians and Philistines controlled the coast of the Mediterranean, while the Gulf of Aqaba was far from the centers of population, and its port-city, Ezion-geber, was held consistently by the Hebrews only during the reigns of David and Solomon. The ships of the Bible, therefore, were built and sailed by non-Israelites. For "ships of Tarshish," *see* TARSHISH.

Paul used ships more than any other Bible character, and his companion on the journey to Rome wrote the best account of a sea voyage that has come down to us from ancient times. On Paul's earlier missionary journeys the ships he used would have been wretched (by today's standards) little coastal commercial vessels, whose captains would accept a few passengers, but whose business was carrying goods from one port-town or city to another along the coast—staying within the harbor if a storm threatened, and within sight of land as far as possible. Navigation, if done at night, was by the stars only—another reason for staying in port when sky-darkening storms threatened. The compass had not yet been invented. On his journey to Rome, from Myra westward, Paul was aboard a heavier and much more substantial ship, one of the many that plied between wheat-producing Egypt and Rome's principal wheat port, Puteoli, the lifeline of the Roman populace. His first ship was wrecked at Malta; a similar vessel took him on the final lap three months later. The dangers of travel on the Mediterranean are vividly described in Acts 27 and the strategies for avoiding the worst conditions for sailing are made clear.

Shiphrah, One of the two midwives of the Hebrews who were commanded by the Pharaoh to kill off all the new-born boys of the Hebrews while letting the girls live. For fear of God they did not obey the Pharaoh's command, and when the latter sent for them, they pleaded that the Hebrew women, unlike the Egyptians, were hardy and gave birth before the midwife came . The Bible account says that God was kind to the midwives for this (Ex. 1:15-20). *See* PUAH.

Shishak, Pharaoh in Egypt (935-914 B.C.) founder of the twenty-second dynasty. He gave asylum to Jeroboam when he fled after his revolt against Solomon failed (1 Kgs. 11:26-40). When Solomon died Shishak invaded Palestine captured many cities and reached Jerusalem, where he took the treasures of the Temple, as well as all the gold shields Solomon had made (1 Kgs. 14:25-28). This information is confirmed by what we learn from a stele found at Megiddo and erected by Shishak to commemorate his campaign, and from inscriptions on the walls of the temple of Karnak which enumerate 156 cities that were conquered. The account of the event in 2 Chronicles 12:2-9 tells that Shemaiah intervened to communicate to Solomon's son, King Rehoboam, that the invasion was a punishment for his sins. When he repented, Yahweh announced through Shemaiah: "In a little while I will grant them deliverance; my wrath shall not fall on Jerusalem through the power of Shishak."

Shitrai (shit′-rye), A servant of David in charge of the king's herds in the plain of Sharon (1 Chron. 27:29).

Shittim, 1. A region in Transjordan on the plains of Moab where the Israelites encamped before crossing the Jordan (*see* Num. 33:49). From there Joshua sent two scouts to Jericho (Josh. 2:1), and from there also the Israelites struck camp to set out for the passage across the Jordan (Josh. 3:1). Shittim was the scene of the last episodes recorded in Numbers (Num. 25:1). *See* Micah 6:5.

2. Joel, describing the restoration of Israel in 4:18, reads as follows: "A fountain shall issue from the house of the Lord to water the Valley of Shittim." It is a probable reference to the lower part of the Kidron Valley, southeast of Jerusalem.

Shoa, A region east of Babylonia (Ezek. 23:23) .

Shobab (show′-bab), Son of David and Bathsheba, the former wife of Uriah, born in Jerusalem (2 Sam. 5:14; 1 Chron. 3:5).

Shobach (show′-bak), Chief of the army of Hadadezer, king of the Aramaeans. Shobach came with an army to the aid of the Ammonites at Helam, but David routed them, killing seven hundred of their chariot teams and forty thousand of their men. Shobach was also killed in that battle (2 Sam. 10:15-19; 1 Chron. 19:16-18).

Shobi (show′-by), Son of the Ammonite king Nahash from Rabbah. When David was in Mahanaim in flight from Absalom, Shobi, Barzillai and Machir generously offered him whatever he needed for himself or his men (2 Sam. 17:27-29).

Show bread, A translation of **lehem happanim,** literally, "breads of the face," but better translated "bread of the presence," Leviticus 24:5-9 prescribed that wheaten flour should be baked in twelve cobs to be arranged in two rows of six on the pure table that stood in front of the Holy of Holies. Each Sabbath they were changed. These sacred breads, when replaced with a new baking, were eaten by the priests, but by way of exception Ahimelech, a priest of Nob, gave them to David and his men who were famished. First however he ascertained that the men were in a state of legal purity, and that they had not had sexual relationships (1 Sam. 21:5-7). Exodus 25:23-30 tells us that the breads were placed on a wooden table that was plated with pure gold. According to Leviticus 24:8 the breads served as a memorial of the covenant of the twelve tribes with Yahweh.

Shua (shoo′-ah), The father of the Canaanite wife of Judah (Gen. 38:2, 12; 1 Chron. 2:3).

Shuah (shoo′-ah), Son of Abraham and Keturah (Gen. 25:2; 1 Chron. 1:32); also an Arab tribe from which came Bildad, one of Job's disputants (Job 2:11; 8:1; 18:1; 25:1; 42:9).

Shuham, A son of Dan (Num. 26:42).

Shulamite. The bride of the Song of Songs is called a Shulamite in 7:1: "Return, return, O maid of Shulam, return, return that we may gaze on you." The name gets different interpretations; it either denotes the place of origin, as in the case of Abishag, the girl who warmed David's aging bones (1 Kgs. 1:3) or it is a symbolic name made from the substantive **Shalom,** "peace," as "she who has peace," or again, it might be the feminine form of **selomo,** Solomon, who is often mentioned in the Song, and to whom the Song is attributed.

Shunem, A city in the land of Issachar (Josh. 19:18), today Solem on the Esdraelon plain. There the Philistines camped before the battle of the Mountains of Gilboa (1 Sam. 28:4). Shunem was the native place of Abishag, the girl who lived with David during his last months (1 Kgs. 1:3). It was also the name of the woman who gave hospitality to the prophet Elisha, and whose son the prophet raised to life (2 Kgs. 4).

Shuni (shoo′-nie), A son of Gad (Gen. 46:16; Num. 26:15).

Shur, A desert region southwest of Palestine, between Egypt to the west and the Sinai desert to the south. The appearance of the angel to the fleeing Hagar took place at the spring on the road to Shur (Gen. 16:7). Abraham camped between Kadesh and Shur (Gen. 20:1). Various nomadic groups camped in the region, among them the Ishmaelites and Amalekites (Gen. 25:18; 1 Sam. 15:7; 27:8). The Israelites passed through it after escaping from Egypt (Ex. 15:22).

Shuthelah (shoo′-the-lah), A son of Ephraim (Num. 26:35, 36).

Shuthites, Together with the Moabites and Edomites, the sons of Sheth or Shuthites will suffer defeat at the hands of the Israelites, according to a prophecy of Balaam (Num. 24:17). Perhaps the name designates a nomadic people south of Palestine that is known from documents of the period.

Sibbecai (sib′-e-kie), Sibbecai from Husha was one of the Thirty warriors of David (2 Sam. 23:27). He slew one of the giant Rephaim called Saph in a battle against the Philistines at Gob (2 Sam. 21:18; 1 Chron. 20:4).

Sibmah, A city of Transjordan in the land of Reuben (Num. 32:3, 38; Josh. 13:19) but in Moabite hands at the time of Isaiah and Jeremiah (Isa. 16:8, 9; Jer. 48:32).

Sicyon (sish′-i-on), A city of Greece on the shore of the Gulf of Corinth (1 Mac. 15:23).

Siddim, The valley of Siddim is the scene of the battle between the four Mesopotamian kings and the five kings of the Pentapolis that lay south of the Dead Sea (Gen. 14:3, 8). "The valley of Siddim was full of bitumen pits" (Gen. 14:10). In 14:3 the valley of Siddim is the Salt Sea, that is, the Dead Sea. This identification does not apply to the whole present Dead Sea, but at most to its southern part, south of the peninsula of Lisan. This part of the sea is much shallower, due to a recent geological formation.

Sidon, A city and seaport on the Mediterranean coast half way between Tyre and Beirut. Today it is Saida, in the Republic of Lebanon. The city is accounted for in Egyptian documents as early as the first half of the second millenium B.C. It was one of the principal commercial centers of Phoenicia. It often figures with Tyre in the oracles of the prophets against the nations (Isa. 23; Jer. 25:22; 27:3-6; Ezek. 28:20-23). Sidon, like Tyre, suffered from the Assyrian expansion in Syria and Palestine. It was taken by Sennacherib (705-681 B.C.) and later again by Esarhaddon, who destroyed it. Under the Persians it revived, its people constructing ships for the exploits of the Persians against the Greeks. Sidon surrendered without a struggle to Alexander the Great and succeeded in maintaining its prosperity and commercial independence until the Roman domination (63 B.C.) which signaled its decline, though Herod the Great adorned it.

Sidon is mentioned in the Old Testament as the northern limit of Canaanite territory, of the northern Israelite tribes and of David's kingdom (Gen. 10:9; 49:13; Josh. 19:28; 2 Sam. 24:6). Jezebel (*see* JEZEBEL) was the daughter of Ethbaal, king of the Sidonians, who were enthusiasts of the cult of Baal and Ashtoreth. Solomon found Sidonians to be superior woodcutters (1 Kgs. 5:6; *see* Ezra 3:7). Jesus made a journey to the region of Tyre and Sidon (Matt. 15:21; Mk. 7:24, 31) and many people of this region came to hear his words (Matt. 3:8; Lk. 6:17). Of Tyre and Sidon Jesus said that had the miracles been worked there that had been performed in Bethsaida and Chorazin, "they would have reformed in sackcloth and ashes long ago" (Matt. 11:21, 2; Lk. 10:13, 14). It was in that region that the famous conversation took place between Jesus and the Canaanite woman, who asked for her daughter's cure, "since even the dogs can eat the leavings that fall from their masters' table" (Matt. 15:21-28). While being taken prisoner to Rome, Paul stopped there (Acts 27:3).

Siege, Siege warfare was brought to a fine art by the Assyrians. It was however in general use throughout the Near East. A walled city under siege was surrounded by the Israelites with a further mound, siegeworks or wall (2 Sam. 20:15; 2 Kgs. 19:32; Isa. 37:33), from which the besiegers could better attack the defenders. The Assyrians would force the gates or walls with a battering ram, while attempting to weaken or undermine it by tunneling. Other weapons against the besieged city were catapults for bombarding the city with large boulders or even with fire. Hunger and thirst were of course the implacable enemies of the besieged, to which eventually they would have to cede.

Sign, Sign translates the Hebrew 'oth. In the use of the term in the Bible one must underline its poetic value as a means to know the existence and character of an unseen reality, and its function as a memorial of a past event as well as a pledge or guarantee for the future.

In the case of pacts, contracts, promises and so on, the sign is the pledge or guarantee that is seen and can be verified that certain terms were agreed to; and at the same time the pledge remains on as a reminder to the contracting parties of the pact that has been entered into. The rainbow was the sign of the covenant of God with Noah: "As the bow appears in the clouds, I (God) will see it and recall the everlasting covenant that I have established between God and all the living things" (Gen. 9:16). Circumcision is the sign, memorial and pledge of the covenant of God with Abraham (Gen. 17:11; *see* CIRCUMCISION). The sabbath is the sign of the covenant with the Israelites (Ex. 31:13, 17). Rahab asks and obtains a sign which is the pledge and guarantee of her safety when the Israelites capture the city of Jericho (Josh. 2:12).

The prodigies performed to guarantee the divine origin of a message to be given or a mission to be accomplished are also called signs. Such are the prodigies that Moses must perform to prove to the Israelites that it is God who sends him to save them (Ex. 4:1-9). Samuel gives to Saul signs which should convince him that "The Lord has anointed you (Saul) as commander over his heritage" (1 Sam. 10:2-13). When Isaiah had announced to Ahaz the imminent end of the two kings who had invaded Judah, he invited the king to ask for a sign to confirm the truth of the oracle (Isa. 7:11). Some of the scribes and pharisees also asked Jesus for a sign from heaven, "to put him to the proof," but Jesus refused to give them the type

of sign that they were asking, and answered that they should have no other sign but the sign of Jonah (Matt. 12:38-40; 16:1-4; Mk. 8:11, 12; Lk.
11:29, 30; *see* JONAH).

In the Exodus tradition and the texts that refer to it, the signs ('oth)
and prodigies (**mosphet**) were the ten plagues which struck Egypt (*see* Ex.
10:1, 2; Josh. 24:17, etc.). They are called signs for they are events which
reveal the active presence of God in the exercise of his work of saving
judgment. It should be noted that this notion of sign is not to be confused
with the theological notion of miracle. According to the usual definition, a
miracle is a fact that outstrips all the forces of nature and is therefore to be
attributed alone to a direct intervention by God. The Bible does not have
this scientific notion of God and of the laws of nature. Its view of nature
sees it totally penetrated by God's action and certainly did not catalogue
all his interventions, as we might, into acts of ordinary concourse or providence, and acts miraculously performed. This is why it is necessary to
proceed with caution when giving a judgment on the miraculous nature of
an event.

A very similar use of the term "signs and miracles" can be found in
Detueronomy 28:46 in the conclusion of the curses that will befall the
transgressors of the covenant. They are nothing more than calamities and
disasters of the natural order: "They will light on you and your descendants as a sign and a wonder for all time." In both cases they are seen as
natural facts but viewed as disposed that way by God and the result of his
judgment. The person who believes cannot but see present in them the
hand of God who had warned the transgressor and threatened him: "This
is the finger of God" (Ex. 8:15).

"Signs and prodigies" (**semeia kai terata**) are what the New Testament
often calls miracles worked by Jesus and by the apostles. They confirm the
truth of his words and the authenticity of his mission (Matt. 16:7, 9; Acts
2:22; 2:43; 4:30; 5:12; 6:8; Rom. 15:19; 1 Cor. 12:28; Gal. 3:5, etc.). The
miracles of Jesus are moreover signs of the coming of the Kingdom of
God. The exorcism and curses worked by Jesus reveal that God is bringing about in Jesus definitive salvation. (*See* MIRACLES OF JESUS.) This aspect
of the miracles has been particularly developed by John in his gospel. In
20:31 John says that he has gathered into his writing some of the many
signs that Jesus had worked in front of his disciples so that we might believe that Jesus is the Son of God. These words recall what he had written
in 12:37 at the conclusion of the public ministry of Jesus: "Despite his
many signs performed in their presence, they refused to believe in him."

John is clearly referring to the miracles described in the first part of his
gospel (cc. 1-12), which for that reason has been called the "Booklet of
Signs," *see* John 2:11; 4:54. These are signs for they reveal the divine glory of Jesus: "Jesus performed this first of his signs at Cana in Galilee.
Thus did he reveal his glory, and his disciples believed in him" (Jn. 2:11).
This text recalls Numbers 14:22 where it states that the Israelites who
went out of Egypt were those "who have seen my (God's) glory and the
signs I worked in Egypt." Jesus' signs reveal his glory, that is, his divine
vivifying power, and not just in a generic fashion. In fact, for some time
now scholars have noticed the tight link between the signs and the discourses that follow them in John's gospel. From this point of view, the
signs of Jesus approach the symbolic actions of the prophets. (*See* PROPH-
ETS.) They were not just simple plastic representations of the content of
the discourses, but efficacious prefigurements of what God intended to
achieve. Analogously the signs ratify the declarations of Jesus in which he
claims to be the light of the world, the bread of life, resurrection and life.
These signs reveal the divine power already in action, albeit in inchoate

fashion. They show forth the vivifying, enlightening and saving power of Jesus which will be revealed without limits after his exaltation.

Sihon (sy′-hon), King of the Amorites from Heshbon in Transjordan. On their way to Canaan the Israelites asked permission to pass through his territories, promising not to use up the fruits of the land or do any other damage. Sihon's answer was to attack Israel, but he suffered a great defeat (Num. 21:21-32). The Old Testament makes frequent mention of this victory together with that over Og king of Bashan (Deut. 1:4; Josh. 2:10; Pss. 135:11; 136:19). The Israelites took possession of the territory and cities of Sihon which were then consigned to the tribes of Reuben, Gad and half the tribe of Manasseh (Num. 32:33; Josh. 13:21, 27).

Silas, Also called Silvanus. He was a member of the Church at Jerusalem and sent by the apostolic Council of Jerusalem with Paul and Barnabas to communicate to the Christians of Antioch its decisions (Acts 15:22-29). Later he accompanied Paul on his second apostolic journey (Acts 15:40) and suffered imprisonment with him in Philippi (16:16-40). He was constrained by difficulties with the Jews to flee from Thessalonica to Beroea where he remained on with Timothy while Paul continued on to Athens. Later he and Timothy rejoined Paul at Corinth (Acts 17:10-15; 18:5; 2 Cor. 1:19). His and Timothy's names are read in the inscriptions of 1 and 2 Thessalonians which were written from Corinth. Later he was in Peter's company (1 Pet. 5:2): "I write these few words to you through Silvanus, who is a brother I know and I can trust."

Siloam (sy-loe′-am), *See* SHILOAH.

Silvanus, *See* SILAS.

Silver, A precious metal well known and often referred to in the Bible. It was more plentiful and therefore less valuable than gold and was in common use as currency (e.g. Gen. 20:16; Matt. 25:18, 27; 28:12; Mk. 14:11; Lk. 22:5). Silver, like gold, denoted riches (Gen. 24:35). It was a malleable material, and so the Israelites were forbidden to shape it into gods (Ex. 20:3). Utensils were made from the precious metal. Numbers 7 lists the offerings for the altar, among which there were silver dishes and bowls in abundance. God told Moses to make two trumpets of beaten silver (Numbers 10:2). Silver and its processing is a frequent symbol on the lips of the psalmist. In Psalm 66:10 the psalmist sings that God has tested him like silver. Psalm 68:13 hymns silver's brightness. Proverbs states that the tongue of a just man is purest silver (10:20).

In the New Testament, Revelation complains of those who refuse to abandon their idols of silver (9:20). Peter tells the cripple: "I have neither silver nor gold, but what I have I give you" (Acts 3:6), namely healing and salvation in Christ. Demetrius, the silversmith of Ephesus, incited a riot against Paul, whose preaching was hurting his sale of silver miniature models of the great shrine of Diana.

Simeon (sim′-e-on), Second son of Jacob and Leah (Gen. 29:33; 35:23) and founding father of the tribe of Simeon. With Levi he vindicated the insult offered to their sister Dinah by killing the men of Shechem. For this he was reproved by his father (Gen. 34). This event is again thrown up to them in the blessing of Jacob (Gen. 49:5-9) which turns out to be a curse related to their division and dispersal in the Israelite confederacy. This account is interpreted by the authors as a fact in the history of the tribe which amounted to an unsuccessful attempt on their part to establish themselves in central Palestine near Shechem. (*See* DINAH, GENEALOGY.) Later Simeon appears with Judah in the synthesis of the conquest of Palestine in Judges 1 (vv. 3,17) and his territory is placed near that of

Judah (Josh. 19:1-9). It does not seem, however, that they retained for long their consistency and independence as a tribe. Simeon is not included in the blessing of Moses (Deut. 33) and his territory is presented as part of Judah in Josh. 15:21-32.

Simon, 1. Simon II, high priest (220-195 B.C.), son of Onias II and father of Onias III. Ben Sira praises him in Sirach 50:1-21.

2. Simon, who was called Thassi, the second son of Mattathias and brother of Jonathan and Judas Maccabeus (1 Mac. 2:4). While his brothers were still living, Simon engaged in several military actions against the Seleucids (1 Mac. 9:62-68; 10:82; 11:59; 11:65; 12:33-38) and against the Nabataeans (1 Mac. 9:33-42). When Jonathan was treacherously killed by Trypho, Simon took command. The story of his rule (143-134 B.C.) is recounted in cc. 13-16. Simon sided with Demetrius II Nicator, Trypho's rival, and from him he got important concessions, including tax relief and a recognition of Simon's initiative in fortifying Judea. In practice Simon became independent sovereign of Judea. The concession of these privileges was celebrated as the end of the yoke of the Gentiles, and all documents were dated from that event, which was called "the first year of Simon, high priest, governor and leader of the Jews" (1 Mac. 13:31-42). Another step in the direction of a fuller freedom was the expulsion of the Seleucid garrison from the citadel of Jerusalem (13:39-53). Simon reconfirmed the alliance struck by Jonathan with Rome and Sparta (14:16-24). An inscription in honor of Simon and his brothers on bronze tablets that were set up on pillars on Mount Zion, while copies were put in the treasury and made available to Simon and his family, appears in 1 Maccabees 14:25-49.

Demetrius died in the war against the Parthians and his son Antiochus VII Sidetes succeeded him to the throne. He continued to pass over Trypho, but later he turned against Simon whose position was becoming ever more dangerous to the Seleucid interests. He fitted out an army which invaded Palestine under its general Cendebaeus, but this was defeated by the army of the Jews under the leadership of Simon's sons Judas and John Hyrcanus at Modein (1 Mac. 15:38-16:10).

Simon died treacherously at the hands of his son-in-law Ptolemy, governor of the plain of Jericho. The latter was moved by ambition to kill off Simon and his sons, and so invited them to a banquet in their honor at the fortress of Dok, near Jericho. Simon, Mattathias and Judas fell into the trap but John Hyrcanus arrived in time to kill those who would have been his assassins. He then succeeded Simon as high priest and ruler of the Jews (134-104 B.C.).

3. Simon, of the priestly line of Bilgah, superintendent of the Temple at the time of the High Priest Onias III (195-175 B.C.). Out of enmity of Onias, Simon told Apollonius, governor of Coelesyria, about the Temple treasures, and he in turn informed the king, who sent Heliodorus to take them by force. Heliodorus was struck down in terror by the vision of a mysterious horseman; the experience converted him. Then Simon began to insinuate that it was the high priest Onias who had contrived these startling events (2 Mac. 3:4-4:3).

4. Simon son of Jonah, the "first" of the Twelve (Matt. 10:2) called Peter by Jesus (Matt. 16:16; Jn. 1:42). *See* PETER.

5. Simon the Canaanite (Matt. 10:4; Mk. 3:18) or the Zealot (Lk. 6:15; Acts 1:13; *see* ZEALOT), one of the twelve Apostles.

6. One of the brothers of the Lord (Matt. 13:55; Mk. 6:3). *See* BRETHREN OF THE LORD.

7. Simon the Leper. While Jesus was at supper in his house, a woman anointed his head with precious ointments (Matt. 26:6-13; Mk. 14:3-9).

8. The father of Judas Iscarot, one of the Twelve (Jn. 6:71; 12:4; 13:2, 26).

9. Simon of Cyrene, father of Alexander and Rufus, the man who was forced to carry the cross of Jesus to Calvary (Matt. 2:32; Mk. 15:21; Lk. 23:26).

10. Simon the Pharisee who invited Jesus to his home. During the dinner a woman who was a sinner washed Jesus' feet with her tears and anointed them with ointment. Simon began to think within himself that if Jesus were a true prophet he would know that this was a sinner. Jesus however defended his action and hers, and forgave her sins, while he pointed out to Simon how she in her love was giving him the courtesies that Simon had failed to provide to his guest (Luke 7:36-50).

11. Simon the tanner, a Christian at Jaffa in whose house Peter stayed. There Peter had the celebrated vision before meeting the centurion Cornelius, which led to the conversion of the first Gentile to the Church (Acts 9:43; 10:6; 10:17, 32).

12. Simon Magos, the magician who in Samaria exercised his art to the confusion of the people who believed him to be the divine power that is called Great. He received baptism from Philip. Then came the Apostles Peter and John to impose hands and confer the Holy Spirit on the newly baptized. When Simon saw the extraordinary power of the apostles, he offered them money in exchange for the power of conferring the Holy Spirit. Peter rebuked him severely, whereupon Simon asked them to pray for him so that none of the evil threatened by the apostles would befall him. This incident has given the sin of simony its name (*see* Acts 8:9-24).

Sin, 1. A desert region on the Sinai peninsula between Elim and Sina (Ex. 16:1; 17:1; Num. 33:11-12) along the way taken by the Israelites on their flight from Egypt.

2. A city of Egypt. The context of Ezekiel 30:15, 16 suggests as its probable identification Pelusium. See SYENE.

Sinai (sy′-nye, sy′-ni-eye), According to the Yahwist and Priestly documents in the Pentateuch, Sinai was the place where the theophany took place in which God gave Israel the law through Moses, and where the Covenant was made (Ex. 19–Num. 10:11). In the Elohist source and in Deuteronomy it is called Horeb. There is no doubt but that both J/P and E/D are describing the same event, even though they use different names for the place. There are several instances in the Bible of different names for the same place. It might be that there is reference to a different zone or peaks of the same mountain range. Where exactly Sinai-Horeb was, however, is a much discussed question. Tradition situates it in Jebel Musa, in the southern corner of the modern Sinai peninsula. The name Jebel Musa, "mountain of Moses," points in this direction. At the foot of the mountain is the famous monastery of Saint Catherine where the Codex Sinaiticus was found. (*See* TEXT, NEW TESTAMENT.) This identification however does not go back beyond the Christian era. The biblical indications of its whereabouts are scarce and do not give enough information to decide the question. Deuteronomy 1:2 reads: "it is a journey of eleven days from Horeb to Kadesh-barnea by way of the highlands of Seir." This would fit the traditional identification, but would not exclude other localities, also within the same range of march. Nothing can be concluded from the words of 1 Kings 19:8 that Elijah walked for forty days and forty nights until he came to Horeb the mountain of God. The principal objection to placing the mountain in the traditional way comes from some poetic texts of the Bible which describe the coming of God to Canaan from Seir and Edom (Jgs. 5:4), or from Seir, from the desert of Paran (Hab. 3:3). All these texts suggest a place east of the Gulf of Aqaba (*see* Gal. 4:24). Of less value is the reason often given that the theophany of Exodus 19 evokes the idea of a volcanic eruption. In the traditional Sinai there are no volcanoes, whereas there are volcanoes east of Aqaba. It must be remembered that c. 19 depends directly on the cult and should not therefore be taken as a reconstruction of the event as it took place. *See* THEOPHANY.

Sinaiticus Codex (sin′-a-it′-a-kus), A biblical manuscript of the fourth century found in 1859 in the monastery of St. Catherine at the foot of Mt. Sinai. It contains the Greek text of the Septuagint, and all of the New Testament as well as numerous ancient writings. It is one of the chief witnesses to recension B. (*See* TEXT, NEW TESTAMENT; SEPTUAGINT.) It was first kept in Leningrad, and then in 1933 purchased for 100,000 pounds sterling by the British Museum, where it is now kept.

Siphmoth, A city of Judah, one of the beneficiaries of the booty that David captured from the Amalekites (1 Sam. 30:28).

Sirach (sy′-rak), *See* ECCLESIASTICUS.

Sirion (sir′-i-on), The Sidonian name for Mount Hermon (Deut. 3:9; 4:48; Ps. 29:6). *See* HERMON.

Sisera (sis′-e-ra), The commander of the army of the Canaanite king, Jabin, who reigned at Hazor. Sisera came from Harosheth-hagoiim. His army of nine hundred iron-plated chariots and other troups was routed by Barak near Mt. Tabor. Sisera succeeded in fleeing to the tent of Jael, wife of Heber the Kenite. At her invitation he went into the tent and fell asleep, whereupon Jael took a mallet and drove a peg into his temple right through to the ground. Then she invited the pursuing Barak to come and see the corpse of the man he was chasing (Jgs. 4:1-22; 5:19-31).

Sitnah, One of the wells sunk by Isaac's servants near Gerar (Gen. 26:21). The name means "quarrel," "because they quarrelled over it" with the shepherds of Gerar.

Sivan (sy′-van), Third month in the Hebrew calendar, corresponding to our May-June. *See* MONTH.

Slavery, Slavery was an essential component of the social life and economy of the whole of antiquity, and to this Israel was no exception. Jewish legislation is ample evidence to this fact. Slavery was the inevitable lot of prisoners of war (Num. 31:26-47; Deut. 21:10-14; 20:10-18; 2 Sam. 8:2; 12:31). Such prisoners made up the chief merchandise for the slave-traffic (Amos 1:6, 9; Ezek. 27:13; 1 Mac. 3:41; 2 Mac. 8:10-11) and also supplied the state with its slaves, who were put to forced labor in the building of temples and other public edifices, or in industrial or mineral endeavors of king or state (2 Sam. 12:31; 1 Kgs. 9:15-21).

Jewish legislation in regard to slaves is complex and underwent development with the passage of time. The most ancient dispositions are found in the "Book of the Covenant" (Ex. 21:23). It is typical to distinguish between foreign and Israelite slaves. Israelites are favorably treated in that they are enslaved only temporarily. Their slavery could not last longer than six years unless they freely wished to continue in that state (Ex. 21:2-11; *see* Deut. 15:12-18; 21:10-14). It is clear that this disposition was not always observed. In fact the one recorded case (Jer. 34:15, 16) also tells that the Jews went back on their decision. For this fault Yahweh threatens to hand over Zedekiah (598-587 B.C.) to his enemies (*see* Jer. 34:8-22).

The book of Leviticus further mitigates the law on Israelite slaves. There it is laid down that it is licit to have slaves bought from among the neighboring nations, and even "from among the aliens who reside with you," but "you shall not lord it harshly over any of the Israelites, your kinsmen" (Lev. 25:44-46). When then "your countryman becomes so impoverished beside you that he sells you his services, do not make him work as a slave. Rather, let him be like a hired servant or like your tenant, working with you, until the jubilee year, when he . . . shall be released" (Lev. 25.39-41). This is clearly a mitigation, not an abolition of slavery, and still left the possibility of being sold into slavery. Poverty was without a doubt the principal reason why some Israelites became slaves of others. To this there is frequent reference (Deut. 15:2-3; 2 Kgs. 4:1-7; Neh. 5:1-5), and payment of debts immediately freed the slave (Lev. 25:48; Neh. 5:8). Liberation was automatic after six years, or in the jubilee year.

A general principle governing slavery was this: the slave is the thing or property of the owner. This principle governed all the slave's duties, the use that could be made of him, and his death. The legislation places the extreme limits within which the proprietor or master must keep himself. Should he beat the slave to death, the master must pay the penalty. If however the slave lives for a day or two, then there was no penalty "because the slave is his own property" (Ex. 21:20, 21). Should the master blind the slave or break a tooth, then he was obliged to free him on account of the mutilation (Ex. 21:26, 27). Should an ox gore a slave, the owner had to pay over to the slave's master thirty shekels. These extreme cases, however, do not allow one to form a good picture of the slave's existence. Slaves were considered a part of the family, and if they were foreigners, they had to submit to circumcision (Gen. 17:12-13). The decalogue prescribed that they rest on the Sabbath (Ex. 20:10), and they also took part in the religious life of the family (Deut. 16:11, 14; 12:12, 18). They were admitted to the paschal banquet (Ex. 12:44). In the last analysis the slave's treatment and condition in the family depended on the character and disposition of the master, who, even if he was not by nature bent on kindness to them, would at least be so for his own interests (Sir. 33:25-33; Job 31:13-15). The women slaves were given in marriage by the master (Ex. 21:4), who could also take one as concubine or wife (Deut. 21:10-14). The sons of the slaves were themselves slaves to their fathers' master (Ex. 21:4; Lev. 22:11).

Christian revelation proclaimed to the world the principles that would eventually put an end to slavery, but the church did not confront the problem directly. Christian faith proclaims the equality of all men before God. Men are established in sin and salvation to the degree that any social, ethnic or national difference between them is of little or no account (*see* 1 Cor. 12:13; Gal. 3:28; Col. 3:11). Christianity erects charity as the link between men (Jn. 13; Matt. 20:27; Mk. 10:44). The apostolic church however, while diffusing itself throughout the Greek and Roman world, had no intention of starting a social revolution. Paul exhorted people to remain in the condition in which they found themselves when they embraced the faith: "Were you a slave when your call came? Give it no thought. Even supposing you could go free, you would be better off making the most of your slavery" (1 Cor. 7:21; *see* 22-24). Moreover he works to see that the relationships between slaves and masters are transformed by the demands of faith in Christ (Eph. 6:5-9; Col. 3:22-4:1; *see* 1 Pet. 2:18). The case of Philemon is enlightening in this respect: Paul sends back to Philemon his slave Onesimus with the recommendation that his master receive him "if then you regard me as a partner, welcome him as you would me. If he has done you an injury or owes you anything, charge it to me" (v. 17).

The term 'ebed, servant or slave, is not only used in its juridical sense; it has also many other usages. When an inferior presents himself to a superior to whom he owes obedience, he speaks in the third person as "Your servant" (*see* Gen. 44:7; Num. 32:25; Ruth 3:9; 1 Sam 25:41). The "king's servants" are his ministers (1 Sam. 19:1), among whom is distinguished his "servant," a kind of vizier or prime minister (2 Kgs. 22:12).

In religious language there are two different meanings. Servants are the adorers of a divinity, the faithful of a god: they are Yahweh's servants, or servants of God. The term is also used more specifically for those among God's people who are chosen for a particular mission. The prophets are the servants of God (Amos. 3:7; Jer. 25:4) and above all there is the anonymous personage of the poem of Deutero-Isaiah (*see* SERVANT OF THE LORD), the prophetic figure of which Jesus is the fulfilment (Acts 3:13; 3:26; 4:27; 12:18). The apostles and ministers of the Lord are called the Lord's servants in this sense. Paul claims as an honorific title, alongside that of apostle, "the servant of Jesus Christ" in several of his letters (*see* Rom. 1:1; Phil. 1:1; Tit. 1:1; *see* James 1:1; 2 Pet. 1:1; Jude 1:1; Rev. 1:1; 22:6).

In the New Testament the notions of slavery and liberty serve to illustrate the moral and religious condition of man and the fruits of Jesus' redemptive work. Man is the slave of sin (Jn. 8:34; Rom. 6:17, 20). Christ has liberated us from the slavery of sin, from death and from the law, and so has made us truly free (Rom. 8:1-4; Gal. 5:1). The Christian is not one who has received a spirit of slavery and fear, but a spirit of adoption on account of which he calls God his father (Gal. 4:4; Rom. 8:15). Paul wishes to prevent a false interpretation of his doctrine on the liberty of the Christian (*see* Rom. 6:1), and paradoxically transforms this liberty into the service of a new Lord, who is God and Christ (Rom. 6:22), to whom he belongs (1 Cor. 6:19) and for whom he must live and die, for, both living and dying, he is totally Christ's (2 Cor. 5:15).

Sling, A sling was part of the equipment of every warrior (Jgs. 20:16; 1 Kgs. 3:25; 1 Chron. 12:2; 2 Chron. 26:14) and shepherd (1 Sam. 17:40, 49). David killed Goliath with a slingshot. With it he felt most at ease on account of his shepherd life, and so he rejected in its favor the heavy armor offered to him by Saul. The Benjaminites were celebrated for their proficiency with the sling. According to Judges 20:18 the warriors of the tribe numbered "seven hundred picked men who were left-handed, every one of them able to fling a stone at a hair without missing."

Smith, Gold, silver, copper, lead, tin and iron were in use in ancient Palestine. According to Genesis 4:22 Tubalcain, son of Lamech, was the ancestor of all metalworkers in bronze and iron. Tubal (*see* Gen. 10:2) was the name of a northern race which inhabited a region noted for its metal deposits, while Cain in Arabic means smith. 1 Samuel 13:19 tells us that the Israelites had not one smith among them so that they were totally dependent on the Philistines for metal and metal-work, military and otherwise. This placed them at a disadvantage. When however the monarchy was set up, metal workers were in demand for the building projects of King Solomon. Hiram, the son of a Tyrian bronze-worker is celebrated for his achievements in this field in 1 Kings 7:12 ff. (*see* 1 Kgs. 6:7). The remains of the huge copper works at Tell el-Kheleifeh at the south end of the Wadi Arabah were discovered in 1938-40, and are very probably Solomon's work of the tenth century B.C.

References to the smith are found in Sirach 38:29 ff., where the author asserts that he is too bent on his task to have leisure for wisdom. Isaiah pillories the idolatry of those who, like the smith, beat their gods out on the anvil only to fall down and adore the work of their own hands (Isa. 44:12 ff.; *see* Isa. 54:16).

smooth

and I am *s.*-skinned	Gen. 27:11	the rough ways *s.*	Lk. 3:5
David selected five *s.* stones		with *s.* and flattering	Rom. 16:18
	1 Sam. 17:40		

Smyrna, A city and seaport on the west coast of Asia Minor. It was one of the most flourishing of Greek colonies and a commercial center for the Aegean Sea. It retained its importance even under the Roman domination. Smyrna had its Christian community very early. To it is addressed one of the seven letters of Revelation, which has nothing but praise for it (Rev. 1:11; 2:8-11).

snare

they will become a *s.*	Ex. 34:12	and a *s.* lays hold	Job 18:9
shall become a *s.*	Jgs. 2:3	be a *s.* before them	Ps. 69:23
her to him to become a *s.*		the *s.* of the fowler	Ps. 91:3
	1 Sam. 18:21		

Snow, Snow is a rare phenomenon of the climate of Palestine (2 Sam. 23: 20; 1 Mac. 13:22). There is constant snow only on the mountains of Lebanon and Hermon to the north (Jer. 18:14). In the central highlands light snows usually fall in January and February each year. An occasional heavy snowfall of several inches surprises the central highlands or the Transjordan plateau every 6 or 8 years. Snow is mentioned in the Bible most of all in figurative and poetic language, and more or less in the same way as in today's languages (*see* Ex. 4:6; Ps. 51:9; Isa. 1:18; Job 9:30; Sir. 43:18). According to popular biblical cosmology, which was more fanciful than realistic, snow, with hail and rain, was stored up in heaven's chambers (Job 38:22; Ps. 147:16) to descend on the earth at the Lord's command (Ps. 148:8; Isa. 55:10).

Soap, Lye, Soap is only mentioned twice in the Bible (Jer. 2:22; Mal. 3:2). It was compounded by fullers from vegetable alkalies.

Soco, Socoh (so′-koe), 1. A city of Judah (Josh. 15:35) in the valley of the Terebinth beside Azekah where Goliath was slain by David (1 Sam. 17:1-4). It was taken by the Philistines during the reign of Ahaz king of Judah (735-715 B.C.; 2 Chron. 28:18). Today it is called Khirket Abbad.

2. A city of Judah (Josh. 15:48) fortified by Rehoboam (2 Chron. 11:7).

3. A city in the third district of the administrative division of Solomon (1 Kgs. 4:10).

Sodom, With Gomorrah, Admah, Zeboiim and Bela, or Zoar, Sodom made up the five cities of the Pentapolis of the Dead Sea (Gen. 14:2). When Lot and Abraham separated, the former chose "the whole Jordan Plain . . . and settled among the cities of the Plain, pitching his tents near Sodom" (Gen. 13:10-13). Genesis 14 recounts the punitive expedition of the four kings of Mesopotamia against the five kings of the Pentapolis. The Pentapolis kings were defeated and Lot and his family, together with the king of Sodom, were taken prisoners. Abraham mustered three hundred and eighteen men, fell on the victorious kings by night, and defeated them, thus liberating Lot. The king of Sodom offered Abraham the booty with the exception of the people, but Abraham refused.

Genesis 18-19 tells of the destruction of Sodom and the other four cities. It was a divine judgment on the corruption of the inhabitants of the region, from which only Lot was immune. Abraham's intercession with God to spare the place failed, for there were not found in the whole region ten just men (Gen. 18:15-33). Lot gave hospitality to the three mysterious messengers who had previously visited Abraham. At the risk of his own life and the honor of his daughters he prevented them falling victims to the perverse passions of the inhabitants of the city (Gen. 19:1-11). On orders from these messengers Lot and his wife and daughters took flight at dawn while "the Lord rained down sulphurous fire upon Sodom and Gomorrah" (Gen. 19:24).

The story of the destruction of Sodom and the other cities is the story of a divine judgment on sin. In the Bible tradition it became almost the type of every divine judgment (*see* Deut. 29:22; 32:32; Isa. 1:9, 10; Jer. 20:16; 23:14; 49:18; Amos 4:11; Wis. 10:6; Matt. 10:15; 11:23; Lk. 10:12; 17:29; 2 Pet. 2:6; Rev. 11:8). From the historical point of view, the same can be said of this as was said in regard to the Flood. (*See* FLOOD, THE.) Here a popular tradition was used for religious purposes. In all probability the tradition came from outside Israel, but became part of its patrimony through Lot's people who made their founding father the center of the story. (*See* LOT.) According to the biblical account the cities, with the exception of Zoar, have left no trace of themselves (Gen. 19:19-22). It is commonly held that the story's origins are not unconnected with the formation of the most southerly part of the Dead Sea, south of the Lisan peninsula on the eastern coast. This is a geological formation of recent date. The beds of the Jordan and Arabah are geologically unstable. The catastrophe would however have taken place long before Abraham's time, for which reason it is necessary to consider both Abraham and Lot as extraneous to the beginnings of the account.

Soldier, *See* ARMY, WAR.

soldiers

the priest told the *s.*	Num. 31:21	The procurator's *s.*	Matt. 27:27
counted up the *s.*	Num. 31:49	giving the *s.*	Matt. 28:12, 13
all the *s.* left	2 Kgs. 25:4	The *s.* now led	Mk. 15:16

solemn

On that *s.* closing	Lev. 23:36	on our *s.* feast	Ps. 81:4

Solomon, Son and successor of David as king of Judah and Israel (c. 960-922 B.C.). He was born of Bathsheba, who had been the wife of Uriah, and at his birth had been called Jedidiah, that is, "Beloved of the Lord" (2 Sam. 12:24, 25). His succession to the throne was not easy. Solomon had an important rival in Adonijah, the eldest son of David, who was counting on the support of Joab, general of David's army, and Abiathar the priest. Bathsheba with the assistance of Nathan the prophet and Zadok the priest, and Benaiah head of the personal guard of the king, intervened with David, reminding him of his promise to leave the throne to Solomon. Adonijah wished to force the will of the old king by anticipating his designation with a ceremony of enthronement, but David was warned in time by Nathan. David decided for Solomon and gave instructions that he should be immediately anointed king by Zadok (1 Kgs. 1).

The new reign was started with revenge. David left to Solomon the task of settling some accounts which he for one reason or another had failed to. Joab was executed (1 Kgs. 2:5, 6; 2:29:35) as was Shimei, the man who had insulted the king while he was fleeing Jerusalem (1 Kgs. 2:8, 9; 2:36-46). Solomon also lost no time in liquidating his rival Adonijah (1 Kgs. 2:12-25) and in replacing the priest Abiathar who had supported Adonijah with his faithful priest Zadok (2 Kgs. 2:26-27), while even before he had Joab executed, he appointed Benaiah as commander-in-chief of the army (2 Kgs. 2:35).

Solomon reaped the fruits of the seeds David had planted in riches, power and splendor. All David's military exploits and political maneuvers now paid off. With Solomon's reign Israel reached a summit of glory she was never more to enjoy throughout her history. The description of Solomon's reign in 1 Kings 3-10 is full of admiration and enthusiasm. The negative aspects from the religious point of view are left for 1 Kings 11, but other equally negative aspects were to come to the fore immediately after the death of Solomon.

Solomon is above all presented as a wise king and judge (1 Kgs. 3:12). The celebrated judgment of Solomon has parallels in all ancient literature and so must not be taken as history. It does however illustrate Solomon's characteristics of perception and wisdom in the exercise of his judicial function, which cannot be denied. The wisdom tradition of Israel venerates Solomon as its most illustrious representative and patron, and has placed under his name some of its most important writings. (*See* QOHELETH, PROVERBS.) 1 Kings 5:9-14 gives concrete information on the personal culture and creativity of Solomon with his surpassing wisdom. According to this laudation he composed three thousand proverbs and over a thousand songs. People came from all nations to hear Solomon discourse. Solomon undoubtedly wanted for his kingdom the splendor of the culture of the time, and the wisdom that was on the other hand so intimately connected with the organization of the kingdom. *See* SCRIBE, WISDOM.

Solomon did honor to his name, which is derived from **shalom,** peace. His was an interregnum between the wars of conquest of his father and the wars of survival of his successors. The earlier half of his reign was fortunate in that neither of the great world powers, Egypt and Assyria, was stirring. Soloman could therefore concentrate on international trade as well as administration. He substituted for the old tribal organization a new distribution of people and territories according to criteria that were inspired by the necessities of his political and fiscal administration (1Kgs. 4:7-5:3). During his administration the kingdom achieved the boundaries that were to remain but an ideal and an aspiration for successive reigns: "Judah and Israel lived in security, every man under his vine or under his fig tree, from Dan to Beer-sheba, as long as Solomon lived" (1 Kgs. 5:5).

What emerges in sharp detail from the account is the development of commerce and industry and the building enterprises of the king. He imported horses and chariots from Egypt and Cilicia, and mustered a force of 1400 war chariots and 12,000 horses which he distributed in the chariot cities and near the capital Jerusalem (*see* 1 Kgs. 10:26-29). With the collaboration of Hiram, Solomon built a fleet at Ezion-geber to set up commercial relationships with Ophir (1 Kgs. 9:26-28: 10:22). At Ezion-geber have been found the ruins of the foundry set up by Solomon to process the copper of Arabah. Solomon maintained regular commercial contact above all with Arabia. 1 Kings 10:10-13 has conserved the account of one of the missions received by Solomon in Jerusalem, that of the Queen of Sheba. *See* SHEBA.

Outstanding among Solomon's building undertakings was the construction of the Temple. (*See* TEMPLE.) He also constructed at Jerusalem a splendid palace (1 Kgs. 7:1-12) and fortified numerous other cities (1 Kgs. 9:15-23).

All these undertakings were undoubtedly made possible by the riches that flowed from the commercial and industrial enterprises of the king. The author of 1 Kings evidently exaggerates when he states "The king made silver as common in Jerusalem as stones and cedars as numerous as the sycamores of the foothills" (1 Kgs. 10:27). It is also necessary to add to these the annual tributes of the vassal countries since the time of David (1 Kgs. 10:24, 25). The works, however, would not have been possible if it were not for the perfectly organized forced labor system imposed by Solomon (1 Kgs. 9:15-23). Even in the enthusiastic account of the sacred author can be sensed the burden that this placed on a poor people, which was to explode with violence at Solomon's death. When Rehoboam went to Shechem to take over the kingdom of Israel, he heard them say: "Your father put on us a heavy yoke. If you now lighten the harsh service and the heavy yoke your father imposed on us, we will serve you" (1 Kgs. 12:3, 4). Rehoboam refused the request, and so Israel and Judah came to a split that was to last until the end of both kingdoms (722 B.C. and 587 B.C.).

The reign of Solomon brought to conclusion the assimilation of the Israelite monarchy to the oriental type of monarchy of neighboring countries. Solomon drew especially on Egypt to give his kingdom effective administration. Nor did he hesitate to gather to himself a harem which in number and quality showed the splendor of his reign. "He had seven hundred wives of princely rank and three hundred concubines" (1 Kgs. 11:3). This is an obviously exaggerated account, but it fits easily into the enthusiasm of the description of the preceding chapters. However the author passes a very negative judgment on this point on account of its deleterious effects on the religious order of things (1 Kgs. 11:4-13).

Solomon's long reign, even before it ended, experienced the unequivocal signs of its own decomposition. Solomon had had to make territorial concessions to Hiram of Tyre to pay for his services in the building projects (1 Kgs. 10:14-15). There were also other losses. Hadad the Edomite, with the protection of the Pharaoh of Egypt, made himself an independent king of Edom (1 Kgs. 11:14-22, 25). Rezon did the same thing in Damascus (1 Kgs. 11:23-24) while Jeroboam, after the failure of the revolt of the forced laborers, fled to Egypt waiting for the opportune moment when Rehoboam, Solomon's son, was rejected as king of Israel (1 Kgs. 11:25-40; 12:2, 20). Shishak, founder of a new Egyptian dynasty, stood in the background of these secessionist movements, and when Solomon died he moved in and with one blow succeeded in impoverishing Solomon's heirs (1 Kgs. 14:25-28).

Solomon's Portico, The eastern side of the portico which surrounded the outer courtyard of the Temple of Herod in Jerusalem. (*See* TEMPLE.) Jesus taught there (Jn. 10:23), and there Peter preached to the people after the cure of the paralytic who had begged for alms at the gateway to the Temple (Acts 3:11). The Christians used to gather in the portico of Solomon in the Temple (Acts 5:12).

Son of God, The title "son of God" has different applications in the Bible that for the most part are linked up with one another. One independent line that quickly vanished, and was found mostly in poetical texts, referred to the "sons of God" who were celestial beings belonging to the heavenly court. (*See* Gen. 6:2; Pss. 29:1; 87:7; Job 1:6; 2:1; 38:7.) In texts such as Job 1:6; 2:1; 38:7 they are identical with the angels of later Judaism (*see* 1 Kgs. 22:19). In other texts their relationship with God is no different, but in them it is easier to see the origin of the concept. It can be said that these are the Yahwist's polemic answer to the richness and multiplicity of the world of the gods of Canaan. In the Ugaritic religious texts, the "sons of God" are gods of inferior rank, subject to the father El. (*See* BAAL, UGARIT.) Israel entered Canaan bringing with her the experience and explicit prohibition of Yahweh in regard to any other gods (Ex.

20:3). Though Yahweh was intolerant of the existence of other gods, it does not seem to have stopped all speculation about the "world of gods": Yahweh is the one God of Israel who lords it over all the other gods of the nations, who cannot even be compared to him (Ex. 15:11). With the ever more explicit monotheistic faith, the existence of other gods is more and more attacked (Deut. 32:37) and they are reduced to ever more modest proportions as slaves or ministers of Yahweh. By continuing to call themselves sons of God or of the Most High they reveal the ultimate origin of this concept (Deut. 32:8, 9; 82:1-8).

With this exception, the Old Testament links the title "son of God" with the historical relationships which God deigned to establish with his people. In Exodus 4:22 God through Moses tells Pharaoh: "Israel is my son, my first born . . . let my son go, that he may serve me." "Son of God" in this sense is a title of election. One might speak of adoptive sonship. This transfers to a more intimate sphere the historical relationships between Yahweh and Israel, which were sanctioned in the covenant (*see* COVENANT) and unfolded in a fatherly providence over Israel on the part of God which was reciprocated by her obedience to him (Deut. 14:1; Isa. 2:1; Jer. 3:19; 31:9; Hos. 11:1; 13:13). This order of ideas and relationships is also lived out between God and the individual (*see* Ps. 73:15) and so is applied to the just Israelite who is the special object of the enmity of the impious (Wis. 2:13, 18; 5:5; 12:19-21).

The king is called the son of God in a particular way (Pss. 2:7; 89:28; 2 Sam. 7:14; 2 Chron. 22:10). This does not depend on the divine affiliation of kings that was frequent among the Middle Eastern peoples, especially in Egypt. Rather it is the particular application of the divine affiliation of Israel to the king, in the explained sense. The king is son of God because he is head and representative of the people who is "son of God." This divine sonship of the king is based on the historical election of the Davidic dynasty (2 Sam. 7; 2 Sam, 23; Ps. 89), and sums up the special relationship of protection and obedience that exists between God and the king. This election is also called covenant (2 Sam. 23:1; Ps. 132:11; Jer. 33:21; Ps. 89:4 ff.). It was not just to favor David's family, singling it out from among the people. David's election was first and foremost for the sake of the people of whom David was king. By choosing the Davidic dynasty God wished to associate the lot and destiny of Israel with the lot and destiny of the house of David. The hopes for the future would in this way assume messianic dimensions.

The New Testament applies the title "Son of God" primarily to Jesus, and in him to all who believe in him. Jesus however is not always called "Son of God" in the same sense.

The title has a messianic sense. This is true in the statements of the devils expelled by Jesus: "Why meddle with us, Son of God?" (*see* Matt. 8:29; Lk. 4:41). This also holds for the greeting Nathanael gave to Jesus: "Son of God, king of Israel." Psalm 2:7 produces the formula that was used to signify the divine adoption of the king at the moment of his enthronement: "You are my son, this day have I begotten you." This is applied to Jesus at the moment of his resurrection, that is, when he is exalted to the right hand of God in the heavens, thus taking possession of his universal saving power (Acts 13:13; Heb. 1:5; Rom. 1:4). Son of God in these texts is a royal title and is in line with the oracle of Nathan to David (2 Sam. 7).

The title however is applied to Christ in a more profound sense: it is meant to convey the intimate and eternal personal relationship that exists between Jesus and God. This follows on the custom of Jesus who called himself Son without any other addition (*see* Matt. 11:27; Lk. 10:22; Matt. 21:33-41; Mk. 12:1-9; Lk. 20:9-16; Mk. 13:32; Matt. 24:36). This relation of sonship is ineffable (Lk. 10:22; Matt. 11:25-27). Jesus takes pains to distinguish his sonship from that of other men, which cannot be placed on the same level (Matt. 15:13; 16:17; 18:10; 20:23; 26:39-43 and parallel texts).

John marks the difference by using two different Greek terms that are both translated in English by "Son." Only Jesus, however, is **hyios** (Jn. 1:18) or "son, natural son, son properly so called," while other men who believe in him are **tekna**, children (Jn. 1:12; 3:1). Jesus is in fact the only-begotten son (Jn. 1:18). He lives from the life of the Father (Jn. 6:57) and is one with the Father (Jn. 10:30). His divine sonship lies at the center of his saving mission. It is in fact because he is Son and has life in himself that he has been sent by the Father to share the divine life with men (Jn. 5:26; 10:10). Jesus is the revelation of the Father because the Father is in him and he in the Father (Jn. 1:18; 14:10). This sonship is revealed in time, but it is transcendental and timeless (Jn. 3:16-19). Because he is Son, Jesus can empower men to become the sons of God (Jn. 1:12, 13).

This link between Jesus' divine sonship and ours, which however does not eliminate the difference between them, is often expounded by Paul. In the Christological hymns of his epistles Paul confesses the preexistence and transcendence of Jesus' divine sonship (*see* Col. 1:14 ff.; Eph. 1:3 ff.). He is the source and the finality of all that is created: for him are all things created, and in him all things have their consistency while to him they tend (1 Cor. 15:28; *see* Heb. 1:1-4).

God sent his Son into the world so that we might receive the Spirit of adoption. Through being inserted into Christ, we share through adoption in his natural condition as Son of God. For this reason we can address God as Jesus did: "Abba! Father!" (Gal. 4:4; Rom. 8:15). Our union with Jesus makes us his coheirs to the kingdom of the Father (Rom. 8:18). The gift of the Son is the proof of the love of the Father (Rom. 8:32; *see* Jn. 3:16) who wishes to shape us to his image (Rom. 8:29). Our adoptive sonship is already real, but hidden, awaiting its perfect fulfilment or revealing when glory will cover up our mortal bodies and our transformation in Christ will be complete (Rom. 8:23; *see* 1 Jn. 3:2).

We have indicated several senses in which the title "Son of God" is applied to Christ. This may seem to give rise to ambiguity. This ambiguity however is only apparent or at least superficial. The history of the relationship between God and his people, which is the history of salvation, is summed up in the terms in which God reveals himself: as Father to his son Israel. What was prophetic in the Old Testament was brought to fulfilment in the New, when God revealed his only-begotten Son. Thus the texts that were interpreted in a "messianic" sense get a much deeper meaning, for the universal domination that was promised was such that it could not be conferred on a man as instrument or minister but only on him who was the Son of God incarnate. He, by despoiling himself of his power, wished to win for himself through obedience and death that glory that as divine Son was his (*see* Matt. 17:5; Mk. 9:7; Lk. 9:35; 2 Pet. 1:17; Phil. 2:15 ff.).

Son of Man, "Son of Man" is the literal translation of the Aramaic expression **bar nasha**, in Hebrew **ben adam**, which in the ordinary use of language means "man" or "a man," with or without the definite article. Often in the gospels Jesus speaks of the "Son of Man" with definite reference to himself. Indeed except for Acts 7:55 (the words of the dying Stephen), the expression "Son of Man" is only read on the lips of Jesus. Revelation 1:13 and 14:14 are rather quotations of Daniel 7:13. The title "Son of Man" is absent from the letters of the New Testament, and the evangelists never apply the title to Jesus when they are speaking in their own words.

Some authors have thought that when Jesus used this title he had no implicit reference to any prophetic figure of the Old Testament, but was simply making a veiled reference to himself, using the third person. Against this opinion stands the undeniable fact that the title was no invention of Jesus. It had in fact behind it a long tradition, which gave to it very definite function. It is also a fact that Jesus does not use the title indiscriminately but only in very specific contexts.

When we search for the origin of the term we can immediately discount the Book of Ezekiel in which God often addresses the prophet as Son of Man without however the term acquiring any particular importance. Such an origin could only be taken into consideration of those words which Jesus speaks in reference to the actual situation of the Son of Man, in the humility of his state (Matt. 8:20; Lk. 9:58; Matt. 11:19; Lk. 7:34). Most of the sayings of Jesus on the Son of Man speaks of the "power of the Son of Man" (Matt. 9:6; Mk. 2:10; Lk. 5:24; Matt. 12:8; Mk. 2:28; Lk. 6:5), and of his position as judge, and of his future glory. This usage obviously depends on other biblical and extrabiblical sources.

In the Old Testament we find its full sense only in the vision of Daniel 7. In this chapter the author follows the usual scheme of apocalyptic visions: after the vision (7:2-14) which is certainly of eschatological content, Daniel asks for an explanation of its meaning (7:15-16). This is given by an interpreting angel (7:17-27). The vision tells the story of the universe in symbols, according to the four great empires, that is, the Babylonians (7:4), the Medes (7:5), the Persians (7:6) and Alexander and his successors (7:7), among whom Antiochus IV Ephiphanes is highlighted with obvious allusions to his persecution of God's people. Then follows without any interval the conclusion of history. In the heavens are placed thrones, on one of which is seated the venerable Ancient who is to judge the empires. Only then does Daniel see "one like a son of man coming, on the clouds of heaven; when he reached the Ancient One and was presented before him, he received dominion, glory, and kingship. . . . His dominion that shall not be taken away, his kingship shall not be destroyed" (Dan. 7:13, 14). In the interpretation of the vision there is reference to the "holy ones of the Most High" (7:22) or to "the holy people of the Most High," to whom "the kingship and dominion and majesty of all the kingdoms under the heavens shall be given" (7:27). Daniel 7 does not present any individual figure of judge or eschatological savior. The Son of Man is a symbol of God's people and of its glorious destiny. It is also obvious, however, that the Book of Daniel is not the source of the speculations on the Son of Man, but only offers for it an interpretation, with polemic tones, which reduces it to a symbolic figure of the people of God and thus deprives it of that position as judge and savior which it reserves exclusively to the "Ancient of Days."

Although it is of most recent date, the figure of the Son of Man that is presented in the apocryphal work, 1st Book of Enoch, is more genuine. The Book of Enoch speaks of the Son of Man in cc. 37:71, which form the so-called "Booklet of Parables." Much discussion has gone on over the presumed Christian origin of these chapters, or at least over a Christian elaboration of them. However, one must acknowledge that the "Booklet of Parables" lacks all the genuinely Christian elements, e.g. there is no allusion to the incarnation, the passion and death of the Son of Man, etc. It is therefore unthinkable that it should have stemmed from a Christian pen.

In 1 Enoch the Son of Man is also called the Just One of the Elect. He is an eschatolocgical figure, that is, his appearance will take place at the end of time and it will be his function to save the just and condemn the wicked. He is therefore Savior and Judge.

The Son of Man already exists. He was created before the creation of the world and is one of the central elements in God's eternal plan for the universe and history. His manifestation, however, will take place only at the end of time. This manifestation or epiphany will be glorious. It will in fact be his enthronement accompanied by the conferral on him of a universal and quasi-divine power by God for judgment and salvation. After the judgment, his dominion will last forever. Until the day of judgment the Son of Man is held hidden in the heavens with God, but before the end of the world his existence and glorious destiny will be revealed to some chosen ones, that is, to those who will have been temporarily admitted to heaven (Enoch) and who will have had visions (Daniel) and who pass on this experience to others who are worthy of it. The wicked however will be denied this. We have noticed in another place how Jesus conducted himself in regard to the revelation of the mystery of the Son of Man and in regard to the mystery of his own person. *See* MESSIANIC SECRET.

Both in the Book of Enoch and in other apocryphal texts that speak of the Son of Man (4 Ezra, The Apocalypse of Baruch) there is the absence of all allusion to the passion and redemptive death of the Son of Man. This was to be the most original element that Jesus added to the image of the concept of the Son of Man, the glorious judge of the last times.

Jesus spoke of the Son of Man above all to reveal his future glory as Judge and Lord exalted at the right hand of God in heaven. He also used it to explain the salvific meaning of his passion and death as the way to that glory and the means of salvation for the multitude.

"If anyone in this faithless and corrupt age is ashamed of me and my doctrine, the Son of Man will be ashamed of him when he comes with the holy angels in his Father's glory" (Mk. 8:38; *see* Lk. 9:26; Matt. 16:27; Matt. 10:33; Lk. 12:8,9). The decision of faith or incredulity which men will take for or against Jesus will be ratified as his sentence of salvation or damnation by the Son of Man. Some scholars have thought to see in this sentence a distinction between Jesus and the Son of Man, but this interpretation is excluded by other authentic words of Jesus, and moreover is open to the accusation of superficiality. A decision for or against Jesus anticipates the eschatological judgment, not because the Son of Man, distinct from Jesus, will ratify the decision taken as his sentence, but because the eschatological judgment will be the inversion of the present situation in which the sentence has already been issued. The eschatological sentence will be an inversion of the present situation because those who today seem to be judges, that is, men, will then be the judged, and the person who today seems to be the judged one, will himself be the Judge, the Son of Man. This has the same meaning as the response that Jesus gave to the Sanhedrin (Matt. 26:64; Mk. 14:62; Lk. 22:69), where there is no possibility of drawing a distinction between Jesus and the Son of Man (*see* also, on the coming or parousia of the Son of Man: Matt. 24:30-31; Mk. 13:24-27; Lk. 17:22-31; 21:25-28; and on the judgment Matt. 25:31-46). *See* JESUS CHRIST.

Jesus has introduced into the figure of the Son of Man as it was in the apocalyptic literature an innovation without parallel. This is his passion and death as part of the mission of the Son of Man, and indeed a central part as it is the way of glory and the instrument of salvation. Jesus brought about this innovation by fusing the Isaian figure of the Servant of the Lord and the Son of Man. This fusion is above all seen in the prophecies of the passion (Mk. 8:31=Matt. 16:21=Lk. 9:22; Mk. 9:31=Matt.

17:22=Lk. 9:43; Mk. 10:45=Matt. 20:28; Mk. 9:12 and 14:21, 41. *See* SERVANT OF THE LORD.

The existence of Jesus as the Son of Man before his death and exaltation is clouded in mystery, somewhat as is the heavenly existence of the Son of Man in the apocalyptic literature. The mystery of his person is only revealed to a few (Matt. 13:10, 13; Mk. 4:10-12; Lk. 8:9, 10). To the rest it is spoken in parables. It is a revelation that takes place in the veils of mystery, and only happens within the circle of the faith that it creates. The deep reason for this surprising attitude of Jesus is identical with the mystery of his redemptive incarnation which saw him come in the humble vesture of a man like other men, despoiled of the divine glory which was properly his. *See* MESSIANIC SECRET.

Song of Songs, The title is a Hebrewism to indicate the superlative, meaning the "Song among Songs" or "the greatest of songs." The title mentions Solomon as the author or the person to whom it is addressed, but this is obviously a fiction arising from the frequent mention of Solomon in the verses (1:5; 3:7, 9, 11; 8:11), and from the statement in 1 Kings 5:12 that Solomon's songs numbered a thousand and five. The book, at least in its present form, dates from the postexilic age, as one can deduce from the peculiarity of its language. It is not possible, however, to be more precise than to say that it stems from the fifth or fourth century B.C. The canonicity of the work was never seriously questioned among Christians. The Talmudic tradition tells of a discussion that arose over its authenticity at the Synod of Jamnia around 100 A.D. The question was resolved in favor of the book, thanks especially to the intervention of the Rabbi Aqiba who proclaimed: "All the universe is not as valuable as the day in which the Song of Songs was given to Israel, for while all scripture is holy, the Song of Songs is the Holy of Holies."

At first sight the work seems nothing more than a profane love poem or a collection of them, since it sings only of the natural love between a man and a woman. God is not even mentioned, and at no point in the book is there reference to moral or religious matters. Everything surrounds the love theme. From this the big question arises: how did a book treating of human love in a profane (but by no means immoral or illicit) way, achieve canonical status among the sacred Scriptures? This surprising fact seems to be the only reason for the allegorical interpretation of the book. This kind of interpretation is very ancient. It was fairly common in Judaism of old (4 Ezra 5:24-26; 7:26, around 90 A.D.), and explained texts in terms of God's treatment of Israel, his spouse. This was the line of Aqiba and his disciples. Aqiba in fact takes severe exception to those who use the Song of Songs at marriage feasts. This by reflection indicates that the allegorical interpretation at that time may have been an innovation, an answer to the problem of the book's sacredness that was then being questioned. This would mean that formerly the book was understood in a literal way: a collection of love lyrics.

Christian tradition confronted the same problem and followed in the footsteps of the Jews in giving the book an allegorical interpretation with many variations on the theme, such as Christ and the Church, Christ or God and the Christian soul. Christian tradition has always upheld the spiritual meaning of the Song of Songs, and mystical writers like St. John of the Cross found in it their delight.

It must be kept in mind that the legitimacy of the allegorical interpretation was never seriously called into doubt. The first centuries of Christendom found an allegorical escape from the embarassingly evident and obvious love-lyrics. This tradition could bring to its support Hosea 2; Jeremiah 2,

Ezekiel 16 and 23, where the relationship between God and Israel is described in terms of a marriage. These parallel texts however could only be validly called on to point towards an allegorical interpretation of the Song of Songs if this had already been demonstrated, but not before.

The Song itself does not offer the least support for an allegorical interpretation, nor does it afford even the slightest indication in this regard. This is borne out by the exegetes themselves who attempt the allegory. While they agree on the general allegorical context, they differ when it comes to the interpretation of the text itself. The resulting impression is that the exegete discovered the allegory more in his own approach than in the book. While the Song of Songs has occasioned the growth of a rich spiritual doctrine, the actual exegesis of the Song does not really provide the elements that caused this growth.

It is wiser then to stick to the text: it is a collection of love poems and should be interpreted and judged in the light of analogous literary traditions. How did it find its way into the canon? There is no ready answer available as we do not know what concrete use was made of it in the biblical tradition. In the biblical canon, the collection of love lyrics has found its place beside a collection a sacred lyrics. This is the most unequivocal and decisive recognition that human love between man and woman is itself sacred.

Up to this point we have spoken of the traditional allegorical interpretation. Recently some French exegetes have proposed a new type of allegory (A. Robert, A. Feuillet, R. Tournay), which starts off with a criticism of the traditional allegorical interpretation, which they hold to be too polemic in tone, arbitrary and unproven. Then they attempt to discover the literary tradition to which the Song of Songs could have belonged. For these authors the Song belongs to the anthological style which characterized the post-exilic age. After the exile the prophetic charism quickly disappeared and the great creative epoch of Israel had passed. Now Israel was bent on the faithful conservation and application to the new circumstances of the patrimony she had received. The anthological style is the method that responded best to this new spiritual environment. This style picks up the classical texts and themes to adapt them to new circumstances, without however quoting explicitly. They went by way of allusions and rereadings of the central themes.

These authors would hold that the Song of Songs took up many classical themes such as the figure of bride and groom, shepherd and flock to illustrate the relationship between Yahweh and his people, while waking and sleeping, searching and finding were used to expound the religious dispositions of the people towards Yahweh. Each of these themes, even when isolated by a precise context, evoked a definite religious teaching. The author of Song of Songs takes up these themes and subordinates them to a central governing theme: the relationship of love between bride and groom, so that everything that is said is transposed in a certain way. Thus for example, the image of the shepherd and the flock is confused with the central theme, where the groom is the shepherd and the flock as it were stands in place of the bride. The awakening, which in the Deutero-Isaian tradition evoked the interior conversion of the people and the arising of hope in its heart, here becomes the awakening of the bride. The exegetes · in question insist on the absurdities or inelegance in some parts of the poem, which arise, according to them, from the fact that the author's intent is not faithfully to mirror human love, but to give religious teaching in the guise of human love.

For these authors, the Song of Songs is divided into five poems: 1:5-2:7; 2:8-3:5; 3:6-5:1; 5:2-6:3; 6:4-8:3. Each of the poems evolves in three stages. First there is the animated description and the desire of one of the two. Then comes the meeting. Third comes the anxious search by the bride for the groom of whom she has been unexpectedly deprived. Between the poems can be noticed a true, double progression. First there is a psychological progression in the sense that the invitation of the groom becomes ever more pressing, and the invitation is reciprocated ever more readily by the bride. Then there is a historical progression in that the poems reflect so many phases of the history of the post-exilic community, not in terms of external events but in view of how its spiritual renewal is coming along. In this history the Song of Songs underlines two elements: on the one hand there is the untiring initiative on God's part who again and again draws his people to himself, and on the other the continued delusions of the bride which reflect the people's delusions because of full and perfect salvation failing to arrive. The author suggests the motive for these deluded hopes, namely, that the people were not interiorly prepared. The sleepiness and negligence of the bride is the reason why the groom cannot come and take her to himself. In the last analysis the Song of Songs is an invitation to hope and interior renewal while also being a song about the untiring love of God whose demands should be seriously responded to.

Songs of Degrees, *See* PSALMS.

Sons of Prophets, The members of the prophetic guilds which were instituted in Israel at the time of Samuel and Saul (1 Sam. 10:5; 19:20) and afterwards around Elijah and Elisha (1 Kgs. 18:4, 19; 22:6; 2 Kgs. 2:3; 3:11; 4:1; 6:1-2). They were charismatics whose possession of the spirit was expressed in orgiastic ecstasies that were very contagious. (*See* PROPHETS.)

Sons of Thunder, A translation of **Boanerges,** the name Jesus conferred on the brothers John and James (Mk. 3:17) probably because of their over-impulsive zeal, which would have fire come down from heaven to consume the Samaritan village that refused to receive Jesus on his way to Jerusalem (*see* Luke 9:51-56). *See* BOANERGES.

Sopater (soe′-pa-ter), Son of Pyrrhus of Beroea. With others he accompanied Paul from Greece to Jerusalem at the conclusion of his third apostolic journey (*see* Acts 20:4).

sorcery, *See* MAGIC.
there is no *s.*   Num. 23:23

Sorek (sor′-ek), A valley of Shephelah (*see* SHEPHELAH) where Delilah, Sampson's mistress, lived (Jgs. 16:4). The town of the same name in the valley is today's Sarar on the railway line between Jaffa and Jerusalem.

sorrow, *See* MOURNING.
s. take hold   Isa. 13:8

Sosipater (soe-sip′-a-ter), 1. One of the generals of the army of Judas Maccabeus, who with Dositheus defeated and destroyed the force that Timotheus had left behind in the fortress, amounting to more than ten thousand men. They later made Timotheus a prisoner but let him go free for fear that reprisals would be taken on the Jewish hostages who were in the hands of Timotheus' men. An arrangement was reached by which these should be freed upon his liberation (2 Mac. 12:17-25).

2. A Jewish Christian whom Paul salutes from Corinth in Romans 16:21. He is probably to be identified with Sopater in Acts 20:4. *See* SOPATER.

Sosthenes (sos′-the-neez), 1. The head of the synagogue of the Jews at

Corinth after his predecessor Crispus became a Christian through Paul's preaching. The Jews at Corinth took Paul before the tribunal of Gallio, proconsul of Achaia. Gallio however refused to hear the case as it was "quibbles about words and names, and about your own law." The frustrated Jews turned on Sosthenes and beat him in front of the court house, but Gallio refused to intervene (Acts 18:12-17).

2. A Christian companion to Paul (1 Cor. 1:1).

Sostratus (sos/-tra-tus), The commander of the Seleucid garrison of the citadel at Jerusalem. He was entrusted with collecting the taxes. When he was unable to extract from Menelaus the money the latter promised in exchange for nomination as high priest, both he and Menelaus were summoned to Antioch by Antiochus IV Epiphanes. Sostratus left as his substitute Crates, commander of the Cypriots (2 Mac. 4:27-29).

Soul, Soul is the conventional translation of the Hebrew **nephes,** and of the Greek **psyche.** The translations of biblical anthropology into Greek or modern terms must however always remain approximative, for biblical anthropology was not systematically elaborated, nor was its terminology fixed. The result is that terms enjoy a great mobility and attempts at definitions turn out to be precarious. The only satisfactory insight can be gained by examining the concrete use made of the various terms.

First of all it would be vain to seek the line of demarcation between the terms **basar,** flesh, and **nephes,** soul in the sense of body and soul such as they have been understood in the anthropology of the Platonic and Aristotelian philosophical traditions. In the Israelite mentality this type of distinction is rejected as an attempt to dissolve the concrete living unity of man, even if doing so it makes for problems in trying to understand survival after death. **Basar** and **nephes** can both designate the human person in his indivisible unity, in which there is underlined, but not distinguished, one aspect at one time and another at another.

The primitive sense of **nephes** seems to be throat, as in Isaiah 5:14: "the nether world enlarges its throat and opens its maw," and in such expressions as to have at one's throat water (Ps. 69:2; Jonah 2:6) or the sword (Jer. 4:10). To pass from this to mean breath is easy, even though there are not many texts with this meaning (*see* Job 11:20; 31:39; Job 6:11; 21:4 and others).

In the Hebrew way of seeing things, breath and blood are associated with the vital principle and energy much more than in our way of thinking today. They are more than mere biological functions. It is not easy to define the relationship between them, but one could say that the breath like the blood (*see* BLOOD) is the vehicle or seat of the vital principle. **Nephes** at times, then, assumes this sense, but it would be erroneous to think of a vital principle in the western sense of the term. 2 Samuel 1:9 or 1 Kings 17:21, 22 show Saul fatally injured asking to be put to death because he still felt his life in him. In 1 Kings 17:21-22 Elijah raises the son of the widow of Sarephta by making his life return to him. The connection with the biological symptoms of life becomes looser in many other texts, in which the translation is simply "life" in the full sense that it has in common expressions even in today's languages, such as "to save one's life" (1 Kgs. 1:12; Ps. 72:14), to fear for one's life (Ezek. 32:10), to place one's life in danger (Jgs. 12:3; 1 Sam. 19:5), to swear by one's life (Amos 6:8; Isa. 45:23; Jer. 22:5).

Finally **nephes** can mean the individual concrete living person, or men (Ex. 1:5; Deut. 10:22; Josh. 10:28) or even animals (Gen. 1:20; 2:19). The term is often used in this sense in the laws (Lev. 4:2; 5:1; 24:17, 18).

This is the meaning of the word in the classical text of biblical anthropology in the creation account of Genesis 2:7. God forms man from the dust of the earth and breathes into the nostrils the breath of life and man becomes a living person. The account, rather than suggest two integral elements for the whole man, describes two stages of his creation. Man drawn from the dust was inert, but at God's breathing the breath of life into him, man passes on to be **nephes,** a living thing. That **nephes** cannot mean soul is evident from texts such as Leviticus 19:28; 21:1; 22:4, etc. where one reads of a dead **nephes,** in the obvious sense of a dead man, a deceased person, a cadaver.

The Greek translators of the Old Testament used the word **psyche,** soul, to translate **nephes.** Their example was followed by Jewish authors who wrote in Greek. In the Greek writings, Wisdom of Solomon and the New Testament the word **psyche** should be understood in the light of the Old Testament meaning of **nephes** and not as the philosophical **psyche,** at least unless the contrary is evidently demanded in a particular case. One of these exceptions is Wisdom 8:19, 20 where some have thought to see the platonic doctrine of the preexistence of souls. The author is attempting an ingenious description of the excellent qualities of Solomon through the providential harmony between a well disposed body and a good soul. (*See* also 9:5.) Even though the book speaks only of "souls," one should not confuse its eschatological doctrine with the thesis of the natural immortality of the soul. Wisdom is in the line of the biblical tradition of Daniel 12:1-3 and the apocalyptic writings. *See* RESURRECTION.

The New Testament takes up many of the Old Testament uses of **nephes** (*see* Matt. 20:28; Mk. 10:45; Acts 20:24; 27:10, 20; Rom. 16:4; 1 Cor. 15:45; Phil. 2:30). Although the New Testament keeps to the traditional line of the Old Testament, it characteristically uses the word **psyche** to denote in man the central core of his concrete humanity which is the subject of the drama of his perdition or salvation. One could also speak of life and man's supernatural life in his soul. However it is not so important to define this, since the word "soul" to designate the person has passed into the Christian language of all times and places. So one speaks of saving or losing one's soul; parishioners are called "souls" without thereby despising their bodies. It designates the human person from the point of view of what is important for the faith and for salvation. Christ and the apostles are pastors of souls in this sense (1 Pet. 2:25; 2 Cor. 12:15). Christ sums up the Christian life thus: "Whoever would save his life will lose it; but whoever loses his life for my sake will find it" (Matt. 16:25; *see* Lk. 14:26; Mk. 8:35; Matt. 16:26; Mk. 8:36; Matt. 10:39, etc.). The word used for "life" is soul, which is saved if surrendered to Christ and lost if hoarded for oneself.

south

the north and *s.*	Gen. 13:14	on the *s.* side	Ex. 36:23
on the *s.* side	Ex. 26:18	the queen of the *S.*	Matt. 12:42
On the *s.* side	Ex. 27:9	Head *s.* toward	Acts 8:26

sow, sowing

seed for *s.* the land	Gen. 47:23	Then may I *s.*	Job 31:8
you may *s.* your land	Ex. 23:10	a farmer went out *s.*	Matt. 13:3
do not *s.* a field	Lev. 19:19	they do not *s.*	Lk. 12:24
and *s.* trouble	Job 4:8	you never *s.*	Lk. 19:21

Spain, 1 Maccabees 8:3 refers to the conquest of Spain, which was begun by Rome in 209 B.C. as a part of the military operations against the Carthaginians and completed in 133 B.C. In Romans 15:24, 28 Paul speaks of his intention of continuing his journey from Rome to Spain. When however he arrived in Rome, Paul was no longer a free apostle, but a prisoner in chains. It is not known whether, after his liberation, he carried out his intention. The letter of Clement of Rome to the Corinthians (*see* 95; c. 1, 5) asserts that Paul arrived at the extreme limit of the west, which would seem to suggest that he did arrive in Spain. One suspects, however, that these and other allusions stem from the text of Romans 15:24, 28 rather than from independent historical traditions.

sparrow, sparrows

the *s*. finds a home	Ps. 84:4	flock of *s*.	Matt. 10:31
I am like a *s*.	Ps. 102:8	Are not five *s*. sold	Lk. 12:6
Are not two *s*. sold	Matt. 10:29	than a flock of *s*.	Lk. 12:7

Sparta, A Greek city on the Peloponnesian peninsula, capital city of the Lacedaemonians and successor to Athens in leadership over all Greece in the fourth century B.C. Under the Romans it preserved a precarious independence. To this period belongs the alliance between Jonathan Maccabeus and Arius king of Sparta (1 Mac. 12:2-23) which was renewed by Simon Maccabeus (1 Mac. 14:16-23). Jonathan brought forward as a reason for the alliance the common ethnic origin of the two nations (1 Mac. 12:7; *see* also 2 Mac. 5:9). This however does not hold up under critical scrutiny. Rather must it be understood as a usual maneuver in diplomacy to create a benevolent atmosphere. Today, similarly, one hears of the "traditional friendship" between two nations who enter into political or other alliances.

Spear, The word "spear" in earlier English translations of the Bible was used loosely for all varieties of this long-shafted, pointed weapon. Now spear and javelin are recognized as two distinct types of one weapon, differing in size and the way they are employed. The javelin was shorter and lighter, a medium-range weapon thrown by the arm. A javelin-thrower would be armed with several, carried like arrows, in a quiver. Both spear and javelin had a body or shaft of wood and a head of metal, locked together by a tang fitting into the split or bored end of a shaft, or by some sort of socket, depending on the era, the metals available, the metal-working and welding expertise, etc. A spear carrier, on the other hand, carried but one—a longer, stouter, heavier thrusting weapon. Sometimes the tips were barbed, so that the extraction of the weapon caused further ripping injuries to the victim. Some translators prefer "lance" to "spear," thus retiring "spear" to a generic term, with "javelin" for the lighter, hurled type, and "lance" for the heavier, thrusted type, as well as for the ceremonial type of spear.

speckled

s. one among the goats		The *s*. animals shall	Gen. 31:8
	Gen. 30:32	were streaked, *s*. and mottled	
brought forth streaked, *s*.			Gen. 31:10
	Gen. 30:39		

spectacle

a *s*. to the universe   1 Cor. 4:9

spices

s. for the anointing oil	Ex. 25:6	large quantity of *s*.	1 Kgs. 10:10
Take the finest *s*.	Ex. 30:23	to prepare *s*. and perfumes	
s. for the anointing oil	Ex. 35:8		Lk. 23:56
camels bearing *s*.	1 Kgs. 10:2		

Spirit, Spirit translated the Hebrew **ruh,** the Greek **pneuma,** and the Latin **spiritus.** In Hebrew and Greek the word has a much wider range of meaning than the English word spirit. **Ruh** is the movement of air, the wind

(Gen. 3:8; Ex. 10:13, 19) and also the sign of breathing. Both meanings combine in audacious expressions, which make the wind the "breath from Yahweh's nostrils" (Ex. 15:18; 2 Sam. 22:16; Ps. 18:16), thus making it the agent of God's will, or the instrument of his designs (Ps. 104:4).

Man's ruh is above all his breath, in which is reechoed his inner movements of mind or soul, and his passion (Ex. 6:9; Gen. 41:8; Ezek. 3:14; Eccl. 7:8; Sir. 5:11; Job 7:11; 21:4). Like nephes, meaning soul, ruh also signifies breath as the vehicle or seat of life. (*See* SOUL.) God is the absolute lord and only dispenser of this "breath of life" (Gen. 6:7; 7:15). He grants the breath of life to all men and animals (Ps. 104:27) and he withdraws it when he wills. For this reason it can be called God's spirit or breath (Job 27:3; 33:4; Isa. 42:5). When God withdraws his spirit, all flesh dies and returns to dust (Job 34:14, 15). When man dies, his spirit returns to the God who gave it. One must beware of injecting into these expressions the idea of an independently existing spirit or soul. Spirit is the vital force and returns to God because God is its master. The same holds for the animals. Only Qoheleth seems to suggest a destiny for man's spirit that is different from that of the animals, but even he does not go beyond the horizons that he held in common with the rest of the Jews (*see* Eccl. 3:19-21; 12:7).

As man's vital principle, spirit appears as the seat and subject of his affective, intellectual and moral life. It is not possible however to trace a neat distinction between what the "heart" does and what the "soul" does. God too has his spirit. God's spirit however is not taken to be his vital principle. It is his omnipotent and irresistible power which operates in man and in the world. God's spirit raises up the judges of Israel, charismatic leaders who save with their prowess the people when they are threatened by their enemies. (*See* JUDGE; Jgs. 3:10; 6:34; 11:29; 13:25.) Saul, the first king of Israel, retains many of the charismatic traits of the judges who preceded him (1 Sam. 11:5).

The Spirit of Yahweh works on the prophets and gives rise to their ecstatic exaltation (1 Sam. 10:5-13; 19:20-24; 1 Kgs. 22:10-12; *see* Num. 11:25). The spirit of God is not so frequently found in relationship with the great prophets from Amos on. The prophet is a "man of the spirit" (Hos. 9:7) and the spirit's action is at the origin of his oracles (2 Chron. 16:1, 7; 20:14-17; 24:20). The word of Yahweh however takes first place as an organ of revelation. *See* PROPHETS, WORD.

God's spirit is the constant though less obvious companion of those who have a particular mission to fulfil in the history of salvation. Moses (Num. 11:17, 25) transmits his spirit to his successor Joshua (Num. 27:18; Deut. 34:9). The spirit of God is associated with the kings' mission (1 Sam. 16:13) and will be with the ideal Davidic king of the future in his work of justice and salvation (Isa. 11:2). The spirit of Yahweh also rests on the "Servant of the Lord" (Isa. 42:1) and on the messenger charged with the preaching of the gospel to the poor (Isa. 61:1), a text that Jesus applied to himself in the synagogue at Nazareth. (Lk. 4:14)

The Spirit of Yahweh is the principle of newness of life in the prayer of Psalm 51:12-14, and the teacher of souls in the wisdom tradition, in which it assumes to itself the functions of wisdom (*see* Wis. 1:4-6). The Psalmist's prayer anticipates the eschatological hopes of the prophets Jeremiah and Ezekiel. Jeremiah saw into the inner constitution of sin, and foresaw the future renewal of Israel in the form of a new alliance which will rest on the interior renewal of man. Man will be made capable of hearing the voice of God, and carry written in his heart God's law, that is, man will surrender to God's will with an interior spontaneity and freedom (Jer. 31:31-34; 32:38-40). Ezekiel emphasizes more the function of the spirit in this renewal. God will remit men's sins and replace his hard, unlistening heart of stone with a new heart of flesh. He will give them a new spirit, or rather, he will put into them his own spirit which will be in them a dynamic principle of a holy life so that all will walk in accordance with the Lord's precepts (Ezek. 36:23-28). The gift of God's spirit, then, is a compendium of the gifts of eschatological salvation which will come at the last times: "After this I will pour out my spirit on all mankind. . . ." (Joel 3:1-2).

The spirit of God is not mentioned as much in the synoptic gospels as it is in John and Paul. The spirit's action however is marked in the crucial moments of Jesus' work. The virginal conception of Jesus is the work of the Holy Spirit (Matt. 1:18, 20; Lk. 1:35). In baptism the Spirit descends on Jesus (Matt. 3:13-17; Mk. 1:9-11; Lk. 3:12, 13) and rests on him (Jn. 1:33). This confirms Jesus in his humanity and marks him for his mission as Servant of Yahweh according to Isaiah 42:1. This is expressly stated by Peter in Acts 10:38: "God has anointed him with the Holy Spirit and with power, and because God was with him, Jesus went about doing good and curing all who had fallen into the power of the devil." The Spirit drives Jesus into the desert so that he can withstand the attack of Satan the tempter (Mk. 1:12; Lk. 4:1). The miracles and exorcisms of Jesus are signs that the kingdom has come; they are worked through the power of the Spirit (Matt. 12:28; see Lk. 11:2). Jesus' enemies who attribute his powers to Beelzebub blaspheme against the Holy Spirit, and their sin will be unforgiven (Matt. 12:32; Mk. 3:29; Lk. 12:10). The Spirit sums up the gifts of salvation in Luke 11:13, and his outpouring through baptism will take place through Jesus who accomplishes more than the preparatory baptism of John (Matt. 3:11; Mk. 1:8; Lk. 3:16). The only text of the synoptics in which the Holy Spirit is unambiguously called a divine person is the baptismal formula of Matthew 28:19. The other texts in themselves do not go beyond the Old Testament usage. In the light of the whole New Testament, however, they acquire a much deeper meaning.

The Spirit is the principal agent in the Acts. The phenomena of Pentecost fulfil the prophecy of Joel 3:1-2 (Acts 2:14-21). Jesus has been raised to the right hand of God, and having received from the Father the promise of the Spirit, he has poured out this Spirit on mankind (Acts 2:32, 33). Whoever converts and is baptized receives the gift of the Spirit (Acts 2:38) through the imposition of the hands of the Apostles (Acts 8:18). The Spirit descends on Cornelius and his family, and convinces Peter that he should be admitted to baptism and the Church (Acts 10:44-48). The Spirit moves the apostles (Acts 4:8) and the other members of the Church (Acts 13:2; 15:28; 20:28). Through them he accomplishes his work in creating the Church. The Spirit's presence is evidenced in extraordinary gifts and charisms (Acts 2:3-5; 10:47; 11:17; 15:8).

In Paul's theology the Spirit occupies a particularly important post. Here we underline just two aspects. First, the Holy Spirit is associated more intimately with the glorified humanity of Christ. Jesus through his resurrection has been constituted Son of God is power, "according to the spirit of holiness" (Rom. 1:4). Christ is a vivifying spirit, capable of conferring the Spirit to transform to his own image those who through faith and baptism are inserted into him (1 Cor. 15:35-45). This must in the last analysis be the interpretation of Paul's phrase: "the Lord the Spirit is" (2 Cor. 3:17). Secondly, the Holy Spirit becomes, in the Christians who receive him, the principle of a new life. They walk according to the Spirit (Gal. 5:25), they are led by the Spirit (Rom. 8:4) who produces in them his fruits (Gal. 6:8). The Holy Spirit teaches us to pray and intercedes for us (Rom. 8:26) crying out on our lips, Abba, Father!, establishing us in the adoption of sons (Rom. 8:23). The Spirit animates our life of charity (Rom. 5:5; 15:30; Gal. 5:13; Col. 1:8) and of faith (2 Cor. 4:13). The Spirit opens our minds to the mysteries of God (1 Cor. 2:10-16). He is the pledge of our hope in the future (2 Cor. 1:22; 5:5); since the Spirit of him who raised Jesus to life lives in us, then he (the Father) who raised Christ will also restore life to our mortal bodies through the indwelling Spirit he has given us (Rom. 8:11) and whose temples we are (1 Cor. 3:16; 6:19).

Paul undoubtedly sees the Holy Spirit as a divine person, equal to the Father and to Christ. The numerous trinitarian formulae do not allow one to think otherwise (*see* 2 Cor. 13:13; Gal. 4:6; Rom. 8:9, 11; 1 Cor. 12:4-6, etc.). The difficulty remains, however, in the interpretation of Paul's writings. For it is hard to establish when Paul is writing of the spirit as a divine gift or of the spirit of the believer transformed by this divine gift, or when he is speaking of the Person of the Holy Spirit or the Holy Spirit's gift which is the spirit in us. These are not weaknesses in the doctrine itself, but rather a faithful reflection of the intimate relationship that is established between the person renewed by the Spirit and the renewing Spirit who makes himself over in gift.

John often speaks of the Spirit and the Paraclete, the Spirit of truth. The Paraclete is only spoken of in the last discourse (Jn. 14-17) while the Spirit is spoken of in the first chapters. Both these series reflect different traditions, but they are fused together in John 14:26: "But the Paraclete, the Holy Spirit, whom the Father will send in my name, will instruct you in everything and remind you of all I have told you." On the Paraclete *see* PARACLETE. The texts on the Spirit follow in the footsteps of the synoptic and Pauline texts. The Spirit descended on Jesus to bring him to the fulfilment of his mission as Lamb of God who abolishes the sin of the world (Jn. 1:29; *see* 1 Jn. 3:9). The relationship between Christ and the Spirit is enunciated in John 7:37-39; the gift of the Spirit comes from the glorified humanity of Christ, just as in 1 Corinthians 15:45. John 19:34 in all probability alludes to this gift of the Spirit: "one of the soldiers thrust a lance into his side and immediately blood and water flowed out." Water is used to express the outpouring, of the Spirit in John 7:38. To describe Jesus' death, John chose the form: "he delivered over his spirit," as a sign of the outpouring of the Spirit to which this death led (Jn. 19:30).

Rebirth takes place for the Christian through water and the Spirit (Jn. 3:5; *see* 1:33; 1 Jn. 5:5-7). So Christians can adore the Father in spirit and truth, thus opposing and supplanting the cult of the Old Testament. This new cult in spirit (or the Spirit) and truth is the Christian life, especially that lived out in faith and charity.

spirit

the *s.* of God	Gen. 41:38	*S.* begets *s.*	Jn. 3:6
a divine *s.*	Ex. 31:3	I spoke to you are *s.*	Jn. 6:63
the *s.* of God	Num. 24:2	the *S.* gives wisdom	1 Cor. 12:8
he saw the *S.* of God	Matt. 3:16	mysteries in the *S.*	1 Cor. 14:2
S. of God that I expel demons	Matt. 12:28	to pray with my *s.*	1 Cor. 14:16

spit, spits

If the afflicted man *s.*	Lev. 15:8	began to *s.* in his face	Matt. 26:67
her father had *s.*	Num. 12:14	They also *s.* at him	Matt. 27:30
and *s.* in his face,	Deut. 25:9	and *s.* at him	Mk. 10:34
hesitate to *s.* in	Job 30:10	began to *s.* on him	Mk. 14:65

spoils

he distributes the *s.*	Gen. 49:27	you take its *s.*	Josh. 8:2
together with the *s.*	Num. 31:11	divide these *s.*	Josh. 22:8
Having heaped up all its *s.*	Deut. 13:17	dividing the *s.*	Jgs. 5:30

Spring Gate, A gate in the southeast section of Jerusalem, reconstructed by Nehemiah (Neh. 2:14; 3:15; 12:37).

spy, spies, spying

secretly sent out two s.	Josh. 2:1	s. it out	1 Chron. 19:3
to s. on it,	2 Sam. 10:3	into the group to s.	Gal. 2:4

squandered

s. his money   Lk. 15:13

Stachys (stay´-kis), A Christian greeted by Paul as "my beloved" in Romans 16:9.

Staff, The translation of different words in the Old and New Testament that could be rendered, as the occasion demanded, into sceptre (2 Sam. 22:19; Ps. 18:18), walking stick (Ex. 21:19; Matt. 10:10; Mk. 6:8; Lk. 9:3), wand (Ex. 7:9 ff.; Num. 17:5), rod for punishment (Isa. 10:5), flail for reaping (Isa. 28:27), shepherd's crook (Ps. 23:4; Mic. 7:14). Its uses as a defensive or offensive weapon were obvious (1 Sam. 14:27). It was a symbol of rule or power, and this found its way into language. Tobiah was the staff of his parents, their support in their old age (Tob. 5:23). God breaks the staff, that is, the power of the wicked (Isa. 14:5) while the staff is also the expression of God's own anger (Isa. 10:5). Since the poor traveler's only riches were his staff (Gen. 32:10), the variation between Jesus' command to take no staff in Luke (9:3) and to take one staff only in Mark (6:8) is minimal.

stammering

with s. lips   Isa. 28:11   s. in a language   Isa. 33:19

Stars, The author of Genesis 1:14-19 is making a point against the astral cult that was typical of Mesopotamia when he expressly underlines that God set the sun, the moon and the stars in the dome of the sky "to shed light upon the earth, to govern the day and the night, and to separate the light from the darkness" (1:18). In this way the stars are dethroned from their divine state and reduced to the condition of faithful servants commissioned by God their creator with their own task and function in the universe. God calls them by name and at his call they present themselves (Pss. 147:4; 148:3). Before God's majesty they darken and tremble (Isa. 13:10; Ezek. 37:7; Joel 2:10; 4:15), and like good servants, they can intervene, on God's command, to save his people when they are in danger (Jgs. 5:20). On the day of judgment they will be caught up in the cosmic upheaval that will agitate the whole universe and mark the passage from this era to a new heaven and a new earth (Matt. 24:29; Mk. 13:25; Lk. 21:25; Rev. 8:10-12; 12:5).

The stars which Jesus holds in his hand in the vision of Revelation 1:16, 20 are the symbols of the seven churches and their angels to which the author is writing his seven letters (Rev. 2:1; 3:1). The rising of the "star of Jacob" (Num. 24:17) is the sign in the heavens that Israel will prevail over the Moabites. The text however has a messianic resonance. Tradition has seen in it prefigured the future glory of Israel in the person of its Savior. The star of the Magi (Matt. 2:2, 7, 9-10) can only with difficulty be called an astronomical phenomenon. It is called "his (Christ's) star," that is, the sign that should announce his birth, according to the mentality of the Magi themselves, and the realization of Numbers 24:17, according to the mentality of one versed in the scriptures. The account has given too literal a translation to the messianic import of Numbers 24:17.

stars

and he made the s.   Gen. 1:16   and count the s.   Gen. 15:5

stars (cont.)

as numerous as the *s.*	Gen. 26:4	all you shining *s.*	Ps. 148:3
the morning *s.* sang	Job 38:7	the moon and the *s.*	Lk. 21:25

Stater (stay′-ter), A Greek coin, equivalent to two drachmas of silver. The stater of which Matthew speaks in 17:27 is equal to the tetradrachma, that is 4 drachmas. The didrachma, or 2 drachmas was the annual Temple tax for each person. Jesus commanded Peter to catch a fish in whose mouth he would discover the stater with which to pay the tax for both of them.

steal, stealing

by *s.* away secretly	Gen. 31:27	You shall not *s.*	
would we *s.* silver	Gen. 44:8		Deut. 5:19; Mk. 10:19
You shall not *s.*	Ex. 20:15	against *s.*, do you *s.*	Rom. 2:21
You shall not *s.*	Lev. 19:11	The man who has been *s.*	
			Eph. 4:28

Stele, From the Greek meaning "upright stone," it was usually carved with illustrations in word and picture, providing invaluable documentary evidence of the past to archaeologists and biblical scholars. Though no Israelite stele has been found, several from biblical and pre-biblical times have been discovered in Palestine. One famous one is that of Mesha, king of Moab, c. 835 B.C., inscribed with a record of a triumph over Israel, found in 1868 at Beth-shan.

Stephanas (stef′-a-nas), A Christian woman of Corinth who, with her family, was baptized by Paul himself (1 Cor. 1:16). Paul calls her the "first fruits of Achaia," that is, the first of that region to be received into the church. He recommends her to the church at Corinth on account of her services to it, and expresses his delight at her visit when she came to him at Ephesus with Acaicus and Fortunatus (1 Cor. 16:15-18). In all probability it was they who brought to Paul the letter of that church to which he alludes in 1 Corinthians 7:1.

Stephen, A Hellenist Jewish Christian, that is, Greek-speaking, and therefore from the Diaspora. Stephen is the first of the "seven" chosen by the apostles to attend to the service of the poor in the community at Jerusalem. He is described as a man full of faith and of the Holy Spirit (*see* Acts 6:1-6). Stephen became the spokesman for the Hellenist Jewish Christian thesis, and the first to draw from the Christian message the consequences that Paul was to develop and preach against the Judaizers. (*See* GALATIANS, EPISTLE TO THE.) This thesis is summed up in the words of Stephen's adversaries: "This man is always speaking against this Holy Place and the Law. We have heard him say that Jesus of Nazareth is going to destroy this Place and alter the traditions that Moses handed down to us" (Acts 6:13-14). The first accusation re-echoes what was charged against Jesus himself in his trial (*see* Matt. 26:62-66). In both cases, the words of Jesus and those of Stephen went further than a simple prediction of the destruction of the Temple. In reality they announced the abolition of the Temple as such, which had been emptied of meaning after the resurrection of Christ. This is why the veil of the Temple was rent in two at the death of Jesus, a symbol that the Holy of Holies had finished its function. Stephen is possibly even more radical. He calls to his support a celebrated text of Isaiah 66:1-2 and proclaims that "the Most High does not dwell in buildings made by man" (Acts 7:48; *see* Acts 17:24; Heb. 9:11, 24). A similar position must be understood in those words against the law of Moses of which his adversaries accuse him (Acts 6:14; *see* similar accusation against Paul in Acts 15:15; 21:21, 28; 28:17).

Stephen had disputes with Jews from Cyrene and Alexandria and with members of the Synagogue of the Freedmen, and with people from Cilicia and Asia. He was accused and brought before the Sanhedrin, where he gave a long speech (Acts 7:1-53). The speech recorded in Acts obviously does not give the exact words of Stephen. Luke puts in his mouth a discourse that gathers together the most abrasive points of the dispute between the young church and the Jews. It is an implacable accusation of the age-old rebellion of the Jews against the voice of God, a rebellion which climaxed in the murder of "the Just One." The speech also repeats some of the invective Jesus used against the Pharisees (*see* Matt. 23:34-35; Mk. 12:1-11).

Stephen did not conclude the speech. He was brought outside the walls of the city. There he was stoned to death as a blasphemer. A youth by the name of Saul held the clothes of those who threw the stones (Acts 7:55-60).

Stephen's death unleashed a persecution against the nascent Christian church. This persecution proved providential, for it forced the church out of its enclave at Jerusalem and stimulated mission activity in Judea, Samaria and outside the confines of Palestine among the Gentiles (Acts 8:1-6; 11:19-24).

steps

by *s.* to my altar	Ex. 20:26	go back ten *s.*	2 Kgs. 20:11
had advanced six *s.*	2 Sam. 6:13	and number all my *s.*	Job 31:4
	nor our *s.* turned	Ps. 44:19	

steward

the *s.* of my house	Gen. 15:2	wife of Herod's *s.*	Lk. 8:3
his head *s.* these	Gen. 44:1	faithful, farsighted *s.*	Lk. 12:42
	The bishop as God's *s.*	Tit. 1:7	

stick

Elisha cut off a *s.*	2 Kgs. 6:6	Take another *s.*	Ezek. 37:16
take a single *s.*	Ezek. 37:16	Then join the two *s.*	Ezek. 37:17
	to the *s.* of Judah	Ezek. 37:19	

stiff-necked

you are a *s.* people	Deut. 9:6	and be no longer *s.*	Deut. 10:16
how *s.* this people is	Deut. 9:13	how rebellious and *s.*	Deut. 31:27

stocks

my feet in the *s.*	Job 33:11	Jeremiah from the *s.*	Jer. 20:3
and placed in the *s.*	Jer. 20:2	into the *s.*	Jer. 29:26

Stoic

Epicurean and *S.* philosophers	
Acts 17:18	

stomach

the jowls and the *s.*	Deut. 18:3	and fill your *s.*	Ezek. 3:3
Yet in his *s.* the food	Job. 20:14	into the *s.*	Matt. 15:17
	Food is for the *s.*	1 Cor. 6:13	

stones

So they got some *s.*	Gen. 31:46	He took twelve *s.*	1 Kgs. 18:31
you have the two *s.*	Ex. 28:11	wear away the *s.*	Job 14:19
order the infected *s.*	Lev. 14:40	his throne upon these *s.*	Jer. 43:10

Stoning, For some particularly heinous crimes Jewish law inflicted death by stoning. Under this punishment fell such crimes as idolatry (Deut. 13:10-11; 17:5-7), blasphemy (Lev. 24:14, 23), the profanation of the sabbath (Num. 15:35, 36), contumacious rebellion against one's parents (Deut. 21:21), fornication (Deut. 22:21). Stoning is the only method of execution that is explicitly established. It was probably used also in other crimes for which unspecified capital punishment was the punishment. The witnesses who had testified against the guilty one had also to throw the first stones, and then all the others present (Deut. 17:7; *see* Jn. 8:7).

For not having observed the ban against Jericho, Achan was condemned to be stoned (Josh. 7:25). Jesus was often accused of blasphemy and of profaning the sabbath and was therefore threatened with stoning (Jn. 8:59; 10:31-33; 11:8). Stephen was also accused of blasphemy and executed by stoning (Acts 7:55-60) while Paul escaped different attempts to stone him (Acts 14:19; 2 Cor. 11:25). Jesus saved a woman caught in the act of adultery from the punishment of stoning (Jn. 8:1-8).

stood

I s. between	Deut. 5:5	s. facing them	2 Kgs. 2:7
He s. and shouted	1 Sam. 17:8	a manlike figure s.	Dan. 8:15

Stranger, Stranger translates the Hebrew **ger,** a term not applicable to every passing stranger but to those who live more or less stably in a land or among a people not their own. This was the condition of the patriarchs (Gen. 23:4), the Israelites in Egypt (Gen. 15:13), Moses with the Midianites (Ex. 2:22), the family of Naomi at Moab (Ruth 1:1). Israelite legislation has numerous laws concerning these strangers living in Canaan. Like the Levites (Jgs. 19:1) they generally did not possess any land (Deut. 24:14-15) and for that reason they are often recommended to the piety and generosity of the Israelites (Deut. 12:12; 26:12). They may have the produce of the sabbatical year (Lev. 25:6) and what is left in the field after the harvesting (Lev. 19:10; Deut. 24:19-21). To move the Israelites to generosity towards the stranger the law reminds them that "you were once yourselves strangers in the land of Egypt" (Deut. 10:19; *see* Lev. 19:34; Ex. 22:20). Strangers are equal before the law (Deut. 1:16) and also have a part in the religious life of Israel. They are circumcised, and can celebrate the Pasch (Ex. 12:48-49). They should observe the sabbath (Ex. 20:10) which was instituted precisely to alleviate their condition as workers (Deut. 5:12-15; Deut. 24:14). They can also take part in the sacrificial cult (Lev. 22:18) and in other festivities (Lev. 16:29; Deut. 16:11, 14).

stranger

I am a s.	Ex. 2:22	Because no s. lodged	Job 31:32
treat me as a s.	Job 19:15	a s. to my mother's sons	Ps. 69:9

stubborn

a s. and unruly son	Deut. 21:18	practices or s. conduct	Jgs. 2:19
a s. and unruly fellow	Deut. 21:20	Israel is as s.	Hos. 4:16

stumbling block

a s. b. in front of the blind		remove the s. b.	Isa. 57:14
	Lev. 19:14	a s. b. to the Jews	1 Cor. 1:23
there is no s. b.	Ps. 119:165		

stumbling stone

They stumbled over the s. s.	
	Rom. 9:32

stupid

and the s. pass away	Ps. 49:11	advisers give s. counsel	Isa. 19:11
hates reproof is s.	Prov. 12:1	Every man is s.	Jer. 10:14

stutterer

and the s. will speak	Isa. 32:4

subdue, subduing

fill the earth and s. it	Gen. 1:28	I will s. all	1 Chron. 17:10
	S. nations before him,	Isa. 45:1	

subject

the demons are *s*.	Lk. 10:17	not *s*. to God's law	Rom. 8:7
the devils are *s*.	Lk. 10:20	by his power to *s*.	Phil. 3:21

submissive, submit

s. to her	Gen. 16:9	Wives should be *s*.	Eph. 5:22
	be *s*. to your husbands	Col. 3:18	

subverting

this man *s*. our nation   Lk. 23:2   as one who *s*. the people Lk. 23:14

succeed, success

brought him *s*.	Gen. 39:3	*s*. in whatever you do	1 Kgs. 2:3
	for you will not *s*.	2 Chron. 13:12	

Succoth (suk′-oth), 1. A city of Transjordania in the territory of Gad (Josh. 13:27). It is situated in the Jordan valley beside the confluence of the river Jabbok with the Jordan. On his return from Aram, Jacob stopped there (Gen. 33:17). Gideon took severe revenge on the people of Succoth for not coming to his aid when he pursued the Midianite chiefs (Jgs. 8:5-16). Near Succoth were established the factories for the production of the bronze ornaments for the Temple of Solomon (1 Kgs. 7:46; 2 Chron. 4:17).

2. A city in northeastern Egypt. It marked the first stage of the Exodus of the Israelites (Ex. 12:37; 13:30; Num. 33:5, 6).

Sud, A river near Babylon, probably a canal of the Euphrates (Baruch 1:4).

suddenly

someone dies very *s*.	Num. 6:9	*S*. there shall come	Isa. 47:11
at how *s*. this had been		then *s*. I took action	Isa. 48:3
	2 Chron. 29:36		

suffering, sufferings

what they are *s*.	Ex. 3:7	a man of *s*.	Isa. 53:3
saw how great was his *s*.	Job 2:13	the *s*. I endure for you	Col. 1:24

Sumerians, The Sumerians are not mentioned in the Bible. They were however the founders of the Mesopotamian civilization which was inherited by the people of Akkad and the other semitic peoples who settled in Mesopotamia. The origin of the Sumerians is still unknown. They occupied Lower Mesopotamia as early as the fourth millenium and achieved their greatest splendor during the third millenium. The principal city of the Sumerians was Ur. With the Semite and Elamite invasions the Sumerian people as such disappeared at the beginning of the second millenium by fusing with the invaders.

Sun, The sun, like the other stars, was often divinized and adored in antiquity. King Josiah ordered the destruction of the sacred objects dedicated to the worship of the sun, a cult that was very popular in Assyria, and had been introduced to Jerusalem during the vassalage of Kings Menahem and Amon (2 Kgs. 23:11; *see* Ezek. 8:16). To be noted is the insistence of the author of Genesis that the sun was created by God and received from him the humble task of illumination and measuring time. This was obviously due to the author's interest in attacking sun and star cult (*see* Gen. 1:16).

When however there is no apologetic preoccupation with heretical worship the Biblical author does stand astonished at this giant of light in the arc of the heavens, which he sings in epic tone and colors (Ps. 19:5-7). The sun has a central part to play in two well-known episodes. When

Joshua went after the king of Jerusalem and his allies during the descent from Beth-horon, "the sun stood still" (Josh. 10:13). There are the words with which the sacred author comments on a piece of epic poetry from the "Book of Jashar" which he had quoted immediately before: "Joshua prayed to the Lord and said in the presence of Israel: Stand still, O sun, at Gibeon; O moon, in the valley of Aijalon! And the sun stood still and the moon stayed, while the nation took vengeance on its foes" (Josh. 10:12-13). Taken in itself, without the comment, the text really says no more than other texts which have nature, the mountains or trees, standing mute with amazement at what God has done with his people.

In Isaiah 38:7 Isaiah gives to Hezekiah as a sign that God has heard his prayer and has conceded to the sick king another fifteen years of life, the fact that "the shadow cast by the sun on the stairway to the terrace of Ahaz go back the ten steps it has advanced," a figurative expression of the prolongation of life as a new concession of the time that has already been lived.

The sun, moon and stars all figure in the usual descriptions of the "Day of the Lord," the day of judgment, and the interventions of God in history. The sun is darkened (Isa. 13:10; Ezek. 32:7; Joel 3:4; 4:15; Matt. 24:29; Rev. 8:12). These phenomena accompany the death of Christ (Matt. 27:45-50; 15:33; Lk. 23:44-49; Jn. 19:28-30). These signs also indicate the end of the present era which will take place at the end of time.

sunrise
the Jordan, toward *s.*   Num. 34:15

Suph (soof), The Hebrew name for the Red Sea or the Sea of Reeds. *See* RED SEA, REED SEA.

Suphah (soo'-fah), A region of Moab (Num. 21:14).

Supper, *See* MEALS.

Supper, Lord's, *See* LORD'S SUPPER; EUCHARIST.

suppose, supposed
they *s.* they would   Matt. 20:10 She *s.* he was the gardener
                                                          Jn. 20:15

surely
you are *s.* doomed   Gen. 2:17 he would *s.* come out   2 Kgs. 5:11

Susa (soo'-sa), A city in present-day Iran, today called Shush. It is a very ancient city, stemming from the fourth millenium before Christ. It was the capital of the kingdom of Elam, and was conquered by the Assyrian king Assurbanipal in 640 B.C. and later by the Persians. It was the royal residence of the kings of Persia (Dan. 8:2), Xerxes I (485-465 B.C.; Esth. 1:2) and of Artaxerxes I (445-433 B.C.). Nehemiah lived in Susa (Neh. 1:1).

The excavations carried out there at the end of the last century and in this one (1898-1912; 1912-1934; 1946 on) have brought to light the splendid ruins of the palaces of Darius I (521-485 B.C.) and Artaxerxes II (404-358 B.C.). During these excavations was also discovered the famous code of Hammurapi (*see* HAMMURAPI) sculpted on a basalt column, which had been brought to Susa as a war-trophy from Babylon.

Susanna, The heroine of the story of Daniel 13. This chapter is found only in the Greek version of Daniel, not in the original Hebrew-Aramaic of the work. Its canonicity was under dispute during the first centuries but was explicitly defined at the Council of Trent. Susanna, wife of Joakim, "a very beautiful and God-fearing woman," is falsely accused of adultery by two wicked old men who were judges of Israel at Babylon. They had tried without success to seduce her. When the two brought evidence in public against her she was condemned to death. Susanna, however, trusted to the Lord the defense of her innocence. While she was being led to execution Daniel intervened. With astute questions he discovered the calumny of the two vicious elders who were thereupon condemned to death. The story has really no pretensions to historicity, but was meant to inculcate, through artful description, trust in God who is the savior and protector of the oppressed and of those whose rights are abused.

swamps
its marshes and *s.*   Ezek. 47:11

swarm, swarms
let loose *s.* of flies   Ex. 8:17 Thick *s.* of flies   Ex. 8:20
                                a *s.* of bees and honey Jgs. 14:8

swear, *See* OATH.
s. to me by God   Gen. 21:23 or *s.* by them   Josh. 23:7
You shall not *s.*   Lev. 19:12 do not *s.* by your head   Matt. 5:36

sweet
smelled the *s.* odor   Gen. 8:21 How *s.* to my palate   Ps. 119:103
a *s.*-smelling oblation   Ex. 29:18 *s.* to the taste   Prov. 16:24

Swine, The pig is numbered among the impure animals (Lev. 11:7; Deut. 14:8). For this reason it could neither be eaten nor used as a victim in sacrifice (Isa. 66:3). This ritual law acquired particular importance during the Hellenistic period, perhaps in reaction to the generous use that the Greeks made of the pig in their sacrificial rites. This was one of the Greek usages that Antiochus IV Epiphanes wished to impose on the Jews in Palestine (1 Mac. 1:44-49). Those who refused to take part in it were guilty of death (1 Mac. 1:50). According to 2 Mac. 6:18 Eleazar refused to eat pork and offered himself freely for torture, "preferring a glorious death to a life of torture." The same lot awaited the seven anonymous brothers of 2 Maccabees 7.

Sword, Before the bronze age, the sword's predecessor was a flint knife or dagger. The swords of the patriarchs were bronze (Gen. 22:6, 10; 27:40; 31:26; 48:22). The Philistines had a monopoly on the blacksmith's trade which for some time kept iron swords from the Israelites. At the battle of Michmash, only Saul and Jonathan, of the whole Israelite army, were equipped with an iron sword or spear (1 Sam. 14:19-22). Goliath's sword was unique in the land (1 Sam. 21:9).

The sword in Israel was either straight for thrusting and cutting, or curved, scimitar-shaped for slicing. The straight sword was two-edged (Jgs. 3:16). The curved or sickle-like sword was worn by Goliath slung across his shoulders (1 Sam. 17:6, 45). The straight sword was worn in a sheath in the belt.

A good sword was a precious possession. Judas Maccabeus seized as a trophy the sword of Apollonius the mysarch (1 Mac. 1:29) and used it in battle the rest of his life (1 Mac. 3:12).

When Adam and Eve were expelled from the garden of Paradise, God put as guard over the gate the cherubs "and the fiery revolving sword" (Gen. 3:24). Besides its obvious reference, as in all languages, to war and death, in the Hebrew language bitter words were a sword (Ps. 56:5), the sharp tongue was whetted like a sword (Ps. 63:4). God's word penetrates like a two-edge sword "Indeed, God's word is living and effective, sharper than any two-edged sword. It penetrates and divides soul and spirit, joints and marrow;" (Heb. 4:12; *see* Rev. 2:16). To Christians is given the sword of the Spirit (Eph. 6:17).

When the Apostles wished to defend Jesus with force, he ordered them to put away the sword (Jn. 18:11) and announced the principle: "Those who use the sword are sooner or later destroyed by it" (Matt. 26:52). God's kingdom is neither advanced nor defended by the use of physical force.

sycamore

as numerous as the s.	1 Kgs. 10:27	and their *s.* with frost	Ps. 78:47
olive trees and *s.*	1 Chron. 27:28	then climbed a *s.* tree	Lk. 19:4

Sychar (sy′-kar), A village in Samaria "near the field that Jacob gave to his son Joseph," where Jesus met the Samaritan woman with whom he held the discourse recounted in John 4:5-42. There was situated Jacob's well, to which there is no reference in the Old Testament. Genesis 33:18-19 merely states that when Jacob arrived from Shechem, he bought from the sons of Hamor the plot of ground on which he had pitched his tent (*see* also Gen. 48:22). Sychar is probably the ancient Shechem (*see* SHE-CHEM), and the New American Bible reads "Shechem" in John 4:5 instead of "Sychar." In so doing the translators adopted the comment of St. Jerome, who stated that copyists had corrupted "Shechem" to "Sychar."

Syene (sy-ee′-ne), According to Ezekiel 29:10 and 30:6, the southern limit of Egypt. Syrene is the modern Aswan, the frontier between Egypt and Nubia of old.

Symeon, "Symeon known as Niger," a Jewish Christian, prophet and teacher in the church at Antioch (Acts 13:1).

Symmachus (sim′-a-kus), An Ebionite Jewish Christian, the author of a Greek translation of the Hebrew Old Testament, made during the reign of Septimius Severus (193-211 A.D.). Only fragments remain of his version. It was a rather free translation and is included by Origen in his Hexapla. *See* SEPTUAGINT.

Synagogue, Synagogue is a Greek word which signifies a gathering or an assembly. It translates the Aramaic **kenishta,** a word which through use had acquired a more precise meaning: the meetings (and also the place where these were held) which the Jews held on the sabbath for the public reading of Scripture, prayer and instruction. The earliest writings on the synagogue date from around the beginning of the Christian era. By that time it appears to have been an institution solidly rooted in all the Jewish communities in Palestine and outside of it. In the larger cities there were more than one synagogue. Acts 6:9 refers to several in Jerusalem: that of the Freedmen, the Cyreneans, the Alexandrians, and that of those from Cilicia and Asia. There were at least thirteen in Rome.

Although there are no precise traditions on the point, scholars are agreed that the beginnings of the synagogue are to be sought in the time of the Babylonian exile. The exiled Jews did not have their Temple nor their cult, and so their noncultic meetings which were held on the sabbath and on other occasions took on more importance (*see* Zech. 7:5). On their return from Babylonia this practice was not abandoned. Instead the usage grew, as it was found to be a most efficacious instrument for restoring the national conscience, an indispensable condition for survival. The synagogue was not a temple, nor was it considered God's dwelling. God, it was known, had made only Jerusalem his dwelling. The synagogue was a place of prayer and instruction in religious matters. Sometimes one hears of "synagogue cult" but the expression is inexact, for no cult was held in the synagogue. However in a broad sense the term applied, for in the synagogue was offered prayer and the "sacrifice of praise, that is, the words of our lips which celebrate his name" (Heb. 13:15), which was more and more used and assimilated in the theological evaluation of the sacrificial cult.

The central part of the synagogue worship was the reading of the Bible. First of all the Pentateuch was read and then a passage from the prophets. Since the Hebrew language was not understood by the people, there was a translator there with the reader, a **meturgeman** who put the text into Aramaic as it was read in the Hebrew. This was the beginning of the Targumim (*See* TARGUM.) In Babylonia the cycle of readings was so disposed that the whole Pentateuch was read in the course of the year. In Palestine the cycle got the Pentateuch read in the course of three years, but later the Babylonian cycle was adopted and is still used today. When the reading was over, the head of the synagogue or archisynagogus (Lk. 8:41) invited from among those present a person who was particularly qualified to deliver a discourse or exhortation (*see* Lk. 4:20). The Acts of the Apostles recounts that at Antioch, when the readings were over, the presidents of the synagogue sent Paul and Barnabas a message: "Brethren, if you have something to exhort the congregation, speak." It was occasions like these that Paul took to expound the Christian message to the Jewish communities of the Greek world. When the exhortation was over, any priest present would be invited to bless the assembly.

Besides the archisynagogus, there was also an assistant (Lk. 4:20) whose task it was to bring the scroll of the Law or the Prophets to the reader and then replace it, and to invite the priest to pronounce a blessing. The synagogue had various powers, depending on where it was. It could also inflict the punishment of flagellation, and this too was entrusted to the assistant (Matt. 5:25; 10:17; 23:30; 2 Cor. 11:24). A third minister was the person whose function it was to guide the common prayer, that is, the recitation of the **shema'** (Deut. 6:4-6) and the accompanying blessings which began the synagogal worship.

The building was rectangular, often with two lateral naves. At the end was a repository in which the scrolls of the sacred books were kept. It was the most sacred place of the whole building, and the repository or ark was on that account very ornate. A veil hung in front of it. Moreover there was a tribune for the reader and the preacher. Grouped around the central building were minor edifices for storage and other services, and later for the school. Worthy of special mention is the Genizah, where were kept the scrolls that were no longer serviceable or had become defective through use. These were periodically buried. Through good fortune the **Genizah** of the Synagogue of Cairo remained closed and its contents did not perish. It was discovered in 1896, and among the texts discovered there was the Hebrew text of Sirach. *See* ECCLESIASTICUS.

The synagogue was a providential means through which Judaism survived after the destruction of the Temple in 70 A.D. It also served powerfully to diffuse Christianity in the Greco-Roman world. Jesus had already made use of the synagogue to proclaim the "good news of the kingdom" (Matt. 4:23; Mk. 1:39; Matt. 9:35; Mk. 3:1, etc.). Luke has painted for us a very vivid picture of one of these appearances of Jesus in the synagogue at Nazareth (Lk. 4:16-21). Paul made of the synagogue an essential instrument in his strategy for the spread of the Gospel wherever there were synagogues (*see* Acts 17:1, 10) and in their sabbath meetings preached the word (*see* Acts 13:15; 17:2). Often this preaching did not last long, for his message was not well received by the majority of his listeners. However he did gather a nucleus of Jews and especially of Gentile proselytes (*see* PROSELYTES) who would then become centers from which to spread out into the surrounding Hellenistic-pagan world (*see* Acts 17:4; 17:12).

This was Paul's manner of preaching, not simply to make headway in the Hellenistic world, but above all to respect the privilege of the Jews: "The word of God has to be declared to you first of all, but since you reject it and thus convict yourselves as unworthy of everlasting life, we now turn to the Gentiles" (Acts 13:46). Acts 13:14-48 has an account of the preaching of Paul in the synagogue of Antioch of Pisidia, which however tells us also what happened at Salamis (Acts 13:5), Iconium (Acts 14:1), Thessalonica (Acts 17:1), Beroea (Acts 17:10), Corinth (Acts 18:4) and Ephesus (Acts 19:8). Paul on five occasions underwent flagellation at the hands of the synagogue authorities (2 Cor. 11:24).

Synoptic Question, A comparison of the first three gospels, Matthew, Mark and Luke immediately reveals a remarkable likeness between the three in content, the order of events, the words of Jesus, and even the terminology employed. At the same time there are surprising differences at the same levels. What we have is a discordant concordance. The evidence for this is clear when the three gospels are placed in parallel columns so that all three can be taken in at a glance, or **synopsis.** This singular phenomenon is the synoptic fact, and the problem to be explained is the synoptic question. The synoptic question is extremely complex and technical, and this article can be only a brief summary. First a broad outline of the facts of the case, and then a listing of the more notable attempts at explanation.

Mark's gospel, the shortest, has 661 verses, Matthew's 1068 and Luke's 1150. All three have 330 verses in common, the so-called triple tradition. Matthew and Luke have 240 verses in common which are absent from Mark: this is the double tradition. The single tradition comprises that material which is found only in one or other of the gospels. Moreover all three present one and the same scheme of events which is then filled with material that is partly the same and partly different. On the order of events in the gospels when compared with Mark *see* MARK, GOSPEL OF; MATTHEW, GOSPEL OF; LUKE, GOSPEL OF. Two facts must be recalled, however: Luke more faithfully preserves the order of Mark's gospel. Mark's material is inserted in two great blocks without disturbing Mark's order. Matthew however is more systematic, and changes the order of Mark's material accordingly: e.g. the Galilean ministry is ordered differently in Mark 1:21-6:13 and Matthew 4:23-13:58, while they coincide, for example, in Mark 1:21-45 and Matthew 7:28-8:16, and Mark 2:1-22 and Matthew 9:1-17, etc.

The first three evangelists seem to use a common vocabulary and style. There are obvious differences, but these differences are less than those that distinguish the three from John's gospel. The verses in which the synoptic gospels completely coincide are few in number: 8 between Matthew and Mark, 6 between Matthew and Luke, 3 between Mark and Luke. The similitude however, especially in the Lord's words, is extensive and surprising.

Numerous are the attempts to explain this convergence that is at the same time divergent. The very number of these efforts is an index of the complexity of the problem, which poses to the critics contradictory demands. When one theory seems to explain well the convergence it ends up compromising the divergence, and vice versa.

Oral tradition was at one time called on to explain the differences. While oral tradition was a means of conserving intact a patrimony, it was also exposed to minor changes of all kinds as it spread through time and space. No author today holds that oral tradition is the one and exclusive factor explaining the synoptic question. The coincidence is such that it demands a literary link between the gospels themselves and their sources. Equally unjustified however was the attempt to shelve oral tradition, forgetting that it was coextensive with the written tradition: before the Word was written it was preached.

The theories that postulate a literary dependence have covered all possible combinations. The theory supported by most exegetes, especially among the Germans and English, is the two-source theory. This theory places Mark's gospel at the origin of the triple tradition. Mark was used by Matthew and Luke but independently of one another. The source of the double tradition was a hypothetical document or fount, denoted by the sign Q, from the German **Quelle**, which means source. Luke and Matthew drew on this. Q would have been an Aramaic collection of the words of Jesus. The theory is expressed in the following scheme

This theory is enticingly simple, but on scrutiny is exposed to grave criticism. Recently its authority is being seriously questioned. The document Q is a postulate of the critics, but when attempts are made to give the document a more precise visage so as to determine its nature, scope, function and so on, the results are so numerous and diverse that they begin to call into question whether Q really has any other significance than the material that is common to both Matthew and Luke. It is certain that Mark depends neither on Matthew nor Luke, and that Matthew and Luke are independent of each other, and do not know of each other's existence. When however it is stated that Matthew and Luke depend on Mark, then it is also necessary to offer a plausible explanation for all the cases in which Matthew and Luke decide to depart from their source. There is in fact a multiplicity of cases scattered throughout the gospels where the divergencies seem to exclude Matthew's or Luke's having at hand Mark's gospel.

The simplicity of the two-source theory, to which undoubtedly it owes its success, begs the complexity of the synoptic fact. It is oversimplification. Perhaps the day is gone in which one could ask for a scheme comprising and explaining the multiplicity and diversity of the first three gospels. The existence of an oral tradition that was still extant when the first gospels were penned must not be forgotten: this also shaped the written tradition, which however was more complex than the two sources Mark and Q, and came before the first three gospels.

Some authors speak of a multiple document, that is of numerous collections of gospel traditions from which, through different channels, our gospels depend. One must resist the temptation to reduce all material to a universal scheme that explains everything, nor take refuge in an imprecise and comfortable "multiple document." What is being attempted is a more precise determination of the relationships that exist between the recensions of the individual episodes proposed by the different evangelists, without hurrying to universal conclusions that are not warranted by the evidence.

Syntyche (sin′-ti-ki), A woman of the church of Philippi. Paul greets her and exhorts her to make up her differences with Evodia (Phil. 4:2).

Syracuse, A city and seaport on the east coast of Sicily. The ship taking Paul to Rome stopped there for three days (Acts 28:12).

Syria, For the Old Testament *see* ARAMAEANS and SELEUCIDS. The region of Syria, in the strict sense of the term, lay between Asia Minor and the Euphrates, bordered on the south by Palestine, and on the west by the Mediterranean. It became a Roman province in 64 B.C., and was the capital and residence of the Roman legate in Antioch. The Roman prefects and later procurators in Palestine depended on the Syrian legate. Ancient historians distinguished Upper Syria, which comprised the northern regions as far as Lebanon, and Lower Syria, or Coelesyria, that is, the districts between Lebanon and Anti-Lebanon. According to Luke 2:2 Quirinius was legate of Syria when the census took place which accounted for Jesus being born in Bethlehem. (*See* CENSUS.) The Christian church soon spread through Syria. (*See* ANTIOCH.) The decree of the Apostolic Council of Jerusalem was also addressed to the churches of Syria (Acts 15:23, 41).

Syriac Versions of the Holy Scriptures, Syriac is a semitic language derived from classical Aramaic. It has two principal dialects, one eastern and the other western. Christianity spread through Syria from the first century, and the translations of the sacred books into that language are among the oldest made.

Old Testament: the official version of the Syrian Bible used by the Christians is the so-called Peshitta (or Peshitto, depending on the dialect). Peshitta means "simple," but it is not known why the word was applied to the version—perhaps it meant the popular, common, simple Bible to distinguish it from the complex Hexapla of Origen or the Targum paraphrases. It was made in the second, or perhaps even in the first century A.D. The most common opinion is that the version was made from the Hebrew text, but some believe, on good indications, that the Peshitto is the Syrian version of a Palestinian Targum, emended by frequent paraphrases in accordance with the Hebrew Text. In the fifth and sixth centuries a new version of the Old Testament was made from the Septuagint Greek on the orders of Philoxenus, bishop of Mabbug (485-532 A.D.). In the seventh century Paul of Tella made a new translation from the Greek text contained in Origen's Hexapla.

New Testament: The oldest versions of the New Testament have come down only in fragments. The first of these was found in 1842 by William Cureton in the monastery of Santa Maria Deipara in Nitria, Egypt. The second was found by Mrs. Agnes Smith Lewis in the monastery of St. Catherine on Mt. Sinai. The first is called the Syro-Curetonian version, the second the Syro-Sinaitic version. Both versions are very near the western type of Mss. D. *See* TEXT, NEW TESTAMENT.

The Peshitta version of the New Testament probably dates from the fourth century, before the Nestorian and monophysite schism, seeing that both these churches accept it. The text is Antiochian in type.

A particular type of translation is found in the Diatessaron of Tatian, which is a harmony or fusion of the four gospels in one continuous account. It was almost certainly composed in Greek, but immediately translated into Syrian. It is conserved in an Arabic version with a commentary by St. Ephraem of Syria.

Syrophoenician, Mark 6:24-30 tells of a visit of Jesus to Tyre during which a Syrophoenician woman begged him to chase the devil from her daughter. While the apostles were displeased at her vociferous insistence Christ was delighted with her, praised her faith and granted her request (*see* Matt. 15:21-28). Matthew calls her a Canaanite, the ancient name for the semite people who occupied the strip of land along the Mediterranean known to Greeks as Phoenicians. In New Testament times Tyre and Sidon belonged to the Roman province of Syria, hence the appellation Syrophoenician.

Syrtis (sur′-tis), Syrtis Major, a gulf on the north coast of Africa west of Cyrenaica. It is mentioned in the account of Paul's journey to Rome in Acts 27:17.

T

Taanach (tay′-a-nak), A city of Canaan that was conquered by Joshua according to Joshua 12:17, but nevertheless still belonged to Canaan throughout the period of the judges, according to Judges 1:27. It was situated in the land of Manasseh (Josh. 17:11) and was made a Levite city (Josh. 21:25). It was built on the site of the modern Tell-Taannek on the southern limit of the plain of Jezreel on the road that goes from central Palestine to the plain, through the mountains of Carmel. For this reason it was of great strategic importance. In the territorial organization of Solomon, Taanach was included in the fifth district (1 Kgs. 4:12). Egyptian sources speak of an occupation of Taanach by the Pharaoh Shishak during his expedition into Palestine after Solomon's death (1 Kgs. 14:25).

Taanath-shiloh (tay′-a-nath-shy′-lo), A village in Ephraim (Josh. 16:6).

Tabbath, A place in Transjordan to which Gideon went in his pursuit of the Midianites who had invaded Palestine, and whom he had routed in a surprise attack (Jgs. 7:19-22).

Tabeel (tab′-e-el), 1. The son of Tabeel was the person chosen by Pekah son of Remaliah, king of Israel (737-732 B.C.) and by Rezin of Damascus to occupy the throne of Judah in place of Ahaz (735-715 B.C.) according to Isaiah 7:5. Pekah and Rezin had invaded Judah to oblige Ahaz to enter into an alliance with them against Tiglath-pileser III, or, if they failed to do that, to depose him and put on the throne a person more in tune with their anti-Assyrian policy. Ahaz made himself a vassal to Tiglath-pileser and asked his help against the invaders (2 Kgs. 16:5-10).

2. An Aramaean resident in Samaria and an official of the Persian administration who wrote to the Persian king Artaxerxes I in an attempt to block the reconstruction of the walls of Jerusalem (Ezra 4:7).

Taberah (tab′-e-rah), An encampment on the journey of the Israelites through the desert. The people began to murmur, upon which Yahweh's anger blazed, and the fire of Yahweh burned among them and it destroyed one end of the camp (Num. 11:1-3). At Moses' intercession however Yahweh was appeased. The episode is deduced from an approximative etymology of the name of the place which is interpreted in the sense of burning (*see* Num. 11:3; Deut. 9:22).

Tabernacle, Tabernacle is the usual translation of the terms used in the Bible to designate the sanctuary of the Israelites during the journey through the desert. The Old Testament uses two terms: **'ohel mo'ed,** which means the "Tent of Meeting" between God and Israel, and **mishkan** which means dwelling.

The Tabernacle is minutely described in the Priestly source of the Pentateuch. The description is found twice there: first in the instructions that God gave to Moses for its construction (Ex. 25-31) and then in the account of the faithful implementation of God's instructions (Ex. 35-39). In c. 40 is narrated the solemn dedication of the Tabernacle and the descent of God's glory on it in the form of a splendid cloud, which filled it, to show that God was taking possession of it as his habitation.

The description of the Tabernacle in these chapters does not draw on precise and contemporaneous traditions of the events. It amounts to a "mobile" version of Solomon's Temple. It comprises two rooms divided by a veil. In the first is the seven branched candlestick and the table of the breads of the presence, while the Ark resides in the second. The altar is situated in front of the door. All around the altar, leaving however an ample court, is to be placed a fence or rail separating it from the people.

The Pentateuch contains other more ancient traditions on the Tent. These tell us nothing of its appearance but do describe its function. The Tent seems to have been above all the place where Moses consulted God and spoke with him, and where any Israelite could consult God through Moses (Ex. 33:7-11). The divine presence was visibly experienced through a cloud that blocked the door of the Tent (Num. 12:4-10).

It is then evident that the Priestly tradition has conserved faithfully the information about a tent-sanctuary which dated from Israel's nomadic period, but it conceived of it in terms of a collapsible Temple of Solomon. When however it is reduced to more modest dimensions this tent is seen to be akin to the religious usages of modern and ancient nomadic Arabs. They too had in their encampments a small tent or palanquin in which were kept the idols and sacred objects of the tribe and where oracles were sought.

The Tent of Meeting was set up at Shiloh in the time of Joshua (Josh. 18:1; 19:51) and later, under David and Solomon, at Gibeon (1 Chron. 16:39; 21:29; 2 Chron. 1:3-6). These data however are suspect and seen born of the desire to link up Solomon's Temple with the Tent of the desert. It is certain that the Ark at Shiloh was in a building (1 Sam. 1:7, 9; 2: 22; 3:15). On the other hand, when David brought the Ark to Jerusalem, he erected a tent to receive it (2 Sam. 6:17) as was the ancient custom (2 Sam. 7:6). This was not however the Tent of the desert.

According to a legendary tradition recorded in 2 Maccabees 2:4-8, before the siege of Jerusalem by Nebuchadnezzar, Jeremiah the prophet hid the tent, the Ark and the altar of incense in a cave on Mt. Nebo; the place was to remain unknown "until God gathers his people together again and shows them mercy."

In Hebrews 9:1-5 is read a description of the Tabernacle in the context of the rite of the Great Day of Expiation, which was a type of the expiation carried out by Jesus. Jesus however did not offer his expiation in this tabernacle but in a much greater and more perfect one that was not made by human hands, that is, in the very dwelling of God in the heavens (9:11). The function of the Tabernacle as the seat of God's presence is again recorded in Revelation 21:3 where the new Jerusalem is spoken of, where God will dwell with the just. (*See* also Rev. 15:5.) *See* ARK OF THE COVENANT.

Tabernacles, Feast of, Tabernacles is the conventional translation of the Latin **tabernacula**, the Hebrew **sukkot**, the name by which is designated the feast in the religious calendars of Deuteronomy 16:13-15 and Leviticus 23:34 (*see* Ezra 3:4; Zech. 14:16, 18). The word **sukkot** means huts or booths, and it refers to the huts built with branches in which the people lived during the feast. Exodus 23:16 and 34:22 has the most ancient mention of the feast. There it is called the harvest festival, and it was to be celebrated at the year's end when from the field were gathered the fruits of one's labors (Ex. 23:16).

At its beginning the feast certainly had an agrarian character: it celebrated the end of the year and the harvest. Deuteronomy 16:13-15 repeats the prescriptions of Exodus 23:16 and insists on the joy of the feast which was to be marked with merrymaking and thanksgiving. The feast was to be celebrated at Jerusalem and to last seven days. Leviticus 23:33-43 specifies with precision the date: the fifteenth day of the seventh month (September-October), to last seven days, with yet another added. Numbers 29:12-38 specifies the sacrifices that should be offered on the different days of the feast. Leviticus 23:40-41 adds what was a characteristic of the Feast of Tabernacles, namely the processions with palms and fruits (*see* 2 Mac. 10:6-8).

While this feast kept its fundamentally agrarian character it was very soon associated, like the feasts of the Pasch and Pentecost, with the celebration of the mystery of salvation. Now this element, though it is present, is not easy to identify with precision. Leviticus 23:42, 43 prescribes: "For seven days you are to live in huts so that your descendants may know that I made the sons of Israel live in huts when I brought them out of the land of Egypt. I am the Lord your God." The Israelites, however, lived not in huts but in tents when they journeyed through the desert. It is clear then that we have here a secondary interpretation of something that had quite a different origin and meaning: the farmers were wont to build huts or shelters made of branches in the vineyards and fields in which to collect the harvest. There is, then, a vacuum that no explicit text succeeds in filling.

For this reason an attempt was made to try another road. First of all it was thought that since the feast ended and began the year, it had the same meaning and function as the Feast of the New Year in the neighboring Middle Eastern civilizations. The Feast of Tabernacles would then be the feast of the enthronement of Yahweh, impersonated by the figure of the king, after the model of the feast of Akitu in Babylon. On the difficulties of this theory *see* NEW YEAR.

Other scholars, with more reason, and without minimizing the importance of the coincidence of the feast with the beginning of the year, try to find in the feast something more specifically Israelite. The following are the two attempts that enjoy the greatest probability, and they are not exclusive of one another.

Deuteronomy 31:10 ff. prescribes the reading of the law every seven years, to take place during the Feast of Tabernacles. On the other hand Deuteronomy on the whole, and particularly some of its parts such as 27:11-26 ring with a liturgical sound. This leads one to think that they are elements taken from a periodic celebration centered around the commemoration of the covenant and the proclamation of the law. Some of the psalms point in the same direction (Ps. 81:50). It should be kept in mind that the proclamation of the law through Ezra took place during the Feast of Tabernacles (Neh. 8).

Basing themselves on these elements some scholars feel warranted in supposing that the Feast of Tabernacles was already in premonarchic times a celebration of the covenant that took place in the central sanctuary of the amphictyony or tribal league. The rite of this feast can be gathered from the texts already cited, and from Exodus 19-24 which is obviously not an account of the Sinai events but depends on a liturgical celebration of those events. Other authors however direct their attention to different elements, namely, the solemn dedication of the Temple described in 1 Kings 8, which took place during the Feast of Tabernacles. This account, like that of the transferral of the Ark to Jerusalem (2 Sam. 6), would describe the ritual of a periodic commemoration of the events rather than the events themselves. What the Bible describes, then, would be the rite, which however in turn would serve to hand down the memory of the event itself. In this opinion, then, the Feast of Tabernacles would be the framework in which was commemorated God's choice of Sion for his habitation and the election of the dynasty of David (2 Sam. 7) which is intimately connected with the transferral of the Ark to Jerusalem.

On this occasion a solemn procession with the Ark would be repeated annually, and at its entry would be proclaimed the kingship of God over Israel and the world (*see* Psalms of the kingdom of God: Pss. 46; 93-98; Zech. 14:15-19), together with the election of David and his line. Indications of this rite are in fact found in Psalms 24 and 132.

Obviously this feast had meaning only in Judah and Jerusalem, where alone these traditions were alive. It is for this reason that it was earlier remarked that the two theories do not exclude one another, but represent the differing forms the same feast took on in different environments. In the northern kingdom where the monarchy was not fully integrated into the theocracy (*see* KING), the religious traditions of the premonarchic amphictyony remained active with their center in the periodically renewed alliance with God celebrated at the tribal league's central sanctuary. In Judah and Jerusalem, however, the choice by God of David's dynasty and of the city of Sion constituted the beginning of a religious and theological tradition that was also commemorated in the Feast of Tabernacles.

The Feast of Tabernacles is also the backdrop of one of the most significant episodes of John's gospel (cc. 7 and 8; *see* 7:1-10, 14, 37). John is not merely referring to a chronological date but he is painting the backdrop against which must be understood some of Jesus' declarations. Jesus cries: "I am the light of the world" in a liturgical situation in which the Temple was illuminated as part of the Feast. In the rite, water was taken from the spring of Gihon and taken in procession to the Temple where it was poured at the foot of the altar. Against this can be appreciated Jesus' words on the last and greatest day of the festival: "If anyone thirsts, let him come to me; let him drink." And John adds: Scripture has it "From within him rivers of living water shall flow" (Jn. 7:37-39). These words quote Ezekiel 41:1 ff., Zechariah 13:1 and 14:8. They are drawn from the Jewish tradition to justify the rite of the waters and are given, beside the immediate sense of prayer for rain to ensure growth, a more specifically religious interpretation. They are interpreted as referring to the Holy Spirit. Jesus in 7:37, 38 proclaims himself as the only person through whom the gift of the Spirit can be received.

Tabitha, *See* DORCAS.

table

make a *t.* of acacia	Ex. 25:23 He put the *t.* in	Ex. 40:22
poles to carry the *t.*	Ex. 25:27 come to the king's *t.*	1 Sam. 20:29

Table of Nations, This is the name given to the genealogy of the sons of Noah in Genesis 10. (*See* 1 Chron. 1:4-24.) The chapter belongs to the Priestly document, and its intent is to show how the new command to "increase and multiply" was carried out by Noah and his sons, who had survived the deluge. They then became the fathers of the post-diluvian people of the earth. The chapter sets out to show the power of the divine blessing that was given them in order to put the command into practice. The chapter also sets out the author's convictions concerning the origins of humanity and its relationships as creature to the one true God, Yahweh.

The author follows a genealogical schema, but it is clear that here it is not a question of individuals but of peoples and geographical regions. (*See* GENEALOGY.) The whole of humanity coheres in a common ancestry through the three sons of Noah—Shem, Ham and Japheth. Peoples are grouped in common lines of descent, not with ethnographic and linguistic criteria, but through geographical and historical vicinity to one another. Nearness to one another, then, and historical relationships with one another are translated into terms of descent. While the lines are not clearly drawn, in general terms the division of peoples is into Semites, descendants of Shem, Indo-Europeans from Japheth and African or Hamites from Ham. The children of Japheth, the Indo-Europeans, occupy Asia Minor and the islands of the Mediterranean, while the Hamites possess the southern regions: Egypt, Ethiopia, Arabia. In between are the children of Shem, from Palestine to Babylon and Elam. One can see the remains of a Yahwistic Table of Nations in Gen. 10:18, 19, 21, 24-30.

This document represents the geographic and ethnic knowledge that might exist in Palestine around the time of Solomon's reign. In fact the division of peoples that is there described reaches back into about the end of the second millenium.

tablet, tablets
take a clay *t*.   Ezek. 4:1   not on *t*. of stone   2 Cor. 3:3

Tabor (tay′-bor), 1. A Levitical city in the land of Zebulun (1 Chron. 6:62).

2. A mountain on the northeast extremity of the plain of Jezreel, today Jebel-et-Tor. It is 1850 feet high, and rises in isolation from the plain. On Tabor camped the Jews who accompanied Barak in his struggle against Jabin king of Hazor and his general Sisera (Jgs. 4:6, 12, 14) and there too Gideon's brothers were slain by the Midianites (Jgs. 8:18). Tabor is recorded in poetic texts together with Carmel (Jer. 46:18) and Hermon (Ps. 89:13). Tradition has placed the Transfiguration of Jesus on this mountain, but there are no proofs to sustain the opinion (*see* Mk. 9:2-8; Matt. 17:1-8; Lk. 9:28-36 — "a high mountain," but nameless). The gospel context would rather suggest Hermon. *See* TRANSFIGURATION.

3. A village in Benjamin near Bethel, mentioned in the story of Saul's election as king of Israel (1 Sam. 10:3). Its terebinth (large shade tree) was a landmark.

Tabrimmon, The father of Ben-hadad I, the Aramaean king of Damascus, a contemporary of Asa of Judah (913-873 B.C.; *see* 1 Kgs. 15:18). *See* ASA.

Tadmor, According to 2 Chronicles 8:4 Solomon rebuilt the city of Tadmor in the desert. Tadmor is without doubt the famous city of Palmyra of the Hellenistic and Roman age, a commercial and caravan center in the desert of Syria. This information in the Bible is probably legendary. The Chronicler, according to many scholars, has identified without justification the city of Tamar, of which the parallel text in 1 Kings 9:18 speaks, with the more celebrated Tadmor-Palmyra.

Tahan (tay′-han), A son of Ephraim (Num. 26:35).

Tahash (tay′-ash), The third son of Nahor, brother of Abraham (Gen. 22:24), born from his concubine Reumah. *See* REUMAH.

Tahath (tay′-hath), 1. An encampment of the Israelites on their journey through the desert to Canaan (Num. 33:26-27).

2. The name of several people who are recorded in the genealogies of Ephraim (1 Chron. 7:20) and of Levi (1 Chron. 6:24).

Tahpanhes (tah′-pa-neez), A city of Egypt in the eastern region of the Nile delta (Jer. 2:16; Ezek. 30:18), today called Tell Dafna. Some of the Jews who fled before the onslaught of Nebuchadnezzar settled there, bringing with them the prophet Jeremiah (Jer. 43:5-7). At Tahpanhes

Jeremiah received an order from the Lord to perform a symbolic action: he was to take some large stones and bury them in the presence of the men of Judah in the cement of the square in front of Pharaoh's palace in Tahpanhes. This was a prediction, as God's word through Jeremiah explained, of the imminent invasion by Nebuchadnezzar of Egypt (Jer. 43:8-13).

Tahpenes (tah′-pe-neez), The queen of Egypt, wife of the Pharaoh who gave asylum to Hadad of Edom who escaped the slaughter of the Edomites carried out by Joab, David's general. The Pharaoh gave to Hadad as wife a sister of Queen Taphenes. Hadad returned to Edom after the death of David and rebelled against Solomon (1 Kgs. 11:14-22).

tail

take hold of its *t*.	Ex. 4:4	He carries his *t*.	Job 40:17
not the *t*.	Deut. 28:13	to do for head or *t*.	Isa. 19:15

take

T. your son Isaac,	Gen. 22:2	*T*. my yoke	Matt. 11:29
t. our vengeance	Jer. 20:10	to *t*. it up again	Jn. 10:17

talent, *See* WEIGHTS AND MEASURES.

Use a *t*. of pure gold	Ex. 25:39	A *t*. of pure gold	Ex. 37:24
	It weighed a *t*.	2 Sam. 12:30	

Talitha koum (tal′-i-tha koom), An Aramaic expression, translated by Mark as "little girl, get up"; it was used by Jesus when he raised to life Jairus's daughter (Mk. 5:41).

Talmai (tal′-my), 1. Son of Anak, a resident of Hebron (Num. 13:22), defeated with his two brothers by Caleb who captured the city (Josh. 15:14; Jgs. 1:10).

2. King of Geshur, whose daughter Maacah was one of David's wives and mother of Absalom (2 Sam. 3:3; 13:37; 1 Chron. 3:2).

Talmon, Head of a Levitical family (1 Chron. 9:17; Ezra 2:42; Neh. 7:45; 12:25).

Talmud, In Hebrew Talmud means study, and the name covers the whole rabbinical literature that developed as a commentary to the **Mishna.** Mishna means "repetition," "(oral) tradition" or "study," and it is the name given to a collection of oral traditions stemming from the most ancient doctors of Judaism. This collection was made during the third century A.D. by Judah ha-Nasi. This compilation is marked with a definite juridic bent (*see* HALAKHA), and it is a compendium of the so-called oral tradition or law, of which there is mention in the gospels. (*See* e.g. Mk. 7:5.) The Mishna is divided into "orders" called **seder,** and these are subdivided into tracts (**masseket**) which together come to sixty-three. Strictly speaking the Talmud is a commentary on the Mishna. It is a compilation of discussions and opinions expressed by generations of rabbis, called **amoraim,** that is, interpreters.

There are two **Talmuds,** one Palestinian and the other Babylonian. These were confected by the rabbinical schools, respectively of Palestine (Jamnia) and Babylon (Sura and Pumbedita). The first dates from the fifth century and is not a complete commentary: it contains only 39 of the 63 tracts. The Babylonian Talmud was finished around 500 A.D. but in the following two centuries new material was added by another generation of doctors called **Saboraim** or "thinkers."

The Mishna is written in a Hebrew somewhat different from that of the Old Testament. The Talmud is in Aramaic and in the Palestinian and Babylonian dialects.

Tamar (tay′-mar), 1. The wife of Er the son of Judah. On Er's death Onan his brother was bound to marry his widow in keeping with the levirate law. (*See* LEVIRATE.) He refused however to procreate an offspring in the name of his dead brother. For this reason God struck him dead. (*See* ONAN.) Judah refused Tamar his third son Shelah. Tamar thereupon disguised herself as a prostitute and awaited Judah at the point where the road to Timnah branches off from the road to Enaim. Judah had intercourse with her from which she conceived. When later she was denounced as a prostitute Judah ordered her to be buried alive, but she then showed him the cord and stick she had taken from him as a pledge at the time of intercourse. He acknowledged then that he was more guilty than she in not giving his son Shelah to be her husband, in keeping with the levirate law. From her relationship with Judah were born twins, Perez and Zerah (Gen. 38). Tamar's name is mentioned in the genealogy of Jesus in Matthew 1:3.

2. Daughter of David and Maacah (2 Sam. 13:1; 1 Chron. 3:9). David's son by Ahinoam, Amnon, fell in love with her, and by a ruse had her bring food to his room while he feigned sickness. When he got her in, he raped her despite her protests. David was angry but did not wish to harm his own son, his first-born (2 Sam. 13:21). Tamar's full brother Absalom, however, invited him to a banquet and there murdered him (2 Sam. 13:2-29).

3. Absalom's daughter. The Bible remarks: "[she] was a beautiful woman" (2 Sam. 14:27).

4. A borderland town in the southern wilderness, rebuilt and fortified by Solomon (1 Kgs. 9:18; Ezek. 47:19; 48:28). In the parallel text (2 Chron. 8:4) it is confused with Tadmor, that is, the famed city of Palmyra. *See* TADMOR.

tambourine, tambourines

the sound of *t.* and harps   Aaron's sister, took a *t.*   Ex. 15:20
                                 Gen. 31:27   dancing with *t.*   1 Sam. 18:6

Tammuz (tam′-uz, or tah′-mooz), A Mesopotamian deity of Sumerian origin. This god belongs to the vegetation deities whose alternating rhythms represent the myth of the death and resurrection of the god. Ezekiel 8:14 alludes to rites of lamentation which formed part of the cult of the god that was celebrated at Jerusalem.

Tanach, *See* TAANACH.

Tanhumeth (tan-hue′-meth), Father of Seraiah, one of the army chiefs of the Judean army who joined Gedaliah in Mizpah and who was named by Nebuchadnezzar governor of Judah (2 Kgs. 25:23; Jer. 40:8).

Tanis (tay′-nis), A city of Egypt in the eastern region of the Nile delta, also called Zoan (Isa. 19:11-13; 30:4; Ezek. 30:14). It was founded seven years before Hebron (Num. 13:22) and was the capital of the Hyksos kings with the name Avaris. It was rebuilt by Ramses II (1301-1234 B.C.) who made it his residence with the name of Pi-Ramses. Before the Exodus the Israelites took part in these works (Ex. 1; Ps. 78:12, 14). It afterwards got the name of Tanis, and was the residence of the Pharaohs of the 21st to the 23rd dynasties (1085-715 B.C.).

Taphath (tay′-fath), Daughter to Solomon and wife of Ben-Abinadab, an official of the king (1 Kgs. 4:11).

Tappuah (tap′-you-ah), 1. The son of Hebron in the genealogy of Caleb (1 Chron. 2:43).

2. A city of Judah (Josh. 15:34), today Beit-Nettif, west of Bethlehem.

3. A city of Ephraim (Josh. 16:8) on the border with Manasseh (Josh. 17:8). It was first Canaanean and then conquered by Joshua (Josh. 12:17). Menahem king of Israel (745-738 B.C.) punished the city by killing all its citizens and devastating the entire territory but it did not wish to submit to him (2 Kgs. 15:16). The Hebrew text reads Tiphsa, which all the scholars correct with the Septuagint to Tappuah. It is to be identified with today's Sheikh Abu Zared, south of Shechem. The city of Tephon which was fortified by Bacchides should be identified with Tappuah 2 or 3 (1 Mac. 9:50).

Taralah (tar′-a-lah), A town of Benjamin north of Jerusalem (Josh. 18:27).

Targum, An Aramaic word which means "translation" and is reserved for the Aramaic translations of the Old Testament. These translations became necessary for, after the Exile, Hebrew was little by little abandoned as a spoken language and its place taken among the people by Aramaic, so that the sacred books were no longer understood in their original tongue. In the synagogue readings of Scripture, each verse, once it was read in Hebrew, was then rendered in Aramaic. At the beginning, these translations were more or less improvised, but as time passed a true tradition was formed and consigned to writing in the Targum that today we possess. These Targumim did not rest satisfied with a faithful translation but aimed at making the text really intelligible to the listeners. So often the translation becomes paraphrase, or clarifications are inserted or interpretative traditions are gathered here. For this reason the study of the Targumim is very important for the Bible, as they give access to the most common interpretation of the Bible at the time of the New Testament, and not just the interpretation of some particular sect. Even though they were consigned to writing in the centuries after Christ, they contain an interpretation and translation that is contemporary with him, and even ante-dates the Christian era.

Targumim have been preserved for all the proto-canonical books of the Old Testament with the exception of Ezra, Nehemiah and Daniel. The principal Targumim of the Pentateuch are the following:

1. The Targum Onqelos of the Pentateuch, originating in Palestine, received its definitive form in Babylon. It is more literal. Onqelos is a corruption of Aquila, a translator of the Old Testament into Greek; he is not however the author of the Targum.

2. Targum Palestinense I or Pseudo-Jonathan. It is paraphrastic.

3. Targum Palestinense II or the Fragmentary Palestinian Targum. They are the fragments of another Targum tradition coming from Palestine.

4. Targum Neofiti so called because it was found in the manuscript **Neofiti I** of the Vatican Library in 1956. It is a complete Palestinian Targum.

There is also a Targum to the prophets of Jonathan ben Uzziel. Jonathan is not the author; this Targum is a Hebrew transcription of Theodotion, another translator of the Old Testament into Greek. This comes from Babylon.

There also exists an Aramaic Targum of the Samaritan Pentateuch.

Tarshish, 1. A son of Bilhan of the tribe of Benjamin (1 Chron. 7:10).

2. A prince at the court of Ahasuerus (Xerxes) (Esth. 1:14).

3. In the Table of Nations he is son of Javan and a descendant of Japheth (Gen. 10:4; 1 Chron. 1:7). It is a geographic designation which probably means refinery, and therefore applies to a mining center of importance. The more probable attempts at identification of his tribe find the ancient Tarshish at the later Greek colony on the Atlantic coast in southwest Spain near Gibraltar, or the Phoenician colonies of Sardegna. Tarshish maintained very important commercial relationships with the Phoenicians of Tyre (Isa. 23:10; Ezek. 27:12). It was a very important metal-producing center (Jer. 10:9; Ezek. 27:12). The ships of Tarshish were a particular type of ship, perhaps larger and stronger to make the long journey to and from Tarshish, or adapted to commerce in metal. Solomon had ships of this type made in the Red Sea in order to carry on commerce with Ophir (1 Kgs. 10:22). Jehoshaphat (873-849 B.C.) built a Tarshish ship to go to Ophir for gold but it never got there; it was wrecked at Ezion-geber (1 Kgs. 22:49). Jonah embarked on a ship bound for Tarshish (Jonah 1:3; 4:2). Often Tarshish simply expresses some distant idealized place (Ps. 72:10 e.g.) such as one today might refer to "the islands."

Tarsus, A city in Cilicia in the southeastern corner of Asia Minor. The city is situated on the river Cydnus, 20 miles from the Mediterranean coast. During the Roman epoch it was the capital of the Roman province of Cilicia (67 B.C.) and an important cultural center, for here converged Hellenistic and oriental civilizations. Paul was born at Tarsus, which he boasts is no mean city (Acts 21:39), during the first years of the first century. After his conversion and first journey to Jerusalem, where he was badly received by a section of the Christian community, Paul returned to his own city of Tarsus (Acts 9:30). Barnabas went to Tarsus to fetch him to Antioch to share in his apostolic work of evangelization amongst the Gentiles (Acts 11:25). Whether he made further visits to Tarsus is not recorded.

Tartak, A divinity venerated by the Avvites, one of the peoples settled in Samaria after the deportation of the Israelite population (722 B.C.; 2 Kgs. 17:31).

Tartan, An official of the Assyrian army, commander-in-chief of one of its divisions (2 Kgs. 18:17; Isa. 20:1).

Tassel, According to the law of Deuteronomy 22:12 the Jews were to make tassels for the four corners of the cloak in which they wrapped themselves. These were originally intended in an apotropaic sense, but are interpreted in Numbers 15:38-39 as reminders of all the commandments the Lord has given so that they might be put into practice.

taste

| or cannot my *t*. | Job 6:30 | *T.* and see | Ps. 34:9 |

tasted

| which *t*. like cakes | Num. 11:8 | which he *t*. but | Matt. 27:34 |
| the people *t*. food | 1 Sam. 14:24 | The waiter in charge *t*. | Jn. 2:9 |

Tattenai (tat´-e-nie), The name of the satrap of the "province beyond the river," Transeuphrates, belonging to the Persian empire of King Darius Hystaspes. When the Jews after the return from exile began to reconstruct the Temple, Tattenai asked them on what authority they were doing it. He also notified King Darius of what was happening. Darius ordered a search to be made in the royal archives. This brought to light Cyrus' edict authorizing the Jews to repatriate and to rebuild the Temple. Darius ratified the decree and ordered Tattenai to allot state funds for the continuation of the work, and to make other gifts for the cult and sacrifices of the new Temple (Ezra 5:3-6:13).

tattoo
do not *t.* yourselves   Lev. 19:28

taught
and he *t.* it   Deut. 31:22   *t.* by the Lord   Isa. 54:13
you have *t.* me   Ps. 71:17   he *t.* with authority   Matt. 7:29
Who *t.* him the path   Isa. 40:14   because he *t.*   Mk. 1:22

taunt
a fool's *t.*   Ps. 39:9   take up this *t.*-song   Isa. 14:4
a *t.* and a curse   Jer. 24:9

Taw, The 22nd letter of the Hebrew alphabet (t).

tax
the *t.* which Moses,   2 Chron. 24:9   the temple *t.* approached
t. collectors do   Matt. 5:46   Matt. 17:24
take *t.* or toll   Matt. 17:25

Tax Collector, *See* PUBLICAN.

teach
t. the Israelites   Lev. 10:11   Lord, *t.* us to pray   Lk. 11:1
T. it to the Israelites   Deut. 31:19   The Holy Spirit will *t.*   Lk. 12:12

teacher
No pupil outranks his *t.*   (means *T.*), where do you   Jn. 1:38
          Matt. 10:24   a *t.* come from God   Jn. 3:2
t. of the nations   1 Tim. 2:7

tear
T. down their altars   Ex. 34:13   I will *t.* them   Ezek. 13:20
t. their hearts   Hos. 13:8

Tebah (tee′-bah), Son of Nahor, Abraham's brother, by his concubine Reumah, whose other children were Gaham, Tahash and Maacah (Gen. 22:24).

Tebeth (tee′-beth), The tenth month of the year in the Hebrew calendar (*see* MONTH), and corresponding to our December-January.

Tekel (tee′-kel or tek′-el), One of the three words that Belshazzar king of Babylon saw being written by human fingers on the plaster of the wall behind the lampstand at the banquet he had given for his noblemen. This was a sacrilegious banquet, for they quaffed wine from the sacred vessels of the Temple. On seeing the writing the king grew pale and called for his enchanters, Chaldaeans and wizards, but they were unable to read what was written. Daniel was then called and interpreted the three words for the king: "Mene, God has numbered your kingdom and put an end to it; Tekel, you have been weighed on the scales and found wanting; Peres, your kingdom has been divided and given to the Medes and the Persians" (Dan. 5).

Tekoa (te-ko′-a), A city of Judah (1 Chron. 2:24; 4:5) fortified by Rehoboam (2 Chron. 11:6). It was the birthplace of the prophet Amos (Amos 1:1) and of one of the Thirty warriors of David, Ira son of Ikkesh (2 Sam. 23:26). It was also the birthplace of the woman chosen by Joab to persuade David to forgive Absalom and be reconciled with him after he had killed Amnon over the rape of his sister Tamar (2 Sam. 14:2). Today it is Khirbeth Teqoa, south of Bethlehem.

Tel-abib, A colony of exiled Jews in Babylon, beside the river Chebar, where the prophet Ezekiel came after the vision of the scroll and where he stayed for seven days like a man stunned (Ezek. 3:15).

Telaim (te-lay′-im), A city of Judah (Josh. 15:24) where Saul camped in his military campaign against the Amalekites. There he reviewed his army, which amounted to two hundred thousand foot soldiers and ten thousand men of Judah (1 Sam. 15:4).

Telassar, An Aramaean city of northern Mesopotamia conquered by the Assyrians before the campaign of Sennacherib against Jerusalem (2 Kgs. 19:12; Isa. 37:12).

Tell, A mound artificially created, at least in part, by the remains of a succession of towns or cities built on the same site. For defense purposes it was customary to build on a hill, but if the town was abandoned as a result of war or natural disaster the abandoned and often ruined buildings eventually served to create an even bigger hill. The natural advantages of the site (easy defense, a water supply, a trade route) would dictate the reuse of the old location. An unoccupied tell looks like a truncated cone, with its sides smoothed by rain and weather, so that it is easily recognizable.

tell

Do not *t.* anyone	Matt. 17:9	*T.* us, when will	Matt. 24:3
T. the daughter	Matt. 21:5	he will *t.*	Jn. 4:25

Tell el-Amarna, A site in Egypt 200 miles south of Cairo on the eastern bank of the Nile where the ancient city of Akhetaton stood. Akhetaton was the capital of Egypt during the reign of the Pharaoh Amenophis IV (Akhen-Aton) of the Eighteenth dynasty (1377-1358 B.C.). In the ruins at Tell el-Amarna have been found numerous letters from the diplomatic correspondence between the Pharaohs Amenophis III and Amenophis IV and the Assyrian kings, and Syrian and Palestinian vassals. They are written in the Akkadic tongue which was the **lingua franca** of the epoch. These letters were discovered in 1887 and have thrown new light on the political and ethnic condition of Palestine in the second half of the 2nd millenium, about one and a half centuries before the Israelites began to move into it.

Tel-melah (tel-me′-lah), A colony of exiled Jews in Babylonia (Ezra 2:59; Neh. 7:61).

Tema (tee′-ma), Son of Ishmael (Gen. 25:15; 1 Chron. 1:30). Tema was also an Arab tribe in the desert which lived off caravan commerce (Job 6:19; Isa. 21:14).

Temah (tee′-mah), Ancestor of a family of temple servants (Ezra 2:53; Neh. 7:55).

Teman (tee′-man), Son of Eliphaz and a descendant of Esau (Gen. 36:11, 15, 42; 1 Chron. 1:36, 53). It is the name of a region in Edom (Amos 1:12; Ezek. 25:13; Hab. 3:3) which was celebrated for its wise men (Jer. 49:7). It was the birthplace of Eliphaz, one of Job's friends (Josh. 2:11).

tempest

With a *t.* he	Job 9:17	in a time of *t.*	Amos 1:14

Temple, The Jews had no temple for their God Yahweh until the time of King Solomon (960-922 B.C.). The question of a temple was not even posed until the time of David. He transferred the Ark of the Covenant to Jerusalem (2 Sam. 6) and made his city the religious center of Israel. He constructed a royal palace (2 Sam. 7:2), and only then did he think of building a "house" for Yahweh. This pious proposal, from the implementation of which Yahweh prevented him through the mouth of Nathan the prophet, was the occasion of the oracle of divine election of David's dynasty (2 Sam. 7; *see* MESSIANISM).

The Temple was to be built by his successor (2 Sam. 7:13). David had been impeded from building the Temple because he had spilled too much blood and waged great wars (1 Chron. 22:8-10). Nevertheless he took important steps towards building it: he gathered the materials and the necessary funds and left precise dispositions in regard to its construction, its furniture and even its personnel. This exaggeration is due to the particular concept of history that the Chronicler worked under. (*See* CHRONICLES, BOOKS OF THE.) 1 Kings 5:17-19 and 8:15-21 merely states that David was in fact prevented from getting on with the work by his many military campaigns.

The Temple was erected on the site of the threshing floor of Araunah the Jebusite, where David had had an altar built to commemorate the cessation of the plague that hit the people after the census ordered by David (1 Chron. 22:1; 2 Chron. 3:1; 2 Sam. 24:18-25). The threshing-floor was on the highest part of the hill of Ophel (*see* JERUSALEM) where later were constructed the post-exilic Temple and that of Herod, that is, on the site of the present-day Mosque of Omar.

Solomon asked the help of Hiram king of Tyre in the construction of the Temple. The latter provided the necessary materials and the specialized workmen. Labor was levied amongst the tribes of Israel (1 Kgs. 5). Preeminent among the specialized workmen was one Hiram, son of a widow of the tribe of Naphtali with a Tyrian father, a bronzeworker. To him was committed the metal work for the Temple (1 Kgs. 7:13-47).

The Temple was modelled on Syro-Phoenician temples. It was a stone structure with its interior walls panelled with finely carved cedar wood. Its form was rectangular. The door was in one of its lesser sides. On either side of the door was a large bronze pillar with a cast bronze capital. These were called by Hiram, their builder, Jakin and Boaz. *See* JAKIN and BOAZ.

Inside the Temple were three chambers of different dimensions. The first of these was the atrium or **Ulam,** ten cubits long and twenty wide. From this one passed into the great central chamber for worship, called **Hekal** or Holy Place, forty cubits long by twenty wide. The **Debir** or sanctuary, the Holy of Holies, was the innermost section, twenty cubits by twenty. On the raised floor of the **Debir** was placed the Ark of the Covenant under two large figures of cherubim with outspread wings, carved from olive wood (1 Kgs. 6:23-28; 8:6-7).

In the **Hekal** was the altar of incense (1 Kgs. 6:20-21; 7:48), the table for the breads of the presence and the ten lampstands, five at the right and five at the left in front of the **Debir** (1 Kgs. 7:48-49). In the courtyard in front of the Temple was the altar of holocausts or bronze altar (1 Kgs. 8:64; 9:25; 2 Kgs. 16:10), and the sea of bronze, a great basin containing water for the cult services, in particular for the ablutions of the priests (1 Kgs. 7:23-26) and ten other smaller basins erected on wheeled stands (1 Kgs. 7:27-39).

Around three sides of the Temple he built an annex attached to the outside walls of the **Debir** and **Hekal**: this served as storerooms (*see* 1 Kgs. 6:5-10).

The Temple was in a spacious courtyard, called the internal courtyard (1 Kgs. 6:36) to distinguish it from the great courtyard that embraced the Temple and the royal palace (1 Kgs. 7:8).

The building was begun in the fourth year of the reign of Solomon and completed in seven years. It was solemnly dedicated by Solomon during the Feast of Tabernacles (1 Kgs. 8:65). A minute account of this event can be read in 1 Kings 8.

Solomon's Temple was destroyed by the Babylonians under Nebuchadnezzar (587 B.C.; 2 Kgs. 25:8-17). Throughout its four centuries of history it underwent only minor alterations. It figured several times in the political and religious upheavals of the kingdom.

During the reign of Jehoshaphat (873-849 B.C.) a new courtyard was made (2 Chron. 20:5). Joash, the only surviving son of Ahaziah after the slaughter of the princes by Queen Athaliah, was hidden in the Temple, then proclaimed king, giving rise to the revolt that ended with the death of the queen (2 Kgs. 11). When Ahaz became vassal to Tiglath-pileser III he had the altar of holocausts removed and replaced by one that he had constructed after a model he had seen in Damascus (2 Kgs. 16:10-16). Vassalage brought with it repercussions on the religious level, for non-Yahwistic cults were introduced into the Temple, especially during the reign of Manasseh (2 Kgs. 21:4-7). The religious reforms of Hezekiah (2 Kgs. 18:4; 715-687 B.C.) and above all those of Josiah (640-609 B.C.; 2 Kgs. 23:4-12) aimed first of all at restoring the legitimate cult of Yahweh to its original purity.

The Temple was despoiled after Solomon's death, during the Pharaoh Shishak's invasion (1 Kgs. 14:26). While Amaziah was king of Judah (800-783 B.C.) it was plundered by Joash of Israel (2 Kgs. 14:14). Finally in the first conquest of the city by Nebuchadnezzar the Temple was again the object of plunder (597 B.C.; 2 Kgs. 24:13). After its destruction in 587 B.C. the Temple area remained desolate until the return from exile. Cyrus' decree that ordered repatriation also permitted the reconstruction of the Temple (Ezra 6:3-5). The first to return erected an altar (Ezra 3:2-6) and set to work (Ezra 5:16) but were soon blocked by the jealousy of the Samaritans (Ezra 4:1-5). Once it became clear that the Jews were legally authorized to construct their Temple the work started again and the Temple was completed in 515 B.C. There is nothing known of its shape and form, but it is more than probable that it was structured after the model of Solomon's Temple, though less splendid (*see* Hag. 2:3; Ezra 3:12-13). This was the Temple profaned by Antiochus IV Epiphanes in 167 B.C. (1 Mac. 1:48-49; 2 Mac. 6:1-6) but purified and again solemnly dedicated by Judas Maccabeus in 164 B.C. (1 Mac. 4:36-59). This is commemorated in the **Hannukah**, the Feast of the Dedication. *See* DEDICATION, FEAST OF.

In 19 B.C. Herod I the Great began a complete rebuilding of the Temple. The chief part of the work was completed in ten years, but the final touches were not completed until 64 A.D., that is, just a few years before the total destruction of the Temple during the first Judaic war (70 A.D.; *see* Jn. 2:20) Herod's building retained the same basic structure, but it was richly decorated both within and without with marbles and gold. It arose from the middle of a courtyard surrounded by structures and porches. This courtyard was divided into two unequal parts: the most easterly was the women's court, while the other smaller one, the court of Israel, was for men only. In this courtyard was an area completely surrounding the Temple reserved for the priests. Non-Jews were banned entry into this whole area under pain of death (Acts 21:28-30). Beyond these courts was a further area known as the atrium of the Gentiles, surrounded by porches and a colonnade (*see* Jn. 10:22; Acts 3:11; 5:12). From the northeast corner of the whole complex rose the fortress Antonia. *See* ANTONIA.

The Temple of Jerusalem, throughout its long and exciting history, was at the center of the religious life of Israel. The Temple was God's dwelling in the midst of his people. What this meant for the religious soul of Israel is excellently summed up in the prayer that is put on Solomon's lips at the solemn dedication (1 Kgs. 8:23-53). This presence of God is a sign of election and a pledge of salvation (Pss. 68:17; 132:13). This was borne out in an unexpectedly wonderful way during the siege by Sennacherib, which failed, during the reign of King Hezekiah (2 Kgs. 19; Isa. 37). It is probably over this event that Psalms 46, 48 and 76 break out into lyrics. A similar protection in critical times happened during the reign of Ahaz (Isa. 7; 2 Kgs. 16:5). On each occasion god revealed himself as his people's protector from Zion, who from his holy dwelling place brought about their salvation (Ps. 76:10).

Deuteronomy has in a special way emphasized the Temple as the habitation of the "Name of God," an expression to be understood in the light of the biblical conception of the "Name of God." (*See* NAME.) The experience of this protection did induce a false sense of security in the inviolability of the Temple, something nearer to magic than to piety. Jeremiah upbraids this false sense of security: "Put not your trust in the deceitful words: This is the temple of the Lord! The temple of the Lord! The temple of the Lord! We are safe; we can commit all these abominations again" (7:4, 10). Nothing can substitute for the surrender to Yahweh's will, and without this there is no security, not even in the Temple, which after all, is an expression of man's acceptance of God's covenant.

Notwithstanding this universal "Temple spirituality," shared by prophets and psalmists alike, there was in the biblical tradition a current that was not very favorable to the Temple. Perhaps this current was adverse to deviations such as those described in Jeremiah 7:1-5, but its affirmations were much more radical. Already in 1 Samuel 7:6, 7 in the divine answer to David's proposal to build a Temple can be sensed a certain derogation from the transcendence and autonomy of the divine person, which up to that point had been linked with its itinerant condition in the Tent of the desert (*see* 1 Kgs. 8:16, 27).

With Deutero-Isaiah, however, the objections changed tone and became much more forthright: "Thus says the Lord: The heavens are my throne, the earth is my footstool. What kind of house can you build for me; what is to be my resting place? My hand made all these things when all of them came to be, says the Lord. This is the one whom I approve; the lowly and afflicted man who trembles at my word" (Isa. 66:1-2). This was to pass into Stephen's discourse to the Sanhedrin with the conclusion, "Yet the Most High does not dwell in buildings made by human hands" (Acts 7:48). This same tendency can be seen in Hebrews 9: the expiation carried out by the High Priest Jesus did not take place in the Temple, but in one "which is better than the one made by men's hands because it is not of this created order" (Heb. 9:11)—the heavenly sanctuary where God truly dwells.

Jesus' position on the Temple is one of great respect (Matt. 21:12 ff.; Mk. 11:15-17; Lk. 19:45, 46). It is the house of God (Matt. 12:4; Lk. 6:4), the house of prayer (Matt. 21:13; Lk. 19:46). Nevertheless he decisively points out its transitory character—indeed his very presence puts the Temple in a new dimension (Matt. 12:6). Jesus predicted the destruction of the Temple (Matt. 24:2; Mk. 13:2; Lk. 21:6). He spoke in an enigmatic manner of its forthcoming destruction and its rebuilding in three days (Matt. 26:61 and Mk. 14:58). This prediction was quoted against him at his trial. John 2:18-22 frames this saying in the episode in which Jesus drove the sellers from the Temple.

The form in which the saying is quoted by Mark 14:58—"I will destroy this temple made by human hands, and in three days I will construct another, not made by human hands"—points toward the interpretation John gave the saying: "He was speaking of the temple of his body." Jesus' humanity is the new Temple because it is the place of God's salvific presence to man, and the place where man can find God. Only however with the glorification of Jesus can its salvific efficacy be fully unfolded and put into effect (Jn. 7:39).

The new Temple is Christ's glorified humanity. For this reason the moment of his death which coincides with his glorification was marked by the rending of the Temple veil: that is, the Temple is discounted, becomes irrelevant to the religious point of view and its place is taken by the "temple not made with hands," that is, the humanity of Christ now glorified. (*See* Mk. 14:58 and 15:38.) Christians share in Christ's glorified life and are "the body of Christ" which is the Church. They constitute God's temple, for he lives there through his Spirit (1 Cor. 6:19; 1 Jn. 3:24). The whole Church, animated by the Spirit of God, is the temple where God dwells and works out man's salvation (Eph. 2:19-22; 2 Cor. 6:16).

Temptation, The word **to tempt** is used in the Bible with different subjects and objects, so that while it keeps the same fundamental meaning, it acquires different emphases according to the case. To tempt means to test a person to ascertain what he can do or wishes to do. The most significant uses of the word from the religious point of view are the following:

1. Man tempts God, that is, he wishes to put God's omnipotence or salvific will to the test. This amounts to an act of disbelief, or at least distrust. This type of temptation arises from incredulity and is severely reprimanded in Scripture. It is one of the constantly recurring themes of the journey through the desert (Ex. 17:1-7; Num. 14; Ps. 78:18, 40, 41; 95:8, 9; 106:4; Deut. 6:16; 1 Cor. 10:9). In this meaning the invitation not to tempt God is an invitation to believe in him. Another way of tempting God however is to provoke him with an unwarranted reliance on his power while giving no care to his demands. This is the type of temptation of God that Satan suggests to Jesus in Matthew 4:5-7.

2. God puts man to the test to "know what he has in his heart" (Deut. 8:2), that is to prove the rightness and sincerity of the dispositions he nourishes towards God. The person approved through this testing time obviously comes out fortified, and so this type of temptation is often presented as one of the devices by which God teaches and brings man to greater perfection. Abraham received the order to sacrifice his own son, who was also his only son and heir to the promise. By his obedience Abraham showed that he "truly feared God" (Gen. 22:12). The pedagogic character of temptation is especially put into relief by the wisdom literature (Prov. 3:11, 12; Sir. 2:5; Wis. 3:5). The story of Job is the story of a temptation: God is provoked by Satan into permitting Job to be tempted, that is, to be placed in circumstances that seem openly to contradict what his religion teaches him. The point is to find out just how sincere Job is in his attachment to God (Job 1:2).

3. Then there is the case of Satan's tempting man. Under the form of a serpent in Genesis 3 is hidden, according to Wisdom 2:24, the devil who tempts on account of jealousy. He induces to evil with the intention of destroying what was made good. God is never the tempter in this type of temptation (James 1:13). Instead he gives the strength to overcome this kind of temptation (1 Cor. 10:13). Satan is in these cases the tempter (1 Thess. 3:5; 1 Cor. 7:5). Jesus warns his disciples to be watchful and prayerful so as not to succumb to temptation (Mk. 14:38; Matt. 26:41; Lk. 22:46). This prayer is incorporated into the Our Father which he taught us (Matt. 6:21; Lk. 11:4).

4. The New Testament often speaks of temptations (**peirasmoi**) in an almost impersonal sense. These temptations are the inherited lot of the

Christian. The term is more or less a generic word for all kinds of suffering that plague man. These sufferings are the sign of the incompatibility that exists between Christ and Christians and the world taken in its pejorative sense. Thus into sufferings are interwoven the benevolent designs of God who through them brings the Christian to maturity and the malevolence of the devil who through them wishes to bring everything to destruction (Rev. 3:10; 2:10).

It is of this type of temptation that Hebrews 2:18, 4:15 and 5:7-9 speak. 4:15 states that Jesus was tempted in every way that we are, though without sin. Jesus' temptation in this context was the passion (*see* Lk. 4:13; 22:40, 46, 53) which he sustained to the end and which brought his mission to its consummation: "Since he was himself tested through what he suffered, he is able to help those who are tempted" (Heb. 2:18). Through his "temptation" he has become for all who obey him the source of eternal salvation (5:9).

temptation
in time of *t*.   Lk. 8:13

Temptation of Jesus, Jesus' temptation is recounted in Matthew 4:1-11, Luke 4:1-13 and is briefly alluded to by Mark 1:12, 13. Even though one can draw from this episode a moral lesson and an example of prompt and decisive opposition to temptation, it is obvious that this was not the principal aim of the story. To understand the episode it is necessary to remember that the mission and work of Jesus are unfolded, according to the gospel witness, on two fronts at the same time, and these fronts are related to one another. On the one hand Jesus must suffer and confront those who do not believe in his mission, who eventually take him to his death. On the other, at a deeper level Jesus must undergo and confront Satan's attacks. These fronts, or levels, are related since one reflects on the other. Satan is the prince of this world (Jn. 12:31) who enters into the body of the traitor Judas (Jn. 13:27; Lk. 22:3). It is Satan who wishes to sift the apostles like wheat so that they would succumb in the hour of temptation at the Passion (Lk. 22:31), which is the hour of darkness (Lk. 21:53) in which Satan intends to bring to a definitive climax the attack on Jesus which was begun at the temptations (Lk. 4:13). These temptations must be understood in the framework of Jesus' messianic mission. In them are confronted two different concepts on this mission. One is sufficiently suggested in the baptism of Jesus and is linked with the obedience of the servant of Yahweh, that is, with austerity and suffering as the way to glory. The other concept is Satan's, a terrestrial messianism which, in Jesus' eyes, was a challenge to God, a temptation of God and an act of apostasy from him.

The temptations are presented as a dispute between doctors, one of whom, Jesus, calls on the witness of Scripture to correct the suggestions of the other, Satan, who also can invoke Scripture. They are set in an external framework: the place of fasting, the pinnacle of the Temple and a very high mountain. The more recent authors are in agreement on two points. The first is that the account of the temptations came from Jesus himself and was aimed at clarifying for the apostles the nature of his mission, when they seemed demoralized by the poverty of its external appearances and the tragic end that was awaiting it, which seemed to contradict the hopes they had placed in him (*see* Matt. 16:21-23 and parallel texts). This is borne out by the frequent allusions to the failure of the disciples to understand. Secondly Jesus recounted his experiences in a form that might be called parabolic or figurative. This places out of question all discussion of how in space and time the events took place. Jesus chose places and things to give concrete and live form to an episode that took place in the secret of his own spirit.

Ten Commandments, *See* DECALOGUE.

Tent, Nomads are wont to live in tents: the nomadic existence demands this type of habitation. To live in tents is a current expression for the nomadic type of life. The nomadic past of Israel is reflected in several expressions involving pitching and striking tent which survived even after they settled down to a sedentary existence. "Tent" is used in the sense of home or habitation even when there were already houses. To set out on a journey is to pull up the tent, and to die is to fold one's tent (2 Cor. 5:1, 4). The Word pitched his tent among men (Jn. 1:14). The Ark, which was the seat of God's presence in the desert, remained in a tent, and even when David brought it to Jerusalem he pitched a tent to receive it (2 Sam. 6:17). When David decided to build a Temple for Yahweh, he had this dissuading word through the mouth of Nathan the prophet: "I have not dwelt in a house from the day on which I led the Israelites out of Egypt to the present, but I have been going about in a tent under cloth. In all my wanderings everywhere among the Israelites, did I ever utter a word to any one of the judges whom I charged to tend my people Israel, to ask; Why have you not built me a house of cedar? Now then, speak thus to my servant David" (2 Sam. 7:6-8). In fact Yahweh's dwelling in a tent seemed to suggest even more clearly his transcendence and his perfect autonomy even when he freely determined to live among men.

The nomads' tents were made out of cloth woven from camel or goat hair. Paul was by trade a tent-maker (Acts 18:3). The cloth was stretched on cords tied to poles driven into the earth. The interior was divided into two or more sections by curtains. Tents were used for military encampments (2 Sam. 11:11; 2 Kgs. 7:7; Jer. 37:10) but only in unusual circumstances such as during a prolonged campaign or the long siege of a town.

Tent of Meeting, A translation of **'ohel mo'ed,** which is normally called the Tabernacle. *See* TABERNACLE.

tents

who dwell in *t*.	Gen. 4:20 the *t*. of Shem	Gen.9:27
	herds and *t*. Gen. 13:5	

Tephon (tee′-fon), A city of Judea which was fortified by Bacchides (1 Mac. 9:50), to be identified with Tappuah of Judah (Josh. 15:34) or of Ephraim (Josh. 16:8). *See* TAPPUAH, 2 and 3.

Terah (ter′-ah), 1. The father of Abraham, Nahor and Haran. He emigrated from Ur in Babylon to Haran in northern Mesopotamia where he died (Gen. 11:24-32; 1 Chron. 1:26; Josh. 25:2). His name is read in Jesus' genealogy (Lk. 3:34).

2. An encampment on the journey of the Israelites through the desert towards Canaan (Num. 33:27-28).

Teraphim, Small statuettes of the household gods mentioned in the story of Jacob's departure from the home of Laban. In this episode the possession of the teraphim seems to be connected with the inheritance rights (Gen. 31). Judges 17:5 also speaks of teraphim (*see* 18:14-20): they form part of the cult of the Israelites. These images in human form may be a survival of ancestor worship, or perhaps they were statues of the local genii, but they certainly were not graven images of Yahweh. 1 Samuel 19:11-13 leads one to believe that they might be of considerable size, for Michal was able to place one in bed to dupe Saul's men into believing it was David. In later texts the teraphim are condemned as idolatrous (1 Sam. 15:23; 2 Kgs. 23:24; Hos. 3:4-5). They were used to obtain oracles from the divinity (Ezek. 21:21; Zech. 10:2).

Terebinth, *See* OAK.

Teresh (ter'esh), One of the eunuchs at the court of King Ahasuerus who conspired against the king's life. Mordecai discovered the plot and made it known to the king through his adopted daughter, Esther. Teresh and his fellow-conspirator Bigthan were sent to the gallows (Esth. 2:21-23; 6:2).

terrible

you with *t*. woes   Lev. 26:16   *T*. and dreadful   Hab. 1:7
an angel of God, *t*. indeed
                       Jgs. 13:6

terror

a *t*. from God   Gen. 35:5   a *t*. to the Egyptians   Isa. 19:17
by sheer *t*. at home   Deut. 32:25   How *t*. siezes Moab   Jer. 48:39

Tertius, A Christian at Corinth to whom Paul dictated the epistle to the Romans (Rom. 16:22; *see* LETTER).

Tertullus, A lawyer engaged by Ananias the high priest to bring charges against Paul before the tribunal of the Roman procurator of Judea, Felix (Acts 24:1-9).

Testament, The name of the two major parts into which the Bible is divided. Testament comes from the Latin **testamentum,** translating the Greek diatheke, which was the word chosen by the Septuagint to translate the Hebrew **berith,** which strictly speaking means **covenant.** The Greek word diatheke means covenant or agreement, and also last will. The ambivalence in the meaning is exploited in Hebrews 9:16; 17 to underscore the validity of the New Covenant sealed by the sacrificial death of Christ. Ordinarily however it is used in the sense of covenant, alliance—that is, to denote the religious economy established by God for man's salvation. The Old Covenant was established on Sinai; the New Covenant is sanctioned by the death of Jesus. The Old Testament, as part of the Bible, is the collection of sacred and inspired books which refer to the first covenant. The New Testament comprises the sacred and inspired books that describe the new covenant.

Teth, The 9th letter of the Hebrew alphabet (emphatic t).

Tetrarch, Literally this means the ruler of a quarter of a territory. In Hellenistic use it came to mean a ruler of rank lower than a king, and therefore a prince who was more or less vassal with less autonomy from the Roman power than a king had in his territory. Herod I the Great, was first tetrarch, and then received the title of king. The title however was denied by the Romans to his sons and successors, who appear as tetrarchs: Herod Antipas, tetrarch of Galilee (Matt. 14:1; Lk. 3:19; 9:7; Acts 13:1) and Philip, tetrarch of Ituraea and Trachonitis (Lk. 3:1) while Lysanias was tetrarch of Abilene (Lk. 3:1).

Text Criticism, None of the books of the Bible has come down to us in the manuscript of its author. We only have manuscripts that date from several centuries after the books were written. In this work of transmission there was the possibility of copyists' errors, which in fact took place, as well as deliberate modifications introduced into the text. Textual criticism is the art of recovering and establishing the authentic text of a writing on the basis of the manuscripts that we possess. The fruit of the application of textual criticism is called a recension. A recension, then, is the text that emerges when an expert in textual criticism applies his art—the text, that is, that he judges to be nearest to the authentic one.

The first step in textual criticism is to gather the manuscript material that exists and study the interdependence between them. This means creating a genealogical tree of manuscripts. This is very important to facilitate the work, for if it can be proved that fifty manuscripts depend on one single one and another fifty on another, then it is sufficient to compare these two which are the sources of all the rest.

For textual criticism work it is also necessary to know the most common changes that occur in the transcription of the manuscripts. These changes are of two kinds, deliberate and indeliberate. Involuntary changes arise from the weakness of the human faculties, from fatigue, monotony and so on. Thus the scribe might write only once what was repeated in the original text (haplography) or vice versa (dittography). Again the scribe or amanuensis, having paused at one word, might take up again at the same word in a different place, either before or after, and in the latter case, might omit all that went between (homoeoteleuton). Confusion can arise between letters that look alike, or if the writing is done on dictation, the sounds can be confused. In copying ancient manuscripts that did not separate the words, the copyist could decide on a wrong division or badly interpret the abbreviations that abounded in those times.

Other changes however could be deliberate, such as corrections of style, grammar or orthography. Sometimes the scribe is anxious to clarify the text by additions, or to change it because of theological scruples.

The principal rules of textual criticism have been worked out by a study of the most common changes and the expert opinion of the critics. If then one finds that different manuscripts have a different text, a variant reading, the authentic one is: a. the reading that makes it possible to explain the others; in other words an attempt is made to reconstruct the very process which led in the first place to the variety of reading in the manuscripts.

b. the more difficult reading both in content and form. This rule arises from a study of scribes who tend always to write in the better, easier, more intelligible text. Obviously this rule is only applied to variant texts that come from deliberate corrections.

c. the shorter reading. This rule also holds for deliberate changes, and stems from the fact that scribes are more prone to add to the text than just leave it as it is. When it is not possible to give a judgment from a comparison of the texts among themselves, then it is necessary to have recourse to authority. Those texts are presumed to be authentic that are found in the better and more numerous manuscripts. It is for the student of text history to determine which are the better manuscripts.

Text, New Testament, The history of the text of the New Testament is very different from that of the Old Testament. First and foremost the conformity that is found in the Old Testament manuscripts is lacking in the New; and the number of manuscripts is much greater (more than 5000), some of which date from soon after the writing of the books themselves. Here, a brief note on the principal manuscripts, the recensions or types of text one finds in the manuscripts, and the printed texts of the New Testament.

The chief manuscripts of the New Testament can be divided into papyri, codices and lectionaries, which are the parts of the gospels and epistles that were read in the liturgy.

1. Papyri: The Chester Beatty papyri (P 45-47), found in Egypt in 1931, stem from the third century, and contain fragments of the gospels, Paul's epistles and Revelation.

The Rylands papyrus contains John 18:31-33, 37, 38. It dates from 130-150 A.D. and is the most ancient witness of the New Testament. It comes from Egypt and was found in 1920.

The Bodmer papyri, among which P 66, from about 200 A.D., contains John 1-14, is the most recent important discovery. Other papyri of the same collection contain other writings of the New Testament—1 and 2 Peter from the third century and others from a more recent date.

2. Codices: The Sinaitic Codex was found in the monastery of St. Catherine on Mt. Sinai. It was located at first in St. Petersburg, but was bought from the Soviet Government by the British Museum in 1933. It comes from the fourth century and was made in Egypt. It also contains the Septuagint Greek version and some ancient Christian writings. The Codex Vaticanus; now in the Vatican Library; comes from the beginning of the fourth century, and also stems from Egypt.

The Bezae Codex (D) is in the library of Cambridge University. It comes from the fifth century and contains the gospels and the Acts of the Apostles in Latin and Greek.

The Washington Codex (W) in the Freer Gallery in Washington was bought in 1906 in Egypt. It dates from the beginning of the fifth century.

All these are uncial manuscripts, that is, written with capital letters. The minuscule manuscripts are more recent and very numerous.

Textual criticism of the last two centuries has set out to organize the many manuscripts of the New Testament into families. Four principle families have been identified. Under this quadruple division can be grouped all the known manuscripts. These families are the fruit of recensions, that is, of critical work of text restoration carried out in different environments of the ancient church from the second to the sixth centuries. St. Jerome has handed down some historical information on these labors of text criticism carried out in the ancient church. He speaks of Hesychius of Alexandria and Lucianus of Antioch who made editions or recensions of the New Testament. The labors of Origen on the Bible text are also well known.

The Antiochian recension of Lucianus forms a family of many uncial manuscripts and the greater part of the minuscules. It is an intelligible text and stylistically correct. Its value is secondary. Erasmus used manuscripts from this family for his critical edition, and from this the text went into almost all printed editions up to the last century. Because of this large diffusion it is called the "textus receptus" (received text).

The Alexandrian recension of Hesychius is found in the Vatican and Sinaitic manuscripts. It contains the purest original text and is ordinarily taken as the basis for critical editions. It is more critical and objective than the Antiochian text, as was to be expected from a cultural center of such long tradition as was Alexandria.

The so-called Western recension is the most ancient; it is found in manuscript D and W but also in the ancient Latin version and in the Syrian version. It is a popular text, and has its own additions, especially in Acts.

The Caesarean recension is the most recently discovered one. It appears to be the result of Origen's labors at Caesarea in Palestine, from which it gets its name.

The first printed edition of the Greek New Testament was prepared by Erasmus and was published in 1516 in Basel in Johannes Froben's printing press. Then followed the Polyglot Bible of Alcalá in 1520. Recent editions used, above all, manuscripts of the Antiochian family. The modern critical editions begin with the work of Westcott and Hort in England

(1882) and H. von Soden (1902) in Germany. These are called the major editions as they contain a long list of variant readings taken from different manuscripts. The most used modern editions, with a reduced critical apparatus, are above all E. Nestle (from 1898 on) and A. Merk, S. J. (from 1933), Vogels (from 1920) and Bover (from 1947). The most recent of the minor editions has been prepared with new criteria by Metzger, Aland in 1967.

Text, Old Testament, This can be but a brief note on the history of the books of the Old Testament written and preserved in Hebrew or Aramaic. For the others *see* SEPTUAGINT. The following are the most ancient manuscripts of the Old Testament:

a. The Bible manuscripts found in the caves at Qumran and Murrabba'at. *See* DEAD SEA SCROLLS.

b. The **Nash papyrus,** a 24-line fragment found in 1902 in Fayum in Egypt, containing Exodus 20:2-17 and Deuteronomy 5:6-21, and stemming from the second century after Christ. All the other 700 manuscripts are from the middle ages. All these show a great uniformity. Indeed the history of the Old Testament text can be presented from this point of view: how this uniformity was arrived at. This uniformity is a rather recent phenomenon, that is, it rose after the Christian era. This can be proved by comparing the Hebrew text with the Greek version known as the Septuagint, made in the third to the first centuries before Christ, with the manuscripts from Qumran and with the Samaritan Pentateuch.

According to a tradition preserved in the Talmud, at the end of the first century A.D., a Hebrew text was made on the basis of three highly esteemed manuscripts. In case of discrepancy the text on which two of the manuscripts agreed against the other was taken to be the authentic one. Once this version was completed, all the others that did not agree with it were proscribed. Some authors hold that this story is a legend, but the fact remains that between 70 and 120 A.D. a recension was made of the Hebrew text that was imposed as the only legitimate one. This can be seen from the way in which all the texts thereafter, even those very close to the period, agree among themselves and with the consonant text that we possess.

This text contained only the consonants, for Hebrew script up to that time did not have any signs for the vowels. From the beginning of the second century to the tenth, which is the date of the manuscripts used in our critical editions of the Old Testament, the history of the text can be summed up as one long struggle to conserve unchanged and immune from any corruption the consonant text, and to find a precise system to express the vowel sounds.

This work was brought systematically to completion by specialized scribes called **Massoretes,** from the word **massora,** meaning tradition. The text that is the fruit of their work is known as the Massoretic text. There were different schools of Massoretes. The Palestinian Massoretes had as early as the sixth century worked out a system of signs to be placed over the consonants to express the vowels. This was, in general, a very simple system. In the meantime in the flourishing Babylonian schools another system was being used, also of signs placed above the consonants. Neither of these systems prevailed.

From the ninth to the tenth centuries in Tiberias in Palestine two Massorete families, that of Ben Asher and that of Ben Naphtali, brought to completion a most accurate system of vocalization or vowel sounds to be placed under the consonants, which noted, with several accent sounds, the traditional pronunciation of the text down to the last detail. The manuscripts that today are used in the critical edition of the Hebrew Bible, edited by G. Kittel and P. Kahle, are based on mansucripts that were elaborated by the family of Ben Asher. These are:

a. The Cairo Codex of the prophets written by Moshe ben Asher in 895 A.D.

b. The Petropolitanus Codex, 1008 A.D., written by the disciples of the last member of the family of Asher, Aaron ben Moshe ben Asher. This manuscript is the basis of the edition mentioned.

c. The Codex of Aleppo (around 950 A.D.) is the best of all, but up to this time has not been used in any critical edition. Its vocalization is the work of Aaron ben Asher.

The Massoretic text contains numerous marginal annotations (**Massora marginalis**) and at the end of each book (**Massora finalis**). In these can be found many useful and curious observations: variant readings, Qere or corrected reading in the margin of the Kethibh or uncorrected text as the Massoretes found it, the number of times a certain word is used, the number of words to a book, and so on. All these observations are the fruits of many generations of work, and their aim is to secure the faithful transmission of the text.

For the Pentateuch there is a tradition independent of the Massoretes' work and of the uniform text of 70-120 A.D. This is the Pentateuch text preserved by the Samaritans who separated from the Judeans in the fourth century before Christ. *See* SAMARITAN PENTATEUCH.

Thaddaeus (tha-dee′-us or thad′-e-us), One of the twelve disciples chosen by Jesus according to the lists in Matthew 10:3 and Mark 3:18: Luke's lists, on the other hand, speak of Judas son of James (Lk. 6:16 and Acts 1:13). Only with difficulty can the identity between these two be denied. The form that Matthew and Mark use seems to have been born of the desire to avoid confusing Thaddaeus with Judas Iscariot the betrayer. Luke therefore always adds "of James." "Judas, not the Iscariot" is probably Thaddaeus in John 14:22, where he asks Jesus: "Lord, why is it that you will reveal yourself to us and not to the world?" Some manuscripts of Matthew have Lebbaeus instead of Thaddaeus. *See* LEBBAEUS.

thank, thanks

to celebrate, *t.* and praise	Give *t.* to the Lord,	1 Chron. 16:8
1 Chron. 16:4	and give *t.* to God	Lk. 17:18
	Father, I *t.* you Jn. 11:41	

Thanks Offering, A translation of **todah** in the ritual of sacrifice (Lev. 7:12-13). It was a special type of sacrifice. *See* SACRIFICE.

Thassi (thas′-eye), Surname of Simon Maccabee (1 Mac. 2:3).

Theater, The Greek theater of old was not just destined for theatrical performances of plays. Originally it was also used for the whole cult of Dionysius, and in it public meetings were also held (*see* Acts 19:29, 31). The theater had three parts: there was the theater strictly so called, the place where the spectators sat on semicircular concentric steps rising from the middle, for which often a suitable, naturally contoured piece of land would be chosen. Then there was the stage which closed the semicircle and where the drama or other activity took place. In the orchestra between the stage and the spectators was the choir. In the larger Hellenistic cities of Palestine there were theaters. Herod had them built in Caesarea, Damascus, Gadara, Jerusalem and elsewhere. In the New Testament the theater at Ephesus is mentioned in the silversmith's riot against Paul (Acts 19:29-31). Paul states that he has become a spectacle, in Greek, a "theater" to the whole world (1 Cor. 4:9; *see* Heb. 10:33).

Thebes, A city of Upper Egypt, capital and residence of the Pharaohs during long periods from 2000 B.C. until the Assyrian conquest (663 B.C.). The city rose in the present-day region of Karnak and Luxor, where are preserved the ruins of once magnificient temples. Near the city on the other side of the river was the Valley of the Kings, the burial place of the Pharaohs, the Burial Temples of Deir-el-Bahri and the funeral monument of Ramses II. Thebes was the capital of Egypt during the period of the empire's greatest splendor. The Old Testament has some mention of the city, especially in the prophetic oracles against Egypt (Jer. 46:25; Ezek. 30:15-16). Nahum 3:8 alludes to its destruction during the Assyrian conquest. In Hebrew it was called **No'.** The Greeks named it Diospolis, the city of Zeus.

Thebez (the'-bez), A town near Shechem, probably today's Tubas, ten miles to the north. Abimelech, son of Jerubbaal attacked it and took it, but in the assault of the citadel or fortified tower a woman threw down a millstone on his head and crushed his skull. He ordered his armor-bearer to run him through with his sword so that it should not be said that a woman had slain him (Jgs. 9:50-55; 2 Sam. 11:21).

theft
to pay for his *t*.   Ex. 22:2

Theodotion (thee'-o-doe'-tion), A Jewish proselyte of Ephesus who lived under the emperor Commodus (180-192 A.D.). He was the translator from Hebrew into Greek of a version of the Old Testament. His work is rather a revision of the Greek version known as the Septuagint to adjust it to the Hebrew. The version of Daniel made by Theodotion was used by the church and found its way into the Septuagint. *See* SEPTUAGINT.

Theodotus (the-od'-o-tus), One of the ambassadors sent by Nicanor, head of the Seleucid army, to Judas Maccabeus to talk peace (2 Mac. 14:19).

Theophany (the-off'-a-nee), From the Greek **theos,** God, and **phainein** to appear. Theophany is, then, an apparition of God. The word, for Bible scholars, means a particular type of manifestation of God in the Old Testament with consistent and typical characteristics. The stage-setting of these manifestations is one of terrifying storms, great winds, lightning, thunder, earthquakes, smoke and other such upheavals. In the Bible tradition the original theophany, both logical and chronological, and the very type of all others, is the Sinai revelation of God (Ex. 19:20) when Yahweh first came to meet his people. The principal descriptions of theophanies are read in Psalm 18:68; Isaiah 6; Habakkuk 3; Ezekiel 1; Nahum 1; Deuteronomy 33, but allusions to them are numerous in the Psalms, the prophets and the historical books.

Theophany is a typical literary genre of the Bible. Its frequency and characteristics are, in the last analysis, explained by the altogether particular nature of the God of Israel in the religious context of the Middle East. The theophany and the natural phenomena that accompany it undoubtedly reveal Yahweh as the Lord of nature. In fact these upheavals which accompany the theophany are at times interpreted as revealing the sacred terror which possesses creatures at the approach of their Lord.

At the same time they reveal a God who is perfectly and absolutely above nature. Yahweh is radically other than his creatures. Between the cosmos and God there is not that ontological continuity that myth discovers in other divinities (*see* MYTH), so that nature itself becomes a manifestation of the sacred. God breaks into his world to bring into effect his designs in which the background is the history of mankind. God "comes" or "appears" in order to save, judge or communicate with men.

The theophany, then, reveals a God who wishes to enter into historical contact with man, and who intervenes in his history.

Theophilus (the-off'-a-lus), The name of the Christian to whom Luke dedicated his gospel and the Acts of the Apostles (Lk. 1:3; Acts 1:1). Luke addresses him as "Most Excellent," a title he reserves in other places for Roman governors (*see* Acts 23:26; 24:2; 26:25). For this reason Theophilus is believed to have been a personage of considerable public importance.

There is, however, a second possibility—that Theophilus, which in Greek means "loved by God," is intended to cover all Christians in a symbolic way. However, as the name is in the prologue context, one would rather expect it to refer to a real person.

Thessalonians, Epistles to, Among the epistles handed down under the name of Paul are two directed to the church of Thessalonica. (*See* THESSALONICA.) Paul has to interrupt his ministry in Thessalonica because of an agitation against him organized by the Jews. When he reached Athens he was still worried about that community whose instruction he had been forced to leave incomplete, so he sent Timothy to strengthen their faith and sustain them in a time of persecution. Timothy rejoined Paul at Corinth and brought good news about the situation of the community at Thessalonica (1 Thess. 3:1-13).

Paul thanks God for their faith, hope and charity (1 Thess. 1:2-10) and reminds them of his selfless activity in their midst and his dedication to them (2:1-12). He goes on to exhort them to sanctity of life which is a demand of the Christian life (4:1-12). In answer to questions that perhaps were brought to him by Timothy, he clarifies some points in eschatology. Those who will have died when the Lord comes will arise in glory, while the others—and he writes "we" (4:15)—who will be alive will be changed. All will go to meet the Lord, and all, the living and the dead, will remain with him always (4:13-18).

It cannot be denied that this passage is written by one who is intimately persuaded that the second coming of the Lord is not far off, so that there is a possibility that he will be still alive when the event occurs. This is not the point the apostle is making, but nevertheless, it seems to have been his strong conviction. He does not develop the subject clearly with arguments and proofs, but at the time of writing the epistle, this is his thought. Paul adds exhortations that fit in with his eschatological teaching (5:1-11) and admonitions on the smooth running of the community.

The first epistle to the Thessalonians, whose Pauline authenticity is generally admitted, was written during the apostle's second missionary journey, and from Corinth around 50/51 A.D., a little after his first visit to the community. The most commonly held chronology for the epistles of St. Paul holds this to be his first.

The second letter to the Thessalonians once more takes up the question of the **parousia** or second coming of Christ, and "how we shall all be gathered around him" (2 Thess. 2:1). The occasion of this second letter was the excitement and alarm of the community over certain predictions, rumors, and a letter that claimed to come from Paul in regard to the second coming of Christ (2:2). Paul severely admonishes the community and corrects the disorders that followed (3:6-16). First however he clarifies his own position on eschatology, expounding which events should precede *the* event: "It cannot happen until the Great Revolt has taken place and the Rebel, the Lost One has appeared" (2:3-4). This Enemy claims to be greater than God but is being held in check by some one not clearly specified in the letter. When the Rebel does come, Satan will set to work with signs and portents to bring to destruction those who refused to believe (2:4-12).

2 Thessalonians gives the impression that it was written a little after 1 Thessalonians. It cannot however be denied that there is a real difference between 1 and 2 Thessalonians. In the first Paul is intimately persuaded that he will be still living, or possibly so, at the time of the second coming. The second letter is precisely to discuss this theme of the imminence of the second coming. It offers no unequivocal response to the burning question, but it is clear from the signs indicated that the present generation would not be live spectators to the happening. Because of these and other differences between the two letters, some scholars hold that the author of the first cannot be the author of the second, and so they attribute the second to one of Paul's disciples who wished to correct some false interpretations and clarify some of the difficulties that arose from Paul's teachings.

Other scholars, however, while admitting the differences, hold that they are not incompatible with the Pauline authorship of both. These differences are not on the doctrinal level but on the more delicate level of changing personal hopes and horizons.

Thessalonica, A city and seaport on the Termaic Gulf, now the Gulf of Salonica. It was founded, in 315 B.C. on the Via Egnatiana which linked Rome with the eastern provinces. From 148 B.C. it was the capital of the Roman province of Macedonia. Today it is called Saloniki. There existed at Thessalonica a Jewish synagogue where Paul preached during his second apostolic journey (Acts 17:1-4). His preaching produced abundant fruit but it was brought to a sudden end by an agitation organized by the Jews. These came to the house of Jason where Paul and Silas, as well as Timothy, were staying (*see* 1 Thess. 3:1). They failed however to find Paul and Silas, and instead dragged Jason and some of the brothers before the city council, accusing them of breaking every one of Caesar's edicts by claiming that Jesus was another emperor. The citizens were alarmed, and Jason and the rest had to put up bail before being freed (Acts 17:5-9). When dark fell Paul and Silas were spirited out of the city and made for Beroea (v. 10) where they immediately began to preach the word to a more open-minded audience. The Jews of Thessalonica, however, soon heard of this and went down there to stir up trouble as well, so that Paul had to flee again, this time to Athens, leaving Silas and Timothy behind (vv. 13-15). To these persecutions Paul alludes in 1 Thessalonians 1:13-17.

Paul remained preoccupied for the community there and sent Timothy back once more to keep them strong in the faith and prevent the Thessalonians from being unsettled by troubles. Timothy rejoined Paul at Corinth and gave a good report of his visit to Thessalonica (1 Thess. 3:1-13). Paul has much praise for the faith, charity and courage of the Thessalonians (1 Thess. 1:2-10; 2:13-16) to whom he wrote two epistles which form part of the New Testament. *See* THESSALONIANS, EPISTLES TO.

Theudas (thoo′-das), One of the several pseudo-messiahs in the Judaism of the first century. Josephus Flavius dates his messianic movement during the consulate of Cuspius Fadius (44 A.D.). He announced that he would renew the miracle of the dividing of the waters in the Jordan river to prove his mission, but he was arrested and beheaded by the Romans.

Acts 5:17 recounts how the high priest had the apostles arrested. They were brought before the Sanhedrin who wished to put them to death. Gamaliel intervened, citing the case of Theudas, who became notorius and collected four hundred followers, but whose followers scattered and came to nothing after his death. So, concluded Gamaliel, if God is with the apostles, their work will be permanent; if not it will break up of its own accord (5:33-39).

The two Theudases are probably the same person, but Acts 5:36 dates the episode before the revolt of Judas the Galilean, who lived at the time of the census. This would date him around the time of Christ's birth.

Either there were two Theudases, or more probably the dates put in Gamaliel's discourse are confused.

thicket, thickets

in wait in the *t.*	Job 38:40	in the *t.* of the Jordan　Jer. 12:5
	up from the *t.*　Jer. 49:19; 50:44	

thief

If a *t.* is caught	Ex. 22:1	that against a *t.*	Job 30:5
the *t.*, if caught,	Ex. 22:6	when the *t.* was coming	Lk. 12:39
	The *t.* comes only　Jn. 10:10		

thigh, thighs

Put your hand under my *t.*	and your *t.* waste away　Num. 5:22
	Gen. 24:2

thirst

in their *t.* for water,	Ex. 17:3	Must I now die of *t.*	Jgs. 15:18
therefore in hunger and *t.*		are parched with *t.*	Isa. 41:17
	Deut. 28:48	they who hunger and *t.*	Matt. 5:6

Thisbe, A place south of Kedesh Naphtali in Upper Galilee, above Hazor, some distance to the west, north of Shephat. It was the birthplace of Tobit, from which he was exiled by Shalmaneser, king of Assyria, to Nineveh (Tob. 1:2).

thistle, thistles

Thorns and *t.* shall it bring	The *t.* of Lebanon sent
Gen. 3:18	2 Chron. 25:18
thorns and *t.* shall　Hos. 10:8	

Thomas, One of the Twelve (Matt. 10:3; Mk. 3:18; Lk. 6:15; Acts 1:13). In Aramaic the name means twin, and appears with the Greek translation of the term Didymus in John 11:16; 20:24; 21:2. John's is the only gospel that recounts two episodes in which Thomas has a leading part. Thomas, in one, exhorts the other disciples to face with Jesus the dangers of the intended journey to Jerusalem, albeit in a somewhat fatalistic attitude: "Let us go along, to die with him" (11:16). In the other which took place after the resurrection, Thomas was absent when Jesus appeared. Upon being told of the apparition, Thomas made his famous statement: "without probing the nailprints in his hands, without putting my finger in the nailmarks and my hand into his side." One week later Jesus again appeared and offered to Thomas his proof, upon which Thomas made his confession of faith: "My Lord and my God!" (Jn. 20:24-29). Thomas is again mentioned among the disciples to whom Jesus appeared while they fished on the Sea of Tiberias (Jn. 21:2).

The tradition of the apocalyptic acts of Thomas tells us that Thomas preached the gospel in Mesopotamia and in India where he suffered martyrdom.

Thorn, The Greek word **akantha** means thorn-plant, a very frequent example of which was the common thorny weed, Ononis spinosa, cammock or rest-harrow. Thorns are used in a pejorative sense in the Old and New Testament, for while they grew on cultivated land, they harmed the grain

(Matt. 13:7, 22; Mk. 4:7, 18). Part of Adam's punishment for the fall was that thorns and thistles should plague his husbandry (Gen. 3:18). The wicked are like desert thorns, never to be touched with the hand, but to be gathered with iron or the shaft of a spear and then burned with fire, according to 2 Samuel 23:6, 7.

The crown of thorns with which the soldiers tortured Jesus during his passion is mentioned by Matthew 27:29, Mk. 15:16-20, and Jn. 19:2-7, but not by Luke. The crown was probably not a wreath, but a radical type of crown with the sprongs directed outwards from the center, such as was used by the Ptolemies and the Seleucids: it would have been very difficult to weave the thorns into any other shape.

thorn

a tearing *t.* for the house	a *t.* in the flesh	2 Cor. 12·7
Ezek. 28:24		

thousand

a *t.* shekels	Gen. 20:16	increase you a *t.* times	Deut. 1:11
one *t.* men to war	Num. 31:4	one *t.* seven hundred	2 Sam. 8:4

Thrace, A region in Europe south of the river Danube between Macedonia and the Black Sea. It was a Roman province from the year 46 A.D. Mercenaries from Thrace were present in Gorgias' army in his struggles with Judas Maccabeus (2 Mac. 12:35).

Three Taverns, A place on the Via Appia 33 miles south of Rome. While Paul was being taken prisoner to the capital the brethren from Rome came there to meet him, upon which Paul "thanked God and took fresh courage" (Acts 28:15).

Threshing, The separation of the kernels of the corn from the rest, the chaff, was an operation carried out in biblical times on the threshing floor, a flat, terraced surface of rock or pounded earth. Araunah the Jebusite had his own threshing floor (2 Sam. 24:16), but more often it was common property built at the gate of the city in a place exposed to the wind, for winnowing.

Several methods of threshing are referred to in the Bible. Gideon beat the kernel out with a flail on a stone wine-press floor (Jgs. 6:11). Deuteronomy legislates that one must not muzzle the ox when it is treading out the corn, that is, being driven through it to beat out the kernels with its hooves (Deut. 25:4). Paul interprets this text as referring to the minister of religion having a right to a livelihood from his flock, even though Paul himself did not exercise this right (1 Cor. 9:8 ff.; 1 Tim. 5:18). The most commonly used method was however a threshing sledge, made of a frame of wood with sharp points of stone or metal on the underpart, which were drawn by animals over the corn until the kernels were sufficiently separated.

Throne, The official king's chair. Solomon had his throne made out of ivory and the purest gold. "It had six steps, a back with a round top and an arm on each side of the seat. Next to each arm stood a lion, and twelve other lions stood on the steps, two to a step, one on either side of each step" (1 Kgs. 10:18, 20). In front of the throne was a footstool (Ps. 110:2). In Scripture as in other literature the throne is a symbol of royalty, its functions and powers, and especially the judiciary powers (Isa. 14:13; 16:5; Lk. 1:32; Acts 2:30, etc.). The ark of the covenant, and in particular the two cherubim with extended wings on the cover of the ark, were conceived of as the throne of God, the place of his invisible presence in the midst of his people. (*See* ARK OF COVENANT.) These ideas are transformed into glorious dimensions in some of the visions of the prophets (Isa. 6:1-

3; Ezek. 1:4-28) and in apocalyptic literature (Dan. 7:9-10; Rev. 4). Eventually the concept is extended to enfold the whole universe: the heavens are God's throne and the earth the footstool under his feet (Isa. 66:1; *see* Matt. 5:34).

In Colossians 1:16 "thrones" is the name of a special category of angels, a terminology that mirrors the angelology of the apocalyptic tradition.

thumb, thumbs
and on the *t.* of   Ex. 29:20 on the *t.* of his right hand
                                                        Lev. 8:23

Thummim, *See* URIM AND THUMMIM.

Thunder, Thunder and lightning are a common phenomenon in Palestine especially in spring and autumn. Its awesomeness and power were naturally impressive and often became signs of the divine presence or power in the Bible. When the commandments were given, Yahweh spoke with a great voice from the heart of the fire in cloud and thick darkness (Deut. 5:22), while Exodus 19:16-19 describes the scene on Sinai: "On the morning of the third day there were peals of thunder and lightning."

The Hebrew word for thunder is the common one for sound or voice: **kol,** and thunder was often interpreted as God's voice (e.g. Ps. 29:3-9; Sir. 43:16). John reports in 12:29 that a voice from heaven came in answer to Jesus' prayer to the Father to glorify his name. The people standing by said it was a clap of thunder, while others took it for the voice of an angel. Thunder is a frequent part of the stage-effects of Revelation (4:5; 8:5; 11:19; 16:18). *See* THUNDER, SONS OF; BOANERGES.

Thunder, Sons of, A translation of the Aramaic word, **Boanerges** meaning sons of thunder. This was the name given by Jesus to the sons of Zebedee, as recorded in Mark 3:17. Luke records in 9:54 that these "sons of thunder" wished to call down fire from heaven (lightning?) on a Samaritan village that refused to receive Jesus. *See* BOANERGES.

Thyatira (Thie′-a-tie′-ra), A city of Lydia in western Asia Minor on the river Lycus. It was the home town of Lydia, a merchant in purple (dye). She is described in Acts 16:14 as a devout woman: she was a proselyte of Judaism who listened to Paul and Luke and accepted Paul's preaching. She and her entire household were converted.

Thyatira had a flourishing industry of wool and linen textiles, both weaving and dyeing. To the community at Thyatira the author of Revelation addressed one of his seven letters (Rev. 2:18-29). While in it the community is praised for its charity, it is reproved for tolerating in its midst a pseudo-prophetess who is symbolically referred to as Jezebel (*see* 1 Kgs. 16:31, *see* JEZEBEL). This woman was preaching immorality, idolatry (*see* Rev. 2:14) and the knowledge of the "secrets of Satan" (2:23), and so had seduced many Christians. Similar heterodox movements had been noted at Ephesus (2:6) and Pergamum (2:14).

Tiamat (ti-ah′-mat), The goddess-monster of the abyss of waters, wife of the god Apsu, conquered by Marduk, who out of her body made heaven and earth, according to the Babylonian creation poem, Enuma Elish. *See* CREATION.

Tiberias, A city of the western coast of the lake of Gennesaret, which is also called the Sea of Tiberias and the Sea of Galilee, today Tabarijah.

The city got its name from its founder Herod Antipas, who built it in honor of the emperor Tiberius (Jn. 6:1; 6:23; 21:1).

Tiberius, Roman emperor from 14 to 37 A.D. He was born in 42 B.C. to Livia, who was later the wife of Augustus. Tiberius was then adopted as son and heir to Augustus. Luke dates the beginning of John the Baptist's ministry in the fifteenth year of Tiberius, which would be 28/29 A.D. according to the most probable computation.

Tibni (tib′-nie), Son of Ginath, a rival of Omri as successor to Zimri (876 B.C.) on the throne of Israel (1 Kgs. 16:21-22). For four years the people were divided in a civil war between the two rivals, but the partisans of Omri prevailed (1 Kgs. 16:22).

Tidal, Tidal was king of Goiim and one of the four kings of the east who carried out a punitive expedition against the cities of the Pentapolis south of the Dead Sea in the time of Abraham (Gen. 14:1, 9). Attempts to identify him with Tudhalia I, king of the Hittites, remain dubious

Tiglath-pileser (tig′-lath-pil-eez′-er), Tiglath-pileser III, king of Assyria (745-727 B.C.), was successor to Adad-Nirari III. Tiglath-pileser III was the creator of the great Assyrian empire. He conquered Babylon, of which he made himself king with the name of Pul (2 Kgs. 15:19), and after an unsuccessful campaign against Armenia he advanced against Syria and Palestine. King Rezin of Damascus and Pekah of Israel wanted to force Ahaz of Judah into an alliance against the advance of Tiglath-pileser III. The prophet Isaiah advised Ahaz to remain neutral (Isa. 7:1-14). Ahaz, however, was dismayed at seeing his territories invaded by the Aramaeans and the Israelites, and so declared himself a vassal to Tiglath-pileser whose help he asked (2 Kgs. 16:7-9; 2 Chron. 28:20). This act had repercussions on the religious life of Judah, for Ahaz had Uriah the priest build an altar similar to the one he had seen at Damascus, and on it he burned incense and offered gifts (2 Kgs. 16:10-18). Tiglath-pileser advanced against Ahaz's enemies. Pekah submitted and succeeded in saving Samaria and the surrounding lands but left Galilee and Gilead in Assyrian hands (2 Kgs. 15:19; 734 B.C.). A year later (732 B.C.) Tiglath-pileser moved against Damascus itself, which fell into his hands. Rezin was killed and the inhabitants of the Syrian capital were transported in great numbers to Assyria.

It was Tiglath-pileser III who initiated the Assyrian policy of mass deportations of conquered peoples. This was intended to strike at the roots of national sentiment and eradicate any movement towards revolt; and this was further assured by the installation of Assyrian governors instead of keeping the conquered chieftains in the condition of vassals and tributaries.

On his death Tiglath-pileser was succeeded by his son, Shalmaneser V.

Tigris (tie′-gris), A river of Mesopotamia, modern Iraq. It rises in Armenia on the southern slopes of the Malatya Mountains, and runs in a southwesterly direction towards the Gulf of Persia. Before it reaches the Gulf however, it joins the Euphrates to form the Shatt-el-Arab. On its banks are the cities of Mosul (facing the ancient Nineveh, the Assyrian capital), Qal'at Shergat (the site of the ancient Asshur), Baghdad and Basra, which is situated at a point below the river's meeting with the Euphrates. The principal tributaries flow into it from the eastern mountains. They are the Upper and Lower Zab and the Kerkhah. The Tigris is named in Genesis 2:14 as one of the four rivers of paradise. Daniel 10:4 makes it the scene of one of Daniel's visions. From the Tigris came the fish which Tobiah used to heal his father's blindness and to free the young Sarah from the demon (Tob. 6:1).

Tikvah, Father-in-law of Huldah, the Jerusalem prophetess who was consulted by Josiah about the book of the law which was discovered in the Temple (2 Kgs. 22:14; 2 Chron. 34:22).

Timaeus (ti-mee'-us), Father of the blind man cured by Jesus (Mk. 10:46). *See* BARTIMAEUS.

timbrel

They sing to the *t*.	Job 21:12	praise to him with *t*.	Ps. 149:3
and sound the *t*.	Ps. 81:2	With harp and lyre, *t*..	Isa. 5:12

time

this *t*. next year	Gen. 18:10	our savior in *t*.	Jer. 14:8
the *t*. when the women go		My appointed *t*. draws near	
	Gen. 24:11		Matt. 26:18
wither before its *t*.	Job. 15:32		

Timna, A sister of Lotan, daughter of Seir the Horite (Gen. 36:22). She was a concubine of Esau's son Eliphaz, and mother of Amalek (Gen. 36:12).

Timnah, 1. A city in the territory of Dan (Josh. 15:10; 19:43) but occupied by the Philistines in the time of Samson (Jgs. 14:1-20). Samson married a Philistine woman of Timnah. Later however he abandoned her, for she told the Philistine chieftains the solution of the riddle he had proposed to them. Timnah passed over to Philistine dominion once more in the time of Ahaz (2 Chron. 28:18). Today it is Tell el-Batashi.

2. A town of Judah (Josh. 15:57) mentioned in the traditions concerning the patriarch Judah (Gen. 38:12-14).

Timnath-serah, A locality in the highlands of Ephraim which fell by lot to Joshua and where he built a city (Josh. 19:50; 24:30). Joshua was buried there (Jgs. 2:9). Its site is the present Khirbet Tibneh, southwest of Shechem.

Timon (tie'-mon), One of the seven "deacons" chosen by the Apostles to look after the daily distribution of food and alms (Acts 6:1-6).

Timothy, 1. The head of the Ammonites, defeated by Judas Maccabeus (1 Mac. 5:6-13; 2 Mac. 8:20; 9:3; 10:24; 12:2).

2. A disciple and companion of Paul who was born at Lystra in Lycaonia, Asia Minor, the son of a pagan father and a Jewish-Christian mother called Eunice, the daughter of Lois, who was also a Jewish Christian (2 Tim. 1:5). Paul took Timothy with him while passing through Lystra on his second missionary journey, and, because of the Jews, had him circumcised (*see* Acts 16:1-3). From then on Timothy was in the almost constant company of the apostle. He was the companion throughout the rest of the second missionary journey and was sent on a mission to Thessalonica, to rejoin Paul at Corinth a little later (1 Thess. 3:1-6).

On the third missionary journey Timothy was sent by Paul to Corinth to take care of the disturbances in that community (1 Cor. 4:17; 16:10). That Timothy was Paul's almost constant companion can be gathered from the epistles, four of which have Timothy's name beside that of the apostle at the beginning (1 and 2 Thess., 2 Cor., Col., Phil. and Philem.). We learn from the inscription of Colossians and Philemon that Timothy was with Paul during his first Roman imprisonment. From 1 Timothy 1:3 it can be gathered that Paul left Timothy in Ephesus with the task of assisting in the organization of that community and combating the heresies springing up there. In 2 Corinthians 4:9, 21 Paul presses Timothy to come as soon as possible, before winter, as he had only Luke for a companion. We know nothing of Timothy's further ministry.

Timothy, Epistles to, *See* PASTORAL EPISTLES.

Tiphsah, A city on the northern boundry of the kingdom of Solomon (1 Kgs. 5:4) on the river Euphrates, today known as Dibseh. There was a city of the same name in the vicinity of Tirzah, mentioned in 2 Kings 15:16, but it is probably correctly read in some Greek manuscripts as Tappuah.

Tiras (tie′-ras), Son of Japheth in the Table of Nations (Gen. 10:2; 1 Chron. 1.5).

Tirhakah (tir-hay′-kah), King of Ethiopia and Egypt who advanced as far as Judah to do battle with Sennacherib during the latter's campaign against Hezekiah (2 Kgs. 19:9; Isa. 37:9).

Tirshatha (tir-shay′-tha), The title of the Persian governor of Judah (Esdras 2:63; Neh. 7:65; 8:9; 10:1).

Tirzah, A Canaanite city taken by Joshua (Josh. 12:24) and assigned to Manasseh (*see* Josh. 17:3). It was the residence of the king for the kingdom of Israel from the time of Jeroboam I (922-901 B.C. 1 Kgs. 14:17) until Omri who, in the sixth year of his reign, transferred the seat of residence to Samaria (1 Kgs. 16:23). King Zimri died at Tirzah (1 Kgs. 16:15-17). Tirzah was the native place of Menahem king of Israel (745-738 B.C.; 2 Kgs. 15:14). Today it is Tell el Farah, 6 or 7 miles north of Shechem.

Tishbe (tish′-be), Traditionally this has been regarded as the name of a locality in Gilead, birthplace of the prophet Elijah (1 Kgs. 17:1; 21:17; 2 Kgs. 1:3; 8; 9:36), today Khirbet Listib. But many modern scholars hold that the Hebrew means "one of the settlers in Gilead," a reading carried in the margin of RSV.

Tishri (tish′-re), The name of the seventh month of the Hebrew calendar, corresponding to September-October. *See* MONTH.

Tithes, A tax consisting of a tenth part of a product. According to the law of Deuteronomy 14:22-27, the tithes of grain, wine and oil, as well as the first-born of the animals, should each year be consecrated "before the Lord." Every third year the tithes should be distributed to the poor (Deut. 14:28-29). In Numbers 18:21-32 the tithes are prescribed for the maintenance of the Levites of the Temple, who in their turn give over a tenth part of them to the priests (*see* Lev. 27:30-32). After the exile Malachi 3:8-12 reproved the Jews for failing to pay the tithes. In Nehemiah 10:37 the community commits itself to observe the law in regard to the tithes of Numbers 18:21. In New Testament times Jesus blamed the scribes and Pharisees for tithing mint and dill and cummin, that is, observing the minutiae of the law, while neglecting its weightier precepts (Matt. 23:23; Lk. 18:12).

Titius Justus, *See* JUSTUS.

Titus, 1. A disciple and companion of Paul. He accompanied Paul and Barnabas to Jerusalem to meet with the other apostles and examine together the question of the obligation of the Mosaic law for Christians converted from paganism. On that occasion Paul took a stand against the circumcision of Titus, who was not a Jew. To yield would have been against the principles for which he was fighting (Gal. 2:1-5). Titus was commissioned by Paul to intervene in the crisis that was tearing apart the church at Corinth. He succeeded in restoring peace (2 Cor. 2:13; 7:6-13). Paul sent him once more to Corinth to take up a collection for the faithful in Jerusalem. On this occasion he called him "my companion and fellow worker in your behalf" (2 Cor. 8:23; 12:18). The letter from Paul to Titus was written to him while he was in Crete, sent there by Paul to organize the church of the island. According to 2 Timothy 4:10 he was also in Dalmatia.

2. **Titus Flavius Sabinius Vespasianus**, son and successor of Vespasian as Emperor of Rome (79-81 A.D.). Before becoming emperor, Titus took part in the war against the Jews (66-70 A.D.), first as the commanding officer of a legion and later directing the siege that led to the fall of Jerusalem, Sept. 8, A.D. 70. Bernice was his mistress. *See* BERNICE.

Titus, Epistle to, *See* PASTORAL EPISTLES.

Titus Manius, A Roman legate who sent to the Jews at the time of Judas Maccabeus a letter (2 Mac. 11:34-38) concerning the peace arrived at with Lysias (164 B.C.).

Tob, Name of a region and of a town in it, northeast of Gilead, in Aramaean territory. When Jephthah, the son of Gilead and a harlot, was driven out by Gilead's sons by his legitimate wife on a question of inheritance, he took refuge in Tob where he formed a gang of bandits with whom he made raids (Jgs. 11:3-5). When, however the Ammonites attacked Israel, the elders of Gilead were constrained to come and beg Jephthah's help in defending them. He accepted the role of defender provided that he should then become their leader, which was agreed to.

The Aramaeans of Tob came to the help of the Ammonites against the army of David, but they were defeated by Joab (2 Sam. 10:6-13). Tob appears again at the time of Judas Maccabeus, who came to the defense of the Jews of the region when they were attacked by the neighboring Greek cities (1 Mac. 5:13; 2 Mac. 12:17).

Tobiah, 1. The head of one of the families repatriated from Babylon, but who were unable to prove that their ancestral house and their descent were Israelite (Esd. 2:60; Neh. 7:62). Perhaps he is the same person as in 2, below.

2. **Tobiah**, governor of the province of Ammon in Transjordan, a contemporary of Nehemiah and his enemy, who calls him "the Ammonite slave," thus derogating his title as "servant" or official of the king (Neh. 2:10). He allied himself with Sanballat the Horonite and Geshem the Arab in ridiculing Nehemiah's reconstruction of the walls of Jerusalem (Neh. 2:19; 4:1; 6:1). Tobiah maintained close relationships with the nobles of Judah, with whom he was linked by marriage (Neh. 6:17-19), and with the priests of Jerusalem. Eliashib the priest was another connection, and when he become supervisor of the chambers of the Temple he furnished Tobiah with a spacious apartment which had previously served as a storeroom. Nehemiah, away at the time, on his return became very angry at what had happened. He threw Tobiah's household furniture out of the chamber and had it purified and once more used as a storeroom for the Temple oblations, utensils and incense (Neh. 13:4-9).

Members of the same family held exalted positions in the government of Transjordan under the Ptolemies of Egypt and under Seleucus IV (2 Mac. 3:11).

3. Son of Tobit. *See* TOBIT.

Tobijah, With Heldai, Jedaiah and Josiah, one of the returned Jews asked to make a crown and place it on the head of Zerrubabel (Zech. 6:9-14).

Tobit, A deuterocanonical book of the Old Testament, narrative in style, aimed however at doctrination and edification. The story is one of the most popular among Christians. Its chief character is Tobit, a rich and religious Jew of the tribe of Naphthali, married to Anna, and father of Tobiah. During the reign of Shalmaneser king of Assyria, Tobit was exiled from Thisbe to Nineveh (c. 1:2). God looked with benevolence on his piety and granted him favor and status with Shalmaneser, so that he became purchasing agent for all his needs (1:14).

Tobit is presented as a typical model of Israelite piety, an observer of the law, intent on good works, patient in adversity (cc. 1-2), under the weight of which he asked the Lord to be allowed to die (3:1-6). It happened that at the same time Sarah, daughter of Raguel in Ecbatana in Media, made the same prayer. She had suffered the persecution of Asmodeus, the worst of demons, who had killed off her seven husbands even before they could have intercourse with her (3:7-15). God heard both their prayers and sent Raphael to heal them.

Tobit remembered that he had left money with Gabael at Rages in Media. He sent his son Tobiah to collect it. Tobiah met the angel Raphael, whom he took to be a fellow Israelite, who agreed to show him the way to Media. Then follows the story of how Tobiah was instructed in the curative properties of the large fish (c. 6). In Media Tobiah was brought to Raguel's house where he asked for Sarah's hand.

While Tobiah was sleeping with Sarah, Raguel had a grave dug for him, expecting that to Tobiah would happen the same tragedy that had ended the lives of the previous seven husbands of Sarah. Thanks to the angel's counsel, however, a remedy was found against the demon's designs in the reeking smell of the liver and heart of the fish burning in the bridal chamber on some incense (c. 6, 7).

There followed the wedding feast and the journey back to Tobit, who was then cured of the blindness he had contracted (c. 2) by means of the fish's gall, which on the advice of the angel was spread on his eyes, and drew off them a white filmy skin (c. 11). Raphael then, with due solemnity, revealed himself: "I am Raphael, one of the seven angels who enter and serve before the Glory of the Lord" (12:15). There follows a song of promise for Zion (c. 12) followed by the dying Tobit's exhortation to his children to leave Nineveh (c. 13).

The author offers his story in a rather loose historical context, which already suggests that it has no real historical intent. It is impossible to determine whether the author based his story on some actual person or not; nor is it necessary for the interpretation of the work. Its point is to present a model of authentic piety, as conceived by the post-exilic wisdom tradition. This meant the observance of the law, almsgiving, thoughtfulness for the dead, respect for parents, patience in adversity, trust in God born of conviction that he does not abandon his people but intervenes in their favor even in extraordinary ways. All these religious sentiments are illustrated in the story and find a place in the prayers that are scattered through the book (3:1-6; 3:11-15; 9:15-17; 13:1-18). They are condensed into maxims for living (4:3-19; 12:6-10; 14:7, 9).

The author weaves into his account non-Israelite folklore, such as the demon Asmodeus, adapted from a Persian demon, the curative powers of the fish, the rite of exorcism and so on.

The book has come down in its complete form only in the Greek, but it is undoubtedly a translation from the Hebrew or Aramaic. The differences that exist in the Greek manuscripts lead one to suppose that the book was known in several forms. Hebrew and Aramaic fragments of the work have been discovered at Qumran. The author of the book is unknown, but it is supposed that he wrote in Palestine around 200 B.C.

Togarmah (toe-gar'-mah); Son of Gomer and descendant of Japheth in the Table of Nations (Gen. 10:3; 1 Chron. 1:6). It was also the name of a region in Asia Minor near headwaters of the Euphrates which had commercial dealings with Tyre (*see* Ezek. 27:14; 38:6).

Toi (toy or toe'-i), King of Hamath at the time of David, (2 Sam. 8:9-10), also known as Tou (1 Chron. 18:9-10). *See* TOU.

Tomb, A natural or artificially created cave for the burial of the dead. Cemeteries were located as a rule near cities in terrain unsuited for cultivation, but suitable for excavating caverns or already provided with them. They are often mentioned in the Bible. *See* BURIAL.

Tongue, Often in the Bible the tongue indicates speech itself and to it there are attached the epithets that refer to speech, its effects, and the motives that inspire it. Thus one reads of a "lying tongue" (Pss. 109:2; 120:3), a "seductive tongue" (Prov. 6:24), a "proud tongue" (Ps. 12:4). The ancients were more sensitive to the force of speech than are we today, and so used comparisons that today sound exaggerated, e.g., "their tongue is a sharp sword" (Ps. 57:4), "sharpening their tongues like swords, shooting bitter words like arrows" (Ps. 64:3, 4) (*see* Ps. 140:4; Prov. 18:21; Jer. 18:18). A favorite theme of the masters of wisdom is the right use of the tongue, the benefits that are born of it, the evils that flow from it, and proverbs in its regard abound. "The man of discretion keeps his knowledge hidden, the heart of fools proclaims their folly" (Prov. 12:23; *see* vv. 13-22; Sir. 6:1; 20:1-7; 20:18-23; 23:7-15; 28:13-16). To this tradition belongs the series of severe warnings about the abuse of the tongue that James speaks of in his epistle (James 1:26; 3:2-12).

Outstanding among the charismatic gifts in the apostolic church, perhaps the most remarkable and the one on which is available the most information, is glossolaly or the gift of tongues. The manifestations of this gift had brought disorder and rivalry into the church at Corinth. Paul takes exception to this and issues apt dispositions for good order in the Christian assembly (1 Cor. 14). From Paul's words it can be deduced that the "speaking of tongues" took place in a certain ecstatic state. Members of the assembly broke out into words or sounds unintelligible to the other members of the congregation. So it was necessary to find someone with the charism of interpretation of tongues so that the community could draw profit from what was being said.

This description is not applicable to the miracle of the tongues that took place on Pentecost day (Acts 2:4-11), even though that too is described as the "speaking of tongues." As Luke describes it, it seems it must be taken more as a piece of theology than a report of the facts. The apostles proclaimed the "great works of God" and each person heard them in "the tongue in which each was born." Luke then gives a long list of the regions from which the audience hailed, a kind of reduced Table of Nations from Genesis 10.

The sense of this passage and the surprising phenomenon it describes is the universality of salvation and the mission of the Church which is destined for all peoples.

On the other hand, the miracle of the tongues reverses the story of Genesis 11 concerning the Tower of Babel, the division of tongues and the scattering of the nations. Now once more the peoples are gathered from the ends of the earth: a new people embracing the whole of humanity is formed, and so the story of Genesis 11:1 becomes a reality: "The whole world spoke the same language, using the same words"—something sin had destroyed.

Acts 10:46 and 19:6, in connection with the baptism of Cornelius and of the disciples at Ephesus, speak once more of the gift of tongues. These texts should be understood in the sense of 1 Corinthians 14 (Acts 2:4-11; *see* also Mark 16:17).

Tongues, Gift of, Glossolaly, a charismatic gift frequently evidenced in the early church, in which members of the community, caught up in some sort of ecstatic religious state, broke out into sounds or words, often unintelligible to the audience for whose benefit they were meant (1 Cor. 14). This is not to be confused with the miracle of the tongues described in Acts 2:4-11. *See* TONGUE.

Toparchy, Each of the administrative divisions or districts in a territory. In the time of Jonathan Maccabeus the toparchies of Aphairema, Lydda and Ramathaim were annexed to Judea from Samaritan territory (1 Mac. 11:34).

Topheth (toe'-feth), The "high place" of the Valley of Hinnom near Jerusalem where, in the lifetime of Isaiah and Jeremiah, at least, human sacrifices to Molech were occasionally held. King Josiah "defiled" (destroyed) the furnace there, putting an end temporarily to the sacrifices (2 Kgs. 23:10). Jeremiah cursed the place bitterly (Jer. 7:32; 19:6-13).

Torah, The name of the first part of the Hebrew canon of the Old Testament, comprising the five books of Moses, from Genesis to Deuteronomy. *See* LAW, PENTATEUCH.

torment
dead where he was in *t.*   Lk. 16:23

Tou (too, or toe'-oo), King of Hamath who sent his son Hadoram to David to congratulate him on his victory over Hadadezer, who was also Tou's enemy. He sent gifts of gold, silver and bronze to David who consecrated them to Yahweh (1 Chron. 18:9-10; *see* 2 Sam. 8:9-12 and TOI).

touch

eat it or even *t.* it	Gen. 3:3	and *t.* his bones Job 2:5
or even to *t.* its base	Ex. 19:12	he shall not *t.* you 2 Sam. 14:10
	more than *t.* the tassel Matt. 14:36	

Tower, The tower is a brick or stone structure frequently mentioned in the Bible by different names and covering a variety of sizes and purposes, but chiefly for refuge and defense. The most celebrated tower in the Bible is the tower of Babel (*see* BABEL), but others are mentioned, such as the tower of David, to which the neck of the beloved in the Songs of Songs is compared (S. of S. 4:4), the tower of Eder (Gen. 35:21), the Oven tower or Corner Tower (Neh. 3:11). In the story of the wicked husbandmen, the vineyard is described as having a tower (Mk. 12:1; *see* Isa. 5:1) serving as a watchtower and perhaps as a refuge against wild beasts. Judges 9:51 however talks of a city tower or citadel in Thebez in which all the inhabitants took refuge against the attack by Abimelech. With such an image in mind, God is called a strong tower against the enemy (Ps. 61:3).

Tower of Babel, According to Genesis 11 the Tower of Babel was to be built in the land of Shinar. God however confused the people's language and scattered them over the whole earth. *See* BABEL.

Tower of Shechem, *See* SHECHEM, TOWER OF.

Town
worthy citizen in every *t*.
                              Matt. 10:11

Trachonitis (trak′-o-ny′-tis), A region of Transjordan south of Damascus and Hermon on the volcanic highlands around Gebel ed-Druz. Together with the neighboring Galaunitis, Auranitis and Batanea, it corresponds roughly with the territory called Bashan in the Old Testament. Trachonitis was given by Augustus to Herod I the Great, who at his death left it to his son Philip, with the title of tetrarch (Lk. 3:1).

Tradition, The word tradition can be taken in an active or in a passive sense. In the active sense it means the faithful transmission from one generation to the next of a doctrinal patrimony. In the passive sense it refers to the patrimony itself which is passed on. For Christian revelation tradition has a very important part to play. In the last analysis this importance arises from the historic character of this revelation. For Christian revelation is not a body of doctrine that is timeless; it is rather the solemn witness given to the salvific impact of the life, death and resurrection of a historic figure, Jesus of Nazareth.

Accepting this witness carries with it the urgency and obligation to conserve it faithfully and hand it on unimpaired. Before it becomes an object of theological reflection, tradition in the New Testament is transparently an operative mentality that inspires veneration for what has been received and faithfulness to it (*see* 1 Cor. 11:2; 15:3; 2 Thess. 2:15; 3:6). It makes use of the techniques and resources that were used in the faithful transmission of an oral patrimony.

This traditional mentality has not been sufficiently appreciated by some schools of modern exegetes, who as a consequence show an exaggerated reserve in regard to large strata of the gospel tradition. These authors would have it that tradition was created by the primitive church and that it hands down in the first place information on the situation, interests and beliefs in that community, and only in the second place and by indirect means does it hand on knowledge about Jesus. This judgment is strongly influenced by rather antiquated sociological theories which give great importance to the creative power of the anonymous community in giving birth and sustenance to religious, literary and artistic movements. A recent author, Th. Boman, has examined this thesis in the light of the modern science of folklore, and remarks that the idea of a community that creates tradition is based on romantic old ideas that are left behind by the science of folklore, and so the idea of a collective and anonymous handing down of the words and works of Jesus should also be abandoned.

Reacting to the excesses of these authors some Scandinavian scholars, such as H. Riesenfeld and B. Gerhardsson, sustain that the environment in which the elaboration and transmission of the gospel tradition took place made use of techniques and means similar to those used in the Pharasaical school for the handing on of their oral tradition. It is in fact known that alongside the law of Moses, and on the same level of authority as it, there existed an oral tradition that interpreted and extended the written law. This oral law is in part gathered in the Mishna, and for centuries was handed down orally with the help of mnemonic techniques and other devices. *See* PHARISEES.

This thesis is acceptable provided it is not proposed as a unique and exclusive theory. It can be held that in the apostolic church there were circles who took care to preserve faithfully the traditons concerning Jesus. These were probably the "didaskaloi" or masters of whom Paul writes in 1 Corinthians 4:17; 12:28 and Galatians 6:6. In the gospels also can be discovered traces of this school work, such as the rhythmic form, the assonance and the parallelism in which many of the sayings of Jesus are preserved, even though these may have been Jesus' own way of saying them. Then there is fusion of discourses according to theme, or grouped around one key word that appears in different sayings, of which an evident example is Mark 9:41-48, or according to numerical schemes of which there are several examples in the Sermon on the Mount, Matthew 5-7. A recent scholar of New Testament Judaism remarks, in regard to this theory, that it can no longer be doubted that the process of tradition in Christianity is to be largely understood in the light of the Pharisaic usage in handing down oral traditions. So he concludes that a "traditionalist" emphasis marked the Church from its very beginning, and this is amply evidenced by the Pauline epistles.

One must however add that the gospel tradition carries within it evident traces that it was also used in the liturgy, in catechesis, in anti-Jewish polemics and so on.

Gospel tradition was at the center of the life of the Church in her different manifestations. It was handed down not only with scholastic precision but also as a live and life-giving patrimony. The Church, then, is not a wall between its members and Christ. She received the tradition from Jesus, and living it out in her own life, she handed it on faithfully.

traitor
who turned *t*.   Lk. 6:16

Transfiguration, The transfiguration of Jesus is recounted by the three synoptic gospels (Matt. 17:1-8; Mk. 9:2-8; Lk. 9:28-36) and to it 2 Peter 1:16-18 alludes. The scene of this episode was the top of a high mountain, according to Matthew 17:1. Tradition has identified this mountain with Mount Tabor which rises from the center of the plain of Jezreel. If however one attends to the context into which the episode is inserted, it becomes more probable that the evangelists were referring to Mount Hermon or to some other peak among the highlands of the Anti-Lebanon mountains. In fact the gospel account of the transfiguration follows Peter's confession of Christ at Caesarea Philippi, which was at the extreme north of Palestine, near the headwaters of the Jordan.

In the transfiguration Jesus allowed some part of the glory that was his as "beloved Son of the Father" to appear (*see* Matt. 17:5). This revelation took place in front of only three witnesses, chosen among Jesus' intimates. This is to be understood as part of the "revelation in mystery" which governed all Jesus' mission, and especially the mystery of his person. Moses and Elijah appeared with him, witnesses on the part of the Law and the Prophets to Christ.

The transfiguration episode came after one of the most enigmatic sayings of Jesus: "I assure you, among those standing here there are some who will not experience death before they see the Son of Man coming in his kingship" (Matt. 16:28). It is probable that the evangelists wished to point out the realization of that prophecy in the transfiguration. There is however a strict relationship between the transfiguration and the first prediction of the passion which had just taken place (Matt. 16:21-23) and which had provoked Peter's scandal. In Luke's version this connection between prediction and transfiguration is more evident. The third evangelist writes: suddenly there were two men there talking to him; they were Moses and Elijah appearing in glory, and they were speaking of his passing which he was to accomplish in Jerusalem (Lk. 9:30-31). The transfiguration throws its light on the passion and reveals the mystery of glory to which it will lead. Thus the passion loses that sense of ineluctability which

it might seem to have when viewed merely from an extrinsic point of view."
Now the predicted passion is revealed as a voluntary gift of self which the
Son of God makes, and which, through his surrender, becomes the way to
the glory of which the transfiguration was a momentary vision.

Though John does not recount the transfiguration, the essence of this
mystery is present in his gospel. This mystery pervades his whole gospel
as one of its major themes, always present in his writing, and no longer
confined to a brief passing experience as in the synoptics. The apostles
have seen the glory of the enfleshed Word (Jn. 1:4). They have caught
sight of his glory through the signs he performed, and have believed
(2:11). This revelation of his glory is still in mystery and will not fully appear until his exaltation, which is the cross as the way to full glory, glory
that Jesus had in the company of the Father before the world began
(17:5).

Transjordan, A generic name of the region on the other side of the Jordan
and the Dead Sea, that is, east of the river as far as the desert. From north
to south it comprised Bashan, Gilead and the kingdoms of Moab, Ammon and Edom. *See* AMMON; BASHAN; GILEAD; MOAB.

trap
in on you like a *t*.   Lk. 21:34

tribe, tribes
any other *t*. of Israel   Gen. 49:16   the twelve *t*. of Israel   Ex. 24:4
the twelve *t*. of Israel   Gen. 49:28   among your *t*.   Deut. 12:14
                    The chiefs of her *t*.   Isa. 19:13

Trinity, The term in Christian dogma means that there are three Persons,
the Father, the Son and the Holy Spirit in the one God. The word itself is
not biblical: rather it is the result of development through controversy
The reality described by the term is, however, New Testament revelation.
The oneness of God is the accepted doctrine of the Old and New Testament (*see* MONOTHEISM). The New Testament provides the revelation that
the Son is God, and that the Spirit is God. They nevertheless do not fuse
into one divine person, for the Father sends the Son (e.g. Jn. 20:21), and
the Son sends the Spirit (Jn. 16:7; Gal. 4:4-8) who prays in the Christian
spirit the Abba of the Son to the Father (Rom. 8:15). For a fuller exposition on the Persons of the Trinity, *see* FATHER, SON, SPIRIT.

Tripolis, A city and seaport on the Phoenician coast north of Byblos
(2 Mac. 14:1).

Troas (tro′-as), A city and seaport on the northwest corner of Asia Minor
near the ruins of ancient Troy. Paul visited the city on several occasions,
but it does not seem that he spent much time there. During his second
missionary journey Paul embarked at Troas to cross to Macedonia after
he had received, in a noctural vision, the invitation of a Macedonian
youth to come to his land (Acts 16:7-11). He passed through Troas once
more on his third apostolic journey, both while going (2 Cor. 2:12-13)
and coming back (Acts 20:1-12). On this latter occasion Paul broke bread
with the Christians of the place. It was the first day of the week and Paul
was about to set out next day. His sermon went on and on until the middle
of the night. A young man named Eutychus was sitting in the casement of
the upper chamber where the community was meeting, but grew drowsy
and fell asleep, with the result that he fell to the ground, three floors below. The young man was picked up dead, but Paul came down, clasped
the boy to him and reassured the people that the boy would live. He then
went back up, broke bread and ate and continued talking until morning
(Acts 20:1-12). On one occasion, probably different from the above two,

Paul left in the house of Carpus some scrolls and a cloak which he asked Timothy to bring to him at Rome (2 Tim. 4:13).

Trophimus (trof′-i-mus), A Christian of Ephesus who accompanied Paul as far as Jerusalem at the end of his third apostolic journey (Acts 20:4-5). Some Jews of Asia had seen Paul and Trophimus together in the city, and later found Paul in the Temple. They took this occasion to accuse Paul of having brought into the atrium of the Temple reserved for the Jews an uncircumcised gentile. Paul was thereupon arrested, and so began the long process that eventually brought Paul to Rome (Acts 21:27-29). According to 2 Timothy 4:20 Trophimus became sick at Miletus and was left there by Paul, but it is impossible to determine if this is the same person, or in what circumstances this occurred.

trouble

our salvation in time of *t*.	Isa. 33:2	Sir, do not *t*. yourself	Lk. 7:6

trumpet

the *t*. blast and	Ex. 20:18	When the *t*. blows,	Isa. 18:3
let the *t*. sound	Lev. 25:9	Blow the *t*. through	Jer. 4:5

trust

Lo, he puts no *t*.	Job 4:18	And put your *t*. in	Isa. 30:12
T. in the Lord	Isa. 26:4	I *t*. that you will	Rom. 15:24
	so that we might *t*.,	2 Cor. 1:9	

Truth, Truth translates the Hebrew word 'emet which is the substantive of the root 'mn whose primary meaning is to be solid, stable, firm. "Truth" then is said of what is solid, secure, something in which one can place his hope or confidence, for it neither fails nor defrauds. God's truth, then, is his fidelity, the guarantee of the truth of his words and promises, and the power which overcomes all obstacles, even that of man's sin, to bring to fulfilment what he pledged to do. To truth in the sense explained is opposed lying, which is tantamount to what is inconsistent and therefore defrauds. God in this sense is truth and man a lie. These two notions are maintained more or less unaltered in the Old and New Testament, and have many applications.

In the Old Testament—in some Psalms, wisdom and apocalytic literature —a variation of the same notion of truth can be discovered that has its own development. Truth is here the wisdom doctrine and the law given by God, for they have their origin in God who revealed them. Both notions combine, in that the law and wisdom have the guarantee of their truth, their trustworthiness, in God. In the same way truth is related to the "mysteries of God," that is, with his salvific design in man's favor (*see* Wis. 3:6; Dan. 9:13; 8:26; 11:2, etc.).

In the Dead Sea Scrolls "truth" is a central notion and practically designates the religious convictions of the sect. Its members say they possess a knowledge of God's truth, that is, of God's mysteries revealed to the sect's founder, who by God's gift was introduced into the true interpretation of the word of God. In this tradition then, the truth is the same as the authentic revelation of God, with a polemic accent against any other doctrine that might be proposed as such.

This is the fundamental sense of the word "truth" in John's gospel, but this meaning is not unknown to other New Testament authors. Paul (*see* Rom. 2:20) speaks of the truth of the gospel (Gal. 2:5, 14), of the word of truth (Col. 1:5; Eph. 1:13) which is nothing more than the authentic word of God preached by the apostle (2 Cor. 4:2). To arrive at the knowledge of the truth is to believe the word of the gospel (1 Tim. 2:4; 2 Tim. 3:7;

Tit. 1:1). On the regenerative power of the truth *see* James 1:18; 1 Peter 1:23; 2 Peter 1:12.

For John the truth is the word of God which Jesus heard from the Father and repeats to us, to which he gives witness and in which he invites belief from us (Jn. 8:40). To the question, then, what this word of truth is which Jesus reveals and in which he invites belief, the best answer can be found in Martha's words: "I have come to believe that you are the Messiah, the Son of God; he who is to come into the world" (Jn. 11:27). Jesus is the Son of God who has come into the world; he perfectly reveals to us the Father and leads us to him. In this sense the Son of God who has come into the world is himself the truth, that is, the supreme, perfect and authentic revelation of God. This is suggested by texts such as John 1:17 and 17:6 and is explicitly affirmed in John 14:6: "I am the way, the truth and the life," that is, he is the way, the salvation, for being Son of God, He is the revelation of the Father and communicates the divine life that he possesses in himself.

For John, the truth or word of Jesus received with faith becomes a dynamic principle which irradiates from within the whole Christian life. In 2 John 2:3 Christians are those who know the truth because the truth is in them. The truth, then, is an active principle which teaches us from within so that we have no further need of a teacher (1 Jn. 2:20, 27). These affirmations are much like those one reads in Jeremiah 31:31-34, from which, in the last analysis, they stem. Jeremiah states that the New Covenant will consist in a renewal of heart brought about by God; he will write his law into man's heart. Ezekiel 36:25-27 underscores the work of the Holy Spirit in this work of renewal.

One must be wary of understanding John's statements in a purely intellectual sense. The knowledge of God has an affective aspect and involves adhesion of the will. It is, in other words, the complete surrender of the whole person to God which is expressed above all in charity. *See* KNOWLEDGE.

John 8:31-34 states that the truth makes us free. The freedom referred to is freedom from sin (8:34). This freedom is granted by the Son to all those who receive with faith his word which is the truth. This reception of the word is not just a condition for the reception of freedom. When we open ourselves to the truth we receive into ourselves the creator of freedom. Truth is the dynamism which enables us to overcome sin (1 Jn. 2:4). Further, if the truth, which is God's seed in man, remains in the Christian, he cannot sin (1 Jn. 3:9).

John then makes use of the concept of truth to drive home a doctrine common to the whole New Testament, and especially dear to Paul. The interior renewal of man takes place through faith, through which he receives into himself an internal dynamism which guides him from within to the full knowledge of the mystery of Christ and to the fulfilment of his precepts, especially that of charity.

Tryphaena (try-fee′-na), A Christian woman at Rome, who with Tryphosa works "hard for the Lord," and is saluted by Paul in Romans 16:12.

Trypho (try′-foe), A general of Alexander Balas. When Demetrius II Nicator conquered Alexander and became king, Trypho took with him Alexander's young son and proclaimed him king while he took over the regency (1 Mac. 11:39; 54). Jonathan Maccabeus took advantage of the rivalries that were disturbing the Seleucid kingdom. First he supported Demetrius, but when he failed to keep his promises (1 Mac. 11:57), Jonathan took the side of Trypho from whom he got confirmation in his dignity as high priest (1 Mac. 11:57-59). Trypho decided to get rid of the young king Antiochus VI, but for fear that Jonathan would not support this move he decided first of all to take care of that end of things. He prepared an army and penetrated into Jonathan's territories as far as Beth-shan. Jonathan came to meet him with a superior army. Trypho then decided to act with astuteness. He received Jonathan with great honor and convinced him to let his men go and to accompany him to Ptolemais. Jonathan fell into the trap. As soon as they got into Ptolemais the men of the city closed the gates and seized him. All who entered with him were also taken and all were killed (1 Mac. 12:39-48). Trypho then returned to Antiochia, had Antiochus VI assassinated, and thus became king. His triumph was of brief duration, however. He was expelled from Antiochia by Antiochus VII Sidetes, brother of Demetrius II. Boarding a ship he escaped to Orthosia and from there reached Apamea, where he was put to death (1 Mac. 15:10-37).

Tubal, Son of Japheth, son of Noah, in the Table of Nations (Gen. 10:2; 1 Chron. 1:5). It was a region and a people south of the Black Sea in Asia Minor, noted for its commerce (Ezek. 27:13). It is often linked with Meshech, which means Ionia or the western peoples in general (Ezek. 27:13; 32:26; 38:2-3; 39:1). Ezekiel 38:2 ff. contains a bitter prophecy against Tubal and Meshech.

Tubalcain, In the Yahwist genealogy for Cain, he was the son of Lamech by his second wife Zillah. He was a brother of Naamah. Genesis 4:22 calls him the ancestor of all metalworkers in bronze or iron.

tumors
Egyptian boils and with *t.*
                                        Deut. 28:27

tumult
your enemies raise a *t.*   Ps. 83:3

tunics
t. and sashes and turbans   and clothe them with *t.*   Ex. 29:8
                              Ex. 28:40

turbans
tunics and sashes and *t.*   Ex. 28:41   the ornate *t.* of fine linen
and tie the *t.* on them   Ex. 29:9   Ex. 39:28

turn
your enemies *t.* from you   Every man shall *t.*   Isa. 13:14
                              Ex. 23:27   and *t.* back to me,   Matt. 13:15
t. my hand against you   Isa. 1:25   to *t.* the hearts   Lk. 1:17

Turtledove, This term covered smaller pigeons in general. The cooing of the turtledove with the appearance of the flowers signals the departure of winter and heralds the season of glad songs (S. of S. 2:12; *see* Jer. 8:7). Leviticus prescribes that, for ritual purification after birth, a poorer person who could not afford to offer a lamb should instead bring two turtledoves, which is what Joseph and Mary did in Luke 2:24. *See* Lev. 12:7-8.

Twelve, The, *See* APOSTLE.

twice
had the same dream *t.*   Gen. 41:32   *t.* as much as he had   Job 42:10
gathered *t.* as much   Ex. 16:22   before the cock crows *t.*,
perhaps once, or even *t.*   Job 33:14   Mk. 14:30

two-edged

And let *t.* swords be	**Ps.** 149:6 sharper than any *t.* sword
as sharp as a *t.* sword	Prov. 5:4 Heb. 4:12

Tychicus (tik'-a-kus), A Christian of the Roman province of Asia. With others he accompanied Paul from Troas at the end of the third missionary journey (Acts 20:4). Later, probably from Rome, he brought the letter from Paul to the Colossians and to the Ephesians (Col. 4:7; Eph. 6:21). Paul calls him a beloved brother and loyal helper in the Lord (Eph. 6:21). In 2 Timothy 4:12 Tychicus is once more sent to Ephesus and Titus 3:12 speaks of the possibility of sending him to Titus in Crete.

type

that *t.* of the man   Rom. 5:14

Typical Sense, Besides the literal sense which the Bible has like any other human writing, its altogether special origin (*see* INSPIRATION) gives it a pattern of meanings all its own. Of these the most important is the so-called typical sense. The typical sense arises when a thing, such as the tabernacle described in Exodus cc. 25-27, 35-38 (*see* Heb. 9:1-11), or a fact, such as the miracle of the manna (*see* Jn. 6) or an institution such as the law on expiation (Lev. 16; *see* Heb. 9:1-11) points—in the mind at least of the principle author, who is God—to a future reality in the history of salvation. The thing, fact or institution becomes then a figure, prefiguration or type (*see* Rom. 5:12; 1 Cor. 10:6) of the second reality which is sometimes referred to as the anti-type (e.g. 1 Peter 3:21).

So that a thing might have a typical sense, the thing, fact or institution must have a historical or at least literary reality with its own complete meaning and function in the time and circumstances in which it occurs. We speak of a reality that is at least literary, for the typical sense does not demand that the type be historically a fact in the critical sense. It is enough that it has been consigned to the Bible as such. Thus, for example, from the fact that the lot of Jonah is a type of Christ one may not argue to the historical fact of Jonah; for a typical sense it is enough that it is described in the Bible as such.

Moreover the type gets its meaning as such from the particular way in which the Bible presents it, not from what really happened. The typical sense is different from the literal sense in that the things, persons or institutions are also signs of other realities; the typical sense is however rooted in the literal sense in which the Bible presents the typical things, persons, or institutions.

A typical sense is not just conjecture or similarity between things or persons of different ages. It arises from the divine intention of its author God. God wishes to seal in this way, through a marvelous correspondence between the different stages of his revelatory and salvific action, the fact that salvation history is of a piece. God's designs are worked out through history. There is continuity and correspondence between promise and fulfilment.

The type arises because God intends it: the material in which this intention is expressed will show a certain similarity between the reality that signifies, the type, and the reality that is signified. This similarity must be established in the Bible testimony on both realities. This does not demand a perfect similarity or adherence between type and anti-type, but it does demand at least that degree of similarity that makes the first type a sign of the second.

Tradition has often expressed itself on the value and usefulness of the typical sense. It is, moreover, based on the Apostles' own exegesis as this

710

emerges in the New Testament (*see* e.g. Rom. 5:12-21; 1 Cor. 10:1-11; Rom. 4; 1 Pet. 3:20-21; Heb. 9, etc.). The traditional doctrine has been summed up brilliantly by Pius XII in his encyclical **Divino afflante Spiritu.** Keeping to the terminology of the Fathers, the Pope speaks of the spiritual sense, but he is clearly treating of the typical sense: "What was said and done in the Old Testament was most wisely ordered and disposed by God so that what happened in the past would presignify what was to happen in the New Covenant of grace. . . . Only God could have known this spiritual sense and reveal it to us."

Tyrannus (tie-ran′-us), A citizen at Ephesus who owned a lecture hall that Paul made use of daily for two years after he had broken with the Jews for their stubborn unbelief and their open attack on Christianity (Acts 19:9).

Tyre, A city in Phoenicia on the Mediterranean coast south of Beirut, today called Sur. Of old the city was on a little island separated from the mainland by a narrow strait. Today the town is part of the mainland. Although the city existed from the third millenium, it only became an important commercial and industrial city in the eleventh century B.C. Colonists from Tyre established commercial centers along the whole Mediterranean coast from Cyprus to Spain, in Sardegna and North Africa (Carthage).

King Hiram of Tyre (*see* HIRAM), a contemporary of Solomon, had an important part to play in the construction of the Temple and the royal palace in Jerusalem (1 Kgs. 5). Previously he had had commercial dealings with David (2 Sam. 5:11; 2 Chron. 14:1). From Tyre, too, came Hiram the bronzeworker, "a highly intelligent craftsman, skilled in all types of bronzework" (1 Kgs. 7:14) who made an important contribution to the building program of Solomon (1 Kgs. 7:13-45).

Ahab king of Israel (874-853 B.C.) married Jezebel, daughter of Ethbaal, king of Tyre, also called "king of the Sidonians" (1 Kgs. 16:31). Although this alliance was very advantageous from the economical, political and commercial point of view, it turned out to be disastrous for the religious life of the land, for it led to the introduction of the Canaanite cult of Baal under the queen's protection. She in turn fought against the sustainers of Yahwism. *See* ELIJAH, AHAB, JEZEBEL.

Tyre is often mentioned in the Old Testament for its riches and commerce, but was destined to divine condemnation of which several oracles of the prophets speak (Isa. 23:1-17; 25:22; 27:3-6; 47; Ezek. 26:2-29:18; Amos 1:9; Joel 4:4; Zech. 9:3).

Throughout its history Tyre was obliged to undergo the domination of the great kingdoms of the Middle East, but it was not conquered by outsiders until Alexander the Great took it in 332 B.C. by building a causeway nearly ¼ mile long, from mainland to the island-city. It fell to the Romans under Pompey, but its ancient importance as a commercial center had diminished with the Greek and the Roman expansion throughout the Mediterranean.

Tyre existed still in New Testament times. Tyre and Sidon often figure in the gospels (Matt. 11:21-22; Matt. 15:21; Mk. 3:8; 7:24, 31; Lk. 6:17; 10:13, 14). Paul stopped there on his journey to Jerusalem and found some Christians in the place (Acts 21:3-7).

Tyropoeon (tie-roe′-pe-on), A valley in Jerusalem between the hill of Zion or Ophel and the most westerly hill. The Greek name means "valley of the cheesemaker" and figures in the writings of Josephus. Today it is almost completely filled in with the residue accumulated through the centuries. *See* JERUSALEM.

U

Ucal (you′-kal), One of the people to whom Agur addressed his collection of proverbs (*see* Proverbs 30:1).

Ugarit (oo′-ga-rit), A Phoenician city on the Syrian coast, today called Ras Shamra. The place is not mentioned in the Bible, but the chance discovery of its ruins in 1928 and the numerous texts discovered there have proved invaluable to Scripture scholars, both for the historical material and for the religious and mythological information they supply about the Canaanite religion which, according to the Bible, was the principle rival to the Hebrew Yahwism. The principle texts are about the popular Canaanite deity, Baal, even though he was not the chief deity in the Canaanite pantheon: this was El (*see* BAAL). The study of these texts has also provided the identification of one of the main literary traditions which marked the Biblical tradition. The texts were composed in the Canaanite language but with a cuneiform alphabet that was hitherto unknown. Ugaritic literature has given a more precise impression of the Canaanite culture into which the Jews were inserted when they settled in Palestine.

Ulai (you′-lie), A man-made canal near Susa on the banks of which Daniel saw in a vision the ram with the different-sized horns and the he-goat with the one majestic horn who had covered the entire earth without touching the ground (Dan. 8:2-16).

Ulam (you′-lam), A proper name (1 Chron. 7:16, 17; 8:39, 40).

Ummah, A town in the territory of Asher (Josh. 19:30).

unbelieving

an *u*. and perverse lot	Matt. 17:17	the *u*. husband is	1 Cor. 7:14
	the *u*. wife is	1 Cor. 7:14	

uncircumcised

outpost of the *u*.	1 Sam. 14:6	lest these *u*. come	1 Sam. 31:4
Who is this *u*. Philistine		their ears are *u*.	Jer. 6:10
	1 Sam. 17:26	*u*. in heart and ears	Acts 7:51

Unclean, *See* CLEAN.

understood

Joseph *u*. what they said		Have you not *u*.	Isa. 40:21
	Gen. 42:23	Have you *u*. all	Matt. 13:51
	They *u*. nothing	Lk. 18:34	

unjust

on the just and the *u*.	Matt. 5:45	anyone *u*. in a slight matter	Lk. 16:10

Unleavened Bread, This translates the Greek **azyma**, unleavened, which in turn translates the Hebrew **Massot**, meaning unleavened bread. Unleavened bread was mandatory in the offerings that accompanied the sacrifices (Ex. 23:18; 34:25), except for those destined to be eaten by the priests or others (Lev. 7:13; 23:17). Unleavened bread was moreover prescribed at all times during the Feast of Unleavened Bread and the Pasch. These two feast are closely related so as to form almost one and the same celebration in the priestly tradition of the Pentateuch (Ex. 12:1-20, 40-51; Lev. 23:5-8; Num. 28:16-25). This relationship, however, does not appear in the more ancient texts (Ex. 23:15 and 34:18), which speak only of the Feast of Unleavened Bread and not of the Pasch. This, combined with a study of the characteristics of the feast, prove that originally the two festivities had different origins and aims, and that only in a later period were they joined together.

The Feast of Unleavened Bread was originally an agrarian feast and celebrated at the beginning of the harvesting (Deut. 16:9); it was a religious
celebration for the new harvest. It lasted seven days during which bread
made from new corn was consumed. This new corn was unmixed with
anything from the previous year, and so it was unleavened (Ex. 23:15;
34:20). The agricultural feast as such was not adopted by the Israelites
before they settled in Canaan (*see* Lev. 23:10). Already in ancient times
however it had been associated with the Exodus from Egypt (Ex. 23:15;
34:20). The Feast of Unleavened Bread was a pilgrimage feast, and its
date of celebration depended on the time of harvest (the month of Abib).
The paschal feast had originally been a feast of shepherds or pastoral
feast, also linked to the memory of the Exodus. The fusion between the
two must have taken place during the period of centralization of worship
in Jerusalem (Deut. 12). Then the Pasch was made a pilgrimage feast to be
celebrated at the time of the full moon of the month Nisan-Abib. The
convergence of the two feasts was motivated by the fact that they coincided in time, they commemorated the Exodus, and during both of them unleavened bread was eaten. In this way the Feast of Unleavened Bread got
a more precise calendar; it was celebrated for one week beginning with
the day after the Pasch (Lev. 23:5-8). This was its dating in the New Testament as is clear from Matthew 27:17; Mark 14:12; Luke 22:1-7; Acts
12:3; 20:6; 1 Corinthians 5:7, 8.

unleavened bread
you must eat *u. b.*	Ex. 12:15	and baked *u. b.*	1 Sam. 28:24
	u. b. is to be	Ezek. 45:21	

unpunished
he will not go *u.*	Prov. 16:5	will not go *u.*	Prov. 19:5
will not go *u.*	Prov. 17:5	let you go *u.*	Jer. 46:28

uphold
and *u.* you with my	Isa. 41:10	my servant whom I *u.*	Isa. 42:1

upper
of the *u.* pool	Isa. 7:3

upstairs
u. room
    Mk. 14:15; Lk. 22:12; Acts 1:13

Ur, A city in lower Mesopotamia on the Euphrates, center of the Sumerian civilization (2500-1950 B.C.), today called El-Muqeiyer. With the rise
of Babylonia, Ur fell into decline. According to Genesis 11:28-31 the
family of Terah, Abraham's father, migrated from Ur to Haran in upper
Mesopotamia. Genesis 15:7 situates the calling of Abraham in Ur (*see*
Neh. 9:7). In the Bible it is always called Ur of the Chaldees, which does
not mirror the facts in Abraham's time, but refers to the neo-Babylonian
empire (*see* CHALDAEANS).

Urbanus, A Roman Christian and one of Paul's collaborators (Rom.
16:9).

urged, urging
they kept *u.* him	2 Kgs. 2:17	despite Naaman's *u.*	2 Kgs. 5:16
who *u.* him to dine	2 Kgs. 4:8	Gemariah *u.* the king	Jer. 36:25

Uri (yoor*'*-eye), Personal name (Ex. 31:2; 35:30; Ezra 10:24).

Uriah (you-rie*'*-a), 1. A Hittite, an officer in David's army and one of his
Thirty warriors (2 Sam. 23:39; 1 Chron. 11:41). While Uriah was engaged
in the war against the Ammonites, David seduced his wife Bathsheba, as a

result of which she became pregnant. David recalled Uriah from active duty, sent him home to enjoy himself and sent a present after him—all aimed at covering up the adultery. Uriah however did not go home, so David sent him back to the siege of Rabbah with a letter to Joab, the general of the army, ordering Joab to place Uriah in the thick of the fight where he should certainly die. After his death, David married Bathsheba, but the child born of the adultery died, as had been predicted by the prophet Nathan, in punishment of the double crime committed (2 Sam. 11:2-12:20).

2. A priest at Jerusalem, a contemporary of Isaiah, chosen by the prophet to be witness to an oracle announcing the imminent ruin of Damascus and Israel who had invaded Judah (Isa. 8:1-4). On Ahaz's orders Uriah had built for the Temple an altar modelled after an Assyrian one the king had seen in Damascus when he went there to pay homage to Tiglath-pileser III, whose vassal he was (2 Kgs. 16:10-16).

3. A prophet of Jerusalem, King Jehoiakim's contemporary (609-598 B.C.), who was slain by the king, after an attempted flight, for having spoken like Jeremiah of the impending ruin of Jerusalem (Jer. 26:20-23).

Urim and Thummim (yoor'-im and thum'-mim), The meaning of these words is uncertain. They were objects worn or carried by the priest to ask God for an answer to problems (Deut. 33:8; Num. 27:21). There is no description of them in the Bible, but one supposes that they were small stones or chips, drawn at random, and presumed to indicate God's answer to a precisely placed question. To discover, for instance, why God was silent, Saul set out to find who sinned. Urim would point the finger at Saul and Jonathan, while Thummim would declare the people guilty. Urim was drawn and again lots were drawn, so that Jonathan's fault was disclosed (*see* 1 Sam. 14:41, 42; 28:6). The objects were in the ephod, one presumes from 1 Samuel 23:10; 30:8. After the time of Saul and David, they no longer seem to have been used to consult God (*see* Ezra 2:63; Neh. 7:65). The pectoral of the high priest's sacred vestments had the urim and thummim sewn into them (Ex. 28:30; Lev. 8:8). Already however they seem to have lost their oracular function.

us

with *u*., all of *u*.	Deut. 5:3	to cut *u*. down	Isa. 14:8
a sortie against *u*.	Josh. 8:5	Inquire for *u*.	Jer. 21:2

use

may be put to any other *u*.		No *u*. to multiply remedies	
	Lev. 7:24		Jer. 46:11
you shall *u*. in assembling		who make *u*. of the world	
	Num. 10:2		1 Cor. 7:31

Uthai (you'-thie), Personal name (1 Chron. 9:4; Ezra 8:14).

utter, utters

I will *u*. mysteries	Ps. 78:2	and your tongue *u*. deceit Isa. 59:3

Uz, 1. Son of Aram (Gen. 10:23) or of Nahor (Gen. 22:21), an Aramaean clan of northern Mesopotamia, about whom no more is known.

2. A clan or territory of Edom (Gen. 38:28; Lam. 4:21) which is Job's home (Job 1:1).

Uzal (you'-zal), An Arabian region listed among the sons of Shem in the Table of Nations (Gen. 10:27; 1 Chron. 1:21).

Uzzah, 1. Son of Shimei, a Levite of the Merari family (1 Chron. 6:14, 15).

2. Son of Abinadab and brother to Ahio. When David was having the ark of the covenant transported by cart from Kiriath-jearim to Jerusalem, Uzzah walked beside the cart while Ahio led it. When they came to the threshing floor of Nodan Uzzah reached out to steady the ark as the oxen were making it tilt, for which crime the anger of God struck him dead on the spot (2 Sam. 6:1-8). The place where he died was called on that account Perez-uzzah, that is "the breaking forth upon Uzzah." David became fearful, so instead of taking the ark to his citadel at Jerusalem, he housed it with Obed-edom of Gath, where it remained three months (2 Sam 6:9-11).

3. The garden of Uzzah in Jerusalem was probably thus called after its owner. It was the burial place of King Manasseh and his murdered son, King Amon of Judah (2 Kgs. 21:18, 26).

Uzzen-sheerah, A town in Ephraim built by Sheerah, daughter of Ephraim (1 Chron. 7:24).

Uzzi (uz′-eye), A proper name (1 Chron. 7:7; 9:8; Ezra 7:4; Neh. 12:19, 42).

Uzziah (uh-zie′-ah), King of Judah (783-742 B.C.), also known as Azariah, son and successor of Amaziah (1 Kgs. 14:21). At sixteen years of age he became king (1 Kgs. 15:1, 2). He reorganized the army and provided his soldiers with shields, spears, helmets, coats of mail, bows and sling stones, while he constructed several defense turrets around the city. On these he mounted war-engines capable of firing arrows and great stones. He also interested himself in the home economy, dug many cisterns, had large herds, peopled the land with farmers and vine-dressers.

He was victorious in his campaign against the Philistines and recaptured Elath in the Gulf of Aqaba (2 Chron. 26:1-15). In his later years he contracted a disease the Bible calls "leprosy" (*see* LEPROSY) and his son Jotham became regent (1 Kgs. 15:5). The Chronicler explains this disease as a punishment from God for having usurped some of the functions of the priest by offering incense. While the first part of his life is praised for his godliness, he is condemned for his pride at the end (2 Chron. 26:16-23).

Uzziel (uz′-i-el), 1. The name of a grandson of Levi (Ex. 6:18; Num. 3:19; 6:3).

2. Several other men in the Old Testament (1 Chron 4:42; 7:7; 25:4; 2 Chron. 29:14; Neh. 3:8).

V

Vaizatha (vye′-za-tha), A son of Haman the vizier of King Ahasuerus (Esth. 9:9). *See* HAMAN; AHASUERUS; XERXES.

valley

in the *V.* of Siddim	Gen. 14:3	the wheat in the *v.*	1 Sam. 6:13
greet him in the *V.*	Gen. 14:17	overlooks the *V.*	1 Sam. 13:18

Vanity, Vanity translates the Hebrew word **hebel** and its synonyms. In the Hebrew original it does not have the meaning given to it by Christian asceticism and everyday use. This would be the search after notoriety based on futile motives. The term in the Bible is nearer the physical meaning of emptiness, being without consistency or content, and therefore being a delusion.

Vanity is one of the favorite expressions of Qoheleth: "Vanity of vanities! All things are vanity" (Eccl. 1:2). This is the implacable verdict passed by the author on the different concepts of life that come under review and reflection. Vain it is to seek after durable celebrity (1:9-11), or wisdom (7:13-17) or riches (2:18-23), etc. This is not properly speaking a moral verdict, but it is diametrically opposed to those who proclaim celebrity, wisdom or virtue to be the unfailing source of happiness and joy. On the interpretation of Qoheleth's thought, *see* QOHELETH.

In an analogous sense other texts propose as vain the cult of idols (Jer. 16:19) and the gods of other people (Isa. 57:13; Jer. 2:5; 8:18; 14:22, etc.). Even the seemingly happy life of the impious and transgressors of the law (Pss. 78:33; 94:11) is vanity. While its exterior splendor might for a moment blind one, in reality this is a life without consistency, and therefore, in the last analysis, a life of delusion destined to ruin, just as the idols, which are themselves vain and empty, delude the hopes of those who place in them their trust (Acts 14:15).

The third commandment of the Decalogue is a prohibition: "You shall not take the name of the Lord your God in vain" (Ex. 20:7; Deut. 5:11). This excludes all abuse of God's name, and in particular it prohibits perjury (*see* Jer. 7:9), swearing in the name of other gods (Deut. 6:13), magic (*see* MAGIC) and similar cases.

Vashti (vash′-tie), The wife of Ahasuerus, king of Persia (Xerxes I, 486-465 B.C.), who was repudiated and her place taken by Esther. During the celebration of a royal banquet, the king ordered his eunuchs "to bring Queen Vashti into his presence wearing the royal crown, that he might display her beauty to the populace and the officials, for she was lovely to behold" (Esth. 1:11). The queen refused to come. The king was thrown into a rage and called together his counselors to know how she should be punished for such an affront, in accordance with the law. The counselors emphasized the social repercussions of Vashti's conduct "for the queen's conduct will become known to all the women, and they will look with disdain upon their husbands" (Esth. 1:17). So it was decided to deprive her of her queenly dignity and thus leave place for the king to "give her royal dignity to one more worthy than she" (Esth. 1:19). Thus Esther became queen.

The account is a legend. According to Herodotus, the Greek historian, Xerxes' wife was called Amestris, and there is no indication that she was ever dethroned. The episode however serves the purpose of the author of the Book of Esther, and helps form the framework for his message. *See* ESTHER, BOOK OF.

Vaticanus, Codex, A manuscript of the Greek Bible containing both Old and New Testaments. It stems from the fourth century, and comes from Egypt. Today it is preserved in the Vatican Library. Together with the Sinaiticus (*see* SINAITICUS) it is one of the principle witnesses t the recension by Hesychius. *See* TEXT, NEW TESTAMENT; SEPTUAGINT. It is indicated by the sign B.

Vau (vaw), The sixth letter of the Hebrew alphabet (w).

vehemently
keep reasserting *v.*   Mk. 14:31   to accuse him *v.*   Lk. 23:10

Veil of Temple, According to Exodus 26:31-37 the innermost c amber of the Tabernacle was closed off with a veil woven of violet, purple and scarlet yarn, and finely embroidered with cherubim. Behind the rtain was the Holy of Holies, in which was kept the Ark of the Covenan , covered by the Throne of Mercy. The Tabernacle was but a stylized version of Solomon's Temple, where the innermost chamber was also cut off by a curtain of "violet, crimson and fine linen, which had cherubim embroidered upon it" (2 Chron. 3:14).

Only Aaron and his sons were permitted to penetrate beyond the veil into the Holy of Holies (Num. 18:7), and later this was again limited, to the High Priest alone, once a year, on the Day of Atonement. (*See* ATONEMENT, DAY OF.) On that occasion the High Priest went in with a censer and incense which he burned so that a cloud of smoke formed over the Throne of Mercy where God was present, and "if he does this, he shall not die" (Lev. 16:13). He then took the blood of the bull and sprinkled it with his finger to the eastern side of the Throne of Mercy, and then seven times in front of it (Lev. 16:14; *see* Heb. 9:1-10). In other sacrifices of expiation the victim's blood was sprinkled on the veil itself, without the priest entering into the Holy of Holies. In Hebrews 10:20 the veil of the Temple is a type of the humanity of Christ, which is the new way to the throne of God's mercy and grace.

According to Matthew 27:51; Mark 15:38; Luke 23:45, at Jesus' death the veil of the Temple was rent in two, from top to bottom. Often this is interpreted in the sense that with Christ's death the Holy of Holies is open to all. In reality however the meaning is rather the opposite: the Temple has been disowned, emptied and its place now taken by Christ, the new Temple not made by human hands (Mk. 14:58). The risen and glorified humanity of Jesus has become the one and exclusive point of meeting between man and God.

Veil of Women, The Old Testament clearly alludes to the custom of women of covering their faces with a veil (Gen. 24:65; 38:14, 19; Isa. 3:23; S. of S. 4:1, 3; 6:7), but this seems to have been the case only on certain occasions, and probably only referred to the marriage ceremony (*see* MARRIAGE) or to later periods in Judaism. In ancient times girls were not secluded nor were they veiled. Nor did the veiling of women ever reach the universality it achieved among the Arabs.

In 1 Corinthians 11:2-16 Paul censures the conduct of some women who attended the meetings of the Christian community without veiling their head. Paul is not against this practice per se, but because the custom of veiling was then held to be of significance: the veil was a symbol of the subjection of woman to man (1 Cor. 11:10). This passage however provides no conclusions of universal validity of Paul's admonition. It was a disciplinary question that was subject to change with time and circumstances. For the apostle the correctness and modesty that the veil expressed was clearly more important than the veil itself.

Vengeance, Vindictiveness or revenge are rare concepts in the Bible (*see* Jer. 20:10; Prov. 6:34; Ezek. 25:12, 15). It was not a question of personal revenge for a wrong received but the restoration of the good order in social and religious relationship that had to be accomplished. This is the point of the legislation on Avenger of Blood (*see* Num. 35:9-34). In the New Testament God reserves vengeance to himself (*see* Rom. 12:19; Deut. 32:35; Heb. 10:30). Christ reassures his faithful that God will see justice done to his chosen who cry to him day and night. Even when he seems to delay, a speedy deliverance is at hand (Lk. 18:7-8). *See* AVENGER; MURDER.

venom

the *v.* of reptiles	Deut. 32:24	the *v.* of asps	Ps. 140:4
the *v.* of dragons	Deut. 32:33	the *v.* of asps lies	Rom. 3:13

vermilion

and paints it with *v.*	Jer. 22:14	Chaldeans drawn with *v.*	
			Ezek. 23:14

Versions of Holy Scripture. *See* ENGLISH VERSIONS OF THE BIBLE, SEP-

TUAGINT, SYRIAC VERSIONS OF THE BIBLE, TARGUM, TEXT CRITICISM, VULGATE.

Vespasian, Titus Flavius Vespasianus, Roman Emperor from 69 to 79 A.D. Before he became emperor at Nero's death, Vespasian, with his son and successor Titus, had led the Roman legions in suppressing the Jewish revolt in Palestine. Vespasian left the command to Titus who brought Judea into submission and captured Jerusalem.

village, villages

Go into the *v.* straight	through towns and *v.*	Lk. 8:1
Mk. 11:2; 21:2	Jesus entered a *v.*	Lk. 10:38
As he was entering a *v.*	Lk. 17:12	

Vine, Israelite folklore attributed the beginnings of viniculture to Noah, the father of humanity after the deluge (Gen. 9:20). Viniculture was widespread in the ancient East, and the fruit of the vine, together with oil and grain was one of the chief products of Canaan (Deut. 11:14; Josh. 24:13; Jer. 5:17).

The allegory of the vine in Isaiah 5:1-7 affords many details on the cultivation of the vine. The vines were normally planted on hills (Isa. 5:1; Amos 9:13). The terrain had first to be spaded and cleared of stones (Isa. 5:2). The vineyard was surrounded by a ditch or moat to protect it from animals or robbers (Jer. 49:9; S. of S. 2:15). A watchtower was built in the vineyard, as well as a wine press (Isa. 5:2). The vines could be raised from the ground by means of stakes (Ezek. 19:11) or allowed to spread out on the ground. September was the vintage month and an occasion for festivity and dancing (Jgs. 21:19). The grapes were taken to the press to have the juice stamped out of them (Isa. 63:3). They could also however be preserved and dried in the sun to make raisins (1 Sam. 25:18; 30:12; 2 Sam. 16:1).

Vines and viniculture have given rise to many figurative expressions in the language. Isaiah 5:1-7 refers to Israel as the vineyard of the Lord, the object of his continual care, yet refusing to produce good fruit. The Lord, who is deluded by the sterility of the vine, will "take away its hedges, give it to grazing; . . . it shall not be pruned or hoed, but overgrown with thorns and briers" (Isa. 5:5-7; *see* Ezek. 15:1-8). The wife of the man who fears the Lord will be "like a fruitful vine" (Ps. 128:3). Wisdom too compares herself to a vine for the abundance and quality of her fruits (Sir. 24:17).

The most noted application of this figure however is the allegory of the vine in John 15:1-8. Jesus is the vine that gives life to the branches. If they are separated from the vine they cannot bear fruit and are good for nothing but to be gathered into bunches and burned. The Father is the vinedresser who prunes the branches so that they can bear more fruit and cuts off the branches that bear none. The person who lives on in the vine that is Jesus will bear much fruit. The fruit of the vine is charity which becomes a reality when one keeps Christ's commandments (Jn. 15:9-10). Tradition has seen in this text the Johannine version of Paul's doctrine of the incorporation of Christians into Christ who is the source of life and salvation.

Vinegar, Wine gone sour or overfermented produces vinegar. which is several times mentioned in the Old Testament. Since the Nazirite was under vow, he was not only forbidden alcohol but also its derivatives, such as vinegar (even though some translations, in Num. 6:3, read "strong drink"). Vinegar was a condiment for food. Ruth was invited by Boaz to dip her bread in vinegar sauce (Ruth 2:14).

Virgin, Virginity, A virgin is a woman who has not had sexual relationships. In Hebrew the word is **betulah,** and in Greek **parthenos.** In the ordinary language of the people the word is generally applied to every unmarried girl.

In Isaiah 7:14, however, the Hebrew reads **almah,** "mature," one of marriageable age, a word that says nothing about sexual experience. Matthew (1:22 f) uses the verse to confirm the virgin birth of our Lord, or perhaps better, as a prophetic reinterpretation of Isaiah 7:14 in the light of the manifestations of God's plan.

The virginity of the promised bride was highly prized by the Israelites as can be seen in their legislation. Should a bridegroom discover upon marrying a girl that she is not a virgin, the law states that he should denounce her to the elders of the city, who should then take her to the entrance of her father's house and there stone her to death (Deut. 22:20, 21). If however a husband should unjustly accuse a girl of misconduct, then the parents' task was to prove her virginity, whereupon her accusing husband was taken and flogged, and fined one hundred shekels of silver, to be handed over to the girl's father in recompense for "defaming a virgin of Israel." Moreover the husband in this case could never dismiss by divorce such an unjustly accused wife (Deut. 22:13-19).

Should a man seduce a virgin who is not betrothed, he would be fined fifty shekels (Deut. 22:29), to be paid to the girl's father, and was bound to marry the girl with no liberty later to divorce her (Deut. 22:28, 29). Even if her father refuses to give her to him, he must still pay him the customary price for virgins (Ex. 22:15, 16). Leviticus 21:13, 14 prescribes that the priest should marry a virgin, "otherwise he will have base offspring among his people."

One will however search the Old Testament in vain for any trace of esteem for virginity as a perpetual life condition. The epilogue of the story of Jephthah's daughter is significant on this point. Her father's imprudent vow destined her to die in sacrifice. She asked for two months of life to go down the mountains to mourn her virginity, i.e. her fate not to bear sons, with her companions (Jgs. 11:29-40). The only case that in some way anticipates the Christian ideal of virginity is that of Jeremiah, who received this command from the Lord: "Do not marry any woman, you shall not have sons or daughters in this place." The reason, however, was a prophetic and religious one, to make of Jeremiah a living warning to the people of the lot that awaited them: "the sons and daughters who will be born in this place . . . of deadly disease they shall die" (Jer. 16:1-4).

The New Testament proposes the ideal of virginity without detriment to the sanctity of marriage. Mary's virginity is explained both by Matthew and Luke in the light of her calling to be the mother of the Son of God, and not the other way around. Both in word and example Jesus proposed an ideal that renounced matrimony for the kingdom. Celibacy and virginity, like poverty and the renouncing of goods, is an expression of one dimension of complete dedication to the kingdom of God and the following of Christ. Matthew 19:12, on eunuchs who have made themselves so for the sake of the kingdom, has traditionally been taken as an invitation to those called to live a life of celibacy. Some exegetes however believe that the text refers back to the previous passage (Matt. 19:1-11) on marriage and divorce, so that eunuchs for the kingdom would be those who, though innocent, are abandoned by their spouses, and who nevertheless refuse to remarry as a living expression of God's loyalty to his people who are often disloyal (*see* Hos. 2).

"The unmarried man is busy with the Lord's affairs, concerned with pleasing the Lord" (1 Cor. 7:32-35). In this chapter Paul offers some doctrine and advice on marriage and virginity. The passage is much discussed, and problems arise because Paul's words are addressed to precise questions put by the Corinthians, which unfortunately we do not know. The whole difficulty seemed to arise from a mistaken notion of the "newness of life" to which baptism introduced one. Some were interpreting this as if it also entailed the complete rupture with family relations and the social condition in which one had been before conversion. Paul's general principle was: "The general rule is that each one should lead the life the Lord has assigned him, continuing as he was when the Lord called him" (to the faith through baptism) (1 Cor. 7:17). He may have been called from being a circumcised Jew or otherwise (1 Cor. 7:18-20), from being a slave or free man (1 Cor. 7:21-24). Paul reasserts the indissolubility of marriage (1 Cor. 7:10-11) and "counsels" the unmarried to remain so. It is however no sin to marry (1 Cor. 7:25-28). This is a counsel to respect the gift that each person received from the Lord, just as he advises the widow not to remarry, while at the same time raising no difficulties about remarriage (1 Cor. 7:39, 40).

While Christ was celibate, his relationship with the Church is expressed in terms of the intimate union between husband and wife, which is derived from, and becomes a sacramental and symbolic expression of, the union in which the celibate Christ embraces his bride the Church. Paul's thought oscillates between the two in Ephesians 5:25 ff. *See* MARRIAGE.

Vision, Among the means by which revelation is made to man in the Bible, visions also figure. It is not easy to define the phenomenon in psychological terms, seeing that the data supplied by the Bible on this score are not abundant. In itself, a vision is an interior phenomenon, that is, there is no corresponding reality present that can be perceived by the five senses. Nevertheless it is no hallucination, for what really takes place, while not striking the external senses, does meet the imagination and intellect. The ordinary exercise of these faculties is suspended while the visionary is interiorly encountered by ideas and images which appear with such spontaneity and unequivocation that he is convinced that they are not his own, but are placed there by some other power. The vision always stimulates and concentrates psychic powers, sometimes to the point of ecstasy in the strict sense of the term, that is, complete physical insensibility and psychic unconsciousness. The most minute description of the psychological process of vision is read in the introduction to the third and fourth ora les of Balaam: "The utterance of Balaam, son of Boer, the utterance of the man whose eye is true. The utterance of one who knows what the Almighty sees, enraptured and with eyes unveiled" (Num. 24:15-16).

According to 1 Samuel 9:9 "he who is now (in Saul's time) called prophet was formerly called seer." This text links vision and prophecy very closely together, even though the "seer" was better known, in all probability, for his gifts of clairvoyance and telepathy than for visions in the sense explained above. This would seem to follow from the question Saul projected to the "seer," that is, where did his father's donkeys go (1 Sam. 9:20)? Elisha the prophet had evident gifts of clairvoyance and telepathy (2 Kgs. 6:9; 6:12; 6:32; 5:26; 3:6).

Visions, in the sense explained above are infrequent in the prophetic books, even though these bear the stereotyped title: "Vision of the prophet N." (*see* Isa. 1:1; Amos 1:1). One could quote the vision in which Isaiah received his mission (Isa. 6:1-6) which is noteworthy for its sobriety and solemnity. Amos 8 and Jeremiah 1:11-14 have a particular type of vision, which, in the terminology of some authors, is a "symbolic perception." This means that an external object stimulates the prophetic inspiration, such as, for example, a pot boiling (Jer. 1:3), a basket of figs (Amos

8:1), which become "significant," that is, they carry a message that vividly imprinted itself on the mind of the prophet

In Ezekiel visions are more numerous. They are complex and more charged with content than in previous prophets (e.g. Ezek. 1: God's throne; Ezek. 2-3: Ezekiel eats a scroll; Ezek. 28: vision of the abominations in the Temple at Jerusalem, etc.). Ezekiel was undoubtedly a visionary in the good sense of the word. It is legitimate, however, to suspect that in his account of the visions there is literary elaboration that does not keep strictly to the experience it is describing. Frequent visions are also described in Zechariah (*see* Zech. 1-6). In fact visions are not only frequent but also seem to be the most characteristic trait of the last phase of prophetism, after the exile, and with this the apocalyptic era is already announced. *See* ZECHARIAH, BOOK OF.

In apocalyptic literature visions are the ordinary organ of revelation. They are, however, literary constructions. The real author of the book expresses himself in visions that were had in the past by great personages of the Bible such as Enoch, Moses, Daniel, Ezra, and Baruch. They are nothing more than contrived speculations on the constitution and working of the universe, on the wonders of the heavens, or allegorical versions of the past. The literary construction makes use of a repertory of symbols that is in part drawn from the prophetic books.

The New Testament is very meager on visions. Jesus states in Luke 10:18: "I watched Satan fall from the sky like lightning": this probably alludes to a visionary phenomenon. At Joppa Peter had a vision to prepare him for the reception into the Church of the first Gentile (Acts 10:10-16). Paul alludes to numerous "visions and revelations" that he had received (2 Cor. 12:1). Paul speaks of another type of vision, which will have God himself as object. This will be when God will no longer have to be viewed "as through a mirror in a dark manner" but face to face. This vision however will be on the other side of death's river; now however it is the object of Christian hope (1 Cor. 13:12-13) which is promised by Christ to the pure of heart (Matt. 5:8).

visit, visited

you shall be *v*.	Isa. 29:6	he has *v*. and ransomed me	
you come to *v*. me	Matt. 25:36		Lk. 1:68
When did we *v*. you	Matt. 25:39		

voice

hear my *v*.	Gen. 4:23	her *v*. could not be	1 Sam. 1:13
the *v*. is Jacob's	Gen. 27:22	heard the *v*. of the Lord	Isa. 6:8

Vow, A deliberate promise made to God of a free, supererogatory good. Often a vow accompanied prayer in a conditional form. Hanna promised to consecrate to God her child should God grant her one (1 Sam. 1:11). The sailors who were companions to Jonah made vows to God to get him to calm the sea (Jonah 1:16). There are numerous allusions to vows with unspecified objects in the Psalms (Pss. 56:12-13; 61:5, 8; 65:1; 66:13-15). To this kind of vow belongs Jephthah's, in which he pledged to God, in return for victory over the Ammonites, to offer in holocaust the first person he should meet at the door of his house when he returned in triumph. To his dismay it was his only child, an unmarried daughter who met him. She asked for two months to wander in the mountains "to weep for her virginity,"—i.e., would be unable to fulfill her function and desire to bear sons—after which the vow was fulfilled (Jgs. 11:29-40).

Israelite legislation has something to say on vows. The law on sacrifices makes provision for "voluntary" sacrifices, that is, the offering of unpre-

Vulgate   **BIBLE DICTIONARY**

scribed gifts which were then often the object of vows (Lev. 7:16-17; 22:17-25). A particular type of vow was the Nazirite vow, a temporary consecration that involved the abstention from alcoholic drink and keeping himself ritually clean, allowing his hair to grow long until the period of the consecration was over and he made his sacrifice (Num. 6; *see* NAZIRITE). The vows taken by unmarried women depended on the approval of their fathers and those of married women on the approval of their husbands (Num. 30). When the vow proved more difficult than was foreseen, the law in Leviticus 27:1-8 makes provision for a financial commutation —an adult male was valued for this purpose at fifty silver shekels, an adult female at thirty, a boy at twenty, a girl at ten, an infant boy at five, an infant girl at three, and an old person, man or woman at ten; but should the person be unable to meet this sum, the priest was to set a sum proportionate to their means (Num. 27:1-8).

Wisdom tradition has also its contribution in this important aspect of religious practice. Sirach warns against precipitation in making vows, not vowing something without giving it thought in view of the seriousness of the obligation assumed (Sir. 18:23; Prov. 20:25). Moreover one is exhorted by example quickly to fulfil one's vows (Sir. 18:22).

Vulgate, The Latin version of the Bible done by St. Jerome in the fourth century and destined to become the most widely distributed edition in the Latin church from the sixth century on.

As early as the second century there were Latin translations from the Bible, the Old Testament based on the Greek of the Septuagint and the New Testament staying close to the so-called "Western Text." (*See* TEXT, NEW TESTAMENT.) That there was more than one translation is very probable, and a distinction is usually drawn between the more ancient African form and the Italian form which was really no more than a revision of the former. With the imperfection in the existing translations with their often arbitrary changes and the variety of texts in the different codices, a drastic intervention was called for. This step was taken by Pope Damasus (366-384 A.D.) who commissioned St. Jerome in 382 to undertake the correction of the Latin text of the Bible. Thus St. Jerome commenced his work on the Bible text, a work that was to last for 24 years. To Jerome we owe:

a. The correction of the ancient Latin translation of the gospels on the basis of the original Greek. St. Jerome corrected only when the meaning in the Latin did not correspond to the meaning in the Greek. This is the text that is printed in the Vulgate editions of the New Testament (383 A.D.)

b. Jerome probably undertook a similar correction procedure for the rest of the books of the New Testament, but there is no proof of this.

c. While still at Rome Jerome undertook the correction of the Psalter on the basis of the Greek text of the Septuagint, without taking into account Origen's corrections. (*See* SEPTUAGINT.) This is called the Roman Psalter and is used only in the choral recitation of the Divine Office in St. Peter's Basilica in Rome.

d. After Pope Damasus' death in 384 A.D. Jerome went to Palestine where he found the Septuagint text corrected by Origen, in the light of which he again revised the Psalter which is now known as the Gallican Psalter and is found in the printed editions of the Vulgate.

e. From 390 A.D. on Jerome began to work on a Latin translation from the Hebrew Old Testament.

The Vulgate translation then comprises: the Old Testament books from the Hebrew made by Jerome; the translation of the Old Testament Greek books or deuterocanonical works in the ancient Latin, not by Jerome; the

722

Gallican Psalter, a correction of the old Latin translation made by Jerome on the basis of the Septuagint Greek, which had previously been corrected by Origen; the old Latin version of the gospels corrected on the basis of the original Greek by Jerome, and the rest of the New Testament from the old Latin, probably corrected by Jerome.

It took Jerome's translation two centuries to establish itself in the Latin church on account of its contrasts with the ancient Latin versions. From the time of Bede (735 A.D.), however, it reigned supreme in the liturgy, in preaching and in teaching. Alcuin of York, who from 796 had been Abbot of the monastery of St. Martin of Tours, made at the beginning of the ninth century the first and best of the ancient recensions of the Vulgate text, which had become crowded with glosses and deformations.

During the thirteenth century at Paris the need was felt for a uniform Latin text of the Vulgate which could easily be quoted. This was the birth of the Paris Bible, with its division into chapters by Stephen Langton in 1214. From a critcal point of view however the text was horrible. This factor gave rise to the **Correctoria,** lists of corrections to be made in the text, which eventually succeeded in adding more confusion to the issue.

The Vulgate was the first printed book and before 1500 A.D. it had run through 100 editions. The first printing was the work of Gutenberg, and came out in two volumes, without the year being indicated. In all probability it dates back to 1452.

The Council of Trent (1545-1563) took up the question of the Vulgate from a disciplinary, not a dogmatic, point of view. The Council was concerned about the Latin versions only, and among them it chose the Vulgate as the authentic Latin translation. (The use of the term "authentic" provoked many discussions that were eventually settled in a definitive manner by Pius XII in his encyclical **Divino afflante Spiritu,** 1943). Aware of the sorry state of his sacred text, the Council also ordered that a new, corrected version be prepared. This came out in 1592 and is known as the Sixto-Clementine edition, from the names of Popes Sixtus V (1585-1590) and Clement VIII (1592-1605) who had parts to play in its publication. In 1907 Pius X created a special commission to publish a new critical edition of the Vulgate of St. Jerome, making use of today's critical methods. The work was confided to the Benedictines of the monastery of St. Jerome in Rome, which was erected for this purpose. Most of the volumes of the Old Testament have been brought to completion.

vulture
the *v,* the osprey
> Lev. 11:13; Deut. 14:12

W

wafers
unleavened *w.* spread   Ex. 29:2

wages

what your *w.* should be	what *w.* you want	Gen. 30:28
	Gen. 29:15 and changed my *w.*	Gen. 31:7
	The *w.* of sin is death Rom. 6:23	

Wagon, *See* CART.

Waheb (way'-eb), A region in Moab (Num. 21:14).

wail, wails

Moab *w.*	Isa. 15:2	Everywhere they *w.*	Isa. 16:7
everyone *w.*	Isa. 15:3	*W.,* O ships of Tarshish	Isa. 23:1

723

wail, wails, (cont.)

w., you vinedressers	Joel 1:11	w., O ministers	Joel 1:13

wait

W. here for us until	Ex. 24:14	I would w.	Job 14:14
If we w. until morning	2 Kgs. 7:9	or lie in w.	Job 38:40

wall, walls

the water like a w.	Ex. 14:22	into the city w.	Josh. 2:15
infection on the w.	Lev. 14:37	cubits of the w.	Neh. 3:13
surface of the w.	Lev. 14:37	and its stone w.	Prov. 24:31
	the w. of daughter Zion	Lam. 2:8	

wanderer

a restless w.	Gen. 4:12

War, Among the peoples of the ancient East, war was not an exclusively politico-military affair. In its motivation and execution religion had its part to play, and the gods were directly involved. To this Israel was no exception, and so Israel's God was also invested with the qualities of a warrior-God. Only with time did these warrior characteristics disappear.

Before the time of the monarchy wars were fought by the people who took up arms for the occasion. There was no regular army nor any professional soldiers. (*See* ARMY.) The people would be rallied by the sound of the trumpet (Jgs. 3:27; 6:34; 1 Sam. 13:3, 4) and drawn up for war so to as become the "People of the Lord" (Jgs. 5:13) or the "hosts of the Lord" (Ex. 12:41; *see* HOSTS, LORD OF). Seeing that God is present in the midst of his people and that it is he who conducts the battle by means of his intervention, war was a kind of theophany, for which the people had to prepare themselves with purification rites so as to have ritual purity. The nation must "sanctify" itself (Josh. 3:5; 1 Sam. 21:6), abstain from sexual intercourse (1 Sam. 21:6; 2 Sam. 11:11), and purify the camp itself (Deut. 23:9-14).

Since God is the principal agent, and to him the victory properly belongs, war is not engaged in without consulting him, that is, without obtaining a positive oracle which guarantees the effective intervention of God (*see* 1 Sam. 7:9; 23:9-12; 30:7, 8). God's positive answer often takes the form: "God has given the land of the people of N. into our hands" (*see* Deut. 2:24; 3:2; 20:13; Josh. 2:24; 6:2; 8:1; 10:8, etc.). God goes out at the head of his people to fight its enemies (Deut. 20:4; Jgs. 4:14; 2 Sam. 5:24) and it is he who fights (Ex. 14:14; Deut. 1:30; Josh. 11:6; 1 Sam. 14:23) and gives victory (Ex. 15:14-16; 23:27, 28). His are not the arms of the people: he sows in the enemy terror and panic that leaves them in disarray and flight (Ex. 15:16; 23:27; Josh 10:10, 11; 24:7; Jgs. 4:15; 7:22; 1 Sam. 5:11). God's intervention is accompanied by the usual backdrop of the theophanies. (*See* THEOPHANY.) In this concept of war the role of Israel's arms is almost superfluous. More than once it is stated that the people of Israel should do nothing but stay calm and trust in God (Ex. 14:13; Deut. 20:3; Josh. 10:8, 25; Jgs. 7:3). Sometimes the number of combatants is reduced so that it will be all the more clear who the true Victor is, namely God and not the people (Jgs. 7:2; 1 Sam. 14:6; 17:45, 47). Even the concluding act of the war has a sacred character. The booty is consecrated to God, and in practice, totally destroyed (Josh. 6:18-24; 1 Sam. 15). The Israelites were under obligation to observe this practice, called *herem* or ban, in regard to all the peoples of Canaan (Deut. 7:5, 25). Sometimes the population would be destroyed but not their goods (*see* e.g. Deut. 3: 6-7; 20:14; Josh. 8:27) or a certain category of people would be spared (*see* e.g. Num. 31:14-18).

Here obviously we have a "concept" of war, not an account of military tactics in battle or war. It is also clear that the wars of the monarchy were progressively more "profaned," that is, taken more as political and military exploits, even though the sacral element did not completely disappear. On the other hand the "holy war" passed into the realm of ideology and helped give a theological interpretation to Israel's history in the context of the covenant. This idea of a holy war is re-evoked in the laws for war given in Deuteronomy 20. Holy wars were no longer fought, but a theology of war evolved, through which the omnipotence of God is seen, as well as his fidelity to the covenant and the need of the people to stay loyal if they are to live.

This fact explains why the Bible provides so little information on the tactics of war, and why it is so difficult to reconstruct in detail how the various battles were fought or the wars waged. The sources are intent on presenting examples of a theological thesis rather than a detailed account of a struggle.

The ideology of the sacred war was, after the monarchy, detached from war as it was really waged. It had its purpose however in pointing out God's interventions in history, in which he played the part of Judge and Master of its events. Moreover it served to illustrate what the eschatological intervention would be like. In the prophetic and apocalyptic tradition the ultimate events of history are filled with wars and political upheavals, and God's action takes the shape of the warrior schemes in the holy war, in which God of old intervened peremptorily to bring his designs to realization. It is not possible to take these visions as literal accounts of what is to happen. They are conventional presentations which originate in the ideology of the holy war, which served to show God's dominion in history and in the world.

warrior

The Lord is a w.	Ex. 15:3	me like a w.	Job 16:14
every valiant w.	2 Chron. 32:31	like a w. he stirs	Isa. 42:13

Wars of the Lord, Book of the, An ancient Israelite book mentioned in Numbers 21:14 and from which some excerpts are transcribed in 21:15, 17-18, 23-30. It is presumed to have been a collection of poetic compositions of the epic genre, celebrating the "wars of the Lord," that is, the wars fought by Israel in which God gloriously and victoriously intervened. (*See* WAR.) A similar collection called the Book of Jashar is quoted in Joshua 10:13 and 2 Samuel 1:18. *See* JASHAR, BOOK OF.

wash

slave to w. the feet	1 Sam. 25:41	W. yourselves clean	Isa. 1:16
If I should w. myself	Job 9:30	When I did go and w.	Jn. 9:11
	If I do not w. you Jn. 13:8		

watch
W. the wholehearted man   Ps. 37:37

Water, The land of Palestine is a "good country, a land with streams of water, with springs and fountains welling up in the hills and valleys" (Deut. 8:7). It "is not like the land of Egypt . . . where you would sow your seed and then water it by hand, as in a vegetable garden. No, the land into which you are crossing for conquest is a land of hills and valleys that drinks in rain from the heavens" (11:10,11). It is superfluous to note that no impartial traveller would praise Palestine for its abundance of water. These texts however do serve to illustrate the value that was given to water by a people who had thirsted for it in the desolate wastes of the desert. The rain that makes the earth fertile was a gift from God (Deut. 11:14) and drought the just punishment for the people's infidelity (Deut. 28:23, 24; 1 Kgs. 17:1-6).

In Palestine water is scarce. For the most part the waters of the Jordan flow in a deep ravine, and so could not be led off in irrigation ditches for agriculture. The other streams were more or less winter torrents rather than constant water-supplies. Cities were built beside springs to ensure water, and hydraulic engineering did make notable progress as at Gezer, where cisterns in honeycombed rocks were connected by shafts into a considerable water-storage system. (*See* SILOAM.) Everywhere rainwater was caught on flat roofs. The nomadic shepherds followed the route of the wells, about the proprietorship and use of which there was minute legislation (Gen. 26:15-25). The Nabataeans, as N. Glueck has shown, were masters of preserving rain water in desert lands in S. Palestine. *See* WELLS.

In the Jewish ritual, water is used in the rite of purification (*see* CLEANSING) and in the New Testament it is the material for the sacrament of Baptism. (*See* BAPTISM.) It also has in the Bible other symbolic uses. Water is the gift of God and the bearer of life, and so symbolized the gift of salvation (Isa. 12:3; 55:1; Jer. 2:13; Ezek. 47:1) and the eschatological outpouring of the Spirit (Jn. 7:37-39).

"Live water" was running water, as opposed to water in pools and wells: this is how the Samaritan woman at the well understood Jesus' words (Jn. 4:10). As the discourse develops however, Jesus explains in which sense he speaks of living water, namely, as a symbol for eternal life (Jn. 4:13-14).

Wisdom and the law which give life are compared to the beneficent action of water in Prov. 13:14; 16:22; Ps. 1:3; Sir. 24:23-29.

way

by *w*. of the Philistines'	Ex. 13:17	understand the *w*.	Ps. 119:27
cloud to show them the *w*.		How can we know the *w*.	Jn. 14:5
	Ex. 13:21	I am the *w*.	Jn. 14:6
keep to the ancient *w*.	Job 22:15	according to the new *w*.	Acts 9:2

Wealth, In the Old Testament wealth or riches—that is, an abundance of the good things this world has to offer, such as property, land, livestock, slaves—were the tangible evidence of the blessings of God on people who had been loyal to him. The Promised Land abounded with good things, and blessings in kind poured down on those who, like Solomon, were heirs to the promise (1 Kgs. 3:13). God, through Nathan, upbraided David for his murder of Uriah, and reminded him of how he had favored him with his master's house, and wives, and the house of Israel and of Judah, and if this were too little, he would add as much more (2 Sam. 12:8 ff.). Nevertheless the dishonest pursuit of riches was severely reproved, as was pride in one's own possessions (2 Sam. 12; Isa. 10:3; Jer. 5:27; Hos. 12:8). The book of Job however shows that sometimes the good can become impoverished (*see* JOB), even though at the end Job has everything restored to him as a sign and expression of God's blessing. The psalms (10; 12; 14; 37; 40; 41; 72; 74) theologize a little more, and more realistically, even to the point of holding the rich to be the wicked and the poor to be holy. *See* POVERTY.

The attitude of the New Testament towards wealth and riches is in general negative. Christ solemnly warns of the difficulty the rich will find in entering heaven (Mark 10:23). The rich man hoards his possessions and comes to a feeling of self-sufficiency in them that is totally at variance with the attitude of the Christian, whose riches are in God from whom at each moment he depends (*see* Lk. 12:16-21). In the Sermon on the Mount Jesus warns his disciples not to store up treasures on earth where they can be broken into and stolen (Matt. 6:19-21). Money itself can enslave a man so that God's grace cannot get to him (Matt. 6:24). While the beatitudes in Matthew 5:2 speak of the happiness of the poor in spirit, Luke 6:20, probably with an eye to the real conditions of the Christian community of the time, speaks simply of the poor. Nevertheless poverty is not praised for its own sake. Penny-pinching poverty was not then nor is it now an aid to virtue. When Mary poured out the costly ointment over Jesus at the dinner in Bethany, Judas complained of the waste in the name of the poor, only to be rebuked by Jesus himself. The poverty of the New Testament is related to the doctrine of the psalms: it is the felt need, not just of material goods, but of God and salvation. Riches can take the edge from this hunger and give man a feeling of self-sufficiency which is fatal (*see* Lk. 16:9-13).

weaned, weaning

of the child's *w*.	Gen. 21:8	Once the child is *w*.	1 Sam. 1:22
	she had *w*. him	1 Sam. 1:23	

weapon, weapons

everyone kept his *w*.	Neh. 4:17	No *w*. fashioned against you	
escape the iron *w*.	Job 20:24		Isa. 54:17
and forges *w*.	Isa. 54:16		

wearing

was *w*. the ephod	1 Sam. 14:3	Jesus came out *w*. the crown	
			Jn. 19:5

Weaving, This was a very ancient art. In Egypt the Israelites would have encountered it developed to a comparatively high state, and the Canaanites, among whom the Israelites settled, could have continued their education, with the Babylonians completing it during the Exile. Spinning was the preliminary to weaving, and the two skills by necessity grew side by side. Spinning involved the transformation of the fibers of the raw material at hand (wool, goat's hair, camel's hair, flax, hemp, etc.) into an even, strong, weavable thread rolled on a spindle. The spun yarn (dyed or not) was woven into fabric on a loom by intersecting threads of the warp ("That which is thrown across") and the weft or woof ("that which is woven"). (*See* Lev. 13:48-59). The whole operation survives basically unchanged today and can be observed wherever native arts are practiced, while modern industrial textile looms are but sophisticated developments of the ancient trade. The "beam" to which the warp was fixed is alluded to in 1 Samuel 17:7; the shuttle which carried the woof and was thrown to and fro by the hand of the weaver in Job 7:6; and also the pin on which the finished web was rolled in Judges 16:14. Among the Israelites the great part of woven goods were simple woolens for clothing, coarse fabrics such as tent-cloth, sackcloth and the cheap hairy garments of the poor. But materials for the Tabernacle were woven by men and women (Ex. 26:1-13; 35:35), and such cities as Lachish and Tell Beit Mirsim have, in their uncovering by archaeologists, provided evidences of a considerable weaving industry. Later various guilds would appear in the larger market centers, from which retail merchants (e.g. Lydia of Thyatira) secured their stocks. Paul learned his art of tent-making in the region of the Taurus Mountains, famous for goat's hair cloth.

Weeks, *See* SABBATH.

Weeks, Feast of, The Feast of Pentecost was also called the Harvest Festival (Ex. 23:16; 34:22). It was celebrated seven weeks after the "sickle is first put to the standing grain" (Deut. 16:9, 10), that is, after the Passover, or Feast of Unleavened Bread. *See* PENTECOST.

Weights and Measures, Here is a list of the principal weights and measures. It is not always easy to determine the equivalent weight in our system, and it must not be forgotten that the same measure could have had different values according to region or time.

Weights: The basic unit was the shekel, around 11.5 grams. 50 shekels made 1 mina and one mina made 1 talent (Ex. 38:25, 26). Ezekiel 45:12 gives another proportion, which makes 1 mina equal to sixty shekels. The smallest unit was the beqa, equal to one half shekel.

Capacity: The names are taken from the vessels used to measure the goods. The 'homer contained 10 ephah (Ex. 16:36) and the ephah contained 10 omer. The ephah is also called bat (Ezek. 45:11). The seah is one third of an ephah (Ex. 16:36; Isa. 5:10). From a jar discovered at Qumran one can deduce that 1 seah was equal to about fourteen quarts.

Length: As in many other tongues the names are those of the human body. 1 cubit, about 18 inches, had two spans, 6 palm and 24 fingers. The reed was 6 cubits. The Greek-Roman measures mentioned in the Bible are the Roman mile (4860 feet) of 8 furlongs, one furlong being about 200 yards.

Wells, Wells as a crucial factor in the life of the people in Bible lands is better understood if one starts with the broader term, water. In Egypt, water, in the form of the Nile, was truly indispensable. In the valley of the Tigris and Euphrates rivers the harnessing of the waters brought down from regions far to the northwest into otherwise too-arid lands made the Assyrian-Babylonian civilization possible. In Palestine the Jordan and its major tributaries performed less cooperatively, often plunging at breakneck speed and for much of their lengths running through deep gorges and ultimately down the Jordan Rift, making it impossible to distribute their waters for irrigation purposes in the plateau regions on either side of the river valleys. No region in Palestine receives a truly ample supply of rainfall except a small oval area southeast of Mount Carmel. The next best region for rainfall is a narrow strip running almost due north from Hebron, passing just westward of Jerusalem, and extending approximately to Thebez—a strip of hill country about 65 miles long and only 5 to 15 miles wide; this strip catches the moisture brought in by clouds from the Mediterranean. Of the rest of the country, perhaps one-third is marginal at best for agriculture, with rainfalls apt to be poorly distributed through the year; and this category is largely along the coastline, in territories occupied by Phoenicians and Philistines. The remaining sections were either submarginal or nearly totally dry, notably the vast area south of the Dead Sea and along its shores. From east and south pressed the desert, whose only water was at scattered oases.

Because of the life-giving qualities of water, wells had a great importance to the Hebrews that is plainly reflected in nearly every O.T. book. Without water there was no survival for man or beast. Great concern for wells, springs, cisterns, pits, reservoirs—anything that dealt with obtaining and conserving water—runs through the entire history, from Abraham to the woman at the well at Sychar. All the connotations of water, poetic, prophetic and Wisdom, are good.

Technically a well is a natural spring curbed by man and equipped to make easy the delivery of water to the seeker, or a water supply found and made available by digging holes below the level of the supply. A sure water supply was a blessing, wherever it could be found, in the wilderness (Gen. 16:14), in valleys (Gen. 26:17), near cities (Gen. 24:11), in fields (Gen. 29:2), in a courtyard (2 Sam 17:18). Wells were a form of wealth; they were fought over; enemies destroyed them; the digging of a new one was a cause for rejoicing.

The importance of wells to agricultural, and pastoral and nomadic folk is obvious. As for wells, springs, and streams in urban life, the archaeologist Nelson Glueck has stated the case convincingly: "He who would rediscover the sites of ancient villages and towns and fortresses must find first where springs and wells or perennial streams exist or once existed, and where cisterns and reservoirs were built. It is a truism . . . that the location of an early settlement is almost always determined by the presence of an adequate supply of water." Deep-shafted wells inside fortified cities, added to the security of its inhabitants. In Judah and Israel very deep wells, or long horizontal shafts, or a combination, have been found in Lachish, Jerusalem, Gibeon, Gezer and Hazor—all key cities, strategic sites. Similarly deep and protected wells have also been found in Shobek and Kerak in Moab. Wells dug down to a level of 200 feet below the grade of the city were not uncommon at a later period. The Nabataeans were masters of water location and conservation, and they made large areas of the Negev fertile by their water-conservation expertise—an art lost to later residents of the old Edomite territories, until the modern state of Israel brought new dedication to the use of water in sub-marginal rainfall areas.

went

we w. to Samuel	1 Sam. 10:14	as they w. their own	Isa. 57:17
Saul also w. home	1 Sam. 10:26	each w. straightforward	Ezek. 1:9

west

with Bethel to the w.	Gen. 12:8	very strong w. wind	Ex. 10:19
spread out east and w.	Gen. 28:14	On the w. side	Ex. 27:12
	and the ambush w. of it	Josh. 8:13	

Western Sea, The Mediterranean Sea (Deut. 11:24; 34:2; Joel 2:20; Zech. 14:8).

wheat

during the w. harvest	Gen. 30:14	cream of its finest w.	Deut. 32:14
the w. and the spelt were	Ex. 9:32	was beating out w.	Jgs. 6:11

wheels

four bronze w.	1 Kgs. 7:30	like chariot w.	1 Kgs. 7:33
The four w. were	1 Kgs. 7:32	I saw w. on the ground	Ezek. 1:15
	The w. had a sparkling	Ezek. 1:16	

whitewash

cover it with w.	Ezek. 13:10	you have w.	Ezek. 13:14
Where is the w.	Ezek. 13:12	covered them with w.	Ezek. 22:28

whole

the surface of the w.	Ex. 10:15	but roasted w.	Ex. 12:9
the w. assembly Israel	Ex. 12:6	the w. head is sick	Isa. 1:5
	the w. heart faint	Isa. 1:5	

wick

and quenched like a w.	Isa. 43:17

wicked

do not be so w.	Jgs. 19:23	innocent and the w.	Job 9:22
There the w. cease from	Job 3:17	But the w. will be	Prov. 2:22
	the w. man will	Prov. 5:22	

Widow, The widow is permitted to remarry in both the Old and the New Testament (*see* Lev. 21:14; Ruth 1:9; 1 Cor. 7:8). In Old Testament law, should the widow be childless, she could benefit from the levirate law. (*See* LEVIRATE.) She did not inherit from her husband, but returned, if she

remained without support, to her paternal home (Lev. 22:13; Ruth 1:8).
By way of exception Ruth wished to remain on with her mother-in-law,
Naomi, and she lived with her until she married Boaz (Ruth 1:16). Should
a widow who was poor be left without parents, she was abandoned to easy
exploitation and all kinds of injustice (2 Kgs. 4:1-7). The prophets denounced these abuses (Isa. 1:17; Jer. 7:6; 22:3; Zech. 7:10). Jesus warns
his disciples to guard themselves from the scribes who devour the houses
of widows and pretend to pray long prayers (Mk. 12:40; Lk. 20:28).
Deuteronomy includes widows among the disinherited (Deut. 14:29), to
whom then must go a portion of the tithes (Deut. 26:12), and who are
permitted to glean what they can from the fields after the harvest (Deut.
24:19-21; Ruth 2).

Because the widow is so defenseless God takes special care of her (Deut.
10:18; Jer. 49:11; Mal. 3:5; Ps. 146:9). Whoever abuses her will be ac-
cursed (Deut. 27:19).

The churches of Palestine did not neglect to care for their widows (Acts
6:1; 9:39). This practice was also inherited by the Hellenistic churches:
Paul sends Timothy precise instructions in this regard. If widows should
have children and grandchildren, they should attend to the eduction of
the children and take care to govern their own homes (1 Tim. 5:4, 8).
Those however who were truly widows, that is, who had nobody to be the
support of their old age, should put their hope in the Lord and stay vigilant in prayer and good works (1 Tim. 5:5, 6). Because danger surrounds
them Paul advises the young widows to remarry, have children and look
after their own home; in 1 Corinthians 7:8, 40 however, he invites them,
in general, not to remarry. In regard to assistance for widows who have
no resources, Paul advises that they look to their own relatives, or failing
that, to the Church (1 Tim. 5:10). There is moreover a further category,
those inscribed in the register of widows. To qualify one had to be at least
sixty years old, to have married but once, and be distinguished for piety
and good works. This was then a kind of perpetual consecration, from
which the younger widows were excluded because of the danger of turning out unfaithful when an opportunity for remarrying presented itself (1
Tim. 5:9-12). Paul does not specify in what exactly this consecration consisted nor which services these widows rendered the Christian community.

Wife, *See* FAMILY, MARRIAGE, WIDOW; WOMAN.

wilderness, *See* DESERT.

close by the *w.*	Gen. 14:6	aimlessly in the *w.*	Gen. 21:14
a spring in the *w.*	Gen. 16:7	He lived in the *w.*	Gen. 21:20

wind

God made a *w.* sweep	Gen. 8:1	suddenly a great *w.* came	Job 1:19
wings of the *w.*	2 Sam. 22:11	tremble in the *w.*	Isa. 7:2
the blast of the *w.*	2 Sam. 22:16	The *w.* blows	Jn. 3:8
	a strong driving *w.*	Acts 2:2	

Wine, Wine made from grapes, also called metaphorically "the blood of
the grape" (Gen. 49:11; Deut. 32:14) was throughout the history of Palestine one of its principal and most prized products (Deut. 8:8). As the
grapes were picked they were put in the wine press, which was generally
situated within the vineyard itself (Isa. 5:1-5). The press consisted of two
basins excavated in the rock, one higher than, and communicating with,
the other. The grapes were placed in the upper one and there stamped out
with the feet, at times of several people (Isa. 63:2, 3). The juice of the
grape thus flowed down into the lower basin where fermentation began.
The must was later poured out into amphorae (Jer. 13:12) or skins (Josh.
9:13) which had to be in good condition so that they would not burst un-

der the pressure of the fermentation (Mk. 2:22; Matt. 9:17; Lk. 5:37, 38).

Wine was held at a premium as is abundantly evidenced in the Bible. Sirach 39:26 states that "chief of all needs for human life are water and fire, iron and salt, the heart of the wheat, milk and honey, the blood of the grape, and oil and cloth." And he goes on to add: "For the good all these are good, but for the wicked they turn out evil" (39:27). Besides bread to sustain the heart of man and oil which makes his face resplendent, God gave him wine to rejoice his heart (Ps. 104:15; Jgs. 9:13; Prov. 31:6-7). Wine was also noted for some of its therapeutic qualities, for example, in stomach upsets (1 Tim. 5:23; *see* also Lk. 10:34).

The Bible however is severe in condemning excesses that lead to intoxication. Drunkenness is one of the sins that exclude from eternal life (Rom. 13:13; 1 Cor. 5:11; 6:10; Gal. 5:21), and brings with it grave moral consequences when it becomes a vice. It leads to dissoluteness (Hos. 4:11) and insensibility of conscience (Amos 6:6; Isa. 5:11, 12; 56:11, 12) and can cause economic and social ruin to a family (Prov. 20:1; 23:20-21, 23, 29-35). Paul advises Titus and Timothy to choose as ministers in the churches persons who are not lovers of wine (Tit. 1:7; 1 Tim. 3:3).

wine press

| or the *w. p.* | Num. 18:30 | and hewed out a *w. p.* | Isa. 5:2 |
| or the *w. p.* | 2 Kgs. 6:27 | the *w. p.* I have | Isa. 63:3 |

Winnowing, The work of separating the grain from the chaff after the threshing. (*See* THRESHING.) It was done by tossing the mixture in the air against the wind, so that the lighter straw would be carried away leaving the heavier corn on the ground where it fell separately (Ruth 3:2). It is an image of the judgment. John the Baptizer awaits the Messiah who holds in his hand the winnowing-fan to clean well his threshing floor and gather the corn into his granary while the straw is burnt with unquenchable fire (Lk. 3:17; *see* Isa. 41:15, 16; Jer. 15:7).

Wisdom, Wisdom (in Hebrew **hokmah**) is a cultural phenomenon of the whole middle east. Israel did not create it: in fact the concept was imported into Israel from abroad. Wisdom is practical knowledge that is the fruit of observation and experience. What perhaps most of all characterizes it is its bent on practice or the practical life. It is not sought for itself, for the sole purpose of knowledge, but in order to succeed well in the affair or action which is being spoken of. Being born of observation and experience already suggests the ways in which it is cultivated and communicated. Wisdom is a heritage handed down from generation to generation, each succeeding generation enriching in its turn what it hands on to the next.

Wisdom groups under this definition a vast array which appears in very different concrete forms. The ability of the artisan, for instance, is called wisdom (1 Kgs. 7:13; Isa; 40:20), which, if it is truly expert, is considered to be of divine origin: the workers chosen for the construction of the Temple are filled with God, "with a divine spirit of skill and understanding and knowledge in every craft" (Ex. 31:3; *see* Ex. 28:3; 35:31). Wisdom is also the name given to what in ancient times most approched encyclopedic knowledge: so Solomon is said to have "surpassed all the Cedemites and all the Egyptians in wisdom. . . . He discussed plants from the cedar on Lebanon to the hyssop growing out of the wall, and he spoke about beasts, birds, reptiles, and fishes" (1 Kgs. 5:10, 13). The type of wisdom here referred to did not consist precisely in composing tracts on the nature and habits of the various objects but rather in drawing up ever more complete and well-ordered lists of animals and plants, more or less as Linnaeus and Buffon did with more scientific criteria to work with, a work which formed the basis for the scientific study of zoology and botany. Here then it is a question of trying to put order into the world that was man's environment, giving its contents their proper esteem and use. This type of knowledge was considered so valuable, and indeed so fundamental that the author of Genesis 2, to bring out Adam's unsurpassed wisdom, shows him naming all the living creatures of the earth (Gen. 2:19, 20). *See* NAME.

In the Bible the wisdom that most comes to the fore is not skill or science, however, but what might be termed the art of living, or conducting one's own life with ability and success. This wisdom is gathered up into maxims and proverbs which establish a practical norm of conduct in the multiple circumstances of life. Wisdom is not imposed from without by the authority of a law. Rather it seeks to become established in the heart of the youth as a solid conviction that plays its part in his practical judgment. Wisdom, then, is a type of humanism, and its most ancient type. It sought to perfect an ideal of life that still attracts for its extraordinary good sense, by the modesty of its aspirations, mingling as its does a tone of confidence and gaiety with a little resignation which permits those who follow it to overcome disappointment.

At times, it is true, this wisdom can seem egoistic, or at least ungenerous. It avoids on the one hand avarice, but on the other it eschews gratuitous heroism and supererogatory renouncements, avoiding precipitousness and keeping to the just mean in all things, be it in the search for riches, the treatment of friends or the government of one's own home (e.g. Prov. 6; Sir. 12; 30). It never, however, hides its purpose of giving man what happiness is possible for him in life by serving God and enjoying the goods he gives. Wisdom is a manual of good sense.

Wisdom is particularly necessary for the person in authority. A special type of wisdom is the art of conducting public affairs and promoting the common good while governing subjects. In Israel and among other peoples the wise addressed their instructions to the kings, while at times the king himself is a "wise man" or seer (*see* Prov. 3:1; Eccl. 2; Wis. 1; 6).

All peoples, no matter what their stage of cultural evolution, have their own type of popular wisdom. The elders and parents are the privileged repositories of this wisdom, which is spontaneously summed up in popular proverbs that are transmitted in the people's language. What however we find in the wisdom books of the Bible is not just a simple collection of this type of wisdom. This is a wisdom developed by specialists in the art, the wise men, with the precise aim of instruction and education. Wisdom in this sense paid homage to the popular wisdom by adopting its vehicle for transmission, namely the proverb. This proverb, however, was polished, and artificaly assumed the role of father or mother admonishing their children. This is how a wise man expresses himself when he wants to pass on to his disciples his wisdom: "Hear, my son, your father's instructions and reject not your mother's teaching; a graceful diadem will they be for your head; a torque for your neck" (Prov. 1:8, 9).

The initiator and great patron of this wisdom in Israel was Solomon. Under his name and patronage have come down to us the greater part of the wisdom books, even though he was not their author. These are the books of Proverbs, Ecclesiastes and Wisdom. Nevertheless the tradition that makes Solomon the initiator of Israelite wisdom is rooted in solid historical foundations. In fact, before David the organization and culture of the Israelite people had not progressed beyond the tribal stage. With the affirmation however of the monarchy under David, Israel began to organize along the lines of the neighboring states. David and Solomon created a truly royal court in Jerusalem, in imitation above all of the royal court of Pharaoh. Experts in administration and government were brought from

Egypt (*see* 2 Sam. 20:23-26; 1 Kgs. 4:1-6). These were the scribes, people not only able to read and write, but with secretarial and organizational abilities that made them indispensable. It is more important however to understand the process by which wisdom assumed a new face once it was interpenetrated with typical Jewish faith. This can be summed up in two points. First, true wisdom was a gift of God, so that true wisdom could not ignore God, indeed the beginning of wisdom is the fear of God (Prov. 1:7). This doctrine was to find its most perfect expression in the personification of wisdom. (*See* WISDOM, PERSONIFICATION OF.) Secondly, wisdom is the Law. Wisdom propose a way of conducting oneself in order to obtain life. Life however is God's gift to those who observe his law and keep his word. The true art of living, then, is the observance of the law. This identification had important repercussions. On the one side, the exposition of the law lost a little of its rigidity and apodictic severity, and drew nearer to man to draw from him a full consent. This effort to draw the law near to the heart of man is everywhere present in Deuteronomy, where it is explicitly stated: "Observe them (the laws) carefully, for thus will you give evidence of your wisdom and intelligence to the nations, who will hear of all these statutes and say, 'this great nation is truly a wise and intelligent people' " (Deut. 4:6). On the other side, the wisdom tradition is concerned for administrative functions of the kingdom. Scribes took their place beside the king as his counselors and secretaries. The art of writing was handed down in schools that also specialized in the art of administration. Here, too, no effort was spared in giving the young scribe a fully human formation that would prove indispensable to him in the exercise of his delicate future mission. These schools are the real source of cultivated wisdom and of the notion of the wise man as a born educator, who knew how to make of anybody entrusted to his care a fully capable person, equipped to make headway in life.

The wisdom heritage that was introduced into Israel at the fringes of the sacred traditions could not but come into contrast with these latter. Some traces of these conflicts can be gleaned from the prophetic writings. According to Isaiah 29:14 the nation had allowed itself to be guided by a wisdom that practically ignored Israel's God, for which God himself threatened Israel's wise men: "The wisdom of its wise men shall perish and the understanding of its prudent men be hid (*see* also Jer. 18:18; 8:8 ff.; 50:35; 51:57; *see* KNOWLEDGE, TREE OF).

Ben Sira, having made an elegy on wisdom, concludes: "All this is true of the Book of the Most High's covenant, the Law which Moses commanded us as an inheritance for the community of Jacob" (Sir. 24:22). Sira thinks of his work as a "rivulet from its (the Law's) stream, channeling the waters into a garden" (Sir. 24:28-31). He conceives of his profession as a wise man as that of studying the law of the Most High (Sir. 38:24-39). The scribe has become a man expert in the law, and this is how he appears in the gospels.

Wisdom, Book of, A deuterocanonical wisdom book of the Old Testament. The author presents himself as Solomon (1:1; 6:1-11; 8:9-16), but this is obviously a literary artifice. The book was written in Greek, and in all probability in Alexandria during the first half of the first century B.C., perhaps 80-50 B.C. The author is acquainted with popular Greek philosophy, especially with Plato and Epicurus. He carries on a polemic against those Jews who have become apostates to a crass form of Epicurianism. The book is divided into three clearly distinguished parts:

a. cc. 1-5: the final destiny of the just and the wicked according to the plan of God. The author has in mind the thesis of the Jewish apostates who denied the providence of God and his power over death, while also denying any life beyond this one (2:1-5), so that their conclusion is: "Let us enjoy the good things that are real" (2:6-9). These apostates lash out at the just who reprove their conduct and repudiate their thesis, persecuting and killing them (2:10-20). In retort, the author unfolds the mystery ef God, that is, his plan of salvation as it is propounded in Scripture, especially in Genesis 3: "God formed man to be imperishable; the image of his own nature he made him. But by the envy of the devil, death entered the world, and they who are in his possession experience it" (2:23, 24). Even though, then, the just man might seem to die at the hands of the wicked, in reality God takes him to himself where he comes into an inheritance that is glory-filled (3:1-6). The folly of the wicked will be made evident to all on the day of visitation (3:7), that is, on the day of judgment. On that day those who had been despised and killed will come forward in triumph, crowned with glory while the wicked will be punished (3:7-12). Wisdom 1-5 is the clearest Old Testament witness to the resurrection. *See* RESURRECTION.

b. cc. 6-9: The eulogy on true wisdom. This is recommended for its origins, for it is in truth derived from God. It is a spirit that is intelligent, holy, unique, manifold, subtle, agile (7:22). "She is an aura of the might of God and a pure effusion of the glory of the Almighty" (7:25). (*See* WISDOM, PERSONIFICATION OF.) Wisdom is moreover recommended for her works. To wisdom Solomon owes everything that he is. While Solomon was like every other man, conceived and formed in the manner of men (7:1-6), he asked God for wisdom and avidly sought after it until it was granted him (7:7-12). With wisdom came to him all gifts (8:2-21). At the end the author puts in Solomon's mouth a prayer to God for wisdom (c. 9).

c. cc. 10-19 The works of salvation in history. The author cites most of all the preeminent salvific interventions, such as the exodus from Egypt and the plagues. In cc. 13-15 he once more takes up the cudgel against the apostates, upbraiding them for their idolatry in the sarcasm that the prophets had heaped on the idols. (*See* IDOL, IDOLATRY.) Some themes of Greek philosophy are brought together to form a little natural theology, going from a contemplation of creatures to the existence and nature of God.

The book of Wisdom is a first-class example of Hellenistic Judaism with its theology and proselytic aspirations. Judaism is dressed out as a universal religion accessible to all men with a true answer to the eternal problems of life and death. It is thus related to the missionary literature of Alexandrine Judaism (Philo, Josephus and others) which did not disdain to absorb into itself whatever it found suitable in Greek wisdom.

Wisdom, Personification of, In some of the Old Testament wisdom texts (*see* Prov. 1:20-33; 8; 9; Sir. 24:1-24; Wis. 7:24-8:1), wisdom is presented as a person speaking of itself, its origins and its action. This unusual presentation is partly explained by a literary genre that was in common use in the whole East. The wisdom writers are accustomed to praise wisdom in general, its value and the goods it confers, or also to praise the doctrine expounded in their writings. It was thus an easy passage to personification, placing the praise in the mouth of Lady Wisdom, a purely literary personification. This however is not sufficient, seeing that here the wisdom that is singing its own praises is not simply a compendium of doctrine.

In Proverbs 1:20-33 wisdom like a prophet speaks to all in the streets and on the squares of the city. Its speech is vehement: threats, reproofs, accusations and condemnations appear throughout. It addresses itself to sinners, even though they give no heed, and so the final ruin is announced.

All this brings to mind the more dramatic moments in the prophetic ministry (*see* e.g. Isa. 6; 58:1; 65:1; Jer 7:2; 17:19, 20). It speaks moreover of an outpouring of its spirit so that its words may be understood: "I will pour out to you my spirit. I will acquaint you with my words" (1:23), a statement that closely approaches the promise of the new covenant in Jeremiah 31:31 and Ezekiel 36:27. In Proverbs 8:1-38 wisdom speaks of herself and of the gifts that she has ready for those who will allow themselves to be guided by her. Vv. 14-16 is much like Isaiah 11:1-6 where the Spirit is made the source of these same gifts. Wisdom must be loved and sought after, just as in other places God is loved and sought after (Deut. 4:29; Jer. 29:13).

These considerations permit a first attempt at interpretation. Wisdom exercises a similar office to that of the prophets, but speaks in her own name and on her own authority, unlike the prophets who explicitly affirm that their words have been received from God. Moreover, to wisdom are attributed actions that belong properly and exclusively to God, such as the outpouring of the Spirit. Again, wisdom herself gives to her followers what elsewhere is described as the fruit of the Spirit. This is conceded to wisdom's followers in the form of human wisdom, which is a gift of salvation and thus the way to life. In other words the whole economy of salvation in Israelite tradition, with its double aspect of moral will and salvific action of God, is now put forward in the vocabulary and typical concepts of the widsom tradition. Wisdom takes the part and the place of God, and mediates salvation; on the other hand it is the supreme gift of God which brings with it salvation. In this way a perfect fusion has been effected between Israelite religious tradition and the wisdom tradition, reaching a unitary and coherent exposition unparalleled except for Deuteronomy. God's revelation is propounded in the clear categories of the wisdom tradition.

Proverbs 8:22-31 and Sirach 24:1-24 speak of the origins of wisdom's relationship with God: "The Lord begot me, the firstborn of his ways," that is, I hold first place among his created works, and I was created in view of the creation of the universe. When God created, wisdom was with him as his craftsman (8:30). Wisdom proceeds from God like the breath from his mouth (Sir. 24:3), holding sway over every people and nation (24:6). Of these he chose one for his dwelling place (24:10-12). In this expression converge the doctrines on Israel's election and on the dwelling of God among his people. Wisdom too comes to dwell among the people and distribute its gifts. 24:22 concentrates on one of these gifts and one aspect of wisdom's activity: wisdom has brought with itself the law of the Most High, which is the doctrine of life so that he who follows it will have life (24:22-31).

Wisdom is the mediatrix of the works of God: it creates, saves, directs history, chooses his people, and guides individuals along the way of salvation, and is given to them as a gift. Is it then a divine person, together with and distinct from the Lord? Christian tradition has seen in the personification of wisdom a first revelation of the Second Person of the Blessed Trinity. Viewed from the full light that the New Testament throws on the Old through the Incarnation, this conclusion is legitimate. If however we take the stance of the author of the Old Testament, it seems obvious that he did not think of wisdom as a second divine Person. Wisdom is rather the new face in which God wishes to be sought and found. Wisdom is then neither another person nor a simple literary personification. The personality that wisdom is given is the personality of God. The personification of wisdom has very close parallels in the personification of the spirit, the word (Isa. 55:10, 11; Wisdom 18:14) and the name of God (Deut. 14:23). These personifications are nothing other than God himself and his action seen in his relationships with the world and with men.

wise
they are *w.* in evil   Jer. 4:22

Wise Men, The Three, *See* MAGI.

Witness, A witness is a person called before the tribunal to speak the truth he knows in a given case. There were in the Old Testament witnesses for the defense and witnesses for the prosecution (Prov. 14:25; 1 Kgs. 21:10, 13). To hand down a verdict the concordant testimony of at least two witnesses was necessary (Deut. 19:15; Matt. 26:59-60; 1 Tim. 5:19). This was above all true in capital offenses (Num. 35:30; Deut. 17:6). Evidence could be controlled, and if it was found false the witness was subjected to the same punishment allotted to the crime for which he falsely witnessed against another person (Deut. 19:16-29; Dan. 13:62). If the accused was found guilty and condemned to be stoned, the witnesses were the first to throw the stones at him (Deut. 17:7; Jn. 8:7; Acts 7:58).

Contracts and commercial transactions, as well as other assumed duties, were carried out in front of witnesses who could eventually guarantee fulfilment of the terms of the contracts (Gen. 23; Ruth 4; Isa. 8:1, 2). The witnesses could sign the contract document (Jer. 32). In an alliance document both parties called on the gods to witness the terms of the alliance. In this case even the mountains, the sea and so forth were invoked as witnesses of the duties assumed. (*See* COVENANT.) In the covenant between God and Israel the sea and the mountains are called to the stand, and invited to judge the infidelity of Israel in carrying out the terms of the alliance (*see* Mic. 6:2). In Deuteronomy the function of witness is outlined in the canticle that Moses taught to the children of Israel (Deut. 31:19) and in the alliance of Shechem, the rock erected by Joshua is witness "for it has heard all the words which the Lord spoke to us. It shall be a witness against you, should you wish to deny your God" (Josh. 24:27). Obviously Joshua does not think that the rock will speak in the future against Israel, but the rock will remain a visible sign of the duties assumed, and its very presence will be a mute witness of accusation against every infidelity (*see* also Gen. 31:44-54). In an oath God is called to witness the truth of the words spoken and the sincerity of the duties assumed, thus sealing the oath (*see* OATH; 1 Sam. 12:5, 6; Rom. 1:9; 2 Cor. 1:23).

The apostles are the witnesses of Jesus (Acts 1:8, 22; 2:32; 13:31), qualified witnesses, that is, endowed with a solemn mission from Jesus to give witness to him. It was not sufficient to be acquainted with the facts—it was necessary to have an official mandate from Jesus to give public witness to his death and resurrection (1:22). Paul was called by Jesus to be a witness, and to make him capable to fill this office, Jesus came to him on the road to Damascus (Acts 22:15; 26:16; Gal. 1:15, 16; 1 Cor. 9:1; 15:5-8).

John 1:6 tells us that the mission of John the Baptizer was to render testimony to the Light. This testimony he gave when he proclaimed that he had seen the Spirit descend from heaven like a dove and repose on Jesus (1:31). This led him to assert that "This is God's chosen One" (1:34). Jesus calls to his side the witness of Scripture (Jn. 5:39) but has a still more powerful witness for himself, namely the works which the Father gave him to accomplish which tell that the Father is in him and he in the Father (Jn. 5:34-37; *see* WORK). The Spirit of Truth, the Paraclete, will give witness to him before the disciples (Jn. 15:26, 27) as well as accuse the world in regard to judgment, justice and sin (Jn. 16:8-11; on this text *see* PARACLETE). The apostle witnesses to what he has seen and knows that his witness is true (Jn. 21:24). In Revelation 2:13 and 17:6 the witnesses are those who have shed their blood for Jesus. From these texts, then, is derived what was later to be known as martyrdom, from the Greek word **martyrco** meaning "to witness." *See* MARTYR.

woe

W. to you, O Moab	Num. 21:29	*W.* to the Pharisees	Lk. 11:43
W. to them	Isa. 3:9	*W.* to you lawyers also	
W. to the wicked man	Isa. 3:11		Lk. 11:46, 52

Wolf, Although the wolf was well known in ancient Palestine, almost all references to the animal in the Bible are figurative. Benjamin is a rapacious wolf, so called because of the fierce, war-like qualities of the tribe (Gen. 49:27). The wolf for his fierceness is poles apart from the meekness of the lamb, and so the peace and harmony of eschatological times will see them both lie down together (Isa. 11:6; 65:25). Christ sends his disciples like sheep into a pack of wolves (Matt. 10:16) but he himself will not, like the hireling, abandon his own when he sees the wolf approach (Jn. 10:12).

Woman, The story of the creation of woman (Gen. 2:18-25) offers an ideal picture of the relationship between man and woman, an ideal, however, which unfortunately was belied by the facts, as the author ruefully recounts in 3:16. The point of the creation account is not to describe how the first woman came into being but rather to define woman's condition and role in the world. She, for the Bible author, was formed to be a support or prop to man (*see* Sir. 36:24-26). When Adam found no helper like unto himself among the animals, God shaped woman from a part of his body and brought her to him to be named. The whole account surrounds the naming, which will sum up all that Adam will see in her in relationship to himself. Adam sees in her a person like himself and expresses his discovery in a phrase that was often to recur in the Bible: "She is bone of my bones and flesh of my flesh," thus expressing a link of parity and familiarity (*see* Jgs. 9:2; 2 Sam. 5:1; 2 Sam. 19:12-13; Isa. 58:7). The name that suits her is woman ('issah,) seeing that she has been taken from man ('is,) just as Adam was named because of his parentage in the earth, 'adamah, from which he was taken.

Genesis 2:24, 25 adds further considerations: Adam went in search of a helpmate and found the possibilities of a communion of life and union in the flesh. Adam's reflections are an etiology: the attraction that a man feels for a woman is explained by this presumed unity of origin, which was somehow restored by the marital act. It would be absurd to see here any attempt at explaining the biological origins of the body of the first woman. The author is far from scientific enquiry: he is answering questions on the essence of things by explaining their presumed origin in a way that reveals what they are, what they are for, why they exist. In this portrait of the first couple the mutual and intimate adhesion of the partners above all stands out. This arises from their having the same nature, the same ends and destiny. The adhesion of man to woman and woman to man arises spontaneously from the depths of their flesh: a man, says St. Paul, loves his wife like his own flesh (Eph. 5:28).

The picture here painted is of course in large part an ideal. The author saw and experienced the ideal only through its deformation by sin which burdened the woman in her natural functions and upset the equilibrium of relationships between her and her husband (Gen. 3:16) until the original unity and indissolubility were watered down (Gen. 4:19). The author had to delve deep behind the actual social conditions of his time to paint his ideal picture. In fact Israel is no exception on this point in its social and cultural context.

Woman really had no true autonomy. Before marrying she was under the authority of her father (*see* FAMILY) and when she married she passed under the authority of her husband (*see* MARRIAGE); if she became a widow she was under the rule of her oldest son, while if she had no children she returned to her paternal home or remained defenseless. (*See* WIDOW.) Her task in life was to be wife and mother. Her life unfolded in the home and in the toil of the field.

The law contains various prescriptions aimed at protecting the woman, but even these show that in the last analysis woman was held in less account than man (Lev. 12:1-5). Children should respect father and mother (Ex. 20:12; Lev. 19:3; Deut. 5:16) but the father could divorce his wife while she had no right to do the same (Deut. 24:1). Some dispositions of the law seemed to reduce the daughters almost to the status of mere property (*see* Ex. 21:7; Jgs. 19:24). The vows made by a woman could be blocked by the father or husband (Lev. 27:1-7). (*See* also Deut. 21:10; 22:13; 22:28). From the religious point of view there is no discrimination in Israelite law between men and women, with the exception of the exercise of the priesthood which was reserved to males.

The women were singers and dancers **par excellence** at the agrarian festivals (Jgs. 21:19-21), when victories were being celebrated (Ex. 15:20) and when the victorious soldiers were being welcomed back from battle (1 Sam. 18:6-7). They were also the quasi-official lamenters for the dead (2 Sam. 1:24; *see* MOURNING).

Women were a subject on which the wisdom authors loved to dwell. They warn the young of the dangers of falling into the hands of prostitutes or adulteresses (Prov. 7:5-27), and advise prudence and sagacity in the choice of a life partner, as much of their future happiness will depend on their having made a good choice (Sir. 25:16-25). They also have praise for the good wife (Prov. 31) and know what good this can bring a husband (Sir. 26:1-4). Their overall view of women, however, was gray rather than rosy.

The New Testament does not contain any declarations on the social condition of the woman. There is certainly no discrimination in the order of salvation (Gal. 3:28). Christianity however was not primarily preoccupied with revising social structures, even though the Christian spirit could not leave these untouched for long. Without then touching the family structure, Christianity inspired relationships that were more human between man and woman. If the New Testament demands submission from the woman, it equally demands love and solicitude from the man, just as Christ cares for his Church (Eph. 5:21-28), for woman is "the weaker sex" (1 Pet. 3:7).

Paul (1 Cor. 14:34, 35) tells the women to observe silence and modesty, but they did have an active part in the life of the community, even collaborating with the apostles (Acts 18:26; Rom. 16:1, 3, 6; 1 Cor. 16:19). This custom was founded on the example of Christ himself, who did not disdain the help afforded by some women who followed him about and contributed to his and his apostles' support (Lk. 8:2, 3). The women showed particular loyalty and courage during the Passion (Matt. 27:55-56; Mk. 15:40), taking care to anoint and bury Jesus' body (Matt. 27:57-61; Mk. 15:42-47; Lk. 23:50-55; Jn. 19:38-42). They were the first to discover the tomb emptied by the risen Christ (Matt 28:1-10; Mk. 16:1-8; Lk. 24:1-10; Jn. 20:1).

Jesus never showed that reserve towards women that was frequent among the Jewish doctors of the time (Jn. 4:27). He showed kindness towards the most unfortunate and defended them against the inhuman severity of the "just" (Lk. 7:36-50; Jn. 8:1-11), and was glad to accept from them marks of affection and reverence (Matt. 26:6-13; Mk. 14:3-9). Among the women he found some of his most faithful followers, Mary Magdalene, Mary and Martha of Bethany.

Wood, In Palestine today wood is not to be found in quantity, even though there is reference in the Scriptures to having had to clear land of woods in ancient times (Josh. 17:15-18). Sycamore, pine, cypress and oak, and of course olive wood was available (*see* 1 Kgs. 6:23; Ezek. 27:5; Zech. 11:2). Wood was used in the construction of buildings and ships, and, of course, gibbets for execution (Deut. 21:22; Josh. 10:26). The cedars of Lebanon were the most celebrated trees both for buildings and beauty, and they often figure in the Bible, especially in poetic language (*see* e.g. Ps. 37:35; Rev. 5:15).

Wool, Wool was one of Palestine's most important products. It was used in trade (Ezek. 27:13) and to pay tribute (2 Kgs. 3:4). Wool and linen are often mentioned together, but linen was more expensive to produce (*see* Deut. 22:11; Prov. 31:13). The Israelites raised brown and white sheep, but the white wool was more highly prized and often occurs in figurative speech. God will take away the scarlet of sin and give people wool-white forgiveness (Isa. 1:18) while Daniel saw the Ancient of Days with hair the color of pure wool (Dan. 7:9; *see* Rev. 1:14).

Word, Biblical revelation is both revelation in history and revelation in word. In reality these two aspects can neither be separated nor opposed, for they complement one another and together make up the revelation and salvation event. (*See* SALVATION HISTORY.) This fusion into one indivisible whole is already suggested by the Hebrew term that is translated as "word," namely **dabar,** a term that can also mean "thing" or "deed."

The word of God distinguishes the prophet and in fact constitutes him a prophet (Jer. 18:18). The prophet proclaims the word not as his own but as a messenger who announces what the Lord has confided to him and ordered him to speak: "Thus speaks the Lord God of Israel. . . ." God's word takes possession of the prophet so that he cannot contain it. It pushes him to proclamation that is faithful and exact. This internal experience of the prophet as bearer of the word of God is above all known to us from the "confessions" of Jeremiah: "I say to myself, I will not mention him (God), I will speak in his name no more. But then it becomes like fire burning in my heart, imprisoned in my bones; I grow weary holding it in, I cannot endure it" (Jer. 20:9).

Not only with the prophet however does the word of God reveal itself efficacious and powerful. When God speaks, it expresses his will, and it will not be in vain. He does not issue empty threats, nor does he promise salvation without guaranteeing it. God's word is irrevocable and brings to reality whatever it expresses. It creates a tension that is resolved when the word becomes reality, so that history can be told in accordance with this rhythm of prophecy and fulfilment, thus also revealing its deepest stratum, transcending the interplay of human affairs and passions. (*See* KINGS, BOOKS OF.) The word of God, therefore, is God speaking and acting. It is at times endowed with a certain autonomy and personality. It goes out from God and does not return without having brought to fulfilment its work, like a faithful minister of the Lord: "For just as from the heavens the rain and snow come down and do not return there till they have watered the earth, making it fertile and fruitful . . . so shall my word be that goes forth from my mouth; it shall not return to me void, but shall do my will, achieving the end for I which sent it" (Isa. 55:10, 11). Speaking, for instance, of the salvation from Egypt, Wisdom states: "For when peaceful stillness compassed everything . . . your all-powerful word from heaven's royal throne bounded, a fierce warrior, into the doomed land, bearing the sharp sword of your inexorable decree" (Wisdom 18:14, 15).

God's word is not only an instrument of judgment and salvation, but also a creative word. The idea of creation through a word had a long tradition behind it in the religions of Mesopotamia and Egypt. The way in which the Bible however uses the idea does not seem directly derived from these sources, but rather to have been born from a legitimate extension of the experience of the efficaciousness of the prophetic word. In Isaiah 48:13 creation leaps into being at a call from God: "My hand laid the foundations of the earth, my right hand spread out the heavens. When I call them, they stand forth at once" (*see* also Pss. 33:6, 9; 148:5). Genesis 1 shows the word of God efficacious and omnipotent, for it invites out of nothingness all that is (1:2; *see* CREATION). The idea of creation through the word also wishes to convey the concept of God's utter transcendence in regard to what is created. The world is not an emanation of God, nor is God caught up and immersed in nature's vicissitudes. The world stands before God like a servant who awaits the word of his master. The only link between them is God's word which is his most efficacious instrument, for it contains within itself his omnipotence.

At times the word of God appears as a personified force with God himself. Here Christian tradition has been a first revelation of the Word, which is legitimate when the Old Testament is read in the light of its fulfilment in the New. Read from the point of view of the Old Testament author, however, the word is not a person, nor however is it a mere literary personification. The personality that the word sometimes assumes is the personality of God himself which is now viewed under the guise of his word which calls man and which will inevitably come to realize what it dictates.

The Aramaic translations of the Old Testament (*see* TARGUM) put into even greater relief the "word" of God. A theological scrupulosity about pronouncing the name of God in the Judaism of the centuries before Christ prompted substitute words by which he would be referred to. The Jews were at pains to avoid using the name of God as the subject or complement of an action involving the world. So, for instance, instead of saying, "God lives in the Temple," one spoke of the "habitation" of God in the Temple. Instead of saying "God reigns," one spoke of the advent or revelation of the kingdom of God. And so too, instead of stating that God spoke, one referred to the "word of God" (memra di Yahweh.)

In the prologue of John's gospel the Word (ho logos) is a divine person, with God, and who is God. Through him the whole world was created. He is the light of men. He came into the world and pitched his tent among men. Jesus is the Word of God enfleshed (Jn. 1:1-18). In this way is completed the progressive revelation of the Word of God which was started in the Old Testament.

The question of the origin of the Johannine idea of the Logos-Word has been and is currently much discussed. During the past decades, even if accord has not arisen, there has been an increasing tendency to search for the origins of the idea in the Old Testament and in Christian revelation. So there has been a regression from the attempt to locate its origins in Hellenism or the Plato-colored Judaism of Philo of Alexandria. It is not to be denied that the speculations on the word-logos among the Stoics, the pre-Gnostics and Philo did help to put into relief the Word in the Christian tradition. It must be affirmed, however, that the content of John's idea of the Word cannot be derived from Hellenism, but is rather the ripened fruit of Old Testament and Christian tradition.

In Acts and the letters of Paul the word of God, or simply the word, is the

Christian message, that is, the revelation of God which is the event of Jesus, his appearance, death and resurrection as the ultimate and definitive salvation (*see* 1 Thess. 1:6; 2:13; Acts 6:2, 4, etc.). It is an efficacious word (Heb. 4:12; Eph. 6:17), a saving word (James 1:21) and a sanctifying word (1 Tim. 4:13; 1 Cor. 1:18). It is the word of salvation (Acts 13:26) and of life (Phil. 2:16).

The word of God is the vehicle of the salvific event and through the word is its power transmitted. This word spoken by God is not just a moral or doctrinal discourse. The perfect revelation of God is not a system of notions but is Jesus himself, a person, with his destiny of death and glory. The identification between Jesus and the Word is in the atmosphere. It was John who took the decisive step. In Revelation 19:13 Christ, in his role of future judge, is called "the Word of God." 1 John 1:1, which is parallel to the prologue to John, calls Jesus the "Word of Life": "This is what we proclaim to you; what was from the beginning, what we have heard, what we have seen with our eyes, what we have looked upon and our hands have touched—we speak of the word of life." In the gospel the "Word" makes no more appearance after the prologue. Its point is the preexistence of the Word, equal to God, who has now come among men with the name Jesus Christ.

It can however cause surprise that the title "Word," which fuses revelation and communication, should disappear precisely at the point at which is begun the perfect revelation and communication of God. To this difficulty an answer can be offered by considering what was the point of view and what was the problem John wished to resolve by speaking of the Logos: that is, how can one think of the pre-existence of the Person who came from God and appeared among men to bring them revelation from God. John's answer is this: Christ had preexisted as the subsistent word of God, the creative and salvific word of the whole Old Testament tradition. Precisely because he was the Word of God, to him was confided the perfect realization of the salvation that had been begun by him in the past. Just as in him was life, he came to give life, and just as in him was light, he came to enlighten.(*See* LIFE; LIGHT.) The Word then came among men, was incarnated to take up his dwelling with us (Jn. 1:14). This Word is Jesus Christ.

word

and scorned the *w*.	Isa. 5:24	The *W*. became flesh	Jn. 1:14
In the beginning was the *W*.			

Jn. 1:1

Work, In the use of the term work (Greek **ergon**) two cases demand some elucidation.

a. Paul often speaks, and especially in Galatians and Romans of the "works of the Law." On these he passes a totally negative verdict when speaking of justification: "No one will be justified in God's sight through observance of the law" (Rom. 3:20). The works of the Law are the works which the Law prescribes. According to Paul the Jews think that they will be recognized as just by God through the observance of the Law, and that in this way they will be saved. This however, declares Paul, is an illusion and a presumption. It is an illusion because all men are caught up in sin (Rom. 3:23). The Law brings man to an awareness of sin, but its voice is overcome by the power of sin in man (Rom. 7:7-25). It is also a presumption because the person who pretends to justification through works and presents himself before God with these pretensions shows himself self-sufficient and the author of his own salvation. To this Jewish doctrine Paul opposes Christian justification which has faith as its foundation.

Man acknowledges that he is a sinner and recognizes that he has nothing to boast of before God. In faith he receives the word of the Christian message and opens himself to God's action in him which changes him from being a slave to sin to being a just man. *See* FAITH; JUSTICE; LIBERTY.

b. The gospel of John often speaks of the works or the work of Jesus. The distinction between the singular and the plural is important. The work of Jesus is the object of his mission which he accomplishes through his death and glorification (17:4). The works of Jesus are the signs effected by him. (*See* SIGN.) In its genuine sense, however, the expression is found only on Jesus' lips. Jesus never calls them "my works." He accurately avoids this expression, using paraphrases that at times are quite contorted, such as: "the works the Father has given me to accomplish, these very works which I perform testify on my behalf that the Father has sent me" (Jn. 5:36) or "I have given you glory on earth by finishing the work you gave me to do" (Jn. 17:4).

How must this expression be understood? What does Jesus mean by the works that the Father gave him to do? First it means that the Father gave the Son the mandate and mission to complete them (Jn. 4:34; 15:10). Not only did he give him the mission, but he also gave him the power to accomplish these works, and an autonomy of decision (5:27; 10:18; 17:2). Jesus insists that the Father does the same works (14:10; 9:3; 10:32, 37), without however substituting for Jesus, seeing that it is Jesus himself who does them (5:36). When therefore Jesus affirms that "My Father is at work until now and I am at work as well" (Jn. 5:17), he does not wish to insinuate that there are two parallel actions going on, one coordinated with the other, but that Jesus is the Person in whom and through whom the Father operates, so that all Jesus' works are God's works. It is Jesus who exercises the whole judgment that he has received from the Father (Jn. 5:22). It is also he who vivifies, a power he has also received from the Father (Jn. 5:26, 27).

In this way can be explained some disconcerting phrases in the gospel of John, such as when Jesus states that he cannot do or say anything, or that his doctrine is not his, that he only states what he has heard (Jn. 5:19, 30; 7:16; 8:28). At first these might seem to be the expression of a profound and even excessive humility. In reality they are something altogether different: they contain unheard of pretensions, for they merely state negatively what Jesus affirmed positively when speaking of his works, that is, that there is an intimate communion of action and work between the Father and Jesus. All that men see Jesus doing or hear him saying has no other source than the Father: "I solemnly assure you, the Son cannot do anything by himself—he can do only what he sees the Father doing. For whatever the Father does, the Son does likewise" (Jn. 5:19). For this reason Jesus' works are signs manifesting his divine glory (Jn. 2:11), showing that the Father is in him and he in the Father.

World, There is no exact Hebrew word corresponding to the English word "world." To express the whole of the created universe, the Bible uses the expression "heaven and earth" (Gen. 1:1), or spells out "heaven, earth, the sea and all that is in them" (Ex. 20:11; Neh. 9:6). Apocalyptic literature and rabbinical thelogy, however, have a term, *olam*, which originally meant an indefinite period of time, like "era" or "eon," but came to mean "age," especially when contrasting the present age to the future. In this way it came near to the word *kosmos* or world. The distinction is not just temporal, but qualitative, so that age did not mean just a reach in time but also a definite order or level of creation, and hence too it became equivalent to our "world." Not only is there a chronological succession between the present world and the one to come: the present world is subjected to sin, corruption and death, while the future world is a renewed world where incorruption and glory triumph. The passage from one world to the other is the eschatological event, that is, resurrection and judgment.

This doctrine of the two worlds was adopted as the basic scheme for the eschatology of the New Testament, as we shall presently see, but it introduced some important novelties into the concept.

In the New Testament, world corresponds to the Greek kosmos. When the New Testament authors use the term, they mean it as it was understood in Greek and with the connotation it had gathered by being translated from the Jewish term 'olam, so that when we come across it in the Scripture text, we must search for its nuances from the context.

In the Greek, the world or kosmos is the universe understood as an organized whole. It is then a term that was absent from the Hebrew tongue to designate the totality of what was created, and so is used with no pejorative connotation when it refers to the creation of the world (Acts 17:24), a work God performed through the Word (Jn. 1:3, 10; 17:5, 24). The world is man's dwelling-place, into which he is born (Jn. 1:9; 16:21). By metonymy, world could mean humanity alone to the exclusion of other creatures. In this sense God loves the world (Jn. 3:16), reconciles it with himself through the cross of Christ (2 Cor. 5:19), and sends his Son to abolish the sin of the world (Jn. 1:29 1 Jn. 2:2). In this sense too Jesus is called the Savior (Jn. 4:42), and light (Jn. 8:12; 9:5) of the world to which he gives life and for which he gives his life (Jn. 6:33, 51). These texts already show that the world, needing as it did, redemption and pardon, was not a neutral term from the religious point of view. Thus one passes irresistibly to the concept that apocalyptic literature gave to the term world. The world means the present situation of the created order, and man in it, at enmity with God, doomed to corruption and death, over which the "prince of this world" has dominion (Jn. 12:31; 14:30; 16:11). Christ came to liberate us from this perverse world (Gal. 1:4) and transfer us to "the kingdom of his beloved Son" (Col. 1:13). The novelty introduced by the Christian revelation is the following: in the Jewish eschatology the future world follows on, or is revealed after, the consummation of this world. In Christian eschatology, however, both worlds already exist together. In fact the passage from one to the other is the glorious resurrection, which is, for Christians, something already realized in Christ (Rom. 1:4), from whom life is transmitted to all who are incorporated into him through faith and baptism (Gal. 2:20, 21; Rom. 6:1-11). The Christian has already tasted the goods of the world to come (Heb. 6:5) but awaits the moment when the full glory of the Christ-life will be manifested in him, and he will be fully configurated to the glorious humanity of the Savior (Phil. 3:20, 21). The Christian, then, still lives on in this world, but he no longer belongs to it. He is dead to the world or must die to it (Gal. 6:14). He cannot go out from the world (1 Cor. 5:10), but neither can he settle for it (Rom. 12:2). Here are repeated the paradoxes born of Paul's notion of the "flesh." *See* FLESH.

John went even further. "World" in his writings can also mean the totality of men who willfully closed themselves off from the light, responding with hatred to the mission of love of the Son. "The light came into the world, but men preferred the dark to the light," and "He was in the world, and through him the world was made, yet the world did not know who he was" (Jn. 1:10).

The world, in this sense, hates Jesus and all that belong to him (Jn. 7:7; 15:18). Thus it lies under judgment and is condemned (12:31) and so excluded from Jesus' prayer (17:9). The world does not know the Father

(17:25) and is incapable of receiving the Spirit (14:17). The disciples are not of this world (15:19) even though they still live here. In this meaning the world is the irreconcilable enemy of God. Its hatred however is a sign of salvation, for it can only hate what does not belong to it (15:19). Jesus has overcome this world (16:33) and his disciples too can overcome it with the force of their faith (1 Jn. 5:4).

Worm, In the Bible the worm is associated with destruction and death. Moses threatens the people by prophesying that for their disobedience the worm will eat their crops (Deut. 28:39). Job in his distress cries out that worms and dust are his parents (Job 17:14), while in 25:6 Bildad answers that man is a maggot and the son of man is a worm! Jesus gives an effective description of the sufferings of the damned, who are thrown into hell, "where the worm dies not and the fire is never extinguished" (Mk. 9:48). Luke records that Herod (Agrippa I) was struck down by God "because he did not ascribe the honor to God, and he died eaten by worms" (Acts 12:23).

worrying
Stop w.   Lk. 12:29

worship
that I may w. the Lord   they w. the works   Isa. 2:8
                1 Sam. 15:25 which they made for w.   Isa. 2:20
                You people w. what   Jn. 4:22

wound, wounds
w. for w.   Ex. 21:25 in my w. the arrow   Job 34:6
who inflict w.   Deut. 32:39 my w. is incurable   Jer. 10:19

wrath, *See* ANGER.
he terrifies them in his w.   Ps. 2:5 nor chastise me in your w.   Ps. 6:2
                in your w. chastise me not   Ps. 38:2

wrists
which he put on her w. Gen. 24:22 and the bracelets on her w.
                                                        Gen. 24:47

write, *See* BOOK, PAPYRUS, PARCHMENT, OSTRAKA, CUNEIFORM, INK, SCRIBE.
W. this down in a document   W. them on the doorposts
                Ex. 17:14   Deut. 6:9
                to w. about him   Acts 25:26
                We never w. anything   2 Cor. 1:13

writhe
W. in pain, grow faint   Mic. 4:10

writing
finished w. out   Deut. 31:24 He signaled for a w. tablet
committed to w.   1 Chron. 28:19   Lk. 1:63

written
Tablets on which I have w.   that you have w.   Ex. 32:32
                Ex. 24:12 a letter not w. with ink   2 Cor. 3:3

wrong
but you w. me by   Jgs. 11:27 I have done the Jews no w.
and done w.   2 Chron. 6:37   Acts 25:10
If your brother does w.   Lk. 17:3

wrongfully
they who w. are my enemies   they persecute me w.   Ps. 119:86
                Ps. 69:5

wrote

Moses then *w.* down	Ex. 24:4	for a writing tablet and *w.*
which he *w.*	2 Kgs. 17:37	Lk. 1:63
	he bent down and *w.*	Jn. 8:8

wrought

When he *w.* his signs   Ps. 78:43

X

Xanthicus (zan′-thi-kus), A month in the Macedonian calendar, adopted by the Seleucids, the equivalent of March and April, or Nisan, in the Hebrew calendar (2 Mac. 11:27-38).

Xerxes (zerk′-seez), Xerxes I, King of Persia (486-465 B.C.) son and successor of Darius. He appears in the book of Esther with the name of Ahasuerus. *See* AHASUERUS; ESTHER.

Y

Yahweh (yah′-weh), The proper name of the God of Israel. Exodus 6:2-6 tells us that God had revealed himself to the patriarchs under the name of El Shaddai, God the Almighty, without telling them his own name Yahweh. Exodus 3:13-15 explains the name Yahweh as a form of the verb **hayah**, which means "to be": "I am who am" or "My name is 'I am'." The text continues: "This is what you shall tell the Israelites: I AM sent me to you." These two texts belong, the first to the document P and the second to E. *See* PENTATEUCH.

The name for the Israelites comprised and defined the reality, so that the revelation of this name was for them a true theophany or self-revelation by God himself. On the other hand, by giving his name, a person gives himself, by opening up the possibilities of a direct relationship with others. By unveiling his name God makes himself accessible to his people. The people, for their part, can now praise him, call on him, ask his help. The revelation of God's name is then the sign, means and invitation to enter into interpersonal dialogue between God and man.

The name Yahweh poses problems not easy to resolve. In the Hebrew text there are four consonants to the name YHWH, called the tetragrammaton. The name written with the vowels e-o-a, taken from the name **Adonai**, a Hebrew word meaning lord, master, husband, or god. What emerges is the name **Yehowah** anglicized "Jehovah," which however was never used as a name for God. The name was written this way to warn the reader, for reverence sake, not to pronounce the name of Yahweh, but to say Adonai instead. *See* LORD.

Three questions can be distinguished: philological, historical and theological.

The philological problem is this: what does Yahweh really mean? The Bible links it with the verb **hayah**, to be. It is however practically certain that the form Yahweh cannot be derived from **hayah**. In Hebrew the root **hawah** means to desire, but this renders no meaning. The name is not Hebrew, and it may well be that it underwent transformation when it was adopted into the Hebrew tongue. The name also appears in the form **Yah, Yahu, Yaw.**

The historical problem is the following: was there a cult of Yahweh before the time of Moses? There are some remarkable facts which seem to demand an affirmative answer to this question. a. Some ancient poetic texts call Yahweh the God of Sinai, or he is presented as coming from Sinai or Seir to intervene in Canaan on behalf of his people (Deut. 33:2; Jgs. 5:4,

5; Hab. 3:3: *see* Kgs. 19:8; Ps. 68). It is evident in the Bible that these phrases are interpreted as the God who revealed himself on Sinai. The primitive meaning however seems simply to be: Yahweh is the God who has his dwelling on Sinai, or who has on Sinai his sanctuary.

b. The Bible itself confirms this impression, for in Exodus 3:1-5 Sinai is presented as a place that was sacred even before Moses arrived there, and Moses only came to know Yahweh when he came there.

c. The priest of Midian who gave hospitality and became father-in-law to Moses does not seem to have been a stranger to the cult on Sinai. Moses discovered Sinai while living among the Midianites, and later the priest of Midian offered sacrifices with Moses on Sinai, at his return from Egypt (Ex. 18:10-12).

d. Judges 1:16 tells us that Moses' father-in-law belonged to the Kenites. Genesis however tells us that the Kenites were adorers of Yahweh, and carried on their foreheads the sign of Yahweh. *See* CAIN.

Moses then was given particular religious experiences. To him was communicated an oracle, in which he was commissioned to save his people in Egypt, to bring them to Sinai, and which also guaranteed him success in his undertaking through the help of the God Yahweh, who was venerated on Sinai. Moreover the great deeds of Yahweh in Egypt on Israel's behalf seem to have been the reason why other groups joined with them, such as Judah, Cain and Caleb, who themselves had already been adorers of Yahweh (Ex. 18:8-11).

The revelation of the true God did not take place on the margins of the typical forms of the religions of the time. Nevertheless, it was by means of them that God spoke to make himself understood by men. The form was the channel of revelation, not its content. God dealt with Moses, and later with the people, in a countenance and form that pre-existed the Israelites. The concrete and direct experience of Moses and the people, however, is the determining element which gave the name Yahweh its content.

The theological problem arises from the way in which biblical tradition has interpreted the name Yahweh. It adopted Yahweh as a form of a verb **hayah**, to be. The form **Yahweh** however can be causative: to cause to be, to create, or simply, to be. This last interpretation was preferred by older translations and is in fact to be preferred. One must however understand, concretely, the verb **hayah**, in distinction to the English "to be." It is not passive existence, but taken in the strong sense of being present in an active, dynamic sense, in the exercise of one's powers. The word at least connotes the diverse possible relationships.

When God names himself "I am who am" (Ex. 3:13-15) he evidently wants to suggest a certain indetermination, that is, the indetermination of the divine initiative, which can neither be controlled nor predetermined, but is pure freedom without boundaries within which it must work. The nearest parallel is Exodus 33:19 where the mercy and goodness of God appear as free (not arbitrary) initiatives on God's part, unlimited and omnipotent. What relationship does this presence of God conjure up? If we take 33:19 as a free commentary on the name of God, the name Yahweh suggests the active and uncontrollable presence of God, his unbrookable dynamism in bringing about everywhere salvation and judgment.

To define God in these terms is not perhaps what the reader might expect. It is necessary however to remember that tradition works under a great handicap. First it must interpret in a meaningful way the term Yahweh, the usage and original meaning of which were unknown. Secondly, it has to explain the name in the service of the precise historical and literary context in which the name was preserved, and for which it was both the promise and guarantee of the saving of the people out of Egypt. In this way however it receives its full meaning of active, autonomous, unlimited, saving and judging presence. All this is contained in the name of the Emissary, Yahweh, which thus becomes a secure pledge of the certainty of realization of what has been promised.

The word Yahweh, however, does not appear in the New American Bible; the translators have consistently translated this Hebrew word, wherever it appears, into the English word Lord.

Year, The Israelite year had 12 months (1 Chron. 27:1-15). These were lunar months however, each consisting of 29 days, so that 12 of them only came to 354 days (*see* MONTH). To match this computation with the actuality of the true solar year of 365 days, an extra month was added at the end of the year after a certain period. This intercalated month was called **wea-dar,** but as to the rules that governed its insertion there is no knowledge. In pre-exilic times the year began with the autumn equinox (Ex. 23:16; 34:22). It would seem that in the time of Josiah, and certainly after the exile, the Babylonian method of computing the calendar was adopted, and so the year began with the spring equinox, at least for civil purposes, even though perhaps the old usage was retained for dating the religious feasts. In the book of Jubilees, an apocryphal work of the 2nd century before Christ, the year consisted of 364 days, divided into 52 weeks with 4 seasons of thirteen weeks each: this is probably the chronology adopted by the P tradition in the Penteteuch as well.

year to year

time from *y.* to *y.*	Ex. 13:10	Add *y.* to *y.*,	Isa. 29:1

yearly

Israelite women to go *y.*	Jgs. 11:40	they thought of the *y.* feast	Jgs. 21:19

years

fixed times, the days and the *y.*		For three *y.*,	Lev. 19:23
	Gen. 1:14	for eighteen *y.* had	Lk. 13:11
four hundred and thirty *y.*			
	Ex. 12:40		

yellow

fine *y.* hair on it	Lev. 13:30	no *y.* hair on it	Lev. 13:32
	look for *y.* hair Lev. 13:36		

yes

Say "*y.*" when you mean "*y.*"		*Y.*, of the Gentiles too	Rom. 3:29
	Matt. 5:37		

yesterday

amount of bricks *y.*	Ex. 5:14	The fever left him *y.*	Jn. 4:52
not come to table *y.*	1 Sam. 20:27	killed the Egyptian *y.*	Acts 7:28

yet

anything to him as *y.*	1 Sam. 3:7	*Y.* even now there remains	
y. we have been spared	Ezra 9:15		Ezra 10:2
	Y. Job to no purpose Job 35:16		

yield, yielded

will continue its *y.*	Lev. 19:25	obtained a fruitful *y.*	Ps. 107:37
The earth has *y.*	Ps. 67:7	shall *y.* but one liquid	Isa. 5:10

Yod, The 10th letter of the Hebrew alphabet (y).

Yoke, A stout wooden bar attached to the shoulder and around the neck of the team of oxen by thongs, cords or rods. To the middle was attached a single shaft which at the other end pulled the plough or cart (*see* Jer. 28:10; Deut. 21:3; Num. 19:2). Yokes of iron were not much in use. Jesus and Joseph, as carpenters, would have made yokes.

The yoke was put on captives (Jer. 28:10) and slaves were sometimes placed under the yoke (1 Tim. 6:1). The yoke thus easily suggested itself as a symbol of submission, surrender and servitude. A yoke of iron denoted hard servitude. Sin can be a yoke (Lam. 1:14), but one can also submit oneself to the yoke of Yahweh (Jer. 2:20).

By comparison with the yoke of slavery, or even with the yoke of the law (Matt. 11:29), surrender to Christ is sweet and easy. "My yoke is easy and my burden light" (Matt. 11:30) is one of the best known and most attractive sayings of Christ.

Yom Kippur, *See* ATONEMENT, DAY OF.

yonder
I go on over *y.*   Gen. 22:5

you

y. are my father	Ps. 89:27	*y.* did not step	Ezek. 13:5
y. send forth springs	Ps. 104:10	Do *y.* still not	Matt. 16:9

young

a bird's nest with *y.* birds		When Rehoboam was *y.*	
	Deut. 22:6		2 Chron. 13:7
nor pity for the *y.*	Deut. 28:50	or a *y.* stag	S. of S. 2:9

youngest

but the *y.* one is not	Gen. 42:13	shall lose his *y.* son	Josh. 6:26
from the eldest to the *y.*		Ahaziah, his *y.* son,	2 Chron. 22:1
	Gen. 43:33		

your, yours

and *y.* children	Ps. 115:14	Egypt shall be *y.*	Gen. 45:20
y. country is waste,	Isa. 1:7	set foot shall be *y.*	Deut. 11:24
For *y.* name's sake,	Jer. 14:21	the reign of God is *y.*	Lk. 6:20
The Lord *y.* God	Matt. 4:7	All things are *y.*	1 Cor. 3:22

yourselves

and then rest *y.*	Gen. 18:4	of a like mixture for *y.*	Ex. 30:37
	Come by *y.* Mk. 6:31		

youth

the faults of my *y.*	Job 13:26	taught me from my *y.*	Ps. 71:17
The sins of my *y.*	Ps. 25:7	in the days of your *y.*	Eccl. 11:9

Z

Zaanaim, Zaanannim (zay′-a-nay′-im, zay′-a-nan′-im), A locality in the land of Naphtali (Josh. 19:33) where Heber the Kenite had camped and where his wife Jael killed Sisera, general of the army of Jabin, king of Hazor (Jgs. 4:11).

Zabad (zay′-bad), A proper name (1 Chron. 2:36, 37; 7:21; 11:41; 2 Chron. 24:26; Ezra 10:27, 33, 43).

Zabdi (zab′-die), Personal name (1 Chron. 8:19; 27:27; Neh. 11:17).

Zabdiel (zab′-di-el), Personal name (1 Chron. 27:2; 1 Mac. 11:17).

Zacchaeus (zak-kee′-us), Head of the publicans at Jericho, a man of means, small of stature. He wished to see Jesus, so he climbed a sycamore tree so that he might look over the heads of the crowd. Jesus invited him to come down from the tree and be his host in his home. Zacchaeus was overjoyed and pledged half of his goods to the poor and to restore fourfold whatever he had gained dishonestly (Lk. 19:1-10).

Zaccur, (zak′-ur), 1. An Israelite of the tribe of Reuben (Num. 13:4).

2. Personal name (1 Chron. 4:26; 24:27; 25:2; Neh. 3:2; 10:13; 13:13).

Zacharias, Zachary, *See* ZECHARIAH.

Zadok (zay′-dok), A priest of David and, with Abiathar, chief of the priests during his reign. According to 2 Samuel 8:17 he was the son of Ahitub of Eli's family, and thereby a descendant of Eleazar, who was son of Aaron (1 Chron. 5:29-34). This genealogy however seems to contradict 1 Kings 2:26-27 which sees in the accession of Zadok the fulfilment of the prophecy of 1 Samuel 2:30-35 against Eli's house. During Absalom's rebellion Zadok and Abiathar remained faithful to David (2 Sam. 15: 24-35; 17:15) and on his suggestion intervened with the elders of Judah to have the king return to Jerusalem (2 Sam. 19:12-15). In the division over the succession, Zadok supported Solomon and was commissioned by David to anoint him king (1 Kgs. 1:8, 32-40). Abiathar, who had supported Adonijah, was dismissed by Solomon, who appointed Zadok chief of the priests (1 Kgs. 2:26-27, 35). Zadok's family kept its position throughout the entire monarchy of Judah (*see* 1 Kgs. 4:2; 2 Chron. 31:10). Only descendants of Zadok were legitimate priests of the Temple in the restoration decreed by Ezekiel (Ezek. 40:46; 43:19; 44:15; 48:11). The theology of the Chronicler placed the same conditions for legitimacy in the High Priesthood; he held that Zadok was a descendant of Eleazar (1 Chron. 5:29-34).

Zaham (zay′-ham), A son of Rehoboam, king of Judah (922-915 B.C.; 2 Chron. 11:19).

Zalmon, A mountain near the city of Shechem, probably one of the peaks of Gerizim or Ebal. When Abimelech set out against the men of Migdal-schechem, they took refuge in the crypt of the temple of El-berith. Abimelech and his men went to Mt. Zalmon and cut down branches from the trees which they heaped upon the crypt and set the temple on fire, killing all inside (Jgs. 9:42-49). Psalm 68:15 also refers to a Mt. Zalmon which is not identified.

Zalmonah (zal-moe′-nah), One of the encampments of the Israelites on the way through the desert to Canaan. It lay between Mt. Hor and Punon (Num. 33:41-42).

Zalmunna, *See* ZEBAH AND ZALMUNNA.

Zamzummim (zam-zum′-im), An ancient people in Ammonite territory, belonging to the Rephaim group (Deut. 2:20).

Zanoah (za-noe′-ah), The name of two villages of Judah (Josh. 15:34, 56), one in the Shephelah, north of Adullam, the second in the hill country south of Hebron.

Zaphenath-paneah (zaf′-e-nath-pa-nee′-ah), The Egyptian name Pharaoh gave to Joseph when he made him head of all Egypt (Gen. 41:45). It means "God speaks and he lives."

Zaphon (zay′-fon), A city in the land of Gad in Transjordan (Josh. 13:27) north of Succoth where the Ephraimites waited for Japheth to ask why they had not been invited to take part in the expedition against the Ammonites (Jgs. 12:1). The name suggests that it was a shrine of Baalzephon, a Canaanite deity.

Zarephath (zar′-e-fath), A Phoenician town (Obad. 20) south of Sidon, on the site of today's Sarafand, where Elijah, at God's word, dwelled for a time in the house of a widow while Palestine suffered a severe drought during the reign of King Ahab (869-850 B.C.; 1 Kgs. 17:8-24; Lk. 4:26).

Zarethan (zar′-e-than), A city on the east side of the Jordan valley beside the ford of Adam (Josh. 3:16). Between Succoth and Zarethan, by a process of sand-casting, were made the bronze furnishings for Solomon's temple (1 Kgs. 7:45-47). Joshua 3 describes a stoppage of the flow of the Jordan from Adam, opposite Jericho, as far north as Zarethan, allowing Joshua and the Israelites to cross.

Zayin (zah′-yin), The 7th letter of the Hebrew alphabet (z).

Zeal, *See* JEALOUSY.

Zealots, A group of Jewish fanatics who combined religion and nationalism, and existed during the first and second centuries A.D. They held that God's reign was incompatible with the Roman domination of Israel. They would tolerate no compromise or passivity towards the foreign power. Instead they promoted direct action to put an end to the Roman occupation. They were undismayed by their poor military strength, convinced as they were that their initiative would unchain the massive forces of the heavens to fight on their side. They were called **sicarii** by the Romans (from **sica,** a short dagger) on account of the concealed weapon they carried for use when opportunity presented itself on Romans or less fervent co-nationals. The movement originated as an uncoordinated revolt by various groups at the time of the census order by Quirinius (e.g. Judas of Gamela, the Galilean, Acts 5:37). Although they were discounted by other more moderate groups, including the Pharisees, they nevertheless succeeded in involving the whole nation in the Jewish War (66-70 A.D.) which saw the destruction of Jerusalem and the Temple. They continued the resistance in dispersed groups and provoked the second rebellion against the Romans during the reign of Hadrian in 132-135 A.D. Simon, one of the twelve, is called the Zealot in the lists of the evangelists; Mark 3:18 names him Simon the Canaanean, which is the Aramaic equivalent of "Zealot" (*see* Luke 6:15; Matt. 10:4; Acts 1:13). There is however no other indication linking Simon with the Zealot party. The fanatic group who vowed to kill Paul during his trial at Jerusalem were very likely Zealots (Acts. 23:12-15).

Zebadiah, (zeb′-a-die′-ah), Personal name of nine men in the O.T. (1 Chron. 8:15, 17; 12:8; 26:2; 27:7; 2 Chron. 17:8; 19:11; Ezra 8:8; 10:20).

Zebah and Zalmunna (zee′-bah, zal-mun′-na), Kings of Midian, who at the head of fifteen thousand men, were defeated by Gideon at Karkor in the Sirhan Valley east of the Dead Sea. They fled but were captured and killed by Gideon in revenge for the death of his brothers (Jgs. 8:4-21; Ps. 83:12).

Zebedee (zeb′-e-dee), Father of the apostles John and James (Matt. 4:21; Mk. 1:19-20; Lk. 5:10). He was husband to Salome (Mk. 15:40; Matt. 27:56). He was apparently a man of means: he had servants (Mk. 1:20); his wife apparently contributed to Jesus' support (Mk. 15:40; *see* Lk. 8:2-3).

Zebidan (ze-by′-dah), The mother of King Jehoiakim of Judah (2 Kgs. 23:36).

Zeboiim (ze-boy'-im), One of the cities of the valley of Siddim, south of the Dead Sea, against which the punitive expedition of the kings of the east was directed in the time of Abraham (Gen. 14:2). It was later destroyed with Sodom and Gomorrah (Gen. 19:24-26; *see* 10:19; Deut. 29:22; Hos. 11:8).

Zebul (zee'-bul), Governor of Shechem who remained loyal to Abimelech when Gaal, son of Ebed, tried to rouse the people against him. Zebul sent a message to Abimelech advising him to come by night with his men and surprise Gaal. Gaal and his party were routed (Jgs. 9:30-41).

Zebulun (zeb'-you-lun), The tenth of Jacob's sons, a younger son of Leah (Gen. 30:20; 35:23; 46:15; Ex. 1:3). He was the founding father of the Israelite tribe that went by his name. The tribe of Zebulun established itself in Galilee north of Carmel and the plain of Jezreel towards the Mediterranean coast (Josh. 19:10-16; Gen. 49:13; Deut. 33:18). With Barak, the tribe fought against Jabin's army under his general Sisera (Jgs. 4:6; 5:18) and with Gideon against the alliance of Midian, Amalek and the men from the East (Jgs. 6:35). The territory was occupied by Tiglath-pileser III of Assyria in the reign of Pekah in Israel (734 B.C.; Isa. 8:23).

Zechariah (zek'-a-rye'-ah), 1. King of Israel (746 B.C.), son and successor of Jeroboam II, killed after six months of reign by the usurper Shallum, who in turn reigned only one month (2 Kgs. 14:29; 15:8-13).

2. A prophet of Judah, son of the priest Jehoiada, killed in the porch of the Temple by order of King Joash (837-800 B.C.; 2 Chron. 24:20-22). This assassination was revenged by the king's own officers who killed him in his bed (2 Chron. 24:25). The murder of this prophet is recalled by Matthew 23:35 and by Luke 11:51. Here he is called son of Berachiah instead of Jehoiada, through confusion with the better known Zedekiah the prophet.

3. The eleventh of the minor prophets in the Hebrew canon of the Old Testament. *See* ZECHARIAH, BOOK OF.

4. A priest of the division of Abijah, Elizabeth's husband and father of John the Baptist. An angel announced the birth of John the Baptist while he was offering incense in the inner sanctuary. He asked for some sign, as his wife was already advanced in years and conception seemed now impossible. Zechariah was struck dumb for his incredulity until the day came for the circumcision of the new-born child (Lk. 1:5:25). Zechariah chose for the child the name John, which he wrote on a slate, as he was unable to speak it. This name had been communicated to him by the angel. With this, his tongue was loosed and he broke into the canticle now known as the **Benedictus**, from the first word in Latin of the song (Lk. 1:57-79). This account of John's birth draws freely on analogous Old Testament accounts of prodigious births (*see* e.g. Jgs. 13; 1 Sam. 1:2) and the aim is to establish a parallelism between it and the similar events surrounding Jesus' conception and birth, in order to underline and define their correlated missions. It must not be taken as a chronicle of actual events, but a story which made use of the literary style of Midrash, which is history in a broad sense.

Zechariah, Book of, The eleventh of the minor prophets in the Hebrew canon of the Old Testament. The first verse of the Book describes Zechariah as son of Berechiah, son of Iddo (1:1), while Ezra 5:1; 6:14; Nehemiah 12:16 simply call him "Son of Iddo"; Iddo was the head of one of the priestly families who returned from the exile to Jerusalem. That he belonged to the priestly class is also evidenced from the importance he attaches in his book to cult, priesthood, and the way in which he highlights the high priest Joshua alongside the Davidic Zerubbabel. Ezra 5:1, 2 and 6:14 recalls once more the work of Zechariah and Haggai in the reconstruction of the Temple after the exile.

The book consists of two parts which can be distinguished in their origin, authorship, historic background and aim. Cc. 1-8 contain the oracles of Zechariah, but the rest of the book is by unknown authors and belongs to an age much later than that of the prophet.

Cc. 1-8 are written in the first person, and the prophecies can be dated with precision: in the eighth month of the second year of Darius (1:1—October/November 520 B.C.), on the 24th of the 11th month of the same year (1:7—February 519 B.C.), the fourth of the 9th of the 4th year of Darius (November 518 B.C.). They contain 8 visions, nearer in style to apocalyptic literature than to the classical pre-exilic prophecies, and starting with a general exhortation to penance (1:2-6), and closing with a discourse on the sins of the past and a promise of the glorious messianic restoration which will put an end to the actual miserable condition of those who returned to Palestine (cc. 7-8).

The visions also refer to the historic and messianic restoration of the post-exilic community: the reconstruction of the Temple (1:7-17) and of the city (2:5-17), and the punishment of those people who provoked such a catastrophe (2:1-4). Zechariah's messianic ideal is inspired by the Davidic theme but it is complemented by the role assigned to the high priest (3:1-10) alongside the royal descendant of David (3:8-10; 4:6-10). United these two stand before the Lord of all the earth (4:1-6, 10-14). The visions conclude with the account of the symbolic coronation of Zerubbabel, a text later applied to the high priest Joshua and interpreted as the divine confirmation of the exaltation of the priesthood of Jerusalem (6:9-14; *see* ZERUBBABEL).

The second part of the book belongs to more than one author and contains no clear allusions to the problems of the post-exilic restoration. Some allusions to Egypt and the Assyrians (10:11) seem to demand a pre-exilic origin, but are in fact evident archaisms, which is also true of the reference to the Philistines (9:1-8). The invasion described in 9:1-8 is better explained as recounting the conquest of Alexander the Great (9:13); this is the probable historic background of a collection of oracles which are presented without any clear order and which revolve around the messianic and eschatological theme. The coming of a mild Messiah is announced: he will preach peace (9:9-10); this text is cited for the triumphal entry of Jesus into Jerusalem (Matt. 21:1-9; Mk. 11:1-10; Lk. 19:28-38). The mysterious announcement "They shall look on him whom they have thrust through" (12:10) is tied up with the restoration of Jerusalem, and referred by John to Jesus on the Cross (Jn. 19:37). Then will come the final victory of God, when all Jerusalem's enemies will be gathered there to be destroyed and when the King of all the earth will be enthroned there, and on it will converge every year the nations of the whole world to celebrate the feast of Tabernacles (cc. 13-14).

Zedekiah, (zed′-e-kie′-ah), 1. Chenaanah's son, one of Ahab's 400 prophets who promised him success in his campaign against Ramoth-gilead. Zedekiah had made himself horns of iron, a symbol of power. "With these," he said, "you will gore Aram until you have destroyed them" (1 Kgs. 22:11-12). Micaiah, son of Imlah, accused them, and particularly Zedekiah, of trying to trick Ahab, and of being led by a lying spirit. Zedekiah struck Micaiah on the jaw, and Ahab imprisoned him, but nevertheless Micaiah proved right (1 Kgs. 22:13-38).

2. Son of Maaseiah, and prophet at the time of Jeremiah, who was accused by him of giving false prophecy in Yahweh's name (Jer. 29:21-23).

3. King of Judah (597-587 B.C.), uncle and successor of Jehoiachin. He was the third son of Josiah and brother of Jehoahaz and Jehoiakim (2 Kgs. 24:17; 1 Chron. 3:15). After only three months of reign Jehoiachin was deported with his family and many Jews by Nebuchadnezzar, who made Mattaniah, Jehoiachin's uncle, king with the name of Zedekiah (2 Kgs. 24:17) as a sign of vassalage. Zedekiah rebelled against Nebuchadnezzar, contrary to the advice of Jeremiah (Jer. 27). This probably took place after the Pharaoh succeeded in blocking the Babylonians (Jer. 44:30). Nebuchadnezzar sent his army from Riblah to lay siege to Jerusalem (589 B.C.; 2 Kgs. 25:1; Jer. 39:1; 52:1). Jeremiah counseled the king not to offer resistance, but Zedekiah would not listen (Jer. 38:17). In July of 587 the city fell. Zedekiah tried to flee but was captured at Jericho, brought to Riblah before Nebuchadnezzar who ordered that he be blinded and brought chained to Babylonia. The king's sons and many other ranking citizens of Judah were executed by the Babylonian king at Riblah (2 Kgs. 25:2-20; Jer. 39:2-10; 52:2-30).

Zeeb, *See* OREB AND ZEEB.

Zela (zee′-la), A city of Benjamin (Josh. 18:28) where the remains of Saul and Jonathan were interred (2 Sam. 21:14) in the family sepulchre.

Zelek (zee′-lek), An Ammonite, one of the Thirty warriors of David (2 Sam. 23:37; 1 Chron. 11:39).

Zelophehad (ze-loe′-fa-had), Son of Hepher of the tribe of Manasseh. He died in the desert without male heirs. His five daughters therefore asked Moses to have his inheritance divided among them so that the family name might not be wiped out. This provided the opportunity for legislation regarding the inheritance of heads of families who die without male heirs (Num. 27:1-11).

Zelzah, A place in the territory of Benjamin near the tomb of Rachel (1 Sam. 10:2). The site is unknown, and some suspect that the name is a corruption, for 1 Samuel 10:2 and Jeremiah firmly suggest that Rachel was buried near Ramah.

Zenas (zee′-nas), A Christian lawyer, probably from the island of Crete. Paul asked Titus to make all traveling arrangements for him, and see to it that he and Apollos had everything they needed. (Tit. 3:13).

Zephaniah (zef′-a-nie′-ah), 1. The ninth of the minor prophets in the Hebrew Canon of the Old Testament. *See* ZEPHANIAH, BOOK OF.

2. Son of Maaseiah, a priest contemporary of Jeremiah (Jer. 21:1; 37:3; 29:25). After the conquest of Jerusalem Zephaniah was brought to Riblah and killed on Nebuchadnezzar's orders (2 Kgs. 25:18; Jer. 52:24).

Zephaniah, Book of, The ninth of the minor prophets in the Hebrew canon of the Old Testament. All we know about him is contained in the inscription of the book in his name. He claims descendancy from Hezekiah who, some would hold, without telling evidence, to be King Hezekiah of Judah (715-687 B.C.). Zephaniah's ministry is placed in the reign of Josiah (640-609 B.C.). This date is generally accepted by all the critics. However it is necessary to limit the prophet's activity to the first years of Josiah, and to terminate it at least by 622 B.C., the year of the discovery of the book of the law and the religious reform that temporarily abolished the idolatrous deviations and abuses denounced by the prophet (1:4, 5, 9) which had endured from the reigns of Manasseh and Amon.

The book is a collection of his oracles, clearly distributed according to themes. 1-2:3 announces the coming of the "day of Yahweh" which will explode as an implacable judgment against the impiety of Judah. This part, especially 1:14-16, inspired the author of the celebrated medieval sequence **Dies irae.** The political crisis tied up with this announcement seems to be the prodigious growth of the neo-Babylonian empire, which soon put an end to the Assyrian empire and made its appearance in Judah during Josiah's reign. 2:4-15 is a collection of oracles against the nations hostile to God's people: the Philistines (2:4-7), Moab and Ammon (2:8-11); the Ethiopians (2:2) and the Assyrians (2:13-15). 3:1-8 is an oracle against Jerusalem for its persistence in evil despite the warning contained in the judgments of God on other nations.

The book concludes with the promises of restoration (3:9-20), of which some of the elements reflect better a later composition (3:9, 10 and 3:19-20), since they seem to suppose the conditions experienced at the Exile.

Zephath (zee'-fath), The ancient name for Hormah (Jgs. 1:17), a town in southwest Judah at the time of the Conquest.

Zephon (zee'-fon), Eldest son of Gad (Num. 26:15).

Zer, A fortified town in the territory allotted to Naphtali (Josh. 19:35).

Zerah (zir'-ah), 1. Son of Reuel and grandson of Esau (Gen. 36:13, 17).

2. Son of Judah and Tamar, and twin brother of Perez (Gen. 38:27-30). He was founder of a clan of Judah (Num. 26:20; 1 Chron. 9:6). His name figures in Matthew's genealogy for Jesus (Matt. 1:3).

3. An Ethiopian chieftain who attempted to invade Judah but was defeated by Asa of Judah at Mareshah (2 Chron. 14:8-14).

Zered (zer'-ed), The biblical name of Wadi el-Hesa, which flows into the southeast end of the Dead Sea (Num. 21:12; Deut. 2:13). It falls 3,900 feet in its 35-mile course.

Zeredah (zer'-e-dah), A city of Ephraim, Jeroboam's place of origin and residence (1 Kgs. 11:26; 2 Chron. 4:17) before his rebellion against Solomon.

Zeresh (zer'-esh), Wife of Haman, King Ahasuerus' minister who was hostile to the Jews (Esth. 5:14; 6:13).

Zeror (zer'-or), An ancestor of King Saul (1 Sam. 9:1).

Zeruah (zir-oo'-ah), The mother of King Jeroboam I of Israel (1 Kgs. 11:26).

Zerubbabel (ze-rub'-a-bel), The son of Shealtiel (Ezra 3:2; 5:2; Hag. 1:1-12, etc.) or (much less likely) of Pedaiah (1 Chron. 3:19). He was governor of Judah under the Persian domination at the time of Darius I (522-486 B.C.). Encouraged by the prophets Haggai and Zechariah, Zerubbabel started once more the reconstruction of the Temple (Hag. 1:1-2; Zech. 4:9). His Davidic lineage (Esd. 3:2; Matt. 1:12) reawakened the messianic and monarchic hopes of the Jewish community after the exile (Hag. 2:21-23; Zech. 4:6-10). Zechariah 6:9-14 originally spoke of a coronation of Zerubbabel, even though later his name was replaced in the text by that of the high priest Joshua. The silence that shrouds the continuation and end of Zerubbabel's government is taken to mean that the Persian authorities deposed him on account of the awakened messianic enthusiasm that centered on his person. In the absence of evidence, this remains but a hypothesis.

Zeruiah (ze-roo'-yah), David's sister, mother of Joab, Abishai and Asahel (2 Sam. 2:18; 1 Chron. 2:16), who are always identified as her sons; the father is ignored.

Zethar, (zee'-thar), One of the seven eunuchs who served King Ahasuerus as chamberlains (Esth. 1:10).

Zeus, The supreme god in the Greek pantheon, the equivalent of the Roman Jupiter. One of the provocations of the Seleucid king which led to the Maccabean revolt was the proposal to dedicate the Temple at Jerusalem to the Olympian Zeus and that of Mt. Gerizim to Zeus Xenios. The last measure was at the request of the inhabitants of the place (2 Mac. 6:2). At Lystra Paul healed a cripple only to find that the people were taking him for the god Hermes and Barnabas his companion for the god Zeus, with the priests urging the people to offer sacrifices to them (Acts 14:118).

Ziba (zie'-ba), A servant of Saul's household who survived Saul's overthrow. To him David committed the care of Mephibosheth (also called Meribbaal, 2 Sam. 4:4), Jonathan's crippled son (2 Sam. 9:1-13). Ziba gave David provisions when he had to abandon Jerusalem on account of Absalom's revolt. He also told David that Mephibosheth was confident that the kingdom would be his. David pledged all Mephibosheth's properties to Ziba (2 Sam. 16:1-4) but on David's return to power, Mephibosheth in his turn accused Ziba of deception and slander, and pleaded his lameness as an excuse for not having gone out to David. Nonplussed, David decreed to divide the properties between Ziba and Mephibosheth, but the latter responded: "Let him have it all, now that my lord and king has returned safely to his palace" (2 Sam. 19:25-31).

Zibiah (zib'-i-ah), The mother of King Joash of Judah (2 Kgs. 12:1).

Zichri (zik'-rye), Personal name of a dozen O.T. men (Ex. 6:21; 1 Chron. 8:19, 23, 27; 9:15; 26:25, 27:16; 2 Chron. 17:16; 23:1; 28:7; Neh. 11:9; 12:17).

Ziklag, A frontier town in the territory of Simeon, east of Gath (Josh. 19:5), given to David as a fief by the Philistine king of Gath (1 Sam. 27:6; 2 Sam. 1:1). The desert-dwelling Amalekites took advantage of David's absence and burned the city, carrying off the women and children. David overtook the raiders, defeated them and recaptured the prisoners (1 Sam. 30).

Zillah, Lamech's second wife, mother of Tubalcain and of Naamah (Gen. 4:19-24).

Zilpah, A maidservant of Leah from whom, with Leah's permission, Jacob had two sons, Gad and Asher (Gen. 30:9-12; 35:26).

Zimran, An Arabian people or region listed among the sons of Abraham and Keturah, his second wife (Gen. 25:2; 1 Chron. 1:32).

Zimri (zim'-rye), King of Israel (876 B.C.), an officer in the army of his predecessor Elah, whom he murdered. He reigned for seven days at Tirzah. He butchered Elah's entire family. The army, which was encamped in front of the Philistine town of Gibbethon, on hearing the news of the assassination, proclaimed Omri, their general, king. Omri laid siege to Tirzah, whereupon Zimri lost hope of escape and put fire to the royal palace, in which he too died (1 Kgs. 16:9-20)

Zin, A desert southeast of the Dead Sea (Num. 13:21; 20:1; 34:3-4; Josh. 15:1-3), through which the Israelites passed en route to Canaan.

Zion, *See* JERUSALEM.

Zior (zie'-or), A village of Judah near Hebron (Josh. 15:54).

Ziph, 1. A town in Judah in the Negeb (Josh. 15:24), southwest of the Dead Sea.

2. A town in the hill country of Judah south of Hebron (Josh. 15:55), to-day called Tell Zif. David took refuge from Saul in the desert that takes its name from the town, and was later betrayed by the inhabitants who took Saul's side (1 Sam. 23:26).

Zippor, The father of Balak, king of Moab (Num. 22:2; 23:18; Josh. 24:9; Jgs. 11:25).

Zipporah (zip′-o-rah), One of the seven daughters of Jethro, the priest of Midian, who became Moses' wife; mother of Gershom and Eliezer (Ex. 2:15, 21-22). She remained with her father and children when Moses returned to Egypt (Ex. 18:2-4).

Ziv, The second month of the Hebrew calendar (1 Kgs. 6:1, 37). *See* MONTH.

Ziza (zie′-za), A son of King Rehoboam of Judah (2 Chron. 11:20).

Zoan (zoe′-an), A city of Egypt in the eastern region of the delta (Isa. 19:11-13; 30:4; Ezek. 30:14). It was founded 7 years before Hebron (Num. 13:22). It was the capital of the Hyksos kings with the name Avaris, and rebuilt by Ramses II who made it his residence, with the name Pi-Ramses. The Israelites took part in these works before the Exodus (*see* Ex. 1; Ps. 78:12, 43). *See* RAAMSES. Later it was known as Tanis, and was the residence of the Pharaohs of the 21st to the 23rd dynasties. It declined when Alexander built Alexandria.

Zoar (zoe′-ar), One of the cities of the Pentapolis, south of the Dead Sea, against which the kings of the east gathered in the time of Abraham (Gen. 14:2, 8). Zoar, which was also called Bela, was, at the request of Lot who wished to take refuge there, spared in the catastrophe which enveloped the other four cities (Gen. 19:18-23).

Zobah (zoe′-bah), An Aramaean state in Syria in the valley of Beqa' between Lebanon and Anti-Lebanon. At one time (c. 1000 B.C.) its territories extended to the Euphrates River and pressed upon the Assyrians. Hostilities erupted between Zobah and Israel as early as Saul's time (1 Sam. 14:47). Hadadezer, king of Zobah, a contemporary of David, went to the help of the Ammonites, against whom David had sent Joab with an army to avenge the insult offered to his messengers. Hadadezer and his allies however were defeated (2 Sam. 10). Another defeat of Hadadezer, (2 Sam. 8:3-8) seems to be a different one from 2:10: David made a raid on the kingdom of Zobah and made off with a rich booty. Zobah was rich in silver. Its more sophisticated army used horses and chariots. Though subjugated by Assyria in c. 732 B.C., its traders continued to prosper in western Asia.

Zohar (zoe′-har), The father of Ephron the Hittite, who sold to Abraham the cave of Machpelah (Gen. 23:8; 25:9).

Zophar, A man from Naamath, friend of Job and one of the principal disputant-friends of Job in the book of Job (Job 2:11; 11:1; 20:1; 42:9).

Zorah, A town in the territory of Dan (Josh. 19:41) before the tribe moved north. It was Samson's homeland (Jgs. 13:2; 16:31), and his family buried him nearby. Its valley provides an easy approach from the coastal plain to Jerusalem; the railroad from Tel Aviv-Jaffa runs through it.

Zuzim (zoo′-zim), A pre-Israelite people in Transjordan, in the city of Ham, defeated by Chedorlaomer and the kings of the east in the time of Abraham (Gen. 14:5). Perhaps they are the Zamzummim (Deut. 2:20), described as a great and numerous people, tall as the Anakim.